lonely planet

KU-443-145

discover EUROPE

LISA DUNFORD, OLIVER BERRY
BRETT ATKINSON, ALEXIS AVERBUCK, JAMES BAINBRIDGE, NEAL BEDFORD, GEERT COLE, DAVID ELSE, STEVE FALLON, DUNCAN GARWOOD, LEANNE LOGAN, VESNA MARIC, VIRGINIA MAXWELL, CRAIG McLACHLAN, TIM RICHARDS, CAROLINE SIEG, DAMIEN SIMONIS, RYAN VER BERKMOES, MARA VORHEES, NICOLA WILLIAMS, NEIL WILSON

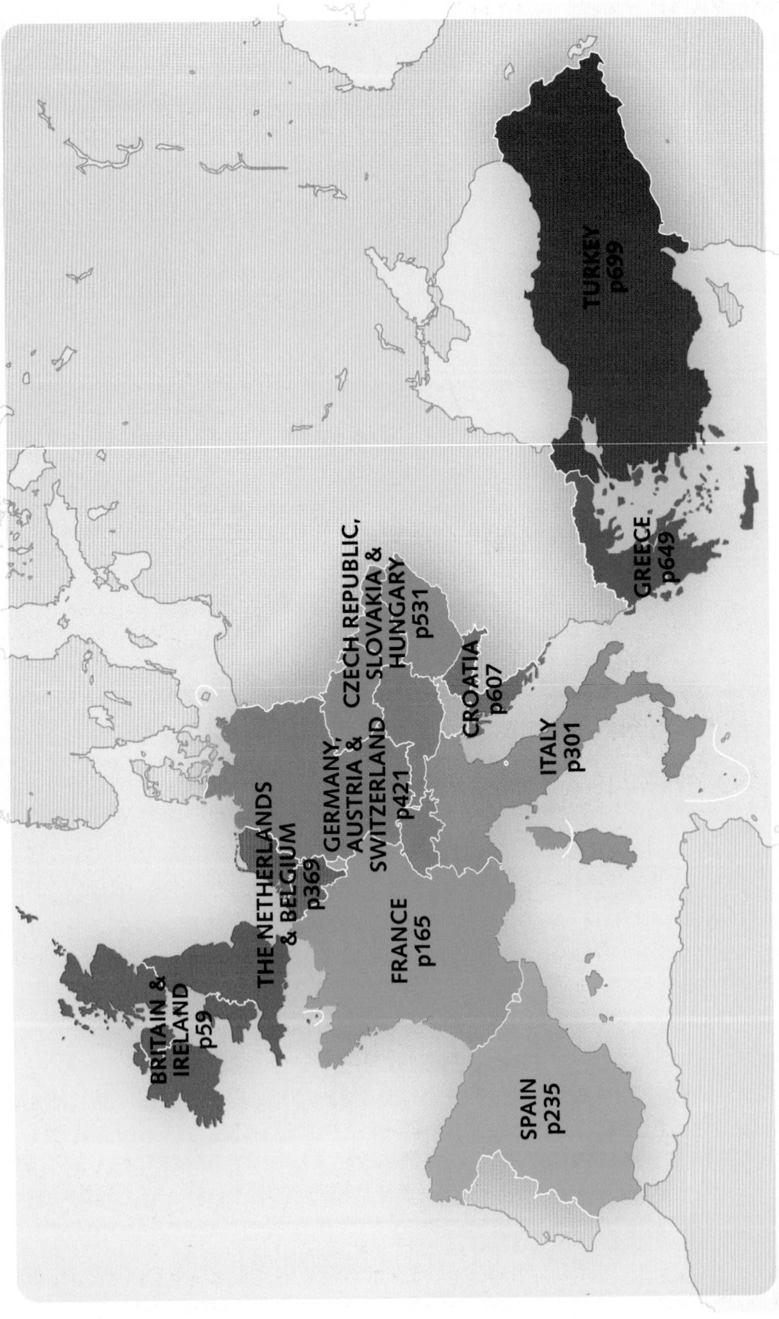
BRITAIN & IRELAND p59
THE NETHERLANDS & BELGIUM p369
FRANCE p165
SPAIN p235
GERMANY, AUSTRIA & SWITZERLAND p421
CZECH REPUBLIC, SLOVAKIA & HUNGARY p531
CROATIA p607
ITALY p301
GREECE p649
TURKEY p699

DISCOVER EUROPE

Europe's Top 25 Experiences (p13) The best bits of a great continent.

Britain & Ireland (p59) Ancient history and modern culture.

France (p165) A country filled with food, wine and joie de vivre.

Spain (p235) Flamenco, beaches, cathedrals and Modernista monuments.

Italy (p301) Artistic beauty in the museums, towns and hills nationwide.

The Netherlands & Belgium (p369) A quirky mix of art, business and pleasure.

Germany, Austria & Switzerland (p421) Big cities and bigger mountains.

Czech Republic, Slovakia & Hungary (p531) Old towns with old-world feel.

Croatia (p607) Endless coastline dotted with medieval stone towns.

Greece (p649) Archaeological sites and breathtaking beaches.

Turkey (p699) Markets and minarets mix with Mediterranean resort towns.

Europe in Focus (p745) Handy information to help you on your way.

CONTENTS

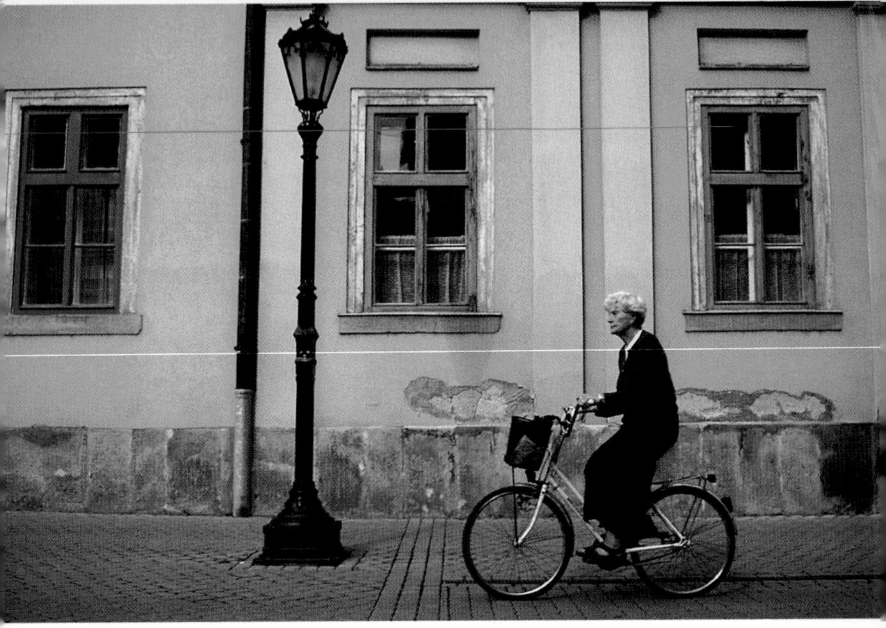

BRITAIN & IRELAND p59
THE NETHERLANDS & BELGIUM p369
GERMANY, AUSTRIA & SWITZERLAND p421
CZECH REPUBLIC, SLOVAKIA & HUNGARY p531
FRANCE p165
CROATIA p607
SPAIN p235
ITALY p301
TURKEY p699
GREECE p649

DUBLIN p142
Pubs by the pint-load in a city that's synonymous with black beer and great literature
LONDON p72
Britain's world-in-a-city capital, a vivacious hub of cultural goings-on
PARIS p178
Refined, romantic, sexy and street smart, the French capital exudes savoir faire
SWISS ALPS p505
Europe's most spectacular mountain range demands the attention of any serious skier, climber or hiker
BARCELONA p267
Gaudí's surreal architecture blows the mind in this buzzing modern metropolis
VENICE p341
Four hundred bridges and 150 canals serve as routes around this atmospheric town
BERLIN p436
Nightclubs, bars and ever-changing exhibits reflect the Zeitgeist in this modern chameleon
ICELAND
58°N
50°N
42°N
34°N
8°W
0°
NORWEGIAN SEA
Faroe Islands (DEN)
Shetland Islands
Orkney Islands
Outer Hebrides
NORWAY
SWEDE
DENMARK
NORTH SEA
ATLANTIC OCEAN
Northern Ireland
Scotland
Inverness
Aberdeen
Oban
Dundee
Glasgow
Edinburgh
Derry
Belfast
Isle of Man
Newcastle-upon-Tyne
Middlesborough
Galway
Dublin
IRELAND
Irish Sea
York
Liverpool
Manchester
Killarney
Cork
Rosslare
BRITAIN
Wales
England
Swansea
Cardiff
Oxford
London
Portsmouth
Frisian Islands
Stralsund
Lübeck
Hamburg
NETHERLANDS
Den Haag
Amsterdam
Hanover
Berlin
Düsseldorf
Leipzig
Brussels
GERMANY
BELGIUM
Dresden
Channel Islands
English Channel
Le Havre
Caen
Brest
Quimper
Frankfurt
Prague
Rheims
Paris
Rennes
CZECH REPUBL
Bavaria
St Nazaire
Nantes
Blois
Strasbourg
Stuttgart
Tours
Loire
Dijon
Munich
Český Krumlov
La Rochelle
Freiburg
Salzburg
Vien
FRANCE
Bern
Zürich
Geneva
SWITZERLAND
AUSTRI
Limoges
Bay of Biscay
Bordeaux
Lyon
Mt Blanc (4807m)
Clermont-Ferrand
Milan
Venice
SLOVEN
Zagreb
CROATI
La Coruña
Vigo
Gijón
Santander
Bilbao
Bayonne
León
San Sebastián
Toulouse
Avignon
Provence
Turin
Genoa
Po
Pyrenees
Marseille
Nice
Alps
Rhône
Pamplona
Golfe de Lion
Douro
Salamanca
Pisa
Florence
Split
ADRIATIC
PORTUGAL
Tajo
Zaragoza
ANDORRA
Toledo
Madrid
Barcelona
Corsica
Elba
Ajaccio
Badajoz
SPAIN
Rome
Valencia
ITALY
Mallorca
Menorca
Seville
Córdoba
Ibiza
Palma
Sassari
Naples
Balearic Islands
Sardinia
Granada
Alicante
Cádiz
Murcia
Taran
Cagliari
TYRRHENIAN SEA
Strait of Gibraltar
Málaga
Almería
MEDITERRANEAN SEA
Palermo
Sicily
Pantelleria
Catania
Isole Pelagie
MALTA
ALGERIA
TUNISIA
MOROCCO
LIBYA

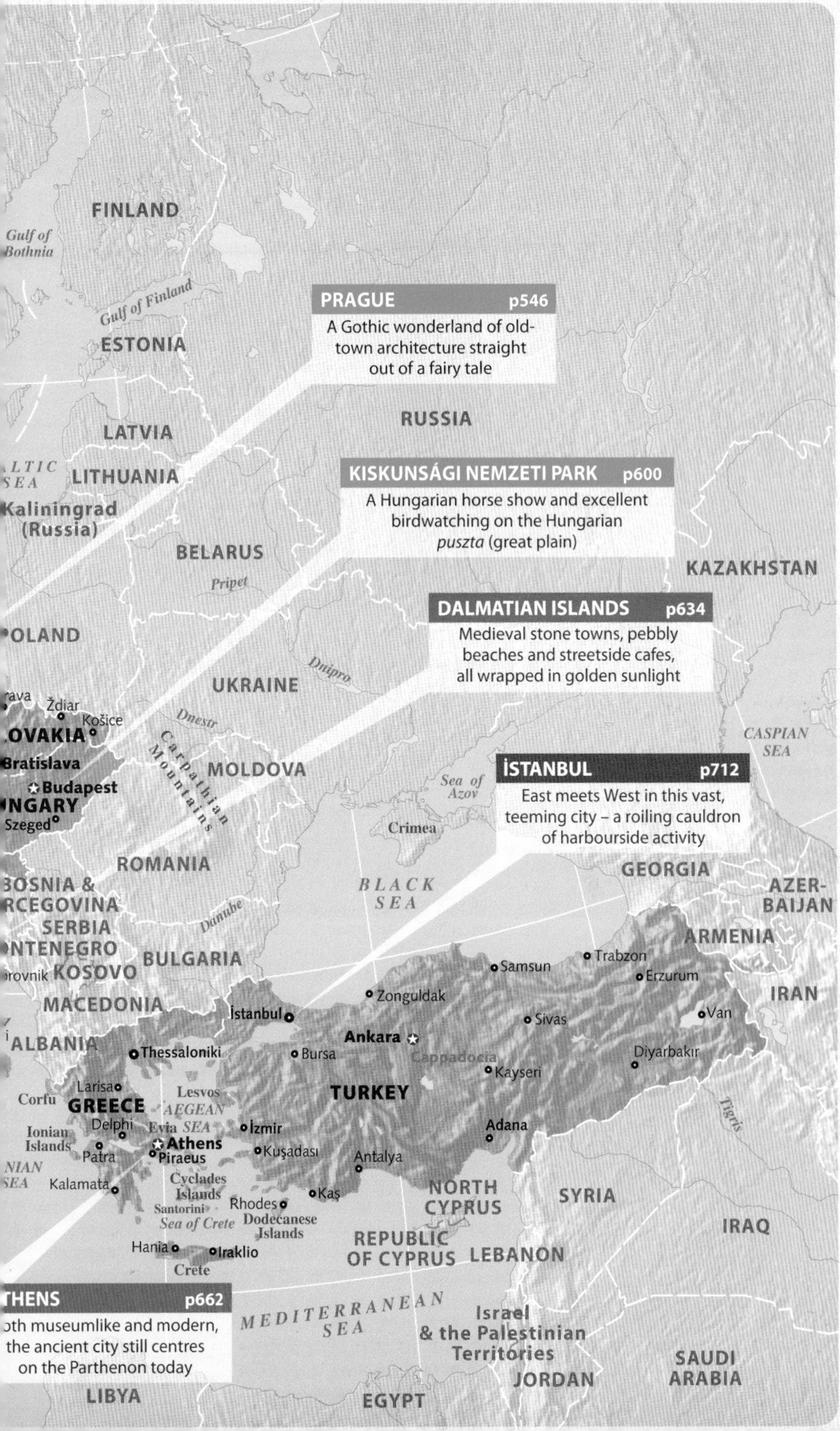
PRAGUE p546
A Gothic wonderland of old-town architecture straight out of a fairy tale
KISKUNSÁGI NEMZETI PARK p600
A Hungarian horse show and excellent birdwatching on the Hungarian *puszta* (great plain)
DALMATIAN ISLANDS p634
Medieval stone towns, pebbly beaches and streetside cafes, all wrapped in golden sunlight
İSTANBUL p712
East meets West in this vast, teeming city – a roiling cauldron of harbourside activity
THENS p662
oth museumlike and modern, the ancient city still centres on the Parthenon today
FINLAND
Gulf of Bothnia
Gulf of Finland
ESTONIA
LATVIA
LITHUANIA
LTIC SEA
Kaliningrad (Russia)
BELARUS
Pripet
RUSSIA
KAZAKHSTAN
OLAND
UKRAINE
Dnipro
Dnestr
ava
Ždiar
Košice
OVAKIA
Bratislava
Budapest
NGARY
Szeged
Carpathian Mountains
MOLDOVA
Sea of Azov
Crimea
CASPIAN SEA
ROMANIA
BLACK SEA
GEORGIA
AZER-BAIJAN
ARMENIA
BOSNIA &
RCEGOVINA
SERBIA
NTENEGRO
Danube
BULGARIA
rovnik
KOSOVO
MACEDONIA
ALBANIA
İstanbul
Samsun
Trabzon
Erzurum
Zonguldak
IRAN
Van
Sivas
Ankara
Cappadocia
Diyarbakır
Kayseri
Thessaloniki
Bursa
TURKEY
Tigris
Corfu
Larisa
Lesvos
GREECE
AEGEAN SEA
Delphi
Evia
İzmir
Ionian Islands
Patra
Athens
Piraeus
Kuşadası
Antalya
Adana
NIAN SEA
Kalamata
Cyclades Islands
Santorini
Kaş
Rhodes
NORTH CYPRUS
SYRIA
Sea of Crete
Dodecanese Islands
REPUBLIC OF CYPRUS
LEBANON
IRAQ
Hania
Iraklio
Crete
MEDITERRANEAN SEA
Israel & the Palestinian Territories
JORDAN
SAUDI ARABIA
LIBYA
EGYPT

↘ THIS IS EUROPE

The Parthenon, Big Ben, the Eiffel Tower and the Grand Bazaar – Europe is indeed filled with iconic sights. But it's also about celebrating in a piazza, hiking the wild coastlines and eating in a neighbourhood taverna. Here the layers of experience run as deep as the continent's history.

Tourist hordes may be the only invaders now, but for millennia conquerors came and went, leaving their legacy: pre-classical-culture stonework and statuary; Roman ruins scattered from England to the Aegean; and Ottoman minarets and mosques as far north as Hungary. Seeking out these treasures could take a lifetime, but there are also medieval walled cities, Gothic cathedrals, Renaissance town squares and baroque monuments to explore.

So many great thinkers, artists, musicians and writers hail from Europe that it is rightly called the cradle of Western civilisation. Plato, da Vinci, Descartes; Michelangelo, Monet, Van Gogh; Bach, Beethoven, Mozart; Shakespeare, Sartre, Kafka…the list goes

on. Their works, influence and more can be experienced at the incredible museums, ornate concert halls and bustling theatres across the continent.

Arrive in one of the urban centres, however, and you'll know that Europe isn't all about the past. Pulsing nightlife, trendy eateries and postmodern monuments are part of city life. And there's plenty of sun to soak up in pebbly coves and on sugar-sand beaches. Though each country retains its distinct flavour, 13 of the 16 nations represented in this book are members of the EU. Age-old racial and religious differences do still cause tensions, but with relaxed (or nonexistent) border controls and 10 of these countries using the euro, there's no better time to beat it to Europe. The proliferation of low-cost carriers and high-speed trains means you can cover more territory in less time. So come, sift through Europe's many layers – for your first time or your fifth. But throw a coin in the Trevi Fountain, because we bet you'll be back.

'each country retains its distinct flavour'

LAST DROP
WELCOME
CROESO
BENVENUTI
Bienvenido
ようこそ
TO
THE
LAST
DROP

EUROPE'S TOP 25 EXPERIENCES

1

THAMES-SIDE WANDERINGS, LONDON

My favourite place and time in London is strolling along the **South Bank** (p82) early on a sunny day. From Westminster Bridge down to Tower Bridge, I walk past 1000-year-old Lambeth Palace and the new-millennium London Eye, later getting views of St Paul's Cathedral and the Tower of London.

David Else, Lonely Planet Author, Britain

MONUMENTAL SIGHTS, PARIS

Stroll the boulevards, shop till you drop and drink in the sights of France's unforgettable capital city. Clamber to the top of the **Eiffel Tower** (p182), marvel at the architectural ambition of **Notre Dame** (p187) and seek out celebrity graves in the **Cimetière du Père Lachaise** (p190).

Oliver Berry,
Lonely Planet Author, Britain

2

3

TRAIN TRAVEL

We got to Barcelona late at night and found a night **train** (p298) going our way. The next morning we awoke and the entire train was empty. Curtains flapped as wind blew through the open windows and the train meandered through the plains of central Spain. It was like being in a Sergio Leone movie.

Ryan Ver Berkmoes, Lonely Planet Author, USA

1 DAVID TOMLINSON; 2 JEAN-PIERRE LESCOURRET; 3 AGSTOCKUSA/ALAMY

1 St Paul's Cathedral (p81) from the Millennium Bridge, London, Britain; 2 Arc de Triomphe (p187), Paris, France; 3 Train passing a sunflower field, Spain

BEERFEST IN BAVARIA

Are you a beer lover? Then **Oktoberfest** (p455) is for you. Twenty-odd beer halls hold thousands of like-minded people. I spent my first day sitting with some locals who were there for their 27th straight year and after 10 minutes they treated me like a lifelong friend.

Damian Hughes, Traveller, Australia

4

5

EATING IN ITALY

By chance we walked into a little restaurant in **Italy** (p314) and had the most amazing meal of our lives. Cheese drizzled in honey, prosciutto, cherry tomatoes, anchovies and fresh bread. But then there was dessert: succulent figs washed down with a complimentary glass of *limoncello* (lemon liqueur).

Diana Steicke, Traveller

CLIFFTOPS OF SANTORINI, GREECE

The startling sight of the submerged caldera of **Santorini** (p680) grabbed our attention as we wandered along the path to Oia. Recovering from our exertions in a caldera-facing taverna, we sank ice-cold Mythos beer and wondered at the seeming precariousness of our spectacular surroundings.

Craig McLachlan, Lonely Planet Author, New Zealand

6

4 KRZYSZTOF DYDYNSKI; 5 MASSIMO PIZZOTTI / ALAMY; 6 PAOLO CORDELLI

4 Oktoberfest (p455) celebrations, Munich, Germany; 5 Restaurant in Sicily (p362), Italy; 6 Rooftops of Santorini (p680), Greece

FAIRY CHIMNEYS, CAPPADOCIA, TURKEY

Even after an overnight bus trip, the sight of **Göreme** (p736) in Cappadocia is unlike any other. Its fairy chimneys and Flintstones-like setting is amazing. The cave pensions are a highlight, hiking through the valleys is a must, and there are many historic sites in the area.

Warren Harrower, Traveller, Australia

7

8

A PINT IN A PUB

If you really want to know what makes the Irish tick, there's nothing like a pint of stout in a village pub. You'll find gorgeous inns and cosy ale houses dotted all over the Emerald Isle (p142), and if you're really lucky, you might be treated to a spot of traditional music, too.

SKIING IN SWITZERLAND

The first time my sister and I ever skied was on the slopes of the Swiss Alps (p505). I gave up and tried, unsuccessfully, to have hot cocoa (it's *chocolat*, I learnt later); she got stuck in the powder snow and had her picture taken by tourists. But, oh, the scenery – unforgettable!

Kate Showalter, Traveller, USA

9

7 JOHN ELK III; 8 HOLGER LEUE; 9 CHERYL FORBES

7 Hot-air balloon over Göreme (p736), Turkey; 8 A pub in Temple Bar, Dublin (p142), Ireland; 9 The Matterhorn (p505), Zermatt, Switzerland

10

WORLD-CLASS MUSEUMS

The highlights of my trip to Europe were the magnificent **Louvre** (p189), **Musée d'Orsay** (p182) and **Uffizi** (p354). I was surrounded by such exquisite beauty, I laughed and cried simultaneously. The display of man's creative ability filled me with great hope.

Catherine Navarro, Traveller, USA

THE MEZQUITA, CÓRDOBA

Spain's southern coastline is only a hop, skip and jump from North Africa, and for centuries the clash of Moorish and Christian cultures has given this corner of Spain a uniquely exotic flavour. Nowhere sums this up more than the mighty **Mezquita** (p292) in Córdoba – halfway between a Moorish mosque and a Christian cathedral.

Oliver Berry,
Lonely Planet Author, Britain

11

CAFE CULTURE

12

Whiling away the afternoon with a cake and a coffee in an old world **Viennese kaffeehaus** (p480) may be the ultimate in indulgence, but much of Europe has a lively cafe culture. Paris' streetside tables are epic for people-watching, then there's Zagreb, Budapest… even tiny little Bratislava in Slovakia has outdoor tables galore.

13

RED ROOFS OF DUBROVNIK

Walking around **Dubrovnik** (p640) on the city walls offers beautiful views of grassy mountains, rocky islands and shimmering seas, along with domestic views of women pegging out their washing and winding it along on lines between buildings.

Lisa Citaris, Traveller, Australia

10 IZZET KERIBAR; 11 JOHN ELK III; 12 OLIVER STREWE; 13 JEAN-PIERRE LESCOURRET

10 Musée du Louvre (p189), Paris, France; 11 Interior of the Mezquita (p292), Córdoba, Spain; 12 Outdoor cafe crowd, Paris (p178), France; 13 Dubrovnik (p640), Croatia

14

DAWN AT THE TREVI FOUNTAIN

Rome was quiet in the wee morning hours. When we sat down on the steps of the fountain, we joined six others, including one man sweeping the previous day's coin haul into a pile. We tossed coins into the **Trevi** (p323), the first of the day.

Bon & Alicia Smith, Travellers, Canada

EXPLORING EDINBURGH

Edinburgh (p130) is a city rich in history. The city buzzes with the sound of locals, travellers and the bagpipes on Princes St. Look up to see the castle watching over the city, walk on cobbled streets, and visit underground Edinburgh to get an insight into the history of the city.

Louise Griffiths, Traveller, Australia

15

14 WILL SALTER; 15 IZZET KERIBAR

14 The Trevi Fountain (p323), Rome, Italy; 15 The Royal Mile, Edinburgh (p130) , Britain

COFFEE SHOPS & CANALS

When you step into a **coffee shop** (p389) in Amsterdam, coffee is not the first thing on the menu. Back outside, the canals seem so serene. I recommend taking one of the many boat tours on offer; it's a great way to see the city without getting lost while in your coffee-shop haze.

Erin Cavarretta, Traveller, USA

16

17 SEASIDE IDYLLS

Explore another side of Europe on the islands and waterfront promenades of Croatia (p620), Greece (p662) and Turkey (p712), where the pace of life is gentle and the sun seems to shine every day. Amid olive groves, lavender fields and pristine beaches you're sure to find your own Mediterranean idyll.

Will Gourlay, Lonely Planet Staff

18 FOLKSY ŽDIAR, SLOVAKIA

Whether snow is lying on the hillsides or heather is blooming in the fields, there's something tranquil about Ždiar (p580), a traditional Slovak village beneath the High Tatras. Hand-painted designs on the log cottages and blazing fireplaces in each of the handful of restaurants make it all the more welcoming.

Lisa Dunford,
Lonely Planet Author, USA

16 WILL SALTER; 17 RACHEL LEWIS; 18 WAYNE WALTON

16 Canals of Amsterdam (p382), the Netherlands; 17 Banje Beach, Dubrovnik (p640), Croatia;
18 Traditional house, Ždiar (p580), Slovakia

MEDIEVAL KNIGHTS, ČESKÝ KRUMLOV

If I had been wearing armour and riding a horse I would have felt right at home in Czech Český Krumlov (p566). It doesn't take much to imagine King Arthur, Sir Lancelot and a golden dragon battling in the main square. The medieval charm of the town is alluring. Don't forget to pack your sword.

Piero Liguori, Traveller, New Zealand

19

20

MARKETPLACE MAYHEM

Shopping in general – for fruit and veg in France, leatherwork in Greece, handbags in Italy etc – is just more fun in the open air. But the granddaddy of all markets is the **Grand Bazaar** (p717) in İstanbul, a maze of nearly 4000 shops on dozens of streets.

19 JOHN ELK III; 20 IZZET KERIBAR

19 Český Krumlov (p566), Czech Republic; 20 Grand Bazaar (p717), İstanbul, Turkey

21

HUNGARIAN HOT SPRING SPAS

The neoclassical buildings of **Széchenyi Baths** (p589) in Budapest go on forever. My cousin pulled me out of my shyness and into the sprawling indoor-outdoor complex of pools, saunas and walk-through steam rooms. From then on I was hooked; I went to every thermal bath I could across Hungary.

Lisa Dunford, Lonely Planet Author, USA

GRECIAN ANTIQUITIES, DELPHI

Visit the Greek archaeological remains scattered across the beautiful hillside at **Delphi** (p675), once the site of the most important oracle of the god Apollo. In the 8th century BC the oracle was consulted before any major undertakings, such as war or the founding of colonies.

sunphlower, Traveller

22

GRAND PLACE, BRUSSELS

I wandered for the first time along Rue des Harengs, a dark, cobbled alley in downtown Brussels (Belgium), and suddenly stepped out into the magnificence of the city's **Grand Place** (p403). In those few seconds I was transported back centuries; on every trip I make to Brussels, I always repeat this experience.

Leanne Logan, Lonely Planet Author, Australia

23

24

CYCLING IN HAMBURG, GERMANY

Immediately upon my arrival in **Hamburg** (p469), the wide network of manicured cycling trails beckoned to me. The next day I hired a bike and zipped along sparkling waterways and tooled through neighbourhoods such as trendy St Georg. I felt like a true local.

Caroline Sieg, Lonely Planet Author, Germany

21 DAVID GREEDY; 22 ANDREW BAIN; 23 PASCALE BEROUJON; 24 MARK DAFFEY

21 Chess players at Széchenyi Baths (p589), Budapest, Hungary; 22 Ruins at Delphi (p675), Greece;
23 Brussels' Grand Place (p403), Belgium; 24 Cycling along the Alster Lakes, Hamburg (p469), Germany

PROVENCE, FRANCE

Follow in the footsteps of countless painters, poets and expats in idyllic **Provence** (p217). From sleepy southern villages to buzzy fishing ports and fragrant lavender fields, this sultry southern region sums up what French joie de vivre is all about.

25

BILL WASSMAN

Abbey and lavender field in Provence's Avignon (p221), France

➘ EUROPE'S TOP ITINERARIES

FOUR CITIES & SOME MOUNTAINS

10 DAYS LONDON TO ROME

Ten days isn't much time to cover a continent so we've picked some of Europe's most popular cities and most breathtaking scenery. The train can take the strain all the way, so you can just sit back, enjoy the view and hit the ground running.

❶ LONDON

Europe's greatest city? There's so much to do in the British capital that you probably won't even have time to ponder that question as you try to fit in a visit to the **Tower of London** (p82), a night at a **West End show** (p92) and a meal in one of the city's cool **restaurants** (p89).

❷ PARIS

Just a couple of hours on the train from London and you can be strolling the streets of irresistible Paris. Show the Mona Lisa your own enigmatic smile at the **Louvre** (p189), try snails for the first time at a chic **bistro** (p193), and shop in the city's **grands magasins** (department stores; p198).

❸ SWISS ALPS

To slow the pace after your own Tale of Two Cities, head south from Paris to the Swiss Alps. Easily reached on the train (head for Geneva and then pick up a connecting service), top destinations include **Montreux** (p504), **Lucerne** (p510) and the **Jungfrau Region** (p513).

DAVID TOMLINSON

View of Jungfrau (p513), Switzerland

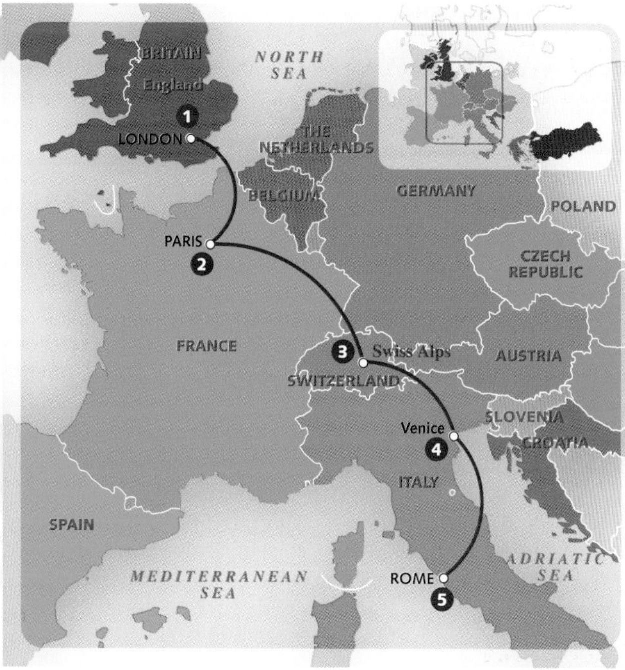

Climb every mountain, explore the chocolate-box villages, and breathe in that fresh Alpine air.

❹ VENICE

Venice's unique beauty hardly makes it an undiscovered gem, but many visitors are day-trippers so a night or two here can allow you to enjoy *La Serenissima* in (relative) peace. The big sights – **Basilica di San Marco** (p341), the **Palazzo Ducale** (p344) etc – are all worth seeing, but one of the best things you can do in Venice is simply get lost in the quiet backstreets where you'll find that there *are* some undiscovered gems still to be found.

❺ ROME

Last stop the Eternal City. Magnificent monuments recalling the Italian capital's illustrious history include the **Colosseum** (p318), the **Trevi Fountain** (p323) and the **Vatican** (p319), and are reason enough to come here. But throw in exceptional food, a great nightlife and some classy shopping and you've got the perfect place to finish off your whistle-stop trip.

MEDITERRANEAN MEANDERING

TWO WEEKS BARCELONA TO ATHENS

Once home to Europe's first civilisations and now home to many of its best beaches and seaside cities, the Mediterranean oozes charm. This trip takes you from buzzing cities to quiet resorts, skipping from one to the next by train, plane, bus or ferry.

❶ BARCELONA

Amazing architecture, stylish inhabitants, exciting nightlife and city beaches – what's not to love about Barcelona? Spain's most European city has enough to fill a week's exploration, but on a quick trip top choices should be the **Sagrada Familia** (p273), **La Rambla** (p268) and the **restaurants** (p276) and **bars** (p277) around La Ribera. Not forgetting a half day on the sand to get your first taste of the Med itself.

❷ NICE

A quick flight or an enjoyable two-train journey (change in Montpellier) and you're in Nice, the cosmopolitan capital of France's chic Côte d'Azur. Explore the **Old Town** (p223) and either Nice's own pebbly **beach** (p225) or the cool nearby sands of **Cannes** (p226) and **St Tropez** (p227).

❸ CINQUE TERRE

Five cliff-hugging towns give their name to this scenic strip of Italian **coastline** (p337). A train line runs the length of the area, offering stunning views of sea and land, or tackle the **Blue Trail** (p337) hiking route for equally impressive panoramas and a dose of healthy exercise.

GEORGE TSAFOS

Caryatids of Erechtheion at the Acropolis (p663), Athens, Greece

❹ VENICE

By boat is the best way to go when you're in this historic island city. In a couple of days you can indulge in a **gondola ride** (p346), get lost among the bridges and back streets, and board a *vaporetto* to the neighbouring **islands** (p345) to see Venetian glass-making and pastel-coloured townhouses.

❺ DUBROVNIK

Ferry and bus combinations along Croatia's stunning coast will soon get you to the country's most beautiful city, **Dubrovnik** (p640). Stroll the **ancient walls** (p642), hit the local **beaches** (p644) or just enjoy a drink amid the baroque splendour.

❻ ATHENS

The cradle of western civilisation is also a thoroughly modern city, meaning you can admire the ruins of the **Acropolis** (p663) before dining out in a fancy Michelin-star restaurant. And if time is on your side, the nearby port of **Piraeus** (p672) is the gateway to the Greek islands where you can continue your Mediterranean odyssey.

COUNTRYSIDE RETREATS

TWO WEEKS PROVENCE TO THE DANUBE

The rural and natural areas of Europe deserve just as much attention as the glittering cities. This central-ish tour takes you through parts of France, Italy, Switzerland, Germany and Austria. Though entirely possible to do by public transport, some regional car hire would add flexibility.

❶ PROVENCE

Enjoy three days surrounded by lavender fields, atmospheric villages, fine French food and wine. **Avignon** (p221), with its ancient stone ramparts and bridges, is a good place to start. Then you can explore your artistic side in Cézanne's hometown of **Aix-en-Provence** (p221). South in **Marseille** (p218), explore the old port and its eateries.

❷ TUSCANY

Tuscany's famous rolling hills and medieval towns warrant at least a few days. To get to the magnificent museums and churches of **Florence** (p352), you'll have to take an overnight bus unless you want to transfer trains. From there the countryside is at your disposal, but don't miss an excursion to the 14th-century walled centre of **Siena** (p358).

❸ SWISS ALPS

Central Switzerland and Bernese Oberland are home to some the most stunning peaks and towns. From Florence transfer by train to **Lucerne**

LEFT: PASCALE BEROUJON; RIGHT: DIANA MAYFIELD

Left: Fort St-Jean at Vieux Port (p219), Marseille, France; Right: House and vineyards in Tuscany (p352), Italy

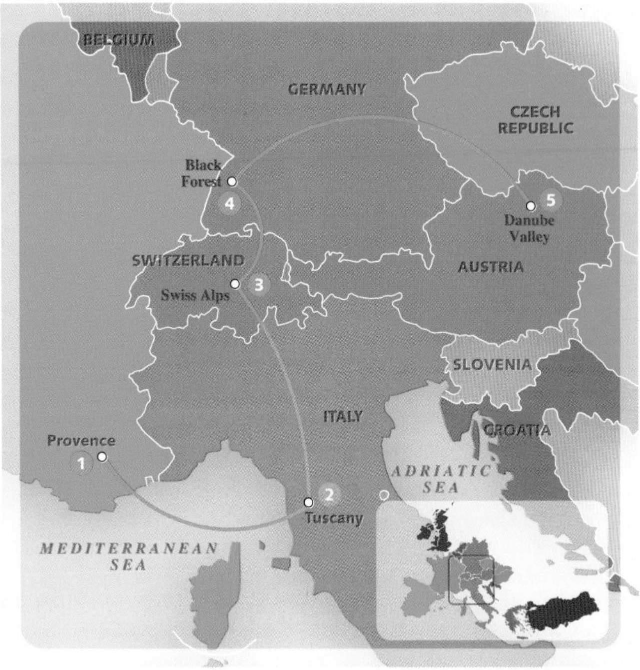

(p510). Divide three days between this gorgeous old lakeside city ringed by mountains and **Interlaken** (p512), mountain-sport central. From the latter you can ride to the continent's highest train station, **Jungfraujoch** (p516).

❹ BLACK FOREST

Go cuckoo for the bucolic countryside where evergreens intersperse with farmland. **Freiburg** (p466) is a good base for two days exploring the Black Forest. Take the cable car up and hike the highlands or make excursions to little local towns like **Schiltach** (p466).

❺ DANUBE VALLEY

A full day and two trains later and you're in Austria's picturesque Danube Valley, or Wachau. Stay a night in the old town of **Krems an der Donau** (p484), before boarding a pleasure boat the next day. Your Danube River excursion passes beneath castles and vineyards before finishing in **Melk** (p484). Its imposing fortified abbey on a hill is well worth your third afternoon. From here the major transport hub of **Vienna** (p472) is just over an hour away.

THE BEER & WINE ROUTE

THREE WEEKS DUBLIN TO VIENNA

Drink up the local culture of six countries in 21 days – from a pint in a pub to new wine in a garden. Oh, and you'll see some sights. Based upon your preferences, spend three or four days in each town.

❶ DUBLIN

One of the joys of the Irish capital is the opportunity to spend your days in literary pursuits, learning about Joyce, Wilde and Beckett at the **Dublin Writers Museum** (p145), and then spend your evenings enjoying locally made Guinness at the **Stag's Head** (p148) pub where Joyce drank, or in the raucous Temple Bar district.

❷ LONDON

London's vast variety of attractions can be pretty exhausting, so for a pit stop after tackling the Tower, St Paul's and the Eye the city's historic pubs are perfect. Some to check out include the **Coach & Horses** (p92), once frequented by artist Francis Bacon; the **Princess Louise** (p92), a late Victorian beauty; and the **George Inn** (p92), a 1677 coaching inn tucked up a small side street.

❸ PARIS

Pop over to Paris, where after seeing the **Sacré Cœur** (p188) and braving the lines at the **Eiffel Tower** (p182) you can sip famous French

LEFT: DIANA MAYFIELD; RIGHT: MICAH WRIGHT

Left: Vineyards on the outskirts of Vienna (p472), Austria; Right: Pulling pints of Guinness in Ireland

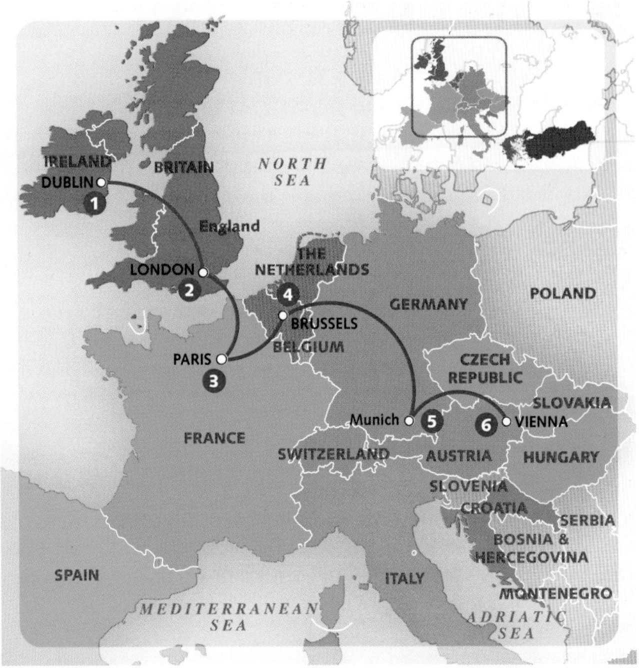

wines at a musical bistro like **Le Limonaire** (p198). Spend an extra night so you can take a day trip to the **Burgundy** (p218) wine region.

❹ BRUSSELS

No Brussels trip is complete without shopping for **chocolate** (p407), touring the **Grand Place** (p403) and wondering what all the fuss is about with **Manneken Pis** (p405). As for beers, Belgium brews more than 8000. Choose from at least 2000 at **Delirium Café** (p406).

❺ MUNICH

If Bavaria is beerland then its capital, Munich, is lager central. See the **Glockenspiel** (mechanical clock; p456) on Marienplatz, then stop into the kitsch **Hofbräuhaus** (p458) beer hall. The next day visit one, or three, of the beer gardens in **Englischer Garten** (p458).

❻ VIENNA

Just a few hours' train-ride east across the border and you're in Vienna where, after the fall harvest, the city's **Heurigen** (wine taverns vending 'new wine' made on-site; p480) are especially lively. Sit out in the garden and enjoy the effervescent vino and buffet victuals.

THE BIG ONE

THREE WEEKS LONDON TO İSTANBUL

This transcontinental grand tour is a lot to cram into three weeks, but the following cities offer more than enough masterpiece-filled museums, chic shopping, mouth-watering food and pulsing nightlife to make up for sore feet and lack of sleep.

❶ LONDON

Two days isn't a huge amount of time in a city with so much to do, but you should still be able to see highlights like the Tower, Tate Modern, Big Ben and Buckingham Palace as well as attend a **West End theatre show** (p92) and enjoy the ethnic eateries of the **East End** (p91).

❷ PARIS

A high-speed Channel Tunnel train takes you to the sights in **Paris** (p178). Overlooking the avenues from the Arc de Triomphe, seeing the Louvre or Versailles and a beautiful church or two is the least you can do. Try lively **Montmartre** (p195) for dinner.

❸ BARCELONA

An overnight ride of the rails and you're at your next stop, colourful Barcelona, where the organic Modernista architecture and Gaudí's **Sagrada Familia** (p273) will wow you. Don't miss the **Catalan cooking** (p274). Your first flight of the trip moves you along to…

LEFT: OLIVER STREWE; RIGHT: WILL SALTER

Left: Spires of La Sagrada Família (p238), Barcelona, Spain; Right: St Peter's Basilica (p320), Vatican City, Rome, Italy

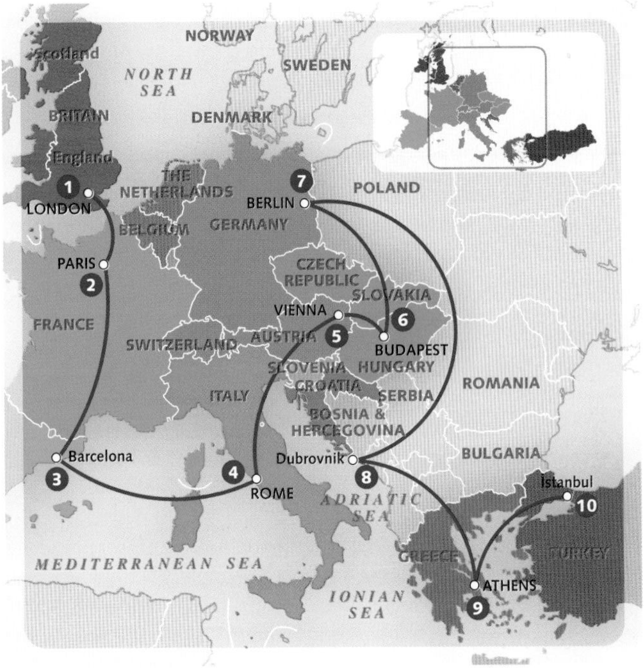

❹ ROME

The Eternal City; they say a lifetime isn't enough to know it. During two days sightseeing in **Rome** (p314), choose from among the monumental attractions of the Colosseum, Vatican City, Pantheon, Spanish Steps and the Trevi Fountain. Evenings you'll be eating out in the **centro storico** (p331) and **Trastevere** (p331).

❺ VIENNA

Overnight on the train to the imperial city of Vienna, where you'll linger in a **coffee house** (p480), watch the **Lipizzaner stallions** (p482), wander the pedestrian shopping streets and see a performance at the **Staatsoper** (p481).

❻ BUDAPEST

Just three hours away, Budapest also has a lively cafe culture, plus a vibrant mix of old and new. Be sure to visit **Castle Hill** (p585) and take a soak in one of the city's **thermal baths** (p587).

❼ BERLIN

A full day riding the rails brings you to the sights of **Berlin** (p436); must-sees include all the Berlin Wall galleries, memorials and museums, plus new city sights like the Sony Centre and Filmmuseum. To check out local **bars** (p444), Kreuzberg is the alternative nightlife hub, while Prenzlauer Berg is more grown up.

❽ DUBROVNIK

You'll have to board a plane in order to be dazzled by the marble streets and red roofs of Dubrovnik, Croatia. By all means, first walk the **city walls** (p642); the views over the town and sea are great. Explore the rest of the old town and take a seat at a cafe or along one of the **beaches** (p644).

❾ ATHENS

The Greek capital is a treasure trove of ancient ruins with the magnificent buildings of the hill-top **Acropolis** (p663) heading the list. Below it stand more impressive remains, plus bustling flea markets and lively tavernas giving you a taste of more modern Athenian life.

❿ İSTANBUL

Once you've touched down you've reached the edge of Europe, where East meets West. In **Old İstanbul** (p717) explore the Blue Mosque, Topkapı Palace and Aya Sofya. Then shop and dine in modern Beyoğlu, centre of the city's nightlife. A **boat ride** (p720) on the Bosphorus gives you the chance to step foot in Asia, looking back at the Europe you've just explored.

JOHN SONES

Houses and boats along the Bosphorus, İstanbul (p712), Turkey

➘ PLANNING YOUR TRIP

EUROPE'S BEST…

SACRED SPACES

- **Sistine Chapel** (p332) Michelangelo's masterpiece frescos in Vatican City, Rome.
- **Blue Mosque** (p717) Slender minarets and a cascade of domes surround a dramatic blue-tile interior in İstanbul.
- **Ancient Delphi** (p675) Where the oracle sat at the centre of the ancient Greek world.
- **Matthias Church** (p586) Colourful mosaic tile roof and interior murals on Castle Hill in Budapest.
- **Notre Dame** (p187) Paris' glorious Gothic cathedral with stained-glass rose windows.
- **Temple Bar** (p143) Dublin's party district, where the holy grail is Guinness.

BATHING BEAUTIES

- **Bath** (p104) Tour the ancient Roman Baths Museum in England.
- **Budapest** (p584) Bathe in the city's thermal hot spring spas.
- **Piešťany** (p576) Treat your skin to a thermal mud wrap or mirror pool soak in Slovakia.
- **İstanbul** (p719) Be massaged on marble in age-old *hammams*.
- **Baden-Baden** (p468) Take the cure at Germany's ritzy spa town.
- **Karlovy Vary** (p564) The Czech answer to Baden-Baden.

STONES THAT ROCK

- **Meteora** (p676) Rock pinnacle–topping monasteries in central Greece.
- **Stonehenge** (p103) A 5000-year-old indecipherable ring of giant stones.

RACHEL LEWIS

Cathédrale de Notre Dame de Paris (p187), Paris, France

- **Cappadocia** (p735) Houses and churches carved into startling rock pyramids and cones.
- **Carnac** (p209) More than 3000 ancient stones scattered across the French countryside.
- **Pompeii** (p360) A 2000-year-old southern Italian town frozen in time beneath volcanic pumice.
- **Mt Nemrut** (p739) Gigantic godhead statues carved atop a mountain in central Turkey.

PLACES YOU MAY NOT HAVE HEARD OF

- **Ghent, Belgium** (p410) A beautiful Belgian waterfront promenade, minus the crowds.
- **Zadar, Croatia** (p628) Marble-paved seaside Old Town with a hip, young vibe.
- **Kecskemét, Hungary** (p598) Art-nouveau architecture near a famous Hungarian horse show.
- **Safranbolu, Turkey** (p734) Unesco-recognised town filled with Ottoman half-timber houses.
- **Bratislava, Slovakia** (p571) A rabbit-warren Old Town filled with outdoor cafes.
- **Bern, Switzerland** (p506) Europe's most underrated capital.

GREEK & ROMAN RUINS

- **Acropolis** (p663) These hillside temples were at the centre of ancient Athenian society.
- **Diocletian's Palace** (p631) Dozens of bars, restaurants and shops inhabit an ancient, walled palace in Split, Croatia.
- **Colosseum** (p318) Ancient Rome's entertainment, this theatre once seated 50,000.
- **Pont du Gard** (p217) A 50m-long, intact aqueduct from 19 BC.
- **Ephesus** (p727) The best-preserved classical city in Turkey.
- **Hadrian's Wall** (p121) Remnants of the northernmost boundary of the Roman Empire, in England.

TOP-NOTCH MUSEUMS

- **British Museum, London** (p81) A treasure trove of Egyptian, Etruscan, Greek, Oriental and Roman artefacts.
- **Louvre, Paris** (p189) Mind-boggling array of art inside an equally impressive palace.
- **Rijksmuseum, Amsterdam** (p385) A master-filled collection valued in the billions.
- **Uffizi Gallery, Florence** (p354) The world's greatest assembly of Italian Renaissance art.
- **National Archaeological Museum, Athens** (p665) A vast collection from all the ancient civilisations across Greece.
- **Prado, Madrid** (p249) A seemingly endless parade of priceless art works from Spain and beyond.

LITERARY & ARTISTIC HAUNTS

- **Paris, France** (p196) What bar in Paris didn't Ernest Hemingway haunt?
- **Figueres, Spain** (p279) Home to Salvador Dalí and several of his surreal sights.
- **Salzburg, Austria** (p485) Native son Wolfgang Mozart's music is one of the town's claims to fame.
- **Prague, Czech Republic** (p546) Follow in Milan Kundera and Franz Kafka's footsteps.
- **Liverpool, England** (p124) The Beatles, the formative years.
- **Weimar, Germany** (p449) Bach, Liszt, Goethe and Nietzsche – just some of the luminaries who lived and worked here.

OFFBEAT BUILDINGS

- **KunstHausWien, Vienna** (p477) A colourful mishmash of purposely uneven floors, misshapen windows and industrial materials.
- **La Pedrera, Barcelona** (p275) Rooftop sculpture and organic lines from Antoni Gaudí.
- **Leaning Tower of Pisa** (p358) Tilting in Tuscany since 1173.
- **Overblaak, Rotterdam** (p397) Geometric houses, a bit like giant ice cubes tumbled together.
- **Atomium, Brussels** (p405) A 102m-tall molecule replica, complete with escalators in the connection tubes.
- **House of the Black Madonna, Prague** (p550) A cubist monument and museum.

ON THE WILDER SIDE

- **High Tatras, Slovakia** (p577) A pocket-size range of rocky alpine peaks and pine forests.
- **Ring of Kerry, Ireland** (p152) The circuit of Inverness Peninsula passes the Atlantic coast, beaches, mountains and lakes.
- **Mljet Island, Croatia** (p638) More than 70% forested, with two saltwater lakes.
- **Black Forest, Germany** (p465) Forests interspersed with bucolic farmers' fields.
- **Lesvos, Greece** (p690) A mountainous and fertile northeastern Aegean Island.
- **The Jura, Switzerland** (p523) Low, green mountains laced with 1200km of walking paths.

SHOPPING

- **Milan** (p338) Designer garb at the Golden Quad, cut rates at street markets.
- **Grand Bazaar, İstanbul** (p717) Four thousand shops, enough said.
- **Nuremberg** (p461) Germany's premier Christmas market.
- **Portobello Rd, London** (p95) Crowded street market filled with antiques.
- **Prague** (p546) Bohemian Moser crystal and more, in Nové Město.
- **Brussels** (p407) Chocolate, comics and lace all widely available.

MUSICAL MAYHEM

- **Flamenco, Spain** (p260, p284) Catch the passionate, foot-tapping music and dance in Madrid and across Andalucía.
- **Rembetika, Greece** (p670) Hear the blues-like Greek folk music in Athens and beyond.
- **Traditional Folk, Ireland** (p142) Listen to Irish folk at musical pubs across the green isle.
- **Fasıl, Turkey** (p722) Rousing Romani music played in İstanbullu clubs.
- **Sziget, Hungary** (p591) Budapest hosts Sziget, one of the biggest outdoor modern music festivals in Europe.
- **Edinburgh Military Tattoo, Scotland** (p131) Bag pipes and marching bands play a month-long schedule at Edinburgh Castle.

ICONIC EXPERIENCES

- **A trip around the London Eye** (p83) Touristy, but great South Bank views from a giant Ferris wheel.
- **Tasting French wine where it grows** (p218) Bordeaux, Burgundy, Champagne… Let your palate be your guide.
- **Island hopping in Greece** (p696) Take a ferry from Piraeus to the Cyclades, Crete, Corfu and more.
- **Puffing pot in Amsterdam** (p389) Mellow out in a 'coffee shop'.
- **Balloon ride over Cappadocia** (p737) Float over the ethereal fairy chimney rock formations in central Turkey.
- **An idle cafe day in Vienna** (p480) Idle over coffee and cake for hours at a turn-of-the-20th-century cafe.

ROBERTO GEROMETTA

High Tatras (p577), Slovakia

THINGS YOU NEED TO KNOW

AT A GLANCE

- **ATMS** Widely available in cities and towns, may be scarce in villages.
- **Credit cards** Visa and MasterCard more widely accepted than others; the smallest places may not accept any cards.
- **Currency** euro (€; Austria, Belgium, France, Germany, Greece, Ireland, Italy, Netherlands, Slovakia, Spain), pound (£; Britain), Swiss franc (Sfr; Switzerland), Czech crown (Kč; Czech Republic), forint (Ft; Hungary), kuna (KN; Croatia), Turkish lira (TL; Turkey)
- **Language** English spoken fairly widely in big cities, especially among the young, with the possible exception of France. See p797.
- **Tipping** Varies by country, 10% is a good general guideline.
- **Visas** Not required in most countries for most nationals; Turkey is the exception (see p741).

ACCOMMODATION

For more information on accommodation, see p746.

- **Pensions and guesthouses** Usually the most character-filled places; may be city centre or on the fringe, exude the owners' personality or be more businesslike.
- **Backpacker hostels** The boutique version of the dormitory fave; loads of services (sheets included, breakfast, laundry, internet, sightseeing), some private rooms.
- **Hotels** What you lose in character, you make up for in amenities, central location – and price.

ADVANCE PLANNING

- **Three months ahead** Start researching airfares to Europe. If you plan on travelling in July or August, book even further in advance. In other seasons, a month ahead might still get you a good deal.
- **One month ahead** Depending on how scheduled you plan to be, make hotel reservations. If you're winging it, at least book ahead your first and last nights in Europe.
- **Two weeks ahead** Book intra-European flights, but know that reserving even earlier will snag you a better fare.

BE FOREWARNED

- **Travel light** Flying within Europe, most airlines charge for the number of bags and the weight. On budget carriers the cost of lugging that Czech crystal along may be three times as much as your seat fare. Know the regulations.
- **Misplacing things happens** Keep a copy of your passport and drivers licence in a separate place from the real things. Of all the items we've lost, these are the trickiest two to replace.
- **August slowdown** Countries in the sunny climes, especially France, take their vacations in August; some restaurants and businesses close. In Athens, some

in-town bars and restaurants close up shop and move to the shore.

COSTS

- **under €100** You'll be staying in cheaper places, including some hostels, occasionally eating meals from food markets and choosing your museum admissions wisely.
- **€120** For this, or the equivalent, you can get around in comfort. Stay in pensions, eat at restaurants, take public transport and see the sights. You'll pay more in London and Switzerland, less in Turkey. Provincial areas cost generally at least 20% less than metropolises.
- **€300+** The sky's the limit when you want to stay in posh digs, eat at five-stars, rent a vehicle or add in a lot of last-minute flights.

EMERGENCY NUMBERS

- **European Union–wide emergency hotline** (☎ 112)

GETTING AROUND

For more information on getting around Europe, see p791.

- **Air** The proliferation of low-cost carriers across Europe has made it easier to cover a lot of ground in a short space of time.
- **Train** With the exception of Greece and Turkey, most of the countries in this book are really well connected by rail.
- **Buses** Long distances by bus may be a tad cheaper, but you'll trade in comfort. Buses are best used for mountainous or coastal routes not covered by rail, as in Croatia.

GETTING THERE & AWAY

For more information on getting to Europe, see 791.

- **European gateway airports** The airports in London, Frankfurt, Paris, Rome and Athens are among the major gateways, but most major European cities receive flights from abroad.

TECH STUFF

- **Electricity** Europe runs on 220-240V, 50Hz AC. This varies from that in the US and Canada; converters for appliances from those countries are necessary.

CHRISTOPHER GROENHOUT

Metro station entrance, Paris (p178), France

THINGS YOU NEED TO KNOW

- **Plugs** Most of Europe uses the two, round pin plug. Greece, Italy and Switzerland use a third round pin/receptacle in a way that the two-pin plug usually fits. The UK and Ireland use three-pin, square plugs. Adapters are available at airports.
- **Wi-fi** Wireless internet access is becoming more common across the continent – in hotels, bars, cafes and even on some public squares.
- **Internet cafes** As laptop computer and wi-fi use increases, the number of internet cafes decrease. Hotels often have business centres with computer access.

TRAVEL SEASONS

- **Skiing** The ski season in the Alps and in Slovakia's High Tatras runs from roughly December to March. Higher elevations may have slopes open earlier and later.
- **Summer holidays** July and August are the busiest times to travel in Europe; expect queues and booked-solid hotels. Plan ahead.

PAUL BERNHARDT

Flamenco dancer, Spain

WHAT TO BRING

- **Swiss Army knife** A multi-use tool often comes in handy for cutting bread or salami and opening beer and wine… Just remember to keep it in your checked luggage.
- **Antibacterial gel or wipes** Avoid swapping surface germs with a hoard of other travellers.
- **Travel-size detergent** You'll often wish you could wash something out in the sink.
- **Our language section** Saying *Jo napot* in Hungarian or toasting *prost* in German goes a long way towards making friends (p797).

WHEN TO GO

- **Spring** For most of Europe, April and May are springtime. Crowds are fewer, costs sometimes less, and the weather pleasant. (Though the mountains will still be cool.)
- **Autumn/fall** September and October are good, when crowds are down and seasonal attractions haven't closed for the winter yet.
- **Christmas** OK, so Christmas is an expensive, chilly, busy time to visit. But we just love all the Christmas markets and decorations, and there are usually added concerts this time of year.

GET INSPIRED

BOOKS

- **A Tramp Abroad** Mark Twain's humorous 1870s look at Europe on foot (free online at www.mtwain.com).
- **Europe 101: History and Art for the Traveller** Insight into all those artworks and churches.
- **Europe: A History** Professor Norman Davies boils European history down to one book.
- **In Europe: Travels through the 20th Century** Journalist Geert Mak travelled the continent the final year of the millennium.
- **Neither Here nor There** Bill Bryson retraces his European backpacking trip of 20 years before.
- **The Europe Book** Lonely Planet's full-colour grand pictorial tour.

FILMS

- **A Room with a View** (1985) EM Forrester's classic tale about an Englishwoman in the 1900s who travels to Italy and back.
- **Europe Trip** (2004) Youthful comedy about a post–break up, cross-Europe trip to meet a German pen pal.
- **European Vacation** (1985) Chevy Chase and the Griswalds' usual zaniness. 'Look, kids – Big Ben!'
- **From Russia with Love** (1963) James Bond 007 spy flick filmed in Turkey, Italy, England and Scotland.
- **Murder on the Orient Express** (1974) Inspector Poirot solves the puzzle en route from İstanbul to London.

MUSIC

- **European Jazz Masters** Tropical jazz, French pop, a Tuscan orchestra…
- **François-René Duchâble plays Bach, Beethoven, Scarlatti and Mozart** Classical music by Austrian, German and Italian composers.
- **German Drinking & Beer Garden Songs: 14 All-time Favorites** Learn 'em by heart.
- **Mediterranean Sunset** Blends traditional eastern instruments like the mandolin and bouzouki with Spanish guitar.
- **Putumayo Presents: Music from the Wine Lands** Sounds from southern countries like France, Spain and Italy.

WEBSITES

- **Arts in Europe** (www.artsineurope.com) On exhibits and art in Belgium, the Netherlands, Switzerland, Hungary, Spain and Germany.
- **Eurocheapo** (www.eurocheapo.com) Budget-friendly ideas for European travel.
- **Lonely Planet Community Blog** (www.lonelyplanet.com) Tips from the traveller community.
- **Restaurants in Europe** (www.foodeu.com) Articles, recipes, and those Michelin stars explained.
- **The Man in Seat 61** (www.seat61.com) Dream about travelling by train anywhere in Europe.

CALENDAR

CONOR CAFFREY

St Patrick's Day Parade, Dublin, Ireland

JANUARY

CAMEL WRESTLING TURKEY

Hoof it to **Selçuk** (p726) for camel wrestling on the last Sunday in January. The animals' natural inclination during mating season is to try to knock other male competitors down, which some say looks a bit like Sumo wrestling.

MARCH–APRIL

ST PATRICK'S DAY IRELAND

On March 17 towns big and small in Ireland celebrate St Patty's Day with parades and parties. But it's **Dublin** (p142) that really does it up, in a three-day-long cacophony of processions, fireworks and light shows.

SEMANA SANTA SPAIN

The week before Easter in **Seville** (p289), thousands of members of religious brotherhoods parade in penitents' garb with tall, pointed *capirotes* (hoods) accompanying sacred icons through the city, while huge crowds look on.

CARNAVAL/CARNEVALE/KARNEVAL/FASCHING PAN-EUROPEAN

The pre-Lenten season prior to Ash Wednesday is celebrated across Europe. **Venice** (p346) is known for its decorated masques and balls, in Germany the areas that celebrate the most are along the Rhine and in the Black Forest.

ORTHODOX EASTER GREECE

Easter (p694), which takes place on different days than those of the Western Christian church, is the most important festival on the Greek Orthodox calendar. Candle-lit processions happen all across the country on the Saturday before. Fireworks even figure into the joyful celebration.

MAY JUN JUL AUG SEP OCT NOV DEC

PLANING YOUR TRIP

CALENDAR

MAY–JUNE

PRAGUE SPRING
CZECH REPUBLIC

Czech composer Bedřich Smetana inspired this Prague classical music festival (p557), which kicks off with a parade from his grave to the performance hall where his opera, *Má vlast*, is staged. Performances are scheduled from mid-May to early June.

VIENNA FESTIVAL
AUSTRIA

Nearly 200 performances, representing 27 countries, are presented during this wide-ranging program of arts held in Vienna (p479) from mid-May to mid-June. The opening festivities involve a grand open-air presentation on stage in the Rathausplatz (City Hall Sq).

MARTIN MOOS

Semana Santa parade (p289), Seville, Spain

RICHARD CUMMINS

Cannes Film Festival, Cannes, France

CANNES FILM FESTIVAL
FRANCE

The uberfamous flock to Cannes (p226) for 11 glittering days in May. In addition to those films participating in the official competition, nearly 1000 more are screened in conjunction with the Marché du Film, the commercial arm of the festival.

KHAMORO
CZECH REPUBLIC

An annual festival of Romani music, dance and culture in Prague (p557). Music and dance play out in a colourful flourish for five days in May.

INMUSIC FESTIVAL
CROATIA

Two days in early June, rock, indie and punk bands take the stage in Zagreb (p624). Book your camping online, Jarun Island really fills up. Expect international acts like Moby and Artic Monkeys.

CALENDAR

CHRISTOPHER STREET DAY GERMANY

Begun in 1978, this celebration in **Berlin** (p444) is one of the oldest gay and lesbian festivals in the world. Events on the last weekend in June include a parade, stage shows and a disco corner.

İSTANBUL INTERNATIONAL MUSIC FESTIVAL TURKEY

Popular artists and orchestras perform in **İstanbul** (p720) throughout the month of June. Recent headliners have included the prestigious Italian philharmonic Dela Scala, and U2. Some of the venues – like the Aya İrini Kilisesi, a Byzantine church – are not open the rest of the year.

JULY–AUGUST

IL PALIO ITALY

Siena (p359) stages a pageant-filled bareback horse race on 2 July and 16 August. On the tight turns in the packed Piazza del Campo, the jockey is lucky to hang on. No worries, it's the horse that wins – with or without a rider.

SUMMER FESTIVALS CROATIA

Dubrovnik, Split and **Zagreb** (p624) host month-long events, with music, dance and theatre performances at venues around the towns.

HELLENIC FESTIVAL GREECE

Music, theatre, dance – July and August in **Athens** (p665) are chock full of performances. Many are made even more special by the ancient Greek outdoor theatre venues.

HISTORIC KIRKPINAR OIL WRESTLING FESTIVAL TURKEY

Muscular men, naked except for a pair of heavy leather pants, coat themselves with olive oil and throw each other around for three early-July days

DALLAS STRIBLEY

Parade at Il Palio (p359), Siena, Italy

TIM HUGHES

Sziget Music Festival (p591), Hungary

in Edirne (p723). The tradition started back in 1640; today about 1000 wrestlers compete.

MONTREUX JAZZ FESTIVAL

SWITZERLAND

Since 1967, for a fortnight in early July, big-name rock and jazz acts have played at the Montreux Jazz Festival (p504). An all-inclusive week pass (just Sfr1500) gets you into every sold-out show.

KARLOVY VARY INTERNATIONAL FILM FESTIVAL

CZECH REPUBLIC

International celebrities often appear at this Czech Republic festival in Karlovy Vary (p564). More than 200 films are screened each year in early July. Concurrent world-music concerts, food stands and street performances liven up what is usually a pretty sleepy town.

RUNNING OF THE BULLS

SPAIN

Risk life and limb as Hemingway did at the *Sanfermines*, or Running of the Bulls, in Pamplona (p283) from 6 to 14 July. Though the daily race lasts only three minutes, the bulls' hooves get little traction on cobblestone and injuries to man and animal are common. Find a hotel room with a balcony view.

SZIGET MUSIC FESTIVAL

HUNGARY

The week-long music bash in Budapest (p591) features bands from around the world playing at more than 60 venues on Óbuda Island in late July or early August.

CHRISTIAN ASLUND

Running of the Bulls (p283), Pamplona, Spain

CALENDAR

JAN FEB MAR APR

STREET PARADE SWITZERLAND

Zürich (p520) lets its hair down with an enormous techno parade. Peace and love are the themes at this ove r-the-top August event.

NOTTING HILL CARNIVAL BRITAIN

This massive, multicultural street fair in **London** (p87) takes over for two days in August. The carnival shows off its Caribbean colours with vibrant costumes and dance.

EDINBURGH FESTIVAL FRINGE BRITAIN

Three weeks in late August, the biggest festival of the performing arts anywhere in the world plays out in **Edinburgh** (p131). Experimental theatre is complimented by mainstream drama, comedy and dance.

JONATHAN SMITH

Edinburgh Festival Fringe (p131), Britain

KRZYSZTOF DYDYNSKI

Musicians at Oktoberfest (p455), Munich, Germany

SEPTEMBER–OCTOBER

OKTOBERFEST GERMANY

Some six million people guzzle five million litres of beer and gobble 400,000 sausages each September in **Munich** (p455). Music and madness abound in ginormous tents, each with their own character.

VENICE INTERNATIONAL FILM FESTIVAL ITALY

The Mostra del Cinema di Venezia is a huge indie film fest held during 11 September days in **Venice** (p346). More than 200 screenings take place annually.

REGATA STORICA ITALY

The first weekend in September, a flotilla of carved dragonhead boats parades down the Grand Canal in **Venice** (p346). The races follow as men, women and boys in period costumes row two- to eight-person boats across the finish line.

FESTES DE LA MERCÈ SPAIN

On and around 24 September, **Barcelona** (p273) celebrates in honour of its patron saint. Fireworks, concerts, jugglers and acrobats are just the beginning. Here *castellers* climb aloft one another to create human 'castles' and the *correfocs* parade features fireworks-spitting dragons and devils.

GALWAY OYSTER FESTIVAL IRELAND

Thousands of visitors converge on the town of **Galway** (p154) during late September to drink Guinness and eat oysters. Festival events include an oyster-opening contest, balls, parties and tastings.

NOVEMBER–DECEMBER

CHRISTMAS MARKETS PAN-EUROPEAN

Winter Christmas markets are held in places across Europe. The most famous ones are in **Vienna** (p479) and **Nuremberg** (p461) but even smaller towns host crafts-and-food fairs from mid-November to Christmas. Drink mulled wine, munch on sausages and hunt for that perfect unique (or kitschy) present.

NATALE ITALY

Churches in **Italy** (p301) set up intricate cribs or *presepi* (nativity scenes) in the lead-up to the Christmas celebrations. Parishes within a town often compete with each other for who has the best displays, and visitors go from church to church comparing.

ROBERTO GEROMETTA

Regata Storica (p346), Venice, Italy

BRITAIN & IRELAND

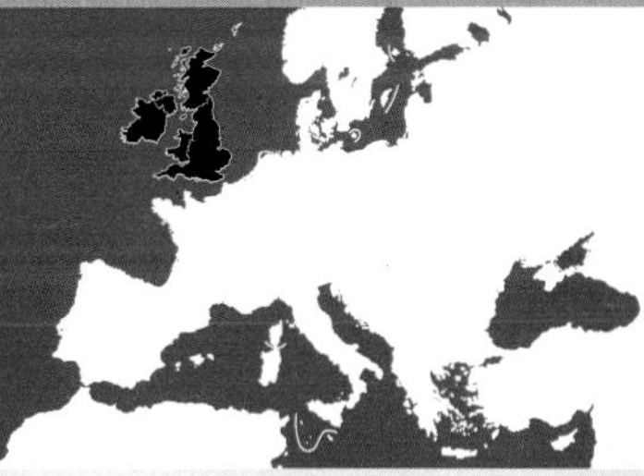

BRITAIN

0 — 100 km
0 — 50 miles

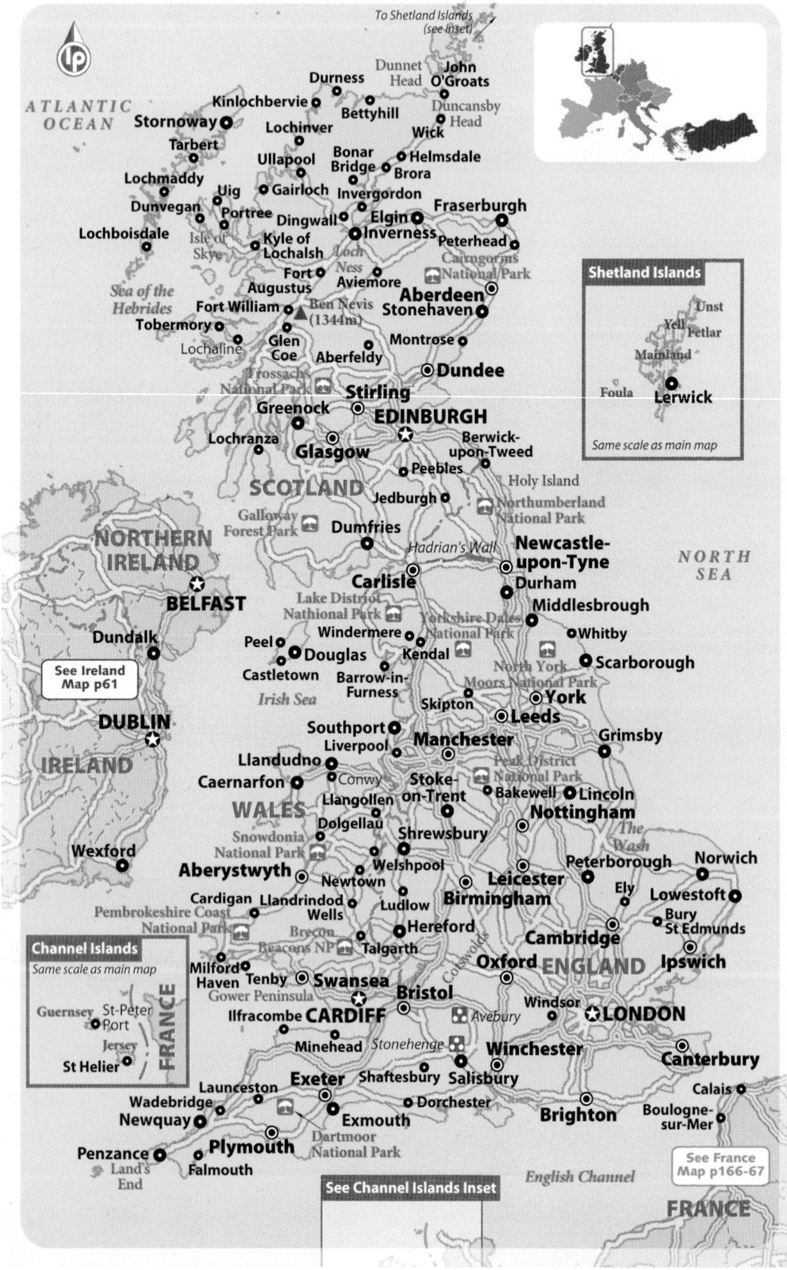

IRELAND

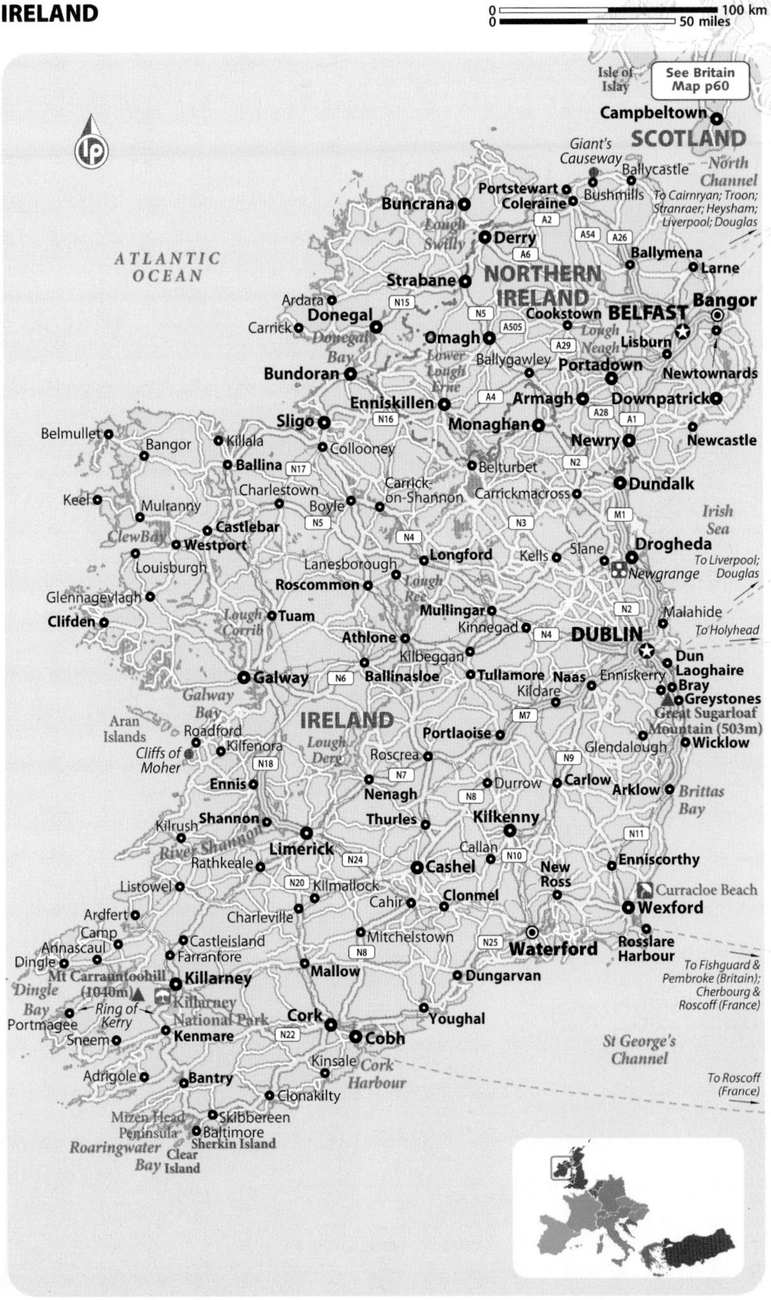
0
0
100 km
50 miles
Isle of Islay
See Britain Map p60
Campbeltown
SCOTLAND
Giant's Causeway
Ballycastle
North Channel
Portstewart
Bushmills
Coleraine
To Cairnryan; Troon; Stranraer; Heysham; Liverpool; Douglas
Buncrana
A2
Lough Swilly
Derry
A54
A26
A6
Ballymena
Larne
ATLANTIC OCEAN
Strabane
NORTHERN IRELAND
Ardara
N15
Bangor
Donegal
N5
Cookstown
BELFAST
Carrick
A505
Lough Neagh
Donegal Bay
Omagh
A29
Lisburn
Lower Lough Erne
Ballygawley
Portadown
Bundoran
Newtownards
A4
Armagh
Downpatrick
Enniskillen
A28
Sligo
N16
A1
Monaghan
Belmullet
Killala
Newry
Newcastle
Bangor
Collooney
Ballina
N17
Belturbet
N2
Dundalk
Carrick-on-Shannon
Charlestown
Carrickmacross
Keel
Boyle
Mulranny
N5
M1
Irish Sea
Castlebar
N3
Clew Bay
N4
Westport
Drogheda
Slane
Longford
Kells
Louisburgh
Lanesborough
Newgrange
To Liverpool; Douglas
Lough Ree
Roscommon
Glennagevlagh
Mullingar
N2
Malahide
Lough Corrib
Tuam
Clifden
Kinnegad
N4
DUBLIN
To Holyhead
Athlone
Kilbeggan
Dun Laoghaire
Galway
N6
Ballinasloe
Tullamore
Naas
Enniskerry
Bray
Kildare
Greystones
Galway Bay
Great Sugarloaf Mountain (503m)
Aran Islands
IRELAND
M7
Roadford
Portlaoise
Lough Derg
Wicklow
Cliffs of Moher
Kilfenora
Glendalough
Roscrea
N18
N9
N7
Ennis
Durrow
Carlow
Nenagh
Arklow
Brittas Bay
N8
Shannon
Thurles
Kilkenny
Kilrush
Limerick
N11
River Shannon
Callan
Rathkeale
N24
N10
Cashel
New Ross
Enniscorthy
N20
Kilmallock
Listowel
Curracloe Beach
Clonmel
Cahir
Ardfert
Wexford
Charleville
Camp
Mitchelstown
Annascaul
Castleisland
Rosslare Harbour
N25
Waterford
Dingle
Farranfore
N8
To Fishguard & Pembroke (Britain); Cherbourg & Roscoff (France)
Mallow
Mt Carrauntoohill (1040m)
Killarney
Dungarvan
Dingle Bay
Killarney National Park
Ring of Kerry
Youghal
Portmagee
Cork
Kenmare
N22
Cobh
Sneem
St George's Channel
Kinsale
Cork Harbour
Adrigole
Bantry
To Roscoff (France)
Clonakilty
Mizen Head Peninsula
Skibbereen
Baltimore
Sherkin Island
Roaringwater Bay
Clear Island

HIGHLIGHTS

1 THE TOWER OF LONDON

BY JOHN KEOHANE, CHIEF YEOMAN WARDER AT THE TOWER OF LONDON

The Yeomen Warders (or Beefeaters, as we're often known) have been a part of the Tower's history since at least 1485. To qualify, you must have served at least 22 years in the armed forces and have earned a Long Service and Good Conduct medal.

↘ JOHN KEOHANE'S DON'T MISS LIST

❶ A TOWER TOUR

To understand the Tower and its history, a guided tour with one of the Yeomen Warders is essential. The tower is actually our home as well as our place of work; all the Warders live inside the outer walls, which once housed stables and workshops. It's rather like a miniature village – visitors are often surprised to see our washing hanging out!

❷ THE CROWN JEWELS

Visitors often think the Crown Jewels are the Queen's personal jewellery collection, but they're actually the ceremonial regalia used during the coronation. Highlights are the sceptre and the Imperial State Crown. The Crown Jewels aren't insured (as they could never be replaced).

❸ THE WHITE TOWER

The White Tower is the original royal palace of the Tower of London, but it

Clockwise from top: Sightseers, Tower of London; Close-up of the Tower; Guard on alert; Changing of the guard; Tower view from the Thames

CLOCKWISE FROM TOP: WAYNE WALTON; NEIL SETCHFIELD; BRIAN CRUICKSHANK; VERONICA GARBUTT; DOUG MCKINLAY

hasn't been used as a royal residence since 1603. It's the most iconic building in the Tower complex – inside you can see various exhibits from the Royal Armouries, including a suit of armour belonging to Henry VIII.

❹ THE RAVENS

Legend states that if the Tower's resident ravens ever leave, the monarchy will topple, so a royal decree states that we must keep a minimum of six ravens at any time. We currently have nine ravens, looked after by the Ravenmaster and his two assistants.

❺ THE CEREMONY OF THE KEYS

We hold three daily ceremonies: the official opening at 9am, the Ceremony of the Word (when the day's password is issued), and the Ceremony of the Keys at 10pm, when the gates are locked after the castle has closed to the public. Visitors are welcome to attend the Ceremony of the Keys, but they must apply directly to the Tower in writing.

➘ THINGS YOU NEED TO KNOW

Top tip Booking online will allow you to dodge the queues **Photo op** Standing on the battlements overlooking the Thames **Did you know?** The Yeoman Warders' famous red-and-gold ceremonial outfits cost around £7000 **See our author's review on p82**

HIGHLIGHTS

2

↘ THE TATE MODERN

Housed in a converted warehouse on the south bank of the Thames, this amazing **art gallery** (p82) has become one of London's best-loved landmarks since it opened in 2000. Works by all the big names of modern art (from Andy Warhol to Mark Wallinger) appear somewhere on the gallery's five floors, and you can't possibly miss the gigantic exhibitions in the great Turbine Hall.

3

↘ BATH

Say what you like about the Romans, but one thing's for sure – they knew how to build a hot tub. Bath's **hot springs** (p104) have been a tourist magnet for over two millennia, but this bewitching city has so much more to offer than a soothing soak: great restaurants, lively bars, top-notch shopping and some of the finest Georgian streets in all of England.

4

↘ CASTLE HOWARD

If you've only got time to visit one stately home, make it **Castle Howard** (p119). The Duke of Devonshire's ancestral seat is a showstopper, and has served as an architectural benchmark for the rest of the nation since the 18th century.

5

↘ DUBLIN

What's not to love about **Dublin** (p142)? Ireland's capital city has galleries galore, museums aplenty and pubs by the pint-load, and if you've got a soft spot for the black stuff, there's nowhere better to down a few draughts of Guinness

6

↘ EDINBURGH

If it's historical clout you're after, you won't want to miss **Edinburgh** (p130). Built around the remains of a long-extinct volcano, the city's elegant streets are packed with fascinating sights. If you happen to pitch up in August, you'll find yourself smack-bang in the middle of the world's largest arts festival.

2 NEIL SETCHFIELD; 3 JON DAVISON; 4 JOE CORNISH/PHOTOLIBRARY.COM; 5 DOUG MCKINLAY; 6 JONATHAN SMITH

2 Turbine Hall, Tate Modern (p82); 3 Sign to Bath's hot springs (p104); 4 Castle Howard (p119); 5 View of Edinburgh from Arthur's Seat (p131); 6 Traditional Irish music performance in a pub in Dublin (p142)

THE BEST…

BEAUTY SPOTS

- **The Lake District** (p126) Where the Romantics got inspired.
- **The Cairngorms** (p140) Scotland's wildest landscape.
- **The Ring of Kerry** (p152) Scenic driving in southern Ireland.
- **Snowdonia** (p129) Wales' highest peaks.
- **The Yorkshire Dales** (p118) Green, grand and gorgeous.

LANDMARKS

- **The Eden Project** (p109) Space-age biomes in a Cornish claypit.
- **The Houses of Parliament** (p80) Britain's political seat of power.
- **Stonehenge** (p103) The world's most famous stone circle.
- **The Angel of the North** (p120) Antony Gormley's winged icon.
- **The Giant's Causeway** (p156) Northern Ireland's geological oddity.

CASTLES

- **Windsor Castle** (p98) The Queen's weekend retreat.
- **Leeds Castle** (p101) England's finest fortress? You decide.
- **Edinburgh Castle** (p130) Climb the battlements for panoramic views.
- **Conwy Castle** (p129) The quintessential Welsh castle.
- **Blarney Castle** (p152) Stop yer blabbing and kiss the stone.

URBAN EXPERIENCES

- **Brighton** (p101) Party till dawn in Brighton's bars.
- **Newcastle** (p119) Get artistic at the Baltic, cultural at the Sage and tipsy in Ouseburn.
- **Glasgow** (p135) Admire Charles Rennie Mackintosh's home town.
- **Oxford** (p109) Visit Oxford's celebrated colleges.
- **Galway** (p153) Catch an Irish jig in Galway's pubs.

LEFT: GLENN BEANLAND; RIGHT: MICAH WRIGHT

Left: Stonehenge (p103); Right: Conwy Castle (p129)

THINGS YOU NEED TO KNOW

AT A GLANCE

- **Population** 66 million
- **Official languages** English, Cymraeg (Welsh), Gàidhlig (Scotland), Gaelige (Ireland)
- **Currency** Pound (£; UK), euro (€; Ireland)
- **Telephone codes** ☎44 (UK), ☎353 (Ireland)
- **When to go** Spring and autumn are best for travelling, but bring rain gear
- **Tipping** 10% to 15% in restaurants
- **Tax** VAT (Value Added Tax) is included in most purchases at 17.5%

REGIONS IN A NUTSHELL

- **London** (p72) The big smoke has big thrills to match.
- **Southeast England** (p98) From Dover's white cliffs to Brighton's non-stop nightlife.
- **Southwest England** (p103) Coast and countryside.
- **Central England** (p109) The cradle of English industry.
- **Northern England** (p116) Rolling dales, windswept hills and revitalised cities.
- **Southern & Central Scotland** (p129) Castle and abbey country.
- **The Highlands** (p140) Picture-postcard Scotland: lochs, mountains and glens galore.
- **Ireland** (p142) Explore the Emerald Isle.
- **Northern Ireland** (p156) Ireland with a difference.

ADVANCE PLANNING

- **Two months before** Book hotels for London, Bath, York, Edinburgh and Dublin.
- **One month before** Arrange train tickets, ferry travel and car hire.
- **Two weeks before** Confirm opening times, prices and tours.

BE FOREWARNED

- **Train travel** Buy in advance and travel off-peak for cheapest fares.
- **Traffic** Rush hour, ring roads and bank holidays equal traffic jams.
- **Nightlife** City centres get rowdy after dark on weekends.
- **Public holidays** Christmas and Easter are the main ones.

BUSINESS HOURS

- **Offices and banks** (9am-5pm Mon-Fri)
- **Shops** (9am-5pm Mon-Sat, many also open 10am-4pm on Sun)
- **Restaurants** (lunch 11am-3pm, dinner 6pm-10pm)
- **Pubs** (11am-11pm Mon-Sat, to 10pm Sun)

COSTS

Britain

- **Under £100 per day** Budget B&Bs and restaurants.
- **£100 to £200** Quality B&Bs and hotels, with cash to spare for attractions.
- **More than £200** Top-notch hotels, top-rated restaurants and top-dollar sights.

THINGS YOU NEED TO KNOW

Ireland

- **Under €120 per day** Ireland on a shoestring
- **€120 to €200** Should cover most mid-range hotels and restaurants
- **€200+** The Emerald Isle with top-end trimmings

EMERGENCY NUMBERS

- **Police/Fire/Ambulance** (☎ 999)
- **Samaritans** (☎ 0845-790 9090)

GETTING AROUND

- **Air** (p161) Britain's major airports are London Heathrow and London Gatwick; budget carriers often use the capital's smaller airports (London City, Luton and Stansted), or regional airports (Newcastle, Liverpool, Manchester, Glasgow, Edinburgh). Ireland's main airports are in Dublin, Belfast and Cork.
- **Bus** (p162) Intercity coaches and buses are cheap but slow. Coverage can be patchy outside towns.
- **Car** Be prepared for parking headaches and traffic jams. See p162 for information on car travel around Britain and Ireland.
- **Train** (p163) The Eurostar connects London St Pancras with Paris and Brussels, or you can travel with your car on the train using Eurotunnel.
- **Sea** (p160) Car ferries serve ports including Dover, Portsmouth, Weymouth, Newcastle and Liverpool, plus Dublin and Rosslare in Ireland.

MEDIA

- **TV** Major UK broadcasters are BBC, ITV, C4 and satellite-only Sky; Ireland's big boys are RTE and TV3.
- **Radio** BBC Radio 1–4 (FM) & Five Live (MW) plus digital stations; commercial stations include Virgin Radio and Classic FM.
- **Newspapers** Tabloids (*The Sun, Daily Star*), serious 'broadsheets' (*The Guardian, The Times, The Independent*) and in-betweens (*Daily Mail, Daily Express*).

RESOURCES

- **Visit Britain** (www.visitbritain.com) Britain's tourism body.
- **Fáilte Ireland** (www.discoverireland.ie) The Irish tourist board.
- **Northern Ireland Tourist Board** (NITB; www.discovernorthernireland.com) Ditto for Northern Ireland.
- **Tourism Ireland** (www.tourismireland.com) Both Irish tourist boards.

VISAS

- **EU nationals** Free to work or visit Britain and Ireland.
- **Citizens of Australia, Canada, New Zealand, South Africa and the US** Can stay for three to six months without a visa.
- **Citizens of other countries** Will need a visa. See www.ukvisas.gov.uk or www.ukba.homeoffice.gov.uk

GET INSPIRED

BOOKS

- **Oliver Twist** (1837) Fagin, the Artful Dodger – need we say more?
- **Cider with Rosie** (1959) Laurie Lee's childhood memoir.
- **McCarthy's Bar** (1998) McCarthy drinks in bars that bear his name.
- **The English** (1999) Journo Jeremy Paxman on Englishness.
- **White Teeth** (2000) Zadie Smith on multicultural London.

FILMS

- **Brief Encounter** (1945) David Lean's tale of unrequited love.
- **Withnail & I** (1986) Cult comedy about out-of-work thesps.
- **Trainspotting** (1996) Irvine Welsh's heroin classic gets the cinematic treatment.
- **Shaun of the Dead** (2004) Brit zombie-comedy.
- **The Commitments** (1991) Irish no-hopers form a band.
- **Once** (2007) Heart-warming Dublin-set rom-com.

MUSIC

- **Sergeant Pepper's Lonely Hearts Club Band** (The Beatles) The Fab Four's finest moment.
- **The Village Green Preservation Society** (The Kinks) Poppy melodies and wry observations.
- **Different Class** (Pulp) Tales of English eccentricity from Jarvis Cocker.
- **Astral Weeks** (Van Morrison) Van's yer man.
- **Tonight: Franz Ferdinand** (Franz Ferdinand) Latest album from innovative Scot rockers.

WEBSITES

- **BBC** (www.bbc.co.uk) News and entertainment.
- **British Council** (www.britishcouncil.org) British culture, arts and science.
- **National Rail** (www.nationalrail.co.uk) Online train travel.
- **Traveline** (www.traveline.org.uk) UK-wide public transport.
- **UK Tea Council** (www.tea.co.uk) The national tipple.

LEFT: NEIL SETCHFIELD; RIGHT: STEPHEN SAKS

Left: Police box and warden, Glasgow (p135); Right: Giant's Causeway (p156)

ITINERARIES

THE BIG SMOKE & BEYOND Three Days

Let's face it – every British adventure simply has to begin in **(1) Londo** (p72). The capital is stuffed with attractions to suit all sorts, but ther are a few mustn't-miss essentials: on the first day you could just abou fit in **Westminster** (p77), **St Paul's** (p81), the **Tower of London** (p82, **Trafalgar Square** (p77) and the **British Museum** (p81), and spen the evening catching a performance at **Shakespeare's Globe** (p83). On day two, concentrate on exploring another area: perhaps chich **Kensington** and **Knightsbridge** (p83) for shopping and muse-ums, the **West End** (p76) for theatre and retail therapy, or gracefu **Greenwich** (p85) for maritime history. On the last day, pack a picni and hop on a boat down the Thames to Henry VIII's country pad a **Hampton Court** (p86), or brush up on your botanical knowledge a **Kew Gardens** (p86).

NORTHERN ADVENTURE Five Days

This northerly trip begins with a day in either **(1) Manchester** (p122 or **(2) Liverpool** (p124). After decades in the post-industrial doldrums both cities have smartened up their act and now boast some of th nation's top museums, galleries and restaurants. On day two, detou via the gorgeous Viking city of **(3) York** (p116) and **(4) Castle Howar** (p119), the stunning stately home, before spending a couple of day hiking the hills and valleys of the **(5) Yorkshire Dales** (p118) and th fells of the **(6) Lake District** (p126). While away a day in revitalise **(7) Newcastle** (p119). Make sure you allow plenty of time for the art a the **Baltic** (p119), the refurbished **Great North Museum** (p120) and pilgrimage to Antony Gormley's world-renowned **Angel of the Nort** sculpture (p120) before heading across the Scottish border for a visi to either **(8) Edinburgh** (p130) or **(9) Glasgow** (p135).

THREE NATIONS One Week

This three-country itinerary begins in the city of dreaming spires **(1) Oxford** (p109). This stately beauty has been setting the academi standard for the nation for well over eight centuries, but these days it' as well known for its lively nightlife as its scholarly credentials. Ther it's on to the birthplace of the Bard, **(2) Stratford-upon-Avon** (p111) where you'll find a host of Shakespeare-themed sights as well as th home base for the world-renowned **Royal Shakespeare Company** (p113). Once you've had your Shakespeare fix, cross over the Welsh border and drink in the stunning scenery as you drive through the **(3) Brecon Beacons** (p128). In nearby **(4) Snowdonia** (p129), steely legged walkers can tackle Wales' loftiest summit, **(5) Mt Snowdon** (p129), while less energetic types can catch a ride to the top courtesy

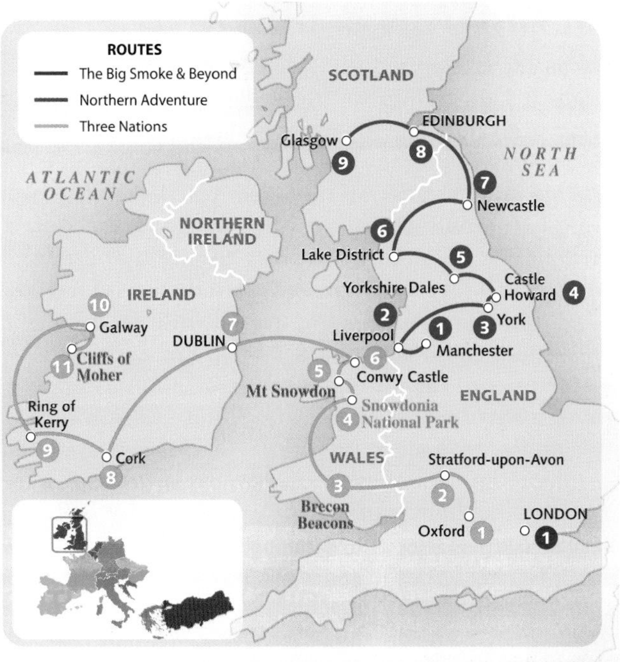

›f the Snowdon Mountain Railway (p129). After a wander along the ›attlements of (6) Conwy Castle (p129), head for Holyhead and catch ›he ferry across the Irish Sea to delightful (7) Dublin (p142), where you ›an easily spend a couple of days exploring the museums and guzzling ›uinness in Temple Bar. Head down for a day in Ireland's 'real capital', ›8) Cork (p150), before heading west to the idyllic (9) Ring of Kerry ›p152) and the quintessentially Celtic town of (10) Galway (p153) ›efore reaching journey's end at the (11) Cliffs of Moher (p153). *Slán ›gat*, Ireland – next stop, America…

DISCOVER BRITAIN & IRELAND

Few countries are as cliché-plagued as Britain and Ireland. On one side of the Irish Sea, it's all shamrocks and shillelaghs, Guinness and 40 shades of green; over in Britain, it's double-decker buses and red telephone boxes, buttoned-up emotions and stiff upper lips. But while some of the old stereotypes still ring true, you'll soon discover these neighbouring island nations have a whole lot more to offer.

Whether it's ancient history or contemporary culture that draws you to these shores, you'll find you're never more than a train ride away from the next national park, historic castle, world-class gallery or stately home. London, Edinburgh and Dublin are as exciting as ever; York, Cork, Oxford and Cambridge are chock-full of history; and up-and-coming towns such as Newcastle, Cardiff, Glasgow and Galway have a life and energy all of their own. There are museums aplenty, galleries galore and some of Europe's most stunning coastlines and countryside. Buckle up, chaps – you're in for an awfully big adventure.

BRITAIN

LONDON

☎ 020 / pop 7.5 million

One of the world's greatest cities, London has enough history, vitality and cultural drive to keep most visitors occupied for weeks. In recent years this most cosmopolitan of capitals has led international trends in music, fashion and the arts, riding a wave of 21st-century British confidence. The downside of this renaissance, of course, is increasing cost: London is now Europe's most expensive city for visitors, but with some careful planning and a bit of common sense, you can find great bargains and freebies among the attractions.

HISTORY

London first came into being as a Celtic village, possibly called Lundyn, near a ford across the River Thames. In the Roman era the settlement – now called Londinium – became properly established, enclosed in protective walls with four main entrances still echoed today in the shape of the City financial district, and the areas of Ludgate, Aldgate, Bishopsgate and Newgate.

London grew prosperous and increased in global importance throughout the medieval period, surviving devastating challenges like the 1665 Plague and 1666 Great Fire. By 1720 London had 750,000 inhabitants and was the centre of a growing world empire. In contrast, WWII was London's darkest hour, with the city on the edge of destruction after relentless bombing.

The ugly postwar rebuilding phase of the 1950s gave way to the cultural renaissance of the 1960s when London became the planet's undisputed swinging capital. Things dipped again during the 1970s, while the 1980s heralded a time of great plenty for some Londoners and hardship for others.

In 2000 the modern metropolis of London got its first elected mayor and is set to host the Olympic Games in 2012.

WAYNE WALTON

Boys play on bikes outside a London pub

ORIENTATION

The busy M25 circular ring road encompasses the area broadly regarded as Greater London. Cutting the circle in two is the city's main geographical feature – the famous River Thames. To the north of the river is the highly walkable **Westminster** area. To the east of Westminster, the **City** (note the big 'C') is the capital's financial district, covering roughly a square mile bordered by the Thames and the ancient (but long gone) city walls. The areas to the east of the City are collectively known as the **East End**. The **West End**, on the City's other flank, is effectively the centre of London nowadays.

MAPS

No Londoner would be without a handy, pocket-sized *London A-Z* map book. For getting around the London Underground system (also known as the 'tube') pick up a 'tube map' for free at underground stations.

INFORMATION

INTERNET RESOURCES

BBC London (www.bbc.co.uk/london)
Evening Standard (www.thisislondon.co.uk)
Londonist (www.londonist.com)
Time Out (www.timeout.com/london)
View London (www.viewlondon.co.uk)

MEDIA

It's hard to avoid London's free press, with vendors pushing freebies in your face outside every central tube stop on weekdays. The city's only real paper is the tabloid *Evening Standard,* which comes out in early and late editions. *Time Out* (£2.95) is the excellent local listing guide, published every Tuesday.

MEDICAL SERVICES

Royal Free Hospital (Map pp74-5; ☎ 7794 0500; Pond St NW3; ⊖ Belsize Park)
St Thomas' Hospital (Map pp78-9; ☎ 7188 7188; Lambeth Palace Rd SE1; ⊖ Waterloo)
University College Hospital (Map pp78-9; ☎ 0845 155 5000; 235 Euston Rd WC1; ⊖ Euston Sq)

GREATER LONDON

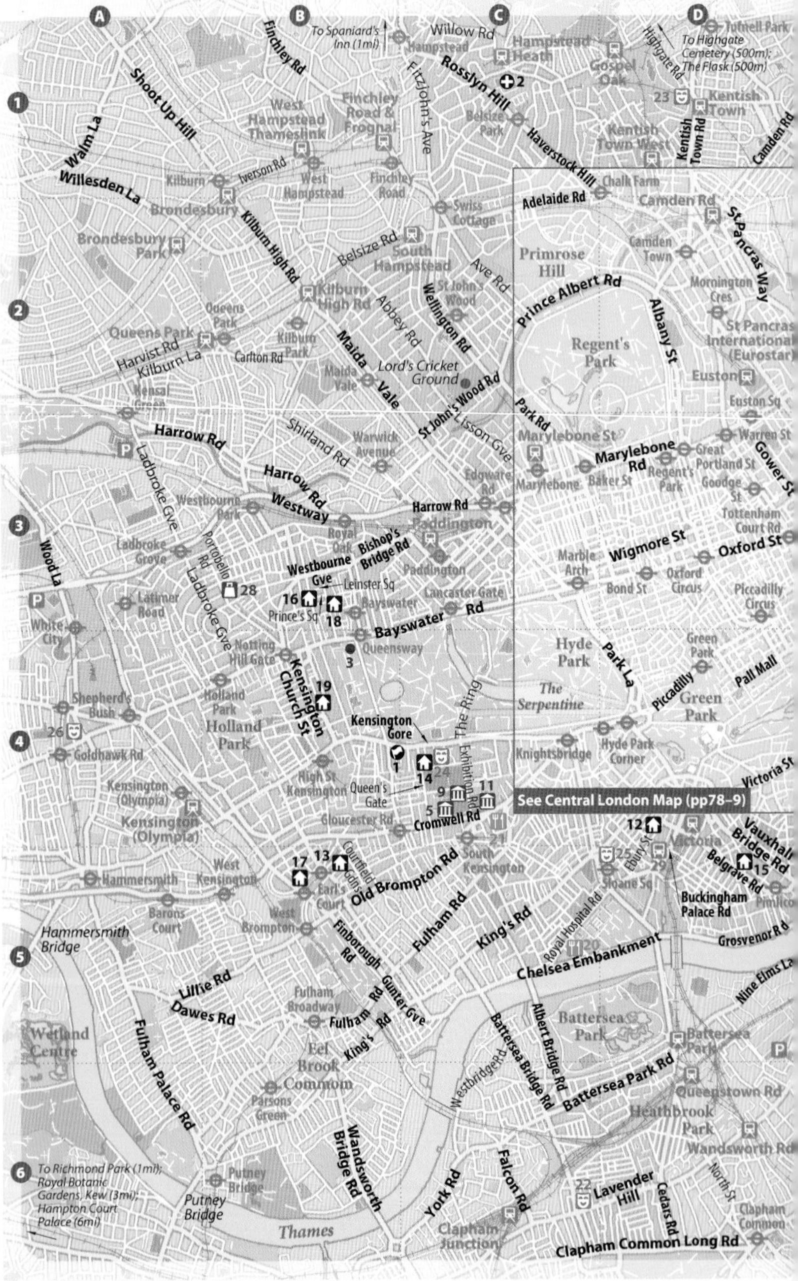

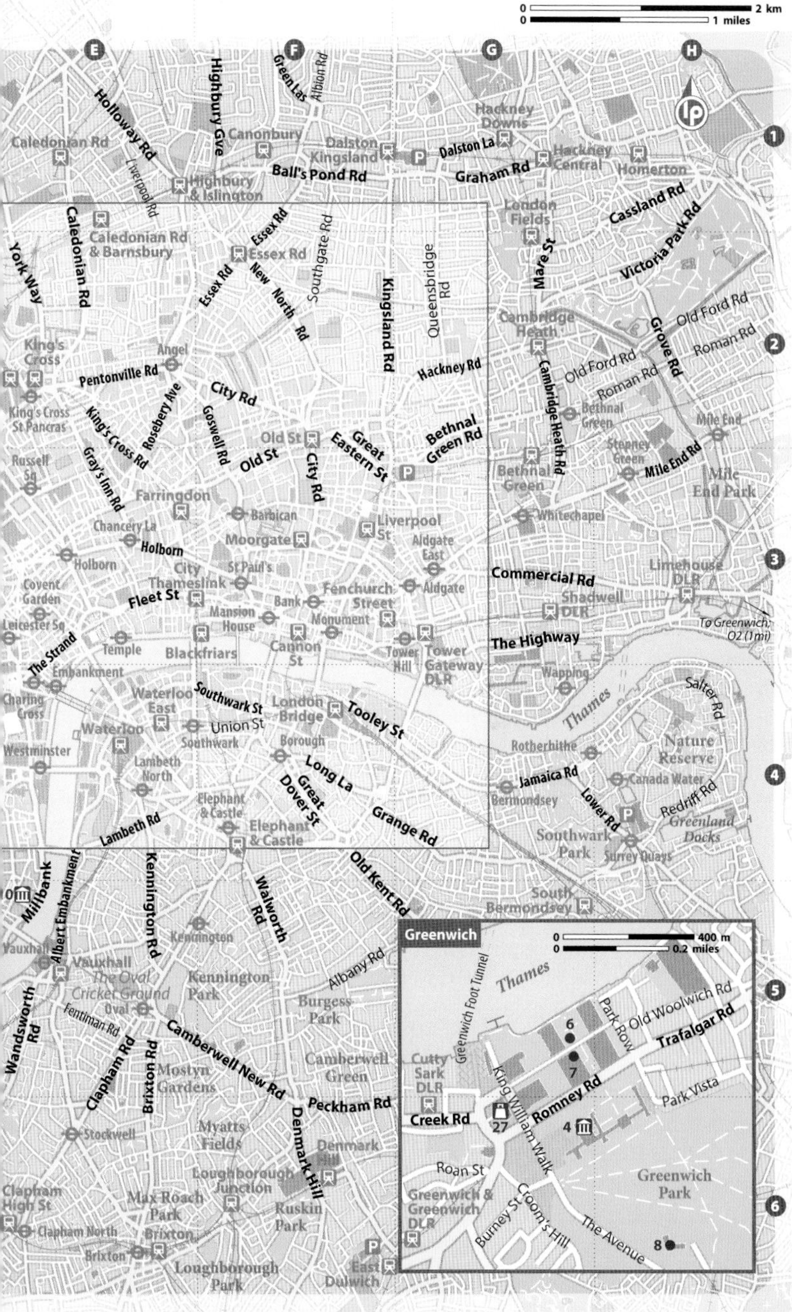
0 2 km
0 1 miles
E
F
G
H
1
2
3
4
5
6
Holloway Rd
Highbury Gve
Green Las
Albion Rd
Hackney Downs
Caledonian Rd
Canonbury
Dalston Kingsland
Dalston La
Hackney Central
Homerton
Liverpool Rd
Highbury & Islington
Ball's Pond Rd
Graham Rd
London Fields
Cassland Rd
Victoria Park Rd
Caledonian Rd & Barnsbury
Essex Rd
Southgate Rd
Queensbridge Rd
Mare St
York Way
Caledonian Rd
New North Rd
Kingsland Rd
Cambridge Heath
Old Ford Rd
Roman Rd
Grove Rd
King's Cross
Angel
Pentonville Rd
City Rd
Hackney Rd
Cambridge Heath Rd
Bethnal Green
Mile End
King's Cross St Pancras
King's Cross Rd
Rosebery Ave
Goswell Rd
Old St
Great Eastern St
Bethnal Green Rd
Stepney Green
Mile End Rd
Russell Sq
Gray's Inn Rd
City Rd
Mile End Park
Farringdon
Barbican
Liverpool St
Whitechapel
Chancery La
Holborn
Moorgate
Aldgate East
Holborn
City Thameslink
St Paul's
Commercial Rd
Limehouse DLR
Covent Garden
Fleet St
Fenchurch Street
Aldgate
Shadwell DLR
Leicester Sq
Mansion House
Bank
Monument
To Greenwich; O2 (1mi)
The Strand
Temple
Blackfriars
Cannon St
Tower Hill
Tower Gateway DLR
The Highway
Embankment
Wapping
Charing Cross
Waterloo East
Southwark St
London Bridge
Tooley St
Thames
Salter Rd
Waterloo
Union St
Southwark
Borough
Westminster
Rotherhithe
Nature Reserve
Lambeth North
Long La
Jamaica Rd
Canada Water
Bermondsey
Lower Rd
Great Dover St
Redriff Rd
Elephant & Castle
Elephant & Castle
Grange Rd
Greenland Docks
Lambeth Rd
Southwark Park
Surrey Quays
Millbank
Albert Embankment
Kennington Rd
Walworth Rd
Old Kent Rd
South Bermondsey
Kennington
Vauxhall
Vauxhall
Albany Rd
The Oval Cricket Ground
Kennington Park
Oval
Burgess Park
Fentiman Rd
Wandsworth Rd
Camberwell New Rd
Camberwell Green
Clapham Rd
Brixton Rd
Mostyn Gardens
Peckham Rd
Denmark Hill
Stockwell
Myatts Fields
Denmark Hill
Loughborough Junction
Clapham High St
Max Roach Park
Ruskin Park
Clapham North
Brixton
Brixton
Loughborough Park
East Dulwich
Greenwich
0 400 m
0 0.2 miles
Thames
Greenwich Foot Tunnel
Park Row
Old Woolwich Rd
Trafalgar Rd
6
7
Cutty Sark DLR
King William Walk
Romney Rd
Park Vista
Creek Rd
27
4
Roan St
Greenwich Park
Greenwich & Greenwich DLR
Burney St
Croom's Hill
The Avenue
8

INFORMATION	Victoria & Albert Museum........11 C4	**ENTERTAINMENT**
Dutch Embassy........1 B4		Battersea Arts Centre........22 C6
Royal Free Hospital........2 C1	**SLEEPING**	Forum........23 D1
	B&B Belgravia........12 D4	Royal Albert Hall........24 C4
SIGHTS & ACTIVITIES	base2stay........13 B5	Royal Court Theatre........25 D5
Diana, Princess of Wales Memorial Playground........3 B4	Gore........14 C4	Shepherd's Bush Empire........26 A4
National Maritime Museum........4 G6	Luna & Simone Hotel........15 D5	
	New Linden Hotel........16 B3	**SHOPPING**
Natural History Museum........5 C4	Twenty Nevern Square........17 B5	Greenwich Market........27 G6
Old Royal Naval College........6 G5	Vancouver Studios........18 B3	Portobello Road Market........28 B3
Painted Hall........7 G5	Vicarage Private Hotel........19 B4	
Royal Observatory........8 H6	**EATING**	**TRANSPORT**
Science Museum........9 C4	Gordon Ramsay........20 C5	Victoria Coach Station........29 D5
Tate Britain........10 E5	Orsini........21 C4	

MONEY

ATMs (called cash machines in Britain) are plentiful in central London. You can also change cash easily at banks, travel agents, change bureaus and post offices.

In central London, the following are reliable (both have many other branches):

American Express (Amex; Map pp78-9; ☎ 7484 9610; 30-31 Haymarket SW1; 🕑 9am-6pm Mon-Sat, 10am-4pm Sun; ⊖ Piccadilly Circus)

Thomas Cook (Map pp78-9; ☎ 0845 308 9570; 30 St James's St SW1; 🕑 9am-5.30pm Mon, Tue, Thu & Fri, 10am-5.30pm Wed; ⊖ Green Park)

TOURIST INFORMATION

Britain & London Visitor Centre (Map pp78-9; www.visitbritain.com; 1 Regent St SW1; 🕑 9.30am-6.30pm Mon, 9am-6.30pm Tue-Fri, 10am-4pm Sat & Sun, longer hr in summer; ⊖ Piccadilly Circus) Books accommodation, theatre and transport tickets, and has a money exchange, international telephones and terminals for accessing tourist information on the web.

City of London Information Centre (Map pp78-9; ☎ 7332 1456; www.cityoflondon.gov.uk; St Paul's Churchyard EC4; 🕑 9.30am-5.30pm Mon-Sat; ⊖ St Paul's) Tourist information, fast-track tickets to attractions and guided walks (£6, daily in summer). Open Sunday during summer.

DANGERS & ANNOYANCES

Considering the city's size and its disparities in wealth, London is generally a safe place. That said, do keep your wits about you and don't flash your cash around unnecessarily. When travelling by tube, choose a carriage with other people in it and avoid deserted suburban stations. The main annoyance to avoid is pickpockets, whose haunts include bustling areas like Oxford St and Leicester Sq. As a visitor *never* leave your bag unattended – you may trigger a security alert.

SIGHTS

WEST END

Westminster may be the brains of London, while the parks are the lungs and the City the pockets, but if anywhere is the beating heart of London, it's the West End – a strident mix of culture and consumerism. More a concept than a fixed geographical area it none the less takes in **Piccadilly Circus** and **Trafalgar Sq** to the south, elegant **Regent St** to the west, frantic **Oxford St** to the north, with **Covent Garden** and the **Strand** to the east. **Soho** is a grid of narrow streets with gay bars, strip clubs, cafes and advertising agencies. The area around Lisle St and Gerrard St is **Chinatown**, full of reasonably priced restaurants and unfairly hip youngsters. Nearby **Leicester Sq** is dominated by large cinemas, sometimes hosting star-studded premieres.

TRAFALGAR SQUARE

Trafalgar Square is a great place to start any visit to London. Dominating the square is 43.5m-high **Nelson's Column** (Map pp78-9), erected in 1843 to commemorate Nelson's 1805 victory over Napoleon off Cape Trafalgar in Spain. At the edges of the square are four plinths, three of which have permanent statues while the fourth is given over to temporary modern installations.

NATIONAL GALLERY

Gazing grandly over Trafalgar Square through its Corinthian columns, the **National Gallery** (Map pp78-9; ☎ 7747 2885; www.nationalgallery.org.uk; Trafalgar Sq WC2; admission free; 10am-6pm Sat-Thu, to 9pm Fri; Charing Cross) is the nation's most important art repository. Seminal paintings from every epoch are here, including works by Giotto, Leonardo da Vinci, Michelangelo and Van Gogh.

NATIONAL PORTRAIT GALLERY

The excellent **National Portrait Gallery** (Map pp78-9; ☎ 7312 2463; www.npg.org.uk; St Martin's Pl WC2; admission free; 10am-6pm Sat-Wed, to 9pm Thu-Fri; Charing Cross) is like stepping into a picture book of English history or, if you're trashy, an *OK* magazine spread on history's celebrities.

PICCADILLY

Named after the elaborate collars called *picadils*, the sartorial staple of a 17th-century tailor who lived nearby, Piccadilly became the fashionable haunt of the well-heeled (and collared) and still boasts upmarket icons such as the Ritz Hotel and Fortnum & Mason department store (p94). Neon-lit, turbo-charged **Piccadilly Circus** is home to the popular but unremarkable **Eros statue** (Map pp78-9; Piccadilly Circus).

COVENT GARDEN

A hallowed name for opera fans due to the presence of the esteemed Royal Opera House (p94), Covent Garden is one of London's biggest tourist traps, where chain restaurants, souvenir shops, balconied bars and street entertainers vie for the punters' pound. It *was* once a garden, and then a famous fruit, vegetable and flower market, immortalised in the film *My Fair Lady*.

WESTMINSTER & PIMLICO

WESTMINSTER ABBEY

Not merely a beautiful place of worship, **Westminster Abbey** (Map pp78-9; ☎ 7222 5152; www.westminster-abbey.org; 20 Dean's Yard SW1; adult/child £12/9, tours £5, audio guides £4; 9.15am-4.30pm Mon, Tue, Thu & Fri, to 6pm Wed, to 2.30pm Sat; Westminster) serves England's history cold on slabs of stone. This is where most British monarchs have been crowned since 1066 (look out for the incongruously ordinary-looking **Coronation Chair**), and for centuries the great and the good have been interred here; in **Poet's Corner** you'll find the resting places of Chaucer, Dickens, Hardy, Tennyson, Dr Johnson and Kipling as well as memorials to Shakespeare, Jane Austen, Emily Brontë and more.

WESTMINSTER CATHEDRAL

Not to be confused with the eponymous abbey, the neo-Byzantine **Westminster Cathedral** (Map pp78-9; ☎ 7798 9055; www.westminstercathedral.org.uk; Victoria St SW1; admission free; 7am-7pm; Victoria) dates from 1895, and is the headquarters of Britain's Roman Catholic Church. The distinctive 83m red-brick and white-stone **tower** (adult/child £5/2.50) offers splendid views of London and, unlike St Paul's, you can take the lift.

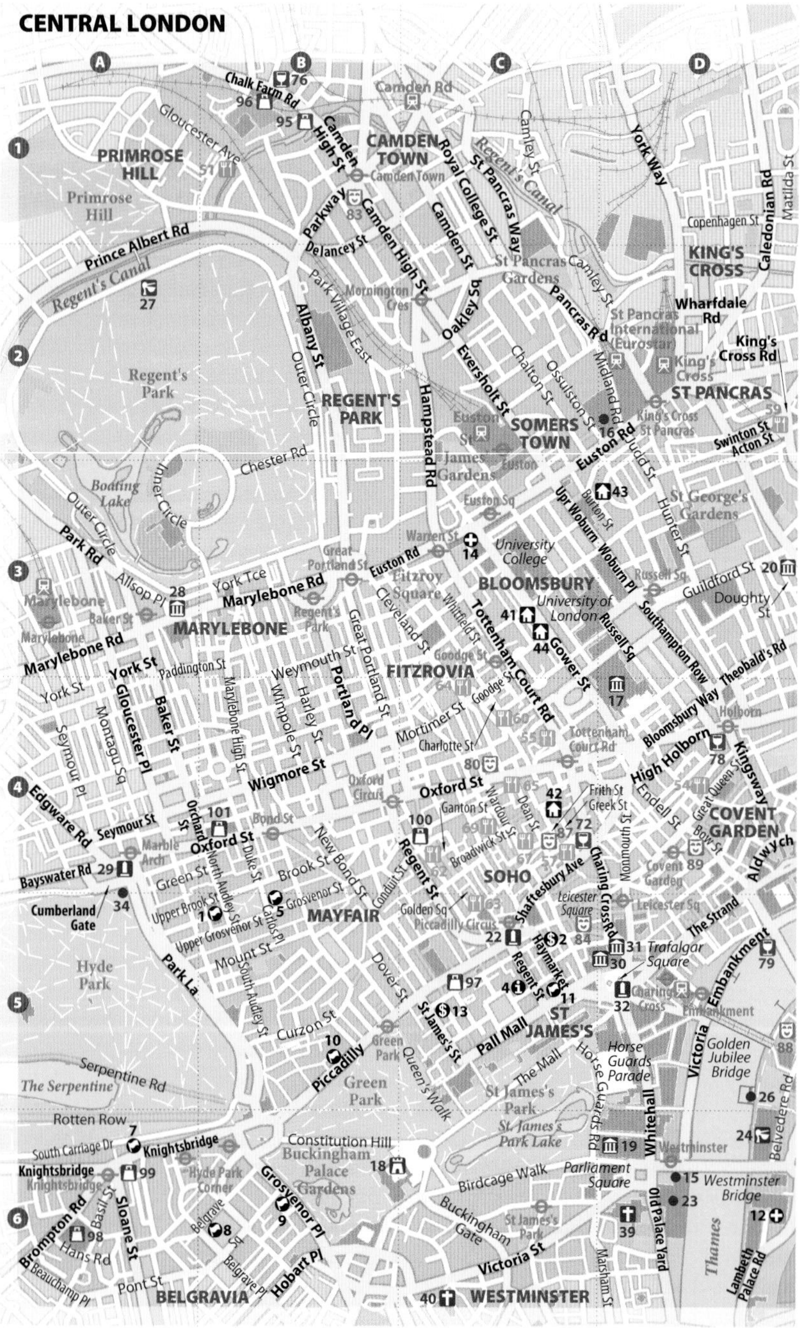
CENTRAL LONDON
A
B
C
D
1
2
3
4
5
6
PRIMROSE HILL
Primrose Hill
Chalk Farm Rd
Gloucester Ave
Camden Rd
Camden High St
CAMDEN TOWN
Camden Town
Royal College St
St Pancras Way
Regent's Canal
Camley St
York Way
Caledonian Rd
Matilda St
Copenhagen St
KING'S CROSS
Prince Albert Rd
Parkway
Delancey St
Camden St
St Pancras Gardens
Pancras Rd
Wharfdale Rd
King's Cross Rd
St Pancras International (Eurostar)
King's Cross
ST PANCRAS
Regent's Park
Albany St
Outer Circle
Park Village East
Mornington Cres
Oakley Sq
Eversholt St
Chalton St
Ossulston St
Midland Rd
REGENT'S PARK
Hampstead Rd
Euston
SOMERS TOWN
Euston Rd
Judd St
King's Cross St Pancras
Swinton St
Acton St
St James Gardens
Chester Rd
Boating Lake
Inner Circle
Euston Sq
Upr Woburn Pl
Burton St
Hunter St
St George's Gardens
Park Rd
Warren St
University College
Great Portland St
Euston Rd
Fitzroy Square
BLOOMSBURY
Woburn Pl
Russell Sq
Guildford St
Doughty St
Marylebone
Allsop Pl
York Tce
Marylebone Rd
Baker St
Regent's Park
Cleveland St
Whitfield St
Tottenham Court Rd
University of London
Southampton Row
MARYLEBONE
Great Portland St
Goodge St
Gower St
Russell Sq
Theobald's Rd
Marylebone Rd
York St
Paddington St
Weymouth St
FITZROVIA
York St
Gloucester Pl
Baker St
Marylebone High St
Wimpole St
Harley St
Portland Pl
Goodge St
Mortimer St
Bloomsbury Way
Holborn
Seymour Pl
Montagu Sq
Charlotte St
Tottenham Court Rd
High Holborn
Kingsway
Wigmore St
Oxford Circus
Oxford St
Wardour St
Dean St
Frith St
Greek St
Great Queen St
Edgware Rd
Seymour St
Orchard St
Bond St
Ganton St
Endell St
COVENT GARDEN
Marble Arch
Oxford St
Duke St
New Bond St
Regent St
Broadwick St
Monmouth St
Bow St
Aldwych
Bayswater Rd
Green St
North Audley St
Brook St
Conduit St
SOHO
Shaftesbury Ave
Charing Cross Rd
Covent Garden
Cumberland Gate
Upper Brook St
Grosvenor St
Carlos Pl
MAYFAIR
Golden Sq
Piccadilly Circus
Leicester Square
Leicester Sq
The Strand
Upper Grosvenor St
Mount St
Haymarket
Trafalgar Square
Embankment
Hyde Park
Park La
South Audley St
Dover St
Regent St
Charing Cross
Embankment
Curzon St
Green Park
St James's St
Pall Mall
ST JAMES'S
Victoria
Golden Jubilee Bridge
Serpentine Rd
The Serpentine
Piccadilly
Queen's Walk
The Mall
Horse Guards Parade
Green Park
St James's Park
Belvedere Rd
Rotten Row
St James's Park Lake
Horse Guards Rd
Whitehall
South Carriage Dr
Knightsbridge
Constitution Hill
Buckingham Palace Gardens
Westminster
Knightsbridge
Hyde Park Corner
Birdcage Walk
Parliament Square
Westminster Bridge
Basil St
Sloane St
Grosvenor Pl
Belgrave Sq
Buckingham Gate
St James's Park
Old Palace Yard
Brompton Rd
Hans Rd
Beauchamp Pl
Pont St
Belgrave Pl
Hobart Pl
Victoria St
Marsham St
Thames
Lambeth Palace Rd
BELGRAVIA
WESTMINSTER
1
2
4
5
7
8
9
10
11
12
13
14
15
16
17
18
19
20
22
23
24
26
27
28
29
30
31
32
34
39
40
41
42
43
44
51
54
55
57
59
60
62
63
64
65
67
69
72
76
78
79
80
83
84
87
88
89
95
96
97
98
99
100
101

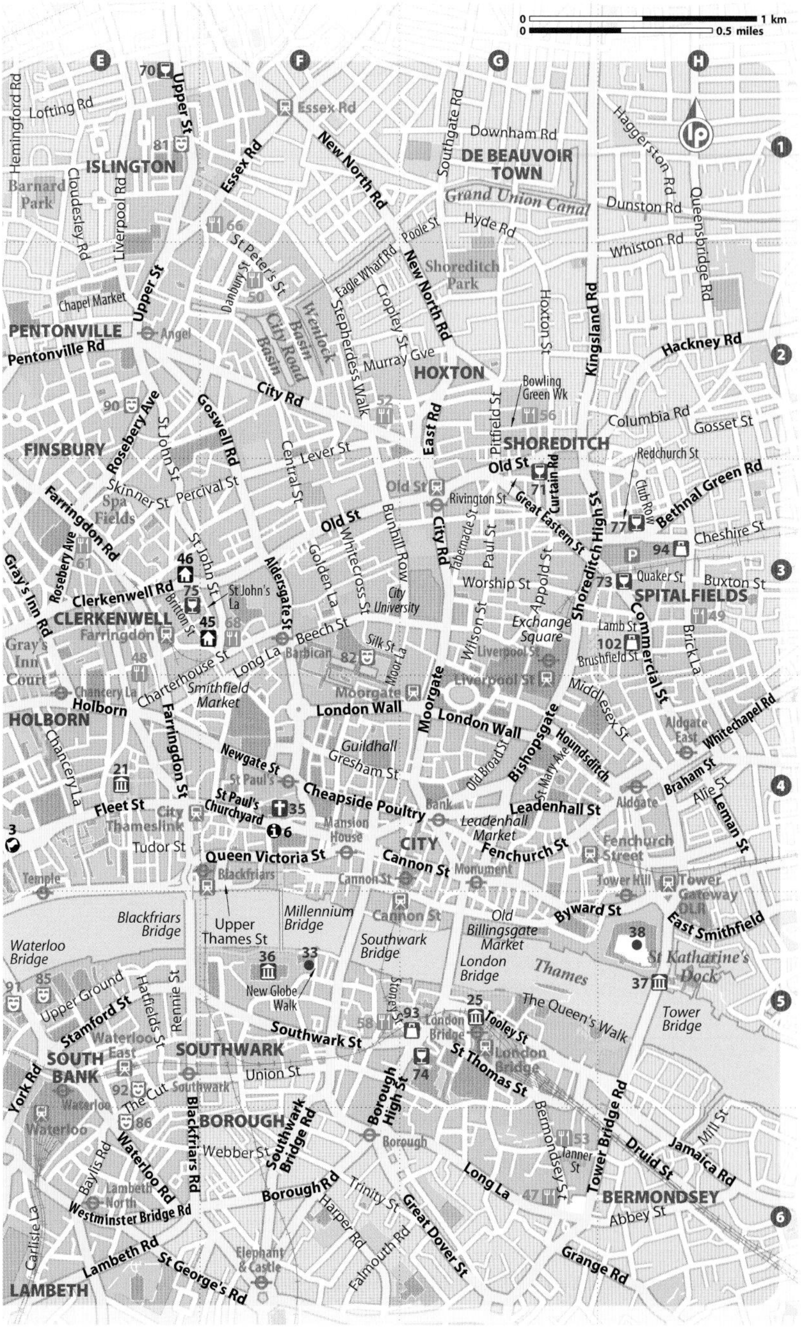
0 1 km
0 0.5 miles
E
F
G
H
1
2
3
4
5
6
70
Upper St
Hemingford Rd
Lofting Rd
Essex Rd
New North Rd
Southgate Rd
Downham Rd
DE BEAUVOIR TOWN
Haggerston Rd
81
ISLINGTON
Barnard Park
Cloudesley Rd
Liverpool Rd
Essex Rd
Grand Union Canal
Dunston Rd
Queensbridge Rd
Hyde Rd
Poole St
66
St Peter's St
Whiston Rd
Shoreditch Park
Eagle Wharf Rd
Danbury St
50
Chapel Market
Upper St
Wenlock Basin
City Road Basin
Stepherdess Walk
Cropley St
New North Rd
Hoxton St
Kingsland Rd
PENTONVILLE
Angel
Pentonville Rd
Murray Gve
HOXTON
Hackney Rd
City Rd
Bowling Green Wk
90
52
East Rd
Pitfield St
56
Columbia Rd
Gosset St
FINSBURY
Rosebery Ave
St John St
Goswell Rd
Central St
Lever St
SHOREDITCH
Redchurch St
Skinner St
Percival St
Spa Fields
Old St
71
Curtain Rd
Old St
Rivington St
Great Eastern St
Club Row
Bethnal Green Rd
Farringdon Rd
Tabernacle St
Paul St
Shoreditch High St
77
94
Cheshire St
Gray's Inn Rd
Rosebery Ave
61
46
St John St
Aldersgate St
Golden La
Whitecross St
Bunhill Row
City Rd
Appold St
P
73
Quaker St
Buxton St
SPITALFIELDS
Clerkenwell Rd
75
St John's La
Britton St
City University
Worship St
CLERKENWELL
45
68
Farringdon
Beech St
Wilson St
Exchange Square
Lamb St
49
Commercial St
Brick La
Gray's Inn Court
48
Charterhouse St
Long La
Barbican
Silk St
82
Moor La
Liverpool St
102
Brushfield St
Chancery La
Smithfield Market
Moorgate
Liverpool St
Middlesex St
Holborn
HOLBORN
Farringdon St
London Wall
Moorgate
London Wall
Bishopsgate
Houndsditch
Aldgate East
Whitechapel Rd
Chancery La
Guildhall
Gresham St
Old Broad St
St Mary Axe
Braham St
Newgate St
21
St Paul's
Cheapside
Poultry
Bank
Leadenhall St
Aldgate
Alie St
Leman St
Fleet St
City Thameslink
St Paul's Churchyard
35
Mansion House
Leadenhall Market
3
6
Tudor St
Queen Victoria St
CITY
Cannon St
Fenchurch St
Fenchurch Street
Temple
Blackfriars
Cannon St
Monument
Tower Hill
Tower Gateway DLR
Byward St
East Smithfield
Blackfriars Bridge
Upper Thames St
Millennium Bridge
Cannon St
Old Billingsgate Market
38
Waterloo Bridge
Southwark Bridge
Thames
St Katharine's Dock
36
33
London Bridge
37
91
85
Upper Ground
Hatfields St
Rennie St
New Globe Walk
Stoney St
25
The Queen's Walk
Tower Bridge
Stamford St
58
93
London Bridge
Tooley St
Waterloo East
Southwark St
SOUTH BANK
SOUTHWARK
74
St Thomas St
London Bridge
Union St
92
The Cut
Southwark
Borough High St
York Rd
Waterloo
Blackfriars Rd
Southwark Bridge Rd
Tower Bridge Rd
Mill St
86
BOROUGH
Bermondsey St
53
Tanner St
Waterloo
Borough
Druid St
Jamaica Rd
Baylis Rd
Waterloo Rd
Webber St
Long La
Lambeth North
Borough Rd
Trinity St
47
BERMONDSEY
Westminster Bridge Rd
Abbey St
Harper Rd
Great Dover St
Carlisle La
Elephant & Castle
Falmouth Rd
Grange Rd
Lambeth Rd
St George's Rd
LAMBETH

INFORMATION

American Embassy	1	B5
American Express	2	C5
Australian High Commission	3	E4
Britain & London Visitor Centre	4	C5
Canadian High Commission	5	B5
City of London Information Centre	6	F4
French Embassy	7	A6
German Embassy	8	B6
Irish Embassy	9	B6
Japanese Embassy	10	B5
New Zealand Embassy	11	C5
St Thomas's Hospital	12	D6
Thomas Cook	13	C5
University College Hospital	14	C3

SIGHTS & ACTIVITIES

Big Ben	15	D6
British Library	16	D2
British Museum	17	D4
Buckingham Palace	18	B6
Cabinet War Rooms	19	D6
Dickens House Museum	20	D3
Dr Johnson's House	21	E4
Eros Statue	22	C5
Houses of Parliament	23	D6
London Aquarium	24	D6
London Duck Tours Departure Point	(see 24)	
London Dungeon	25	G5
London Eye	26	D5
London Zoo	27	A2
Madame Tussauds	28	A3
Marble Arch	29	A4
National Gallery	30	D5
National Portrait Gallery	31	D5
Nelson's Column	32	D5
Shakespeare's Globe	33	F5
Speaker's Corner	34	A5
St Paul's Cathedral	35	F4
Tate Modern	36	F5
Tower Bridge Exhibition	37	H5
Tower of London	38	H5
Westminister Abbey	39	D6
Westminster Cathedral	40	C6

SLEEPING

Arosfa Hotel	41	C3
Hazlitt's	42	C4
Jenkins Hotel	43	D3
Ridgemount Private Hotel	44	C3
Rookery	45	F3
Zetter Hotel	46	E3

EATING

Bermondsey Kitchen	47	G6
Bleeding Heart Restaurant & Bistro	48	E3
Café Bangla	49	H3
Duke of Cambridge	50	F2
Engineer	51	B1
Fifteen	52	F2
Garrison	53	G6
Great Queen Street	54	D4
Hakkasan	55	C4
Hoxton Apprentice	56	G2
Kettners	57	C4
Konditor & Cook	58	F5
Konstam at the Prince Albert	59	D2
La Perla	60	C4
Little Bay	61	E3
Mother Mash	62	C4
Nordic Bakery	63	C5
Ooze	64	C4
Red Veg	65	C4
S&M Café	66	F1
Spiga	67	C4
St John	68	F3
Yauatcha	69	C4

DRINKING

Albert & Pearl	70	E1
Bricklayers Arms	71	G3
Coach & Horses	72	C4
Commercial Tavern	73	H3
George Inn	74	G5
Jerusalem Tavern	75	E3
Lock Tavern	76	B1
Loungelover	77	H3
Princess Louise	78	D4
Queen Mary	79	D5

ENTERTAINMENT

100 Club	80	C4
Almeida Theatre	81	E1
Barbican Centre	82	F3
Jazz Café	83	B1
Leicester Square Half-Price Ticket Booth	84	C5
National Theatre	85	E5
Old Vic	86	E6
Purcell Room	(see 91)	
Queen Elizabeth Hall	(see 91)	
Ronnie Scott's	87	C4
Royal Festival Hall	88	D5
Royal Opera House	89	D4
Sadler's Wells	90	E2
Southbank Centre	91	E5
Young Vic	92	E5

SHOPPING

Borough Market	93	G5
Brick Lane Market	94	H3
Camden Lock Market	95	B1
Camden Stables Market	96	B1
Fortnum & Mason	97	C5
Harrods	98	A6
Harvey Nichols	99	A6
Liberty	100	C4
Selfridges	101	B4
Spitalfields Market	102	H3

HOUSES OF PARLIAMENT

Coming face to face with one of the world's most recognisable landmarks is always a surreal moment, but in the case of the **Houses of Parliament** (**Map pp78-9; ☎ 0870 906 3773; www.parliament.uk; Parliament Sq SW1; ⊖ Westminster**) it's a revelation.

Officially called the Palace of Westminster, the oldest part of the interior is **Westminster Hall** (dating from 1097), but much of the visible building today dates from 1840. The palace's most famous feature is its clock tower, known (erroneously) as **Big Ben** – actually the name of the 13-ton bell inside the tower, named after Benjamin Hall, commissioner of works when the tower was completed in 1858.

When parliament is in recess (three months over the summer, and a couple of weeks over Easter and Christmas) there are guided **tours** (**75min tour adult/child £12/5**) of the **House of Commons**, the **House of Lords** and other historic areas.

TATE BRITAIN

Unlike at the National Gallery, it's Britannia that rules the walls of **Tate Britain** (**Map pp74-5; ☎ 7887 8008; www.tate.org.uk; Millbank SW1; admission free; ⌚ 10am-5.50pm; ⊖ Pimlico**). Reaching through the time from 1500 to the present, it's crammed with local heavyweights such as Blake, Hogarth, Gainsborough, Whistler, Spencer and, especially, Turner, whose 'interrupted visions' – unfinished canvasses of moody skies – wouldn't look out of place in the contemporary section, alongside works by David Hockney, Francis Bacon, Tracey Emin and Damien Hirst.

There are free hour-long guided tours taking in different sections of the gallery daily at midday and 3pm, plus additional tours at 11am and 2pm on weekdays.

CABINET WAR ROOMS

Now a wonderfully evocative and atmospheric museum, the **Cabinet War Rooms** (Map pp78-9; ☎ 7930 6961; www.iwm.org.uk; Clive Steps, King Charles St SW1; adult/child £12/free; 9.30am-6pm, last entry 5pm; ⊖ Westminster) were Prime Minister Winston Churchill's underground military HQ during WWII.

ST JAMES'S & MAYFAIR

BUCKINGHAM PALACE

Built in 1803, **Buckingham Palace** (Map pp78-9; ☎ 7766 7302; www.royalcollection.org.uk; The Mall SW1; adult/child £16/8.75; 9.45am-6pm late Jul-late Sep; ⊖ St James's Park) replaced St James's Palace as the monarch's London home in 1837. When she's not off giving her one-handed wave in far-flung parts of the Commonwealth, Queen Elizabeth II splits her time between here, Windsor and Balmoral. A handy way of telling whether she's home is to check whether the 'royal standard' flag is flying on the roof. The gaudily furnished **State Rooms** are open in summer for the hordes of Royal-loving tourists, but it's more fun outside watching the **changing of the guard** (11.30am daily May-Jul, alternate days for the rest of the year, weather permitting).

PARKS

With its manicured flowerbeds and ornamental lake, **St James's Park** is a wonderful place to stroll and take in the views of Westminster, Buckingham Palace and St James's Palace. The expanse of **Green Park** links St James's Park to Hyde Park and Kensington Gardens, creating a green corridor from Westminster all the way to Kensington.

BLOOMSBURY & FITZROVIA

BRITISH MUSEUM

London's most visited attraction, the **British Museum** (Map pp78-9; ☎ 7323 8000; www.thebritishmuseum.org; Great Russell St WC1; admission free; 10am-5.30pm Sat-Wed, to 8.30pm Thu & Fri; ⊖ Tottenham Court Rd or Russell Sq) is the largest in the country and one of the finest in the world, boasting vast Egyptian, Etruscan, Greek, Oriental and Roman galleries. A latter-day wonder is the museum's spectacular **Great Court**, the largest covered public square in Europe.

HOLBORN & CLERKENWELL

DICKENS HOUSE MUSEUM

The great writer's sole surviving London residence is now the **Dickens House Museum** (Map pp78-9; ☎ 7405 2127; www.dickensmuseum.com; 48 Doughty St WC1; adult/child £5/3; 10am-5pm Mon-Sat, 11am-5pm Sun; ⊖ Russell Sq). The *Pickwick Papers, Nicholas Nickleby* and *Oliver Twist* were all written here, and today visitors can stroll through rooms choc-a-block with fascinating memorabilia.

THE CITY

ST PAUL'S CATHEDRAL

Dominating the City with a dome second in size only to St Peter's in Rome, **St Paul's Cathedral** (Map pp78-9; ☎ 7236 4128; www.stpauls.co.uk; adult/child £10/3.50; 8.30am-4pm Mon-Sat; ⊖ St Paul's) was built by 'London's architect' Christopher Wren between 1675 and 1710. Inside, attractions include the **Whispering Gallery** – if you talk close to the wall it carries your words around to the opposite side – and the **Golden Gallery** at the very top, and an unforgettable view of London.

TOWER OF LONDON

If you only pay one admission fee while you're in London, make it to the **Tower of London** (Map pp78-9; ☎ 0844 482 7777; www.hrp.org.uk; Tower Hill EC3; adult/child £17/9.50; 10am-5.30pm Sun-Mon, 9am-5.30pm Tue-Sat Mar-Oct, 10am-4.30pm Sun-Mon, 9am-4.30pm Tue-Sat Nov-Feb; ⊖ Tower Hill), one of the city's three World Heritage sites (joining Westminster Abbey and Maritime Greenwich). After the obligatory **Crown Jewels** visit, leave plenty of time to explore the walls, dungeons and museum rooms.

TOWER BRIDGE

The south bank of the Thames was a thriving port in 1894 when elegant Tower Bridge was built. So the ships could reach the port, the bridge was designed so the roadway could be raised to allow ships to pass. For more insights, the **Tower Bridge Exhibition** (Map pp78-9; ☎ 7403 3761; www.towerbridge.org.uk; adult/child £6/3; 10am-6.30pm Apr-Sep, 9.30am-6pm Oct-Mar; ⊖ Tower Hill) recounts the story with videos and animatronics.

DR JOHNSON'S HOUSE

The 18th-century residence of this most famous of Londoners, **Dr Johnson's House** (Map pp78-9; ☎ 7353 3745; www.drjohnsonshouse.org; 17 Gough Sq EC4; adult/child £4.50/1.50; 11am-5.30pm Mon-Sat May-Sep, 11am-5pm Mon-Sat Oct-Apr; ⊖ Chancery Lane) is where the rotund raconteur and his assistants compiled the first English dictionary.

SOUTH BANK

TATE MODERN

It's hard to miss this surprisingly elegant former power station on the side of the river, which is fortunate as the tremendous **Tate Modern** (Map pp78-9; ☎ 7887

DAVID TOMLINSON

Wendy Taylor's sundial sculpture *Timepiece* and Tower Bridge

EYE IN THE SKY

Originally designed as a temporary structure to celebrate the year 2000, the giant revolving wheel that is the **London Eye** (**Map pp78-9; ☎ 0870 5000 600; www.londoneye.com; adult/child £15.50/7.75; ⌚ 10am-8pm Jan-May & Oct-Dec, 10am-9pm Jun & Sep, 10am-9.30pm Jul & Aug; ⊖ Waterloo**) is now a permanent addition to the cityscape, joining the tower of Big Ben as one of London's most distinctive landmarks. For budget travellers it's not cheap, but on a clear day the views are spectacular, and give you a real feel for London's size and the delightfully random layout of the city's historic streets (no grid pattern here!). Passengers ride in enclosed egg-shaped pods, and rides take 30 minutes. It's popular, and queues can be long, but you can book online (you'll also get a 10% discount), or pay an additional £10 to jump the queue. For more savings, joint tickets for the London Eye and Madame Tussauds cost adult/child £35/25.

8888; www.tate.org.uk; Queen's Walk SE1; admission free; ⌚ 10am-6pm Sun-Thu, to 10pm Fri & Sat; ⊖ Southwark) really shouldn't be missed. Focussing on modern art in all its wacky and wonderful permutations, it has been extraordinarily successful in bringing challenging work to the masses, becoming one of London's most popular attractions.

SHAKESPEARE'S GLOBE

An authentic 1997 rebuild of the original London theatre where many Shakespeare plays were performed, the **Globe** (**Map pp78-9; ☎ 7401 9919; www.shakespeares-globe.org; 21 New Globe Walk SE1; adult/child £9/6.50; ⌚ 10am-6pm, last entry 5pm, May-Sep, 10am-5pm Oct-Apr; ⊖ London Bridge**) has become a pilgrimage destination for fans of the Bard.

Admission includes a guided tour of the open-roofed theatre, faithfully reconstructed from oak beams, handmade bricks, lime plaster and thatch. Plays are still performed here (seats are £15 to £35); as in Elizabethan times, 'groundlings' can watch proceedings for a modest price (£5), but there's no protection from the elements and you'll have to stand.

LONDON DUNGEON

Older kids love the **London Dungeon** (**Map pp78-9; ☎ 0871 423 2240; www.thedungeons.com; 28-34 Tooley St SE1; adult/child £19.95/14.95; ⌚ 10.30am-5pm; ⊖ London Bridge**), as the terrifying queues during school holidays and weekends testify. It's all spooky music, ghostly boat-rides, macabre hangman's drop-rides, fake blood and actors dressed up as torturers and gory criminals (including Jack the Ripper and Sweeney Todd).

LONDON AQUARIUM

One of the largest in Europe, the **London Aquarium** (**Map pp78-9; ☎ 7967 8000; www.londonaquarium.co.uk; County Hall SE1; adult/child £14/9.75; ⌚ 10am-6pm, last entry 5pm; ⊖ Waterloo**) has three levels of fish organised by geographical origin, but you'll be peering over children's excited heads during holidays.

CHELSEA, KENSINGTON & KNIGHTSBRIDGE

It's called the Royal Borough of Kensington and Chelsea, and residents are certainly paid royally, earning the highest incomes in the UK. Knightsbridge is where you'll find some of London's best-known department stores, while Kensington High St has a lively mix of chains and boutiques.

VICTORIA & ALBERT MUSEUM

A vast, rambling and wonderful museum of decorative art and design, the **Victoria & Albert** (V&A; Map pp74-5; ☎ 7942 2000; www.vam.ac.uk; Cromwell Rd SW7; admission free; 🕑 10am-5.45pm Sat-Thu, to 10pm Fri; ⊖ South Kensington) is a bit like the nation's attic, comprising four million objects collected from Britain and around the globe.

NATURAL HISTORY MUSEUM

A sure-fire hit with kids of all ages, the **Natural History Museum** (Map pp74-5; ☎ 7942 5725; www.nhm.ac.uk; Cromwell Rd SW7; admission free; 🕑 10am-5.50pm; ⊖ South Kensington) is crammed full of interesting stuff, starting with the giant dinosaur skeleton that greets you in the main hall. The Earth Galleries are equally impressive. An escalator slithers up and into a hollowed-out globe where two main exhibits – *The Power Within* and the *Restless Surface* – explain how wind, water, ice, gravity and life itself impact on the earth.

NEIL SETCHFIELD

People flocking to Camden Market (p95)

SCIENCE MUSEUM

With seven floors of interactive and educational exhibits, the **Science Museum** (Map pp74-5; ☎ 0870 870 4868; www.sciencemuseum.org.uk; Exhibition Rd SW7; admission free; 🕑 10am-6pm; ⊖ South Kensington) covers everything from the Industrial Revolution to the exploration of space.

HYDE PARK

At 145 hectares, **Hyde Park** (🕑 5.30am-midnight; ⊖ Marble Arch, Hyde Park Corner or Queensway) is central London's largest open space. Near Marble Arch is **Speaker's Corner** (Map pp78-9) for oratorical acrobats, although these days it's largely total nutters and religious fanatics who maintain the tradition begun in 1872 as a response to rioting.

Blending in with Hyde Park, **Kensington Gardens** (admission free; 🕑 dawn-dusk; ⊖ Queensway) are part of Kensington Palace and hence also associated with Princess Diana. Devotees can visit the **Diana, Princess of Wales Memorial Playground** (Map pp74-5) in its northwest corner.

MARBLE ARCH

London's version of the Arc de Triomphe, and the city's grandest bedsit – there really is a one-room flat inside – **Marble Arch** (Map pp78-9) was designed by John Nash in 1828 as the entrance to Buckingham Palace. It was moved here in 1851.

MARYLEBONE

REGENT'S PARK

A former royal hunting ground, **Regent's Park** (⊖ Baker St or Regent's Park) was designed by John Nash early in the 19th century, although what was actually laid out is only a fraction of the celebrated architect's grand plan. **Open Air Theatre** (☎ 7935 5756; www.openairtheatre.org) hosts performances of Shakespeare here on summer evenings, along with comedy and concerts.

LONDON ZOO

A huge amount of money has been spent to bring **London Zoo** (Map pp78-9; ☎ 7722 3333; www.londonzoo.co.uk; Regent's Park NW1; adult/child £15.40/11.90; 10am-5.30pm Mar-Oct, to 4pm Nov-Feb; ⊖ Camden Town), established in 1828, into the modern world. The humane conditions include a swanky new £5.3-million gorilla enclosure. Feeding times, reptile handling and the petting zoo are guaranteed winners with the kids.

MADAME TUSSAUDS

With so much fabulous free stuff to do in London, it's a wonder that people still join lengthy queues to visit **Madame Tussauds** (Map pp78-9; ☎ 0870 400 3000; www.madame-tussauds.co.uk; Marylebone Rd NW1; adult/child £25/21; 9.30am-5.30pm Mon-Fri, 9am-6pm Sat & Sun; ⊖ Baker St), but in a celebrity-obsessed world the opportunity to pose beside Prince Charles and Camilla, or that other regal couple, Posh and Becks, is not short on appeal.

NORTH LONDON

BRITISH LIBRARY

You need to be a 'reader' (ie member) to use the vast collection of the **British Library** (Map pp78-9; ☎ 7412 7332; www.bl.uk; 96 Euston Rd NW1; admission free; 9.30am-6pm Mon & Wed-Fri, 9.30am-8pm Tue, 9.30am-5pm Sat, 11am-5pm Sun; ⊖ King's Cross St Pancras), but the Treasures gallery is open to everyone. Here you'll find St Thomas Moore's last letter to Henry VIII, Shakespeare's first folio, Leonardo da Vinci's notebooks, and the lyrics to *A Hard Day's Night* scribbled on the back of Julian Lennon's birthday card.

CAMDEN

Technicolour hairstyles, facial furniture, intricate tattoos and ambitious platform shoes are the look of bohemian Camden, a lively neighbourhood of pubs, music venues, quirky boutiques and, most famously, **Camden Market** (p95).

GREENWICH

Greenwich is easily reached from the City via the Docklands Light Railway (a great trip in its own right for a bird's-eye view of London) or by boat with **Thames River Services** (☎ 7930 4097; www.westminsterpier.co.uk) departing half-hourly from Westminster Pier.

OLD ROYAL NAVAL COLLEGE

Designed by the omnipresent Wren, the **Old Royal Naval College** (Map pp74-5; ☎ 8269 4747; www.oldroyalnavalcollege.org; 2 Cutty Sark Gardens SE10; admission free; 10am-5pm Mon-Sat; DLR Cutty Sark) is a magnificent example of monumental classical architecture. Parts are now used by the University of Greenwich and Trinity College of Music, but you can visit the extraordinary **Painted Hall**, which took artist Sir James Thornhill 19 years of hard graft to complete.

NATIONAL MARITIME MUSEUM

Directly behind the old college, the **National Maritime Museum** (Map pp74-5; ☎ 8858 4422; www.nmm.ac.uk; Romney Rd SE10;

admission free; 10am-5pm, last entry 4.30pm; DLR Cutty Sark) completes Greenwich's trump hand of historic buildings, housing a massive collection of paraphernalia recounting Britain's seafaring history. Highlights include Nelson's uniform complete with a hole from the bullet that killed him.

Nearby, **Greenwich Park** climbs up the hill, affording great views of London, and is capped by the **Royal Observatory**, built in 1675 to help solve the riddle of longitude. Success was confirmed in 1884 when Greenwich was designated as the prime meridian of the world, and Greenwich Mean Time (GMT) became the universal measurement of standard time.

WEST LONDON

KEW GARDENS

In 1759 botanists began rummaging around the world for specimens they could plant in the 3-hectare plot known as the **Royal Botanic Gardens, Kew** (**off Map pp74-5; 8332 5655; www.kew.org.uk; Kew Rd; adult/child £13/free; 9.30am-6.30pm Mon-Fri, to 7.30pm Sat & Sun, earlier closing in winter; Kew Gardens**). They never stopped collecting, and the gardens have bloomed to 120 hectares – the most comprehensive botanical collection on earth.

From central London, the gardens are easily reached by tube but you might prefer to take a cruise on a riverboat from the **Westminster Passenger Services Association** (**7930 2062; www.wpsa.co.uk; adult/child return £16.50/8.25**) departing from Westminster Pier (90 minutes, several daily April to October).

HAMPTON COURT PALACE

Built by Cardinal Thomas Wolsey in 1514 but 'given' to King Henry VIII just before the cardinal fell from favour, **Hampton Court Palace** (**off Map pp74-5; 0844 482 7777; www.hrp.org.uk/HamptonCourtPalace; adult/child £13.50/6.65; 10am-6pm Apr-Oct, to 4.30pm Nov-Mar; Hampton Court**) is the largest and grandest Tudor structure in England.

You can take a themed **tour** led by costumed historians or, if you're in a rush, visit the highlights: **Henry VIII's State Apartments**, including the Great Hall with its spectacular hammer-beamed roof; the **Tudor Kitchens**, staffed by 'servants'; and the **Wolsey Rooms**. You could easily spend a day exploring the palace and its 60 acres of riverside gardens, especially if you get lost in the 300-year-old **maze**.

Hampton Court is 13 miles southwest of central London and easily reached by train from Waterloo. Alternatively, the Westminster to Kew **riverboats** (return adult/child £19.50/9.75, 3½ hours) continue to here.

TOURS

One of the best ways to get oriented when you first arrive in London is with a 24-hour hop-on-hop-off pass for the double-decker bus tours operated by the **Original London Sightseeing Tour** (**8877 1722; www.theoriginaltour.com; adult/child £22/12**) or the **Big Bus Company** (**7233 9533; www.bigbustours.com; adult/child £24/10**). The buses loop around interconnecting routes throughout the day, providing a commentary as they go, and the price includes a river cruise and three walking tours.

There are loads of walking tours you can take, including **Citisights** (**8806 3742; www.chr.org.uk/cswalks.htm**), focussing on the academic and literary, and **London Walks** (**7624 3978; www.walks.com**), including Harry Potter tours, ghost walks and the ever-popular Jack the Ripper tours.

Other unusual tour options:

Black Taxi Tours of London (**7935 9363; www.blacktaxitours.co.uk; 8am-6pm £95,**

6pm-midnight £100, plus £5 on weekends) A two-hour spin past the major sights with a chatty cabbie as your guide.

City Cruises (☎ 7740 0400; www.citycruises.com; single/return trips from £6.40/7.80, day pass £10.50; 10am-6pm, later Jun-Aug) Ferry service between Westminster, Waterloo, Tower and Greenwich piers.

London Duck Tours (Map pp78-9; ☎ 7928 3132; www.londonducktours.co.uk; County Hall; adult/child £21.50/15.50; ⊖ Waterloo) Cruise the streets in an amphibious landing craft before making a dramatic plunge into the Thames.

FESTIVALS & EVENTS

Chinese New Year Late January or early February sees Chinatown snap, crackle and pop with fireworks, a colourful street parade and eating aplenty.

Camden Crawl (www.thecamdencrawl.com; day/2-day pass £30/50) Your chance to see the next big thing or a secret gig by an established act, with 28 of Camden's intimate venues given over to live music for two full days in April.

Chelsea Flower Show (www.rhs.org.uk; Royal Hospital Chelsea; admission £18-41) Held in May, this renowned horticultural show attracts the globe's green fingers.

Meltdown (www.southbankcentre.co.uk/festivals-series/meltdown) The Southbank Centre hands over curatorial reigns to a legend (eg David Bowie, Morrissey or Patti Smith) to pull together a full program of concerts, talks and films; late June.

Pride (www.pridelondon.org) The big event on the gay and lesbian calendar. A technicolour West End street parade and Trafalgar Sq concert; June/July.

Notting Hill Carnival (www.nottinghillcarnival.biz) This is Europe's largest and London's most vibrant outdoor carnival. For two days in August the Caribbean community shows the city how to party.

SLEEPING

No matter what your budget, London is a horribly pricey city to sleep in. Anything below £80 for a double is pretty much 'budget', and at the top end how does a £3500 penthouse sound?

BARBARA VAN ZANTEN

Double-decker bus passing the Houses of Parliament (p80)

ALAIN EVRARD

Dancers at Notting Hill Carnival (p87)

WEST END

Hazlitt's (Map pp78-9; ☎ 7434 1771; www.hazlittshotel.com; 6 Frith St W1; d/ste from £205/300; ⊖ Tottenham Court Rd; 💻) Staying in this charming Georgian house (1718) is a trip back into a time when four-poster beds and claw-footed baths were the norm for gentlefolk.

WESTMINSTER & PIMLICO

Luna & Simone Hotel (Map pp74-5; ☎ 7834 5897; www.lunasimonehotel.com; 47-49 Belgrave Rd SW1; s £45-65, d/tw/tr/q £95/95/115/140; ⊖ Pimlico) The ensign of Luna (the moon) and Simone (the owner) is etched into the glass porch and this personal touch continues inside with the friendly service.

B&B Belgravia (Map pp74-5; ☎ 7259 8570; www.bb-belgravia.com; 64-66 Ebury St SW1; s/d/tw/tr/q £99/115/125/145/155; ⊖ Victoria) This small hotel's unassuming facade belies a chic, contemporary interior comprising stylish bathrooms and floor-to-ceiling dark wood cupboards. There's wi-fi access.

BLOOMSBURY & FITZROVIA

Ridgemount Private Hotel (Map pp78-9; ☎ 7636 1141; www.ridgemounthotel.co.uk; 65-67 Gower St WC1; s/d/tr/q with shared bathroom £42/58/78/92, with private bathroom £54/75/93/104; ⊖ Goodge St) There's a comfortable, welcoming feel at this old-fashioned, slightly chintzy place. Wi-fi access.

Jenkins Hotel (Map pp78-9; ☎ 7387 2067; www.jenkinshotel.demon.co.uk; 45 Cartwright Gardens WC1; s with shared bathroom £52, s/d/tr with private bathroom from £72/89/105; ⊖ Russell Sq) This modest hotel has featured in the TV series of Agatha Christie's *Poirot*. Rooms are small but the hotel has charm.

Arosfa Hotel (Map pp78-9; ☎ 7636 2115; www.arosfalondon.com; 83 Gower St WC1E; s £60-65, d/tr/q £90/102/110; ⊖ Goodge St) While the decor of the immaculately presented rooms is unremarkable, recent refurbishments have added en suites to all 15 bedrooms, but they're tiny. Wi-fi access.

HOLBORN & CLERKENWELL

Rookery (Map pp78-9; ☎ 7336 0931; www.rookeryhotel.com; Peter's Lane, Cowcross St EC1; s £175, d £210-495; ⊖ Farringdon) This antique-strewn luxury hotel re-creates an early 19th-century ambience with none of the attendant grime or crime. Wi-fi access.

Zetter Hotel (Map pp78-9; ☎ 7324 4444; www.thezetter.com; 86-88 Clerkenwell Rd EC1M; d £188-400; ⊖ Farringdon) A slickly beautiful 21st-century conversion of a Victorian warehouse; the furnishings are an enticing blend of old and new, and the facilities cutting edge. Wi-fi access.

CHELSEA, KENSINGTON & KNIGHTSBRIDGE

Vicarage Private Hotel (Map pp74-5; ☎ 7229 4030; www.londonvicaragehotel.com; 10 Vicarage Gate W8; s/d/tr/q with shared bathroom £52/88/109/116, with private bathroom £88/114/145/160; ⊖ High St Kensington) This grand Victorian townhouse has quiet and simply furnished rooms. The cheaper ones (without bathrooms) are on the upper floors, so you get a view as well as a workout. Wi-fi access.

Gore (Map pp74-5; ☎ 7584 6601; www.gorehotel.com; 190 Queen's Gate SW7; r £187-390; ⊖ Gloucester Rd) A short stroll from the Royal Albert Hall, this place serves up British grandiosity (antiques, carved four-posters, a secret bathroom in the Tudor room) with a large slice of camp. Wi-fi access.

NOTTING HILL, BAYSWATER & PADDINGTON

Vancouver Studios (Map pp74-5; ☎ 7243 1270; www.vancouverstudios.co.uk; 30 Prince's Sq W2; apt £85-170; ⊖ Bayswater) Technically apartments, it's only the addition of kitchenettes and a self-service laundry that differentiate these smart but reasonably priced studios (sleeping from one to three people) from a regular hotel. Wi-fi access.

New Linden Hotel (Map pp74-5; ☎ 7221 4321; www.newlinden.co.uk; 58-60 Leinster Sq W2; s £95, d £129-179, tr/f/ste £210/250/289; ⊖ Bayswater) Cramming in a fair whack of style for the price, this place has interesting modern art in the rooms and carved wooden fixtures from India combined with elegant wallpaper in the guest lounge. Wi-fi access.

EARL'S COURT

Twenty Nevern Square (Map pp74-5; ☎ 7565 9555; www.twentynevernsquare.co.uk; 20 Nevern Sq SW5; s £79-140, d £85-189; ⊖ Earl's Court) A contemporary townhouse hotel, where a mix of wooden furniture and natural light helps maximise the limited space. Wi-fi access.

base2stay (Map pp74-5; ☎ 0845 262 8000; www.base2stay.com; 25 Courtfield Gardens SW5; s £93, d £107-127, tw £127; ⊖ Earl's Court) With smart decor, power showers, and kitchenettes, this boutique establishment feels like a four-star hotel without the hefty price tag. Wi-fi access.

HEATHROW & GATWICK AIRPORTS

Yotel (☎ 7100 1100; www.yotel.com; r per 4/5/6hr £38/45/53, 7-24hr £59; 💻) The best news for early-morning or late-night flyers since coffee machines, Yotel's smart 'cabins' offer pint-sized luxury: comfy beds, soft lights, internet-connected TVs, monsoon showers and fluffy towels. Wi-fi access.

EATING

WEST END

Nordic Bakery (Map pp78-9; ☎ 3230 1077; 14a Golden Sq W1; snacks £2.80-5; 🕑 8am-8pm Mon-Fri, 11am-7pm Sat, 11am-6pm Sun; ⊖ Piccadilly Circus) As simple and stylish as you'd expect from the Scandinavians, this small cafe has bare wooden walls and uncomplicated snacks.

Yauatcha (Map pp78-9; ☎ 7494 8888; 15 Broadwick St W1; dishes £3.30-18; ⊖ Piccadilly Circus) Dim sum restaurants don't come much cooler than this and the menu is fantastic and Michelin-starred.

Mother Mash (Map pp78-9; ☎ 7494 9644; 26 Ganton St W1; mains £6.95-7.10; ⊖ Oxford Circus) Comfort food central, with four types of mashed potato, eight varieties of sausage (including a vegetarian), six choices of pie and five types of gravy.

Spiga (Map pp78-9; ☎ 7734 3444; 84-86 Wardour St W1; mains £9-18; ⊖ Piccadilly Circus) With warm, colourful decor and a tasty menu of pastas, pizzas, fish and meat dishes, this popular restaurant is a winner.

Kettners (Map pp78-9; ☎ 7734 6112; 29 Romilly St W1; mains £9.15-19.90; ⊖ Leicester Sq) This historic place dishes up pizza and burgers, which you can wash down with champagne while soaking in the gently fading grandeur and tinkling piano music.

Red Veg (Map pp78-9; ☎ 7437 3109; 95 Dean St W1; ⊖ Tottenham Court Rd) Everyone's favourite communist vegetarian burger bar.

BLOOMSBURY & FITZROVIA

Tucked away behind busy Tottenham Court Rd, Fitzrovia's Charlotte and Goodge Sts form one of central London's most vibrant eating precincts.

Ooze (Map pp78-9; ☎ 7436 9444; 62 Goodge St W1; mains £6.95-14.50; ⊖ Goodge St) The humble risotto gets its moment on the catwalk in this breezy Italian restaurant.

La Perla (Map pp78-9; ☎ 7436 1744; 11 Charlotte St W1; mains £9-17; closed Sun lunch; ⊖ Goodge St) The service is lovely, but it's the street tacos that have us infatuated at this great place.

Hakkasan (Map pp78-9; ☎ 7907 1888; 8 Hanway Pl W1; mains £10-58; ⊖ Tottenham Court Rd) Hidden down a lane like all fashionable haunts need to be, the first Chinese restaurant to get a Michelin star combines celebrity status, stunning design and persuasive cocktails.

HOLBORN & CLERKENWELL

Little Bay (Map pp78-9; ☎ 7278 1234; 171 Farringdon Rd EC1; mains before/after 7pm £6.45/8.45; ⊖ Farringdon) The decor is bonkers but fun. The hearty food is very good value.

Bleeding Heart Restaurant & Bistro (Map pp78-9; ☎ 7242 8238; Bleeding Heart Yard EC1; bistro £8.45-16, restaurant £13-25; ⊖ Farringdon) Choose from formal dining in the downstairs restaurant or more relaxed meals in the buzzy bistro – wherever, the French food is divine.

Great Queen Street (Map pp78-9; ☎ 7242 0622; 32 Great Queen St WC2; mains £10-14; lunch Tue-Sat, dinner Mon-Sat; ⊖ Holborn) This place serves the best of British, including brawn, lamb that melts in the mouth and Arbroath smokie (a whole smoked fish with creamy sauce).

St John (Map pp78-9; ☎ 7251 0848; 26 St John St EC1; mains £14-23; ⊖ Farringdon) Bright whitewashed brick walls, high ceilings and simple wooden furniture keep diners free to concentrate on its world-famous nose-to-tail offerings.

SOUTH OF THE THAMES

Konditor & Cook (Map pp78-9; ☎ 7407 5100; 10 Stoney St SE1; snacks £2.10-5.25; ⊖ London Bridge) The original location of arguably the best bakery in London, it serves excellent muffins, sweets, bread and coffee.

Bermondsey Kitchen (Map pp78-9; ☎ 7407 5719; 194 Bermondsey St SE1; mains £10-15; ⊖ London Bridge) Smart but informal, this place sits somewhere between restaurant and gastropub, serving cocktails and tapas all day.

Garrison (Map pp78-9; ☎ 7089 9355; 99-101 Bermondsey St SE1; mains £12-15; ⊖ London Bridge) It may be a gastropub but the ambience is more French country kitchen than London boozer, with great options for vegetarians and carnivores.

CHELSEA, KENSINGTON & KNIGHTSBRIDGE

Orsini (Map pp74-5; ☎ 7581 5553; 8a Thurloe Pl SW3; snacks £1.50-5.50, mains £7.50-12; ⊖ South Kensington) Marinated in authentic Italian charm, this tiny family-run eatery serves excellent espresso and deliciously fresh baguettes stuffed with Parma ham and mozzarella.

Gordon Ramsay (Map pp74-5; ☎ 7352 4441; 68 Royal Hospital Rd SW3; set lunch/dinner £40/90; ⊖ Sloane Sq) One of Britain's finest restaurants and the only one in the capital with three Michelin stars. The food is, of course, blissful, and perfect for a luxurious treat. The only quibble is the specific eat-it-and-beat-it time slots.

NORTH LONDON

Allow at least an evening to explore Islington's Upper St, along with the laneways leading off it. Camden's great for cheap eats, while neighbouring Chalk Farm and Primrose Hill are salted with gastropubs and upmarket restaurants.

S&M Café (Map pp78-9; ☎ 7359 5361; 4/6 Essex Rd N1; mains £6-10; ⊖ Angel) The S&M refers to sausages and mash in this cool diner (featured in the movie *Quadrophenia*) that won't give your wallet a spanking.

Konstam at the Prince Albert (Map pp78-9; ☎ 7833 5040; 2 Acton St WC1; mains £11-17; closed Sunday; ⊖ Kings Cross) As London a restaurant as you can get, Chef Oliver Rowe sources all but a few of his ingredients from within the tube map.

Duke of Cambridge (Map pp78-9; ☎ 7359 3066; 30 St Peter's St N1; mains £12-17; ⊖ Angel) Pioneers in bringing sustainability to the table, this tucked-away gastropub serves only organic, sustainable and locally sourced food, wine and beer.

our pick **Engineer** (Map pp78-9; ☎ 7722 0950; 65 Gloucester Ave NW1; mains £13-17; ⊖ Chalk Farm) One of London's original gastropubs, serving up consistently good international cuisine to hip north Londoners. The courtyard garden is a real treat on balmy summer nights.

HOLGER LEUE

Fish and chips

EAST END

From the hit-and-miss Bangladeshi restaurants of Brick Lane to the Vietnamese strip on Kingsland Rd and the Jewish, Spanish, French, Italian and Greek eateries in between, the East End's cuisine is as multicultural as its residents.

our pick **Fifteen** (Map pp78-9; ☎ 0871 330 1515; 15 Westland Pl N1; breakfast £2-8.50, trattoria £9-18, restaurant £22-24; ⊖ Old St) It can only be a matter of time before Jamie Oliver becomes Sir Jamie. His culinary philanthropy original is where Italian food is beyond excellent, and unemployed young people have a shot at a career in the kitchen.

Café Bangla (Map pp78-9; ☎ 7247 7885; 128 Brick Ln E1; mains £4.15-13; ⊖ Liverpool St) Among the hordes of practically interchangeable restaurants, this one stands out for its murals of scantily-clad women riding dragons, alongside a tribute to Princess Di.

Hoxton Apprentice (Map pp78-9; ☎ 7749 2828; 16 Hoxton Sq N1; mains £9-17; ⊖ Old St) Professionals and trainees work the kitchen in this restaurant, housed appropriately enough in a former Victorian primary school.

DRINKING

As long as there's been a city, Londoners have loved to drink – and, as history shows, often immoderately.

WEST END

Coach & Horses (Map pp78-9; ☎ 7437 5920; 29 Greek St W1; ⊖ Leicester Sq) This Soho institution has been patronised by Sigmund Freud, Francis Bacon, Dylan Thomas, Peter Cooke and Peter O'Toole. The Wednesday night East End sing-along is tops.

Queen Mary (Map pp78-9; ☎ 7240 9404; Waterloo Pier WC2; ⊖ Embankment) Climb aboard this steamer for a welcoming pub-like atmosphere with great views of the London Eye and the South Bank.

HOLBORN & CLERKENWELL

Jerusalem Tavern (Map pp78-9; ☎ 7490 4281; 55 Britton St; ⊖ Farringdon) Pick a wood-panelled cubby hole at this former 18th-century coffee shop, and choose from a selection of St Peter's beers straight from the barrel.

Princess Louise (Map pp78-9; ☎ 7405 8816; 208 High Holborn WC1; ⊖ Holborn) This late-19th-century Victorian boozer is arguably London's most beautiful pub.

SOUTH OF THE THAMES

George Inn (Map pp78-9; ☎ 7407 2056; Talbot Yard, 77 Borough High St SE1; ⊖ London Bridge or Borough) Tucked away in a cobbled courtyard is London's last surviving galleried coaching inn, dating from 1677 and now belonging to the National Trust.

CAMDEN & ISLINGTON

Albert & Pearl (Map pp78-9; ☎ 7354 9993; 181 Upper St; ⊖ Highbury & Islington) This chic cocktail-filled pie is a cut above your average Camden boozer – expect beautiful people and boutique beers.

Lock Tavern (Map pp78-9; 35 Chalk Farm Rd NW1; ⊖ Camden Town) The archetypal Camden pub, with a rooftop terrace, garden, interesting crowd, ready conviviality and regular live music.

EAST END

Commercial Tavern (Map pp78-9; ☎ 7247 1888; 142 Commercial St E1; ⊖ Liverpool St) The zany decor's a thing of wonder in this reformed East End boozer.

Loungelover (Map pp78-9; ☎ 7012 1234; 1 Whitby St E1; 🕑 6pm-midnight Sun-Thu, to 1am Fri & Sat; ⊖ Liverpool St) Book a table, sip a cocktail and admire the Louis XIV chairs, the huge hippo head and the loopy chandeliers.

Bricklayer's Arms (Map pp78-9; ☎ 7613 0469; 63 Charlotte Rd EC2; ⊖ Old St) Backstreet pub with an interesting crowd.

ENTERTAINMENT

THEATRE

London is a world capital for theatre and there's a lot more than mammoth musicals to tempt you into the West End. The term 'West End' – as with Broadway –

generally refers to the big-money productions like musicals, but also includes such heavyweights as the **Royal Court Theatre** (Map pp74-5; ☎ 7565 5000; www.royalcourttheatre.com; Sloane Sq SW1; ⊖ Sloane Sq), the patron of new British writing; the **National Theatre** (Map pp78-9; ☎ 7452 3000; www.nationaltheatre.org.uk; South Bank SE1; ⊖ Waterloo), which has cheaper tickets for both classics and new plays from some of the world's best companies; and the **Royal Shakespeare Company** (RSC; ☎ 0870 609 1110; www.rsc.org.uk), with productions of the Bard's classics and other quality stuff. Kevin Spacey continues his run as artistic director (and occasional performer) at the **Old Vic** (Map pp78-9; ☎ 0870 060 6628; www.oldvictheatre.com; The Cut SE1; ⊖ Waterloo).

On performance days you can buy half-price tickets for West End productions (cash only) from the official **Leicester Square Half-Price Ticket Booth** (Map pp78-9; Leicester Sq; 10am-7pm Mon-Sat, noon-3pm Sun; ⊖ Leicester Sq), on the south side of Leicester Sq.

Off West End – where you'll generally find the most original works – includes venues such as the **Almeida Theatre** (Map pp78-9; ☎ 7359 4404; www.almeida.co.uk; Almeida St N1; ⊖ Highbury & Islington), **Battersea Arts Centre** (Map pp74-5; ☎ 7223 2223; www.bac.org.uk; Lavender Hill SW11; ⊖ Clapham Junction) and the **Young Vic** (Map pp78-9; ☎ 7922 2920; www.youngvic.org; 66 The Cut SE1; ⊖ Waterloo).

For a comprehensive look at what's being staged where, visit www.officiallondontheatre.co.uk or www.theatremonkey.com.

LIVE MUSIC

ROCK & JAZZ

100 Club (Map pp78-9; ☎ 7636 0933; www.the100club.co.uk; 100 Oxford St W1; ⊖ Oxford Circus)

JULIET COOMBE

Statue beside the National Theatre, South Bank

Legendary London venue, once the centre of the punk revolution, now divides its time between jazz, rock and even a little swing.

Forum (Map pp74-5; ☎ 0844 847 2405; www.kentishtownforum.com; 9-17 Highgate Rd NW5; ⊖ Kentish Town) The Forum is a grand old theatre and one of London's best large venues.

Jazz Café (Map pp78-9; ☎ 7485 6834; 5 Parkway NW1; ⊖ Camden Town) Jazz is just part of the picture at this intimate club that stages a full roster of rock, pop, hip hop and dance.

Ronnie Scott's (Map pp78-9; ☎ 7439 0747; www.ronniescotts.co.uk; 47 Frith St W1; ⊖ Leicester Sq) London's legendary jazz club has been pulling in the hep cats since 1959.

Shepherd's Bush Empire (Map pp74-5; ☎ 8354 3300; www.shepherds-bush-empire.co.uk; Shepherd's Bush Green W12; ⊖ Shepherd's Bush) A slightly dishevelled, midsize theatre that hosts some terrific bands.

CLASSICAL

Southbank Centre (Map pp78-9; ☎ 0871 663 2509; www.southbankcentre.co.uk; South Bank; ⊖ Waterloo) This is home to the London Philharmonic Orchestra, London Sinfonietta and the Philharmonia Orchestra, among others, and has three premier venues: the **Royal Festival Hall**, smaller **Queen Elizabeth Hall** and **Purcell Room**, which host classical, opera, jazz and choral music.

Barbican Centre (Map pp78-9; ☎ 0845 120 7500; www.barbican.org.uk; Silk St EC2; ⊖ Barbican) Hulking complex with a full program of film, music, theatre, art and dance, including concerts from the London Symphony Orchestra, which is based here.

Royal Albert Hall (Map pp74-5; ☎ 7589 8212; www.royalalberthall.com; Kensington Gore SW7; ⊖ South Kensington) Splendid circular Victorian arena that hosts classical concerts and the occasional contemporary act, but is best known for the Proms.

OPERA & DANCE

Royal Opera House (Map pp78-9; ☎ 7304 4000; www.royaloperahouse.org; Royal Opera House, Bow St WC2; tickets £5-190; ⊖ Covent Garden) Attracting a younger audience since its £213-million redevelopment, which also breathed new life into programming, the Royal Opera House is the home of the Royal Ballet.

Sadler's Wells (Map pp78-9; ☎ 0844 412 4300; www.sadlers-wells.com; Rosebery Ave EC1; tickets £10-49; ⊖ Angel) Glittering modern venue, though established in the 17th century, bringing modern dance to the mainstream.

SHOPPING

From world-famous department stores to quirky backstreet retail revelations, London is a mecca for shoppers with an eye for style and a card to exercise.

Harrods (Map pp78-9; ☎ 7730 1234; 87 Brompton Rd SW1; ⊖ Knightsbridge) An overpriced theme park for fans of Britannia, Harrods is always crowded with slow tourists.

Harvey Nichols (Map pp78-9; ☎ 7235 5000; 109-125 Knightsbridge SW1; ⊖ Knightsbridge) Beloved as 'Harvey Nicks', this is London's temple of high fashion, jewellery and perfume.

Liberty (Map pp78-9; ☎ 7734 1234; 214-220 Regent St W1; ⊖ Oxford Circus) This landmark store is an irresistible blend of contemporary styles and indulgent pampering in a mock-Tudor fantasyland of carved dark wood.

Fortnum & Mason (Map pp78-9; ☎ 7734 8040; 181 Piccadilly W1; ⊖ Piccadilly Circus) The byword for quality and service from a bygone era, especially noted for its old-world food hall.

Selfridges (Map pp78-9; ☎ 0870 837 7377; 400 Oxford St W1; ⊖ Bond St) Funkiest and most vital of London's one-stop shops, where fashion runs the gamut from street to formal, the food hall is unparalleled and the cosmetics area is the largest in Europe.

GETTING THERE & AWAY

London is the country's major gateway. See p160 for further transport information (including London's airports and airlines flying to/from Britain).

BUS

Most long-distance buses and coaches *leave* London from **Victoria Coach Station**

MARKET FEVER

London has more than 350 markets selling everything from antiques and curios to flowers and fish.

Borough Market (Map pp78-9; cnr Borough High & Stoney Sts SE1; ⌚ 11am-5pm Thu, noon-6pm Fri, 9am-4pm Sat; ⊖ London Bridge) A farmers market has been here in some form since the 13th century.

Brick Lane Market (Map p79-9; Brick Lane E1; ⌚ early-2pm Sun; ⊖ Liverpool St) Sprawling East End bazaar featuring everything from fruit to paintings and bric-a-brac.

Camden Market (Map pp74-5; ⌚ 10am-5.30pm; ⊖ Camden Town) A series of markets spread along Camden High St and Chalk Farm Rd. It's been quieter since the major fire in 2008, but the Lock and Stables markets are still the place for punk fashion, cheap food, hippy shit and a whole lotta craziness.

Greenwich Market (off Map pp74-5; College Approach SE10; ⌚ 11am-7pm Wed, 10am-5pm Thu-Fri, 10am-5.30pm Sat & Sun; DLR Cutty Sark) Antiques, vintage clothing and collectibles on weekdays, arts and crafts on weekends, or just chow down in the food section.

Portobello Road Market (Map pp74-5; Portobello Rd W10; ⌚ 8am-6.30pm Mon-Sat, closes 1pm Thu; ⊖ Ladbroke Grove) One of London's most famous (and crowded) street markets.

Spitalfields Market (Map pp78-9; 105a Commercial St E1; ⌚ 10am-4pm Mon-Fri, 9am-5pm Sun; ⊖ Liverpool St) Thursdays are devoted to antiques and Fridays to fashion and art, but Sunday's the big day.

Map pp74-5; ☎ 7824 0000; 164 Buckingham Palace Rd SW1; ⊖ Victoria). The *arrivals* terminal is in a separate building across Elizabeth St from the main coach station.

TRAIN

London's main-line rail terminals (and their main destinations) include:

Charing Cross (Map pp78-9) Canterbury.

Euston (Map pp78-9) Manchester, Liverpool, Carlisle, Glasgow.

King's Cross (Map pp78-9) Cambridge, Hull, York, Newcastle, Scotland.

Liverpool Street (Map pp78-9) Stansted airport, Cambridge.

London Bridge (Map pp78-9) Gatwick airport, Brighton.

Marylebone (Map pp78-9) Birmingham.

Paddington (Map pp74-5) Heathrow airport, Oxford, Bath, Bristol, Exeter, Plymouth, Cardiff.

St Pancras (Map pp78-9) Gatwick and Luton airports, Brighton, Nottingham, Sheffield, Leicester, Leeds, Paris and Brussels (Eurostar).

Victoria (Map pp74-5) Gatwick airport, Brighton, Canterbury.

Waterloo (Map pp78-9) Windsor, Winchester, Exeter, Plymouth.

GETTING AROUND

TO/FROM THE AIRPORTS

HEATHROW

Transport connections between Heathrow and the city centre are excellent. The cheapest option is the Piccadilly line (accessible from every terminal) of the

Underground (£4, one hour to central London, departing from Heathrow every five minutes 5am to 11.30pm).

The fastest and easiest way to central London is the **Heathrow Express** (☎ 0845 600 1515; www.heathrowexpress.co.uk), an ultra-modern train to Paddington station (£15, 15 minutes, every 15 minutes from 5am to 11.25pm).

There are taxi ranks outside every terminal at Heathrow. A black cab to/from the centre of London costs £40 to £70.

GATWICK

There are regular train services (£9.50, 37 minutes) from Gatwick's South Terminal to London Victoria, running every 15 minutes during the day and hourly through the night. Other trains head to St Pancras (£9, one hour) via London Bridge, City Thameslink, Blackfriars and Farringdon.

If you're racing to make a flight, from Victoria you can jump on the **Gatwick Express** (☎ 0845 850 1530; www.gatwickexpress.co.uk): the 30 minute one way trip costs £18 (return £31), with departures every 15 minutes from 5am to about 1am).

Prices start very low, depending when you book, on **EasyBus** (www.easybus.co.uk) minibus service between Gatwick and Victoria (return from £11, allow 1½ hours, departs every 30 minutes from 3am to 1am. You'll be charged extra if you have more than one carry-on and one check-in bag.

Gatwick's taxi partner, **Checker Cars** (www.checkercars.com), has a counter in each terminal. Fares are quoted and paid for in advance (about £83 for the 65-minute ride to central London). A black cab costs similar, a minicab around £55.

STANSTED

Stansted Express (☎ 0845 600 7245; www.stanstedexpress.com) connects Stansted airport with Liverpool St train station (one way/return £17/26, 46 minutes, every 15 min utes between about 5am and 11pm).

EasyBus (www.easybus.co.uk) has service between Stansted and Victoria via Bake St (return from £13, allow 1¾ hours, ever 30 minutes from 3am to 1am).

Airbus A6 (☎ 0870 580 8080; www.national press.com) runs to/from Victoria coach statio (one way/return £10/16, allow 1¾ hour departing at least every 30 minutes).

A black cab to/from central Londo costs about £100, a minicab around £5

LONDON CITY

The Docklands Light Railway connect London City airport to the tube networ taking 22 minutes to reach Bank statio (£4). A black taxi costs around £25 to/fro central London.

CAR

Driving in London is a nightmare (heav traffic, limited/expensive parking, plus a £8 per day anticongestion charge) bu thankfully totally unnecessary, due to th excellent public transport system. If you'r hiring a car to continue your trip, take th tube to Heathrow or another major ai port and pick up the car from there.

PUBLIC TRANSPORT

Although locals love to complai London's public transport is excellen with frequent buses, trains (overgroun and underground – the latter called th 'tube') and boats to get you pretty muc anywhere. **Transport for London** (www.tf gov.uk) is the glue that keeps the networ together. The only downside: the crush a peak rush hours (roughly 7.30am to 9am and 5pm to 6.30pm).

BUS

Buses run regularly during the day, whil less-frequent night buses (prefixed wit

LONDON'S YOUR OYSTER

London's transport system is divided into six concentric zones, with nearly all the places covered by this book in Zones 1 and 2. If you're here just for a few days, get an off-peak daily Travelcard (£5.30 per day for Zones 1 and 2, valid after 9.30am Monday to Friday and all day on weekends), which covers all tubes, buses and local trains.

For five days or more, the best and cheapest option is an Oyster card, a reusable smartcard on which you can load either a season ticket (weekly/monthly £24.20/93) or prepaid credit. This gives you unlimited transport on tubes, buses and most train services.

the letter 'N') run after about 11pm. At stops with yellow signs you have to buy your ticket from the automatic machine *before* boarding. Buses stop on request, so clearly signal the driver with an outstretched arm.

LONDON UNDERGROUND & DLR

The Underground (or 'tube') extends its subterranean tentacles throughout London and into the surrounding suburbs, with services running every few minutes from 5.30am to roughly 12.30am (from 7am on Sunday).

Also included within the tube network is the driverless Docklands Light Railway (DLR), linking the City to Docklands, Greenwich and London City airport.

TAXI

London's famous black cabs are available for hire when the yellow light above the windscreen is lit. To get a licence, cabbies must do 'The Knowledge', which tests them on their knowledge of around 25,000 streets in central London. Fares are metered, starting at £2.20 and the additional rate depends on time of day, distance travelled and taxi speed. To order a black cab by phone, try **Dial-a-Cab** (☎ 7253 5000); you must pay by credit card and will be charged a premium.

Minicabs are a cheaper alternative to black cabs. They're still licensed (recognisable by the 't' symbol displayed in the window), but not metered (so get a quote first), and drivers don't have to do The Knowledge (so be prepared to show them the way). To find a local minicab firm, visit www.tfl.gov.uk/tfl/gettingaround/findaride. Only use drivers from proper agencies; licensed minicabs aren't allowed to tout for business.

WATERBUS

The public-service boats plying the Thames are ideal for avoiding traffic jams and getting great views. **Thames Clippers** (☎ 0871 781 5049; www.thamesclippers.com) run regular commuter services between Embankment, Waterloo, Bankside, London Bridge, Tower, Canary Wharf, Greenwich and Woolwich piers (adult £2.50 to £6.50, children £1.25 to £3.25), from 7am to midnight (from 9am weekends). Passengers with daily, weekly or monthly travelcards (Oyster or otherwise) get one-third off all fares.

AROUND LONDON

'When you're tired of London, you're tired of life' opined 18th-century Londoner Samuel Johnson. But he wasn't living in an age when too many days on the tube can leave you exhausted and grouchy. Luckily, the capital is surprisingly close to some excellent day escapes.

WINDSOR & ETON

☎ 01753 / pop 31,000

One of Britain's largest and most imposing medieval palaces, **Windsor Castle** (☎ 020-7766 7304; www.royalcollection.org.uk; adult/child £15/8.50; 🕒 9.45am-4pm Mar-Oct, to 3pm Nov-Feb) is still lived in by the Queen. Highlights include Queen Mary's giant dolls house designed by Sir Edward Lutyens, and St George's Chapel containing the tombs of several monarchs, including Henry VIII.

A short walk through Windsor and across the River Thames brings you to **Eton College** (☎ 01753-671177; www.etoncollege.com; adult/child £4.20/3.45; 🕒 school holidays 10.30am-4.30pm Mar-Apr & Jul-Sep, term-time 2-4.30pm), the famous public school – which in Britain means a *private* school – that educated 18 prime ministers and many royals. As you wander round you may recognise some of the buildings; *Chariots of Fire, The Madness of King George, Mrs Brown,* and *Shakespeare in Love* are just some of the classics filmed here.

Windsor and Eton have two train stations, both easily reached from London.

HATFIELD HOUSE

Home to the Cecil family, one of England's most influential dynasties for over 400 years, **Hatfield House** (☎ 01707-287010; www.hatfield-house.co.uk; house & garden adult/child £10/4.50, park only £2.50/1.50; 🕒 noon-4pm Wed-Sun & public holidays, gardens 11am-5.30pm Easter-Sep) is England's most celebrated Jacobean edifice – a graceful stone and red-brick mansion teeming with period tapestries, paintings and furniture. The surrounding park is 800 hectares of tranquil woodland with dozens of walking trails – it's a great place to bring a picnic and spend the day.

The entrance to the grounds is just across the street from Hatfield train station, reached by train from London King's Cross (£7, 20 minutes, every half-hour).

SOUTHEAST ENGLAND

Traditionally a day-trip playground for Londoners escaping overcrowded streets, England's southeast (often dubbed the 'Home Counties') offers fascinating historic towns, sweeping greenbelt vistas and some vibrant seaside resorts – most less than an hour by train from London. For visitor information, see www.visitsoutheastengland.com.

CANTERBURY

☎ 01227 / pop 43,600

The Church of England could not have built a more imposing mother ship than the extraordinary **Canterbury Cathedral** (☎ 762862; www.canterbury-cathedral.org; adult/concession £7/5.50; 🕒 9am-6.30pm Mon-Sat Easter-Sep, 9am-4.30pm Mon-Sat Oct-Easter, plus 12.30-2.30pm & 4.30-5.30pm Sun year-round). It is easy to spend a couple of hours marvelling at the early English architecture. If you would like to hear the stories behind the stonework, it is worth taking a one-hour **tour** (adult/child £5/3; 🕒 tours 10.30am, noon & 2.30pm Mon-Fri, 10.30am, noon & 1.30pm Sat Apr-Sep, noon & 2pm Mon-Sat Oct-Mar).

SLEEPING

Castle House (☎ 761897; www.castlehousehotel.co.uk; 28 Castle St; s/d/f from £50/70/90) This historic guest house sits opposite the ruined castle, and incorporates part of the old city walls. Wi-fi access.

Abode Canterbury (☎ 766266; www.abodehotels.co.uk; 30-33 High St; s/d from £89/109) The only boutique hotel in town, rooms here are graded from 'comfortable' to 'fabulous' and for the most part they live up to their names, with little features such as handmade beds, cashmere throws, velour bathrobes and beautiful modern bathrooms.

HOLGER LEUE

Interior of Canterbury Cathedral

IF YOU LIKE...

Been bowled over by cathedrals such as **Canterbury** (p98), **York Minster** (p116) and **Winchester** (p102)? Then here are some of Britain's other ecclesiastical wonders:

- **Exeter Cathedral** (☎ 01392-255573; www.exeter-cathedral.org.uk; admission £4; 9.30am-6.30pm Mon-Fri, 9am-5pm Sat, 7.30am-6.30pm Sun) A wonderful honey-stoned cathedral framed by half-timbered buildings and a stately green.
- **Wells Cathedral** (☎ 01749-674483; www.wellscathedral.org.uk; adult/child £5.50/2.50; 7am-7pm Apr-Sep, 7am-dusk Oct-Mar) Famous for its sculpture-strewn west front, scissor arches and a 14th-century mechanical clock.
- **Salisbury Cathedral** (☎ 01722-555120; www.salisburycathedral.org.uk; adult/child £5/3; 7.15am-6.15pm Sep-May, 7.15am-7.15pm Jun-Aug) Climb to the top of the tallest spire in England for panoramic views over Salisbury.
- **Durham Cathedral** (☎ 0191-386 4266; www.durhamcathedral.co.uk; admission free, tower £3; 9.30am-8pm mid-Jun–Aug, 9.30am-6.15pm Mon-Sat & 12.30-5pm Sun Sep–mid-Jun). A Unesco-listed landmark, Durham Cathedral's rib-vaulted architecture was an engineering breakthrough. Don't miss seeing the city from the top of the 66m tower.
- **Ely Cathedral** (☎ 01353-667735; www.cathedral.ely.anglican.org; admission £5.50; 7am-7pm Easter-Aug, 7.30am-6pm Mon-Sat & 7.30am-5pm Sun Sep-Easter) Dubbed the 'Ship of the Fens', Ely's cathedral boasts a glorious early-12th-century nave, while the 14th-century octagon and lantern towers soar upwards in shimmering colours.
- **Peterborough Cathedral** (☎ 01733-355300; www.peterborough-cathedral.org.uk; requested donation £3; 9am-5.15pm Mon-Fri, 9am-5pm Sat, noon-5pm Sun) Few cathedrals can rival the instant 'wow' factor of Peterborough, with its elaborate Gothic west front, three-storeyed Norman nave and breathtaking 13th-century timber ceiling.

LEFT: ADINA TOVY AMSEL; RIGHT: CHRISTOPHER GROENHOUT

Left: Cafe at Brighton's Royal Pavilion; Right: Seaside carousel, Brighton

EATING & DRINKING

Tiny Tim's Tearoom (☎ 450793; 34 St Margaret's St; mains £7-13; ⏰ 9.30-5pm Tue-Sat, 10.30am-4pm Sun) Not a hint of chintz in this English tearoom – just pure 1930s elegance.

Goods Shed (☎ 459153; Station Rd West; lunch £8-12, dinner £10-16; ⏰ market 10am-7pm Tue-Sat, to 4pm Sun, restaurant lunch & dinner Tue-Sun) Farmers market, food hall and fabulous restaurant all rolled into one, this converted station warehouse is a hit with everyone from self-caterers to sit-down gourmets.

Old Brewery Tavern (☎ 826682; High St) This trendy pub has historic prints of brewery workers, soft leather sofas, a great choice of beers, and smart versions of pub classics like fish pie or gammon, egg and chips.

GETTING THERE & AWAY

Hourly buses run to/from London Victoria (£12.70, two hours) and Dover (35 minutes).

There are two train stations: Canterbury East, accessible from London Victoria; and Canterbury West, accessible from London's Charing Cross and Waterloo East stations.

DOVER

☎ 01305 / pop 34,100

One of England's mightiest fortresses, **Dover Castle** (☎ 211067; admission £10.30; ⏰ 10am-6pm Apr-Sep, to 5pm Oct, to 4pm Thu-Mon Nov-Jan, 10am-4pm Feb-Mar) occupies a spectacular hilltop promontory dripping with history.

Immortalised in song, film and literature, the iconic **White Cliffs of Dover** are embedded in the national consciousness – a big welcome-home sign to generations of travellers and soldiers. The Langdon Cliffs (their proper name) are managed by the National Trust, which has a **visitor centre** (☎ 01304-202756; admission free; ⏰ 10am-5pm Mar-Oct, 11am-4pm Nov-Feb) 2 miles east of Dover, from where you can take a windy stroll along a 5-mile stretch of marked coastal trail.

For details of ferry services from mainland Europe, and the Channel Tunnel, see p160.

There are more than 40 trains daily to/from London Victoria and Charing Cross (£26, two hours).

LEEDS CASTLE

One of Britain's most-visited historic attractions, **Leeds Castle** (☎ 01622-765400; www.leeds-castle.com; adult/child £11/9.50; 10.30am-6pm Apr-Oct, to 4pm Nov-Mar) never fails to impress. Near Maidstone (not the northern city of the same name), it's situated on two islands surrounded by woodlands, and began life as a Norman stronghold before housing six of England's medieval queens. Today the castle is stuffed with medieval furnishings, has an aviary of endangered birds and even displays an odd collection of antique dog collars. Save time for the elaborate maze.

BRIGHTON & HOVE

☎ 01273 / pop 247,900

While some British seaside resorts are paint-peeled reminders of an earlier era, Brighton and Hove – two towns combined to form a new city in 2000 – has successfully moved on. It's now a cosmopolitan centre with a bohemian spirit, exuberant gay community, dynamic student population and a healthy number of ageing and new-age hippies.

At the **TIC** (☎ 0906-711 2255; www.visitbrighton.com; Royal Pavilion; 9.30am-5.30pm) overworked staff and a 50p-per-minute telephone line provide local information.

SIGHTS

An absolute must is the **Royal Pavilion** (☎ 290900; www.royalpavilion.org.uk; adult/child £8.50/5.10; 10am-4.30pm Oct-Mar, 9.30am-5pm Apr-Sep), the exotic palace and party-pad of Prince George, later King George IV. The flamboyant Indian-style domes and Moorish minarets are only a prelude to the palace's lavish oriental-themed interior, where no colour is deemed too strong, dragons swoop from gilt-smothered ceilings and gem-encrusted snakes slither down pillars.

Brighton's original fishing-village heart is the **Lanes**, a cobblestone web of 17th-century cottages housing a gentrified cornucopia of independent shops, pubs and one-of-a-kind eateries. The adjacent **North Laine** has a funkier, alternative vibe with streets of multicoloured shops, used-record stores and vegetarian cafes for local hipsters.

Formerly named Palace Pier, the landmark **Brighton Pier** (www.brightonpier.co.uk; admission free) is a suitably brash reminder of England's simple, seaside-loving past. Its white-painted exterior houses noisy arcades, greasy takeout food stands, and – like a fairground on a stick – a clutch of thrill rides and traditional attractions, including a stripy helter-skelter. Nearby, the skeletal remains of the **West Pier** shimmer in the haze.

FESTIVALS

There's always something fun going on in Brighton, from **Gay Pride** (www.brightonpride.org) in late July to food fests, but the showpiece is May's three-week **Brighton Festival** (☎ 709709; www.brighton-festival.org.uk), the biggest in Britain after Edinburgh.

SLEEPING

Snooze (☎ 605797; www.snoozebrighton.com; 25 St George's Terrace; s/d incl breakfast from £35/65) This eccentric Kemp Town pad is very fond of retro styling. Rooms are comfortable and spotless, and feature vintage posters, patterned wallpaper, flying wooden ducks, floral sinks and mad clashes of colour.

Hotel Pelirocco (☎ 327055; www.hotelpelirocco.co.uk; 10 Regency Sq; s £50-65, d £90-140; ste £300) One of Brighton's first theme hotels, this is still the nuttiest place in town, with a range of individually designed rooms, some by artists, some by big-name sponsors, from a basic single done up like a boxing ring, to the Motown room full of gold satin and a vintage record player.

Hotel Una (☎ 820464; www.hotel-una.co.uk; 55/56 Regency Sq; s/d from £70/110) This is a simple, unpretentious place, devoid of the themes or kitsch decor that are popular in so many of the city's hotels.

Blanch House (☎ 603504; www.blanchhouse.co.uk; 17 Atlingworth St; d from £100) Themed rooms are the name of the game in this boutique hotel, but there's nothing tacky – plush fabrics and a Victorian roll-top bath rule in the Decadence suite, while the Alice room is an ice-cool vision of silver and white.

EATING

The Lanes is a good area for foodie exploring; eye-opening culinary surprises feature in many other parts of the city.

Infinity Foods Cafe (☎ 670743; 50 Gardner St; mains £5-8; 🕑 9.30am-5pm Mon-Sat) The sister establishment of Infinity Foods wholefoods shop, a Brighton institution, serves a wide variety of vegetarian and organic food, including many vegan options.

Food For Friends (☎ 202310; www.foodforfriends.com; 17a Prince Albert St; mains £8-13; 🕑 lunch & dinner) This airy glass-sided restaurant attracts passers-by as much as it does loyal customers with its ever-inventive choice of vegetarian and vegan food.

Terre á Terre (☎ 729051; 71 East St; mains £10-15; 🕑 noon-10.30pm Tue-Fri, to 11pm Sat, to 10pm Sun) Even staunch meat eaters will come out raving about this legendary vegetarian restaurant: a sublime dining experience, from the vibrant, modern space, to the entertaining menus, to the delicious, inventive dishes, full of rich robust flavours.

Red Roaster (☎ 686668; 1d St James' St; mains £4-5; 🕑 7am-7pm Mon-Fri, 8am-7pm Sat, 9am-6.30pm Sun) You can smell the great coffee from across the street.

Tea Cosy (☎ 677055; 3 George St; Diana Spencer memorial tea £8; 🕑 noon-5pm Wed, 11am-6pm Thu-Sat, noon-6pm Sun) Barmy tearoom full of strict etiquette rules and royal family memorabilia.

GETTING THERE & AWAY

National Express coaches run hourly to/from London Victoria (£11, two hours 20 minutes) and regularly to all London airports. There are trains to/from London Victoria and King's Cross stations (£19, 1¼ hours, four per hour).

WINCHESTER

☎ 01962 / pop 107,300

Glorious **Winchester Cathedral** (☎ 857200; www.winchester-cathedral.org.uk; adult/child £5/free; 🕑 8.30am-5.30pm) is not only the city's star attraction but one of southern England's most inspirational buildings. A magnificent, multicolumned melange of architectural styles, it's also the final resting place of Jane Austen, whose discreet gravestone resides in the nave.

Winchester's other showpiece is the cavernous **Great Hall** (☎ 846476; 🕑 10am-5pm), all that remains of a gargantuan 11th-century castle destroyed by Oliver Cromwell in 1651.

Rest your head at the **Wykeham Arms** (☎ 853834; www.accommodating-inns.co.uk; 75 Kingsgate St; s £90-100, d £105-150), an inn which, at 250-odd years old, is bursting with history – it used to be a brothel and also put Nelson up for the night (some say the two events coincided). Across the river is **Black Boy** (☎ 861754; 1 Wharf Hill; £8-10; noon-11pm), an adorable old pub that dishes up decent grub in a doolally environment filled with freaky collections, from pocket watches to bear traps.

Get a taste of French cooking in the English countryside at **Brasserie Blanc** (☎ 810870; 19 Jewry St; mains £13; lunch & dinner), a supersleek chain. The celebrity chef may not necessarily sauté your starter himself, but the food is full of Gallic charm.

National Express has several direct coaches to/from London Victoria (£13, 2¼ hours). Trains run every 20 minutes to/from London Waterloo (£24, one hour) and hourly to/from Portsmouth (£8.60, one hour).

SOUTHWEST ENGLAND

Southwest England offers the pick of Britain's cities, coast and countryside – all on one verdant, sea-fringed platter. Here you'll find the golden sands and surging waves of Cornwall, your very own fossil on Dorset's Jurassic Coast, Wiltshire's prehistoric sites, Bath's exquisite Georgian cityscape, Bristol's buzzing nightlife, Somerset's hippy-chic ambience and Devon's beguiling blend of moors and shores. For information, see www.visitsouthwest.co.uk.

STONEHENGE

Britain's most iconic archaeological site, **Stonehenge** (☎ 01980-624715; adult/child £6.50/3.30; 9am-7pm Jun-Aug, 9.30am-6pm mid-Mar–May & Sep–mid-Oct, 9.30am-4pm mid-Oct–mid-Mar) has attracted a steady stream of pilgrims, poets and philosophers for millennia. Most visitors today seek spooky mysticism or marvel at the prehistoric engineering project that brought these huge rocks from Wales about 5000 years ago. The reality is a ring of stones, ringed by barbed wire in a field next to a noisy main road, so the best time to arrive is morning when the crowds are small, and with luck it may be misty, disguising modern trappings. Even better, and even closer, evening and early morning **Stone Circle Access Visits**

GLENN BEANLAND

Stonehenge

(☎ 01722-343834; adult/child £13/6) can be arranged; with only 26 people allowed, you'll need to book well in advance

The **Stonehenge Tour** (☎ 01983-827005; www.thestonehengetour.info; adult/child return £11/5) leaves Salisbury's train and bus stations half-hourly in June and August, hourly between September and May.

AVEBURY

Older, bigger and more tranquil than Stonehenge, **Avebury stone circle** (☎ 01672-539250; admission free) is one of the largest megalithic monuments in Britain, completely surrounding the pretty village of the same name.

The fascinating **Alexander Keiller Museum** (☎ 01672-539250; adult/child £4.20/2.10; 10am-6pm Apr-Oct, to 4pm Nov-Mar) provides useful context on the region's mysterious past and other nearby features, including pyramid-shaped **Silbury Hill**, Europe's largest prehistoric construction, a couple of (walkable) miles away.

To reach Avebury, buses run hourly from Salisbury (£6.50 return).

BATH

☎ 01225 / pop 90,200

Getting lost is the first thing any visitor to Bath should do. Its grand streets and teeming alleys, lined with honey-coloured stone buildings, are a stroller's delight and encourage unplanned exploration.

Bath's enduring popularity for visitors is based on a stroke of geological luck. Hot springs bubble to the surface here, and legend has it King Bladud, father of King Lear, founded the city some 2800 years ago after he was cured of leprosy by a dip in the waters. A few centuries later, the Romans created Aquae Sulis, an enormous complex of public baths and temples. The hot springs were rediscovered in the early 18th century when Bath began attracting the fashionable glitterati for restorative sojourns.

The **TIC** (☎ 0906-711 2000, per min 50p; www.visitbath.co.uk; Abbey Churchyard; 9.30am-5pm Mon-Sat, 10am-4pm Sun) is on the southern side of the abbey.

SIGHTS

ROMAN BATHS

The unmissable heart of any visit, the **Roman Baths Museum** (☎ 477785; www.romanbaths.co.uk; Abbey Churchyard; adult/child £11/6.80; 9am-6pm Mar-Jun & Sep-Oct, 9am-10pm Jul & Aug, 9.30am-5.30pm Nov-Feb) offers a tangible link with Britain's historic past. While you may not want to dive into the steaming green pools, the largely intact Roman engineering is fascinating. It gets very busy in summer; you can usually dodge the worst crowds by visiting early on a midweek morning.

BATH ABBEY

Edgar, the first king of united England, was crowned in a church here in 973, but the present **Bath Abbey** (☎ 422462; www.bathabbey.org; admission £2.50; 9am-6pm Mon-Sat Easter-Oct, to 4.30pm Nov-Easter, afternoons only Sun) dates from 1499 to 1616, making it the last great medieval church built in England.

ROYAL CRESCENT & THE CIRCUS

The crowning glory of Georgian Bath and the city's most prestigious address is the **Royal Crescent**, a semicircular terrace of majestic houses overlooking a private lawn and the green sweep of Royal Victoria Park. Built between 1767 and 1775, the houses would have originally been rented for the season by wealthy socialites.

For a glimpse into the splendour of Georgian life, head for **No 1 Royal Crescent** (☎ 428126; www.bath-preservation-trust.org.uk; adult/child £5/2.50; 10.30am-5pm Tue-Sun Feb-Oct, to 4pm Nov), which contains an astonishing amount of period furniture. A walk along Brock St leads to the **Circus**, a magnificent circle of 30 houses. Plaques on the houses commemorate famous residents such as Thomas Gainsborough, Clive of India and David Livingstone.

ASSEMBLY ROOMS

Opened in 1771, the city's glorious **Assembly Rooms** (**☎ 477789; Bennett St; admission free; ⏰ 11am-6pm Mar-Oct, to 5pm Nov-Feb**) were where fashionable Bath socialites once gathered to waltz, play

BATH

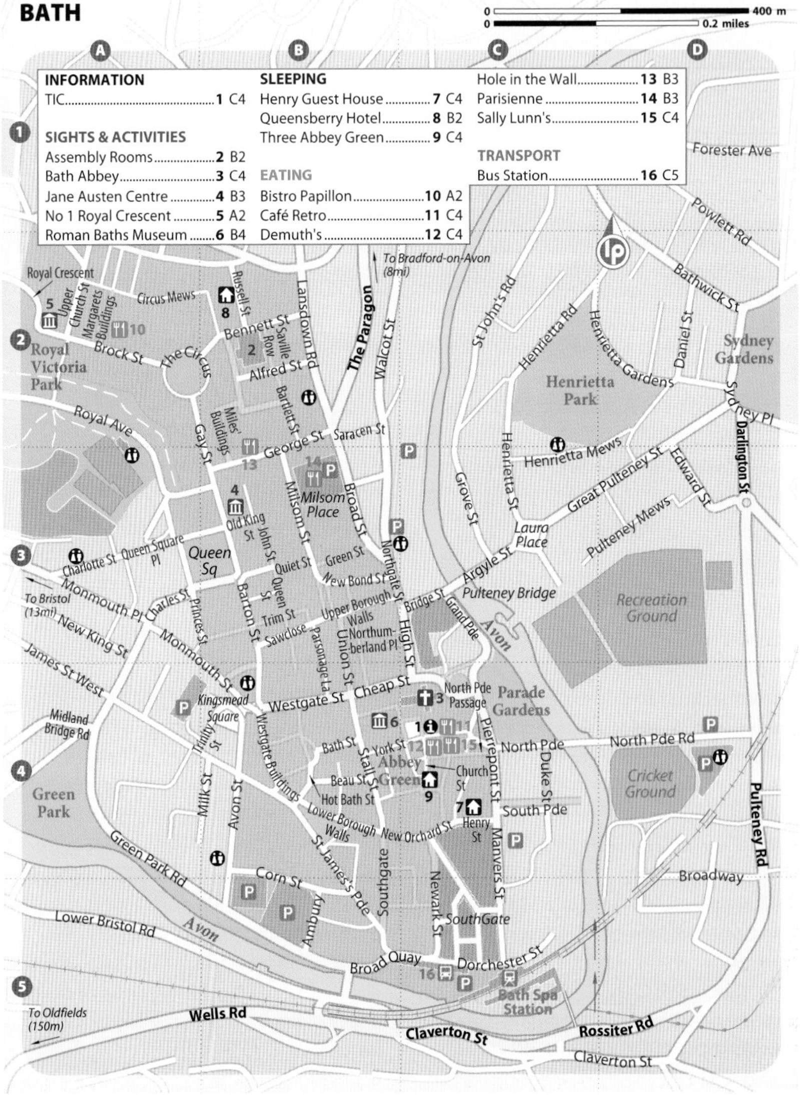

GLENN BEANLAND

Bath Abbey and Roman Baths (p104)

cards and listen to the latest chamber music. You're free to wander as long as they haven't been reserved for a special function; highlights include the card room, tearoom and the truly splendid ballroom – all lit by their original 18th-century chandeliers.

JANE AUSTEN CENTRE

Celebrating the life and times of Bath's most famous resident – she lived here for only five years, but keep that to yourself – the **Jane Austen Centre** (☎ 443000; www.janeausten.co.uk; 40 Gay St; adult/child £6.50/3.50; hours vary) is a must for lit lovers.

TOURS

Bath City Sightseeing (☎ 330444; www.city-sightseeing.com; adult/child £10/6; 9.30am-5pm Mar-Nov, to 6.30pm Jun-Sep) Runs hop-on hop-off tours on an open-top bus.

Bizarre Bath Comedy Walk (☎ 335124; www.bizarrebath.co.uk; adult/student £8/5; 8pm Mar-Sep) A chaotic and frequently hilarious blend of street theatre, live performance and guided tour. Tours leave from outside the Huntsman Inn on North Pde Passage and last about 1½ hours.

Mayor's Guide walking tours (☎ 477 411; www.thecityofbath.co.uk; tours free) A good introduction, running 10.30am and 2pm Sunday to Friday, and 10.30am on Saturday. From May to September there are additional tours at 7pm on Tuesday, Friday and Saturday.

SLEEPING

Henry Guest House (☎ 424052; www.thehenry.com; 6 Henry St; s £35-65, d £70-130, f from £105) Some of the best-value rooms in town are just five minutes' walk from the centre, at this stylish Georgian terrace.

Oldfields (☎ 317984; www.oldfields.co.uk; 102 Wells Rd; s £49-99, d £65-135, f from £85) This has to be one of the best deals in Bath: spacious rooms and soft beds for comfort; brass bedsteads and antique chairs for character. All wrapped up in a lemon-stone house with views over Bath.

Three Abbey Green (☎ 428558; www.threeabbeygreen.com; 3 Abbey Green; d £85-125, f £125-175) A great-value B&B in a secluded square near the abbey. Simplicity and smartness sees plain whites offset by tartan checks or colour-tints.

Queensberry Hotel (☎ 447928; www.thequeensberry.co.uk; 4 Russell St; s £95-300, d £105-425) The Queensberry is one to save your pennies for. This boutique barnstormer is sexy, swanky and super. Prepare to be pampered.

EATING & DRINKING

Sally Lunn's (☎ 461634; 4 North Pde Passage; lunch £5-6, dinner mains from £8) People have been taking afternoon tea here since the 1680s, and it's still high on many a tourist to-do list. The atmosphere is quintessential English chintz.

Café Retro (☎ 339347; 18 York St; mains £5-11; breakfast, lunch & dinner, closed Sun & Mon eve) Making a stand against bland coffee-shop chains, here you can munch a burger, linger over lunch or sink a salad in this quirky gem.

Parisienne (☎ 447147; Milsom Place; mains £7-13; breakfast & lunch) This delightful cafe has a Left Bank air thanks to its lovely courtyard terrace and an authentic menu of baguettes, croissants and more.

Bistro Papillon (☎ 310064; 2 Margarets Bldgs; 2-course lunch £8.50, mains £11-15; Tue-Sat) Rustic Mediterranean dishes dominate at this Gallic bistro, with a thoroughly French ambience of checked tablecloths, sunbaked colours and clattering pans.

Demuth's (☎ 446059; 2 North Pde Passage; mains £11.50-16; lunch & dinner) Delighting vegetarians for more than 20 years. If the asparagus tart or spinach and chickpea curry sounds too healthy, finish off with the devilish apricot and calvados tart.

Hole In The Wall (☎ 425242; 16 George St; mains £15-20; lunch & dinner Mon-Sat) This longstanding favourite with Bath's gourmands takes you on a cook's tour through Anglo-French flavours – check the Chew Magna lamb with potato fondant.

GETTING THERE & AWAY

Useful bus services include buses 173/773 to Wells (1¼ hours, hourly Monday to Saturday, seven on Sunday).

Trains run to/from London Paddington (£20 advance to £60 peak, 1½ hours, half-hourly) and Cardiff (£15, 1¼ hours, four hourly), plus several each hour to/from Bristol (£5.50, 11 minutes) to connect with services to northern and southwest England.

EXMOOR NATIONAL PARK

Straddling the counties of Somerset and Devon, and perched on the coast, exquisite Exmoor offers lovely beaches and dramatic sea cliffs, as well as verdant valleys, tumbling streams, peaceful farmland and expansive moors grazed by horned sheep and England's last herd of wild red deer.

Main towns with tourist offices include Lynton and Porlock, and there are several **National Park visitor centres**: Dulverton (☎ 01398-323841; NPCDulverton@exmoor-nationalpark.gov.uk; 7-9 Fore St; 10am-5pm Apr-Oct, 10.30am-3pm Nov-Mar); Dunster (☎ 01643-821835; NPCDunster@exmoor-nationalpark.gov.uk; Dunster Steep; 10am to 5pm Easter-Oct, limited hr Nov-Easter); Lynmouth (☎ 01598-752509; Lyndale Car Park; 10.30am-3pm Easter-Oct). Two good websites are www.exmoor-nationalpark.gov.uk and www.visit-exmoor.info.

DARTMOOR NATIONAL PARK

Dartmoor is an ancient and compelling landscape, very different from the rest of Devon. Exposed granite hills (called tors) dot the horizon, each linked by swathes of honey-tinged moorland. Moody and utterly empty, you'll find its desolate beauty exhilarating or chilling – or quite possibly a bit of both.

For local information, the **High Moorland Visitor Centre** (☎ 01822-890414; www.dartmoor-npa.gov.uk; 10am-5pm Apr-Oct, to 4pm Nov-Mar) is in Princetown, a large village at the heart of the moor. There are smaller centres at **Haytor** (☎ 01364-661520; 10am-5pm Easter-Oct, to 4pm Sat & Sun Nov & Dec) and **Postbridge** (☎ 01822-880272; 10am-5pm Easter-Oct, 10am-4pm Sat & Sun Nov & Dec).

ST IVES

☎ 01736 / pop 9870

Once a busy fishing port, St Ives is now best known for its wonderful beaches and as a centre for the arts, with cobbled alleyways lined with galleries, shops and cafes catering for thousands of summer visitors.

Like a tasty, overstuffed Cornish pasty, the streets are full of tiny artist-run galleries, but **Tate St Ives** (☎ 796226; www.tate.org.uk/stives; Porthmeor Beach; adult £5.75; 10am-5pm Mar-Oct, to 4pm Tue-Sun Nov-Feb) is the focal point. From its striking beachfront setting, the southwest satellite of the popular London gallery showcases the works of local legends like Barbara Hepworth and John Wells. There's a panoramic top-floor cafe, and an array of free talks and tours that keep the place livelier than a hungry seagull.

A beautifully finished B&B that's far beyond lace doilies, **Treliska** (☎ 797678; www.treliska.com; 3 Bedford Rd; s £40-60, d £64-80) is all clean lines, chrome bath-taps and elegant wooden furniture. Or, sleep with a clear conscience (and in style) at supersleek B&B **Organic Panda** (☎ 793890; www.organicpanda.co.uk; 1 Pednolver Tce; d £80-120), where spotty cushions, technicolour artwork and timber-salvage beds keep the funk factor high, while sea views steal the show outside.

PENZANCE

☎ 01736 / pop 21,200

The end of the train line from London, and the westernmost town in Britain, Penzance is larger and a bit scruffier than St Ives and other Cornish neighbours, but some might say it's better for it.

Looming up from the sea, the island abbey of **St Michael's Mount** (☎ 710507; adult/child £6.60/3; 10.30am-5pm Sun-Fri Mar-Oct) is one of Cornwall's iconic landmarks. Set on a collection of craggy cliffs and connected to the mainland by a cobbled causeway, there's been a monastery here since at least the 5th century. You can walk across at low tide and there are ferries at high tide in summer.

Intercity trains run to/from London Paddington (£90, cheaper if bought in advance, six hours, eight daily), while local trains go to St Ives (£5, 20 minutes, hourly).

LAND'S END

At the extreme southwesterly point of mainland Britain, the coal-black cliffs, heather-covered headlands and booming Atlantic surf should steal the show. Unfortunately, the view is rather spoilt by a tawdry theme park called **Legendary Land's End** (☎ 0870 458 0099; www.landsend-landmark.co.uk; adult/child £11/7; 10am-5pm summer, to 3pm winter). But you can bypass the kitsch and tat, and opt for an exhilarating clifftop stroll instead. On a clear day the Isles of Scilly are visible, 28 miles out to sea.

Land's End is 9 miles from Penzance (and 874 miles from John O'Groats; see p142). Bus 1/1A travels to/from Penzance (around seven daily Monday to Saturday), while bus 300 serves St Ives (four daily May to October).

EDEN PROJECT

If any one thing is emblematic of Cornwall's regeneration, it would be the **Eden Project** (☎ 01726-811911; www.edenproject.com; Bodelva; adult/child £15/5; ⏲ 10am-6pm Apr-Oct, 10am-4.30pm Nov-Mar). Ten years ago the site was a dusty, exhausted clay pit; a symbol of the county's industrial decline. Now it's home to the largest plant-filled greenhouses in the world and is effectively a superb, monumental education project about how much man depends on the natural world.

CENTRAL ENGLAND

The geographic heartland of England is a mix of wildly differing scenes, with historic towns like Stratford-upon-Avon, Oxford and Shrewsbury, the flower-decked villages of the Cotswolds and the lush dales and peaty moors of the Peak District.

For local information, see www.visitheartofengland.com (covering Birmingham and around, Warwickshire and Shropshire), www.oxfordshirecotswolds.org and www.visitpeakdistrict.com.

OXFORD

☎ 01865 / pop 134,300

Renowned as one of the world's most famous university towns, Oxford lives up to its advance billing as a fascinating, colourful, history-flavoured place. It's also a crowded tourist hot spot in summer – so bypass jostling tour groups by coming early or late in the season if you can.

Oxford University is the oldest university in Britain, with the first of its 39 separate colleges dating from the early 13th century. Its plethora of notable graduates includes William Morris, Oscar Wilde, Lewis Carroll and, the evidence suggests, Sherlock Holmes. Women were not admitted to Oxford's closeted halls until 1878 and even then were not allowed to receive degrees until the 1920s.

The **TIC** (☎ 252200; www.visitoxford.org; 15-16 Broad St; ⏲ 9.30am-5pm Mon-Sat, to 6pm Thu-Sat Jul & Aug, 10am-4pm Sun) is packed with maps and brochures.

SIGHTS

OXFORD UNIVERSITY

The largest and grandest of all of Oxford's colleges, **Christ Church** (☎ 276492; www.chch.ox.ac.uk; St Aldate's; adult £4.90; ⏲ 9am-5pm Mon-Sat, 1-5pm Sun) is also its most popular. The magnificent buildings, illustrious history and latter-day fame as a *Harry Potter* location has tourists coming in droves.

Arguably Oxford's prettiest college, **Magdalen** (☎ 276000; www.magd.ox.ac.uk; High St; adult/under 16yr £4/3; ⏲ noon-6pm Jul-Sep, 1-6pm/dusk Oct-Jun) combines stately buildings with a verdant tapestry of landscaped grounds. Enhance your credentials by pronouncing it properly: *mawd-len*.

From the high street follow wonderfully named Logic Lane to **Merton College** (☎ 276310; www.merton.ox.ac.uk; Merton St; admission free; ⏲ 2-4pm Mon-Fri, 10am-4pm Sat & Sun), one of Oxford's original three colleges.

BODLEIAN LIBRARY & RADCLIFFE CAMERA

Oxford's **Bodleian Library** (☎ 277224; www.bodley.ox.ac.uk; Broad St) is one of the oldest public libraries in the world, with more than seven million items on 118 miles of shelving and seating for 2500 readers.

Nearby is the **Radcliffe Camera** (Radcliffe Sq; ⏲ no public access), a quintessential Oxford landmark and one of the city's most photographed buildings, boasting Britain's third-largest dome.

MUSEUMS

A vast collection of art and antiquities is on display at the **Ashmolean Museum** (☎ 278000; www.ashmolean.org; Beaumont St; admission free; 10am-5pm Tue-Sat, noon-5pm Sun), Britain's oldest public museum, including European, Egyptian, Islamic and Chinese art, rare porcelain, tapestries, silverware and priceless musical instruments.

In a glorious Victorian Gothic building with cast-iron columns, ornate capitals and a soaring glass roof, the **University Museum** (☎ 272950; www.oum.ox.ac.uk; Parks Rd; admission free; 10am-5pm) is worth a visit for its architecture alone. But the real draw is the mammoth natural-history collection ranging from exotic insects and fossils to a towering T-Rex skeleton.

TOURS

The informative folk at Oxford's TIC run two-hour tours of the city and colleges (£7, tours 11am and 2pm year-round, also 10.30am, and 1pm July and August), and a selection of themed tours (£7.50) on various dates throughout the year. Other options include:

City Sightseeing (☎ 790522; www.citysightseeingoxford.com; adult/under 16yr £11.50/6; every 10-15min, 9.30am-6pm Apr-Oct) Has hop-on hop-off bus tours from the bus or train stations.

Oxon Carts (☎ 07747 024600; www.oxoncarts.com; 15min taster tour £10, 1hr tour £30) A fleet of pedicabs touring Oxford's narrow lanes where the buses simply can't go.

Salter Bros (☎ 243421; www.salterssteamers.co.uk; Folly Bridge; boat trips adult/child £8.50/4.80; mid-May–mid-Sep) has boat trips along the River Isis.

SLEEPING & EATING

Beaumont (☎ 241767; www.oxfordcity.co.uk/accom/beaumont; 234 Abingdon Rd; s £45-55, d £60-78) A class above most B&Bs at this price; all crisp white linen, trendy wallpaper, mosaic bathrooms and beautiful furniture.

Tilbury Lodge (☎ 862138; www.tilburylodge.com; 5 Tilbury Lane; s £70, £d £80-90;) Spacious and plush rooms and excellent bathrooms make this stylish B&B worth the trip outside the centre of town.

our pick **Old Parsonage Hotel** (☎ 310210; www.oldparsonage-hotel.co.uk; 1 Banbury Rd; r £170-250;) Wonderfully quirky and instantly memorable, this place has the right blend of old-world character, period charm and modern luxury.

Vaults (☎ 279112; St Mary's Church; mains £3.25-4.95; 10am-5pm) With a great selection of soups, salads, pastas and paellas, plus great views and a historic setting, this is one of the best lunch venues in town.

Jericho Café (☎ 310840; 112 Walton St; mains £7-9) Chill out and relax over a coffee and cake, or go for the wholesome lunch and dinner specials, which encompass everything from sausages and mash to Lebanese lamb kibbeh.

Café Coco (☎ 200232; 23 Cowley Rd; mains £7-14) This Cowley Rd institution is a hip hang-out, with classic posters on the walls, a vaguely Mediterranean menu and a lively atmosphere.

Jam Factory (☎ 244613; www.thejamfactoryoxford.com; 27 Park End St; mains £8-12) Arts centre, bar and restaurant rolled into one, this is a laid-back place with exhibitions, hearty breakfasts and excellent-value modern British dishes.

DRINKING

Turf Tavern (☎ 243235; 4 Bath Pl) Hidden down narrow alleyways, this often crowded medieval pub is one of the best loved in town.

Eagle & Child (☎ 302925; 49 St Giles) This atmospheric pub has been serving ale since 1650 and is still a hotchpotch of nooks and crannies.

GETTING THERE & AWAY

BUS

Competition on the Oxford-London route is fierce, with two companies running buses (£15 return, 90 minutes) up to every 10 to 15 minutes at peak times.

Oxford Espress (☎ 785400; www.oxfordbus.co.uk)

Oxford Tube (☎ 772250; www.oxfordtube.com)

TRAIN

There are half-hourly services to/from London Paddington (£22.50, one hour), and roughly hourly trains to Birmingham (£22, 1¼ hours). Hourly services also run to/from Bath (£19.60, 1¼ hours) and Bristol (£21.40, 1½ hours), via a change at Didcot Parkway.

BLENHEIM PALACE

About 8 miles from Oxford, and often combined with the university city on tour itineraries, **Blenheim Palace** (☎ 08700 602080; www.blenheimpalace.com; adult £16.50; 10.30am-5.30pm mid-Feb–Oct, Wed-Sun Nov–mid-Dec, park open year-round) is a monumental baroque fantasy that's well worth the trip. Now a Unesco World Heritage site, Blenheim (pronounced blen-um) is home to the 11th Duke of Marlborough, and is the historic birthplace of Winston Churchill in 1874. The **Churchill Exhibition** explores the life of this still-revered wartime leader. Additional highlights include the aptly named **Long Library**, the painted ceilings of the **Great Hall** and the **private apartments** of the current duke, accessible via a special 30-minute tour. Save plenty of time for the beautifully landscaped **gardens**.

To get here from Oxford, bus 20 (£4.20 return, 30 minutes, twice hourly) runs from train and bus stations to Woodstock village, from where the palace is a short walk.

STRATFORD-UPON-AVON

☎ 01789 / pop 22,200

Few towns are so dominated by one man's legacy as Stratford is by William Shakespeare. Be prepared to fight the tourist masses for breathing space in the historic buildings associated with England's most famous wordsmith – especially during summer.

GLENN BEANLAND

Blenheim Palace

BRITAIN

CENTRAL ENGLAND

You can book accommodation, buy theatre tickets and exchange currency at the **TIC** (☎ 0870 160 7930; www.shakespeare-country.co.uk; Bridgefoot; 9am-5pm Mon-Sat, 10am-4pm Sun Apr-Oct, 10am-3pm Sun Nov-Mar).

SIGHTS & ACTIVITIES

THE SHAKESPEARE HOUSES

Like artefacts in glass cases, there's an unreal quality to the five timber-framed Shakespeare-related houses on Stratford's mostly modern streets. All are managed by the **Shakespeare Birthplace Trust** (☎ 204016; www.shakespeare.org.uk; all 5 properties £15, 3 townhouses £9; 9am-5pm Mon-Sat, 10am-5pm Sun Jun-Aug, variable at other times). Three of the houses are central, one is an easy walk away, and the fifth a drive or bike ride out; a combination ticket costs about half as much as the individual admission fees combined.

The most worthy of a visit is **Shakespeare's Birthplace**, a scrubbed-clean Tudor building reputed to be where the Bard entered the world mewling and puking, where now chatty interpreters explain the history.

Shakespeare's daughter Susanna married doctor John Hall, and their fine Elizabethan townhouse, **Hall's Croft** (☎ 292107), stands near Holy Trinity Church. The main exhibition offers a fascinating insight into medicine in the 16th century.

Nash's House, where Shakespeare's granddaughter lived, describes the town's history and contains a collection of 17th-century oak furniture and tapestries.

A mile from the centre, **Anne Hathaway's Cottage** is an idyllic thatched farmhouse where Shakespeare's wife grew up. The garden includes sculptures of Shakespearian characters and a maze.

Mary Arden's House, the childhood home of Shakespeare's mother, is at Wilmcote, 3 miles west of Stratford. It's now the **Shakespeare Countryside Museum**, with exhibits tracing local rural life over the past four centuries.

OTHER SIGHTS

You can see where the Bard is now at the immaculate **Holy Trinity Church** (☎ 266316; Old Town; 8.30am-6pm Mon-Sat, 12.30-5pm Sun Apr-Oct, 9am-4pm Mon-Sat,

GLENN BEANLAND

Shakespeare's Birthplace

12.30-5pm Sun Nov-Mar; admission to church free, Shakespeare's grave £1.50). The stained-glass windows are highlights, but most people come to see Will's grave – a discreet stone slab in the floor of the chancel.

Seeing the **Royal Shakespeare Company** (☎ 0844 800 1110; www.rsc.org.uk; tickets £8-38; 9.30am-8pm Mon-Sat) is an absolute must. Major stars have trod the boards here and production standards are very high. The main Royal Shakespeare Theatre reopens after renovations in 2010. In the meantime, performances are held in the striking temporary Courtyard Theatre.

SLEEPING

Moonraker House (☎ 268774; www.moonrakerhouse.com; 40 Alcester Rd; s/d incl breakfast from £47/70;) Pristine rooms behind the whitewashed facade of this memorable B&B have a Shakespeare theme.

Swan's Nest Hotel (☎ 0844 879 9140; www.macdonaldhotels.co.uk/SwansNest; Swan's Nest Lane; d incl breakfast from £120;) In a 17th-century house near the Avon, this hotel has airy rooms, many overlooking the gardens, a wood-panelled bar and a terrace for summer evenings.

EATING & DRINKING

Edward Moon's (☎ 267069; 9 Chapel St; mains £10.95-16.95; lunch & dinner) English food spiced with local ingredients inspires the food at this charming, glass-fronted brasserie.

Lambs (☎ 292554; 12 Sheep St; mains £11-18; noon-2pm Mon-Sun, plus 5-10pm Mon-Sat, 6-9.30pm Sun) The classiest joint in town – from the imposing manor-house door and aristocratic interior to delectable cuisine and fancy wine list.

Dirty Duck (☎ 297312; Waterside) Officially called the Black Swan, this enchanting riverside alehouse is a favourite post-performance thespian watering hole, and the adjoining restaurant (open from 11am to 10pm) is good value.

Cox's Yard (☎ 404600; Bridgefoot) This large riverside complex with a pub, cafe and music venue is a lovely place to enjoy a drink or meal.

GETTING THERE & AROUND

National Express destinations include Birmingham (£7, one hour, twice daily), Oxford (£9, one hour, daily) and London Victoria (£16, 3½ hours, five daily). Trains run to/from London Marylebone (£16, 2¼ hours).

PEAK DISTRICT NATIONAL PARK

Between the industrial Midlands, Manchester and Sheffield, the 555-sq-mile Peak District is one of the finest areas in England for walking, cycling and other outdoor activities. As well as the natural landscape and the pretty villages, the Peak District boasts some stately homes, most famous of which is sumptuous **Chatsworth House** (☎ 01246-582204; www.chatsworth.org; adult/child £11.25/6; 11am-5.30pm Mar-Dec). Known as the 'Palace of the Peak', this vast edifice has been occupied by the dukes of Devonshire for centuries. The house sits in 25 sq miles of **gardens** (adult/child £7.50/4.50), where you can marvel at a high fountain and modern sculptures.

EASTERN ENGLAND

Apart from the bustling magnet of Cambridge, few visitors to the UK see the eastern part of England – or East Anglia, as it's usually called. But Norfolk, Suffolk and Lincolnshire are picturesque counties, and the absence of tourists belies a region well worth exploring, with pretty market towns, gently undulating farm-strewn landscapes, winding rivers and lakes, swaths of beautifully desolate coastline and gallons of colourful

GLENN BEANLAND

Burghley House

↘ IF YOU LIKE...

Britain's famous for its country houses, such as **Chatsworth House** (p113), **Blenheim Palace** (p111), **Castle Howard** (p119) and the following:

- **Stourhead** (☎ 01747-841152; Stourton; house or garden adult/child £6.30/3.80, house & garden £10.50/5.80; ⏰ house 11.30am-4.30pm Fri-Tue mid-Mar–Oct, garden 9am-7pm or sunset year-round) Overflowing with vistas, temples and follies, this is 18th-century English landscaping at its finest. Find it in Wiltshire, 8 miles south of Frome.
- **Longleat** (☎ 01985-844400; www.longleat.co.uk; house & grounds adult/child £10/6, safari park £11/8, all-inclusive passport £22/16; ⏰ house 10am-5pm year-round, safari park 10am-4pm Apr-Nov, other attractions 11am-5pm Apr-Nov) This half country house, half drive-through safari park is 3 miles from Frome and Warminster.
- **Chartwell** (☎ 01732-868 381; Westerham; adult/child £11.20/5.60, garden & studio only £5.60/2.80; ⏰ 11am-5pm Wed-Sun Apr-Jun, Sep & Oct, Tue-Sun Jul & Aug) Six miles east of Sevenoaks, Winston Churchill's former home offers an intimate insight into England's famous cigar-chomping bombast.
- **Erddig** (☎ 01978-355314; adult/child/family £9.40/4.70/23.50; ⏰ grounds 10am-6pm Sat-Thu Jul & Aug, 11am-6pm Sat-Wed Apr-Jun & Sep, to 4pm Mar, Oct & Nov, house noon-5pm Sat-Thu Jul & Aug, noon-5pm Sat-Wed Apr-Jun & Oct, to 4pm Mar, to 4pm Sat & Sun Nov & Dec) Twelve miles northeast of Llangollen, this Welsh beauty offers a glimpse into the upstairs-downstairs life of the British upper class.
- **Burghley House** (☎ 01780-752451; www.burghley.co.uk; adult/child incl sculpture garden £10.90/5.40; ⏰ 11am-5pm Sat-Thu Easter-Oct) Built by Elizabeth I's adviser William Cecil, Burghley is a filmic favourite, featuring in *The Da Vinci Code* and *Elizabeth: The Golden Age*. Near Stamford in Lincolnshire.
- **Sandringham House** (☎ 01553-612908; www.sandringhamestate.co.uk; adult/child 5-15yr £9/5, gardens & museum only £6/3.50; ⏰ 11am-4.45pm late Mar-Oct unless royal family is in residence) The Queen's country getaway languishes in 25 hectares of landscaped gardens. 6 miles northeast of King's Lynn, Norfolk.

history. For information check out www.visiteastofengland.com.

CAMBRIDGE

☎ 01223 / pop 108,900

Hallowed home of one of the world's most prestigious centres of learning, Cambridge is steeped in exquisite architecture and scholarly ambience. The university was founded in the 13th-century by a splinter group from Oxford – still known locally as the 'other place'.

The **TIC** (☎ 0871 266 8006; www.visitcambridge.org; Wheeler St; 10am-5.30pm Mon-Fri, 10am-5pm Sat, 11am-3pm Sun Apr-Sep, 10am-5.30pm Mon-Fri, 10am-5pm Sat Oct-Mar) is crowded in summer.

SIGHTS

Cambridge University comprises 31 colleges, five of these – King's, Queen's, Clare, Trinity and St John's – charge tourists admission. Some other colleges deem visitors too disruptive and simply deny entry. Most colleges close to visitors for the Easter term and all are closed for exams from mid-May to mid-June.

Among the unmissable highlights is **King's College Chapel** (☎ 331212; www.kings.cam.ac.uk/chapel; King's Pde; adult £5; during term 9.30am-3.30pm Mon-Fri, 9.30am-3.15pm Sat, 1.15-2.30pm Sun, outside term 9.30am-4.30pm Mon-Sat, 10am-5pm Sun), a dazzling Tudor testament to Christian devotion with the power to impress even ardent atheists.

Nearby **Trinity College** (☎ 338400; www.trin.cam.ac.uk; Trinity St; adult Mar-Oct £2.50; library noon-2pm Mon-Fri, hall 3-5pm, chapel 10am-5pm) is one of the university's grandest and most attractive academic piles. Don't miss the **Wren Library**; its collection includes AA Milne's original *Winnie the Pooh*.

Echoing its history as a centre of discovery, many Cambridge colleges have their own museums, our favourite being the **Fitzwilliam Museum** (☎ 332900; www.fitzmuseum.cam.ac.uk; Trumpington St; admission free; 10am-5pm Tue-Sat, noon-5pm Sun), where highlights include Egyptian, Greek and Roman artefacts, a kaleidoscope of artworks from Titian, Rembrandt and Monet, and a treasure trove of ceramics, glass and silverware.

TOURS

Time-challenged visitors should consider a TIC-arranged **walking tour** (☎ 457574; tours@cambridge.gov.uk; tickets incl entry to King's/St John's Colleges £10; 11.30pm & 1.30pm, with extra tours at 10.30am & 2.30pm Jul-Aug).

City Sightseeing (☎ 423578; www.city-sightseeing.com; adult/child £10/5; 10am-4pm) has hop-on hop-off tour buses with 21 stops around town, and **Riverboat Georgina** (☎ 307694; www.georgina.co.uk; per person £16-24) has two-hour cruises including a cream tea or boatman's lunch.

SLEEPING & EATING

Victoria Guest House (☎ 350086; www.cambridge-accommodation.com; 55-57 Arbury Rd; s £35-60, d £50-75) A central option worth seeking out, with friendly owners and a hint of period character.

Tenison Towers (☎ 363924; www.cambridgecitytenisontowers.com; 148 Tenison Rd; s/d £35/60) An exceptionally friendly and homely B&B especially recommended if you're arriving by train.

Hotel Felix (☎ 277977; www.hotelfelix.co.uk; Whitehouse Lane, Huntingdon Rd; s/d incl breakfast from £145/180;) This luxurious boutique hotel occupies a lovely villa in landscaped grounds a mile from the city centre.

our pick **Michaelhouse** (☎ 309167; Trinity St; mains £3.55-6.35; 9.30am-5pm Mon-Sat) Sup fair-trade coffee and nibble focaccia among soaring medieval arches at this stylishly converted church.

CB2 (☎ 508503; 5-7 Norfolk St; mains £4-13) Internet cafe, bistro, music venue and cinema, dishing up global cuisine in a relaxed atmosphere.

our pick **Rainbow Vegetarian Bistro** (☎ 321551; www.rainbowcafe.co.uk; 9a King's Pde; mains £8.50-9.50; 10am-10pm Tue-Sat) A snug subterranean gem decorated in funky colours and serving organic dishes with a hint of the exotic.

Chop House (☎ 359506; 1 Kings Pde; mains £9-15) This is a great place to enjoy classic British cuisine, including sausages and mash or fish pie.

Midsummer House (☎ 369299; www.midsummerhouse.co.uk; Midsummer Common; set lunch £30, 3-course dinner £60; lunch Wed-Sun, dinner Tue-Sat) This sophisticated place serves up what is possibly the best food in East Anglia.

GETTING THERE & AROUND

Buses to/from Oxford (£9, 3¼ hours) are regular but take a very convoluted route. The handiest transport is the train, with services at least every 30 minutes to/from London's King's Cross and Liverpool St stations (£17.90, 45 minutes to 1¼ hours).

NORTHEAST ENGLAND

By turns wild and pretty, rural and urban, modern and historic, this part of England contains the large and varied counties of Yorkshire and Northumberland, and three of Britain's great cities: historic York and Durham, and resurgent postindustrial Newcastle. For general information, see www.yorkshirevisitor.com and www.visitnortheastengland.com.

YORK

☎ 01904 / pop 180,000

York has been a military, political, religious and commercial settlement dating back to the Roman era, and time-travellers from the city's medieval past would still recognise much of its wonderfully preserved buildings, such as the spectacular Minster and the stout wall girding the centre's ancient alleyways – although they might be surprised at the modern profusion of gift shops and tea rooms, not to mention the mass of sightseeing visitors.

The city centre is relatively small, though a tangle of medieval alleys is further confused by the fact that here 'gate' means street, and 'bar' means gate. The **TIC** (☎ 550099; www.visityork.org; Exhibition Sq; 9am-6pm Mon-Sat, 10am-5pm Sun) can help with accommodation (£3 booking fee).

SIGHTS

YORK MINSTER

Northern Europe's largest Gothic cathedral, **York Minster** (☎ 557200; www.yorkminster.org; adult £5.50; 9am-5pm Mon-Sat, noon-3.45pm Sun) is the city's highlight – a 1000-year-old treasure house of architecture and richly coloured stained-glass windows. Take an audio tour of the **Undercroft** (£3) for subterranean Roman, Norman and Viking remains, or climb the Minster's 275-step **Tower** for a spectacular view past gargoyles and over the city.

CITY WALLS

If the weather's good, a walk around the **City Walls** (admission free; 8am-dusk) gives a whole new perspective on the city. The full circuit is 4.5 miles (allow two hours); if you're pushed for time, the stretch from Bootham Bar to Monk Bar is best.

SHAMBLES

The cobbled lane called the **Shambles** (www.yorkshambles.com), lined with 15th-century Tudor buildings that overhang so much they almost meet above your head, is the most visited street in Europe. Quaint and picturesque, it hints at what a

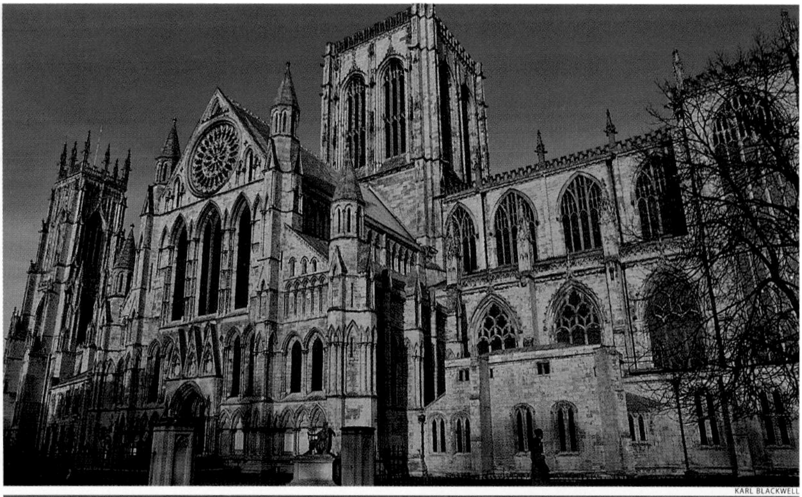
KARL BLACKWELL

York Minster

medieval street may have looked like – if you forget the boutiques and gift shops.

JORVIK CENTRE

Interactive multimedia exhibits aimed at 'bringing history to life' often achieve just the opposite, but the much-hyped **Jorvik** (☎ 543403; www.vikingjorvik.com; Coppergate; adult/child £8.50/6; 10am-5pm), a smells-and-all reconstruction of the original Viking settlement that gave York its name, manages to pull it off.

DIG

Under the same management as Jorvik, and aimed mainly at kids, **Dig** (☎ 543403; www.digyork.co.uk; St Saviourgate; adult/child £5.50/5, Dig & Jorvik combined £11.25/8.50; 10am-5pm) cashes in on the popularity of TV archaeology programs, and lets you 'unearth the secrets' of York's distant past.

OTHER SIGHTS

The **National Railway Museum** (☎ 621261; Leeman Rd; admission free; 10am-6pm) is a homage to train travel, especially the age of steam, but there's also a Japanese bullet train, and a nod to the Channel Tunnel. Even for nontrainspotters it's surprising fun. Nearby is the **Yorkshire Wheel** (a smaller version of the London Eye) with great views over the city.

TOURS

The Association of Voluntary Guides offers free two-hour **walking tours** (10.15am & 2.15pm Apr-Oct, plus 6.45pm Jun-Aug), departing across the street from the TIC. There's a bewildering range of **ghost tours** – York is reputed to be England's most haunted city. For your own wanderings, check the tourist office's suggestions for walking itineraries at www.visityork.org/explore.

SLEEPING & EATING

Elliotts B&B (☎ 623333; www.elliottshotel.co.uk; 2 Sycamore Pl; s/d from £38/75;) Leaning towards the boutique end of the guesthouse market, this place has stylish rooms and hi-tech touches such as flat-screen TVs and free wi-fi.

Dairy Guesthouse (☎ 639367; www.dairyguesthouse.co.uk; 3 Scarcroft Rd; s/d from £55/75) This lovely Victorian home has many original features, but the real treat is the flower-filled courtyard.

Arnot House (☎ 641966; www.arnothouseyork.co.uk; 17 Grosvenor Tce; r £75-80) With four-poster beds and heavy Victorian floral patterns, this place sports an authentically old-fashioned look.

STEPHEN SAKS

Peacock in the grounds of Castle Howard

➘ CASTLE HOWARD

There are big posh houses, there are stately homes – and then there's **Castle Howard**, a work of theatrical grandeur and audacity, instantly recognisable from its starring role in *Brideshead Revisited*. The ostentatious Renaissance exteriors are complemented by sumptuous interiors of priceless art and artefacts, while the surrounding landscaped parkland boasts temples, fountains and strutting peacocks. Castle Howard is about 15 miles from York, and is a popular tour excursion. Or you can get there on Yorkshire Coastliner bus 840 (40 minutes, one daily).

Things you need to know: ☎ 01653-648333; www.castlehoward.co.uk; adult/child house & grounds £10.50/6.50, grounds only £8/5; house 11am-4.30pm, grounds 10am-4.30pm Mar-Oct & 1st three weeks of Dec

Blake Head Vegetarian Café (☎ 623767; 104 Micklegate; mains £4-6; 9.30am-5pm Mon-Sat, 10am-5pm Sun) A bright and airy space at the back of a bookshop, filled with modern oak furniture and funky art.

Betty's (☎ 659142; www.bettys.co.uk; St Helen's Sq; mains £6-11, afternoon tea £15; 9am-9pm) This branch of the Yorkshire chain serves afternoon tea, old-school style, with white-aproned waitresses and crisp linen tablecloths.

Melton's Too (☎ 629222; 25 Walmgate; mains £9-13; 10.30am-10.30pm Mon-Sat, to 9.30pm Sun) A comfortable, chilled-out, booth-lined cafe-bar and bistro; serves everything from cake and cappuccino to three-course dinner of Whitby crab, beef with Yorkshire pudding and local strawberries.

Melton's (☎ 634341; www.meltonsrestaurant.co.uk; 7 Scarcroft Rd; mains £15-18; lunch Tue-Sat, dinner Mon-Sat) This is one of Yorkshire's best restaurants, attracting foodies from far and wide. There's a good-value lunch and early dinner set menu (£18.50 for two courses).

DRINKING

our pick **Blue Bell** (☎ 654904; 53 Fossgate) Typical English pub with a smouldering fireplace, beer-stained decor, real ale and friendly staff.

King's Arms (☎ 659435; King's Staith) Creaky old place with a fabulous riverside location – a perfect spot for a summer's evening.

GETTING THERE & AWAY

National Express coaches run to/from London (£24, 5¼ hours, four daily), and many other destinations including Birmingham (£25, 3¼ hours, one daily) and Newcastle (£14, 2¾ hours, four daily).

On the train, York is a major railway hub with frequent direct services to London King's Cross (£20 to £100 depending when you book and travel, two hours), Birmingham (£40, 2¼ hours), Newcastle (£25, one hour), Leeds (£10, 25 minutes) and Manchester (£20, 1½ hours).

HAWORTH

☎ 01535 / pop 6080

Famous as home of the Brontë novelists, and a hugely popular literary shrine to Emily, Anne and Charlotte, Haworth is a pretty town of cobbled streets and hillside vistas. Most visitors to Haworth head for the **Brontë Parsonage Museum** (☎ 642323; Church St; adult/child/concession £4.90/1.60/3.60; 10am-5.30pm Apr-Sep, 11am-5pm Oct-Mar), which offers a fascinating trip back in time for literature buffs.

YORKSHIRE DALES NATIONAL PARK

Probably the most scenic and certainly the most popular part of the Yorkshire uplands, the Dales is a region of rolling hills, lush valleys and craggy limestone cliffs.

The 700-sq-mile Yorkshire Dales National Park can be broken into two parts: in the north, the main dales run east-west, and include Wensleydale and Swaledale; in the south they run north-south and include Wharfedale and Ribblesdale.

For walkers, the **Dales Way** (www.thedalesway.co.uk) winds through the national park from Ilkley to Windermere in the Lake District; the whole distance takes about a week, and the trail is a great focus for shorter loops from a couple of hours to a day.

A fantastically useful service is the railway line between Settle and Carlisle, cutting through the heart of the park, providing access to small villages and great walking country, which would otherwise be hard to reach. This historic line is also worth riding for its own sake; for details see www.settle-carlisle.co.uk.

NEWCASTLE-UPON-TYNE

☎ 0191 / pop 470,000

Once synonymous with postindustrial decline and decay, today's Newcastle is reborn and brimming with confidence. All of a sudden, this unfailingly friendly city, with its distinctive Geordie accent thicker than molasses, has kick-started a brand-new arts and entertainment scene – while riotous nightlife remains an established tradition.

ORIENTATION & INFORMATION

The Tyne River is a focal point, and also the boundary between Newcastle to the north and the separate entity of Gateshead to the south, although the local tourism authorities bill the area as Newcastle-Gateshead or even NewcastleGateshead.

Newcastle has two main **TICs** Grainger St (☎ 277 8000; 132 Grainger St; 9.30am-5.30pm Mon-Wed, Fri & Sat, to 7.30pm Thu year-round, plus 10am-4pm Sun Jun-Sep); Guildhall (☎ 277 8000; 11am-6pm Mon-Fri, 9am-6pm Sat, 9am-4pm Sun).

SIGHTS

Make sure you take a stroll along the quays beside the Tyne River, under the famous **Tyne Bridges** – including a mini-proto–Sydney Harbour Bridge – where many of Newcastle's and Gateshead's great buildings jostle for your attention.

On the Gateshead side, you can't miss **Baltic** (☎ 478 1810; www.balticmill.com; admission free; 10am-6pm), a former flourmill, now a contemporary art centre, and the north's answer to London's Tate Modern. It's reached from the Newcastle side via the **Millennium Bridge**, a pedestrian walkway that opens like an eye for passing ships.

Nearby, and in sharp architectural contrast, is **Sage** (☎ 443 4666; www.thesagegates

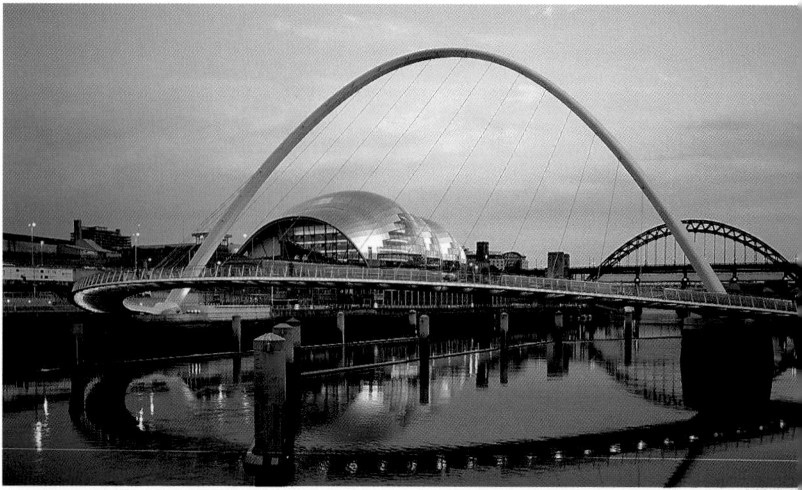

CHRIS MELLOR

Millennium Bridge (p119)

head.org), a magnificent chrome-and-glass concert hall designed by Norman Foster.

Opened in May 2009, the new **Great North Museum** (☎ 222 8996; www.greatnorthmuseum.org) is set to be the north's foremost museum of the natural sciences, archaeology, history and culture.

South of Newcastle, on the outer edge of Gateshead, the towering **Angel of the North** (admission free) is artist Antony Gormley's best-known and most successful work, and Britain's largest sculpture – 20m high with a wingspan wider than a Boeing 767.

SLEEPING

Adelphi Hotel (☎ 281 3109; www.adelphihotelnewcastle.co.uk; 63 Fern Ave; s/d £39/60) Just off Osborne Rd, this attractive hotel has nice floral rooms that are clean and very neat – a rare thing around here for this price range.

Whites Hotel (☎ 281 5126; www.whiteshotel.com; 38-42 Osborne Rd; s/d £45/75) First impressions don't promise a great deal, but this is our favourite of the Osborne Rd hotels, with uniformly modern rooms and first-rate service.

Waterside Hotel (☎ 230 0111; www.watersidehotel.com; 48-52 Sandhill, Quayside; s/d £75/80) Elegant rooms, lavish furnishings, a heritage-listed building and an excellent location make this a great choice in this price bracket.

Copthorne (☎ 222 0333; www.millenniumhotels.com; The Close, Quayside; s/d from £75/85; 🏊) Pick a river-view room at this modern, waterside hotel; book online for the best rates.

New Northumbria Hotel (☎ 281 4961; www.newnorthumbriahotel.co.uk; 61-73 Osborne Rd; s/d from £85/95) Trendy, clean and fairly pleasant, with decent rooms and a good breakfast.

EATING

Café Royal (☎ 231 3000; 8 Nelson St; cafe mains £4-5, restaurant mains £8-12; 🕑 lunch & dinner Mon-Sat, to 7pm Sun) Downstairs is a pleasant cafe, while the upstairs dining room has a Mediterranean menu with vaguely Pacific Rim influences.

Big Mussel (☎ 232 1057; www.bigmussel.co.uk; 15 The Side; mains £6-12; lunch & dinner) Mussels and other shellfish – with chips – are a very popular choice at this informal diner. There are pasta and vegetarian options as well.

Café 21 (☎ 222 0755; Trinity Gardens, Quayside; mains £14.50-22; lunch & dinner Mon-Sat) This elegant restaurant offers new interpretations of old favourites: pork and cabbage, liver and onions and beef and chips.

Jesmond Dene House (☎ 212 3000; www.jesmonddenehouse.co.uk; Jesmond Dene Rd; mains £18-22) A gourmet delight with exquisite menu and northeast specials including County Durham venison and Lindisfarne oysters.

DRINKING

Trent House Soul Bar (1-2 Leazes Lane) Totally relaxed and utterly devoid of pretentiousness, this old-school boozer out-cools every other bar because it isn't trying to.

Free Trade Inn (Lawrence Rd) This no-nonsense boozer overlooking the Tyne attracts students and long-standing patrons.

Cumberland Arms (off Byker Bank) This 19th-century bar has a sensational selection of ales as well as a range of Northumberland meads.

Cluny (36 Lime St) Cool bar by day, superb musical venue by night, this superpopular spot defines the independent spirit of the Ouseburn Valley.

GETTING THERE & AWAY

Newcastle International airport (☎ 286 0966; www.newcastleairport.com) is 7 miles north of the city, with services to a host of UK and European destinations.

Ferries sail from Newcastle to the Netherlands and several Scandinavian ports. See p160 or check out www.newcastleferry.co.uk for more details.

National Express coaches depart and arrive from the Gallowgate coach station. There are services to/from London (£27, seven hours, six daily) and Manchester (£17.50, five hours, six daily) and many other cities in England and Scotland. Local and regional buses operate from Haymarket and Eldon Sq bus stations.

Newcastle is on the main rail line between London and Edinburgh, via York (£20, 45 minutes, every 20 minutes) or Berwick-upon-Tweed (£23, 45 minutes, every two hours). There's also the scenic Tyne Valley Line west to Carlisle.

HADRIAN'S WALL

Built to mark the edge of the Roman Empire, and to separate the civilised colony of Britannia from the savages of Scotland, this 73-mile coast-to-coast barrier across England is mightily impressive to this day. Very little remains in some parts, while other stretches are remarkably well preserved and simply spectacular, notably the section between Hexham and Brampton. The best portal site for information is www.hadrians-wall.org.

Chesters (☎ 01434-681379; admission £4.50; 9.30am-6pm Apr-Sep, 10am-4pm Oct-Mar), situated near Chollerford, is a well-preserved fortification that includes an impressive bathhouse. Its museum displays a fascinating array of Roman sculptures and drawings that have been found in the area.

Vindolanda (☎ 01434-344277; www.vindolanda.com; admission £5.20; 10am-6pm Apr-Sep, to 5pm Feb-Mar & Oct-Nov), 1.5 miles north of Bardon Mill, and 1 mile from Once Brewed, is an extensive site offering a fascinating glimpse into the daily life of a Roman garrison town.

Housesteads (☎ 01434-344363; adult/concession £3.80/2.90; 10am-6pm Apr-Sep, to 4pm Oct-Mar) is the area's most dramatic and popular ruin. The carefully preserved foundations include a famous public latrine, and a gateway overlooking wild Northumbrian countryside, little changed since the legionaries pulled out in AD 410. It's 2.5 miles north of Bardon Mill, or a spectacular walk (3 miles) along the wall from Once Brewed.

GETTING THERE & AWAY

The Newcastle–Carlisle train line runs parallel to the Wall a mile or two to the south, with stations at Hexham, Haydon Bridge, Bardon Mill, Haltwhistle and Brampton. There are hourly buses between Carlisle and Newcastle, via most of the same towns. From June to September the hail-and-ride Hadrian's Wall Bus (number AD 122 – gedit?) shuttles between all the major sites, towns and villages along the way.

NORTHWEST ENGLAND

A place of two halves, Northwest England offers popular culture, arts, music and big nights out in the sprawl of urban conurbations around the world-famous cities of Manchester and Liverpool, alongside peace, quiet, fresh air and high peaks in the mountainous Lake District.

MANCHESTER

☎ 0161 / pop 390,000

Two historical double acts neatly encapsulate Manchester's modern history, for this is where Mr Rolls met Mr Royce and where Mr Marx worked with Mr Engels on the *Communist Manifesto*. Manchester's day as the crucible of industrialisation and political ferment is long gone, however, and today we can enjoy a lively, modern city with ample public space, strikingly juxtaposed modern and Victorian architecture, and a buzzing nightlife, including a vibrant gay scene.

ORIENTATION & INFORMATION

Shoe power and the excellent Metrolink tram are the only things you'll need to get around the compact city centre. All public transport converges at Piccadilly Gardens. Directly north is the on-the-up boho Northern Quarter. A few blocks southeast is the Gay Village, and next to that is Chinatown. Further west again is recently developed Salford Quays, and Old Trafford football stadium, where Manchester United's stars earn their fabulous keep.

The **TIC** (☎ 0871 222 8223; www.visitmanchester.com; Town Hall Extension, St Peter's Sq; 🕑 10am-5.15pm Mon-Sat, 10am-4.30pm Sun) sells tickets for all sorts of guided walks, which operate almost daily year-round and cost £5 for adults.

SIGHTS & ACTIVITIES

Explore the city centre on foot and you'll find some grand Victorian architecture, most notably in Albert Sq, home of the enormous Victorian Gothic **Town Hall**.

Further south, the **Castlefield** district (now dubbed 'urban heritage park') offers a fascinating mosaic of solid old civic structures, warehouses, Roman ruins, serene canalside paths and old pubs – with modern skyscrapers jostling for space in between. The area also contains the excellent **Museum of Science & Industry** (☎ 832 1830; www.msim.org.uk; Liverpool Rd; admission free; 🕑 10am-5pm) with interactive displays on the city's textile and engineering industries, excellent live demonstrations and working steam engines.

Manchester Art Gallery (☎ 235 8888; www.manchestergalleries.org; Mosley St; admission free; 🕑 10am-5pm Tue-Sun) houses an impressive collection ranging from early Italian, Dutch and Flemish painters to Gainsborough, Blake, Constable and the Pre-Raphaelites.

Out in Manchester's rapidly regenerating **Salford Quays** area (take the Metrolink to Broadway or Harbour City), the **Imperial War Museum North** (☎ 836 4000; www.iwm.org.uk/north; Trafford Wharf Rd; admission free; ⏲ 10am-5pm) is visually stunning and truly thought provoking.

Nearby is the architecturally bold **Lowry Complex** (☎ 876 2020; www.thelowry.com; Salford Quays; ⏲ 11am-8pm Tue-Fri, 10am-8pm Sat, 11am-6pm Sun-Mon), which attracts more than one million visitors a year to its myriad functions, from art exhibits and theatre to bars, restaurants and, inevitably, shops. It's also home to more than 300 paintings and drawings by northern England's favourite artist, LS Lowry (1887–1976), visual chronicler of urban working-class landscapes and their 'matchstick' inhabitants.

You may begin to understand why fans of the city's most famous football club treat its home as hallowed ground if you head to **Old Trafford** stadium, the home of **Manchester United** (www.manutd.com). There's a great **museum** (£8.50), but for fans the **stadium tours** (☎ 0870 442 1994; incl museum entry £12; ⏲ tours every 10min 9.40am-4.30pm except match days) are most rewarding.

SLEEPING & EATING

New Union Hotel (☎ 228 1492; www.newunionhotel.com; 111 Princess St; s/d from £40/50) In the heart of the Gay Village, but not exclusively pink, this terrific little hotel is all about affordable fun.

Castlefield (☎ 832 7073; www.castlefield-hotel.co.uk; 3 Liverpool Rd; s/d from £70/99; 🅿) This warehouse conversion results in a thoroughly modern business hotel overlooking the canal basin.

Palace Hotel (☎ 288 1111; www.principal-hotels.com; Oxford St; r from £80) An elegant refurbishment of one of Manchester's most magnificent Victorian palaces has resulted in a pretty special boutique hotel, combining the grandeur of the public areas with the modern look of the bedrooms.

Trof (☎ 832 1870; 5-8 Thomas St; sandwiches £4, mains around £8; ⏲ 9.30am-midnight) Great music, top staff and a fab selection of

NEIL SETCHFIELD

Bridge at Salford Quays

sandwiches, roasts and other dishes plus a broad selection of beers and tunes.

Eighth Day (☎ 273 4878; 111 Oxford Rd; mains around £5; 9.30am-5pm Mon-Sat) This ecofriendly hang-out is a favourite with students and sells everything to make you feel good about your place in the world.

Love Saves the Day (☎ 832 0777; Tib St; salads £5.50) The Northern Quarter's most popular cafe is a New York–style deli and eatery in one large, airy room.

Yang Sing (☎ 236 2200; 34 Princess St; mains £9-16; lunch & dinner) A serious contender for best Chinese restaurant in England, Yang Sing attracts diners from all over with its exceptional Cantonese cuisine.

Market Restaurant (☎ 834 3743; www.market-restaurant.com; 104 High St; mains £11-16; lunch & dinner Wed-Fri, dinner Sat) Beyond the shabby exterior you'll find excellent British cuisine on a changing monthly menu.

GETTING THERE & AWAY

Manchester airport (☎ 489 3000; www.manchesterairport.co.uk) is the largest airport outside London, with flights to around 20 other British cities, plus many more European and long-haul destinations.

National Express coaches serve most major cities from Chorlton St coach station in the city centre, including Liverpool (£5, 1¼ hours, hourly), Leeds (£7.60, one hour, hourly) and London (£23, 3¾ hours, hourly).

Manchester Piccadilly is the main station for trains to and from the rest of the country, including London (£115 on the spot, from £20 with advance booking, three hours, seven daily), Liverpool (£8.80, 45 minutes, half-hourly) and Newcastle (£41.20, three hours, six daily).

LIVERPOOL

☎ 0151 / pop 510,000

Visually more striking than Manchester, with some fantastic architecture, a grand waterfront facing the broad Mersey River, towering cathedrals and a busy nightlife, infectiously friendly Liverpool is on the up – finally emerging from decades of economic depression and industrial decline.

ORIENTATION & INFORMATION

Liverpool is simple to get around. The main attractions are Albert Dock, west of the city centre, and the trendy Ropewalks area, south of Hanover St. Lime St station, the bus station, the tourist office and the Cavern Quarter – a mecca for Beatles fans – lie just to the north.

There's a central **TIC** (☎ 233 2008; 08 Place, Whitechapel; 9am-8pm Mon-Sat, 11am-4pm Sun Apr-Sep, 9am-6pm Mon-Sat, 11am-4pm Sun Oct-Mar) and another branch at Albert Dock.

SIGHTS

In the city centre, **St George's Hall** (☎ 707 2391; admission free; 10am-5pm Tue-Sat, 1-5pm Sun) is arguably Liverpool's most impressive building, built in 1854 and recently restored to former glory.

At the vastly entertaining **World Museum** (☎ 478 4399; www.liverpoolmuseums.org.uk/wml; William Brown St; admission free; 10am-5pm) exhibits range from live insect colonies to space exploration.

Liverpool's two cathedrals, at either end of Hope St, are well worth visiting. The Roman Catholic **Metropolitan Cathedral of Christ the King** (8am-6pm Mon-Sat) was completed in 1967 with a wonderfully serene and uplifting interior, washed with a celestial blue when the sun lights the stained glass. The neo-Gothic **Liverpool Cathedral** (8am-6pm) is the largest Anglican cathedral in the world, with unrivalled city views from its 100m-high **tower** (admission £4.25; 11am-5pm Mon-Sat).

A £100 million renovation helped make **Albert Dock** (www.albertdock.com) Liverpool's number-one tourist attraction, with sights including the **Merseyside Maritime Museum** (☎ 478 4499; www.liverpoolmuseums.org.uk/maritime; admission free; 10am-5pm), which celebrates this city's place as a world port, while the **International Slavery Museum** (☎ 478 4499; www.liverpoolmuseums.org.uk/ism; admission free; 10am-5pm) reveals slavery's unimaginable horrors – including Liverpool's own role in the trade – in a clear and uncompromising manner. For something lighter, **Tate Liverpool** (☎ 702 7400; www.tate.org.uk/liverpool; admission free, 10am-6pm Tue-Sun & bank holiday Mon) displays a roll-call of 20th-century artistic talent; while the **Beatles Story** (☎ 709 1963; www.beatlesstory.com; Albert Dock; adult/child £12.50/6.50; 9am-7pm) is a sanitised version of the rise of Liverpool's most famous sons, with plenty of genuine memorabilia.

SLEEPING & EATING

Feathers Hotel (☎ 709 9655; www.feathers.uk.com; 119-125 Mt Pleasant; s/d from £55/80) A better choice than most of the similar-priced chain hotels, with comfortable rooms, satellite TV and a great buffet breakfast.

Premier Inn (☎ 0870 990 6432; www.premierinn.co.uk; Albert Dock; r from £55) As chain hotels go, this is perfectly fine; what makes it is the location – right in the heart of the Albert Dock action.

Crowne Plaza Liverpool (☎ 243 8000; www.cpliverpool.com; St Nicholas Pl, Princes Dock, Pier Head; r from £82;) The paragon of the modern and luxurious business hotel, listed here thanks to its marvellous waterfront location.

GLENN BEANLAND

Night views of Albert Dock and the city

GLENN BEANLAND

Statue of John Lennon in the Cavern Quarter

Lucy in the Sky with Diamonds (☎ 236 0096; 8 Cavern Walks; mains around £4; 8am-5pm Mon-Sat) Hard to imagine that a cafe with this name in this touristy part of town could be authentic in any way, but Lucy is. And we love her.

Everyman Bistro (☎ 708 9545; www.everyman.co.uk; 13 Hope St; mains £5-8; noon-2am Mon-Fri, 11am-2am Sat, 7-10.30pm Sun) Out-of-work actors and other creative types favour this great cafe-restaurant beneath the Everyman Theatre.

Tea Factory (☎ 708 7008; 79 Wood St; mains £7-12; 11am-late) The wide-ranging menu covers all bases from typical Brit fare to international tapas, but it's the room, darling, that makes this place so popular. Rock stars' favourite.

Quarter (☎ 707 1965; 7-11 Falkner St; mains £9-13; ⏰ lunch & dinner) A gorgeous little bistro with outdoor seating for that elusive summer's day, perfect for a plate of pasta or just a coffee and a slice of mouthwatering cake.

Pan-American Club (☎ 709 7097; Britannia Pavilion, Albert Dock; mains £13-24) A truly beautiful warehouse conversion has created this top-class restaurant and bar, easily one of the best dining addresses in town.

GETTING THERE & AWAY

National Express coaches connect Liverpool with most major towns, including Manchester (£5, 1¼ hours, hourly), London (£24, five to six hours, seven daily), Birmingham (£10.20, 2¾ hours, five daily) and Newcastle (£20.50, 6½ hours, three daily).

Trains run hourly services to almost everywhere, including Chester (£4.45, 45 minutes), London (£25 to £60 depending on time of travel, 3¼ hours) and Manchester.

LAKE DISTRICT NATIONAL PARK

A dramatic landscape of high peaks, dizzying ridges and huge lakes gouged by the march of Ice Age glaciers, the Lake District is a beautiful corner of Britain. Not surprisingly, the awe-inspiring geography here shaped the literary persona of one of Britain's best-known poets, William Wordsworth. Often called simply the Lakes (but never – note, Australians – the 'Lakes District'), the national park and surrounding area attract around 15 million visitors yearly who come for serious hiking or to potter gently around the tearooms and souvenir shops of the countless pretty villages. Principal gateways and bases include the twin towns of Windermere and Bowness in the south, Ambleside slightly nearer the centre, and Keswick in the north. Portal websites include www.lake-district.gov.uk and www.golakes.co.uk.

Via train, Windermere is at the end of a branch off the main line between London Euston and Glasgow. For getting around, the handiest bus service is the 555, cruising regularly through the park via Kendal, Windermere, Ambleside, Grasmere and Keswick.

SOUTH & WEST WALES

South Wales extends north, west and east from Cardiff, and includes the former industrial heartland of the Valleys, and the ports of Swansea and Newport. Beyond Swansea is the delightful Gower Peninsula – with quiet villages and sandy beaches, and then you get into West Wales, a rural area with a stunning coastline.

CARDIFF

☎ 029 / pop 285,000

The Welsh capital labours under many sobriquets these days, but one thing is certain: Cardiff feels very much alive, and is currently emerging as one of Britain's leading urban centres of the 21st century.

The **TIC** (☎ 0870 1211258; www.visitcardiff.com; Old Library, The Hayes; ⏰ 9.30am-6pm Mon-Sat, 10am-4pm Sun; 💻) has piles of information covering all Wales and an accommodation-booking service.

SIGHTS

CITY CENTRE

Dazzling Victorian and mock-Gothic folly make **Cardiff Castle** (☎ 2087 8100; www.cardiffcastle.com; Castle St; grounds only £3.50, with castle tour £8.95; ⏰ 9am-6pm Mar-Oct, 9.30am-5pm Nov-Feb) an entertaining visit. Nearby, the **National Museum Cardiff** (☎ 2039 7951; www.museumwales.ac.uk; Cathays Park; admission free; ⏰ 10am-5pm Tue-Sun) has in-

:ernational-quality galleries, enthralling ıatural history exhibits, as well as a handy :rash course in Welsh culture.

Cardiff's spectacular **Millennium Stadium** (☎ **tours 2082 2228, box office 0870 558 2582; www.millenniumstadium.co.uk; tours adult/child £6.50/4;** 🕐 **10am-5pm Mon-Sat, to 4pm Sun & bank holidays**), on the site of the famous Arms Park, sits smack bang in the middle of town like an invading spaceship, and in this rugby-mad nation, somehow gets away with it.

CARDIFF BAY

Of the many stunning new buildings at Cardiff Bay, the **Wales Millennium Centre** (☎ **box office 0870 040 2000; www.wmc.org.uk; Bute Pl**) stands out the most, with its golden roof and mauve slate panelling. This is Wales' premier arts complex and home to the Welsh National Opera. Next door, **Y Senedd** (☎ **0845 010 5500; www.assemblywales.org**), the National Assembly for Wales, is another distinctive structure of glass, steel and slate.

SLEEPING

Big Sleep (☎ **2063 6363; www.thebigsleephotel.com; Bute Tce; d £45-120**) This wannabe design hotel has minimalist and self-consciously cool ambience, but with rates set according to availability it can be a hit-and-miss experience.

Barceló Angel Hotel (☎ **2064 9200; www.barceloangelcardiff.com; Castle St; s/d from £65/115;** 💻) Longstanding hotel, now under new management and refurbished, with stately rooms and castle (or stadium) views.

St David's Hotel (☎ **2045 4045; www.thestdavidshotel.com; Havannah St; r from £260;** 💻) Epitomising Cardiff Bay's transformation from wasteland to style zone, this landmark hotel offers top-notch rooms and fabulous views.

EATING & DRINKING

our pick Café Minuet (☎ **2034 1794; 42 Castle Arcade;** 🕐 **10am-5pm Mon-Sat**) A classical-music-themed cafe with Italian-influenced dishes named after the great composers. A true one-off.

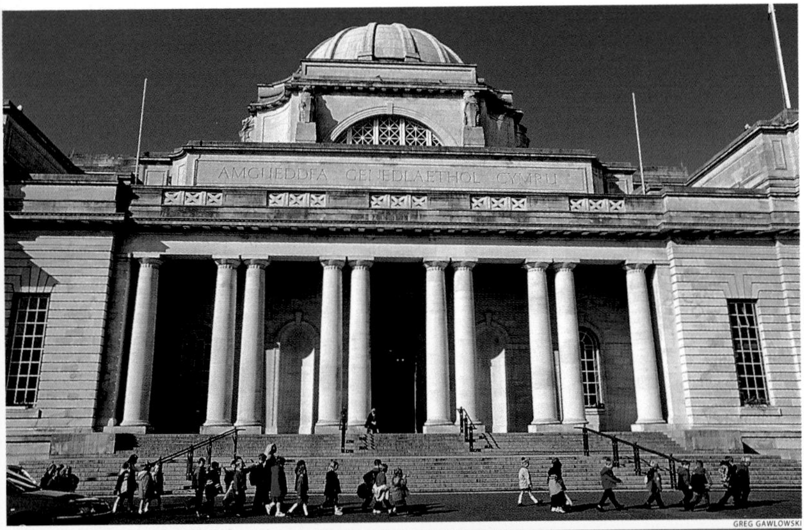

GREG GAWLOWSKI

National Museum Cardiff

Yard (☎ 2022 7577; 42-43 St Marys St) The stand-out option in the chain-heavy Brewery Quarter, this 'bar and kitchen' attracts a chilled-out daytime crowd, cranking up the music and the vibe by night.

Zerodegrees (☎ 2022 9494; www.zerodegrees.co.uk; 27 Westgate St) A bright and buzzy bar-restaurant (and microbrewery) with all-day food and artisan beers.

Woods Bar & Brasserie (☎ 2049 2400; www.woods-brasserie.com; Pilotage Bldg, Stuart St; mains £13-16; lunch & dinner Mon-Sat year-round, lunch & dinner Sun Jun-Sep, dinner Sun Oct-May) Featuring floor-to-ceiling windows and light-wood touches, the menu at this very classy eatery in a converted dockside building includes numerous fish specialities.

GETTING THERE & AWAY

Regular train services include to/from Birmingham (£13.50, two hours, at least half-hourly) and London Paddington (£24, two hours, at least half-hourly).

BRECON BEACONS NATIONAL PARK

The Brecon Beacons National Park covers 519 sq miles of high grassy hills and mountains, marking the traditional and geographical border between South and mid-Wales. For information on the park, you can access the main **National Park Visitor Centre** (☎ 01874-623366), located in the village of Libanus, about 4 miles from Brecon. Or see www.visitbreconbeacons.com.

HAY-ON-WYE

☎ 01497 / pop 1600

On the Wales–England border, at the northeastern tip of the Brecon Beacons, Hay-on-Wye is an eccentric town known as the world centre for secondhand books; there are over 35 shops here, and more than one million books on sale, everything from £1000 first editions to books by the yard (literally).

The town is well served with B&Bs and pubs. The **Start** (☎ 821391; www.thestart.net; s/d £35/70), peacefully set on the fringes of town, is a beautifully comfortable 18th-century house a five-minute walk from the centre.

Popular and welcoming, **Granary** (☎ 820790; Broad St; 9am-5.30pm;) is a bustling country-kitchen cafe and the staple choice for breakfasts, snack lunches and coffees. **Oscars Bistro** (☎ 821193; High Town; 10am-4.30pm) is a popular option for lunch or snacks in the heart of town.

PEMBROKESHIRE COAST NATIONAL PARK

Rocky, sandy, sparkling and remote, the wonders of the Pembrokeshire Coast National Park are unmissable. The stunning coastline is typified by soaring cliffs and vast swaths of golden beach, encompassed within the park's boundaries and set against a backdrop of boiling surf or sheltered crystal coves. For information on the park and surrounding area, see www.pcnpa.org.uk and www.visitpembrokeshirecoast.org.uk.

Preseli Venture (☎ 01348-837709; www.preseliventure.com) has coasteering, kayaking and mountain-biking weekends in stunning ecofriendly accommodation.

TYF Adventure (☎ 01437-721611; www.tyf.com) has coasteering, kayaking, surfing and rock climbing, also with an ecofriendly base.

Bird-spotting, whale-watching, fishing trips, island cruises and landings can be done with **Thousand Islands Expeditions** (☎ 01437-721721; www.thousandislands.co.uk).

MID- & NORTH WALES

Many visitors see Mid-Wales as a staging post en route to elsewhere, but this rich, rural region abounds in hidden gems and is the crucible for new Welsh movements championing green issues and top-notch local food.

SNOWDONIA NATIONAL PARK

The jagged peaks of the mountains of Snowdonia loom over the coast and offer easily the most spectacular scenery in Wales. The most popular region is in the north around Snowdon (at 1085m the highest peak in Britain south of the Scottish Highlands). For more information see www.visitsnowdonia.info and www.snowdonia-npa.gov.uk.

Good bases and gateways include the busy village of **Betws-y-Coed** on the eastern side of the park. Pretty **Beddgelert** and former slate-mining town **Blaenau Ffestiniog** are handy for the south. Most convenient for Snowdon itself is the town of **Llanberis** – less attractive, but with all the facilities you need.

The handiest train line runs along the North Wales coast between Chester and Holyhead, via Llandudno Junction and Bangor (from where you can get buses into the park itself), with a branch line down to Betws-y-Coed and Blaenau Ffestiniog.

An excellent local bus network called the **Snowdon Sherpa** serves the park, with connections to Llandudno, Betws-y-Coed, Bangor and Llanberis.

LLANBERIS

☎ 01286 / pop 2000

This former slate mining village is now outdoor-activity central, attracting walkers, climbers and mountain bikers year-round. If *walking* up mountains isn't for you, from Llanberis you can take the **Snowdon Mountain Railway** (☎ 0870 4580033; www.snowdonrailway.co.uk; ⏰ 9am-5pm Mar-Oct) to the top of Wales' highest peak. The 5-mile journey takes an hour, schedules are weather-dependent and summertime queues can be long.

CENTRE FOR ALTERNATIVE TECHNOLOGY

A couple of miles outside Machynlleth is the **Centre for Alternative Technology** (CAT; ☎ 01654-705950; www.cat.org.uk; adult/child £8.40/4.20; ⏰ 10am-5.30pm Easter–mid-Jul, Sep & Oct, 10am-6pm mid-Jul–Aug, 10am-dusk Nov-Easter), established in the 1970s as a virtually self-sufficient cooperative, and now an impressive (and extensive) series of displays showing how wind, water and solar power provide food, heat and telecommunications. To explore the whole site takes about two hours – take rainwear as it's primarily outdoors.

CONWY

☎ 01492 / pop 3900

Conwy is all about **Conwy Castle** (☎ 592358; adult/child £4.70/4.20; ⏰ 9am-5pm Apr-Oct, 9.30am-4pm Mon-Sat & 11am-4pm Sun Nov-Easter), another great bastion of Edward I's defences, one of Wales's finest and a Unesco World Heritage site. From the battlements, views across the estuary and to the peaks of Snowdonia – when not veiled in cloud – are exhilarating.

SOUTHERN & CENTRAL SCOTLAND

North of the border with England, and below the Central Belt of Edinburgh and Glasgow, sits the broad region of Southern

Scotland. The western side of this region offers some fine scenery – high hills, moors, forests and a craggy coastline – without the attendant tour buses and crowds you might find in the Highlands.

MELROSE

☎01896 / pop 1650

Melrose Abbey (☎822562; admission £5.20; 9.30am-5.30pm Apr-Sep, to 4.30pm Oct-Mar) is perhaps the most beautiful of the Border abbeys, and a potent nationalist symbol for many Scots; the heart of Robert the Bruce is buried here.

There are buses to/from Jedburgh (30 minutes, at least hourly Monday to Saturday) and Edinburgh (£6, 2¼ hours, half-hourly Monday to Saturday).

JEDBURGH

☎01835 / pop 4090

Jedburgh is a classic, historic Border town. Dominating the town skyline, **Jedburgh Abbey** (☎863925; admission £5.20; 9.30am-5.30pm Apr-Sep, 9.30am-4.30pm Oct-Mar) was founded in 1138 by David I as a priory for Augustinian canons. The red-sandstone walls are roofless, and the ingenuity of the master mason can be seen in some of the rich (if somewhat faded) stone carvings in the nave.

Jedburgh has good bus connections to/from Melrose (30 minutes, at least hourly Monday to Saturday) and Edinburgh (£6, two hours, at least hourly Monday to Saturday, five Sunday).

EDINBURGH

☎0131 / pop 440,000

Scotland's proud and historic capital city is a visual delight, built on a grand scale around two hills – one topped by its impressive castle, the other by a big chunk of undeveloped mountain seemingly helicoptered in for effect. And with the UK's most popular and comprehensive summer festival scene, visitors who plan a brief stopover often end up staying longer.

INFORMATION

Edinburgh & Scotland Information Centre (☎0845 225 5121; info@visitscotland.com; 3 Princes St; 9am-9pm Mon-Sat, 10am-8pm Sun Jul & Aug, 9am-7pm Mon-Sat, 10am-7pm Sun May, Jun & Sep, 9am-5pm Mon-Wed, 9am-6pm Thu-Sun Oct-Apr) Offers an accommodation booking service, a currency exchange, a gift and bookshop, internet access, and tickets for Edinburgh city tours and Scottish Citylink bus services.

SIGHTS

Dominating the skyline like a city in the clouds, the hilltop complex of **Edinburgh Castle** (☎225 9846; www.edinburghcastle.gov.uk; Castlehill; adult/child £12/6; 9.30am-6pm Apr-Oct, to 5pm Nov-Mar) should be the first stop for any visitor. It's a hodge-podge of architectural styles, representing centuries of myriad historic uses, and highlights include **St Margaret's Chapel** (the oldest building in Edinburgh) and the **Royal Palace** (including the Stone of Destiny and the Scottish Crown Jewels).

Also in the castle is the **National War Museum of Scotland** (☎225 7534; admission incl in Edinburgh Castle ticket; 9.45am-5.30pm Apr-Sep, to 4.45pm Oct-Mar), a fascinating account of how war and military service have shaped the nation.

Sealed off for 250 years beneath the City Chambers, **Real Mary King's Close** (☎0870 243 0160; 2 Warriston's Close; adult/child £10/6; 9am-9pm Aug, 10am-9pm Apr-Jul, Sep & Oct, 10am-4pm Sun-Fri, to 9pm Sat Nov-Mar) is a spooky, subterranean labyrinth giving a fascinating insight into the daily life of 16th- and 17th-century Edinburgh.

Costumed characters give tours (that must be booked in advance).

The controversial **Scottish Parliament Building** (☎ 348 5200; www.scottish.parliament.uk; Holyrood Rd; admission free, tours adult/concession £6/3.60; 9am-6pm Tue-Thu, 10am-5pm Mon & Fri in session, 10am-5pm Mon-Fri in recess Apr-Oct, 10am-4pm Mon-Fri in recess Nov-Mar) opened for business in 2005. The strange forms of the exterior are all symbolic in some way, right down to the ground plan of the whole complex (best seen from Salisbury Crags), which represents a 'flower of democracy rooted in Scottish soil'.

The **Palace of Holyroodhouse** (☎ 556 5100; www.royal.gov.uk; Canongate; adult/child £9.80/5.80; 9.30am-6pm Apr-Oct, to 4.30pm Nov-Mar, last admission an hr before closing) is the royal family's official residence in Scotland, but is most famous as the 16th-century home of the ill-fated Mary, Queen of Scots.

In **Holyrood Park**, Edinburghers can enjoy a little bit of wilderness in the heart of the city. The highest point is the 251m summit of **Arthur's Seat**, the deeply eroded remnant of a long-extinct volcano; you can hike from Holyrood to the summit in 30 to 45 minutes.

FESTIVALS & EVENTS

Edinburgh Festival Fringe (☎ 226 0026; www.edfringe.com) Originally an adjunct to the main festival, it's now *the* biggest festival of the performing arts anywhere in the world. Held in August, the last two weeks overlapping with the first two of the Edinburgh International Festival.

Edinburgh International Festival (☎ 473 2099; www.eif.co.uk) Hundreds of the world's top musicians and performers congregate for three weeks of diverse and inspirational music, opera, theatre and dance. Late August, early September.

Edinburgh Military Tattoo (www.edintattoo.co.uk) A spectacular display of marching bands, massed pipes and drums, acrobats, cheerleaders and motorcycle display teams, with the magnificent backdrop of the floodlit castle.

SLEEPING

OLD TOWN & SOUTH OF THE ROYAL MILE

Cluaran House (☎ 221 0047; www.cluaran-house-edinburgh.co.uk; 47 Leamington Tce; s/d & tw from £50/80) Bright and arty, this stylish guesthouse is known for its welcoming owners. Breakfasts are also good, particularly the veggie option.

WILL SALTER

Visitors on Royal Mile

EDINBURGH

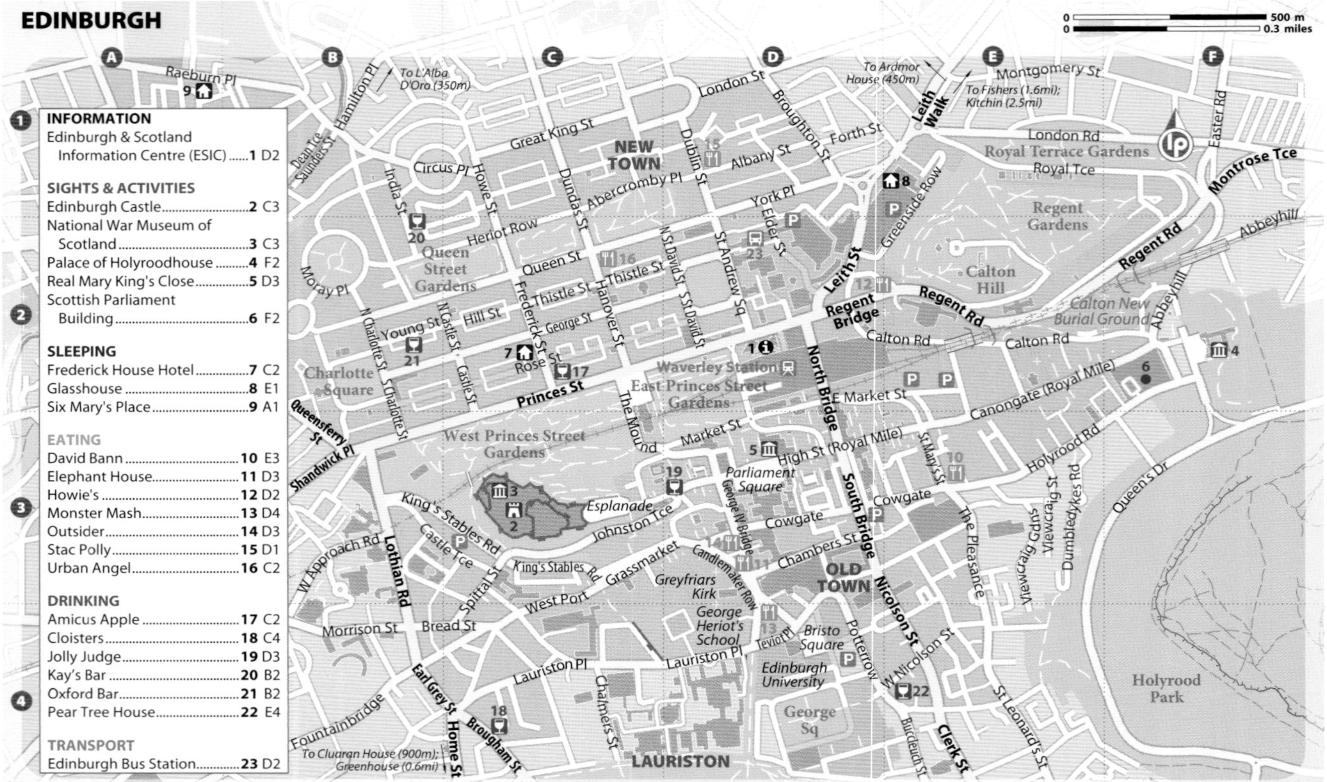

INFORMATION

Edinburgh & Scotland Information Centre (ESIC) 1 D2

SIGHTS & ACTIVITIES

Edinburgh Castle 2 C3
National War Museum of Scotland 3 C3
Palace of Holyroodhouse 4 F2
Real Mary King's Close 5 D3
Scottish Parliament Building 6 F2

SLEEPING

Frederick House Hotel 7 C2
Glasshouse 8 E1
Six Mary's Place 9 A1

EATING

David Bann 10 E3
Elephant House 11 D3
Howie's 12 D2
Monster Mash 13 D4
Outsider 14 D3
Stac Polly 15 D1
Urban Angel 16 C2

DRINKING

Amicus Apple 17 C2
Cloisters 18 C4
Jolly Judge 19 D3
Kay's Bar 20 B2
Oxford Bar 21 B2
Pear Tree House 22 E4

TRANSPORT

Edinburgh Bus Station 23 D2

Greenhouse (☎ 622 7634; www.greenhouse-edinburgh.com; 14 Hartington Gardens; s/d from £65/70) Highly deserved award-winning vegetarian and vegan guest house – even the soap and shampoo are free of animal products.

NEW TOWN & NORTHERN EDINBURGH

our pick **Six Mary's Place** (☎ 332 8965; www.sixmarysplace.co.uk; 6 Mary's Pl, Raeburn Pl; s/d/f from £45/94/150) An attractive Georgian townhouse with a designer mix of period features, contemporary furniture and modern colours. Wi-fi access.

Frederick House Hotel (☎ 226 1999; www.townhousehotels.co.uk; 42 Frederick St; s/d from £50/70) This well-positioned hotel has roomy double beds and large baths to soak away the day's sightseeing aches. Wi-fi access.

Ardmor House (☎ 554 4944; www.ardmorhouse.com; 74 Pilrig St; s/d from £50/75) The 'gay-owned, straight-friendly' Ardmor is a stylishly renovated house with en suite bedrooms, and all those little touches that make a place special – open fire, thick towels, crisp white bed linen and free newspapers at breakfast.

Glasshouse (☎ 525 8200; www.theetoncollection.com; 2 Greenside Pl; d/ste £295/450) A palace of cutting-edge design with luxury rooms, floor-to-ceiling windows, leather sofas, marble bathrooms and a rooftop garden.

EATING

OLD TOWN & SOUTH OF THE ROYAL MILE

Elephant House (☎ 220 5355; www.elephanthouse.biz; 21 George IV Bridge; snacks £3-6; 🕒 8am-11pm; 💻) Brilliant cafe with baguettes, pastries and coffees powerful enough to inspire JK Rowling (she used to write in the back room, overlooking Edinburgh Castle).

our pick **Monster Mash** (☎ 225 7069; www.monstermashcafe.co.uk; 4a Forrest Rd; mains £5-7; 🕒 8am-10pm Mon-Fri, 9am-10pm Sat, 10am-10pm Sun) Classic British grub of the 1950s – bangers and mash, shepherd's pie, fish and chips – all freshly prepared from local produce, including Crombie's gourmet sausages.

Outsider (☎ 226 3131; 15 George IV Bridge; mains £8-12; 🕒 noon-11pm) Edinburgh stalwart known for its rainforest interior and brilliant menu that jumps straight in with mains such as chorizo and chickpea casserole.

David Bann (☎ 556 5888; www.davidbann.com; 56-58 St Mary's St; mains £8-12; 🕒 11am-10pm Sun-Thu, to 10.30pm Fri & Sat) On a one-man mission to convince the world that vegetarian food doesn't have to mean alfalfa and tofu, Bann has been thrilling locals with his sophisticated vegetarian cuisine for years.

NEW TOWN & NORTHERN EDINBURGH

our pick **Urban Angel** (☎ 225 6215; www.urban-angel.co.uk; 121 Hanover St; snacks £3-7, mains £8-11; 🕒 10am-10pm Mon-Thu, to 11pm Fri & Sat, to 5pm Sun) A wholesome deli and cafe-bistro with the emphasis on fair-trade, organic and locally sourced produce.

L'Alba D'Oro (☎ 557 2580; www.lalbadoro.com; 5-7 Henderson Row; fish supper £6-7; 🕒 5-11pm) Pronouncing any place as Edinburgh's best chippie is always contentious, but this place gets the nod from many locals.

Fishers (☎ 554 5666; 1 The Shore, Leith; mains £9-22; 🕒 noon-10.30pm) This cosy little bar-turned-restaurant is one of the city's best seafood places and the handwritten menu (you might need a calligrapher to decipher it) rarely disappoints.

Howie's (☎ 556 5766; 29 Waterloo Pl; mains £10-15; ⏰ lunch & dinner) This bright and airy Georgian corner house is the most central of Howie's four hugely popular Edinburgh restaurants. The recipe for success includes fresh Scottish produce, good-value, fixed-price menus, and eminently quaffable house wines.

Stac Polly (☎ 556 2231; www.stacpolly.co.uk; 29-33 Dublin St; mains £18-20; ⏰ lunch Mon-Fri, dinner daily) Sophisticated twists to fresh Highland produce (think loin of venison with redcurrant and rosemary jus) keep the punters coming back for more at this great restaurant.

our pick **Kitchin** (☎ 555 1755; www.thekitchin.com; 78 Commercial Quay; mains £24-34; ⏰ noon-2.30pm Tue-Sat, 7.30-10pm Tue-Thu, 6.45-10.30pm Fri & Sat) Fresh, seasonal Scottish produce, locally sourced, is the philosophy that has won a Michelin star for this elegant but unpretentious restaurant.

DRINKING

OLD TOWN & SOUTH OF THE ROYAL MILE

Jolly Judge (☎ 225 2669; 7a James Court) Tucked away down an Old Town close, with its low, timber-beamed, painted ceilings and numerous nooks and crannies, the Jolly Judge's convivial atmosphere is undisturbed by TV, music or gaming machines. It has a log fire in cold weather.

Cloisters (☎ 221 9997; 26 Brougham St) Furnished with well-worn wooden tables and chairs, this great old place serves drinks, decent grub and coffee to a mixed congregation of students, locals and real-ale connoisseurs.

Pear Tree House (☎ 667 7533; 38 West Nicolson St) The Pear Tree is a student favourite, with comfy sofas and board games inside, plus the city centre's biggest beer garden outside.

NEW TOWN & NORTHERN EDINBURGH

Kay's Bar (☎ 225 1858; 39 Jamaica St West) This former wine merchant's office (walls are decorated with old wine barrels) is the cosy little pub whose rustic ambience is designed not to get in the way of sampling real ales and malt whiskies.

Amicus Apple (☎ 226 6055; 15 Frederick St) Cream leather sofas and dark brown armchairs, bold design and funky lighting make this laid-back cocktail lounge the hippest hang-out in the New Town.

Oxford Bar (☎ 539 7119; 8 Young St) The Oxford is that rarest of things these days, a real pub for real people, with no 'theme', no music, no frills and no pretensions – immortalised by Ian Rankin, author of the Inspector Rebus novels, who is a regular here, as is his fictional detective.

GETTING THERE & AWAY

Edinburgh **airport** (☎ 333 1000; www.edinburghairport.com), 8 miles west of Edinburgh, has flights to many parts of the UK, Ireland and Continental Europe.

National Express coaches run to/from London (from £34, nine hours, three daily), Newcastle (£17, 2¾ hours, three to five daily) and York (£34, 5¾ hours, one daily). **Scottish Citylink** (☎ 08705 505050; www.citylink.co.uk) buses connect Edinburgh with all of Scotland's major cities and towns, including Aberdeen (£24, 3¼ hours, hourly), Fort William (£24, four hours, three daily), Glasgow (£6, 1¼ hours, four an hour), Inverness (£10, four hours, hourly), and Stirling (£6, one hour, hourly).

Trains run at least hourly between Edinburgh and London Kings Cross (from £25 if you book in advance, £126 on the spot, 4½ hours) via Newcastle (£20 to £40, 1½ hours) and York (£30 to £70, 2½ hours). There are frequent daily services to Scottish cities, including Aberdeen (£38,

NEIL SETCHFIELD

Kelvingrove Art Gallery & Museum (p137), Glasgow

2½ hours) and Inverness (£38, 3¼ hours), and a regular shuttle between Edinburgh and Glasgow (£11, 50 minutes, every 15 to 30 minutes).

GETTING AROUND

The **Airlink** (www.flybybus.com) service 100 runs from Waverley Bridge, outside the train station, to the airport (one way/return £3/5, 30 minutes, every 10 to 15 minutes) via the West End and Haymarket.

Around town, the two main bus operators are **Lothian Buses** (☎ 554 4494; www.lothianbuses.co.uk) and **First Edinburgh** (☎ 08708 72 72 71; www.firstedinburgh.co.uk). Buy your ticket as you board – on Lothian services you need the exact change. A Day Saver ticket (£2.50) covers a whole day's travel.

GLASGOW

☎ 0141 / pop 581,000

Not as picturesque as Edinburgh, the former industrial powerhouse of Glasgow is grittier, edgier and arguably more fun than the capital, with the best nightlife in Scotland and a lively arts scene – kept vibrant by the presence of a good art school – plus many fine museums and galleries.

The excellent **TIC** (☎ 204 4400; www.seeglasgow.com; 11 George Sq; 9am-6pm Mon-Sat Oct-Jan & Easter-May, 9am-7pm Mon-Sat Jun & Sep, 9am-8pm Mon-Sat Jul-Aug, 10am-6pm Sun Easter-Sep) can help with local and national accommodation bookings (£3).

SIGHTS

Glasgow's main square is **George Sq**, a grand public space, built in the Victorian era to show off the city's wealth and dignified by statues of notable Glaswegians and Scots, including Robert Burns, James Watt, John Moore and Sir Walter Scott.

A shining example of pre-Reformation Gothic architecture, **Glasgow Cathedral** (☎ 552 6891; www.glasgowcathedral.org.uk; admission free; 9.30am-6pm Mon-Sat, 1-5pm Sun Apr-Sep, 9.30am-4pm Mon-Sat, 1-4pm Sun Oct-Mar) is the only mainland cathedral in Scotland to survive the Reformation.

The **People's Palace** (☎ 271 2951; Glasgow Green; admission free; 🕑 10am-5pm Mon-Thu & Sat, 11am-5pm Fri & Sun) showcases what it means to be Glaswegian. From the goofy 1970s portrait of Billy Connolly to dance cards from the former Barrowland dance hall, this place is a monument to social history, with displays on language, comedy and more, charting the city's development from the 1750s to the present day. The neighbouring **Winter Gardens** is an elegant Victorian glasshouse where

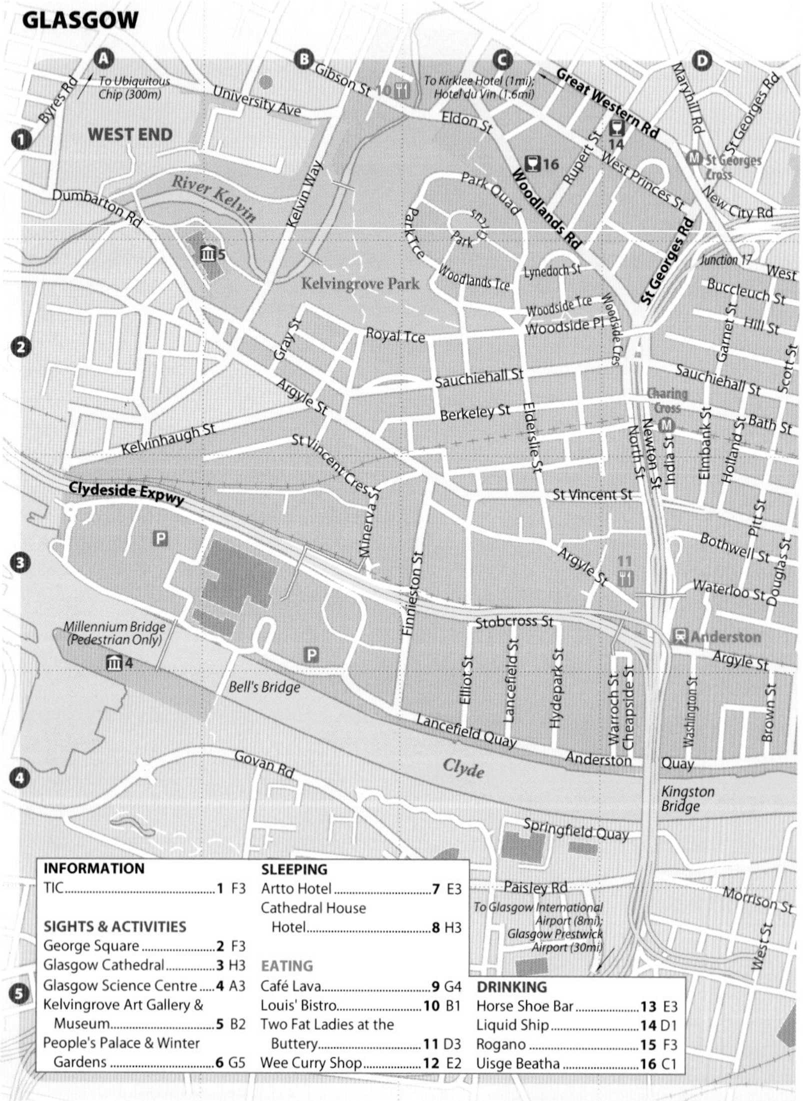

you can enjoy a cup of coffee among the tropical palms.

Recently reopened after an enormous refurbishment program, Glasgow's much-loved cultural icon, the **Kelvingrove Art Gallery & Museum** (☎ 276 9599; Argyle St; admission free; 10am-5pm Mon-Thu & Sat, 11am-5pm Fri & Sun), is the most visited museum in the UK outside of London. Its magnificent Edwardian building houses a superb collection of Scottish and European art as well as a fascinating series of natural

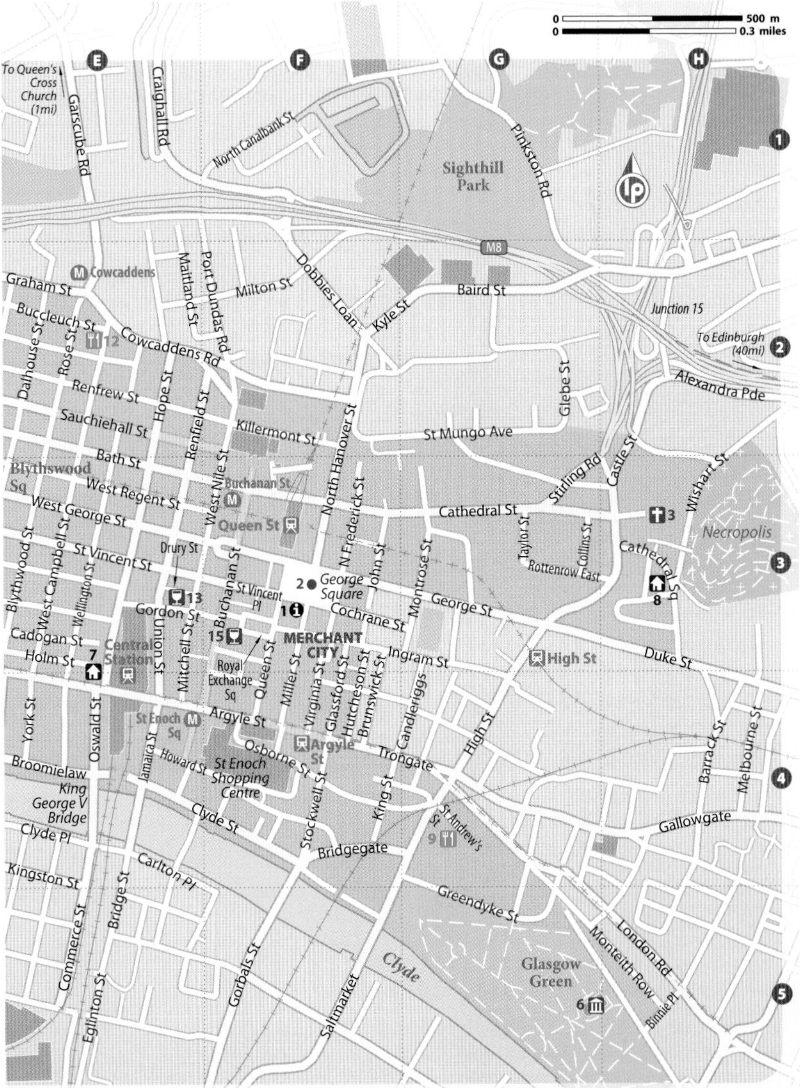

history exhibits, and plenty on Scottish history including the Viking influence.

Strolling along the **Clyde River** gives two very different insights into the city: one of fading glory and another of new prosperity in the redevelopment that some locals call the 'silver city'. The flagship project is **Glasgow Science Centre** (☎ 420 5000; www.glasgowsciencecentre.org; 50 Pacific Quay; adult/child £7.95/5.95; ⏰ 10am-6pm), bringing science and technology alive through hundreds of interactive exhibits and kid-friendly activities.

SLEEPING

Kirklee Hotel (☎ 334 5555; www.kirkleehotel.co.uk; 11 Kensington Gate, West End; s/d £59/75) A grand Edwardian townhouse, combining the luxury of a classy hotel with the warmth of staying in someone's home.

our pick **Cathedral House Hotel** (☎ 552 3519; www.cathedralhousehotel.org; 28-32 Cathedral Sq; s/d from £60/90) In the heart of the leafy, dignified East End stands this 19th-century Scottish baronial-style hotel, complete with turrets and eight individual and beautifully furnished rooms. Wi-fi access.

Artto Hotel (☎ 248 2480; www.arttohotel.com; 37 Hope St; s/d £70/90) Everything is squeaky clean and gleaming in this fashionable hotel. Modish decor and sparkling en suites with power showers complete the happy picture. Wi-fi access.

Hotel du Vin (☎ 339 2001; www.hotelduvin.com; 1 Devonshire Gardens, West End; r from £145, ste from £395) Made famous as One Devonshire Gardens – Glasgow's first boutique hotel – new management has maintained this sumptuous spot's reputation as the favourite place for celebrity guests to hang their hat when visiting Glasgow. Wi-fi access.

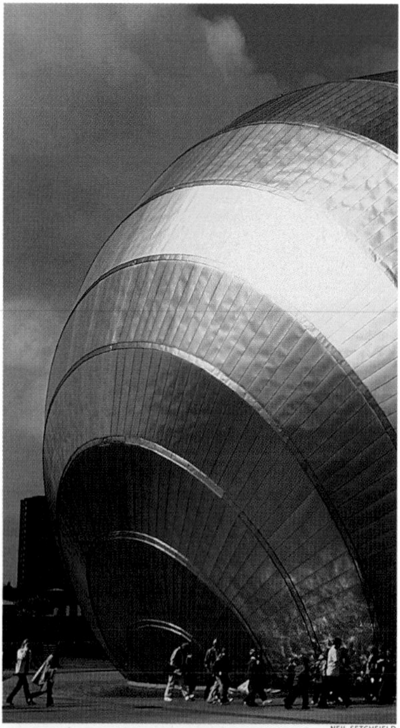

NEIL SETCHFIELD

Glasgow Science Centre

EATING

Café Lava (☎ 553 1123; 24 St Andrew's St; mains £2-6; ⏰ 8am-6pm Mon-Fri, 10am-5pm Sat & Sun) Everyone wants to live next door to a cafe like this. The understated menu delivers delicious home cooking, the coffee is the best in town, and the carrot cake the best in Scotland. Wi-fi access.

Wee Curry Shop (☎ 353 0777; 7 Buccleuch St; 2-course lunch £6, dinner mains £11; ⏰ lunch Mon-Sat, dinner daily) Could there be a better illustration of Scotland's infatuation with Indian cuisine than a curry shop decked out in tartan?

Louis' Bistro (☎ 339 7915; 18 Gibson St; mains £8-13; ⏰ lunch & dinner Tue-Sat) Well placed to take the award for best burger in town, this unpretentious neighbourhood bistro also serves perfectly prepared steaks.

Two Fat Ladies at the Buttery (☎ 221 8188; 652-4 Argyle St; mains £18-22; ⏰ lunch & dinner) Now under new management, Glasgow's oldest restaurant (opened 1856) has toned down the tartan and shrugged off its air of formality. The modern Scottish cuisine is still first class, though.

Ubiquitous Chip (☎ 334 5007; 12 Ashton Lane, West End; 3-course lunch/dinner £30/40; ⏰ lunch & dinner) The original champion of quality Scottish produce, this restaurant has won lots of awards with several dining areas spread around a covered, cobbled courtyard filled with tropical greenery.

DRINKING

Rogano (☎ 248 4055; 11 Exchange Pl) A gem of art-deco design, based on the decor in the *Queen Mary* ocean liner, and the place for classic cocktails.

Horse Shoe Bar (☎ 221 3051; 17 Drury St) This legendary city pub dates from the late 19th century and has hardly changed its appearance since then. Tops for real ale and the best-value three-course lunches (£3.50) in town.

Uisge Beatha (☎ 564 1596; 232-246 Woodlands Rd) Named 'water of life' (the Gaelic for Scotland's national drink), this traditional boozer has more than a hundred single malts on offer.

Liquid Ship (☎ 332 2840; 171-175 Great Western Rd) The best of Glasgow's style bars distilled into a single venue. Breakfasts from 10am, a great range of wines, and live acoustic music most evenings add to the allure.

GETTING THERE & AWAY

AIR

Ten miles west of the city, **Glasgow International airport** (☎ 887 1111; www.baa.co.uk/glasgow) handles international routes, domestic UK traffic and most flights to/from the Scottish islands. Do not confuse it with **Glasgow Prestwick airport** (☎ 0871 223 0700; www.gpia.co.uk), 30 miles southwest of Glasgow near Ayr.

BUS

National Express coaches run to and from London (£34, nine hours, at least four daily) Birmingham (£30, six to seven hours, four daily), Manchester (£28, five hours, four daily), Newcastle (£30, four hours, one daily), and York (£34, seven hours, one daily).

Scottish Citylink (☎ 0870 550 5050; www.citylink.co.uk) has buses to/from most major towns in Scotland, including Edinburgh (£8.40 return, 1¼ hours, every 20 minutes), Stirling (£6, 45 minutes, hourly), Inverness (£23, 3¾ hours, one daily) and Aberdeen (£24, three hours, hourly).

TRAIN

There are direct trains from London's King's Cross and Euston stations (from £25 for advance bookings, up to £125 on the spot, 5½ hours, 12 daily). Within Scotland, trains run to/from Aberdeen (£38, hourly, 1¾ hours) and Inverness (£38, three hours, one direct service daily), and along the scenic West Highland line to Oban and Fort William. There are trains every 15 to 30 minutes to/from Edinburgh (£11, 50 minutes).

STIRLING

☎ 01786 / pop 41,300

With an impregnable position atop a mighty rocky crag, Stirling's beautifully preserved Old Town is a treasure of noble buildings and cobbled streets winding up to the ramparts of its dominant castle, offering views for miles around. Clearly visible is the brooding **Wallace monument**, honouring the giant freedom fighter of *Braveheart* fame. Nearby is **Bannockburn**, scene of Robert the Bruce's major triumph over the English.

Stirling Castle (☎ 450000; admission £8.50; 9.30am-6pm Apr-Sep, to 5pm Oct-Mar) has existed here since prehistoric times, and the location, architecture and historical significance combine to make it a grand and memorable visit today.

For onward travel, trains run half-hourly to Edinburgh (£6.50, 55 minutes) and Glasgow (£6.70, 40 minutes), and hourly to Dundee (£15, 55 minutes) and Aberdeen (£36.60, 2¼ hours). Citylink coach services include Dundee (£10.20, 1½ hours, hourly), Edinburgh (£5.40, one hour, hourly) and Glasgow (£5.40, 45 minutes, hourly).

CAIRNGORMS NATIONAL PARK

The **Cairngorms mountain range** (www.cairngorms.co.uk) is Britain's newest national park, a starkly beautiful place combining wild mountain tundras, secluded old pinewoods, ancient castles, unique wildlife and lush colours year-round. The town of **Aviemore** is a great base and gateway, frequented by active outdoor types, with excellent visitor amenities.

A highlight is the **Cairngorm Mountain Railway** (☎ 01479-861261; Cairngorm Ski Area; adult/concession £8.75/7.50; 10am-4.30pm), the UK's highest and longest funicular. In winter it's the centre of the country's skiing and snowboarding action. Check ski.visitscotland.com for the latest conditions.

WESTERN & NORTHERN SCOTLAND

It's a long way north, and takes effort to reach, but this is by far the best bit of Scotland, and one of the best bits of the whole of Britain, too. Famous name-checks include Loch Lomond, the port of Oban, the rugged Isle of Mull, and Ben Nevis, Britain's highest peak.

LOCH LOMOND

Loch Lomond forms the western half of the **Loch Lomond & the Trossachs National Park** (www.lochlomond-trossachs.org). The eastern half of the park, the Trossach hills, is best reached from Stirling, as there's virtually no road link between the west and east sides. At Balloch you'll find the main 'gateway' centre for the park, **Loch Lomond Shores** (☎ 01389-721500; www.lochlomondshores.com; 9.30am-5.30pm Apr-Sep, 10am-5.30pm Oct-Mar;), with information, an aquarium and audiovisual entertainment.

The more isolated eastern shore is better territory for exploration. The road only runs as far as Rowardennan; beyond there, walkers can follow the West Highland Way for a few miles along the shore or through beautiful woodland.

FORT WILLIAM

☎ 01397 / pop 9900

Fort William is a jumping-off point dubbed 'Outdoor Capital of the UK', and there's much to do in the surrounding area. Trot up **Ben Nevis** and you can look down on everyone in Britain. Or, if downhill's more your thing, go to the nearby **Nevis Range** for mountain biking or skiing. For info on the latter see ski.visitscotland.com.

For walking info, especially if you're considering Ben Nevis, a good place to aim for is the **Glen Nevis Visitor Centre** (☎ 705922; www.bennevisweather.co.uk; 9am-5pm Easter-Oct, to 4pm Nov-Easter) about 2 miles from town.

ISLE OF SKYE

☎ 01478

Skye's romantic and lofty reputation is well deserved, as the scenic splendour of Scotland's largest island rarely disappoints. Even if your stay is marked by the typical mist and drizzle (Skye owes its

EOIN CLARKE

Cairn on the summit of Ben Nevis

name to a Norse word for 'cloud'), you'll likely feel the magic, especially around the striking Cuillin Hills at the island's southern end.

Portree, the island's capital, has the largest selection of accommodation, eating places and other services.

Bayview House (☎ 613340; www.bayviewhouse.co.uk; Bayfield; d £45-50) Solid comfort is the keyword at this great-value stalwart. Wi-fi access.

Braeside B&B (☎ 612613; www.braesideportree.co.uk; Stormy Hill; d £54-60; ⌚ Jan-Oct) A bright and friendly place with good breakfasts.

Ben Tianavaig (☎ 612152; www.ben-tianavaig.co.uk; 5 Bosville Tce; d £60) Has memorable views, friendly hosts and an antipodean flavour.

Marmalade (☎ 611711; www.marmaladehotels.com; Home Farm Rd; s/d/f £100/120/125) Modern cafe chic, above-average breakfasts, and laid-back staff, not to mention large light rooms, superspacious bathrooms and long views. Lovely. Wi-fi access.

Most visitors arrive across the bridge from Kyle of Lochalsh on the mainland. Citylink runs buses to Portree and on to Uig from Glasgow (£31.40, 6½ hours, three daily) and Inverness (£18.60, 3¼ hours, three daily).

On the island, the Skye Roverbus ticket gives unlimited travel for one/three days for £6/15, although Sunday services are scant.

INVERNESS

☎ 01463 / pop 44,500

By far the region's largest settlement, friendly Inverness is an important service centre for Highlanders and visitors, as well as a transport hub. On a riverside hillock, **Inverness Castle** is a lightweight compared with more ancient Highland fortifications, but its rosy walls are beautiful at sunset. Inverness is also a fine gateway: Loch Ness is on the doorstep; tours and buses serve the Highlands; and you can even take a day trip to the Orkneys if time's limited.

SLEEPING

Ivybank Guest House (☎ 232796; www.ivybankguesthouse.com; 28 Old Edinburgh Rd; s/d £25/60) This noble heritage-listed building brims with welcome and character.

Alexander (☎ 231151; www.thealexander.net; 16 Ness Bank; s/d £55/90) A big makeover has left this Georgian riverside house free to express itself, with sensitive contemporary styling enhancing noble original features.

our pick **Rocpool Reserve** (☎ 240089; www.rocpool.com; Culduthel Rd; d £195-365) A far cry from the antlers and creaky wooden staircases of most upmarket Highland hotels, this luxury boutique option is slick, modern and sexy. Wi-fi available and wheelchair accessible.

EATING

Mustard Seed (☎ 220220; 16 Fraser St; 2-course lunch £5.95, mains £11-19) This visionary conversion of a riverside church combines open-plan dining, cordial service and smart Med-Scottish cuisine. Wheelchair accessible.

Riva (☎ 237377; 4 Ness Walk; meals £9-14; lunch & dinner Mon-Sat) This sophisticated riverside Italian choice is a chic destination for great pasta combinations.

Café 1 (☎ 226200; 75 Castle St; mains £9-16; lunch & dinner Mon-Sat) Classy, imaginative food and champers by the glass opposite the castle.

GETTING THERE & AWAY

Ten miles east of town, **Inverness airport** (☎ 01667-464000) has flights to London, Edinburgh, Glasgow and island destinations including Orkney, Shetland and Stornoway.

National Express coaches run to/from London (£40, 13 hours, one daily). Citylink coaches serve Edinburgh and Glasgow (both £21.20, four hours, hourly) via Aviemore; and go to/from Fort William (£11.30, two hours, five to seven daily).

Train destinations include Edinburgh and Glasgow (£38, 3½ hours, six and three daily services respectively), Aberdeen (£23, 2¼ hours, five to 10 daily). The service to Kyle of Lochalsh (£17.30, 2½ hours, around three daily), for Skye, is one of Britain's great scenic rail journeys.

JOHN O'GROATS

☎ 01955 / pop 500

Mainland Britain's northeasterly extreme, John O'Groats should be an epic location. Instead it's a car park surrounded by tourist shops, offering little of interest apart from ferries to Orkney, and a signpost indicating the endpoint of the 874-mile trek from Land's End (p108) – a popular if arduous route for cyclists and walkers, many raising money for charity.

IRELAND

DUBLIN

☎ 01 / pop 1.1 million

Sitting in a tapas bar on Great George's St, nursing a Guinness or a hangover (or both), you think about what your favourite experience has been in Dublin so far. Was it drinking in Temple Bar with people from dozens of other countries or was it buying fresh vegies at the Asian food market? Was it admiring the Georgian houses along St Stephen's Green or was it wandering the grounds of Trinity College? You never come to an answer, but you do realise that, just as the waters on the banks of the Liffey River seem to rise every day, so does your affection for this city.

ORIENTATION

Dublin is neatly divided by the Liffey River into the more affluent 'south side' and the less prosperous 'north side'.

North of the river landmarks are O'Connell St, with its needle-shaped Monument of Light, and Gardiner St, with its B&Bs and guesthouses. Henry St, the main shopping precinct, runs west off O'Connell.

Immediately south of the river is the bustling Temple Bar district, Dame St, Trinity College and, just below it, the lovely St Stephen's Green.

INFORMATION

MEDICAL SERVICES

Doctors on Call (☎ 453 9333; 24hr) Request a doctor to come to your accommodation (€60 to €75).

St James Hospital (☎ 410 3000; James's St) Dublin's main 24-hour accident and emergency department.

TOURIST INFORMATION

All Dublin tourist offices provide walk-in services only – no phone inquiries.

Dublin Tourism Centre (☎ 605 7700; www.visitdublin.com) Main office (St Andrew's Church, 2 Suffolk St; 9am-7pm Mon-Sat, 10.30am-3pm Sun Jul & Aug, 9am-5.30pm Mon-Sat, 10.30am-3pm Sun Sep-Jun); City Centre (14 O'Connell St; 9am-5pm Mon-Sat); Dun Laoghaire (Dun Laoghaire ferry port; 10am-1pm & 2-6pm) Ask about the Dublin Pass (www.dublinpass.ie), which allows entrance into over 30 of Dublin's attractions, as well as tours and special offers.

Fáilte Ireland (☎ 1850 230 330; www.ireland.ie; Baggot St; 9am-5pm Mon-Fri) Tourist information for the whole Republic of Ireland.

Northern Ireland Tourist Board (NITB; ☎ 679 1977; www.discovernorthernireland.com; 16 Nassau St; 9.15am-5.30pm Mon-Fri, 10am-5pm Sat)

SIGHTS

TRINITY COLLEGE & BOOK OF KELLS

Ireland's premier university was founded by Elizabeth I in 1592. Its full name is the University of Dublin, but **Trinity College** (College Green) is the institution's sole college.

Student-guided **walking tours** (per person €10) take place twice an hour from 10.45am to 3.40pm Monday to Saturday and 10.45am to 3.15pm Sunday from mid-May

OLIVER STREWE

Long Room of the Old Library (p144), Trinity College

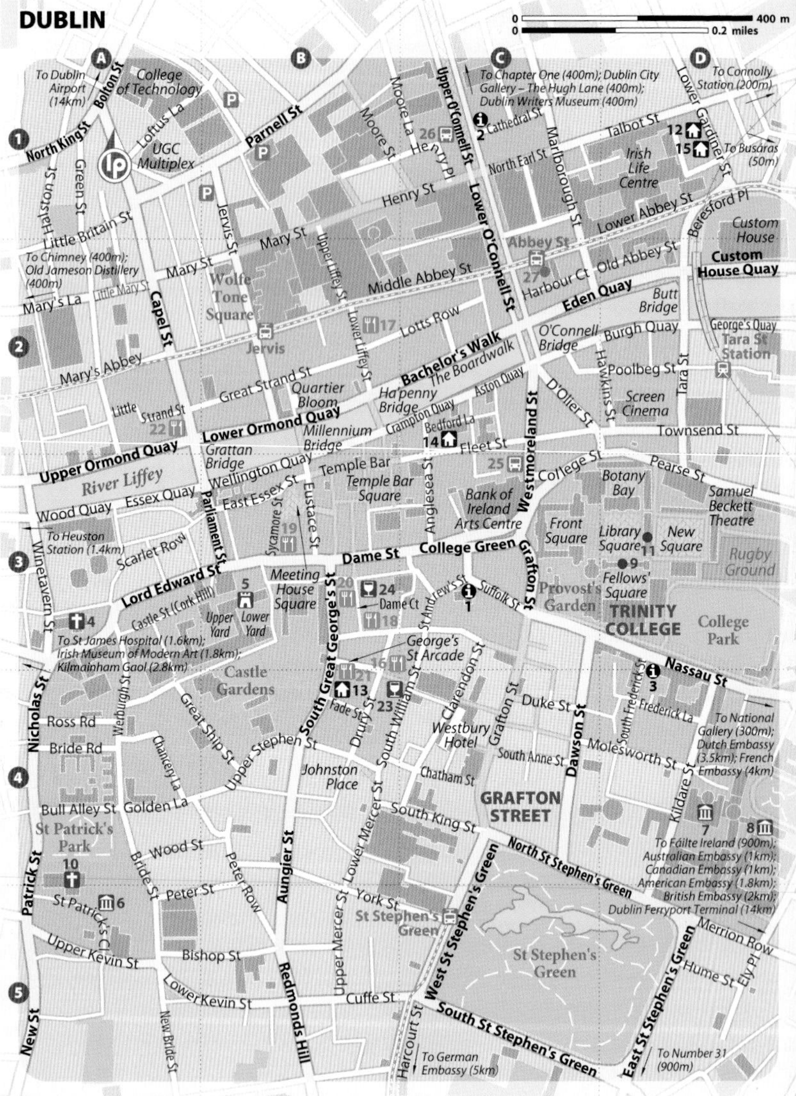

to September, departing from inside the main gate on College St. The tour is a good deal since it includes admission to see the *Book of Kells*, an elaborately illuminated manuscript dating from around AD 800, and one of Dublin's prime attractions. It's displayed in the **Old Library** (☎ 896 2320; www.tcd.ie/Library/heritage; adult/child €9/free; 🕑 9.30am-5pm Mon-Sat year-round, 9.30am-4.30pm Sun May-Sep, noon-4.30pm Sun Oct-Apr), together with the 9th-century *Book of Armagh*.

MUSEUMS

Among the highlights of the impressive **National Museum** (☎ 667 7444; www.museum.ie; Kildare St; admission free; 10am-5pm Tue-Sat, 2-5pm Sun) are its superb collection of prehistoric gold objects; the exquisite 12th-century Ardagh Chalice, the world's finest example of Celtic art; the skeleton of a once-tall, mighty Viking; and the incredibly well-preserved 'Bog Body'. The nearby **Natural History Museum** (☎ 677 7444; www.museum.ie; Merrion St; admission free; 10am-5pm Tue-Sat, 2-5pm Sun), aka the 'dead zoo', has hardly changed since it opened in 1857.

The **Dublin Writers Museum** (☎ 872 2077; www.writersmuseum.com; 18-19 Parnell Sq; adult/child €7.25/4.55; 10am-5pm Mon-Sat, 11am-5pm Sun year-round, to 6pm Mon-Fri Jun-Aug), north of the river, celebrates the city's long and continuing role as a literary centre, with displays on Joyce, Swift, Yeats, Wilde, Beckett and others.

GALLERIES

The **National Gallery** (☎ 661 5133; www.nationalgallery.ie; West Merrion Sq; admission & guided tours free; 9.30am-5.30pm Mon-Wed, Fri & Sat, 9.30am-8.30pm Thu, noon-5.30pm Sun) has a fine collection, strong in Irish art. Guided **tours** are held at 3pm on Saturday, and 2pm, 3pm and 4pm on Sunday.

North of the river on Parnell Sq, **Dublin City Gallery – The Hugh Lane** (☎ 222 5550; www.hughlane.ie; North Parnell Sq; admission free; 10am-6pm Tue-Thu, 10am-5pm Fri & Sat, 11am-5pm Sun) has works by French Impressionists and 20th-century Irish artists, and is wheelchair accessible.

The **Irish Museum of Modern Art** (IMMA; ☎ 612 9900; www.imma.ie; Military Rd; admission free; 10am-5.30pm Tue & Thu-Sat, 10.30am-5.30pm Wed, noon-5.30pm Sun), at the old Royal Hospital Kilmainham, is renowned for its conceptual installations and temporary exhibitions. It has wheelchair access. Bus 51 or 79 from Aston Quay will get you there.

CHRIST CHURCH CATHEDRAL

The mother of all of Dublin's cathedrals is **Christ Church Cathedral** (☎ 677 8099; www.cccdub.ie; Christ Church Pl; adult/concession €6/4; 9am-6pm Jun-Aug, 9.45am-5pm Sep-May), a simple wood structure until 1169, when the present church was built. In the southern aisle is a monument to Strongbow, a 12th-century Norman warrior. Note the precariously leaning northern wall (it's been that way since 1562).

ST PATRICK'S CATHEDRAL & AROUND

A church was on the site of **St Patrick's Cathedral** (☎ 475 4817; www.stpatrickscathedral.ie; St Patrick's Close; adult/concession €5.50/4.20; 9am-6pm Mon-Sat, 9-11am, 12.45-3pm & 4.15-6pm Sun Mar-Oct, 9am-5pm Sat, 10-11am & 12.45-3pm Sun Nov-Feb, closed during times of worship) as early as the 5th century, but the present building dates from 1191.

The oldest public library in the country, **Marsh's Library** (☎ 454 3511; www.marshlibrary.ie; St Patrick's Close; adult/concession €2.50/1.50; 10am-1pm & 2-5pm Mon & Wed-Fri, 10.30am-1pm Sat), contains 25,000 books dating from the 16th to the early 18th centuries, as well as numerous maps and manuscripts.

KILMAINHAM GAOL

The grey, threatening **Kilmainham Gaol** (☎ 453 5984; www.heritageireland.com; Inchicore Rd; adult/child €5.30/2.10; 9.30am-6pm Apr-Sep, 9.30am-5.30pm Mon-Sat, 10am-6pm Sun Oct-Mar), 2km west of the city centre, played a key role in Ireland's struggle for independence and was the site of mass executions following the 1916 Easter Rising. An excellent audiovisual introduction to the building is followed by a thought-provoking tour. Buses 79, 78A and 51B from Aston Quay all pass by here.

OTHER SIGHTS

The centre of British power in Ireland and dating back to the 13th century, **Dublin Castle** (☎ 677 7129; www.dublincastle.ie; adult/concession €4.50/2; 10am-4.45pm Mon-Fri, 2-4.45pm Sat & Sun) is more higgledy-piggledy palace than castle.

The **Old Jameson Distillery** (☎ 807 2355; www.jamesonwhiskey.com/ojd; Bow St; adult/concession €12.50/9) has tours (9.30am to 6pm) covering the entire whiskey-distilling process; tastings follow. At the back of the distillery is the **Chimney** (☎ 817 3838; Smithfield Village; adult/concession €5/3.50; 10am-5pm Mon-Sat, 11am-5.30pm Sun), an old distillery chimney converted into a 360-degree observation tower.

TOURS

Tour companies **City Sightseeing** (www.city-sightseeing.com), **Irish City Tours** (☎ 872 9010; www.irishcitytours.com) and **Dublin Bus** (☎ 872 0000; www.dublinbus.ie/sightseeing) run a variety of 1½-hour bus tours around Dublin, including hop-on hop-off services from €15 (tickets valid for 24 hours).

It's worth considering one of the many walking tours and guided pub crawls of the city. Two of the best are the **Dublin Literary Pub Crawl** (☎ 670 5602; www.dublinpubcrawl.com), led by actors performing pieces from Irish literature, and the well-reviewed **1916 Rebellion Walking Tour**

HOLGER LEUE

City Sightseeing tour bus

(☎ 086 858 3847; www.1916rising.com), which visits key sites of the rebellion. Others include the **Musical Pub Crawl** (☎ 475 3313; www.discoverdublin.ie) and **Historical Walking Tours of Dublin** (☎ 087 688 9412; www.historicalinsights.ie). Each lasts about two hours and costs around €12.

SLEEPING

Dublin is *always* bustling, so call ahead to book accommodation, especially on weekends.

Townhouse (☎ 878 8808; www.townhouseofdublin.com; 47-48 Lower Gardiner St; s/d from €70/115) Elegant but unpretentious, the Georgian Townhouse has beautiful, individually designed bedrooms named after plays by the famous 19th-century playwrights who once lived here (Dion Boucicault and Lafcadio Hearn).

Anchor Guesthouse (☎ 878 6913; www.anchorguesthouse.com; 49 Lower Gardiner St; s/d from €75/90; P) This lovely Georgian guesthouse, with its delicious wholesome breakfasts and an elegance you won't find in many of the other B&Bs along this stretch, comes highly recommended by readers. Free wi-fi.

Grafton Guesthouse (☎ 679 2041; www.graftonguesthouse.com; 26-27 South Great George's St; s/d from €80/110) This heritage-building hotel has bright and funky rooms with contemporary fittings, stylish walnut furniture, retro wallpaper and all mod must-haves, including free wi-fi and vegie breakfasts.

Morgan Hotel (☎ 643 7000; www.themorgan.com; 10 Fleet St; s/d from €115/150; 💻) Falling somewhere between *Alice in Wonderland* and a cocaine-and-hooker-fuelled rock-and-roll fantasy, the ubercool Morgan sports a sexy colour scheme of white floors and walls with dark blue and pink lighting that extends into the bar, the rooms and even the cigar patio.

our pick **Number 31** (☎ 676 5011; www.number31.ie; 31 Leeson Close; s/d/tr from €120/175/230) The coach house and former dwelling of architect Sam Stephenson (of Central Bank fame) still feels like a 1960s designer pad with sunken sitting room, leather sofas, mirrored bar and floor-to-ceiling windows. Children under 10 are not allowed.

EATING

Epicurean Food Hall (Lower Liffey St; mains €3-12; 🕑 9.30am-5.30pm Mon-Sat) You'll be spoilt for choice in this bustling arcade that houses more than 20 food stalls.

Simon's Place (☎ 679 7821; cnr George's St Arcade & South Great George's St; sandwiches €4-5; 🕑 9am-5.30pm Mon-Sat) Simon hasn't had to change his menu of doorstep sandwiches and wholesome vegetarian soups since he first opened shop two decades ago – the grub here is as heartening and legendary as he is.

Soup Dragon (☎ 872 3277; 168 Capel St; soups €5-10; 🕑 8am-5.30pm Mon-Fri, 11am-5pm Sat) Eat in or take away one of 12 tasty varieties of homemade soups, including shepherd's pie or spicy vegetable gumbo.

Fallon & Byrne (☎ 472 1000; Exchequer St; deli mains €6-9, brasserie mains €17-28; 🕑 deli 9am-8pm Mon-Sat, 11am-6pm Sun, brasserie noon-4.30pm & 6.30-10.30pm Mon-Wed, to 11.30pm Thu-Sat, 11am-4pm Sun) Queue for delicious sandwiches at the deli counter in this trendy New York–style food hall, or head upstairs to the chic, buzzy brasserie with its long red banquettes and diverse menu of creamy fish pie, beef carpaccio and roast turbot.

our pick **Gruel** (☎ 670 7119; 68a Dame St; mains €7-13; 🕑 7am-9.30pm Mon-Fri, 10.30am-10.30pm Sat & Sun) The best budget eatery in town, whether it's for the superfilling lunchtime roast-in-a-roll or the exceptional evening menu, where pasta, fish and chicken are given an exotic once-over.

Bistro (☎ 671 5430; 4-5 Castle Market; mains €11-19; 🕑 noon-10pm) An excellent menu of fish, pasta and meat specials, a well-stocked wine cellar and efficient service make this a great warm-weather choice for alfresco dining.

Odessa (☎ 670 7634; 13 Dame Ct; mains €17-26; ⌚ noon-3pm Mon-Fri, 11.30am-4.30pm Sat & Sun, 6pm-late daily) Odessa's loungy atmosphere, with comfy sofas and retro standard lamps, attracts the city's hipsters who flock here for the excellent weekend brunches (€9 to €11), homemade burgers, steaks and daily fish specials.

Chapter One (☎ 873 2266; 18-19 North Parnell Sq; mains €38-42; ⌚ 12.30-2.30pm Tue-Fri, 6-11pm Tue-Sat) Savour fresh Irish produce cooked in classic French style – like veal terrine with pear and mustard puree, or hake and langoustine with roast fennel – to the tinkle of a grand piano in the vaulted basement of the Dublin Writers Museum.

DRINKING

Stag's Head (☎ 679 3701; 1 Dame Ct) Built in 1770, and remodelled in 1895, the Stag's Head is possibly the best traditional pub in Dublin (and therefore the world).

Grogan's Castle Lounge (☎ 677 9320; 15 South William St) A city-centre institution, Grogan's has long been a favourite haunt of Dublin's writers and painters, as well as others from the bohemian, alternative set.

GETTING THERE & AWAY

AIR

About 13km north of the city centre, **Dublin airport** (DUB; ☎ 814 1111; www.dublinairport.com) is Ireland's major gateway, with direct flights from Europe, North America and Asia. Budget airlines including Ryanair and Flybe land here. See also p161.

BOAT

There are two ferries from Holyhead on the northwestern tip of Wales: one to **Dublin Ferryport terminal** (☎ 855 2222; Alexandra Rd) and the other to Dun Laoghaire at the southern end of Dublin Bay. Boats also sail direct to Dublin Port from Liverpool and Douglas (Isle of Man). See also p160.

BUS

Busáras (☎ 836 6111; www.buseireann.ie; Store St), Dublin's main bus station, is just north of the Liffey. Standard one-way fares from Dublin include to Belfast (€15, three hours, 16 daily), Cork (€12, 3½ hours, six daily), Galway (€15, 3¾ hours, 16 daily) and Killarney (€16, three hours, 13 daily).

The private company **Citylink** (☎ 626 6888; www.citylink.ie) has daily services from Dublin (departing from both the airport and city centre) to Galway for €15.

TRAIN

North of the Liffey is **Connolly station** (☎ 703 2358), for trains to Belfast, Derry, Sligo, other points north and Wexford. **Heuston station** (☎ 703 3299), south of the Liffey and west of the city centre, is the station for Cork, Galway, Killarney, Limerick, Waterford, and most other points to the south and west. For travel information and tickets, contact the **Iarnród Éireann Travel Centre** (☎ 836 6222, bookings 703 4070; www.irishrail.ie; 35 Lower Abbey St).

GETTING AROUND

TO/FROM THE AIRPORT

A frequent Airlink Express service is available with **Dublin Bus** (Bus Átha Cliath; ☎ 873 4222; www.dublinbus.ie; 59 O'Connell St) to/from Busáras, Heuston train station and various points around the city (€5, 30 to 40 minutes from the stations). Alternatively, take the slower bus 16A, 230 or 746 (€2, one hour).

Aircoach (☎ 844 7118; www.aircoach.ie) offers a service from the airport to various destinations throughout the city (one way/return €7/12, every 10 to 15 minutes from 6am to midnight).

IRELAND DUBLIN

A taxi to the city centre should cost around €22. Some Dublin airport taxi drivers can be unscrupulous, so make sure the meter is on and mention up front that you'll need a meter receipt.

CAR

All the major car-hire companies have offices at Dublin airport and in the city centre. See p162 for details.

PUBLIC TRANSPORT

Dublin Bus local buses cost from €1.50 to €2 for a single trip. You must pay the exact fare when boarding; you don't get change.

Dublin Area Rapid Transport (**DART; www.irishrail.ie**) provides quick rail access as far north as Howth and south to Bray; Pearse station is handy for central Dublin.

The **Luas** (**www.luas.ie**) tram system runs on two (unconnected) lines; the green line runs from the eastern side of St Stephen's Green southeast to Sandyford, and the red line runs from Tallaght to Connolly station, with stops at Heuston station, the National Museum and Busáras.

Taxis in Dublin are expensive, and flag fall costs €3.80, plus €1.50 per kilometre. For taxi service, call **National Radio Cabs** (**☎ 677 2222**).

AROUND DUBLIN

DUN LAOGHAIRE

☎ 01

Dun Laoghaire (pronounced dun-leary), 13km south of central Dublin, is a seaside resort and busy harbour with ferry connections to Britain. On the southern side of the harbour is the **Martello Tower** where James Joyce's epic novel *Ulysses* opens. It now houses the **James Joyce Museum** (**☎ 280 9265; Sandycove; adult/child €7.25/4.55; 10am-1pm & 2-5pm Mon-Sat, 2-6pm Sun Apr-Sep, by arrangement only Oct-Mar**). If you fancy a cold saltwater dip, the nearby **Forty Foot Pool** (also mentioned in *Ulysses*) is the place.

Take the DART rail service (€3.80 return, 25 minutes, every 10 to 20 minutes) from Dublin to Dun Laoghaire, then bus 59 to Sandycove Rd, or walk (1km).

MALAHIDE CASTLE

☎ 01

Despite the vicissitudes of Irish history, the Talbot family managed to keep **Malahide Castle** (**☎ 846 2184; www.malahidecastle.com; adult/child €7.25/4.55; 10am-5pm Mon-Sat year-round, 10am-6pm Sun Apr-Sep, 11am-5pm Sun Oct-Mar**) from 1185 through to 1973. The castle is packed with furniture and paintings, and Puck, the family ghost, is still in residence. The extensive **Fry Model Railway** (**☎ 846 2184; adult/child €7.25/4.55; 10am-1pm & 2-5pm Mon, Tue & Thu-Sat, 1-5pm Sun Apr-Sep, closed Wed & Oct-Mar**) in the castle grounds covers 240 sq metres and

MARTIN MOOS

Malahide Castle

IRELAND

AROUND DUBLIN

re-creates Ireland's rail and public transport system (it's better than it sounds). Combined tickets (adult/child €12.50/7.70) give admission to the model railway, castle and the James Joyce Museum.

Malahide is 13km northeast of Dublin; take the DART rail service from Dublin Connolly to Malahide station (€3.80 return, 22 minutes, every 10 to 20 minutes).

BRÚ NA BÓINNE

☎ 041

A thousand years older than Stonehenge, the extensive Neolithic necropolis known as Brú na Bóinne (Boyne Palace) is one of the most extraordinary prehistoric sites in Europe. The complex, including the Newgrange and Knowth passage tombs, can only be visited on a guided walk from the **Brú na Bóinne visitor centre** (☎ 988 0300; Donore; adult/child visitor centre only €2.90/1.60, visitor centre & Newgrange €5.80/2.90, visitor centre & Knowth €4.50/1.60; 9am-7pm Jun–mid-Sep, 9am-6.30pm May & late Sep, 9.30am-5.30pm Mar, Apr & Oct, 9.30am-5pm Nov-Feb).

The site is 50km north of Dublin, signposted off the M1. Take Bus Éireann's 100X or 101 service to Drogheda, then the 163 to Donore (total journey €10 return, 1½ hours, five daily), which stops at the gates of the visitor centre. Or use the **Newgrange Shuttlebus** (☎ 1800 424252; www.overthetoptours.com; return €18).

Guided day tours from Dublin by **Mary Gibbons** (☎ 01-283 9973; www.newgrangetours.com; tour incl admission €35; Mon-Sat) are excellent.

SOUTHWEST IRELAND

The southwest comes closest to the misty-eyed vision of Ireland many visitors imagine – blue lakes and green mountains, blustery beaches, bird-haunted sea cliffs, picturesque hamlets, and welcoming towns with live music every night.

CORK

☎ 021 / pop 119,400

There's a reason the locals call Cork (Corcaigh) 'The Real Capital' or 'The People's Republic of Cork'; something special is going on here. The city has long been dismissive of Dublin, and with a burgeoning arts, music and restaurant scene it's now getting a cultural reputation to rival the capital's.

The **tourist office** (☎ 425 5100; www.corkkerry.ie; Grand Pde; 9am-6pm Mon-Sat, 10am-3.40pm Sun Jul & Aug, 9.15am-5pm Mon-Fri, 9.30am-4.30pm Sat Sep-Jun) has plenty of brochures, books and maps.

SIGHTS

Cork City Gaol (☎ 430 5022; www.corkcitygaol.com; Convent Ave; adult/child €7/3.50, 9.30am-6pm Mar-Oct, 10am-5pm Nov-Feb) closed down in 1923 and is now a terrific museum about a terrifying subject. Restored cells, mannequins representing prisoners and guards, and an impressive 35-minute audio tour bring home the horrors of 19th-century prison life. Housed in the same building is the **National Radio Museum** (adult/child €6/3.50), which details the history of broadcast radio in Cork.

Crawford Municipal Art Gallery (☎ 490 7855; www.crawfordartgallery.com; Emmet Pl; admission free; 10am-5pm Mon-Sat) combines the 18th-century Cork Customs House with 21st-century Dutch design, and it's a must-see for anyone who enjoys art and architecture.

Just south of the city centre sits the Protestant **St Finbarre's Cathedral** (☎ 496 3387; www.cathedral.cork.anglican.org; Bishop St; adult/child €3/1.50; 9.30am-5.30pm Mon-Sat, 12.30-5pm Sun Apr-Sep, 10am-12.45pm & 2-5pm Mon-Sat Oct-Mar). Built in 1879, this beautiful Gothic Revival structure has a multitude of notable features, including a Golden Angel who sits on the eastern side of the

OLIVER STREWE

Olive varieties at the English Market, Cork

cathedral, and whose job it is to blow her horn at the onset of the Apocalypse.

The **Cork Public Museum** (☎ 427 0679; Fitzgerald Park; admission free; ⏰ 11am-1pm & 2.15-5pm Mon-Fri, 11am-1pm & 2.15-4pm Sat year-round, 3-5pm Sun Apr-Sep) has a fine collection of artefacts that trace Cork's past from prehistory to the present, including the city's role in the fight for independence.

SLEEPING & EATING

our pick **Garnish House** (☎ 427 5111; www.garnish.ie; Western Rd; s €60-80, d €90-140) With charming rooms (think flowers and fresh fruit), gourmet breakfasts and hosts who are eager to please, Garnish House is possibly the perfect B&B.

Crawford House (☎ 427 9000; www.crawfordguesthouse.com; Western Rd; s €75-85, d €110-120) A top-notch B&B, Crawford House has spacious rooms with king-size beds, gracious furnishings and some bodacious jacuzzis to splash around in.

Café Paradiso (☎ 427 7939; 16 Lancaster Quay; mains lunch €9-15, dinner €24-25; ⏰ 12.30-3pm & 6.30-10.30pm Tue-Sat) Arguably the best vegetarian restaurant in Ireland, the inventive dishes on offer here will seduce even the most committed carnivore.

our pick **Farmgate Café** (☎ 427 8134; English Market; mains €10-15; ⏰ 8.30am-10pm Mon-Sat) An unmissable Cork experience at the heart of the English Market, the Farmgate is perched on a balcony overlooking the market below, the source of all that fresh local produce on your plate.

For self catering, head for the well-stocked food stalls at the **English Market** (⏰ 9am-5.30pm Mon-Sat).

DRINKING

Locally brewed Murphy's is the stout of choice here, not Guinness.

Mutton Lane Inn (☎ 427 3471; 3 Mutton Lane) With Victorian wallpaper, rock-and-roll posters, and a covered outdoor area for drinking and smoking, Cork's oldest pub is the type of place that you'll wish you had in your home town.

Sin É (☎ 450 2266; Coburg St) There are no frills or fuss here – just a comfy, sociable pub long on atmosphere and short on pretension.

There's music most nights, much of it traditional but with the odd surprise.

GETTING THERE & AWAY

Eight kilometres south of the city centre on the N27, **Cork airport** (☎ 431 3131) has direct flights to many major cities, including Edinburgh, London, Manchester, Amsterdam, Barcelona, Milan, Paris, Warsaw and Prague.

The **Cork bus station** (☎ 450 8188; cnr Merchants Quay & Parnell Pl) is east of the city centre. You can get to most places in Ireland from Cork: Dublin (€12, 4½ hours, six daily), Killarney (€14, 1¾ hours, 14 daily), Waterford, Wexford and more. For a direct service to Dublin city and airport, take **Aircoach** (www.aircoach.ie) from St Patrick Quay (€14, four hours, eight daily), right behind the Gresham Metropole hotel.

JOHN ELK III

Blarney Castle

Kent train station (☎ 450 4777; Glanmire R[d] Lower) is across the river. Trains go to Dubli[n] (€60, 2¾ hours, hourly), Galway (€60, fiv[e] to six hours, seven daily) and Killarne[y] (€24, 1½ to two hours, nine daily).

For ferries, see p160.

GETTING AROUND

Frequent buses head from the bus statio[n] to the airport (€3.80, 25 minutes) fro[m] April to September (fewer in the low season). Otherwise, a taxi costs around €16 Buses also run fairly often to the ferry terminal (€5, 40 minutes).

BLARNEY

☎ 021 / pop 2150

Lying just northwest of Cork, the village of Blarney (An Bhlarna) receives a *gazillion* visitors a year, for one sole reason: **Blarney Castle** (☎ 438 5252; www.blarneycastle.ie; adult/child €10/3.50; 9am-7pm Mon-Sat, 9am-5.30pm Sun May-Sep, to dusk daily Oct-Apr) They come to kiss the castle's legendary **Blarney Stone** and get the 'gift of the gab' (Queen Elizabeth I, exasperated with Lord Blarney's ability to talk endlessly without agreeing to her demands, invented the term 'to talk Blarney' back in the 16th century). The stone is up on the battlements, and bending over backwards to kiss it requires a head for heights, although there's someone there to hold you in position. It also helps if you're not germophobic – there's a greasy mark where millions of lips have been before.

Buses run regularly from Cork bus station (€5 return, 30 minutes).

RING OF KERRY

☎ 066

This 179km circuit of the Iveragh Peninsula pops up on every self-respecting tourist itinerary, and for good reason. The road winds past pristine beaches, the island- dotted tlantic, medieval ruins, mountains and ughs (lakes). Even locals stop their cars o gawk at the rugged coastline – particu-rly between Waterville and Caherdaniel in ne southwest of the peninsula, where the eauty dial is turned up to 11. The shorter **ing of Skellig**, at the end of the peninsula, as fine views of the Skellig Rocks and is ee of tourist coaches.

South of Cahirciveen the R565 branches est to the 11km-long **Valentia Island**, ne jumping-off point for an unforget-able experience: the **Skellig Rocks**, two ny islands 12km off the coast.

Calm seas permitting, boats run from oring to late summer from Portmagee, ist before the bridge to Valentia, to kellig Michael. The standard fare is round €40 return. Advance booking is es-ential; there are half-a-dozen boat opera-ors, including **Casey's** (☎ **947 2437; www.kelligislands.com**) and **Sea Quest** (☎ **947 214; www.skelligsrock.com**).

INGLE PENINSULA

☎ **066**

emote and beautiful, the Dingle eninsula ends in the Irish mainland's most esterly point. This is a Gaeltacht area – if ou're driving, don't bother looking for oad signs that say 'Dingle Town'; they all ay 'An Daingean', the Gaelic equivalent. ingle Town (population 1647), the pe-insula's capital, is a special place whose harms have long drawn runaways from cross the world, making the port town surprisingly cosmopolitan and creative lace. There are loads of cafes, bookshops nd art and craft galleries, and a friendly olphin called Fungie who has lived in the ay for 25 years.

Dingle Boatmen's Association (☎ **915 526**) operates one-hour boat trips to visit ungie the dolphin. The cost is €16/8 per dult/child (free if Fungie doesn't show, but he usually does). There are also two-hour trips where you can swim with him (€25 per person, wetsuit hire €25 extra).

Dingle Oceanworld (☎ **915 2111; www.dingle-oceanworld.ie; adult/child €12/7;** ⏲ **10am-8.30pm Jul & Aug, to 6pm Sep-Jun**) is a state-of-the-art aquarium with walk-through tunnel and touch pool, and is wheelchair accessible; look out for the spectacularly ugly wreck fish.

THE WEST COAST

The west coast is Ireland at its wildest and most remote, a storm-battered seaboard of soaring sea cliffs and broad surf beaches. Along its length you can explore the eerie lunar landscape of the Burren's limestone plateau, party on in the music pubs of bohemian Galway, and hike the heather-clad hills and bogs of Connemara.

CLIFFS OF MOHER

About 8km south of Doolin are the towering 200m-high Cliffs of Moher, one of Ireland's most famous natural features. The landscaped **Cliffs of Moher Visitor Centre** (☎ **065-708 1171; www.cliffsofmoher.ie; car park per vehicle €8, exhibition €4;** ⏲ **8.30am-7.30pm Jun-Aug, 9am-6pm Mar-May, Sep & Oct, 9am-5pm Nov-Feb**) has exhibitions about the cliffs and the environment called the 'Atlantic Edge'. Nearby is **O'Brien's Tower**, which you can climb for €1.

GALWAY

☎ **091 / pop 72,400**

Arty and bohemian, Galway (Gaillimh) is legendary around the world for its entertainment scene. Students make up a quarter of the city's population, and brightly painted pubs heave with live music on any given night. Cafes spill out onto cobblestone streets filled with a frenzy of fiddles, banjos, guitars and *bodhráns*, and jugglers, painters, puppeteers and magicians in outlandish masks enchant passers-by.

The **tourist office** (☎ 537700; www.irelandwest.ie; Forster St; 9am-5.45pm Jun-Oct, 9am-5.45pm Mon-Sat, 9am-12.45pm Sun Jan-May, Nov & Dec) is an efficient information centre.

SIGHTS

Little remains of Galway's old city walls apart from the **Spanish Arch**, which is right beside the river. Nearby **Galway City Museum** (☎ 532460; Spanish Pde; admission free; 10am-5pm daily Jun-Sep, to 5pm Tue-Sat Oct-May) has exhibits on the city's history from 1800 to 1950.

The focal point of the city centre is **Eyre Square**, a pleasant green space dotted with statues. In the centre of the square is **Kennedy Park**, honouring a visit by John F Kennedy in 1963. Southwest of the square, the **Collegiate Church of St Nicholas of Myra** (Shop St) dates from 1320 and has several tombs.

Across the road, in the Bowling Green area, is the **Nora Barnacle House Museum** (☎ 564743; www.norabarnacle.com; 8 Bowling Green; admission €3; 10am-5pm mid-May–mid-Sep or by appointment), the former home of the wife and lifelong muse of James Joyce. The small museum is dedicated to the couple.

Feel like petting slimy sea creatures? Stop by the **Atlantaquaria** (☎ 585100; www.nationalaquarium.ie; Salthill Promenade; adult/child €9.75/6; 9am-5pm Mon-Fri, to 6pm Sat & Sun) and see the hands-on exhibit at Ireland's National Aquarium. It's roughly 2km from the city centre.

FESTIVALS & EVENTS

Galway Arts Festival (www.galwayartsfestival.com) Held in July, this is the main event on Galway's calendar.

Galway Oyster Festival (www.galwayoysterfest.com) Going strong for 50 years now, this festival draws thousands c visitors in late September.

SLEEPING & EATING

Griffin Lodge (☎ 589440; griffinlodge@eircom.net; 3 Father Griffin Pl; s €35-50, d €55-70) You' be welcomed like a long-lost friend a this completely renovated B&B, whic has eight immaculate rooms in soothin shades of spearmint and moss green.

St Martin's B&B (☎ 568286; stmartins@gmail.com; 2 Nun's Island Rd; s/d €45/60) S Martin's is in a great location, with back window views overlooking the William O'Brien Bridge and a simple garden on th banks of the Corrib.

Spanish Arch Hotel (☎ 569600; www.spanisharchhotel.ie; Quay St; s €75-85, d €99-14 In a sensational spot on the main drag this 20-room boutique hotel is housed in 16th-century former Carmelite convent

Goya's (☎ 567010; 2 Kirwan's Lane; main €5-10; 9.30am-6pm Mon-Sat) Goya's is Galway treasure hidden down a narrow back alley, with cool pale-blue deco Segafredo coffee, superb cakes, and ho lunchtime specials.

Druid Lane (☎ 563015; 9 Quay St; main lunch €10-20, dinner €15-26; 5pm-late daily, plu 1-4pm Sat & Sun) Signature main courses a this intimate restaurant include saddle c rabbit, and roasted duck breast.

our pick **Nimmo's** (☎ 561114; www.nimmo.ie; Spanish Arch; mains €17-26; cafe 10am-3.30pm Mon-Sat, noon-3.30pm Sun, restaurant 6-10.30pm Tucked behind the Spanish Arch, thi informal, cottage-style restaurant wit whitewashed interior and mismatche furniture serves some of the finest foo in the west of Ireland, from scallops an sea bass to roast Irish lamb.

DRINKING & ENTERTAINMENT

Most of Galway's pubs see musician performing at least a couple of nights veek, whether in an informal session or ıs a headline act.

Róisín Dubh (☎ 586540; www.roisindubh.et; Upper Dominick St) A superpub complete vith vast roof terrace, Róisín Dubh is *the* lace to see emerging indie bands before hey hit the big time.

Séhán Ua Neáchtain (☎ 568820; 17 Upper ross St) Known simply as Neáchtains (*nock-ans*), this dusty old pub has a fabulous tmosphere and attracts an eccentric, nixed crowd.

Good spots to hear trad sessions in-:lude **Monroe's Tavern** (☎ 583397; Upper ominick St), which has set dancing on Tuesday, **Taaffe's Bar** (☎ 564066; 19 Shop t), **Taylor's Bar** (☎ 587239; Upper Dominick t) and the **Crane Bar** (☎ 587419; 2 Sea Rd).

GETTING THERE & AROUND

Bus Éireann buses depart from next to **Ceannt train station** (☎ 561444). Private ous companies use a **new coach station** cnr Forster St & Fairgreen Rd) a block northeast.

Bus Éireann (☎ 562000) operates services to Doolin (€13, 1½ hours, seven daily Monday to Saturday in summer, twice on Sunday), Dublin (€13, 3¾ hours, hourly), Killarney (€20, 4¾ hours, three daily), Limerick, Sligo and beyond. **Citylink** (☎ 564163; www.citylink.ie) runs buses to Dublin (€15, three hours, hourly), and Clifden (€11) in Connemara.

Trains run to and from Dublin (€15, 2¾ hours, five daily).

CONNEMARA

☎ 095

With its shimmering black lakes, pale mountains, lonely valleys and more than the occasional rainbow, Connemara in the northwestern corner of County Galway is one of the most gorgeous corners of Ireland. Connemara is prime hiking country with plenty of wild terrain, none more so than the **Twelve Bens**, a ridge of rugged mountains that form part of **Connemara National Park** (☎ 41054; www.connemaranationalpark.ie; Letterfrack; adult/child €2.90/1.30; 🕒 visitor centre 9.30am-6.30pm Jun-Aug, 10am-5.30pm Mar-May, 10am-5.30pm Sep-early Oct). Located on the park's northern edge is **Kylemore Abbey** (☎ 41146; www.kylemoreabbey.com; adult/child €12/free; 🕒 9am-5pm),

GARETH MCCORMACK

Glassillaun Beach, Connemara

a 19th-century neo-Gothic mansion set beside a lake; the abbey's scenic grounds offer much easier walking.

Galway–Westport buses stop in Clifden, as well as Oughterard, Maam Cross and Recess. There are four express buses daily between Clifden and Galway (two on Sunday).

NORTHERN IRELAND

☎ 028 / pop 1.7 million

When you cross from the Republic into Northern Ireland you notice a couple of changes: the accent is different, the road signs are in miles, and the prices are in pounds sterling. Dragged down for decades by the violence and uncertainty of the Troubles, Northern Ireland today is a nation rejuvenated. The 1998 Good Friday Agreement laid the groundwork for peace and raised hopes for the future, and since then the province has seen a huge influx of investment and redevelopment.

GLENS OF ANTRIM

The Antrim Coast between Larne and Ballycastle is characterised by a series of nine beautiful valleys known as the Glens of Antrim, with lush green fields slung between black basalt crags, and picturesque harbour villages such as **Cushendall** and **Cushendun**. **Glenariff**, with its forest park and waterfalls, has been dubbed 'Queen of the Glens'.

CARRICK-A-REDE ROPE BRIDGE

The 20m-long **rope bridge** (☎ 2076 9839; adult/child £3.70/2; 10am-7pm Jun-Aug, to 6pm Mar-May, Sep & Oct) that connects Carrick-a-Rede Island to the mainland, swaying some 30m above the pounding waves, is a classic test of nerve. The island is the site of a salmon fishery and is a scenic 1.25km walk from the car park. Note that the bridge is closed in high winds.

GIANT'S CAUSEWAY

This spectacular rock formation – Norther Ireland's only Unesco World Heritage site is one of Ireland's most impressive an atmospheric landscape features. Whe you first see it you'll understand why th ancients thought it wasn't a natural fea ture – the vast expanse of regular, close packed, hexagonal stone columns look for all the world like the handiwork c giants.

The more prosaic explanation is tha the columns are contraction crack caused by a cooling lava flow some 6 million years ago. The phenomenon i explained in an audiovisual (£1) at th **Causeway Visitors Centre** (☎ 2073 185 www.giantscausewaycentre.com; 10am-6p Jul & Aug, 10am-5pm Mar-Jun, Sep & Oct, 10am 4.30pm Nov-Feb). It costs nothing to visit th site, but car parking is £5. Try to visit th Causeway midweek or out of season t avoid the crowds.

DIRECTORY

ACTIVITIES

Walking, hiking and cycling are the mos popular and accessible activities – thing you can do virtually on a whim, and th perfect way to open up some beautifu corners of the country. **Visit Britain** (www visitbritain.com) has special sections devote to holiday ideas and outdoor activities.

CYCLING

Getting around by bike is a brilliant wa to see Britain and Ireland, but you're no going to get away without tackling few hills! Popular regions to tour includ southwest England, the Yorkshire Dales Derbyshire's Peak District, Mid-Wale and the Scottish Borders. The 10,000 mile **National Cycle Network** (www nationalcyclenetwork.org.uk) offers cyclists web of quiet roads and traffic-free tracks that pass through busy cities and remote rural areas.

SURFING & KITESURFING

Despite the chilly seas, surfing's a popular pastime in many of Britain's coastal corners, including Southwest Wales, Cornwall and Devon. For info, see www.britsurf.co.uk – and don't forget your wetsuit!

Kitesurfing is one of the fastest-growing water sports in the world. Brisk winds, decent waves and great beaches once again make Cornwall and Pembrokeshire favourite spots, but it's possible on other beaches along the British coastline. See www.kitesurfing.org.

WALKING & HIKING

Britain's picturesque terrains are great for walking and hiking. Every country town is surrounded by a network of footpaths, with even more choice in the national parks and mountain areas such as the Lake District, North Wales and the Highlands of Scotland. Some long routes are designated National Trails (see www.nationaltrails.co.uk) but you don't have to do the *whole* route; many people follow sections of the classics for a day or two, or just a few hours.

The **Ramblers Association** (☎ 020-7339 8500; www.ramblers.org.uk) is the country's leading organisation for walkers, and its website is a mine of background information. For keen walkers and hikers, Britain boasts many multiday routes:

Coast to Coast Popular hike across three northern England national parks.
Cotswold Way Delightful ramble through southern hills and countryside.
Dales Way Through Yorkshire's charming countryside to the Lake District.
Pembrokeshire Coast Path Rollercoaster romp around the West Wales peninsula.
West Highland Way Classic route through southern Scotland.
Wicklow Way 132km of wonderful Irish walking.

DANGERS & ANNOYANCES

Britain's booze culture means that many city centres get rowdy late on Friday and Saturday nights. Beware drunken fights, vandalism, and the odd patch of vomit.

EMBASSIES & CONSULATES

BRITAIN

Most of the major foreign diplomatic missions are based in London; for a complete list consult the **Foreign & Commonwealth Office** (www.fco.gov.uk).

Australia (Map pp78-9; ☎ 020-7379 4334; www.australia.org.uk; The Strand, WC2B 4LA)
Canada (Map pp78-9; ☎ 020-7258 6600; www.canada.org.uk; 1 Grosvenor Sq, W1X 0AB)
France (Map pp78-9; ☎ 020-7073 1000; www.ambafrance-uk.org; 58 Knightsbridge, SW1 7JT)
Germany (Map pp78-9; ☎ 020-7824 1300; www.london.diplo.de; 23 Belgrave Sq, SW1X 8PX)
Ireland (Map pp78-9; ☎ 020-7235 2171; www.embassyofireland.co.uk;17 Grosvenor Pl, SW1X 7HR)
Japan (Map pp78-9; ☎ 020-7465 6500; www.uk.emb-japan.go.jp; 101 Piccadilly, W1J 7JT)
Netherlands (Map pp74-5; ☎ 020-7590 3200; www.netherlands-embassy.org.uk; 38 Hyde Park Gate, SW7 5DP)
New Zealand (Map pp78-9; ☎ 020-7930 8422; www.nzembassy.com/uk; 80 Haymarket, SW1Y 4TQ)
USA (Map pp78-9; ☎ 020-7499 9000; www.usembassy.org.uk; 24 Grosvenor Sq, W1A 1AE)

IRELAND

The following countries have diplomatic offices in Dublin:

Australia (off Map p144; ☎ 01-664 5300; www.ireland.embassy.gov.au; 2nd fl, Fitzwilton House, Wilton Tce, Dublin 2)

Canada (off Map p144; ☎ 01-234 4000; www.canada.ie; 7-8 Wilton Tce, Dublin 2)
France (off Map p144; ☎ 01-277 5000; www.ambafrance.ie; 36 Ailesbury Rd, Dublin 4)
Germany (off Map p144; ☎ 01-269 3011; www.dublin.diplo.de; 31 Trimleston Ave, Booterstown, Co Dublin)
Netherlands (off Map p144; ☎ 01-269 3444; www.netherlandsembassy.ie; 160 Merrion Rd, Dublin 4)
New Zealand Contact the NZ High Commission in London.
UK (off Map p144; ☎ 01-205 3700; www.britishembassy.ie; 29 Merrion Rd, Ballsbridge, Dublin 4)
USA (off Map p144; ☎ 01-668 8777; http://dublin.usembassy.gov; 42 Elgin Rd, Ballsbridge, Dublin 4)

FESTIVALS & EVENTS

JANUARY

Hogmanay/New Year (www.edinburghshogmanay.org; Princess St, Edinburgh) Huge, raucous party from 31 December to 1 January echoed by smaller versions throughout the UK.

MARCH

St Patrick's Day Parades and fireworks and light shows for three days around 17 March in Dublin, Cork, and Belfast.

APRIL

Grand National (www.aintree.co.uk) Britain's top annual horse race. Held in Aintree, Liverpool, in early April.

MAY

FA Cup Final (www.thefa.com) Nail-biting conclusion to England's annual knockout football club competition at Wembley Stadium in London. Held mid-May.

JULY

Llangollen International Musical Eisteddfod (www.international-eisteddfod.co.uk) A 60-year-old celebration of international folk music and dance. Held early July in Llangollen, Wales.
Galway Arts Festival (www.galwayartsfestival.com) Artistic types congregate on Galway for one of Ireland's main cultural happenings.
Orangeman's Day Orangemen take to the streets throughout Northern Ireland on the 'glorious 12th'.

AUGUST

Edinburgh Fringe Festival (www.edfringe.com) Sprawling, three-week comedy and avant-garde performance fest in Edinburgh from early August.

SEPTEMBER

Braemar Gathering (www.braemargathering.org) Caber tossing and other Highland sports come to Braemar in early September.

NOVEMBER

Guy Fawkes Night Bonfires and fireworks recalling a failed antigovernment plot from the 1600s. Held nationwide on 5 November.

GAY & LESBIAN TRAVELLERS

Most major cities have gay and lesbian scenes – especially London, Brighton, Manchester and Glasgow. **Gay Britain Network** (www.gaybritain.co.uk), **Gay Times** (www.gaytimes.co.uk) and **Diva** (www.divamag.co.uk) provide resources and information in print and online versions.

Despite the decriminalisation of homosexuality for people over 17 years of age, gay life in Ireland is generally neither acknowledged nor understood. Only the larger cities and towns have open gay and lesbian communities. The monthly **Gay Community News** (www.gcn.ie) is a free publication of the **National Lesbian & Gay Federation** (☎ 01-671 9076; www.nlgf.ie; Unit 2, Scarlet Row, West Essex St, Dublin 8).

HOLIDAYS

Called 'bank holidays' in Britain, public holidays affect most businesses, although larger shops often stay open. If a public holiday falls on a weekend, the nearest Monday is usually taken instead.

New Year's Day 1 January
New Year's Holiday 2 January (Scotland only)
St Patrick's Day 17 March
Good Friday March/April
Easter Monday March/April (except Scotland)
May Day First Monday in May
Spring Bank Holiday Last Monday in May
Summer Bank Holiday First Monday in August (Scotland); last Monday in August (England and Wales)
Christmas Day 25 December
Boxing Day 26 December

Northern Ireland's holidays include the **Spring Bank Holiday** (last Monday in May), **Orangemen's Day** (12 July, following Monday if 12th is at weekend) and **August Bank Holiday** (last Monday in August).

In the Republic, there's also the **June Holiday** (first Monday in June), the **August Holiday** (first Monday in August) and the **October Holiday** (last Monday in October).

MONEY

Britain's currency is the pound sterling (£); banks in Scotland and Northern Ireland issue their own banknotes, which are legal tender across the UK. The Irish Republic uses the euro (€).

Tipping is usually expected in restaurants, bars and pubs that serve food – somewhere around 10% is the norm. Taxi drivers do not have to be tipped, but if you do, 10% is more than generous.

CREDIT CARDS & DEBIT CARDS

MasterCard and Visa are the most widely accepted cards, with Amex not far behind. Britain recently launched 'Chip & Pin', a debit and credit-card payment system that requires a security number to be entered (instead of a signature). Many overseas card providers have also adopted the system; if you use a PIN number back home, chances are you will in the UK, too.

TRAVELLERS CHEQUES

Travellers cheques have largely been superseded by credit and debit cards; very few businesses will accept them as payment, although they can still be exchanged for cash at most banks or bureaux de change.

POST

There are two classes of post within Britain: a standard letter costs 36p 1st-class (normally delivered next day) and 27p 2nd-class (up to three days). Stamps are available at post offices and many shops and newsagents. For details on all prices, see www.postoffice.co.uk.

Post offices (An Post) throughout the Republic are generally open 9am to 5.30pm Monday to Friday, and 9am to 1pm Saturday. Letters weighing less than 100g cost €0.82 to anywhere in the world.

TELEPHONE

BRITAIN

To call outside the UK dial ☎ 00, then the country code, the area code (you usually drop the initial zero) and the number. To call within the UK, you use the area code and the number, although if you're dialling locally you can drop the area code.

☎0500 or ☎0800 numbers are free. ☎0845 numbers are charged at local rate, ☎087 are charged at national-call rate, ☎089 or ☎09 are premium rate (and very expensive). Mobile numbers begin ☎07 and are more expensive than landlines.

For the operator, call ☎100. For directory inquiries, a host of agencies compete for your business and charge from £0.10 to £0.40; numbers include ☎118 192, ☎118 118, ☎118 500 and ☎118 811.

Most public phoneboxes take coins, credit cards, phonecards or all three. Coin phones do not give change and charge a minimum of £0.20 or £0.40.

Britain and Ireland use the GSM 900/1800 mobile network, which is compatible with Europe and Australia but not all phones from North America or Japan. Alternatively, you could buy a local SIM card (around £30) or a pay-as-you-go phone (from around £50, including SIM and number). Both options use 'top-up' cards (available at shops, supermarkets and newsagents) to add credit to your phone.

IRELAND

Local telephone calls from a public phone in the Republic cost a minimum of €0.50 for three minutes; in Northern Ireland a local call costs a minimum of £0.30. Some payphones in the North accept euro coins. Prepaid phonecards by Eircom or private operators are available in newsagencies and post offices.

To call Northern Ireland from the Republic, do not use ☎0044 as for the rest of the UK. Instead, dial ☎048 and then the local number. To dial the Republic from the North, however, use the full international code ☎00-353, then the local number.

Mobiles in the Republic begin with 085, 086 or 087. A local pay-as-you-go SIM will cost from around €10.

TRANSPORT

GETTING THERE & AWAY

AIR

Britain's major airports are **London Heathrow** (LHR; ☎0870 000 0123; www.heathrowairport.com) and **London Gatwick** (LGW, ☎0870 000 2468; www.gatwickairport.com). Budget carriers often use the capital's smaller airports (London City, Luton and Stansted), or regional airports (eg Newcastle, Liverpool, Manchester, Glasgow, Edinburgh). Ireland's main airports are **Dublin** (DUB; ☎01-814 1111; www.dublinairport.com) and **Belfast International** (BFS; ☎028-9448 4848; www.belfastairport.com), plus Cork, Kerry, Shannon and Derry.

BUS

Eurolines (www.eurolines.com) is an umbrella company comprising around 30 bus/coach operators across Europe. Services to/from Britain are operated by **National Express** (☎08717 818181; www.nationalexpress.com).

National Express and **Bus Éireann** (☎01-836 6111; www.buseireann.ie) operate services direct to Dublin, Belfast and other cities via various ferry crossings.

SEA

Britain has frequent ferry connections to Ireland and mainland Europe. For tickets and routes check out **Ferry Booker** (www.ferrybooker.com), **DirectFerries** (www.directferries.co.uk) or **Ferry Savers** (☎in UK 0844-5768835; www.ferrysavers.com), and book as early as possible for the best fares. The main ferry operators include the following:

Brittany Ferries (☎in UK 0871-2440744, ☎in France 825 828 828; www.brittany-ferries.com) Routes include Portsmouth to Caen, Cherbourg, St-Malo and Santander; Poole to Cherbourg; Plymouth and Cork to Roscoff.

Celtic Link Ferries (☎ in UK 0844-5768834; www.celticlinkferries.com) Cherbourg to Portsmouth and Rosslare (Ireland).
DFDS Seaways (☎ in UK 0871-5229955; www.dfds.co.uk) Newcastle to Amsterdam; Harwich to Esbjerg (Norway).
Irish Ferries (☎ in UK & Ireland 0818 300 400, ☎ in France 01 70 72 03 26; www.irishferries.co.uk) Dublin to Holyhead; Rosslare to Pembroke, Cherbourg and Rosscoff.
Norfolkline (☎ 0844 847 5042; www.norfolkline.com) Dover to Dunkirk; Liverpool to Belfast and Dublin; Rosyth to Zeebrugge.
P&O Ferries (☎ in the UK 08716-645645, ☎ in France 0825 120 156; www.poferries.com) Dover to Calais; Hull to Zeebrugge and Rotterdam; Portsmouth to Bilbao.
P&O Irish Sea (☎ in Ireland 01 407 3434, ☎ in the UK 0871-6644999; www.poirishsea.com) Dublin to Liverpool; Larne to Troon and Cairnryan.
Stena Line (☎ in Ireland 01 204 7777, ☎ in the UK 08705-707070; www.stenaline.com) Several routes between Wales and Ireland, including Fishguard to Rosslare, Fleetwood to Larne and Holyhead to Dublin. Other options include Stranraer to Belfast, and Harwich to Hook of Holland.
Transmanche (☎ in the UK 0800 917 1201, ☎ in France 0800 650 100; www.transmancheferries.com) Newhaven to Dieppe, Portsmouth to Le Havre, Dover to Boulogne, and Rosslare to Cherbourg.

TRAIN

The Channel Tunnel allows direct train travel between Britain and Continental Europe. High-speed **Eurostar** (☎ 08705 186186; www.eurostar.com) passenger services hurtle at least 10 times daily between London St Pancras and Paris (2¼ hours) or Brussels (two hours).

If you're travelling by car, you'll use **Eurotunnel** (☎ 08705 353 535; www.eurotunnel.com). At Folkestone (England) or Calais (France) you drive onto a train, go through the tunnel, and drive off at the other end. Trains run four times an hour from 6am to 10pm, then hourly. The journey takes 35 minutes.

In addition to Eurostar, there are also many combo tickets combining train travel and ferry crossing – see www.raileurope.co.uk for ideas.

GETTING AROUND

For getting around Britain and Ireland, a car will make the best use of your time and help you reach remote places. Hire costs, fuel, parking and incessant traffic jams can all spoil the fun, however, so if you're sticking to the major cities public transport is usually a better way to go.

For public transport, **Traveline** (☎ 0871 200 2233; www.traveline.org.uk) provides details of bus, coach, taxi and train services nationwide.

AIR

If you're pushed for time, flying around Britain and Ireland can be a useful option, especially with the advent of budget carriers – but on most domestic routes you'll probably find train durations compare favourably with planes, especially once you've factored in airport downtime. Budget flights also connect many regional airports with cities all over Europe, but destinations and routes change frequently. Major operators include:
Aer Arann (☎ in Ireland 08 18 210 210, ☎ in the UK 0870 876 76 76)
Aer Lingus (☎ in Ireland 0818 365000, ☎ in the UK 0871 718 5000)
Air Southwest (WOW; ☎ 0870 241 8202; www.airsouthwest.com)
bmibaby (WW; ☎ 0870 224 0224; www.bmibaby.com)
easyJet (EZY; ☎ 0870 600 0000; www.easyjet.com)

Flybe (BE; ☎ 0871 700 2000; www.flybe.com)
Ryanair (FR; ☎ 0871 246 0000; www.ryanair.com)

BUS

If you're on a tight budget, long-distance buses (called coaches) are nearly always the cheapest (and slowest) way to travel. Many towns have separate bus and coach stations – make sure you go to the right place!

Bus Éireann (☎ 01-836 6111; www.buseireann.ie) Ireland's inter-city operator.
Megabus (www.megabus.com) Budget coaches serving about 30 UK destinations.
National Express (☎ 08717 818181; www.nationalexpress.com) The major British coach operator.
Scottish Citylink (☎ 08705 505050; www.citylink.co.uk) For buses north of the border.
Ulsterbus (☎ 028-9066 6630; www.translink.co.uk) Buses within Northern Ireland.

BUS PASSES

National Express offers discount passes to full-time students and under 26s called Young Persons Coachcards; a pass costs £10 and gets 30% off standard adult fares. There are also coachcards for over 60s, families and travellers with disabilities.

For touring Britain, National Express **Brit Xplorer** passes allow unlimited travel for seven days (£79), 14 days (£139) and 28 days (£219). Many local bus companies in Britain and Ireland offer **Rover** or **Ranger** tickets that cover multi-day trips and sometimes include local train travel, too.

Open Road passes are available from Bus Éireann for bus-only travel in the Republic. They cost €49 (for travel on four out of eight consecutive days), €119 (eight out of 16 days) or €217 (15 out of 30 days). **Irish Rover** tickets combine services on Bus Éireann and Ulsterbus; they cost €76 (for three days' travel out of eight consecutive days), €172 (eight out of 15 days) and €255 (15 out of 30 days).

CAR & MOTORCYCLE

AUTOMOBILE ASSOCIATIONS

Automobile association members should ask for a Card of Introduction entitling you to services offered by sister organisations, usually free of charge.

Automobile Association (AA; www.aaireland.ie) Northern Ireland (☎ 0870-950 0600, breakdowns 0800-667 788); The Republic (☎ 01-617 9999, breakdowns 1800-667788)
Royal Automobile Club (RAC; www.rac.ie) Northern Ireland (☎ 0800-029 029); The Republic (☎ 1890-483 483)

DRIVING LICENCE

Most overseas driving licences are valid in Britain and Ireland for up to 12 months from the date of entry.

HIRE

Whether you're driving in Britain, Ireland or both, hiring a car is relatively expensive: plan on around £200 to £250 per week for a small car in the UK (€200 to €350 in Ireland) including insurance, unlimited mileage and collision damage waiver. Package deals booked at home usually offer the best deals.

Small, local car-hire companies can often undercut the big boys; consult the **Yellow Pages** (www.yell.com) or rental-brokers such as **UK Car Hire** (www.ukcarhire.net) or **Nova Car Hire** (www.rentacar-ireland.com) in Ireland.

Manual transmissions are the norm in Britain and Ireland; you'll have to ask specifically if you're after an automatic. You'll normally need to be over 21 and have held a valid driving licence for at least one year, although some firms require drivers to be aged 25+. Your own local licence is usually sufficient to hire a car for up to three months.

Some main UK players:

1car1 (☎ 0113-263 6675; www.1car1.com)
Avis (☎ 0844 581 0147; www.avis.co.uk)
Budget (☎ 0844 581 9998; www.budget.co.uk)
Europcar (☎ 0870 607 5000; www.europcar.co.uk)
Sixt (☎ 08701 567567; www.sixt.co.uk)
Thrifty (☎ 01494-751540; www.thrifty.co.uk)

ROAD RULES

Road rules are similar in Britain and Ireland; one of the major differences to remember is that while the UK measures distances and speed-limits in miles/mph, Ireland uses kilometres/kph.

The *Highway Code,* available in bookshops or online at www.direct.gov.uk/en/TravelAndTransport/Highwaycode/DG_069889, contains everything you need to know about Britain's road rules. The Irish equivalent is The Rules of the Road (www.rulesoftheroad.ie).

Drinking and driving is taken very seriously in all parts of the UK and the Republic of Ireland; the maximum blood-alcohol level allowed is 80mg/100mL.

Car parks, street parking and many other designated areas are regulated by 'pay and display' tickets. Make sure you stick to the rules of the car park and don't overstay your time, otherwise you might find yourself clapped with an expensive parking ticket or wheel-clamp. Double yellow lines in Britain and Ireland mean no parking at any time, while single yellow lines indicate restrictions (which will be signposted).

The main rules to remember:

- always drive on the left
- wear fitted seat belts in cars, or use child seats/child restraints for children aged under 12/under 1.35m in height
- in Ireland, children under 12 cannot sit in the front
- wear crash helmets on motorcycles
- give way to your right at junctions and roundabouts
- use the left-hand lane on motorways and dual-carriageways, and overtake on the right
- dip your headlights at night to avoid dazzling oncoming traffic
- don't use a mobile phone while driving unless it's fully hands-free.

SPEED LIMITS

Unless otherwise indicated, national speed limits are:

- 30mph (50km/h in Ireland) in built-up areas
- 60mph (100km/h in Ireland) on main roads
- 70mph (110km/h in Ireland) on motorways and most dual carriageways.

TRAIN

For long-distance travel, trains are faster and more comfortable than coaches but can be substantially more expensive. The UK rail network is provided by around 20 companies, while Network Rail operates tracks and stations. If you have to change trains, or use two train operators, you usually still buy one ticket, valid for the whole journey. Train times and fares are provided by **National Rail Enquiries** (☎ 08457 484950; www.nationalrail.co.uk).

The Republic of Ireland's railway system, **Iarnród Éireann** (☎ 1850-360 222, 01-836 6222; www.irishrail.ie), has routes radiating out from Dublin, but there is no direct north-south route along the west coast. **Northern Ireland Railways** (☎ 028-9066 6630; www.translink.co.uk) has four lines from Belfast, one of which links up with the Republic's rail system.

CLASSES

There are two classes of rail travel: 1st and standard. Travelling 1st class costs around 50% more than standard and, except on crowded trains, is not really worth it. At weekends some train operators offer 'upgrades' for an extra £10 to £15.

COSTS & RESERVATIONS

For short journeys (less than about 50 miles), it's usually fine to buy tickets on the spot at rail stations. For longer journeys tickets are much, much cheaper if bought in advance – the earlier you book, the bigger the discount. You also save if you travel off-peak (ie avoiding commuter times, Fridays and Sundays). The cheapest fares are usually non-refundable, so if you miss your train you'll have to buy a new ticket.

If you buy online, you can have the ticket posted to you (UK addresses only), or collect it at the station on the day of travel, either at the ticket desk or via automatic machines.

TRAIN PASSES

In Britain, Railcards (available from most mainline stations) cost around £25 and get you 33% off most train fares. They're valid for one year; for details, see www.railcard.co.uk.

16-25 Railcard For those aged 16 to 25, or full-time UK students.

Family & Friends Railcard Covers up to four adults and four children.

Senior Railcard For anyone over 60 years.

For countrywide travel, **BritRail Passes** (**www.britrail.com**) are good value, but only for visitors from overseas and they're not for sale *in* Britain. Some passes allow you to add train travel in Ireland for an extra fee (including ferry transit). There are also lots of **regional passes** (usually known as Ranger or Rover tickets) covering specific areas of Britain; it's always worth asking to see what might be available, or consult www.nationalrail.co.uk/times_fares/promotions/rangers_and_rovers.html.

For train travel only in Ireland, **Iarnród Éireann Explorer** tickets cost €138 within the Republic only, or €171 including Northern Ireland (five days' travel out of 15).

In Northern Ireland the **Freedom of Northern Ireland** ticket is good for unlimited travel on Ulsterbus and Northern Ireland Railways for one day (£15), three days' travel out of eight (£36) or seven consecutive days (£53). **Irish Explorer** Rail and Bus tickets (€210) allow you eight days' travel out of 15 consecutive days on trains and buses in the Republic.

Eurail passes are valid for train travel in the Republic of Ireland, and will get you a 50% discount on Irish Ferries crossings to France. **InterRail** passes give you a 50% reduction on train travel within Ireland and on Irish Ferries and Stena Line services. Eurail cards are not accepted in Britain and Northern Ireland, and InterRail cards are only valid if bought in another mainland European country.

FRANCE

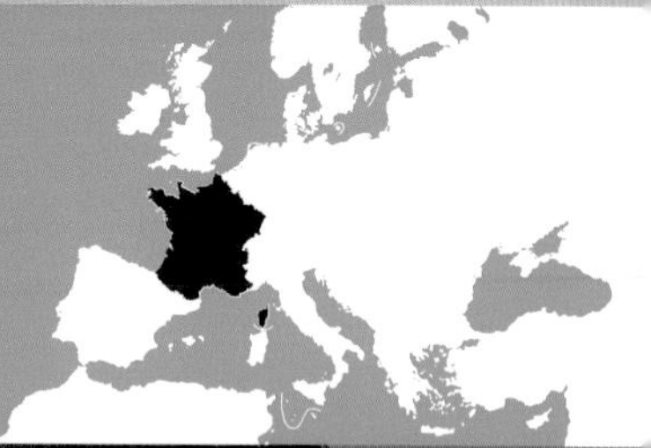

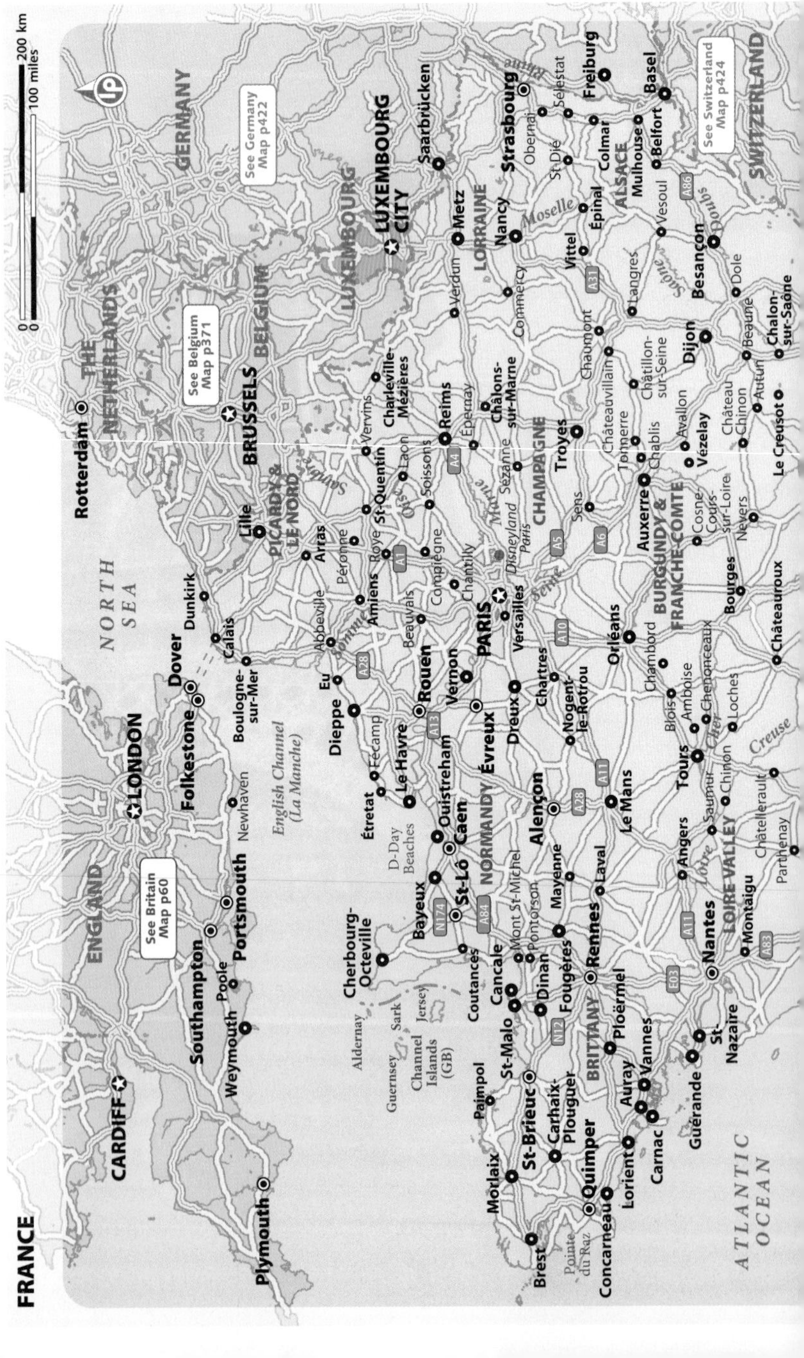
FRANCE
0 200 km
0 100 miles
NORTH SEA
English Channel (La Manche)
ATLANTIC OCEAN
ENGLAND
THE NETHERLANDS
BELGIUM
LUXEMBOURG
GERMANY
SWITZERLAND
See Britain Map p60
See Belgium Map p371
See Germany Map p422
See Switzerland Map p424
LONDON
CARDIFF
BRUSSELS
LUXEMBOURG CITY
PARIS
Rotterdam
Plymouth
Weymouth
Poole
Southampton
Portsmouth
Newhaven
Folkestone
Dover
Dunkirk
Calais
Boulogne-sur-Mer
Lille
Arras
PICARDY & LE NORD
Abbeville
Amiens
Péronne
St-Quentin
Vervins
Charleville-Mézières
Laon
Soissons
Reims
Épernay
Châlons-sur-Marne
Verdun
Metz
Saarbrücken
Nancy
LORRAINE
Strasbourg
Obernai
Sélestat
St-Dié
Colmar
ALSACE
Freiburg
Mulhouse
Basel
Belfort
Épinal
Vittel
Commercy
Chaumont
Langres
Vesoul
Besançon
Doubs
Dole
Dijon
Beaune
Chalon-sur-Saône
Châtillon-sur-Seine
Châteauvillain
Troyes
CHAMPAGNE
Sézanne
Disneyland Paris
Compiègne
Chantilly
Beauvais
Roye
Eu
Dieppe
Fécamp
Étretat
Le Havre
Rouen
Vernon
Évreux
Versailles
Dreux
Chartres
Nogent-le-Rotrou
Orléans
Chambord
Blois
Amboise
Chenonceaux
Loches
Tours
Saumur
Chinon
Châtellerault
Parthenay
Angers
LOIRE VALLEY
Montaigu
Nantes
St-Nazaire
Guérande
Vannes
Auray
Carnac
Lorient
Quimper
Concarneau
Pointe du Raz
Brest
Morlaix
Carhaix-Plouguer
St-Brieuc
Paimpol
St-Malo
Dinan
Cancale
Fougères
Rennes
Ploërmel
BRITTANY
Mont St-Michel
Pontorson
Mayenne
Laval
Le Mans
Alençon
NORMANDY
Caen
Ouistreham
Bayeux
St-Lô
Coutances
D-Day Beaches
Cherbourg-Octeville
Alderney
Guernsey
Sark
Jersey
Channel Islands (GB)
Sens
Auxerre
Tonnerre
Chablis
Avallon
Vézelay
BURGUNDY & FRANCHE-COMTÉ
Cosne-Cours-sur-Loire
Nevers
Bourges
Châteauroux
Le Creusot
Autun
Château Chinon
Seine
Somme
Loire
Cher
Creuse
Moselle
Saône
A1
A4
A5
A6
A10
A11
A13
A28
A31
A83
A84
A86
N12
N174
E03

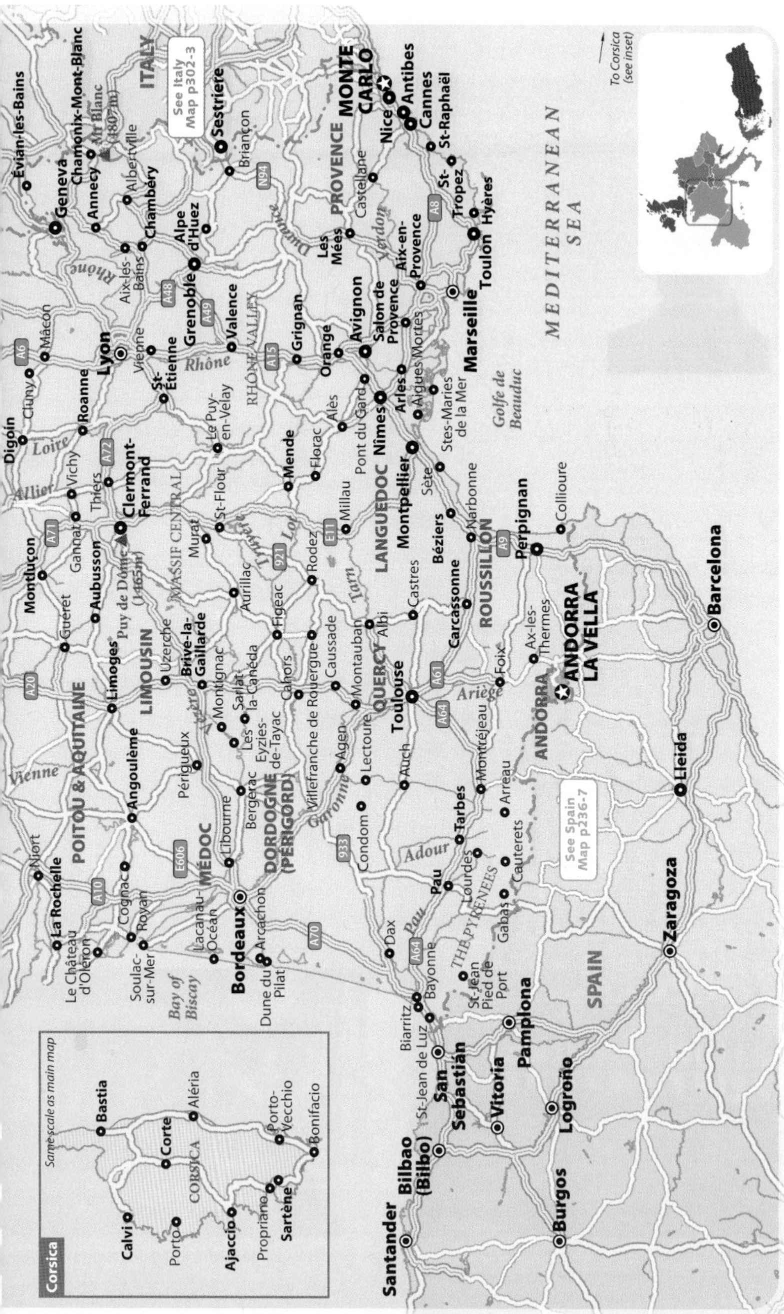
FRANCE
Corsica
Same scale as main map
Bastia
Calvi
Corte
Aléria
CORSICA
Porto
Ajaccio
Propriano
Sartène
Porto-Vecchio
Bonifacio
Évian-les-Bains
Geneva
Chamonix-Mont-Blanc
Mt Blanc (4807m)
Annecy
Albertville
Chambéry
Aix-les-Bains
ITALY
See Italy Map p302-3
Sestrière
Briançon
Alpe d'Huez
Grenoble
Valence
Lyon
Mâcon
Cluny
Digoin
Roanne
Vichy
Thiers
Clermont-Ferrand
St-Étienne
Vienne
Le Puy-en-Velay
Loire
Allier
Rhône
RHÔNE VALLEY
Durance
Verdon
PROVENCE
Les Mées
Castellane
Grignan
Orange
Avignon
Salon de Provence
Aix-en-Provence
Marseille
Toulon
Hyères
St-Tropez
St-Raphaël
Cannes
Antibes
Nice
MONTE CARLO
To Corsica (see inset)
MEDITERRANEAN SEA
Golfe de Beauduc
Arles
Aigues Mortes
Stes-Maries de la Mer
Nîmes
Pont du Gard
Alès
Montpellier
Sète
Béziers
Narbonne
Perpignan
Collioure
LANGUEDOC
ROUSSILLON
Mende
Florac
Millau
Rodez
MASSIF CENTRAL
St-Flour
Murat
Aurillac
Figeac
Montluçon
Gannat
Puy de Dôme (1465m)
Aubusson
Guéret
Limoges
LIMOUSIN
Uzerche
Brive-la-Gaillarde
Montignac
Sarlat-la-Canéda
Les Eyzies-de-Tayac
Cahors
Caussade
Montauban
Albi
Castres
Carcassonne
QUERCY
Toulouse
Villefranche de Rouergue
Agen
Lectoure
Auch
Condom
Foix
Ariège
Ax-les-Thermes
ANDORRA
ANDORRA LA VELLA
Barcelona
Lleida
Montréjeau
Arreau
Tarbes
Lourdes
Cauterets
Gabas
THE PYRENEES
Pau
Adour
Garonne
Tarn
Lot
Dordogne
Vézère
Vienne
POITOU & AQUITAINE
Niort
La Rochelle
Le Château d'Oléron
Cognac
Angoulême
Royan
Soulac-sur-Mer
Bay of Biscay
MÉDOC
Périgueux
Libourne
Bergerac
DORDOGNE (PÉRIGORD)
Lacanau-Océan
Bordeaux
Arcachon
Dune du Pilat
Dax
Bayonne
Biarritz
St-Jean de Luz
St-Jean Pied de Port
San Sebastián
Pamplona
Vitoria
Logroño
Bilbao (Bilbo)
Santander
Burgos
Zaragoza
SPAIN
See Spain Map p236-7
A6
A20
A10
A71
A72
A48
A49
A15
A7
A8
N94
A9
A61
A64
A62
A70
E11
E606
933
921

HIGHLIGHTS

1 VERSAILLES

BY SYLVAIN POSTOLLE, OFFICIAL GUIDE, CHÂTEAU DE VERSAILLES

Versailles, as official residence of the kings of France, is magnificent – the only place where the daily life of the monarchy before the French Revolution can really be felt. My favourite time of day is the evening, after the crowds have gone, when I quietly walk from room to room lecturing to just a small group. Extraordinary.

SYLVAIN POSTOLLE'S DON'T MISS LIST

❶ THE KING'S PRIVATE APARTMENT

This is the most fascinating part of the palace, as it shows the king as a man and very much reflects his daily life in the 18th century. Of the 10 or so rooms the most famous is his bedroom, where he not only slept but also held ceremonies. He had lunch here each day at 1pm and also supper, which up to 150 courtiers and people invited from outside the court would watch! By the 1780s, the king's life had become more private – he had an official supper just once a week on Sunday.

❷ KING LOUIS XVI'S LIBRARY

This is a lovely room. Full of books, it's a place where you can really imagine the king coming to read for hours and hours. Louis XVI loved geography, and his copy of *The Travels of James Cook* – in English! – is still here.

Clockwise from top: *Parterre d'eau* sculpture; State Apartments; Geometric gardens; Hall of Mirrors; Gardens and chateau

CLOCKWISE FROM TOP: JOHN ELK III; JOHN ELK III; RUSSELL MOUNTFORD; DENNIS JOHNSON; GLENN BEANLAND

❸ HERCULES SALON

I love one particular perspective inside the palace: from the Hercules Salon you can see all the rooms that comprise the King's State Apartment, and to the right you can see the gallery that leads to the opera house. The salon served as a passage for the king to go from his apartment to the chapel for daily mass.

❹ THE ROYAL CHAPEL

This is an exquisite example of the work of architect Jules Hardouin-Mansart (1646–1708). The paintings are also stunning: they evoke the idea that the French king was chosen by God and was his lieutenant on earth. This is the chapel where the future Louis XVI wed Marie Antoinette in 1770.

❺ ENCELADE GROVE

Versailles' gardens are extraordinary but my favourite spot is this grove, typical of the gardens created by André Le Nôtre for Louis XIV. A gallery of trellises surrounds a pool with a statue of Enceladus, chief of the Giants, who was punished for his pride by the gods from Mt Olympus.

↘ THINGS YOU NEED TO KNOW

Nightmare queues Arrive first thing or after 4pm **Day to avoid** Tuesday, when many museums close, rendering Versailles' queues even more nightmarish **Absolute must** Buy tickets in advance from www.chateauversailles.fr, a branch of Fnac or an SNCF train station **See our author's review on p203**

HIGHLIGHTS

2

THE LOUVRE

Europe certainly isn't short on museums, but there aren't many that can top the **Louvre** (p189) in terms of size and scope. In just a single day you could take in the wonders of ancient Egypt, the treasures of the Renaissance or the pinnacle of pop art, but for many people it's da Vinci's enigmatic masterpiece *La Joconde* (otherwise known as the *Mona Lisa*) that steals the show.

3

THE LOIRE VALLEY

Everyone knows about Versailles, but for many people it's the chateaux of the **Loire Valley** (p208) that really illustrate the pomp and power of the French aristocracy. If you've ever wondered what it was that got the revolutionaries' goat, the architectural extravagance of **Chambord** (p208) and **Chenonceau** (p212) provides an eloquent answer.

4

MONT ST-MICHEL

Second only to the Eiffel Tower in terms of iconic importance, the otherworldly abbey of **Mont St-Michel** (p206), off the Normandy coastline, is one of the unmissable sights of northern France. Set atop a rocky island connected to the mainland by a slender causeway, it looks like it could have dropped straight from the pages of *The Lord of the Rings*.

5

THE CÔTE D'AZUR

The Azure Coast certainly lives up to its name: sprinkled with glittering bays, super-exclusive beaches and sunbaked Mediterranean towns, it's been one of Europe's favourite seaside retreats for as long as anyone cares to remember. **Nice** (p223) is an essential stop, but for glitzy Mediterranean glamour you can't beat **St-Tropez** (p227) and **Monaco** (p228).

6

THE VÉZÈRE VALLEY

Some of the world's most complete prehistoric paintings ever found were discovered in the limestone caves of the Dordogne. Antelope, aurochs, horses, bears and even woolly mammoths all make an appearance. Don't miss the fabulous **Grotte de Lascaux** (p215).

2 JOHN HAY; 3 CHRISTOPHER WOOD; 4 JOHN ELK III; 5 JON DAVISON; 6 PASCALE BEROUJON

2 Pyramide du Louvre (p189); 3 Château de Chenonceau (p212) ; 4 Mont St-Michel (p206); 5 Pebble beach at Nice (p223); 6 Cave entrance in the Vézère Valley (p215)

THE BEST...

HISTORICAL HIGHLIGHTS

- **Alignements de Carnac** (p209) The world's largest prehistoric monument.
- **The D-Day Beaches** (p206) The liberation of Europe began on Normandy's beaches.
- **Cathédrale de Notre Dame de Paris** (p187) Unforgettable views, but no sign of Quasimodo.
- **The Bayeux Tapestry** (p205) Trace the Norman conquest of England.
- **Nîmes** (p216) See one of France's finest Roman amphitheatres.

ICONIC BUILDINGS

- **The Eiffel Tower** (p182) Climb the metal asparagus.
- **Arc de Triomphe** (p187) Where all roads in Paris lead.
- **Chartres Cathedral** (p203) One of the great Gothic landmarks.
- **Centre Pompidou** (p188) The world's first inside-out building.
- **Mont St-Michel** (p206) The subject of a million postcards.

SEASIDE RETREATS

- **Nice** (p223) The Côte d'Azur classic.
- **Cannes** (p226) Roll out the red carpet.
- **Biarritz** (p213) The surfers' choice.
- **St-Malo** (p207) Brittany's fortified port.
- **Corsica** (p229) Some of the Med's best beaches.

ARTISTIC SPOTS

- **Musée d'Orsay** (p182) Second only to the Louvre.
- **Montmartre** (p188) Get your portrait painted on Place du Tertre.
- **Aix-en-Provence** (p221) Follow in the footsteps of Van Gogh and Cézanne.
- **Giverny** (p207) Visit Monet's beloved gardens.
- **Mamac** (p223) Nice's fabulous modern art museum.

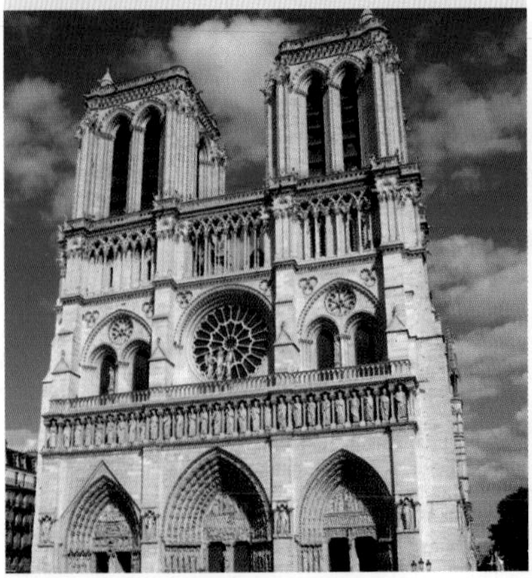

LEFT: GLENN BEANLAND; RIGHT: ROCCO FASAN

Left: Cathédrale de Notre Dame de Paris (p187); Right: Sun lovers in St-Malo (p207)

THINGS YOU NEED TO KNOW

AT A GLANCE

- **Population** 63.4 million
- **Official language** French
- **Currency** Euro (€)
- **Telephone code** ☎ 33
- **When to go** Summer if you can handle the heat, spring or autumn if you can't
- **Tipping** 10% to 15% in cafes and restaurants

REGIONS IN A NUTSHELL

- **Paris & Around** (p178) The city of lights.
- **Brittany & Normandy** (p204) Rural coast and countryside.
- **Loire Valley** (p208) Chateau splendour.
- **Atlantic Coast** (p213) Beaches and bordeaux.
- **Languedoc-Roussillon** (p214) The sunbaked south begins.
- **Provence** (p217) Fragrant France.
- **Cote d'Azur & Monaco** (p223) France's favourite seaside retreat.

ADVANCE PLANNING

- **Two months ahead** Book hotels for Paris, Provence, the Côte d'Azur and Corsica.
- **Two weeks ahead** Check out SNCF train timetables online; see p234 before you buy.
- **When you arrive** Pick up a Paris Museum Pass (p178) or a Paris Visite Pass (p202).

BE FOREWARNED

- **Dog poo** Watch where you step, especially in Paris.
- **Holidays** Most of France goes on holiday during July and August.
- **Manners** It's polite to say *bonjour* (hello) and *au revoir* (goodbye) when entering and leaving shops.
- **Public transport** On most public transport, you must time stamp your ticket in a *composteur* (validating machine).

BUSINESS HOURS

- **Banks** (🕑 **9am-1pm & 2pm-4.30pm Mon-Fri or Tue-Sat**)
- **Bars & cafes** Cafes usually open all day, while bars close around 1am.
- **Restaurants** (🕑 **noon-2pm & 7-10pm**) Closed at least one day a week.
- **Shops** (🕑 **9am or 9.30am-6pm or 7pm**) Hours generally include a lunch break from noon to 2pm or 3pm. Many places close on Sunday and/or Monday.

COSTS

- **Up to €100 per day** Will limit you to hostels, good-value *chambres d'hôtes* (B&Bs), cheap hotels and cut-price cafes.
- **€100 to 200** High-quality hotels and bistros.
- **More than €200** Michelin-starred restaurants and luxury accommodation.

THINGS YOU NEED TO KNOW

EMERGENCY NUMBERS

- **Ambulance** (☎ 15)
- **Fire** (☎ 18)
- **Police** (☎ 17)

GETTING AROUND

- **Air** (p232) France's busiest airport is Paris' Roissy Charles de Gaulle; budget airlines generally use Orly or Paris-Beauvais. Most big French cities have their own airports offering domestic and international flights.
- **Bus** (p233) Bus coverage in France is very patchy – you're nearly always better off catching a train.
- **Car** (p233) The country's road network is excellent, but note that you will have to pay a toll on most *autoroutes*.
- **Sea** (p233) Cross-Channel ferries service French ports including Roscoff, St-Malo, Cherbourg and Calais. Nice and Marseille both have ferry services to Corsica and Italy.
- **Train** (p234) The state-sponsored SNCF (www.sncf.com) is fantastically efficient. Flagship TGVs serve most French cities, while smaller areas are served by slower TERs. The Eurostar links Paris' Gare du Nord and London's St Pancras.

MEDIA

- **Newspapers** Centre-left *Le Monde*, right-leaning *Le Figaro*, left-leaning *Libération*.
- **Radio** Radio France Info (105.5MHz), multilingual RFI (738kHz/89kHz in Paris), NRJ (www.nrj.fr), Skyrock (www.skyrock.fm), Nostalgie (www.nostalgie.fr).
- **TV** The channels of the national public broadcaster, France Télévisions, include France 2, 3 and 5; commercial stations include TF1 and M6.

RESOURCES

- **France Tourisme** (**www.tourisme.fr**) The official site, in French.
- **France Guide** (**www.franceguide.com**) More official info, but in English.
- **SNCF** (**www.sncf-voyages.com**) Plan any train travel and buy tickets online.
- **Météo France** (**www.meteo.fr**) The latest weather forecasts.

VISAS

- **EU nationals, Iceland, Norway, Switzerland** Free to live and work in France.
- **Citizens of Australia, Canada, Israel, Hong Kong, Japan, Malaysia, New Zealand, Singapore, the USA** Do not require visas for stays of fewer than 90 days.
- **Other countries** Will need a visa. See www.diplomatie.gouv.fr for more info.

GET INSPIRED

BOOKS

- **A Moveable Feast** (Ernest Hemingway) Hemingway captures Paris in the interwar years.
- **A Motor Flight Through France** (Edith Wharton) The Whartons' automobile adventures.
- **Chéri** (Colette) Classic novel from France's controversial authoress.
- **Another Long Day on the Piste** (Will Randall) Hilarious account of life on the slopes.
- **A Year in the Merde** (Stephen Clarke) Expat life in France.

FILMS

- **Breathless** (1960) Godard's love letter to Paris.
- **The 400 Blows** (1959) Truffaut's New Wave masterpiece.
- **Before Sunset** (2004) Richard Linklater's free-wheeling rom-com.
- **Amélie** (2001) Charming Parisian fable by Jean-Pierre Jeunet.
- **The Chorus** (2004) Sweet tale set in a French school.

MUSIC

- **Pocket Symphony** (Air) Latest album from electronica super-duo.
- **The Best of Edith Piaf** The Little Sparrow's greatest hits.
- **Alive** (Daft Punk) Electronic noodlings from Daft Punk.
- **Histoires ExtraOrdinaires d'un Jeune de Banlieue** (Disiz La Peste) Hard-hitting French hip-hop.
- **Initials S.G.** (Serge Gainsbourg) The archetypal French crooner.

WEBSITES

- **Go Go Paris! Culture!** (www.gogoparis.com) All things Parisian.
- **Alliance Française** (www.alliancefr.org) Learn French in France.
- **Cours de Cuisine Olivier Berté** (www.coursdecuisineparis.com) Parisian cooking school.
- **Chocolate & Zucchini** (www.chocolateandzucchini.com) Montmartre-based food blog.
- **Libération** (www.liberation.fr) French news and views.

KEVIN CLOGSTOUN

Buskers in Paris (p178)

ITINERARIES

LA BELLE PARIS Three Days

Every French adventure begins with a few days in the capital city of **(1) Paris** (p178). This sexy, sophisticated and ever-so-slightly self-important city still has a special atmosphere all of its own. With just three days, you won't get much beyond the essentials. The **Louvre** (p189) will take up most of day one, so start out early: to avoid museum fatigue, break your visit with a lunchtime picnic in the nearby **Jardin des Tuileries** (p187). Head up the **Eiffel Tower** (p182) for dusk, when the lights of Paris start to twinkle, followed by supper at **Brasserie Lipp** (p195) or **Chez Allard** (p195).

On day two, start out with an early-morning visit to **Notre Dame** (p187), followed by the main attractions of the Left Bank: the **Panthéon** (p183), a wander around St-Germain and the Latin Quarter, the **Musée d'Orsay** (p182) and the **Musée Rodin** (p183). Chill out in the **Jardin des Plantes** (p186) before taking an early-evening cruise on the **Seine** (p190), followed by supper at posh **Perraudin** (p194) or cosy **Le Petit Pontoise** (p194).

The final day is left for the **Marais** (p188) or **Montmartre** (p188); with more time, you could add in day trips to **(2) Giverny** (p207), **(3) Rouen** (p204) or **(4) Chartres** (p203).

NORTHERN HIGHLIGHTS Five Days

This five-day itinerary makes an ideal post-Paris trip. Start with a day in the lovely medieval city of **(1) Rouen** (p204), renowned for its half-timbered buildings and as the location of Joan of Arc's trial and execution. Swing north along the beautiful coastline of Normandy (p204), famous for its connections with Impressionism and the momentous events of 6 June 1944, forever after known as D-Day. Get some historical perspective at the **(2) Caen Mémorial** (p206), before heading for the **(3) D-Day Beaches** (p206) themselves, either on a guided tour or under your own steam. Overnight in **(4) Bayeux** (p205), factoring in time for a visit to the town's famous **tapestry** (p205), before venturing west to **(5) Mont St-Michel** (p206), where late afternoon's the best time to avoid the tourist crush. The gorgeous walled town of **(6) St-Malo** (p207) is only a short drive away and makes a great place to conclude your northern trip; with a few more days to spare you could set out to explore the rest of **Brittany** (p204), including the great stone alignments of **(7) Carnac** (p209).

THE DEEP SOUTH One Week

France's sun-drenched south is the perfect place for an extended road trip. This week-long itinerary begins in medieval **(1) Carcassonne** (p214) followed by a spin along the Mediterranean coastline to

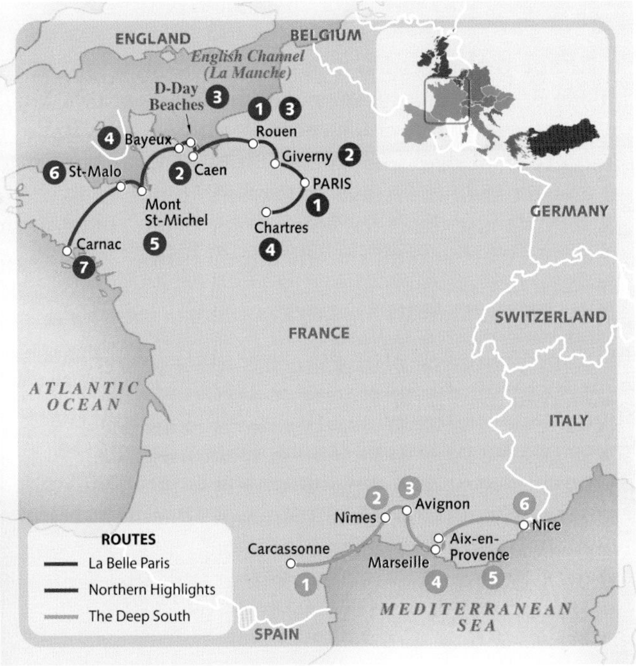

(2) Nîmes (p216), once one of the great centres of Roman Gaul, where you can still see the remains of the massive amphitheatre and Roman walls. Nearby, (3) Avignon (p221) boasts one of the most amazing examples of medieval architecture in southern France, the mighty Pont St-Bénézet (p221).

After a few days in the countryside, multicultural (4) Marseille (p218) comes as something of a shock: it's noisy and chaotic, but if you've ever wanted to taste authentic bouillabaisse, this is definitely the place to do it. When the city din gets too much, beat a retreat for the Château d'If (p219) or artistic (5) Aix-en-Provence (p221). Wind things up in (6) Nice (p223), the Côte d'Azur's quintessential resort, where you can while away a few days bronzing yourself on the beach and exploring the alleyways of the old town.

DISCOVER FRANCE

Few countries in Europe provoke such a passionate panoply of responses as La Belle France. Snooty, sexy, superior, chic, infuriating, arrogant, officious and inspired in equal measures, the French have long lived according to their own idiosyncratic rules, and if the rest of the world doesn't always see eye to eye with them, well, *tant pis* (too bad) – that's just the price you pay for being culinary trendsetters, artistic pioneers and all-round cultural icons.

In many ways France is a deeply traditional place: castles, chateaux and ancient churches litter the landscape; centuries-old principles of rich food, fine wine and *joie de vivre* underpin everyday life; and any decision to meddle with the status quo is guaranteed to bring out half the nation in a placard-waving protest. But it's also a place that never seems to rest on its historic laurels. France has one of the most multicultural make-ups of any European country, not to mention a well-deserved reputation for artistic experimentation and architectural invention.

PARIS

pop 2.15 million

What can be said about the sexy, sophisticated City of Lights that hasn't already been said a thousand times before? Quite simply, this is one of the world's great metropolises: a trendsetter, market leader and cultural capital for over a thousand years and still going strong.

HISTORY

The Parisii, a tribe of Celtic Gauls, settled the Île de la Cité in the 3rd century BC. Paris prospered during the Middle Ages and flourished during the Renaissance, when many of the city's most famous buildings were erected. The excesses of Louis XVI and his queen, Marie-Antoinette, led to an uprising of Parisians on 14 July 1789, and the storming of the Bastille prison – kick-starting the French Revolution.

In 1851 Emperor Napoleon III oversaw the construction of a more modern Paris, complete with wide boulevards, sculptured parks and a sewer system. Following the disastrous Franco-Prussian War and the establishment of the Third Republic, Paris entered its most resplendent period, the belle époque, famed for its art-nouveau architecture and artistic and scientific advances. By the beginning of the 1930s, Paris had become a centre for the artistic avant-garde until the Nazi occupation of 1940–44.

ORIENTATION

Paris is divided into 20 *arrondissements* (districts), which spiral clockwise from the centre. City addresses always include the number of the *arrondissement*. The city has 372 metro stations and there is almost always one within 500m of where you need to go.

INFORMATION

DISCOUNT CARDS

The **Paris Museum Pass** (www.parismuseumpass.fr; 2/4/6 days €30/45/60) is valid for around 38 Parisian sights, including the Louvre, Centre Pompidou and the

Musée d'Orsay, plus the St-Denis basilica and parts of Versailles and Fontainebleau. You can buy it online, from the Paris Convention & Visitors Bureau (right), Fnac outlets, major metro stations and all participating venues.

MEDICAL SERVICES

American Hospital of Paris (Map pp180-1; ☎ 01 46 41 25 25; www.american-hospital.org; 63 blvd Victor Hugo, 92200 Neuilly-sur-Seine; Ⓜ Pont de Levallois Bécon)

Hertford British Hospital (Map pp180-1; ☎ 01 46 39 22 22; www.british-hospital.org; 3 rue Barbès, 92300 Levallois-Perret; Ⓜ Anatole France)

Hôpital Hôtel Dieu (Map pp184-5; ☎ 01 42 34 82 34; www.aphp.fr; 1 place du Parvis Notre Dame, 4e; Ⓜ Cité)

MONEY

Post offices with a Banque Postale offer the best exchange rates in Paris, and accept banknotes (commission €4.50) as well as travellers cheques issued by Amex (no commission) or Visa (1.5%, minimum €4.50).

TOURIST INFORMATION

The main branch of the **Paris Convention & Visitors Bureau** (Office de Tourisme et de Congrès de Paris; Map pp180-1; ☎ 08 92 68 30 00; www.parisinfo.com; 25-27 rue des Pyramides, 1er; 9am-7pm Jun-Oct, 10am-7pm Mon-Sat & 11am-7pm Sun Nov-May, closed 1 May; Ⓜ Pyramides) is 500m northwest of the Louvre. There are also branches at **Anvers** (Map pp180-1; opp 72 blvd de Rochechouart, 18e; 10am-6pm, closed Christmas Day, New Year's Day & 1 May; Ⓜ Anvers), **Gare de Lyon** (Map pp184-5; Hall d'Arrivée, 20 blvd Diderot, 12e; 8am-6pm Mon-Sat, closed Sun & 1 May; Ⓜ Gare de Lyon) and **Gare du Nord** (Map pp180-1; 18 rue de Dunkerque, 10e; 8am-6pm, closed Christmas Day, New Year's Day & 1 May; Ⓜ Gare du Nord).

DANGERS & ANNOYANCES

Paris is generally a safe city, but as always keep your wits about you. Take extra care on the metro after dark. Thefts from handbags and rucksacks are a particular problem around Montmartre, Pigalle, Forum des Halles, the Latin Quarter, the Eiffel Tower, and on the metro during rush hour.

WILL SALTER

Arc de Triomphe (p187) and Av des Champs-Élysées (p188)

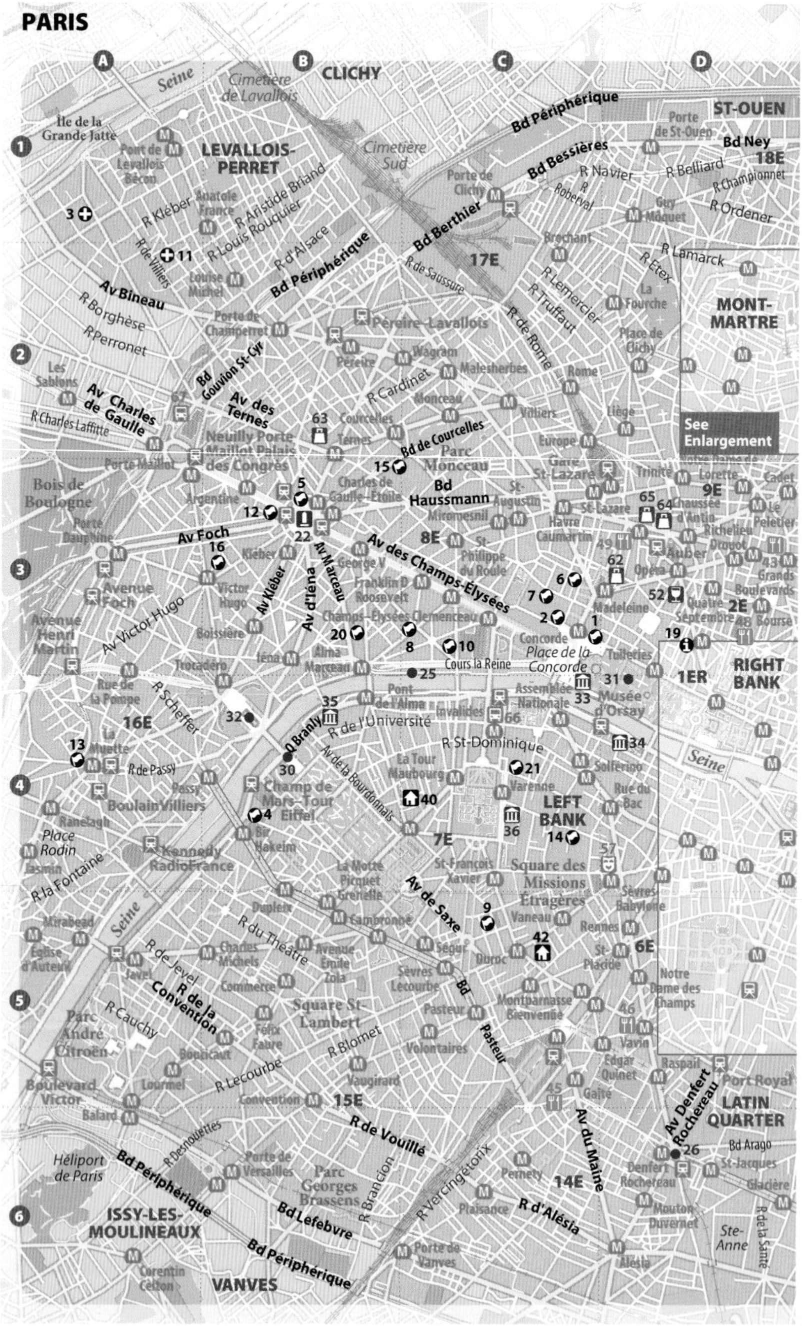
PARIS
A
B
C
D
1
2
3
4
5
6
Seine
Cimetière de Levallois
CLICHY
Bd Périphérique
ST-OUEN
Porte de St-Ouen
Bd Ney
18E
Île de la Grande Jatte
Pont de Levallois Bécon
LEVALLOIS-PERRET
Cimetière Sud
Bd Bessières
R Navier
R Belliard
R Championnet
R Roberval
Guy Môquet
R Ordener
Porte de Clichy
Anatole France
R Kléber
R Aristide Briand
R Louis Rouquier
Bd Berthier
Brochant
R Lamarck
R Etex
R de Villiers
R d'Alsace
17E
Louise Michel
Bd Périphérique
R de Saussure
R Lemercier
La Fourche
MONTMARTRE
Av Bineau
R Borghèse
Porte de Champerret
Pereire-Levallois
R Truffaut
R Perronet
Pereire
Wagram
R de Rome
Place de Clichy
Les Sablons
Bd Gouvion St-Cyr
Malesherbes
Rome
Av Charles de Gaulle
Av des Ternes
R Cardinet
Monceau
Villiers
Liège
R Charles Laffitte
Courcelles
Ternes
See Enlargement
Neuilly Porte Maillot Palais des Congrès
Bd de Courcelles
Parc Monceau
Europe
Porte Maillot
Gare St-Lazare
Trinité
Notre Dame de Lorette
Cadet
Bois de Boulogne
Argentine
Charles de Gaulle-Étoile
Bd Haussmann
St-Augustin
St-Lazare
Chaussée d'Antin
9E
Le Peletier
Porte Dauphine
Miromesnil
Havre Caumartin
Richelieu Drouot
Av Foch
Kléber
8E
St-Philippe du Roule
Av des Champs-Élysées
Aubert
Opéra
Grands Boulevards
George V
Av Marceau
Av d'Iéna
Av Kléber
Victor Hugo
Franklin D Roosevelt
Madeleine
Quatre Septembre
2E
Avenue Foch
Bourse
Avenue Henri Martin
Av Victor Hugo
Boissière
Champs-Élysées Clemenceau
Concorde
Place de la Concorde
Tuileries
Iéna
Alma Marceau
Cours la Reine
RIGHT BANK
1ER
Trocadéro
Rue de la Pompe
R Scheffer
Pont de l'Alma
Assemblée Nationale
Musée d'Orsay
16E
Q Branly
R de l'Université
Invalides
La Muette
R St-Dominique
Av de la Bourdonnais
La Tour Maubourg
Solférino
Seine
R de Passy
Passy
Champ de Mars-Tour Eiffel
Varenne
Rue du Bac
Boulainvilliers
LEFT BANK
Ranelagh
Place Rodin
Bir Hakeim
7E
Jasmin
Kennedy RadioFrance
La Motte Picquet Grenelle
St-François Xavier
Square des Missions Étrangères
R la Fontaine
Av de Saxe
Sèvres Babylone
Dupleix
Cambronne
Vaneau
Mirabeau
Seine
R du Théâtre
Rennes
Ségur
Duroc
St-Placide
6E
Église d'Auteuil
Charles Michels
Avenue Émile Zola
R de Javel
Javel
Sèvres Lecourbe
Notre Dame des Champs
R de la Convention
Commerce
Bd Pasteur
Parc André Citroën
R Cauchy
Square St-Lambert
Pasteur
Montparnasse Bienvenüe
Félix Faure
Vavin
Boucicaut
R Blomet
Volontaires
Edgar Quinet
Raspail
Boulevard Victor
Lourmel
R Lecourbe
Vaugirard
Gaîté
Port Royal
Av Denfert Rochereau
LATIN QUARTER
Balard
Convention
15E
Av du Maine
R de Vouillé
Bd Arago
R Desnouettes
Héliport de Paris
Porte de Versailles
Parc Georges Brassens
R Brancion
R Vercingétorix
Pernety
14E
Denfert Rochereau
St-Jacques
Glacière
Bd Périphérique
ISSY-LES-MOULINEAUX
Bd Lefebvre
Plaisance
R d'Alésia
Mouton Duvernet
R de la Santé
Ste-Anne
Bd Périphérique
Porte de Vanves
Alésia
Corentin Celton
VANVES
1
2
3
4
5
6
7
8
9
10
11
12
13
14
15
16
19
20
21
22
25
26
30
31
32
33
34
35
36
40
42
43
45
46
48
49
52
57
62
63
64
65
66

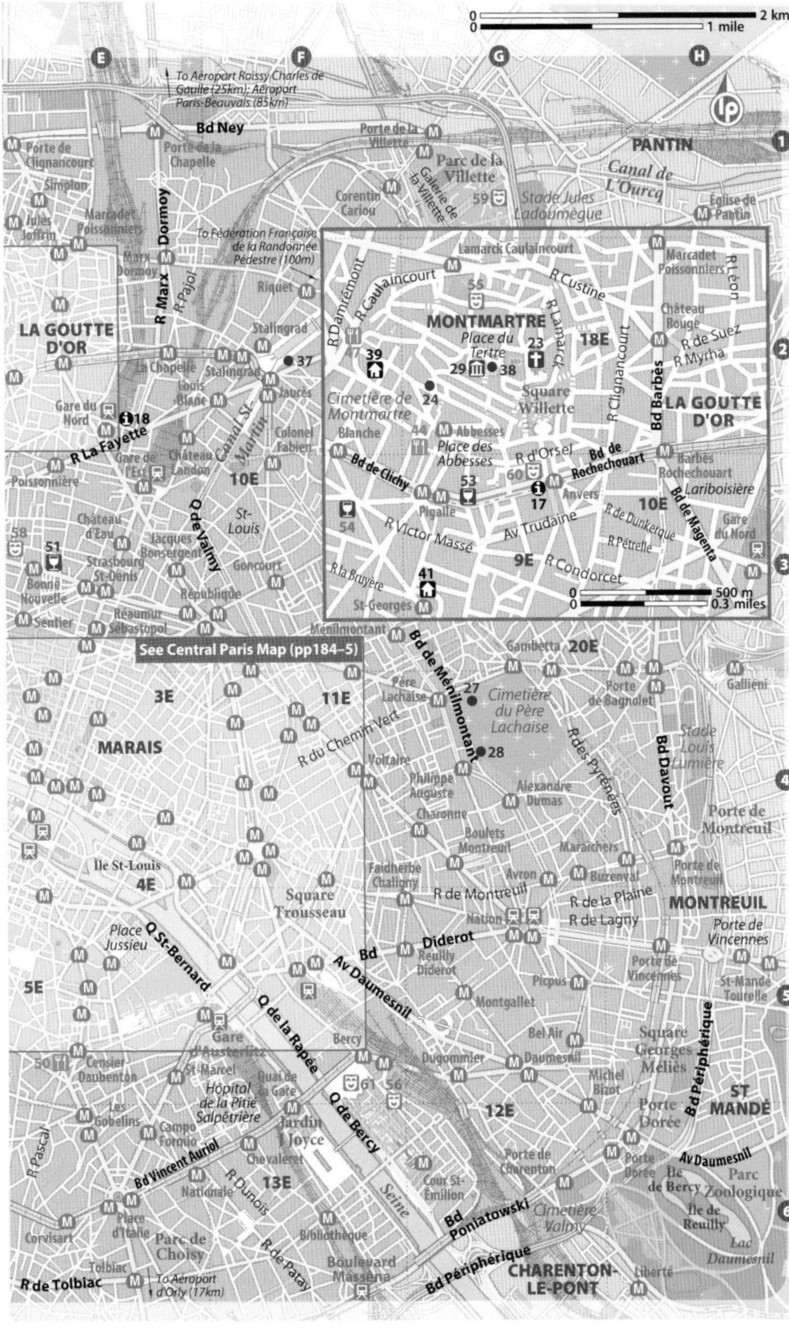
To Aéroport Roissy Charles de Gaulle (25km); Aéroport Paris-Beauvais (85km)
Bd Ney
Porte de Clignancourt
Porte de la Chapelle
Porte de la Villette
Parc de la Villette
PANTIN
Canal de L'Ourcq
Stade Jules Ladoumègue
Église de Pantin
Corentin Cariou
Galerie de la Villette
Simplon
Jules Joffrin
Marcadet Poissonniers
Dormoy
Marx Dormoy
R Marx Dormoy
R Pajol
To Fédération Française de la Randonnée Pédestre (100m)
Riquet
Stalingrad
Jaurès
LA GOUTTE D'OR
La Chapelle
Louis Blanc
Gare du Nord
R La Fayette
Gare de l'Est
Château Landon
Canal St-Martin
Colonel Fabien
10E
Poissonnière
St-Louis
Q de Valmy
Château d'Eau
Jacques Bonsergent
Strasbourg St-Denis
Bonne Nouvelle
Goncourt
République
Sentier
Réaumur Sébastopol
Ménilmontant
Lamarck Caulaincourt
R Caulaincourt
R Damrémont
R Custine
MONTMARTRE
Place du Tertre
R Lamarck
18E
R Clignancourt
Marcadet Poissonniers
R Léon
Château Rouge
R de Suez
R Myrha
Bd Barbès
LA GOUTTE D'OR
Cimetière de Montmartre
Square Willette
Blanche
Abbesses
Place des Abbesses
Bd de Clichy
R d'Orsel
Bd de Rochechouart
Barbès Rochechouart
Lariboisière
Pigalle
Anvers
10E
Bd de Magenta
R de Dunkerque
Gare du Nord
R Victor Massé
Av Trudaine
R Pétrelle
9E
R Condorcet
R la Bruyère
St-Georges
500 m
0.3 miles
2 km
1 mile
See Central Paris Map (pp184–5)
Gambetta
20E
3E
11E
Bd de Ménilmontant
Père Lachaise
Cimetière du Père Lachaise
Porte de Bagnolet
Gallieni
MARAIS
R du Chemin Vert
Voltaire
R des Pyrénées
Stade Louis Lumière
Bd Davout
Philippe Auguste
Alexandre Dumas
Charonne
Porte de Montreuil
Boulets Montreuil
Maraîchers
Île St-Louis
Faidherbe Chaligny
Avron
Buzenval
Porte de Montreuil
4E
Square Trousseau
R de Montreuil
R de la Plaine
MONTREUIL
Place Jussieu
Q St-Bernard
Nation
R de Lagny
Porte de Vincennes
Bd Diderot
Reuilly Diderot
Av Daumesnil
Porte de Vincennes
Picpus
St-Mandé Tourelle
5E
Montgallet
Bd Périphérique
Gare d'Austerlitz
Q de la Rapée
Bercy
Bel Air
Square Georges Méliès
Censier Daubenton
St-Marcel
Quai de la Gare
Dugommier
Daumesnil
Hôpital de la Pitié Salpêtrière
Michel Bizot
ST MANDÉ
Les Gobelins
Campo Formio
Jardin Joyce
Q de Bercy
12E
Porte Dorée
R Pascal
Bd Vincent Auriol
Chevaleret
Porte de Charenton
Porte Dorée
Av Daumesnil
Île de Bercy
Parc Zoologique
Nationale
R Dunois
13E
Cour St-Émilion
Île de Reuilly
Place d'Italie
Seine
Bd Poniatowski
Cimetière Valmy
Corvisart
Parc de Choisy
Bibliothèque
R de Patay
Lac Daumesnil
Tolbiac
Boulevard Massena
Bd Périphérique
CHARENTON-LE-PONT
Liberté
R de Tolbiac
To Aeroport d'Orly (17km)

INFORMATION
American Consulate 1 C3
American Embassy 2 C3
American Hospital of Paris 3 A1
Australian Embassy 4 B4
Belgian Embassy 5 B3
British Consulate 6 C3
British Embassy 7 C3
Canadian Embassy 8 C3
Dutch Embassy 9 C5
German Embassy 10 C3
Hertford British Hospital 11 A2
Irish Embassy & Trade Office 12 B3
Italian Consulate 13 A4
Italian Embassy 14 C4
Japanese Embassy 15 B3
New Zealand Embassy 16 B3
Paris Convention & Visitors Bureau (Anvers) 17 G3
Paris Convention & Visitors Bureau (Gare du Nord) 18 E2
Paris Convention & Visitors Bureau (Main Branch) 19 D3
Spanish Embassy 20 B3
Swiss Embassy 21 C4

SIGHTS & ACTIVITIES
Arc de Triomphe 22 B3
Basilique du Sacré Cœur 23 G2
Bateau Lavoir 24 G2
Bateaux Mouches 25 C3
Catacombes 26 D6
Cimetière du Père Lachaise 27 G4
Cimetière du Père Lachaise Conservation Office 28 G4
Dalí Espace Montmartre 29 G2
Eiffel Tower 30 B4
Jardin des Tuileries 31 D4
Jardins du Trocadéro 32 B4
Musée de l'Orangerie 33 C4
Musée d'Orsay 34 D4
Musée du Quai Branly 35 B4
Musée Rodin 36 C4
Paris Canal Croisières 37 F2
Place de l'Étoile (see 22)
Place du Tertre 38 G2

SLEEPING
Hôtel des Arts 39 F2
Hôtel du Champ-de-Mars 40 C4
Hôtel Résidence des 3 Poussins 41 G3
Mayet Hôtel 42 C5

EATING
Chartier 43 D3
Chez Toinette 44 G2
La Cagouille 45 C5
La Coupole 46 D5
Le Café Qui Parle 47 F2
Le Grand Colbert 48 D3
Le Roi du Pot au Feu 49 D3
Marché Rue Mouffetard 50 E5

DRINKING
De La Ville Café 51 E3
Harry's New York Bar 52 D3
La Fourmi 53 G3
Le Dépanneur 54 F3

ENTERTAINMENT
Au Lapin Agile 55 G2
Cinémathèque Française 56 F5
La Cigale 57 D4
Le Limonaire 58 E3
Le Zénith 59 G1
L'Élysée-Montmartre 60 G3
Palais Omnisports de Paris-Bercy 61 F5

SHOPPING
Fauchon 62 D3
Fromagerie Alléosse 63 B2
Galeries Lafayette 64 D3
Le Printemps 65 D3

TRANSPORT
Aérogare des Invalides 66 C4
Parking Pershing Express Bus 67 A2

SIGHTS

LEFT BANK

EIFFEL TOWER

It's impossible now to imagine Paris (or France, for that matter) without La Tour Eiffel, the **Eiffel Tower** (**Map pp180-1; ☎ 01 44 11 23 23; www.tour-eiffel.fr; lifts to level 1 adult/child €4.80/2.50, level 2 €7.80/4.30, top level €12/6.70; lifts 9am-midnight mid-Jun–Aug, 9.30am-11pm Sep–mid-Jun, stairs 9am-midnight mid-Jun–Aug, 9.30am-6pm Sep–mid-Jun; M Champ de Mars-Tour Eiffel or Bir Hakeim**), but the 'metal asparagus', as some Parisians snidely called it, faced fierce opposition from Paris' artistic elite when it was built for the 1889 Exposition Universelle (World Fair). The tower was almost torn down in 1909, and was only saved by the new science of radiotelegraphy (it provided an ideal spot for transmitting antennas). The city should be thankful it's still standing – some 6.9 million people make the 324m trek up to the top each year, and it's as synonymous with France these days as fine cooking and smelly cheese. If you're feeling steely legged and sturdy-lunged, you can dodge the lift fees by taking the stairs (€4/3.10 over/under 25 years old) to the 1st and 2nd platforms, but be warned: it's steep. Really, really steep.

Since the millennium, the tower has been lit up every hour after dusk by a spectacular flashing light display, but it's recently been announced that the city has decided to halve the time the bulbs are left on in an effort to reduce the electricity bill – and with over 20,000 bulbs to power, you can't really blame them.

Spreading out around the Eiffel Tower are the **Jardins du Trocadéro** (**Map pp180-1; M Trocadéro**), whose fountains and statue garden are grandly illuminated at night.

MUSÉE D'ORSAY

The **Musée d'Orsay** (**Map pp180-1; ☎ 01 40 49 48 14; www.musee-orsay.fr; 62 rue de Lille, 7e; adult/under 18yr/18-30yr €8/free/5.50, 1st Sun of**

month free; ⌚ 9.30am-6pm Tue, Wed & Fri-Sun, 9.30am-9.45pm Thu; Ⓜ Musée d'Orsay or Solférino), housed in a turn-of-the-century train station overlooking the Seine, displays France's national collection of paintings, sculptures and artwork produced between the 1840s and 1914.

Tickets are valid all day. The reduced entrance fee of €5.50 applies to everyone after 4.15pm (6pm on Thursday). A combined ticket including the Musée Rodin costs €12.

PANTHÉON

The domed landmark now known as the **Panthéon** (**Map pp184-5; ☎ 01 44 32 18 00; www.monuments-nationaux.fr; place du Panthéon, 5e; adult/under 18yr/18-25yr €7.50/free/4.80, 1st Sun of month Oct-Mar free; ⌚ 10am-6.30pm Apr-Sep, to 6.15pm Oct-Mar; Ⓜ Luxembourg**) was commissioned around 1750 as an abbey church, but because of financial and structural problems it wasn't completed until 1789 (the start of the French Revolution – not a good year for opening churches in France). The crypt houses the tombs of Voltaire, Jean-Jacques Rousseau, Victor Hugo, Émile Zola, Jean Moulin and Nobel Prize winner Marie Curie, among many others.

MUSÉE RODIN

The **Musée Rodin** (**Map pp180-1; ☎ 01 44 18 61 10; www.musee-rodin.fr; 79 rue de Varenne, 7e; permanent or temporary exhibition plus garden adult/18-25yr €6/4, both exhibitions plus garden €9/7, garden only €1, under 18yr free, 1st Sun of month free; ⌚ 9.30am-5.45pm Tue-Sun Apr-Sep, 9.30am-4.45pm Tue-Sun Oct-Mar; Ⓜ Varenne**) is both a sublime museum and one of the most relaxing spots in the city, with a lovely sculpture garden in which to rest. The 18th-century house displays some of Rodin's most famous works, including *The Burghers of Calais (Les Bourgeois de Calais)*, *Cathedral*, *The Thinker (Le Penseur)* and *The Kiss (Le Baiser)*.

MUSÉE DU QUAI BRANLY

It's been a long time coming, but the **Musée du Quai Branly** (**Map pp180-1; ☎ 01 56 61 70 00; www.quaibranly.fr; 37 quai Branly, 7e; adult/under 18yr/student & 18-25yr €8.50/free/6, admission free for 18-25yr after 6pm Sat, 1st Sun of month free; ⌚ 11am-7pm Tue, Wed & Sun, to 9pm Thu-Sat; Ⓜ Pont de l'Alma or Alma-Marceau**) has finally been installed in a fantabulous glass, wood and turf structure beside the Seine, designed by renowned architect Jean Nouvel. It's an immersive experience, closer to an artwork than a museum, making use of video, music, audio and ambitious displays exploring the cultures of Africa, Oceania, Asia and the Americas.

CATACOMBES

There are few spookier sights in Paris than the **Catacombes** (**Map pp180-1; ☎ 01 43 22 47 63; www.catacombes.paris.fr, in French; 1 av Colonel Henri Roi-Tanguy, 14e; adult/under 14yr/14-26yr €7/free/3.50; ⌚ 10am-5pm Tue-Sun; Ⓜ Denfert Rochereau**), one of three underground cemeteries created in the late 18th century to solve the problems posed by Paris' overflowing graveyards. Twenty metres below street level, the catacombs consist of 1.6km of winding tunnels stacked from floor to ceiling with the bones and skulls of millions of Parisians – guaranteed to send a shiver down your spine.

ÉGLISE ST-GERMAIN DES PRÉS

Paris' oldest church, the Romanesque **Église St-Germain des Prés** (**Map pp184-5; ☎ 01 55 42 81 33; 3 place St-Germain des Prés, 6e; ⌚ 8am-7pm Mon-Sat, 9am-8pm Sun; Ⓜ St-Germain des Prés**) was built in the 11th century on the site of a 6th-century abbey and was the dominant church in Paris until the arrival of Notre Dame.

CENTRAL PARIS

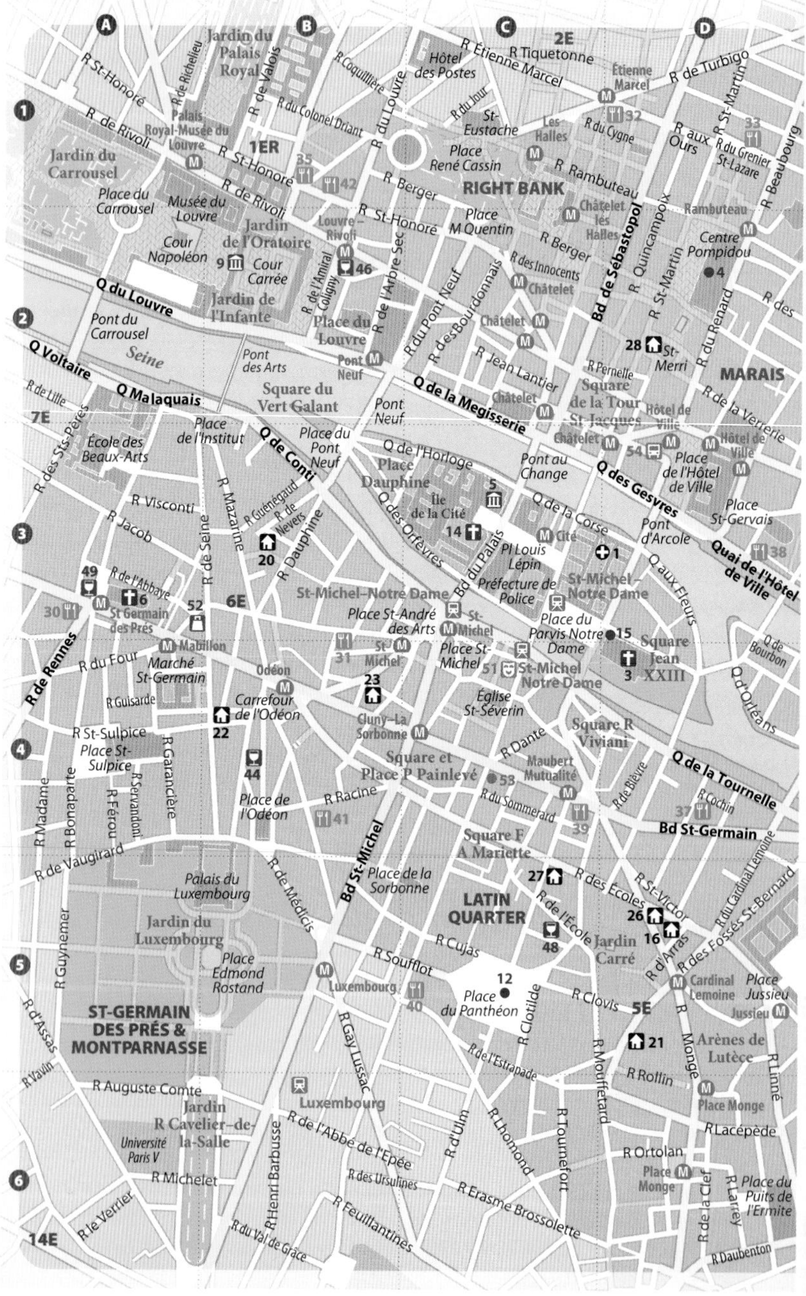

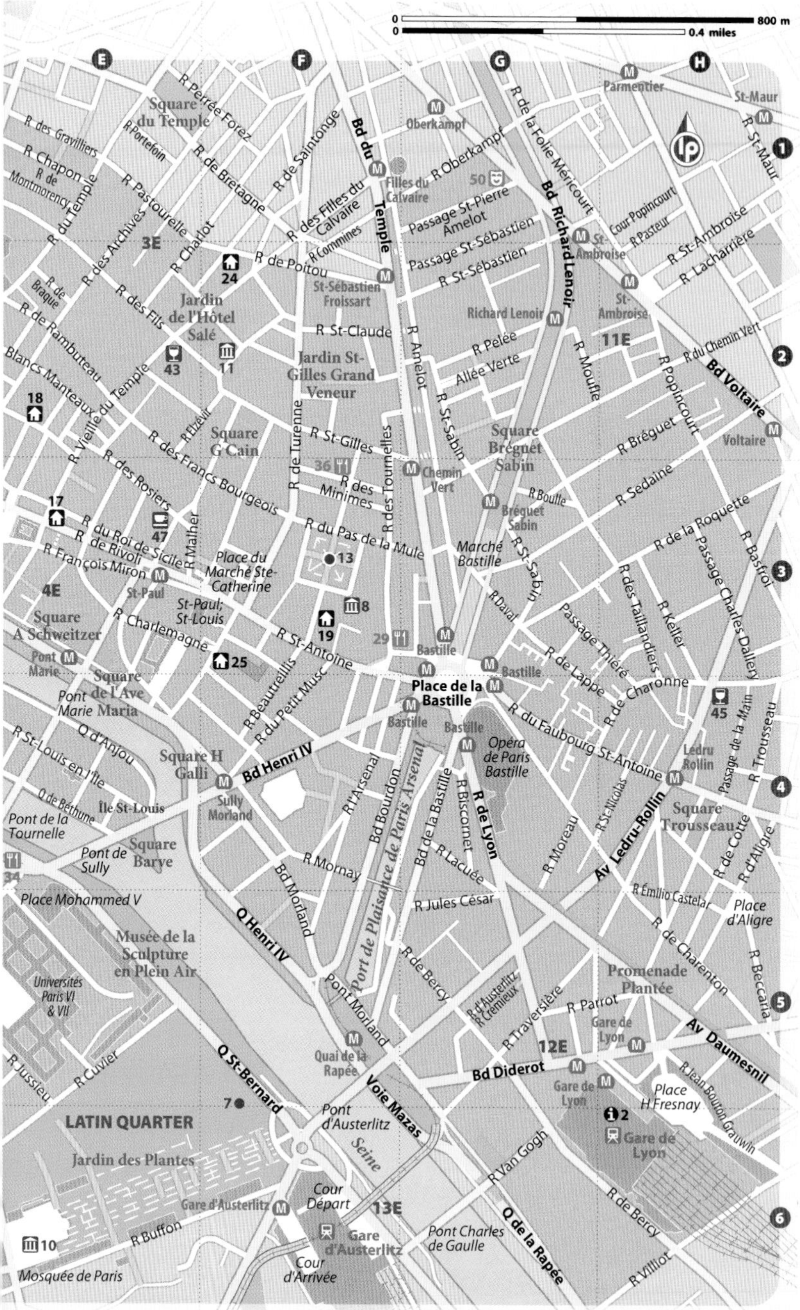
0
800 m
0
0.4 miles
E
F
G
H
1
2
3
4
5
6
Square du Temple
R Perrée
Forez
R des Gravilliers
R Portefoin
R Chapon
R de Montmorency
R du Temple
R Pastourelle
R de Bretagne
R de Saintonge
Bd du Temple
Oberkampf
Filles du Calvaire
R Oberkampf
50
R de la Folie Méricourt
Parmentier
St-Maur
R St-Maur
R des Archives
3E
R Charlot
24
R de Poitou
R des Filles du Calvaire
R Commines
Passage St-Pierre Amelot
Passage St-Sébastien
R St-Sébastien
St-Sébastien Froissart
Bd Richard Lenoir
St-Ambroise
Cour Popincourt
R Pasteur
R St-Ambroise
R Lacharrière
R de Braque
R de Rambuteau
R des Fils
Jardin de l'Hôtel Salé
43
11
R St-Claude
Jardin St-Gilles Grand Veneur
R Amelot
Richard Lenoir
R Pelée
Allée Verte
R Moufle
11E
R du Chemin Vert
Bd Voltaire
R Popincourt
Blancs Manteaux
18
R Vieille du Temple
R Elzévir
Square G Cain
R de Turenne
R St-Gilles
R des Tournelles
R St-Sabin
Square Bréguet Sabin
R Bréguet
Voltaire
R des Rosiers
R des Francs Bourgeois
36
R des Minimes
Chemin Vert
R Boulle
Bréguet Sabin
R Sedaine
17
47
R du Roi de Sicile
R de Rivoli
R François Miron
R Mahler
Place du Marché Ste-Catherine
R du Pas de la Mule
13
Marché Bastille
R St-Sabin
R de la Roquette
Passage Charles Dallery
R Basfroi
4E
St-Paul
St-Paul; St-Louis
8
19
R Daval
R des Taillandiers
R Keller
Passage Thiéré
Square A Schweitzer
R Charlemagne
29
Bastille
Pont Marie
25
R St-Antoine
Place de la Bastille
R de Lappe
R de Charonne
Square de l'Ave Marie Maria
Pont Marie
R Beautreillis
R du Petit Musc
45
Q d'Anjou
R St-Louis en l'Île
Square H Galli
Bd Henri IV
Sully Morland
R l'Arsenal
Bd Bourdon
Port de Plaisance de Paris Arsenal
Bd de la Bastille
R Biscornet
R de Lyon
Opéra de Paris Bastille
R du Faubourg St-Antoine
Ledru Rollin
Passage de la Main
R Trousseau
Q de Béthune
Île St-Louis
Pont de la Tournelle
R St-Nicolas
R Moreau
Av Ledru-Rollin
Square Trousseau
R de Cotte
R d'Aligre
Pont de Sully
Square Barye
34
Place Mohammed V
R Mornay
Bd Morland
R Lacuée
R Jules César
R Émilio Castelar
Place d'Aligre
Q Henri IV
Musée de la Sculpture en Plein Air
R de Charenton
R Beccaria
Universités Paris VI & VII
R de Bercy
Pont Morland
R d'Austerlitz
R Crémieux
Promenade Plantée
R Traversière
R Parrot
Gare de Lyon
Av Daumesnil
Quai de la Rapée
12E
Bd Diderot
R Jussieu
R Cuvier
Q St-Bernard
Voie Mazas
Gare de Lyon
Place H Fresnay
R Jean Bouton
Grauwin
7
Pont d'Austerlitz
2
LATIN QUARTER
Seine
R Van Gogh
Jardin des Plantes
Cour Départ
13E
Gare d'Austerlitz
Gare d'Austerlitz
Pont Charles de Gaulle
R de Bercy
Q de la Rapée
10
R Buffon
Cour d'Arrivée
Mosquée de Paris
R Villiot

INFORMATION
- Hôpital Hôtel Dieu **1** D3
- Paris Convention & Visitors Bureau **2** H6

SIGHTS & ACTIVITIES
- Cathédrale de Notre Dame de Paris **3** D4
- Centre Pompidou **4** D2
- Conciergerie **5** C3
- Église St-Germain des Prés **6** A3
- Jardin Alpin .... (see 7)
- Jardin des Plantes **7** F5
- Jardin d'Hiver .... (see 7)
- Maison de Victor Hugo **8** F3
- Ménagerie du Jardin des Plantes .... (see 7)
- Musée du Louvre **9** B2
- Musée National d'Art Moderne .... (see 4)
- Musée National d'Histoire Naturelle **10** E6
- Musée Picasso **11** F2
- Panthéon **12** C5
- Place des Vosges **13** F3
- Ste-Chapelle **14** C3
- Tours de Notre Dame Entrance **15** D3

SLEEPING
- Familia Hôtel **16** D5
- Hôtel Caron de Beaumarchais **17** E3
- Hôtel de la Bretonnerie **18** E2
- Hôtel de la Place des Vosges **19** F3
- Hôtel de Nesle **20** B3
- Hôtel des Grandes Écoles **21** D5
- Hôtel du Globe **22** B4
- Hôtel du Lys **23** B4
- Hôtel du Petit Moulin **24** F2
- Hôtel du Septième Art **25** F3
- Hôtel Minerve **26** D5
- Hôtel St-Jacques **27** C5
- Hôtel St-Merry **28** D2

EATING
- Bofinger **29** F3
- Brasserie Lipp **30** A3
- Chez Allard **31** B4
- Joe Allen **32** D1
- L'Ambassade d'Auvergne **33** D1
- Le Baba Bourgeois **34** E4
- Le Petit Mâchon **35** B1
- Le Petit Marché **36** F3
- Le Petit Pontoise **37** D4
- Le Trumilou **38** D3
- Marché Maubert **39** C4
- Perraudin **40** C5
- Polidor **41** B4
- Scoop **42** B1

DRINKING
- La Perle **43** E2
- Le 10 .... **44** B4
- Le Bistrot du Peintre **45** H4
- Le Fumoir **46** B2
- Le Loir dans la Théière **47** E3
- Le Piano Vache **48** C5
- Les Deux Magots **49** A3

ENTERTAINMENT
- Le Bataclan **50** G1
- Le Caveau de la Huchette **51** C4

SHOPPING
- Cacao et Chocolat **52** A3

TRANSPORT
- Eurolines **53** C4
- Noctilien (Night Bus) Stop (Châtelet) **54** D3

JARDIN DES PLANTES

Paris' 24-hectare **Jardin des Plantes** (**Botanical Garden; Map pp184-5; ☎ 01 40 79 56 01/54 79; 57 rue Cuvier & 3 quai St-Bernard, 5e; 🕑 8am-5.30pm, to 8pm summer; Ⓜ Gare d'Austerlitz, Censier Daubenton or Jussieu**) was founded in 1626 as a medicinal herb garden for Louis XIII.

Here you'll find the famous **Jardin d'Hiver** (Winter Garden; Map pp184-5) and the **Serres Tropicales** (Tropical Greenhouses), renovated in 2008; the **Jardin Alpin** (**Map pp184-5; weekend admission adult/under 4yr/4-15yr €1/free/0.50; 🕑 8am-4.30pm Mon-Fri, 1-5pm Sat & Sun Apr-Oct**), and the **Ménagerie du Jardin des Plantes** (**Botanical Garden Zoo; Map pp184-5; adult/under 4yr/4-15yr €7/free/5; 🕑 9am-5pm**), a historic zoo founded in 1794.

The gardens also contain the city's main natural history museum, the **Musée National d'Histoire Naturelle** (**Map pp184-5; ☎ 01 40 79 30 00; www.mnhn.fr, in French; 57 rue Cuvier, 5e; 🕑 10am-5pm Wed-Mon; Ⓜ Censier Daubenton or Gare d'Austerlitz**), with several galleries covering evolution, geology, palaeontology and the history of human evolution. You can buy individual tickets, but the two-day combo ticket is much better value at €20/15 adult/child.

THE ISLANDS

ÎLE ST-LOUIS

The smaller of the Seine's twin islands, **Île St-Louis** (**Map pp184-5; Ⓜ Pont Marie**) is just downstream from the Île de la Cité. The streets and quays of Île St-Louis are lined with 17th-century houses, art galleries and upmarket shops, and it feels a world away from the hustle of the rest of the city.

ÎLE DE LA CITÉ

The site of the first settlement in Paris around the 3rd century BC and later the Roman town of Lutèce (Lutetia), the Île de la Cité (Map pp184-5) remained the centre of royal and ecclesiastical power throughout the Middle Ages. The seven decorated arches of Paris' oldest bridge, **Pont Neuf** (**Map pp184-5; Ⓜ Pont Neuf**) have linked the Île de la Cité with both banks of the Seine since 1607.

CATHÉDRALE DE NOTRE DAME DE PARIS

The **Cathédrale de Notre Dame de Paris** (Map pp184-5; ☎ 01 42 34 56 10; www.cathedraledeparis.com; place du Parvis Notre Dame, 4e; audio guide €5; 7.45am-6.45pm; M Cité) is one of the masterpieces of French Gothic architecture, famed for its stunning stained-glass rose windows, leering gargoyles and elegant flying buttresses, as well as a monumental 7800-pipe organ.

The entrance to the famous **tours de Notre Dame** (Map pp184-5; ☎ 01 53 10 07 02; rue du Cloître Notre Dame; adult/under 18yr/18-25yr €7.50/free/4.80, 1st Sun of month Oct-Mar free; 10am-6.30pm daily Apr-Jun & Sep, 9am-7.30pm Mon-Fri, 9am-11pm Sat & Sun Jul & Aug, 10am-5.30pm daily Oct-Mar) is from the North Tower. The 422 spiralling steps take you to the top of the west facade for face-to-face views of countless gargoyles, the massive 13-tonne 'Emmanuel' bell in the South Tower and an unforgettable bird's-eye view of Paris. No hunchbacks, though, despite what you may have heard from Victor Hugo.

STE-CHAPELLE & THE CONCIERGERIE

Paris' most exquisite Gothic monument is **Ste-Chapelle** (Holy Chapel; Map pp184-5; ☎ 01 53 40 60 97; www.monuments-nationaux.fr; 4 blvd du Palais, 1er; adult/under 18yr/18-25yr €6.50/free/4.50, 1st Sun of month Oct-Mar free; 9.30am-6pm Mar-Oct, 9am-5pm Nov-Feb; M Cité), tucked within the Palais de Justice (Law Courts). The chapel was conceived by Louis IX to house his sacred relics, now kept in the treasury of Notre Dame.

Nearby, the 14th-century palace known as the **Conciergerie** (Map pp184-5; ☎ 01 53 40 60 97; www.monuments-nationaux.fr; 2 blvd du Palais, 1er; adult/under 18yr/18-25yr €8/free/6, 1st Sun of month Oct-Mar free; 9.30am-6pm Mar-Oct, 9am-5pm Nov-Feb; M Cité) became the city's main prison during the Reign of Terror (1793–94). A joint ticket with Ste-Chapelle costs €11.50/9 adult/18 to 25 years.

RIGHT BANK

JARDIN DES TUILERIES

Joggers and picnickers congregate in the 28-hectare **Jardin des Tuileries** (Map pp180-1; ☎ 01 40 20 90 43; 7am-9pm Apr, May & Sep, 7am-11pm Jun-Aug, 7.30am-7.30pm Oct-Mar; M Tuileries or Concorde), laid out in the mid-17th century by André Le Nôtre, designer of the gardens at Versailles.

In the gardens' southwestern corner is the **Musée de l'Orangerie** (Map pp180-1; ☎ 01 44 77 80 07; www.musee-orangerie.fr; Jardin des Tuileries, 1er; adult/senior, student & 13-18yr €6.50/4.50, 1st Sun of month free; 12.30-7pm Wed, Thu & Sat-Mon, 12.30-9pm Fri; M Concorde), which exhibits some important Impressionist works, including a series of Monet's *Water Lilies*, as well as works by Cézanne, Matisse, Picasso, Renoir, Sisley and Utrillo.

ARC DE TRIOMPHE

The **Arc de Triomphe** (Map pp180-1; ☎ 01 55 37 73 77; www.monuments-nationaux.fr; viewing platform adult/under 18yr/18-25yr €9/free/6.50, 1st Sun of month Nov-Mar free; 10am-11pm Apr-Sep, to 10.30pm Oct-Mar; M Charles de Gaulle-Étoile) stands in the middle of the world's largest traffic roundabout, **place de l'Étoile** (Map pp180-1; M Charles de Gaulle Étoile), officially known as place Charles de Gaulle. The 'triumphal arch' was commissioned in 1806 by Napoleon to commemorate his victories, but remained unfinished when he started losing battles, and wasn't completed until 1836. Since 1920, the body of an **unknown soldier** from WWI has lain beneath the arch; a memorial flame is rekindled each evening around 6.30pm.

The **viewing platform** affords wonderful views of the dozen avenues that radiate out from the arch, many of which are named after Napoleonic generals. **Av Foch** is Paris' widest boulevard, while **av des Champs-Élysées** leads south to **place de la Concorde** and its famous 3300-year-old pink granite obelisk, which once stood in the Temple of Ramses at Thebes (present-day Luxor).

CENTRE POMPIDOU

Opened in 1977, the **Centre National d'Art et de Culture Georges Pompidou** (**Map pp184-5; ☎ 01 44 78 12 33; www.centrepompidou.fr; place Georges Pompidou, 4e; Ⓜ Rambuteau**) – Centre Pompidou for short, and also known as the Centre Beaubourg – is one of central Paris' most iconic modern buildings; it was one of the first structures to have its 'insides' turned out. It's now a huge cultural and artistic centre; the main attraction is the **Musée National d'Art Moderne** (**MNAM, Map pp184-5; adult €10-12, senior & 18-25yr €8-10, under 18yr free, free 6-9pm Wed for 18-25yr, 1st Sun of month free; 11am-9pm Wed-Mon**), on the 4th and 5th floors, which contains France's national collection of post-1905 art, with surrealists, cubists, fauvists and pop artists all amply represented.

PLACE DES VOSGES

The **Marais**, the area of the Right Bank north of Île St-Louis in the 3e and 4e, was originally a marsh before it was transformed into one of the city's most fashionable districts by Henri IV, who constructed the elegant *hôtels particuliers* around place Royale – today known as the **Place des Vosges** (**Map pp184-5; Ⓜ St-Paul or Bastille**).

The novelist Victor Hugo lived here from 1832 to 1848, and the **Maison de Victor Hugo** (**Map pp184-5; ☎ 01 42 72 10 16; www.musee-hugo.paris.fr, in French; permanent collections admission free, temporary exhibitions adult/under 14yr/senior & student/14-26yr €7.50/free/3.50/5.50; 10am-6pm Tue-Sun**) now houses drawings, paintings and memorabilia relating to the author.

MUSÉE PICASSO

The **Musée Picasso** (**Map pp184-5; ☎ 01 42 71 25 21; www.musee-picasso.fr, in French; 5 rue de Thorigny, 3e; adult/under 18yr/18-25yr €7.70/free/5.70, 1st Sun of month free; 9.30am-6pm Wed-Mon Apr-Sep, 9.30am-5.30pm Wed-Mon Oct-Mar; Ⓜ St-Paul or Chemin Vert**) contains more than 3500 of the *grand maître*'s engravings, paintings, ceramics and sculptures, as well as works from his own art collection by Braque, Cézanne, Matisse, Modigliani, Degas and Rousseau.

MONTMARTRE & PIGALLE

During the late 19th and early 20th centuries, bohemian Montmartre attracted a number of important writers and artists, including Picasso, who lived at the studio called **Bateau Lavoir** (**Map pp180-1; 11bis place Émile Goudeau; Ⓜ Abbesses**) from 1908 to 1912.

Montmartre's most famous landmark is the **Basilique du Sacré Cœur** (**Map pp180-1; ☎ 01 53 41 89 00; www.sacre-coeur-montmartre.com; place du Parvis du Sacré Cœur, 18e; 6am-10.30pm; Ⓜ Anvers**), whose gleaming white **dome** (**admission €5; 9am-7pm Apr-Sep, 9am-6pm Oct-Mar**) has one of the most spectacular city panoramas anywhere in Paris.

Nearby **place du Tertre** (**Map pp180-1; Ⓜ Abbesses**) was once the main square of the village of Montmartre; these days it's filled with cafes, restaurants, endless tourists and a concentrated cluster of caricaturists and painters – if you want to get your portrait painted in Paris, this is definitely the place.

WILL SALTER

Interior of Pyramide du Louvre

MUSÉE DU LOUVRE

The vast Palais du Louvre was constructed as a fortress by Philippe-Auguste in the 13th century and rebuilt in the mid-16th century for use as a royal residence. In 1793 the Revolutionary Convention transformed it into the **Musée du Louvre**, the nation's first (and foremost) national museum.

The collection is mind-bogglingly diverse, ranging from Islamic artworks and Egyptian artefacts through to a fabulous collection of Greek and Roman antiquities (including the *Venus de Milo* and the *Winged Victory of Samothrace*). But it's the celebrated paintings that draw most visitors; highlights include signature works by Raphael, Botticelli, Delacroix, Titian, Géricault and of course Leonardo da Vinci's slyly smiling *La Joconde*, better known as the *Mona Lisa*.

The gallery's main entrance and ticket windows in the Cour Napoléon are covered by the iconic 21m-high **Pyramide du Louvre**. You can avoid the queues outside the pyramid or the Porte des Lions entrance by entering via the Carrousel du Louvre shopping centre, at 99 rue de Rivoli, or by following the 'Musée du Louvre' exit from the Palais Royal-Musée du Louvre metro station.

Machines in the Carrousel du Louvre sell advance tickets, or for an extra €1.10 you can buy online (www.louvre.fr), from Fnac ticket offices, or by ringing ☎ 08 92 68 36 22 or 08 25 34 63 46. Tickets remain valid for the whole day.

Things You Need to Know: Map pp184-5; ☎ 01 40 20 53 17; www.louvre.fr; permanent collections/permanent collections & temporary exhibits €9/13, after 6pm Wed & Fri €6/11, permanent collections free for under 18yr & after 6pm Fri for under 26yr, 1st Sun of month free; 9am-6pm Mon, Thu, Sat & Sun, 9am-10pm Wed & Fri; M Palais Royal-Musée du Louvre

View across the Seine to Cathédrale de Notre Dame de Paris (p187)

Only a few blocks southwest of the tranquil residential streets of Montmartre is lively, neon-lit Pigalle (9e and 18e), one of Paris' two main sex districts. It's connected to the top of Butte de Montmartre (Montmartre Hill) by a funicular.

DALÍ ESPACE MONTMARTRE

More than 300 works by Salvador Dalí (1904–89), the flamboyant Catalan surrealist printmaker, painter, sculptor and self-promoter, are on display at the **Dalí Espace Montmartre** (Map pp180-1; ☎ 01 42 64 40 10; www.daliparis.com; 11 rue Poulbot, 18e; adult/under 8yr/student & 8-26yr/senior €10/free/6/7; 10am-6.30pm; M Abbesses), a surrealist-style basement museum west of place du Tertre.

CIMETIÈRE DU PÈRE LACHAISE

The world's most-visited graveyard, **Cimetière du Père Lachaise** (Map pp180-1; ☎ 01 55 25 82 10; admission free; 8am-6pm Mon-Fri, 8.30am-6pm Sat, 9am-6pm Sun mid-Mar–early Nov, 8am-5.30pm Mon-Fri, 8.30am-5.30pm Sat, 9am-5.30pm Sun early Nov–mid-Mar; M Philippe Auguste, Gambetta or Père Lachaise) opened its one-way doors in 1804. Among the 800,000 people buried here are Chopin, Molière, Balzac, Proust, Gertrude Stein, Colette, Pissarro, Seurat, Modigliani, Sarah Bernhardt, Yves Montand, Delacroix, Édith Piaf and even the 12th-century lovers Abélard and Héloïse. The graves of **Oscar Wilde** (Division 89) and **Jim Morrison** (Division 6) are perennially popular. Free maps are available from the **conservation office** (Map pp180-1; 16 rue du Repos, 20e).

ACTIVITIES

BOAT TRIPS

There's no finer way to appreciate the City of Lights than a cruise on the River Seine. The most famous riverboat company is **Bateaux Mouches** (Map pp180-1; ☎ 01 42 25 96 10; www.bateauxmouches.com, in French; Port de la Conférence, 8e; adult/under 4yr/senior & 4-12yr €9/free/4; mid-Mar–mid-Nov; M Alma Marceau), based just east of the Pont de l'Alma. From April to September, 1000-seater cruises (70 minutes) depart eight times daily between 10.15am and 3.15pm and then every 20 minutes till 11pm. They depart 10 times a day between 10.15am and 9pm the rest of the year. Commentary is in French and English.

Alternatively, **Paris Canal Croisières** (**Map pp180-1; ☎ 01 42 40 96 97; www.pariscanal.com; Bassin de la Villette, 19-21 quai de la Loire, 19e; adult/under 4yr/4-11yr/senior & 12-25yr €17/free/10/14; Ⓜ Jaurès**) has daily 2½-hour cruises via the charming Canal St-Martin and Canal de l'Ourcq. Departures are at 9.30am from quai Anatole France and at 2.30pm from Bassin de la Villette.

WALKING

Paris Walks (**☎ 01 48 09 21 40; www.paris-walks.com; adult/under 15yr/student under 21yr from €10/5/8**) has English-language tours of several districts, including Montmartre at 10.30am on Sunday and Wednesday (leaving from Abbesses metro station, Map pp180-1) and the Marais at 10.30am on Tuesday and at 2.30pm on Sunday (departing from St-Paul metro station, Map pp184-5). There are other tours focusing on themes including Hemingway, medieval Paris, the Latin Quarter, fashion, the French Revolution and even chocolate.

SLEEPING

The Paris Convention & Visitors Bureau (p179) can nearly always find you a room and doesn't charge for reservations, although you'll need a credit card, and queues can be horrendously long in high season.

MARAIS & BASTILLE

our pick **Hôtel du Septième Art** (**Map pp184-5; ☎ 01 44 54 85 00; www.paris-hotel-7art.com; 20 rue St-Paul, 4e; s €65, d €90-145; Ⓜ St-Paul;** 💻) Filmic fun place for cinema buffs (*le septième art*, or 'the seventh art', is what the French call cinema), with a black-and-white-movie theme throughout the 23 rooms, right down to the tiled floors and bathrooms.

Hôtel de la Place des Vosges (**Map pp184-5; ☎ 01 42 72 60 46; www.hotelplacedesvosges.com; 12 rue de Birague, 4e; r €90-95, ste €150; Ⓜ Bastille;** 💻) This superbly situated 17-room hotel is an oasis of tranquillity near sublime place des Vosges. The public areas are impressive and the rooms warm and cosy – floors one to four have a lift, but beyond that it's stairs only.

Hôtel de la Bretonnerie (**Map pp184-5; ☎ 01 48 87 77 63; www.bretonnerie.com; 22 rue Ste-Croix de la Bretonnerie, 4e; r €125-160, ste €185-210; Ⓜ Hôtel de Ville;** 💻) With 17th-century architecture, a central Marais location, and a smattering of four-poster and canopy beds, this hotel is a real find.

our pick **Hôtel Caron de Beaumarchais** (**Map pp184-5; ☎ 01 42 72 34 12; www.carondebeaumarchais.com; 12 rue Vieille du Temple, 4e; r €125-162; Ⓜ St-Paul;** ❄ 💻) An 18th-century pianoforte, gaming tables, gilded mirrors and candelabras set the tone in the palatial lobby, but the 19 rooms are smallish and the welcome's rather frosty.

our pick **Hôtel St-Merry** (**Map pp184-5; ☎ 01 42 78 14 15; www.hotelmarais.com; 78 rue de la Verrerie, 4e; d & tw €160-230, tr €205-275, ste €335-407; Ⓜ Châtelet;** 💻) Beamed ceilings, church pews and wrought-iron candelabras make this a goth's dream (or should that be nightmare?) come true. Standing side by side with next-door Église St-Merry, the 11 rooms and single suite are crammed with Gothic character, but there's no lift or air-con.

Hôtel du Petit Moulin (**Map pp184-5; ☎ 01 42 74 10 10; www.hoteldupetitmoulin.com; 29-31 rue de Poitou, 3e; r €180-280, ste €350; Ⓜ Filles du Calvaire;** ❄ 💻) Scrumptious boutique hotel designed from top to bottom by Christian Lacroix. Its 17 rooms, named after Parisian neighbourhoods, range from medieval and rococo Marais

WILL SALTER
Patrons at Les Deux Magots (p196)

to more modern *quartier* with contemporary murals and heart-shaped mirrors.

LATIN QUARTER

Familia Hôtel (**Map pp184-5; ☎ 01 43 54 55 27; www.familiahotel.com; 11 rue des Écoles, 5e; s €86, d & tw €103-124, tr €161-173, q €184; Ⓜ Cardinal Lemoine;**) Family-run hotel with sepia-tinted murals of Paris' landmarks in 21 of its 30 rooms. Eight have balconies with distant glimpses of Notre Dame.

Hôtel Minerve (**Map pp184-5; ☎ 01 43 26 26 04; www.parishotelminerve.com; 13 rue des Écoles, 5e; s €90-125, d €106-136, tr €156-158, all incl breakfast; Ⓜ Cardinal Lemoine;**) Run by the owners of the Familia, this two-building hotel is decked out in oriental carpets, antique books, frescoes of French monuments and reproduction 18th-century wallpapers.

Hôtel St-Jacques (**Map pp184-5; ☎ 01 44 07 45 45; www.hotel-saintjacques.com; 35 rue des Écoles, 5e; s €92, d €105-137, tr €168; Ⓜ Maubert Mutualité;**) Stylish 38-room hotel overlooking the Panthéon. Audrey Hepburn and Cary Grant, who filmed *Charade* here in the 1960s, would appreciate the mod cons that now complement the *trompe l'œil* ceilings and iron staircase.

our pick **Hôtel des Grandes Écoles** (**Map pp184-5; ☎ 01 43 26 79 23; www.hotel-grandes-ecoles.com; 75 rue du Cardinal Lemoine, 5e; d €110-135, tr €125-155; Ⓜ Cardinal Lemoine or Place Monge**) Wonderful hotel with one of the loveliest situations in the Latin Quarter, tucked away off a medieval street around its own courtyard.

ST-GERMAIN, ODÉON & LUXEMBOURG

The well-heeled St-Germain des Prés is the quintessential place to stay in central Paris, but you'll need to bring your spare change – budget places just don't exist in this part of town.

Hôtel de Nesle (**Map pp184-5; ☎ 01 43 54 62 41; www.hoteldenesleparis.com; 7 rue de Nesle, 6e; s €55-85, d €75-100; Ⓜ Odéon or Mabillon**) The Nesle is a relaxed, colourful place with 20 rooms, half of which are painted with murals taken from classic literature.

Hôtel du Globe (**Map pp184-5; ☎ 01 43 26 35 50; www.hotel-du-globe.fr; 15 rue des Quatre Vents, 6e; s €95-140, d €115-150, ste €180; Ⓜ Odéon;**) The Globe is an eclectic caravanserai with 14 small but completely renovated rooms just south of the blvd St-Germain.

Hôtel du Lys (**Map pp184-5; ☎ 01 43 26 97 57; www.hoteldulys.com; 23 rue Serpente, 6e; s/d/tr €100/120/140; Ⓜ Odéon**) This 22-room hotel is situated in a former 17th-century *hôtel particulier*. Beamed ceiling and chinoiserie wallpaper in the lobby, and a tempting choice of rooms including blue-toned No 13 and terracotta-themed No 14.

FAUBOURG ST-DENIS & INVALIDES

The 7e is a lovely *arrondissement* in which to stay, but it's a little removed from the action.

Hôtel du Champ-de-Mars (Map pp180-1; ☎ 01 45 51 52 30; www.hotelduchampdemars.com; 7 rue du Champ de Mars, 7e; s/d/tw/tr €84/90/94/112; Ⓜ École Militaire; 💻) This charming 25-room hotel in the shadow of the Eiffel Tower is on everyone's wish list, so book a good month in advance.

Mayet Hôtel (Map pp180-1; ☎ 01 47 83 21 35; www.mayet.com; 3 rue Mayet, 6e; s €95-120, d €120-140, tr €160; Ⓜ Duroc; 💻) Light-hearted and loads of fun, this 23-room boutique hotel has a penchant for oversize clocks and primary colours, plus good-sized rooms and complimentary breakfasts.

MONTMARTRE & PIGALLE

Montmartre is one of the most charming neighbourhoods in Paris, with a clutch of midrange and top-end hotels.

Hôtel des Arts (Map pp180-1; ☎ 01 46 06 30 52; www.arts-hotel-paris.com; 5 rue Tholozé, 18e; s €75-95, d & tw €95-105, tr €160; Ⓜ Abbesses or Blanche; 💻) The 'Arts Hotel' is a friendly and attractive 50-room place convenient to both place Pigalle and Montmartre. Towering over it is the old-style windmill Moulin de la Galette.

our pick **Hôtel Résidence des 3 Poussins** (Map pp180-1; ☎ 01 53 32 81 81; www.les3poussins.com; 15 rue Clauzel, 9e; s/d €137/152, 1- or 2-person studio €187, 3- or 4-person studio €222; Ⓜ Pigalle or St-Georges; ✲ 💻) Due south of place Pigalle, the 'Hotel of the Three Chicks' is a lovely property with 40 rooms, half of them small studios with their own cooking facilities.

EATING

LOUVRE & LES HALLES

Le Petit Mâchon (Map pp184-5; ☎ 01 42 60 08 06; 158 rue St-Honoré, 1er; starters €7-12.50, mains €14-22; 🕑 lunch & dinner Tue-Sun; Ⓜ Palais Royal-Musée du Louvre) An upbeat bistro with Lyon-inspired specialities. Try the *saucisson de Lyon* (Lyon sausage) studded with pistachios.

Joe Allen (Map pp184-5; ☎ 01 42 36 70 13; 30 rue Pierre Lescot, 1er; starters €7.50-10.30, mains €15.50-26, lunch menus €13.90-22.50, dinner menus €18-22.50; 🕑 noon-1am; Ⓜ Étienne Marcel) An institution in Paris since 1972, Joe Allen is a little bit of New York in Paris. There's an excellent brunch (€19.50 to €23.50) from noon to 4pm at the weekend.

Le Grand Colbert (Map pp180-1; ☎ 01 42 86 87 88; 2-4 rue Vivienne, 2e; starters €10-21.50, mains €19.50-30, lunch menus €32-39, dinner menus €39; 🕑 noon-3am; Ⓜ Pyramides) This former workers' *cafétéria* transformed into a fin de siècle showcase is a convenient spot for lunch when visiting the nearby *passages couverts* (covered arcades).

Scoop (Map pp184-5; ☎ 01 42 60 31 84; 154 rue St-Honoré, 1er; dishes €10.90-16.90; 🕑 11am-7pm; Ⓜ Palais Royal-Musée du Louvre) This American-style ice-cream parlour has been making quite a splash with its wraps, burgers, tarts and soups and central, trendy location.

MARAIS & BASTILLE

The Marais, filled with small restaurants of every imaginable type, is one of Paris' premier neighbourhoods for eating out.

Le Trumilou (Map pp184-5; ☎ 01 42 77 63 98; 84 quai de l'Hôtel de Ville, 4e; starters €4.50-13, mains €15-22, menus €16.50 & €19.50; 🕑 lunch & dinner; Ⓜ Hôtel de Ville) This no-frills bistro is a Parisian institution known for its classic French cooking: try *confit aux pruneaux* (duck with prunes) and the *ris de veau grand-mère* (veal sweetbreads in mushroom cream sauce).

Le Petit Marché (Map pp184-5; ☎ 01 42 72 06 67; 9 rue de Béarn, 3e; starters €8-11, mains €15-25, lunch menus €14; 🕑 lunch & dinner; Ⓜ Chemin Vert) This great little bistro just up from place des Vosges attracts a mixed crowd with its hearty cooking and friendly service.

our pick **L'Ambassade d'Auvergne** (Map pp184-5; ☎ 01 42 72 31 22; 22 rue du Grenier St-Lazare, 3e; starters €8-16, mains €14-22, lunch menus €20-28, dinner menus €28; lunch & dinner; M Rambuteau) The 100-year-old 'Auvergne Embassy' is the place to go if you're hungry; the sausages and hams of this region are among the best in France.

Bofinger (Map pp184-5; ☎ 01 42 72 87 82; 5-7 rue de la Bastille, 4e; starters €8-18.50, mains €15.50-31.50, lunch menus €24-31.50, dinner menus €31.50; lunch & dinner to 12.30am; M Bastille) Glimmering in art-nouveau brass and polished mirrors, Bofinger is reputedly the oldest brasserie in Paris (founded in 1864). Specialities include *choucroute* (sauerkraut; €18 to €20) and seafood.

LATIN QUARTER & JARDIN DES PLANTES

From cheap student haunts to chandelier-lit palaces, the 5e has something to suit every budget and culinary taste.

Le Petit Pontoise (Map pp184-5; ☎ 01 43 29 25 20; 9 rue de Pontoise, 5e; starters €8-13.50, mains €15-25; lunch & dinner; M Maubert Mutualité) This charming bistro offers a blackboard menu of seasonal delights: *rognons de veau à l'ancienne* (calf's kidneys), *boudin campagnard* (black pudding) and roast quail with dates.

Perraudin (Map pp184-5; ☎ 01 46 33 15 75; 157 rue St-Jacques, 5e; starters €10-20, mains €15-30, lunch menus €19-29, dinner menus €29; lunch & dinner Mon-Fri; M Luxembourg) Ubertraditional Perraudin has barely changed since it first opened in 1910 – if you're after classic French dishes such as *boeuf bourguignon* (beef stew) and *gigot d'agneau* (leg of lamb), this frayed old place is tough to top.

Le Baba Bourgeois (Map pp184-5; ☎ 01 44 07 46 75; 5 quai de la Tournelle, 5e; mains €15-20; lunch & dinner Wed-Sat, 11.30am-5pm Sun; M Cardinal Lemoine) Contemporary dining on the Seine in a former architect's studio. Its *tartines* (open-face sandwiches), terrines, *tartes salées* (savoury tarts) and salads are delicious, and there's an all-you-can-eat Sunday buffet.

WILL SALTER

Enjoying Paris in Montmartre (p188)

Place Maubert becomes the lively food market **Marché Maubert** (Map pp184-5) on Tuesday, Thursday and Saturday mornings, while **rue Mouffetard** (Map pp180-1; 8am-7.30pm Tue-Sat, 8am-noon Sun; M Censier Daubenton) and **place Monge** (Map pp184-5; place Monge, 5e; 7am-2pm Wed, Fri & Sun; M Place Monge) both have their own street markets.

ST-GERMAIN, ODÉON & LUXEMBOURG

Polidor (Map pp184-5; ☎ 01 43 26 95 34; 41 rue Monsieur le Prince, 6e; starters €4.50-17, mains €11-22, menus €22-32; lunch & dinner to 12.30am Mon-Sat, to 11pm Sun; M Odéon) A meal at this quintessentially Parisian bistro is like taking a quick trip back to Victor Hugo's Paris – the restaurant and its decor date from 1845 – but everyone knows about it and it's pretty touristy.

our pick **Chez Allard** (Map pp184-5; ☎ 01 43 26 48 23; 41 rue St-André des Arts; starters €8-20, mains €25, menus €25-34; lunch & dinner Mon-Sat; M St-Michel) One of our favourite Left Bank eateries, always busy and always superb. Try 12 snails, some *cuisses de grenouilles* (frogs' legs) or *un poulet de Bresse* (France's most legendary chicken, from Burgundy) for two.

Brasserie Lipp (Map pp184-5; ☎ 01 45 48 53 91; 151 bd St-Germain, 6e; starters €10-15, mains €15.50-25; noon-2am; M St-Germain des Prés) Expect politicians, celebs, media moguls and plenty of waistcoated waiters at the lovely Lipp, one of Paris' most beloved of brasseries.

MONTPARNASSE

La Coupole (Map pp180-1; ☎ 01 43 20 14 20; 102 blvd du Montparnasse, 14e; starters €6.50-20, mains €12.50-35, lunch menus €24.50-31.50, dinner menus €31.50; 8am-1am Sun-Thu, to 1.30am Fri & Sat; M Vavin) This 450-seat brasserie, which opened in 1927, has mural-covered columns painted by such European artists as Brancusi and Chagall. You can book for lunch, but you'll have to queue for dinner.

our pick **La Cagouille** (Map pp180-1; ☎ 01 43 22 09 01; 10 place Constantin Brancusi, 14e; starters €11-15, mains €18-33, menus €26-42; lunch & dinner; M Gaîté) Chef Gérard Allemandou, one of the best seafood cooks (and cookbook writers) in Paris, gets rave reviews for his fish and shellfish.

OPÉRA & GRANDS BOULEVARDS

Chartier (Map pp180-1; ☎ 01 47 70 86 29; 7 rue du Faubourg Montmartre, 9e; starters €2.20-12.40, mains €6.50-16, menus incl wine €20; lunch & dinner; M Grands Boulevards) Chartier is a real gem for the budget traveller, justifiably famous for its 330-seat belle époque dining room and its excellent-value menu. Reservations are not accepted and lone diners will have to share a table.

Le Roi du Pot au Feu (Map pp180-1; ☎ 01 47 42 37 10; 34 rue Vignon, 9e; starters €5-7, mains €17-20, menus €24-29; noon-10.30pm Mon-Sat; M Havre Caumartin) The typical Parisian bistro atmosphere adds immensely to the charm of the 'King of Hotpots', where the dish of the day is always *pot au feu*, a stewed stockpot of beef, root vegetables and herbs. No bookings.

MONTMARTRE & PIGALLE

You'll still find some decent eateries in Montmartre, but beware the tourist traps.

Chez Toinette (Map pp180-1; ☎ 01 42 54 44 36; 20 rue Germain Pilon, 18e; starters €6-9, mains €15-20; dinner Tue-Sat; M Abbesses) This convivial French restaurant has somehow managed to keep alive the tradition of old Montmartre in one of the capital's most touristy neighbourhoods.

Le Café Qui Parle (Map pp180-1; ☎ 01 46 06 06 88; 24 rue Caulaincourt, 18e; starters €7-14,

mains €13.50-20, menus €12.50-17; lunch & dinner Thu-Tue; M Lamarck Caulaincourt or Blanche) 'The Talking Cafe' offers inventive, reasonably priced dishes prepared by owner-chef Damian Mœuf. We love the art on the walls.

DRINKING

Paris is justly famous for its cafe culture, but these days there's a huge range of drinking establishments, especially in the Marais and along the Grands Boulevards.

LOUVRE & LES HALLES

Le Fumoir **(Map pp184-5; ☎ 01 42 92 00 24; 6 rue de l'Amiral Coligny, 1er; 11am-2am; M Louvre-Rivoli)** The 'Smoking Room' is a huge, stylish colonial-style bar-cafe opposite the Louvre. It's a fine place to sip top-notch gin while nibbling on olives; during happy hour (6pm to 8pm) cocktails, usually €8.50 to €11, drop to €6.

MARAIS & BASTILLE

La Perle **(Map pp184-5; ☎ 01 42 72 69 93; 78 rue Vieille du Temple, 3e; 6am-2am Mon-Fri, 8am-2am Sat & Sun; M St-Paul or Chemin Vert)** This is where *bobos* (bohemian bourgeois types) come to slum it over *un rouge* (glass of red wine) until the DJ arrives and things liven up.

Le Bistrot du Peintre **(Map pp184-5; ☎ 01 47 00 34 39; 116 av Ledru-Rollin, 11e; 8am-2am; M Bastille)** Lovely belle époque bistro and wine bar, with a 1902 art nouveau bar, elegant terrace and spot-on service.

our pick **Le Loir dans la Théière** **(Map pp184-5; ☎ 01 42 72 90 61; 3 rue des Rosiers, 4e; 9.30am-7pm; M St-Paul)** The dim and cosy 'Dormouse in the Teapot' is filled with retro toys and comfy couches, while scenes of *Through the Looking Glass* decorate the walls.

LATIN QUARTER & JARDIN DES PLANTES

Le Piano Vache **(Map pp184-5; ☎ 01 46 33 75 03; 8 rue Laplace, 5e; noon-2am Mon-Fri, 9pm-2am Sat & Sun; M Maubert Mutualité)** Just downhill from the Panthéon, the 'Mean Piano' is effortlessly underground and a huge favourite with students, with bands and DJs playing mainly rock, plus some goth, reggae and pop.

ST-GERMAIN, ODÉON & LUXEMBOURG

Le 10 **(Map pp184-5; ☎ 01 43 26 66 83; 10 rue de l'Odéon, 6e; 5.30pm-2am; M Odéon)** A local institution, this cellar pub groans with students, smoky ambience and cheap sangria.

Les Deux Magots **(Map pp184-5; ☎ 01 45 48 55 25; www.lesdeuxmagots.fr; 170 blvd St-Germain, 6e; 7am-1am; M St-Germain des Prés)** The favoured hang-out of Sartre, Hemingway, Picasso and André Breton. Everyone has to sit on the terrace here at least once and have a coffee or the famous hot chocolate served in porcelain jugs.

OPÉRA & GRANDS BOULEVARDS

De la Ville Café **(Map pp180-1; ☎ 01 48 24 48 09; 34 blvd de Bonne Nouvelle, 10e; 11am-2.30am; M Bonne Nouvelle)** This one-time brothel has an alluring mix of restored history and modern design. DJs play most nights, so it's popular with the preclub crowd.

our pick **Harry's New York Bar** **(Map pp180-1; ☎ 01 42 61 71 14; 5 rue Daunou, 2e; 10.30am-4am; M Opéra)** Lean upon the bar where F Scott Fitzgerald and Ernest Hemingway drank and gossiped, while white-smocked waiters mix killer martinis and Bloody Marys.

MONTMARTRE & PIGALLE

La Fourmi **(Map pp180-1; ☎ 01 42 64 70 35; 74 rue des Martyrs, 18e; 8am-2am Mon-Thu, 8am-**

WILL SALTER

Jardin des Tuileries (p187)

4am Fri & Sat, 10am-2am Sun; M Pigalle) A Pigalle stayer, 'The Ant' always hits the mark: hip but not snobby, with a laid-back crowd and a rock-orientated playlist.

Le Dépanneur (**Map pp180-1; ☎ 01 44 53 03 78; 27 rue Pierre Fontaine, 9e; ⏰ 10am-2am Mon-Thu, 24hr Fri-Sun; M Blanche**) An American-style diner-cum-bar open (almost) round the clock, 'The Repairman' specialises in tequila and fancy cocktails (€7.50). DJs play after 11pm from Thursday to Saturday.

ENTERTAINMENT

It's impossible to sample Paris' entertainment scene without first studying *Pariscope* (€0.40) or *Officiel des Spectacles* (€0.35), both published every Wednesday.

Tickets for concerts, theatre performances and events are sold at *billeteries* (ticket offices) in **Fnac** (**☎ 08 92 68 36 22; www.fnacspectacles.com, in French**) outlets or **Virgin Megastores** (**☎ 08 25 12 91 39; www.virginmega.fr, in French**).

CINEMAS

Going to the cinema in Paris is not cheap: expect to pay up to €10 for a first-run film. Students, under 18s and over 60s get discounted tickets (usually just under €6), except Friday night, all day Saturday and on Sunday matinees. Wednesday yields discounts for everyone.

Cinémathèque Française (**Map pp180-1; ☎ 01 71 19 33 33; www.cinemathequefrancaise.com; 51 rue de Bercy, 12e; adult/under 12yr/student €6/3/5; ⏰ box office noon-7pm Mon, Wed, Fri & Sat, noon-10pm Thu, 10am-8pm Sun; M Bercy**) This national institution is a veritable temple to the 'seventh art', and always screens its foreign offerings in their original language.

LIVE MUSIC

ROCK & POP

The city's big gig venues are the **Palais Omnisports de Paris-Bercy** (**Map pp180-1; ☎ 08 92 39 01 00; www.bercy.fr, in French; 8 blvd de Bercy, 12e; M Bercy**) in Bercy; the **Stade de France** (**off Map pp180-1; ☎ 08 92 70 09 00; www.stadedefrance.fr, in French; rue Francis de Pressensé, ZAC du Cornillon Nord, St-Denis La Plaine;**

M St-Denis-Porte de Paris) in St-Denis; and **Le Zénith** (Map pp180-1; ☎ 08 90 71 02 07; www.le-zenith.com, in French; 211 av Jean Jaurès, 19e; M Porte de Pantin).

For smaller acts, head along to **La Cigale** (Map pp180-1; ☎ 01 49 25 89 99; www.lacigale.fr; 120 blvd de Rochechouart, 18e; admission €25-60; M Anvers or Pigalle), a music hall dating from 1887 that prides itself on its avant-garde program, and **L'Élysée-Montmartre** (Map pp180-1; ☎ 01 44 92 45 47; www.elyseemontmartre.com; 72 blvd de Rochechouart, 18e; admission €15-45; M Anvers), another old music hall that specialises in one-off rock and indie concerts.

Meanwhile, **Le Bataclan** (Map pp184-5; ☎ 01 43 14 00 30; www.bataclan.fr, in French; 50 blvd Voltaire, 11e; admission €20-45; M Oberkampf or St-Ambroise) was Maurice Chevalier's debut venue in 1910 and today draws some French and international acts.

JAZZ & BLUES

Le Baiser Salé (Map pp184-5; ☎ 01 42 33 37 71; www.lebaisersale.com, in French; 58 rue des Lombards, 1er; admission free-€20; M Châtelet) 'The Salty Kiss' is one of several jazz clubs on the same street.

Le Caveau de la Huchette (Map pp184-5; ☎ 01 43 26 65 05; www.caveaudelahuchette.fr; 5 rue de la Huchette, 5e; admission Sun-Thu/Fri & Sat €11/13; ⏲ 9.30pm-2.30am Sun-Wed, to 4am Thu-Sat; M St-Michel) Housed in a *caveau* (cellar) used as a courtroom and torture chamber during the Revolution, this club has hosted all the jazz greats.

FRENCH CHANSONS

French music has come a long way since the days of Édith Piaf, Jacques Brel and Georges Brassens, but you'll still find traditional *chansons* at lots of Parisian venues.

Au Lapin Agile (Map pp180-1; ☎ 01 46 06 85 87; www.au-lapin-agile.com; 22 rue des Saules, 18e; adult €24, student except Sat €17; ⏲ 9pm-2am Tue-Sun; M Lamarck Caulaincourt) This historic cabaret venue in Montmartre still hosts *chansons* and poetry readings. Admission includes one drink.

Le Limonaire (Map pp180-1; ☎ 01 45 23 33 33; http://limonaire.free.fr; 18 cité Bergère, 9e; admission free; ⏲ 7pm-midnight Mon, 6pm-midnight Tue-Sun; M Grands Boulevards) This wine bar is one of the best places to listen to traditional French bistro music.

SHOPPING

DEPARTMENT STORES

Paris' *grands magasins* (department stores) include the vast **Galeries Lafayette** (Map pp180-1; ☎ 01 42 82 34 56; 40 blvd Haussmann, 9e; ⏲ 9.30am-7.30pm Mon-Wed, Fri & Sat, 9.30am-9pm Thu; M Auber or Chaussée d'Antin) and **Le Printemps** (Map pp180-1; ☎ 01 42 82 57 87; 64 blvd Haussmann, 9e; ⏲ 9.35am-7pm Mon-Wed, Fri & Sat, 9.35am-10pm Thu; M Havre Caumartin). Le Printemps, 'The Spring' (as in the season), is actually three separate stores: one for women's fashion, one for men and one for beauty and household goods.

FOOD

Cacao et Chocolat (Map pp184-5; ☎ 01 46 33 77 63; 29 rue du Buci, 6e; ⏲ 10.30am-7.30pm Mon-Sat, 11am-7pm Sun; M Mabillon) This place is a contemporary take on chocolate, showcasing the cocoa bean in all its guises.

Fauchon (Map pp180-1; ☎ 01 70 39 38 00; 26 & 30 place de la Madeleine, 8e; ⏲ 8.30am-7pm Mon-Sat; M Madeleine) Paris' most famous caterer has a half-dozen departments in two buildings selling the most incredibly mouth-watering delicacies, from pâté de foie gras and truffles to *confitures* (jams).

Fromagerie Alléosse (Map pp180-1; ☎ 01 46 22 50 45; 13 rue Poncelet, 17e; ⏲ 9.30am-1pm & 4-7pm Tue-Thu, 9am-1pm & 3.30-7pm Fri & Sat, 9am-1pm Sun; M Ternes) The best cheese shop in Paris, bar none.

RUSSELL MOUNTFORD

Cakes on display in a Paris patisserie

GETTING THERE & AWAY

AIR

Aéroport d'Orly (ORY; off Map pp180-1; ☎ 3950, 01 70 36 39 50; www.aeroportsdeparis.fr), the older and smaller of Paris' two major airports, is 18km south of the city.

Aéroport Roissy Charles de Gaulle airport (CDG; off Map pp180-1; ☎ 3950, 01 70 36 39 50; www.aeroportsdeparis.fr), 30km northeast of Paris, consists of three terminal complexes and two train stations, linked to the TGV network.

International airport **Aéroport Paris-Beauvais** (BVA; off Map pp180-1; ☎ 08 92 68 20 66, 03 44 11 46 86; www.aeroportbeauvais.com), 80km north of Paris, is used by charter companies as well as Ryanair and other budget airlines.

BUS

The central **Eurolines office** (Map pp184-5; ☎ 01 43 54 11 99; www.eurolines.fr; 55 rue St-Jacques, 5e; 9.30am-6.30pm Mon-Fri, 10am-1pm & 2-5pm Sat; Ⓜ Cluny-La Sorbonne) takes reservations and sells tickets.

TRAIN

Paris has six major train stations:

Gare d'Austerlitz (Map pp184-5; blvd de l'Hôpital, 13e; Ⓜ Gare d'Austerlitz) Spain and Portugal; Loire Valley and non-TGV trains to southwestern France.

Gare de l'Est (Map pp180-1; blvd de Strasbourg, 10e; Ⓜ Gare de l'Est) Luxembourg, parts of Switzerland (Basel, Lucerne, Zürich), southern Germany (Frankfurt, Munich) and points further east; regular and TGV Est trains to areas of France east of Paris (Champagne, Alsace and Lorraine), and Luxembourg.

Gare de Lyon (Map pp184-5; blvd Diderot, 12e; Ⓜ Gare de Lyon) Parts of Switzerland (eg Bern, Geneva, Lausanne), Italy and points beyond; regular and TGV Sud-Est and TGV Midi-Méditerranée trains to areas southeast of Paris, including Dijon, Lyon, Provence, the Côte d'Azur and the Alps.

Gare Montparnasse (Map pp180-1; av du Maine & blvd de Vaugirard, 15e; Ⓜ Montparnasse Bienvenüe) Brittany and places en route from Paris (eg Chartres, Angers,

DOOR-TO-DOOR TRANSPORT

If you want to get into (or out of) the city in a hurry, you could catch a private minibus such as **Allô Shuttle** (☎ 01 34 29 00 80; www.alloshuttle.com), **Paris Airports Service** (☎ 01 55 98 10 80; www.parisairportservice.com) or **PariShuttle** (☎ 01 53 39 18 18; www.parishuttle.com). Count on around €25 per person (€40 between 8pm and 6am) for Orly or Roissy Charles de Gaulle and €150 for one to four people to/from Beauvais. Book ahead and allow time for pick-ups and drop-offs.

Nantes); TGV Atlantique Ouest and TGV Atlantique Sud-Ouest trains to Tours, Nantes, Bordeaux and other destinations in southwestern France.

Gare du Nord (Map pp180-1; rue de Dunkerque, 10e; Ⓜ Gare du Nord) UK, Belgium, northern Germany, Scandinavia etc (terminus of the high-speed Thalys trains to/from Amsterdam, Brussels and Cologne and Eurostar to London); trains to northern France, including TGV Nord trains to Lille and Calais.

Gare St-Lazare (Map pp180-1; rue St-Lazare & rue d'Amsterdam, 8e; Ⓜ St-Lazare) Normandy (eg Dieppe, Le Havre, Cherbourg).

GETTING AROUND

TO/FROM THE AIRPORTS

AÉROPORT D'ORLY

Air France bus 1 (☎ 08 92 35 08 20; www.cars-airfrance.com; one way/return €9/14; ⏲ from Orly 6am-11.30pm, from Invalides 5.45am-11pm) This shuttle bus runs every 15 minutes to/from the eastern side of **Gare Montparnasse** (Map pp180-1; rue du Commandant René Mouchotte, 15e; Ⓜ Montparnasse Bienvenüe) as well as **Aérogare des Invalides** (Map pp180-1; Ⓜ Invalides) in the 7e.

Noctilien bus 31 (☎ 08 92 68 77 14, in English 08 92 68 41 14; adult/4-9yr €6/3; ⏲ 12.30am-5.30pm) Part of the RATP night service, Noctilien bus 31 runs once an hour, linking Gare de Lyon, Place d'Italie and Gare d'Austerlitz with Orly-Sud. It takes 45 minutes.

Orlybus (☎ 08 92 68 77 14; adult/4-11yr €6.10/3.05; ⏲ from Orly 6am-11.50pm, from Paris 5.35am-11.25pm) This RATP bus runs every 15 to 20 minutes to/from metro Denfert Rochereau (Map pp180-1) and stops in the eastern 14e. It takes 30 minutes.

Orlyval (☎ 08 92 68 77 14; adult/4-10yr €9.30/4.65; ⏲ 6am-11pm) This RATP service links Orly with the city centre via a shuttle train and the RER. An automated shuttle train (every 4 to 12 minutes) runs between the airport and Antony RER station (eight minutes) on RER line B, from where it's an easy journey into the city; to get to Antony from the city (26 minutes), take line B4 towards St-Rémy-lès-Chevreuse. Orlyval tickets are valid for travel on the RER and metro.

AÉROPORT ROISSY CHARLES DE GAULLE

Roissy Charles de Gaulle has two train stations: Aéroport Charles de Gaulle 1 (CDG1) and the sleek Aéroport Charles de Gaulle 2 (CDG2). Both are served by RER line B3. A free shuttle bus links the terminals with the train stations.

Air France bus 2 (☎ 08 92 35 08 20; www.cars-airfrance.com; one way/return €13/18; ⏲ 5.45am-11pm) Links the airport with two locations on the Right Bank every 15 minutes: near the Arc de Triomphe just outside 2 av Carnot, 17e (Map pp180-1; Ⓜ Charles de Gaulle-Étoile) and the Palais des Congrès de Paris (**Map pp180-1; blvd Gouvion St-Cyr, 17e; Ⓜ Porte Maillot**). The trip takes 35 to 50 minutes.

Air France bus 4 (☎ **08 92 35 08 20; www.cars-airfrance.com; one way/return €14/22; 🕒 7am-9pm from Roissy Charles de Gaulle, 6.30am-9.30pm from Paris**) Air France bus 4 links the airport with Gare de Lyon (**Map pp184-5; 20bis blvd Diderot, 12e; Ⓜ Gare de Lyon**) and Gare Montparnasse (**Map pp180-1; rue du Commandant René Mouchotte, 15e; Ⓜ Montparnasse Bienvenüe**) **every 30 minutes; it takes 45 to 55 minutes.**

Noctilien buses 120, 121 & 140 (☎ **08 92 68 77 14, in English 08 92 68 41 14; adult/4-9yr €7.50/3.75; 🕒 12.30am-5.30pm**) Noctilien buses 120 and 121 link Montparnasse, Châtelet (Map pp184-5) and Gare du Nord with Roissy Charles de Gaulle, and bus 140 links Gare du Nord and Gare de l'Est with the airport. They run once an hour.

RATP bus 350 (☎ **08 92 68 77 14; adult/4-9yr €4.50/2.25 or 3 metro/bus tickets; 1hr; every 30min 🕒 5.45am-7pm**) This public bus links Aérogares 1 & 2 with Gare de l'Est (**Map pp180-1; rue du 8 Mai 1945, 10e; Ⓜ Gare de l'Est**) and with Gare du Nord (**Map pp180-1; 184 rue du Faubourg St-Denis, 10e; Ⓜ Gare du Nord**).

RATP bus 351 (☎ **08 92 68 77 14; adult/4-9yr €4.50/2.25 or 3 metro/bus tickets; 🕒 7am-9.30pm from Roissy Charles de Gaulle, 8.30am-8.20pm from Paris**) Links place de la Nation (**Map pp180-1; av du Trône, 11e; Ⓜ Nation**) with the airport every 30 minutes (1 hour).

RER B (☎ **08 90 36 10 10; adult/4-11yr €8.20/5.80; 🕒 5am-midnight**) RER line B3 links CDG1 and CDG2 with the city every 10 to 15 minutes (30 minutes).

AÉROPORT PARIS-BEAUVAIS

The special **Express Bus** (☎ **08 92 68 20 64; €13; 🕒 8.05am-10.40pm from Beauvais, 5.45am-8.05pm from Paris**) leaves **Parking Pershing** (**Map pp180-1; 1 blvd Pershing, 17e; Ⓜ Porte Maillot**), just west of Palais des Congrès de Paris, three hours before Ryanair departures (you can board up to 15 minutes before a flight) and leaves the airport 20 to 30 minutes after each arrival, dropping off just south of Palais des Congrès on Place de la Porte Maillot. Tickets can be purchased online (http://ticket.aeroportbeauvais.com), at the airport from Ryanair (☎ 03 44 11 41 41), or at a car-park kiosk. The trip takes one to 1¼ hours.

PUBLIC TRANSPORT

Paris' public transit system, operated by the **RATP** (**Régie Autonome des Transports Parisians; ☎ 32 46, 08 92 69 32 46; www.ratp.fr; 🕒 7am-9pm Mon-Fri, 9am-5pm Sat & Sun**), is one of the most efficient in the Western world. The same RATP tickets are valid on the metro, the RER, buses, the Montmartre funicular and Paris' three tramlines.

BUS

Paris' bus system runs between 5.45am and 12.30am Monday to Saturday. Services are drastically reduced on Sunday and public holidays (when buses run from 7am to 8.30pm) and from 8.30pm to 12.30am daily when a *service en soirée* (evening service) of 20 buses runs, followed by **Noctilien** (**www.noctilien.fr**) night buses, departing every hour between 12.30am and 5.30am.

Short bus rides (ie rides in one or two bus zones) cost one metro/bus ticket (€1.50); longer rides require two. Remember to cancel *(oblitérer)* single-journey tickets in the *composteur* (cancelling machine) next to the driver.

METRO & RER NETWORK

Paris' underground network consists of two interlinked systems: the Métropolitain (metro), with 14 lines and 372 stations;

and the RER (Réseau Express Régional), a network of suburban train lines. The last metro train on each line begins sometime between 12.35am and 1.04am, before starting up again around 5.30am. Some of Paris' attractions, particularly those on the Left Bank, can be reached more easily by the RER than by metro.

TOURIST PASSES

The Mobilis card allows unlimited travel for one day in two to six zones (€5.60 to €15.90; €4.55 to €13.70 for children aged four to 11 years), while the Paris Visite pass allows unlimited travel (including to/from airports) plus discounted entry to museums and activities. The version covering one to three zones costs €8.50/14/19/27.50 for one/two/three/five days.

OLIVIER CIRENDINI

Castle, Disneyland Paris

TRAVEL PASSES

If you're staying for a while, a combined travel pass might be a good investment. The **Navigo system** (**www.navigo.fr, in French**), similar to London's Oyster or Hong Kong's Octopus cards, consists of a weekly, monthly or yearly pass that can be recharged at Navigo machines in metro stations; you simply swipe the card across the electronic panel as you go through the turnstiles. The Navigo Découverte costs €5 and can be recharged for one week or more; you'll need a passport photo.

TAXI

To order a taxi, call Paris' **central taxi switchboard** (**☎ 01 45 30 30 30, passengers with reduced mobility 01 47 39 00 91; 🕑 24hrs**). The first piece of baggage is free; additional pieces over 5kg cost €1 extra, as do pick-ups from SNCF mainline stations. Most drivers won't carry more than three people, for insurance reasons.

Alpha Taxis (**☎ 01 45 85 85 85; www.alphataxis.com**)

Taxis Bleus (**☎ 01 49 36 29 48, 08 91 70 10 10; www.taxis-bleus.com**)

Taxis G7 (**☎ 01 47 39 47 39; www.taxisg7.fr, in French**).

AROUND PARIS

Bordered by five rivers – the Epte, Aisne, Eure, Yonne and Marne – the area around Paris is rather like a giant island, which explains why it's often referred to as the Île de France. In past centuries, this was where you'd find the country retreats of the French kings – most notably at the extravagant chateaux of Versailles and Fontainebleau. These days the royal castles have been joined by a kingdom of a rather more magical kind.

DISNEYLAND PARIS

In 1992, Mickey Mouse, Snow White and chums set up shop on reclaimed sugar-beet fields 32km east of Paris at a cost of €4.6 billion. Though not quite as over-the-top as its American cousins, **Disneyland Paris** (☎ 01 60 30 60 30; www.disneylandparis.com) is still capable of packing in the crowds – some 12 million visitors strolled through its gates in 2008.

The main **Disneyland Park** (🕐 9am-11pm daily mid-Jul–Aug, 10am-8pm Mon-Fri, 9am-8pm Sat & Sun Sep-Mar, 9am-8pm daily Apr-early May, 10am-8pm Mon-Fri, 9am-8pm Sat & Sun early May–mid-Jun, 9am-8pm daily mid-Jun–early Jul) is divided into five *pays* (lands), including an idealised version of an American **Main St**, a recreation of the American Wild West in **Frontierland**, futuristic **Discoveryland**, and the exotic-themed **Adventureland**, complete with *Indiana Jones* and *Pirates of the Carribean* connections. Unsurprisingly, the candy-coated heart of the park is **Fantasyland**, where you'll come face-to-face with fairy-tale characters such as Sleeping Beauty, Pinocchio, Peter Pan and Snow White.

The adjacent **Walt Disney Studios Park** (adult/under 3yr/3-11yr €46/free/38; 🕐 9am-6pm daily Jul-Sep, 10am-6pm Mon-Fri, 9am-6pm Sat & Sun Oct-Mar, 10am-6pm Apr-Jun) has a sound stage, backlot and animation studios illustrating how films, TV programs and cartoons are produced.

Standard **admission fees** (adult/under 3yr/3-11yr €46/free/38) only cover one park – to visit both you'll need a **Passe-Partout** (adult/under 3yr/3-11yr €56/free/48) ticket, or the two-/three-day **Hopper Ticket** (adult €103/128, child €84/105) if you want to spread your visit.

Marne-la-Vallée/Chessy, Disneyland's RER station, is served by line A4; trains run every 15 minutes or so from central Paris (€7.50, 35 to 40 minutes). The last train back to Paris leaves just after midnight.

VERSAILLES

pop 85,300

The **Château de Versailles** (☎ 08 10 81 16 14; www.chateauversailles.fr; adult/under 18yr €13.50/free, from 4pm/3pm in low/high season €10/free; 🕐 9am-6.30pm Tue-Sun Apr-Oct, to 5.30pm Tue-Sun Nov-Mar) was built in the mid-17th century by Louis XIV – the Roi Soleil (Sun King) – to project the absolute power of the French monarchy. Jointly designed by the architect Louis Le Vau (later replaced by Jules Hardouin-Mansart), the painter and interior designer Charles Le Brun, and the landscape artist André Le Nôtre, it's a fabulous monument to the wealth and ambition of the French aristocracy.

Guided tours (☎ 08 10 81 16 14; adult with/without palace ticket, Passeport or ticket to the Domaine de Marie-Antoinette €7.50/14.50, under 18yr €5.50; 🕐 9.45am-3.45pm Tue-Sun) explore several themes – life at court, classical music, 'Versailles splendours', the private apartments of Louis XV and Louis XI – although only a few are in English. Versailles is currently undergoing an enormous €370 million restoration program, so at least one part of the palace is likely to be clad in scaffolding until 2020.

RER line C5 (€2.80, every 15 minutes) goes from Paris' Left Bank RER stations to Versailles-Rive Gauche, 700m southeast of the chateau. SNCF operates up to 70 trains daily from Paris' Gare St-Lazare (€2.80) to Versailles-Rive Droite, 1.2km from the chateau. Versailles-Chantiers is served by half-hourly SNCF trains daily from Gare Montparnasse (€2.80); trains continue to Chartres (€10.90, 45 to 60 minutes).

CHARTRES

pop 40,250

The magnificent 13th-century **Cathédrale Notre Dame de Chartres** (☎ 02 37 21 22 07; www.diocese-chartres.com, in French; place de la Cathédrale; 🕐 8.30am-7.30pm) rises from rich farmland 88km southwest of Paris and dominates the medieval town. The original Romanesque cathedral was devastated in a fire in 1194, but remnants of it remain in the **Portail Royal** (Royal Portal) and the 103m-high **Clocher Vieux** (Old Bell Tower, also known as the South Tower). The rest of the cathedral predominantly dates from the 13th century, including many of the 172 glorious **stained-glass windows**, which are renowned for the depth and intensity of their 'Chartres blue' tones.

A platform emerges some 70m up the 112m-high **Clocher Neuf** (**new bell tower; adult/under 18yr/18-25yr €6.50/free/4.50, 1st Sun of certain months free; 9.30am-noon & 2-5.30pm Mon-Sat, 2-5.30pm Sun May-Aug, 9.30am-noon & 2-4.30pm Mon-Sat, 2-4.30pm Sun Sep-Apr**), with superb views of the cathedral's three-tiered flying buttresses and 19th-century copper roof.

More than 30 SNCF trains a day (20 on Sunday) link Paris' Gare Montparnasse (€12.90, 70 minutes) with Chartres via Versailles-Chantiers (€10.90, 45 minutes to one hour).

BRITTANY & NORMANDY

Famous for cows, cider and Camembert, the largely rural region of Normandy (www.normandie-tourisme.fr) is one of the most traditional areas of France, home to the historic D-Day beaches, the otherworldy spires of Mont St-Michel and the half-timbered houses and Gothic cathedral of Rouen, as well as the world's largest comic-strip – the Bayeux Tapestry.

Neighbouring Brittany has long considered itself a separate nation from the rest of France, with its own history, customs and Breton language; chuck in some scenic coastline, windswept islands and the eeriest stone circles this side of Stonehenge and you'll discover one of France's most fascinating corners.

ROUEN

pop 108,800

With its elegant spires, beautifully restored medieval quarter and soaring Gothic cathedral, the ancient city of Rouen is one of Normandy's highlights. The old city's

CHRISTOPHER WOOD

Cathédrale Notre Dame, Rouen

main thoroughfare, rue du Gros Horloge, runs from the cathedral west to **place du Vieux Marché**, where 19-year-old Joan of Arc was executed for heresy in 1431. Dedicated in 1979, the modernist **Église Jeanne d'Arc** (10am-noon & 2-6pm Apr-Oct, to 5.30pm Nov-Mar) marks the spot where Joan was burned at the stake.

Rouen's stunning Gothic **Cathédrale Notre Dame** (8am-6pm Tue-Sun, 2-6pm Mon) is the famous subject of a series of paintings by Monet, although the great man would hardly recognise the place these days – an ongoing restoration project has polished up the soot-blackened stone to its original brilliant-white colour.

The **Musée des Beaux-Arts** (02 35 71 28 40; esplanade Marcel Duchamp; adult/under 18yr/student €3/free/2; 10am-6pm Wed-Mon), housed in a grand structure erected in 1870, features canvases by Caravaggio, Rubens, Modigliani, Pissarro, Renoir, Sisley (lots) and (of course) several works by Monet, including a study of Rouen's cathedral (in room 2.33).

SLEEPING & EATING

Hôtel des Carmes (02 35 71 92 31; www.hoteldescarmes.com, in French; 33 place des Carmes; d €49-65, tr €67-77;) This sweet little hotel has 12 rooms decked out with patchwork quilts and vibrant colours; some even have cerulean-blue cloudscapes painted on the ceilings.

Le Vieux Carré (02 35 71 67 70; www.vieux-carre.fr; 34 rue Ganterie; d €58-62) Set around a cute little garden courtyard, this quiet half-timbered hotel has a delightfully old-fashioned *salon de thé* and 13 smallish rooms decorated with old postcard blowups and threadbare rugs.

Thé Majuscule (02 35 71 15 66; 8 place de la Calende; plats du jour €10.50; restaurant noon-2pm Mon-Sat, salon de thé 2.30-6.30pm Mon-Sat) Downstairs it's a typically chaotic French secondhand bookshop, upstairs a homey tearoom with homemade *tartes*, salads, cakes and exotic teas (€3.30).

Pascaline (02 35 89 67 44; 5 rue de la Poterne; menus €14.90-26.90; lunch & dinner) A top spot for a great-value *formule midi* (lunchtime menu), this bustling bistro serves up French cuisine in typically Parisian surroundings – think net curtains, white tablecloths and chuffing coffee machines.

Les Maraîchers (02 35 71 57 73; www.les-maraichers.fr, in French; 37 place du Vieux Marché; menus €16-25; lunch & dinner) All gleaming mirrors, polished wood and colourful floor tiles, this bistro – established in 1912 – has a genuine zinc bar and a warm and very French ambience.

GETTING THERE & AWAY

From **Gare Rouen-Rive Droite** (rue Jeanne d'Arc), trains go direct to Paris' Gare St-Lazare (€19.30, 1¼ hours, 25 daily Monday to Friday, 14 to 19 daily weekends), Caen (€21.80, 1½ hours, eight daily), Dieppe (€9.90, 45 minutes, 10 to 15 daily Monday to Saturday, five Sunday) and Le Havre (€12.90, 50 minutes, 18 daily Monday to Saturday, 10 Sunday). Tickets are sold at the **Boutique SNCF** (20 rue aux Juifs; 10am-7pm Mon-Sat).

BAYEUX

pop 14,600

The world's most celebrated embroidery, the **Bayeux Tapestry** (02 31 51 25 50; www.tapisserie-bayeux.fr; rue de Nesmond; adult/student incl audio guide €7.80/3.80; 9am-6.30pm mid-Mar–mid-Nov, to 7pm May-Aug, 9.30am-12.30pm & 2-6pm mid-Nov–mid-Mar) recounts the conquest of England from an unashamedly Norman perspective. The final showdown at the Battle of Hastings is depicted in graphic fashion, complete with severed limbs and decapitated heads (along the bottom of scene 52), while Halley's Comet, which blazed across the sky in 1066, appears in scene 32. Scholars believe that the 68.3m-long tapestry was commissioned by Bishop Odo of Bayeux, William the Conquerer's half-brother, for the opening of Bayeux cathedral in 1077.

Bus Verts (☎ 08 10 21 42 14; www.busverts.fr) runs to Caen (bus 30; €4, one hour, three or four daily Monday to Friday except holidays) and provides regular buses to the D-Day beaches. The most useful train link from Bayeux is Caen (€5.50, 20 minutes, 13 to 19 daily Monday to Saturday, eight Sunday), from where there are connections to Paris' Gare St-Lazare (€32) and Rouen (€24.60).

D-DAY BEACHES

Early on 6 June 1944, Allied troops stormed ashore along 80km of beaches north of Bayeux, code-named (from west to east) Utah, Omaha, Gold, Juno and Sword. The landings on D-Day – called Jour J in French – were followed by the Battle of Normandy, which ultimately led to the liberation of Europe from Nazi occupation.

The most brutal fighting on D-Day took place 15km northwest of Bayeux along the stretch of coastline now known as **Omaha Beach**, where you'll find the huge **American Military Cemetery** (☎ 02 31 51 62 00; www.abmc.gov; Colleville-sur-Mer; 9am-6pm mid-Apr–mid-Sep, 9am-5pm mid-Sep–mid-Apr) at Colleville-sur-Mer, the largest American cemetery in Europe.

To make it possible to unload cargo without having to capture one of the heavily defended Channel ports, the Allies established two prefabricated breakwaters code-named Mulberry Harbours. One of them can still be viewed at low tide at **Arromanches**, a seaside town 10km northeast of Bayeux. Nearby **Juno Beach**, 12km east of Arromanches, was stormed by Canadian troops on D-Day, while original bomb craters and German gun emplacements can be seen at the nearby **Pointe du Hoc Ranger Memorial** (☎ 02 31 51 90 70; admission free; 24hr).

Caen's hi-tech museum, **Mémorial – Un Musée pour la Paix** (Memorial – A Museum for Peace; ☎ 02 31 06 06 45; www.memorial-caen.fr; esplanade Général Eisenhower; adult/under 10yr & war veteran/student €16/free/15; 9am-7pm Mar-Oct, 9.30am-6pm Nov-Feb, closed last 3 weeks Jan) uses sound, lighting, film, animation and lots of exhibits to explore the events of WWII, the D-Day landings and the ensuing Cold War.

TOURS

Caen Mémorial (☎ 02 31 06 06 45; www.memorial-caen.fr; adult/under 18yr €69/55; tours 1pm Oct-Mar, 9am & 2pm Apr-Sep) Excellent four- to five-hour minibus tours around the landing beaches. The price includes entry to the Mémorial.

Normandy Sightseeing Tours (☎ 02 31 51 70 52; www.normandywebguide.com) From May to October (and on request the rest of the year), this experienced outfit offers morning (adult/under 10 years/student €40/25/35) and afternoon tours (€45/30/40) of various beaches and cemeteries. These can be combined into an all-day excursion (€75/45/65).

Normandy Tours (☎ 02 31 92 10 70; www.normandy-tours-hotel.com; 26 place de la Gare; adult/student €41/36; year-round) Bayeux-based operator offering four- or five-hour tours of the main sites at 8.15am and 1.15pm.

MONT ST-MICHEL

On a rocky island opposite the coastal town of Pontorson, connected to the mainland by a narrow causeway, the sky-scraping turrets of the abbey of

Mont St-Michel (☎ 02 33 89 80 00; www.monuments-nationaux.fr; adult/under 18yr/18-25yr incl guided tour €8.50/free/5; ⌚ 9am-7pm May-Aug, 9.30am-6pm Sep-Apr, last entry 1hr before closing) provide one of France's iconic sights. The surrounding bay is notorious for its fast-rising tides: at low tide the Mont is surrounded by bare sand for miles around, but at high tide, barely six hours later, the bay, causeway and nearby car parks can be submerged.

At the base of the mount, just inside Porte de l'Avancée as you enter the abbey, the **Mont St-Michel tourist office** (☎ 02 33 60 14 30; www.ot-montsaintmichel.com; ⌚ 9am-7pm Jul & Aug, 9am-12.30pm & 2-6.30pm Mon-Sat, 9am-noon & 2-6pm Sun Apr-Jun & Sep, 9am-noon & 2-6pm Mon-Sat, 10am-noon & 2-5pm Sun Oct-Mar) sells detailed visitor maps (€3). From here, a winding cobbled street leads up to the **Église Abbatiale** (Abbey Church), incorporating elements of both Norman and Gothic architecture. Other notable sights include the arched **cloître** (cloister), the barrel-roofed **réfectoire** (dining hall), and the Gothic **Salle des Hôtes** (Guest Hall), dating from 1213. A one-hour tour is included in the ticket price: English tours are run twice a day (11am and 3pm) in winter, hourly in summer. From Monday to Saturday in July and August, there are illuminated *nocturnes* (night-time visits) with music from 7pm to 10pm.

ST-MALO

pop 49,600

The pretty port of St-Malo is inextricably tied up with the briny blue: the town became a key harbour during the 17th and 18th centuries as a base for merchant ships and government-sanctioned privateers, and these days it's a busy cross-Channel ferry-port and summertime getaway.

The city's sturdy ramparts were constructed at the end of the 17th century by the military architect Vauban, and afford fine views of the old walled city – you can access them from all of the main city *portes* (gates). From their northern stretch, you'll see the remains of the former prison, the **Fort National** (adult/child €4/2; ⌚ Jun-Sep), and the rocky islet of **Île du Grand Bé**, where the great St-Malo–born 18th-century writer Chateaubriand is buried. You can walk across at low tide, but check the tide times with the tourist office.

The battle to liberate St-Malo destroyed around 80% of the old city during August 1944; damage to the **Cathédrale St-Vincent** (place Jean de Châtillon; ⌚ 9.30am-6pm except during Mass) was particularly severe.

Within **Château de St-Malo**, built by the dukes of Brittany in the 15th and 16th centuries, is the **Musée du Château** (☎ 02

MAISON DE CLAUDE MONET

Monet's home for the last 43 years of his life is now the delightful **Maison et Jardins de Claude Monet** (☎ 02 32 51 28 21; www.fondation-monet.com; adult/7-12yr/student €5.50/3/4, gardens only €4; ⌚ 9.30am-6pm Tue-Sun Apr-Oct), where you can view the famous gardens and lily ponds that often featured in his canvases.

The gardens are in Giverny, 66km southeast of Rouen. Several trains (€9.60, 40 minutes) leave Rouen before noon; with hourly return trains between 5pm and 10pm (till 9pm on Saturday). From Paris' Gare St-Lazare two early-morning trains run to Vernon (€11.90, 50 minutes), 7km west of Giverny.

99 40 71 57; adult/child €5.20/2.60; ⌚ 10am-noon & 2-6pm daily Apr-Sep, Tue-Sun Oct-Mar).

The attractions at the fantastic **Grand Aquarium** (☎ 02 99 21 19 00; av Général Patton; adult/child €14/10; ⌚ at least 10am-6pm Feb-Dec, to 8pm Jul & Aug) include a minisubmarine descent and a *bassin tactile* (touch pool), where you can fondle rays, turbots – even a baby shark. The aquarium is 4km south of the city.

SLEEPING & EATING

Hôtel San Pedro (☎ 02 99 40 88 57; www.sanpedro-hotel.com; 1 rue Ste-Anne; s €46-48, d €53-70; ⌚ Feb-Nov; 💻) Tucked at the back of the old city, the San Pedro has cool, crisp, neutral-toned decor with subtle splashes of colour, plus friendly service and superb sea views.

Hôtel de l'Univers (☎ 02 99 40 89 52; www.hotel-univers-saintmalo.com, in French; place Chateaubriand; s €48-78, d €63-95) Right beside Porte St-Vincent, this cream-coloured two-starrer is perfectly poised for St-Malo's attractions and boasts its own maritime-themed bar.

Le Biniou (☎ 02 99 56 47 57; 3 place de la Croix du Fief; crêpes €2-8, menus €10; ⌚ 10am-1am summer, closed Thu winter) St-Malo has no shortage of crêperies, but this one – with cute little illustrations of Breton *biniou* (bagpipes) – is a time-honoured fave. Savour 100 galettes and crêpes, including the house speciality: apples flambéed in Calvados.

Côté Jardin (☎ 02 99 81 63 11; 36 rue Dauphine, St-Servan; menus €25; ⌚ lunch Tue-Sun, dinner Tue & Thu-Sun) The charming, friendly Côté Jardin presents regional and traditional French cuisine, with a scenic terrace overlooking the marina and St-Malo's walled city.

GETTING THERE & AWAY

Brittany Ferries (☎ reservations in France 08 25 82 88 28, in UK 0870 556 1600; www.brittany-ferries.com) sails between St-Malo and Portsmouth, and **Condor Ferries** (☎ France 08 25 13 51 35, UK 0870 243 5140; www.condorferries.co.uk) runs to/from Poole and Weymouth via Jersey or Guernsey.

From April to September, **Compagnie Corsaire** (☎ 08 25 13 80 35) and **Vedettes de St-Malo** (☎ 02 23 18 41 08; www.vedettes-saint-malo.com) run a **Bus de Mer** (Sea Bus; adult/child return €6/4; ⌚ hourly) shuttle service (10 minutes) between St-Malo and Dinard.

TGV train services run between St-Malo and Rennes (€11.60, one hour), and there are direct trains to Paris' Gare Montparnasse (€58, three hours).

LOIRE VALLEY

One step removed from the French capital and poised on the frontier between northern and southern France, the Loire was historically the place where princes, dukes and notable nobles established their country getaways, and the countryside is littered with some of the most extravagant architecture outside Versailles.

For full-blown chateau splendour, you can't top **Chambord** (☎ 02 54 50 50 20; www.chambord.org; adult/under 18yr/18-25yr €9.50/free/7.50, €1 reduction Jan-Mar & Oct-Dec; ⌚ 9am-7.30pm mid-Jul–mid-Aug, to 6.15pm mid-Mar–mid-Jul & mid-Aug–Sep, to 5.15pm, Jan–mid-Mar & Oct-Dec), constructed from 1519 by François I as a lavish base for hunting game in the Sologne forests, but eventually used for just 42 days during the king's 32-year reign (1515-47). The chateau's most famous feature is the double-helix staircase, attributed by some to Leonardo da Vinci, who lived in Amboise (34km southwest) from 1516 until his death three years later.

Several times daily there are 1½-hour **guided tours** (€4) in English. Free *son et lumière* (sound and light) shows, known

THE MORBIHAN MEGALITHS

Predating Stonehenge by 100 years, the **Alignements de Carnac** (Garnag in Breton) consist of more than 3000 upright stones scattered across the countryside between **Carnac-Ville** and the village of **Locmariaquer** in southern Brittany. They were erected between 5000 BC and 3500 BC, but academics are still divided about their original purpose. Were they a sacred site? A phallic fertility cult? A celestial calendar? Or something else altogether?

Guided tours (€4) run in French year-round and in English at 3pm Wednesday, Thursday and Friday from early July to late August. Sign up for guided visits at the **Maison des Mégalithes** (☎ 02 97 52 89 99; rte des Alignements; admission free; 9am-8pm Jul & Aug, to 5.15pm Sep-Apr, to 7pm May & Jun).

as **Les Clairs de Lune**, are projected onto the chateau's facade nightly from July to mid-September.

Chambord is 16km east of Blois, 45km southwest of Orléans and 17km northeast of Cheverny.

LYON

pop 467,400

Gourmets, eat your heart out: Lyon is *the* gastronomic capital of France, with a lavish table of piggy-driven dishes and delicacies to savour. The city has been a commercial, industrial and banking powerhouse for the past 500 years, and is still France's second-largest conurbation, with outstanding art museums, a dynamic cultural life, a busy clubbing and drinking scene, green parks and a Unesco-listed Old Town.

INFORMATION

Tourist office (☎ 04 72 77 69 69; www.lyon-france.com; place Bellecour, 2e; 9am-6pm; M Bellecour)

SIGHTS

VIEUX LYON

Old Lyon, with its cobblestone streets and **medieval and Renaissance houses** below Fourvière hill, is divided into three quarters: St-Paul at the northern end, St-Jean in the middle and St-Georges in the south. Lovely old buildings languish on **rue du Bœuf**, **rue St-Jean** and **rue des Trois Maries**. The partly Romanesque **Cathédrale St-Jean** (place St-Jean, 5e; 8am-noon & 2-7.30pm Mon-Fri, 8am-noon & 2-7pm Sat & Sun; M Vieux Lyon), seat of Lyon's 133rd bishop, was built from the late 11th to the early 16th centuries. The **astronomical clock** chimes at noon, 2pm, 3pm and 4pm.

FOURVIÈRE

Over two millennia ago, the Romans built the city of Lugdunum on the slopes of Fourvière. Today, Lyon's 'hill of prayer' – topped by a basilica and the **Tour Métallique**, an Eiffel Tower–like structure built in 1893 and used as a TV transmitter – affords spectacular views of the city and its two rivers. Footpaths wind uphill but the funicular departing from place Édouard Commette is the least taxing way up; a return ticket costs €2.20.

Crowning the hill is the 27m-high **Basilique Notre Dame de Fourvière** (☎ 04 78 25 86 19; www.fourviere.org; 7am-7pm), a superb example of exaggerated 19th-century ecclesiastical architecture. **Rooftop tours** (adult/under 12yr €5/3;

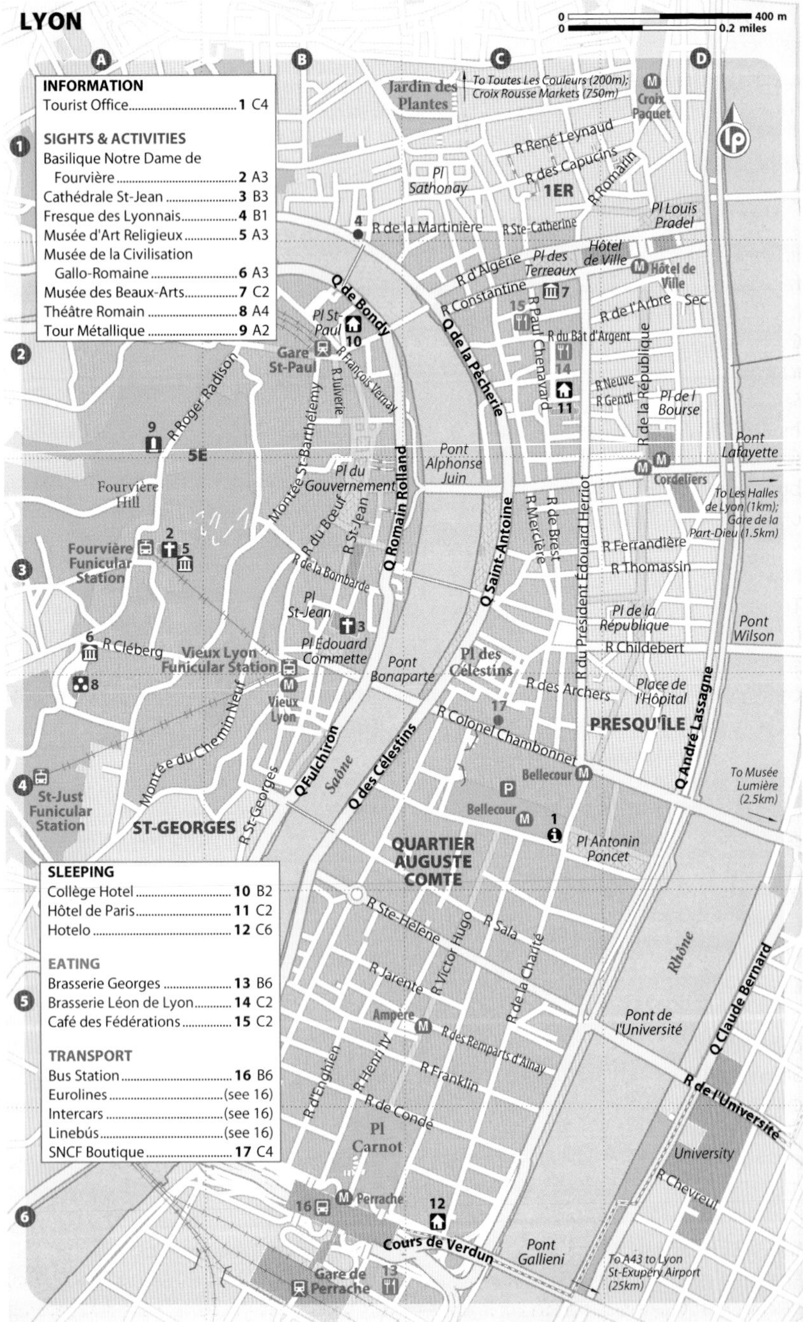
LYON
0 400 m
0 0.2 miles
INFORMATION
Tourist Office 1 C4
SIGHTS & ACTIVITIES
Basilique Notre Dame de Fourvière 2 A3
Cathédrale St-Jean 3 B3
Fresque des Lyonnais 4 B1
Musée d'Art Religieux 5 A3
Musée de la Civilisation Gallo-Romaine 6 A3
Musée des Beaux-Arts 7 C2
Théâtre Romain 8 A4
Tour Métallique 9 A2
SLEEPING
Collège Hotel 10 B2
Hôtel de Paris 11 C2
Hotelo 12 C6
EATING
Brasserie Georges 13 B6
Brasserie Léon de Lyon 14 C2
Café des Fédérations 15 C2
TRANSPORT
Bus Station 16 B6
Eurolines (see 16)
Intercars (see 16)
Linebús (see 16)
SNCF Boutique 17 C4
Jardin des Plantes
To Toutes Les Couleurs (200m); Croix Rousse Markets (750m)
Croix Paquet
R René Leynaud
R des Capucins
R Romarin
Pl Sathonay
1ER
Pl Louis Pradel
R de la Martinière
R Ste-Catherine
Hôtel de Ville
Pl des Terreaux
R d'Algérie
R Constantine
Hôtel de Ville
R de l'Arbre Sec
Q de Bondy
Pl St-Paul
Gare St-Paul
R François Vernay
R Juiverie
Q de la Pêcherie
R Paul Chenavard
R du Bât d'Argent
R Neuve
R Gentil
R de la République
Pl de l Bourse
R Roger Radisson
5E
Montée St-Barthélemy
Pont Alphonse Juin
Pont Lafayette
Cordeliers
To Les Halles de Lyon (1km); Gare de la Part-Dieu (1.5km)
Fourvière Hill
Pl du Gouvernement
R du Bœuf
R St-Jean
Q Romain Rolland
Q Saint-Antoine
R Mercière
R de Brest
R du Président Édouard Herriot
R Ferrandière
R Thomassin
Fourvière Funicular Station
R de la Bombarde
Pl St-Jean
Pl de la République
Pont Wilson
R Childebert
R Cléberg
Vieux Lyon Funicular Station
Pl Édouard Commette
Pont Bonaparte
Pl des Célestins
R des Archers
Place de l'Hôpital
Vieux Lyon
Montée du Chemin Neuf
R Colonel Chambonnet
PRESQU'ÎLE
Q André Lassagne
St-Just Funicular Station
Q Fulchiron
Saône
Q des Célestins
Bellecour
To Musée Lumière (2.5km)
R St-Georges
ST-GEORGES
Bellecour
Pl Antonin Poncet
QUARTIER AUGUSTE COMTE
R Ste-Hélène
R Sala
R Victor Hugo
R de la Charité
Rhône
R Jarente
Ampère
R des Remparts d'Ainay
Pont de l'Université
Q Claude Bernard
R Henri IV
R Franklin
R d'Enghien
R de Condé
R de l'Université
Pl Carnot
University
R Chevreul
Perrache
Cours de Verdun
Pont Gallieni
To A43 to Lyon St-Exupéry Airport (25km)
Gare de Perrache

(🕑 2.30pm & 4pm daily Jun-Sep, 2.30pm & 4pm Wed & Sun Apr, May & Oct, 2.30pm & 3.30pm Wed & Sun Nov) climax on the stone-sculpted roof.

Sacred treasures are showcased in the **Musée d'Art Religieux** (☎ 04 78 25 13 01; 8 place de Fourvière, 5e; adult/under 26yr €6/4; 🕑 10am-12.30pm & 2-5.30pm daily; Ⓜ Fourvière funicular station), while Gallo-Roman artefacts take centre stage at the **Musée de la Civilisation Gallo-Romaine** (Museum of Gallo-Roman Civilisation; ☎ 04 72 38 39 30; www.musees-gallo-romains.com, in French; 17 rue Cléberg, 5e; adult/under 18yr/18-25yr €3.80/free/2.30, free Thu; 🕑 10am-6pm Tue-Sun; Ⓜ Fourvière funicular station). Next door, the **Théâtre Romain**, built around 15 BC, once sat an audience of 10,000.

PRESQU'ÎLE

The centrepiece of **place des Terreaux** (Ⓜ Hôtel de Ville) is the 19th-century fountain sculpted by Frédéric-Auguste Bartholdi, creator of the Statue of Liberty.

Nearby, the **Musée des Beaux-Arts** (☎ 04 72 10 17 40; www.mba-lyon.fr; 20 place des Terreaux, 1er; adult/under 18yr €6/free; 🕑 10am-6pm Wed, Thu & Sat-Mon, 10.30am-6pm Fri; Ⓜ Hôtel de Ville) showcases France's finest collection of sculptures and paintings outside Paris. West of place des Terreaux, well-known Lyonnais peer out from the seven-storey **Fresque des Lyonnais** (cnr rue de la Martinière & quai de la Pêcherie, 1er; Ⓜ Hôtel de Ville) – look out for the yellow-haired Little Prince, created by Lyon-born author Antoine de St-Exupéry (1900–44), amid the frescoed characters on the wall.

OTHER ATTRACTIONS

Cinema's glorious beginnings are showcased at the **Musée Lumière** (☎ 04 78 78 18 95; www.institut-lumiere.org; 25 rue du Premier Film, 8e; adult/under 18yr €6/5, audio guide €3; 🕑 11am-6.30pm Tue-Sun; Ⓜ Monplaisir-Lumière), 3km southeast along cours Gambetta. The museum is housed inside the art nouveau home of Antoine Lumière, whose sons Auguste and Louis shot the world's first motion picture, *La Sortie des Usines Lumières* (Exit of the Lumières Factories) in 19 March 1895.

SLEEPING

Hôtel de Paris (☎ 04 78 28 00 95; www.hoteldeparis-lyon.com; 16 rue de la Platière, 1er; s/d from €48/62; Ⓜ Hôtel de Ville; ❄ 💻) This fantastic-value hotel resides in a 19th-century bourgeois building. The funkiest rooms sport retro 1970s decor with chocolate-and-turquoise or candyfloss-pink colour schemes.

Hotelo (☎ 04 78 37 39 03; www.hotelo-lyon.com; 37 cours de Verdun, 2e; s/d/tr from €79/90/97; Ⓜ Perrache) Our hot choice around Gare de Perrache, this striking newbie with a refreshingly contemporary design. Studios have a kitchenette and one room is perfectly fitted out for travellers with disabilities.

OUR PICK **Collège Hotel** (☎ 04 72 10 05 05; www.college-hotel.com; 5 place St-Paul, 5e; d €110-140; Ⓜ Vieux Lyon; ❄ 💻) Superstylish hotel, although those with a dislike of white might not appreciate it. Reception is decked out in warm, ochre tones, while the white minimalism of the bedrooms is dazzling. Enjoy a balcony breakfast, savour the schoolroom-style breakfast room, or lounge on the roof garden.

EATING

The traditional place to eat is the *bouchon* (literally meaning 'bottle stopper' or 'traffic jam', but in Lyon a small, friendly bistro).

Toutes les Couleurs (☎ 04 72 00 03 95; 26 rue Imbert Colomès, 1er; plats du jour €9.50, 2-course menus €13 & €16.50, 3-course menus €18, €21 & €25; 🕑 lunch Tue-Fri, lunch & dinner Fri &

SALLY DILLON

Detail of a tapestry at Château de Cheverny

IF YOU LIKE...

The sheer number of **Loire chateaux** can be daunting. Here are our must-sees.

- **Cheverny** (☎ 02 54 79 96 29; www.chateau-cheverny.fr; adult/7-14yr €7/3.40; 9.15am-6.45pm Jul & Aug, 9.15am-6.15pm Apr-Jun & Sep, 9.45am-5.30pm Oct, 9.45am-5pm Nov-Mar) Thought by many to be the most perfectly proportioned chateau of all.
- **Chenonceau** (☎ 02 47 23 90 07; www.chenonceau.com; adult/student & 7-18yr €10/7.50, incl audio guide €14/11.50; 9am-8pm Jul & Aug, 9am-7.30pm Jun & Sep, 9am-7pm Apr & May, 9.30am-5pm or 6pm Oct-Mar) One of the most architecturally attractive (and busiest) of the Loire chateaux, famous for its 60m-long Grande Gallerie spanning the Cher River.
- **Azay-le-Rideau** (☎ 02 47 45 42 04; adult/18-25yr €7.50/4.80; 9.30am-7pm Jul & Aug, 9.30am-6pm Apr-Jun & Sep, 10am-12.30pm & 2-5.30pm Oct-Mar) A moat-ringed wonder, decorated with geometric windows, turrets and a famous loggia staircase.
- **Langeais** (☎ 02 47 96 72 60; adult/under 10yr/10-17yr €7.50/free/4; 9.30am-7pm Jul & Aug, to 6.30pm Feb-Jun & Sep-mid-Nov, 10am-5pm mid-Nov-Jan) Classic medieval fortress, complete with drawbridge, battlements and ruined donjon (keep).
- **Château Royal d'Amboise** (☎ 02 47 57 00 98; place Michel Debré, Amboise; adult/7-14yr/15-25yr €9/5.30/7.50; 9am-7pm Jul & Aug, to 6.30pm Apr-Jun, to 6pm Sep & Oct, to 5.30pm Mar & early Nov, to 12.30pm Jan, Feb & mid-Nov-Dec) Highlights include the Flamboyant Gothic wing and the Chapelle St-Hubert, da Vinci's final resting place.
- **Clos Lucé** (☎ 02 47 57 00 73; www.vinci-closluce.com; adult/6-15yr/student Mar-mid-Nov €12.50/7/9.50, mid-Nov-Mar €9.50/6/7; 9am-8pm Jul-Aug, 9am-7pm Feb-Jun & Sep-Oct, 9am-6pm Nov-Jan) Inventions at da Vinci's former home include an automobile, tank, parachute, turbine and helicopter.
- **Château Royal de Blois** (☎ 02 54 90 33 32; place du Château, Blois; adult/6-17yr/student €7.50/3/5; 9am-7pm Jul & Aug, 9am-6.30pm Apr-Jun & Sep, 9am-12.30pm & 1.30-5.30pm Oct-Mar) Blois' historic castle showcases all the key periods of French architecture.

Sat; M Croix-Paquet) Vegetarians in France for a while will be in seventh heaven at this 100% authentic *restaurant bio.*

Brasserie Georges (☎ 04 72 56 54 54; www.brasseriegeorges.com; 30 cours de Verdun, 2e; breakfasts €11.50-14, menus €20-25, seafood platters €36.50-66; 8am-11.15pm Sun-Thu, to 12.15am Fri & Sat; M Perrache) At this huge art deco brasserie, up to 2000 punters tuck into hearty portions of onion soup, mussels, sauerkraut and seafood.

Brasserie Léon de Lyon (☎ 04 72 10 11 12; www.leondelyon.com; 1 rue Pléney, 1er; plats du jour €15, 2-/3-course menus du jour €23/26; lunch & dinner; M Hôtel de Ville) Legendary Lyonnais chef Jean-Paul Lacombe has turned his Michelin-starred gastronomic restaurant into a soulful brasserie – same 1904 decor, similar culinary products, more-affordable prices.

Café des Fédérations (☎ 04 78 28 26 00; www.lesfedeslyon.com, in French; 8 rue Major Martin, 1er; lunch/dinner menus €19.50/24; lunch & dinner Mon-Fri; M Hôtel de Ville) B&W photos of old Lyon speckle the wood-panelled walls of the city's best-known *bouchon.*

Lyon has two superb outdoor food markets: **Presqu'île** (quai St-Antoine, 2e; Tue-Sun morning; M Bellecour or Cordeliers) and **Croix Rousse** (blvd de la Croix Rousse, 4e; Tue-Sun morning; M Croix Rousse), as well as a legendary indoor market, **Les Halles de Lyon** (102 cours Lafayette, 3e; 8am-7pm Tue-Sat, 8am-2pm Sun; M Part-Dieu).

GETTING THERE & AWAY

Flights to/from European cities land at **Lyon St-Exupéry airport** (☎ 08 26 80 08 26; www.lyon.aeroport.fr), 25km east of the city. **Satobus** (☎ 04 72 68 72 17; www.satobus.com) runs city-centre shuttles (single/return €8.60/15.20) every 20 minutes between 5am or 6am and midnight.

In the Perrache complex, **Eurolines** (☎ 04 72 56 95 30), **Intercars** (☎ 04 78 37 20 80) and Spain-oriented **Linebús** (☎ 04 72 41 72 27) have offices on the bus-station level of the Centre d'Échange.

Lyon has two mainline train stations: **Gare de Perrache** (M Perrache) and **Gare de la Part-Dieu** (M Part-Dieu), which mainly handles long-haul trains. Tickets are sold at the **SNCF Boutique** (2 place Bellecour, 2e; 9am-6.45pm Mon-Fri, 10am-6.30pm Sat; M Bellecour).

GETTING AROUND

Buses, trams, a four-line metro and two funiculars linking Vieux Lyon to Fourvière are run by **TCL** (☎ 08 20 42 70 00; www.tcl.fr, in French; 5 rue de la République, 1er; 7.30am-6.30pm Mon-Fri, 9am-noon & 1.30-5pm Sat; M Bellecour). Public transport runs from around 5am to midnight. Tickets for all forms of public transport cost €1.50/12.50 for one/carnet of 10. Remember to time-stamp your ticket.

ATLANTIC COAST

Though the Côte d'Azur is the most popular beach spot in France, the many seaside resorts along the Atlantic coast are fast catching up.

BIARRITZ

pop 30,700

As ritzy as its name suggests, this stylish coastal town, 8km west of Bayonne, took off in the mid-19th century when Napoleon III visited regularly. It glimmers with architectural treasures from the belle époque and art deco eras, but these days its big waves and beachy lifestyle are more popular with European surfers.

Biarritz' fashionable beaches, particularly the **Grande Plage** and **Plage Miramar**, are end-to-end bodies on hot summer days. North of Pointe St-Martin, the adrenaline-pumping surf beaches of **Anglet** (the final *t* is pronounced) continue northwards for more than 4km. Beyond long, exposed **Plage de la Côte des Basques**, some 500m south of Port Vieux, are **Plage de Marbella** and **Plage de la Milady**.

SLEEPING & EATING

La Maison du Lierre (☎ 05 59 24 06 00; www.maisondulierre.com; 3 av du Jardin Public; r €56-139) This place has 23 exquisitely decorated rooms named for local plants in the adjacent Jardin Public, and many rooms have garden views.

Hôtel Mirano (☎ 05 59 23 11 63; www.hotelmirano.fr, in French; 11 av Pasteur; r €70-110) Squiggly purple, orange and black wallpaper and oversize orange perspex light fittings are some of the rad '70s touches at this boutique retro hotel, a 10-minute stroll from the town centre.

Le Corsaire (☎ 05 59 24 63 72; Port des Pêcheurs; mains €11-23.50; lunch & dinner Tue-Sat) Down by the water's edge, sit out on the terrace to savour dishes like grilled cod with chorizo. The neighbouring seafood restaurants in this little harbourside setting offer similar quality and prices.

Bistrot des Halles (☎ 05 59 24 21 22; 1 rue du Centre; mains €14.50-17; lunch & dinner) One of a cluster of decent restaurants along rue du Centre that get their produce directly from the nearby covered market, this bustling place serves excellent fish and other fresh fare from the blackboard menu.

GETTING THERE & AWAY

Biarritz-La Négresse train station is about 3km south of the town centre, and is served by buses 2 and 9 (B and C on Sundays).

LOURDES

pop 15,700 / elev 400m

Lourdes has been one of the world's most important pilgrimage sites since 1858, when 14-year-old Bernadette Soubirous (1844–79) saw the Virgin Mary in a series of 18 visions that came to her in a grotto. The most revered site is the **Grotte de Massabielle** (Massabielle Cave), lit by flickering candles left by previous pilgrims. The 19 holy **baths** (generally 9-11am & 2.30-4pm Mon-Sat, 2-4pm Sun & holy days) are said to cure all kinds of diseases and ailments – the most recent confirmed case was that of an Italian, Anna Santaniello, who was apparently cured of chronic rheumatism in 2005.

The main 19th-century section of the **sanctuaries** is divided between the neo-Byzantine Basilique du Rosaire, the crypt and the spire-topped Basilique Supérieure (Upper Basilica). All four places of worship open 6am to 10pm in summer and 7am to 7pm in winter.

Lourdes is well connected by train; destinations include Bayonne (€18.90, 1¾ hours, up to four daily) and Toulouse (€22.20, 1¾ hours, six daily). There are four daily TGVs to Paris' Gare Montparnasse (€91.80, six hours).

LANGUEDOC-ROUSSILLON

Languedoc-Roussillon is three separate regions rolled into one. Bas Languedoc (Lower Languedoc) is known for bullfighting, rugby and robust red wines, and is home to all the major sights, including the Roman amphitheatre at Nîmes and the turret-topped town of Carcassonne.

CARCASSONNE

pop 45,500

With its witch's hat turrets and walled city, Carcassonne looks like some fairytale fortress from afar – but the medieval magic's more than a little tarnished by an annual influx of over four million visitors.

ANCIENT ART & ARCHITECTURE COLLECTION LTD/ALAMY

Cave painting in Grotte de Lascaux

IF YOU LIKE...

The Dordogne is home to some of Europe's finest **prehistoric art**, especially around the Vézère Valley. Many of the caves are closed in winter, and get very busy in summer, so reserve tours well ahead and ask about the availability of English-language tours.

- **Grotte de Lascaux** (☎ 05 53 51 95 03; www.semitour.com; adult/6-12yr €8.30/5.30, joint ticket with Le Thot €11.50/7.80; 9am-8pm Jul & Aug, 9.30am-6.30pm Sep & Apr-Jun, 10am-12.30pm & 2-6pm Oct–mid-Nov, 10am-12.30pm & 2-5.30pm mid-Nov–Mar) France's most celebrated cave paintings, near Montignac, were closed in 1963 to prevent damage, but the most famous sections have been recreated in a second cave nearby. Look out for the huge 5.5m bull, the largest cave drawing ever found.
- **Grotte de Font de Gaume** (☎ 05 53 06 86 00; www.leseyzies.com/grottes-ornees; adult/under 18yr/18-25yr €6.50/free/4.50; 9.30am-5.30pm mid-May–mid-Sep, 9.30am-12.30pm & 2-5.30pm mid-Sep-mid-May) Bison, reindeer, horses, mammoths, bears and wolves all feature in this cave 1km northeast of Les-Eyzies-de-Tazac.
- **Abri du Cap Blanc** (☎ 05 53 06 86 00; adult/under 18yr €6.50/free; 9.30am-5.30pm mid-May–mid-Sep, 9.30am-12.30pm & 2-5.30pm mid-Sep–mid-May, closed Sat year-round) An unusual sculpture gallery of horses, bison and deer about 7km east of Les-Eyzies.
- **Grotte de Rouffignac** (☎ 05 53 05 41 71; www.grottederouffignac.fr; adult/child €6.20/3.90; tours in French 9-11.30am & 2-6pm Jul & Aug, 10-11.30am & 2-5pm Mar-Jun, Sep & Oct) An electric train ventures deep underground into the 'Cave of 100 Mammoths', 15km north of Les-Eyzies-de-Tazac.

You can borrow an audio guide to **La Cité** (The Old City; €3 for 2hr) at the **tourist office** (☎ 04 68 10 24 30; www.carcassonne-tourisme.com; 28 rue de Verdun; 9am-7pm Jul & Aug, to 6pm Mon-Sat, to 1pm Sun Sep-Jun) or one of the summer annexes: **La Cité** (Porte Narbonnaise; year-round) or **Ville Basse** (av Joffre; mid-Apr–Oct).

The old city is dramatically illuminated at night and enclosed by two **rampart walls** punctuated by 52 stone towers, Europe's largest city fortifications. A drawbridge leads to the old gate of **Porte Narbonnaise** and rue Cros Mayrevieille en route to place Château and the 12th-century **Château Comtal** (**adult/under 18yr/18-25yr €7.50/free/4.80; 10am-6.30pm Apr-Sep, 9.30am-5pm Oct-Mar**). South of place du Château is **Basilique St-Nazaire** (**9-11.45am & 1.45-5.30pm Mon-Sat, 9-10.45am & 2-6pm Sun**), with its delicate medieval rose windows.

NÎMES

pop 145,000

The buzzy city of Nîmes boasts some of France's best-preserved classical buildings. The magnificent **Roman Amphitheatre** (**adult/under 7yr/7-17yr incl audio guide €7.70/free/5.90; 9am-7pm Jun-Aug, 9am-6pm or 6.30pm Mar-May, Sep & Oct, 9.30am-5pm Nov-Feb**), the best preserved in the whole of the Roman Empire, was built around AD 100 to seat 24,000 spectators.

DIANA MAYFIELD

Pont du Gard

The **Maison Carrée** (**place de la Maison Carrée; adult/under 7yr/7-17yr €4.50/free/3.70; 10am-7pm or 7.30pm Apr-Sep, 10am-6.30pm Mar & Oct, 10am-1pm & 2-5pm Nov-Feb**) is a rectangular Roman temple, constructed around AD 5 to honour Emperor Augustus' two adopted sons.

A 10- to 15-minute uphill walk to the top of the gardens brings you to the crumbling shell of the **Tour Magne** (**adult/under 7yr/7-17yr €2.70/free/2.30; 9.30am-6.30pm or 7pm Jun-Sep, 9.30am-1pm & 2-4.30pm or 6pm Oct-Mar**), raised around 15 BC and the largest of a chain of towers that once punctuated the city's 7km-long Roman ramparts.

A **combination ticket** (**adult/child €9.80/7.50**), valid for three days, covers all three of Nîmes' major sights.

SLEEPING

Hôtel Amphithéâtre (**04 66 67 28 51; http://page sperso-orange.fr/hotel-amphitheatre; rue des Arènes; s €41-45, d €53-70; Feb-Dec;**) The welcoming, family-run Amphithéâtre is just up the road from its namesake. Once a pair of 18th-century mansions, it has 15 rooms decorated in warm, woody colours, each named after a writer or painter.

Royal Hôtel (**04 66 58 28 27; www.royal hotel-nimes.com, in French; 3 blvd Alphonse Daudet; s €60-65, d €75-85**) This boho hotel's a treat: rooms are furnished with flair, and some overlook pedestrian place d'Assas, a work of modern art in its own right – although light sleepers might not appreciate the traffic noise.

EATING

Look out for *cassoulet* (pork, sausage and white bean stew, sometimes served with duck), aïoli and *rouille* (a spicy chilli mayonnaise).

Haddock Café (☎ 04 66 67 86 57; www.haddock-café.fr, in French; 13 rue de l'Agau; daily specials €8, mains €10-14.50, menus €15-20; lunch & dinner Mon-Fri, 7pm-2am Sat) This cheerful cafe began life as a convent. Traditional food, local wines and live music at least twice a week.

Le Marché sur la Table (☎ 04 66 67 22 50; 10 rue Littré; mains €15-18; Tue-Sun) You *could* just pop in for a glass of wine at this up-and-coming bistro, but you'd be missing out on Éric Vidal's market-fresh food. Eat in the attractively furnished interior or quiet rear courtyard.

Le 9 (☎ 04 66 21 80 77; 9 rue de l'Étoile; lunch menus €15, mains €15-18; Mon-Sat & lunch Sun May-Sep, dinner Fri & Sat only Oct-Apr) Tucked away behind high green doors you'll find a converted stables and a vine-clad courtyard.

GETTING THERE & AWAY

Nîmes airport (☎ 04 66 70 49 49), 10km southeast of the city on the A54, is served by Ryanair to/from London (Luton), Liverpool and Nottingham East Midlands.

The **bus station** (☎ 04 66 38 59 43; rue Ste-Félicité) connects with the train station. International operators **Eurolines** (☎ 04 66 29 49 02) and **Line Bus** (☎ 04 66 29 50 62) both have kiosks. Regional destinations include Pont du Gard (€6.50, 30 minutes, five daily) and Alès (€8, 1¼ hours, five daily).

More than 12 TGVs daily run to/from Paris' Gare de Lyon (€68.50 to €96, three hours), while regional trains run to/from Avignon (€8.10, 30 minutes), Marseille (€17.90, 1¼ hours) and Montpellier (€8.20, 30 minutes).

PONT DU GARD

The Pont du Gard, a Unesco World Heritage site, is an exceptionally well-preserved, three-tiered Roman aqueduct. It's part of a 50km-long system of canals built about 19 BC by the Romans to bring water from near Uzès to Nîmes.

From car parks (€5) either side of the Gard River, you can walk along the road bridge, built in 1743. The best view of the Pont du Gard is from upstream, beside the river, where you can swim on hot days.

PROVENCE

Provence conjures up images of rolling lavender fields, blue skies, gorgeous villages, wonderful food and superb wine. It certainly delivers on all those fronts, but it's not just worth visiting for its good looks – dig a little deeper and you'll also discover the multicultural metropolis of Marseille, the artistic haven of Aix-en-Provence and the old Roman city of Arles.

MARSEILLE

pop 826,700

There was a time when Marseille was the butt of French jokes and on the receiving end of some pretty bad press. No longer. Marseillais will tell you that the city's rough-and-tumble edginess is part of its charm and that, for all its flaws, it is a very endearing place. They're right: Marseille grows on you with its unique history, souklike markets, millennia-old port and spectacular *corniches* (coastal roads).

INFORMATION

There are banks and exchange bureaux on La Canebière near the Vieux Port.

Tourist office (☎ 04 91 13 89 00; www.marseille-tourisme.com; 4 La Canebière, 1er; 9am-7pm Mon-Sat, 10am-5pm Sun; M Vieux Port)

DANGERS & ANNOYANCES

Marseille isn't a hotbed of crime, but petty crimes and muggings are commonplace. There's no need for paranoia but you

FRENCH WINES

Practically every corner of France has its own vineyards (even Paris!), but the seven principal regions are Alsace, Bordeaux, Burgundy, Champagne, Languedoc, the Loire and the Rhône.

Winemaking in France is a serious business, with a wealth of rules and regulations governing every step of the process from vine to bottle. Top-quality wines are governed by their own *appélations d'origine contrôlée* (AOCs; literally 'label of inspected origin'), specific production areas whose soils and microclimates give the wines particular qualities. Wines are further divided into a bewildering range of classifications, from top-quality *grands crus* (literally 'great growth') down to blended *vin de table* (table wine). Some wine regions only have a single AOC, such as Alsace, while Burgundy is chopped into scores of individual AOCs.

Local tourist offices in each region can provide comprehensive listings of local growers, organised tours and tasting sessions; the offices in **Bordeaux** (☎ 05 56 00 66 00; www.bordeaux-tourisme.com), **Reims** (☎ 03 26 77 45 00, 08 92 70 13 51; www.reims-tourisme.com) and **Beaune** (☎ 03 80 26 21 30; www.beaune-burgundy.com) are all well stocked with information, while **French Wines** (http://uk.wines-france.com) is a great online resource.

should avoid the Belsunce area. Women *will* get unsolicited attention, ranging from wolf-whistling to sometimes aggressive chat-up routines – but keep your wits about you and you should be fine.

SIGHTS

MUSEUMS

Built as a charity shelter for the town's poor, the stunning **Centre de la Vieille Charité** (☎ 04 91 14 58 80; 2 rue de la Charité, 2e; Ⓜ Joliette) now houses Marseille's **Musée d'Archéologie Méditerranéenne** (Museum of Mediterranean Archeology; ☎ 04 91 14 58 59) and **Musée d'Arts Africains, Océaniens & Amérindiens** (Museum of African, Oceanic & American Indian Art; ☎ 04 91 14 58 38). An all-inclusive ticket costs €5/2.50 adult/student.

A fascinating insight into Marseille's cultural heritage, the **Musée d'Histoire de Marseille** (☎ 04 91 90 42 22; ground fl, Centre Bourse shopping centre, 1er; adult/child €2/1; ⏲ noon-7pm Mon-Sat; Ⓜ Vieux Port) has some extraordinary exhibits, including the remains of a merchant vessel discovered in the Vieux Port in 1974.

BASILIQUE NOTRE DAME DE LA GARDE

Be blown away by the celestial views and knock-out 19th-century architecture at the hilltop **Basilique Notre Dame de la Garde** (☎ 04 91 13 40 80; montée de la Bonne Mère; admission free; ⏲ basilica & crypt 7am-7pm, longer hr summer), the resplendent Romano-Byzantine basilica 1km south of the Vieux Port that dominates Marseille's skyline.

CHÂTEAU D'IF

Immortalised in Alexandre Dumas' 1840 novel *Le Comte de Monte Cristo* (The Count of Monte Cristo), the 16th-century island prison of **Château d'If** (☎ 04 91 5[illegible] 02 30; adult/student €5/3.50; ⏲ 9.30am-6.30pm May-Aug, 9.30am-5.30pm Tue-Sun Sep-Mar

9.30am-5.30pm daily Apr) sits 3.5km west of the Vieux Port.

Boats run by **Frioul If Express** (☎ **04 91 46 54 65; www.frioul-if-express.com; 1 quai des Belges, 1er)** leave from the Vieux Port (€10 return, 20 minutes, 15 boats daily in summer, fewer in winter).

VIEUX PORT

Ships have docked for more than 26 centuries at Marseille's colourful Vieux Port. Guarding the harbour are **Fort St-Nicolas** on the southern side and, across the water, **Fort St-Jean**, founded in the 13th century by the Knights Hospitaller of St John of Jerusalem. Standing guard between the old and the 'new' port is the striking Byzantine-style **Cathédrale de la Major**. Its 'stripy' facade is made of Cassis stone (local white stone) and green marble from Florence.

SLEEPING

Hôtel Péron (☎ **04 91 31 01 41; www.hotel-peron.com; 119 corniche Président John F Kennedy, 7e; d €60-85;** 💻) This unusual 1920s period piece has touches including original art deco bathrooms and geometric parquet floors. Balconies have sea views, although you'll have to put up with road noise.

Hôtel St-Louis (☎ **04 91 54 02 74; www.hotel-st-louis.com; 2 rue des Récollettes, 1er; d €65-90;** 🚊 **Canebière Garibaldi,** Ⓜ **Noailles;** ❄ 💻) Behind the scarlet 1800s facade and pale-green shutters, this gorgeous boutique place reveals character-filled rooms – round windows, high or sloping ceilings, four-poster beds, expensive mattresses and discreet vintage furniture.

EATING

our pick **Chez Madie Les Galinettes** (☎ **04 91 90 40 87; 138 quai du Port, 2e; menus €15-27, mains €25-50;** 🕑 **lunch & dinner Mon-Sat, closed Sat lunch summer)** They're so friendly at Madie's that you'll leave feeling as though you've just had dinner with friends. The portside terrace is perfect for those long summer evenings, and the menu's stocked with fish and a fantastic bouillabaisse that you'll need to order in advance.

Chez Jeannot (☎ **04 91 52 11 28; 129 rue du Vallon des Auffes; mains €15-22;** 🕑 **lunch & dinner Tue-Sat, lunch Sun, closed Mon)** An institution among Marseillais, the rooftop terrace is booked out days in advance. The atmosphere is jovial and uncomplicated, just like the thin-crust pizzas, *grillades* (grilled meats) and seafood on your plate.

Le Souk (☎ **04 91 91 29 29; 100 quai du Port, 2e; menus €20-30;** 🕑 **lunch & dinner Tue-Sat, lunch Sun;** Ⓜ **Vieux Port)** Thanks to Marseille's heritage, you'll eat some of the best North African food this side of the Med, and Le Souk does the town's top *tajines* (slow-cooked meat and vegetable stews).

Chez Fonfon (☎ **04 91 52 14 38; 140 rue du Vallon des Auffes, 7e; mains around €40;** 🕑 **lunch & dinner Tue-Sat, dinner Mon)** Overlooking the enchanting little harbour Vallon des Auffes, Chez Fonfon is famed for its bouillabaisse. The place is quite formal, although the wonderful views brighten things up.

The small but enthralling **fish market** **(quai des Belges;** 🕑 **8am-1pm;** Ⓜ **Vieux Port)** is a daily fixture at the Vieux Port docks. Cours Julien hosts a Wednesday-morning organic fruit and vegetable market.

Stock up on fruit and vegetables at **Marché des Capucins** **(place des Capucins, 1er;** 🕑 **8am-7pm Mon-Sat;** 🚊 **Canebière Garibaldi,** Ⓜ **Noailles)**, one block south of La Canebière, and at the **fruit and vegetable market** **(cours Pierre Puget, 6e;** 🕑 **8am-1pm Mon-Fri;** Ⓜ **Estrangin Préfecture)**.

GETTING THERE & AWAY

Aéroport Marseille-Provence (☎ **04 42 14 14 14; www.marseille.aeroport.fr)**, also known as Aéroport Marseille-Marignane, is 25km

BRUCE BI

Panier Quarter, Marseille

GLENN BEANLAND

Fish market in Marseille's Vieux Port

northwest of town. **Navette shuttle buses** (☎ Marseille 04 91 50 59 34, airport 04 42 14 31 27; €8; 25min) run to Marseille's train station every 20 minutes between 5.30am and 10.50pm.

The **bus station** (☎ 08 91 02 40 25; 3 rue Honnorat, 3e; Ⓜ Gare St-Charles SNCF) is at the back of the train station. Buses travel to Aix-en-Provence (€4.60, 35 minutes, every five to 10 minutes), Avignon (€18.50, two hours, one daily), Cannes (€25, two hours, up to three daily), Nice (€26.50, three hours, up to three daily) and other destinations.

Marseille's train station, **Gare St-Charles**, is served by both metro lines. Useful destinations include Paris' Gare de Lyon (€80.20, three hours, 21 daily), Nice (€27.80, 2½ hours, 21 daily), Avignon (€23.10, 35 minutes, 27 daily) and Lyon (€57.60, 1¾ hours, 16 daily).

GETTING AROUND

Marseille has two metro lines (Métro 1 and Métro 2), two tram lines (yellow and green) and an extensive bus network. Most leave from **Espace Infos RTM** (☎ 04 91 91 92 10; 6 rue des Fabres, 1er; 🕑 8.30am-6pm Mon-Fri, 9am-12.30pm & 2-5.30pm Sat; Ⓜ Vieux Port), where you can obtain information and tickets. Bus, metro or tram tickets (€1.70) are valid for one hour after being time-stamped.

AIX-EN-PROVENCE

pop 141,200

Aix-en-Provence is to Provence what the Left Bank is to Paris: a pocket of Bohemian chic with an edgy student crowd. Art, culture and architecture abound in Aix, especially thanks to local lad Paul Cézanne (1839–1906). To see where he ate, drank, studied and painted, you can follow the **Circuit de Cézanne**, marked by footpath-embedded bronze plaques inscribed with the letter C.

The trail takes in Cézanne's last studio, **Atelier Paul Cézanne** (☎ 04 42 21 06 53; www.atelier-cezanne.com; 9 av Paul Cézanne; adult/student €5.50/2; 🕑 10am-noon & 2-5pm Oct-Mar, to 6pm Apr-Jun & Sep, 10am-6pm Jul & Aug), 1.5km north of the tourist office, as well as the **Bastide du Jas de Bouffan**, the family home where Cézanne started painting, and the **Bibémus quarries**, where he did most of his Montagne Ste-Victoire paintings.

Cézanne also features at the **Musée Granet** (☎ 04 42 52 88 32; place St-Jean de Malte; adult/student €4/2; 🕑 11am-7pm Wed-Mon Jun-Sep, noon-6pm Wed-Mon Oct-May), which houses nine of the artist's canvases alongside works by Picasso, Léger, Matisse, Tal Coat and Giacometti.

GETTING THERE & AWAY

Aix' **bus station** (☎ **08 91 02 40 25; av de l'Europe**) is 10 minutes southwest from La Rotonde. Routes include Marseille (€4.60, 30 to 50 minutes, every 10 minutes, every 20 minutes on Sunday), Arles (€10.40, 1½ hours, six daily Monday to Saturday) and Avignon (€14, 1¼ hours, six daily Monday to Saturday).

The only useful train from Aix' city-centre **train station** (⏰ **7am-7pm**) goes to Marseille (€6.50, 50 minutes). For other routes, you'll have to travel to the **TGV station**, 8km from the city centre.

Half-hourly shuttle buses run from the bus station to the TGV station (€3.70) and Aéroport Marseille-Provence (€7.90) from 4.40am to 10.30pm.

ARLES

pop 52,400

If the winding streets and colourful houses of Arles seem familiar, it's hardly surprising – Vincent van Gogh lived here late in his life in a yellow house on place Lamartine, and the town regularly featured in his canvases. Van Gogh's original house was destroyed during WWII, but you can still follow in his footsteps on the **Van Gogh Trail**, marked out by footpath plaques and a brochure handed out by the **tourist office** (☎ **04 90 18 41 20; www.tourisme.ville-arles.fr; esplanade Charles de Gaulle;** ⏰ **9am-6.45pm Apr-Sep, 9am-4.45pm Mon-Sat, 10am-12.45pm Sun Oct-Mar**; train station ☎ **04 90 43 33 57;** ⏰ **9am-1.30pm & 2.30-4.45pm Mon-Fri Apr-Sep**).

Two millennia ago, Arles was a major Roman settlement. The town's 20,000-seat amphitheatre and 12,000-seat theatre, known as the **Arénes** and the **Théâtre Antique**, are nowadays used for cultural events and bullfights.

Telleschi (☎ **04 42 28 40 22**) runs buses to/from Aix-en-Provence (€10.40, 1½ hours) and Nîmes (€6.60, one hour), and there are regular trains from Nîmes (€7.20, 30 minutes), Marseille (€12.70, 55 minutes) and Avignon (€6.30, 20 minutes).

AVIGNON

pop 90,800

Hooped by 4.3km of superbly preserved stone ramparts, this graceful city is the belle of Provence's ball. Famed for its annual performing arts festival and its fabled bridge, the Pont St-Bénezet (aka the Pont d'Avignon), Avignon is an ideal spot from which to step out into the surrounding region.

SIGHTS

The **Pont St-Bénezet** (☎ **04 90 27 51 16; adult/under 8yr/student & 8-18yr €4.50/free/3.50;** ⏰ **9am-9pm Aug, 9am-8pm Jul & early–mid-Sep, 9am-7pm Apr-Jun & mid-Sep–Oct, 9.30am-5.45pm Nov-Mar**), immortalised in the French nursery rhyme *Sur le Pont d'Avignon*, was completed in 1185. The 900m-long wooden bridge was repaired and rebuilt several times before all but four of its 22 spans were washed away in the mid-1600s.

Wrapping around the city, Avignon's ramparts were built between 1359 and 1370. They were restored during the 19th century, minus their original moats. Within the walls is a wealth of fine museums, including the **Palais des Papes** (☎ **04 90 27 50 00; place du Palais; adult/under 12yr/student & 12-18yr €6/free/3;** ⏰ **9am-9pm Aug, 9am-8pm Jul & early–mid-Sep, 9am-7pm Apr-Jun & mid-Sep–Oct, 9.30am-5.45pm Nov-Mar**).

The **Musée Lapidaire** (☎ **04 90 86 33 84; 27 rue de la République; adult/under 12yr/pass €2/free/1;** ⏰ **10am-6pm Wed-Mon Jun-Sep, 10am-1pm & 2-6pm Wed-Mon Oct-May**) houses a collection of Egyptian, Roman, Etruscan and early Christian pieces, while works by Cézanne, Manet, Degas, Modigliani and the only

Van Gogh painting in Provence can be seen at the charming **Musée Angladon** (☎ 04 90 82 29 03; www.angladon.com; 5 rue Laboureur; adult/under 7yr/pass, student & 7-18yr €6/free/4; 1-6pm Tue-Sun mid-Mar–mid-Nov, 1-6pm Wed-Sun mid-Nov–mid-Mar).

Fine views of the old city are afforded by the **Tour Philippe-le-Bel** (☎ 04 32 70 08 57; adult/pass €2/1.50; 10am-12.30pm & 2-6.30pm Tue-Sun Apr-Sep, 10am-noon & 2-5pm Tue-Sun Oct, Nov & Mar), 3km across the Rhône in neighbouring Villeneuve-lès-Avignon.

FESTIVALS & EVENTS

Hundreds of artists take to the stage and streets during the world-famous **Festival d'Avignon** (www.festival-avignon.com), held every year from early July to early August. The more experimental (and cheaper) fringe event **Festival Off** (☎ 04 90 85 13 08; www.avignonleoff.com, in French) runs alongside the main festival.

SLEEPING & EATING

You'll need to book months ahead for a room during the festival.

Hôtel Boquier (☎ 04 90 82 34 43; www.hotel-boquier.com, in French; 6 rue du Portail Boquier; d €45-66;) Run by new owners, this great little hotel is bright, airy, spacious and central, and the themed rooms are particularly attractive (try for Morocco or Lavender).

our pick **Le Limas** (☎ 04 90 14 67 19; www.le-limas-avignon.com; 51 rue du Limas; d incl breakfast €100-160, tr incl breakfast €150-180;) A state-of-the-art kitchen and minimalist white decor jostle for space with antique fireplaces and an 18th-century spiral staircase, and breakfast is served on a sun-drenched summer terrace. Lovely.

Numéro 75 (☎ 04 90 27 16 00; 75 rue Guillaume Puy; mains from €10; lunch & dinner Mon-Sat) Lodged inside the house of absinthe inventor Jules Pernod, the food at Numéro 75 screams Mediterranean cuisine: superfresh, packed with flavours, and ever so cheap.

Au Tout Petit (☎ 04 90 82 38 86; 4 rue d'Amphoux; lunch menus €10, dinner menus €18-24; lunch & dinner Mon-Sat, closed Wed night) The menu of 'The Teeny Tiny' is a foodies' treat – asparagus ravioli, salmon lasagne,

JOHN ELK II

Pont St-Bénezet (p221)

apricot *tarte Tatin* with rosemary-and-madeleine ice cream. Food poetry.

GETTING THERE & AWAY

The **bus station** (☎ 04 90 82 07 35; blvd St-Roch; ⏰ information window 8am-7pm Mon-Fri, to 1pm Sat) is near the train station. Services include Aix-en-Provence (€14, one hour), Arles (€7.10, 1½ hours), Marseille (€18.50, two hours) and Nîmes (€8.10, 1¼ hours).

Long-haul bus companies **Linebús** (☎ 04 90 85 30 48) and **Eurolines** (☎ 04 90 85 27 60; www.eurolines.com) have offices at the far end of the bus platforms.

Avignon has two train stations: **Gare Avignon Centre** (42 blvd St-Roch) has local trains to/from Arles (€6.30, 20 minutes) and Nîmes (€8.10, 30 minutes), while **Gare Avignon TGV**, 4km southwest of town, has TGV connections to/from Marseille (€23.10, 35 minutes) and Nice (€51.80, three hours). *Navette* (shuttle) buses (€1.10, 10 to 13 minutes, half-hourly between 6.15am and 11.30pm) link Gare Avignon TGV with the stop in front of the post office on cours Président Kennedy.

CÔTE D'AZUR & MONACO

With its glistening seas, idyllic beaches and lush hills, the Côte d'Azur (Azure Coast) – otherwise known as the French Riviera – has long been a symbol of exclusivity, extravagance and excess, and it's still a favourite getaway for the European jet set, especially around the chichi resorts of St-Tropez, glamorous Cannes and super-rich, sovereign Monaco.

NICE

pop 346,900

Nice is the Côte d'Azur's most complex and cosmopolitan city. It's noisy, it's smelly and it's insanely touristy throughout the summer, but somehow Nice still manages to be irresistible, with a charming old city and a clutch of fantastic museums to explore.

INFORMATION

Main tourist office (☎ 08 92 70 74 07; 5 promenade des Anglais; ⏰ 8am-8pm Mon-Sat, 9am-7pm Sun Jun-Sep, 9am-6pm Mon-Sat Oct-May) Right by the beach.

Train station tourist office (☎ 08 92 35 35 35; av Thiers; ⏰ 8am-8pm Mon-Sat, 9am-7pm Sun Jun-Sep, 8am-7pm Mon-Sat, 10am-5pm Sun Oct-May)

SIGHTS

VIEUX NICE

Go off-map in the Old Town's tangle of tiny 18th-century pedestrian passages and alleyways, where you'll find several historic churches including the baroque **Cathédrale Ste-Réparate** (place Rossetti) and the mid-18th-century **Chapelle de la Miséricorde**, next to place Pierre Gautier.

At the eastern end of quai des États-Unis, steep steps and a **cliffside lift** (per person €1; ⏰ 9am-8pm Jun-Aug, 9am-7pm Apr, May & Sep, 10am-6pm Oct-Mar) climb to the **Parc du Château**, a beautiful hilltop park with great views over the old city and the beachfront.

MUSEUMS

The excellent **Mamac** (☎ 04 97 13 42 01; www.mamac-nice.org; Promenade des Arts; admission free; ⏰ 10am-6pm Tue-Sun) is worth a visit for its stunning architecture alone, but it also houses some fantastic avant-garde art from the 1960s to the present, including iconic pop art from Roy Lichtenstein, and Andy Warhol's 1965 *Campbell's Soup Can*.

The small **Musée National Message Biblique Marc Chagall** (☎ 04 93 53 87 20; www.musee-chagall.fr, in French; 4 av Dr Ménard; permanent collection adult/student €6.50/4.50, temporary exhibitions additional €1.20; ⏰ 10am-5pm Wed-Mon Oct-Jun, to 6pm Jul-Sep) houses the largest

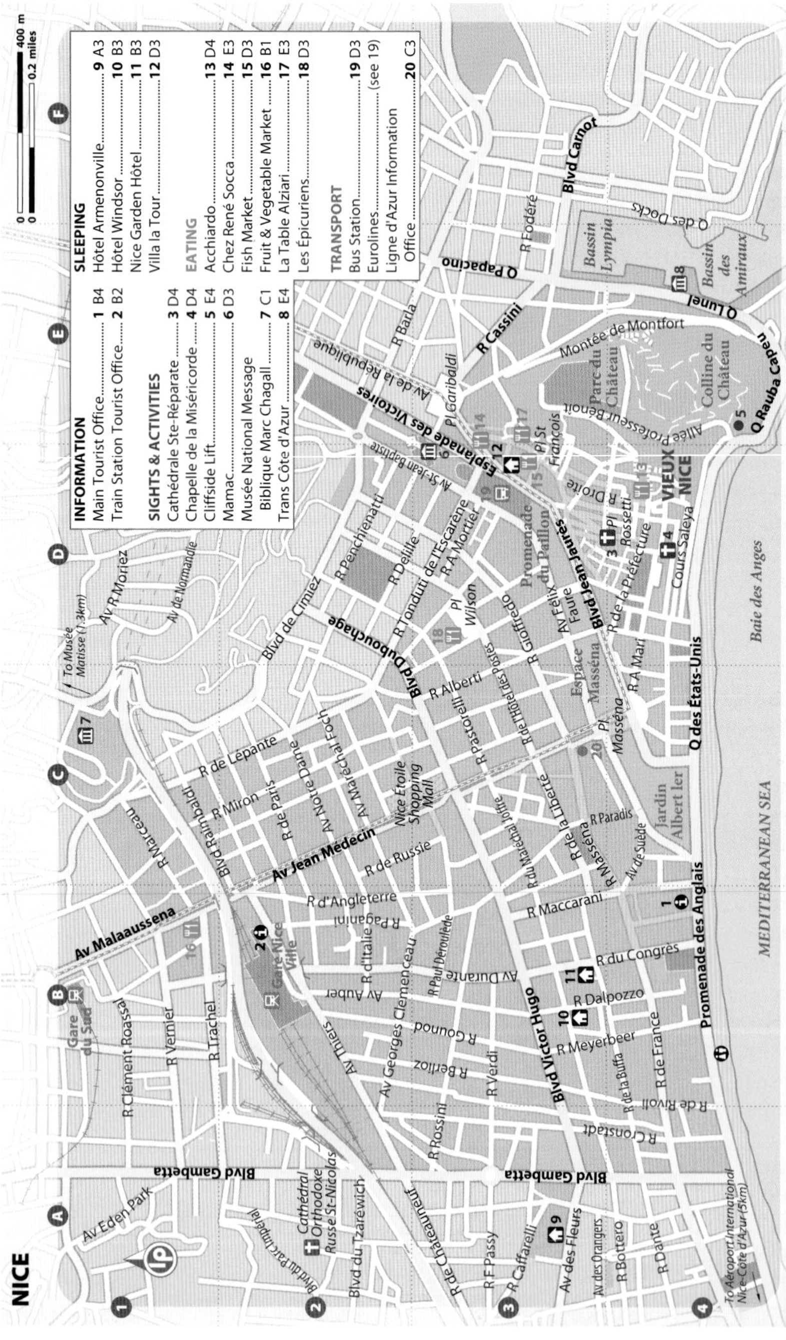
NICE
0 400 m
0 0.2 miles
INFORMATION
Main Tourist Office 1 B4
Train Station Tourist Office 2 B2
SIGHTS & ACTIVITIES
Cathédrale Ste-Réparate 3 D4
Chapelle de la Miséricorde 4 D4
Cliffside Lift 5 E4
Mamac 6 D3
Musée National Message Biblique Marc Chagall 7 C1
Trans Côte d'Azur 8 E4
SLEEPING
Hôtel Armenonville 9 A3
Hôtel Windsor 10 B3
Nice Garden Hôtel 11 B3
Villa la Tour 12 D3
EATING
Acchiardo 13 D4
Chez René Socca 14 E3
Fish Market 15 D3
Fruit & Vegetable Market 16 B1
La Table Alziari 17 E3
Les Épicuriens 18 D3
TRANSPORT
Bus Station 19 D3
Eurolines (see 19)
Ligne d'Azur Information Office 20 C3

public collection of the Russian-born artist's seminal *Old Testament* paintings.

Heading northeast from the Chagall museum (about 2.5km from the city centre) brings you to the **Musée Matisse** (☎ 04 93 81 08 08; www.musee-matisse-nice.org; 164 av des Arènes de Cimiez; admission free; 10am-6pm Wed-Mon), which contains a fantastic collection of exhibits and paintings spanning Matisse's entire career, including his famous paper cut-outs *Blue Nude IV* and mixed-media *Woman with Amphora*.

BEACHES

You'll need at least a beach mat to cushion your tush from Nice's pebbly **beaches**. Free sections of beach alternate with 15 sun-lounge-lined **plages concédées** (private beaches; late Apr or early May-15 Sep), for which you have to pay by renting a chair (around €15 a day) or mattress (around €10).

TOURS

Trans Côte d'Azur (☎ 04 92 00 42 30; www.trans-cote-azur.com; quai Lunel; Apr-Oct) runs scenic one-hour coastal cruises (adult/child under 10 years €14/8.50) as well as day trips to the offshore islands of Îles de Lérins (adult/child €32/23), as well as St-Tropez (adult/child €52/39) and Monaco (adult/child €29/21).

FESTIVALS & EVENTS

Carnaval de Nice (www.nicecarnaval.com) Two-week carnival with flower floats and fireworks.

Nice Jazz Festival (www.nicejazzfestival.fr) In July, Nice swings to the week-long jazz festival at the Arènes de Cimiez, amid the Roman ruins.

SLEEPING

Villa la Tour (☎ 04 93 80 08 15; www.villa-la-tour.com; 4 rue de la Tour; s €45-129, d €48-139;) Small but perfectly formed, the Villa la Tour offers romantic Provençal rooms, a stellar Old Nice location, and a flower-decked terrace with views of Nice's rooftops.

Nice Garden Hôtel (☎ 04 93 87 35 63; www.nicegardenhotel.com; 11 rue du Congrès; d €60-98;) Behind heavy iron gates hides this little gem of a hotel: nine beautifully appointed rooms overlooking an exquisite garden with a glorious orange tree. Amazingly, it's just two blocks from the promenade.

Hôtel Armenonville (☎ 04 93 96 86 00; www.hotel-armenonville.com; 20 av des Fleurs; d €62-98, tr €79-112; P) Tucked down an alleyway and shielded by its large garden, this grand early-20th-century mansion has sober rooms, three of them (12, 13 and 14) with a huge terrace overlooking the garden. There is a free car park and wi-fi.

Hôtel Windsor (☎ 04 93 88 59 35; www.hotelwindsornice.com; 11 rue Dalpozzo; d €90-175;) Wherever you look in this boutique hotel, you'll be treated to real wit and imagination – from the graffiti mural by the pool, the weird and wonderful artist-designed rooms, or the luxurious garden with its exotic plants.

EATING

Niçois nibbles include *socca* (a thin layer of chickpea flour and olive oil batter), *salade niçoise* and *farcis* (stuffed vegetables). Restaurants in Vieux Nice are a mixed bag, so choose carefully.

Chez René Socca (☎ 04 93 92 05 73; 2 rue Miralhéti; dishes from €2; 9am-9pm Tue-Sun, to 10.30pm Jul & Aug, closed Nov) Forget about presentation; here, it's all about taste. Grab a portion of *socca* or a plate of *petits farçis* and head across the street for a *grand pointu* (glass) of red, white or rosé.

La Table Alziari (☎ 04 93 80 34 03; 4 rue François Zanin; mains €8-14, noon-2pm & 7.30-10pm Tue-Sat) Run by the grandson of the

Alziari olive oil family, this citrus-coloured restaurant does local specialities such as *morue à la niçoise* (cod served with potatoes, olives and a tomato sauce), *daube* (stew) or grilled goat's cheese.

Acchiardo (☎ **04 93 85 51 16; 38 rue Droite; mains €14-20;** ⏰ **lunch & dinner Mon-Fri)** Locals flock to historic Acchiardo for the simple, tasty food – think lamb chops with green beans or steak with homemade French fries.

Les Épicuriens (☎ **04 93 80 85 00; 6 place Wilson; mains €18-45.50;** ⏰ **lunch & dinner Mon-Fri, dinner Sat)** Nice's rising star is famous for its *cocottes* (casseroles cooked in cast-iron dishes), but you could find yourself tucking into anything from foie gras to *brandade de cabillaud* (oven-cooked cod).

Pack the ultimate picnic hamper from cours Saleya's **fruit and vegetable market** (⏰ **6am-1.30pm Tue-Sun)** and pick up fresh seafood from the **fish market** **(place St-François;** ⏰ **6am-1pm Tue-Sun)**.

GETTING THERE & AWAY

AIR

Nice's international airport, **Aéroport International Nice-Côte d'Azur** (☎ **08 20 42 33 33; www.nice.aeroport.fr)**, is about 6km west of the city centre. Its two terminals are connected by a free **shuttle bus** (⏰ **every 10min 4.30am-midnight)**.

Ligne d'Azur runs two airport buses (€4). Route 99 shuttles approximately every half-hour direct between Gare Nice Ville and both airport terminals daily from around 8am to 9pm. Route 98 takes the slow route and departs from the bus station every 20 minutes (every 30 minutes on Sunday) from around 6am to around 9pm.

BUS

Buses stop at the **bus station** **(gare routière;** ☎ **08 92 70 12 06; 5 blvd Jean Jaurès)**. There are services to Antibes (one hour), Cannes (1½ hours), Menton (1½ hours) and Monaco (45 minutes).

Eurolines (☎ **04 93 80 08 70)** operates from the bus station.

TRAIN

Nice's main train station, **Gare Nice Ville** **(av Thiers)** has fast and frequent services (up to 40 trains a day in each direction) to coastal towns including Antibes (€3.80, 30 minutes), Cannes (€5.70, 30 to 40 minutes), Menton (€4.30, 35 minutes) and Monaco (€3.20, 20 minutes). Direct TGVs link Nice with Paris' Gare de Lyon (€110, 5½ hours).

GETTING AROUND

Travelling on the **Ligne d'Azur** (☎ **08 10 06 10 07; www.lignedazur.com; 3 place Masséna;** ⏰ **7.45am-6.30pm Mon-Fri & 8.30am-6pm Sat)** transport network costs €1 per trip (except to the airport); the fare includes one connection. Tickets can be purchased from the driver or from ticket machines at tram stops.

Nice's much delayed tram launched in November 2007. Line 1 runs from 4.30am to 1.30am, taking in useful areas such as the train station,`the Old Town, and the Acropolis in the centre.

CANNES

pop 70,400

Everyone's heard of Cannes and its celebrity film festival, which runs for around 11 days every May and attracts big-name stars to the red carpets and flashy hotels of the blvd de la Croisette. But outside the festival season, Cannes retains a genuine small-town feel, with pleasant shops, sparkling beaches and buzzy markets, as well as the idyllic Îles de Lérins just offshore.

SLEEPING

Hotel prices in Cannes fluctuate wildly according to the season, and soar during the film festival, when you'll need to book months in advance.

Hôtel des Orangers (☎ 04 93 39 99 92; www.hotel-orangers.com; 1 rue des Orangers; s/d from €74/81; P) Perched at the edge of the Old Town, the water views from the bright, west-facing rooms on the 2nd and 3rd floors are an unexpected treat, and the restaurants of rue du Suquet (five minutes) are steps away.

Hôtel Splendid (☎ 04 97 06 22 22; www.splendid-hotel-cannes.com; 4-6 rue Félix Faure; s/d from €115/128;) This elaborate 1871 building has everything it takes to rival Cannes' posher palaces: beautifully decorated rooms, fabulous location and stunning views, as well as 15 rooms with self-catering kitchenettes.

EATING

Aux Bons Enfants (80 rue Meynadier; menus €23; lunch & dinner Tue-Sat) This familial place doesn't have a phone, but it doesn't seem to matter – it's always full. The lucky ones who get a table (get there early or late) can feast on top-notch regional dishes.

Barbarella (☎ 04 92 99 17 33; 16 rue St-Dizier; mains €25-35; 7-11.30pm Tue-Sun) You've seen the film, now go to the err…restaurant. It's as kitsch as the movie (trompe l'œil–painted building, see-through chairs, psychedelic lighting, groovy atmosphere) and its fusion food is fine.

our pick **Mantel** (☎ 04 93 39 13 10; 22 rue St-Antoine; lunch menus €25, dinner menus €36-58; lunch & dinner, closed Wed & lunch Tue & Thu) The Italian maître d' will make you feel like a million dollars and you'll melt for Noël Mantel's divine cuisine and great-value prices.

The **Marché Forville** (rue du Marché Forville; Tue-Sun mornings) is where many of the city's restaurants shop and where you should get your picnic supplies. The **food market** (place Gambetta; morning) is another good address for fruit and veg.

CHRIS MELLOR

Harbour at St-Tropez

GETTING THERE & AWAY

Regular buses go to Nice (bus 200, €1, 1½ hours) and Nice airport (bus 210, €14.20, 50 minutes, half-hourly from 8am to 6pm). Trains serve Nice (€5.70, 30 to 40 minutes), Grasse (€3.60, 25 minutes) and Marseille (€24.80, two hours).

Boats for the islands travel from quai des Îles on the western side of the harbour. **Riviera Lines** (☎ 04 92 98 71 31; ww.riviera-lines.com) runs ferries to Île Ste-Marguerite (adult/child €11/5.50 return), while **Compagnie Planaria** (☎ 04 92 98 71 38; www.cannes-ilesdelerins.com) operates boats to Île St-Honorat (adult/child €11/5.50 return).

ST-TROPEZ

In the soft autumn or winter light, it's hard to believe that the pretty terracotta fishing village of St-Tropez is yet another stop

ISLAND ESCAPES

The rugged island of **Corsica** (**Corse in French; www.visit-corsica.com**) is officially a part of France, but remains fiercely proud of its own culture, history and language. It's one of the Meditteranean's most dramatic islands, with a bevy of beautiful beaches, glitzy ports and a mountainous, *maquis* (thicket)-covered interior to explore. It's hugely popular with French tourists between July and August, but visit in early spring or late autumn and you might well find you have the island practically to yourself.

There are regular ferries and flights from Nice, Marseille and Toulon to the island's main ports in Ajaccio, Bastia and Calvi. There are also direct flights from Paris and several other French cities in season, plus seasonal ferries from Porto Torres on Sardinia and Genoa, Livorno and Savona in Italy.

on the Riviera celebrity circuit. It seems far removed from its glitzy siblings further up the coast, but come spring or summer, it's a different world: the town's population increases tenfold, prices triple and celebrities (including Gallic crooner Johnny Hallyday) monopolise town.

The panoramas of St-Tropez' bay from the elevated 17th-century **Citadelle de St-Tropez** (**☎ 04 94 97 59 43; admission €2.50; 10am-6.30pm Apr-Sep, 10am-12.30pm & 1.30-5.30pm Oct-Mar**) are definitely worth the climb. The glistening **Plage de Tahiti**, 4km southeast of town, morphs into the 5km-long **Plage de Pampelonne**, which in summer incorporates a sequence of exclusive restaurant/clubs.

Trans Côte d'Azur (p225) runs day trips from Nice and Cannes between Easter and September.

MONACO

☎ 377 / pop 32,000

After all the gorgeous medieval hilltop villages, glittering beaches and secluded peninsulas of the surrounding area, Monaco's concrete high-rises and astronomic prices might come as a shock. In its 1.95 sq km, the world's second-smallest state (a smidgen bigger than the Vatican) has managed to squeeze in not only a thriving performing-art and sport scene, but also a world-famous circus festival, a world-class aquarium, a beautiful Old Town, stunning gardens, interesting architecture throughout and a royal family on a par with British royals for best gossip fodder.

Monaco is a sovereign state but there is no border control. It has its own flag (red and white), national holiday (19 November), postal system and telephone code (☎ 377), but the official language is French and the country uses the euro even though it is not part of the European Union.

SIGHTS & ACTIVITIES

At 11.55am every day, guards are changed at Monaco's **Palais du Prince** (**☎ 93 25 18 31**) in Monaco Ville. For a glimpse into royal life, you can tour the **state apartments** (**adult/child €7/3.50; 9.30am-6.30pm May-Sep, 10.30am-6pm Apr, 10am-5.30pm Oct**) with an 11-language audio guide. A combined ticket also covers the **Musée des Souvenirs Napoléoniens** (**10.30am-5pm Dec-Mar, to 5.30pm Oct & Apr, 9.30am-6.30pm May-Sep**), costs €9 (children €4.50).

Propped on a sheer cliff-face, the graceful 1910 **Musée Océanographique de Monaco** (**☎ 93 15 36 00; av St-Martin; adult/student €12.50/6; 9.30am-7pm Jul & Aug, to 6.30pm Apr-Jun & Sep, to 6pm Oct-Mar**) houses an aquarium stocked with sharks, tropical fish, and a tactile basin where you can get hands-on with local sea creatures.

Flowering year-round, over 1000 species tumble down the slopes of the **Jardin Exotique** (☎ 93 15 29 80; 62 blvd du Jardin Exotique; adult/student €6.90/3.60; 9am-7pm mid-May-mid-Sep, 9am-6pm mid-Sep-mid-May). Admission includes a half-hour visit to the stalactites and stalagmites in the **Observatory Caves**.

SLEEPING

Hôtel Le Versailles (☎ 93 50 79 34; 4-6 av Prince Pierre; s €70-90, d €100-160;) Run by a gregarious family, this sun-filled hotel is good value for Monaco: refurbished rooms have wooden floors, simple decor, flat-screen TVs, wi-fi and minifridges.

Hôtel de France (☎ 93 30 24 64; fax 92 16 13 34; 6 rue de la Turbie; s/d/tr €80/90/108) The cheapest place in town is certainly no-frills, but it's handily plonked in La Condamine.

Hôtel Alexandra (☎ 93 50 63 13; fax 92 16 06 48; 35 blvd Princesse Charlotte; s €100-125, d €120-160, tr €170-190;) This turn-of-the-century hotel is conveniently located in Monte Carlo, close to the train stations, but its 56 rooms are in dire need of a revamp. Breakfast is a whopping €15.

EATING

Bilig (☎ 97 98 20 43; 11bis rue Princesse Caroline; mains €6-12; 11am-6pm Mon-Sat winter, to 10pm summer) A small cafe serving big portions of salads, crêpes and the odd meat dish.

Vecchia Firenze (☎ 93 30 27 70; 4-6 av Prince Pierre; mains €12-27; lunch & dinner Tue-Fri, dinner Sat) Authentic pizza, pasta and Italian cooking at the Hôtel Le Versailles' inhouse restaurant.

Le Castelroc (☎ 93 30 36 68; place du Palais; mains €22-27; 9am-3pm daily, dinner Tue-Sat May-Sep) Right across from the palace, Le Castelroc's alfresco terrace is the perfect place to try genuine Monégasque specialities like *barbajuan* (a beignet filled with spinach and cheese) and *cundyun* (Monaco's version of *salade niçoise*).

GETTING THERE & AWAY

Monaco's **train station** (av Prince Pierre) has frequent trains to Nice (€3.20, 20 minutes), and east to Menton (€1.80, 10 minutes), and the Italian town of Ventimiglia (€3.20, 20 minutes).

DIRECTORY

ACTIVITIES

CYCLING

The French take cycling very seriously – the country practically grinds to a halt during the annual Tour de France. Mountain-biking (known in France as VTT, or *vélo tout-terrain)* is gaining popularity around the Alps and Pyrenees, but road-cycling still rules the roost.

Association Française de Développement des Véloroutes et Voies Vertes (www.af3v.org) has a database of 250 signposted *véloroutes* (bike paths) and *voies vertes* (greenways).

Fédération Française de Cyclotourisme (www.ffct.org, in French) promotes bicycle touring and mountain biking.

HIKING

The French countryside is criss-crossed by a staggering 120,000km of *sentiers balisés* (marked walking paths), including the *sentiers de grande randonnée* (GR) trails, long-distance footpaths marked by red-and-white-striped track indicators.

The **Fédération Française de la Randonnée Pédestre** (FFRP; French Ramblers' Association; www.ffrp.asso.fr, in French) has an **information centre** (Map pp180-1; ☎ 01 44 89 93 93; 64 rue du Dessous des Berges, 13e, Paris; M Bibliothèque François Mitterrand) in Paris.

SKIING & SNOWBOARDING

France has over 400 ski resorts, which are located in the Alps, the Jura, the Pyrenees, the Vosges and Massif Central. The season generally lasts from mid-December to late March or April, but the slopes get very crowded during the February/March school holidays.

Paris-based **Ski France** (www.skifrance.fr) has information and an annual brochure covering more than 90 ski resorts.

WATER SPORTS

The beautifully sandy beaches along the Atlantic coast are less crowded than their counterparts on the Côte d'Azur and Corsica, while Brittany, Normandy and the Channel coast are also popular, albeit cooler, beach destinations. The best surfing in France is on the Atlantic coast around Biarritz.

EMBASSIES & CONSULATES

All foreign embassies are in Paris.

Australia Paris (Map pp180-1; ☎ 01 40 59 33 00; www.france.embassy.gov.au; 4 rue Jean Rey, 15e; M Bir Hakeim)

Belgium Paris (Map pp180-1; ☎ 01 44 09 39 39; www.diplomatie.be/paris; 9 rue de Tilsitt, 17e; M Charles de Gaulle-Étoile)

Canada Paris (Map pp180-1; ☎ 01 44 43 29 00; www.amb-canada.fr; 35 av Montaigne, 8e; M Franklin D Roosevelt); Nice consulate (☎ 04 93 92 93 22; 10 rue Lamartine, Nice)

Germany Paris Embassy & Consulate (Map pp180-1; ☎ 01 53 83 45 00; www.paris.diplo.de, in French & German; 13 av Franklin D Roosevelt, 8e; M Franklin D Roosevelt)

Ireland Paris (Map pp180-1; ☎ 01 44 17 67 00; www.embassyofirelandparis.com; 12 av Foch, 16e; M Argentine)

Italy Paris Embassy (Map pp180-1; ☎ 01 49 54 03 00; www.amb-italie.fr; 51 rue de Varenne, 7e; M Rue du Bac); Paris Consulate (Map pp180-1; ☎ 01 44 30 47 00; 5 blvd Émile Augier, 16e; M La Muette)

Japan Paris (Map pp180-1; ☎ 01 48 88 62 00; www.amb-japon.fr; 7 av Hoche, 8e; M Courcelles)

Netherlands Paris (Map pp180-1; ☎ 01 40 62 33 00; www.amb-pays-bas.fr; 7 rue Eblé, 7e; M St-François Xavier)

New Zealand Paris (Map pp180-1; ☎ 01 45 01 43 43; www.nzembassy.com; 7ter rue Léonard de Vinci, 16e; M Victor Hugo)

Spain Paris (Map pp180-1; ☎ 01 44 43 18 00; www.amb-espagne.fr; 22 av Marceau, 8e; M Alma-Marceau)

Switzerland Paris Embassy (Map pp180-1; ☎ 01 49 55 67 00; www.amb-suisse.fr; 142 rue de Grenelle, 7e; M Varenne)

UK Paris Embassy (Map pp180-1; ☎ 01 44 51 31 00; www.amb-grandebretagne.fr; 35 rue du Faubourg St-Honoré, 8e; M Concorde); Paris Consulate (Map pp180-1; ☎ 01 44 51 31 00; 18bis rue d'Anjou, 8e; M Madeleine); Marseille Consulate (☎ 04 91 54 92 00; place Varian Fry, 6e)

USA Paris Embassy (Map pp180-1; ☎ 01 43 12 22 22; http://france.usembassy.gov; 2 av Gabriel, 8e; M Concorde); Paris Consulate (Map pp180-1; ☎ 01 43 12 26 71; 4 av Gabriel, 8e; 9am-noon Mon-Fri except US & French holidays; M Concorde)

FESTIVALS & EVENTS

Carnaval de Nice (www.nicecarnaval.com) Merrymaking in Nice during France's largest street carnival (last half of February).

May Day Across France, workers' day is celebrated with parades and protests.

Festival d'Aix-en-Provence (www.festival-aix.com) Attracts some of the world's best classical music, opera, ballet and buskers (late June to mid-July).

Bastille Day Fireworks, balls, processions – including a military parade down Paris' Champs-Élysées – for France's National Day (14 July).

Festival d'Avignon (www.festival-avignon.com) Avignon has an official and fringe festival (mid-July).
Nice Jazz Festival (www.nicejazzfest.fr) Jazz cats among the Roman ruins of Nice (mid-July).
Christmas Markets in Alsace Last weekend in November through Christmas or New Year.
Fête des Lumières (www.lumieres.lyon.fr) France's biggest and best light show transforms Lyon (8 December).

HOLIDAYS

The following *jours fériés* (public holidays) are observed in France:
New Year's Day (Jour de l'An) 1 January
Easter Sunday & Monday (Pâques & lundi de Pâques) Late March/April
May Day (Fête du Travail) 1 May – traditional parades
Victoire 1945 8 May – commemorates the Allied victory in Europe that ended WWII
Ascension Thursday (Ascension) May – celebrated on the 40th day after Easter
Pentecost/Whit Sunday & Whit Monday (Pentecôte & lundi de Pentecôte) Mid-May to mid-June – celebrated on the seventh Sunday after Easter
Bastille Day/National Day (Fête Nationale) 14 July – *the* national holiday
Assumption Day (Assomption) 15 August
All Saints' Day (Toussaint) 1 November
Remembrance Day (L'onze Novembre) 11 November – marks the WWI armistice
Christmas (Noël) 25 December

LEGAL MATTERS

French police have wide powers of stop-and-search and can demand proof of identity at any time. Foreigners must be able to prove their legal status in France (eg passport, visa, residency permit). Don't leave baggage unattended at airports or train stations.

MONEY

The official currency of France is the euro. *Bureaux de change* are available in most major cities, and most large post offices offer currency exchange and cash travellers cheques. Most ATMs are linked to the Cirrus, Plus and Maestro networks.

Visa and MasterCard (Access or Eurocard) are widely accepted at shops, restaurants and hotels; you'll need to know your *code* (PIN number).

For lost cards, call:
Amex (☎ 01 47 77 72 00)
Diners Club (☎ 08 10 31 41 59)
MasterCard, Eurocard & Access (Eurocard France; ☎ 08 00 90 13 87, 01 45 67 84 84)
Visa (Carte Bleue; ☎ 08 00 90 20 33)

POST

Post offices have a yellow or brown sign reading 'La Poste'. All mail to France *must* include the five-digit *code postal* (postcode/ZIP code), which begins with the two-digit number of the *département*.

TELEPHONE

Area codes are an integral part of phone numbers in France and are included in the phone numbers listed this chapter.

INTERNATIONAL DIALLING

To call someone outside France, dial the international access code (☎ 00), the country code, the area code (without the initial zero if there is one) and the local number.

Numbers beginning ☎ 08 00 or ☎ 08 05 are free but other ☎ 08 numbers are not.

For France Telecom's *service des renseignements* (directory inquiries) dial ☎ 11 87 12 (€1.18 per call from a fixed-line phone). Not all operators speak English.

For help in English with France Telecom's services, see www.francetelecom.com or call ☎ 08 00 36 47 75.

MOBILE PHONES

French mobile phone numbers begin ☎ 06. Dialling from a fixed-line phone or another mobile can be very expensive. France uses GSM 900/1800, which is compatible with the rest of Europe and Australia but not with Japanese or North American systems. You can buy your own French SIM card (€20 to €30), rechargeable at most *tabacs* and newsagents.

SIMs are available from all three of France's mobile companies: **Bouygues** (☎ 08 10 63 01 00; www.bouyguestelecom.fr), France Telecom's **Orange** (www.orange.fr, in French) and **SFR** (☎ 08 11 70 70 73; www.sfr.com).

PUBLIC PHONES & TELEPHONE CARDS

Most public phones operate using a credit card or two kinds of *télécartes* (phonecards): *cartes à puce* (cards with a magnetic chip) and *cartes à code* (which use a free access number and a scratch-off code). Both types are sold at *tabacs*, newsagents and post offices in various denominations; phonecards with codes offer *much* better international rates than their chip equivalents.

TRANSPORT

GETTING THERE & AWAY

AIR

France's two major international airports, both outside Paris, are **Roissy Charles de Gaulle** (CDG; off Map pp180-1; ☎ 3950, 01 48 62 22 80; www.aeroportsdeparis.fr) and **Orly** (ORY; off Map pp180-1; ☎ 3950, 01 49 75 15 15; www.aeroportsdeparis.fr). A third airport, **Aéroport Paris-Beauvais** (BVA; off Map pp180-1; ☎ 08 92 68 20 66, 03 44 11 46 86; www.aeroportbeauvais.com), 80km north of Paris, is used by some budget airlines.

Most major international airlines fly into Paris, while budget carriers including **bmibaby** (BD; www.bmibaby.com), **easyJet** (U2; www.easyjet.com), **Flybe** (BE; www.flybe.com), **germanwings** (4U; www.germanwings.com), **Ryanair** (FR; www.ryanair.com) and **Transavia.com** (HV; www.transavia.com) operate from several regional airports. There are airports in major French cities including Bordeaux, Lyon, Marseille, Nantes and Nice.

LAND

BUS

Eurolines (☎ 08 92 89 90 91; www.eurolines.eu) provides bus services to various destinations throughout France.

Buses run by London-based **Busabout** (☎ in UK 0207-950 1661; www.busabout.com; 1/2/3 loops US$639/1069/1319) link 29 Continental European cities from early May to October. In France, stops are in Bordeaux, Tours, Paris, Avignon and Nice.

CAR & MOTORCYCLE

Arriving in France by car is easy. At some border points you may need a passport or EU national identity card (your driver's licence will not be sufficient ID).

From the UK, the Channel Tunnel runs high-speed **Eurotunnel trains** (☎ in UK 08705-35 35 35, in France 08 10 63 03 04; www.eurotunnel.com) from Folkestone to Coquelles, 5km southwest of Calais.

TRAIN

Rail services link France with virtually every country in Europe. In France ticketing is handled by **SNCF** (☎ in France 36 35, from abroad 08 92 35 35 35; www.sncf.com).

Certain services between France and its neighbours are marketed under separate names: **Alleo** heads to Germany; **Artésia** (www.artesia.eu) serves Italian cities such as

Milan, Venice, Florence and Rome; **Elipsos** (www.elipsos.com) has luxury services to Spain; and **TGV Lyria** (www.tgv-lyria.fr) takes passengers to Switzerland. **Thalys** (www.thalys.com) links Paris' Gare du Nord with destinations including Brussels-Midi, Amsterdam CS and Cologne's Hauptbahnhof (€91, 3¾ hours, six per day).

The civilised **Eurostar** (☎ in UK 08705-186-186, in France 08 92 35 35 39; www.eurostar.com) whisks you between London St Pancras and Paris Gare du Nord in just 2¼ hours, with onward connections to Calais, Lille and Disneyland Resort Paris.

SEA

For details of ferries between the UK and France, see p160. For ferries to Italy, see p366.

GETTING AROUND

AIR

Air France (☎ 36 54; www.airfrance.com) and its subsidiaries **Brit Air** (www.britair.fr) and **Régional** (☎ 36 54; www.regional.com) control the lion's share of France's domestic airline industry, although budget airlines including **easyJet** (www.easyjet.com), **Airlinair** (www.airlinair.com) and **Twin Jet** (www.twjet.net) are steadily making inroads.

Students, people aged 12 to 24 and the over 60s receive hefty discounts. Special last-minute offers appear on the Air France website every Wednesday.

BUS

You're nearly always better off travelling by train in France if possible, as the SNCF domestic railway system is heavily subsidised by the government and is much more reliable than local bus companies. Nevertheless, buses are widely used for short-distance travel within *départements*, especially in rural areas with relatively few train lines (eg Brittany and Normandy).

CAR & MOTORCYCLE

Many French motorways *(autoroutes)* are fitted with toll *(péage)* stations that charge a fee based on the distance you've travelled.

Foreign motor vehicles entering France must display a sticker or licence plate identifying its country of registration. All drivers must carry a national ID card or passport; a valid driving licence *(permis de conduire)*; car-ownership papers, known as a *carte grise* (grey card); and proof of third party (liability) insurance.

To hire a car you'll usually need to be over 21 and in possession of a valid driving licence and a credit card. Auto transmissions are *very* rare in France. When comparing rates check the *franchise* (excess), which is usually €350 for a small car. Your credit card may cover CDW if you use it to pay for the car rental.

Cars drive on the right in France. All passengers must wear seat belts, and children who weigh less than 18kg must travel in backward-facing child seats. The speed limits on French roads are 50km/h in built-up areas, 90km/h (80km/h if it's raining) on N and D highways, 110km/h (100km/h if it's raining) on dual carriageways and 130km/h (110km/h if it's raining) on *autoroutes*. Under the *priorité à droite* (priority to the right) rule, any car entering an intersection from a road on your right has the right-of-way, unless the intersection is marked *'vous n'avez pas la priorité'* (you do not have right of way) or *'cédez le passage'* (give way). It is illegal to drive with a blood-alcohol concentration over 0.05% – the equivalent of two glasses of wine for a 75kg adult.

Since July 2008, all French vehicles must carry a reflective safety jacket and a reflective triangle; the fine for not carrying one/both is €90/135.

TRAIN

France's superb rail network is operated by the state-owned **SNCF** (www.sncf.com). The flagship trains on French railways are the superfast TGVs, which reach speeds in excess of 320km/h and can whisk you from Paris to the Côte d'Azur in as little as three hours. Otherwise you'll find yourself aboard a non-TGV train, referred to as a *corail* or TER *(train express régional)*.

TGV Nord, Thalys & Eurostar Paris' Gare du Nord to Arras, Lille, Calais, Brussels, Amsterdam, Cologne and London St Pancras.

TGV Est Européen New line connecting Paris' Gare de l'Est with Reims, Nancy, Metz, Strasbourg, Zürich and Germany, including Frankfurt, Stuttgart and Luxembourg. At the time of writing, the high-speed section of the line only stretched as far east as Lorraine; plans to extend the superfast line all the way to Strasbourg are scheduled for completion in 2012.

TGV Sud-Est & TGV Midi-Méditerranée Paris' Gare de Lyon with the southeast, including Dijon, Lyon, Geneva, the Alps, Avignon, Marseille, Nice and Montpellier.

TGV Atlantique Sud-Ouest & TGV Atlantique Ouest Paris' Gare Montparnasse to western and southwestern France, including Brittany (Rennes, Brest, Quimper), Nantes, Tours, Poitiers, La Rochelle, Bordeaux, Biarritz and Toulouse.

COSTS

Full-fare tickets can be quite expensive, and are always pricier during peak periods, eg workday rush hours, on Friday evening and at the beginning and end of holiday periods. Special deals are published online every Tuesday at www.sncf.com, and the new website www.idtgv.com sells tickets for as little as €19 for TGV travel on 20 routes to/from Paris.

Reductions of between 25% and 60% are available with several discount cards:

Carte 12-25 (www.12-25-sncf.com; €49) For travellers aged 12 to 25.

Carte Enfant Plus (www.enfantplus-sncf.com, in French; €65) For one to four adults travelling with a child aged four to 11.

Carte Sénior (www.senior-sncf.com, in French; €55) For over 60s.

Carte Escapades (www.escapades-sncf.com, in French; €85) For people aged 26 to 59. Gets you discounts on return journeys of at least 200km that include a Saturday night away or only involve travel on a Saturday or Sunday.

TICKETS

Buying online at the various SNCF websites can reward with you some great reductions on fares, but be warned – these are generally intended for domestic travellers, and if you're buying abroad it pays to be aware of a few pitfalls. Many tickets can't be posted outside France, and if you buy with a non-French credit card, you might not be able to use it in the automated ticket collection machines at many French stations. Buying from a ticket office may not secure you the cheapest fare, but at least you'll be sure of being able to pick up your ticket…

TRAIN PASSES

The **InterRail One Country Pass** (www.interrailnet.com), valid in France, entitles nonresidents to unlimited travel on SNCF trains for three to eight days over a month. For three/four/six/eight days, the cost is €189/209/269/299 for adults and €125/139/175/194 for young people aged 12 to 25.

➘ SPAIN

SPAIN

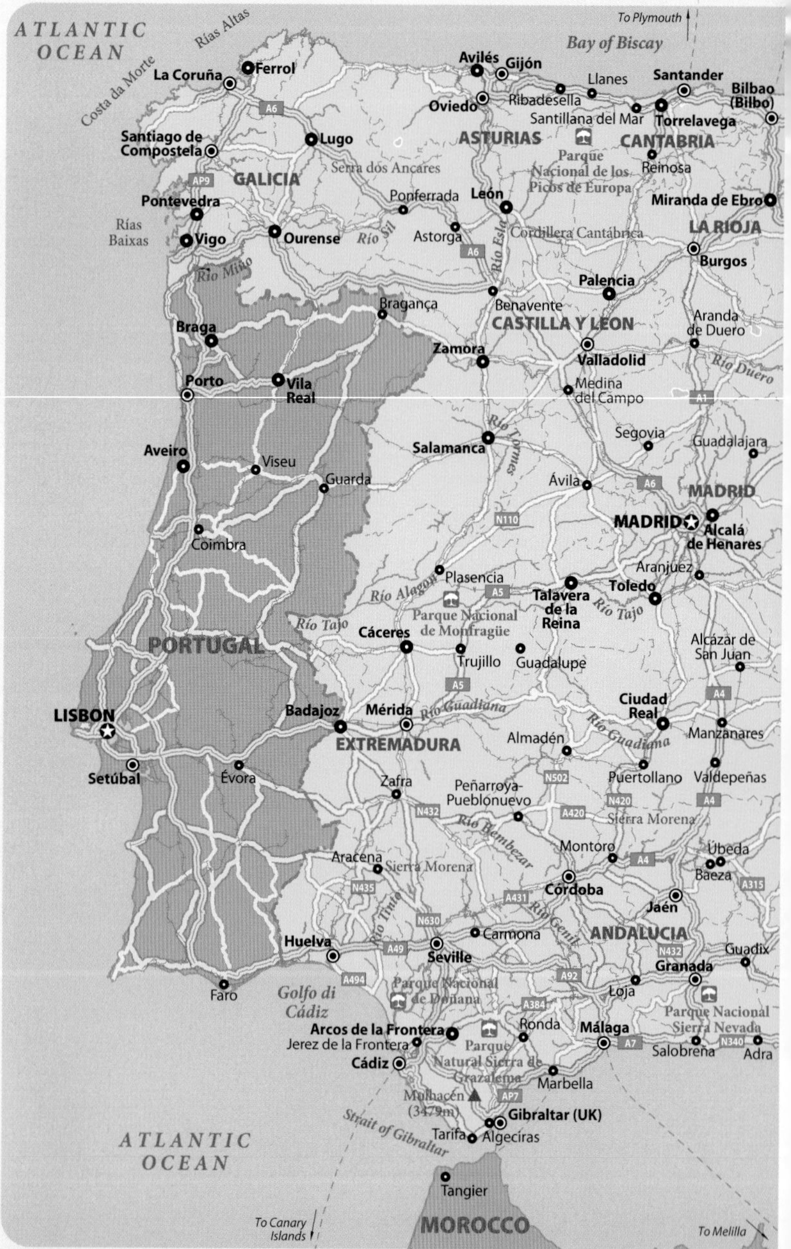
ATLANTIC OCEAN
Rías Altas
Costa da Morte
Bay of Biscay
To Plymouth
La Coruña
Ferrol
Avilés
Gijón
Llanes
Santander
Bilbao (Bilbo)
Oviedo
Ribadesella
Santillana del Mar
Torrelavega
ASTURIAS
CANTABRIA
Parque Nacional de los Picos de Europa
Reinosa
Santiago de Compostela
Lugo
Serra dos Ancares
GALICIA
Pontevedra
Ponferrada
León
Miranda de Ebro
Rías Baixas
Vigo
Ourense
Río Sil
Astorga
Río Esla
Cordillera Cantábrica
LA RIOJA
Burgos
Río Miño
Palencia
Bragança
Benavente
Aranda de Duero
CASTILLA Y LEÓN
Braga
Zamora
Valladolid
Río Duero
Porto
Vila Real
Medina del Campo
Río Tormes
Segovia
Aveiro
Viseu
Salamanca
Guadalajara
Guarda
Ávila
MADRID
MADRID
Alcalá de Henares
Coimbra
Aranjuez
Plasencia
Río Alagón
Talavera de la Reina
Toledo
Río Tajo
Parque Nacional de Monfragüe
Cáceres
PORTUGAL
Trujillo
Guadalupe
Alcázar de San Juan
LISBON
Badajoz
Mérida
Río Guadiana
Ciudad Real
EXTREMADURA
Almadén
Manzanares
Setúbal
Évora
Puertollano
Valdepeñas
Zafra
Peñarroya-Pueblonuevo
Sierra Morena
Río Bembézar
Montoro
Úbeda
Aracena
Sierra Morena
Baeza
Córdoba
Jaén
Río Tinto
Río Genil
Carmona
ANDALUCÍA
Huelva
Seville
Guadix
Granada
Faro
Golfo di Cádiz
Parque Nacional de Doñana
Loja
Parque Nacional Sierra Nevada
Arcos de la Frontera
Ronda
Málaga
Jerez de la Frontera
Parque Natural Sierra de Grazalema
Salobreña
Adra
Cádiz
Marbella
Mulhacén (3479m)
Gibraltar (UK)
Strait of Gibraltar
Tarifa
Algeciras
ATLANTIC OCEAN
Tangier
To Canary Islands
MOROCCO
To Melilla
A6
AP9
A6
A1
A6
N110
A5
A5
A4
N502
N420
A4
N432
A420
A4
N435
A431
A315
N630
A49
N432
A494
A92
A384
A7
N340
AP7

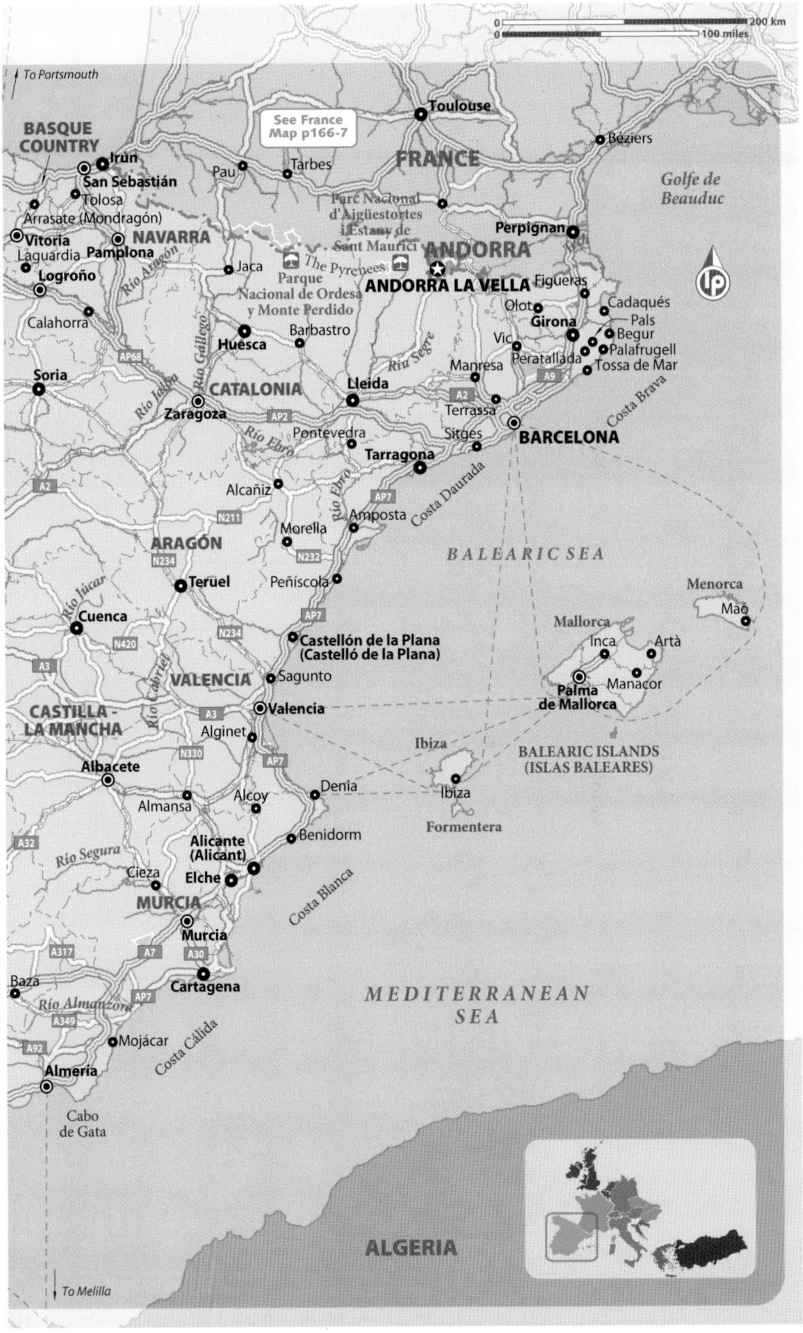
0 200 km
0 100 miles
To Portsmouth
See France Map p166-7
BASQUE COUNTRY
Irún
San Sebastián
Tolosa
Arrasate (Mondragón)
Vitoria
NAVARRA
Laguardia
Pamplona
Logroño
Calahorra
Soria
Pau
Tarbes
Toulouse
FRANCE
Béziers
Golfe de Beauduc
Parc Nacional d'Aigüestortes i Estany de Sant Maurici
ANDORRA
ANDORRA LA VELLA
Perpignan
The Pyrenees
Parque Nacional de Ordesa y Monte Perdido
Jaca
Río Aragón
Río Gállego
Huesca
Barbastro
Figueras
Olot
Girona
Cadaqués
Pals
Begur
Palafrugell
Peratallada
Tossa de Mar
Vic
Manresa
Riu Segre
CATALONIA
Lleida
Río Jalón
Zaragoza
Terrassa
BARCELONA
Costa Brava
Sitges
Río Ebro
Pontevedra
Tarragona
Costa Daurada
Alcañiz
Amposta
Morella
ARAGÓN
BALEARIC SEA
Teruel
Peñíscola
Menorca
Maó
Río Júcar
Cuenca
Mallorca
Inca
Artà
Castellón de la Plana (Castelló de la Plana)
Sagunto
Manacor
VALENCIA
Río Cabriel
Palma de Mallorca
CASTILLA - LA MANCHA
Valencia
Alginet
Ibiza
BALEARIC ISLANDS (ISLAS BALEARES)
Albacete
Denia
Almansa
Alcoy
Formentera
Benidorm
Alicante (Alicant)
Río Segura
Cieza
Elche
MURCIA
Murcia
Costa Blanca
Cartagena
Baza
MEDITERRANEAN SEA
Río Almanzora
Mojácar
Costa Cálida
Almería
Cabo de Gata
ALGERIA
To Melilla
AP68
AP2
A2
N211
AP7
N232
N234
A9
A3
N420
N330
A32
A317
A7
A30
A349
A92

HIGHLIGHTS

1 LA SAGRADA FAMÍLIA

BY JORDI FAULÍ, DEPUTY ARCHITECTURAL DIRECTOR FOR LA SAGRADA FAMÍLIA

The Temple Expiatori de la Sagrada Família is Antoni Gaudí's masterpiece, on which he worked for 43 years. It's a slender structure devoted to geometric perfection and sacred symbolism. It's also a work-in-progress spanning the generations but never losing Gaudí's breathtaking originality and architectural synthesis of natural forms.

JORDI FAULÍ'S DON'T MISS LIST

❶ PASSION FACADE

Among the Fachada de la Pasión's highlights are the angled columns, scenes from Jesus' last hours, a rendering of the Last Supper and a bronze door that reads like a sculptured book. The most surprising view is from inside the door on the far right (especially in the afternoon with the sun in the west).

❷ MAIN NAVE

The majestic Nave Principal showcases Gaudí's use of tree motifs for columns to support the domes: he described this space as a forest. But it's the skylights that give the nave its luminous quality, even more so once the scaffolding is removed in 2010, when light will flood down onto the apse and main altar from the skylight 75m above the floor.

❸ SIDE NAVE & NATIVITY TRANSEPT

Although beautiful in its own right, with windows that project light into the interior and onto the Doric-style

Clockwise from top: Crafting plaster for construction of the church interior; Passion Facade; Script on bronze door in the Passion Facade; Detail of the Nativity Facade; Two of the towers

CLOCKWISE FROM TOP: DENNIS JOHNSON; JOHN ELK III; KRZYSZTOF DYDYNSKI; KRZYSZTOF DYDYNSKI; KRZYSZTOF DYDYNSKI

columns, this is the perfect place to view the sculpted tree-like columns and get an overall perspective of the main nave. Turn around and you're confronted with the inside of the Nativity Facade, an alternative view that most visitors miss; the stained-glass windows are superb.

❹ NATIVITY FACADE

The Fachada del Nacimiento is Gaudí's grand hymn to Creation. Begin by viewing it front-on from a distance, then draw close enough (but to one side) to make out the details of its sculpted figures. The complement to the finely wrought detail is the majesty of the four parabolic towers that reach for the sky and are topped by Venetian stained glass.

❺ MODEL OF COLONIA GÜELL

Among the many original models used by Gaudí in the Museu Gaudí, the most interesting is the church at Colonia Güell. From the side you can, thanks to the model's ingenious use of rope and cloth, visualise the harmony and beauty of the interior. It's upside down because that's how Gaudí worked to best study the building's form and structural balance.

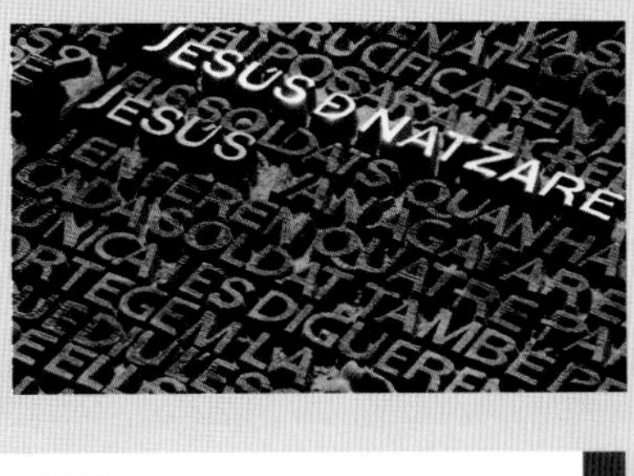

THINGS YOU NEED TO KNOW

How it's done Gaudí spent his last 12 years preparing plans for finishing the building **Expected completion date** 2020 to 2040 **Best photo op** Take a lift (€2) up one of the towers **Metro** Sagrada Família **Admission** €8 **Guided tours** €3.50 **Audioguides** €3.50 **See our author's review on p273**

HIGHLIGHTS

2

MUSEO NACIONAL DEL PRADO

Housed in a glorious 18th-century palace (now enhanced by a modern extension), this Madrid **museum** (p249) houses Spain's top artistic treasures. Around 7000 pieces are on show: Rubens, Rembrandt and Van Dyck are all represented, but it's the Spanish boys, Goya and el Greco, who take the prize.

3

BARCELONA

Beautiful **Barcelona** (p267) is the jewel in Catalonia's crown. Awash with world-class museums, stately squares and Modernista masterpieces, this is a city that's crying out to be explored. Shop till you drop, feed yourself silly and dance till dawn – Barcelona's one nonstop party.

4

ALHAMBRA

This Moorish **palace** (p293) is one of Spain's architectural marvels, built for the Muslim rulers of Granada between the 13th and 15th centuries. Parts of the structure date back to the 11th century, but it's the medieval **Palacio Nazaríes** (Nasrid Palace) which really takes your breath away.

5

TEATRE-MUSEU DALÍ

The surrealist Salvador Dalí is Spain's best-known artistic export, and his **museum** (p279) in Figueres is a surreal sculpture in its own right. Look out for a menagerie of monsters in the courtyard, a room upholstered in red velvet and a 'Wind Palace' decorated with Dalíesque murals.

6

SEVILLE

Few cities sum up the Spanish spirit better than **Seville** (p287). From the bullring to the *barrios,* this vibrant Andalucían city is a delight: don't miss the amazing Alcázar and the landmark cathedral, and make sure you leave time for exploring.

2 Gallery in Museo Nacional del Prado (p249); 3 Plaça Reial (p268); 4 Patio de los Leones, Palacio Nazaríes (p293), Alhambra; 5 Teatre-Museu Dalí (p279); 6 Views over the Alcázar from the Catedral (p288)

THE BEST...

FOOD

- **Tapas** Snack Spanish style in Madrid (p257).
- **Pintxos** Savour Basque tapas in San Sebastian (p280).
- **Paella** Taste the nation's best paella in Valencia (p284).
- **Cochinillo asado** Try suckling pig in Segovia (p263).
- **Seafood** Fans of seafood should try San Sebastian (p280) and Barcelona (p274), Spain's seafood meccas.

FESTIVALS

- **Semana Santa** (p297) One of the highlights of the pre-Easter calendar.
- **Sanfermines** (p283) Pamplona's hair-raising bull-run – brave, barking or both?
- **Feria de Abril** (p289) Seville's April street party.
- **Carnaval** Cadiz (p297) hosts Spain's wildest carnival.
- **Festes de la Mercè** (p273) Barcelona shakes its booty in September.

SACRED SITES

- **Santiago de Compostela** (p283) Join the pilgrims on the holy trail.
- **Seville Cathedral** (p288) See Christopher Columbus' tomb.
- **The Mezquita** (p292) Córdoba's Moorish mosque-cum-cathedral.
- **Burgos Cathedral** (p290) View El Cid's tomb.
- **Montserrat** (p279) Visit this mountain monastery.

SPANISH EXPERIENCES

- **Bullfighting** Watch top *toreros* strut their stuff (p289).
- **Flamenco** Experience flamenco in an Andalucían *tablao* (p291).
- **Nightlife** Drink till daybreak in Madrid (p258) and Barcelona (p276).
- **Football** Watch the superstars at the Camp Nou (p277).
- **Zarzuela** Catch this Spanish blend of dance, music and theatre (p259).

LEFT: ROBERTO GEROMETTA; RIGHT: JOHN BANAGAN

Left: *Pintxos* (Basque tapas); Right: The Mezquita (p292), Córdoba

THINGS YOU NEED TO KNOW

AT A GLANCE

- **Population** 45 million
- **Official languages** Spanish (Castilian or *castellano*), Catalan, Basque, Galician *(gallego)*
- **Currency** Euro (€)
- **Telephone code** ☎34
- **When to go** Spain is sunny year-round, although central and northern Spain can be chilly outside summer
- **Tipping** 10% to 15% in restaurants and cafes

REGIONS IN A NUTSHELL

- **Castilla Y León** (p262) The Spanish heartland.
- **Castilla La Mancha** (p265) Don Quixote's stomping ground.
- **Catalonia** (p266) From ancient ruins to Modernista masterpieces.
- **Basque Country** (p280) Nation within a nation.
- **Cantabria, Asturias & Galicia** (p283) Spain's greenest corner.
- **Andalucía** (p287) Flamenco country.

ADVANCE PLANNING

- **Three months before** Book hotels and travel tickets, especially during festival season.
- **One month before** Arrange theatre, opera and flamenco tickets.
- **Two weeks before** Confirm travel plans and check opening hours.

BUSINESS HOURS

- **Banks** (8.30am-2pm Mon-Fri & Sat mornings)
- **Offices & shops** (9am-2pm & 4.30-8pm Mon-Fri, some also open Sat)
- **Supermarkets** (9am-9pm Mon-Sat)
- **Department stores** (10am-10pm Mon-Sat)
- **Museums** (often closed Mon)
- **Restaurants** (1.30-4pm & 8.30-11pm)
- **Bars** Around 6pm to 2am Monday to Thursday, and 6pm to 3am Friday and Saturday.

BE FOREWARNED

- **Public holidays** Most of Spain goes on holiday during August and Semana Santa (the week before Easter Sunday).
- **Smoking** 'Officially' banned in most public places.
- **Scams** See p296 for common scams, and watch for pickpocketing and bag snatching.

COSTS

- **Under €100 per day** Budget pensions or *hostales*, cheap meals.
- **€100 to €200** Should cover most midrange hotels and restaurants.
- **More than €200** Top-drawer travel, including the best hotels and restaurants.
- **Tax** Accommodation and restaurants charge IVA *(impuesto sobre el valor añadido)* at 7%. On retail goods and car hire, it's 16%.

THINGS YOU NEED TO KNOW

EMERGENCY NUMBERS

- Ambulance (☎ 061)
- Fire (☎ 080)
- Police (☎ 091)

GETTING AROUND

- Air International flights serve Spanish airports including Barcelona (BCN), Bilbao (BIO), Girona (GRO), Madrid (MAD), Málaga (AGP), Palma de Mallorca (PMI), Seville (SVQ), Valencia (VLC) and Zaragoza (ZAZ). The big Spanish carriers include Iberia (IB; ☎ 902 40 05 00; www.iberia.es) and Spanair (JK; ☎ 902 13 14 15; www.spanair.com).
- Bus Spain's bus network is extensive but chaotic. ALSA (☎ 902 42 22 42; www.alsa.es) is one of the largest companies.
- Car Traffic and parking are worst around the big cities. Major motorways are called *autopistas;* tolls are compulsory on many routes.
- Sea Frequent ferries connect Spain with the UK, Italy, Morocco and Algeria. Major ports are in Santander, Bilbao and Barcelona.
- Train Spain's railways are run by Renfe (☎ 902 24 02 02; www.renfe.es). High-speed AVE trains link Madrid, Barcelona and major towns in between, and travel across the Pyrenees into France.

MEDIA

- Newspapers Left-wing *El País,* conservative *ABC,* populist *El Mundo,* Catalonia-focused *La Vanguardia.*
- Radio There's a broad mix of talk radio and music stations. The national pop-rock station, RNE 3, has varied programming.
- TV Most TVs receive at least eight channels: two state-run (TVE1 and La2), five private (Antena 3, Tele 5, Cuatro, La Sexta and Canal Plus) and one regional.

RESOURCES

- Turespaña (www.spain.info, www.tourspain.es) National tourism body.
- Renfe (www.renfe.es) Plan your train travel.
- EuroResidentes (www.euroresidentes.com) Multi-lingual advice on living and working in Spain.

VISAS

- EU nationals Free to enter Spain with their national ID card or passport.
- Australia, Canada, Israel, Japan, New Zealand, US Can stay visa-free for 90 days.
- Other nations Will need visas from their home country.

GET INSPIRED

FILMS

- **Volver** (2006) Multi-generational melodrama from Pedro Almodóvar.
- **Jamón, Jamón** (1992) Saucy, sexy and very Spanish.
- **Flamenco** (2000) Carlos Saura's flamenco documentary.
- **Mar Adentro** (2004) Oscar-winning drama by Alejandro Amenábar.
- **Vicky Cristina Barcelona** (2008) Woody Allen rom-com set in Barcelona.

BOOKS

- **Death in the Afternoon** Hemingway's bullfighting classic.
- **Ghosts of Spain** Fascinating study of Spain by Giles Tremlett.
- **The New Spaniards** Illuminating account of contemporary Spain by John Hooper.
- **The Shadow of the Wind** Spanish-set mystery by novelist Carlos Ruíz Zafón.
- **Spanish Steps** Tim Moore tackles the Santiago de Compostela trail.

MUSIC

- **Zapatillas** (Canto del Loco) Spanish power-pop band.
- **Carlos Nunez Y Amigos** (Carlos Nunez) Trad music with a Galician flavour.
- **No Es Lo Mismo** (Alejandro Sanz) Grammy award-winning balladeer.
- **Noche de Flamenco y Blues** (Raimundo Amador) Flamenco fusion from one of Spain's most inventive musicians.
- **Gold** (Paco de Lucía) Popular flamenco guitarist's compilation.

WEBSITES

- **Spain for Visitors** (www.spainforvisitors.com) Online travel guide.
- **Wines from Spain** (www.winesfromspain.com) Top Spanish tipples.
- **Wild Spain** (www.wild-spain.com) Nature and outdoor activities.
- **Fiestas.net** (www.fiestas.net) Pick your party.
- **Andalucía** (www.andalucia.com) The home of flamenco.

LEFT: MARK AVELLINO; RIGHT: OLIVER STREWE

Left: FC Barcelona in action at Camp Nou (p277); Right: Plate of mussels

ITINERARIES

THE HEART OF SPAIN Three Days

If you've only got a few days, nowhere captures the Spanish soul as much as **(1) Madrid** (p248). Start with incredible art at the **Museo Nacional del Prado** (p249), the **Museo Thyssen-Bornemisza** (p253) and the **Caixa Forum** (p253), followed by some people-watching on the **Plaza Mayor** (p254) and an after-dark visit to the *tabernas* and tapas bars of **La Latina** (p259), **Chueca** (p259) and **Los Austrias and Centro** (p258).

On day two, spend the morning exploring the **Palacio Real** (p254), the monarch's official Madrid residence, then pack a picnic and pass the afternoon at the **Parque del Buen Retiro** (p254). Book yourself a spot at one of the city's top *tablaos* for some late-night flamenco: **Casa Patas** (p260) and **Las Tablas** (p260) are both recommended.

The last day's reserved for a day trip to either historic **(2) Toledo** (p265) or the 'hanging houses' of **(3) Cuenca** (p266).

ANDALUCÍAN ADVENTURE Five Days

For passion, energy and Spanish atmosphere, it's tough to top **(1) Seville** (p287). You'll need a couple of days to do it justice: this gorgeous city knows how to live life to the full, with some of the liveliest *barrios*, buzziest nightlife and most frenetic festivals in southern Spain. The centuries-old clash of Moorish and Christian cultures has left an enduring mark on this part of Spain, and the meeting of worlds is clearly evident in Seville's landmarks, the **Catedral** (p288) and the **Alcázar** (p288). After nightfall, catch some authentic flamenco in Seville's traditional **tablaos** (p291).

On day three, hop in the car or catch a train to **(2) Córdoba** (p292), where you'll find more Moorish culture at the beautiful **Mezquita** (p292) and the **Medina Azahara** (p292), a 10th-century Muslim city-palace. Even more spectacular is the **Alhambra** (p293) in nearby **(3) Granada** (p292), one of the crowning architectural achievements of the ancient Muslim world. Take your time exploring, and arrive early to avoid the worst crowds.

The last day is set aside for another fascinating Andalucían city, **(4) Cádiz** (p294), which for centuries served as the gateway to southern Spain for merchants, seafarers and globetrotting explorers – including a chap by the name of Christopher Columbus, who set out on two of his landmark voyages from here.

BARCELONA & BEYOND One Week

This trip begins with two days in beautiful **(1) Barcelona** (p267), celebrated for its big-city style and Modernista architecture. Top of the sightseeing list is the **Sagrada Família** (p273), Gaudí's fantasy

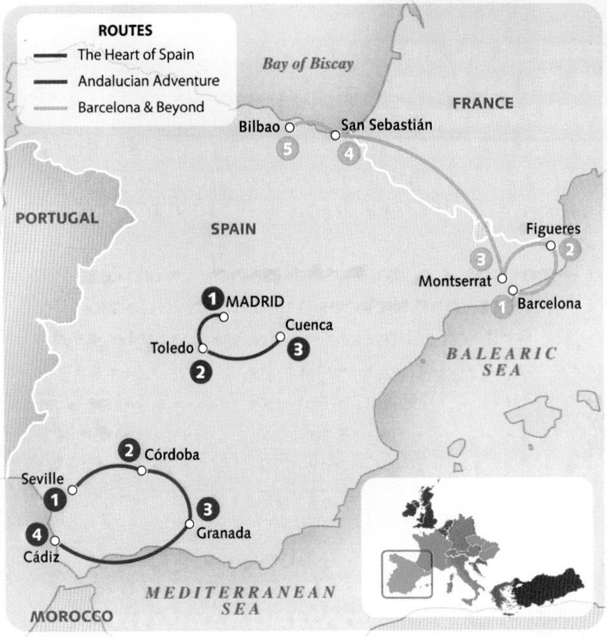

cathedral (currently scheduled for completion sometime around 2020), followed by a tour around Barcelona's other modernist landmarks (p275). Spend the evening exploring the bars and restaurants of the Barrí Gòtic (p268).

On day two, head for the Museu Picasso (p269) and the Museu d'Art Contemporani de Barcelona (p268), have a wander around the shops and boutiques of El Raval (p268) and La Ribera (p269) or chill out in Gaudí's surreal hilltop Park Güell (p275). Round things off with sophisticated Spanish dining in L'Eixample (p276) or La Barceloneta (p276).

On day three, take a day trip into the surreal world of Salvador Dalí at the fantastic Teatre-Museu Dalí (p279) in (2) Figueres. Follow it up with a pilgrimage to the mountain monastery of (3) Montserrat (p279) and a final day exploring the stylish cities of (4) San Sebastián (p280) or (5) Bilbao (p281).

DISCOVER SPAIN

Stretching sun-drenched and untamed to the south of the wild and majestic Pyrenees, this passionate nation works a mysterious magic. Spain is littered with hundreds of glittering beaches, flamenco *bailaors* (dancers) swirl in flounces of colour, and *toreros* (bullfighters) strut their stuff in the bullrings. Summer holidaymakers gather around great pans of steaming paella (at its tasty best in Valencia) and pitchers of sangria...

From its Roman amphitheatres to Muslim palaces, from Gothic cathedrals and Modernista constructions, the country is a treasure chest of artistic and architectural marvels across a matchless cultural palette. Up and down the country, a zest for life creates an intense, hedonistic vibe in its effervescent cities. Indeed, if there is one thing Spaniards love, it is to eat, drink and be merry, whether gobbling up tapas over fine wine in Madrid and the south, or the elaborate Basque Country equivalent, *pintxos,* over cider in the north.

MADRID

pop 3.13 million

Madrid has a raw, infectious energy. Explore the old streets of the centre, relax in the plazas, soak up the culture in its excellent art museums, and take at least one evening to experience the city's legendary nightlife scene.

HISTORY

Madrid was little more than a muddy, mediocre village when King Felipe II declared it Spain's capital in 1561. Despite being home to generations of nobles, the city was a squalid grid of unpaved alleys and dirty buildings until the 18th century, when King Carlos III turned his attention to public works.

The post–civil war 1940s and '50s were trying times for the capital, with rampant poverty. When Spain's dictator, General Franco, died in 1975, the city exploded with creativity and life, giving *madrileños* the party-hard reputation they still cherish.

Terrorist bombs rocked Madrid in March 2004, just before national elections, and killed 191 commuters on four trains. In 2007, two people died in a Basque terrorist bomb attack at the city's airport. With remarkable aplomb, the city quickly returned to business as usual on both occasions.

ORIENTATION

In Spain, all roads lead to Madrid's Plaza de la Puerta del Sol. Radiating out from this busy plaza are roads – Calle Mayor, Calle del Arenal, Calle de Preciados, Calle de la Montera and Calle de Alcalá – as well as a host of metro lines and bus routes.

South of the Puerta del Sol is the oldest part of the city, with Plaza Mayor and Los Austrias to the southwest and the busy streets of the Huertas *barrio* (district or quarter) to the southeast.

North of the plaza is a modern shopping district and, beyond that, the east–west thoroughfare Gran Vía and the gay *barrio* Chueca, gritty Malasaña, then Chamberí and Argüelles. East of the Puerta del Sol, across the Paseo del Prado and Paseo de los Recoletos, lie El Retiro park and chichi Salamanca.

INFORMATION

Like all Spanish cities, Madrid is fairly crawling with bank branches equipped with ATMs. As a rule, exchange bureaux have longer hours but worse rates and steeper commissions.

Anglo-American Medical Unit (Map pp250-1; ☎ 91 435 18 23; www.unidadmedica.com; Calle del Conde de Aranda 1; 9am-8pm Mon-Fri, 10am-1pm Sat for emergencies; M Retiro)

Farmacia del Globo (Map p252; ☎ 91 369 20 00; Calle de Atocha 46; 24hr; M Antón Martín)

Madrid Card (☎ 91 360 47 72; www.madridcard.com; 1/2/3 days €42/55/68) It includes free entry to more than 40 museums in and around Madrid. There's also a cheaper version (€28/32/36 for one/two/three days) that covers just cultural sights.

Municipal tourist office (Centro de Turismo de Madrid; Map p252; ☎ 91 429 49 51; www.esmadrid.com; Plaza Mayor 27; 9.30am-8.30pm)

Regional tourist office (Map p252; ☎ 91 429 49 51, 902 100 007; www.turismomadrid.es; Calle del Duque de Medinaceli 2; 8am-8pm Mon-Sat, 9am-2pm Sun) There are also tourist offices at Barajas airport (T1 & T4), and Chamartín and Atocha train stations.

Servicio de Atención al Turista Extranjero (Foreign Tourist Assistance Service; Map p252; ☎ 91 548 85 37, 91 548 80 08; satemadrid@munimadrid.es; Calle de Leganitos 19; 9am-10pm; M Plaza de España or Santo Domingo)

DANGERS & ANNOYANCES

Madrid is a generally safe city although you should, as in most European cities, be wary of pickpockets in the city centre, on the Metro and around major tourist sights.

Prostitution along Calle de la Montera and in the Casa del Campo park means that you need to exercise extra caution in these areas.

SIGHTS & ACTIVITIES

MUSEO NACIONAL DEL PRADO

Spain's premier art museum, the **Prado** (Map p252; ☎ 91 330 28 00; http://museoprado

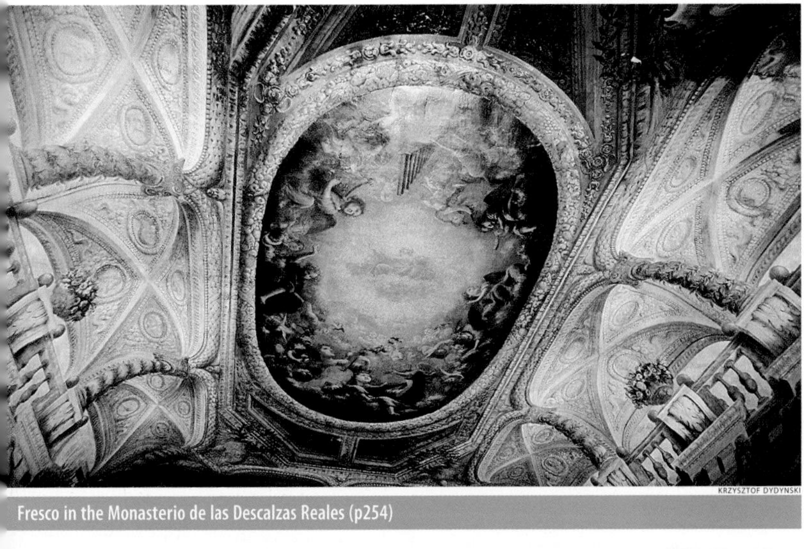
KRZYSZTOF DYDYNSKI

Fresco in the Monasterio de las Descalzas Reales (p254)

SPAIN

MADRID

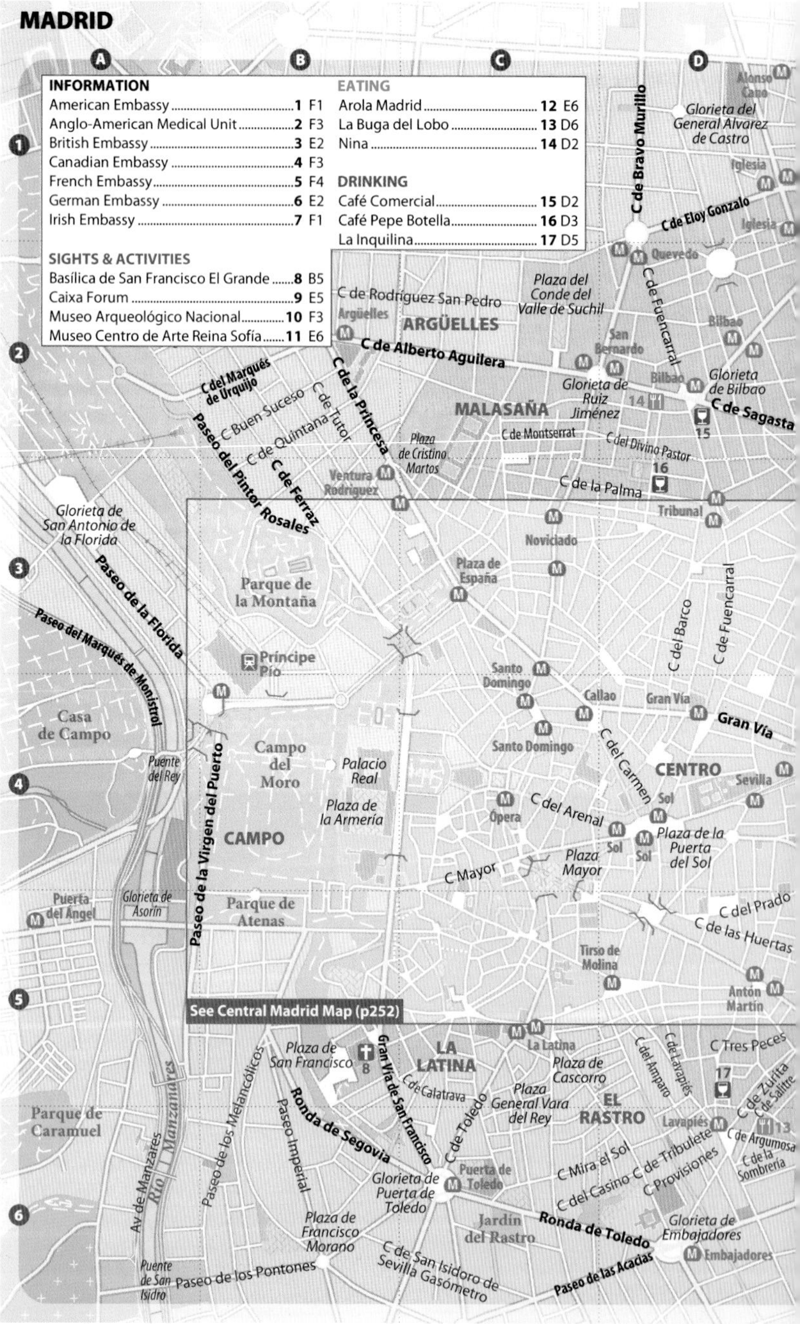
MADRID
A
B
C
D
1
2
3
4
5
6
INFORMATION
American Embassy 1 F1
Anglo-American Medical Unit 2 F3
British Embassy 3 E2
Canadian Embassy 4 F3
French Embassy 5 F4
German Embassy 6 E2
Irish Embassy 7 F1
SIGHTS & ACTIVITIES
Basílica de San Francisco El Grande 8 B5
Caixa Forum 9 E5
Museo Arqueológico Nacional 10 F3
Museo Centro de Arte Reina Sofía 11 E6
EATING
Arola Madrid 12 E6
La Buga del Lobo 13 D6
Nina 14 D2
DRINKING
Café Comercial 15 D2
Café Pepe Botella 16 D3
La Inquilina 17 D5
C de Bravo Murillo
Glorieta del General Alvarez de Castro
Iglesia
C de Eloy Gonzalo
Quevedo
C de Fuencarral
Plaza del Conde del Valle de Suchil
C de Rodríguez San Pedro
Argüelles
ARGÜELLES
San Bernardo
Bilbao
C de Alberto Aguilera
Glorieta de Bilbao
Glorieta de Ruiz Jiménez
C de Sagasta
MALASAÑA
C del Marqués de Urquijo
C de la Princesa
C Buen Suceso
C de Tutor
C de Quintana
Paseo del Pintor Rosales
C de Ferraz
Plaza de Cristino Martos
C de Montserrat
C del Divino Pastor
Ventura Rodríguez
C de la Palma
Tribunal
Glorieta de San Antonio de la Florida
Paseo de la Florida
Noviciado
Plaza de España
Parque de la Montaña
C del Barco
Paseo del Marqués de Monistrol
Príncipe Pío
Santo Domingo
Callao
Gran Vía
Casa de Campo
Puente del Rey
Campo del Moro
Palacio Real
Paseo de la Virgen del Puerto
C del Carmen
CENTRO
Sevilla
Sol
Plaza de la Armería
CAMPO
Ópera
C del Arenal
Plaza de la Puerta del Sol
Plaza Mayor
C Mayor
Puerta del Ángel
Glorieta de Asorín
Parque de Atenas
C del Prado
C de las Huertas
Tirso de Molina
Antón Martín
See Central Madrid Map (p252)
Plaza de San Francisco
Gran Vía de San Francisco
LA LATINA
La Latina
C de Calatrava
Plaza de Cascorro
C del Amparo
C de Lavapiés
C Tres Peces
Paseo de los Melancólicos
Ronda de Segovia
Paseo Imperial
C de Toledo
Plaza General Vara del Rey
EL RASTRO
Lavapiés
C de Zurita
C de Salitre
C de Argumosa
C de la Sombrería
Parque de Caramuel
Río Manzanares
Av de Manzanares
Glorieta de Puerta de Toledo
Puerta de Toledo
C Mira el Sol
C del Casino
C de Tribulete
C Provisiones
Jardín del Rastro
Ronda de Toledo
Glorieta de Embajadores
Embajadores
Plaza de Francisco Morano
C de San Isidoro de Sevilla
Gasómetro
Paseo de las Acacias
Puente de San Isidro
Paseo de los Pontones

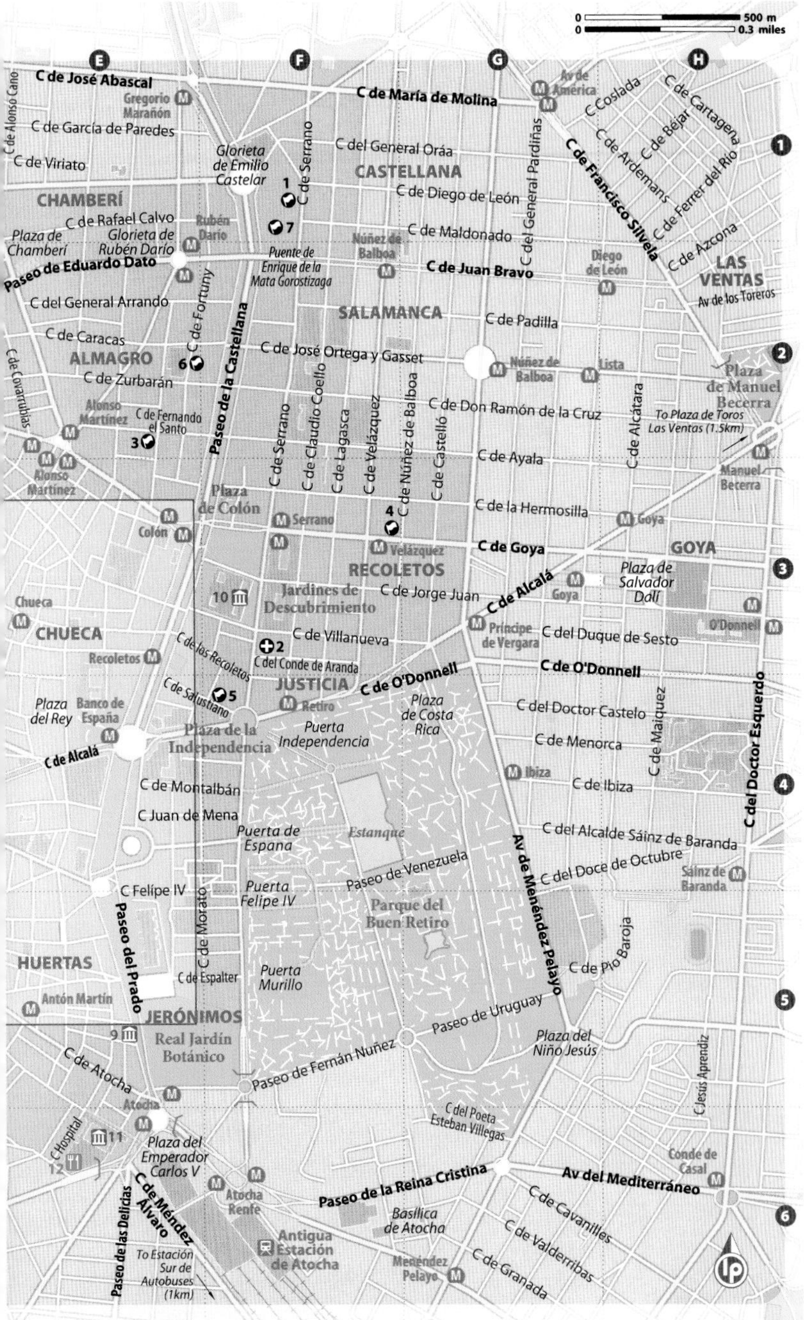

SPAIN

MADRID

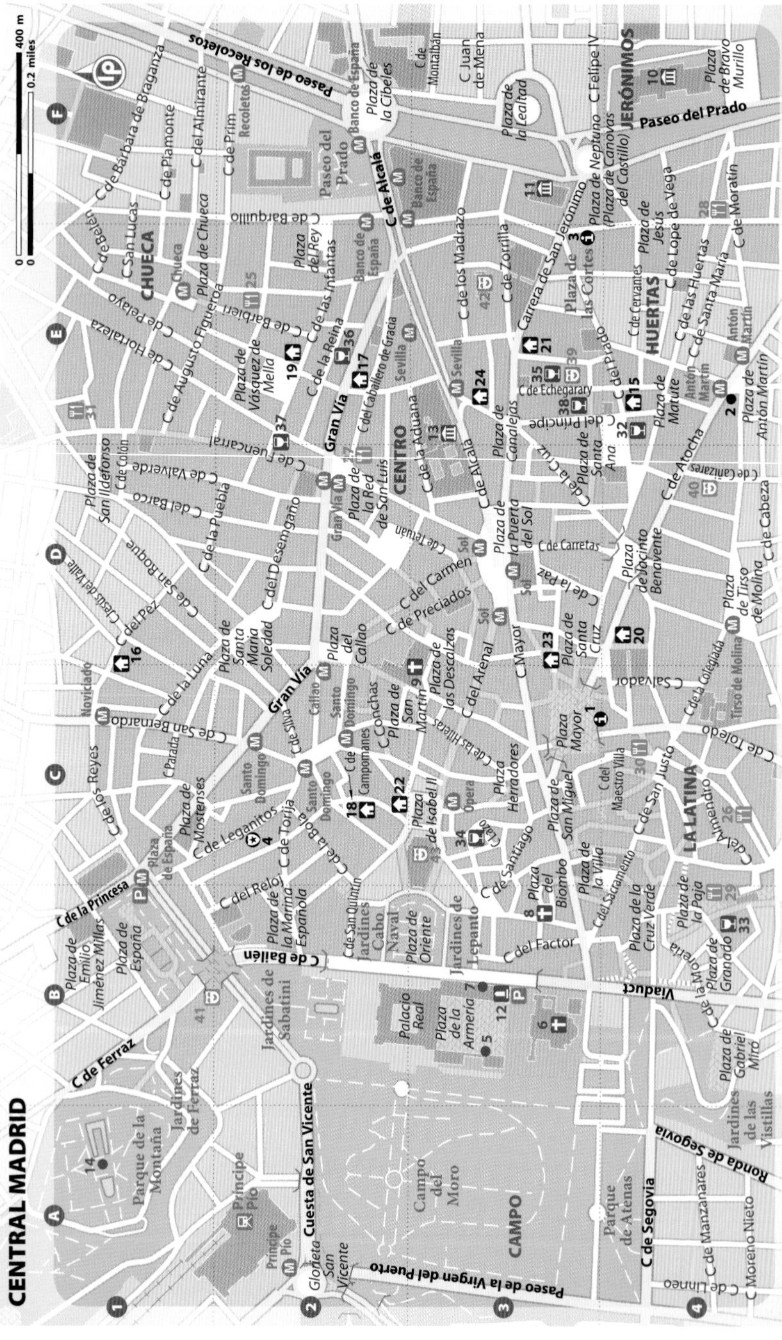
CENTRAL MADRID
0 400 m
0 0.2 miles
CHUECA
CENTRO
HUERTAS
JERÓNIMOS
LA LATINA
CAMPO
Paseo de los Recoletos
Paseo del Prado
Plaza de la Cibeles
Plaza de la Lealtad
C de Alcalá
Gran Vía
Paseo de la Virgen del Puerto
Cuesta de San Vicente
C de Bailén
C de la Princesa
C de Ferraz
Ronda de Segovia
C de Segovia
Viaduct
Parque de la Montaña
Jardines de Ferraz
Príncipe Pío
Campo del Moro
Parque de Atenas
Jardines de Sabatini
Palacio Real
Plaza de la Armería
Plaza de Oriente
Jardines Cabo Naval
Jardines de Lepanto
Plaza de España
Plaza de Isabel II
Plaza Mayor
Plaza de la Puerta del Sol
Plaza de Santa Ana
Plaza de Tirso de Molina
Plaza de Jacinto Benavente
Plaza de Antón Martín
Plaza de las Cortes
Plaza de Neptuno (Plaza de Cánovas del Castillo)
Plaza de Chueca
Plaza de Vásquez de Mella
Plaza del Rey
Plaza de San Ildefonso
Plaza de Santa María Soledad
Plaza del Callao
Plaza de Santo Domingo
Plaza de San Miguel
Plaza de la Villa
Plaza de la Paja
Plaza de la Cruz Verde
Plaza de Gabriel Miró
Jardines de las Vistillas
Plaza de Bravo Murillo
Banco de España
Sol
Sevilla
Ópera
Callao
Santo Domingo
Noviciado
Tirso de Molina
Antón Martín
Gran Vía
Recoletos
Chueca

INFORMATION
Centro de Turismo de Madrid ... **1** C3
Farmacia del Globo ... **2** E4
Regional Tourist Office ... **3** E3
Servicio de Atención al Turista Extranjero ... **4** C2

SIGHTS & ACTIVITIES
Armería Real ... **5** B3
Catedral de Nuestra Señora de la Almudena ... **6** B3
Farmacia Real ... **7** B3
Iglesia de San Nicolás ... **8** B3
Monasterio de las Descalzas Reales ... **9** C3
Museo Nacional del Prado ... **10** F4
Museo Thyssen-Bornemisza ... **11** F3
Palacio Real ... **12** B3
Real Academia de Bellas Artes de San Fernando ... **13** E3
Templo de Debod ... **14** A1

SLEEPING
Alicia Room Mate ... **15** E4
Hotel Abalú ... **16** D1
Hotel de Las Letras ... **17** E2
Hotel Meninas ... **18** C2
Hotel Óscar ... **19** E2
Hotel Plaza Mayor ... **20** D4
Hotel Urban ... **21** E3
Mario Room Mate ... **22** C2
Petit Palace Posada del Peine ... **23** D3
Quo ... **24** E3

EATING
Bazaar ... **25** E2
Casa Lucio ... **26** C4
La Gloria de Montera ... **27** D2
Maceiras ... **28** F4
Naïa Restaurante ... **29** B4
Restaurante Sobrino de Botín ... **30** C4
Ribeira Do Miño ... **31** E1

DRINKING
Cervecería Alemana ... **32** E4
Delic ... **33** B4
Gaia Cocktail Lounge ... **34** C3
La Venencia ... **35** E3
Museo Chicote ... **36** E2
Stop Madrid ... **37** E2
Viva Madrid ... **38** E3

ENTERTAINMENT
Cardamomo ... **39** E3
Casa Patas ... **40** D4
Las Tablas ... **41** B1
Teatro de la Zarzuela ... **42** E3
Teatro Real ... **43** C3

mcu.es; Paseo del Prado s/n; adult/under 18yr & over 65yr/student €6/free/4, Sun free, headset guide €3.50; 9am-8pm Tue-Sun; M Banco de España) is a seemingly endless parade of priceless works from Spain and beyond. Aside from works by Velázquez and other Siglo de Oro (Golden Century) painters, you'll find two of the Prado's greatest masterpieces, Goya's *El Dos de Mayo* and *El Tres de Mayo*, which bring to life the 1808 anti-French revolt and subsequent execution of insurgents in Madrid. Showing Goya's darker side is the well-known *Saturno Devorando a Un Hijo* (Saturn Devouring his Son); the name says it all.

MUSEO THYSSEN-BORNEMISZA

Opposite the Prado, the **Museo Thyssen-Bornemisza** **(Map p252; ☎ 91 369 01 51; www.museothyssen.org; Paseo del Prado 8; adult/concession €6/4; 10am-7pm Tue-Sun; M Banco de España)** is an eclectic collection of international masterpieces. Begin your visit on the 2nd floor, where you'll start with medieval art, and make your way down to modern works on the ground level, passing paintings by Titian, El Greco, Rubens, Rembrandt, Anton van Dyck, Canaletto, Cézanne, Monet, Sisley, Renoir, Pissarro, Degas, Constable, Van Gogh, Miró, Modigliani, Matisse, Picasso, Gris, Pollock, Dalí, Kandinsky, Toulouse-Lautrec, Lichtenstein and many others on the way.

CENTRO DE ARTE REINA SOFÍA

A stunning collection of mainly Spanish modern art, the **Museo Nacional Centro de Arte Reina Sofía** **(Map pp250-1; ☎ 91 774 10 00; www.museoreinasofia.es; Calle de Santa Isabel 52; adult/child & senior/student €6/free/4, 2.30-9pm Sat & 10am-2.30pm Sun free, audio guide €3; 10am-9pm Mon & Wed-Sat, 10am-2.30pm Sun; M Atocha)** is home to Picasso's *Guernica* – his protest against the German bombing of the Basque town of Guernica during the Spanish Civil War in 1937 – in addition to important works by surrealist Salvador Dalí and abstract paintings by the Catalan artist Joan Miró.

CAIXA FORUM

The **Caixa Forum** **(Map pp250-1; ☎ 91 330 73 00; www.fundacio.lacaixa.es, in Spanish; Paseo del Prado 36; admission free; 10am-10pm; M Atocha)**, opened in 2008, seems to hover above the ground. On one wall is the *jardín colgante* (hanging garden), a lush vertical wall of greenery almost four storeys high. Inside are four floors used to hold top-quality art exhibitions.

PALACIO REAL & AROUND

Still King Juan Carlos I's official residence (though no one actually lives here), Madrid's 18th-century royal palace, **Palacio Real** (Map p252; ☎ 91 542 69 47; www.patrimonionacional.es; Calle de Bailén s/n; adult/student & EU senior €10/3.50, Wed EU citizens free; 9am-6pm Mon-Sat, to 3pm Sun & holidays Apr-Sep, closes 1hr earlier Oct-Mar; M Ópera), is used mainly for important events of pomp and state. Look out for the 215 clocks of the royal clock collection and the five Stradivarius violins, used occasionally for concerts and balls.

Outside the main palace, poke your head into the **Farmacia Real** (Map p252; Royal Pharmacy), where apothecary-style jars line the shelves. Continue on to the **Armería Real** (Map p252; Royal Armoury), where you'll be impressed by the shiny (and surprisingly tiny!) royal suits of armour, most of them from the 16th and 17th centuries.

PLAZA MAYOR

Ringed with numerous cafes and restaurants and packed with people day and night, the 17th-century arcaded Plaza Mayor (Map p252) was traditionally used as a market but is now an elegant and bustling square.

Colourful frescoes decorate the **Real Casa de la Panaderia** (Royal Bakery), which predates the plaza and was restored after a 1790 fire.

CHURCHES

The **Catedral de Nuestra Señora de la Almudena** (Map p252; ☎ 91 542 22 00; Calle de Bailén; 9am-9pm; M Ópera) is just across the plaza from the Palacio Real. It's worth a quick peek but is much less captivating than the imposing 18th-century **Basílica de San Francisco El Grande** (Map pp250-1; ☎ 91 365 38 00; Plaza de San Francisco 1; admission €3; 8-11am Mon, 8am-1pm & 4-6.30pm Tue-Fri, 4-8.45pm Sat; M La Latina). Also worth a visit is the largely 15th-century **Iglesia de San Nicolás** (Map p252; ☎ 91 548 83 14; Plaza San Nicolás 6; M Ópera).

MONASTERIO DE LAS DESCALZAS REALES

Opulent inside though with a rather plain Plateresque exterior, the **Monasterio de las Descalzas Reales** (Convent of the Barefoot Royals; Map p252; ☎ 91 542 69 47; www.patrimonionacional.es; Plaza de las Descalzas 3; adult/child €5/2.50, Wed EU citizens free, combined ticket with Convento de la Encarnación €6/3.40; 10.30am-12.45pm & 4-5.45pm Tue-Thu & Sat, 10.30am-12.45pm Fri, 11am-1.45pm Sun; M Ópera or Sol) was founded in 1559 by Juana of Austria. Daughter of Spain's King Carlos I and Isabel of Portugal, Juana transformed one of her mother's palaces into the noblewomen's convent of choice. On the obligatory guided tour you'll see a gaudily frescoed Renaissance stairway, a number of extraordinary tapestries based on works by Rubens, and a wonderful painting entitled *The Voyage of the 11,000 Virgins*. Some 33 nuns still live here and there are 33 chapels dotted around the convent.

PARQUE DEL BUEN RETIRO

A stroll in the **Parque del Buen Retiro** (Map pp250-1; 7am-midnight May-Sep, 7am-10pm Oct-Apr; M Retiro), or simply El Retiro, is an integral part of Madrid life. Come on a weekend for street performers, clowns, puppet shows and the occasional theatre performance.

Just outside the park is the **Real Jardín Botánico** (Map pp250-1; ☎ 91 420 30 17; Plaza de Bravo Murillo 2; adult/child/concession €2/free/1; 10am-dusk), equally pleasant for strolling.

KRZYSZTOF DYDYNSKI

Monument to King Alfonso XII in Parque del Buen Retiro

OTHER SIGHTS

The frescoed ceilings of the **Ermita de San Antonio de la Florida** (Map pp250-1; ☎ 91 542 07 22; Glorieta de San Antonio de la Florida 5; admission free; 9.30am-8pm Tue-Fri, 10am-2pm Sat & Sun, varied hr Jul & Aug; M Príncipe Pío) are one of Madrid's most surprising secrets. In the southern of the two small chapels you can see Goya's work in its original setting, created in 1798. The painter is buried in front of the altar.

Highlights of the **Museo Arqueológico Nacional** (National Archaeology Museum; Map pp250-1; ☎ 91 577 79 12; http://man.mcu.es, in Spanish; Calle de Serrano 13; admission €3, free after 2.30pm Sat & Sun; 9.30am-8pm Tue-Sat, to 3pm Sun & holidays; M Serrano) include stunning mosaics taken from Roman villas across Spain; a gilded Mudéjar domed ceiling; and the ancient *Dama de Ibiza* and *Dama de Elche* sculptures that reveal a flourishing artistic tradition among the Iberian tribes, influenced by contact with Greek and Phoenician civilisations.

The authentically ancient **Templo de Debod** (Map p252; ☎ 91 366 74 15; www.munimadrid.es/templodebod; Paseo del Pintor Rosales; admission free; 10am-2pm & 6-8pm Tue-Fri, 10am-2pm Sat & Sun Apr-Sep, 9.45am-1.45pm & 4.15-6.15pm Tue-Fri, 10am-2pm Sat & Sun Oct-Mar; M Ventura Rodríguez) was transferred here stone by stone from Egypt in 1972 as a gesture of thanks to Spanish archaeologists who helped save Egyptian monuments from the rising waters of the Aswan Dam.

The somewhat fusty **Real Academia de Bellas Artes de San Fernando** (Map p252; ☎ 91 524 08 64; http://rabasf.insde.es, in Spanish; Calle de Alcalá 13; adult/senior & under 18yr/student €3/free/1.50; 9am-7pm Tue-Fri, 9am-2.30pm & 4-7pm Sat, 9am-2.30pm Sun & Mon Sep-Jun, varied hr Jul & Aug; M Sevilla) offers a broad collection of old and modern masters, including works by Zurbarán, El Greco, Rubens, Tintoretto, Goya, Sorolla and Juan Gris.

El Rastro (Map pp250-1; Calle Ribera Curtidores; 8am-2pm Sun; M La Latina) A bustling flea market, the chaotic El Rastro sells a bit of everything. The madness begins at Plaza Cascorro and worms its way downhill. Watch your wallet.

TOURS

The Municipal tourist office (p249) offers **Descubre Madrid** (**Discover Madrid; ☎ 91 588 29 06; www.esmadrid.com/descubremadrid/portal .do; walking tours adult/child, student, under-25 or senior €3.30/2.70, bus tours €6.45/5.05, bicycle tours €3.30/2.70 plus €6 bike rental**), with dozens of guided walking, cycling and bus itineraries.

FESTIVALS & EVENTS

Fiesta de San Isidro Street parties, parades, bullfights and other fun events honour Madrid's patron saint on and around 15 May.

Summer Festivals Small-time but fun, the neighbourhood summer festivals, such as San Cayetano in Lavapiés, and San Lorenzo and La Paloma in La Latina, allow hot and sweaty *madrileños* to drink and dance the night away in the streets.

SLEEPING

LOS AUSTRIAS & CENTRO

Hotel Plaza Mayor (**Map p252; ☎ 91 360 06 06; www.h-plazamayor.com; Calle de Atocha 2; s/d from €65/85; M Sol or Tirso de Molina; ❄**) Stylish decor, charming original elements of an 150-year-old building and helpful staff are selling points here. The attic rooms have great views.

Mario Room Mate (**Map p252; ☎ 91 548 85 48; www.room-matehoteles.com; Calle de Campomanes 4; s €90-120, d €100-140; M Ópera; ❄ 💻**) Mario's offers sleek designer boutique chic. Rooms are spacious, with high ceilings and simple furniture, light tones contrasting smoothly with muted colours and dark surfaces.

Hotel Meninas (**Map p252; ☎ 91 541 28 05; www.hotelmeninas.com; Calle de Campomanes 7; s/d from €109/129; M Ópera; 💻**) Inside a refurbished 19th-century mansion, the Meninas combines old-world comfo with modern, minimalist style.

Petit Palace Posada del Peine (**Ma p252; ☎ 91 523 81 51; www.hthotels.com; Calle d Postas 17; d €115-150; M Sol; ❄**) Combinin a splendid historic building (1610) wit brilliant location, this enticing hotel als has hi-tech rooms. The bathrooms spark and many historical architectural feature remain in situ.

Hotel de Las Letras (**Map p252; ☎ 91 52 79 80; www.hoteldelasletras.com; Gran Vía 11; from €165; M Gran Vía**) Hotel de las Letra started the rooftop hotel bar in Madri The bar's wonderful, but the whole hote is excellent. The individually styled room each have literary quotes scribbled on th walls.

SOL, HUERTAS & ATOCHA

Quo (**Map p252; ☎ 91 532 90 49; www.hotelesqu com; Calle de Sevilla 4; s €90-160, d €90-195; M Se villa; ❄ 💻**) Quo is one of Madrid's home of chic, with black-clad staff, minimalis designer furniture, high ceilings and hug windows. Rooms have black-and-whit photos of Madrid, dark-wood floors and comfy armchairs.

Alicia Room Mate (**Map p252; ☎ 91 389 6 95; www.room-matehoteles.com; Calle del Prad 2; d €90-200; M Sol, Sevilla or Antón Martín; 💻**) With beautiful, spacious rooms, Alici overlooks Plaza de Santa Ana. It has a ultramodern look and the downstairs ba is oh-so-cool.

Hotel Urban (**Map p252; ☎ 91 787 77 70 www.derbyhotels.com; Carrera de San Jerónimo 34 d €200-350; M Sevilla; ❄ 💻 🏊**) The towering glass edifice of Hotel Urban is the epitome of art-inspired designer cool. Dark-wood floors and dark walls are offset by plenty of light, while the bathrooms have wonderful designer fittings. The rooftop swimming pool is Madrid's best.

MALASAÑA & CHUECA

Hotel Abalú (Map p252; ☎ 91 531 47 44; www.hotelabalu.com; Calle del Pez 19; s/d from €74/105, ste €140-200; Ⓜ Noviciado) Each room in this boutique hotel has its own design drawn from the imagination of Luis Delgado, from retro chintz to Zen, Baroque and pure white.

our pick **Hotel Óscar** (Map p252; ☎ 91 701 11 73; www.room-matehoteles.com; Plaza Vázquez de Mella 12; d €90-200, ste €150-280; Ⓜ Gran Vía) Hotel Óscar's designer rooms ooze style and sophistication. Some have floor-to-ceiling murals, the lighting is always funky and the colour scheme is asplash with pinks, lime greens, oranges or a more minimalist black-and-white.

EATING

From the chaotic tapas bars of La Latina to countless neighbourhood favourites, you'll have no trouble tracking down specialities like *cochinillo asado* (roast suckling pig) or *cocido madrileño* (a hearty stew made of beans and various animals' innards).

LOS AUSTRIAS & CENTRO

La Gloria de Montera (Map p252; ☎ 91 523 44 07; Calle del Caballero de Gracia 10; meals €20-25; Ⓜ Gran Vía) Minimalist style, tasty Mediterranean dishes and great prices mean that you'll probably have to wait in line to eat here.

Restaurante Sobrino de Botín (Map p252; ☎ 91 366 42 17; www.botin.es; Calle de los Cuchilleros 17; meals €35-45; Ⓜ La Latina or Sol) Reputedly opened in 1725, this is the oldest restaurant in Madrid. The secret of their staying power is fine *cochinillo* (€21.10) and *cordero asado* (roast lamb; €21.10) cooked in wood-fired ovens.

SOL, HUERTAS & ATOCHA

our pick **Maceiras** (Map p252; ☎ 91 429 15 84; Calle de Jesús 7; meals €20-25; ⏰ lunch & diner Tue-Sun, dinner Mon; Ⓜ Antón Martín) Galician

KRZYSZTOF DYDYNSKI
Atrium of Hotel Urban

tapas (think octopus, green peppers etc) never tasted so good as in this agreeably rustic bar down the bottom of the Huertas hill, especially when washed down with a crisp white Ribeiro.

Arola Madrid (Map pp250-1; ☎ 91 467 02 02; www.arola-madrid.com, in Spanish; Calle de Argumosa 43; meals €50; ⏰ 10am-9pm Mon & Wed-Sat, to 5pm Sun; Ⓜ Atocha) Fashionable chef Sergi Arola serves up nouvelle cuisine with an emphasis on presentation and variations on a traditional Spanish base in this design den.

LA LATINA & LAVAPIÉS

This area is best known for its tapas bars.

La Buga del Lobo (Map pp250-1; ☎ 91 467 61 51; www.labocadellobo.com; Calle de Argumosa 11; meals €25-30; ⏰ 11am-2am Wed-Mon;

M Lavapiés) It's hard to get a table in this bohemian eatery filled with funky, swirling murals, contemporary art exhibitions and jazz or lounge music.

Naïa Restaurante (**Map p252; ☎ 91 366 27 83; www.naiarestaurante.com, in Spanish; Plaza de la Paja 3; meals €25-30; Mon-Sat; M La Latina)** Naïa has a real buzz, with delightful modern Spanish cooking and a chill-out lounge downstairs.

Casa Lucío (**Map p252; ☎ 91 365 32 52; www.casalucio.es, in Spanish; Calle de la Cava Baja 35; meals €35-45; lunch & dinner Sun-Fri, dinner Sat Sep-Jul; M La Latina)** Lucio has been wowing *madrileños* with his light touch, quality ingredients and home-style local cooking for ages – think seafood, roasted meats and, a Lucio speciality, eggs in abundance.

MALASAÑA & CHUECA

Some of the city's best (and best-priced) eateries can be found along the side streets of the trendy Chueca district.

Ribeira Do Miño (**Map p252; ☎ 91 521 98 54; Calle de la Santa Brigida 1; meals €20-25; Tue-Sat; M Tribunal)** The *mariscada de la casa* (€30 for two) is a platter of seafood so large that even the hungriest of visitors will leave satisfied. Leave your name with the waiter and be prepared to wait for a table.

Bazaar (**Map p252; ☎ 91 523 39 05; www.restaurantbazaar.com; Calle de la Libertad 21; meals €25-30; M Chueca)** Bazaar's pristine-white interior design with theatre lighting may draw a crowd that looks like it stepped out of the pages of *Hola!* magazine, but the food is extremely well-priced and innovative. Note it doesn't take reservations.

Nina (**Map pp250-1; ☎ 91 591 00 46; Calle de Manuela Malasaña 10; meals €30-35; M)** The cooking is as cool as the dining area. The *foie fresco a la plancha* (grilled foie gras) is divine. Popular with a sophisticated crowd, Nina can be a hard place to get a table.

DRINKING

Madrid lives life on the streets and plazas. If you're after the more traditional, with tiled walls and flamenco tunes, head to the *barrio* of Huertas. Malasaña caters to a grungy, funky crowd, while La Latina has friendly bars that guarantee atmosphere most nights of the week. The bulk of Madrid bars open to 2am Sunday to Thursday, and to 3am or 3.30am Friday and Saturday.

LOS AUSTRIAS & CENTRO

Museo Chicote (**Map p252; www.museo-chicote.com; Gran Vía 12; 8am-4am Mon-Sat; M Gran Vía)** A timeless classic popular with socialites and film stars, the Museo Chicote has a lounge atmosphere late at night and a stream of famous faces all day.

Gaia Cocktail Lounge (**Map p252; www.gaiacocktail.com in Spanish; Calle de Amnistía 5; 10pm-3am Tue-Thu, 8.30pm-3.30am Fri & Sat; M Ópera)** Gaia serves up delicious cocktails to a DJ-soundtrack of jazz, funk, lounge and occasional house music.

SOL, HUERTAS & ATOCHA

Cervecería Alemana (**Map p252; Plaza de Santa Ana 6; 10.30am-12.30am Sun-Thu, to 2am Fri & Sat, closed August; M Antón Martín or Sol)** A classic and classy watering hole, this place is famous for its cold, frothy beers and delicious tapas. It was one of Hemingway's haunts.

our pick **La Venencia** (**Map p252; Calle de Echegarary 7; M Sol)** Your sherry (in several varieties) is poured straight from dusty wooden barrels and your tab is literally chalked up on the bar itself.

Viva Madrid (**Map p252; www.barvivamadrid.com; Calle de Manuel Fernández y González 7;**

Ⓜ Antón Martín or Sol) A landmark smothered in beautiful coloured tiles, Viva Madrid does tapas earlier in the evening and drinks late into the night.

LA LATINA & LAVAPIÉS

Delic (**Map p252; Costanilla de San Andrés 14; Ⓜ La Latina**) Nursing a fine mojito on a warm summer's evening at Delic's outdoor tables on one of Madrid's prettiest plazas is one of life's great pleasures.

La Inquilina (**Map pp250-1; Calle del Ave María 39; 🕑 7pm-2am Tue-Thu, 1-4pm & 8pm-3am Fri-Sun; Ⓜ Lavapiés**) With its cool-and-casual vibe, this locals bar is run by women and there's sports art by budding local artists on the walls.

MALASAÑA & CHUECA

Café Comercial (**Map pp250-1; Glorieta de Bilbao 7; Ⓜ Bilbao**) The faded elegance of this classic cafe appeals to intellectuals and the artsy crowd.

Café Pepe Botella (**Map pp250-1; Calle de San Andrés 12; Ⓜ Bilbao or Tribunal**) The cosy velvet benches and marble-topped tables give 'Joe Bottle' a retro feel. It's best known for its sherry.

Stop Madrid (**Map p252; Calle de Hortaleza 11; Ⓜ Gran Vía**) This terrific old *taberna* is friendly, invariably packed and serves up a wicked sangria.

ENTERTAINMENT

The *Guía del Ocio* (€1) is the city's classic weekly listings magazine. Better are **Metropoli** (**www.elmundo.es**) and **On Madrid** (**www.elpais.com**), respectively *El Mundo*'s and *El País'* Friday listings supplements. **La Netro** (**http://madrid.lanetro.com**) is a comprehensive online guide.

THEATRE

Teatro Real (**Map p252; ☎ 902 244848; www.teatro-real.com in Spanish; Plaza de Oriente; Ⓜ Ópera**) The Teatro Real is the city's grandest stage for elaborate operas and ballets.

Teatro de la Zarzuela (**Map p252; ☎ 91 524 54 00; http://teatrodelazarzuela.mcu.es; Calle de Jovellanos 4; Ⓜ Banco de España**) Come here for *zarzuela*, a very Spanish mixture of dance, music and theatre.

BRUCE BI

Plaza de Toros Las Ventas (p260)

BRUCE BI

Flamenco performance at Casa Patas

LIVE MUSIC

Many of flamenco's top names perform in Madrid, making it an excellent place to see interpretations of this Andalucian art.

Casa Patas (**Map p252; ☎ 91 369 04 96; www.casapatas.com; Calle de Cañizares 10; admission about €35; Ⓜ Antón Martín**) One of the best *tablaos* (flamenco venues) in the city, this is a great place to see passionate dancing, although it's one of the pricier options.

Las Tablas (**Map p252; ☎ 91 542 05 20; www.lastablasmadrid.com in Spanish; Plaza de España 9; admission €10-30; show 10.30pm; Ⓜ Plaza de España**) Most nights you'll see a classic flamenco show, with plenty of throaty singing and soul-baring dancing.

Cardamomo (**Map p252; ☎ 91 369 07 57; www.carda momo.es, in Spanish; Calle de Echegaray 15; admission €10; 9pm-3.30am, live shows 10.30pm Tue & Wed; Ⓜ Sevilla**) This is a place for those of you who believe that flamenco is best enjoyed in a smoky bar where the crowd is predominantly local and where you can clap, shout '*Olé!*' and sing along.

BULLFIGHTING

Plaza de Toros Las Ventas (**off Map pp250-1; ☎ 91 356 22 00; www.las-ventas.com in Spanish; Calle de Alcalá 237; Ⓜ Las Ventas**) Some of Spain's top *toreros* swing their capes in Plaza de Toros Las Ventas. Fights are held every Sunday afternoon from mid-May through October. Get tickets (from €5 standing in the sun) at the plaza box office or from official ticket agents on Calle Victoria.

GETTING THERE & AWAY

AIR

Madrid's international Barajas airport (MAD), 16km northeast of the city, is a busy place, with flights coming in from all over Europe and beyond. See p298 for more information.

BUS

Estación Sur de Autobuses (**off Map pp250-1; ☎ 91 468 42 00; www.estaciondeautobuses.com, in Spanish; Calle de Méndez Álvaro 83; Ⓜ Méndez Álvaro**), just south of the M-30 ring road, is the city's principal bus station. ALSA has buses to Barcelona (€28 to €39, 7½ to 8½ hours, 27 daily), Zaragoza (€15 to €20, four hours, 28 daily) and many other destinations.

CAR & MOTORCYCLE

If you arrive by car, be prepared to face gridlock traffic. The city is surrounded by three ring roads: the M30, M40 and M50 (still not 100% completed).

Car rental companies abound in Madrid; most have offices both at the airport and in town. **Pepecar** (**www.pepecar.com**) has several locations.

TRAIN

Renfe (www.renfe.es) trains connect Madrid with destinations throughout Spain. There are two main train stations: Atocha, southeast of the city centre, and Chamartín, to the north. Long-distance and *cercanías* (local area trains) trains pass through these two stations.

High-speed AVE trains run to Barcelona (€105 to €124, three hours, up to 18 daily) and Seville (€67 to €74, 2½ hours, up to 20 daily).

GETTING AROUND

TO/FROM THE AIRPORT

Metro line 8 zips you into the city from the airport's T2 and T4 terminals. The 12-minute trip to the Nuevos Ministerios station costs €1; from there, you can easily connect to all other stations.

A taxi ride to the centre should cost about €25 (€35 from Terminal 4) and the trip takes around 20 to 30 minutes.

CAR & MOTORCYCLE

Public transport in Madrid is excellent, so having a car or motorcycle is not necessary (and is usually a big headache!). If you do have a car, be prepared to face plenty of traffic and complicated parking (virtually all meter parking in the streets as well as private parking stations).

PUBLIC TRANSPORT

Madrid's 284km of metro (www.metromadrid.es) is Europe's second-largest metro system, after London. A single-ride costs €1 and a 10-ride ticket is €6.70. You can also get a one-, two-, three-, five- or seven-day travel pass.

The bus system is also good, but working out the maze of bus lines can be a challenge. Contact EMT (www.emtmadrid.es) for more information. Twenty-six night-bus *búhos* (owls) routes operate from midnight to 6am, with all routes originating in Plaza de la Cibeles.

TAXI

Madrid's taxis are inexpensive by European standards. Flag fall is €1.95 from 6am to 10pm daily, €2.15 from 10pm to 6am Sunday to Friday and €2.95 from 10pm Saturday to 6am Sunday.

Among the 24-hour taxi services are Radio-Taxi (☎ 91 405 55 00), Tele-Taxi (☎ 91 371 21 31) and Radio-Teléfono Taxi (☎ 91 547 82 00; www.radiotelefono-taxi.com); the latter runs taxis for people with disabilities.

AROUND MADRID

Get out of the city buzz and explore Comunidad de Madrid, the province surrounding the capital. Places worth exploring include the royal palace complex at San Lorenzo de El Escorial (☎ 91 890 78 18; www.patrimonionacional.es; admission €8, Wed EU citizens free; ⏲ 10am-6pm Apr-Sep, to 5pm Oct-Mar, closed Mon).

Other worthwhile excursions include Aranjuez (☎ 91 891 04 27; www.aranjuez.es, in Spanish), with its royal palace (☎ 91 891 07 40; www.patrimonionacional.es; adult/child, senior & student €5/2.50, Wed EU citizens free, gardens free; ⏲ palace 10am-5.15pm Tue-Sun Oct-Mar, 10am-6.15pm Tue-Sun Apr-Sep, gardens 8am-6.30pm Tue-Sun Oct-Mar, 8am-8.30pm Tue-Sun Apr-Sep), the traditional village of Chinchón (www.ciudad-chinchon.com), and the university town (and birthplace of Miguel de Cervantes) Alcalá de Henares (www.turismoalcala.com). Also interesting is the Valle de los Caídos (www.patrimonionacional.es; Carretera de Guadarrama/El Escorial M-600; admission €8; ⏲ 10am-6pm Tue-Sun Apr-Sep, to 5pm Oct-Mar), Franco's ostentatious civil-war memorial. The basilica and monument are just 9km north of San Lorenzo de El Escorial.

CASTILLA Y LEÓN

The true heart of Spain, Castilla y León is littered with hilltop towns sporting magnificent Gothic cathedrals, monumental city walls and mouth-watering restaurants.

SALAMANCA

pop 156,000

This is a city of rare architectural splendour, awash with sandstone overlaid with Latin inscriptions in ochre and an extraordinary virtuosity of plateresque and Renaissance styles. The monumental highlights are many, especially the Catedral Nueva and grand Plaza Mayor. King Alfonso XI founded what was long Spain's greatest university in 1218 and this is still a university town.

INFORMATION

Municipal tourist office (☎ 923 21 83 42; www.salamanca.es; Plaza Mayor 14; 9am-2pm & 4.30-8pm Mon-Fri, 10am-8pm Sat, 10am-2pm Sun)

Regional tourist office (Casa de las Conchas; ☎ 923 26 85 71; www.turismocastillayleon.com; Rúa Mayor; 9am-2pm & 5-8pm daily Sep-Jun, 9am-8pm Sun-Thu, to 9pm Fri & Sat Jul-Aug)

SIGHTS & ACTIVITIES

The **Catedral Nueva** (New Cathedral; ☎ 923 21 74 76; Plaza de Anaya; admission free; 9am-8pm), completed in 1733, is a late Gothic masterpiece that took 220 years to build. For fine views over Salamanca, head to the southwestern corner of the cathedral facade and the **Puerta de la Torre** (Ieronimus; Plaza de Juan XXIII; admission €3.25; 10am-7.15pm), from where stairs lead up through the tower. Once inside the cathedral, make your way to the largely Romanesque **Catedral Vieja** (Old Cathedral; admission €3.50; 10am-12.30pm & 4-5.30pm Oct-Mar, 10am-1.30pm & 4-7.30pm Apr-Sep), a 12th-century temple with a stunnin 15th-century altarpiece whose 53 panel depict scenes from the life of Christ an Mary, topped by a representation of th Final Judgement.

The **Universidad Civil** (university; ☎ 92 29 44 00; Calle de los Libreros; adult/student €4/ Mon morning free; 9.30am-1pm & 4-7pm Mon Fri, 9.30am-1pm & 4-6.30pm Sat, 10am-1pm Sun) a tapestry in sandstone, bursting with im ages of mythical heroes, religious scene and coats of arms.

Among the other stand-out building are the glorious **Casa de las Concha** (House of Shells; ☎ 923 26 93 17; Calle de Compañia 2; admission free; 9am-9pm Mon-Fr 9am-2pm & 4-7pm Sat & Sun), a city symbo since it was built in the 15th century, an the **Convento de San Esteban**, whos **church** (☎ 923 21 50 00; adult/concession €3/. 10am-2pm & 4-8pm) has an extraordinar altarlike facade with the stoning of Sa Esteban (St Stephen) as its central moti

SLEEPING

Hostal Sara (☎ 923 28 11 40; www.hostalsar org; Calle de Meléndez 11; s/d from €45/50) Th friendly *hostal* opened in 2005 and gets right in all the right places – friendly staf large and well-equipped rooms (unusu ally for this price range, the bathroom have hairdryers) and a fine location.

Rúa Hotel (☎ 923 27 22 72; www.hotelru com; Calle de Sánchez Barbero 11; s incl breakfa €50-57, d incl breakfast €67-115;) This en gaging place has modern decoration an a family-run feel and all rooms are apar ments/suites (with kitchen) of around 3 sq metres. The best rooms are those facin north with terrific views.

EATING & DRINKING

Restaurante La Luna (☎ 923 21 28 8 Calle de los Libreros 4; set menu €11; lunch dinner Tue-Sun, lunch Mon) We like this plac almost as much as Mandala (see below). Downstairs is crowded and intimate, upstairs is bright and modern, and the food is a good mix of hearty meat staples and fresh lighter meals.

Mandala Café (☎ **923 12 33 42; Calle de Serranos 9-11; meals €15-20**) Cool, casual and deservedly popular, Mandala specialises in a wide range of *platos combinados* (€4.20 to €9) and salads, and has plenty of vegetarian choices.

Mesón Las Conchas (☎ **923 21 21 67; Rúa Mayor 16; meals €20-30**) The atmospheric Mesón Las Conchas has a choice of outdoor tables (in summer), an atmospheric bar and an upstairs, wood-beamed dining area; the bar in particular caters less to a tourist crowd than to locals who know their *embutidos* (cured meats).

GETTING THERE & AWAY

The bus station (☎ **923 23 67 17; Avenida de Filiberto Villalobos 71-85**) is northwest of the town centre. Avanza has hourly departures to Madrid (regular/express €11.90/17.40, 2½ to three hours), with other buses going to Ávila (€5.58, 1½ hours) and Segovia (€9.90, 2¾ hours).

Up to eight trains depart daily for Madrid's Chamartín station (€16.50, 2½ hours) via Ávila (€8.40, one hour).

SEGOVIA

pop 56,100 / elev 1002m

This high and, in winter, chilly city warms the traveller's heart with such extraordinary sights as the grand Roman aqueduct and fairytale Alcázar (castle), not to mention steaming serves of hearty suckling pig in many an Old Town restaurant.

SIGHTS

El Acueducto, an 894m-long engineering wonder that looks like an enormous comb of stone blocks plunged into the lower end of old Segovia, is the obvious starting point for a tour of town. This Roman aqueduct is 28m high and was built without a drop of mortar – just good old Roman know-how.

In the heart of town is the resplendent late-Gothic Catedral (☎ **921 46 22 05; Plaza Mayor; adult/concession €3/2, Sunday 9.30am-1.15pm free; 9.30am-5.30pm Oct-Mar, to 6.30pm Apr-Sep**), which was started in 1525 and completed a mere 200 years later.

The fortified Alcázar (☎ **921 46 07 59; www.alcazardesegovia.com; Plaza de la Reina Victoria Eugenia; adult/concession €4/3, tower €2, 3rd Tue of month EU citizens free; 10am-6pm Oct-Mar, 10am-7pm Apr-Sep**) is perched dramatically on the edge of Segovia. Inside is a collection of armour and military gear, but even better are the ornate interiors of the reception rooms and the 360-degree views from the Torre de Juan II.

PICOS DE EUROPA

These jagged mountains straddling Asturias, Cantabria and northeast Castilla y León amount to some of the finest walking country in Spain.

They comprise three limestone massifs, whose highest peak rises 2648m. The 647-sq-km Parque Nacional de los Picos de Europa covers all three massifs and is Spain's second-biggest national park. Check out www.turismopicosdeeuropa.com (in Spanish), www.liebanaypicosdeeuropa.com and also www.picosdeeuropa.com (in Spanish).

If you fancy exploring dramatic mountain country that few foreigners know, consider the 300-sq-km Parque Natural de Somiedo (**www.somiedo.es**), southwest of Oviedo, the capital of Asturias.

MATTHEW SCHOENFELDER
Hiking in the Picos de Europa (p263)

SLEEPING

Hospedería La Gran Casa Mudéjar (☎ 921 46 62 50; www.lacasamudejar.com; Calle de la Infanta Isabel 8; d €60-160;) Spread over two buildings, this place has been magnificently renovated, blending genuine, 15th-century Mudéjar ceilings in some rooms with modern amenities.

Hostería Ayala Berganza (☎ 921 46 04 48; www.partner-hotels.com; Calle de Carretas 5; d €115-150;) This boutique hotel has elegant, individually designed rooms (all have tiled floors, beautiful bathrooms and rustic accents) within a restored 15th-century palace.

EATING & DRINKING

Casa Duque (☎ 921 46 24 87; www.restaurante duque.es; Calle de Cervantes 12; menú del día €21-39.50) They've been serving suckling pig (€19) here since the 1890s. Downstairs is the informal *cueva* (cave), where you can get tapas and yummy *cazuelas* (stews).

Restaurante El Fogón Sefardí (☎ 921 46 62 50; www.lacasamudejar.com; Calle de Isabel La Católica 8; meals €30-40) This is one of the most original places in town, serving Sephardic cuisine (items like aubergine stuffed with vegetables, pine nuts and almonds) in a restaurant with an intimate patio and a splendid dining hall with original, 15th-century Mudéjar flourishes.

Mesón de Cándido (☎ 921 42 59 11; www.mesondecandido.es; Plaza del Azoguejo 5; meals €30-40) Set in a delightful 18th-century building in the shadow of the aqueduct, Mesón del Cándido is famous throughout Spain for its suckling pig and roast lamb.

Cueva de San Esteban (☎ 921 46 09 82; www.lacuevadesanesteban.com, in Spanish; Calle Valdeláguila 15; meals €35; 11am-midnight) One of the only restaurants in Segovia not devoted to suckling pig, this popular spot focuses on seasonal dishes, with a few seafood treats from Galicia.

GETTING THERE & AWAY

The **bus station** (☎ 92 142 77 07; Paseo Ezequiel González 12) is a 15-minute walk from the aqueduct. **La Sepulvedana** buses leave half-hourly from Madrid's Paseo de la Florida bus stop (€5.87, 1½ hours).

Up to nine normal trains run daily from Madrid to Segovia (two hours, one-way €5.90), leaving you at the main train station 2.5km from the aqueduct. The high-speed AVE (€9, 35 minutes) deposits you at the Segovia-Guiomar station, 5km from the aqueduct.

CASTILLA-LA MANCHA

Known as the stomping ground of Don Quixote and Sancho Panza, Castilla-La Mancha conjures up images of lonely windmills, medieval castles and bleak, treeless plains. The characters of Miguel de Cervantes provide the literary context, but the richly historic cities of Toledo and Cuenca are the most compelling reasons to visit.

TOLEDO

pop 55,100 / elev 655m

Toledo is a corker of a city. Commanding a hill rising above the Tajo River, it's crammed with monuments that attest to the waves of conquerors and communities – Roman, Visigoth, Jewish, Muslim and Christian – who have called the city home during its turbulent history.

INFORMATION

Main tourist office (☎ 925 25 40 30; www.toledo-turismo.com; Plaza del Ayuntamiento s/n; 10.30am-2.30pm Mon, 10.30am-2.30pm & 4.30-7pm Tue-Sun)

Tourist office (☎ 925 22 08 43; fax 925 25 26 48; Puerta Nueva de Bisagra s/n; 9am-6pm Mon-Fri, 9am-7pm Sat, 9am-3pm Sun)

SIGHTS

The Catedral (adult/under 12yr €7/free; 10.30am-6.30pm Mon-Sat, 2-6.30pm Sun) is Toledo's major landmark. There's loads to see within its hefty stone walls, including stained-glass windows, tombs of kings and art in the sacristy by the likes of El Greco, Zurbarán, Crespi, Titian, Rubens and Velázquez.

The Museo de Santa Cruz (☎ 925 22 10 36; Calle de Cervantes 3; admission free; 10am-6pm Mon-Sat, to 2pm Sun) contains a large collection of furniture, faded tapestries and paintings. Upstairs is an impressive collection of El Greco's works, including the masterpiece *La Asunción de la Virgen* (Assumption of the Virgin).

In the southwestern part of the old city, the queues outside an otherwise unremarkable church, the Iglesia de Santo Tomé (☎ 925 25 60 98; www.santotome.org; Plaza del Conde; admission €1.90; 10am-6pm), betray the presence of El Greco's masterpiece *El Entierro del Conde de Orgaz* (The Burial of the Count of Orgaz).

The Museo Sefardi (☎ 925 22 36 65; www.museosefardi.net in Spanish; Calle Samuel Leví s/n; adult/under 12yr/12-25yr €2.40/free/1.20, audio guide €3; 10am-6pm Tue-Sat, to 2pm Sun) is housed in the beautiful 14th-century Sinagoga del Tránsito. Toledo's other synagogue, the nearby Santa María La Blanca (☎ 925 22 72 57; Calle de los Reyes Católicos 4; admission €2.30; 10am-6pm), dates back to the beginning of the 13th century.

A little further northwest is San Juan de los Reyes (☎ 925 22 38 02; Calle San Juan de los Reyes 2; admission €1.90; 10am-6pm), a Franciscan monastery and church founded by Fernando and Isabel.

The Alcázar fort, largely destroyed by Republican forces in 1936 and rebuilt under Franco, was closed for renovation at the time of research; it should be open by the time you read this.

SLEEPING & EATING

La Posada de Manolo (☎ 925 28 22 50; www.laposadademanolo.com; Calle de Sixto Ramón Parro 8; s/d incl breakfast from €42/66) This boutique-style hotel has themed each floor with furnishings and decor reflecting one of the three cultures of Toledo. There are stunning views of the Old Town from the terrace.

our pick **Hostal Casa de Cisneros** (☎ **925 22 88 28; www.hostal-casa-de-cisneros.com; Calle Cardenal Cisneros; s/d €50/80;**) Across from the cathedral, this seductive *hostal* is built on the site of an 11th-century Muslim palace, parts of which can be spied via a glass porthole in the lobby floor.

Hostal Alfonso XII (☎ **925 25 25 09; www.hostal-alfonso12.com; Calle de Alfonso XII; r €65;**) A gingerbread cottage of a place with original beams, terracotta tiles and stylish, albeit small, rooms decorated with impeccable taste.

Santa Fe (☎ **670 65 42 16; Calle Santa Fe 6; menú del día €8, tapas €2**) Sit down in the half-tiled dining room to enjoy tapas, tortilla with green pepper, homemade paella and *pollo al ajillo* (chicken in tomato and garlic sauce).

our pick **Palacio** (☎ **925 21 59 72; Calle Alfonso X el Sabio 3; menú del día €14, meals €14-18**) An unpretentious place where stained glass, beams and efficient old-fashioned service combine with traditional no-nonsense cuisine.

Kumera (☎ **925 25 75 53; Calle Alfonso X el Sabio 2; meals €18-25**) The interior here, all golden brick and stone, is complimented by colourful art work; the menu is similarly diverse, with choices such as tuna in soy sauce, crêpes with salmon, spinach and cheese, and venison with roast peppers.

La Abadía (☎ **925 25 11 40; Plaza de San Nicolás 3; meals €25-30, menú del día €28**) Arches, niches and subtle lighting are spread over a warren of brick-and-stone clad rooms, while the menu includes meat and fish plates as well as lightweight dishes such as goat's cheese salad with pumpkin and sunflower seeds.

GETTING THERE & AWAY

Toledo's **bus station** (☎ **925 21 58 50; Avenid de Castilla-La Mancha**) is northeast of the Ol Town. Buses depart for Madrid ever half-hour from about 6am to 10pm dail (8.30am to 11.30pm Sunday and holidays Direct buses (€4.60, one hour) run hourl other services (1½ hours) go via village along the way. There are also services t Cuenca (€10.90, 2¼ hours).

Built in 1920, the **train station** (**Pase Rosa**) is a pretty introduction to the city The high-speed AVE service runs ever hour or so to Madrid's Atocha station (€9 30 minutes).

CUENCA

pop 53,000

A World Heritage site, Cuenca is a curiou spot. Its old medieval centre is set high u on ridges above the modern sprawl. Mos emblematic of its centuries-old build ings are the **casas colgadas**, the hangin houses, which cling precariously to th cliffs above a gorge. To view them, wal over the **Puente San Pablo** (1902), an iro footbridge that crosses the ravine, or wal to the northernmost tip of the Old Tow where a *mirador* offers superb views.

Up to nine buses daily serve Madri (€10.50, two hours). Other bus service include Valencia (€11.95, 2½ hours, up t three daily) and Toledo (€10.90, 2¼ hour one or two daily).

Trains to Madrid's Atocha station de part six times on weekdays and four time on weekends (€10.65, 2½ hours). Train to Valencia leave four times daily (€11.75 3¼ hours).

CATALONIA

Home to stylish Barcelona, ancien Tarragona, romantic Girona, and countles alluring destinations along the coast, in th Pyrenees and in the rural interior, Cataloni

CHRISTOPHER GROENHOUT
Views over the Tajo River to Toledo (p265)

Catalunya in Catalan, Cataluña in Castilian) s a treasure box waiting to be opened.

3ARCELONA

op 1.59 million

3arcelona has two millennia of history but s a forward-thinking place, always on the cutting edge of art, design and cuisine. Whether you explore its medieval palaces and plazas, gawk at the Modernista masterpieces, shop for designer duds along its bustling boulevards, sample its exciting nightlife or just soak up the sun on the beaches, you'll find it hard not to fall in ove with this vibrant city.

ORIENTATION

Central Plaça de Catalunya marks the divide between historic and modern 3arcelona. From here, the long pedestrian boulevard La Rambla shoots southeast to he sea, with the busy Old Town Barrí Gòtic Gothic Quarter) and El Raval districts hugging it on either side. To the northwest of the plaza spreads L'Eixample, the vast grid-like district, laced with Modernista marvels, endless shopping options and plenty of restaurants and bars mixed in with turn-of-the-century apartment and office blocks.

INFORMATION

Banks abounds in Barcelona, many with ATMs, including several around Plaça de Catalunya, on La Rambla and on Plaça de Sant Jaume in the Barrí Gòtic. The foreign-exchange offices that you see along La Rambla and elsewhere are open for longer hours than banks but generally offer poorer rates.

24-hour Pharmacy La Rambla 98 (**Map p272; Ⓜ Liceu**); Passeig de Gràcia 26 (**Map pp270-1; Ⓜ Passeig de Gràcia**). These are two of several 24-hour pharmacies in the city.

Guardia Urbana (**City Police; Map p272; ☎ 092; La Rambla 43; Ⓜ Liceu**)

Hospital Clínic (**Map pp270-1; ☎ 93 227 54 00; www.hospitalclinic.org; Carrer Villarroel 170; Ⓜ Hospital Clínic**) Modern hospital with good services.

Main tourist office (**Map p272; ☎ 93 285 38 32; www.barcelonaturisme.com; Plaça de Catalunya 17-S underground; 🕓 9am-9pm; Ⓜ Catalunya**)

Mossos d'Esquadra (Catalan police; Map pp270-1; ☎ 088; Carrer Nou de la Rambla 80; M Liceu)

DANGERS & ANNOYANCES

Purse snatching and pick pocketing are major problems, especially around Plaça de Catalunya, La Rambla and Plaça Reial. See p296 for common scams.

SIGHTS & ACTIVITIES

LA RAMBLA

Spain's most famous boulevard, the part-pedestrianised La Rambla, explodes with life. The colourful **Mercat de la Boquería** (Map p272; La Rambla; 8am-8pm Mon-Sat; M Liceu), a fresh-food market with a Modernista entrance, is one of La Rambla's highlights. Nearby, stop for a tour of the **Gran Teatre del Liceu** (Map p272; ☎ 93 485 99 00; www.liceubarcelona.com; La Rambla dels Caputxins 51-59; admission with/without guide €8.50/4; guided tour 10am, unguided visits 11.30am, noon, 12.30pm & 1pm; M Liceu), the city's fabulous opera house.

Also stop at the **Plaça Reial**, a grand 19th-century square surrounded by arcades lined with restaurants and bars. At the waterfront end of La Rambla stands the **Monument a Colom** (Map pp270-1; ☎ 93 302 52 24; Plaça del Portal de la Pau; lift adult/under 4yr/senior & 4-12yr €2.50/free/1.50; 9am-8.30pm Jun-Sep, 10am-6.30pm Oct-May; M Drassanes), a statue of Columbus atop a tall pedestal. A small lift will take you to the top for panoramic views.

Just west of La Rambla is the **Museu Marítim** (Map pp270-1; ☎ 93 342 99 20; www.museumaritimbarcelona.org; Avinguda de les Drassanes; adult/senior & student €6.50/3.25; 10am-8pm; M Drassanes). Housed in the city's once mighty medieval shipyards, a gorgeous Gothic creation, the museum takes an in-depth look at Catalonia's seafaring past.

BARRÍ GÒTIC

Barcelona's Gothic **Catedral** (Map p272; ☎ 93 342 82 60; Plaça de la Seu; admission free, special visit €5; 8am-12.45pm & 5.15-8pm, special visit 1-5pm Mon-Sat, 2-5pm Sun & holidays; M Jaume I) was built on top of the ruins of an 11th-century Romanesque church. Highlights include the cool cloister, the crypt tomb of martyr Santa Eulàlia (one of Barcelona's two patron saints), the choir stalls (€2.20), the lift to the rooftop (€2.20) and the modest art collection in the **Sala Capitular** (chapterhouse; admission €2). You only pay the individual prices if you visit outside the special visiting hours.

Not far from the cathedral is pretty **Plaça del Rei** and the fascinating **Museu d'Història de la Ciutat** (Map p272; ☎ 93 256 21 00; www.museuhistoria.bcn.cat; Carrer del Veguer; adult/senior & student €6/4; 10am-2pm & 4-7pm Tue-Sat, 10am-3pm Sun; M Jaume I) where you can visit a 4000-sq-metre excavated site of Roman Barcelona under the plaza. The museum encompasses historic buildings including the **Palau Reial Major** (Main Royal Palace), once a residence of the kings of Catalonia and Aragón, and its **Saló del Tinell** (Great Hall). In summer, outdoor concerts are often held in Plaça del Rei.

EL RAVAL

To the west of La Rambla is El Raval district, a once-seedy, now-funky area overflowing with cool bars and shops. Visit the **Museu d'Art Contemporani de Barcelona** (Macba; Map p272; ☎ 93 412 08 10; www.macba.es; Plaça dels Àngels 1; adult/concession €7.50/6, Wed €3.50; 11am-8pm Mon & Wed, 11am-midnight Thu & Fri, 10am-8pm Sat, 10am-3pm Sun & holidays late Jun-late Sep, 11am-7.30pm Mon & Wed-Fri, 10am-8pm Sat, 10am-3pm Sun & holidays late Sep-May; M Universitat), which has an impressive collection of international contemporary art.

LA RIBERA

Home to Barcelona's bustling textile industry and to its wealthy merchants, La Ribera was the city's most prosperous quarter. Now it's a trendy district full of boutiques, restaurants and bars.

A series of palaces where some of those wealthy merchants lived now house the **Museu Picasso** (Map p272; ☎ 93 256 30 00; www.museupicasso.bcn.es; Carrer de Montcada 15-23; adult/senior & child under 16/student €9/free/3, temporary exhibitions adult €5.80, 1st Sun of month free; 10am-8pm Tue-Sun & holidays; M Jaume I), home to more than 3000 Picassos, most from early in the artist's career. This is one of the most visited museums in the country, so expect queues.

The heart of the neighbourhood is the elegant **Església de Santa Maria del Mar** (Map p272; Plaça de Santa Maria del Mar; admission free; 9am-1.30pm & 4.30-8pm; M Jaume I), a stunning example of Catalan Gothic and arguably the city's most elegant church.

Nearby, the **Mercat de Santa Caterina** (Map p272; www.mercatsantacaterina.net; Avinguda de Francesc Cambó 16; 8am-2pm Mon, to 3.30pm Tue, Wed & Sat, to 8.30pm Thu & Fri; M Jaume I), with its loopily pastel-coloured wavy roof, is a temple to fine foods designed by the adventurous Catalan architect Enric Miralles.

La Ribera is bordered to the northeast by the sprawling **Parc de la Ciutadella** (8am-6pm Nov-Feb, to 8pm Oct & Mar, to 9pm Apr-Sep; M Barceloneta), an ideal park for strolling or picnics. It's home to a small, kid-friendly **zoo** (Map pp270-1; ☎ 93 225 67 80; www.zoobarcelona.com; Passeig de Picasso & Carrer de Wellington; adult/under 4yr/senior/4-12yr €15.50/free/8.50/9.50; 10am-7pm Jun-Sep, to 6pm mid-Mar–May & Oct, to 5pm Nov–mid-Mar; M Barceloneta), which holds about 7500 living thingies, from gorillas to insects.

JOHN ELK III

Cloister walkway of the Catedral, Barrí Gòtic

WATERFRONT

Barcelona has two major ports, **Port Vell** (Old Port) at the base of La Rambla, and **Port Olímpic** (Olympic Port) 1.5km up the coast. Between the two ports sits the onetime factory workers and fishermen's quarter, **La Barceloneta**.

At the end of Moll d'Espanya in Port Vell is **L'Aquàrium** (Map pp270-1; ☎ 93 221 74 74; www.aquariumbcn.com; Moll d'Espanya; adult/under 4yr/4-12yr/over 60yr €16/free/11/12.50; 9.30am-11pm Jul & Aug, to 9.30pm Jun & Sep, to 9pm Mon-Fri, to 9.30pm Sat & Sun Oct-May; M Drassanes), with an 80m-long shark tunnel.

Barcelona boasts 4km of city *platjas* (beaches), beginning with the gritty **Platja de la Barceloneta** and continuing northeast beyond Port Olímpic with a series of cleaner, more attractive strands.

BARCELONA

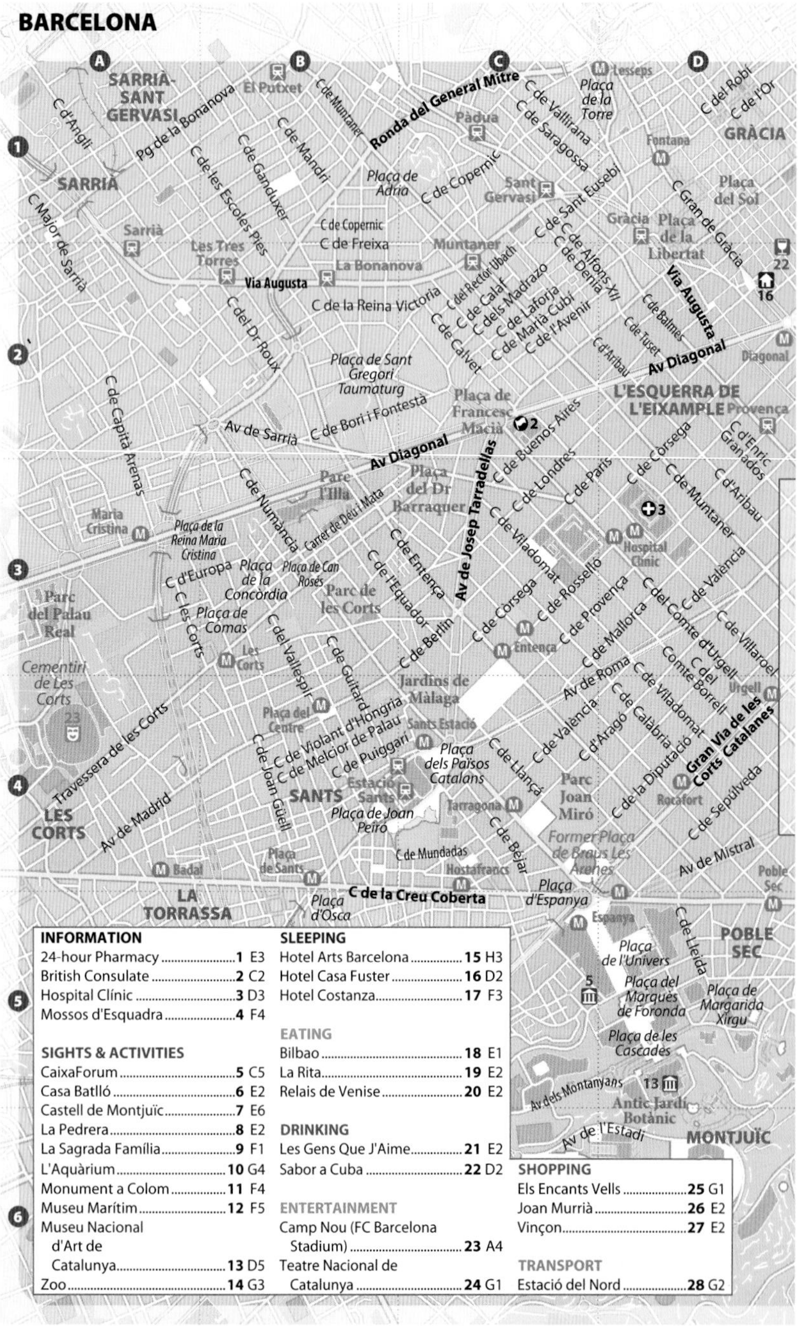

INFORMATION
- 24-hour Pharmacy 1 E3
- British Consulate 2 C2
- Hospital Clínic 3 D3
- Mossos d'Esquadra 4 F4

SIGHTS & ACTIVITIES
- CaixaForum 5 C5
- Casa Batlló 6 E2
- Castell de Montjuïc 7 E6
- La Pedrera 8 E2
- La Sagrada Família 9 F1
- L'Aquàrium 10 G4
- Monument a Colom 11 F4
- Museu Marítim 12 F5
- Museu Nacional d'Art de Catalunya 13 D5
- Zoo 14 G3

SLEEPING
- Hotel Arts Barcelona 15 H3
- Hotel Casa Fuster 16 D2
- Hotel Costanza 17 F3

EATING
- Bilbao 18 E1
- La Rita 19 E2
- Relais de Venise 20 E2

DRINKING
- Les Gens Que J'Aime 21 E2
- Sabor a Cuba 22 D2

ENTERTAINMENT
- Camp Nou (FC Barcelona Stadium) 23 A4
- Teatre Nacional de Catalunya 24 G1

SHOPPING
- Els Encants Vells 25 G1
- Joan Murrià 26 E2
- Vinçon 27 E2

TRANSPORT
- Estació del Nord 28 G2

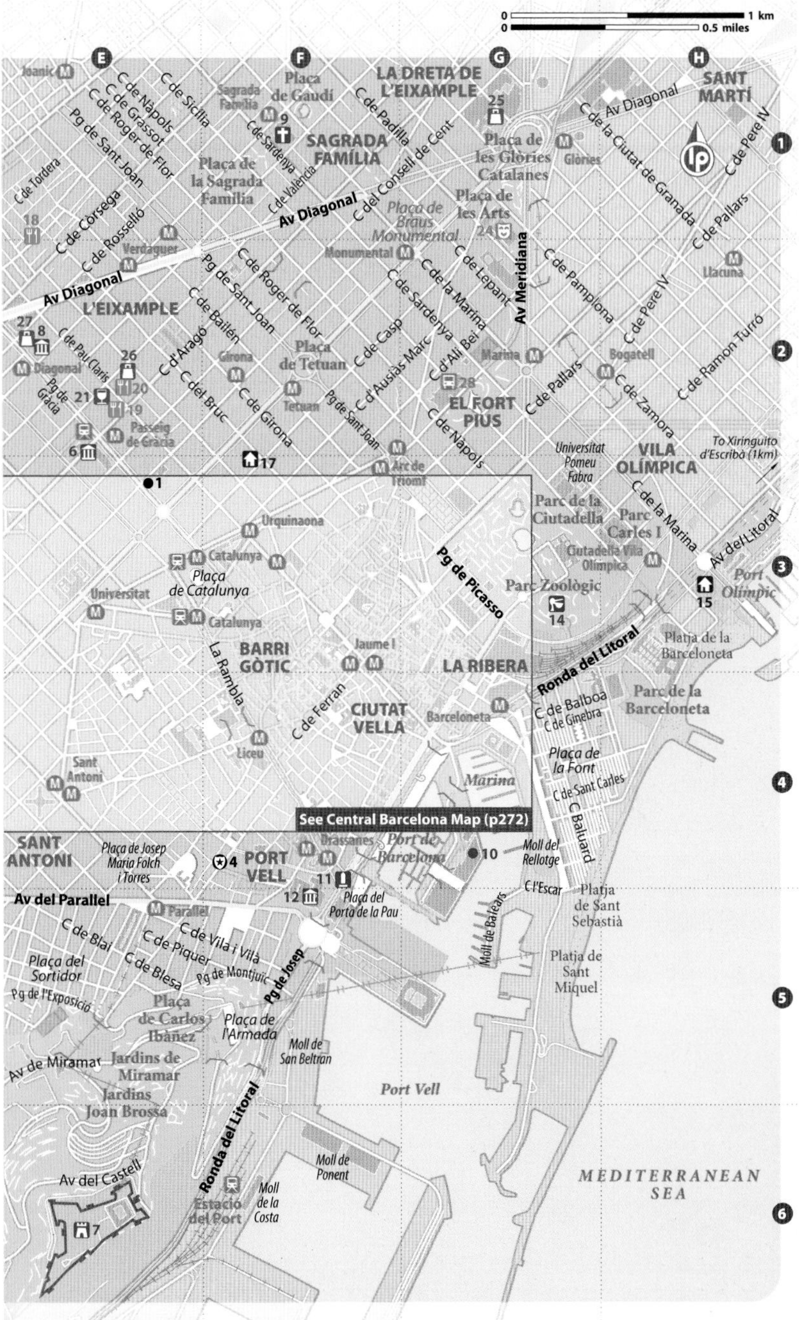

SPAIN

BARCELONA

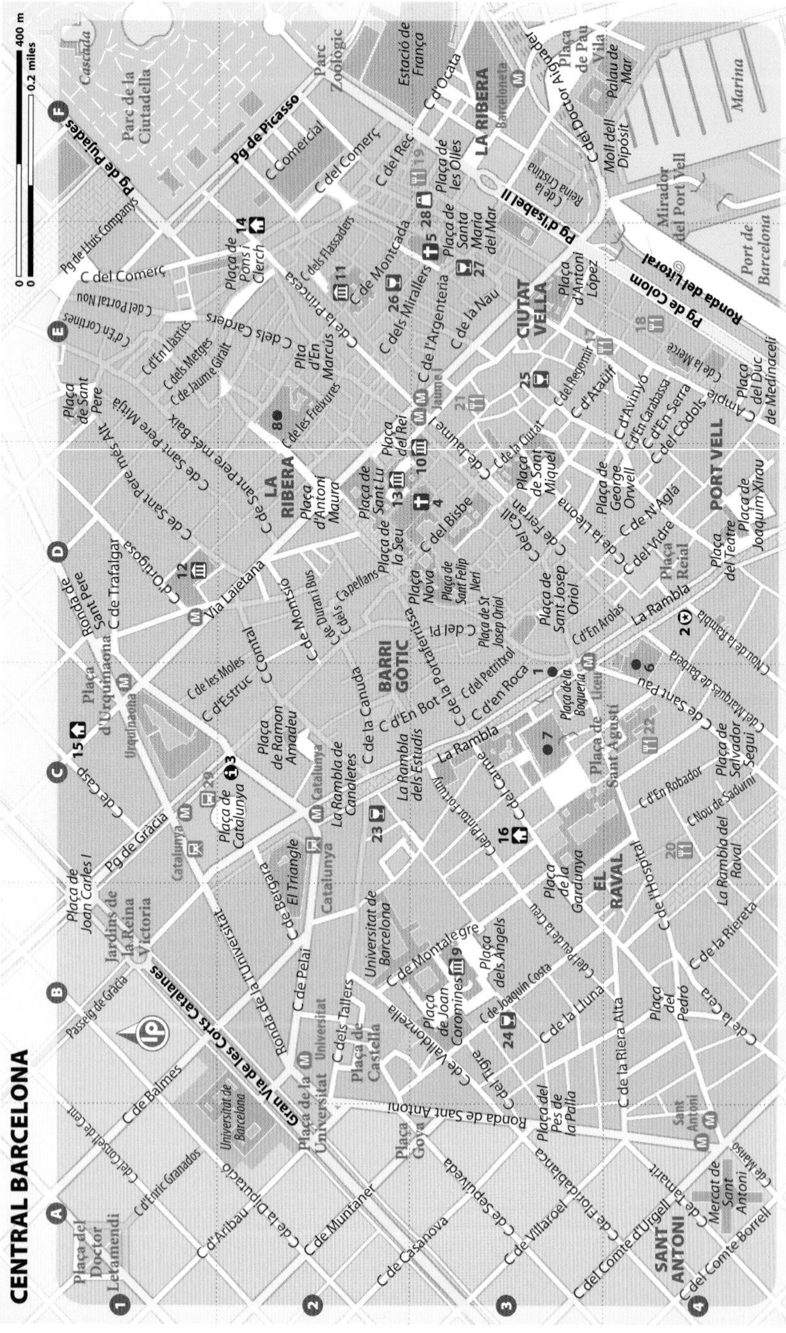
CENTRAL BARCELONA
0 — 400 m
0 — 0.2 miles
Parc de la Ciutadella
Cascada
Parc Zoològic
Estació de França
Pg de Picasso
Pg de Pujades
Pg de Lluís Companys
C del Comerç
C Comercial
C del Rec
C d'Ocata
LA RIBERA
Barceloneta
Plaça de Pau Vila
Palau de Mar
Moll dell Dipòsit
Marina
C del Doctor Aiguader
C de la Reina Cristina
Pg d'Isabel II
Mirador del Port Vell
Port de Barcelona
Ronda del Litoral
Pg de Colom
Plaça d'Antoni López
CIUTAT VELLA
C de la Mercè
Plaça del Duc de Medinaceli
C Ample
C del Còdols
C d'En Serra
C d'En Carabassa
C d'Avinyó
C d'Ataülf
C del Regomir
Plaça de Santa Maria del Mar
Plaça de les Olles
C de la Nau
C de l'Argenteria
C dels Mirallers
C de Montcada
C dels Flassaders
Plaça de Pons i Clerch
C de la Princesa
C dels Carders
C del Portal Nou
C d'En Cortines
C d'En Llàstics
C dels Metges
C de Jaume Giralt
Plta d'En Marcús
Plaça de Sant Pere
C de Sant Pere més Baix
C de Sant Pere més Alt
C de Sant Pere Mitjà
C de les Freixures
LA RIBERA
Plaça d'Antoni Maura
Plaça de Sant Lu
Plaça del Rei
Jaume I
C de Jaume I
C de la Ciutat
Plaça de Sant Miquel
Plaça de George Orwell
C de N'Aglà
C de la Lleona
PORT VELL
Plaça de Joaquim Xirau
Plaça del Teatre
Plaça Reial
C del Vidre
C de Ferran
C del Call
C del Bisbe
Plaça de la Seu
Plaça Nova
Plaça de Sant Felip Neri
Plaça de St Josep Oriol
Plaça de Sant Josep Oriol
C del Pi
C d'En Arolas
La Rambla
C Nou de la Rambla
C del Marquès de Barberà
C de Sant Pau
Liceu
Plaça de la Boqueria
C d'en Roca
C del Petritxol
C de la Portaferrissa
C d'En Bot
BARRI GÒTIC
C de la Canuda
C dels Capellans
C de Duran i Bas
C de Montsió
Via Laietana
C d'Ortigosa
Ronda de Sant Pere
C de Trafalgar
D
E
F
Plaça d'Urquinaona
Urquinaona
C de les Moles
C d'Estruc
C Comtal
Plaça de Ramon Amadeu
La Rambla de Canaletes
La Rambla dels Estudis
Plaça de Catalunya
Catalunya
C de Casp
Pg de Gràcia
Plaça de Joan Carles I
Jardins de la Reina Victoria
El Triangle
C de Bergara
C de Pelai
Universitat de Barcelona
C de Montalegre
Plaça dels Àngels
Plaça de Joan Coromines
C del Pintor Fortuny
C del Carme
Plaça de Sant Agustí
C d'En Robador
C Nou de Sadurní
Plaça de Salvador Seguí
C de l'Hospital
La Rambla del Raval
EL RAVAL
Plaça de la Gardunya
C del Peu de la Creu
C de Joaquín Costa
C de la Riereta
Plaça del Pedró
C de la Cera
C de la Riera Alta
C de la Lluna
C de Valldonzella
C del Tigre
C dels Tallers
Plaça de Castella
Universitat
Plaça de la Universitat
Ronda de la Universitat
Gran Via de les Corts Catalanes
Passeig de Gràcia
B
C
C de Balmes
Universitat de Barcelona
C de Pau Claris
C del Consell de Cent
C d'Enric Granados
C de la Diputació
C d'Aribau
C de Muntaner
C de Casanova
C de Sepúlveda
C de Villarroel
Ronda de Sant Antoni
Plaça Goya
Plaça del Pes de la Palla
C de Floridablanca
Sant Antoni
C del Comte d'Urgell
C de Tamarit
Mercat de Sant Antoni
C de Manso
C del Comte Borrell
SANT ANTONI
A
Plaça del Doctor Letamendi
1
2
3
4

L'EIXAMPLE

Modernisme, the Catalan version of art nouveau, transformed Barcelona's cityscape in the early 20th century. The movement's star architect was the eccentric Antoni Gaudí (1852–1926), a devout Catholic whose work is full of references to nature and Christianity. His masterpiece, **La Sagrada Família** (**Map pp270-1; ☎ 93 207 30 31; www.sagradafamilia.org; Carrer de Mallorca 401; adult/senior & student €10/8; 9am-8pm Apr-Sep, to 6pm Oct-Mar; M Sagrada Família**), is a work in progress and Barcelona's most famous building. Construction began in 1882 and could be completed in 2020. Gaudí spent 40 years working on the church, though he only saw the crypt, the apse and the nativity facade completed. Eventually there'll be 18 towers, all more than 100m high, representing the 12 apostles, four evangelists and Mary, Mother of God, plus the tallest tower (170m) standing for Jesus Christ.

MONTJUÏC

Southwest of the city centre and with views out to sea and over the city, Montjuïc serves as a Central Park of sorts and is a great place for a jog or stroll. It is dominated by the **Castell de Montjuïc** (Map pp270-1), a one-time fortress with great views. Buses 50, 55 and 61 all head up here.

Museu Nacional d'Art de Catalunya (**Map pp270-1; ☎ 93 622 03 76; www.mnac.es; Mirador del Palau Nacional; adult/senior & child under 15/student €8.50/free/6; 10am-7pm Tue-Sat, 10am-2.30pm Sun & holidays**) is a broad panoply of Catalan and European art.

TOURS

The three routes of the **Bus Turístic** (**one day adult/child 4-12yr €19/11, 2 consecutive days €23/15; 9am-7.45pm**) link all the major tourist sights. Buy tickets on the bus or at the tourist office (p267).

The main tourist office also offers various **walking tours** (**€11-15**) in English, Spanish or Catalan.

FESTIVALS & EVENTS

The **Festes de la Mercè** (around 24 September; www.bcn.cat/merce) is the city's biggest party, with four days of concerts, dancing, *castellers* (human castle-builders), fireworks and *correfocs* – a parade of firework-spitting dragons and devils. The evening before the **Dia de Sant Joan** (24 June) is a colourful midsummer celebration with bonfires and fireworks.

SLEEPING

There is no shortage of hotels (with new ones opening seemingly every five minutes) in Barcelona.

EL RAVAL

Hotel Aneto **(Map p272; ☎ 93 301 99 89; www.hotelaneto.com; Carrer del Carme 38; s/d €55/75; M Liceu;)** Nestled in a lively street in one of the nicer parts of El Raval, the Aneto is a good-value, simple midrange base to range out from. The best rooms are the doubles with the shuttered street-side balconies.

LA RIBERA & LA BARCELONETA

our pick **Hotel Banys Orientals** **(☎ 93 268 84 60; www.hotelbanysorientals.com; Carrer de l'Argenteria 37; s/d €89/107; M Jaume I;)** Cool blues and aquamarines combine with dark-hued parquet floors to lend this boutique beauty an understated charm.

Chic & Basic **(Map p272; ☎ 93 295 46 52; www.chicandbasic.com; Carrer de la Princesa 50; d €96-171; M Arc de Triomf;)** The 31 spotlessly white rooms here have high ceilings, enormous beds (room types are classed as M, L and XL!), lots of detailed touches (LED lighting, TFT TV screens) and the retention of many beautiful old features of the original building.

Hotel Arts Barcelona **(Map pp270-1; ☎ 93 221 10 00; www.ritzcarlton.com; Carrer de la Marina 19-21; r €425; M Ciutadella-Vila Olímpica;)** In one of the two sky-high towers that dominate Port Olímpic, these are Barcelona's most fashionable digs, frequented by VIPs from all over the planet. The rooms have unbeatable views.

L'EIXAMPLE

Hostal Goya **(Map p272; ☎ 93 302 25 65; www.hostalgoya.com; Carrer de Pau Claris 74; s €70, d €96-113; M Urquinaona;)** The Goya is a gem of a spot on the chichi side of L'Eixample and a short stroll from Plaça de Catalunya.

Market Hotel **(Map p272; ☎ 93 325 12 05; www.markethotel.com.es; Passatge de Sant Antoni Abad 10; s/d/ste €80/93/112; M Sant Antoni;)** Attractively located in a renovated building along a narrow lane just nort of the grand old Sant Antoni market, thi place has an air of simple chic.

Hotel Constanza **(Map pp270-1; ☎ 93 27 19 10; www.hotelconstanza.com; Carrer del Bruc 33 s/d €90/120; M Urqinaona;)** Constanz is a boutique belle that has stolen th heart of many a visitor to Barcelona. Eve smaller single rooms are made to fee special, with broad mirrors and stron colours (reds and yellows, with blac furniture).

Hotel Casa Fuster **(Map pp270-1; ☎ 9 255 30 00; www.hotelcasafuster.com; Passeig d Gràcia 132; d from €407; M Diagonal;)** A Modernista mansion totally refurbishe to house this luscious five-star hotel, th Casa Fuster is the ultimate splurge. Eve if you don't stay in one of the opulen rooms, come by for a coffee in the beau tiful Café Vienés.

EATING

Although Barcelona has a reputatio as a hot spot of 'new Spanish cuisine' you'll still find local eateries serving u time-honoured local grub, from squid ink *fideuà* (a satisfying paella-like noodl dish) to pigs' trotters, rabbit with snails and *butifarra* (a tasty local sausage).

LA RAMBLA & BARRÍ GÒTIC

Skip the overpriced traps along La Rambl and get into the winding lanes of the Barr Gòtic. Self-caterers should explore the Mercat de la Boquería (p268).

Bar Celta **(Map p272; ☎ 93 315 00 06; Carre de la Mercè 16; meals €20; noon-midnight M Drassanes)** Specialists in *pulpo* (octopus) and other seaside delights from Galicia the waiters waste no time in serving up bottles of crisp white Ribeiro wine to wash down the *raciones* (large tapas servings).

JOHN ELK III

Facade detail of Casa Batlló

IF YOU LIKE...

If you've fallen head over heels for La Sagrada Família (p273), seek out some of Barcelona's other Modernista gems. See www.rutadelmodernisme.com for tips.

- La Pedrera **(Map pp270-1; ☎ 902 40 09 73; www.fundaciocaixacatalunya.es; Carrer de Provença 261-265; adult/concession €8/4.50; 9am-8pm Mar-Oct, to 6.30pm Nov-Feb; M Diagonal)** Formally called the Casa Milà, Gaudí's best-known secular creation is better known as La Pedrera (The Quarry) because of its uneven grey-stone facade. Inside, you can visit a Gaudí museum, a Modernista apartment and the surreal rooftop with its bizarre chimneys.
- Casa Batlló **(Map pp270-1; ☎ 93 216 03 66; www.casabatllo.es; Passeig de Gràcia 43; adult/student & senior €16.50/13.20; usually 9am-8pm; M Passeig de Gràcia)** Just down the street, this building is an architectural allegory for the legend of St George the dragon-slayer (Sant Jordi in Catalan).
- On the same block are two other Modernista gems, Casa Amatller **(Passeig de Gràcia 41)** by Josep Puig i Cadafalch and the Casa Lleó Morera **(Passeig de Gràcia 35)** by Lluís Domènech i Montaner.
- Palau de la Música Catalana **(Map p272; ☎ 902 47 54 85; www.palaumusica.org; Carrer de Sant Francesc de Paula 2; adult/child/student incl guided tour €10/free/9; 50min tours every 30min 10am-6pm Easter & Aug, to 3.30pm Sep-Jul; M Urquinaona)** Designed by Lluís Domènech i Montaner in 1905, this opulent concert hall is one of the city's loveliest Modernista buildings.
- CaixaForum **(Map pp270-1; ☎ 93 476 86 00; www.fundacio.lacaixa.es, in Spanish; Avinguda del Marquès de Comillas 6-8; admission free; 10am-8pm Tue-Fri & Sun, to 10pm Sat; M Espanya)** This art gallery is housed in a former factory designed by Puig i Cadafalch.
- Park Güell **(☎ 93 413 24 00; Carrer d'Olot 7; admission free; 10am-9pm Jun-Sep, to 8pm Apr, May & Oct, to 7pm Mar & Nov, to 6pm Dec-Feb; M Lesseps or Vallcarca, 24)** Gaudí's enchanting park in the Gràcia district is a Dr Seuss–style playground filled with Gaudí-esque mosaics, paths and plazas.

Agut (Map p272; ☎ 93 315 17 09; Carrer d'En Gignàs 16; meals €35; ⏲ lunch & dinner Tue-Sat, lunch Sun; Ⓜ Liceu or Jaume I) Contemporary paintings set a contrast with the fine traditional Catalan dishes offered in this timeless restaurant.

El Café de l'Acadèmia (Map p272; ☎ 93 319 82 53; Carrer de Lledó 1; meals €30-35; ⏲ Mon-Fri; Ⓜ Jaume I) This fine restaurant serves strictly Catalan dishes in a romantic atmosphere.

EL RAVAL

Organic (Map p272; ☎ 93 301 09 02; www.antoniaorganickitchen.com; Carrer de la Junta de Comerç 11; meals €14-20; ⏲ noon-midnight; Ⓜ Liceu) A long sprawl of a vegetarian diner, Organic is always full. Choose from a limited range of options that change from day to day, and tuck into the all-you-can-eat salad bar in the middle of the restaurant.

our pick **Casa Leopoldo** (Map p272; ☎ 93 441 30 14; www.casaleopoldo.com; Carrer de Sant Rafael 24; meals €50; ⏲ lunch & dinner Tue-Sat, lunch Sun Sep-Jul; Ⓜ Liceu) Rambling dining areas with magnificent tiled walls and exposed timber-beam ceilings make this a fine option. The seafood menu is extensive and the local wine list strong.

LA RIBERA & WATERFRONT

La Barceloneta is the place to go for seafood; Passeig Joan de Borbó is lined with eateries but locals head for the back lanes.

Xiringuito d'Escribà (off Map pp270-1; ☎ 93 221 07 29; www.escriba.es; Platja de Bogatell, Ronda Litoral 42; meals €40-50; ⏲ lunch only; Ⓜ Ciutadella-Vila Olímpica) The Barcelona pastry family serves up top-quality seafood at this popular waterfront eatery.

Cal Pep (Map p272; ☎ 93 310 79 61; www.calpep.com; Plaça de les Olles 8; meals €45; ⏲ lunch & dinner Tue-Fri, dinner Mon, lunch Sat Sep-Jul; Ⓜ Barceloneta) This gourmet tapas bar is one of the most popular in town and difficult to snaffle a spot in. Pep recommends *cloïsses amb pernil* (clams and ham – seriously!) or the *trifàsic*, a combo of calamari, whitebait and prawns (€12).

L'EIXAMPLE & GRÀCIA

La Rita (Map pp270-1; ☎ 93 487 23 76; Carrer d'Aragó 279; meals €20; Ⓜ Passeig de Gràcia) For a bit of style, this popular restaurant does the trick. Be prepared to wait in line for its pasta, seafood and traditional dishes.

Relais de Venise (Map pp270-1; ☎ 93 46 21 62; Carrer de Pau Claris 142; meals €30; ⏲ Sep-Jul; Ⓜ Passeig de Gràcia) There's just one dish: a succulent beef entrecote with a secret 'sauce Porte-Maillot' (named after the location of the original restaurant in Paris), chips and salad.

Bilbao (Map pp270-1; ☎ 93 458 96 24; Carrer del Perill 33; meals €40; ⏲ Mon-Sat; Ⓜ Diagonal) The back dining room, with bottle-lined walls, stout timber tables and a yellowing light evocative of distant country taverns, will appeal to carnivores especially.

DRINKING

The city abounds with daytime cafes, laid-back lounges and lively night-time bars. Closing time is generally 2am Sunday to Thursday and 3am on Friday and Saturday.

BARRÍ GÒTIC

La Clandestina (Map p272; Baixada de Viladecols 2bis; ⏲ 10am-10pm Sun-Thu, 9am-midnight Fri & Sat; Ⓜ Jaume I) Opt for tea, a beer or a Middle Eastern *narghile* (the most elaborate way to smoke). You can even get a head massage or eat cake in this chilled tea shop.

EL RAVAL

Boadas (Map p272; Carrer dels Tallers 1; Ⓜ Catalunya) One of the city's oldest cocktai

DALLAS STRIBLEY

Pintxos (Basque tapas) in a local *taberna* (tavern)

bars, Boadas is famed for its daiquiris. The bow-tied waiters have been serving up their poison since 1933.

Casa Almirall (Map p272; Carrer de Joaquín Costa 33; Ⓜ Universitat) In business since the 1860s, this corner drinkery is dark and intriguing, with Modernista decor and a mixed clientele.

LA RIBERA

La Fianna (Map p272; Carrer dels Banys Vells 15; Ⓜ Jaume I) There is something rather medieval Oriental in the style of this bar, with its bare stone walls, forged iron candelabras and cushion-covered lounges. As the night wears on, it's elbow room only.

La Vinya Del Senyor (Map p272; Plaça de Santa Maria del Mar 5; noon-1am Tue-Sun; Ⓜ Jaume I) The wine list here is as long as *War & Peace,* and the terrace lies in the shadow of Santa Maria del Mar.

L'EIXAMPLE & GRÀCIA

Les Gens Que J'Aime (Map pp270-1; Carrer de València 286; Ⓜ Passeig de Gràcia) This intimate relic of the 1960s offers jazz music in the background and a cosy scattering of velvet-backed lounges around tiny dark tables.

Sabor a Cuba (Map pp270-1; Carrer de Francisco Giner 32; Ⓜ Fontana) A mixed crowd of Cubans and fans of the Caribbean island come to drink mojitos and shake their stuff in this home of *ron y son* (rum and sound).

ENTERTAINMENT

There are quite a few venues that stage vanguard drama and dance, including **Teatre Nacional de Catalunya** (Map pp270-1; ☎ 93 306 57 00; www.tnc.es; Plaça de les Arts 1; Ⓜ Glòries).

Football fans can see FC Barcelona play at **Camp Nou** (Map pp270-1; ☎ 902 18 99 00, from overseas 34 93 496 36 00; www.fcbarcelona.com; Carrer Arístides Maillol; Ⓜ Collblanc). Even if you can't score tickets, stop by for a peek at the **museum** (adult/senior & child €8.50/6.80; 10am-8pm Mon-Sat, to 2.30pm Sun & holidays mid-Apr–mid-Oct, to 6.30pm Mon-Sat, to 2.30pm Sun & holidays mid-Oct–mid-Apr).

KRZYSZTOF DYDYNSKI
Custo Barcelona

SHOPPING

Most mainstream fashion stores are along a shopping 'axis' that runs from Plaça de Catalunya along Passeig de Gràcia, then left (west) along Avinguda Diagonal.

The El Born area in La Ribera is awash with tiny boutiques, especially those purveying young, fun fashion. There are plenty of shops scattered throughout the Barrí Gòtic (stroll Carrer d'Avinyò and Carrer de Portaferrissa).

Els Encants Vells (Map pp270-1; ☎ 93 246 30 30; Carrer Dos de Maig 186; 8.30am-6pm Mon, Wed, Fri & Sat; Ⓜ Glòries) Bargain hunters love this free-for-all flea market.

Vinçon (Map pp270-1; ☎ 93 215 60 50; www.vincon.com; Passeig de Gràcia 96; Ⓜ Diagonal) This is a design emporium where home decorators and gadget lovers should head.

Custo Barcelona (Map p272; ☎ 93 268 78 93; www.custo-barcelona.com; Plaça de les Olles 7) Custo bewitches people the world over with a youthful, psychedelic panoply of women's and men's fashion.

Joan Murrià (Map pp270-1; ☎ 93 215 57 89; Carrer de Roger de Llúria 85) The century-old Modernista shop-front ads will draw you into this delicious delicatessen, where the shelves groan under the weight of speciality food from around Catalonia and beyond.

GETTING THERE & AWAY

AIR

Barcelona's airport, **El Prat de Llobregat** (BCN), is 12km southwest of the city centre and Spain's second airport after Madrid. See p298 for airline details.

BUS

The main terminal for most domestic and international buses is the **Estació del Nord** (Map pp270-1; ☎ 902 30 32 22; www.barcelonanord.com; Carrer d'Ali Bei 80; Ⓜ Arc de Triomf). ALSA goes to Madrid (€27, eight hours, 16 daily), Valencia (€24.50, 4½ to 6½ hours, 14 daily) and many other destinations.

CAR & MOTORCYCLE

The AP-7 motorway comes in from the French border, and the AP-2 motorway heads towards Zaragoza. Both are toll roads. The N-II is a nontoll alternative, but it can get choked with traffic at peak times.

TRAIN

Virtually all trains travelling to and from destinations within Spain stop at Estació Sants (**Map pp270-1; Ⓜ Sants-Estació**). High-speed trains to Madrid via Lleida and Zaragoza take as little as two hours 40 minutes (€40 to €163 depending on conditions). Other trains run to Valencia (€32.50 to €38, three to 3½ hours, 15 daily) and Burgos (€38.50, eight to nine hours, four daily).

GETTING AROUND

Information about Barcelona's public transport is available online at www.tmb.net and on ☎ 010.

TO/FROM THE AIRPORT

Renfe's *rodalies* line 10 runs between the airport and Estació de França in Barcelona (about 35 minutes), stopping at Estació Sants and Passeig de Gràcia. Tickets cost €2.60, unless you have a T-10 multitrip public transport ticket.

The A1 Aerobús (**Map p272; ☎ 93 415 60 20**) runs from the airport to Plaça de Catalunya (€4.05, 30 to 40 minutes) via Plaça d'Espanya every six to 15 minutes (depending on the time of day) from 6am to 1am.

CAR & MOTORCYCLE

Street parking in blue and green zones costs €2.35 to €2.85 an hour (generally 8am to 8pm Monday to Saturday).

PUBLIC TRANSPORT

Barcelona's metro system spreads its tentacles around the city in such a way that most places of interest are within a 10-minute walk of a station. A single metro, bus or suburban train ride costs €1.30, but a T-1 ticket, valid for 10 rides, costs €7.20.

TAXI

Barcelona's black-and-yellow taxis are plentiful and reasonably priced. The flag fall is €1.75 weekdays, and €1.85 for nights and weekends. If you can't find a street taxi, call ☎ 93 303 30 33.

MONESTIR DE MONTSERRAT

The monks who built the Monestir de Montserrat (Monastery of the Serrated Mountain), 50km northwest of Barcelona, chose a spectacular spot. The monastery was founded in 1025 and pilgrims still come from all over Christendom to kiss the Black Virgin (La Moreneta), the 12th-century wooden sculpture of the Virgin Mary. If you're around the basilica at the right time, you'll catch a brief performance by the Montserrat Boys' Choir (**Escolania; www.escolania.net; admission free; ⏲ performances 1pm & 6.45pm Mon-Fri, 11am & 6.45pm Sun Sep-Jun**).

The FGC R5 train runs from Plaça d'Espanya station in Barcelona to Monistrol de Montserrat, where it connects with the rack-and-pinion train, or cremallera (**☎ 902 31 20 20; www.cremallerademontserrat.com; one way/return €4.10/6.50**), which takes 17 minutes to make the upwards journey.

FIGUERES

Figueres is home to the zany Teatre-Museu Dalí (**☎ 972 67 75 00; www.salvador-dali.org; Plaça de Gala i Salvador Dalí 5; adult/student €11/8; ⏲ 9am-8pm Jul-Sep, 10.30am-6pm Tue-Sun Oct-Jun**). Housed in a 19th-century theatre converted by Salvador Dalí (who was born here), it has a fascinating collection of his strange creations and is the site of his crypt.

Dalí fans will want to travel south to visit the equally kooky **Castell de Púbol** (☎ 972 48 86 55; www.salvador-dali.org; La Pera; adult/student & senior €7/5; 10.30am-7.15pm mid-Jun–mid-Sep, to 5.15pm Tue-Sun mid-Mar–mid-Jun & mid-Sep–Oct, to 4.15pm Tue-Sat Nov-Dec) at La Pera, 22km northwest of Palafrugell, and his summer getaway at Port Lligat (1.25km from Cadaqués), the **Casa Museu Dalí** (☎ 972 25 10 15; www.salvador-dali.org; Port Lligat; adult/student & senior €10/8; 10.30am-9pm mid-Jun–mid-Sep, to 6pm Tue-Sun mid-Sep–mid-Jan & mid-Mar–mid-Jun).

PORT AVENTURA

Near Salou, 11km west of Tarragona, is **Port Aventura** (☎ 902 20 20 41, 902 20 22 20; www.portaventura.es; adult/senior & child 5-12yr €44/35, 2-day ticket €66/52.50; 10am-midnight Jul & Aug, to 8pm Easter-Jun & Sep, to 7pm Oct), one of Spain's most popular theme parks, fun for the family or the young at heart. Trains run to Port Aventura's own station, about a 1km walk from the site, several times a day from Tarragona (€1.30 to €1.60, 10 to 15 minutes) and Barcelona (from €5.80 to €6.40, around 1½ hours).

BASQUE COUNTRY

The Basques, whose language is believed to be among the world's oldest, claim two of Spain's most interesting cities – San Sebastián and Bilbao – as their own. Stately San Sebastián offers a slick seaside position and some of the best food Spain has to offer. The extraordinary Guggenheim Bilbao museum is that city's centrepiece.

SAN SEBASTIÁN

pop 183,400

Stylish San Sebastián (Donostia in Basque) has the air of an upscale resort, complete with an idyllic location on the shell-shaped Bahía de la Concha.

SIGHTS

San Sebastián's two beautiful city beaches, **Playa de la Concha** and **Playa de Ondarreta**, are popular spots year-round. East of the Urumea River is the somewhat less crowded **Playa de la Zurriola**, popular with surfers. To escape the crowds, you can take the small **boat** (10am-8pm Jun-Sep) to the **Isla de Santa Clara**, an island in the middle of the bay.

The best vista in San Sebastián is from **Monte Igueldo** (www.monteigueldo.es). Drive up or catch the **funicular** (return adult/child €2.30/1.70; 10am-10pm Jul & Aug, 10am or 11am-6pm or 9pm Sep-Jun) from the western end of the seafront *paseo*. At the top, visit the **Parque de Atracciones** (☎ 943 21 02 11; 11am-6pm Mon-Tue & Thu-Fri, to 8pm Sat & Sun), an old-school funfair.

San Sebastián's best museum is the **Museo Chillida Leku** (☎ 943 33 60 06; www.museochillidaleku.com; adult/child/student €8.50/free/6.50; 10.30am-3pm Wed-Mon Sep-Jun, to 8pm Mon-Sat, to 3pm Sun Jul & Aug), 10km outside the city centre. The farmhouse with an outdoor sculpture garden features over 40 large-scale works by the famed Basque artist Eduardo Chillida. The peaceful, 12-hectare place is an ideal spot for picnics. To get here, take the G2 bus (€1.25) for Hernani from Calle de Okendo in San Sebastián and get off at Zabalaga.

Kids and adults alike will have fun at San Sebastián's **aquarium** (☎ 943 44 00 99; www.aquariumss.com; Paseo del Muelle 34; adult/under 3yr/child/student €10/free/6/8; 10am-9pm Jul & Aug, to 8pm Apr-Jun & Sep, to 7pm Mon-Fri & to 8pm Sat & Sun Oct-Mar), which is home to more than 5000 tropical fish, morays, sharks and a variety of other finned creatures.

SLEEPING & EATING

Head to the Parte Vieja for San Sebastián's *pintxos*, Basque-style tapas.

Pensión La Perla (☎ 943 42 81 23; www.pensionlaperla.com; Calle de Loyola 10; s/d/tr €35/55/70) Brisk, old-fashioned service and clean, fairly plain rooms, keep these well-located central digs busy.

Hotel de Londres e Inglaterra (☎ 943 44 07 70; www.hlondres.com; Calle de Zubieta 2; s/d from €175/225;) Queen Isabel II set the tone for this hotel well over a century ago and things have stayed pretty regal ever since. It oozes class, and some rooms have stunning views over Playa de la Concha.

Bar La Cepa (Calle de 31 de Agosto 7) The best *jamón jabugo* does not disappoint here and you eat beneath the blank eyes of a very large bull's head. The kitchens here also produce decent no-frills menus for €13.50.

La Mejillonera (Calle del Puerto) If you thought mussels came only with garlic sauce, come here and discover mussels (from €3) by the thousand in all their glorious forms.

our pick **Astelena** (Plaza de la Constitució/Calle Iñigo 1) The *pintxos* draped across the counter in this bar, tucked into the corner of the plaza, stand out as some of the best in the city.

Arzak (☎ 943 27 84 65; Avenida Alcalde Jose Elosegui 273; meals €150-160) Three–Michelin star chef Juan Mari Arzak is a national institution. The restaurant is about 1.5km east of San Sebastián.

GETTING THERE & AWAY

From San Sebastián airport (EAS), catch the Interbus that runs regularly to the Plaza de Gipuzkoa in town (€1.55, times vary).

The main **Renfe train station** (Paseo de Francia) is just across Río Urumea, on a line linking Paris to Madrid. There are several services daily to Madrid (from €37.20, six hours) and two to Barcelona (from €38.20, eight hours). ET/FV trains run from Amara train station west to Bilbao (€6.50, 2½ hours, hourly) via Zarautz, Zumaia and Durango.

DALLAS STRIBLEY

Playa de la Concha

BILBAO

pop 354,200

The commercial hub of the Basque Country, Bilbao (Bilbo in Basque) is best known for the spectacular **Museo Guggenheim** (☎ 944 35 90 80; www.guggenheim-bilbao.es; Avenida Abandoibarra 2; adult/under 12yr/student €12.50/free/7.50; 🕑 10am-8pm Tue-Sun Sep-Jun, daily Jul & Aug), an architectural masterpiece by Frank Gehry. With its undulating forms covered in titanium

SPAIN

BASQUE COUNTRY

scales, the structure was inspired by the shapes of ships and fish. Many credit this creation with revitalising modern architecture and creating a new standard in vanguard design.

Five minutes from the Museo Guggenheim, the **Museo de Bellas Artes** (**Fine Arts Museum; ☎ 944 39 60 60; www.museobilbao.com; Plaza del Museo 2; adult/student €5.50/4, Wed free; 10am-8pm Tue-Sun**) often seems to exceed its more famous cousin for content.

The **Casco Viejo**, Bilbao's old quarter, is a compact coin of charming streets, boisterous bars and plenty of quirky and independent shops. At its heart are Bilbao's original 'seven streets', Las Siete Calles, which date from the 1400s.

ANGUS OBORN

Views to Museo Guggenheim (p281)

SLEEPING & EATING

The Bilbao tourism authority has a useful **reservations department** (**☎ 902 87 72 98; www.bilbaoreservas.com**) for accommodation.

Pensión Mardones (**☎ 944 15 31 05; www.pensionmardones.com; Calle Jardines 4; s/d €34/48;**) This well-kept number has nice carved wooden wardrobes in the rooms and lots of exposed wooden roof beams. The cheerful owner is very helpful and all up it offers great value.

Pensión Iturrienea Ostatua (**☎ 944 16 15 00; www.iturrieneaostatua.com; Calle de Santa María 14; d/tr €70/96**) Easily the most eccentric hotel in Bilbao, this part farmyard/part old-fashioned toyshop is a work of art in its own right.

Xukeia (**☎ 944 15 97 72; Calle el Perro; pintxos €1-1.50**) One of the more character-infused places in the Old Town. It has something of the look of a small-town French bistro overlaid with raucous Spanish soul. The drool-inducing *pintxos* have won awards and are cheaper than elsewhere.

GETTING THERE & AWAY

Bilbao's airport (BIO) is near Sondika, 12km northeast of the city. **Easyjet** (**www.easyjet.com**) has cheap flights between London and Bilbao. The airport bus Bizkaibus A3247 (€1.25, 30 minutes) runs to/from Termibus (bus station), where there is a tram stop and a metro station.

Two Renfe trains runs daily to Madrid (from €39.80, six hours) and Barcelona (€39.80, nine hours) from the Abando train station.

Bilbao's main bus station (Termibus) is southwest of town. Regular services operate to/from Madrid (€26.20, 4¾ hours), Barcelona (€40.60, seven hours), Pamplona (€12.85, 1¾ hours) and Santander (€9.30, 1½ hours).

CANTABRIA, ASTURIAS & GALICIA

With a landscape reminiscent of parts of the British Isles, 'Green Spain' offers great walks in national parks, seafood feasts in sophisticated towns and oodles of opportunities to plunge into the ice-cold waters of the Bay of Biscay. Even in summer, you can strike four seasons in a day, so be prepared for anything!

SANTIAGO DE COMPOSTELA

pop 88,000 / elev 260m

The supposed burial place of St James (Santiago), Santiago de Compostela is a bewitching city. The Catedral del Apóstol (**www.catedraldesantiago.es; Praza do Obradoiro; 7am-9pm**), a superb Romanesque creation of the 11th to 13th centuries, is the heart and soul of Santiago. It's said that St James' remains were buried here in the 1st century AD and rediscovered in 813. Today, visitors line up to kiss his statue, which sits behind the main altar. The Museo da Catedral (**981 56 05 27; Praza do Obradoiro; adult/child €5/1; 10am-2pm & 4-8pm Jun-Sep, 10am-1.30pm & 4-6.30pm Oct-May, closed Sun afternoon**) includes the cathedral's cloisters, treasury and crypt.

The Museo das Peregrinacións (**981 58 15 58; Rúa de San Miguel 4; admission €2.40; 10am-8pm Tue-Fri, 10.30am-1.30pm & 5-8pm Sat, 10.30am-1.30pm Sun**) explores the pilgrim culture that has so shaped Santiago.

SLEEPING & EATING

our pick Casa-Hotel As Artes (**981 55 52 54; www.asartes.com; Travesía de Dos Puertas 2; r €88-98;**) On a quiet street near the Cathedral, these lovely stone-walled rooms exude a romantic rustic air.

San Francisco Hotel Monumento (**981 58 16 34; www.sanfranciscohm.com; Campillo San Francisco 3; s/d €130/170;**) The stone hallways, with their low lights and stone doorframes, recall the hotel's former life as a 16th-century monastery.

Carretas (**981 56 31 11; Rúa das Carretas 21; mains €10-18, menú del día €18**) On the edge of the Old Town, this classic *marisquería* is known for its shellfish platters (€48 per person) and excellent fish fresh from the *rías* (Galicia's fjord-like inlets).

Restaurante Ó Dezaseis (**981 56 48 80; Rúa de San Pedro 16; mains €11-13, menú del día €11.50**) Wood-beam ceilings and exposed stone walls give an invitingly rustic air to this popular tavern just beyond the touristy buzz.

GETTING THERE & AROUND

Services fan out from the bus station (**981 54 24 16; Rúa San Caetano**) to destinations all over Galicia and the rest of Spain.

THE RUNNING OF THE BULLS

Immortalised by Ernest Hemingway in *The Sun Also Rises*, the city of Pamplona (Iruña in Basque) is famous as the home of the wild Sanfermines (aka Encierro or Running of the Bulls) festival, held on 6 to 14 July. The action begins at 8am daily, when bulls are let loose from the Coralillos Santo Domingo, but the 825m race lasts just three minutes, so don't be late. The safest place to watch the Encierro is on TV; if that's too tame for you, try to sweet-talk your way onto a balcony or book a room in a hotel with views.

Regular Renfe trains run to/from Madrid (€52, three hours, three daily) and San Sebastián (from €14.70, two hours, three daily).

From the train station (Avenida de Lugo), trains travel to/from Madrid (€45) on a daytime Talgo (seven hours) or an overnight Trenhotel (nine hours). Regional trains run to La Coruña (€3.90 to €5.25, 45 to 70 minutes) and other destinations.

VALENCIA & MURCIA

A warm climate, an abundance of seaside resorts, and interesting cities make this area of Spain a popular destination. The beaches of the Costa Blanca (White Coast) draw most of the visitors, but venture beyond the shore to get a real feel for the region.

VALENCIA

pop 805,300

Valencia is where paella first simmered over a wood fire. It's a vibrant, friendly, slightly chaotic place with two outstanding fine-arts museums, an accessible old quarter, Europe's newest cultural and scientific complex – and one of Spain's most exciting nightlife scenes.

INFORMATION

Regional tourist office (☎ 96 398 64 22; Calle Paz 48; 9am-2.30pm & 4.30-8pm Mon-Fri)

Turismo Valencia (VLC) tourist office (☎ 96 315 39 31; www.turisvalencia.es; Plaza de la Reina 19; 9am-7pm Mon-Sat, 10am-2pm Sun) There's also a branch at the train station.

SIGHTS & ACTIVITIES

You'll see Valencia's best face by simply wandering around the Barrio del Carmen, strolling the Jardines del Turia (in what was once the city's river) or people watching in one of the city's many plazas.

Valencia's Romanesque-Gothic-baroque-Renaissance catedral (adult/under 3yr/3-12yr incl audio guide €4/free/2.70; 10am-5.30pm or 6.30pm Mon-Sat, 2-5.30pm Sun) is a compendium of centuries of architectural history and home to the Capilla del Santo Cáliz, a chapel said to contain the Holy Grail, that is the chalice Christ supposedly used in the Last Supper. Climb the 207 stairs of the Micalet (or Miguelete) bell tower (adult/under 14yr €2/1; 10am-7.30pm) for sweeping city views.

Valencia's other architectural pride and joy, the state-of-the-art Ciudad de las Artes y las Ciencias (City of Arts & Sciences; ☎ reservations 902 10 00 31; www.cac.es; Autovía a El Saler; combined ticket for all 3 attractions adult/child €30.60/23.30) is a complex of museums including the L'Oceanográfic aquarium (adult/child €23.30/17.60; 10am-6pm or 8pm Sep–mid-Jul, to midnight mid-Jul–Aug); the Museo de las Ciencias Príncipe Felipe (adult/child €7.50/5.80; 10am-7pm or 9pm) interactive science museum; and L'Hemisfèric (adult/child €7.50/5.80) planetarium, IMAX theatre and L'Umbracle covered garden. Also here is the shimmering, beetle-like Palau de les Arts Reina Sofía performing-arts centre (☎ 902 20 23 83; www.lesarts.com; Autovía a El Saler). Bus 35 goes from Plaza del Ayuntamiento.

Check out the latest exhibitions of contemporary art and the permanent collection of 20th-century paintings at the Instituto Valenciano de Arte Moderno (IVAM; ☎ 96 386 30 00; www.ivam.es; Calle Guillem de Castro 118; adult/student €2/1, Sun free; 10am-8pm or 10pm Tue-Sun).

The Museo de Bellas Artes (Fine Arts Museum; ☎ 96 378 03 00; Calle San Pío V 9; admission free; 10am-8pm Tue-Sun) ranks among Spain's best. Highlights include the grandiose Roman *Mosaic of the Nine Muses*, a collection of late medieval altarpieces and works by El Greco, Goya, Velázquez and Murillo, plus artists such as Sorolla and Pinazo of the Valencian Impressionist school.

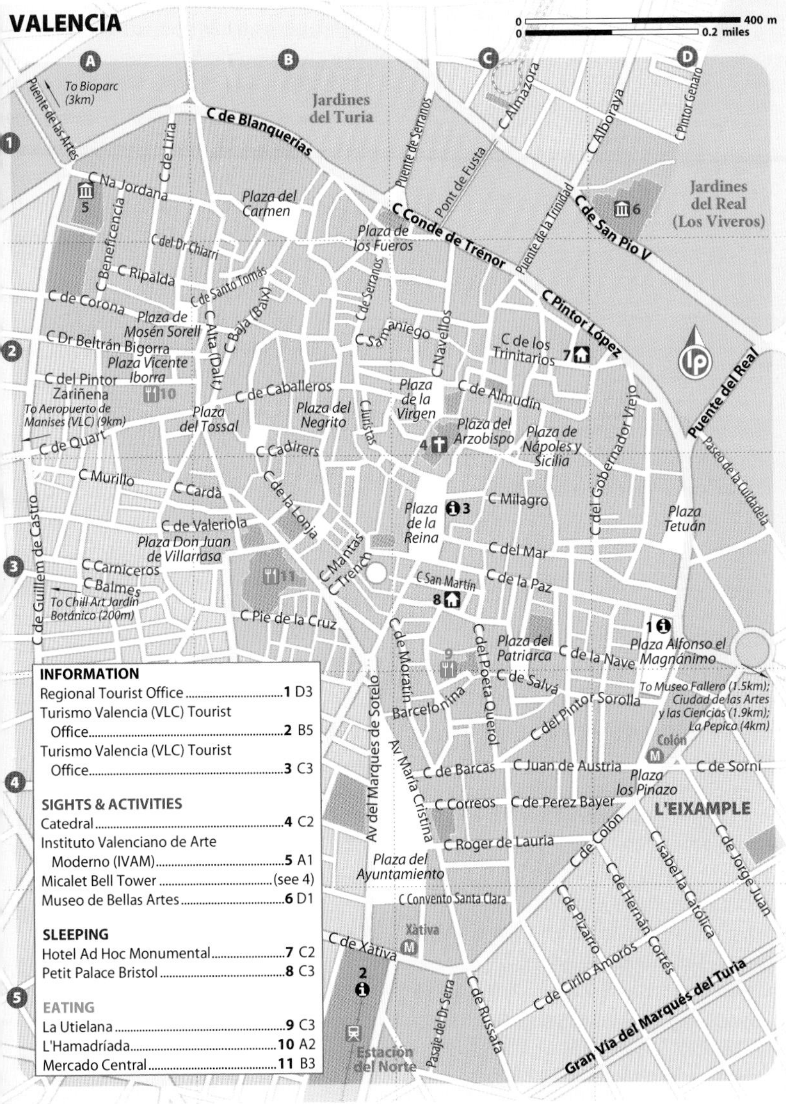

Stretch your towel on broad **Playa de la Malvarrosa**, which runs into **Playa de las Arenas**, each bordered by the Paseo Marítimo promenade and a string of restaurants. Take bus 1, 2 or 19, or the high-speed tram from Pont de Fusta or the Benimaclet Metro junction.

Bioparc (☎ **902 25 03 40; www.bioparcvalencia.es; Avenida Pio Baroja 3; adult/child €20/15;** 🕑 **10am-dusk**) is Valencia's latest attraction, an ecofriendly hypermodern zoo opened in 2008. Take bus 3, 81 or 95 or get off at the Nou d'Octubre metro stop.

BURN BABY BURN

In mid-March, Valencia hosts one of Europe's wildest street parties: Las Fallas de San José (www.fallas. es in Spanish). For one week (12 to 19 March), the city is engulfed by an anarchic swirl of fireworks, music, festive bonfires and all-night partying. On the final night, giant *ninots* (effigies), many of political and social personages, are torched in the main plaza.

If you're not in Valencia then, see the *ninots* saved from the flames by popular vote at the Museo Fallero (Plaza Monteolivete 4; adult/child €2/1, Sat & Sun free; ☺ 10am-2pm & 4.30-8.30pm Tue-Sat, 10am-3pm Sun).

SLEEPING & EATING

Hotel Ad Hoc Monumental (☎ 963 91 91 40; www.adhochoteles.com; Calle Boix 4; s €76-101, d €89-125; ☒) This charming boutique hotel has stencilled ceilings, pretty balconies and fabulous colour schemes.

Petit Palace Bristol (☎ 96 394 51 00; www. hthoteles.com; Calle Abadía San Martín 3; s €80-120, d €90-140; ☒ ☐) Hip, minimalist and friendly, this boutique belle retains the best of its 19th-century past and does a particularly scrumptious buffet breakfast.

Chill Art Jardín Botánico (☎ 96 315 40 12; www.hoteljardinbotanico.com; Calle Doctor Peset Cervera 6; s €94-133, d €94-149; ☒) Welcoming and mega-cool, this intimate hotel is furnished with flair. Candles flicker in the lounge and each bedroom has original art.

L'Hamadríada (☎ 96 326 08 91; www. hamadriada.com; Plaza Vicente Iborra 3; midday menú del día €10; ☺ lunch daily, dinner Wed-Sat) Down a blind alley, this slim white rectangle of a place does an innovative midday

menú, perfectly simmered rice dishes tha change daily and great meat grills.

La Utielana (☎ 96 352 94 14; Plaza Picade dos Aguas 3; meals around €15; ☺ lunch & dinne Mon-Fri & lunch Sat) Tucked away off Cal Prócida, La Utielana is ultra-Valencian It packs in the crowds, drawn by th wholesome fare and exceptional valu for money.

Mercado Central (Plaza del Mercad ☺ 7.30am-2.30pm Mon-Sat) This is a feas of colours and smells, with nearly 100 stallholders crammed under the market' modernist glass domes.

At weekends, locals in their hundred head for Las Arenas, just north of the por where a long line of restaurants overlook ing the beach all serve up authentic pa ella in a three-course meal costing aroun €15. Sprawling beachside La Pepica (☎ 9 371 03 66; Playa de Levante 6; mains €8-20) is on of the locals' favourites.

GETTING THERE & AWAY

Valencia's airport, Aeropuerto de Manise (VLC), is 10km west of the centre.

Valencia's bus station (☎ 96 346 62 66) i beside the riverbed on Avenida Ménéde Pidal. There are regular services to/from Madrid (€23 to €29, four hours), Barcelon (€25.15 to €38.50, four to 5½ hours) anc Alicante (€17.60 to €20, 2½ hours).

From Valencia's Estación del Norte (Calle Jativa), trains also go to/from Madrid Barcelona and Alicante, among othel destinations.

Regular car and passenger ferries go to the Balearic Islands (see opposite).

GETTING AROUND

Valencia has an integrated bus, tram and metro network. EMT buses ply town routes, while MetroBus serves outlying towns and villages.

The high-speed tram leaves from the GV tram station, 500m north of the athedral, at the Pont de Fusta. This is pleasant way to get to the beach, the aella restaurants of Las Arenas and the ort. Metro lines primarily serve the outer uburbs.

COSTA BLANCA

Clean white beaches, bright sunshine and rockin' nightlife have made the Costa Blanca (www.costablanca.org) one of Europe's favourite summer playgrounds. Many resorts are shamefully overbuilt, but it is still possible to discover charming towns and unspoilt coastline. Some of the best towns to explore include: Benidorm, a highrise nightlife hot spot in summer (but filled to the brim with pensioners the rest of the year); Altea, whose church, with its pretty blue-tiled dome, is its crowning glory; and Calpe, known for the Gibraltar-like Peñon de Ifach (332m).

ANDALUCÍA

The tapping feet and clapping hands of a passionate flamenco performance is an Andalucían signature that's as distinctive as the sweet aroma of orange blossom or the voluptuous flavour offered by a glass of chilled summer *gazpacho*.

In years past, armies of Christians and Muslims fought over this sun-drenched part of Spain; these days, tourists are the only visitors to arrive in battalions, lured here by Andalucía's beaches, its incomparable Islamic monuments and its full-blooded culture. Have a look at www.andalucia.org.

SEVILLE

pop 699,200

A completely sexy, gutsy and gorgeous city, Seville is home to two of Spain's most colourful festivals, some fascinating and distinctive *barrios* and a local population that lives life to the fullest. A fiery place (as you'll soon see in its packed and noisy tapas bars), it is also hot climate-wise – try to avoid July and August!

INFORMATION

Municipal tourist office (☎ 954 22 17 14; Calle de Arjona 28; 9am-7.30pm Mon-Fri, 9am-2pm Sat & Sun)

ISLAND ESCAPES

The Balearic Islands (Illes Balears in Catalan) adorn the glittering Mediterranean waters off Spain's eastern coastline. Beach tourism destinations par excellence, each of the four islands has a quite distinct identity. Modern overdevelopment has marred much of the coastline, but you can still experience the islands' traditional side by exploring further inland away from the heavily touristed areas. The archipelago's capital is touristy Mallorca (www.palmademallorca.es), while Ibiza (www.ibiza.travel/en) is notorious for its non-stop clubbing culture; you'll usually find a bit more peace and quiet on the smaller, more traditional islands of Formentera (www.turismoformentera.com) and Menorca (www.visitmenorca.com).

Scheduled flights fly from many major cities across Spain and Europe, while regular ferries travel from Barcelona and Valencia to Ibiza, Menorca and Mallorca; the main companies are Acciona Trasmediterránea (www.trasmediterranea.es) and Baleària (☎ 902 160180; www.balearia.com).

Regional tourist offices Avenida de la Constitución 21 (☎ **954 22 14 04; otsevilla@andalucia.org; 9am-7pm Mon-Fri, 10am-2pm & 3-7pm Sat, 10am-2pm Sun, closed holidays)**; Estación Santa Justa (☎ **954 53 76 26; 9am-8pm Mon-Fri, 10am-2pm Sat & Sun, closed holidays)**.

Turismo Sevilla (☎ **954 21 00 05; www.turismosevilla.org; Plaza del Triunfo 1; 10.30am-7pm Mon-Fri)**

SIGHTS & ACTIVITIES

CATEDRAL & LA GIRALDA

Seville's **Catedral** (☎ **954 21 49 71; adult/under 12yr/student & senior €7.50/free/1.50, Sun free; 11am-6pm Mon-Sat, 2.30-7pm Sun Sep-Jun, 9.30am-4.30pm Mon-Sat, 2.30-7pm Sun Jul & Aug)** was built on the site of Muslim Seville's main mosque between 1401 and 1507. One highlight of the cathedral's lavish interior is Christopher Columbus' supposed tomb, although research indicates he was probably laid to rest in the Caribbean. The adjoining tower, **La Giralda**, was the mosque's minaret and dates from the 12th century. Climb to the top for the city views.

DAN HERRICK

Plaza de España

ALCÁZAR

Seville's **Alcázar** (☎ **954 50 23 23; adult/under 16yr, senior & student €7/free; 9.30am-8pm Tue-Sat, to 6pm Sun & holidays Apr-Sep, to 6pm Tue-Sat, to 2.30pm Sun & holidays Oct-Mar)**, a royal residence for many centuries, was founded in 913 as a Muslim fortress. The Alcázar has been expanded and rebuilt many times in its 11 centuries of existence. The Catholic Monarchs, Fernando and Isabel, set up court here in the 1480s as they prepared for the conquest of Granada.

WALKS & PARKS

Seville's medieval *judería* (Jewish quarter), the **Barrio de Santa Cruz**, east of the cathedral and Alcázar, is a tangle of quaint winding streets and lovely plant-decked plazas perfumed with orange blossom.

A more straightforward walk is along the **river bank** and past Seville's famous bullring, the **Plaza de Toros de la Real Maestranza** (☎ **954 22 45 77; www.realmaestranza.es; Paseo de Cristóbal Colón 12; tours adult/over 65yr €5/4; 9.30am-7pm Nov-Apr, to 8pm May-Oct, to 3pm bullfighting days)**, one of the oldest in Spain. The tour departs half-hourly, and is in English and Spanish.

South of the centre is **Parque de María Luisa**, with its maze of paths, tall trees, flowers, fountains and shaded lawns. Be sure to seek out the magnificent **Plaza de España**, with its fountains, canal and a simply dazzling semicircle of *azulejo* (ceramic tile) clad buildings.

FESTIVALS & EVENTS

The first of Seville's two great festivals is **Semana Santa**, the week leading up to Easter Sunday. Throughout the week, thousands of members of religious brotherhoods parade in penitents' garb with tall, pointed *capirotes* (hoods) accompanying sacred images through the city, while huge crowds look on.

The **Feria de Abril**, a week in late April, is a welcome release after this solemnity: the festivities involve six days of music, dancing, horse riding and traditional dress, plus daily bullfights.

The city also stages Spain's largest flamenco festival, the month-long **Bienal de Flamenco**. It's held in September in even-numbered years.

SLEEPING

The city's accommodation is often full on weekends and is always booked solid during festivals, so book well ahead then.

Hotel Simón (☎ 954 22 66 60; www.hotelsimonsevilla.com; Calle García de Vinuesa 19; s €60-70, d €95-110;) A charming small hotel in a grand old 18th-century house, with spotless and comfortable rooms.

Hotel Puerta de Sevilla (☎ 954 98 72 70; www.hotelpuertadesevilla.com; Calle Puerta de la Carne 2; s/d €66/86;) A small, shiny hotel in a great location, the Puerta de Sevilla is all flower-pattern textiles and wrought-iron beds.

Hotel Amadeus (☎ 954 50 14 43; www.hotelamadeussevilla.com; Calle Farnesio 6; s/d €80/90;) This musician family converted their 18th-century mansion into a stylish hotel with 14 elegant rooms. Five new rooms have been added, one or two soundproofed for piano or violin practice.

Las Casas de la Judería (☎ 954 41 51 50; www.casasypalacios.com; Callejón Dos Hermanas 7; s/d from €140/175;) This charming five-star hotel is in fact a series of luxuriously restored houses and mansions.

DEATH IN THE AFTERNOON

Seville's bullfight season runs from Easter to October, with fights about 7pm most Sundays, and every day during the Feria de Abril and the preceding week. Tickets cost between €32.50 and €110. Tickets can be purchased in advance from **Empresa Pagés** (☎ 954 50 13 82; Calle de Adriano 37) and from 4.30pm on fight days at the bullring.

EATING

Restaurante La Cueva (☎ 954 21 31 43; Calle Rodrigo Caro 18; mains €11-24, menú del día €16) This popular bull's-head-festooned eatery cooks up a storming fish *zarzuela* (casserole; €30 for two people) and a hearty *caldereta* (lamb stew; €14.90).

Restaurante Modesto (☎ 954 41 68 11; Calle Cano y Cueto 5; mains €11-34) This bustling place is famed for its lobster and monkfish stew.

Corral del Agua (☎ 954 22 48 41; Callejón del Agua 6; mains €16.50-22; Mon-Sat) Inventive Al-Andalus and traditional dishes served in a semitropical courtyard under a twining canopy of vines and jacaranda.

Restaurante La Albahaca (☎ 954 22 07 14; Plaza de Santa Cruz 12; mains €20-30) Gastronomic invention is the mainstay of this elegant, gilded restaurant with an azure blue interior.

Restaurante Egaña Oriza (☎ 954 22 72 11; Calle San Fernando 41; mains €22-32; lunch & dinner Mon-Fri, dinner Sat) Regarded as one of the city's best restaurants, Egaña Oriza cooks up superb Andalucian-Basque cuisine, including lasagne with seafood, lobster and truffles.

ALDO PAVAN

A boy playing before the cathedral in León

IF YOU LIKE...

Spain is awash with stunning examples of ecclesiastical architecture, so if you've been inspired by Seville (p287), Salamanca (p262) and Santiago de Compostela (p283), don't miss the following:

- León Léon's 13th-century Gothic cathedral (**☎ 987 87 57 70; www.catedraldeleon.org in Spanish; admission free; 8.30am-1.30pm & 4-7pm Mon-Sat, 8.30am-2.30pm & 5-7pm Sun Oct-Jun, 8.30am-1.30pm & 4-8pm Mon-Sat, 8.30am-2.30pm & 5-8pm Sun Jul-Sep**) is one of Spain's most beautiful churches, with an extraordinary gallery of stained glass.
- Avila This pilgrim town is famous for its 12th-century murallas (**walls; ☎ 920 21 13 87; adult/child €4/2.50; 11am-6pm Tue-Sun Sep-Jun, 10am-8pm Jul & Aug**) and its cathedral (**☎ 920 21 16 41; Plaza de la Catedral; admission €4; 10am-7pm Mon-Fri, to 8pm Sat, noon-6pm Sun Jun-Sep, shorter hours Oct-May**), Spain's earliest Gothic church.
- Burgos The legendary warrior El Cid was born near Burgos and is buried beneath the dome of the cathedral (**☎ 947 20 47 12; Plaza del Rey Fernando; adult/child/senior/pilgrim & student €4/1/2.50/3; 9.30am-7.30pm 19 Mar-Oct, 10am-7pm Nov-18 Mar**).
- Girona (**☎ 972 21 44 26; www.lacatedraldegirona.com; admission €4; 10am-2pm & 4-7pm Tue-Sat Mar-Jun, 10am-8pm Tue-Sat Jul-Sep, 10am-2pm & 4-6pm Tue-Sat Oct-Feb, 10am-2pm Sun & holidays**) boasts Europe's widest Gothic nave (23m), a lovely Romanesque cloister, and a blustering baroque facade.
- Zaragoza The baroque Basílica de Nuestra Señora del Pilar (**☎ 976 39 74 97; admission free; 6.45am-9.30pm**) is the spiritual heart of the Aragón region. The faithful flock to the Capilla Santa to kiss a piece of marble *pilar* (pillar).

DRINKING

Bars usually open until 2am weekdays and 3am at the weekend. Drinking and partying really get going around midnight on Friday and Saturday.

Casa Morales (**☎ 954 22 12 42; Garcia de Vinuesa 11**) Founded in 1850, not much has changed in this defiantly old-world bar, with charming anachronisms wherever you look. Towering clay *tinajas* (wine torage jars) carry the chalked-up tapas hoices of the day.

El Garlochi (Calle Boteros 4) Named after he *gitano* (Roma) word for 'heart', this leeply camp bar hits you with clouds of incense, Jesus and Virgin images displayed on scarlet walls, and potent cocktails with names like Sangre de Cristo Blood of Christ).

Plaza del Salvador is brimful of drinkers rom mid-evening to 1am.

ENTERTAINMENT

Seville is arguably Spain's flamenco capital and you're most likely to catch a pontaneous atmosphere (of unpredictable quality) in one of the bars staging egular nights of flamenco with no admission fee.

La Carbonería (☎ 954 21 44 60; Calle evíes 18; admission free; ⏰ about 8pm-4am) The sprawling converted coal yard throngs with tourists and locals who come to mingle and enjoy live flamenco every night of the week.

Casa de la Memoria Al-Andalus (☎ 954 6 06 70; Calle Ximénez de Enciso 28; adult/child 14/8; ⏰ 9pm & 10.30pm) Book a ticket here or nightly shows with a focus on medieval and Sephardic Al-Andalus styles of music, in a room of shifting shadows.

For flamenco, hotels and tourist offices end to steer you towards *tablaos* (expensive, tourist-oriented flamenco venues). Of these, Los Gallos (☎ 954 21 69 81; www.ablaolosgallos.com; Plaza de Santa Cruz 11; admission incl 1 drink €30; ⏰ 2hr shows 8-10pm & 10.30-12.30pm) is a cut above the average.

GETTING THERE & AWAY

AIR

A range of domestic and international lights lands in Seville's San Pablo airport SVQ), 8.5km from the city centre.

BUS

Regular services run from the Plaza de Armas bus station (☎ 954 90 80 40; Avenida del Cristo de la Expiración). Destinations include Madrid (€18.65, six hours, 14 daily), Mérida (€11, three hours, 12 daily), Cáceres (€15, four hours, six daily) and northwestern Spain.

Buses to other parts of Andalucía use Prado de San Sebastián bus station (☎ 954 41 71 11; Plaza San Sebastián). Twelve or more buses run daily to/from Córdoba (€9.43, two hours) and Granada (€18.57, 3½ hours), and five to Ronda (€10.50, 2½ hours).

TRAIN

From Seville's Estación de Santa Justa (Avenida Kansas City), 1.5km northeast of the centre, there are superfast AVE trains as well as regular trains to Madrid (€59 to €75.10, 2½ to 3½ hours, hourly). Other destinations include Barcelona (€57.50 to €88, 10½ to 13 hours, three daily), Cádiz (€9.80, 1¾ hours, 13 daily), Córdoba (€8.20 to €28.30, 40 minutes to 1½ hours, 21 or more daily) and Granada (€21.65, three hours, four daily).

GETTING AROUND

Amarillos Tours (☎ 902 21 03 17) runs buses between the airport and Puerta de Jerez (€2.20 to €2.50, 30 to 40 minutes, at least 15 daily). A taxi costs about €18.

Local buses are run by Seville's urban transport authority, Tussam (☎ 902 45 99 54; www.tussam.es, in Spanish). The C1, C2, C3 and C4 buses link the main transport terminals and the city centre. Two new tram lines operate between Plaza Nueva (near the Ayuntamiento) and along Avenida de la Constitución to the Archivo de Indias and Puerta de Jerez, then down San Fernando to the bus station at Prado de San Sebastian. Tickets cost €1.10.

A metro line was under construction at the time of writing.

CÓRDOBA

pop 323,600

Córdoba pays graceful testament to its Moorish past. The inside of the famous **Mezquita** (☎ **957 47 05 12; adult/child €8/4; 10am-7pm Mon-Sat Apr-Oct, to 6pm Mon-Sat Nov-Mar, 9-10.45am & 1.30-6.30pm Sun year-round**), which was begun by emir Abd ar-Rahman I in 785 and enlarged by subsequent generations, is a mesmerising sequence of two-tier arches amid a thicket of columns. From 1236, the mosque was used as a church and in the 16th century a cathedral was built right in its centre – somewhat wrecking the effect of the original Muslim building.

It's well worth the 8km trip west of Córdoba to the intriguing **Medina Azahara** (**Madinat al-Zahra;** ☎ **957 32 91 30; Carretera Palma del Río, Km 5.5; adult/EU citizen €1.50/free; 10am-6.30pm Tue-Sat, to 8.30pm May–mid-Sep, to 2pm Sun**), a mighty Muslim city-palace from the 10th century. A taxi costs €37 for the return trip, with one hour to view the site, or you can book a three-hour coach tour for €6.50 to €10 through many Córdoba hotels. Guided visits can also be arranged for around €15.

The **bus station** (☎ **957 40 40 40; Glorieta de las Tres Culturas**) is located 1km northwest of Plaza de las Tendillas, behind the train station. Destinations include Seville (€10, 1¾ hours, six daily), Granada (€12 to €16.60, 2½ hours, seven daily) and Madrid (€14.40, 4½ hours, six daily).

The **train station** (**Avenida de América**) is on the high-speed AVE line between Madrid and Seville. Destinations include Seville (€27.80, 90 minutes, 23 or more daily), Madrid (€49 to €62, 1¾ to 6¼ hours, 23 or more daily) and Barcelona (€56 to €125, 10½ hours, four daily).

GRANADA

pop 300,000 / elev 685m

Granada's eight centuries as a Muslim capital are symbolised in its keynote emblem, the remarkable Alhambra, one of the most graceful architectural achievements in the Muslim world. Islam was never completely expunged here and today it seems more present than ever in the shops, restaurants, tearooms and mosque of a growing North African community in and around the maze of the Albayzín.

INFORMATION

Provincial tourist office (☎ **958 24 71 28; www.turismodegranada.org; Plaza de Mariana Pineda 10; 9am-8pm Mon-Fri, 10am-7pm Sat, 10am-3pm Sun Mar-Oct, 9am-7pm Mon-Fri, 10am-7pm Sat, 10am-3pm Sun Nov-Feb**) Information on Granada province.

Regional tourist office Plaza Nueva (☎ **958 22 10 22; Calle Santa Ana 1; 9am-7.30pm Mon-Sat, 9.30am-3pm Sun & holidays**); Alhambra (☎ **958 22 95 75; ticket-office bldg, Avenida del Generalife s/n; 8am-7.30pm Mon-Fri, 8am-2pm & 4-7.30pm Sat & Sun Mar-Oct, 8am-7.30pm Mon-Fri, 8am-2pm & 4-6pm Sat & Sun Nov-Feb, 9am-1pm holidays**) Information on all of Andalucía.

SIGHTS

After you've explored the Alhambra (opposite), a wander around the narrow, hilly streets of the **Albayzín**, the old Moorish quarter across the river from the Alhambra, is highly enjoyable. When doing this, make sure you keep your wits about you, as muggings sometimes occur around here. After heading uphill to reach the **Mirador de San Nicolás** – a viewpoint with breathtaking vistas and a relaxed scene – you may wish to return to Plaza Nueva via the **Museo Arqueológico** (☎ **958 22 56 03; Carrera del Darro 43; adult/EU citizen €1.50/free; 2.30-8.30pm Tue, 9.30am-8.30pm Wed-Sat, 9.30am-2.30pm Sun**).

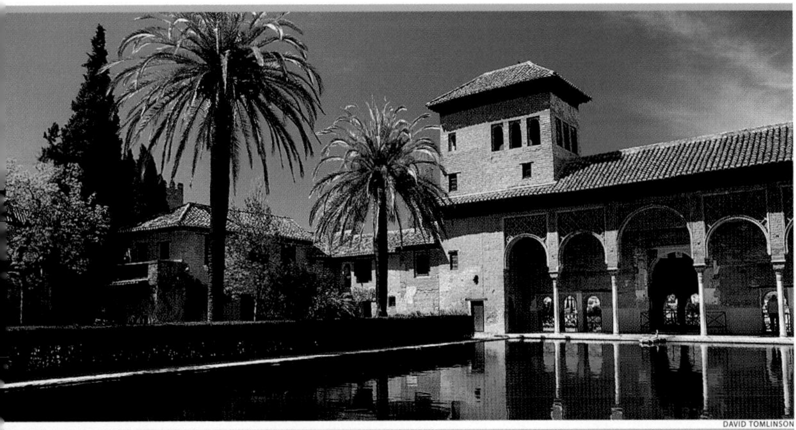

DAVID TOMLINSON

The Palacio del Partal at Alhambra

ALHAMBRA

The mighty Alhambra is breathtaking. Much has been written about its fortress, palace, patios and gardens, but nothing can really prepare you for seeing the real thing.

The Alcazaba, the Alhambra's fortress, dates from the 11th to the 13th centuries. There are spectacular views from the tops of its towers. The Palacio Nazaríes (Nasrid Palace), built for Granada's Muslim rulers in their 13th- to 15th-century heyday, is the centrepiece of the Alhambra. The beauty of its patios and intricacy of its stuccoes and woodwork, epitomised by the *Patio de los Leones* (Patio of the Lions) and *Sala de las Dos Hermanas* (Hall of the Two Sisters), are stunning.

It's good to book in advance (€1 extra per ticket) online from Alhambra Advance Booking, Servicaixa or from Servicaixa cash machines, in the Alhambra grounds. Alhambra tickets are only valid for half a day, so specify whether you wish to visit in the morning or afternoon. The Palacio Nazaríes is also open for night visits.

Things You Need to Know: **Alhambra (☎ 902 44 12 21; www.alhambra.org; adult/under 12yr/student & EU senior €12/free/9, Generalife only €6; 🕑 8.30am-8pm Mar-Oct, to 6pm Nov-Feb, closed 25 Dec & 1 Jan); Alhambra Advance Booking (☎ 902 88 80 01, from overseas 34 93 492 37 50; 🕑 8am-9pm); Servicaixa (www.servicaixa.com); Servicaixa cash machines (🕑 8am-7pm Mar-Oct, to 5pm Nov-Feb); night visits (🕑 10pm-11.30pm Tue-Sat Mar-Oct, 8pm-9.30pm Fri & Sat Nov-Feb)**

It's worth exploring the streets and lanes surrounding Plaza de Bib-Rambla, and visiting the Capilla Real **(Royal Chapel; ☎ 958 22 92 39; www.capillarealgranada.com; Calle Oficios; admission €3.50; 🕑 10.30am-12.45pm & 4-7pm Mon-Sat, 11am-12.45pm & 4-7pm Sun Apr-Oct, 10.30am-12.45pm & 3.30-6.15pm Mon-Sat, 11am-12.45pm & 3.30-6.15pm Sun Nov-Mar)**, where Fernando and Isabel, the Christian monarchs who conquered Granada in 1492, are buried.

Next door to the chapel is Granada's **Catedral** (☎ **958 22 29 59; admission €3.50; 10.45am-1.30pm & 4-8pm Mon-Sat, 4-8pm Sun, to 7pm Nov-Mar**), which dates from the early 16th century.

SLEEPING

Hotel América (☎ **958 22 74 71; www.hotelamericagranada.com; Calle Real de la Alhambra 53; s/d €70/115; Mar-Nov;**) Within the Alhambra grounds, the early 19th-century building creates a restful ambience in contrast to the busy Alhambra foot traffic.

Puerta de las Granadas (☎ **958 21 62 30; www.hotelpuertadelasgranadas.com; Calle Cuesta de Gomérez 14; s/d €77/99, superior r €107-180;**) This 19th-century building, renovated in modern-minimalist style, has wooden shutters and elegant furnishings.

Casa Morisca Hotel (☎ **958 22 11 00; www.hotelcasamorisca.com; Cuesta de la Victoria 9; d interior €118, exterior €148;**) The hotel occupies a late-15th-century Albayzín mansion, with 14 stylish rooms centred on an atmospheric patio with an ornamental pool and wooden galleries.

EATING

Granada is one of the last bastions of that fantastic practice of free tapas with every drink, and some have an international flavour.

Poë (**Calle Paz; media raciones €3**) British-Angolan Poë offers Brazilian favourites such as *feijoada* or chicken stew with polenta, and a trendy multicultural vibe.

Bodegas Castañeda (**Calle Almireceros; raciones from €6**) An institution, and reputedly the oldest bar in Granada, this kitchen whips up traditional food in a typical *bodega* (traditional wine bar) setting. Get a table before 2pm, as it gets busy.

Restaurante Arrayanes (☎ **958 22 84 01; Cuesta Marañas 4; mains €8.50-19; from 8pm**) In the Albayzín, this intimate restauran serves decent Moroccan dishes in a dining area strewn with brocade banquettes rugs and brightly coloured cushions.

Cunini (☎ **958 25 07 77; Plaza de Pescadería 14; mains €11-23, set menu €19**) This place dishes up first-class fish and seafood as tapas if you stand at the bar, or full meals out back.

For fresh fruit and veg, head for the large covered **Mercado Central San Agustín** (**Calle San Agustín; 8am-2pm Mon-Sat**), a block west of the cathedral.

GETTING THERE & AWAY

Autocares J Gonzalez (☎ **95 849 01 64; www.autocaresjosegonzalez.com**) runs a bus service between Granada's airport (GRX) and the city centre, 17km distant. A taxi costs €18 to €22.

The **bus station** (**Carretera de Jaén**) is 3km northwest of the centre. Bus 33 (€1.10) travels between the two. There are buses to Córdoba (€12 to €16.60, 2¾ hours direct, nine daily), Seville (€18.60, three hours direct, eight daily) and Madrid (€15.66, five to six hours, 10 to 13 daily).

The **train station** (**Avenida de Andaluces**) is 1.5km northwest of the centre. Four trains run daily to/from Seville (€21.65, three hours), three to/from Ronda (€12.25, three hours) and Algeciras (€18.35, 4½ hours). One or two trains go to Madrid (€62.20, four to five hours) and Valencia (€46 to €73, 7½ to eight hours).

CÁDIZ

pop 128,600

Cádiz is crammed onto the head of a promontory like an overcrowded ocean liner. Columbus sailed from here on his second and fourth voyages, and after his success in the Americas, Cádiz grew into Spain's richest and most cosmopolitan city in the 18th century. The best time to visit is during the February *carnaval* (carnival), which rivals Rio in terms of outrageous exuberance.

The **municipal tourist office** (☎ **956 24 10 01; Paseo de Canalejas s/n; 8.30am-6pm Mon-Fri, 9am-5pm Sat & Sun**) has helpful staff.

SIGHTS & ACTIVITIES

The yellow-domed 18th-century **Catedral** (☎ **956 28 61 54; Plaza de la Catedral; adult/student €5/3, free during services; 10am-6.30pm Mon-Fri, 10am-4.30pm Sat, 1-6.30pm Sun, services 7-8pm Tue-Fri, 11am-1pm Sun**) is the city's most striking landmark.

Get your bearings by climbing up the baroque **Torre Tavira** (☎ **956 21 29 10; Calle Marqués del Real Tesoro 10; adult/student €4/3.30; 10am-6pm, to 8pm 15 Jun-15 Sep**), the highest of Cádiz' old watchtowers, which features sweeping views of the city.

The **Museo de Cádiz** (☎ **956 20 33 68; Plaza de Mina; admission/EU citizen €1.50/free; 2.30-8.30pm Tue, 9am-8.30pm Wed-Sat, 9.30am-2.30pm Sun**) has a magnificent collection of archaeological remains, as well as a fine-art collection. The city's lively **central market** (**Plaza de las Flores**) is on the site of a former Phoenician temple.

The broad, sandy **Playa de la Victoria**, a lovely Atlantic beach, stretches about 4km along the peninsula from its beginning 1.5km beyond the Puertas de Tierra. Bus 1 'Plaza España-Cortadura' from Plaza de España will get you there.

SLEEPING & EATING

Hostal Fantoni (☎ **956 28 27 04; www.hostalfantoni.net; Calle Flamenco 5; s/d €45/70;**) The Fantoni offers a dozen attractive and spotless rooms in an attractively modernised 18th-century house. The roof terrace catches a breeze in summer.

La Gorda Te Da De Comer (**tapas €2-2.40**) Luque (**Calle General Luque 1; Mon-Sat**); Rosario (**cnr Calle Rosario & Calle Marqués de Valdeiñigo; Tue-Sat**) Incredibly tasty food at low prices amid trendy pop design. Try the *solomillo* in creamy mushroom sauce or the curried chicken strips with Marie-Rose dip.

El Aljibe (☎ **956 26 66 56; www.pablogrosso.com; Calle Plocia 25; tapas €2-3.50, mains €10-15**) *Gaditano* (Cádiz native) chef Pablo Grosso concocts delicious combinations of the traditional and the adventurous. He stuffs his pheasant breast with dates and his *solomillo ibérico* (Iberian pork sirloin) with Emmental cheese, ham and piquant peppers.

GETTING THERE & AWAY

From the Cádiz **bus station** (☎ **95 680 70 59; Plaza de la Hispanidad**), buses head for Seville (€10.70, 1¾ hours, 10 daily), Tarifa (€7.90, two hours, five daily), Ronda (€12.60, three hours, two daily) and Granada (€28, five hours, four daily).

From the **train station** (**Plaza Sevilla**), up to 15 services run to Seville (€9.80, two hours), three to Córdoba (€34 to €43, three hours) and two to Madrid (€63, five hours).

DIRECTORY

ACTIVITIES

CYCLING

The Vuelta de España is one of Europe's great bike races (after the Tour de France and Giro d'Italia) and the country has produced many fine cyclists. Mountain biking is popular; areas such as Andalucía and Catalonia have many good tracks.

SKIING

Skiing is cheaper but less varied than in much of the rest of Europe. The season runs from December to mid-April. The best resorts are in the Pyrenees, especially in northwest Catalonia. The Sierra Nevada in Andalucía offers the most southerly skiing in Western Europe.

SURFING, WINDSURFING & KITESURFING

The Basque Country has good surf spots, including San Sebastián, Zarautz and the legendary left at Mundaka. Tarifa, with its long beaches and ceaseless wind, is generally considered to be the windsurfing capital of Europe.

WALKING

Spain is a trekker's paradise. Throughout Spain you'll find GR (*Grandes Recorridos*, or long-distance) trails. The Camino de Santiago (St James' Way, with several branches) is perhaps Spain's best-known long-distance walk.

DANGERS & ANNOYANCES

Stay alert and you can avoid most thievery techniques. Algeciras, Barcelona, Madrid and Seville are the worst offenders, as are many popular beaches in summer (never leave belongings unattended). Common scams include the following:

- Kids crowding around you asking for directions or help. They may be helping themselves to your wallet.
- A person pointing out bird droppings on your shoulder (some substance their friend has sprinkled on you) – as they help clean it off they are probably emptying your pockets.
- The guys who tell you that you have a flat tyre. While your new friend and you check the tyre, his pal is emptying the interior of the car.
- The classic snatch-and-run. Never leave your purse, bag, wallet, mobile phone etc unattended or alone on a table.

EMBASSIES & CONSULATES

Some 70 countries have their embassies in Madrid. Most embassies' office hours are around 9am to 2pm Monday to Friday.

Australia (off Map pp250-1; ☎ 91 353 66 00; www.spain.embassy.gov.au; Plaza del Descubridor Diego de Ordás 3)

Canada (Map pp250-1; ☎ 91 423 32 50; www.canada-es.org; Calle de Núñez de Balboa 35)

France (Map pp250-1; ☎ 91 423 89 00; www.ambafrance-es.org; Calle de Salustiano Olózaga 9)

Germany (Map pp250-1; ☎ 91 557 90 00; www.madrid.diplo.de; Calle de Fortuny 8)

Ireland (Map pp250-1; ☎ 91 436 40 93; Paseo de la Castellana 46)

Netherlands (off Map pp250-1; ☎ 91 353 75 00; www.embajadapaisesbajos.es; Avenida del Comandante Franco 32)

New Zealand (off Map pp250-1; ☎ 91 523 02 26; www.nzembassy.com; Calle del Pinar 7)

Portugal (off Map pp250-1; ☎ 91 782 49 60; www.embajadaportugal-madrid.org; Calle del Pinar 1)

UK Madrid (Map pp250-1; ☎ 91 700 82 00; www.ukinspain.com; Calle de Fernando el Santo 16); Barcelona (Map pp270-1; ☎ 93 366 62 00; Avinguda Diagonal 477)

USA Madrid (Map pp250-1; ☎ 91 587 22 00; www.embusa.es; Calle de Serrano 75); Barcelona (☎ 93 280 22 27; Passeig de la Reina Elisenda de Montcada 23-25)

FESTIVALS & EVENTS

Spaniards indulge their love of colour, noise, crowds and partying at innumerable local festivals, fiestas and *ferias* (fairs).

JANUARY

Festividad de San Sebastián Held in San Sebastián (p280) on 20 January; the whole town dresses up and goes berserk.

FEBRUARY & MARCH

Carnaval A time of fancy-dress parades and merrymaking celebrated around the country on the eve of the Christian Lent season (40 days before Easter). Among the wildest parties are those in Cádiz (p294) and Sitges, near Barcelona.

Las Fallas (www.fallas.com) Week-long mid-March party in Valencia (p284), with all-night dancing and drinking, mammoth bonfires, first-class fireworks and processions.

APRIL

Semana Santa Parades of holy images and huge crowds, notably in Seville (p289), during Easter week.

Feria de Abril (http://feriadesevilla.andalunet.com) A week-long party held in Seville (p289) in late April.

JULY

Sanfermines (www.sanfermin.com) The highlight of this originally religious festival is the running of the bulls, in Pamplona (p283). It's held in early July.

AUGUST

Semana Grande A week of heavy drinking and hangovers all along the northern coast during the first half of August.

SEPTEMBER

Festes de la Mercè (www.bcn.cat/merce) Barcelona's big annual party, held around 24 September. See p273 for more info.

HOLIDAYS

Spain has at least 14 official holidays a year, some observed nationwide, some very local. When a holiday falls close to a weekend, Spaniards like to make a *puente* (bridge), taking the intervening day off, too.

New Year's Day 1 January
Three Kings' Day 6 January
Good Friday Before Easter Sunday
Labour Day 1 May
Feast of the Assumption 15 August
National Day 12 October
All Saints' Day 1 November
Feast of the Immaculate Conception 8 December
Christmas 25 December

LANGUAGE

Spanish, or Castilian *(Castellano)* as it's more precisely called, is spoken throughout Spain, but there are also three other important regional languages: Catalan *(Català)* – another Romance language with close ties to French – is spoken in Catalonia, and dialects of it are spoken in the Balearic Islands and in Valencia; Galician (*Galego*), similar to Portuguese, is spoken in Galicia; and Basque (*Euskera;* of obscure, non-Latin origin) is spoken in the Basque Country and in Navarra.

LEGAL MATTERS

Spaniards no longer enjoy liberal drug laws. No matter what anyone tells you, it is not legal to smoke dope in public bars. There is a reasonable degree of tolerance when it comes to people having a smoke in their own home, but not in hotel rooms or guest houses.

MONEY

Spain's currency is the euro (€). Banks tend to give better exchange rates than the currency-exchange offices. It's easy to withdraw money – ATMs are ubiquitous.

In Spain, VAT (value-added tax) is known as *impuesto sobre el valor añadido* (IVA). On accommodation and restaurant prices it's 7%, but it's not always included in quoted prices. On retail goods and car hire, IVA is 16%. Non-EU visitors, if they spend €90.16 or more in one store (services don't count), are eligible for a tax refund. Request the appropriate form, fill it out and present it to a customs officer on leaving the European Union. They will stamp it and you can then cash it in or mail it for a refund to your credit card. Find more information at www.spainrefund.com.

In restaurants, tipping is a matter of personal choice – most people leave some small change; 5% is plenty, 10% is generous.

POST

Stamps are sold at post offices and *estancos* (tobacco shops with the Tabacos sign in yellow letters on a maroon background). A postcard or letter weighing up to 20g costs €0.60 from Spain to other European countries, and €0.78 to the rest of the world.

TELEPHONE

Blue public payphones are common and easy to use. They accept coins, phonecards and, in some cases, credit cards. Phonecards come in €6 and €12 denominations and, like postage stamps, are sold at post offices and tobacconists.

Telephone codes in Spain are an integral part of the phone number. Mobile phone numbers in Spain start with the number 6. All numbers prefixed with ☎ 900 are toll-free numbers.

TRANSPORT

GETTING THERE & AWAY

AIR

Flights from all over Europe, including many budget airlines, serve Spanish airports including Barcelona (BCN), Bilbao (BIO), Girona (GRO), Madrid (MAD), Palma de Mallorca (PMI), Seville (SVQ), Valencia (VLC) and Zaragoza (ZAZ). The big Spanish carriers include Iberia (IB; ☎ 902 40 05 00; www.iberia.es) and Spanair **(JK; ☎ 902 13 14 15; www.spanair.com).**

LAND

BUS

There are regular international bus services to Spain from European cities such as Lisbon, London and Paris. From London, the popular megacompany Eurolines **(www.nationalexpress.com/eurolines)** offers regular services to Barcelona (24 to 26 hours), Madrid (25 to 30 hours) and other cities.

CAR & MOTORCYCLE

If you're driving or riding to Spain from England, you'll have to choose between going through France or taking a direct ferry from England to Spain (see oppostite).

TRAIN

For details on long-distance rail travel, contact the Rail Europe Travel Centre **(☎ in UK 08448 484064; www.raileurope.co.uk)** in London.

From France, sleeper trains run from Paris Austerlitz daily to Madrid or Barcelona. The Barcelona service stops at Orléans, Limoges, Perpignan, Figueres, Girona and Barcelona Sants; the Madrid equivalent stops at Orléans, Blois, Poitiers, Vitoria and Burgos.

Two or three TGV trains leave from Paris Montparnasse for Irún, where you change to a normal train for the Basque Country and carry on towards Madrid. Up to three TGVs also put you on the road to Barcelona (leaving from Paris Gare de Lyon), with a change of train at Montpellier or Narbonne. One or two daily direct services connect Montpellier with Barcelona in 4½ hours (and on to Murcia).

SEA

UK

If you drive your own car, a ferry is your best bet. Brittany Ferries (☎ in UK 0870 907 6103; www.brittany-ferries.co.uk) runs Plymouth–Santander ferries (24 hours) twice-weekly from mid-March to mid-November. P&O Ferries (☎ in UK 0871 664 5645; www.poferries.com) runs Portsmouth–Bilbao ferries (35 hours) two or three times weekly year-round.

ITALY

The Grimaldi group's Grandi Navi Veloci (☎ 902 41 02 00, in Italy 010 209 4591; www1.gnv.it; Moll de San Beltran) runs a daily ferry service from Genoa to Barcelona (18 hours). Grimaldi Ferries (☎ 902 53 13 33, in Italy 081 496444; www.grimaldi-ferries.com) has a similar service between Barcelona and Civitavecchia (for Rome, 20 hours) and Livorno (Tuscany, 19½ hours) up to six days a week.

GETTING AROUND

Students and seniors are eligible for discounts of 30% to 50% on almost all types of transport within Spain.

AIR

Iberia has an extensive network covering all of Spain. Competing with Iberia are Spanair and Air Europa, as well as the low-cost companies Clickair (an Iberia subsidiary) and Vueling. EasyJet has a hub in Madrid and offers domestic flights to Oviedo, Ibiza and La Coruña. Ireland's Ryanair also runs a handful of domestic Spanish flights.

BOAT

Regular ferries connect the Spanish mainland with the Balearic Islands. The main companies:

Acciona Trasmediterránea (☎ 902 45 46 45; www.trasmediterranea.es)
Baleària (☎ 902 16 01 80; www.balearia.com)
Iscomar (☎ 902 11 91 28; www.iscomar.com)

BUS

Spain's bus network is operated by countless independent companies, and reaches into the most remote towns and villages. The best-known national company, under whose umbrella many smaller companies operate, is ALSA (☎ 902 42 22 42; www.alsa.es).

It is not necessary, and often not possible, to make advance reservations for local bus journeys. It is, however, a good idea to turn up at least 30 minutes before the bus leaves to guarantee a seat. For longer trips, you can and should buy your ticket in advance.

Other bus companies include the following:

Avanza (☎ 902 02 00 52; www.avanzabus.com)
Comes (☎ 902 19 92 08; www.tgcomes.es)
La Roncalesa (☎ 943 46 10 64)
Larrea/La Sepulvedana (☎ 902 22 22 82; www.lasepulvedana.es)
Los Amarillos (☎ 902 21 03 17; www.losamarillos.es)
PESA (☎ 902 10 12 10; www.pesa.net)
Portillo (☎ 902 14 31 44; www.ctsa-portillo.com)
Socibus/Secorbus (www.socibus.es)

CAR & MOTORCYCLE

Spain's roads vary enormously but are generally good. Fastest are the *autopistas;* on some, you have to pay hefty tolls (from Zaragoza to Barcelona, for example, it's €22.60). Trying to find a parking spot in larger towns and cities can be a nightmare. *Grúas* (tow trucks) can and will tow your car. The cost of bailing out a car can be €200 or more.

Spanish cities do not have US-style parking meters at every spot. Instead, if you park in a blue zone (frequently from 8am to 2pm or from 4pm to 8pm), you have to obtain a ticket from a streetside meter, which may be a block away. Display the ticket on the dash. If you bring your own vehicle into Spain, remember to always carry the vehicle registration document.

All EU member states' driving licences are recognised. Other foreign licences should be accompanied by an International Driving Permit. These are available from automobile clubs in your country and valid for 12 months.

Third-party motor insurance is a minimum requirement and it is compulsory to have a Green Card, an internationally recognised proof of insurance, which can be obtained from your insurer.

Driving in the cities can be a little hairraising at times but, otherwise, Spain doesn't present any special driving difficulties. Speed limits are 120km/h on the *autopistas,* 80km/h or 100km/h on other country roads and 50km/h (sometimes 30km/h) in built-up areas. The bloodalcohol limit is 0.05%. Seat belts must be worn and motorcyclists must always wear a helmet and keep headlights on day and night.

TRAIN

Renfe (☎ **902 24 02 02; www.renfe.es**), the national railway company, runs numerous types of trains. *Regionales* are all-stops trains (think cheap and slow). *Cercanías* provide regular services from major cities to the surrounding suburbs and hinterland, sometimes even crossing regional boundaries. High-speed AVE trains link Madrid with Barcelona (via Zaragoza, Lleida and Tarragona), Burgos and Seville (via Córdoba) – and in coming years with Valencia (via Cuenca) and with Bilbao.

You can buy tickets and make reservations online, at stations, at travel agencies displaying the Renfe logo and in Renfe offices in many city centres.

Rail passes are valid for all long-distance Renfe trains, but Inter-Rail users have to pay supplements on Talgo, InterCity and AVE trains.

ITALY

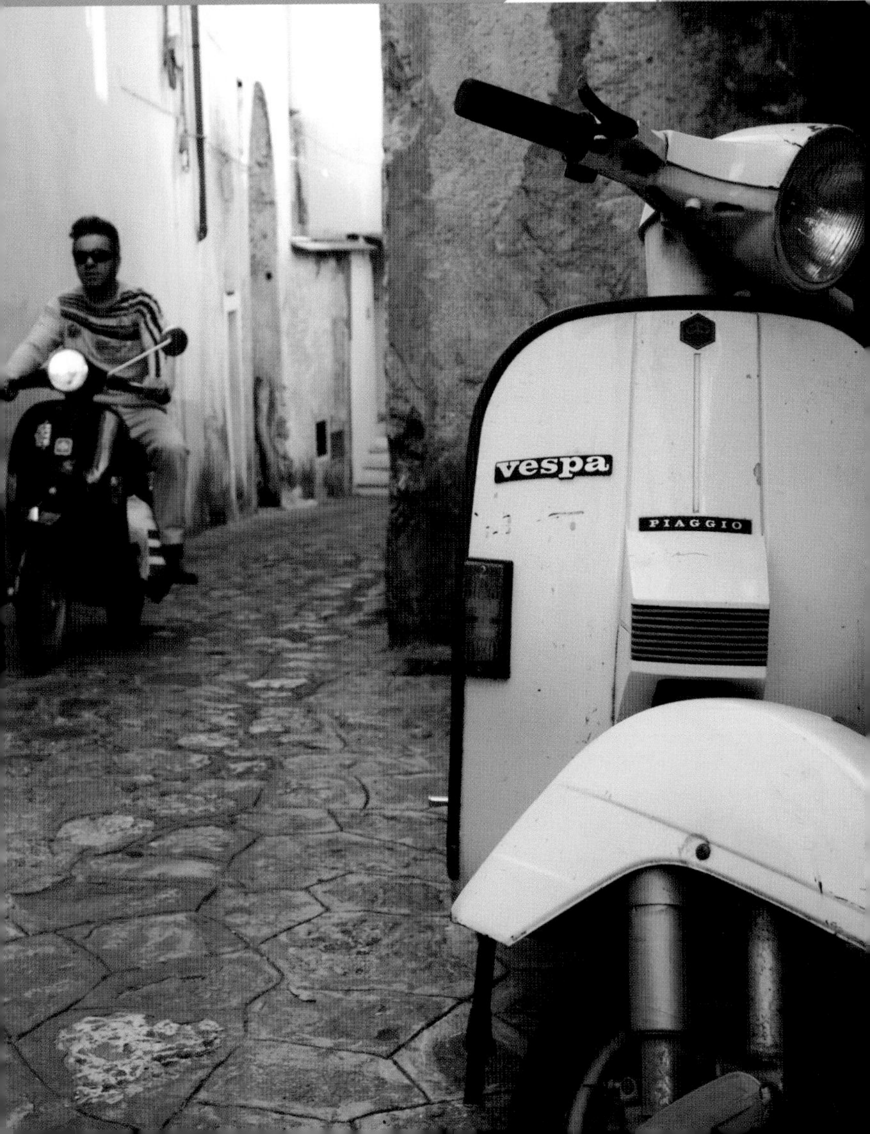

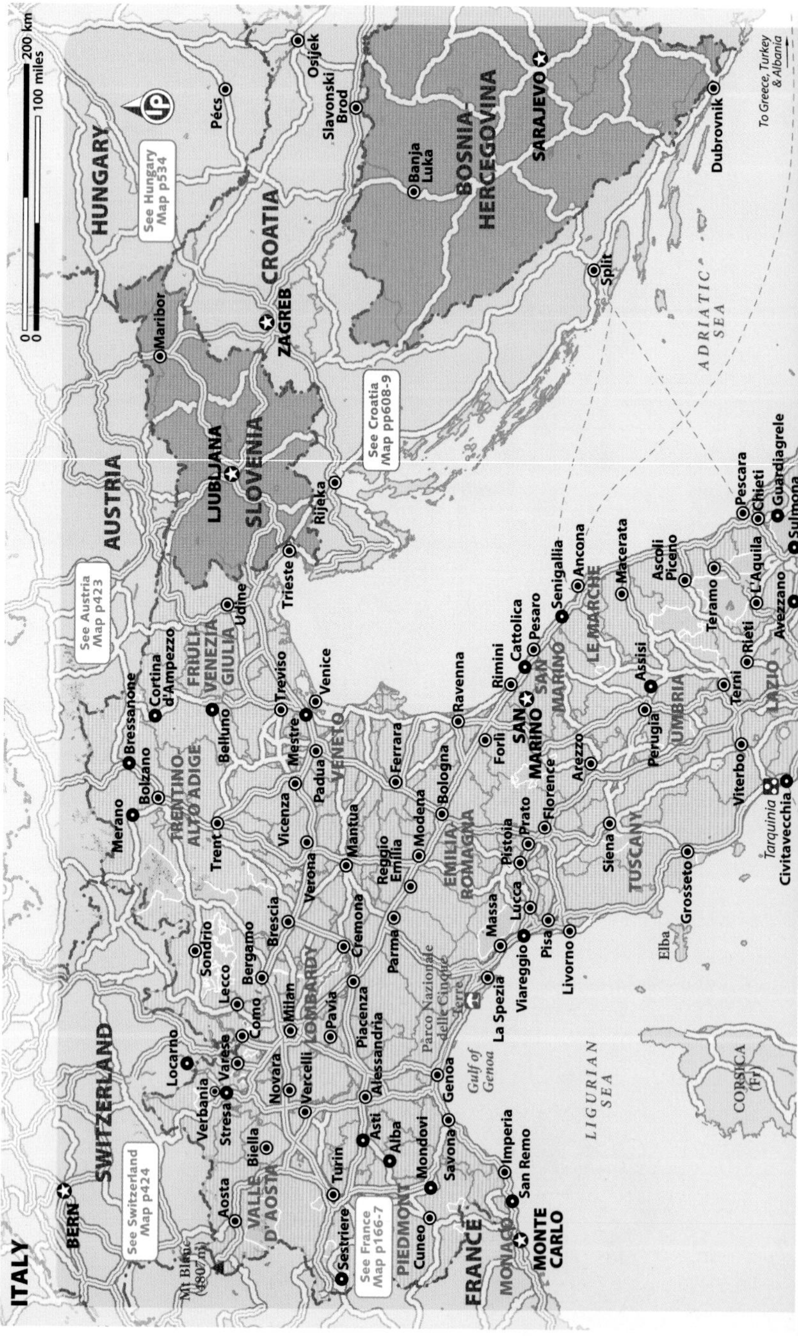
ITALY
0 200 km
0 100 miles
BERN
SWITZERLAND
See Switzerland Map p424
See Austria Map p423
See Hungary Map p534
See Croatia Map pp608-9
See France Map p166-7
AUSTRIA
HUNGARY
SLOVENIA
LJUBLJANA
CROATIA
ZAGREB
BOSNIA-HERCEGOVINA
SARAJEVO
FRANCE
MONACO
MONTE CARLO
SAN MARINO
Mt Blanc (4807m)
Aosta
VALLE D'AOSTA
Biella
Verbania
Stresa
Locarno
Varese
Como
Lecco
Bergamo
Sondrio
Brescia
Novara
Vercelli
Milan
LOMBARDY
Pavia
Piacenza
Alessandria
Asti
Alba
Turin
Sestriere
PIEDMONT
Cuneo
Mondovì
Savona
Genoa
Imperia
San Remo
Gulf of Genoa
LIGURIAN SEA
Parco Nazionale delle Cinque Terre
La Spezia
Massa
Viareggio
Lucca
Pisa
Livorno
Elba
CORSICA (Fr)
Cremona
Parma
Reggio Emilia
Modena
Bologna
EMILIA-ROMAGNA
Mantua
Verona
Vicenza
Trent
TRENTINO-ALTO ADIGE
Merano
Bolzano
Bressanone
Cortina d'Ampezzo
Belluno
FRIULI-VENEZIA GIULIA
Udine
Treviso
Padua
Mestre
Venice
VENETO
Ferrara
Ravenna
Forlì
Rimini
Cattolica
Pesaro
Pistoia
Prato
Florence
Arezzo
Siena
TUSCANY
Grosseto
Perugia
UMBRIA
Assisi
Terni
Viterbo
Tarquinia
Civitavecchia
LAZIO
Rieti
Teramo
L'Aquila
Avezzano
Sulmona
Pescara
Chieti
Guardiagrele
Ascoli Piceno
Macerata
LE MARCHE
Ancona
Senigallia
Trieste
Rijeka
Maribor
Pécs
Osijek
Slavonski Brod
Banja Luka
Split
Dubrovnik
ADRIATIC SEA
To Greece, Turkey & Albania

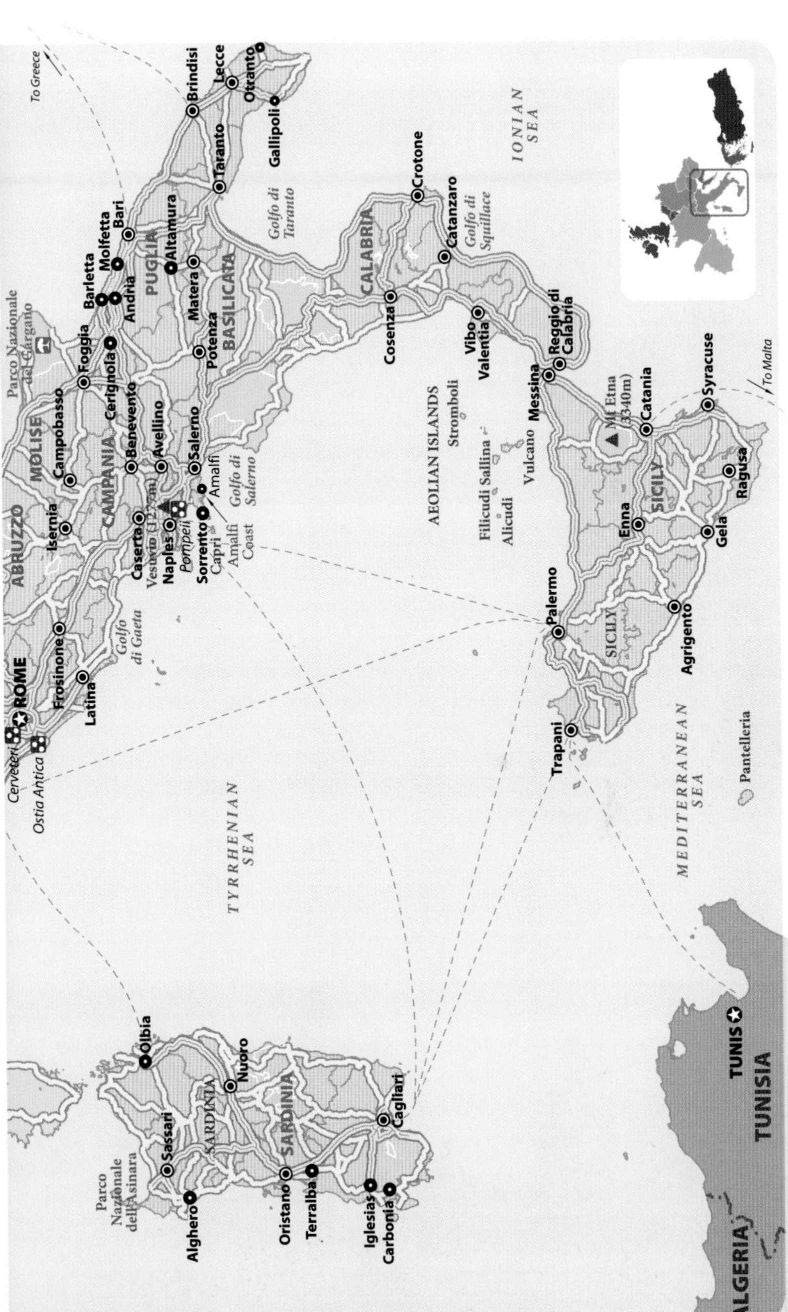

ITALY
To Greece
Brindisi
Lecce
Otranto
Gallipoli
Taranto
Golfo di Taranto
IONIAN SEA
Crotone
Catanzaro
Golfo di Squillace
Bari
Molfetta
Barletta
Andria
Altamura
PUGLIA
Matera
BASILICATA
Potenza
CALABRIA
Cosenza
Vibo Valentia
Reggio di Calabria
Messina
Parco Nazionale del Gargano
Foggia
Cerignola
Campobasso
MOLISE
Benevento
Avellino
CAMPANIA
Salerno
Amalfi
Golfo di Salerno
Amalfi Coast
Sorrento
Capri
Pompeii
Naples
Vesuvio (1277m)
Caserta
Isernia
ABRUZZO
Frosinone
Latina
ROME
Cerveteri
Ostia Antica
Golfo di Gaeta
AEOLIAN ISLANDS
Stromboli
Filicudi
Salina
Alicudi
Vulcano
Mt Etna (3340m)
Catania
Syracuse
To Malta
Ragusa
SICILY
Enna
Gela
Palermo
Agrigento
Trapani
Pantelleria
MEDITERRANEAN SEA
TYRRHENIAN SEA
Olbia
Nuoro
Sassari
SARDINIA
Cagliari
Parco Nazionale dell'Asinara
Alghero
Oristano
Terralba
Iglesias
Carbonia
TUNIS
TUNISIA
ALGERIA

HIGHLIGHTS

1 COLOSSEUM

BY VINCENZO MACCARRONE, COLOSSEUM STAFF MEMBER

Even before stepping foot into the arena, most visitors are gobsmacked to step out of the metro station to find the Colosseum looming before them in all its glory. Not only is this Roman arena impressive for its size and endurance, but its well-preserved condition makes for an evocative insight into ancient life itself.

VINCENZO MACCARRONE'S DON'T MISS LIST

❶ THE ARENA

The fascinating arena had a wooden floor covered in sand to prevent combatants from slipping and to soak up the blood. Gladiators arrived directly from the Ludus Magnus (their training ground) via underground passageways, and were hoisted onto the arena by a complicated system of pullies.

❷ THE CAVEA & THE PODIUM

The cavea, for spectator seating, was divided into three tiers: knights sat in the lowest tier, wealthy citizens in the middle and plebs sat at the top. In front of the tiers, the podium was reserved for emperors, senators and VIPs. Naturally, these were the best seats in the house, close to the action but protected from the wild animals on stage by high nets made of hemp.

❸ THE FACADE

The exterior mimics the Teatro di Marcello and the walls were once clad in travertine, with marble statues filling

Clockwise from top: Walkway near the Colosseum; Roman Forum; Colosseum arena; Passage to lower floors of the Colosseum; Colosseum facade

CLOCKWISE FROM TOP: PHILIP & KAREN SMITH; GREG ELMS; JON DAVISON; MARTIN MOOS; JOHN HAY

the niches on the 2nd and 3rd storeys. On the top level you'll see square holes that held the wooden masts supporting the Velarium, a canvas awning over the arena.

❹ TEMPORARY EXHIBITIONS

The Colosseum's 2nd floor hosts some fantastic exhibitions, either about the Colosseum or on the history of Rome itself. Past exhibitions have explored everything from Roman dynasties to classical theatre. While you're up there, walk past the bookshop to the end of the corridor. From here, look towards the eastern side of the **Roman Forum** (p318) and you'll get a wonderful view of the Tempio di Venere e Roma (Temple of Venus and Rome), hard to view from the ground.

❺ THE PERFECT PHOTO

Towards closing time, the Colosseum is bathed in a beautiful light, which makes for excellent photos. For great views of the building itself, head up Colle Oppio (Oppio Hill) right above the Colosseo metro station, or up Colle Celio (Celio Hill) opposite the Palatino and Colosseum exit.

THINGS YOU NEED TO KNOW

Best time to visit Afternoon **Best route** Take the lift to the 2nd floor for the temporary exhibitions and view of the Palatine (p319) and Forum, then head to the arena **Tickets** Buy online (www.pierreci.it) to skip the queues **Avoid** Unofficial guides outside the entrance **See our author's review on p318**

HIGHLIGHTS

2

VENICE

What else is there to say about Venice (p341)? Quite simply, this is one of the world's unmissable cities, renowned for its glorious architecture, romantic canals, historic churches and stunning museums. Whether it's riding the gondolas, wandering the alleyways or joining the throngs in Piazza San Marco, you'll find it impossible not to fall for this Italian beauty.

3

FLORENCE

If it's art you're after, look no further than Florence (p352). During the Middle Ages the Medicis transformed this merchant town into the centre of the Italian Renaissance, and it's brimful of artistic treasures. Marvel at the canvases of the Uffizi, admire the architecture of the Duomo, or line up to glimpse Michelangelo's masterpiece, *David* – just don't expect to have the city to yourself.

4

POMPEII

You know the story: 2000 years ago, the bustling Roman town of Pompeii (p360) was devastated by a catastrophic eruption from nearby Mt Vesuvius. But nothing can prepare you for the eerie experience of Pompeii itself; its deserted streets, abandoned squares and spooky body casts bring a whole new meaning to the term 'ghost town'.

5

AMALFI COAST

For an Italian road-trip, nowhere can hold a candle to the Amalfi Coast (p360). Stretching for 50km along the southern Sorrento Peninsula, this glittering coastline is one of the most beautiful spots in the Mediterranean – studded with sparkling beaches, secluded bays and clifftop towns.

6

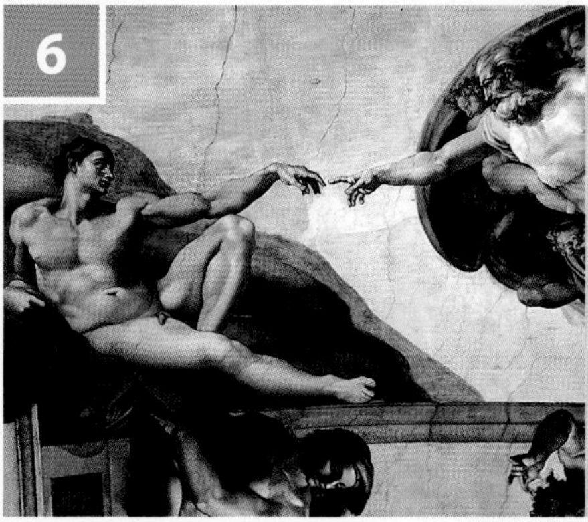

SISTINE CHAPEL

It's a tough call, but if we had to pick out Italy's artistic gem, we'd go for the Sistine Chapel (p322). Michelangelo's celebrated four-year fresco on the chapel's ceiling is the highlight, but his seven-year labour of love, *The Last Judgment,* runs it a close second. Trust us – this is one artwork that lives up to the hype.

2 MAX PAOLI & RUTH EASTHAM; 3 HANNAH LEVY; 4 PHILIP & KAREN SMITH; 5 GLENN BEANLAND; 6 RUSSELL MOUNTFORD

2 Masks for sale, Piazza San Marco (p341); 3 Michelangelo's *David* in Galleria dell'Accademia (p355); 4 Pompeii (p360); 5 View of the Amalfi Coast from Villa Ruffolo in Ravello (p361); 6 Ceiling of the Sistine Chapel (p322)

THE BEST...

ARTISTIC TREASURES

- **Basilica di San Marco** (p341) The Venetian showstopper.
- **David** (p355) Michelangelo's sculptural masterpiece.
- **St Peter's Basilica** (p320) Rome's unmissable landmark.
- **Leaning Tower of Pisa** (p358) Wonkily wondrous.
- **Spring** and **Venus** (p354) Botticelli's finest works are at the Uffizi.

ROMAN REMAINS

- **Colosseum** (p318) Where the gladiators slugged it out.
- **Roman Forum** (p318) The heart of the Roman Republic.
- **Pantheon** (p322) Roman temple turned Christian church.
- **Villa Adriana** (p336) Hadrian's weekend retreat.
- **Ostia Antica** (p336) Ancient Rome's port.

CITY VIEWS

- **Duomo, Florence** (p354) Climb the campanile for the quintessential Florence photo op.
- **Basilica di San Marco** (p341) See the Piazza San Marco from the basilica's bell tower.
- **Pincio Hill** (p326) Fantastic outlook over Rome.
- **Torre del Mangia** (p358) Siena views.
- **Leaning Tower of Pisa** (p358) Erm – where else?

FESTIVALS

- **Carnevale** (p346) Don your costume for Venice's crazy carnival.
- **Settimana Santa** (p364) Easter celebrations.
- **Scoppio del Carro** (p356) Easter Saturday goes off with a bang in Florence.
- **Il Palio** (p364) Siena's annual horse races.
- **Venice International Film Festival** (p346) Italy's answer to Cannes.

KRZYSZTOF DYDYNSKI

View across Piazza San Marco to Basilica di San Marco (p341) and the campanile (p344), Venice

THINGS YOU NEED TO KNOW

AT A GLANCE

- **Population** 59.1 million
- **Official language** Italian
- **Currency** Euro (€)
- **Telephone code** ☎ 39
- **When to go** Spring (April to June) and early autumn (September and October) for settled weather and bearable crowds. November is Italy's wettest month
- **Tipping** Not expected, but leave an optional 10% in restaurants and small change in bars (€0.10 or €0.20)

REGIONS IN A NUTSHELL

- **Rome** (p314) The heart of Italy.
- **Northern Italy** (p337) Sexy, sophisticated and just a little snooty.
- **Tuscany** (p352) Italy's artistic and cultural centre.
- **Southern Italy** (p360) Hot, fiery and unmistakeably Italian.

ADVANCE PLANNING

- **Two months before** Book your hotels early, especially for Rome, Florence and Venice.
- **One month before** Arrange car hire now for the best deals.
- **When you arrive** Pick up the Roma Pass (p318) or Venice Card (p344) for discounted sightseeing, and book for Florence sights with Firenze Musei (p354).

BE FOREWARNED

- **Theft** Watch out for pickpockets and bag-snatchers in touristy areas.
- **Money** Count your change carefully when paying with a note.
- **Driving** Expect the unexpected on Italy's roads – Italians have a relaxed attitude to road rules.
- **Prices** Prices for everything skyrocket during summer and major holidays.

BUSINESS HOURS

- **Banks** (8.30am-1.30pm & 2.45-4.30pm Mon-Fri)
- **Bars & Cafes** (7.30am-8pm) Hours are variable.
- **Post offices** (major offices 8.30am-6.50pm Mon-Fri, to 1.15pm Sat; branches 8.30am-1.50pm Mon-Fri, to 11.50am Sat)
- **Restaurants** (noon-3pm & 7.30-11pm, later in summer)
- **Shops** (9am-1pm & 3.30-7.30pm or 4-8pm Mon-Sat)
- **Supermarkets** (9am-7.30pm Mon-Sat, 9am-1pm Sun) Food shops often close Thursday afternoon; other shops often on Monday morning.

COSTS

- **€80 per day** Hostels, budget hotels (often with shared bathroom) and cheap restaurants.
- **€80 to €200** Mid-range hotels and trattoria.
- **more than €200+** The full-blown luxury Italian experience.

EMERGENCY NUMBERS

- **Ambulance** (☎ 118)
- **Fire** (☎ 115)
- **Police** (☎ 113)

THINGS YOU NEED TO KNOW

GETTING AROUND

- **Air** (p367) Italy's largest airport is the Leonardo da Vinci (better known as Fiumicino) in Rome. International flights also serve Milan, while low-cost carriers use regional airports including Rome's Ciampino, Pisa's Galileo Galilei and Venice's Marco Polo. Domestic flights can be expensive, although budget routes have brought costs down. Gateway airports include Rome and Milan.
- **Train** (p368) Italy has train links to most major European cities; major rail hubs are Rome, Milan and Venice. High-speed services operate on the main line from Milan to Rome/Naples via Bologna and Florence. Other routes operate local *regionale* or faster InterCity (IC) services.
- **Sea** (p366) Dozens of options to France, Spain and various other Mediterranean destinations; main ports are in Rome, Ancona and Genoa.
- **Bus** (p367) Extensive and often the only option to many rural areas.
- **Car** (p367) Italy's roads are generally good, although the same can't be said for Italian drivers. Using the *autostrade* (motorways) is quick, but often incurs a toll; regional roads are better for sightseeing.

MEDIA

- **Newspapers** If your Italian's up to it, try the *Corriere della Sera,* the country's leading daily; *Il Messaggero,* a popular Rome-based broadsheet; or *La Repubblica,* a centre-left daily full of Mafia conspiracies and Vatican scoops.
- **Radio** State-owned Italian RAI-1, RAI-2 and RAI-3 broadcast all over the country. Commercial stations such as Rome's Radio Centro Suono (www.radiocentrosuono.it) and Radio Città Futura (www.radiocittafutura.it), and Milan-based Radio Popolare (www.radiopopolare.it) are good for popular music.
- **TV** State-run RAI-1, RAI-2 and RAI-3 (www.rai.it), plus commercial stations Canale 5, Italia 1, Rete 4 and La 7.

RESOURCES

- **Italian Government Tourist Board** (www.enit.it) Great for festivals and events.
- **Trenitalia** (www.trenitalia.it) Plan your train trips.

VISAS

- **EU nationals** Free to enter Italy with their national ID card or passport.
- **Australia, Canada, Israel, Japan, New Zealand, Switzerland, US** Can stay visa-free for 90 days. For longer stays non-EU nationals will need a *permesso di soggiorno* (permit to stay); application kits are available from post offices.

GET INSPIRED

BOOKS

- Gomorrah (Roberto Saviano) Exposé of the Neapolitan mafia.
- A Small Place in Italy (Eric Newby) Travelogue.
- La Bella Figura (Beppe Severgnini) An Italian journalist examines his nation's foibles.
- The Italian Cookery Course (Katie Caldesi) Bring the taste of Italy home.

FILMS

- La Dolce Vita (1960) Rome's never looked better than in Fellini's classic.
- Don't Look Now (1973) Nic Roeg captures Venice's spookier side.
- Cinema Paradiso (1988) Cockle-warming tale of one boy's cinematic love affair.
- Il Postino (1994) Italian postman meets Chilean poet Pablo Neruda.
- Bicycle Thieves (1948) Neo-realism's finest hour.

MUSIC

- The Ultimate Collection (Pavarotti) Italy's greatest tenor.
- The Voice of the Century (Maria Callas) Queen of arias.
- Corto Circuito (99 Posse) Naples-based hip-hop collective.
- Da Solo (Vinicio Capossela) The Italian Tom Waits.
- Anime Salve (Fabrizio de Alve) Landmark album.

WEBSITES

- Beppe Grillo (www.beppegrillo.it) Italy's most famous blogger.
- Delicious Italy (www.deliciousitaly.com) Whet your appetite.
- Italia Mia (www.italiamia.com) Links to Italy-related sites.
- La Cucina del Garga (www.peggymarkel.com) Book a culinary adventure.
- Life In Italy (www.lifeinitaly.com) Sections on food, art, culture and travel.

LEFT: GREG ELMS; RIGHT: DALLAS STRIBLEY

Left: Street vendor selling pizza; Right: Swimming in Sardinia (p362)

ITINERARIES

THE CANAL CITY Three Days

The crowds are a nightmare, the people are snooty and the prices are sky-high, but no Italian adventure would be complete without a few days in **(1) Venice** (p341). Day one's for the classics: start early to dodge the crowds in the **Piazza San Marco** (p341), the **Basilica di San Marco** (p341) and the **Palazzo Ducale** (p344). Wander westwards and devote the afternoon to the **Galleria dell'Accademia** (p344) or, if you prefer your art modern, the **Collezione Peggy Guggenheim** (p344). Do the tourist thing and take a twilit **gondola ride** (p346), or save your pennies for supper – try **La Bitta** (p347) or **Ristorica Oniga** (p347) before indulging in a late-night tipple around **Campo Santa Margherita** (p348).

Spend day two and three exploring the renovation-in-progress **Palazzo Grassi** (p345) or the city's stunning **churches** (p345). Alternatively, hop on a *vaporetto* to Venice's outer **islands** (p345) – Murano for glass, Burano for lace or the original Venetian settlement of Torcello. Tie things up with a canalside meal at **Da Marisa** (p347), or blow the budget at **Hostaria da Franz** (p348).

ROMA, ROMA Five Days

Its empire may have long since sailed into the sunset, but there's still nowhere better to experience Italy at its passionate, pompous, pizza-spinning best than **(1) Rome** (p314). It makes sense to begin at the mighty **Colosseum** (p318) – a guided tour will give you some historical perspective and allows you to dodge the queues. Spend the afternoon exploring the ruins of the **Roman Forum** (p318), followed by an early evening visit to the **Pantheon** (p322), pizza at **Baffetto** (p331) and a wander around vibrant **Trastevere** (p327).

Devote day two to the **Vatican** (p319), allowing time for **St Peter's Basilica** (p320), the **Vatican Museums** (p322) and the jaw-dropping **Sistine Chapel** (p322). You might be able to squeeze in **Castel' Sant Angelo** (p322) before supper at **Dino e Tony** (p331).

On days three and four, you could explore **Rome's churches** (p328), head for the **Museo Nazionale Romano** (p327) in Termini, or delve into the fascinating area around **Villa Borghese** (p323) – don't miss the Spanish Steps, the Trevi Fountain and the Piazza del Popolo. On the final day, take a day trip to **(2) Ostia Antica** (p336), ancient Rome's great port, or Emperor Hadrian's magnificent country residence, the **(3) Villa Adriana** (p336).

UNDER THE TUSCAN SUN One Week

If anywhere encapsulates the Italian character, it's **Tuscany** (p352). This sunbaked corner of southern Italy is one of the country's most

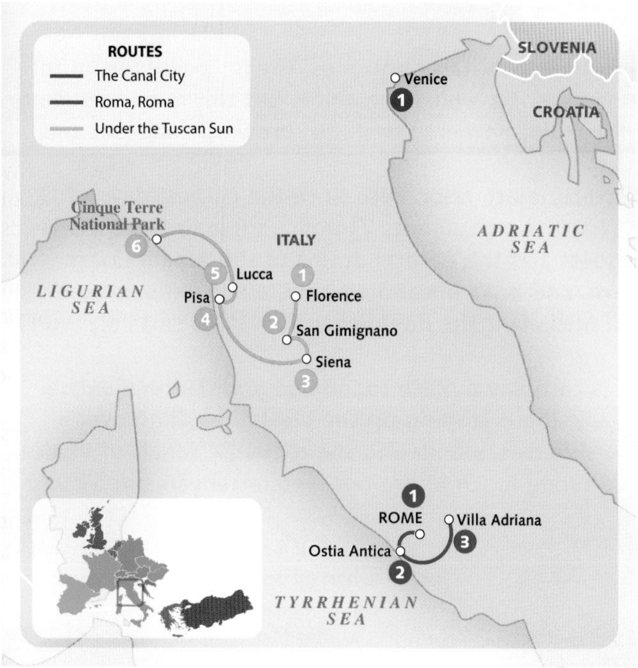

rewarding regions for culture vultures. As long as you can stomach the crowds, (1) Florence (p352) is brimming with architectural treasures, from the Gothic Duomo (p354) to the Palazzo Pitti (p355), while some of the world's most important artworks are housed at the Uffizi (p354) and the Galleria dell' Accademia (p355).

From Florence, veer south via hilltop (2) San Gimignano (p349) to (3) Siena (p358), another classic Tuscan town, renowned for its medieval architecture, delectable restaurants and annual horse race, Il Palio (p359). After Siena, head back up the Tuscan coast to Italy's punch-drunk landmark, the (4) Leaning Tower of Pisa (p358). Add a detour via lovely (5) Lucca (p349) en route to the (6) Cinque Terre National Park (p337), where you can soak up your last few days basking in the Tuscan sun or striking out along the hilltop trails.

DISCOVER ITALY

The world's love affair with Italy continues. The *bel paese* (beautiful country) may no longer be a blushing bride, but this most beguiling of countries still has the power to thrill, to throw up surprises and excite emotion.

Italy's been attracting attention ever since the earliest days of tourism. Rome's martial monuments, Florence's Renaissance glories, Milan's chichi streets and the natural drama of the Amalfi Coast are all well known, and if it's art and architecture that floats your boat, the land of Michelangelo, Raphael and da Vinci certainly won't disappoint.

But while this is certainly a place to indulge your cultural side, a trip to Italy is really about lapping up the lifestyle – idling over a coffee at a street-side cafe, wandering the romantic canals of Venice or lingering over a long lunch in the hot Mediterranean sun. *La vita è bella…*

ROME

pop 2.7 million

An epic, monumental metropolis, Rome has been in the spotlight for close to 3000 years. Fortunately, its reality is every bit as enticing as its reputation. With its architectural and artistic treasures, its romantic corners and its noisy, colourful markets, Rome is a city that knows how to impress.

HISTORY

According to the legend of Romulus and Remus, Rome was founded in 753 BC. Archaeological discoveries have confirmed the existence of a settlement on the Palatine Hill in that period.

In 509 BC the Roman Republic was founded. By AD 100 Rome had a population of 1.5 million and was the Caput Mundi (Capital of the World). But by the 5th century decline had set in, and in 476 Romulus Augustulus, the last emperor of the Western Roman Empire, was deposed. Pope Gregory I (590–604) did much to strengthen the Church's grip over the city, laying the foundations for its later role as capital of the Catholic Church.

Under the Renaissance popes of the 15th and 16th centuries, Rome was given an extensive facelift. The building boom following the unification of Italy and the declaration of Rome as its capital also profoundly influenced the look of the city, as did Mussolini and hasty post-WWII expansion.

ORIENTATION

Rome is a sprawling city but most sights are concentrated in the area between Stazione Termini and the Vatican on the other side of the Tiber River. Halfway between the two, the Pantheon and Piazza Navona lie at the heart of the *centro storico* (historic centre).

Roma Termini, known as Stazione Termini, is the city's main transport hub. International, intercity and local trains stop here and city buses depart from the square outside, Piazza dei Cinquecento. Rome's two airports are well connected with the city centre.

INFORMATION

EMERGENCY

Police station (Questura; Map pp324-5; ☎ 06 468 61; Via San Vitale 15)

INTERNET RESOURCES

Pierreci (www.pierreci.it) Has the latest on museums, monuments and exhibitions. Book tickets online here.

Roma Turismo (www.romaturismo.it) Rome Tourist Board's website lists useful numbers, all official accommodation, sites, transport and much more.

Vatican (www.vatican.va) The Holy See's official website with practical information on Vatican sites.

LEFT LUGGAGE

Stazione Termini (Map pp316-17; 1st 5hr €3.80, 6-12hr per hr €0.60, 13hr & over per hr €0.20; 6am-midnight) On the lower-ground floor under platform 24.

MEDICAL SERVICES

For emergency treatment, go straight to the *pronto soccorso* (casualty) section of an *ospedale* (hospital).

24-hour Pharmacy (Map pp324-5; ☎ 06 488 00 19; Piazza dei Cinquecento 49/50/51)

Ospedale Bambino Gesù (Map pp316-17; ☎ 06 685 92 351; Piazza di Sant'Onofrio 4) For paediatric assistance.

Ospedale G Eastman (Map pp316-17; ☎ 06 84 48 31; Viale Regina Elena 287b) A dental hospital.

Ospedale Santo Spirito (Map pp320-1; ☎ 06 683 51; Lungotevere in Sassia 1) Near the Vatican; multilingual staff.

MONEY

ATM's are liberally scattered around the city.

American Express (Map pp320-1; ☎ 06 676 41; Piazza di Spagna 38; 9am-5.30pm Mon-Fri, 9am-12.30pm Sat) Offers exchange facilities and travel services.

TOURIST INFORMATION

Centro Servizi Pellegrini e Turisti (Map pp320-1; ☎ 06 698 81 662; St Peter's Square; 8.30am-4.15pm Mon-Sat) The Vatican's official tourist office.

Enjoy Rome (Map pp316-17; ☎ 06 445 68 90; www.enjoyrome.com; Via Marghera 8a;

PAOLO CORDELLI

St Peter's Basilica (p320)

ITALY

ROME

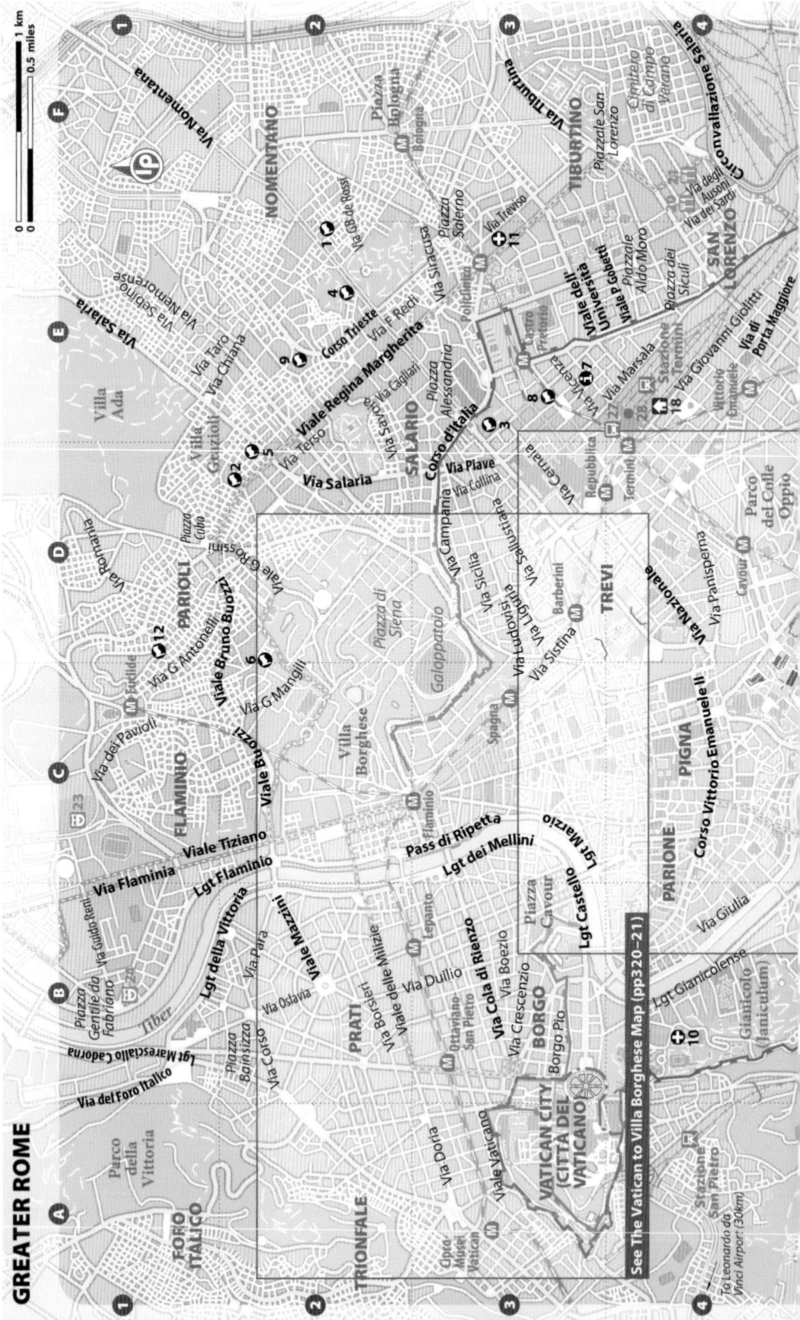
GREATER ROME
0 1 km
0 0.5 miles
A
B
C
D
E
F
1
2
3
4
FORO ITALICO
Parco della Vittoria
Via del Foro Italico
Lgt Maresciallo Cadorna
Piazza Gentile da Fabriano
Tiber
Via Guido Reni
Via Flaminia
Lgt Flaminio
Lgt della Vittoria
Viale Tiziano
FLAMINIO
Via dei Pavioli
Euclide
Via G Antonelli
PARIOLI
Viale Bruno Buozzi
Via Romania
Piazza Cuba
Viale G Rossini
Via G Mangili
Viale Buozzi
Villa Ada
Via Salaria
Via Sebino
Via Nemorense
Via Taro
Via Chiana
Villa Grazioli
Via Tevere
Viale Regina Margherita
Corso Trieste
Via F Redi
Via GB de Rossi
NOMENTANO
Via Nomentana
Piazza Bologna
Bologna
Via Tiburtina
TIBURTINO
Piazzale San Lorenzo
Cimitero di Campo Verano
Circonvallazione Salaria
Piazza Salerno
Via Siracusa
Via Treviso
Policlinico
Castro Pretorio
Viale dell' Università
Viale P Gobetti
Piazzale Aldo Moro
Piazza dei Siculi
SAN LORENZO
Via degli Ausoni
Via dei Sardi
Via Giovanni Giolitti
Via di Porta Maggiore
Via Marsala
Stazione Termini
Termini
Vittorio Emanuele
Via Vicenza
Piazza Alessandria
Via Cagliari
Via Savoia
SALARIO
Corso d'Italia
Via Piave
Via Collina
Via Salaria
Via Cernaia
Repubblica
Parco del Colle Oppio
Cavour
Via Panisperna
Via Nazionale
Via Campania
Via Sicilia
Via Sallustiana
Via Ludovisi
Via Liguria
Barberini
TREVI
Via Sistina
Spagna
Galoppatoio
Piazza di Siena
Villa Borghese
Flaminio
Pass di Ripetta
Lgt dei Mellini
Lgt Marzio
Lgt Castello
Piazza Cavour
PIGNA
Corso Vittorio Emanuele II
PARIONE
Via Giulia
Lgt Gianicolense
Gianicolo (Janiculum)
Viale Mazzini
Via Para
Via Oslavia
Piazza Bainsizza
Via Corso
PRATI
Via Borsieri
Viale delle Milizie
Lepanto
Via Duilio
Via Cola di Rienzo
Via Boezio
Via Crescenzio
Ottaviano-San Pietro
BORGO
Borgo Pio
VATICAN CITY (CITTÀ DEL VATICANO)
Via Doria
Viale Vaticano
Cipro-Musei Vaticani
TRIONFALE
See The Vatican to Villa Borghese Map (pp320–21)
Stazione San Pietro
To Leonardo da Vinci Airport (30km)
1
2
3
4
5
6
7
8
9
10
11
12
18
22
23
27
28

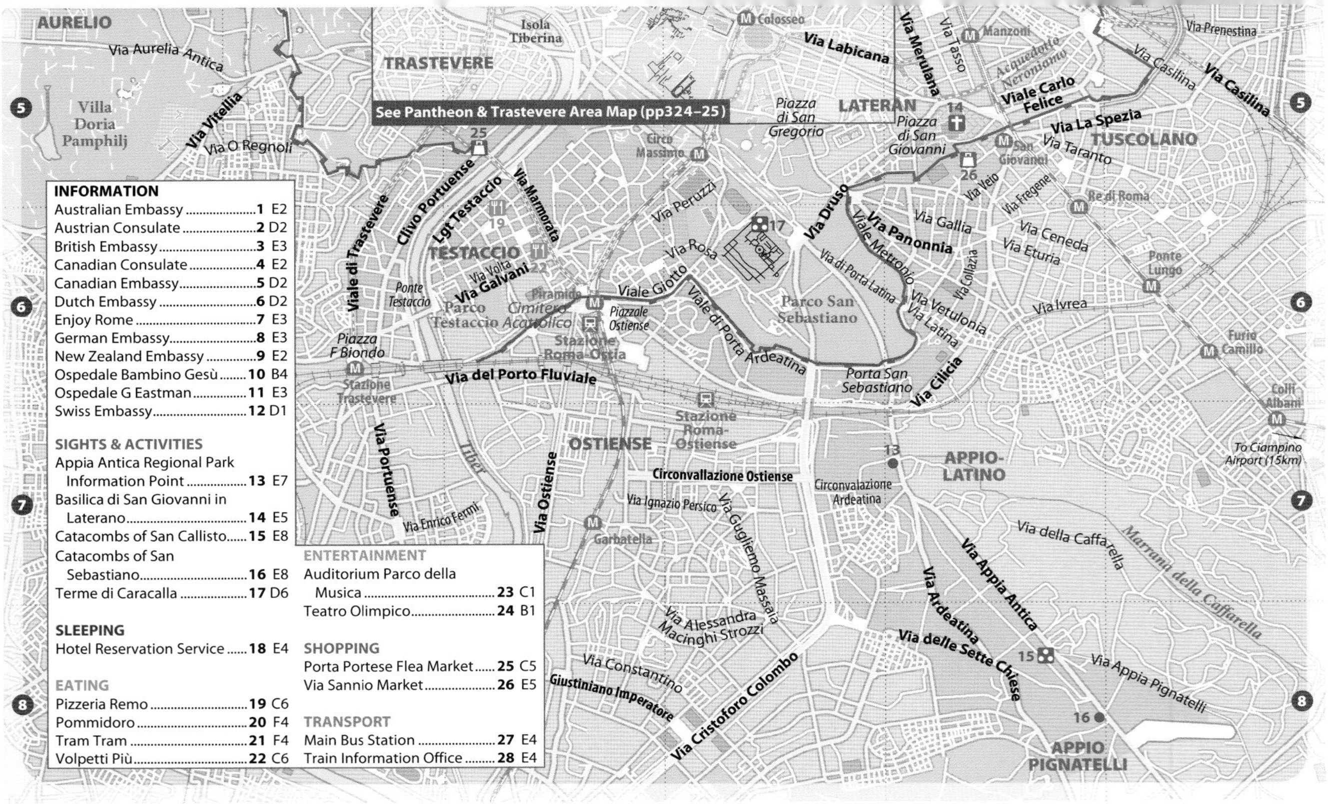

INFORMATION

Australian Embassy.......................**1** E2
Austrian Consulate......................**2** D2
British Embassy..........................**3** E3
Canadian Consulate......................**4** E2
Canadian Embassy........................**5** D2
Dutch Embassy...........................**6** D2
Enjoy Rome..............................**7** E3
German Embassy..........................**8** E3
New Zealand Embassy.....................**9** E2
Ospedale Bambino Gesù..................**10** B4
Ospedale G Eastman.....................**11** E3
Swiss Embassy..........................**12** D1

SIGHTS & ACTIVITIES

Appia Antica Regional Park Information Point..................**13** E7
Basilica di San Giovanni in Laterano...........................**14** E5
Catacombs of San Callisto..............**15** E8
Catacombs of San Sebastiano............................**16** E8
Terme di Caracalla.....................**17** D6

SLEEPING

Hotel Reservation Service..............**18** E4

EATING

Pizzeria Remo..........................**19** C6
Pommidoro..............................**20** F4
Tram Tram..............................**21** F4
Volpetti Più...........................**22** C6

ENTERTAINMENT

Auditorium Parco della Musica......................................**23** C1
Teatro Olimpico........................**24** B1

SHOPPING

Porta Portese Flea Market..............**25** C5
Via Sannio Market......................**26** E5

TRANSPORT

Main Bus Station.......................**27** E4
Train Information Office...............**28** E4

8.30am-7pm Mon-Fri, to 2pm Sat) A private tourist office that arranges walking tours and has a free hotel-reservation service.

Rome Tourist Board **(Map pp324-5; ☎ 06 48 89 91; Via Parigi 5; 9am-7pm Mon-Sat)** Can provide maps and plenty of printed material.

The Comune di Roma runs a multilingual tourist infoline **(☎ 820 59 127; 9am-7pm)** and information points across the city.

SIGHTS & ACTIVITIES

COLOSSEUM

Rome's iconic monument is a thrilling site. The 50,000 seater Colosseum **(Map pp324-5; ☎ 06 399 67 700; admission incl Palatine Hill €11; 9am-1hr before sunset; M Colosseo)** was ancient Rome's most feared arena and is today one of Italy's top tourist attractions. Queues are inevitable but you can usually avoid them by buying your ticket at the nearby Palatine Hill. Alternatively, join a walking tour (€9 on top of ticket price) and use the shorter ticket line.

Originally known as the Flavian Amphitheatre, the Colosseum was started by Emperor Vespasian in AD 72 and finished by his son Titus in AD 80. It was clad in travertine and covered by a huge canvas awning that was held aloft by 240 masts. Inside, tiered seating encircled the sand-covered arena, itself built over underground chambers where animals were caged. Contrary to Hollywood folklore, bouts between gladiators rarely ended in death as the games' sponsor was required to pay the owner of a killed gladiator 100 times the gladiator's value.

ROMAN FORUM & PALATINE HILL

Now a collection of fascinating, if rather confusing, ruins, the Roman Forum **(Map pp324-5; ☎ 06 399 67 700; admission free; 9am-1hr before sunset Mon-Sat; M Colosseo)** was once the showpiece centre of the Roman Republic. The area was systematically excavated in the 18th and 19th centuries and excavations continue.

As you enter at Largo Romolo e Remo, ahead to your left is the Tempio di Antonino e Faustina, built by the senate in AD 141 and transformed into a church in the 8th century. To your right, the Basilica Aemilia, built in 179 BC, was 100m long with a two-storey porticoed facade lined with shops. At the end of the short path Via Sacra traverses the Forum from northwest to southeast. Opposite the basilica stands the Tempio di Giulio Cesare, erected by Augustus in 29 BC on the site where Caesar's body had been burned.

Head right up Via Sacra and you reach the Curia, once the meeting place of the Roman senate and later converted into a

MUSEUM DISCOUNTS

If you're planning to blitz the sights, consider the Roma Pass. Valid for three days, it costs €20 and provides free admission to two museums or sites, as well as unlimited city transport, and reduced entry to other sites, exhibitions and events. It's available at all participating sites and tourist information points.

Note that EU citizens aged between 18 and 25, and students from countries with reciprocal arrangements, generally qualify for a discount (usually half price) at galleries and museums. Under 18s and over 65s often get in free. In all cases you'll need proof of your age, ideally a passport or ID card.

hurch. In front of the Curia is the Lapis liger, a large piece of black marble that urportedly covered Romulus' grave.

At the end of Via Sacra, the Arco di ettimio Severo was erected in AD 203 o honour Emperor Septimus Severus nd his two sons and to celebrate victory ver the Parthians. Nearby, the Millarium ureum marked the centre of ancient ome, from which distances to the city vere measured.

Southwest of the arch, eight granite olumns are all that remain of the Tempio i Saturno, one of ancient Rome's most mportant temples.

To the southeast, you'll see the Piazza lel Foro, the Forum's main market and neeting place, marked by the 7th-century olonna di Foca (Column of Phocus). To our right are the foundations of the asilica Giulia, a law court built by Julius aesar in 55 BC. At the end of the basilica s the Tempio di Castore e Polluce, built n 489 BC in honour of the Heavenly Twins, astor and Pollux.

Back towards Via Sacra, the Casa delle estali was home of the virgins whose job t was to keep the sacred flame alight in he adjoining Tempio di Vesta. They were equired to stay chaste and committed to eeping the flame burning for 30 years.

Continuing up Via Sacra, you come o the vast Basilica di Costantino, also nown as the Basilica di Massenzio, whose mpressive design inspired Renaissance rchitects. The Arco di Tito, at the olosseum end of the Forum, was built n AD 81 in honour of the victories of the mperors Titus and Vespasian against erusalem.

From here, climb the Palatine (**Map p324-5; ☎ 06 399 67 700; entrances Via San regorio 30 or Piazza Santa Maria Nova 53; admission incl Colosseum €11; 9am-1hr before sunset; M Colosseo**), ancient Rome's poshest neighbourhood. Most of the Palatine is covered by the ruins of Emperor Domitian's vast complex, which served as the main imperial palace for 300 years.

CHRISTOPHER GROENHOUT

Spanish Steps (p326)

Among the best-preserved buildings on the Palatine is the Casa di Livia. Home to Augustus' wife Livia, it was decorated with frescoes of mythological scenes, landscapes, fruits and flowers. Also of note is the Tempio della Magna Mater, built in 204 BC.

VATICAN CITY

Covering just 0.44 sq km, the Vatican is all that's left of the Papal States. For more than 1000 years, the Papal States encompassed Rome and much of central Italy, but after Italian unification in 1861 the pope was forced to give up his territorial possessions. As an independent state, the Vatican has its own postal service, currency, newspaper, radio station and army of Swiss Guards.

ST PETER'S BASILICA

In a city of churches, none can hold a candle to **St Peter's Basilica** (**Map pp320-1; ☎ 06 698 85 518; Piazza San Pietro; admission free; 7am-7pm Apr-Sep, to 6.30pm Oct-Mar; Ⓜ Ottaviano-San Pietro**), Italy's biggest, richest, and most spectacular church. Built over the spot where St Peter was buried, the first basilica was consecrated b Constantine in the 4th century. Later, i 1503, Bramante designed a new basilica which took more than 150 years to com plete. Michelangelo took over the projec in 1547, designing the grand dome, whic soars 120m above the altar. The cavernou 187m-long interior contains numerou treasures, including two of Italy's mos celebrated masterpieces: Michelangelo' *Pietà,* the only work to carry his signature and Bernini's 29m-high baldachin ove the high altar.

THE VATICAN TO VILLA BORGHESE

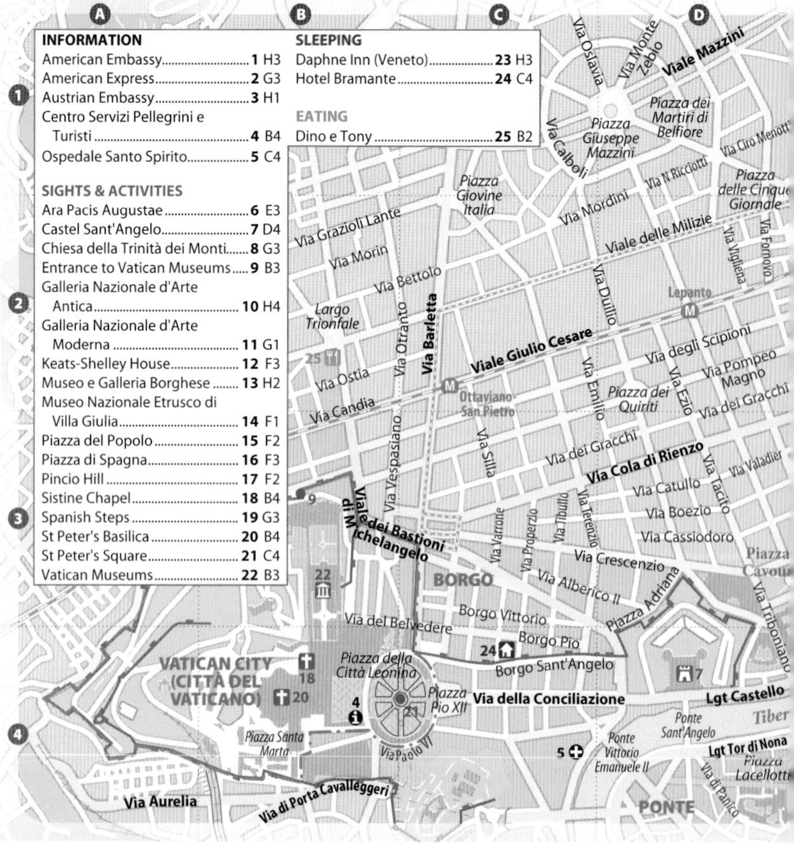

Entrance to the **dome** (🕒 **8am-6pm Apr-Sep, 8am-5pm Oct-Mar)** is to the right as you climb the stairs to the basilica's atrium. Make the climb on foot (€5) or by lift (€7).

Dress rules and security are stringently enforced at the basilica – no shorts, miniskirts or sleeveless tops, and be prepared to have your bags searched.

ST PETER'S SQUARE

The Vatican's central piazza, and one of the world's great public spaces, **St Peter's Square** **(Piazza San Pietro; Map pp320-1; Ⓜ Ottaviano-San Pietro)** was laid out between 1656 and 1667. Seen from above it resembles a giant keyhole: two semicircular colonnades, each consisting of four rows of Doric columns, bound by a giant ellipse that straightens out to funnel believers into the basilica.

In the centre, the 25m obelisk was brought to Rome by Caligula from Heliopolis in Egypt and later used by Nero as a turning post for the chariot races in his circus.

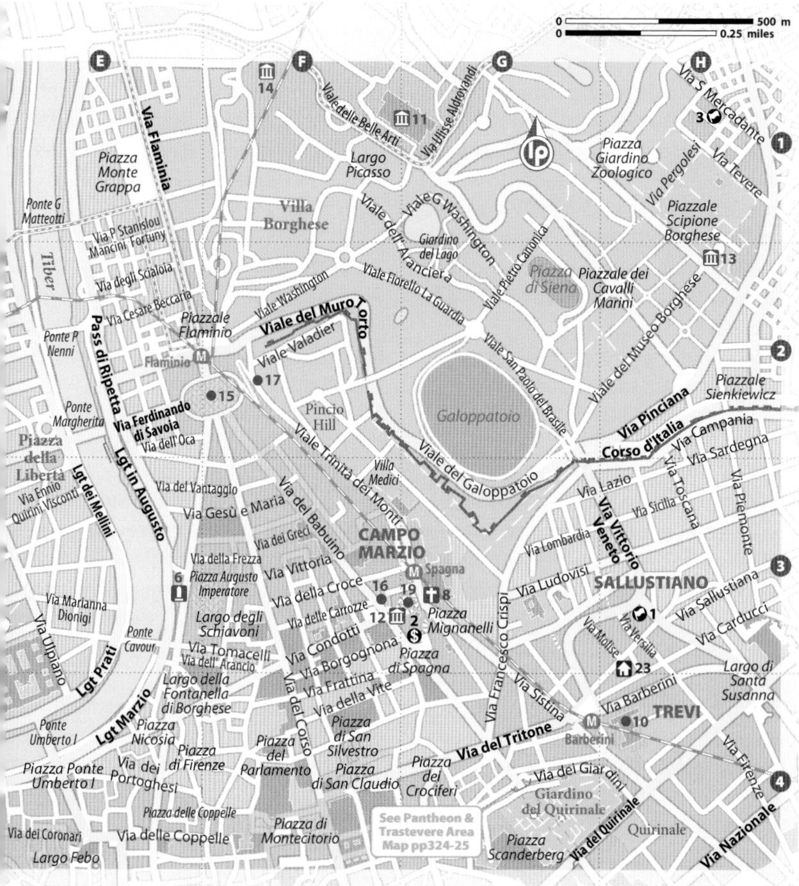

VATICAN MUSEUMS

Boasting one of the world's great art collections, the **Vatican Museums** (**Map pp320-1; adult/concession €14/8, last Sun of month free; 8.30am-4pm Mon-Sat, 8.30am-12.30pm last Sun of month; M Ottaviano-San Pietro**) are housed in the Palazzo Apostolico Vaticano. There are four colour-coded itineraries that take anything from 45 minutes to five hours. Audio guides are available for €6.

The place in the Vatican Museums that not a single one of the four million annual visitors wants to miss is the **Sistine Chapel** (Cappella Sistina; Map pp320-1). The chapel was originally built in 1484 for Pope Sixtus IV, after whom it is named, but it was Julius II who commissioned Michelangelo to decorate it in 1508. Over the next four years, the artist painted the remarkable *Genesis* (Creation; 1508–12) on the barrel-vaulted ceiling. Twenty-two years later he returned at the behest of Pope Clement VII to paint the *Giudizio universale* (Last Judgement; 1534–41) on the end wall.

The other walls of the chapel were painted by artists including Botticelli, Ghirlandaio, Pinturicchio and Signorelli.

CASTEL SANT'ANGELO

An instantly recognisable landmark, the chunky, round-keeped **Castel Sant'Angelo** (**Map pp320-1; ☎ 06 681 91 11; Lungotevere Castello 50; admission €7; 9am-7.30pm Tue-Sun; Piazza Pia**) was commissioned by Emperor Hadrian in 123 BC as a mausoleum for himself and his family. In the 6th century, it was converted into a papal fortress, and it's now a museum with an assorted collection of sculptures, paintings, weapons and furniture. The terrace, immortalised by Puccini in his opera *Tosca*, offers fine views over Rome.

PIAZZA DEL CAMPIDOGLIO & MUSEI CAPITOLINI

The lowest of Rome's seven hills, the Capitoline (Campidoglio) was considered the heart of the Roman Republic. At its summit were ancient Rome's two most important temples: one dedicated to Juno Moneta and another to Jupiter Capitolinus, where Brutus is said to have hidden after assassinating Caesar. Together, Palazzo Nuovo and Palazzo dei Conservatori house the **Musei Capitolini** (**Capitoline Museums; Map pp324-5; ☎ 06 96 74 00; adult/concession €6.50/4.50; 9am-8pm Tue-Sun; Piazza Venezia**), one of the oldest public museums in the world, dating to 1471. Showstoppers include the *Lupa capitolina* (She-Wolf), a sculpture of Romulus and Remus under a wolf, and the *Galata morente* (Dying Gaul), which movingly depicts the anguish of a dying Gaul.

PANTHEON

A striking 2000-year-old temple, now church, the **Pantheon** (**Map pp324-5; ☎ 06 683 00 230; Piazza della Rotonda; admission free; 8.30am-7.30pm Mon-Sat, 9am-6pm Sun, 9am-1pm holidays; Largo di Torre Argentina**) is the best preserved of ancient Rome's great monuments. In its current form it dates to around AD 120 when the Emperor Hadrian built over Marcus Agrippa's original 27 BC temple (Agrippa's name remains inscribed on the pediment). The dome, considered the Romans' most important architectural achievement, is the largest masonry vault ever built, a structure so sophisticated that had it been built with modern concrete it would long ago have collapsed under its own weight. Inside, you'll find the tomb of Raphael, alongside those of kings Vittorio Emanuele II and Umberto I.

WILL SALTER

Villa Borghese

CAMPO DE' FIORI & AROUND

Campo de' Fiori (Map pp324-5; Corso Vittorio Emanuele II), affectionately dubbed 'Il Campo', is a major focus of Roman life: by day it hosts a noisy market, and at night it becomes a vast, open-air pub. For centuries, Il Campo was the site of public executions. The twin fountains in the piazza are enormous granite baths taken from the **Terme di Caracalla** (Baths of Caracalla; see p328).

VILLA BORGHESE

Once the estate of Cardinal Scipione Borghese, **Villa Borghese** (Map pp320-1; Porta Pinciana) is a good spot for a picnic and a breath of fresh air. There are also several museums, including the **Museo e Galleria Borghese** (Map pp320-1; ☎ 06 3 28 10; www.galleriaborghese.it; Piazzale del Museo Borghese; adult/concession €8.50/5.50, plus obligatory booking fee €2; 8.30am-7.30pm Tue-Sun; Via Pinciana), Rome's finest art gallery. With works by Caravaggio, Bernini, Botticelli and Raphael, there are too many highlights to list here, but try not to miss Bernini's *Ratto di Proserpina* (Rape of Persephone) and *Apollo e Dafne*, and the six Caravaggio's in room VII.

In the north of the park is the **Galleria Nazionale d'Arte Moderna** (Map pp320-1; ☎ 06 32 29 81; Viale delle Belle Arti 131; admission €6.50; 8.30am-7.30pm Tue-Sun; Viale delle Belle Arti), a belle époque palace housing 19th- and 20th-century paintings. Nearby, the **Museo Nazionale Etrusco di Villa Giulia** (Map pp320-1; ☎ 06 320 05 62; Piazzale di Villa Giulia; admission €4; 8.30am-7.30pm Tue-Sun; Viale delle Belle Arti) displays Italy's finest collection of Etruscan treasures.

TREVI FOUNTAIN

Immortalised by Anita Ekberg's sensual dip in Fellini's *La dolce vita*, the **Fontana di Trevi** (Map pp324-5; Piazza di Trevi; M Barberini) was designed by Nicola Salvi in 1732 and depicts Neptune's chariot being led by Tritons, with sea horses representing the moods of the sea. The water comes from the *aqua virgo*, a 1st-century BC underground aqueduct, and the name 'Trevi'

PANTHEON & TRASTEVERE AREA

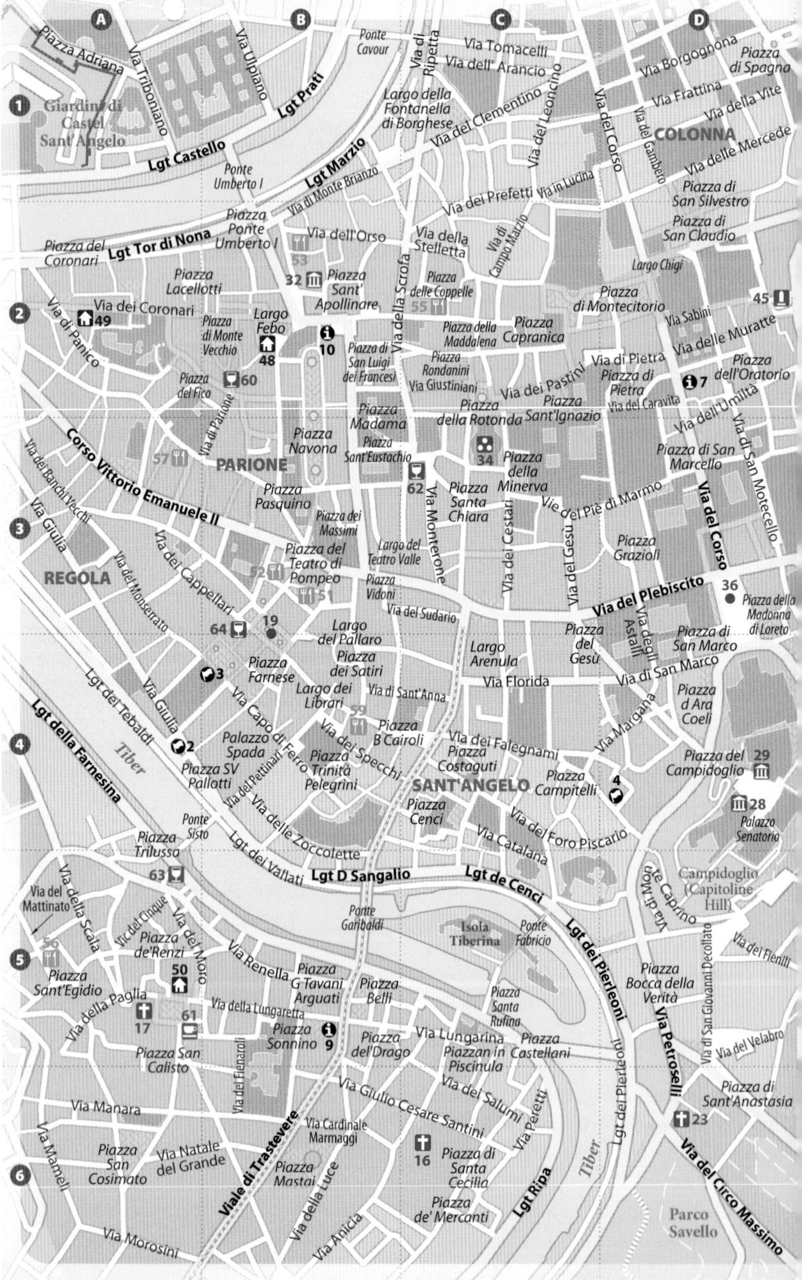

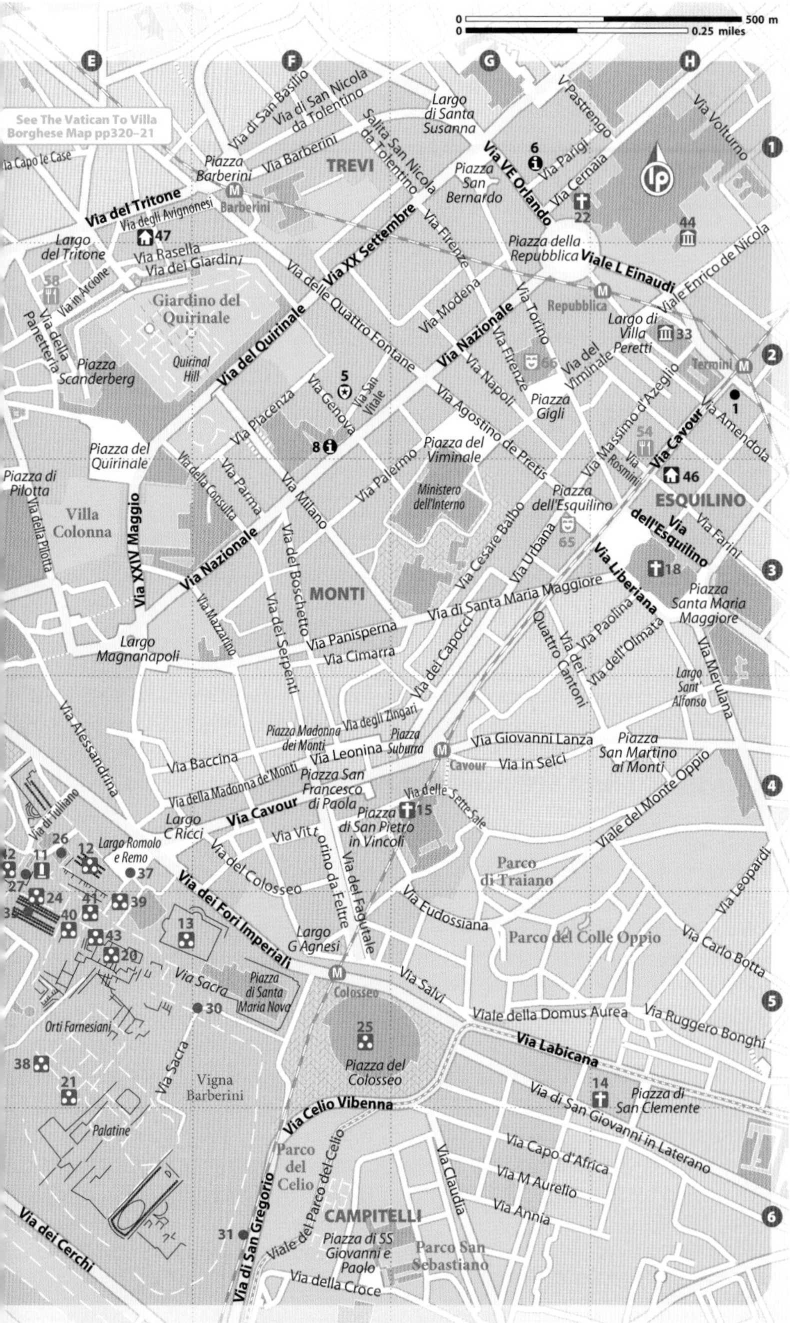
0 500 m
0 0.25 miles
See The Vatican To Villa Borghese Map pp320–21
TREVI
MONTI
ESQUILINO
CAMPITELLI
Giardino del Quirinale
Quirinal Hill
Villa Colonna
Ministero dell'Interno
Parco di Traiano
Parco del Colle Oppio
Vigna Barberini
Palatine
Orti Farnesiani
Parco del Celio
Parco San Sebastiano
Piazza Barberini
Piazza San Bernardo
Piazza della Repubblica
Largo di Santa Susanna
Largo del Tritone
Piazza Scanderberg
Piazza del Quirinale
Piazza di Pilotta
Largo Magnanapoli
Piazza del Viminale
Piazza Gigli
Piazza dell'Esquilino
Largo di Villa Peretti
Piazza Santa Maria Maggiore
Largo Sant Alfonso
Piazza Madonna dei Monti
Piazza Suburra
Piazza San Martino ai Monti
Piazza San Francesco di Paola
Piazza di San Pietro in Vincoli
Largo C Ricci
Largo Romolo e Remo
Largo G Agnesi
Piazza di Santa Maria Nova
Piazza del Colosseo
Piazza di San Clemente
Piazza di SS Giovanni e Paolo
Via del Tritone
Via degli Avignonesi
Via Rasella
Via dei Giardini
Via Barberini
Via di San Basilio
Via di San Nicola da Tolentino
Salita San Nicola da Tolentino
Via VE Orlando
Via Parigi
Via Cernaia
V Pastrengo
Via Volturno
Via XX Settembre
Via Firenze
Viale L Einaudi
Viale Enrico de Nicola
Via delle Quattro Fontane
Via Modena
Via Nazionale
Via Torino
Via del Viminale
Via Napoli
Via Agostino de Pretis
Via Massimo d'Azeglio
Via Cavour
Via Amendola
Via Rosmini
Via dell'Esquilino
Via Farini
Via Liberiana
Via del Quirinale
Via Piacenza
Via Genova
Via San Vitale
Via Palermo
Via della Consulta
Via Parma
Via Milano
Via del Boschetto
Via dei Serpenti
Via Mazzarino
Via XXIV Maggio
Via della Pilotta
Via in Arcione
Via della Panetteria
Via Capo le Case
Via Cesare Balbo
Via Urbana
Via di Santa Maria Maggiore
Via Quattro Cantoni
Via dei Quattro Cantoni
Via Paolina
Via dell'Olmata
Via Merulana
Via Panisperna
Via Cimarra
Via dei Capocci
Via degli Zingari
Via Giovanni Lanza
Via in Selci
Via Leonina
Via Baccina
Via della Madonna de'Monti
Via Alessandrina
Via di Tulliano
Via delle Sette Sale
Viale del Monte Oppio
Via Vittorino da Feltre
Via del Fagutale
Via del Colosseo
Via dei Fori Imperiali
Via Eudossiana
Via Leopardi
Via Carlo Botta
Via Sacra
Via Salvi
Viale della Domus Aurea
Via Ruggero Bonghi
Via Labicana
Via di San Giovanni in Laterano
Via Celio Vibenna
Via Capo d'Africa
Via M Aurelio
Via Annia
Via Claudia
Viale del Parco del Celio
Via di San Gregorio
Via della Croce
Via dei Cerchi
Barberini
Repubblica
Termini
Cavour
Colosseo
A B C D E F G H
1 2 3 4 5 6
1 5 6 8 11 12 13 14 15 18 20 21 22 24 25 26 27 30 31 33 37 38 39 40 41 43 44 46 47 54 58 65 66

INFORMATION		
24-hour Pharmacy	1	H2
French Consulate	2	A4
French Embassy	3	B4
Irish Embassy	4	D4
Police Station (Questura)	5	F2
Rome Tourist Board	6	G1
Tourist Information Point	7	D2
Tourist Information Point	8	F2
Tourist Information Point	9	B5
Tourist Information Point	10	B2
SIGHTS & ACTIVITIES		
Arco di Settimio Severo	11	E4
Basilica Aemilia	12	E4
Basilica di Costantino	13	E5
Basilica di San Clemente	14	H5
Basilica di San Pietro in Vincoli	15	G4
Basilica di Santa Cecilia in Trastevere	16	C6
Basilica di Santa Maria in Trastevere	17	A5
Basilica di Santa Maria Maggiore	18	H3
Bocca della Verità	(see 23)	
Campo de' Fiori	19	B3
Casa delle Vestali	20	E5
Casa di Livia	21	E5
Chiesa di Santa Maria degli Angeli	22	G1
Chiesa di Santa Maria in Cosmedin	23	D6
Colonna di Foca	24	E5
Colosseum	25	F5
Curia	26	E4
Millarium Aureum	27	E4
Musei Capitolini (Palazzo dei Conservatori)	28	D4
Musei Capitolini (Palazzo Nuovo)	29	D4
Palatine Entrance	30	F5
Palatine Entrance	31	F6
Palazzo Altemps	32	B2
Palazzo Massimo alle Terme	33	H2
Pantheon	34	C3
Piazza del Foro	35	E5
Piazza Venezia	36	D3
Roman Forum Entrance	37	E4
Tempio della Magna Mater	38	E5
Tempio di Antonino e Faustina	39	E5
Tempio di Castore e Polluce	40	E5
Tempio di Giulio Cesare	41	E5
Tempio di Saturno	42	E4
Tempio di Vesta	43	E5
Terme di Diocleziano	44	H1
Trevi Fountain	45	D2
SLEEPING		
58 Le Real B&B	46	H3
Daphne Inn (Trevi)	47	E1
Hotel Raphaël	48	B2
Relais Palazzo Taverna	49	A2
Villa della Fonte	50	A5
EATING		
Baffetto 2	51	B3
Ditirambo	52	B3
Il Convivio di Troiano	53	B2
La Gallina Bianca	54	H2
Maccheroni	55	C2
Osteria da Lucia	56	A5
Pizzeria da Baffetto	57	A3
San Crispino	58	E2
Vineria Roscioli	59	B4
DRINKING		
Bar della Pace	60	B2
Bar San Calisto	61	A5
Caffè Sant'Eustachio	62	C3
Freni e Frizioni	63	A5
La Vineria	64	B3
ENTERTAINMENT		
Orbis	65	G3
Teatro dell'Opera	66	G2

refers to the *tre vie* (three roads) that converge at the fountain. The custom is to throw a coin over your shoulder into the fountain, thus ensuring your return to Rome. On an average day about €3000 is chucked away.

PIAZZA DI SPAGNA & SPANISH STEPS

A hang-out for flirting adolescents and footsore tourists, **Piazza di Spagna** (Map pp320-1) and the **Spanish Steps** **(Scalinata della Trinità dei Monti)** have been a magnet for foreigners since the 18th century. Built with a legacy from the French in 1725, but named after the Spanish embassy to the Holy See, the steps were constructed to link the piazza with the well-heeled folks living above it. Looming over the Steps is the **Chiesa della Trinità dei Monti** **(Map pp320-1; ☎ 06 679 41 79; Piazza Trinità dei Monti; ⏲ 10am-noon & 4-6pm; Ⓜ Spagna)**.

To the right as you face the steps is the **Keats-Shelley House** **(Map pp320-1; ☎ 06 678 42 35; Piazza di Spagna 8; ⏲ 9am-1pm & 3-6pm Mon-Fri, 11am-2pm & 3-6pm Sat; Ⓜ Spagna** where Keats spent the last three month of his life in 1821.

PIAZZA DEL POPOLO & AROUND

One of Rome's landmark squares, **Piazz del Popolo** **(Map pp320-1; Ⓜ Flaminio)** wa laid out in 1538 at the point of conve gence of three roads – Via di Ripetta, Vi del Corso and Via del Babuino – that forr a trident at what was once Rome's north ern entrance. Today, this part of centra Rome is known as Il Tridente. Rising abov the piazza is **Pincio Hill**, which afford great views of the city.

South of the piazza on Via di Ripetta the **Ara Pacis Augustae** **(Altar of Peac Map pp320-1; ☎ 06 671 03 887; admissio €6.50; ⏲ 9am-7pm Tue-Sun; Ⓜ Flaminio)** is monument to the peace that Augustu established both at home and abroac Housed in Richard Meier's controversia white pavilion, it is considered one of th most important works of ancient Roma sculpture.

MUSEO NAZIONALE ROMANO

Spread over five sites, the **Museo Nazionale Romano** (National Roman Museum) houses one of the world's most important collections of classical art and statuary. A combined ticket including each of the sites costs €7 and is valid for three days.

Lovers of ancient sculpture should make a beeline for **Palazzo Altemps** (Map pp324-5; ☎ 06 683 37 59; Piazza Sant'Apollinare 44; 🕑 9am-7.45pm Tue-Sun; 🚌 Corso del Rinascimento) near Piazza Navona.

Up near Termini, **Palazzo Massimo alle Terme** (Map pp324-5; ☎ 06 399 67 700; Largo di Villa Peretti 1; 🕑 9am-7.45pm Tue-Sun; Ⓜ Termini) features yet more sculpture, although the highlights are the amazing frescoes and wall paintings on the 2nd floor. Nearby, the **Terme di Diocleziano** (Baths of Diocletian; Map pp324-5; ☎ 06 488 05 30; Via Enrico de Nicola 79; 🕑 9am-7.45pm Tue-Sun; Ⓜ Termini) are a sight in themselves. Built at the turn of the 3rd century, they were Rome's largest baths complex, covering 13 hectares and capable of accommodating 3000 people.

TRASTEVERE

Trastevere is one of central Rome's most vivacious neighbourhoods, a tightly packed district of ochre *palazzi*, ivy-clad facades and photogenic lanes. Taking its name from the Latin *trans Tiberium*, meaning over the Tiber, it was originally a working-class district, but it has since been gentrified and today it's a trendy hang-out full of bars, trattorias and restaurants.

Trastevere's focal point is Piazza Santa Maria. Here, nestled in a quiet corner, is the **Basilica di Santa Maria in Trastevere** (Map pp324-5; ☎ 06 581 48 02; Piazza Santa Maria in Trastevere; 🕑 7.30am-12.30pm & 3.30-7.30pm; 🚌 Viale di Trastevere), believed to be the oldest Roman church dedicated to the Virgin Mary. Inside it's the glittering 12th-century mosaics that are the main drawcard.

Over on the eastern side of Trastevere, the **Basilica di Santa Cecilia in Trastevere** (Map pp324-5; ☎ 06 589 92 89; Piazza di Santa Cecilia; basilica/fresco free/€2; 🕑 basilica 9am-12.30pm & 4-6.30pm, fresco 10.15am-noon Mon-Sat, 11.15am-12.15pm Sun; 🚌 Viale di Trastevere) harbours fragments of a spectacular 13th-century fresco, Pietro Cavallini's *The Last Judgment*.

APPIA ANTICA & THE CATACOMBS

Known to the ancient Romans as the *regina viarum* (queen of roads), Via Appia Antica (Appian Way) was named after Appius Claudius Caecus, who laid the first

MAX PAOLI & RUTH EASTHAM

Piazza del Popolo

90km section in 312 BC. It was extended in 190 BC to reach Brindisi some 540km away on the Adriatic coast.

The easiest way to get to the road is to take Metro Line A to Colli Albani, then bus 660. It's traffic-free on Sunday if you want to walk or cycle it. For information on bike hire or to join a guided tour, head to the **Appia Antica Regional Park Information Point** (Map pp316-17; ☎ 06 513 53 16; www.parcoappiaantica.org; Via Appia Antica 58-60; 9.30am-5.30pm summer, to 4.30pm winter; Via Appia Antica).

Rome's extensive network of catacombs was built as communal burial grounds. A Roman law banned burials within the city walls, and persecution left the early Christians little choice but to dig. On Via Appia Antica, you can visit the **Catacombs of San Callisto** (Map pp316-17; ☎ 06 446 56 10; Via Appia Antica 110; adult/concession €5/3; 9am-noon & 2-5pm Thu-Tue, until 5.30pm Jun-Sep, closed Feb; Via Appia Antica), Rome's largest, most famous and busiest catacombs, and, a short walk away, the **Catacombs of San Sebastiano** (Map pp316-17; ☎ 06 785 03 50; Via Appia Antica 136; adult/concession €5/3; 9am-noon & 2-5pm Mon-Sat, until 5.30pm Jun-Sep, closed mid-Nov–mid-Dec; Via Appia Antica).

TERME DI CARACALLA

The vast ruins of the **Terme di Caracalla** (Baths of Caracalla; Map pp316-17; ☎ 06 39 96 77 00; Via delle Terme di Caracalla 52; admission €6; 9am-1hr before sunset Tue-Sun, to 2pm Mon; M Circo Massimo) are an awe-inspiring sight. Begun by Caracalla and inaugurated in AD 217, the 10-hectare leisure complex could hold up to 1600 people and included richly decorated pools, gymnasiums, libraries, shops and gardens. The baths were used until 537 and the ruins are now used to stage summer opera.

CHURCHES & CATHEDRALS

One of Rome's four patriarchal basilicas the **Basilica di Santa Maria Maggiore** (Map pp324-5; ☎ 06 48 31 95; Piazza Santa Maria Maggiore; 7am-7pm, to 6pm winter; Piazza Santa Maria Maggiore) was built by Pope Liberius in AD 352 after the Virgin Mary instructed him to construct a church on the spot where the next snow fell.

Similarly impressive is the great white **Basilica di San Giovanni in Laterano** (Map pp316-17; ☎ 06 698 86 433; Piazza di San Giovanni in Laterano 4; 7am-7pm, to 6pm winter; M San Giovanni). Consecrated in 324 AD, this was the first Christian basilica to be built in Rome and, until the late 14th century, was the pope's principal residence. Nowadays, it's Rome's official cathedral and the pope's seat as Bishop of Rome.

Just off Via Cavour, the **Basilica di San Pietro in Vincoli** (Map pp324-5; Piazza di San Pietro in Vincoli; 8am-12.30pm & 3-7pm; M Cavour) displays Michelangelo's magnificent *Moses,* as well as the chains worn by St Peter before his crucifixion; hence the church's name (St Peter in Chains).

The **Basilica di San Clemente** (Map pp324-5; ☎ 06 774 00 21; Via di San Giovanni in Laterano; 9am-12.30pm & 3.30-6.30pm; M Colosseo), east of the Colosseum, is a multilayered affair. The 12th-century church at street level was built over a 4th-century church that was, in turn, built over a 1st-century Roman house with a temple dedicated to the pagan god Mithras.

Considered one of the finest medieval churches in Rome, the **Chiesa di Santa Maria in Cosmedin** (Map pp324-5; ☎ 06 678 14 19; Piazza della Bocca della Verità 18; 9am-1pm & 2.30-6pm; Via dei Cerchi) is most famous for the **Bocca della Verità** (Mouth of Truth) in its portico. Legend has it that if you put your right hand into

CHRISTOPHER GROENHOUT

Pantheon (p322)

he stone mouth and tell a lie, it will bite 'our hand off.

Facing onto Piazza della Repubblica, he hulking **Chiesa di Santa Maria degli** **\ngeli** **(Map pp324-5; Piazza della Repubblica; 7am-6.30pm Mon-Sat, to 7.30pm Sun; M Repub-lica)** occupies what was once the central hall of Diocletian's enormous baths com-plex (see p327).

GALLERIA NAZIONALE D'ARTE ANTICA

\ must for anyone into Renaissance and baroque art, the **Galleria Nazionale d'Arte Antica** **(Map pp320-1; ☎ 06 481 45 91; www.galleriaborghese.it; Via Quattro Fontane 13; admission €5; 8.30am-7pm Tue-Sun; M Barberini)** is housed in the spectacular Palazzo Barberini, itself a notable work of art. Inside, you'll find works by Raphael, Caravaggio, Guido Reni, Bernini, Filippo Lippi and Holbein, as well as Pietro da Cortona's breathtaking *Trionfo della Divina Provvidenza* (Triumph of Divine Providence) in the main salon.

FESTIVALS & EVENTS

Easter On Good Friday the pope leads a candlelit procession around the Colosseum. At noon on Easter Sunday he blesses the crowds in St Peter's Square.

Settimana della Cultura Public museums and galleries open free of charge during culture week, held between March and May.

Natale Di Roma (21 April) Rome celebrates its birthday with music and fireworks.

Estate Romana Between June and September, Rome's big cultural festival hosts events ranging from book fairs to raves and gay parties.

Festa dei Santi Pietro e Paolo (June 29) Romans celebrate patron saints Peter and Paul around St Peter's Basilica and Via Ostiense.

Festa di Noantri Trastevere's annual party takes over the neighbourhood for the last two weeks of July.

Romaeuropa Rome's premier music and dance festival runs from late September to November.

Festival International del Film di Roma Rome's film festival rolls out the red carpet for Hollywood big guns in October (from 29 to 6 November in 2010).

SLEEPING

There's no point beating around the bush, Rome is expensive. Always try to book ahead, even if it's just for the first night. If you arrive without a booking, there's a **hotel reservation service** (**Map pp316-17; ☎ 06 699 10 00; booking fee €3; 🕑 7am-10pm**) next to the tourist office at Stazione Termini.

58 Le Real B&B (**Map pp324-5; ☎ 06 482 35 66; www.58viacavour.it; Via Cavour 58; r €70-150;** ❄) This swish 12-room B&B is on the 4th floor of a towering 19th-century

GLENN BEANLAND

Laneway in Trastevere (p327)

townhouse. Room decor is a stylish mi of leather armchairs, plasma TVs, Muran chandeliers, polished-wood bedstead and parquet floors. Topping everythin is a panoramic roof terrace.

Relais Palazzo Taverna (**Map pp324-5 ☎ 06 203 98 064; www.relaispalazzotaverna.com Via dei Gabrielli 92; s €80-150, d €100-210, tr €120 240;** ❄) Boutique style at less than de signer prices is the drawcard here. That and a perfect location in a quiet *centr storico* cul-de-sac.

Hotel Bramante (**Map pp320-1; ☎ 06 68 06 426; www.hotelbramante.com; Via delle Pallin 24; s €100-160, d €150-240;** ❄) Housed in Renaissance *palazzo* by the Vatican Cit wall, this charmer is a model of effortles elegance.

Villa della Fonte (**Map pp324-5; ☎ 06 58 37 97; www.villafonte.com; Via della Fonte dell'Oli 8; s €110-120, d €150-180;** ❄) Near Piazz Santa Maria in Trastevere, this charm ing little hotel is a gem. The five room are simple but tasteful with white walls earth-coloured floors and modern en suite bathrooms.

our pick **Daphne Inn** (**Map pp320-1; ☎ 0 874 50 086; www.daphne-rome.com; Via di Sa Basilio 55 & Via degli Avignonesi 20; s €110-160 d €90-200, ste €320-550;** ❄ 💻) Daphne is star. Spread over two sites near Piazz Barberini, it offers value for money, ex ceptional service and fashionably attire rooms.

Hotel Raphaël (**Map pp324-5; ☎ 06 6 28 31; www.raphaelhotel.com; Largo Febo 2; €200-280, d €250-350;** ❄ 💻) An ivy-clad landmark just off Piazza Navona, th Raphaël is a Roman institution. With it gallery lobby – look out for the Picass ceramics and Miro lithographs – and sleek Richard Meier–designed rooms this place knows how to lay out the re carpet.

EATING

Like all Italians, Romans love eating out. The best places to eat are in the *centro storico* and Trastevere, but there are also excellent choices in San Lorenzo and Testaccio.

Roman specialities include *trippa alla romana* (tripe with potatoes, tomato and pecorino cheese), *fiori di zucca* (fried courgette flowers) and *carciofi alla romana* (artichokes with garlic, mint and parsley). Of the pastas, *cacio e pepe* (with pecorino cheese, black pepper and olive oil) and *all'amatriciana* (with tomato, pancetta and chilli) are Roman favourites.

CITY CENTRE & JEWISH GHETTO

Pizzeria da Baffetto (**Map pp324-5; ☎ 06 686 16 17; Via del Governo Vecchio 114; pizzas €8; ⏲ 6.30pm-1am**) For the full-on, Roman pizza experience get down to this local institution. Meals here are raucous, chaotic and fast, but the thin-crust pizza's good and the vibe is fun. To partake, join the queue and wait to be squeezed in wherever there's room. There's now a Baffetto 2 (☎ 06 682 10 807) on Piazza del Teatro di Pompeo 18 (Map pp324-5) near Campo de' Fiori (note that it's closed Tuesdays).

Maccheroni (**Map pp324-5; ☎ 06 683 07 895; Piazza delle Coppelle 44; meals €35**) Popular with locals and tourists alike, this is the archetypal *centro storico* trattoria. It's boisterous, busy and fancy-free with a classic Roman menu and an attractive setting near the Pantheon.

Ditirambo (**Map pp324-5; ☎ 06 687 16 26; Piazza della Cancelleria 72; meals €40; ⏲ closed Sun lunch**) Beautifully located near Campo dei' Fiori, this hugely popular trattoria has made a name for itself with innovative, organic cooking.

Vineria Roscioli (**Map pp324-5; ☎ 06 687 52 87; Via dei Giubbonari 21; meals €55; ⏲ Mon-Sat**) Under the brick arches, you'll find a mouth-watering array of olive oils, conserves, cheeses and hams, while out back the small restaurant serves classic Italian dishes.

Il Convivio de Troiani (**Map pp324-5; ☎ 06 68 69 432; www.ilconviviotroiani.com; Vicolo dei Soldati 31; meals €100; ⏲ Mon-Sat**) One for a special occasion, this swish restaurant is one of the best in Rome. Menus are seasonal but always luxurious, so you could find yourself sitting down to roasted quails with semolina dumplings, spicy mango and foie gras sauce.

TRASTEVERE, TESTACCIO & THE VATICAN

Pizzeria Remo (**Map pp316-17; ☎ 06 574 62 70; Piazza Santa Maria Liberatice 44; pizzas €6**) This rowdy Testaccio spot is a favourite with young Saturday-nighters. Queues are the norm, but the large, thin-crust pizzas and delicious *bruschette* (toasted bread drizzled with olive oil and selected toppings) make the chaos bearable.

Volpetti Più (**Map pp316-17; ☎ 06 574 43 06; Via A Volta 8; meals €10-15**) A sumptuous *tavola calda*, this is one of the few places in town where you can sit down and eat well for less than €15.

our pick **Dino e Tony** (**Map pp320-1; ☎ 06 397 33 284; Via Leone IV 60; meals €25; ⏲ Mon-Sat**) Something of a rarity, Dino e Tony is an authentic trattoria in the Vatican area. Famous for its *amatriciana*, it serves a monumental antipasto that might well see you through to dessert. If you've got room, finish up with a *granita di caffé*, a crushed ice coffee served with a full inch of whipped cream.

Osteria da Lucia (**Map pp324-5; ☎ 06 580 36 01; Via del Mattinato 2; meals €28; ⏲ Tue-Sun**) In an atmospheric corner of Trastevere, da Lucia is a terrific neighbourhood trattoria. It's a good place to get your teeth into some authentic *trippa alla romano*.

San Crispino (Map pp324-5; Via della Panetteria 42) Near the Trevi Fountain, this place sells the best gelato in Rome. Flavours are natural and seasonal – think *crema* with honey – and served in tubs only.

TERMINI & SAN LORENZO

La Gallina Bianca (Map pp324-5; ☎ 06 474 37 77; Via Rosmini 9; pizzas from €6, meals €30) On a small street off Via Cavour, this choice restaurant offers a welcome respite from the tourist rip-off joints near Termini.

Pommidoro (Map pp316-17; ☎ 06 445 26 92; Piazza dei Sanniti 44; meals €35; Mon-Sat) A much-loved San Lorenzo institution, Pommidoro continues to do what it has always done – serve traditional food to crowds of appreciative diners. Celebs often drop by, including in recent times Nicole Kidman and Fabio Capello, but it's an unpretentious place with a laid-back vibe and excellent food.

Tram Tram (Map pp316-17; ☎ 064 470 25 85; Via dei Reti 44; meals €50; Tue-Sun) Taking its name from the trams that rattle past outside, this is a trendy San Lorenzo eatery. Seafood from southern Italy is the house speciality – if it's on, try the *riso, cozze e patate* (rice, mussels and potato) – and the excellent wine list highlights small producers.

DRINKING

Drinking in Rome is all about looking the part and enjoying the atmosphere. Much of the action is in the *centro storico*, on Campo de' Fiori and around Piazza Navona.

our pick **Caffè Sant'Eustachio** (Map pp324-5; Piazza Sant'Eustachio 82) Aficionados claim that this unassuming cafe serves the best coffee in Rome. And, after extensive research, we agree.

Bar San Calisto (Map pp324-5; Piazza San Calisto; Mon-Sat) Drug dealers, drunks, bohemian diners, foreign students – they al flock to this Trastevere landmark for th cheap prices and laid-back atmosphere It's famous for its chocolate, drunk hot o eaten as ice cream.

La Vineria (Map pp324-5; Campo de'Fiori 15 A good spot to watch the nightly Campo de' Fiori circus, this is the hippest of th square-side bars. It has a small, bottle lined interior and several outside tables.

Bar della Pace (Map pp324-5; Via della Pac 3-7) Style hounds looking for the archetypal *dolce vita* bar should stop here. With its art nouveau interior, ivy-clad facad and well-dressed customers, it's the ver epitome of Italian style.

Freni e Frizioni (Map pp324-5; Piazz Trilussa) In a bohemian corner of Trastevere this is one of the in-spots for *aperitivo*. It' housed in a former garage (hence th name – 'brakes and clutches') and attract a young, fashionable crowd.

ENTERTAINMENT

The best listings guide is *Roma C'* (www.romace.it, in Italian), with a English-language section, publishe on Wednesday (€1.50). Another usefu guide is *Trova Roma*, a free insert with *L Repubblica* newspaper every Thursday.

Two good ticket agencies are **Orbis** (Ma pp324-5; ☎ 06 48 27 403; Piazza dell'Esquilino 37 9.30am-1pm & 4-7.30pm Mon-Fri, 9.30am-1pm Sat) and the online agency **Hello** (☎ 800 9 70 80; www.helloticket.it, in Italian).

CLASSICAL MUSIC & OPERA

Rome's premier concert complex is th **Auditorium Parco della Musica** (Ma pp316-17; ☎ 06 802 41 281; www.auditorium.com Viale Pietro de Coubertin 34). The auditorium i also home to Rome's top classical-musi organisation, the **Accademia di Santa Cecilia** (☎ box office 06 808 20 58; www.sant cecilia.it), which organises a world-clas

WILL SALTER

Exterior of Auditorium Parco della Musica

symphony season and short festivals dedicated to single composers.

The **Accademia Filarmonica Romana** (☎ 06 320 17 52; www.filarmonicaromana.org) concentrates on classical and chamber music, although it also stages ballet, opera and multimedia events at the **Teatro Olimpico** (Map pp316-17; ☎ 06 326 59 91; www.teatroolimpico.it; Piazza Gentile da Fabriano 17).

Rome's opera season runs from December to June. The main venue is the **Teatro dell'Opera** (Map pp324-5; ☎ 06 481 601; www.operaroma.it; Piazza Beniamino Gigli 7), which also houses the city's ballet company. In summer, opera is performed outdoors at the spectacular Terme di Caracalla (see p328).

SHOPPING

Shopping is fun in Rome. With everything from designer flagship stores to antique emporiums, flea markets and bohemian boutiques, there's something for all tastes.

For the big-gun designer names head for Via dei Condotti and the area between Piazza di Spagna and Via del Corso. Moving down a euro or two, Via Nazionale, Via del Corso, Via dei Giubbonari and Via Cola di Rienzo are good for midrange clothing stores. For something more left field, try the small fashion boutiques and vintage clothes shops on Via del Governo Vecchio.

The best places for art and antiques are Via dei Coronari and Via Margutta. A cheaper option is to try one of the city's markets. The most famous, **Porta Portese** (Map pp316-17; 7am-1pm Sun), is held every Sunday morning near Trastevere and sells everything from antiques to clothes, bikes, bags and furniture. Near Porta San Giovanni, the **Via Sannio market** (Map pp316-17; Via Sannio; morning Mon-Sat) sells new and secondhand shoes and clothes.

GETTING THERE & AWAY

AIR

Rome's main international airport **Leonardo da Vinci** (FCO; ☎ 06 6 59 51; www.adr.it), better known as Fiumicino, is on the coast 30km west of the city. The much smaller **Ciampino airport** (CIA; ☎ 06 6 59 51; www.adr.it), 15km southeast of the city centre, is the hub for low-cost carriers including **Ryanair** (www.ryanair.com) and **easyJet** (www.easyjet.com).

BOAT
Rome's main port is at Civitavecchia, about 80km north of Rome. See p366 for more information on ferry companies and routes.

Half-hourly trains depart from Roma Termini to Civitavecchia (€4.50 to €8.50, one hour). On arrival, it's about a 15-minute walk to the port (to your right) as you exit the station.

BUS
Long-distance national and international buses use the bus terminus on Piazzale Tiburtina, in front of Stazione Tiburtina. National companies include the following:

ARPA (☎ 199 166 952; www.arpaonline.it) For L'Aquila and Abruzzo.

Cotral (www.cotralspa.it, in Italian) For the Lazio region.

Interbus (☎ 0935 56 51 11; www.interbus.it, in Italian) For destinations in Sicily, including Messina, Catania and Palermo.

Marozzi (☎ 080 579 01 11; www.marozzivt.it, in Italian) To/from Sorrento, Bari, Matera and Lecce.

SAIS (☎ 091 616 60 28; www.saisautolinee.it, in Italian) For Sicily.

SENA (☎ 0577 20 82 82; www.senabus.it) To/from Siena, Milan and Bologna.

Sulga (☎ 800 099 661; www.sulga.it) For Perugia, Assisi and Ravenna.

CAR & MOTORCYCLE
It's no holiday driving into central Rome. You'll have to deal with traffic restrictions, one-way systems, an almost total lack of street parking and a few hundred thousand lunatics vying for your road space.

Rome is circled by the Grande Raccordo Anulare (GRA) to which all *autostrade* (motorways) connect, including the main A1 north-south artery (the Autostrada del Sole), and the A12, which connects Rome to Civitavecchia and Fiumicino airport.

TRAIN
Almost all trains arrive at and depart from Stazione Termini. On the main concourse, the **train information office** (Map pp316-17; 🕑 7am-9.45pm) is helpful (English is spoken) but often very busy. To avoid the queues, you can get information online at www.trenitalia.com or, if you speak Italian, by calling ☎ 89 20 21.

Rome's other principal train station is Stazione Tiburtina, a short ride away on metro line B.

GETTING AROUND
TO/FROM THE AIRPORT
FIUMICINO
The efficient *Leonardo Express* train service leaves from platform 24 at Stazione Termini and travels direct to the airport every 30 minutes from 5.52am until 10.52pm. It costs €11 and takes about 30 minutes.

During the night, **Cotral** (www.cotralspa.it, in Italian) runs a bus from Stazione Tiburtina via Stazione Termini to Fiumicino. It departs Tiburtina at 12.30am, 1.15am, 2.30am and 3.45am, returning at 1.15am, 2.15am, 3.30am and 5am. Tickets, available on the bus, cost €4.50 to the airport and €7 from the airport.

The set taxi fare to/from the city centre is €40, which is valid for up to four passengers with luggage.

CIAMPINO

Terravision (☎ 06 454 41 345; www.terravision.eu) buses depart from Via Marsala outside Stazione Termini two hours before each scheduled flight and from Ciampino soon after flight arrivals. Get tickets (€8) online, on board, from Agenzia 365 at Stazione Termini or at Ciampino airport.

Alternatively, **SIT** (☎ 06 591 68 26; www.sitbusshuttle.com) covers the same route, with regular departures from Termini between 4.30am and 9.15pm, and from Ciampino between 8.30am and midnight. Buy tickets (€6) on board.

Cotral runs two night services: from Termini at 4.45am and 4.50am, and from Ciampino at 11.50pm and 12.15am. Tickets (€5) are available on the bus.

Regular Cotral buses connect with Anagnina metro station (€1.20, about 15 minutes) where you can get the metro direct to Stazione Termini.

By taxi the set rate to/from Ciampino is €30.

GREG ELMS

Pizza margherita

PUBLIC TRANSPORT

Rome has an integrated public transport system, so the same ticket is valid for all modes of transport: bus, tram, metro and suburban railway. You can buy tickets at *tabacchi*, newsstands and from vending machines at main bus stops and metro stations. Single tickets cost €1 for 75 minutes, during which time you can use as many buses or trams as you like, but only go once on the metro. Tickets must be purchased before you get on the bus/train and validated in the yellow machine, or at the entrance gates for the metro.

Rome's buses and trams are run by **ATAC** (☎ 06 57 003; www.atac.roma.it). The **main bus station** (Map pp316-17; Piazza dei Cinquecento) is in front of Stazione Termini, where there's an **information booth** (🕓 7.30am-8pm). Largo di Torre Argentina, Piazza Venezia and Piazza San Silvestro are also important hubs. Buses generally run from about 5.30am until midnight, with limited services throughout the night.

The Metropolitana has two lines, A and B, which both pass through Termini. Take line A for the Trevi Fountain (Barberini), Spanish Steps (Spagna), and Vatican (Ottaviano-San Pietro); and line B for the Colosseum (Colosseo) and Circus Maximus (Circo Massimo). Trains run on line B between 5.30am and 11.30pm (1.30am on Friday and Saturday) and to 10pm on line A.

TAXI

Rome's taxi drivers are no better or worse than in any other city. Some will try to

WITOLD SKRYPCZAK

Teatro Marittimo, Villa Adriana

IF YOU LIKE...

If Rome (p314) has whetted your appetite for the ancient world, try these Roman ruins:

- **Ostia Antica** (☎ 06 563 58 099; adult/concession €6.50/3.25; ⏲ 8.30am-6pm Apr-Sep, to 5pm Mar & Oct, to 4pm Nov-Feb) Ostia was ancient Rome's port, and the ruins of restaurants, laundries, shops, houses and public meeting places really bring ancient Rome to life. To get to Ostia Antica from Rome take metro line B to Piramide, then the Ostia Lido train (25 minutes, half-hourly).
- **Villa Adriana** (☎ 0774 38 27 33; with/without exhibition €10/6.50; ⏲ 9am-6pm summer, to 3.30pm winter) Set 5km from Tivoli, Emperor Hadrian's holiday villa was the most sumptuous in the Roman Empire. There are frequent trains from Rome to Tivoli, where you can catch CAT bus 4X (€1, 10 minutes, hourly) to the villa.
- **Tarquinia** Ninety kilometres northwest of Rome, Tarquinia's highlights are the Unesco-listed Etruscan **necropolis** (☎ 0766 85 63 08; Via Ripagretta; admission €6, incl museum €8.50; ⏲ 8.30am-6.30pm Tue-Sun summer, to 2pm winter) and a fascinating Etruscan museum, the **Museo Nazionale Tarquiniense** (☎ 0766 85 60 36; Piazza Cavour; admission €6, incl necropolis €8; ⏲ 8.30am-7.30pm Tue-Sun).
- **Ravenna** Once the capital of the Western Roman and Byzantine Empires, Ravenna is famous for its Unesco-listed mosaics: the town's five main **monuments** (www.ravennamosaici.it; adult/under 10yr/concession €8.50/free/7.50) are covered by a single ticket valid for seven days. Regular trains connect the town with Bologna (€5, 1½ hours, 13 daily).

fleece you, others won't. To minimise the risk, make sure your taxi is licensed and metered, and always go with the metered fare, never an arranged price (the set fares to and from the airports are exceptions to this rule). Official rates are posted in taxis.

You can't hail a taxi, but there are major taxi ranks at the airports, Stazione Termini and Largo di Torre Argentina.

Cosmos (☎ 06 8 81 77)
La Capitale (☎ 06 49 94)
Pronto Taxi (☎ 06 66 45)
Radio Taxi (☎ 06 35 70)
Samarcanda (☎ 06 55 51)
Tevere (☎ 06 41 57)

NORTHERN ITALY

Italy's well-heeled north is a fascinating area of historical wealth and natural diversity. Bordered by the northern Alps and boasting some of the country's most spectacular coastline, it also encompasses Italy's largest lowland area, the decidedly nonpicturesque Po Valley plain.

CINQUE TERRE

Named after its five tiny villages (Riomaggiore, Manarola, Corniglia, Vernazza and Monterosso), the Unesco-listed Parco Nazionale delle Cinque Terre (www.parconazionale5terre.it) encompasses some of Italy's most picturesque and environmentally sensitive coastline. The villages are linked by the 12km Blue Trail (Sentiero Azzurro), a magnificent, mildly challenging 9km (five hour) trail. To walk it, you'll need to buy a Cinque Terre Card (**adult/under 4yr/4-12yr 1 day €5/free/2.50, 2 days €8/free/4**), available in all of the park offices. If you prefer, you can buy a Cinque Terre Treno Card (**adult/under 4yr/4-12yr 1 day €8.50/free/4.30, 2 days €14.70/free/7.40**), which includes the walk plus unlimited train travel between Levanto and La Spezia, including all five villages.

Regional train services from Genoa to Riomaggiore stop at each of the Cinque Terre villages (€4.40, two to 2½ hours).

Consorzio Marittimo Turistico 5 Terre (☎ **0187 81 84 40**) runs ferries between four of the villages (not Corniglia) every day in summer (adult/child return €12.50/6.50, one way €8/4).

MILAN

pop 1.3 million

You may love it, you may hate it, but one thing's for sure – you won't remain indifferent to Milan (Milano). Italy's financial and fashion capital is expensive, noisy, dirty and strictly for city lovers – all of whom end up dazzled by its vibrant cultural scene, sensational shopping and wicked nightlife.

INFORMATION

Tourist offices Piazza del Duomo (☎ **02 774 04 343; www.milanoinfotourist.com; Piazza Duomo 19a; 8.45am-1pm & 2-6pm Mon-Sat, 9am-1pm & 2-5pm Sun**); Stazione Centrale (☎ **02 774 04 318; 9am-6pm Mon-Sat, 9am-1pm & 2-5pm Sun**) Pick up the free guides *Hello Milano* and *Milanomese.*

SIGHTS

With a capacity of 40,000 people, Milan's landmark Duomo (**Piazza del Duomo; admission free; 7am-7pm**) is the world's largest Gothic cathedral. Commissioned in 1386 to a florid French-Gothic design and finished nearly 600 years later, it's a fairy-tale ensemble of 3400 statues, 135 spires and 155 gargoyles. Climb up to the roof (**stairs/elevator €5/7; 9am-5.20pm, to 8.30pm high summer**) for memorable views of the city.

Nearby, on the northern flank of Piazza del Duomo, the elegant iron and glass Galleria Vittorio Emanuele II shopping arcade leads towards the famous Teatro alla Scala (☎ **02 720 03 744; www.teatroallascala.org; Piazza delle Scala; admission €5; 9am-12.30pm & 1.30-5.30pm when no performances are scheduled**).

To the west, the dramatic 15th-century Castello Sforzesco (☎ **02 884 63 700; www.milanocastello.it; Piazza Castello 3; admission free; 9am-5.30pm Tue-Sun**) was the Renaissance residence of the Sforza dynasty. It now shelters the Musei del Castello (☎ 02 884 63 703; adult/concession €3/1.50; ☽ 9am-5.30pm), a group of museums dedicated to art, sculpture, furniture, archaeology and music. Entry is free on Friday between 2pm and 5.30pm and from Tuesday to Sunday between 4.30pm and 5.30pm.

Art addicts shouldn't miss the Pinacoteca di Brera (☎ 02 894 21 146; www.brera.beniculturali.it; Via Brera 28; adult/concession €5/2.50; ☽ 8.30am-7.15pm Tue-Sun), whose heavyweight collection includes Andrea Mantegna's masterpiece, the *Dead Christ,* and Raphael's *Betrothal of the Virgin*.

Milan's most famous tourist attraction – Leonardo da Vinci's mural of *The Last Supper* – is in the Cenacolo Vinciano (☎ 02 894 21 146; www.cenacolovinciano.org; Piazza Santa Maria delle Grazie 2; booking compulsory, adult/child €6.50/free, plus booking fee of €1.50; ☽ 8.15am-6.45pm Tue-Sun), just west of the city centre. Although we have been lucky in the past and scored a ticket on the day (go at lunchtime), it's much safer to book ahead.

TOURS

Autostradale (☎ 02 339 10 794; www.autostradale.it) runs three-hour bus tours that take in the Duomo, Galleria Vittorio Emanuele II, La Scala, Castello Sforzesco and the Cenacolo Vinciano. If you haven't booked ahead for your *Last Supper* ticket, this may be the only opportunity you'll have to see it, as the €55 ticket (€45 for children) for this tour includes entry to see the famous mural. The multilingual tours depart from outside the office at 9.30am every morning except Monday.

SLEEPING & EATING

Prepare yourself for a budget blow-out when booking a hotel here – everything is ridiculously expensive, particularly when trade fairs are on (which is often).

Ariston Hotel (☎ 02 720 00 556; www.aristonhotel.com; Largo Carrobbio 2; s €100-220, d €140-320; ☒ ☐) Claiming to be Milan's first 'ecological hotel' (hmm), the Ariston offers comfortable but characterless rooms with jacuzzis and flat-screen TVs.

Alle Meraviglie (☎ 02 805 10 23; www.allemeraviglie.it; Via San Tomaso 8; r from €182; ☒ ☐) Boutique with a capital B, this stylish place has only six rooms, all of which balance simplicity and style to great effect. Breakfast costs €15.

ourpick Peck Italian Bar (☎ 02 869 30 17; Via Cesare Cantù 3; meals €40; ☽ 11.30am-8pm) This place truly encapsulates Milan – chic and sleek surrounds, top-quality produce and a glamorous clientele. The delicious Milanese menu features classics such as *cotolleto* (breaded veal cutlet) and risotto.

Il Brellin (☎ 02 581 01 351; Via Alzaia Naviglio Grande 14; meals €46; ☽ closed Sun) Set around a laundry dating from the 1700s, atmospheric Il Brellin is a great place to linger over dinner. The three-course traditional Milanese tasting menu (€46) is a great idea, and the passing parade makes for an entertaining evening.

After dinner at a pizzeria or Il Brellin, think about sampling the gelato at Rinomata (☎ 02 58113877; Ripa di Porta Ticinese).

SHOPPING

For designer clobber head to the so-called Golden Quad, the area around Via della Spiga, Via Sant'Andrea, Via Monte Napoleone and Via Alessandro Manzoni. Street markets are held around the canals, notably on Viale Papiniano on Tuesday and Saturday mornings.

GETTING THERE & AWAY

Most international flights fly into Malpensa airport (MXP; ☽ 02 748 52 200; www.sea-aeroportimilano.it), about 50km

MILAN

INFORMATION

Central Tourist Office 1 C4
Tourist Office 2 D1

SIGHTS & ACTIVITIES

Castello Sforzesco 3 B3
Cenacolo Vinciano 4 A4
Duomo 5 C4
Galleria Vittorio Emanuele II 6 C4
Museo d'Arte Antica .... (see 3)
Museo degli Strumenti Musicali .... (see 3)
Museo della Preistoria .... (see 3)
Museo Teatrale alla Scala .... (see 7)
Pinacoteca di Brera 7 C3
Teatro alla Scala .... (see 7)

SLEEPING

Alle Meraviglie 8 B4
Ariston Hotel 9 B5

EATING

Il Brellin 10 A6
Peck Italian Bar 11 B4
Rinomata 12 A6

TRANSPORT

Bus Station 13 C2
Bus Stop for Starfly Buses to Linate Airport 14 C4
Malpensa Shuttle, Malpensa Express Bus & Autostradale Shuttle Buses 15 A4

Galleria Vittorio Emanuele II (p337)

PAOLO CORDELL

northwest of Milan. Domestic and some European flights use **Linate airport** (LIN; 02 748 52 200 www.sea-aeroportimilano.it), about 7km east of the city; and low-cost airlines are increasingly using **Orio al Serio airport** (BGY; 035 32 63 23; www.sacbo.it), near Bergamo.

Regular **trains** depart Stazione Centrale for Venice (€22, three hours, hourly), Florence (€26, 3½ hours, hourly), Rome (€45, six hours, hourly) and other Italian and European cities. Most regional trains stop at Stazione Nord in Piazzale Cadorna.

GETTING AROUND

TO/FROM THE AIRPORT

Malpensa Shuttle (☎ 02 585 98 31 85; www.malpensashuttle.it) coaches run to/from Piazza Luigi di Savoia next to Stazione Centrale every 20 minutes between 4.15am and 11.15pm. Tickets for the 50-minute journey cost €7/3.50 per adult/child one way (€12/5 return). **Malpensa Bus Express** (☎ 02 339 10 794) buses depart half-hourly from the same piazza between 4.15am and 11.15pm; tickets cost €7.50 one way and the trip takes 50 minutes.

By train, take the **Malpensa Express** (☎ 02 851 14 382; www.malpensaexpress.it) from Cadorna underground station – there are hourly or half-hourly departures between 5.57am and 8.57pm (buses take over from 10.27pm to 5am). The 50-minute journey costs €11.

For Linate, **Starfly** (☎ 02 585 87 237) buses depart from Piazza Luigi di Savoia half-hourly between 5.40am and 9.30pm; tickets cost €4.50 and journey time is 30 minutes.

Autostradale (☎ 035 31 84 72; www.autostradale.it) run half-hourly buses from Piazza Luigi di Savoia to Orio al Serio between 4am and 11.30pm; the journey lasts one hour and tickets cost €8.90.

BUS & METRO

Milan's excellent public transport system is run by **ATM** (www.atm-mi.it). Tickets (€1), are valid for one underground ride or up to 75 minutes travel on city buses and trams.

VENICE

pop 269,000

Venice (Venezia) is a hauntingly beautiful city. At every turn you're assailed by unforgettable images – tiny bridges crossing limpid canals, delivery barges jostling chintzy gondolas, tourists posing under flocks of pigeons. The reality of modern Venice is, however, a city besieged by rising tides and up to 20 million visitors a year.

HISTORY

Venice's origins date to the 5th and 6th centuries when barbarian invasions forced the Veneto's inhabitants to seek refuge on the lagoon's islands. First ruled by the Byzantines from Ravenna, it wasn't until AD 726 that the Venetians elected their first *doge* (duke). Over successive centuries, the Venetian Republic grew into a great merchant power, dominating half the Mediterranean, the Adriatic and the trade routes to the Levant – it was from Venice that Marco Polo set out for China in 1271.

ORIENTATION

With 117 islands, 150-odd canals and 400 bridges (only three of which – the Rialto, the Accademia and, at the train station, the Scalzi – cross the Grand Canal) it's impossible not to get a bit lost.

It gets worse. Instead of a street and civic number, local addresses often consist of no more than the *sestiere* (Venice is divided into six districts: Cannaregio, Castello, San Marco, Dorsoduro, San Polo and Santa Croce) followed by a long number. Some, however, do have street names and where possible we've provided them. You'll still need to know that a street can be a *calle, ruga* or *salizada;* beside a canal it's a *fondamenta*. A canal is a *rio*, a filled canal-turned-street a *rio terrà*, and a square a *campo* (Piazza San Marco is Venice's only piazza).

INFORMATION

Pick up the free *Shows & Events* guide at tourist offices. It contains comprehensive city listings and a useful public transport map on the inside back cover. The tourist offices also sell a useful map of the city (€2.50).

Azienda di Promozione Turistica (**Venice Tourist Board; ☎ central information line 041 529 87 11; www.turismovenezia.it**) Lido (**Gran Viale Santa Maria Elisabetta 6a; ⌚ 9am-noon & 3-6pm Jun-Sep**); Marco Polo airport (**Arrivals Hall; ⌚ 9am-9pm**); Piazza San Marco (**Piazza San Marco 71f; ⌚ 9am-3.30pm**); Piazzale Roma (**⌚ 9.30am-4.30pm Jun-Sep**); train station (**⌚ 8am-6.30pm**).

Ospedale Civile (**Hospital; ☎ 041 529 41 11; Campo SS Giovanni e Paolo 6777**)

Police station (**Questura; ☎ 041 274 70 70; Fondamenta di San Lorenzo, Castello 5053**)

SIGHTS

PIAZZA SAN MARCO

Piazza San Marco beautifully encapsulates the splendour of Venice's past and its tourist-fuelled present. Flanked by the arcaded **Procuratie Vecchie** and **Procuratie Nuove**, it's filled for much of the day with tourists, pigeons, balloon-vendors and policemen. While you're taking it all in, you might see the bronze *mori* (Moors) strike the bell of the 15th-century **Torre dell'Orologio** (clock tower).

But it's to the remarkable **Basilica di San Marco** (**St Mark's Basilica; ☎ 041 522 52 05; Piazza San Marco; admission free; ⌚ 9.45am-5pm Mon-Sat, 2-4pm Sun Apr-Sep, 9.45am-4.45pm Mon-Sat, 2-4.30pm Sun Oct-Mar**) that all eyes are drawn. Sporting spangled spires, Byzantine domes, luminous mosaics and lavish marble work, it was originally built to house the remains of St Mark. He's since

VENICE

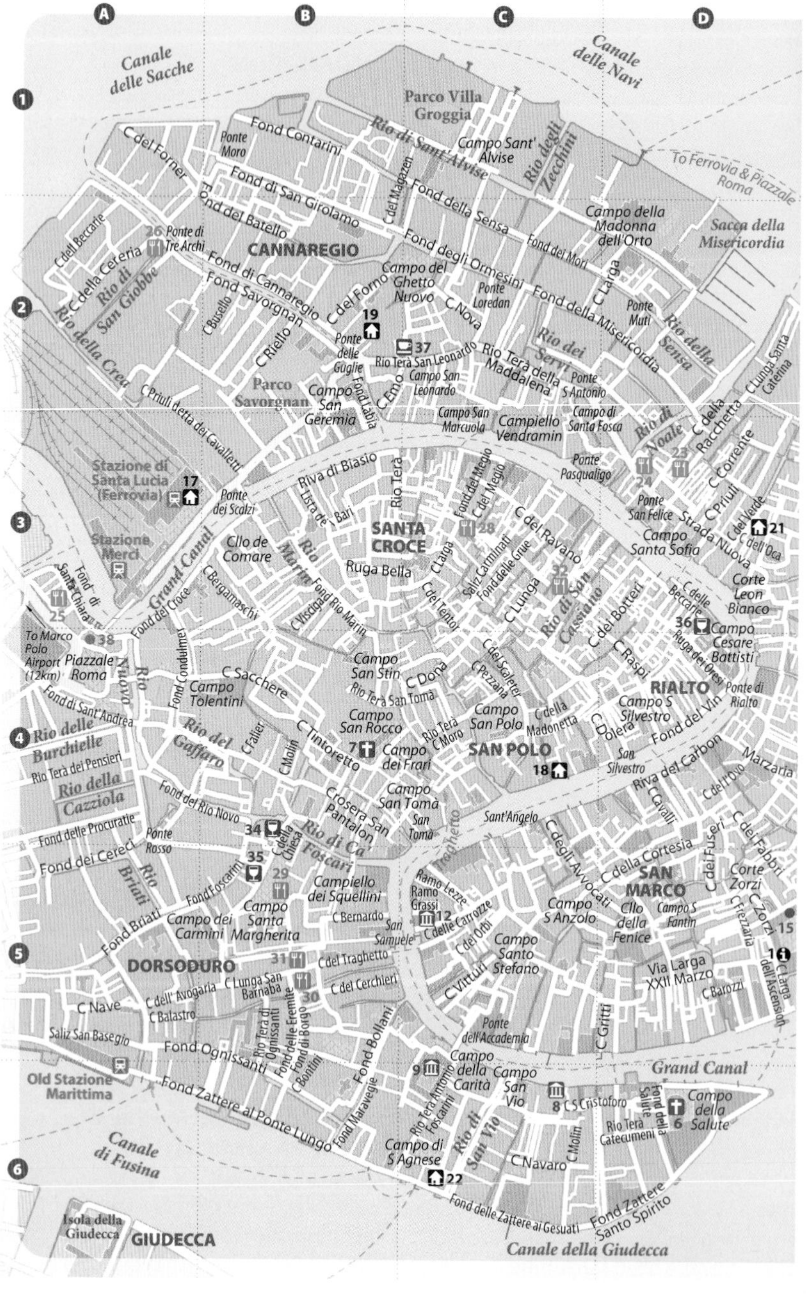
A
B
C
D
1
2
3
4
5
6
Canale delle Sacche
Canale delle Navi
Parco Villa Groggia
Rio di Sant'Alvise
Campo Sant' Alvise
Rio degli Zecchini
To Ferrovia & Piazzale Roma
C del Forner
Ponte Moro
Fond Contarini
Fond di San Girolamo
Fond del Batello
C del Magazen
Fond della Sensa
Campo della Madonna dell'Orto
Sacca della Misericordia
Fond dei Mori
C dell Beccarie
26 Ponte di Tre Archi
C della Ceteria
Rio di San Giobbe
CANNAREGIO
Fond di Cannaregio
Fond Savorgnan
Campo del Ghetto Nuovo
Fond degli Ormesini
Ponte Loredan
C Nova
C Larga
Fond della Misericordia
Ponte Muti
Rio della Sensa
Rio della Crea
C Busello
C Riello
C del Forno
19
Ponte delle Guglie
37
Rio Terà San Leonardo
Campo San Leonardo
Rio Terà della Maddalena
Rio dei Servi
Ponte S Antonio
C Lunga Santa Caterina
C Priuli detta dei Cavalletti
Parco Savorgnan
Campo San Geremia
Fond Labia
C Emo
Campo San Marcuola
Campiello Vendramin
Campo di Santa Fosca
Rio di Noale
C della Racchetta
C Corrente
Stazione di Santa Lucia (Ferrovia)
17
Ponte dei Scalzi
Riva di Biasio
Rio Terà
Fond del Megio
C del Megio
Ponte Pasqualigo
24
23
Ponte San Felice
C Priuli
Strada Nuova
C del Verde
21
C dell'Oca
Campo Santa Sofia
Stazione Merci
Lista de Bari
SANTA CROCE
28
C del Ravano
Cllo de Comare
Rio Marin
Ruga Bella
C Larga
Saliz Carminati
Fond delle Grue
32
Rio di San Cassiano
C dei Botteri
C delle Beccarie
Corte Leon Bianco
Fond di Santa Chiara
25
Grand Canal
Fond del Croce
C Bergamaschi
Fond Rio Marin
C Visciga
C del Tentor
C Lunga
36
Campo Cesare Battisti
Ruga dei Oresi
To Marco Polo Airport (12km)
38
Piazzale Roma
Rio Nuovo
Fond Condulmer
C Sacchere
Campo San Stin
C Dona
C del Scaleter
C Pezzana
C Raspi
RIALTO
Ponte di Rialto
Campo Tolentini
Rio Terà San Tomà
Campo San Rocco
Rio Terà C Moro
Campo San Polo
C della Madonetta
Campo S Silvestro
C Dolera
Fond del Vin
Fond di Sant'Andrea
Rio delle Burchielle
Rio Terà dei Pensieri
Rio del Gaffaro
C Falier
C Molin
C Tintoretto
7
Campo dei Frari
SAN POLO
18
San Silvestro
Riva del Carbon
C dell'Ovo
Marzaria
Rio della Cazziola
Fond del Rio Novo
Crosera San Pantalon
Campo San Tomà
San Tomà
Traghetto
Sant'Angelo
C Cavalli
C dei Fuseri
C dei Fabbri
Fond delle Procuratie
Ponte Rosso
34
C della Chiesa
Rio di Ca' Foscari
C degli Avvocati
C della Cortesia
SAN MARCO
Corte Zorzi
C Zorzi
C Frezzaria
Fond dei Cereci
Rio Briati
35
Fond Foscarini
29
Campiello dei Squellini
Ramo Lezze
Ramo Grassi
12
C delle Carrozze
Campo S Anzolo
Cllo della Fenice
Campo S Fantin
15
Fond Briati
Campo dei Carmini
Campo Santa Margherita
C Bernardo
San Samuele
C dei Orbi
Campo Santo Stefano
1
C Larga dell'Ascension
DORSODURO
31
C del Traghetto
C Vitturi
Via Larga XXII Marzo
C Barozzi
C Nave
C dell' Avogaria
C Balastro
C Lunga San Barnaba
30
C del Cerchieri
Rio Terà di Ognissanti
Fond delle Eremite
Fond di Borgo
C Bontini
Ponte dell'Accademia
C Gritti
Saliz San Basegio
Fond Ognissanti
Fond Bollani
9
Campo della Carità
Campo San Vio
Grand Canal
Old Stazione Marittima
Fond Zattere al Ponte Lungo
Fond Maravegie
Rio Terà Antonio Foscarini
Rio di San Vio
8
C S Cristoforo
Fond della Salute
6
Campo della Salute
Rio Terà Catecumeni
C Molin
Canale di Fusina
Campo di S Agnese
C Navaro
22
Fond delle Zattere ai Gesuati
Fond Zattere Santo Spirito
Isola della Giudecca
GIUDECCA
Canale della Giudecca

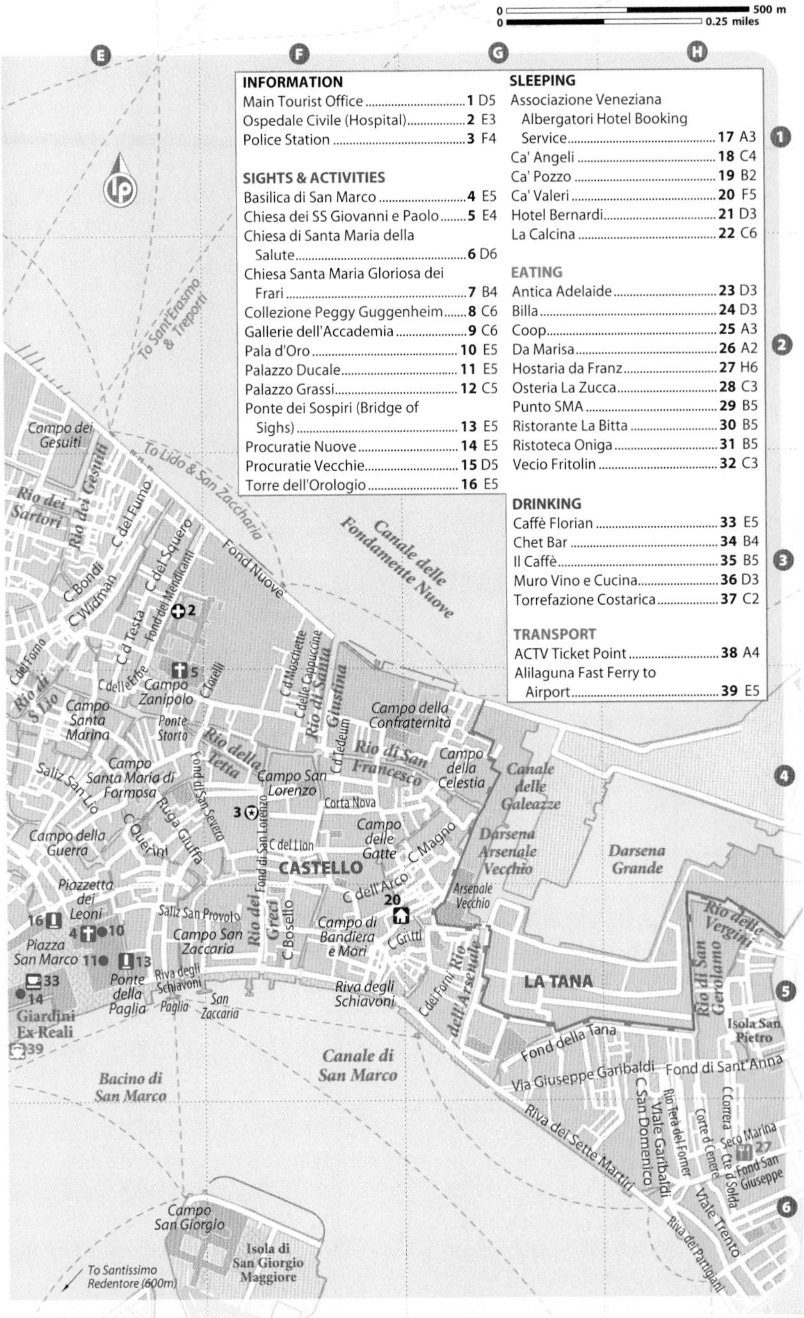

INFORMATION
Main Tourist Office 1 D5
Ospedale Civile (Hospital) 2 E3
Police Station 3 F4

SIGHTS & ACTIVITIES
Basilica di San Marco 4 E5
Chiesa dei SS Giovanni e Paolo 5 E4
Chiesa di Santa Maria della Salute 6 D6
Chiesa Santa Maria Gloriosa dei Frari 7 B4
Collezione Peggy Guggenheim 8 C6
Gallerie dell'Accademia 9 C6
Pala d'Oro 10 E5
Palazzo Ducale 11 E5
Palazzo Grassi 12 C5
Ponte dei Sospiri (Bridge of Sighs) 13 E5
Procuratie Nuove 14 E5
Procuratie Vecchie 15 D5
Torre dell'Orologio 16 E5

SLEEPING
Associazione Veneziana Albergatori Hotel Booking Service 17 A3
Ca' Angeli 18 C4
Ca' Pozzo 19 B2
Ca' Valeri 20 F5
Hotel Bernardi 21 D3
La Calcina 22 C6

EATING
Antica Adelaide 23 D3
Billa 24 D3
Coop 25 A3
Da Marisa 26 A2
Hostaria da Franz 27 H6
Osteria La Zucca 28 C3
Punto SMA 29 B5
Ristorante La Bitta 30 B5
Ristoteca Oniga 31 B5
Vecio Fritolin 32 C3

DRINKING
Caffè Florian 33 E5
Chet Bar 34 B4
Il Caffè 35 B5
Muro Vino e Cucina 36 D3
Torrefazione Costarica 37 C2

TRANSPORT
ACTV Ticket Point 38 A4
Alilaguna Fast Ferry to Airport 39 E5

been buried several times, his body now resting under the high altar. Behind the main altar is the **Pala d'Oro** (**admission €2; 9.45am-5pm Mon-Sat, 2-4.30pm Sun Apr-Sep, to 4pm Oct-Apr**), a stunning gold altarpiece decorated with priceless jewels.

The basilica's 99m freestanding **campanile** (**bell tower; adult/child €8/4; 9am-7pm Apr-Jun, Sep & Oct, to 9pm Jul & Aug, 9.30am-4.15pm Nov-Mar**) dates from the 10th century, although it suddenly collapsed on 14 July 1902 and had to be rebuilt. A lift takes you to the top.

ADMISSION DISCOUNTS

The **Rolling Venice Card** (**€4**) is for visitors aged 14 to 29 years; it offers discounts on food, accommodation, shopping, transport and museums. You'll need ID.

The **Venice Card** (**www.venicecard.it; under 30yr 3/7 days €53.50/76, 30yr & over €62/85**) covers Venice's civic museums, the 16 Chorus churches, use of ACTV public transport, discounted car parking and use of public toilets. It's cheaper online.

To visit the museums on Piazza San Marco you'll need to buy either a **Museum Pass** (**041 240 52 11; www.museicivicivenezia ni.it; adult/under 5yr/6-14yr/EU citizen €18/free/12/12**), which gives entry to the museums on Piazza San Marco and six other civic museums; or a **San Marco Plus Ticket** (**adult/child/student €13/free/7.50**), which gives entry to the San Marco Museums and your choice of one other civic museum.

The **Chorus Pass** (**041 275 04 62; www.chorusvenezia.org; adult/student under 29yr/family €9/6/18**) covers admission to 16 of Venice's major churches.

PALAZZO DUCALE

The official residence of the *doges* from the 9th century and the seat of the Republic's government and bureaucracy, **Palazzo Ducale** (**Doge's Palace; 041 271 59 11; Piazzetta di San Marco; admission with Museum Pass or San Marco Plus Ticket; 9am-7pm Apr-Oct, to 5pm Nov-Mar**) also housed Venice's prisons. On the 2nd floor, the massive **Sala del Maggiore Consiglio** (Grand Council Hall) is dominated by Tintoretto's *Paradiso* (Paradise), one of the world's largest oil paintings, which measures 22m by 7m.

The **Ponte dei Sospiri** (Bridge of Sighs) connects the palace to an additional wing of the city dungeons. It's named after the sighs that prisoners – including Giacomo Casanova – emitted en route from court to cell.

GALLERIA DELL'ACCADEMIA

One of Venice's top galleries, the **Galleria dell'Accademia** (**041 522 22 47; Dorsoduro 1050; adult/child/concession €6.50/free/3.50; 8.15am-2pm Mon, to 7.15pm Tue-Sun**) traces the development of Venetian art from the 14th to the 18th century. You'll find works by Bellini, Titian, Carpaccio, Tintoretto, Giorgione and Veronese.

COLLEZIONE PEGGY GUGGENHEIM

For something more contemporary, visit the **Collezione Peggy Guggenheim** (**041 240 54 11; www.guggenheim-venice.it; Palazzo Venier dei Leoni, Dorsoduro 701; adult/child/student/senior €10/free/5/8; 10am-6pm Wed-Mon**). Housed in the American heiress's former home, the spellbinding collection runs the gamut of modern art with works by, among others, Bacon, Pollock, Picasso and Dalí. In the sculpture garden you'll find the graves of Peggy and her dogs.

ALLAN MONTAINE

Outdoor cafes in Piazza San Marco (p341)

PALAZZO GRASSI

In 2005 French businessman and art collector François Pinault purchased one of the Grand Canal's most impressive buildings, the 18th-century **Palazzo Grassi** (☎ 041 523 16 80; www.palazzograssi.it; Campo San Samuele 3231; adult/student & child €10/6; ⏲ 10am-7pm Wed-Mon), and commissioned Japanese architect Tadeo Ando to renovate the building. Since opening it has housed his extensive and eclectic collection of modern art and hosted impressive temporary exhibitions.

CHURCHES

As in much of Italy, Venice's churches harbour innumerable treasures; unusually, though, you have to pay to get into many of them. See the boxed text, opposite, for details of the Chorus Pass, which gives admission to 16 of the most important.

Scene of the annual Festa del Redentore (see p346), the **Santissimo Redentore** (Church of the Redeemer; Campo del SS Redentore 194; admission €3; ⏲ 10am-5pm Mon-Sat, 1-6pm Sun) was built by Palladio to commemorate the end of the Great Plague in 1577.

Guarding the entrance to the Grand Canal, the 17th-century **Chiesa di Santa Maria della Salute** (☎ 041 522 55 58; Campo della Salute 1/b; sacristy €2; ⏲ 9am-noon & 3.30-6pm) contains works by Tintoretto and Titian. Arguably the greatest of Venice's artists, Titian's celebrated masterpiece the *Assunta* (Assumption; 1518) hangs above the high altar in the **Chiesa di Santa Maria Gloriosa dei Frari** (Campo dei Frari, San Polo 3004; admission €3; ⏲ 9am-6pm Mon-Sat, 1-6pm Sun), the same church in which he's buried.

Some way to the east, the vast Gothic **Chiesa dei SS Giovanni e Paolo** (☎ 041 523 59 13; Campo SS Giovanni e Paolo; admission €3; ⏲ 9.30am-7pm Mon-Sat, 1-6pm Sun) is famous for its glorious 15th-century stained-glass window, the largest in Venice.

ISLANDS

Murano is the home of Venetian glass. Tour a factory for a behind-the-scenes look at production or visit the **Glass**

Museum (☎ 041 73 95 86; Fondamenta Giustinian 8; adult/student €5.50/3; ⏰ 10am-4.30pm Thu-Tue Nov-Mar, 10am-6pm Apr-Oct); you'll find it near the Museo *vaporetto* stop. **Burano**, with its cheery pastel-coloured houses, is renowned for its lace. **Torcello**, the republic's original island settlement, was largely abandoned due to malaria and now counts no more than 80 residents. Its not-to-be-missed Byzantine cathedral, **Santa Maria Assunta** (☎ 041 270 24 64; Piazza Torcello; adult/child €4/3; ⏰ 10.30am-6pm Mar-Oct, 10am-5pm Nov-Feb), is Venice's oldest.

Vaporetto 41 (and *vaporetto* 5 in summer only) services Murano from the San Zaccaria *vaporetto* stop. *Vaporetto* LN services all three islands from the *vaporetto* stop at Fondamente Nuove in the northeast of the city. *Vaporetto* T connects Burano and Torcello.

HOLGER LEUE

Venetian glass, Murano (p345)

ACTIVITIES

Be prepared to pay through the nose for that most quintessential of Venetian experiences, a **gondola ride**. Official rates per gondola (maximum six people) start at €80 (€100 at night) for a short trip including the Rialto but not the Grand Canal, and €120 (€150 at night) for a 50-minute trip including the Grand Canal. Haggling may or may not get you a reduction.

FESTIVALS & EVENTS

Carnevale The major event of the year, when some Venetians and loads of tourists don Venetian-made masks and costumes for a weeklong party in the lead-up to Ash Wednesday.

Palio delle Quattro Repubbliche Marinare Venice, Amalfi, Genoa and Pisa take turns to host this historic regatta. It's in Venice in early June 2011.

Venice Biennale This major exhibition of international visual arts is held every odd-numbered year from June to November.

Festa del Redentore Held on the third weekend in July; celebrations climax with a spectacular fireworks display.

Venice International Film Festival (Mostra del Cinema di Venezia) Italy's top film fest is held in late August and September at the Lido's Palazzo del Cinema.

Regata Storica Costumed parades precede gondola races on the Grand Canal; held on the first Sunday in September.

SLEEPING

Venice is Italy's most expensive city. It's always advisable to book ahead, especially at weekends, in May and September, and during Carnevale and other holidays. At the train station, the **Associazione**

Veneziana Albergatori (☎ 800 843 006; ☻ 8am-10pm Easter-Oct, to 9pm Nov-Easter) will book you a room for a small fee.

Hotel Bernardi (☎ 041 522 72 57; www. hotelbernardi.com; SS Apostoli Calle dell'Oca, Cannaregio 4366; s €55, d with shared bathroom €55-70, d with private bathroom €80-110; ☒) Comfortable rooms, hospitable owners and keen prices mean that this top choice is always heavily booked.

La Calcina (☎ 041 520 64 66; www.lacalcina. com; Fondamenta Zattere ai Gesuati, Dorsoduro 780; s €65-110, d €99-225; ☒ ▯) A charming place with 29 rooms and a small garden, La Calcina offers immaculate and elegant rooms with parquet floors and timber furnishings.

Ca' Valeri (☎ 041 241 15 30; www.locandaca valeri.com; Ramo Corazzieri, Castello 3845; r €69-169, ste €79-179; ☒) The drawcard here is an extremely quiet location and beautifully decorated rooms with excellent bathrooms. And there's only one way to describe the low-season prices – a total steal.

ourpick **Ca' Angeli** (☎ 041 523 24 80; www. caangeli.it; Calle del Tragheto della Madoneta, San Polo 1434; s €80-150, d €105-215, ste €195-315; ☒) A fabulous choice overlooking the Grand Canal, Ca' Angeli is notable for its extremely comfortable rooms, helpful staff and truly magnificent breakfast spread.

Ca' Pozzo (☎ 041 524 05 04; www.capozzo venice.com; Sotoportego Ca'Pozzo, Cannaregio 1279; s €90-175, d €120-205; ☒ ▯) Its motto is 'accommodation and art', and this very stylish boutique hotel in the Ghetto melds the two perfectly. Rooms are decorated with a minimalist aesthetic but have all the mod cons you'll need; some have a private terrace or courtyard.

EATING

Venetian specialities include *risi e bisi* (pea soup thickened with rice) and *sarde di saor* (fried sardines marinated in vinegar and onions).

Antica Adelaide (☎ 041 523 26 29; Calle Priuli, Cannaregio 3728; meals €30) The ancient Adelaide was (under different names) in the food business as far back as the 18th century. You can pop in for a drink and *cicheti* (bar snacks) or tuck into a hearty bowl of pasta or full meal.

Osteria La Zucca (☎ 041 524 15 70; Calle del Tentor, Santa Croce 1762; meals €32; ☻ closed Sun) A wonderful, unpretentious little restaurant in an out-of-the-way spot, 'The Pumpkin' serves a range of innovative Mediterranean dishes prepared with fresh, seasonal ingredients.

Da Marisa (☎ 041 72 02 11; Fondamenta di San Giobbe 652b, Cannaregio; set menu incl wine & coffee €35-40; ☻ lunch daily, dinner Tue & Thu-Sat) You can watch the sun setting over the lagoon from the canal-side tables here. Devotees overlook the fact that service can be brusque, meal times are set (noon and 8pm), credit cards aren't accepted and there's no opportunity to vary the daily menu, which is mostly meat but sometimes seafood.

Ristorante La Bitta (☎ 041 523 05 31; Calle Lunga San Barnaba, Dorsoduro 2753a; meals €40; ☻ closed Sun) The bottle-lined dining room and attractive internal courtyard are a lovely setting in which to enjoy your choice from a small, meat-dominated menu that changes with the season. No credit cards.

Ristoteca Oniga (☎ 041 522 44 10; Campo San Barnaba, Dorsoduro 2852; meals €46; ☻ closed Tue) Its food and ambience are top-class, but its service is possibly the worst we encountered in Venice (and that's saying a lot). In the end, we decided that the superb homemade pasta dishes and piazza setting came up trumps.

Vecio Fritolin (☎ 041 522 28 81; Calle della Regina, Santa Croce 2262; meals €50; ☻ dinner

Tue, lunch & dinner Wed-Mon) Traditionally, a *fritolin* was an eatery where diners sat at a common table and tucked into fried seafood and polenta. This is the modern equivalent, only the food is sophisticated, the menu is varied and the decor is stylish rather than rustic.

our pick **Hostaria da Franz** (**☎ 041 522 70 24; Calle del Pestrin, Castello 3886; meals €70-90)** Expensive? Yes. Elegant? Excessively. Delicious? You said it! This is one of the best seafood restaurants in the city, and it's also world-renowned for its creamy tiramisu.

For fruit and veg, as well as deli items, head for the markets near the Rialto bridge, or on the Rio Terà San Leonardo. There are also supermarkets: **Punto Sma** (**Campo Santa Margherita**), **Billa** (**Strada Nova, Cannaregio 3660**) and **Coop** (**Fondamenta di Santa Chiara, Piazzale Roma 506a**).

DRINKING

Chet Bar (**☎ 041 523 87 27; Campo Santa Margherita, Dorsoduro 3684**) Late at night, patrons at this laid-back drinking den spill out of the bar and sit on the steps of the nearby bridge. It's one of the most popular venues on buzzing Campo Santa Margherita.

Il Caffè (**☎ 041 528 79 98; Campo Santa Margherita, Dorsoduro 2963**) Popular with foreign and Italian students, this is one of Venice's historic drinking spots. Known to locals as Café Rosso because of its red frontage, it's got outdoor seating and great *sprizze* (a type of apéritif).

Muro Vino e Cucina (**☎ 041 523 47 40; Campo Cesare Battisti, San Polo 222; closed Sun**) The centre of a happening nightlife scene in the market squares of the Rialto.

Caffè Florian (**☎ 041 520 56 41; Piazza San Marco 56/59**) If you think it's worth paying up to four times the usual price for a coffee, emulate Byron, Goethe and Rousseau and pull up a seat at Piazza San Marco's most famous cafe.

Torrefazione Costarica (**☎ 041 71 63 71; Rio Terá San Leonardo, Cannaregio 1337**) Connoisseurs come here for Venice's best coffee.

GETTING THERE & AWAY

AIR

Most European and domestic flights land at **Marco Polo airport** (**VCE; ☎ 041 260 92 60; www.veniceairport.it**), 12km outside Venice. Ryanair flies to **Treviso airport** (**TSF; ☎ 0422 31 51 11; www.trevisoairport.it**), about 30km from Venice.

BOAT

Minoan Lines (**☎ 041 240 71 01; www.minoan.gr**) runs ferries to Corfu (€69 to €91, 23½ hours), Igoumenitsa (€69 to €91, 22 hours) and Patra (€69 to €182, 36 hours) daily in summer and four times per week in winter.

BUS

ACTV (**☎ 041 24 24; www.actv.it**) buses service surrounding areas, including Mestre, Padua and Treviso. Tickets and information are available at the bus station in Piazzale Roma.

TRAIN

Venice's Stazione di Santa Lucia is directly linked by regional trains to Padua (€2.90, 45 minutes, every 20 minutes), Verona (€13.50, 1½ hours, half-hourly) and Ferrara (€6.15, two hours, half-hourly).

GETTING AROUND

TO/FROM THE AIRPORT

To get to Marco Polo there are various options: **Alilaguna** (**www.alilaguna.com**) operates a fast ferry service from the San Marco ferry stop (€12, 70 minutes, approximately every hour); alternatively, from Piazzale

SEAN CAFFREY

San Gimignano

IF YOU LIKE...

Fallen for the eye-popping architecture of Venice (p341) and Pisa (p358)? Here are a few more archetypal Italian towns you might like to seek out.

- Caserta Caserta's monumental castle, the Palazzo Reale (**☎ 0823 44 80 84; Corso Pietro Giannone 1; adult/concession €6/3; 8.30am-7pm Wed-Mon**) is known as the Italian Versailles and boasts 1200 rooms, 1790 windows and 34 staircases.
- Verona Shakespeare set *Romeo and Juliet* in romantic Verona, and you can get your picture snapped on Juliet's balcony at the Casa di Giulietta (**☎ 045 803 43 03; Via Cappello 23; courtyard free, museum adult/child/concession €6/1/4.40; 8.30am-7.30pm Tue-Sun, 1.30-7.30pm Mon**).
- San Gimignano This tiny Tuscan town is dubbed 'the medieval Manhattan' thanks to its distinctive 11th-century towers. The tallest, Torre Grossa, offers unforgettable Tuscan views. Regular buses link San Gimignano with Florence and Siena.
- Matera Set atop two rocky gorges, Matera is famous for its *sassi* (cave dwellings), where Mel Gibson filmed *The Passion of the Christ*. Buses run from Rome's Stazione Tiburtina.
- Urbino Birthplace of Raphael and Bramante, this Unesco-listed town boasts one of Italy's oldest universities and a fabulous Palazzo Ducale (**☎ 0722 32 26 25; Piazza Duca Federico; adult/concession €8/4; 8.30am-7.15pm Tue-Sun, to 2pm Mon**). Trains don't run to Urbino, although buses go to Rome.
- Lucca Puccini's birthplace is a love-at-first-sight type of place, founded by the Etruscans and famous for its 12m-high city walls. Regular buses and trains run to Florence and Pisa.
- Lecce The 'Florence of the South' is known for its opulent *barocco leccese* (Lecce baroque) style of architecture. Direct trains go to Rome, Bari and points throughout Puglia.

Roma take either an **ATVO** (☎ **041 520 55 30; www.atvo.it, in Italian**) bus (€3, 20 minutes, every half-hour) or ACTV bus 5d (€2, 25 minutes, every half-hour).

For Treviso airport, take the ATVO Ryanairbus (€5, 70 minutes, 16 daily) from Piazzale Roma two hours and 10 minutes before your flight departure. The last service is at 7.40pm.

BOAT

The city's main mode of public transport is the *vaporetto*. The most useful routes:

1 From Piazzale Roma to the train station and down the Grand Canal to San Marco and the Lido.
2 From S Zaccaria (near San Marco) to the Lido via Giudecca, Piazzale Roma, the train station and the Rialto.
3 From Piazzale Roma to San Marco via the Rialto and Accademia.
17 Car ferry between Tronchetto and the Lido.
LN From Fondamenta Nuove to Murano, Burano and Torcello.
T Runs between Burano and Torcello.

Tickets, available from ACTV booths at the major *vaporetti* stops, are expensive: €6.50 for a single trip; €14 for 12 hours; €16 for 24 hours; €21 for 36 hours; €26 for 48 hours and €31 for 72 hours (€18 if you have a Rolling Venice card).

BOLOGNA

pop 374,000

Boasting a boisterous bonhomie rare in Italy's reserved north, Bologna is worth a few days of anyone's itinerary, not so much for its specific attractions, but for the sheer fun of strolling its animated, arcaded streets. Bologna is also famous as one of the country's foremost foodie destinations. Besides the eponymous bolognese sauce *(ragù)*, classic pasta dishes such as tortellini and lasagne wer invented here, as was mortadella (ak baloney or Bologna sausage).

INFORMATION

Ospedale Maggiore (**Hospital;** ☎ **051 64 81 11**)

Police station (**Questura;** ☎ **051 640 11 11 Piazza Galileo 7**)

Tourist information (☎ **051 23 96 60 www.bolognaturismo.info**) airport (**8am 8pm**); Piazza Maggiore 1 (**9.30am 7.30pm**); train station (**9am-7pm Mon-Sat 9am-3pm Sun**) Ask for a copy of the free *b* 'what's on' booklet.

SIGHTS & ACTIVITIES

Bologna's porticoed *centro storico* is a vibrant and atmospheric place to wander The place to start is pedestrianised **Piazza Maggiore** and adjoining **Piazza del Nettuno**. Here you'll find the **Fontana del Nettuno** (Neptune's Fountain), sculpted by Giambologna in 1566 and featuring an impressively muscled Neptune. On the western flank of Piazza Maggiore is the **Palazzo Comunale** (**Town Hall;** ☎ **051 20 31 11; admission free**), home to the **Collezioni Comunali d'Arte** (**Civic Art Collection; admission free;** **9am-3pm Tue-Fri, 10am-6.30pm Sat & Sun**) and a museum dedicated to the work of artist **Giorgio Morandi** (**admission free,** **9am-3pm Tue-Fri, 10am-6.30pm Sat & Sun**).

To the south, the Gothic **Basilica di San Petronio** (☎ **051 22 54 22; Piazza Maggiore;** **7.45am-12.30pm & 3-6pm**) is dedicated to the city's patron saint, Petronius.

It's a short walk to **Piazza di Porta Ravegnana** and Bologna's two leaning towers, the **Due Torri**. The taller of the two, the 97m **Torre degli Asinelli** (**admission €3;** **9am-6pm, to 5pm winter**), was built between 1109 and 1119 and is now open to the public. Climb the 498 steps for some superb city views.

Of the city's other churches, the **Basilica di San Domenico** (☎ 051 640 04 11; Piazza San Domenico; 8am-12.30pm & 3.30-7.30pm) is noteworthy for the elaborate sarcophagus of San Domenico, founder of the Dominican order.

For tombs of an altogether more sober style, head for the **Museo Civico Archeologico** (☎ 051 275 72 11; Via dell'Archiginnasio 2; admission free; 9am-3pm Tue-Fri, 10am-6.30pm Sat & Sun), which houses one of Italy's best Etruscan collections.

The recently opened **Museo d'Arte Moderna do Bologna** (MAMBO, Museum of Modern Art; ☎ 051 649 66 11; Via Don Minzoni 14; admission free; 10am-6pm Tue, Wed & Fri-Sun, to 10pm Thu) is in a converted bakery in Bologna's new – and very impressive – arts and culture precinct.

SLEEPING & EATING

Hotel Novecento (☎ 051 745 73 11; www.bolognarthotels.it; 3rd fl, Piazza Galileo 4; s €90-230, d €140-328;) Decorated in the Viennese Succession style, this chic boutique offering is one of four hotels and one studio apartment run by Bologna Art Hotels. Of the five, the Orologico is the cheapest.

Hotel Accademia (☎ 051 23 23 18; www.hotelaccademia.it; Via delle Belle Arti 6; s €100-128, d €155-180;) A good option in the thick of the university quarter, the three-star Accademia has fresh, tastefully decorated rooms with wi-fi and satellite TV.

Pizzerie Belle Arti (☎ 051 22 55 81; Via Belle Arti 14; pizzas from €4.50, meals €25) This sprawling place near the university serves delicious thin-crust pizzas that deserve the descriptor 'the best in Bologna'.

Osteria de'Poeti (☎ 051 23 61 66; Via de' Poeti 1b; meals €32; closed Mon, lunch Sun) In the cellar of a 14th-century *palazzo*, this atmospheric place is a bastion of old-style service and top-notch Emilia-Romagna cuisine.

MAX PAOLI & RUTH EASTHAM

Piazza Maggiore

our pick **Drogheria della Rosa** (☎ 051 22 25 29; Via Cartoleria 10; meals €45; Mon-Sat) Its wooden shelves and apothecaries' jars and bottles signal this trattoria's former life as a *drogheria* (pharmacy). Claim a table to enjoy a set menu of antipasto (including mortadella), a selection of excellent pasta dishes and wonderful meat or fish *secondi*. There's no menu, but the friendly English-speaking owner will happily describe the daily offerings.

Two of the best *gelaterie* in Italy can be found here (and yes, we realise that's one heck of a call). Sample the stuff on offer at **Gelateria Stefino** (Via Galleria 49b; noon-12.30am) and **La Sorbetteria Castiglione** (Via Castiglione 44; 8.30am-10.30pm Tue-Fri, 9am-midnight Sat, 9am-10.30pm Sun) and we're sure you'll agree with us.

GETTING THERE & AROUND

European and domestic flights arrive at Bologna's **Guglielmo Marconi airport** (BLQ; ☎ 051 647 96 15; www.bologna-airport.it), 6km northwest of the city. An Aerobus shuttle (€5, 30 minutes, three times hourly) departs from the main train station; buy your ticket at the ACTV office behind the taxi rank. Ryanair flies to **Forlì** (FRL; ☎ 0543 47 49 21; www.forli-airport.it), 70km southeast of Bologna. **Ebus** (☎ 199 11 55 77) buses run between Forlí and the main train station to coincide with flights. The trip takes 1½ hours and costs €10.

From the **main train station** (Piazza delle Medaglie d'Oro), trains run to Venice (€15.10, two hours, half-hourly), and to the following on the fast Eurostar Alta Velocità (ES AV) trains: Florence (€16.20, one hour, hourly), Rome (€45.60, 2¾ hours, hourly) and Milan (€33, one hour, hourly).

THE DOLOMITES

Stretching across Trentino-Alto Adige and into the Veneto, the stabbing sawtooth peaks of the Dolomites provide some of Italy's most thrilling scenery. With their jagged silhouettes and colourful tints (blue-grey turning to red, then purple as the sun sets), they are popular all year – in winter for the skiing, in summer for the superb hiking. The best online resource option is www.dolomiti.org, which has a great deal of useful information.

In Trentino-Alto Adige, **Bolzano airport** (BZO; ☎ 0471 25 52 55; www.abd-airport.it) is served by ski charter flights from the UK in winter and daily year-round flights from Rome and Milan. Otherwise the nearest airports are in Verona or Bergamo.

On terra firma, the area's excellent bus network is run by **Trentino Trasporti** (☎ 0461 82 10 00; www.ttspa.it, in Italian) in Trent; **SAD** (☎ 800 84 60 47; www.sii.bz.it) in Alto Adige; and **Dolomiti Bus** (www.dolomitibus.it, in Italian) in the Veneto. During winte most resorts offer 'ski bus' services.

TUSCANY

Tuscany is one of those places that we and truly lives up to its press. Its fable rolling landscape has long been con sidered the embodiment of rural chic, favourite of holidaying PMs and retire advertising executives, while its citie are home to a significant portfolio of th world's medieval and Renaissance art.

FLORENCE

pop 366,000

Poets of the 18th and 19th centurie swooned at the beauty of Florenc (Firenze), and once here you'll appreci ate why. An essential stop on everyone' Italian itinerary, this Renaissance treasur trove is busy year-round. Fortunately, th huge crowds fail to diminish the city' lustre.

A rich merchant city by the 12th cen tury, its golden age arrived in the 15tl century. Under the Medici prince Lorenz il Magnifico (1469–92), the city's cultura artistic and political fecundity culminate in the Renaissance.

INFORMATION

Police station (Questura; ☎ 055 497 71; Vi Zara 2)

Tourist Medical Service (☎ 055 47 54 11 Via Lorenzo il Magnifico 59; 24hr)

Tourist offices (www.firenzeturismo.it main office (☎ 055 29 08 32; Via Cavour 1r 8.30am-6.30pm Mon-Sat, to 1.30pm Sun) airport (☎ 055 31 58 74; 8.30am-8.30pm) Borgo Santa Croce 29r (☎ 055 234 04 44 9am-7pm Mon-Sat, to 2pm Sun Mar–mid-Nov 9am-5pm Mon-Sat, to 2pm Sun mid-Nov–Feb) Piazza della Stazione 4 (☎ 055 21 22 45 www.commune.fi.it; 8.30am-7pm Mon-Sat to 2pm Sun)

FLORENCE

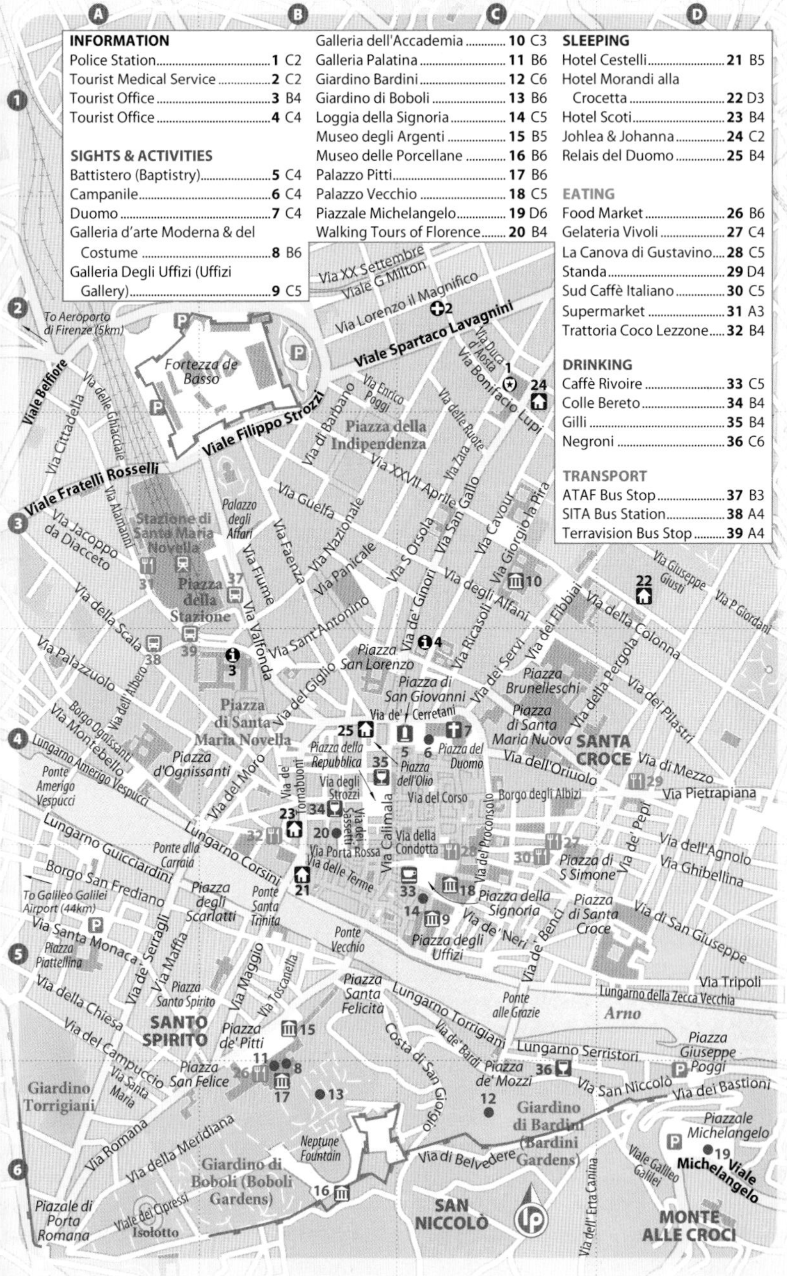

INFORMATION
- Police Station ... 1 C2
- Tourist Medical Service ... 2 C2
- Tourist Office ... 3 B4
- Tourist Office ... 4 C4

SIGHTS & ACTIVITIES
- Battistero (Baptistry) ... 5 C4
- Campanile ... 6 C4
- Duomo ... 7 C4
- Galleria d'arte Moderna & del Costume ... 8 B6
- Galleria Degli Uffizi (Uffizi Gallery) ... 9 C5
- Galleria dell'Accademia ... 10 C3
- Galleria Palatina ... 11 B6
- Giardino Bardini ... 12 C6
- Giardino di Boboli ... 13 B6
- Loggia della Signoria ... 14 C5
- Museo degli Argenti ... 15 B5
- Museo delle Porcellane ... 16 B6
- Palazzo Pitti ... 17 B6
- Palazzo Vecchio ... 18 C5
- Piazzale Michelangelo ... 19 D6
- Walking Tours of Florence ... 20 B4

SLEEPING
- Hotel Cestelli ... 21 B5
- Hotel Morandi alla Crocetta ... 22 D3
- Hotel Scoti ... 23 B4
- Johlea & Johanna ... 24 C2
- Relais del Duomo ... 25 B4

EATING
- Food Market ... 26 B6
- Gelateria Vivoli ... 27 C4
- La Canova di Gustavino ... 28 C5
- Standa ... 29 D4
- Sud Caffè Italiano ... 30 C5
- Supermarket ... 31 A3
- Trattoria Coco Lezzone ... 32 B4

DRINKING
- Caffè Rivoire ... 33 C5
- Colle Bereto ... 34 B4
- Gilli ... 35 B4
- Negroni ... 36 C6

TRANSPORT
- ATAF Bus Stop ... 37 B3
- SITA Bus Station ... 38 A4
- Terravision Bus Stop ... 39 A4

JEAN-PIERRE LESCOURRET

Galleria degli Uffizi

GALLERIA DEGLI UFFIZI (UFFIZI GALLERY)

Home to the world's greatest collection of Italian Renaissance art, the Galleria degli Uffizi attracts some 1.5 million visitors annually. They won't all be there when you visit, but unless you've booked a ticket (see Firenze Musei, below), expect to queue.

The gallery houses the Medici family collection, bequeathed to the city in 1743 on the condition that it never leave the city. Highlights include *La nascita di Venere* (Birth of Venus) and *Allegoria della primavera* (Allegory of Spring) in the Botticelli Rooms (10 to 14); Leonardo da Vinci's *Annunciazione* (Annunciation; room 15); Michelangelo's *Tondo doni* (Holy Family; Room 25); and Titian's *Venere d'Urbino* (Venus of Urbino; Room 28). Elsewhere you'll find works by Giotto and Cimabue, Filippo Lippi, Fra Angelico and Paolo Uccello, Raphael, Andrea del Sarto, Tintoretto and Caravaggio.

Things you need to know: **☎ 055 238 86 51; www.uffizi.firenze.it; Piazza degli Uffizi 6; admission €10; 8.15am-6.35pm Tue-Sun**

SIGHTS & ACTIVITIES

Sightseeing in Florence inevitably means time spent in queues. You'll never avoid them altogether, but by pre-booking museum tickets you'll save time. For €4 extra per museum you can book tickets for the Uffizi, Palazzo Pitti, Galleria dell'Accademia and Cappelle Medicee through **Firenze Musei** (**☎ 055 29 48 83; www.firenzemusei.it; booking service 8.30am-7pm Tue-Sun**). Buy or collect your tickets from the information desks at the Uffizi or Palazzo Pitti.

PIAZZA DEL DUOMO & AROUND

Pictures don't do justice to the exterior of Florence's Gothic **Duomo** (**☎ 055 230 28 85; 10am-5pm Mon-Wed & Fri, 10am-3.30pm Thu, 10am-4.45pm Sat, 10am-3.30pm 1st Sat of every month, 1.30-4.45pm Sun**). Its most famous feature, the enormous octagonal **cupola** (**dome; admission €6; 8.30am-6.20pm Mon-Fri,** to 5pm Sat) was built by Brunelleschi after his design won a public competition in 1420. The interior is decorated with frescoes by Vasari and Zuccari, and the stained-glass windows are by Donatello, Paolo Uccello and Lorenzo Ghiberti. The facade is a 19th-century replacement of the unfinished original, pulled down in the 16th century.

Beside the cathedral, the 82m campanile (admission €6; 8.30am-6.50pm Nov-May, to 10.20pm Jun-Oct) was begun by Giotto in 1334 and completed after his death by Andrea Pisano and Francesco Talenti. The views from the top make the 414-step climb worthwhile.

To the west, the Romanesque battistero (baptistery; Piazza di San Giovanni; admission €3; 12.15-6.30pm Mon-Sat, 8.30am-1.30pm 1st Sat of every month, 8.30am-1.30pm Sun) is one of the oldest buildings in Florence and it was here that Dante was baptised.

PIAZZA DELLA SIGNORIA

Traditional hub of Florence's political life, Piazza della Signoria is dominated by Palazzo Vecchio (☎ 055 276 82 24; adult/child/concession €6/2/4.50; 9am-7pm Fri-Wed, to 2pm Thu), the historical seat of the Florentine government. Visit the Michelozzo courtyard and the lavish upstairs apartments.

To the south, the famous Loggia della Signoria is a 14th-century sculpture showcase. The statue of *David* is a copy of Michelangelo's original, which stood here until 1873 but is now in the Galleria dell'Accademia (right).

PALAZZO PITTI

Built for the Pitti family, great rivals of the Medici, the vast 15th-century Palazzo Pitti (☎ 055 238 86 14; Piazza de' Pitti) was bought by the Medici in 1549 and became their family residence. Today it houses four museums, of which the Galleria Palatina (Palatine Gallery; ☎ 055 238 86 14; adult/concession €12/6, ticket valid 3 days; 8.15am-6.50pm Tue-Sun) is the most important. Works by Raphael, Filippo Lippi, Titian and Rubens adorn lavishly decorated rooms, culminating in the royal apartments. Three other museums – the Museo degli Argenti (Silver Museum), the Museo delle Porcellane (Porcelain Museum) and the Galleria d'arte Moderna & del Costume (Modern Art & Costume Gallery) are also here. A group ticket (adult/EU citizen 18-25yr €10/5) gets you in to all three, as well as the Giardino di Boboli (Boboli Gardens) and Giardino Bardini (Bardini Gardens). All sights covered by the ticket are open from 8.15am to 7.30pm June to August, to 6.30pm March to May and September, to 5.30pm in October, and to 4.30pm November to February.

GALLERIA DELL'ACCADEMIA

The people queuing outside Galleria dell' Accademia (☎ 055 238 86 09; Via Ricasoli 60; adult/concession €6.50/3.25, incl temporary exhibition €10/5; 8.15am-6.50pm Tue-Sun) are waiting to see *David*, arguably the Western world's most famous sculpture. Michelangelo carved the giant figure from a single block of marble, finishing it in 1504 when he was just 29. The gallery also displays paintings by Florentine artists spanning the 13th to 16th centuries and regularly hosts temporary exhibitions.

TOURS

Walking Tours of Florence (☎ 055 264 50 33; www.italy.artviva.com; Via de' Sassetti 1; tours per person from €25) offers a range of city tours, all led by English-speaking guides.

FESTIVALS & EVENTS

Scoppio del Carro (Explosion of the Cart) A cart full of fireworks is exploded in front of the Duomo on Easter Sunday.

Maggio Musicale Fiorentino (**www.maggiofiorentino.com**) Italy's longest-running music festival held from April to June.

Festa di San Giovanni (Feast of St John) Florence's patron saint is celebrated on 24 June with costumed soccer matches on Piazza di Santa Croce.

SLEEPING

Although there are hundreds of hotels in Florence, it's still prudent to book ahead.

Hotel Scoti (**☎ 055 29 21 28; www.hotelscoti.com; Via de' Tornabuoni 7; s €45-75, d €75-125**) On Florence's smartest shopping strip, the friendly Scoti is a gem. Housed in a 16th-century *palazzo,* it has an amazing frescoed living room and comfortable, characterful rooms.

our pick **Relais del Duomo** (**055 21 01 47; www.relaisdelduomo.it, in Italian; Piazza dell'Olio 2; s €50-80, d €60-120;**) Florentine B&Bs don't come much better than this one. Located in the shadow of the Duomo, it has four light and airy rooms with attractive furnishings and lovely little bathrooms.

Hotel Cestelli (**☎ 055 21 42 13; www.hotelcestelli.com; Borgo SS Apostoli 25; s with shared bathroom €60-80, d with private bathroom €100-115;**) The Cestelli gets rave reviews in innumerable guidebooks for good reason. Run by Florentine photographer Alessio and his Japanese partner Asumi, it offers attractively decorated rooms and as much friendly and informed advice about Florence as you could possibly need.

Johlea & Johanna (**☎ 055 463 32 92; www.johanna.it; Via San Gallo 80; s €70-120, d €85-175;**) This highly regarded B&B has more than a dozen tasteful, individually decorated rooms housed in five historic residences.

Hotel Morandi alla Crocetta (**☎ 055 234 47 47; www.hotelmorandi.it; Via Laura 50; s €110-140, d €177-220; P**) This medieval convent-turned-hotel, away from the madding crowds, is a stunner. Rooms are charmingly decorated (try for the frescoed No 29) and extremely well equipped, with added features such as wi-fi. Breakfast costs €12.

EATING

Classic Tuscan dishes include *ribollita,* a heavy vegetable soup, *cannellini* (white beans) and *bistecca alla Fiorentina* (Florentine steak served rare). Chianti is the local tipple.

Sud Caffé Italiano (**☎ 055 28 93 68; Via della Vigna Vecchia; pasta €8-10.50, pizza €9.50; closed Sun & Mon**) An ode to southern-Italian-style casual chic, this place is perfect for a simple meal of pasta or pizza washed down by your choice from an impressive list of wines by the glass.

our pick **La Canova do Gustavino** (**☎ 055 239 98 06; Via della Condotta 29r; meals €20**) There aren't too many opportunities to enjoy a delicious cheap meal in stylish surrounds here in Florence, which is why this friendly *enoteca* is such a find. The adjoining restaurant (meal €42; open for dinner Monday to Friday, lunch and dinner Saturday and Sunday) offers a more sophisticated menu.

Trattoria Coco Lezzone (**☎ 055 28 71 78; Vai Parioncino 26r; meals €25; closed Sun**) The name means 'the slovenly chef', but there's nothing slovenly about this cheerful Florentine institution. Classic Tuscan fare such as *ribollita* (Tuscan soup), *arista di maiale* (roasted pork loin) and *papa al pomodoro* (tomato and bread soup) take centre stage. No credit cards accepted and, bizarrely, no coffee.

Gelateria Vivoli (☎ 055 29 23 34; Via dell'Isola delle Stinche 7; closed Mon & mid-Aug) Ice-cream aficionados rate the gelati here the city's best – we'd go as far as to say that it's up there with the best in the country.

Fresh produce is available at the central **food market** (Piazza San Lorenzo; 7am-2pm Mon-Sat). Alternatively, there's a **supermarket** (Stazione di Santa Maria Novella) at the train station, and a **Standa** (Via Pietrapiana 94) east of Piazza del Duomo.

DRINKING

our pick **Caffè Rivoire** (☎ 055 21 44 12; Piazza della Signoria; closed Mon & 2nd half Jan) Famous for its chocolate (try a cup of the hot stuff), Rivoire's terrace has the best view in the city.

Colle Bereto (☎ 055 28 31 56; Piazza Strozzi 5r) Slip into something Dolce & Gabbana and join the fashionistas at this glam bar. It's known for excellent cocktails and a lavish *aperitivo* spread.

Gilli (☎ 055 21 38 96; Piazza della Repubblica 39r; closed Mon & Tue) The city's grandest cafe, Gilli has been serving excellent coffee and delicious cakes since 1733.

Negroni (☎ 055 24 36 47; Via dei Renai 17r) The famous Florentine cocktail gives its name to this popular bar in the trendy San Nicolò district.

GETTING THERE & AWAY

The main airport serving Florence is Pisa's **Galileo Galilei airport** (PSA; ☎ 050 84 93 00; www.pisa-airport.com). There's also a small city airport 5km north of Florence, **Aeroporto di Firenze** (Aeroporto Vespucci, FLR; ☎ 055 306 13 00; www.aeroporto.firenze.it).

The **SITA bus station** (☎ 800 37 37 60; www.sitabus.it, in Italian; Via Santa Caterina da Siena 17) is just south of the train station. Buses leave for Siena (€6.80, 1½ hours, every 30 to 60 minutes) and San Gimignano (€6, 1¼ hours, 14 daily).

Florence is well connected by train. There are regular services to/from Pisa (Regionale €5.60, 1¼ hours, every 10 to 30 minutes), Rome (Eurostar AV, €36.50,

MARTIN MOOS

Florence skyline, with the Duomo (p354) on the right

70 minutes, hourly), Bologna (Eurostar AV, €16.20, one hour, hourly), Venice (Eurostar €32.30, 2¾ hours, 10 daily) and Milan (Eurostar AV, €16.20, one hour, hourly).

GETTING AROUND

Terravision (☎ **06 321 20 011; www.terravision.it**) runs a bus service between the train station and Galileo Galilei airport (adult/child five to 12 €8/4, 70 minutes, 12 daily). Otherwise there are regular trains (€5.10, 1½ hours, hourly between 6.37am and 8.37pm).

Volainbus (☎ **800 42 45 00; www.ataf.net**) runs a shuttlebus (€4.50, 25 minutes, half-hourly from 5.30am to 11pm) connecting Florence airport with the SITA bus station.

ATAF (☎ **800 42 45 00; www.ataf.net**) buses service the city centre and Fiesole, a small town in the hills 8km northeast of Florence. Take bus 7 for Fiesole, and 12 or 13 for Piazzale Michelangelo. Tickets (70 minute/24 hour €1.20/5) are sold at *tabacchi* and newsstands – you can also buy a 70-minute ticket on board the bus (€2).

PISA

One of Italy's most recognisable monuments, the **Leaning Tower of Pisa** (**Torre Pendente; www.opapisa.it; admission €15, plus booking fee €2; 10am-7pm Nov-Feb, 9am-6pm Mar, 8.30am-8.30pm Apr-Sep, 9am-7pm Oct**) is a genuinely astonishing sight. Bonanno Pisano began building in 1173, but almost immediately his plans came a cropper in a layer of shifting soil. Only three of the tower's seven tiers were completed before it started tilting – continuing at a rate of about 1mm per year. By 1990 the lean had reached 5.5 degrees – a tenth of a degree beyond the critical point established by computer models. Stability was finally ensured in 1998 when a combination of biased weighting and soil drilling forced the tower into a safer position. Visits are limited to groups of 30; entry times are staggered and queuing is predictably inevitable. It is wise to book ahead.

Regular trains run to Florence (Regionale €5.60, 1¼ hours, every 10 to 30 minutes), Rome (Regionale €17.15, four hours, five daily) and Genoa (€15, two hours, half-hourly).

SIENA

pop 53,900

Famous for its annual horse race (Il Palio), Siena is one of Italy's most enchanting medieval towns. Its walled centre, a beautifully preserved warren of dark lanes punctuated by Gothic *palazzi*, piazzas and eye-catching churches, is a lovely place to get lost.

Ever since the 14th century, the slanting, shell-shaped **Piazza del Campo** has been the city's civic centre. Forming the base of the piazza, the **Palazzo Pubblico** (Palazzo Comunale) is a magnificent example of Sienese Gothic architecture. Inside, the **Museo Civico** (☎ **0577 29 26 14; adult/child/concession €7.50/free/4.50; 10am-7pm mid-Mar–Oct, to 6pm Nov-mid–Mar**) houses some extraordinary frescoes, including Simone Martini's famous *Maestà* (Virgin Mary in Majesty) and Ambroglio Lorenzetti's *Allegories of Good and Bad Government*. Soaring above the *palazzo* is the 102m **Torre del Mangia** (**admission €7; 10am-7pm mid-Mar–end Oct, to 4pm Nov-mid–Mar**), which dates from 1297. A combined ticket to the two costs €12 and is only available at the Torre del Mangia ticket office.

The spectacular **Duomo** (☎ **0577 473 21; admission €3; 10.30am-8pm Mon-Sat, 1.30-6pm Sun mid-Mar–Sep, 10.30am-7.30pm Mon-Sat, 1.30-6pm Sun Oct, 10.30am-6.30pm Mon-Sat, 1.30-5.30pm Sun Nov-mid–Mar**) is another Gothic masterpiece. The striking facade of green,

DAVID TOMLINSON
Crowds in Piazza del Campo during Il Palio

red and white marble was designed by Giovanni Pisano, who also helped his dad, Nicola, craft the cathedral's intricate pulpit. Inside, it's the 14th-century **inlaid-marble floor** (viewing €6; 10.30am-7.30pm mid-Aug–Oct), decorated with 56 biblical panels, that's the highlight.

Behind the cathedral and down a flight of stairs, the **battistero** (baptistery; Piazza San Giovanni; admission €3; 9.30am-8pm Mar-Sep, to 7.30pm Oct, 10am-5pm Nov-Feb) has a Gothic facade and a rich interior of 15th-century frescoes.

FESTIVALS & EVENTS

Siena's great annual event is **Il Palio** (2 Jul & 16 August), a pageant culminating in a bare-back horse race round Il Campo. The city is divided into 17 *contrade* (districts), of which 10 are chosen annually to compete for the *palio* (silk banner).

SLEEPING

It's always advisable to book in advance, but for August and the Palio, it's essential.

Hotel Antica Torre (☎ 0577 22 22 55; www.anticatorresiena.it; Via di Fiera Vecchia 7; s €65-90, d €90-120;) Eight pretty rooms with Tuscan-style decor are on offer in a restored 16th-century tower; the two at the top offer spectacular views over the surrounding countryside (no lift).

Il Chiostro del Carmine (☎ 0577 22 34 76; www.chiostrodelcarmine.com; Via della Diana 4; r €129-189;) Sleeping in a 14th-century Carmelite Monastery is good postcard-writing fodder, but this choice just inside the Porta San Marco offers more than just atmosphere.

EATING & DRINKING

Pasticceria Nannini (☎ 0577 23 60 09; 24 Via Banchi di Sopra) For the finest *cenci* (fried sweet pastry), *panforte* (dense fruit and nut cake) and *ricciarelli* (almond biscuits) in town, enjoyed with a cup of excellent coffee, you need go no further than this Sienese institution.

La Chiacchiera (☎ 0577 28 06 31; Costa di Sant'Antonio 4; pasta €7, meals €18) With its rustic wooden tables and stone walls,

POMPEII

An ancient town frozen in its 2000-year-old death throes, Pompeii was a thriving commercial town until Mt Vesuvius erupted on 24 August AD 79, burying it under a layer of *lapilli* (burning fragments of pumice stone) and killing some 2000 people. The skeletal, Unesco-listed **ruins** (**☎ 081 857 53 47; www.pompeiisites.org; adult/concession €11/5.50, audio guides €6.50; 8.30am-7.30pm Apr-Oct, 8.30am-5pm Nov-Mar, last entry 1½ hr before closing**) provide a remarkable model of a working Roman city, complete with temples, a forum, an amphitheatre, apartments, a shopping district and a brothel. Dotted around the 44-hectare site are a number of creepy body casts, made in the late 19th century by pouring plaster into the hollows left by disintegrated bodies.

The easiest way to get to Pompeii is by the Ferrovia Circumvesuviana from Naples (€2.40, 35 minutes, half-hourly) or Sorrento (€1.90, 30 minutes, half-hourly).

this is an atmospheric spot. The food is seasonal, earthy and filling. In summer, there's outdoor seating on a quiet pedestrian street.

Hosteria Il Carroccio (**☎ 0577 411 65; Via del Casato di Sotto 32; meals €30; closed dinner Tue & Wed winter**) Recommended by the prestigious Slow Food movement (always a good sign), Il Carroccio specialises in traditional Sienese cooking.

GETTING THERE & AWAY

Siena is not on a main train line so it's easier to take a bus. From the bus station on Piazza Gramsci, **Train SpA** (**www.trainspa.it**) and SITA buses run to/from Florence (€6.80, 1½ hours, every 30 to 60 minutes), Pisa airport (€14, two daily) and San Gimignano (€5.30, 1¼ hours, hourly), either direct or via Poggibonsi.

Sena (**☎ 0577 28 32 03; www.sena.it**) operates services to/from Rome (€18.50, three hours, 10 daily).

SOUTHERN ITALY

A sun-bleached land of spectacular coastlines, silent, windswept hills and proud towns, southern Italy is an altogether more raw prospect than the manicured north. Its stunning scenery, graphic ruins and fabulous beaches often go hand in hand with urban sprawl and scruffy coastal development, sometimes in the space of a few kilometres.

AMALFI COAST

Stretching 50km along the southern side of the Sorrento Peninsula, the Amalfi Coast (Costiera Amalfitana) is a postcard vision of Mediterranean beauty. Against a shimmering blue backdrop, whitewashed villages and terraced lemon groves cling to vertiginous cliffs backed by the craggy Lattari mountains.

There are two main entry points to the Amalfi Coast: Sorrento and Salerno. Regular SITA buses run from Sorrento to Positano (€3, 50 minutes) and Amalfi (€6, 1½ hours) and from Salerno to Amalfi (€3, 1¼ hours).

Between April and September, **Metrò del Mare** (**☎ 199 600 700; www.metrodelmare.com**) runs boats from Naples to Sorrento (€6.50, 45 minutes), Positano (€14, 55 minutes) and Amalfi (€15, 1½ hours).

POSITANO

pop 3930

The best way to approach Positano, the coast's most expensive and glamorous town, is by boat. As you come into dock, feast your eyes on the unforgettable view of colourful, steeply stacked houses packed onto near-vertical green slopes. In town, the main activities are hanging out on the small beach and browsing the flamboyant shop displays.

Villa Maria Antonietta (☎ 089 87 50 71; Via C Colombo 41; r €80-100) Value for money is not something you can count on in Positano, but you'll get it here. All seven of the sunny, white-walled rooms look over a flower-filled terrace and, beyond that, the sea.

Villa Rosa (☎ 089 81 19 55; www.villarosapositano.it; Via C Colombo 127; d €160-240; Mar-Oct) This stylish little hotel has impeccable rooms decorated in classic coastal style, with white walls and cool, tiled floors. Some have private balconies, but if yours doesn't, just head along to the picturesque terrace.

RAVELLO

The refined, polished town of Ravello commands some of the finest views on the Amalfi Coast. A hairy 7km climb from Amalfi, it has been home to an impressive array of bohemians including Wagner, DH Lawrence, Virginia Woolf and Gore Vidal, whose former home can be seen on the bus ride up from Amalfi. The main attractions are the beautiful gardens at **Villa Cimbrone** and **Villa Ruffolo**. The **tourist office** (☎ 089 85 70 96; www.ravellotime.it; Via Roma 18bis; 9am-8pm) can provide details on these and Ravello's famous summer festival.

Regular SITA buses run from Amalfi to Ravello.

AMALFI

pop 5430

An attractive tangle of souvenir shops, dark alleyways and busy piazzas, Amalfi is the coast's main hub. Large-scale tourism has enriched the town, but it maintains a laid-back, small-town vibe, especially outside of the busy summer months.

Looming over the central piazza is the town's landmark **Duomo** (☎ 089 87 10 59; Piazza del Duomo; admission 10am-5pm €2.50,

STEPHEN SAKS

Marina Grande, Capri (p362)

7.30am-10am & 5pm-7.30pm free; 7.30am-7.30pm), one of the few relics of Amalfi's past as an 11th-century maritime superpower. Between 10am and 5pm, entry is through the adjacent Chiostro del Paradiso.

Four kilometres west of town, the **Grotta dello Smeraldo** (**admission €5; 9am-4pm**) is a haunting sea cave. Boat trips from Amalfi cost €10 return.

SLEEPING & EATING

Hotel Lidomare (**089 87 13 32; www.lidomare.it; Largo Duchi Piccolomini 9; s €50-65, d €70-135;**) Housed in a 14th-century building on a petite piazza, the Lidomare is a lovely, family-run hotel. The spacious rooms are full of character with majolica tiles and fine old antiques. Some also have jacuzzis and sea views.

Residence del Duca (**089 87 36 365; www.residencedelduca.it; Via Mastalo II Duca 3; s €60-70, d €80-160;**) Make it up the tricky staircase to the 3rd floor of this 10th-century *palazzo* and you'll be rewarded with a warm welcome and a smart room.

our pick **Pizzeria Donna Stella** (**338 358 84 83; Salita Rascica 2; pizzas from €5, mains €8; Tue-Sun**) It's well worth searching out this delightful back-alley pizzeria. Not only does it serve superb pizzas, but it also boasts one of Amalfi's loveliest settings – a delightful summer garden enclosed by jasmine-clad walls.

ISLAND ESCAPES

When you feel the urge to escape the mainland, Italy provides easy access to some of the Mediterranean's most fascinating islands.

First up is **Sicily**, a hotbed of rugged hills, sparkling beaches, Roman remains and Italian excess, dominated by the sputtering volcano of Mt Etna (3320m); regular flights and ferries arrive at Palermo, the island's capital and main transport hub. Even more idyllic are the seven **Aeolian Islands** (Isole Eolie), whose windswept mountains, hissing volcanoes and rich waters have been seducing visitors since Odysseus' time.

The traditional holiday island for many Italians is **Sardinia**, synonymous with exclusive beach resorts and sky-high prices. While it's true that the 55km-long Costa Meralda (Emerald Coast) is one of the priciest destinations on the Med, Sardinia's coast stretches for 1850km, and much of it is still undeveloped – but visit out of season unless you're a fan of crowds. The easiest route to the islands is via air: Sardinia's three main airports are in Cagliari, Alghero and Olbia, or you can catch a ferry from various Italian ports, including Civitavecchia, Genoa, Livorno, Naples and Palermo.

The most visited of Naples' Bay islands, **Capri** is far more interesting than a quick day trip would suggest. Get beyond the glamorous veneer of chichi piazzas and designer boutiques and you'll discover an island of rugged seascapes, desolate Roman ruins and a surprisingly unspoiled rural inland. The island's most famous attraction is the **Grotta Azzurra** (**Blue Grotto; admission €4; 9am-1hr before sunset**), a stunning sea cave illuminated by an other-worldly blue light. Year-round ferries to Capri depart from Naples and Sorrento; in summer, hydrofoils connect Capri with Positano and Amalfi.

Trattoria San Giuseppe (☎ 089 87 26 40; Salita Ruggiero II 4; pizzas €6, meals €30; ⏰ Fri-Wed) A long-standing favourite, this bustling trattoria-pizzeria is touristy but the food is good. The menu is typical of the coast, so expect plenty of seafood, thick-crust Neapolitan pizza and calorie-heavy desserts.

DIRECTORY

ACTIVITIES

CYCLING

Italy offers everything from tough mountain biking to gentle valley rides. Tuscany and Umbria are favourite spots, particularly around Florence (p352) and Siena (p358). Further north, the Dolomites (p352) and northern lakes are popular with mountain-bikers, as is Sardinia's rugged interior.

DIVING

Transparent topaz waters and a spiky, volcanic geology make for spectacular diving. Dive hot spots include Lipari, one of Sicily's Aeolian Islands (p362), and the Golfo di Orosei on the eastern coast of Sardinia (p362), where you can investigate caves rich in sea life.

HIKING & WALKING

Thousands of kilometres of *sentieri* (marked trails) criss-cross Italy. In the high season (the end of June to September), the Dolomites (p352) are a favourite destination. Other popular areas include the Cinque Terre (p337), Amalfi Coast (p360) and Mt Etna in Sicily (p362).

SKIING

Most of the country's top ski resorts are in the Alps, although there are excellent facilities throughout the Apennines. Skiing isn't cheap, and high-season (December to March) costs will hit your pocket hard. The best way to save money is to buy a *settimana bianca* (literally 'white week') package deal, covering seven days' accommodation, food and ski passes.

DANGERS & ANNOYANCES

The greatest risk visitors face in Italy is from pickpockets and bag snatchers. Pickpockets follow the tourists, so be on your guard in popular centres such as Rome, Florence and Venice. Be especially vigilant on public transport. Watch out for gangs of dishevelled-looking kids, and for moped thieves.

Another insidious form of theft is short-changing. This takes various forms but typically goes as follows: you pay for a €3 panino with a €20 note. The cashier then distractedly gives you a €2 coin and a €5 note before turning away. The trick here is to wait and chances are that the €10 note you're waiting for will appear without a word being said.

Road rules are obeyed with discretion, so don't take it for granted that cars will stop at red lights.

EMBASSIES & CONSULATES

The embassies and consulates are in Rome.

Australia (Map pp316-17; ☎ 06 85 27 21, emergencies 800 87 77 90; www.italy.embassy.gov.au; Via Antonio Bosio 5; ⏰ 8.30am-5pm Mon-Fri)

Austria Embassy (Map pp320-1; ☎ 06 844 01 41; www.bmeia.gv.at/it/ambasciata/roma; Via Pergolesi 3); Consulate (Map pp316-17; ☎ 06 855 28 80; Viale Liegi 32; ⏰ 9am-noon Mon-Fri)

Canada Embassy (Map pp316-17; ☎ 06 85 44 41; www.international.gc.ca/canada-europa/italy; Via Salaria 243) Consulate (Map pp316-17; ☎ 06 85 44 41; Via Zara 30; ⏰ 8.30am-noon, 2-4pm Mon-Fri)

France Embassy (Map pp324-5; ☎ 06 68 60 11; www.ambafrance-it.org; Piazza Farnese 67) Consulate (Map pp324-5; ☎ 06 68 60 11; Via Giulia 251; 🕑 9am-12.30pm Mon-Fri)
Germany (Map pp316-17; ☎ 06 49 21 31; www.rom.diplo.de; Via San Martino della Battaglia 4; 🕑 8.30-11.30am Mon-Fri)
Ireland (Map pp324-5; ☎ 06 697 91 21; www.ambasciata-irlanda.it; Piazza Campitelli 3; 🕑 10am-12.30pm, 3-4.30pm Mon-Fri)
Netherlands (Map pp316-17; ☎ 06 322 86 001; www.olanda.it; Via Michele Mercati 8; 🕑 9am-noon Mon, Tue, Thu & Fri)
New Zealand (Map pp316-17; ☎ 06 853 75 01; www.nzembassy.com; Via Clitunno 44; 🕑 8.30am-12.45pm & 1.45-5pm Mon-Fri)
Switzerland (Map pp316-17; ☎ 06 80 95 71; www.eda.admin.ch/roma; Via Barnarba Oriani 61; 🕑 9am-noon Mon-Fri)
UK (Map pp316-17; ☎ 06 4220 0001; www.britishembassy.gov.uk/italy; Via XX Settembre 80a; 🕑 9am-5pm Mon-Fri)
USA (Map pp320-1; ☎ 06 4 67 41; www.usis.it; Via Vittorio Veneto 119a; 🕑 8.30am-12.30pm Mon-Fri)

FESTIVALS & EVENTS

FEBRUARY, MARCH & APRIL

Carnevale In the period before Ash Wednesday, many towns stage carnival celebrations. The best known is in Venice (see p346).
Settimana Santa Italy celebrates Holy Week with processions and passion plays. On Easter Sunday, the pope gives a traditional blessing in St Peter's Square, Rome.
Scoppio del Carro A cart full of fireworks is exploded in Florence's Piazza del Duomo on Easter Saturday (see p356).

MAY-SEPTEMBER

Palio delle Quattro Antiche Repubbliche Marinare (Regatta of the Four Ancient Maritime Republics) Boat races between the four historical maritime republics – Pisa, Venice, Amalfi and Genoa. The event rotates between the towns and is usually held in June.
Il Palio On 2 July and 16 August, Siena stages its extraordinary bareback horse race.
Venice International Film Festival (Mostra del Cinema di Venezia) The international film glitterati disembark at Venice Lido for the annual film fest (see p346).

HOLIDAYS

Most Italians take their annual holiday in August. This means that many businesses and shops close down for at least a part of the month, usually around *Ferragosto* (15 August). Easter is another busy holiday.

Public holidays include the following:
New Year's Day (Capodanno) 1 January
Epiphany (Epifania) 6 January
Easter Monday (Pasquetta) March/April
Liberation Day (Giorno delle Liberazione) 25 April
Labour Day (Festa del Lavoro) 1 May
Republic Day (Festa della Repubblica) 2 June
Feast of the Assumption (Ferragosto) 15 August
All Saint's Day (Ognisanti) 1 November
Feast of the Immaculate Conception (Immacolata Concezione) 8 December
Christmas Day (Natale) 25 December
Boxing Day (Festa di Santo Stefano) 26 December

Individual towns also have holidays to celebrate their patron saints:
St Mark (Venice) 25 April
St Janarius (Naples) First Sunday in May, 19 September and 16 December

St John the Baptist (Florence, Genoa and Turin) 24 June
Saints Peter and Paul (Rome) 29 June
St Rosalia (Palermo) 15 July
St Ambrose (Milan) 7 December

MONEY

Italy's currency is the euro. ATMs (known in Italy as *bancomat*) are widespread and will accept cards displaying the appropriate sign. If your credit card is lost, stolen or swallowed by an ATM, telephone toll free to block it:

Amex (☎ 800 914 912)
MasterCard (☎ 800 870 866)
Visa (☎ 800 81 90 14)

POST

Italy's postal system, **Poste** (☎ 803 160; www.poste.it, in Italian), is not the world's most efficient, but it has improved in recent years. The standard service is *posta prioritaria,* which costs €0.60 for a normal letter. Registered mail is known as *posta raccomandata,* insured mail as *posta assicurato.*

Francobolli (stamps) are available at post offices and *tabacchi* (tobacconists) – look for the official sign, a big white 'T' against a black background.

TELEPHONE

Local and long-distance calls can easily be made from public phones by using a phonecard. Peak rates apply from 8am to 6.30pm Monday to Friday and until 1pm on Saturday. To make a reverse-charge (collect) international call, dial ☎ 170. All operators speak English.

MOBILE PHONES

Italy uses the GSM 900/1800 network, which is compatible with the rest of Europe and Australia, but not with the North American GSM 1900 or the Japanese system (although some GSM 1900/900 phones do work here).

Companies offering SIM cards include **TIM** (Telecom Italia Mobile; www.tim.it), **Wind** (www.wind.it) and **Vodafone** (www.vodafone.it).

PHONE CODES

Mobile phone numbers begin with a three-digit prefix such as 330 or 339; toll-free (free-phone) numbers are known as *numeri verdi* and usually start with 800; national call rate numbers start with 848 or 199. Some six-digit national rate numbers are also in use.

Area codes are an integral part of all Italian phone numbers, meaning that you must always use them, even when calling locally.

PHONECARDS

To phone from a public payphone you'll need a *scheda telefonica* (telephone card), although you'll still find some that accept credit cards and coins. You can buy phonecards (€5, €10, €20) at post offices, *tabacchi* and newsstands.

TRAVELLERS WITH DISABILITIES

Italy is not an easy country for disabled travellers. Cobbled streets, blocked pavements and tiny lifts all make life difficult. Rome-based **Consorzio Cooperative Integrate** (COIN; ☎ 06 232 69 231; www.coinsociale.it) is the best point of reference for disabled travellers. You can also check out www.romapertutti.it and www.milanopertutti.it for information on Rome and Milan.

For those travelling by train, **Trenitalia** (www.trenitalia.com) runs a telephone info line (☎ 199 30 30 60) with details of assistance available at stations.

TRANSPORT

GETTING THERE & AWAY

AIR

Alitalia, Italy's national carrier, was saved from bankruptcy in late 2008 by a consortium of private investors who bought the company from the Italian government. It has since merged with Air One, but both Alitalia and Air One continue to operate.

Air One (AP; ☎ 199 207 080; www.flyairone.it)

Alitalia (AZ; ☎ 06 22 22; www.alitalia.it)

LAND

BUS

A consortium of 32 European coach companies, **Eurolines** (☎ 055 35 70 59; www.eurolines.com) operates across Europe with offices in all major European cities. Italy-bound buses head to Ancona, Florence, Rome, Siena and Venice.

CAR & MOTORCYCLE

Traversing the Alps into Italy, the main, year-round routes are the Mont Blanc tunnel from France; the Grand St Bernard tunnel and the new Lötschberg Base tunnel from Switzerland; and the Brenner Pass from Austria. All three connect with major *autostrade* (motorways).

When driving into Italy always carry proof of ownership of a private vehicle. You'll also need third-party motor insurance.

TRAIN

International trains connect with various cities, including the following:

Milan To/from Barcelona, Nice, Paris, Amsterdam, Zürich, Munich, Frankfurt and Vienna.

Rome To/from Paris, Munich and Vienna.

Venice To/from Paris, Zürich, Munich, Vienna, Prague, Ljubljana, Zagreb, Belgrade, Budapest and Bucharest.

There are also international trains from Genoa, Turin, Verona, Bologna, Florence and Naples. Details are available online at www.trenitalia.com. **Cisalpino** (www.cisalpino.com) operates daily fast trains from Milan and Venice to Switzerland.

For details of Eurail and Inter-Rail passes, both valid in Italy, see p796.

SEA

Dozens of ferry companies connect Italy with virtually every other Mediterranean country. For details of routes, companies and online booking log onto **Traghettionline** (www.traghettionline.net). Holders of Eurail and Inter-Rail passes should check with the ferry company if they are entitled to a discount or free passage.

Regional ferry companies:

Agoudimos (☎ 0831 52 90 91; www.agoudimos-lines.com) Bari to Igoumenitsa (€70, 10 to 12 hours), Patra (€70, 16½ hours) and Kefallonia (€70, 15½ hours) in Greece; Brindisi to Corfu (€75, 6½ hours) in Greece.

Corsica Sardinia Ferries (☎ 199 400 500; www.sardiniaferries.com) Rome to Golfo Aranci, Sardinia.

Endeavor Lines/Hellenic Mediterranean Lines (☎ 0831 52 85 31; www.hml.it) Brindisi to Igoumenitsa (€66, eight hours), Patra (€70, 14 hours), Corfu (€66, 11½ hours) and Kefallonia (€80, 12½ hours) in Greece.

Grandi Navi Veloci (☎ 010 209 45 91; www.gnv.it) Genoa to Barcelona (€99, 18 hours) in Spain and Tunis (€151, 24 hours) in Tunisia.

Grimaldi Lines (☎ 091 58 74 04; www.grimaldi.it) Rome to Barcelona, Toulon in France and Tunis in Tunisia.

Jadrolinija (☎ Croatia +385 51 666 111; www.jadrolinija.hr) Ancona to Split (€63.50, 11 hours); Bari to Dubrovnik (€63.50, 7½ hours) in Croatia.
Minoan Lines (☎ 041 504 12 01; www.minoanlines.it) Ancona to Igoumenitsa (€103, 16 hours) and Patra (€103, 22 hours); Venice to Corfu (€106, 22 hours), Igoumenitsa (€106, 23½ hours) and Patra (€106, 29½ hours).
SNAV (☎ 081 428 55 55; www.snav.it) Ancona to Split (€90, 4½ hours) in Croatia; Brindisi to Corfu (€80, 5½ hours) in Greece; Rome to Palermo and Olbia.
Superfast Ferries (☎ 899 92 92 06; www.superfast.com) Ancona to Igoumenitsa (€108, 15 hours) and Patra (€108, 21 hours) in Greece; Bari to Igoumenitsa (€85, 9½ hours) and Patra (€85, 15½ hours) in Greece.
Tirrenia (☎ 892 123; www.tirrenia.it) Genoa to Tunis (€140.50, 24 hours) in Tunisia; Bari to Durrës (€64.70, nine hours) in Albania; Rome to Sardinia.

GETTING AROUND

You can reach almost any destination in Italy by train, bus or ferry – services are generally efficient and cheap. Domestic airlines connect major cities, but flights are still relatively expensive. Your own car gives you more freedom, but comes at a cost – expensive *benzina* (petrol), motorway tolls and a lack of parking are just some of the headaches you'll have to face.

AIR

Italy's major domestic airlines are **Air One** (☎ 199 207 080; www.flyairone.it); **Alitalia** (☎ 06 22 22; www.alitalia.it) and **Meridiana** (☎ 89 29 28; www.meridiana.it).

Ryanair (☎ 899 678 910; www.ryanair.com) also flies a number of domestic routes.

The main airports are in Rome, Pisa, Milan, Bologna, Genoa, Turin, Naples, Venice, Catania, Palermo and Cagliari.

BUS

Italy boasts an extensive and largely reliable bus network. Buses are not necessarily cheaper than trains, but in mountainous areas such as Umbria, Sicily and Sardinia they are often the only choice. In larger cities, companies have ticket offices or operate through agencies, but in most villages and small towns tickets are sold in bars or on the bus. Reservations are usually only necessary for high-season long-haul trips.

CAR & MOTORCYCLE

Roads are generally good throughout the country and there's an excellent system of *autostrade* (motorways). There's a toll to use most *autostrade*, payable in cash or by credit card at exit barriers. Motorways are indicated by an A with a number (eg A1) on a green background; *strade statali* (main roads) are shown by an S or SS and number (eg SS7) against a blue background.

To hire a car in Italy you'll need a valid driving licence (plus International Driving Permit if required). Age restrictions vary from agency to agency but generally you'll need to be 21 or over. Make sure you understand what is included in the price (unlimited kilometres, tax, insurance, collision damage waiver etc) and what your liabilities are. You'll have no trouble hiring a scooter or motorcycle (provided you're over 18); there are rental agencies in all Italian cities. Rates start at about €20 a day for a 50cc scooter.

All EU driving licences are recognised in Italy. Holders of non-EU licences must get an International Driving Permit (IDP) to accompany their national licence. If you're driving your own car, you'll need an international insurance certificate, known as a *Carta Verde* (Green Card), available from your insurance company.

In Italy drive on the right, overtake on the left and give way to cars coming from the right. It's obligatory to wear seat belts, to drive with your headlights on outside built-up areas, and to carry a warning triangle and fluorescent waistcoat in case of breakdown. Wearing a helmet is compulsory on all two-wheeled vehicles. The blood alcohol limit is 0.05%.

Speed limits, unless otherwise indicated, are 130km/h (in rain 110km/h) on *autostrade;* 110km/h (in rain 90km/h) on all main, non-urban roads; 90km/h on secondary, non-urban roads; and 50km/h in built-up areas.

TRAIN

Trenitalia (☎ 89 20 21; www.trenitalia.com) runs most train services in Italy. There are several types of train: local *regionale* or *interregionale* trains; faster InterCity (IC) services; Eurostar (ES) trains; and since December 2008, Eurostar Alta Velocità trains (ES AV). These high-speed services operate on the main line from Milan, via Bologna and Florence, to Rome and Naples. On train timetables, high-speed trains are marked with the following symbols: ES AV (Eurostar Alta Velocità); ES AV Fast (the nonstop Rome–Milan trains) and ES Fast.

COSTS

Ticket prices depend on the type of train and class (1st class costs almost double 2nd class). Regional trains are cheaper than InterCity and Eurostar services, both of which require a supplement determined by the distance you travel. Generally, it's cheaper to buy all local train tickets in Italy – check for yourself on the Trenitalia website.

Tickets must be validated – in the yellow machines at the entrance to platforms – before boarding trains. Children under four years travel free, while kids between four and 12 years are entitled to discounts of between 30% and 50%.

For detailed information on using trains in Italy see www.seat61.com/Italy-trains.htm.

TRAIN PASSES

Available at all major train stations, the *Carta Verde* is available to anyone between 12 and 26. It costs €40 and is valid for a year, entitling holders to discounts of 10% on national trains and up to 25% on international trains. The *Carta d'Argento* (€30) is a similar pass for the over-60s, offering 15% reductions on national routes and 25% on international journeys.

THE NETHERLANDS & BELGIUM

THE NETHERLANDS

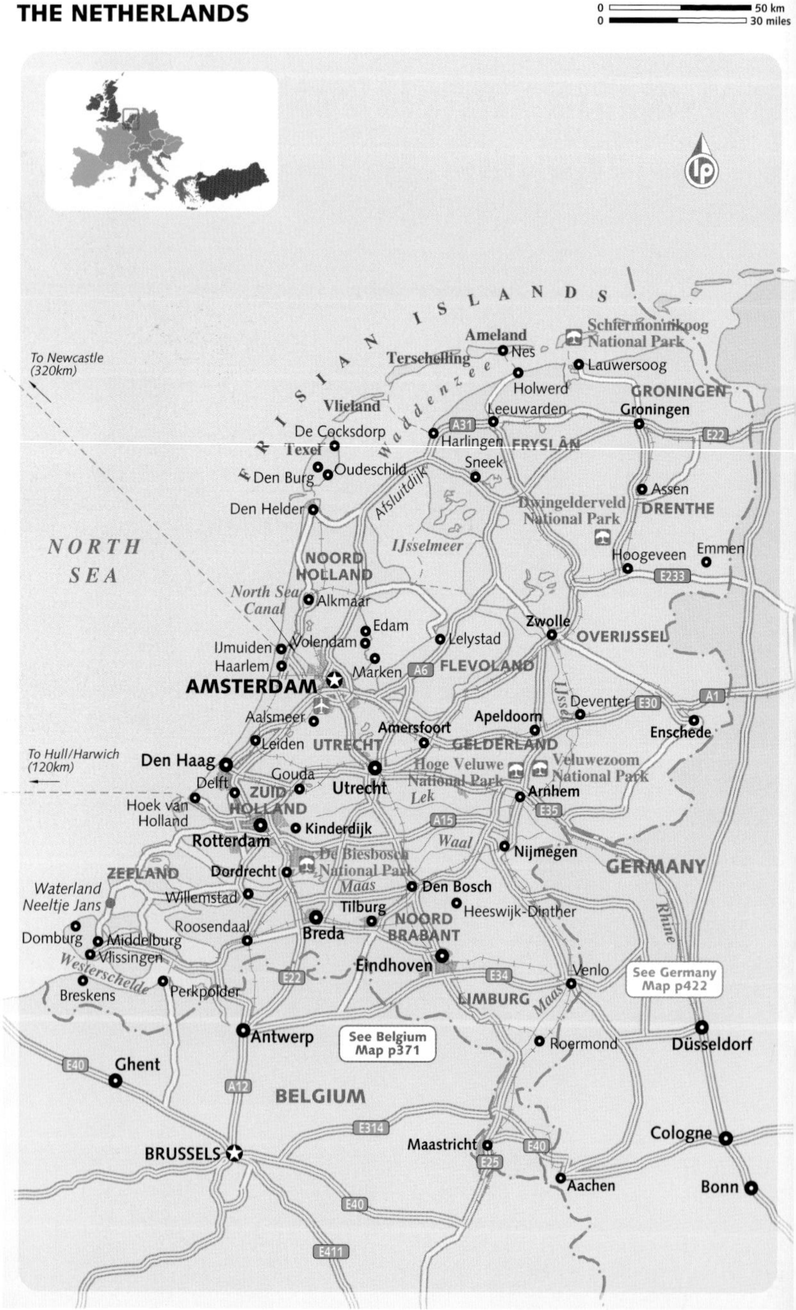

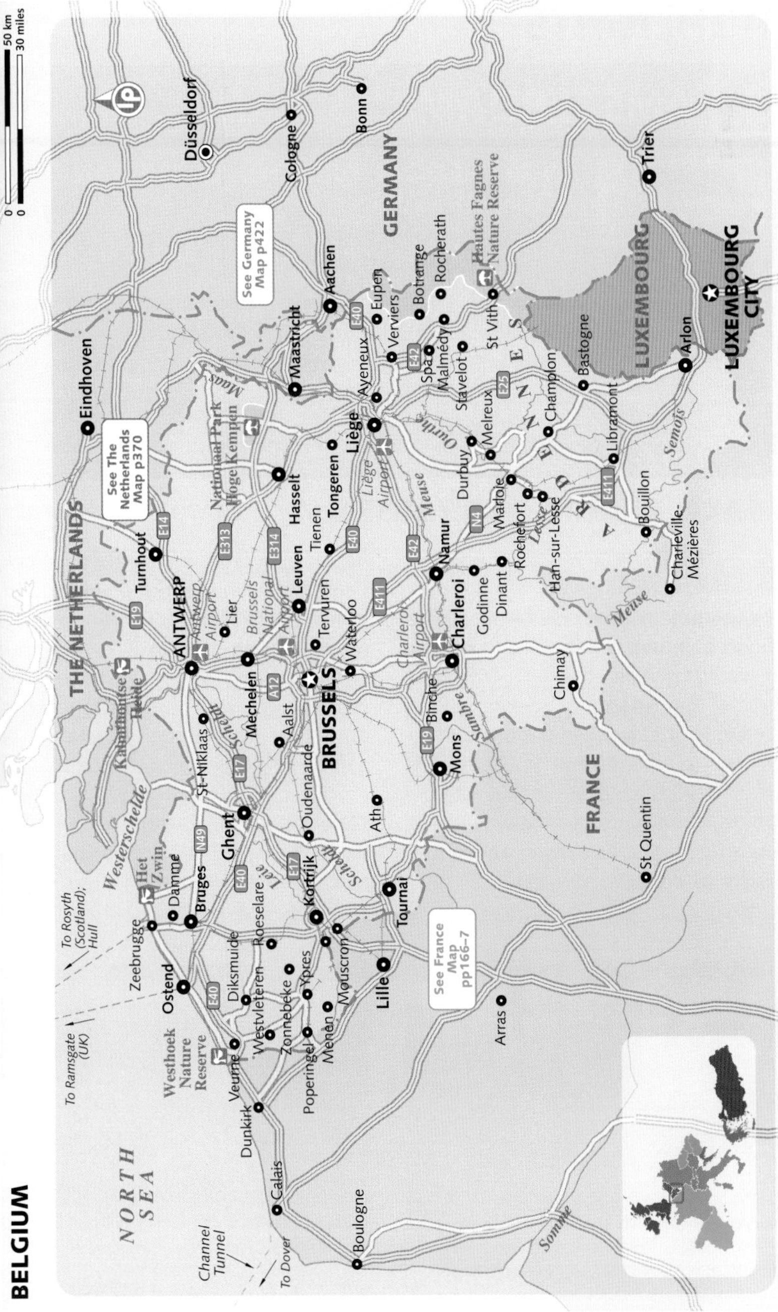
BELGIUM
0
0
50 km
30 miles
NORTH SEA
Channel Tunnel
To Dover
To Ramsgate (UK)
To Rosyth (Scotland); Hull
Boulogne
Calais
Dunkirk
Veurne
Westhoek Nature Reserve
Poperinge
Westvleteren
Zonnebeke
Menen
Ypres
Mouscron
Diksmuide
Ostend
Zeebrugge
Roeselare
Kortrijk
Lille
Tournai
Bruges
Damme
Het Zwin
Westerschelde
Ghent
Leie
Schelde
Oudenaarde
Ath
Arras
See France Map pp166–7
St-Niklaas
Scheldt
Kalmthoutse Heide
THE NETHERLANDS
ANTWERP
Antwerp Airport
Turnhout
Lier
Mechelen
Aalst
BRUSSELS
Brussels National Airport
Leuven
Tervuren
Waterloo
Mons
Binche
Sambre
Charleroi
Charleroi Airport
Chimay
FRANCE
St Quentin
Somme
Namur
Godinne
Dinant
Tienen
Hasselt
Tongeren
Liège
Liège Airport
Meuse
National Park Hoge Kempen
Maas
Maastricht
Eindhoven
See The Netherlands Map p370
Aachen
Eupen
Verviers
Ayeneux
Spa
Malmédy
Botrange
Rocherath
Hautes Fagnes Nature Reserve
Stavelot
St Vith
Durbuy
Melreux
Marloie
Rochefort
Han-sur-Lesse
Lesse
Ourthe
Champlon
Bastogne
Libramont
Bouillon
Semois
Charleville-Mézières
ARDENNES
Arlon
LUXEMBOURG
LUXEMBOURG CITY
Trier
GERMANY
See Germany Map p422
Cologne
Bonn
Düsseldorf
E40
E19
E14
E313
E314
E17
N49
A12
E411
E42
E25
N4

HIGHLIGHTS

1 AMSTERDAM

BY AXEL RÜGER, DIRECTOR OF THE VAN GOGH MUSEUM

I moved to Amsterdam 3½ years ago to become director of the Van Gogh Museum. I'm originally from Germany, but I loved Amsterdam long before moving here – not just for its physical beauty, but also for its cosmopolitan atmosphere and rich cultural heritage.

AXEL RÜGER'S DON'T MISS LIST

❶ VAN GOGH'S WHEATFIELD WITH CROWS

It's tough to pick out my favourite Van Gogh painting; but if I had to choose it would be *Wheatfield with Crows*. It's one of Van Gogh's last works, but its dynamic brushwork and striking blue-yellow colours are full of energy. I'm also fascinated by the ominous atmosphere of the sky above the wheatfield, and the black crows flying above it. A true masterpiece.

❷ THE NEGEN STRAATJES

One of my favourite areas of Amsterdam is the 'Negen Straatjes', or **Nine Streets** (**www.theninestreets.com**). It's bounded by nine cross streets between the Herengracht and the Prinsengracht, and filled with beautiful restaurants, cafes and quirky shops. Look out for **De Witte Tandenwinkel** (**☎ 020 623 3443; Runstraat 5; 🕒 1-6pm Mon, 10am-6pm Tue-Fri, 10am-5pm Sat**), a shop that's entirely devoted to toothbrushes!

Clockwise from top: Canals and bridges in the city centre; Bric-a-brac stall at Noordermarkt; Queue at the Van Gogh Museum (p383); Westerpark; Negen Straatjes

CLOCKWISE FROM TOP: WILL SALTER; RICHARD NEBESKY; WILL SALTER; ILSE SCHRAMA / ALAMY; PICTURE CONTACT / ALAMY

❸ NOORDERMARKT

Beautifully situated on the Prinsengracht, the **Noordermarkt** (**www.amsterdam.info/markets/noordermarkt**) is one of the city's most popular markets. The best day is on Saturdays when you can buy organic products from all over the country. Monday is another good day, especially for antiques.

❹ AMSTERDAM'S CANALS

Amsterdam's **canals** feel a world away from the hustle and bustle of most big cities. One of my favourite times for a wander is the early evening, when the city lights start to reflect off the water – for me, that's when Amsterdam is at its most beautiful.

❺ WESTERPARK

Everyone knows about Vondelpark, but Westerpark is well worth a visit, too. This area has recently been renovated and has some lovely bars and restaurants to discover, as well as a fantastic little cinema called **Het Ketelhuis** (**☎ 020-684 0090; Pazzanistraat 4; www.ketelhuis.nl**). Unfortunately most of the films are in Dutch!

➘ THINGS YOU NEED TO KNOW

Getting around Do as the Dutch do: hire a bike (p391) **Avoid** July and August **Do** Take a canal cruise **Don't** Smoke pot unless you're in a licensed coffee shop **See our author's review on p382**

HIGHLIGHTS

2

ANTWERP

Fashionable and funky, **Antwerp** (p408) is an essential post-Brussels stop. Famous for its art and architecture, Belgium's second city is home to the former **studio of Pieter Paul Rubens** (p408) and the fabulous fashion museum, **MoMu** (p409), but the main pleasure is just wandering the city and soaking up the sights – especially around the grand central square, **Grote Markt** (p408).

3

ROTTERDAM

Rotterdam (p397) may not have Amsterdam's instant wow factor, but this harbour city has plenty of surprises up its sleeve. Rebuilt from the ground up after being levelled during WWII, it's one of the Netherlands' most vibrant, multicultural and architecturally adventurous cities. Don't miss the view from the **Euromast** (p397) or the world-class canvases at the **Museum Boijmans van Beuningen** (p397).

4

BRUGES

With its beautiful medieval centre and charmingly old-world atmosphere, **Bruges** (p412) is a Belgian treasure. The city's most famous landmark is the huge **Belfort** (413; belltower) overlooking the central marketplace – 366 winding steps lead to the top for one of the best views in Belgium.

5

GHENT

Relatively few visitors make the trip to **Ghent** (p410), and that's a real shame, as they're missing out on one of Belgium's secret gems. Much less touristy than its sister cities Brussels, Antwerp and Bruges, this bewitching town is the perfect place to experience Belgium at its most beautiful.

6

HOGE VELUWE NATIONAL PARK

Want to escape the crowds? Look no further than the Netherlands' largest **nature park** (p400), where deer, wild boar and mouflon wander freely through 55 sq km of moorland, forest and dunes. Explore it on foot or by two wheels, or visit its excellent **art museum** (p388) in case the weather takes a turn for the worse.

2 JONATHAN SMITH; 3 GLENN VAN DER KNIJFF; 4 GLENN VAN DER KNIJFF; 5 JONATHAN SMITH; 6 IMAGEBROKER / ALAMY

2 MoMu (p409); 3 Modern architecture near the Erasmusbrug (p397); 4 Markt square (p413); 5 Views across the Leie River to Graslei (p411); 6 Red deer stag in Hoge Veluwe National Park (p400)

THE BEST...

↘ OFFBEAT MUSEUMS

- **SMAK** (p411) Contemporary art in old-world Ghent.
- **Frietmuseum** (p414) Where the French fry becomes an art form.
- **Musée Bruxellois de la Gueuze** (p405) Everything you ever wanted to know about Belgian beer.
- **Condomerie** (p389) Shop-cum-temple to the world's favourite prophylactic.

↘ SHOPPING SPOTS

- **Albert Cuypmarkt** (p390) Amsterdam's biggest street market.
- **Waterlooplein** (p390) Pick up vintage goods at this huge flea market.
- **Aalsmeer** (p391) Shop for flowers of every description.
- **Place du Jeu-de-Balle** (p407) Browse for *brocantes* (bric-a-brac) in Brussels.
- **Galeries St-Hubert** (p403) Brussels' elegant shopping arcade.

↘ PLACES FOR A BEER

- **Delirium Café** (p406) Over 2850 beers and counting!
- **'t Smalle** (p389) Our favourite Amsterdam drinking hole.
- **Graslei** (p411) Grab a beer along Ghent's waterfront.
- **Zuiderterras** (p410) Architect-designed Antwerp cafe.
- **In de Vrede** (p414) Sip beers brewed by Trappist monks.

↘ WEIRD BUILDINGS

- **Rietveld-Schröderhuis** (p399) Super-stark building by Utrecht architect Gerrit Rietveld.
- **Kinderdijk** (p400) Unesco-listed windmill complex.
- **Euromast** (p397) Climb the tower for amazing Rotterdam views.
- **Overblaak** (p397) The future's cube-shaped.
- **Atomium** (p405) Marvel at a giant molecule.

LEFT: WILL SALTER; RIGHT: PASCALE BEROUJON

Left: Figurine for sale at Waterlooplein flea market (p390), Amsterdam; Right: The Atomium (p405), Brussels

THINGS YOU NEED TO KNOW

AT A GLANCE

- **Population** 16.6 million (Netherlands), 10.6 million (Belgium)
- **Official languages** Dutch and Frisian (Netherlands); Dutch, French and German (Belgium)
- **Currency** Euro (€)
- **Telephone codes** ☎31 (Netherlands), ☎31 (Belgium)
- **When to go** May to September is the driest season; July and August are busiest
- **Tipping** Optional, as service and VAT is usually included

REGIONS IN A NUTSHELL

- **Amsterdam** (p382) The definitive Dutch city.
- **Randstad** (p392) Home to half of the Netherlands.
- **Brussels** (p401) Belgium's elegant capital.
- **Flanders** (p408) Flat but full of sights.

ADVANCE PLANNING

- **Two months before** Book accommodation for Amsterdam, Brussels, Antwerp, Bruges and Ghent.
- **One week before** Check the weather forecast and pack accordingly.
- **When you arrive** Pick up a *Museumkaart* (p416), which covers 400 Dutch museums.

BE FOREWARNED

- **Public transport** The prepaid *OV chipkaart* covers all public transport in the Netherlands (p420).
- **Drugs** In the Netherlands, soft drugs are tolerated, but hard drugs are a serious crime. Smoking is banned in public places, but you can smoke pot without tobacco in coffee shops.
- **Languages** Belgium has three official languages – French, German and Dutch (also called Flemish). Many Dutch people speak excellent English.
- **Monday opening hours** On Mondays shops and businesses in the Netherlands usually open late (generally between 11am and 1pm).

BUSINESS HOURS

- **Banks** (**Netherlands 1-4pm Mon, 9am-4pm Tue-Fri; Belgium 9am-4pm Mon-Fri**)
- **Bars, pubs & cafes** Generally close between midnight and 2am.
- **Museums** Often closed on Monday in the Netherlands.
- **Restaurants** (**Netherlands 11am-2.30/3pm & 5.30-10/11pm; Belgium 11.30am-3pm, 5.30pm-10pm**)
- **Shops** (**Netherlands 1-5.30pm Mon, 9am-6pm Tue-Fri, 9am-5pm Sat; Belgium 9am-6pm Mon-Sat**) In the Netherlands many shops are open for late-night shopping till 9pm on Thursday or Friday; some also open from 10am to 4pm on Sunday.

COSTS

- **€80 per day** Should cover cheap meals and B&B digs.
- **€80-150** Midrange hotels and restaurants.
- **€150+** Boutique accommodation and first-rate food.

THINGS YOU NEED TO KNOW

EMERGENCY NUMBERS

- **Ambulance** (☎ 112)
- **Fire** (☎ 112)
- **Police** (☎ 112)

GETTING AROUND

- **Air** (p418) The Netherlands' main airports are at Schiphol (Amsterdam) and Rotterdam, while most Belgian flights land in Brussels, Antwerp, Charleroi or Liège. All airports have shuttle buses and/or trains serving the relevant cities.
- **Bus** (p419) Regular buses serve most major Dutch cities plus Brussels, Antwerp, Ghent and Liège.
- **Car** (p420) Rental costs and petrol can be pricey, but you can hire a car easily in most cities and regional airports.
- **Train** (p420) Belgium and the Netherlands both have good rail networks, with high-speed trains (known as Thalys in Belgium and Hispeed in the Netherlands) connecting several major cities.

MEDIA

- **Newspapers** Local lingo papers include *De Standaard, Grenzecho* and *Le Soir* in Belgium, and *De Telegraaf, NRC Handelsblad* and *De Volkskrant* in the Netherlands. Belgium's English-language paper is *The Bulletin* (www.bulletin.com).
- **Radio** Major Belgian stations include Radio 1 (91.7FM), Studio Brussel (100.6FM), Action FM (106.9FM) and Musiq3 (91.2FM). In the Netherlands, stations include Noordzee FM (100.7FM), Radio 538 (102FM) and 3fm (96.8FM).
- **TV** In Belgium, Flemish channels include TV1, VTM and Ketnet/Canvas, plus La Une and La Deux1 in French. Some of the many Dutch channels are Nederland 1, 2 and 3 and RTL4.

RESOURCES

- **Belgische Spoorwegen** (www.b-rail.be) The Belgian railway.
- **Holland** (www.holland.com/uk) The official Dutch tourist site.
- **KLM** (www.klm.com) The Netherlands' national airline.
- **Nederlandse Spoorwegen** (www.ns.nl) Plan your Dutch train travel.
- **Visit Belgium** (www.visitbelgium.com) Belgium's official touris site.

VISAS

- **EU nationals** Free to work and travel in the Netherlands and Belgium.
- **Citizens of Australia, Canada, Israel, Japan, New Zealand & US** Can enter visa-free for three months.
- **Other countries** Will need a visa issued in their home country.

GET INSPIRED

FILMS

- **Black Book** (2006) Paul Verhoeven's WWII thriller.
- **Crusade in Jeans** (2006) Big-budget time-travel fantasy.
- **Girl with a Pearl Earring** (1999) Hollywood version of the novel.
- **In Bruges** (2008) Irish hit-men kill time in Bruges.
- **L'Enfant** (2005) Palme d'Or winner from the Dardenne brothers.

BOOKS

- **A Tall Man in a Low Land** (Harry Pearson) Belgian travelogue by a lanky-legged Brit.
- **Amsterdam: The Brief Life of a City** (Geert Mak) Historical overview of Amsterdam.
- **My 'Dam Life** (Sean Condon) Expat Aussie's Amsterdam experiences.
- **The Diary of Anne Frank** (Anne Frank) Heart-breaking but essential.
- **The Good Beer Guide Belgium** (Tim Webb) Belgium's best beer.

MUSIC

- **Funked Up!** (Candy Dulfer) The Netherlands' sexiest saxophonist.
- **Gedicht Gezongen** (Denise Jannah) Smooth jazz by Dutch singer.
- **Infiniment: 40 Chansons** (Jacques Brel) Double-CD from the great Belgian balladeer.
- **My Way – The Hits** (Herman Brood) Compilation from the doomed Dutch rock-and-roller.

WEBSITES

- **A Beginner's Guide to Belgian Beer** (www.beermad.org.uk/writings/belgianbeer.shtml) School your tastebuds.
- **Amsterdam.info** (www.amsterdam.info) Useful 'Dam guide with a good coffee-shop section.
- **Cruise Holland** (www.cruiseholland.com) Travel the Netherlands by barge.
- **Dutch Bike Tours** (www.dutchbiketours.nl) Plan a two-wheeled adventure.

WILL SALTER

Condomerie (p389), Amsterdam

ITINERARIES

AMSTERDAM & AROUND Three Days

If there's one spot in the Netherlands you absolutely must not miss, it's **(1) Amsterdam** (p382). Despite its racy reputation, it won't take you long to fall head over heels for this lovely, laid-back city. Amsterdam's renowned for its relaxed lifestyle, so don't try to do too much – with a couple of days you should be able to cover the main attractions.

Start with the essentials on day one, beginning with a comprehensive overview of classical Dutch art at the **Rijksmuseum** (p385), followed by the world's largest collection of V**incents at the Van Gogh Museum** (p383). If time allows, you might also squeeze in a late-afternoon visit to the **Museum het Rembrandthuis** (p383) or Amsterdam's excellent photographic museum, **FOAM** (p383). Spend the evening exploring the lively bars and coffee houses of the **Red Light District** (p383) – just make sure the kids are tucked up tight at the hotel first…

On day two, prepare for a moving couple of hours at **Anne Frank's house** (p383), where the teenager penned her diary during the Nazi occupation. Spend a lazy afternoon exploring some of the city's quirky **shops** (p389) and **markets** (p390). Chill out in **Vondelpark** (p385) and take an early evening **canal cruise** (p390), followed by a slap-up supper at **Van Dobben** (p387) and some late-night beers at **Doelen** (p388) or **Hoppe** (389).

Round things off with a day trip to either **(2) Haarlem** (p392) or **(3) Utrecht** (p399).

THE BEST OF BELGIUM Five Days

Five days is long enough to experience Belgium's belles. Begin with a couple of days exploring the stately capital **(1) Brussels** (p401), factoring in time for the Old Masters at the Musées Royaux des Beaux-Arts (p404), a dose of art nouveau at the **Musée Horta** (p404), some window-shopping around the **Galeries St-Hubert** (p403) and an early-evening coffee on the **Grand Place** (p403), Brussels' glorious central square. Don't forget to pick up some Belgian souvenirs – Brussels has plenty of places where you can stock up on lace, chocolates and Belgian beers.

Post-Brussels, hop on a train across flat Flanders to **(2) Antwerp** (p408) – you'll see the spire of the fabulous **Onze Lieve Vrouwekathedraal** (p408) long before you arrive. See where Rubens worked his magic at the **Rubenshuis** (p408), followed by some cutting-edge fashion at **MoMu** (p409), a wander around the **Grote Markt** (p408) and a meal at one of the city's **estaminets** (taverns, p410).

Spend the last couple of days exploring the peaceful canals and medieval squares of **(3) Bruges** (p412) and **(4) Ghent** (p410).

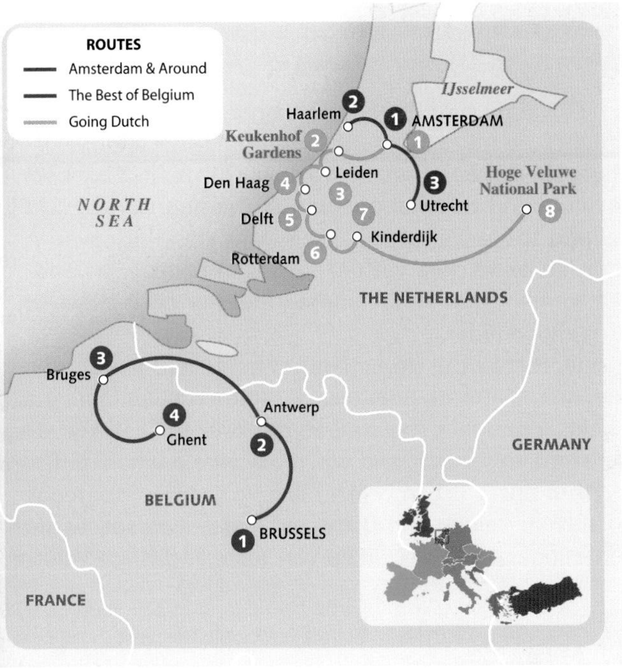

GOING DUTCH One Week

This week-long itinerary covers all of the Netherlands' essential sights. Start with at least two days in (1) Amsterdam (p382), then hire a car and head off to explore the Randstad (p392), with stops at the lovely (2) Keukenhof Gardens (p400), the elegant canal-town of (3) Leiden (p393), the fabulous art museums of (4) Den Haag (p394) and the picture-perfect streets of (5) Delft (p396).

From here it's an easy spin to (6) Rotterdam (p397), the lively Dutch city that has risen from its WWII ashes and reinvented itself as a cultural and architectural centre. Take a detour via the Unesco-listed windmills of (7) Kinderdijk (p400), before venturing east for some hiking and biking in Holland's largest national park, (8) Hoge Veluwe (p400).

DISCOVER THE NETHERLANDS & BELGIUM

They might be next-door neighbours, but Belgium and the Netherlands couldn't be more different in attitude and outlook.

On the one side, there's Belgium: best-known for its bubbly beer, top-quality chocolate and political position at the heart of the EU. But look beyond these well-worn clichés and you'll discover an eccentric little nation packed with centuries of history, art and architecture, not to mention a longstanding identity crisis between its Flemish and Walloon sides.

On the other side, there's the Netherlands: liberal, laid-back and flat as a pancake, famous for its brown cafes, spinning windmills and colourful tulip fields. But again, the stereotypes only tell half the story. Look beyond Amsterdam's canals and you'll discover a whole different side to Holland, from buzzy urban centres like Rotterdam, gorgeous medieval towns such as Leiden and Delft, and wide-open spaces such as the stunning national parks of Duinen van Texel and Hoge Veluwe.

THE NETHERLANDS

AMSTERDAM

☎ 020 / pop 747,000

If Amsterdam were a staid place it would still be one of Europe's most beautiful and historic cities, right up there with Venice and Paris. But add in the qualities that make it Amsterdam: the funky and mellow bars, brown cafes full of characters, pervasive irreverence, whiffs of pot and an open-air marketplace for sleaze and sex and you have a literally intoxicating mix.

ORIENTATION

Centraal Station is the hub. Leidseplein is the centre of (mainstream) Amsterdam nightlife, and Nieuwmarkt is a vast cobblestone square with open-air markets and popular pubs. The Red Light District is bound by Zeedijk, Nieuwmarkt and Kloveniersburgwal in the east, by Damstraat, Oude Doelenstraat and Oude Hoogstraat in the south, and by Warmoesstraat in the west.

INFORMATION

GWK Travelex (Grenswisselkantoor; ☎ 0900 0566; Centraal Station; 8am-10pm Mon-Sat, 9am-10pm Sun) Converts travellers cheques and makes hotel reservations; also at Schiphol.

I Amsterdam Card (per 24/48/72hr €33/43/53) Available at tourist (VVV) offices and some hotels. Gives admission to most museums, canal boat trips, and discounts at shops, attractions and restaurants. Also includes a transit pass.

Tourist office (VVV; ☎ 0900-400 40 40; www.vvvamsterdam.nl) Centraal Track 2 (Centraal Station; 8am-8pm Mon-Sat, 9am-5pm Sun); Stationsplein 10 (7am-9pm Mon-Fri, 8am-9pm Sat & Sun)

SIGHTS & ACTIVITIES

MEDIEVAL CENTRE

Just north of the Royal Palace, the late-Gothic basilica **Nieuwe Kerk** (New Church;

☎ 638 69 09; www.nieuwekerk.nl; Dam; adult/ hild €4/free; 🕑 10am-6pm) is the coronation hurch of Dutch royalty, with a carved ak chancel, a bronze choir screen, a nassive, gilded organ and stained-glass vindows.

Amsterdam's oldest building, the 14th-entury **Oude Kerk** (Old Church; ☎ 625 82 84; www.oudekerk.nl; Oudekerksplein 23; adult/child 5/4; 🕑 11am-5pm Mon-Sat, 1-5pm Sun) was uilt to honour the city's patron saint, St Nicholas.

The **Red Light District** (see the boxed ext, p387) retains the power to make your aw go limp, even if near-naked prostitutes propositioning passers-by from black-lit vindows is the oldest Amsterdam cliché. Note that even in the dark heart of the dis-rict there are charming shops and cafes vhere the only thing that vibrates is your nobile phone.

For a polar opposite, duck into the **Begijnhof** (☎ 622 19 18; www.begijnhofamster dam.nl; admission free; 🕑 8am-5pm), an en-closed former convent from the early 14th century.

Housed in the old civic orphanage, he **Amsterdams Historisch Museum** Amsterdam Historical Museum; ☎ 523 18 22; www.ahm.nl; Kalverstraat 92; adult/child €10/5; 🕑 10am-5pm Mon-Fri, 11am-5pm Sat & Sun) akes you through all the fascinating wists and turns of Amsterdam's convo-uted history.

NIEUWMARKT

You almost expect to find the master him-self at the **Museum het Rembrandthuis** Rembrandt House Museum; ☎ 520 04 00; www. embrandthuis.nl; Jodenbreestraat 4; adult/child €8/1.50; 🕑 10am-5pm), the house where Rembrandt van Rijn ran his painting stu-dio, only to lose the lot when profligacy set in, enemies swooped, and bankruptcy came knocking.

RICHARD NEBESKY

Sign for the modern section of the Van Gogh Museum

VAN GOGH MUSEUM

The outstanding Van Gogh Museum houses the world's largest Van Gogh collection, arranged chrono-logically. Trace the artist's life from his tentative start though to his Japanese phase, and on to the black cloud that descended over him and his work. There are also works by contemporaries Gauguin, Toulouse-Lautrec, Monet and Bernard.

Things You Need to Know: ☎ 570 52 00; www.vangoghmuseum.nl; Paulus Pot-terstraat 7; adult/child under 12yr/child 12-21yr €10/free/2.50; 🕑 10am-6pm Sun-Thu, to 10pm Fri

CANAL BELT

The **Anne Frank Huis** (Anne Frank House; ☎ 556 71 00; www.annefrank.org; Prinsengracht 267; adult/child €8.50/4; 🕑 9am-9pm Apr-Aug, to 7pm Sep-Mar), where Anne wrote her famous diary, lures almost a million visitors annu-ally with its secret annexe, reconstruction of Anne's melancholy bedroom, and her actual diary. Try going in the early morn-ing or evening when crowds are lightest. Look for the newly added photo of Peter Schiff, her 'one true love'.

FOAM (Fotografie Museum Amsterdam; ☎ 551 65 00; www.foam.nl; Keizersgracht 609; adult/child €7/5; 🕑 10am-5pm Sat-Wed, to 9pm Thu & Fri) is an airy gallery devoted to painting with

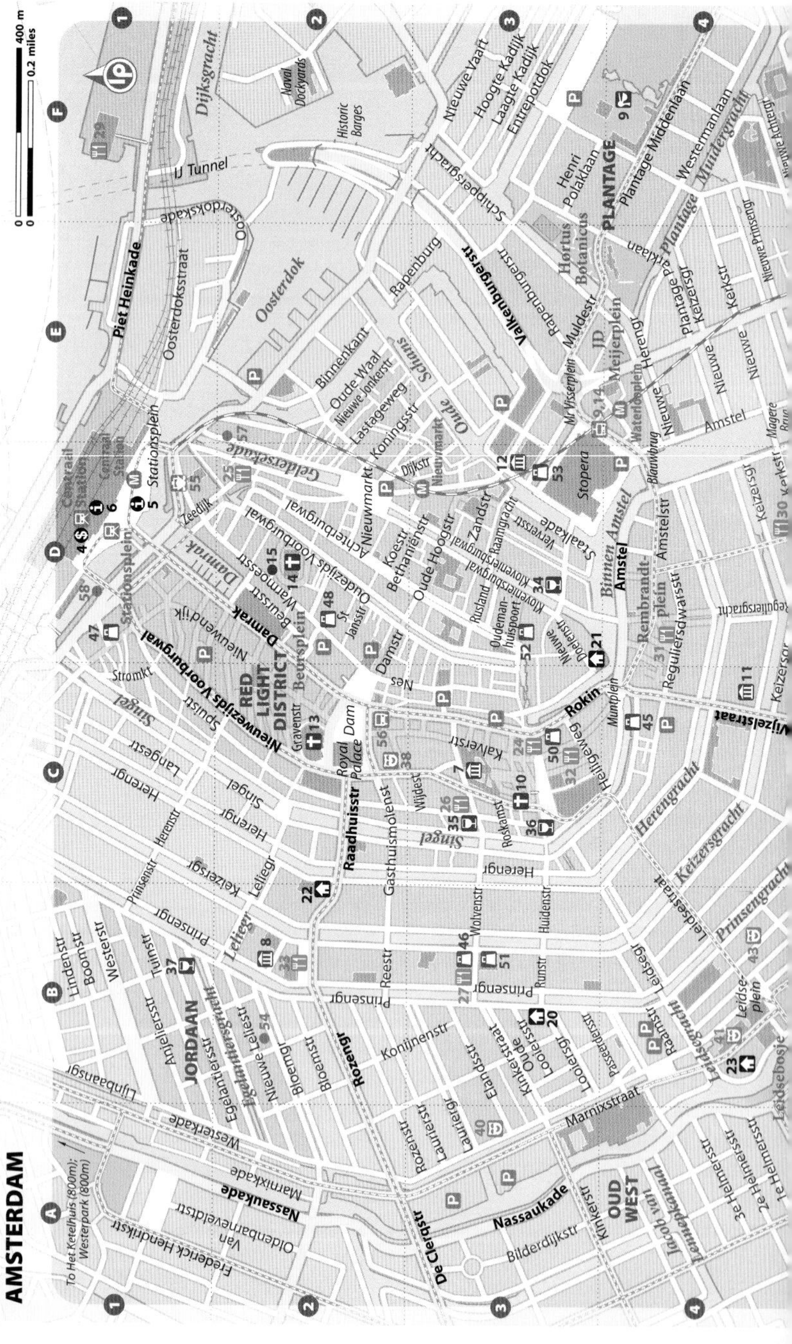
AMSTERDAM
0.2 miles
400 m
To Het Ketelhuis (800m); Westerpark (800m)
Centraal Station
Stationsplein
IJ Tunnel
Piet Heinkade
Oosterdokskade
Oosterdoksstraat
Oosterdok
Dijksgracht
Naval Dockyards
Historic Barges
Nieuwe Vaart
Hoogte Kadijk
Laagte Kadijk
Entrepotdok
Schippersgracht
Henri Polaklaan
PLANTAGE
Plantage Middenlaan
Westermanlaan
Plantage Muidergracht
Hortus Botanicus
Valkenburgerstr
Rapenburgerstr
Rapenburg
Binnenkant
Oude Waal
Nieuwe Jonkerstr
Lastageweg
Koningsstr
Oude Schans
Geldersekade
Zeedijk
Nieuwmarkt
Dijkstr
Achterburgwal
Oudezijds Voorburgwal
Kloveniersburgwal
Raamgracht
Zandstr
Verversstr
Staalkade
Stopera
Waterlooplein
Mr Visserplein
Muiderstr
JD Meijerplein
Nieuwe Herengr
Amstel
Blauwbrug
Binnen Amstel
Amstelstr
Rembrandtplein
Reguliersdwarsstr
Reguliersgracht
Vijzelstraat
Muntplein
Rokin
Nieuwe Doelenstr
Oudemanhuispoort
Rusland
Oude Hoogstr
Koestr
Bethaniënstr
Damstr
Nes
St Jansstr
Warmoesstr
Beursstr
Beursplein
Damrak
RED LIGHT DISTRICT
Nieuwendijk
Nieuwezijds Voorburgwal
Stromkt
Spuistr
Graventsr
Dam
Royal Palace
Kalverstr
Heiligeweg
Raadhuisstr
Gasthuismolensteeg
Wijdesteeg
Singel
Roskamst
Herengr
Keizersgr
Prinsengr
Leliegr
Langestr
Herenstr
Prinsenstr
Wolvenstr
Huidenstr
Reestr
Runstr
Lindenstr
Boomstr
Westerstr
Tuinstr
Anjeliersstr
JORDAAN
Egelantiersgracht
Egelantiersstr
Nieuwe Leliestr
Bloemgr
Bloemstr
Rozengr
Konijnenstr
Rozenstr
Lauriersstr
Lauriergr
Elandsstr
Kinkerstr
Oude Looiersstr
Looiersgr
Passeerdersstr
Raamstr
Leidsegr
Leidsestraat
Leidseplein
Leidsebosje
Lijnbaansgr
Westerkade
Marnixkade
Nassaukade
Marnixstraat
Van Oldenbarneveldtstr
Frederick Hendrikstr
De Clercqstr
Bilderdijkstr
OUD WEST
Jacob van Lennepkanaal
3e Helmersstr
2e Helmersstr
1e Helmersstr
Herengracht
Keizersgracht
Prinsengracht
Kerkstr
Nieuwe Prinsengr
Magere Brug

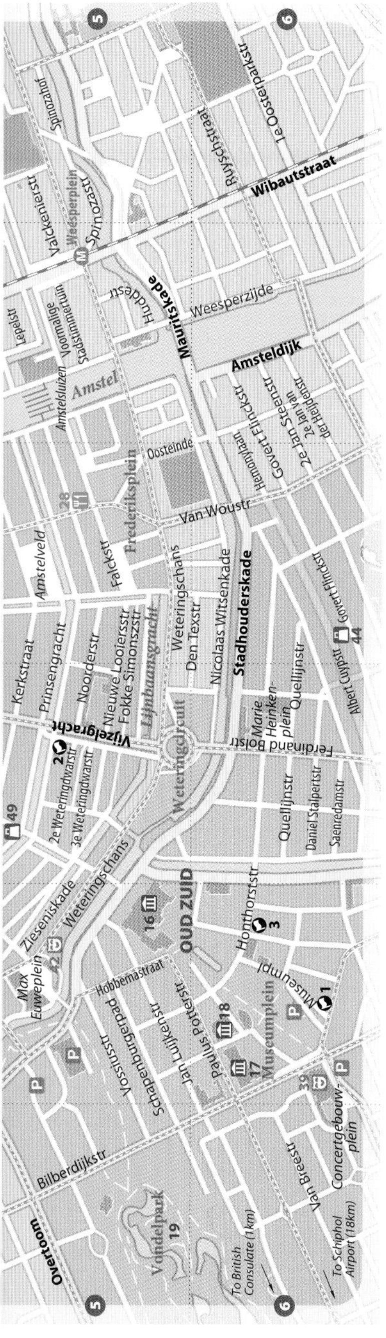

light. Two storeys of changing exhibitions feature world-renowned photographers such as Sir Cecil Beaton, Annie Leibovitz and Henri Cartier-Bresson.

MUSEUMPLEIN

Rijksmuseum (☎ 674 70 00; www.rijksmuseum.nl; Stadhouderskade 42; adult/child €10/free; 10am-6pm, to 8.30pm Fri) boasts a collection valued in the billions, but until renovations finish in 2013 (or later) there are only a few masterpieces displayed, including a couple of Vermeers and the crowning glory, Rembrandt's *Nightwatch* (1650). Save one queue by buying your ticket online.

When open, the **Stedelijk Museum** (☎ 573 29 11; www.stedelijkindestad.nl; Museumplein; 10am-6pm) features around 100,000 pieces including Impressionist works from Monet, Picasso and Chagall; sculptures from Rodin and Moore; De Stijl landmarks by Mondrian; and pop art from Warhol and Lichtenstein. Until renovations are complete (possibly early 2010) a few select works are on display around town, check the website for details.

Vondelpark (www.vondelpark.nl, in Dutch) is an English-style park with free concerts, ponds, lawns, thickets, winding footpaths and three outdoor cafes. It was named after the poet and playwright Joost van den Vondel, the 'Dutch Shakespeare', and is popular with joggers, skaters, buskers and lovers.

JORDAAN

Originally a stronghold of the working class, the Jordaan is now one of the most desirable areas to live in Amsterdam. It's a pastiche of modest old homes and a few modern carbuncles, squashed in a grid of tiny lanes peppered with bite-sized cafes and shops.

PLANTAGE

Besides the well-rounded animal population, **Artis** (**☎ 523 34 00; www.artis.nl; Plantage Kerklaan 38-40; adult/child €18/15; 9am-6pm Jun-Sep, to 5pm Oct-May**) is also home to a planetarium, a petting zoo and themed habitats. The aquarium complex has coral reefs, shark tanks and an Amsterdam canal displayed from a fish-eye view.

SLEEPING

Book ahead for weekends and in summer.

Quentin Hotel (**☎ 626 21 87; www.quentinhotels.com; Leidsekade 89; r €45-100**) The Quentin, decorated with colourful murals, rock-star art and contemporary handmade furniture, offers a variety of rooms: some with balconies and canal views, others small and cramped.

Hotel Nadia (**☎ 620 15 50; www.nadia.nl; Raadhuisstraat 51; r €55-150**) This handsome building has a precipitous set of stairs (go figure) but the energetic staff will tote your luggage up them. Rooms to the front have great views of the Westerkerk.

our pick **Hotel Amsterdam Wiechmann** (**☎ 626 33 21; www.hotelwiechmann.nl; Prinsengracht 328; r €85-180**) This family-run hotel occupies three houses. It has a marvellous canalside location, cosy but lovingly cared-for rooms furnished like an antique shop with country quilts and chintz, and lobby *tchotchkes* (knick-knacks) that have been there for some 50 years.

Hotel de l'Europe (**☎ 531 17 77; www.leurope.nl; Nieuwe Doelenstraat 2-8; r from €250**) Oozing Victorian elegance, L'Europe welcomes visitors with a marble lobby, 100 gloriously large rooms (some with terraces, most with canal views), and a sense of serene calm that makes it a blissful oasis amid the hurly-burly of the city.

EATING

Amsterdam abounds in food choices. Happy streets for hunting include Utrechtsestraat, Spuistraat and any of the little streets lining and connecting the west canals, such as Berenstraat.

RESTAURANTS

Pancakes! (☎ 528 97 97; Berenstraat 38; mains from €3; ⏰ 10am-7pm) A great place to sample Dutch pancakes in an atmosphere free of clogs and other kitsch – and there are just as many locals here as tourists.

our pick **Van Dobben** (☎ 624 42 00; Korte Reguliersdwarsstraat 5; mains from €4) Open since the 1940s, the venerable Van Dobben has white tile walls and white-coated counter men who specialise in snappy banter. Trad Dutch fare is the speciality: try the *pekelvlees* (something close to corned beef). Best *kroquetten* (croquettes) and pea soup in town.

Lucius (☎ 624 18 31; Spuistraat 247; mains from €15; ⏰ dinner) Delicious and consistently full, Lucius is known for simple but expertly prepared fish, such as Dover sole in butter and giant North Sea oysters. The interior, all fish tanks and tiles, is workman-like and professional, just like the service.

Star Ferry (☎ 788 20 90; www.starferry.nl; Piet Heinkade 1; mains from €15) The flash bistro-cafe at the Muziekgebouw aan't IJ is hard to beat for its location and views. Several storeys of glass take in the striking harbour panorama and an acre of outside tables soak up the sun.

Tempo Doeloe (☎ 625 67 18; www.tempodoeloerestaurant.nl; Utrechtsestraat 75; mains from €18; ⏰ dinner) One of the most respected Indonesian restaurants in the city, this tiny place is also more formal than most.

Restaurant De Kroonluchter (☎ 428 1074; Utrechtstraat 141; set meals €35; ⏰ 6pm-1am Tue-Sat) Seafood is served with Asian flair at this stylish bistro on a street with many good choices.

CAFES & QUICK EATS

Gartine (☎ 320 41 32; Taksteeg 7; mains €4-7; ⏰ 8am-6pm Wed-Sun) Makes delectable breakfast pastries, sandwiches and salads from produce grown in its own garden plot. It has impeccable slow-food and organic credentials.

Hofje Van Wijs (☎ 624 04 36; Zeedijk 43; mains €4-8) The 200-year-old coffee and tea vendor Wijs & Zonen maintains this oasis of a courtyard cafe. Many of the teas are from Indonesia and you can get excellent coffees, cakes and meals.

Vlaams Friteshuis (Voetboogstraat 31) The city's best-loved fries since 1887. Go local and drown the golden spudlings in mayo or one of dozens of other sauces.

Wil Graanstra Friteshuis (☎ 624 40 71; Westermarkt 11) This little stall near the Anne Frank Huis has been serving up

VICE SQUAD

Amsterdam's city government caused a stir in 2008 when it unveiled a plan to reduce by roughly half the number of windows used by prostitutes for self-marketing in the Red Light District. It also announced plans to close half of the coffee shops in the same area, or about 20% of the total citywide. Needless to say these plans aroused considerable controversy. Many mocked the city's claim that organised crime controls much of these businesses and expressed fear that it was really a scheme to make Amsterdam's sleazy heart 'upscale'.

Meanwhile, you can learn all you ever wanted to know about the Red Light District on a **Prostitution Information Centre walking tour** (☎ 420 73 28; www.pic-amsterdam.com; Enge Kerksteeg 3; €12.50; ⏰ varies). Tours are led by women who formerly worked as prostitutes and proceeds go to the centre, which helps the women find new work.

CHARLOTTE HINDLE

Groninger Museum

IF YOU LIKE...

If the **Rijksmuseum** (p385), **Rembrandthuis** (p383) and **Van Gogh Museum** (p383) have piqued your interest, you might want to pay a visit to some of the Netherlands' more out-of-the way institutions:

- **Bonnefantenmuseum** (☎ 043-329 01 90; www.bonnefantenmuseum.nl; Ave Céramique 250, Maastricht; adult/child €7.50/4; 11am-5pm Tue-Sun) Maastricht museum mixing Flemish masterpieces with controversial modern works.
- **Groninger Museum** (☎ 050-366 65 55; www.groningermuseum.nl; Museumeiland 1, Groningen; adult/child €10/3; 10am-5pm Tue-Thu, Sat & Sun, to 10pm Fri) Striking polymorphous museum in the lively town of Groningen, hosting everything from photography to Old Masters.
- **Kröller-Müller Museum** (☎ 0318-59 12 41; www.kmm.nl; Houtkampweg 6, Otterlo; adult/child €7/3.50; 10am-5pm Tue-Sun) This art museum in the Hoge Veluwe National Park (p400) features works by Van Gogh, Picasso, Renoir and Manet among many others.
- **Zeeuws Museum** (☎ 0118-65 30 00; www.zeeuwsmuseum.nl; Abdij, Middelburg; adult/child €8/free; 10am-5pm Tue-Sun) Offbeat Middelburg museum housed in a former monks' dormitory, offering 30,000 eclectic items from historic tapestries to 'dragons' preserved in jars.

delectably light and crispy fries with mayo since 1956. Nearby stalls offer local staples such as herring on a stick.

DRINKING

Doelen (☎ 624 90 23; Kloveniersburgwal 125) On a busy crossroads between the Amstel and De Wallen (the Red Light District), this cafe dates back to 1895 and looks it: carved wooden goat's head, stained-glass lamps, sand on the floor. During fine weather the tables spill across the street for picture-perfect canal views.

Gollem (☎ 626 66 45; Raamsteeg 4; j1/2/5 Spui) All the brew-related paraphernalia in this miniscule space barely leaves room for the 200 beers and the connoisseurs who come to try them.

our pick **Hoppe** (☎ 420 44 20; Spuistraat 18) This gritty *bruin café* has been luring drinkers for more than 300 years. Journalists, bums, socialites and raconteurs toss back brews amid the ancient wood panelling.

't Smalle (☎ 623 96 17; Egelantiersgracht 12) There's no more convivial spot than this canalside terrace on a sunny day, and the 18th-century interior is perfect in winter.

ENTERTAINMENT

Find out what's on in Thursday's papers, Wednesday's English-language *Amsterdam Weekly* or the monthly *Time Out Amsterdam.*

COFFEE SHOPS

'Cafe' means 'pub' throughout the Netherlands; 'coffee shops' are where one procures pot. Note that new smoking regs mean you can puff pot but not tobacco.

Abraxas (☎ 625 57 63; Jonge Roelensteeg 12) The Abraxas management knows what stoners want: mellow music, comfy sofas, rooms with different energy levels, and thick milkshakes.

Rokerij (☎ 422 66 43; Lange Leidsedwarsstraat 41) Behind the black hole of an entrance you'll find Asian decor and candlelight for those tired of the Rastafarian vibe. One of several locations.

LIVE MUSIC

Concertgebouw (☎ for tickets 10am-5pm 671 83 45; www.concertgebouw.nl; Concertgebouwplein 2-6) Each year, this neo-Renaissance centre presents around 650 concerts attracting 840,000 visitors, making it the world's busiest concert hall (with reputedly the best acoustics).

Maloe Melo (☎ 420 45 92; Lijnbaansgracht 163) Home to Amsterdam's blues scene, this dingy venue is rowdy and casual, and often adds bluegrass and soul to the calendar.

Melkweg (Milky Way; ☎ 531 81 81; www.melkweg.nl; Lijnbaansgracht 234A) The Milky Way – it's housed in a former dairy – must be Amsterdam's coolest club-gallery-cinema-cafe-concert hall.

Paradiso (☎ 626 45 21; www.paradiso.nl, in Dutch; Weteringschans 6) This converted church has long been a premier rock venue since the '60s.

SHOPPING

The big department stores cluster around the Dam. Chains line the pedestrian (in more ways than one) Kalverstraat. Stray off for more interesting choices like **Laundry Industry** (☎ 420 25 54; Spui 1), a cool Dutch label that specialises in minimalist functional fashion.

The Red Light District buzzes with vibrating latex creations. **Condomerie** (☎ 627 41 74; Warmoesstraat 141) puts the 'pro' back in prophylactic: rarely can you shop for a condom in such a tasteful setting and grapple with so many choices.

Nieumarkt has several good streets for typically eccentric local stores, and you can easily lose a day wandering Reesstraat and Hartenstraat and the blocks south to Runstraat and Huidenstraat. **Mendo** (☎ 612 12 16; Berenstraat 11) has a striking combination of visually stunning books, art, candy and even umbrellas. Nearby, **Boekie Woekie** (☎ 639 05 07; Berenstraat 16) sells books by artists. On the way to the Rijksmuseum, **Eduard Kramer** (☎ 623 08 32; Nieuwe Spiegelstraat 64) is one of many cute little oddball shops on this street. Not too far from Centraal Station is **Chills & Thrills** (☎ 638 00 15; Nieuwendijk 17), where you'll find herbal trips, mushrooms, psychoactive cacti, novelty bongs and life-sized alien sculptures. Remember that importing drugs is illegal.

TO MARKET

Amsterdam's largest and busiest market **Albert Cuypmarkt** (www.decuyp.nl; Albert Cuypstraat; 10am-5pm, closed Sun) is 100 years old. Food of every description, flowers, souvenirs, clothing, hardware and household goods can be found here.

Bloemenmarkt (Singel; 9am-5pm, closed Sun Dec-Feb) is a 'floating' flower market that's actually on pilings. Traders can advise on import regulations. It's notorious for pickpockets.

A favourite with academics, **Oudemanhuispoort book market** (Oudemanhuispoort; 11am-4pm Mon-Fri) is a moody, old, covered alleyway connecting two streets and it's lined with secondhand booksellers.

Waterlooplein flea market (Waterlooplein; 9am-5pm Mon-Fri, 8.30am-5.30pm Sat) is Amsterdam's most famous flea market: curios, secondhand clothing, music, used footwear, ageing electronic gear, New Age gifts, cheap bicycle parts...

GETTING THERE & AWAY

AIR

Most major airlines fly directly to **Schiphol** (AMS; ☎ 0900-0141; www.schiphol.nl), 18km southwest of the city centre.

BUS

For details of regional transport in the Netherlands, call the **transport information service** (☎ 0900-9292; www.9292ov.nl); it costs €0.70 per minute.

Eurolines (☎ 560 87 87; www.eurolines.nl; Rokin 10) tickets can be bought at its office near the Dam, and at most travel agencies and the NS Reisburo (Netherlands Railways Travel Bureau) in Centraal Station. Departures are from the **bus station** (☎ 694 56 31) next to Amstelstation.

Busabout (☎ in UK 020-7950 1661; www.busabout.com) tickets can be bought through its London office or on the coaches themselves. Coaches stop at Stayokay Amsterdam Zeeburg, Timorplein 21, near Centraal Station.

CAR & MOTORCYCLE

Motorways link Amsterdam to Den Haag and Rotterdam in the south, and to Utrecht and Amersfoort in the southeast. Amsterdam is about 480km from Paris, 840km from Munich, 680km from Berlin and 730km from Copenhagen. The Hoek van Holland ferry port is 80km away; IJmuiden is just up the road along the Noordzeekanaal.

TRAIN

Amsterdam's main train station is Centraal Station (CS). See p420 for details about the frequent and fast Dutch train system.

GETTING AROUND

TO/FROM THE AIRPORT

A taxi into Amsterdam from Schiphol airport takes 20 to 45 minutes and costs about €40. Trains to Centraal Station leave every few minutes, take 15 to 20 minutes, and cost €3.80/6.40 per single/return.

BOAT

Canal Bus (☎ 623 98 86; www.canalbus.nl; day pass per adult/child €18/12) does several circuits between Centraal Station and the Rijksmuseum between 10am and 8pm. The day pass is valid until noon the next day. The same company rents canal bikes (pedal boats) for €10 per person per hour (€7 if there are more than two people per canal bike). Docks are by Leidseplein and near the Anne Frank Huis.

Rederij Lovers (☎ 530 10 90; www.lovers.nl; Prins Hendrikkade 25-27; 1hr tour per person €11) offers a variety of night-time cruises.

BICYCLE

Amsterdam is cycling nirvana: flat, beautiful, and with dedicated bike paths. About 150,000 bicycles are stolen each year in Amsterdam alone, so always lock up.

For bicycle rental, try **Bike City** (☎ 626 37 21; www.bikecity.nl; Bloemgracht 68-70; per day/week €15/62) or **Orangebike** (☎ 528 99 90; www.orangebike.nl; Geldersekade 37; per 3hr/day/week €6/10/43), which offers a range of city tours (from €20). Both require a passport/ID and a credit-card or cash deposit.

PUBLIC TRANSPORT

Services – including the iconic trams – are run by the local transit authority, the GVB; national railway (NS) tickets are not valid on local transport. The GVB has a highly useful **information office** (☎ 0900 80 11, per min €0.10; www.gvb.nl; Stationsplein 10; 7am-9pm Mon-Fri, 8am-9pm Sat & Sun) across the tram tracks from the Centraal Station main entrance.

Public transport in Amsterdam, like the rest of the Netherlands, has switched to the *OV-chipkaart* (p420).

TAXI

Amsterdam taxis are expensive, even over short journeys. Try **Taxicentrale Amsterdam** (☎ 677 77 77).

AALSMEER

☎ 0297 / pop 20,000

Here, at the world's biggest **flower auction** (☎ 39 21 85; www.flora.nl; Legmeerdijk 313; adult/child €5/3; 7-11am Mon-Fri), 21 million flowers and plants worth around €6 million change hands daily; the rose is the biggest seller, outselling the tulip three to one. Bidding usually takes place between 7am and 9.30am; Monday, Tuesday and Friday are the best days.

Take Connexxion bus 172 from Amsterdam Centraal Station to the Aalsmeer VBA stop (50 minutes, four times hourly).

WILL SALTER

Bloemenmarkt, Amsterdam

WILL SALTER
Relaxing in Vondelpark (p385), Amsterdam

RANDSTAD

The Randstad is the Netherlands' most densely populated region (and among the world's densest), containing almost half the country's population. It stretches from Amsterdam to Rotterdam and also includes the classically Dutch towns and cities of Den Haag, Utrecht, Haarlem, Leiden, Delft and Gouda.

HAARLEM

☎ 023 / pop 150,000

Haarlem is the Netherlands in microcosm, with canals, gabled buildings and cobblestone streets. Its historic buildings, grand churches, museums, cosy bars, good restaurants and antique shops draw scores of day trippers. It's only 15 minutes by train from Amsterdam, but it can be a serene stopover for a longer stay.

Kept in an almshouse where Frans Hals spent his final, impoverished years, the superb collection at the **Frans Hals Museum** (☎ 511 57 75; www.franshalsmuseum.nl; Groot Heiligland 62; adult/child €10/free; 11am-5pm Tue-Sat, noon-5pm Sun) features Hals' two paintings known collectively as the *Regents & the Regentesses of the Old Men's Alms House* (1664). Five old masters stolen in 2002 were recovered in 2008 and are back on display.

The **Grote Kerk van St Bavo** (☎ 553 20 40; www.grotekerk.nl; Oude Groenmarkt 23; adult/child €2/1.50; 10am-4pm Mon-Sat) is a Gothic cathedral with a 50m-high steeple that can be seen from almost anywhere in Haarlem.

Also known as 'the hiding place', the **Corrie ten Boom House** (☎ 531 08 23; www.corrietenboom.com; Barteljorisstraat; admission free; 10am-3.30pm Tue-Sat) is named for the matriarch of a family that lived in the house during WWII. Using a secret compartment in her bedroom, she hid hundreds of Jews and Dutch resistors until they could be spirited to safety. In 1944 the family was betrayed and sent to concentration camps where three died. Later, Corrie Ten Boom toured the world preaching peace.

EATING & DRINKING

De Haerlemsche Vlaamse (☎ 532 59 91; Spekstraat 3; frites €2) Practically on the doorstep of the Grote Kerk, this *frites* joint, not much bigger than a telephone box, is a local institution.

Jacobus Pieck (☎ 532 61 44; Warmoesstraat; mains from €10; lunch & dinner Mon-Sat) Touches like freshly squeezed OJ put this tidy bistro on a higher plain. The menu bursts with fresh dishes, from salads and sandwiches at lunch to more complex pasta and seafood choices at dinner.

Proeflokaal In den Uiver (☎ 532 53 99; Riviervismarkt 13) This nautical-themed old place has shipping knick-knacks and a schooner sailing right over the bar. It's one of many atmospheric cafes overlooking the Grote Markt.

GETTING THERE & AWAY

Sample train fares from Haarlem's stunning station: Amsterdam (€3.80, 15 minutes, eight per hour), Den Haag (€7.30, 35 minutes, six per hour) and Rotterdam (€10.50, 50 minutes, four per hour).

LEIDEN

☎ 071 / pop 118,000

Leiden is a busy, vibrant town that is another popular day trip from Amsterdam. Claims to fame: it's Rembrandt's birthplace, it's home to the Netherlands' oldest university (and 20,000 students) and it's where America's pilgrims raised money to lease the leaky *Mayflower* that took them to the New World in 1620.

The 17th-century **Lakenhal** (Cloth Hall; ☎ 516 53 60; www.lakenhal.nl; Oude Singel 28-32; adult/under 18yr €4/free; 10am-5pm Tue-Fri, noon-5pm Sat & Sun) houses the Municipal Museum, with an assortment of works by old masters (including a few Rembrandts) as well as period rooms and temporary exhibits.

The **Rijksmuseum van Oudheden** (National Museum of Antiquities; ☎ 516 31 63; www.rmo.nl; Rapenburg 28; adult/under 18yr €8.50/5.50; 10am-5pm Tue-Sun) showcases hieroglyphs and almost 100 human and animal mummies.

Cultural achievements by civilizations worldwide are on show at the **Museum Volkenkunde** (Museum of Ethnology; ☎ 516 88 00; www.volkenkunde.nl; Steenstraat 1; adult/child €7.50/4; 10am-5pm Tue-Sun). Over 200,000 artefacts span China, South America and Africa. There's a rich Indonesian collection; watch for performances by the museum's gamelan troupe.

Leiden's carefully restored windmill, **De Valk** (Falcon; ☎ 516 53 53; www.molenmuseumdevalk.nl; 2e Binnenvestgracht 1; adult/under 15yr €3/2; 10am-5pm Tue-Sat, 1-5pm Sun), features many presentations, including one that laments the fact that local boy Rembrandt, as a miller's son, didn't paint many windmills. The upper levels afford an inspired view of the Old Town.

SLEEPING

Hotel Nieuw Minerva (☎ 512 63 58; www.nieuwminerva.nl; Boommarkt 23; r from €80;) The Minerva has a traditional look and a quiet canalside location. If you want a bit more bang for your buck, try the various theme rooms. The Rembrandt Room features an old-style walled bed with thick privacy curtains.

EATING

Annie's (☎ 512 57 37; Hoogstraat 1a; mains from €8; 11am-1am) At the confluence of canals and pedestrian zones, Annie's has a prime water-level location with dozens of tables on a floating pontoon.

Brasserie FYN (☎ 512 60 66; www.brasseriefyn.nl; Nieuwe Rijn 37; dishes €9; dinner daily, lunch Sat year-round & Wed-Fri Apr-Sep) This cute little bistro is right on a canal and has tables outside when the Dutch weather allows.

Brasserie de Engelenbak (☎ 512 54 40; www.brasseriedeengelenbak.nl, in Dutch; Lange Mare 38; mains from €18) Right in the shadow of the 17th-century octagonal Marekerk, this elegant bistro serves a seasonally changing menu of fresh fare that takes its cues from across the continent.

GETTING THERE & AWAY

Sample train fares: Amsterdam (€8, 35 minutes, six per hour) and Den Haag (€3.20, 10 minutes, six per hour). Regional and local buses leave from the bus station directly in front of Centraal Station.

DEN HAAG

☎ 070 / pop 476,000

Den Haag (The Hague), officially known as 's-Gravenhage (Count's Hedge), is the Dutch seat of government (although Amsterdam's the capital). It's suitably regal and is the kind of place where the musky aftershave of suave men wearing pink cravats mingles with the frilly scents of sachets sold in pricey boutiques.

The **tourist office** (☎ 0900-340 35 05; www.denhaag.com; Hofweg 1; 10am-6pm Mon-Fri, to 5pm Sat, noon-5pm Sun) sells tickets for local events, has internet access and a good reading area.

Grote Markstraat is fittingly the street for large stores. Interesting shops and oddball boutiques can be found in and around Kneuterdijk and Prinsestraat.

SIGHTS & ACTIVITIES

For a painless introduction to Dutch and Flemish Art 101, visit the **Mauritshuis** (☎ 302 34 56; www.mauritshuis.nl; Korte Vijverberg 8; adult/child €12/free; 10am-5pm Tue-Sat, 11am-5pm Sun), a small museum in a jewel-box of an old palace. Highlights include the Dutch Mona Lisa: Vermeer's *Girl with a Pearl Earring*. Rembrandts include a wistful self-portrait from the year of his death, 1669.

Adjoining the Mauritshuis, the **Binnenhof** (☎ 364 61 44; 10am-4pm Mon-Sat) is surrounded by parliamentary buildings that have long been at the heart of Dutch politics. A highlight of the complex is the 13th-century Gothic **Ridderzaal** (Knights' Hall). Stroll around the Hofvijver, where the reflections of the Binnenhof and the Mauritshuis have inspired countless snapshots.

The **Grote Kerk** (☎ 302 86 30; Rond de Grote Kerk 12), dating from 1450, has a fine pulpit that was constructed 100 years later. The neighbouring 1565 **old town hall** is a splendid example of Dutch Renaissance architecture.

Admirers of De Stijl and Piet Mondrian mustn't miss the Berlage-designed **Gemeentemuseum** (Municipal Museum; ☎ 338 11 20; Stadhouderslaan 41; www.gemeentemuseum.nl; adult/under 18yr €8.50/free; 11am-5pm Tue-Sun). It also houses extensive exhibits of applied arts, costumes and musical instruments. Mondrian's unfinished *Victory Boogie Woogie* takes pride of place.

Madurodam (☎ 355 39 00; www.madurodam.nl; George Maduroplein 1; adult/under 11yr €14/10; 9am-8pm) is a miniaturised Netherlands, complete with 1:25 scale versions of Schiphol, Amsterdam, windmills and tulips, Rotterdam harbour, the Delta dikes, and so on.

The long beach at **Scheveningen** (www.scheveningen.nl) attracts nine million visitors per year. Most streets heading west reach Scheveningen, but it's more pleasantly approached at the end of a 15- to 20-minute (4km) bike ride that will take you past the lush homes of some of Den Haag's most well-heeled residents.

SLEEPING

Hotel 't Centrum (☎ 346 36 57; www.hotelhetcentrum.nl; Veenkade 5-6; r €40-85) The 13 rooms here are the best deal close to the centre. Things are basic white but spotless and comfortable; some rooms share bathrooms. Apartments have basic cooking facilities and there's a small cafe. Book ahead.

Corona Hotel (☎ 363 79 30; www.corona.nl; Buitenhof 39-42; r from €90; 💻) This pleasant hotel is across the way from the Binnenhof and has all the usual business facilities and amenities.

EATING

our pick **De Zwarte Ruiter** (The Black Rider; ☎ 364 95 49; Grote Markt 27; snacks from €4) The Rider faces off with the competing Boterwaag across the Markt like rival Kings of Cool. We call this one the winner, with its terrace and art-deco mezzanine – light-filled, split-level and cavernous – and boisterous crowds of commoners, diplomats and no doubt, the odd international jewel thief.

Zebedeüs (☎ 346 83 93; Rond de Grote Kerk 8; meals from €7) Built right into the walls of the Grote Kerk, this bright cafe is a day-tripper's dream, with huge, fresh sandwiches served all day.

Cloos (☎ 363 97 86; www.eetcafecloos.nl; Plein 12a; mains from €8) One of a gaggle of swank cafes on the vast Plein. Rest your gentrified butt on the comfy wicker chairs and watch the pigeons bedevil the solemn statue of Willem I, hero of the Spanish War.

It Rains Fishes (☎ 365 25 98; www.itrainsfishes.nl; Noordeinde 123; mains €15-32) It's the 'restaurant on the sunny side of the street' (quite a feat given the local weather…), a multi-award-winning bistro serving perfectly prepared seafood from the waters just west.

ENTERTAINMENT

Nederlands Dans Theater (☎ 880 01 00; www.ndt.nl; Schedeldoekshaven 60) This world-famous dance company has two main components: NDT1, the main troupe of 32 dancers and NDT2, a small group of 12 dancers under 21.

GETTING THERE & AROUND

Most trains start/stop their journeys from Den Haag Centraal Station. But some through trains only stop at Den Haag HS (Holland Spoor) station just south of the centre. Tram 1 links to both Scheveningen and Delft.

JOHN ELK III

Binnenhof

DELFT

☎ 015 / pop 96,300

Ah, lovely Delft: compact, charming, relaxed. Many of the canalside vistas could be scenes from the *Girl with a Pearl Earring*, the novel about Golden Age painter Jan Vermeer, which was made into a movie (and partially shot here) in 2003. Delft is also famous for its 'delftware', the distinctive blue-and-white pottery originally duplicated from Chinese porcelain by 17th-century artisans.

The **tourist office** (☎ 0900-515 15 55; www.delft.nl; Hippolytusbuurt 4; 11am-4pm Mon, 10am-4pm Tue-Fri, to 5pm Sat, to 4pm Sun) has free internet. Highly recommended is its range of thematic walking guides.

SIGHTS & ACTIVITIES

The 14th-century **Nieuwe Kerk** (☎ 212 30 25; www.nieuwekerk-delft.nl; Markt; adult/child €3.20/1.60; 9am-6pm Apr-Oct, 11am-4pm Nov-Mar, closed Sun) houses the crypt of the Dutch royal family and the mausoleum of Willem the Silent. The fee includes entrance to the **Oude Kerk** (☎ 212 30 15; www.oudekerk-delft.nl; Heilige Geestkerkhof; 9am-6pm Apr-Oct, 11am-4pm Nov-Mar, closed Sun) – and vice versa. The latter, 800 years old, is a surreal sight: its tower leans 2m from the vertical. Among the tombs inside is Vermeer's.

The non-prolific painter (only 35 works are firmly attributed to him) is the star of the **Vermeer Centre Delft** (☎ 213 85 88; Voldersgracht 21; adult/child €6/4; 10am-5pm), which looks at his artistry and life in detail but actually has none of his paintings.

Municipal Museum het Prinsenhof (☎ 260 23 58; www.gemeentemusea-delft.nl; St Agathaplein 1; adult/child €6/free; 10am-5pm Tue-Sat, 1-5pm Sun), a former convent, is where Willem the Silent was assassinated in 1584. The museum displays various objects telling the story of the 80-year war with Spain, as well as 17th-century paintings.

The **Museum Nusantara** (☎ 260 23 58; www.nusantara-delft.nl, in Dutch; St Agathaplein 4; adult/child €3.50/free; 10am-5pm Tue-Sat, 1-5pm Sun) shines a light on the Netherlands' colonial past. There's a collection of furniture and other lifestyle artefacts from 17th-century Batavia (now Jakarta), as well as a 'colonial department' detailing the beginnings of Dutch rule in Indonesia.

See Delft on a **canal boat tour** (☎ 212 63 85; www.rondvaartdelft.nl; adult/under 12yr €6/3; 11am-5pm Apr-Oct) departing from Koornmarkt 113.

SLEEPING & EATING

Hotel de Ark (☎ 215 79 99; www.deark.nl; Koornmarkt 65; r €115-150;) Four 17th-century canalside houses have been turned into this gracious and luxurious small hotel. Out back there's a small garden; nearby are apartments for longer stays.

Stadys Koffyhuis (☎ 212 46 25; www.stads-koffyhuis.nl; Oude Delft 133; mains €7-10) Enjoy drinks, sandwiches and pancakes while admiring possibly the best view in Delft – the Oude Kerk, just ahead at the end of the canal.

our pick **'t Walletje** (☎ 214 04 23; Burgwal 7; mains €7-12) Tables front this small bistro on a pedestrian street near the centre. Lunch has good smoothies, sandwiches and salads. At night three-course specials (€20) are artfully prepared and feature nice accents like pesto sides with seafood and steaks.

GETTING THERE & AWAY

Sample train fares: Den Haag (€2.50, 12 minutes), Rotterdam (€3.20, 12 minutes) and Amsterdam (€11.60, one hour). Tram 1 makes the run to Den Haag.

ROTTERDAM

☎ 010 / pop 605,000

Rotterdam, the second-largest Dutch city, was bombed flat during WWII. The following decades were spent rebuilding the harbour and the centre, often with eye-popping architecture that's unique in Europe. Today, Rotterdam has a crackling energy, with vibrant nightlife, a diverse, multi-ethnic community, an intensely interesting maritime tradition and a wealth of top-class museums.

ORIENTATION & INFORMATION

Rotterdam, split by the vast Nieuwe Maas shipping channel, is crossed by a series of tunnels and bridges, notably the fabulously postmodern Erasmusbrug. The centre is on the north side of the water. From Centraal Station (CS), a 15-minute walk along the canal-like ponds leads to the waterfront. The commercial centre is to the east and most of the museums are to the west.

The Rotterdam Welcome Card offers discounts for sights, hotels and restaurants; it's €5. Buy it from the tourist office.

Tourist office (☎ 271 01 28; www.rotterdam.info; Coolsingel 5; 9am-6pm Mon-Fri, to 5pm Sat & Sun) Free internet, paid wi-fi; excellent cafe with rooftop views.

Use-It (☎ 240 91 58; www.use-it.nl; Schaatsbaan 41-45; 9am-6pm Tue-Sun mid-May–mid-Sep, to 5pm Tue-Sat mid-Sep–mid-May) Offbeat independent tourist organisation all but lost amid the station construction.

SIGHTS & ACTIVITIES

Museum Boijmans van Beuningen (☎ 441 94 00; www.boijmans.nl; Museumpark 18-20; adult/child €9/free, Wed free; 11am-5pm Tue-Sun) is among Europe's very finest museums and has a permanent collection taking in Dutch and European art (Bosch, Van Eyck, Rembrandt, Tintoretto, Titian and Bruegel's *Tower of Babel*). The surrealist wing features ephemera, paraphernalia and famous works from Dalí, Duchamp, Magritte, Man Ray and more.

The **Nederlands Architectuur Instituut** (NAI; ☎ 440 12 00; www.nai.nl; Museumpark 25; adult/child €8/1; 10am-5pm Tue-Sat, 11am-5pm Sun & holidays) offers a full overview of Dutch architecture. Admission includes a tour of the adjoining landmark Modernist gem, the 1933 Huis Sonneveld.

The **Overblaak development** (1978–84), designed by Piet Blom, is marked by its pencil-shaped tower and arresting up-ended, cube-shaped apartments. One unit, the **Kijk-Kubus Museum-House** (☎ 414 22 85; www.kubuswoning.nl; adult/child €2.50/1.50; 11am-5pm), lets you see what its like to live at odd angles.

Chances are something you buy in Europe will have transited through Rotterdam's port, Europe's busiest. **Maritiem Museum Rotterdam** (☎ 413 26 80; www.maritiemmuseum.nl; Leuvehaven 1; adult/child €5/3; 10am-5pm Tue-Sat, 11am-5pm Sun year-round, plus 10am-5pm Mon Jul & Aug) looks at the Netherlands' rich maritime traditions.

At 185m, a shimmy up the **Euromast** (☎ 436 48 11; www.euromast.com; Parkhaven 20; adult/child €8.30/5.40; 10am-11pm) is a must. It offers unparalleled 360-degree views of Rotterdam, with its rotating, glass-walled 'Euroscope' contraption ascending to near the summit, from where you'll fully appreciate just how mighty the harbour is.

Spido (☎ 275 99 88; www.spido.nl; Willemsplein 85; adult/child €9.25/5.30; 9.30am-5pm Jun-Sep, shorter hr Oct-May) offers daily harbour tours.

Historic and appealing, **Delfshaven** is a vibrant, multi-ethnic neighbourhood with many cafes and bars, especially along the canal near the Oude Kerk.

SLEEPING

Hotel Bazar (☎ 206 51 51; www.hotelbazar.nl; Witte de Withstraat 16; r €60-120) Bazar is deservedly popular for its 27 Middle Eastern-, African- and South American-themed rooms: lush, brocaded curtains, exotically tiled bathrooms and more. Top-floor rooms have balconies and views.

Hotel Emma (☎ 436 55 33; www.hotelemma.nl; Nieuwe Binnenweg 6; r €90-145; 💻) Recently refurbished, the Emma is a modern place with 24 rooms close to the centre. There's free wi-fi and touches like posh bathrooms and double-glazed windows.

our pick **Hotel New York** (☎ 439 05 00; www.hotelnewyork.nl; Koninginnenhoofd 1; r €110-220; 💻) The city's most appealing hotel is housed in the former headquarters of the Holland–America passenger-ship line. The 72 art-nouveau rooms – with many original and painstakingly restored decor items and fittings – are worthy of any luxury ocean liner.

EATING

Bazar (☎ 206 51 51; Witte de Withstraat 16; mains €4-15) On the ground floor of the inventive Hotel Bazar, this eatery comes up with creative Middle Eastern fusion fare that compliments the stylised decor.

Toaster (☎ 413 70 81; Pannekoekstraat 38A; meals €6-12; 🕑 closed Mon) Take time out from cruising the trendy shops and little lanes in and around Pannekoekstraat at this neighbourhood hang-out. The name refers to the many toasted sandwiches, there's also tapas and all-day breakfast.

Dudok (☎ 433 31 02; Meent 88; dishes €6-20) There are always crowds at this sprawling brasserie near the centre. Meals range from breakfasts to snacks to cafe fare like soups and pasta.

Stadsbrouwerij De Pelgrim (☎ 477 11 89; Aelbrechtkolk 12, Delfshaven; mains €7-20) It's named for the religious folk who passed through on their way to America and you can make your own voyage through the various beers brewed in the vintage surrounds.

our pick **Het Eethuisje** (☎ 425 49 17; Mathenesserdijk 436, Delfshaven; mains €8-10) Trad Dutch food is served from this little storefront near the canal. Tuck into meaty fare served with rib-sticking starchy sides.

Look (☎ 436 70 00; www.restaurantlook.nl; 's Gravendijkwal; mains €13-20; 🕑 dinner Wed-Sun) It's an orgasm of garlic at this locally loved bistro with a wildly creative menu celebrating the fabulous clove. Needless to say, there's creamy garlic soup on the menu, but you'll also find inventive meat and seafood mains and, yes, desserts with hints of garlic.

DRINKING

Stalles (☎ 436 16 55; Nieuwe Binnenweg 11a) This classic *bruin café* is on a great stretch of road near plenty of good shops, cafes and bars.

Locus Publicus (☎ 433 17 61; Oostzeedijk 364) The listings of the more than 200 beers on offer cover the panelled walls at this outstanding specialist beer cafe.

GETTING THERE & AWAY

The area around Rotterdam Centraal Station will be one big construction site until the stunning new station – set above and below ground – is completed in 2012. The high-speed line to Belgium stops here. Sample train fares: Amsterdam (€13.60, one hour, four every hour) and Utrecht (€9.30, 40 minutes, two every hour).

GETTING AROUND

Rotterdam's trams, buses and metro are provided by **RET** (☎ 447 69 11; www.ret.

nl). Most converge in front of CS, where there is an **information office** (6am-11pm Mon-Fri, 8am-11pm Sat & Sun) that also sells tickets.

UTRECHT

030 / pop 283,000

Utrecht is one of the Netherlands' oldest cities and boasts a beautiful, vibrant, old-world city centre, ringed by striking 13th-century canal wharves. The wharves, well below street level, are unique to Utrecht, and the streets alongside brim with shops, restaurants and cafes. The only blot on the landscape is the hulking Hoog Catharijne shopping centre, a postwar carbuncle that's scheduled for a long-overdue redevelopment over the next few years.

INFORMATION

Tourist office (0900-128 87 32; www.utrecht.nl; Domplein 9; 10am-6pm Mon-Fri, to 5pm Sat, noon-5pm Sun)

SIGHTS

One of Utrecht's favourite sons, Dick Bruna, is honoured at the **Dick Bruna Huis** (236 23 62; www.dickbrunahuis.nl; Agnietenstraat 2; adult/child €8/2; 11am-5pm Tue-Sun). Bruna is the creator of beloved cartoon rabbit Miffy (Nijntje in Dutch) and she naturally takes pride of place, along with an extensive overview of Bruna's career.

Admission also includes entry to the nearby **Centraal Museum** (236 23 62; www.centraalmuseum.nl; Nicolaaskerkhof 10; adult/child €8/2; 11am-5pm Tue-Sun). It has a wide-ranging collection: applied arts dating back to the 17th century as well as paintings by some of the Utrecht School artists.

The museum offers tours of the Unesco-recognised **Rietveld-Schröderhuis** just outside the centre. Built in 1924 by Utrecht architect Gerrit Rietveld, it is a stark example of 'form follows function'.

LEANNE LOGAN

Domtoren

The **Museum Catharijneconvent** (231 72 96; www.catharijneconvent.nl; Nieuwegracht 63; adult/child €10/6; 10am-5pm Tue-Fri, 11am-5pm Sat & Sun) has the finest collection of medieval religious art in the Netherlands, housed in a Gothic former convent and an 18th-century canalside house.

The **Domtoren** (Cathedral Tower; 233 30 36; www.domtoren.nl; Domplein; adult/child €7.50/4.50; 11am-4pm Mon-Sat, noon-4pm Sun) is 112m high, with 465 steps. It's a tough haul to the top, but well worth the exertion: the tower gives unbeatable city views.

SLEEPING

B&B Utrecht (☎ 065 043 48 84; www.hostelutrecht.nl; Lucas Bolwerk 4; dm from €19, r from €55; 💻) Straddling the border between hostel and hotel, this spotless inn in an elegant old building has an internal Ikea vibe.

NH Centre Utrecht Hotel (☎ 231 31 69; www.nh-hotels.com; Janskerkhof 10; r €100-

MANFRED GOTTSCHALK

Tulips in Keukenhof Gardens

IF YOU LIKE...

The Netherlands is one of the most densely populated countries on earth, but if you like escaping the cities, we think you'll enjoy the following:

- **Hoge Veluwe National Park** (☎ 0318-59 16 27; www.hogeveluwe.nl; adult/child €7/3.50, park & museum €14/7, car €6; 🕒 8am-8pm Apr, to 9pm May & Aug, to 10pm Jun & Jul, 9am-8pm Sep, to 7pm Oct, to 6pm Nov-Mar) The Netherlands' largest national park is a mix of forests, woods and heathery moors, along with red deer, wild boar and mouflon (wild sheep). It's also home to the Kröller-Müller Museum (p388), featuring works by Van Gogh, Picasso, Renoir and Manet.
- **Texel** (*tes*-sel) Highlights of this island include the peaceful forest trails of De Dennen and the undulating dunes of the Duinen van Texel National Park. It's 3km off Noord Holland; the ferry crossing from Den Helder takes 20 minutes.
- **Keukenhof Gardens** (www.keukenhof.nl; adult/child under 11yr €13.50/6.50; 🕒 8am-7.30pm mid-Mar–mid-May, last entry 6pm) Near Lisse, these lovely gardens are renowned for their tulip, daffodil and hyacinth displays. Bus 54 travels from Leiden Centraal Station to Keukenhof (25 minutes). A combo ticket costs adult/child €20/11.
- **Kinderdijk** (www.kinderdijk.nl; windmill adult/child €3.50/2; 🕒 windmill 9.30am-5.30pm Apr-Oct, 11am-4pm Sat & Sun Nov-Mar weather permitting) In 1740 a series of windmills was built to drain a polder 12km southeast of Rotterdam. Today 19 of the Dutch icons survive; you can even see inside one of them. Ask at the Rotterdam tourist offices about boat trips and bike hire.

150; 💻) This mannered hotel is housed in an atmospheric old building (1870). The rooms are very comfortable, with good church views and modern, stylish decor.

EATING & DRINKING

When Utrecht groans with visiting mobs, you can escape down to the waterside canal piers with a picnic.

Oudaen (☎ **231 18 64; www.oudaen.nl; Oudegracht 99; mains €8-22**) Set in a restored 14th-century banquet hall, Oedaen has a varied menu of salads, steaks and seafood. Best of all, it brews its own beer, which you can enjoy under the high ceilings or outside on the canal.

Polman's (☎ **231 33 68; cnr Jansdam & Keistraat; mains €12-25**) Diners at this grand cafe are welcomed in an elegant former ballroom with ceiling frescoes and extravagant floral displays. French and Italian flavours dominate the menu *and* the extensive wine list.

our pick **Blauw** (☎ **234 24 63; Springweg 64; set menu from €20;** 🕑 **dinner**) Blauw is *the* place for stylish Indonesian food in Utrecht. Young and old alike enjoy superb rice tables amid the stunning red decor that mixes vintage art with hip minimalism.

Café Ledig Erf (☎ **231 75 77; Tolsteegbrug 3**) This classy pub overlooks a confluence of canals (and other cafes) at the southern tip of town. The terrace vies with the beer list in offering the most joy. The fall bock beer fest is a winner.

GETTING THERE & AROUND

Utrecht is easily walked (once you escape the shopping mall). Its train station is a major connection point and is Holland's busiest. It is on the line linking Amsterdam to Cologne.

BELGIUM

BRUSSELS

pop 1.03 million

Defining Brussels (Brussel in Dutch, Bruxelles in French) is no easy task. Quirky, secretive, surreal – Brussels, like the country it represents, pulls multiple identities into one enigmatic core. Home to superb art-nouveau architecture, the EU headquarters, shabby suburbs and more restaurants, pubs and chocolate shops than you could possibly visit, Brussels subtly seduces.

ORIENTATION

The Grand Place, Brussels' imposing 15th-century market square, is the city's chief landmark. It sits dead centre in the Petit Ring, a pentagon of boulevards enclosing the central Brussels area. The city centre divides into the Lower Town (comprising the medieval core and atmospheric quarters such as Ste-Catherine, St-Géry and the Marolles) and the Upper Town, home to major museums and chic shopping precincts based around the Sablon and Ave Louise. East of the Petit Ring is the real-life Gotham City of the EU headquarters.

Gare Centrale, Brussels' most central train station, is about a five-minute walk from the Grand Place; Gare du Midi, where international trains arrive, is 2.5km from the famous square. To get to the Grand Place from Gare du Midi, take either a train to Gare Centrale or a *premetro* tram (18, 52, 56, 81 or 82) to the stop Bourse.

Unlike anywhere else in Belgium, Brussels is officially bilingual. Everything, from the names of streets to train stations, is written in both Dutch and French.

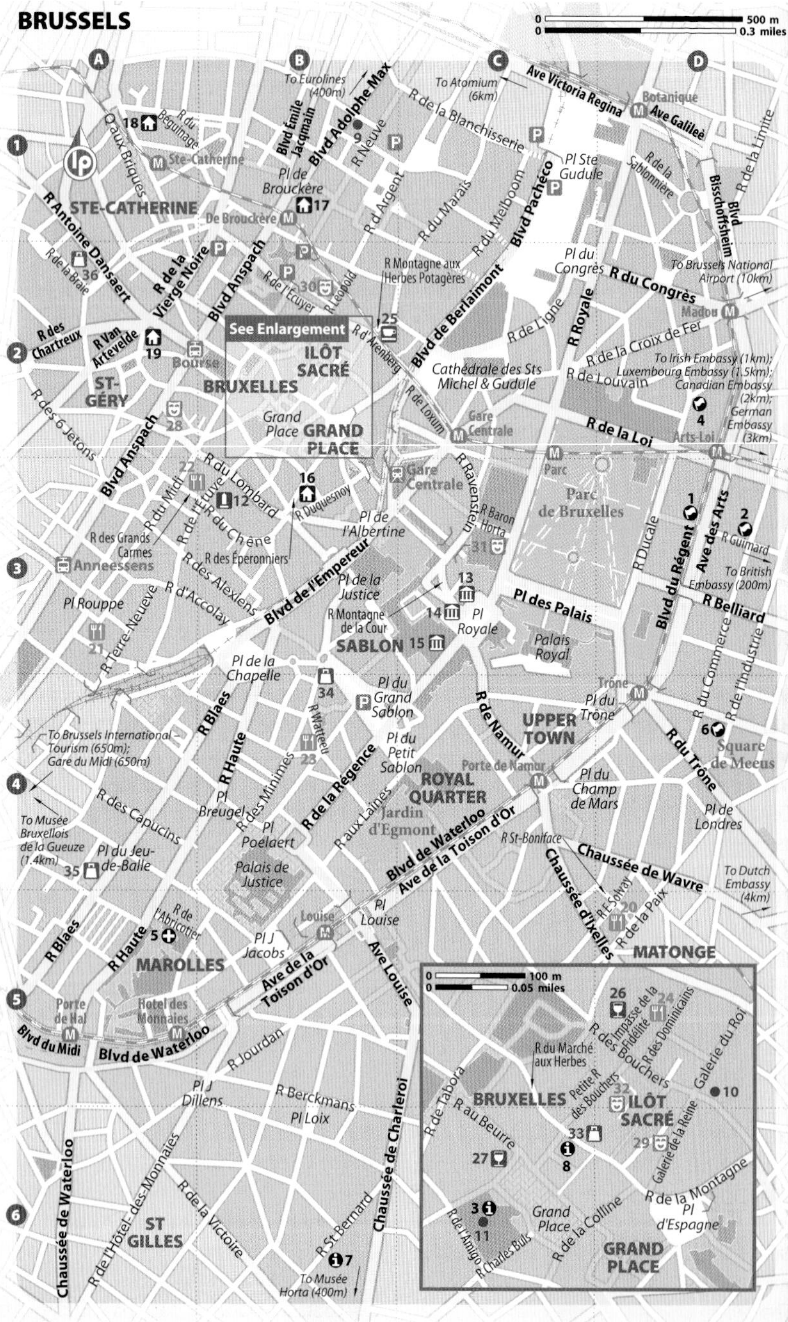
BRUSSELS
0 500 m
0 0.3 miles
A
B
C
D
1
2
3
4
5
6
To Eurolines (400m)
To Atomium (6km)
Ave Victoria Regina
Botanique
Ave Galilée
R du Béguinage
Q aux Briques
Ste-Catherine
Blvd Émile Jacqmain
Blvd Adolphe Max
R Neuve
R de la Blanchisserie
Pl Ste Gudule
R de la Sablonnière
R de la Limite
Blvd Bisschoffsheim
Pl de Brouckère
STE-CATHERINE
De Brouckère
R Antoine Dansaert
R de la Braie
R de la Vierge Noire
Blvd Anspach
R de l'Écuyer
R Léopold
R d'Argent
R du Marais
R du Melboom
Blvd Pachéco
Pl du Congrès
R du Congrès
To Brussels National Airport (10km)
R Montagne aux Herbes Potagères
Madou
R des Chartreux
R Van Artevelde
Bourse
See Enlargement
ILÔT SACRÉ
BRUXELLES
R d'Arenberg
Blvd de Berlaimont
R de Ligne
R Royale
R de la Croix de Fer
R de Louvain
To Irish Embassy (1km); Luxembourg Embassy (1.5km); Canadian Embassy (2km); German Embassy (3km)
ST-GÉRY
Cathédrale des Sts Michel & Gudule
R des 6 Jetons
Grand Place
GRAND PLACE
R de Loxum
Gare Centrale
R de la Loi
Arts-Loi
Parc
Parc de Bruxelles
R du Midi
R de l'Étuve
R du Lombard
R Duquesnoy
R du Chêne
R Ravenstein
R Baron Horta
R Ducale
Blvd du Régent
Ave des Arts
R Guimard
To British Embassy (200m)
R des Grands Carmes
R des Éperonniers
Pl de l'Albertine
Anneessens
R des Alexiens
Blvd de l'Empereur
Pl de la Justice
Pl des Palais
R Belliard
Pl Rouppe
R Terre-Neuve
R d'Accolay
R Montagne de la Cour
Pl Royale
SABLON
Palais Royal
Pl de la Chapelle
Pl du Grand Sablon
R Watteeu
Trône
Pl du Trône
R du Commerce
R de l'Industrie
R de Namur
UPPER TOWN
To Brussels International Tourism (650m); Gare du Midi (650m)
R Blaes
R Haute
Pl du Petit Sablon
Porte de Namur
R du Trône
Square de Meeus
ROYAL QUARTER
To Musée Bruxellois de la Gueuze (1.4km)
R des Capucins
Pl Breugel
R des Minimes
R de la Régence
R aux Laines
Jardin d'Egmont
Pl du Champ de Mars
Pl de Londres
Pl Poelaert
Blvd de Waterloo
Ave de la Toison d'Or
R St-Boniface
Pl du Jeu-de-Balle
Palais de Justice
Chaussée de Wavre
To Dutch Embassy (4km)
Chaussée d'Ixelles
R de l'Abricotier
Louise
Pl Louise
R E Solvay
R de la Paix
Pl J Jacobs
MATONGE
MAROLLES
Ave Louise
Porte de Hal
Hotel des Monnaies
Blvd du Midi
R Jourdan
Pl J Dillens
R Berckmans
Pl Loix
Chaussée de Charleroi
Chaussée de Waterloo
R de l'Hôtel-des-Monnaies
R de la Victoire
R St Bernard
ST GILLES
To Musée Horta (400m)
0 100 m
0 0.05 miles
Impasse de la Fidélité
R des Dominicains
R des Bouchers
Galerie du Roi
R du Marché aux Herbes
Petite R des Bouchers
R de Tabora
R au Beurre
Galerie de la Reine
R de la Montagne
Pl d'Espagne
R de l'Amigo
R Charles Buls
R de la Colline
1
2
3
4
5
6
7
8
9
10
11
12
13
14
15
16
17
18
19
20
21
22
23
24
25
26
27
28
29
30
31
32
33
34
35
36

INFORMATION

DISCOUNT CARDS

Brussels Card (24/48/72hr €20/28/33) Includes admission to many museums plus unlimited use of city public transport and discounts in bars and restaurants. Order online (www.bitc.be) or buy from the tourist offices.

MEDICAL SERVICES

Hôpital St Pierre (☎ 02 535 31 11, emergency 02 535 40 51; cnr Rue Haute & Rue de l'Abricotier; 24hr; M Hôtel des Monnaies) Central hospital offering emergency assistance.

TOURIST INFORMATION

Brussels International (☎ 02 513 89 40; www.brusselsinternational.be; Grand Place; 9am-6pm Easter-Oct, 9am-6pm Mon-Sat, 10am-2pm Sun Nov-Dec, 9am-6pm Mon-Sat Jan-Easter; M Gare Centrale, Bourse) The City of Brussels' tiny tourist office is located inside the town hall and is usually crammed.

Brussels International – Tourism (Gare du Midi; 8am-8pm Sat-Thu, 8am-9pm Fri May-Sep, 8am-5pm Mon-Thu, 8am-8pm Fri, 9am-6pm Sat, 9am-2pm Sun Oct-Apr; M Gare du Midi) For visitors arriving by Eurostar or Thalys.

Office de Promotion du Tourisme de Wallonie et de Bruxelles (OPT; ☎ 070 22 10 21; www.opt.be; Rue St Bernard 30; 9am-5pm; M Horta) For information on Wallonia and Brussels.

Visit Flanders (☎ 02 504 03 90; www.visitflanders.com; Rue du Marché aux Herbes 61; 9am-7pm Jul-Aug, 9am-6pm Mon-Sat, 9am-5pm Sun Apr-Jun & Sep, 9am-5pm Mon-Sat, 9am-4pm Sun Oct-Mar, closed 1-2pm Sat & Sun all year; M Gare Centrale, Bourse) For tourist info on Flanders.

SIGHTS

GRAND PLACE

Brussels' magnificent central square, **Grand Place**, tops every newcomer's itinerary. Here you will find the splendid Gothic-style **Hôtel de Ville**, the only building to escape bombardment by the French in 1695 – an ironic fate, considering that it was the target. The square's splendour is due largely to its antique frame of **guildhalls**, erected by merchant guilds and adorned with gilded statues and symbols.

GALERIES ST-HUBERT & RUE DES BOUCHERS

Galeries St-Hubert, situated one block northeast of Grand Place, is a European

JONATHAN SMITH

Grand Place (p403)

first and a must-visit. Opened in 1847, this *grande dame* of Brussels' shopping arcades contains an eclectic mix of shops, as well as a cinema, theatre, restaurant and cafes. Off one of the galleries is the famous **Rue des Bouchers** (see p405).

MUSÉES ROYAUX DES BEAUX-ARTS

The **Musées Royaux des Beaux-Arts** (Royal Museums of Fine Arts; ☎ 02 508 32 11; www.fine-arts-museum.be; Rue de la Régence 3; adult/concession €6/3.50, admission free 1-5pm 1st Wed of month; 9.30am-5pm Tue-Fri, 10am-5pm Sat & Sun; M Gare Centrale or Parc, 92, 93 or 94) houses Belgium's premier collections of ancient and modern art, and is well endowed with works by Pieter Breugel the Elder, Rubens and the Belgian surrealists. Headphones (for English explanations) cost an extra €2.50.

MUSÉE MAGRITTE

The **Musée Magritte** (☎ tickets 02 508 33 33; www.musee-magritte-museum.be; Place Royale; admission €8; 10am-5pm Tue-Sun, till 8pm Wed; M Gare Centrale or Parc, 92, 93 or 94) should be operating by the time you read this. It will house some 150 works by Belgium's most famous surrealist artist, René Magritte.

MUSÉE DES INSTRUMENTS DE MUSIQUE

The **Musée des Instruments de Musique** (Musical Instrument Museum; ☎ 02 545 01 30; www.mim.fgov.be; Rue Montagne de la Cour 2; adult/child/concession €5/free/4; 9.30am-5pm Tue-Fri, 10am-5pm Sat & Sun; M Gare Centrale or Parc, 92, 93 or 94) boasts one of the world's biggest collections of instruments.

MUSÉE HORTA

A superb introduction to the art-nouveau movement is the **Musée Horta** (☎ 02 543 04 90; www.hortamuseum.be; Rue Américaine 25; adult/child/concession €7/3/5; 2-5.30pm Tue-Sun; M Horta, 91 or 92). It occupies two adjoining houses in St Gilles that Horta designed as his private house and studio in 1898.

MUSÉE BRUXELLOIS DE LA GUEUZE

Anyone with even a vague interest in Belgian beers must not miss the excellent **Musée Bruxellois de la Gueuze** (Brussels' Gueuze Museum; ☎ 02 521 49 28; www.cantillon.be; Rue Gheude 56; admission €5; 9am-5pm Mon-Fri, 10am-5pm Sat; M Gare du Midi). It's about 800m from Gare du Midi – head to Place Bara, take Rue Limnander and then cross into Rue Gheude.

MANNEKEN PIS

Despite being a national symbol, the **Manneken Pis** fountain – a little boy cheerfully taking a leak into a pool – never fails to disappoint visitors because of its diminutive size. It's three blocks from the Grand Place, on the corner of Rue de l'Étuve and Rue du Chêne.

ATOMIUM

More than 50 years old, the **Atomium** (☎ 02 475 47 77; www.atomium.be; Sq de l'Atomium; adult/child/concession €9/free/6; 10am-7pm May-Sep, 10am-6pm Oct-Apr; M Heyzel, 81) is a space-age leftover from the 1958 World Fair – a model of an iron molecule enlarged 165 billion times.

TOURS

Atelier de Recherche et d'Action Urbaines (ARAU; ☎ 02 219 33 45; www.arau.org; Blvd Adolphe Max 55; M De Brouckère), a heritage conservation group, runs tours (either themed walks or coach tours) offering entry into some of Brussels' private art-nouveau showpieces.

SLEEPING

As capital of the EU, Brussels is overflowing with top-end hotels catering to Eurocrats and business people. Many of these hotels (and some midrange hotels as well) drop their rates dramatically on weekends and during the July/August summer holidays to make up for the Eurocrat shortfall.

Hôtel Noga (☎ 02 218 67 63; www.nogahotel.com; Rue du Béguinage 38; s/d/tr €95/110/135, weekend €75/85/110; M Ste Catherine;) Sixty years old and still going strong, this little gem in Ste Catherine mixes modern and old in a self-assured feast for the eyes.

Hotel Alma (☎ 02 502 2828; www.almahotel.be; Rue des Éperonniers 42-44; s/d weekday €125/144, r weekend €86; M Gare Centrale;) Dark decor and modern minimalism is the tone of this new hotel, secreted in a backstreet close to the Grand Place.

Hotel Orts (☎ 02 517 0717; www.hotelorts.be; Rue Auguste Orts 38; d from €150; Bourse;) Hotels rarely come or go in downtown Brussels, so this boutique newcomer is well worth mentioning. Opened in 2006, the Orts occupies a 19th-century building in the city's hip hub of St Gèry.

our pick **Hôtel Métropole** (☎ 02 217 23 00, reservations 02 214 24 24; www.metropolehotel.com; Pl de Brouckère 31; s/d/ste weekday from €330/360/500, s/d weekend from €130/155; M De Brouckère;) The *grande dame* of Brussels' hotel scene, and perfect for a weekend splurge that won't cost an arm or a leg. The lavish French Renaissance-style foyer contrasts with the soberly furnished rooms.

EATING

Restaurants of all persuasions abound in Brussels and the standards are high. The exception to this are the eateries along Rue des Bouchers, a must-see street lined with barking hawkers and tacky tourist restaurants – it's great for a wander, but you're best eating elsewhere.

Le Perroquet (☎ 02 512 99 22; Rue Watteeu 31; light meals €8-10; noon-1am; M Porte de Namur) Art-nouveau cafe in the affluent

Sablon. Salads and stuffed pitas, including vegetarian options, are the mainstay.

Le Cercle des Voyageurs (☎ 02 514 39 49; Rue des Grands Carmes 18; mains €13-17; from 11am Wed-Mon; Bourse) Perfect for the armchair traveller, this stylish cafe/bar has a great array of travel books for browsing and a world kitchen for tasting.

Belgo Belge (☎ 02 511 11 21; Rue de la Paix 20; mains from €15; noon-midnight; M Porte de Namur) Just one of many great eateries in this Ixelles backstreet (check out the options in Rue St Boniface, too). An eclectic crowd keeps this restaurant buzzing day and night, and the lunchtime *menu du jour* (€10) is good value.

our pick **Vincent** (☎ 02 511 26 07; Rue des Dominicains 8; mains €18-29; lunch & dinner; M Gare Centrale) Over a century old, and still drawing in the locals, this Brussels' institution combines classic Belgian cuisine with good-natured waiters and historic decor.

Comme Chez Soi (☎ 02 512 29 21; Pl Rouppe 23; mains €45-65, 4-course menu from €76; lunch & dinner Tue-Sat; M Anneessens) Chef Pierre Wynants' innovative cuisine will bite a good chunk out of your holiday budget, but it'll be worth every cent. Reservations essential.

DRINKING

Cafe culture is ingrained in Brussels.

Delirium Café (www.deliriumcafe.be; Impasse de la Fidélité 4A; 10am-4am, until 2am Sun; M Gare Centrale) This cellar pub guarantees to stock at least 2004 beers – the lion's share are Belgian, of course. When we visited they had 2851 brews on hand. Cheers!

Le Roy d'Espagne (☎ 02 513 08 07; Grand Place 1; M Gare Centrale) Sit and sip (pricey beers) the splendour of the Grand Place in this former guildhall. And, yes, those are inflated dried pigs' bladders above your head.

À la Mort Subite (☎ 02 513 13 18; Montagne aux Herbes Potagères 7; M Gare Centrale) Long cafe with wood panelling, mirrored walls and brusque service.

ENTERTAINMENT

Get past the cafes and Brussels offers everything from unique folkloric pageants to stunning contemporary dance. The weekly English-language magazine *The Bulletin* has entertainment coverage. Also check *Le Soir* on Wednesday.

CINEMAS

Cinéma Arenberg (☎ 02 512 80 63; www.arenberg.be; Galerie de la Reine 26; admission €8; from 1.30pm; M Gare Centrale) Remodelled art-deco cinema located inside Galeries St-Hubert. Foreign and art-house films are the staples.

our pick **Musée du Cinéma** (☎ 02 551 19 19; Rue Baron Horta 9; admission €2.50; from 5pm; M Gare Centrale) One to make cinema buffs swoon. Two auditoriums: silent movies with live piano accompaniment are screened every night of the year in one; the other is devoted to classic talkies.

LIVE MUSIC, DANCE & THEATRE

AB (☎ 02 548 24 24; www.abconcerts.be; Blvd Anspach 110; Bourse) Great venue smack in the heart of the city. AB, or Ancienne Belgique, has two auditoriums accommodating international and home-grown bands.

La Monnaie/De Munt (☎ 02 229 12 00; www.demunt.be; Pl de la Monnaie; M De Brouckère) Brussels' premier venue for opera and theatre is also the place to catch contemporary dance by Anne Teresa De Keersmaeker's innovative company, Rosas.

Théâtre Royal de Toone (☎ 02 511 71 37; www.toone.be; Petite Rue des Bouchers 21; adult/concession €10/7; 8.30pm Thu-Sat; M Gare

PASCALE BEROUJON

Chocolate shop in Brussels

Centrale) Famous marionette theatre, operated for eight generations by the Toone family.

SHOPPING

Chocolate, beer, fashion, comics, lace and bric-a-brac… Brussels has these and many other lines covered.

De Biertempel (☎ 02 502 19 06; Rue du Marché aux Herbes 56; Bourse) A great place that stocks hundreds of Belgian brews, plus matching glasses.

Pierre Marcolini (☎ 02 514 12 06; Pl du Grand Sablon 39; M Porte de Namur) Head here for Belgium's most expensive pralines (€70 per kg).

Stijl (☎ 02 512 03 13; Rue Antoine Dansaert 74; M Ste Catherine) The shop that changed this part of the city. Home to top fashion designers, including members of the Antwerp Six.

Place du Jeu-de-Balle flea market (Pl du Jeu-de-Balle; 7am-2pm; M Porte de Hal) This is the Marolles' famous *brocante* (secondhand) market.

Gare du Midi market (6am-1.30pm Sun; M Gare du Midi) Brussels' biggest general market sprawls next to the train lines and has a distinctly Mediterranean feel.

GETTING THERE & AWAY

For details on air services to and from Brussels, see p418.

The **Eurolines** (☎ 02 274 13 50; www.eurolines.be; Rue du Progrès 80; 5.45am-8.45pm; Gare du Nord) office is located at Gare du Nord train station, from where its buses arrive and depart.

Gare du Midi (☎ 02 528 28 28), often referred to as Brussels Midi, is the main station for international connections: the Eurostar and Thalys fast trains stop here only. For more on international train services, including Eurostar and Thalys trains, see p419.

GETTING AROUND

TO/FROM THE AIRPORT

The Brussels Airport Express train runs between Brussels National airport and the city's three main train stations – Gare du Nord, Gare Centrale and Gare du Midi (one way €2.90). The service runs every 15 minutes from 5.30am to 12.25am and the trip takes 13 to 20 minutes (depending on the station).

A taxi between the airport and central Brussels costs €31.

PUBLIC TRANSPORT

Brussels' efficient public transport system is operated by **Société des Transports Intercommunaux Bruxellois** (☎ 070 23 20 00; www.stib.be), and comprises buses, trains, metro, trams and *premetro* (trams that travel underground). Single tickets cost €1.70, a booklet of five/10 tickets is €6.80/11.50 and a one-day 'Jump' ticket costs €4. Services run from 6am until midnight.

TAXI

Call **Taxis Bleus** (☎ 02 268 00 00) or **Taxis Verts** (☎ 02 349 49 49). Taxes are officially included in the meter price.

FLANDERS

The only thing flat about Flanders is its topography. Belgium's Dutch-speaking northern region is the country's powerhouse, home to vibrant cities, historic gems and contemporary culture.

ANTWERP

pop 457,000

Cosmopolitan, confident and full of contrasts, Antwerp (Antwerpen in Dutch, Anvers in French) is an essential stop on your Belgium travels. Appreciated by art and architecture lovers, mode moguls, club queens and diamond dealers alike, Belgium's second-biggest city once again revels in fame and fortune and what's more, it's now on the high-speed train network.

ORIENTATION

Antwerp's historic centre, based around the Grote Markt, is 1km from the impressive Centraal Station. The two are linked by the pedestrianised Meir (pronounced 'mare'), a bustling shopping thoroughfare. The city basically ends at the Scheldt River, Antwerp's economic lifeline.

INFORMATION

Museumcard (2 days €20) Discount card providing free entrance to many of the city's museums. Sold at tourist offices and museums.

Tourism Antwerp (☎ 03 232 01 03; www.antwerpen.be; Grote Markt 13; 9am-5.45pm Mon-Sat, to 4.45pm Sun; Groenplaats) Main tourist office.

Tourist office (Level 0, Centraal Station; 9am-5.45pm Mon-Sat, to 4.45pm Sun; Diamant) For travellers arriving by train.

SIGHTS

Antwerp's epicentre is the **Grote Markt** (Groenplaats), a pedestrianised market square presided over by the Renaissance-style **Stadhuis** and lined by Renaissance-style **guildhalls**, most of which were reconstructed in the 19th century. Rising from a rough pile of rocks at its centre is the voluptuous, baroque **Brabo Fountain**.

Just a steeple's fall away is Belgium's largest Gothic cathedral, **Onze Lieve Vrouwkathedraal** (☎ 03 213 99 51; www.dekathedraal.be; Handschoenmarkt; adult/child under 12/concession €4/free/2; 10am-5pm Mon-Fri, 10am-3pm Sat, 10am-4pm Sun; Groenplaats). Built between 1352 and 1521, it houses four early canvases by Rubens including the *Descent from the Cross* (1612).

The prestigious **Rubenshuis** (☎ 03 201 15 55; www.museum.antwerpen.be; Wapper 9-11; adult/child under 19/concession €6/free/4, admission free last Wed of month; 10am-5pm Tue-Sun; Meir) was the home and studio of Pieter Paul Rubens, northern Europe's greatest baroque artist. Little more than a ruin when acquired by the city in 1937, it has been superbly restored along original lines.

To immerse yourself in Rubens, head to the **Koninklijk Museum voor Schone Kunsten** (03 238 78 09; www.kmska.be; Leopold De Waelplaats, 't Zuid; adult/child under 19/concession €6/free/4, admission free last Wed of month; 10am-5pm Tue-Sat, to 6pm Sun; 8, 1 or 23 direction Zuid). This fine arts museum houses an impressive permanent collection, from Flemish Primitives to contemporary styles.

Fashion followers must start with Antwerp's mode museum, **MoMu** (03 470 27 70; www.momu.be; Nationalestraat 28; adult/child under 12/concession €6/free/4; 10am-6pm Tue-Sun; Groenplaats). It's located in the much-celebrated **Modenatie** complex, home also to the Flanders Fashion Institute.

Down on the Scheldt is **Zuiderterras** (Groenplaats), a raised promenade built decades ago alongside the city's main dock. It offers a steepled skyline plus an essential pit stop (see p410).

Wander the length of Zuiderterras to arrive at **St Jansvliet**, a small tree-lined square and entry to **St Annatunnel** (Groenplaats). This 570m-long pedestrian tunnel, dug under the Scheldt in the 1930s, links the city centre with the **Linkeroever**, or Left Bank, from where there's a fab city panorama.

Zurenborg, about 2km southeast of Centraal Station, is famed for the eclectic architecture found in a handful of its streets. The showcase is **Cogels-Osylei** (11 direction Eksterlaar), where affluent citizens went wild a century ago.

BRUCE BI

Brabo Fountain and guildhall facade, Grote Markt

SLEEPING & EATING

Hotel Scheldezicht (03 231 66 02; www.hotelscheldezicht.be; St Jansvliet 10-12; s/d/tr from €45/65/90; Groenplaats;) Quaint old-style hotel on a tree-lined square in the historic centre. The spacious rooms have private shower cubicles, but the toilets are shared.

Le Patio (03 232 76 61; www.lepatio.be; Pelgrimstraat 8; r €90;) Smack in the city centre on a pedestrianised street brimming with restaurants and cafes, this friendly B&B has three modern ground-floor rooms built around a small inner courtyard.

Matelote Hotel (03 201 88 00; www.matelote.be; Haarstraat 11; r from €120; Groenplaats;) Discreet new design hotel on a pedestrianised backstreet in the heart of the city, with nine contemporary rooms, tastefully arranged in a 16th-century building. Breakfast costs €12.

Diksmuidse Boterkoeken (☎ 03 227 40 26; Groenplaats; sandwich €3; 8.30am-7.30pm Mon-Sat; Groenplaats) *The* place (really!) in town to buy a sandwich – and not your run-of-the-mill filled baguette either. Ask husband and wife team, Marc and Mia, for a 'Smos' and you'll soon find out why Joe Cocker loved the place (they've an autograph to prove it). It's located in the basement of the Grand Bazar shopping centre.

our pick **Lombardia** (☎ 03 233 68 19; Lombaardenvest 78; light meals €8-12; 7.45am-6pm Mon-Sat; Meir) Legendary health-food-shop-cum-cafe that's been around for nearly four decades. The food's all *bio* (organic) and the decor's bizarre.

Patine (☎ 03 257 09 19; Leopold de Waelstraat 1; quiches €8-12; 9am-1am Mon-Fri, 9am-2am Sat & Sun; 8, 1 or 23 direction Zuid) Bohemian little wine bar/restaurant/tearoom in 't Zuid. The decor's warm and soothing, the clientele includes poodles, and the cuisine is light and healthy – quiche and pasta dishes.

Bistro De Koraal (☎ 03 226 26 70; Leeuwenstraat 1; mains €23-50, 3-/5-course menu €35/60; lunch & dinner Tue-Sat; Groenplaats) Delicious seasonal dishes served in old-fashioned surroundings by a jovial team are the salient features of this intimate restaurant, discreetly located on a quiet backstreet.

DRINKING

Zuiderterras (☎ 03 234 12 75; Ernest van Dijckkaai 37; 9am-midnight; Groenplaats) Landmark cafe/restaurant at the southern end of the riverside promenade and designed by the city's eminent contemporary architect, bOb Van Reeth.

Den Engel (☎ 03 233 12 52; Grote Markt 3; 9am-late; Groenplaats) 'The Angel', as it's known in English, is one of the city's oldest watering holes. A reasonable number of tourists dilute the locals – join them in downing a *bolleke* (little bowl) of De Koninck (The King), the city's favourite ale.

Oud Arsenaal (☎ 03 232 97 45; Pijpelincxstraat 4; 7.30am-7.30pm Sat & Sun, from 9am Mon & Wed-Fri; Meir) Catch the city's most congenial brown cafe while it lasts. Beers are among the cheapest in town – just €2.70 for a Duvel.

GETTING THERE & AROUND

Buses arrive and depart from the **Eurolines** (☎ 03 233 86 62; Van Stralenstraat 8; 9am-6pm Mon-Fri, to 3.30pm Sat & Sun; Diamant) office near Franklin Rooseveltplaats.

Antwerp's beautiful **Centraal Station** (☎ 02 528 28 28; Diamant) is 1.5km from the historic centre. National connections include IC trains every half-hour to Brussels (€6.30, 35 minutes) and Ghent (€8.20, 45 minutes), and hourly trains to Bruges (€12.90, 70 minutes).

De Lijn Antwerpen (☎ 070 22 02 00; www.delijn.be) runs a good network of buses, trams and a *premetro* (trams that run underground for part of their journey). The main bus hubs are Franklin Rooseveltplaats and Koningin Astridplein.

GHENT

pop 235,000

Ghent (known as Gent in Dutch and Gand in French) is Flanders' unsung city. Sandwiched between Brussels, Bruges and Antwerp, this stylish and well-organised city has long been overlooked by visitors on the art-town hop between Belgium's big three.

ORIENTATION & INFORMATION

The city's medieval core contains not one but three central squares. The westernmost square, the Korenmarkt, is the main hub – it's 2km north of the main train station, St Pietersstation.

Museum Pass(ion) (€12.50, valid 3 days) Discount card providing free entrance to many of the city's museums.

Tourist office (☎ 09 266 52 32; www.visitgent.be; Botermarkt 17; 9.30am-6.30pm Apr-Oct, 9.30am-4.30pm Nov-Mar; 1)

SIGHTS

Leave the Korenmarkt behind to reach one of Belgium's most picturesque shots – the view from **St Michielsbrug**, the bridge over the Leie River. Stretching before you is the **Graslei**, the city's favoured waterfront promenade, lined with 'medieval' warehouses and townhouses (largely rebuilt for Ghent's 1913 World Fair) and now home to many restaurants.

Though **St Baafskathedraal** (☎ 09 269 20 45; St Baafsplein; 8.30am-6pm Apr-Oct, 8.30am-5pm Nov-Mar; 1) is unimpressive from the outside, formidable queues form to see the **Adoration of the Mystic Lamb** (adult/child €3/1.50; 9.30am-4.30pm Mon-Sat, 1-4.30pm Sun Apr-Oct, 10.30am-3.30pm Mon-Sat, 1-3.30pm Sun Nov-Mar). This lavish representation of medieval religious thinking is one of the earliest-known oil paintings, executed in 1432 by Flemish Primitive artist Jan Van Eyck.

The 14th-century **Belfort** (☎ 09 233 39 54; Botermarkt; adult/child €3/free; 10am-6pm Easter–mid-Nov; 1) affords spectacular views of the city and is accessible by lift or stairs.

The **Gravensteen** (☎ 09 225 93 06; St Veerleplein; adult/child/concession €6/free/1.20; 9am-6pm Apr-Sep, 9am-5pm Oct-Mar; 1), located smack in the heart of the city, belonged to the 12th-century counts of Flanders and is the quintessential castle.

JONATHAN SMITH

Views past St Baafskathedraal to Belfort

Ghent's highly regarded modern art museum, or **SMAK** (Stedelijk Museum voor Actuele Kunst; ☎ 09 221 17 03; www.smak.be; Citadelpark; adult/child/concession €5/free/3.80, 10am-1pm Sun free; 10am-6pm Tue-Sun; 4), contains works by Karel Appel, Pierre Alechinsky and Panamarenko – three of Belgium's best-known contemporary artists – as well as works by international celebrities.

In the same park you'll find the newly renovated **Museum voor Schone Kunsten** (Fine Arts Museum; ☎ 09 240 07 00; www.mskgent.be; Citadelpark; adult/child/concession €4/free/2.50, 10am-1pm Sun free; 10am-6pm Tue-Sun; 1), whose light and airy rooms house a good selection of Belgian art from the 14th to 20th centuries.

The **Museum voor Vormgeving** (Design Museum; ☎ 09 267 99 99; www.designmuseumgent.be; Jan Breydelstraat 5; adult/child/concession €2.50/free/1.20, 10am-1pm Sun free; 10am-6pm Tue-Sun; 1) is one of Ghent's little-known gems, with a mix of furnishings from the Renaissance through to contemporary styles.

SLEEPING

Brooderie (☎ 09 225 06 23; www.brooderie.be; Jan Breydelstraat 8; s/d/tr €45/65/85; 1) Three simple rooms (shared bathroom facilities) located above a bakery-cum-tea-room. Unpolished wooden floors, earthy furniture, and a fabulous location are the salient features.

Hotel Harmony (☎ 09 324 26 80; www.hotel-harmony.be; Kraanlei 37; s/d from €130/145; 1;) The Harmony occupies two buildings, including a riverfront mansion from 1859, that have been beautifully renovated.

EATING & DRINKING

The canalside Graslei is adorned with terrace restaurants and cafes. The Vrijdagmarkt is a nightlife hub. St Pietersnieuwstraat is good for student hang-outs.

Souplounge (☎ 09 223 62 03; Zuivelbrugstraat 6; small/large soup €3.50/4.50; 10am-7pm; 1) Modern soup kitchen and great for a light, fast meal. The new branch (Overpoortstraat 1) in the student hub is closed on Sundays.

De Orchidee (☎ 09 224 40 49; Vlaanderenstraat 105; mains €7.50; lunch Mon-Fri, dinner daily; 4) Excellent value all-you-can-eat Thai wok restaurant. Choose the filling and sauce, seat yourself in either the purple or pink section, and wait while the chef puts it together.

Belga Queen (☎ 09 280 01 00; Graslei 10; mains €21-35; lunch & dinner; 1) Belga Queen is a few years old but still wears the crown around town. Seafood lovers, vegetarians and carnivores alike are all copiously catered for.

Herberg De Dulle Griet (☎ 09 224 24 55; Vrijdagmarkt 50; noon-1am; 1) Ghent's best-known beer pub. Local brews include Guillotine (9.3%), Delirium Tremens (9.5%) and the city's strongest beer, Piraat (10.5%).

GETTING THERE & AROUND

Ghent's main train station is **St Pietersstation** (☎ 02 528 28 28), situated 2km south of the city centre. Trains run half-hourly to Antwerp (€8.20, 45 minutes), Bruges (€5.60, 20 minutes) and Brussels (€8.20, 45 minutes), and there are hourly connections to Ypres (€9.90, one hour).

The city's public transport network is operated by **De Lijn** (☎ 070 22 02 00). Tram 1 heads to the Korenmarkt in the city centre, and departs from the tram station in the tunnel to the right as you exit the train station.

BRUGES

pop 117,000

Touristy, overcrowded and a tad fake. Describe any other city in these terms and it would be left for dead. But not Bruges (Brugge in Dutch, Bruges in French). Suspended in time centuries ago because of misfortune that drove the townsfolk away, Bruges is one of Western Europe's most visited medieval cities and dreamily evokes a world long since gone.

INFORMATION

Toerisme Brugge (☎ 050 44 46 46; www.brugge.be; 't Zand; 10am-6pm) Tourist office located inside the Concertgebouw.

Train station tourist office (☎ 050 38 80 83; 10am-5pm Mon-Fri, 10am-2pm Sat & Sun)

A CORNER OF A FOREIGN FIELD

The area around **Ypres** was the last bastion of Belgian territory unoccupied by the Germans in WWI. More than 300,000 Allied soldiers were killed here during four years of fighting that left the medieval town flattened. Convincingly rebuilt, the town and its surrounds, known as the Ypres Salient, are dotted with cemeteries and memorials.

The **Menin Gate** (Meensestraat) is inscribed with the names of 54,896 British and Commonwealth troops who were lost in the trenches and have no graves.

Tyne Cot Cemetery, 8km northeast of Ypres, is the largest British Commonwealth war cemetery in the world. In all, 11,956 soldiers are buried here, and the names of a further 35,000 missing soldiers are engraved on the rear wall.

The **Memorial Museum Passchendaele 1917** (☎ 051 77 04 41; www.passchendaele.be; Ieperstraat 5, Zonnebeke; admission €5; 10am-6pm Feb-Nov), 3km south of Tyne Cot Cemetery, provides a chilling dugout experience.

These companies offer bus tours of the Ypres Salient:

- **Over the Top Tours** (☎ 057 42 43 20; www.overthetoptours.be; Meensestraat 41; tour €35)
- **Quasimodo** (☎ 050 37 04 70, freephone 0800 975 25; www.quasimodo.be; adult/under 26 €55/45; mid-Mar–mid-Oct) Located in Bruges.
- **Salient Tours** (☎ 057 21 46 57; www.salienttours.com; 2½/4hr tour €28/35; Thu-Tue Mar-Nov) Run by an Englishman based in Ypres.

SIGHTS

Bruges' nerve centre is the historic **Markt**, a large square from which rises Belgium's most famous **Belfort** (Belfry; Markt; adult/concession €5/4; 9.30am-5pm, last tickets sold 4.15pm). The 366 steps to the top are worth the squeeze.

Smaller but arguably more impressive than the Markt is the adjoining **Burg**. This square is home to the **Basiliek van het Heilig Bloed** (Basilica of the Holy Blood; admission €1.50; 9.30am-noon & 2-5.50pm Apr-Sep, 10am-noon & 2-4pm Oct-Mar), where a few coagulated drops of Christ's blood are kept and cherished.

Belgium's oldest and arguably most beautiful **Stadhuis** (Town Hall; adult/concession €2.50/2; 9.30am-5pm Tue-Sun) also rises from the Burg.

Bruges' prized collection of art dating from the 14th to 20th centuries, including some works by the Flemish Primitives, is housed in the small **Groeningemuseum** (Dijver 12; adult/concession €8/6; 9.30am-5pm Tue-Sun).

The **Onze Lieve Vrouwekerk** (Church of Our Lady; Mariastraat; adult/concession €2.50/2; 9.30am-5pm Tue-Fri, 9.30am-4.20pm Sat, 1.30-5pm Sun) has one remarkable art treasure – Michelangelo's *Madonna and Child* (1504). Although pinched several times by occupying forces, it has always been returned.

The **Begijnhof** (admission free; 6.30am-6.30pm) was home to a 13th-century religious community of unmarried or widowed women, known as *Begijnen* (Beguines). One of Bruges' quaintest spots, it's a 10-minute walk south of the Markt.

The smell of frying chips is the first thing you'll notice in the new **Frietmuseum** (☎ **050 34 01 50; www.frietmuseum.be; Vlamingstraat33; adult/child €6/4; 10am-5pm**). Trace the history of the humble *friet* before indulging in the basement cafe.

Choco-Story (☎ **050 61 22 37; www.choco-story.be; Wijnzakstraat 2; adult/child €6/4; 10am-5pm**) is devoted to telling the story of chocolate and does a good job.

De Halve Maan (☎ **050 33 26 97; www.halvemaan.be; Walplein 26; admission €5; 11am-4pm Apr-Sep, 11am-3pm Oct-Mar**) is a family brewery offering crowded guided tours (45 minutes) that finish with a Brugse Zot (Bruges' Lunatic) beer.

TOURS

Quasimundo (☎ **050 33 07 75; www.quasimundo.eu; adult/under 8/under 26 €24/free/22, with your own bike €15; mid-Mar–mid-Oct**) offers half-day bike tours of Bruges and/or the surrounding countryside. Bookings are necessary.

Canal tours (**adult/child €6.50/3; 10am-6pm Mar-Oct**) are touristy, but what isn't here? Viewing Bruges from the wate gives it a totally different feel than b foot. Boats depart every 20 minute from jetties south of the Burg, includin Rozenhoedkaai and Dijver, and tours las 30 minutes.

Horse-drawn carriages (**5 passenge €34; 10am-10pm**) leave from the Mark and their well-trodden route takes 3 minutes.

↘ THE BEST BELGIAN BEER?

With a love of beer and your own wheels, visit **In de Vrede** (☎ **057 40 03 77; Donkerstraat 13, Westvleteren; 10am-8pm Sat-Thu**), in the hamlet of Westvleteren, 15km northwest of Ypres. This cafe belongs to the **Abdij St Sixtus** (**St Sixtus Abbey; www.sintsixtus.be; not open to visitors**) whose Trappist monks live and work across the road making Westvleteren's three beers, widely regarded by connoisseurs as the best in Belgium.

SLEEPING

our pick Tine's Guesthouse (☎ **050 34 5 18; www.tinesguesthouse.com; Zwaluwenstraa 11; s/d €55/65, €5 extra for one-night stay**) *Th* B&B to choose – providing you don' mind the belfry being 1.5km away. Thi homey place is run by the effervescen Tine whose mission in life is to spoil visi tors – unbelievable breakfast, free packe lunch, free bikes and free pick-up/dro off at the train station! Bus number 3 o 13 stops nearby.

B&B Huyze Hertsberge (☎ **050 33 3 42; www.huyzehertsberge.be; Hertsbergestraat 8 d/tr €140/165;**) Top-end B&B, and a mus for antique aficionados. The four spaciou rooms are all different, and the pristin breakfast room has views to a canal-sid garden.

Hotel De Orangerie (☎ **050 34 16 49 www.hotelorangerie.com; Kartuizerinnenstraat 10 s/d/tr €200/230/265;**) Refined 20-roon hotel that started out as a 15th-centur convent and boasts a canal-side positio that's impossible to beat.

EATING

From cosy *estaminets* (taverns) to 1st class restaurants, Bruges has all base covered.

Het Dagelijks Brood (☎ **050 33 60 50 Philipstockstraat 21; snacks €6-13; 7am-6pn Wed-Mon**) Tearoom offering pies and *boter hammen* (sandwiches), plus the essentia

ig table. This Belgian success story now as branches worldwide.

Sint Barbe (☎ 050 33 09 99; De Dambuderstraat 29; mains €12-20; ⏰ lunch Thu-Tue, inner Thu-Mon) Hidden away in the so-alled Verloren Hoek (Lost Corner), this onfident little restaurant offers a small election of Belgian dishes, including vegtarian options.

't Gulden Vlies (☎ 050 33 47 09; Mallergplaats 17; mains €14-19; ⏰ 7pm-3am Wed-Sun) osy late-night restaurant with old-fashoned decor and excellent Belgian cuisine. he three-course *menu* (€16) is superb alue.

Kaffee Pergola (☎ 050 44 76 50; Steenouwersdijk; mains €22-35; ⏰ lunch Thu-Tue, diner Thu-Mon) Prime position for this discreet atery – secluded among greenery beside picturesque stretch of canal, and next to he city's oldest bridge. A limited range f classic Belgian cuisine is offered, and ookings (for the four canal-side tables) re recommended.

RINKING & ENTERTAINMENT

e Republiek (☎ 050 34 02 29; St Jakobsstraat 6; ⏰ from 11am) Local favourite and one of ruges' most congenial pubs.

De Garre (☎ 050 34 10 29; Garre 1; ⏰ noon-idnight) Hidden in a narrow cul-de-sac, his tiny old *estaminet* is a beer-specialst pub – browse the umpteen-page nenu.

Joey's Café (☎ 050 34 12 64; Zilversteeg 4; ⏰ from 11.30am Mon-Sat Oct-May, daily Jun-Sep) ose the tourists at this muso's haunt, trangely located inside the Zilverpand hopping centre. The candle-lit atmoshere is dark and relaxing.

Concertgebouw (☎ 050 47 69 99; www.oncertgebouw.be; 't Zand 34) Contemporary omes to Bruges in the form of this conert hall.

TTL IMAGES/ALAMY

Christmas time in the Markt (p413)

GETTING THERE & AWAY

Bruges' **train station** (☎ 02 528 28 28) is about 1.5km south of the Markt. Trains run every half-hour to Brussels (€12.30, one hour) and Ghent (€5.60, 20 minutes), and hourly to Antwerp (€12.90, one hour 10 minutes). For Ypres (Ieper in Dutch; €10.50, 1¼ hours) take the train to Kortrijk, from where there are hourly connections.

DIRECTORY

ACTIVITIES

Ice skating, windsurfing, sailing and boating are all popular pastimes in this corner of Europe, and cycling is practically a religion. The Netherlands has

20,000km of cycling paths. Major roads have separate bike lanes, and, except for motorways, there's virtually nowhere bicycles can't go.

Belgians are just as bike-mad as their Dutch neighbours: Flanders is popular for road cycling, while hilly Wallonia is great for mountain bikes (VTT, or *vélo tout-terrain* in French). Check out www.fietsroute.org and www.ravel.wallonie.be (in French).

Many train stations have bicycle facilities including bike rental, secure parking and even repair shops. If you're hiring, you may be required to show some ID and leave a deposit or credit card imprint.

DANGERS & ANNOYANCES

The Netherlands is a safe country, but be sensible all the same: watch for pickpockets in crowded areas and *always* lock your bike. Never buy drugs on the street: you'll get ripped off or mugged and it's illegal. And don't light up joints just anywhere – stick to coffee shops.

DISCOUNT CARDS

Available from participating Dutch museums, a *Museumkaart* gives access to 400 museums across the country for €35 (€17 for under 25s).

EMBASSIES & CONSULATES

THE NETHERLANDS

In Amsterdam:

France (Map pp384-5; ☎ 530 69 69; www.ambafrance.nl; Vijzelgracht 2)
Germany (Map pp384-5; ☎ 574 77 00; Honthorststraat 36-8)
UK (off Map pp384-5; ☎ 676 43 43; www.britain.nl; Koningslaan 44)
USA (Map pp384-5; ☎ 575 53 30; http://thehague.usembassy.gov; Museumplein 19)

In Den Haag:

Australia (☎ 070-310 82 00; www.netherlands.embassy.gov.au; Carnegielaan 4)
Belgium (☎ 312 34 56; www.diplomatie.be/thehague; Alexanderveld 97)
Canada (☎ 070-311 16 00; www.netherlands.gc.ca; Sophialaan 7)
France (☎ 312 58 00; www.ambafrance.nl; Smidsplein 1)
Ireland (☎ 070-363 09 93; www.irishembassy.nl; Dr Kuyperstraat 9)
New Zealand (☎ 070-346 93 24; Carnegielaan10-IV)
UK (☎ 070-427 04 27; www.britain.nl; Lange Voorhout 10)
USA (☎ 070-310 22 09; http://thehague.usembassy.gov; Lange Voorhout 102)

BELGIUM

In Brussels:

Australia (Map p402; ☎ 02 286 05 00; fax 02 230 68 02; Rue Guimard 6, B-1040)
Canada (off Map p402; ☎ 02 741 06 11; fax 02 741 06 43; Ave de Tervuren 2, B-1040)
France (Map Map p402; ☎ 02 548 87 11; fax 02 513 68 71; Rue Ducale 65, B-1000)
Germany (Map p402; ☎ 02 787 18 00; fax 02 787 28 00; Rue Jacques de Lalaing 8-14, B-1040)
Ireland (off Map p402; ☎ 02 235 66 76; fax 02 235 66 71; Rue Wiertz 50, B-1050)
Luxembourg (off Map p402; ☎ 02 735 2[illegible] 60; fax 02 737 56 10; Ave de Cortenbergh 75, B-1000)
Netherlands (off Map p402; ☎ 02 679 1[illegible] 11; fax 02 679 17 75; Ave Herrmann-Debroux 48, B-1160)
New Zealand (Map p402; ☎ 02 512 10 40; fax 02 513 48 56; 7th fl, Sq de Meeus 1, B-1100)
UK (off Map p402; ☎ 02 287 62 11; fax 02 28[illegible] 63 55; Rue d'Arlon 85, B-1040)
USA (Map p402; ☎ 02 508 21 11; fax 02 511 2[illegible] 25; Blvd du Régent 27, B-1000)

FESTIVALS & EVENTS

THE NETHERLANDS

Carnaval Celebrations start on the Friday before Shrove Tuesday and last until the following Wednesday.

Amsterdam Fantastic Film Festival (www.afff.nl) Fantasy, horror and science-fiction fest; held in late April.

Koninginnedag (Queen's Day) Celebrated countrywide on 30 April, but especially in Amsterdam.

Nationale Molendag (National Windmill Day) On the second Saturday in May, nearly every working windmill in Holland opens its doors.

Holland Festival (www.hollandfestival.nl) The country's biggest music, drama and dance extravaganza centres on Amsterdam throughout June.

Gay Pride Canal Parade First Saturday of August.

Uitmarkt (www.uitmarkt.nl) The reopening of Amsterdam's cultural season for three days in late August.

Open Monument Day (www.openmonumentendag.nl) Historic buildings and monuments are opened free of charge in the second weekend in September.

Sinterklaas On 5 December, families exchange small gifts ahead of Christmas.

BELGIUM

Belgium buzzes with music, pageantry and parades.

Concours Musical International Reine Élisabeth de Belgique (www.concours-reine-elisabeth.be) Belgium's most prestigious classical-music event, held in May.

KunstenFestivaldesArts (www.kunstenfestivaldesarts.be) Held in Brussels over three weeks in May, big names in the worlds of music, dance, theatre and opera combine for an international festival to rival all others.

Rock Werchter (www.rockwerchter.be) One of Europe's biggest 'field' rock festivals, held near Leuven in the first weekend of July.

10 Days Off (www.10daysoff.be) One of Europe's biggest techno parties; mid-July.

De Gentse Feesten (www.gentsefeesten.be) Ghent's 10-day music and theatre festival in July.

HOLIDAYS

THE NETHERLANDS

Nieuwjaarsdag New Year's Day
Goede Vrijdag Good Friday
Eerste Paasdag Easter Sunday
Tweede Paasdag Easter Monday
Koninginnedag (Queen's Day) 30 April
Bevrijdingsdag (Liberation Day) 5 May
Hemelvaartsdag Ascension Day
Eerste Pinksterdag Whit Sunday (Pentecost)
Tweede Pinksterdag Whit Monday
Eerste Kerstdag (Christmas Day) 25 December
Tweede Kerstdag (Boxing Day) 26 December

BELGIUM

New Year's Day 1 January
Easter Monday March/April
Labour Day 1 May
Ascension Day Fortieth day after Easter
Whit Monday Seventh Monday after Easter
Flemish Community Festival 11 July (Flanders only)
National Day 21 July
Assumption 15 August
Walloon Community Festival 27 September (Wallonia only)
All Saints' Day 1 November

Armistice Day 11 November
German Community Festival 15 November (Eastern Cantons only)
Christmas Day 25 December

MONEY

The Netherlands and Belgium both use the euro (€). In the Netherlands, banks stick to official exchange rates and charge a sensible commission, as does **GWK Travelex** (www.gwk.nl).

In Belgium, banks are the best place to exchange money. Outside banking hours, exchange bureaux (*wisselkantoren* in Dutch, *bureaux d'échange* in French) operate at Brussels National airport and at main train stations.

POST

The Netherlands postal service has been privatised and is now known as **TNT Post** (www.tntpost.nl). In Belgium, postal services are provided by **De Post** (www.post.be).

TELEPHONE

THE NETHERLANDS

Public phones accept various phonecards available at post offices, train-station counters, VVV and GWK offices and tobacco shops for €5, €10 and €20. The KPN Hi card is the most common; other brands include T-Mobile, Orange, Vodafone, Belnet etc. Train stations have Telfort phone booths that require a Telfort card (available at GWK offices or ticket counters), although there are usually KPN booths nearby. The Netherlands' mobile network is GSM 900/1800.

The country code for calling the Netherlands is ☎31 and the area code for Amsterdam is ☎020. You don't need the city code if you are ringing from the same area.

BELGIUM

Belgium's country code is ☎32. Area codes are incorporated into each phone number. Telephone numbers prefixed with 0900 or 070 are pay-per-minute numbers (€0.20 to €0.50 per minute). Numbers prefixed with 0800 are toll-free calls. Those prefixed with 0472 to 0479, 0482 to 0489 and 0492 to 0499 are mobile numbers. Belgium's mobile network is GSM 900/1800.

TRANSPORT

GETTING THERE & AWAY

AIR

Amsterdam's huge **Schiphol airport** (AMS; www.schiphol.nl) is the country's main air hub, and the centre for the national carrier **KLM** (KL; ☎0900-01 41; www.klm.nl). Most other international and budget carriers also fly to/from Schiphol. **Rotterdam** (RTM; ☎010 446 34 44; www.rotterdam-airport.nl) is much smaller.

Belgium's main international airports are **Antwerp** (ANR; ☎03 285 65 00; www.antwerpairport.be), **Brussels National Airport** (BRU; ☎0900 70 000; www.brusselsairport.be), **Charleroi** (CRL; ☎071 25 12 11; www.charleroi-airport.com) and **Liège** (LGG; ☎04 234 84 11; www.liegeairport.com). **SN Brussels Airlines** (SN; www.brusselsairlines.com), **VLM Airlines** (VG; www.flyvlm.com) and **Air France** (AF; www.airfrance.be) are among the busiest carriers.

LAND

BUS

Eurolines (☎in the UK 08705 143219; www.eurolines.com; ☎in Belgium 02 274 13 50; www.eurolines.be) provides regular intercontinental buses to Belgium and the Netherlands from across Europe. **Busabout** (☎in the UK 020-7950 1661; www.busabout.com) is a UK-based budget alternative.

CAR & MOTORCYCLE

There are no border controls for entering either the Netherlands and Belgium. Main motorways travel into Germany and France.

TRAIN

The Netherlands has good train links to Germany, Belgium and France. All Eurail, Inter-Rail, Europass and Flexipass tickets are valid on the Dutch national train service, **Nederlandse Spoorwegen** (Netherlands Railway, NS; ☎ international inquiries 0900-9296; www.ns.nl). Many international services, including those on the high-speed line to Belgium are operated under the **Hispeed** (www.nshispeed.nl) brand. When it finally opened in 2009, the high-speed line from Amsterdam (via Schipol and Rotterdam) shortened travel times to Antwerp (72 minutes), Brussels (one hour 53 minutes) and Paris (three hours 18 minutes).

In Belgium, **Eurostar** (☎ 02 528 28 28; www.eurostar.com) trains connect Brussels' Gare du Midi and London St Pancras through the Eurotunnel in just under two hours. **Thalys** (☎ 070 66 77 88; www.thalys.com) fast trains link various Belgian cities (including Brussels' Garde du Midi) with France, the Netherlands and Germany. Flexible one-way fares are known as Librys tickets; cheaper, nonflexible return fares are called Smilys tickets. **Belgische Spoorwegen/Société National des Chemins de Fer Belges** (Belgian Railways; ☎ 02 528 28 28; www.b-rail.be) operates services to Luxembourg City and from Brussels to Amsterdam via Antwerp.

Discounts are usually available for advance bookings and weekends. Travellers aged 12 to 26 get a 50% discount and seniors a 30% reduction.

SEA

Car/passenger ferries from the Netherlands:

DFDS Seaways (☎ 08702 52 05 24; www.dfds.co.uk) Newcastle–IJmuiden (near Amsterdam).

P&O Ferries (☎ 08705 20 20 20; www.poferries.com) An overnight ferry links Hull and Europoort (near Rotterdam).

Stena Line (☎ 08705 70 70 70; www.stenaline.co.uk) Harwich–Hoek van Holland.

Ferry services to/from Belgium:

P&O (☎ Belgium 070 70 07 74, UK 0871 664 5645; www.poferries.com) Sails overnight from Zeebrugge (Belgium) to Hull (UK).

Superfast Ferries (☎ Belgium 05 025 22 52, UK 0870 234 0870; www.superfast.com) Ultramodern ferry from Zeebrugge (Belgium) to Rosyth (Scotland).

Transeuropa Ferries (☎ Belgium 059 34 02 60, UK 01843 59 55 22; www.transeuropaferries.com) Eight sailings daily between Ostend (Belgium) and Ramsgate (UK).

GETTING AROUND

AIR

The Netherlands and Belgium are small countries, so domestic air travel's geared mainly towards business users – you'll be better off travelling by train.

BUS

Buses are an important backup to Belgium's excellent rail network, especially in the rural Ardennes. Major bus companies:

De Lijn (☎ 070 22 02 00; www.delijn.be, in Dutch) Buses in Flanders.

Société des Transports Intercommunaux de Bruxelles (☎ 070 23 20 00; www.stib.be, in French & Dutch) Buses in Brussels.

Transport en Commun (☎ 010 23 53 53; www.infotec.be, in French) Buses in Wallonia.

CAR & MOTORCYCLE

To drive in Belgium and the Netherlands, you'll usually need the vehicle's registration papers, third-party insurance and your domestic licence. An international driving permit (IDP) isn't usually required, but it might come in handy for non-EU drivers.

Twenty-three is generally the minimum age for car hire, although some firms levy a surcharge for drivers under 25. Most will require a credit card for deposit. All the major car-hire firms operate concessions at main airports, but rental from airports and the Gare du Midi cost considerably more because of additional taxes.

Road rules in Belgium and the Netherlands are similar. Traffic travels on the right. At roundabouts approaching vehicles have right-of-way unless traffic signs tell you otherwise (and these signs appear at most roundabouts now), and in the Netherlands you must give way to trams and bikes when you turn right. Seat belts are legally required in both countries. Speed limits are usually 30km/h or 50km/h in built-up areas; outside towns, the limit is usually 80km/h in the Netherlands and 90km/h in Belgium; on motorways, it's 120km/h unless signs indicate otherwise. The blood-alcohol limit is 0.05%.

PUBLIC TRANSPORT

In the Netherlands, the old *strippenkaart* (strip card), which used to cover public transport nationwide, is being phased out and replaced by the *OV chipkaart*, a prepaid travel card. When you board trams and buses, you'll use the card on gates or card readers to have the value of the ride deducted. Most rides will cost €2.50. You can buy them at most Dutch tourist offices and train stations. Phone ☎ 0900 9292 or see www.9292ov.nl (in Dutch) for nationwide travel info.

TRAIN

THE NETHERLANDS

The Netherlands' train network is run by **Nederlandse Spoorwegen** (**NS; ☎ national inquiries 0900-9296; www.ns.nl**). First-class sections are barely different from the 2nd-class areas, but they are less crowded. Tickets can be bought at the window (for an extra €0.50 for one ticket, €1 for two or more). Ticket machines have an English option and accept coins and some ATM cards. Credit cards are accepted nowhere on NS.

If you're doing a lot of train travel, a *Voordeelurenabonnement* (€55 per year) entitles you to 40% discount on travel weekdays after 9am, on weekends and public holidays, and all of July and August. Other train passes generally aren't good value as travel distances are so short.

BELGIUM

Trains are run by the **Belgische Spoorwegen/Société National des Chemins de Fer Belges** (**☎ 02 528 28 28; www.b-rail.be**). The levels of service are InterCity (IC, the fastest), InterRegional (IR), local (L) and peak-hour (P) commuter trains. Trains have 1st- and 2nd-class nonsmoking compartments.

Second-class tickets are 50% cheaper than 1st-class, and on weekends (from 7pm Friday) return tickets are 50% cheaper than on weekdays. Belgian railway passes include the following:

Benelux Tourrail Five days' travel in one month in Belgium, Luxembourg and the Netherlands, and costs €219/139 in 1st/2nd class (under 26 years €99, 2nd class only). It can be purchased in Belgium or Luxembourg but not the Netherlands (though it's valid for use there).

Go Pass Ten one-way trips anywhere in Belgium for under 26s (€46, 2nd class).

Rail Pass Ten one-way trips anywhere in Belgium, valid for a year (€109/71 in 1st/2nd class).

GERMANY, AUSTRIA & SWITZERLAND

GERMANY

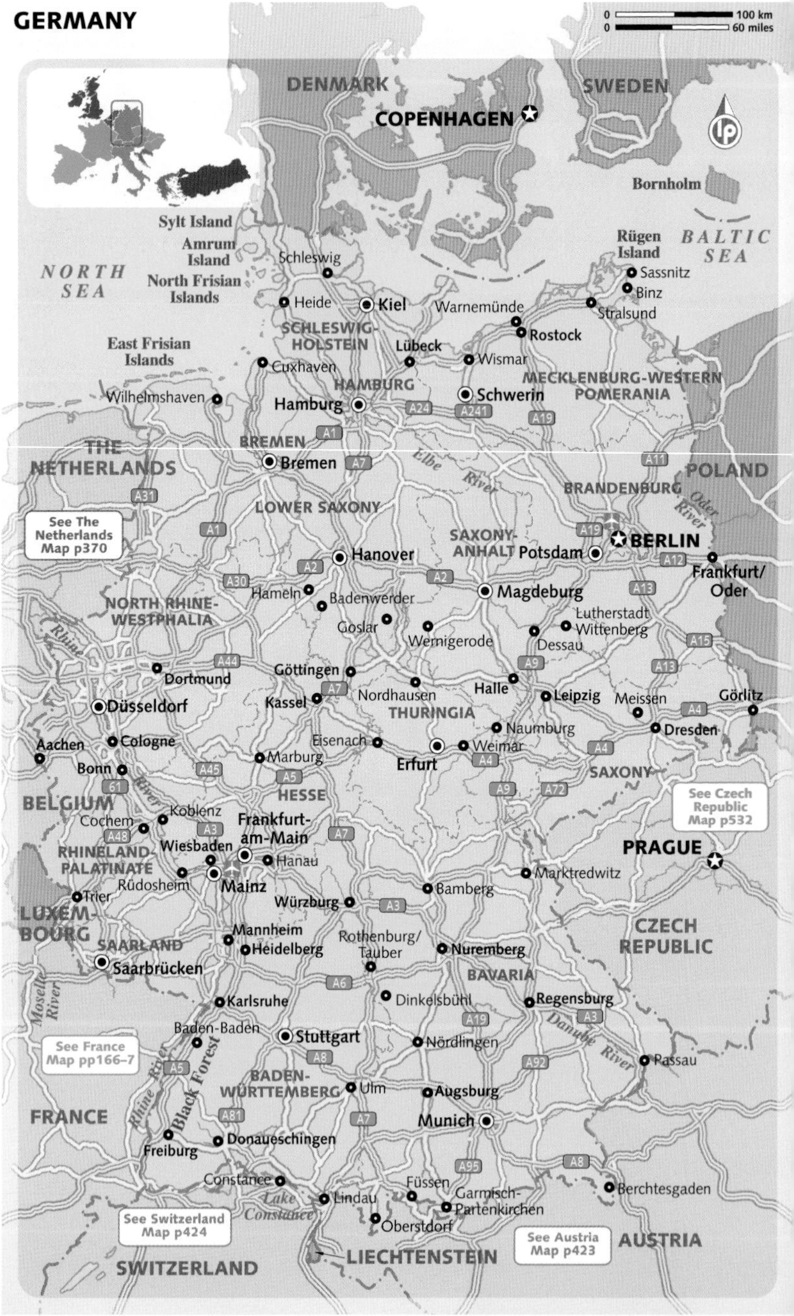
0 100 km
0 60 miles
DENMARK
COPENHAGEN
SWEDEN
Bornholm
BALTIC SEA
Rügen Island
Sassnitz
Binz
Stralsund
Sylt Island
Amrum Island
North Frisian Islands
NORTH SEA
East Frisian Islands
Schleswig
Heide
Kiel
Warnemünde
Rostock
SCHLESWIG-HOLSTEIN
Lübeck
Wismar
Cuxhaven
HAMBURG
MECKLENBURG-WESTERN POMERANIA
Wilhelmshaven
Hamburg
Schwerin
A24
A241
A19
A1
BREMEN
Bremen
A7
Elbe River
A11
THE NETHERLANDS
POLAND
A31
BRANDENBURG
Oder River
See The Netherlands Map p370
LOWER SAXONY
A1
A19
SAXONY-ANHALT
Potsdam
BERLIN
Hanover
A12
Frankfurt/Oder
A2
A2
A30
Hameln
Badenwerder
Magdeburg
A13
NORTH RHINE-WESTPHALIA
Lutherstadt Wittenberg
Goslar
Wernigerode
Dessau
Rhine River
A15
A44
A9
A13
Dortmund
Göttingen
Halle
Görlitz
A7
Nordhausen
Leipzig
Meissen
Düsseldorf
Kassel
THURINGIA
A4
Naumburg
Dresden
Aachen
Cologne
Eisenach
Weimar
A4
Bonn
Marburg
Erfurt
A4
A45
A5
SAXONY
61
HESSE
A9
A72
BELGIUM
Koblenz
See Czech Republic Map p532
Cochem
Frankfurt-am-Main
A3
A48
A7
RHINELAND-PALATINATE
Wiesbaden
PRAGUE
Hanau
Rüdosheim
Marktredwitz
Trier
Mainz
Bamberg
LUXEMBOURG
Würzburg
A3
CZECH REPUBLIC
Mannheim
SAARLAND
Rothenburg/Tauber
Heidelberg
Nuremberg
Saarbrücken
BAVARIA
A6
Moselle River
Karlsruhe
Dinkelsbühl
Regensburg
A19
A3
Danube River
Baden-Baden
Stuttgart
Nördlingen
See France Map pp166–7
A8
A92
Passau
A5
BADEN-WÜRTTEMBERG
Ulm
Augsburg
Rhine River
Black Forest
FRANCE
A81
A7
Munich
Freiburg
Donaueschingen
A95
A8
Constance
Füssen
Berchtesgaden
Lake Constance
Lindau
Garmisch-Partenkirchen
Oberstdorf
See Switzerland Map p424
See Austria Map p423
AUSTRIA
LIECHTENSTEIN
SWITZERLAND

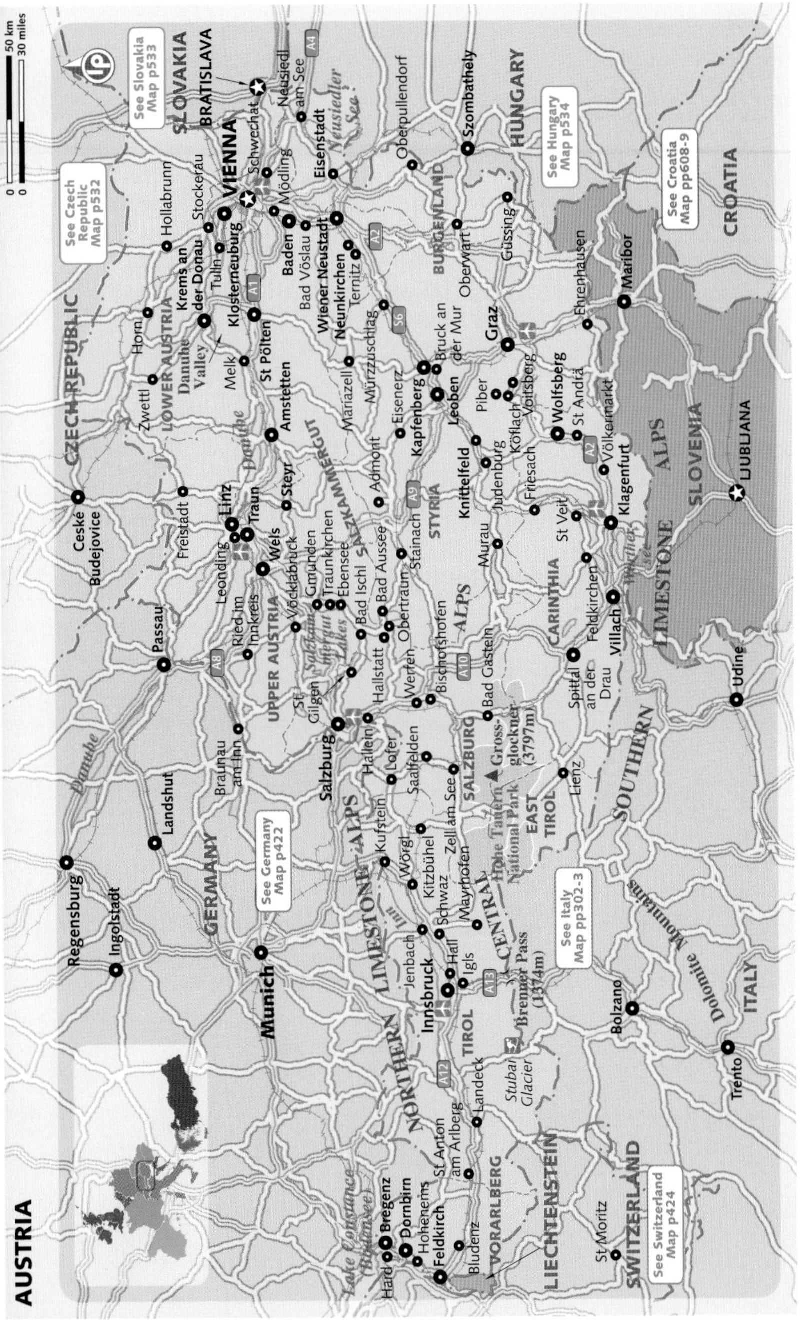
AUSTRIA
0 50 km
0 30 miles
See Czech Republic Map p532
See Slovakia Map p533
See Hungary Map p534
See Croatia Map pp608-9
See Germany Map p422
See Italy Map pp302-3
See Switzerland Map p424
CZECH REPUBLIC
SLOVAKIA
HUNGARY
CROATIA
SLOVENIA
GERMANY
ITALY
SWITZERLAND
LIECHTENSTEIN
BRATISLAVA
VIENNA
LJUBLJANA
LOWER AUSTRIA
UPPER AUSTRIA
BURGENLAND
STYRIA
CARINTHIA
SALZBURG
TIROL
EAST TIROL
VORARLBERG
SALZKAMMERGUT
Danube
Danube Valley
Inn
Neusiedler See
Wörther See
Lake Constance (Bodensee)
NORTHERN LIMESTONE ALPS
CENTRAL ALPS
SOUTHERN LIMESTONE ALPS
Dolomite Mountains
Salzkammergut Lakes
Hohe Tauern National Park
Grossglockner (3797m)
Brenner Pass (1374m)
Stubai Glacier
Ceské Budejovice
Regensburg
Ingolstadt
Landshut
Passau
Munich
Braunau am Inn
Ried im Innkreis
Freistadt
Zwettl
Horn
Hollabrunn
Krems an der Donau
Melk
Tulln
Klosterneuburg
Stockerau
St Pölten
Amstetten
Linz
Leonding
Traun
Wels
Steyr
Vöcklabruck
Gmunden
Traunkirchen
Ebensee
Bad Ischl
Bad Aussee
St Gilgen
Hallstatt
Obertraun
Salzburg
Hallein
Werfen
Bischofshofen
Bad Gastein
Lofer
Saalfelden
Zell am See
Kitzbühel
Kufstein
Wörgl
Mayrhofen
Schwaz
Jenbach
Hall
Innsbruck
Igls
Landeck
St Anton am Arlberg
Bludenz
Feldkirch
Hohenems
Dornbirn
Bregenz
Hard
St Moritz
Bolzano
Trento
Udine
Lienz
Spittal an der Drau
Villach
Feldkirchen
Klagenfurt
St Veit
Friesach
Völkermarkt
St Andrä
Wolfsberg
Murau
Judenburg
Knittelfeld
Köflach
Voitsberg
Piber
Leoben
Kapfenberg
Bruck an der Mur
Graz
Ehrenhausen
Maribor
Stainach
Admont
Eisenerz
Mariazell
Mürzzuschlag
Neunkirchen
Ternitz
Wiener Neustadt
Bad Vöslau
Baden
Mödling
Schwechat
Eisenstadt
Neusiedl am See
Oberpullendorf
Oberwart
Güssing
Szombathely
A1
A2
A4
A8
A9
A10
A12
A13
S6

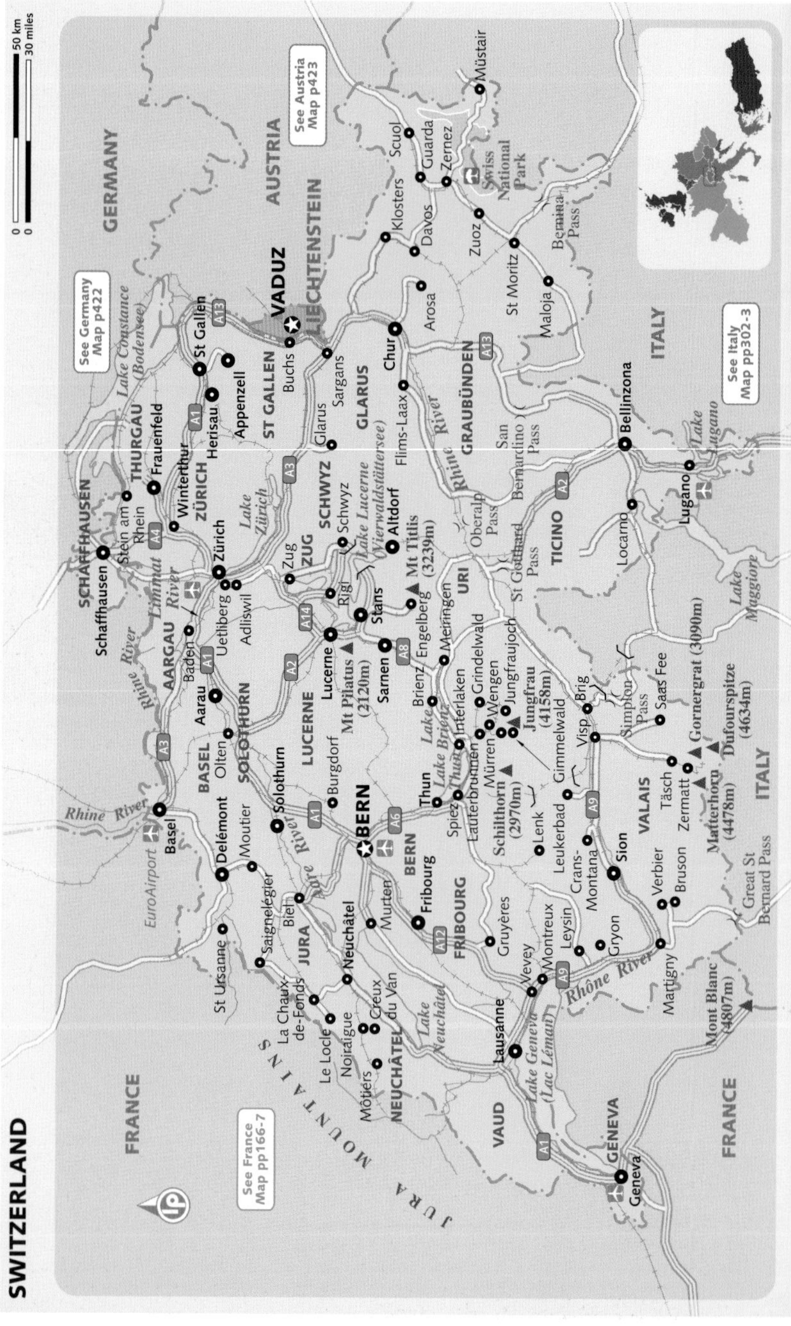
SWITZERLAND
0 50 km
0 30 miles
GERMANY
AUSTRIA
LIECHTENSTEIN
FRANCE
ITALY
See Germany Map p422
See Austria Map p423
See France Map pp166-7
See Italy Map pp302-3
JURA MOUNTAINS
VADUZ
BERN
Lake Constance (Bodensee)
Lake Zürich
Lake Lucerne (Vierwaldstättersee)
Lake Neuchâtel
Lake Geneva (Lac Léman)
Lake Thun
Lake Brienz
Lake Lugano
Lake Maggiore
Rhine River
Aare River
Rhône River
Limmat River
SCHAFFHAUSEN
THURGAU
ZÜRICH
AARGAU
BASEL
SOLOTHURN
LUCERNE
ZUG
SCHWYZ
URI
GLARUS
ST GALLEN
GRAUBÜNDEN
TICINO
VALAIS
BERN
FRIBOURG
VAUD
NEUCHÂTEL
JURA
GENEVA
Schaffhausen
Stein am Rhein
Winterthur
Frauenfeld
Zürich
Uetliberg
Adliswil
Baden
Aarau
Olten
Basel
EuroAirport
Delémont
Moutier
Solothurn
Burgdorf
Biel
Saignelégier
St Ursanne
La Chaux-de-Fonds
Le Locle
Noiraigue
Creux du Van
Môtiers
Neuchâtel
Murten
Fribourg
Gruyères
Lausanne
Vevey
Montreux
Leysin
Gryon
Geneva
Martigny
Verbier
Bruson
Great St Bernard Pass
Mont Blanc (4807m)
Sion
Crans-Montana
Leukerbad
Lenk
Visp
Brig
Simplon Pass
Saas Fee
Täsch
Zermatt
Matterhorn (4478m)
Gornergrat (3090m)
Dufourspitze (4634m)
Gimmelwald
Mürren
Schilthorn (2970m)
Lauterbrunnen
Wengen
Jungfraujoch
Jungfrau (4158m)
Grindelwald
Interlaken
Spiez
Thun
Brienz
Meiringen
Engelberg
Mt Titlis (3239m)
Sarnen
Stans
Mt Pilatus (2120m)
Lucerne
Rigi
Zug
Schwyz
Altdorf
Oberalp Pass
St Gotthard Pass
San Bernardino Pass
Locarno
Lugano
Bellinzona
Flims-Laax
Chur
Arosa
Davos
Klosters
Glarus
Sargans
Buchs
St Gallen
Appenzell
Herisau
Scuol
Guarda
Zernez
Swiss National Park
Zuoz
St Moritz
Bernina Pass
Maloja
Müstair
A1
A2
A3
A4
A6
A8
A9
A12
A13
A14

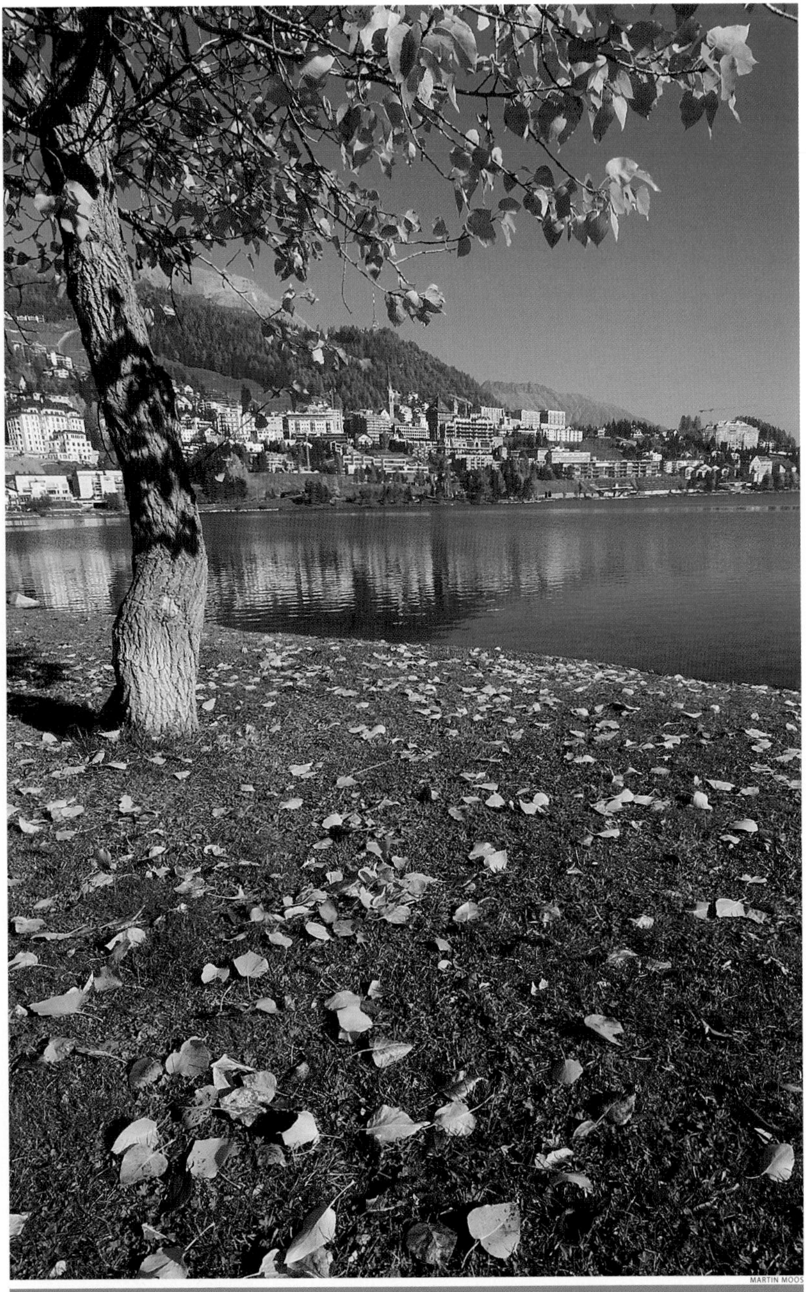

MARTIN MOOS

Lake St Moritz (p522)

HIGHLIGHTS

1 SKIING IN SWITZERLAND

CAROLE JAUFFRET, FORMER GENEVA CHAPTER PRESIDENT OF THE SWISS ACADEMIC SKI CLUB

Wherever you go in Switzerland, there are mountains. From Geneva to Zürich you're never more than two hours from a ski slope. In winter people don't ask what are you doing this weekend, they ask where are you skiing? I love the spirit of it.

CAROLE JAUFFRET'S DON'T MISS LIST

❶ ZERMATT

Because of the glacier, **Zermatt** (p505) is the best for skiing early or late. It's like having two seasons in one – you're skiing up on the mountain and down below people are wearing shorts. There's a good mix of five-star hotels and gastronomic dining along with simpler options. The views of the Matterhorn are nice, too.

❷ APRÈS SKI & NIGHTLIFE

You come in from the slopes still in all your gear and it's happy hour. Later, after dinner, it's time to go out. Nightclubs in Zermatt are a mix, you can still wear your Vans, but you better be dressed stylishly if you expect to be let in to the designer lounges and chichi clubs in places like **Verbier** (p506).

Clockwise from top: Zermatt (p505) and the Matterhorn; Luxury shops, St Moritz (p522); Cow in alpine meadow, Grindelwald (p514); Child tobogganing, Zürich (p516); Lodge in the Lauterbrunnen Valley (p515)

CLOCKWISE FROM TOP: CHRIS MELLOR; CHRIS MELLOR; DAVID TOMLINSON; MARTIN MOOS; WITOLD SKRYPCZAK

❸ GLITZ & GLAMOUR

St Moritz (p522) is where people go to show off their latest fur hats. This is old-style chic, but the slopes are also meticulously prepared. Of course the shopping around the resorts is fabulous if you have a bit of money – maybe more than a bit…

❹ SWISS SKIING HERITAGE

The first international ski races were held in Mürren in 1920 and the quaint towns of the Jungfrau Region (p513) are still firmly rooted in this heritage. The hotels may be a bit out of fashion, but towns like Grindelwald are typically Swiss – and they attract a more local crowd.

THINGS YOU NEED TO KNOW

Travel tip Buy a Swiss Pass (p530) for train travel between resorts, it'll cut your costs and some mountain railways are included **Be prepared to spend** Some resort areas are admirably green – no carbon-emitting cars allowed, so you'll have to shell out for a pricey electric taxi between the station and your hotel

HIGHLIGHTS

2

BAVARIAN BEER DRINKING

A smooth, easy-drinking smoked beverage, anyone? The small town of **Bamberg** (p460) is known for its bacon-flavoured brews, but the entire region take its beer seriously. If you miss the chance to chug-a-lug at **Oktoberfest** (p455) in Munich, meeting new German friends at the shared tables of **Hofbräuhaus** (p458) is the next best thing.

3

VIENNESE COFFEE CULTURE

To escape Vienna's unheated apartments, impoverished artists and intellectuals, like Sigmund Freud, once set up shop at coffee-house tables, writing and holding meetings and debates. A true Viennese **kaffeehaus** (p480) still hosts music, exhibitions and cultural events. You don't have to discuss the id and the ego, but you do have to linger over a coffee for a few hours to feel part of the place.

4

↘ WALL ART

More than 20 years have passed since the **Berlin Wall** (p516) came crumbling down. But the seminal moment is not forgotten. The wall's landmark graffiti has undergone restoration; see the best bits of spray-painted pop art at the Eastside Gallery or follow the 155km of remnants along the Berlin Wall Trail.

5

↘ TOP OF THE WORLD

You're king of the mountain at Europe's highest train station, **Jungfraujoch** (p443). The icy wonderland of glaciers at 3741m inspires scores to make the journey, so start early. And wait for a clear day – the ride's not worth the high price if all you see up there are clouds.

6

↘ PARTY ON

Every August Switzerland's largest city hosts Europe's largest **Street Parade** (p520). Twenty-five or more 'love mobiles' (rolling stages) provide moving entertainment for as many as 800,000 ravers and revellers along the 2.4km parade route. The sounds are mostly techno and the scene's a non-stop dancefest – with peace and love at its thematic heart.

2 KRZYSZTOF DYDYNSKI; 3 GREG ELMS; 4 GREG GAWLOWSKI; 5 KRZYSZTOF DYDYNSKI; 6 MARTIN MOOS

2 Oktoberfest (p455) at Theresienwiese, Munich; 3 *Kaffeehaus* (coffee house; p480), Vienna; 4 Graffiti artist at the Berlin Wall (p443); 5 Jungfrau (p513); 6 Street Parade (p520), Zürich

THE BEST...

CHILL-OUT SPOTS

- **Beach bar, Hamburg** (p470) Toes in the sand, kick back with a cocktail.
- **Jardin Botanique, Geneva** (p499) Peacock-studded lawns and long walks at the Botanical Garden.
- **Beer garden, Munich** (p458) Sitting and sipping among the greenery at one of the Englischer Garten's classic beer gardens.
- **Schloss Mirabell, Salzburg** (p487) Formal landscapes that sing with the *Sound of Music*; free concerts May through August.

DELIGHTFUL DRINKS

- **Bamberg** (p460) Smoked beer in Bavaria.
- **Frankfurt** (p469) *Ebbelwoi* (apple wine) enjoyed in specialized taverns.
- **Vienna** (p480) Effervescent 'new wine' produced on-premises at *heurigen* (wine taverns).
- **Val de Travers** (p523) Absinthe, the infamous green aniseed liqueur is made from wormwood grown in this Swiss valley.

DRIVES OF A LIFETIME

- **Deutsche Alpenstrasse** (p451) Past Füssen it's the Bavarian Alps and Romantic Rd rolled into one.
- **Schwarzwald-Hochstrasse** (p465) Roll along the length of the Black Forest.
- **Grossglockner Hochalpen-strasse** (p496) A winding 2000m ascent through the Austrian Alps.

FREE THRILLS

- **Museums Island** (p440) Free entry the last four hours on Thursday.
- **Schönbrunn Gardens** (p477) The immaculate Viennese gardens of an empress.
- **Jet d'Eau** (p497) Geneva's iconic, dash-through water fountain.

RICHARD NEBESKY

Kunsthistorisches Museum (p477), Vienna

THINGS YOU NEED TO KNOW

AT A GLANCE

- **Population** 83 million (Germany), 8.3 million (Austria), 7.6 million (Switzerland)
- **Official languages** German (Germany, Austria, Switzerland), French (Switzerland), Italian (Switzerland), Romansch (Switzerland); Slovene, Croat and Hungarian are also official languages in some Austrian southern states
- **Currency** Euro (€; Germany, Austria), Swiss franc (Sfr; Switzerland)
- **Telephone codes** ☎ 49 (Germany), ☎ 43 (Austria), ☎ 41 Switzerland
- **When to go** June through September; December through February for skiing
- **Tipping** 10% tip in restaurants

REGIONS IN A NUTSHELL

- **Dresden** (p447) A gem of former East Germany.
- **Bavaria** (p451) Land of legendary clichés: lederhosen, beer halls and impossibly mad castles.
- **Black Forest** (p465) Evergreen forests, country towns and cuckoo clocks.
- **Hamburg** (p469) Germany's shiny new-old port town.
- **Danube Valley** (p484) A romantic Austrian stretch of river.
- **Tirol** (p492) A quintessential Alpine panorama around Innsbruck.
- **Lake Geneva Region** (p503) Lake towns with a distinct French accent.
- **Valais** (p505) Home of the Matterhorn mountain peak, need we say more?
- **Central Switzerland & Bernese Oberland** (p510) Mountain recreation accessed from picture-postcard towns like Lucerne.
- **Jungfrau Region** (p513) Traditional Swiss villages, swirling glaciers and Europe's highest train station.

ADVANCE PLANNING

- **One month before** For December through February book lodging in the Alps at least a month ahead.
- **Two weeks before** Reserve tickets for the State Opera House (p481) or the Spanish Riding School (p482) in Vienna.

BE FOREWARNED

- **Know your airport** Low-cost carriers flying within Europe often do not serve a city's main airport. For example, Ryanair flies to Hahn Airport, 70km from Frankfurt.

BUSINESS HOURS

- **Banks** (8am to 3.30 or 4.30pm Mon-Fri)
- **Post offices** (8am-6pm Mon-Fri, to noon Sat)
- **Shops** (8.30am to 5pm or 6pm Mon-Fri, to noon or 1pm Sat)
- **Grocery stores** (7am-7pm Mon-Fri, to at least to noon on Sat; hypermarkets have extended or non-stop hours)
- **Restaurants** (11am-2.30pm and 6-11pm, varied closing days)
- **Nightclubs** (open between 5pm and 10pm, close between 2am and 5am)

THINGS YOU NEED TO KNOW

COSTS

GERMANY

- **€80 per day** Staying in cheap rooms, doing some self-catering.
- **€120** Eating out, sleeping in median, big-city lodging, visiting museums, taking public transport.
- **€220+** Four-star hotels and restaurants, lots of train travel.

AUSTRIA

- **€70 per day** Staying in low-end lodging, buying some groceries.
- **€110** Midrange accommodation, average eateries, public transport and sightseeing included.
- **€220+** Splashing out at four-star hotels and restaurants.

SWITZERLAND

- **Sfr150 per day** Alternating hostel dorms with hotels with shared bathrooms, occasional restaurant meals.
- **Sfr225** Average (but usually small) hotel rooms, two restaurant meals a day, a sight or two and transport.
- **Sfr450+** The sky's the limit at top-end hotels, eating posh noshes and riding the Swiss rails frequently.

EMERGENCY NUMBERS

- **Germany** (☎ ambulance & fire 112, police 110)
- **Austria** (☎ Alpine rescue 140, ambulance 144, fire 122, police 133)
- **Switzerland** (☎ ambulance 144, fire 118, police 117, Swiss mountain rescue 1414)

GETTING AROUND

- For more on getting around, see p529.
- **Train travel** Extensive and efficient, if expensive, train networks operate in all three nations.
- **Gateway airports**: Frankfurt, Zurich, Vienna
- **Budget carriers** German cities are especially well served by air.

MEDIA

- **German-Times** (http://germantimes.com)
- **Austria News** (http://austrianews.com)
- **Swiss Info** (www.swissinfo.ch)

RESOURCES

- **Austrian National Tourist Office** (ANTO; www.austria.info)
- **Switzerland Tourism** (www.myswitzerland.com)
- **German Tourist Board** (www.cometogermany.com)

VISAS

- **EU citizens** No visa required for EU or Swiss citizens.
- **US, Canadian, Australian and New Zealand citizens** Up to 90-day stays visa free.
- **For more information** Germany (www.auswaertiges-amt.de), Austria (www.immi.gov.au), Switzerland (www.eda.admin.ch)

GET INSPIRED

BOOKS

- **Alpine Points of View** Kev Reynolds' stunning Alpine pictorial.
- **Stalin's Nose** Rory MacLean travels through Germany and beyond weeks after the Berlin Wall falls.
- **Rose of Bern** Paul Desilva set his spy-thriller against the background of Bern.
- **Last Waltz in Vienna** George Claire follows a Jewish family from 1842 until their fate in Nazi hands.

FILMS

- **Sophie Scholl: The Final Days** (2006) A harrowing true story about a woman protesting against the Nazis in Munich.
- **The Sound of Music** (1965) The Austrian icon.
- **Good Bye Lenin!** (2003) A family comically recreates 'communism' when a coma victim wakes to a capitalist world.
- **Heidi** (1935) Cloyingly sweet Heidi searches for her grandfather in the Swiss Alps.

MUSIC

- **Every classical piece** by German composers Bach, Beethoven, Brahms and Wagner.
- **Symphony No 40** A masterpiece from Salzburg's native son, Wolfgang Amadeus Mozart.
- **Dr Schacher Seppli** Rudolf Ryman yodels a Swiss classic.

WEBSITES

- **Gemut** (www.gemut.com) Austrian, German and Swiss features.
- **Toytown Germany** (www.toytowngermany.com) An English-language blogosphere.
- **Glocal** (www.glocals.com) Swiss locals share their tips and parties.
- **Central Cafe** (www.palaisevents.at) History of the landmark Viennese coffee house.

LEFT: GLENN BEANLAND; RIGHT: GLENN BEANLAND

Left: Window-shopping at a bakery, Bern (p506); Right: Detail of a street statue in Innsbruck (p492)

ITINERARIES

BIG CITY BOP Five Days

The big cities of the region dance to their own beat. On a Sunday when all of **(1) Zürich** (p516) seems to be strolling around the lakeshore, you might imagine this a sedate place. Arrive in August during the techno **Street Parade** (p520) and you'll know different. Any weekend of the year you can feel the vibe at nightspots like **Club Q** (p521) or the buzzing bars in **Züri-West** (p521).

After two nights there, the rave continues on in **(2) Berlin** (p436). During the day you can tour museums dedicated to a once-divided city and the **Berlin Wall** (p443), and at night choose from a bevy of underground, edgy or upmarket music-filled **nightlife** (p445). You might want to take a nap in the evening – if you go out before midnight, you'll be dancing solo.

Plan ahead for your last night, in **(3) Vienna** (p472); tickets for the **State Opera** (p481) sell out well in advance. But, oh, does the extravagant music, the gilt theatre, elaborate costumes on stage (and the formal attire off) reward your forethought. Don't miss the chance to drink up some of the **coffee-house culture** (p480) before departing.

ALPINE ADVENTURE One Week

Warning: a week of fresh air and mountain views may leave you breathless. The mind-blowing scenery at **(1) Interlaken** (p512) is a good place to start. Be wowed by the kitsch-filled town beneath Eiger, Mönch and Jungfrau peaks before you head up into the mountains to paraglide, ice-climb or zorb with an outfitter. Day three take a trip to **(2) Jungfraujoch** (p516), the highest train station in Europe at 3741m.

The peaks in the Bavarian Alps may not be quite as high as their sister summits, but **(3) Berchtesgaden** (p463) is still surrounded by six impressive ranges. The hiking in the Berchtesgaden National Park is some of the best in Germany.

Your last two nights are spent south in **(4) Innsbruck** (p492). Stroll the medieval old centre before scaling the surrounding heights. Northpark cable way takes you from town to Hafelekar peak (2256m) in just 25 minutes – via a funicular and two cable cars.

PROVINCIAL CHARMERS 10 Days

Explore the charm of the regions' cities and towns. Baroque buildings fill the quaint and cobbled streets of **(1) Salzburg** (p485), the one-time home of Mozart. It's well worth two days spent touring music museums and castles – and reinacting the *Sound of Music* in situ. Nearby **(2) Munich** (p451) is just as full of character and characters;

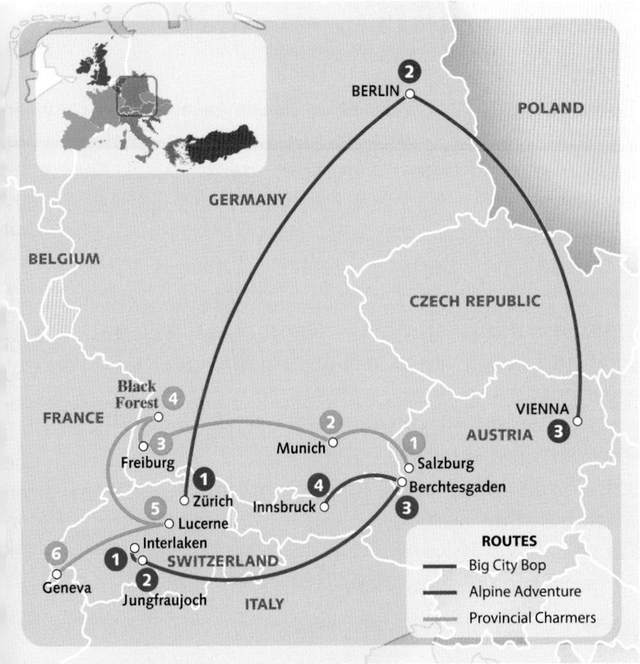

stop at one of the many beer halls or gardens after you've toured the old town and you'll see.

Moving on, the lively university town of **(3) Freiburg** (p466) is a good southern base for excursions into the **(4) Black Forest** (p465). Hike the bucolic hills and go cuckoo for clocks.

South in Switzerland, **(5) Lucerne** (p510) is a gorgeous old Swiss town with atmospheric covered bridges and stunning mountain surrounds. Arrive in June for the **Jodler Fest** (p511) and have some oo-de-lay-ee-hoo Alpine fun. Glittering **(6) Geneva** (p497) is quite the cosmopolitan contrast, though the Alpine lake setting is no less striking. Spend the last evening brushing up on your *français* and indulging in the *gastronomie*.

DISCOVER GERMANY, AUSTRIA & SWITZERLAND

A trifecta of Alpine nations, to a greater or lesser extent, Germany, Austria and Switzerland are all dominated by mountains with a capital M. These are lands of outdoor pursuits: gentle Black Forest walks, strenuous Hohe Tauern National Park hikes and fearless Swiss Alp snowboarding runs.

But don't bypass the cities. Berlin, edgy and vibrant, is a grand capital in a constant state of reinvention, while Bavarian Munich is at the centre of German national traditions. Venture into the backstreets of imperial Vienna and mountain-clad Salzburg and hear the sweet sounds of classical music and opera wafting from open windows. Polyglot Geneva is a cosmopolitan gem on an Alpine lake and Zürich offers cutting-edge art and legendary nightlife.

In the mountains or in town, you'll have plenty of opportunities to imbibe – mid-slope at an après-ski hang-out, in an elegant turn-of-the-20th-century cafe or at raucous oompah-loving Oktoberfest. Great views and good brews? Now that's living the high life.

GERMANY

BERLIN

☎ 030 / pop 3.41 million

Reminders of Berlin's once-divided past sit side by side with its united present – Potsdamer Platz and its shiny Sony Centre host the star-studded Berlin Film Festival each year, a stone's throw from where only 20 years ago you could climb up a viewing platform in the west and peer over the wall to glimpse the alternate reality of the east. Renowned for its diversity and its tolerance, its alternative culture and its night-owl stamina, the best thing about the German capital is the way it reinvents itself and isn't shackled by its mind-numbing history. And the world is catching on – as evidenced by the surge of expatriates and steady increase of out-of-towners coming to see what all the fuss is about. In short, all human life is here, and don't expect to get much sleep.

HISTORY

In the mid-1930s Berlin became a centrepiece of Nazi power and suffered heavily during WWII. The Potsdam Conference took place in August 1945 and split the capital into zones occupied by the four victorious powers – the USA, Britain, France and the Soviet Union. The Berlin Wall, built in August 1961, was originally intended to prevent the drain of skilled labour from the East, but soon became a Cold War symbol. For decades, East Berlin and West Berlin developed separately, until Hungarians breached the Iron Curtain in May 1989 and the Berlin Wall followed on 9 November. The Unification Treaty signed on 3 October 1990 designated Berlin the official capital of Germany.

ORIENTATION

Although wealthier, more mature Berliners still happily frequent the west, the eastern districts are the most happening.

Even Mitte, or the centre, now lies east of the former Wall. As Mitte heads northeast, it merges into the trendy district of Prenzlauer Berg. Friedrichshain, another popular neighbourhood, is found several kilometres east of the centre, around Ostbahnhof.

Kreuzberg, south of Mitte, has two sides: Western Kreuzberg was the alternative hub of West Berlin and is still hanging in there, with some interesting restaurants and bars; eastern Kreuzberg is grungier, hopping and definitely where the 'kool kids' – and adults – hang out.

INFORMATION

Berlin Tourismus (☎ 250 025; www.berlin-tourist-information.de) Alexanderplatz (Alexa Shopping Centre; 🕐 10am-6pm); Brandenburger Tor (🕐 10am-6pm)

Berlin Welcome Card (www.berlin-welcomecard.de; 48/72hr €16.50/21.50, incl Potsdam & up to 3 children €18/24.50) Free public transport, plus museum and entertainment discounts.

Kassenärztliche Bereitschaftsdienst (Public Physicians' Emergency Service; ☎ 310 031; www.kvberlin.de, in German) Phone referral service.

THOMAS WINZ

The Reichstag (p439)

BERLIN IN TWO DAYS

Investigate the **Brandenburg Gate** (p439) area, including the **Reichstag** (p439) and the **Holocaust Memorial** (p439). Walk east along Unter den Linden, stopping at the **Bebelplatz book-burning memorial** (p440). Veer through the **Museumsinsel** (p440) for window-shopping and cafe-hopping through **Hackescher Markt** (p441). In the evening, explore the bars of Prenzlauer Berg, along Kastanieanallee and Pappelallee.

Start the next day at the **East Side Gallery** (p443) remnant of the Berlin Wall, before heading to **Checkpoint Charlie** (p443) and the nearby **Jewish Museum** (p469). Take the U-Bahn to **Kurfürstendamm** (p442) and catch scenic bus 100 back to the **Fernsehturm** (p441). Later, explore Kreuzberg nightlife around Kottbusser Tor and go clubbing – **Berghain/Panoramabar** (p445) is best if you are short on time. Alternatively, head for the **Berliner Ensemble** (p446).

BERLIN

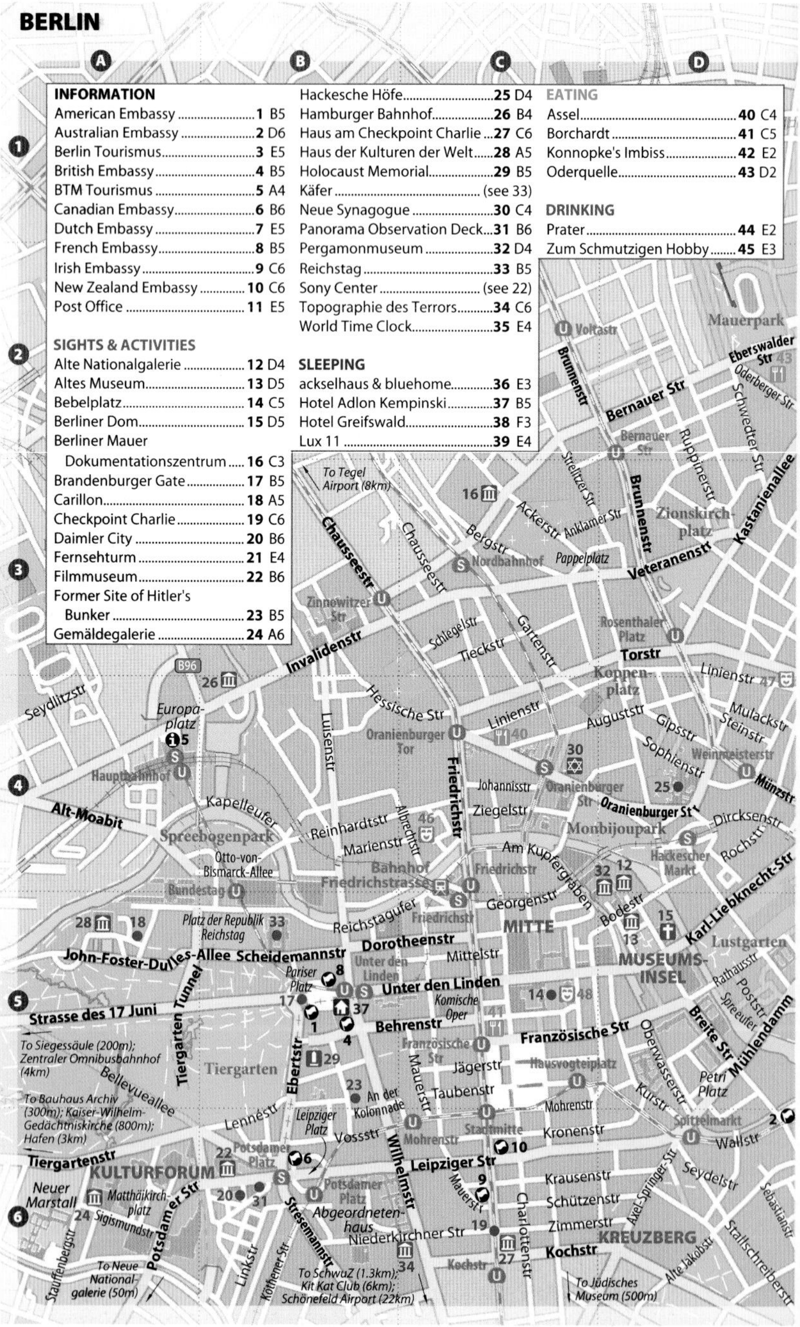

INFORMATION

- American Embassy 1 B5
- Australian Embassy 2 D6
- Berlin Tourismus 3 E5
- British Embassy 4 B5
- BTM Tourismus 5 A4
- Canadian Embassy 6 B6
- Dutch Embassy 7 E5
- French Embassy 8 B5
- Irish Embassy 9 C6
- New Zealand Embassy 10 C6
- Post Office 11 E5

SIGHTS & ACTIVITIES

- Alte Nationalgalerie 12 D4
- Altes Museum 13 D5
- Bebelplatz 14 C5
- Berliner Dom 15 D5
- Berliner Mauer Dokumentationszentrum 16 C3
- Brandenburger Gate 17 B5
- Carillon 18 A5
- Checkpoint Charlie 19 C6
- Daimler City 20 B6
- Fernsehturm 21 E4
- Filmmuseum 22 B6
- Former Site of Hitler's Bunker 23 B5
- Gemäldegalerie 24 A6
- Hackesche Höfe 25 D4
- Hamburger Bahnhof 26 B4
- Haus am Checkpoint Charlie 27 C6
- Haus der Kulturen der Welt 28 A5
- Holocaust Memorial 29 B5
- Käfer ..... (see 33)
- Neue Synagogue 30 C4
- Panorama Observation Deck 31 B6
- Pergamonmuseum 32 D4
- Reichstag 33 B5
- Sony Center ..... (see 22)
- Topographie des Terrors 34 C6
- World Time Clock 35 E4

SLEEPING

- ackselhaus & bluehome 36 E3
- Hotel Adlon Kempinski 37 B5
- Hotel Greifswald 38 F3
- Lux 11 ..... 39 E4

EATING

- Assel 40 C4
- Borchardt 41 C5
- Konnopke's Imbiss 42 E2
- Oderquelle 43 D2

DRINKING

- Prater 44 E2
- Zum Schmutzigen Hobby 45 E3

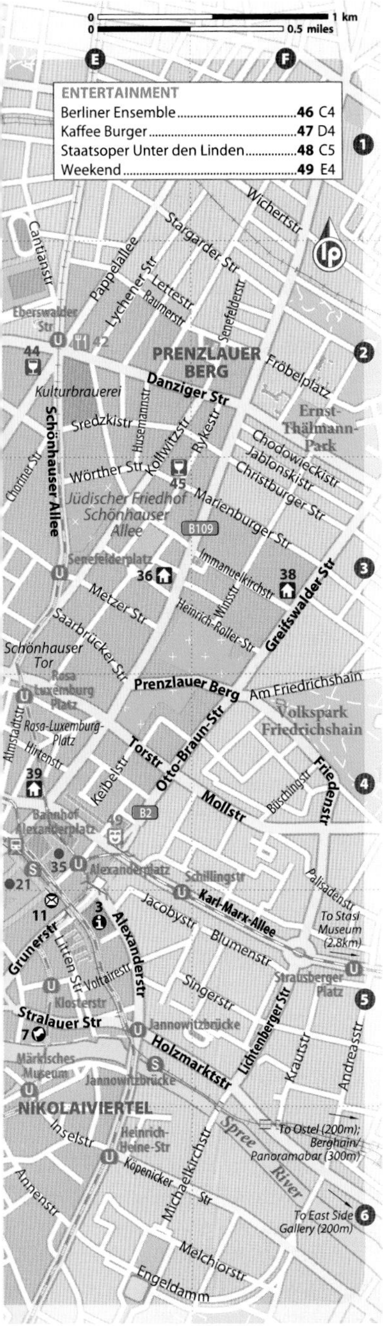

Post office (Rathausstrasse 5; 8am-7pm Mon-Fri, to 4pm Sat; M Alexanderplatz).

SIGHTS

Unless otherwise indicated, where sights are grouped together they are all accessed by the same station listed at the beginning of the section.

BRANDENBURG GATE

Finished in 1791 as one of 18 city gates, the neoclassical **Brandenburg Gate** (Brandenburger Tor; Pariser Platz; M S-Bahn Unter den Linden) became an east–west crossing point after the Berlin Wall was built in 1961. A symbol of Berlin's division, it was a place US presidents loved to grandstand. Ronald Reagan appeared in 1987 to appeal to the Russian leader, 'Mr Gorbachev, tear down this wall!'. In 1989, more than 100,000 Germans poured through it as the wall fell.

Just to the west stands the glass-domed **Reichstag** (Parliament; ☎ 2273 2152; www.bundestag.de; Platz der Republik 1; admission free; 8am-midnight, last admission 10pm), with four national flags fluttering. Today the building is once again the German seat of power, but it's the glass cupola added during the 1999 refurbishment that some 10,000 people a day flock to see. Walking along the internal spiral walkway by British star architect Lord Norman Foster feels like being in a postmodern beehive. To beat the queues, book a table at the rooftop restaurant **Käfer** (☎ 2262 9935; www.feinkost-kaefer.de), which uses a separate entrance.

The Reichstag overlooks the **Tiergarten** (see p441) and further south again is the **Holocaust Memorial** (Denkmal für die ermordeten Juden Europas; ☎ 2639 4336; www.stiftung-denkmal.de; Cora-Berliner-Strasse 1; admission free; field 24hr, information centre 10am-8pm Tue-Sun, last entry

ANDREA SCHULTE-PEEVERS

Bauhaus Archiv

7.15pm Apr-Sep, 10am-7pm Tue-Sun, last entry 6.15pm Oct-Mar; Ⓜ Potsdamer Platz/S-Bahn Unter den Linden) a grid of 2711 'stelae' or differently shaped concrete columns set over 19,000 sq metres of gently undulating ground. For historical background, designer Peter Eisenman has created an underground information centre in the southeast corner of the site. Highly recommended are the weekly **English tours** (€3; tours 4pm Sun).

UNTER DEN LINDEN

Celebrated in literature and lined with lime (or linden) trees, the street **Unter den Linden** was the fashionable avenue of old Berlin. Today, after decades of communist neglect, it's been rebuilt and regained that status.

Stop by **Bebelplatz** (Ⓜ Französische Strasse), opposite the university, where there's a **book-burning memorial** – a reminder of the first major Nazi book-burning, which occurred in May 1933. A transparent window tile in the stone pavement reveals empty bookshelves below.

MUSEUMSINSEL

Lying along the Spree River, the **Museumsinsel** (Museums Island; ☎ all museums 2090 5577; www.smb.museum.de; adult/concession per museum €8/4, combined ticket for all museums €12/6, last 4hr Thu free; 10am-6pm Tue-Sun, to 10pm Thu; Ⓜ S-Bahn Hackescher Markt) contains the **Pergamonmuseum** (Am Kupfergraben 5), which is to Berlin what the British Museum is to London: a feast of Mesopotamian, Greek and Roman antiquities looted by archaeologists. The museum takes its name from the Pergamon Altar inside, but the real highlight of the collection is the Ishtar Gate from Babylon.

Meanwhile, the **Alte Nationalgalerie** (Old National Gallery; Bodestrasse 1-3) houses 19th-century European sculpture and painting; the **Altes Museum** (Am Lustgarten) has art from ancient Rome and Greece.

Overlooking the 'island' is the **Berliner Dom** (Berlin Cathedral; ☎ 2026 9136 www.berliner-dom.de; adult/child under 14/concession €5/free/3; 9am-8pm Mon-Sat, from noon Sun, to 7pm Oct-Mar).

The entire Museumsinsel is currently being renovated and redeveloped – a new main visitor reception area is in the works and construction is expected to last until 2015. One of the most exciting projects is the reopening of the Neues Museum, which was reduced to rubble during WWII. See www.museumsinsel-berlin.de for details.

HACKESCHER MARKT

A complex of shops and apartments around eight courtyards, the **Hackesche Höfe** (M S-Bahn Hackescher Markt) is commercial and touristy, but it's definitely good fun to wander around the big-name brand shops and smaller boutiques or simply people-watch in the cafes and restaurants – the atmosphere is always lively. You'll also find the **Neue Synagogue** (☎ 8802 8300; www.cjudaicum.de; Oranienburger Strasse 28-30; adult/concession €3/2; ⏲ 10am-8pm Sun & Mon, to 6pm Tue-Thu, to 5pm Fri, reduced hr Nov-Apr), with its history of local Jewish life.

Further north, the contemporary art museum **Hamburger Bahnhof** (☎ 3978 3439; www.hamburgerbahnhof.de; Invalidenstrasse 50, Mitte; adult/concession €8/4, last 4hr Thu free; ⏲ 10am-6pm Tue-Fri, 11am-8pm Sat, 11am-6pm Sun; M Hauptbahnhof/Lehrter Stadtbahnhof) is housed in a former neoclassical train station and showcases works by Warhol, Lichtenstein, Cy Twombly and Keith Haring.

TV TOWER

Call it Freudian or call it *Ostalgie* (nostalgia for the communist East or *Ost*), but Berlin's once-mocked socialist **Fernsehturm** (☎ 242 3333; www.berlinerfernsehturm.de; adult/concession €9.50/4.50; ⏲ 9am-midnight Mar-Oct, from 10am Nov-Feb; M Alexanderplatz) is fast becoming its most-loved symbol. That said, ascending 207m to the revolving (but musty) Telecafé is a less singular experience than visiting the Reichstag dome.

The Turm dominates **Alexanderplatz**, a former livestock and wool market that became the low-life district chronicled by Alfred Döblin's 1929 novel *Berlin Alexanderplatz* and then developed as a 1960s communist showpiece.

Even in a city so often described as one big building site, today's Alexanderplatz is an unusual hive of construction activity as it is transformed into the next Potsdamer Platz style development. However, its communist past still echoes through the retro **World Time Clock** and along the portentous **Karl-Marx-Allee**, which leads several kilometres east from the square to Friedrichshain.

TIERGARTEN

From the Reichstag (see p439), the Tiergarten park's **carillon** (🚌 100 or 200) and the **Haus der Kulturen der Welt** (House of World Cultures) are clearly visible. The latter was the US contribution to the 1957 International Building Exposition and it's easy to see why locals call it the 'pregnant oyster'.

Further west, the wings of the **Siegessäule** (Victory Column; 🚌 100 or 200) were the *Wings of Desire* in that famous Wim Wenders film. This golden angel was built to commemorate Prussian military victories in the 19th century.

A short walk south from here is a cluster of interesting embassy buildings and museums, including the **Bauhaus Archiv** (☎ 254 0020; www.bauhaus.de; Klingelhöferstrasse 14; adult/concession Sat-Mon €7/4, Wed-Fri €6/3; ⏲ 10am-5pm Wed-Mon; M Nollendorfplatz) with drawings, chairs and other Modernist objects from the famous Bauhaus school of design – as well as a very tempting shop.

More museums are found a little east in the **Kulturforum**. These include the spectacular **Gemäldegalerie** (Picture Gallery; ☎ 266 2951; www.gemaeldegalerie-berlin.de; Matthäikirchplatz 4-6; adult/concession €8/4; ⏲ 10am-6pm Tue, Wed & Fri-Sun, to 10pm Thu; M S-Bahn Potzdamer Platz) showing European painting from the 13th to the 18th centuries. Nearby is the **Neue Nationalgalerie** (☎ 266 2951; www.neue-nationalgalerie.de; Potsdamer Strasse 50; adult/concession €8/4; ⏲ 10am-6pm Tue, Wed & Fri, to 10pm

Thu, 11am-6pm Sat & Sun; Ⓜ S-Bahn Potzdamer Platz). Twentieth-century works by Picasso, Klee, Munch, Dalì, Kandinsky and many German expressionists are housed in an exquisite 'temple of light and glass' built by Bauhaus-director Ludwig Mies van der Rohe.

POTSDAMER PLATZ

The lid was symbolically sealed on capitalism's victory over socialism in Berlin when this postmodern temple to Mammon was erected in 2000 over the former death strip. Under the big-top, glass-tent roof of the **Sony Center** (**Ⓜ S-Bahn Potsdamer Platz**) and along the malls of the Legolike **Daimler City**, people swarm in and around shops, restaurants, offices, loft apartments, clubs, a cinema, a luxury hotel and a casino – all revitalising what was the busiest square in prewar Europe.

During the International Film Festival Berlin (see p444), Potsdamer Platz welcomes Hollywood A-listers. In between you can rub shoulders with German cinematic heroes – particularly Marlene Dietrich – at the **Filmmuseum** (**☎ 300 9030; www.filmmuseum-berlin.de; Potsdamer Strasse 2, Tiergarten; adult/concession €6/4.50; 🕑 10am-6pm Tue, Wed & Fri-Sun, to 8pm Thu**). There's also 'Europe's fastest' lift to the 100m-high **Panorama Observation Deck** (**www.panoramapunkt.de; adult/concession €3.50/2.50; 🕑 11am-8pm**).

But, as ever in Berlin, the past refuses to go quietly. Just north of Potsdamer Platz lies the **former site of Hitler's Bunker**. A little southeast lies the **Topographie des Terrors** (**☎ 2548 6703; www.topographie.de; Niederkirchner Strasse 8; admission free; 🕑 10am-8pm May-Sep, to dusk Oct-Apr**), a shockingly graphic collection of text and images mounted on the ruins of the Gestapo and SS headquarters.

JEWISH MUSEUM

The Daniel Libeskind building that is the **Jüdisches Museum** (**☎ 2599 3300; www.juedisches-museum-berlin.de; Lindenstrasse 9-14; adult/concession €5/2.50; 🕑 10am-10pm Mon, to 8pm Tue-Sun, last entry 1hr before closing; Ⓜ Hallesches Tor**) is as much the attraction as the Jewish-German history collection within. Designed to disorientate and unbalance with its 'voids', cul-de-sacs, barbed metal fittings, slit windows and uneven floors, this still-somehow-beautiful structure swiftly conveys the uncertainty and sometime terror of past Jewish life in Germany.

KURFÜRSTENDAMM

West Berlin's legendary shopping thoroughfare, the Ku'damm has lost some of its cachet since the wall fell, but is worth visiting. You will find the **Kaiser-Wilhelm-Gedächtniskirche** (**☎ 218 5023; www.gedaechtniskirche-berlin.de; Breitscheidplatz; 🕑 Memorial Hall 10am-4pm Mon-Sat, Hall of Worship 9am-7pm**) here, which remains in ruins – just as British bombers left it on 22 November 1943 – as an antiwar memorial. Only the broken west tower still stands. In 1961 the modern hall of worship was built adjacent to the church.

STASI MUSEUM

This imposing compound, formerly the secret police headquarters, now contains the **Stasi Museum** (**☎ 553 6854; House 1, Ruschestrasse 103; adult/concession €4/3; 🕑 11am-6pm Tue-Fri, 2-6pm Sat & Sun; Ⓜ Magdalenenstrasse**). It's largely in German, but well worth it to get a sense of the impact the Stasi had on the daily lives of GDR citizens through its extensive photos and displays of the astounding range of surveillance devices, as well as exhibits of the tightly sealed jars used to retain cloths containing body-odour samples.

IF WALLS COULD TALK

Today's remnants of the 155km wall are scattered across the city, but you can follow all or sections of its former path along the 160km-long **Berliner Mauerweg** (Berlin Wall Trail; www.berlin.de/mauer), a signposted walking and cycling path that follows the former border fortifications, either along customs-patrol roads in West Berlin or border-control roads used by GDR guards. Along the route, 40 multilingual information stations provide historical context, highlight dramatic events and relate stories about daily life in the divided city.

The longest surviving stretch is the **East Side Gallery** (www.eastsidegallery.com; Mühlenstrasse; Ⓜ S-Bahn Warschauer Strasse) in Friedrichshain. Panels of graffiti and art along this 1.3km section include the famous portrait of Soviet leader Brezhnev kissing GDR leader Erich Hönecker and a Trabant car seemingly bursting through the (now crumbling) concrete.

The sombre **Berliner Mauer Dokumentationszentrum** (Berlin Wall Documentation Centre; ☎ 464 1030; www.berliner-mauer-dokumentationszentrum.de; Bernauer Strasse 111; admission free; 🕘 10am-6pm Tue-Sun Apr-Oct, to 5pm Nov-Mar; Ⓜ U-Bahn Bernauersrasse) is a memorial containing a section of the original wall, photos of the surrounding area (before and during the lifespan of the wall), newspaper clippings and listening stations featuring old West and East Berlin radio programs as well as eyewitness testimonies. Be sure to climb the tower for a view of an artistic recreation of no-man's land as well as the **Kapelle der Versöhnung** (Chapel of Reconciliation), a modern round structure of pressed earth and slim wooden planks built on the site of an 1894 red-brick church blown up in 1985 in order to widen the border strip.

In Kreuzberg, the famous sign at **Checkpoint Charlie** still boasts, 'You are now leaving the American sector'. But it and the reconstructed US guardhouse are just tourist attractions now. For a less light-hearted view of the past, visit **Haus am Checkpoint Charlie** (☎ 253 7250; www.mauer-museum.com; Friedrichstrasse 43-45; adult/concession €12.50/9.50; 🕘 9am-10pm; Ⓜ Kochstrasse/Stadtmitte). Tales of spectacular escape attempts include through tunnels, in hot-air balloons and even using a one-man submarine.

TOURS

Guided tours are phenomenally popular; you can choose Third Reich, Wall, bunker, communist, boat or bicycle tours, as well as guided pub crawls. **New Berlin** (☎ 017-9973 0397; www.newberlintours.com) even offers free (yup, free) 3½-hour introductory walking tours. Guides are enthusiastic, knowledgeable…and accept tips.

Alternatively, you can tool around Berlin in a Trabant car. **Trabi Safari** (☎ 275 2273; www.trabi-safari.de; €30-60) operates from the Berlin Hi-Flyer near Checkpoint Charlie (see above).

Other operators:

Insider Tours (☎ 692 3149; www.insidertour.com)

Original Berlin Walks (☎ 301 9194; www.berlinwalks.com)

FESTIVALS & EVENTS

International Film Festival Berlin (☎ 259 200; www.berlinale.de) The Berlinale, held in February, is Germany's answer to the Cannes and Venice film festivals.

Christopher Street Day (☎ 2362 8632; www.csd-berlin.de) Held on the last weekend in June, Germany's largest gay event celebrated its 30th anniversary in 2008.

B-Parade (www.b-parade.eu) Held each July, Berlin's huge techno street parade is the successor to the Love Parade.

SLEEPING

Ostel (☎ 2576 8660; www.ostel.eu; Wriezener Karree 5; dm/d €9/61, apt €120; Ⓜ Ostbahnhof; 💻) *Ostalgie* – nostalgia for the communist East – is taken to a whole new level at this hostel/hotel with original socialist GDR furnishings and portraits of Honecker and other former socialist leaders. You can even stay in a 'bugged' Stasi Suite.

Hotel Greifswald (☎ 4442 7888; www.hotel-greifswald.de; Greifswalderstrasse 211; s/d/tr/apt from €57/69/90/75; Ⓜ Senefelder Platz; 💻) You'd never guess this informal, quiet hotel set back from the street around a sweet courtyard is regularly home to bands and even rock stars – until you see their photos in the lobby.

our pick ackselhaus & bluehome (☎ 4433 7633; www.ackselhaus.de; Belforter Strasse 21; ste from €90, apt €140-260; Ⓜ Senefelder Platz; 💻) This Zen oasis, spread out across two buildings, offers exquisitely designed suites or apartments (most with kitchenettes); each has a different theme, from Italian to Hollywood.

Lux 11 (☎ 936 2800; www.lux-eleven.com; Rosa-Luxemburg-Strasse 9-13; r/ste from €165/255; Ⓜ Weinmeisterstrasse/Alexanderplatz; 💻) A liberal use of white makes this slick, streamlined hotel a haven of unpretentious minimalism.

Hotel Adlon Kempinski (☎ 226 10; www.hotel-adlon.de, Am Pariser Platz, Unter den Linden 77; r from €450; ❄ 💻 🏊) Still remembered for being the site of Michael Jackson's baby-dangling episode, the luxurious Adlon Kempinski is situated on the doorstep of the Brandenburg Gate.

EATING

Konnopke's Imbiss (Schönhauser Allee 44a; snacks €1.50-5; 🕑 6am-8pm Mon-Fri, noon-7pm Sat; Ⓜ Eberswalder Strasse) The quintessential wurst stand under the elevated U-Bahn tracks. We think Konnopke's serves the best *currywurst* in town.

our pick Assel (☎ 281 2056; Oranienburger strasse 61; mains €5-15; Ⓜ Oranienburger Strasse or Hackescher Markt) One of the few exceptional picks on a particularly touristy and busy stretch of Mitte. Come for coffee, a bite or a full meal and stretch out in the wooden booths made from old S-Bahn seats. Plus, the toilets are entertaining (you'll see).

Oderquelle (☎ 4400 8080; Oderberger Strasse 27; mains €8-16; 🕑 dinner; Ⓜ Eberswalder Strasse) Modern German food in such mellow, convivial digs is rare, almost as rare as snagging a table here after 7pm, so be sure to reserve.

Borchardt (☎ 8188 6250; Französische Strasse 47; mains €18-40; Ⓜ Französische Strasse) On every Berlin *promi*'s (celeb's) speed-dial list, this refined French-German bistro also tolerates ordinary civilians.

DRINKING

Gemütlichkeit, which roughly translates as 'cosy, warm and friendly, with a decided lack of anything hectic', dominates the upmarket bars of the west as well as the hipper, more underground venues in the east. Prenzlauer Berg,

IZZET KERIBAR

Pergamon Altar, Pergamonmuseum (p440)

ıe first GDR sector to develop a happening nightlife, still attracts visitors, ·eative types and gay customers, but ; its residents have aged (and produced ıany, many babies) its nightlife has beome more subdued. Clubs and bars in Aitte around Hackescher Markt cater) a cool, slightly older and wealthier ·owd. Friedrichshain boasts a young ipster feel and Kreuzberg remains the lternative hub, becoming grungier s you move east. Charlottenburg and 'interfeldtplatz are fairly upmarket and ıature, but liberal.

Prater (☎ Kastanienallee 7-9; Ⓜ Eberswalder rasse) A summer institution, Berlin's oldst beer garden (since 1837) invites you ı for a tall chilled draft under the canopy f chestnut trees.

NTERTAINMENT

erlin's legendary nightlife needs little ıtroduction. Whether alternative, underround, cutting edge, saucy, flamboyant r even highbrow, it all crops up here.

NIGHTCLUBS

Few club opens before 11pm (and if you arrive before midnight you may be dancing solo), but they stay open well into the early hours – usually sunrise at least.

Berghain/Panoramabar (www.berghain.de; Wrienzer Bahnhof; from midnight Thu-Sat; Ⓜ Ostbahnhof) If you only make it to one club in Berlin, this is where you need to go. Expect cutting-edge sounds in industrial surrounds.

Kaffee Burger (☎ 2804 6495; www.kaffeeburger.de; Torstrasse 60; Ⓜ Rosa-Luxemburg-Platz) The original GDR '60s wallpaper is part of the decor at this arty bar, club and music venue in Mitte.

Weekend (www.week-end-berlin.de; Am Alexanderplatz 5; from 11pm Thu-Sat; Ⓜ Alexanderplatz) Tear your eyes from the beautiful people and gaze through the 12th-floor windows, across the *Bladerunner* landscape of dug-up Alexanderplatz and over Berlin.

Berlin also has a thriving scene of no-holds-barred sex clubs. The notorious **Kit Kat Club** (☎ 7889 9704; Bessemerstrasse 14; Ⓜ Alt-Tempelhof) is the original and best.

GAY & LESBIAN BERLIN

Berlin boasts a liberal – no, 'wild' is a more accurate description – gay scene where anything goes. Still going strong since the 1920s, Schöneberg is the original gay area, but these days Prenzlauer Berg is the trendiest; Friedrichshain also has a small studenty gay scene. Skim through **Berlin Gay Web** (**http://berlin.gay-web.de, in German**) for all things gay in Berlin or **Girl Ports** (**www.girlports.com/lesbiantravel/destinations/berlin**), a lesbian travel magazine.

SchwuZ (**☎ 693 7025; www.schwuz.de; Mehringdamm 61; from 11pm Fri & Sat; M Mehringdamm**) is one of the longest-running mixed institutions; there's a cafe here all week, too.

Hafen (**☎ 211 4118; Motzstrasse 19; M Nollendorfplatz**) is a Schöneberg staple with a consistent party scene. There's also an eclectic quiz night on Mondays (in English first Monday of the month).

A popular bar attracting a mixed crowd is **Zum Schmutzigen Hobby** (**Rykestrasse 45; from 5pm; M Eberswalder Strasse**) run by well-known drag queen Nina Queer.

MUSIC & THEATRE

Staatsoper Unter den Linden (**☎ information 203 540, tickets 2035 4555; www.staatsoper-berlin.de; Unter den Linden 5-7; M S-Bahn Unter den Linden**) This is the handiest and most prestigious of Berlin's three opera houses, where unsold seats go on sale cheap an hour before curtains-up.

Berliner Ensemble (**☎ information 284 080, tickets 2840 8155; www.berliner-ensemble.de; Bertolt-Brecht-Platz 1; M Friedrichstrasse**) 'Mack the Knife' had its first public airing here, during the *Threepenny Opera's* premiere in 1928. Bertolt Brecht's former theatric home continues to present his plays.

GETTING THERE & AWAY

Berlin has two international airports, re flecting the legacy of the divided city. Th larger one is in the northwestern subur of Tegel (TXL), about 8km from the ci centre; the other is in Schönefeld (SXF about 22km southeast of town. For info mation about either, go to www.berli-airport.de or call ☎ 0180-500 0186.

Berlin will eventually get its own majo international airport, as Schönefeld being expanded into Berlin Brandenbu International (BBI); estimated completio date is 2011.

Most buses arrive at and depart from th **Zentraler Omnibusbahnhof** (**ZOB; ☎ 30 5361; Masurenallee 4-6; M Kaiserdamm/Witzleben**) opposite the Funkturm radio tower.

Regular long-distance train service arrive at the architecturally spectacu lar Hauptbahnhof (also called Lehrte Bahnhof), with many continuing east t Ostbahnhof and Lichtenberg. ICE and I trains leave hourly to every major city i Germany and there are also connection to central Europe.

GETTING AROUND

TO/FROM THE AIRPORT

SCHÖNEFELD

The S9 travels through all the majo downtown stations, taking 40 minutes t Alexanderplatz. The faster 'Airport Expres trains travel the same route half-hourly t Ostbahnhof (15 minutes), Alexanderplat (20 minutes) and Friedrichstrasse (2 minutes).

TEGEL

Tegel (TXL) is connected to Mitte by th JetExpressBus TXL (30 minutes). Tegel i not directly served by the U-Bahn.

THOMAS WINZ

Berlin's Sony Center (p442)

ICYCLE

lat and bike-friendly, with special bike anes, abundant green spaces and peaceul waterways, Berlin is best explored by ooling around on two wheels. Many ostels and hotels rent bicycles to their uests or can refer you to an agency.

UBLIC TRANSPORT

)ne type of ticket is valid on all transport – including the U-Bahn, buses, trams and erries run by **Berliner Verkehrsbetriebe** (☎ 194 49; www.bvg.de) as well as the S-Bahn nd regional RE, SE and RB trains operated y **Deutsche Bahn** (www.bahn.de). If you're aught without a validated ticket, there's €40 on-the-spot fine.

)RESDEN

☎ 0351 / pop 484,000

'roof that there is life after death,)resden has become one of Germany's nost popular attractions, and for good eason. Restorations have returned the ity to its glory when it was famous throughout Europe as 'Florence on the Elbe', owing to the efforts of Italian artists, musicians, actors and master craftsmen who flocked to the court of Augustus the Strong, bestowing countless masterpieces upon the city. But then death came suddenly when, shortly before the end of WWII, Allied bombers blasted and incinerated much of the baroque centre, a beautiful jewel-like area dating from the 18th century. More than 35,000 people died, and in bookstores throughout town you can peruse books showing the destruction (or read about it in Kurt Vonnegut's classic *Slaughterhouse Five*).

The city celebrated its 800th anniversary in 2006 and while much focus is on the restored centre, you should cross the River Elbe to the Neustadt, where edgy new clubs and cafes open every week, joining the 150 already there. The Elbe River splits the town in a rough V-shape, with the Neustadt to the north and the Altstadt (old city) to the south.

Dresden Information Prager Strasse 2 (4919 2100; www.dresden.de; 10am-7pm Mon-Sat); Theaterplatz 2 (10am-6pm Mon-Fri, to 4pm Sat & Sun) Discount cards from €21.

One of Dresden's most beloved icons, the **Frauenkirche** (Church of Our Lady; 439 3934; www.frauenkirche-dresden.org; Neumarkt; 10am-6pm) was rebuilt in time for the city's 800th anniversary celebrations in 2006. Initially built between 1726 and 1743 under the direction of baroque architect George Bähr, it was Germany's greatest Protestant church until February 1945, when bombing raids flattened it. Look for the very few blackened stones on the exterior, these were salvaged from the rubble of the original. The surrounding Neumarkt is part of a massive

ANDREA SCHULTE-PEEVERS

Baroque sculpture on the Zwinger

redevelopment designed to evoke prew
Dresden.

The neo-Renaissance opera hous
Semperoper (491 1496; www.semperope
de; Theaterplatz; tour adult/child €7/3.50; varie
designed by Gustav Semper, *is* Dresder
The best way to appreciate it is throug
one of the many performances.

The **Schloss** (491 4619; Schlossplatz
a massive neo-Renaissance palace, ha
ongoing restoration projects. The Schlos
also houses museums. For information o
most of Dresden's museums, see the wel
site www.skd-dresden.de.

Dresden's elaborate 1728 fortres
Zwinger (491 4622; Theaterplatz 1; 10an
6pm Tue-Sun) is an attraction in its own righ
with a popular ornamental courtyar
and also houses six major museum
The most important is the **Galerie Alt
Meister** (adult/child incl entry to Rüstkamme
€7/4.50), which features masterpieces ir
cluding Raphael's *Sistine Madonna*. Th
Rüstkammer (armoury) has a super
collection of ceremonial weapons. Th
dazzling **Porzelansammlung** (Porcelai
Collection; adult/child €6/3.50) is filled wit
flamboyant breakables.

Cruise the Elbe on the world's old
est fleet of paddle-wheel steamers wit
Sächsische Dampfschiffahrt (866 09
www.saechsische-dampfschiffahrt.de; adult/chil
€16/8). There's also service to villages alon
the river such as Meissen.

Hotel Martha Hospiz (817 60; www
hotel-martha-hospiz.de; Nieritzstrasse 11; s/
€55/120;) Hospitality is taken very se
riously at this lovely quiet inn, which i
close to the lively Königstrasse.

Kempinski Hotel Taschenbergpalai
(491 20; www.kempinski-dresden.de; Tasch
enberg 3; r €200-400;) This restore
18th-century mansion is Dresden's heavy
weight, with views over the Zwinger, in
credibly quiet corridors, and doors tha

seem impervious to anything outside, protecting the 214 rooms and suites.

It's no problem finding somewhere to eat in the Neustadt, with oodles of cafes and restaurants found along Königstrasse and the streets north of Albertplatz. This is definitely the most interesting part of town at night.

Gänsedieb (☎ **485 0905; Weisse Gasse 1; mains €8-15**) One of nearly a dozen choices on Weisse Gasse, the 'Goose Thief' serves hearty schnitzels, goulash and steaks alongside a full range of Bavarian Paulaner beers.

Dresden's **airport** (**DRS; www.dresden-airport.de**), served by Lufthansa and Air Berlin among others, is 9km north of the city centre, on S-Bahn line 2 (€1.70, 30 minutes).

Dresden is well linked with regular services through the day to Berlin-Hauptbahnhof by IC/EC train (€36, 2¼ hours) and Frankfurt-am-Main by ICE (€85, 4½ hours).

Dresden's **public transport network** (**www.dvbag.de**) charges €1.80 for a single-trip ticket; day tickets cost €4.50. Tram 3, 7, 8 and 9 provide good links between the Hauptbahnhof and Neustadt.

THURINGIA

The Nazis had numerous concentration camps here, including the notorious Buchenwald and the nightmare of Mittelbau Dora. But yet again, in contrast, Weimar was the place where Germany tried a liberal democracy in the 1920s and in previous centuries it was home to notables such as Bach, Schiller, Goethe, Thomas Mann and many more.

WEIMAR

☎ 03643 / pop 65,200

Maybe it's because eggheads consider wax museums déclassé that Weimar doesn't have one, otherwise the pantheon of intellectual and creative giants who lived and worked here amounts to a virtual Germanic hall of fame: Cranach the Elder, Johann Sebastian Bach, Wieland, Schiller, Herder, Goethe, Liszt, Nietzsche, Gropius, Feininger, Kandinsky, Klee…the list goes on.

The town is best known as the place where Germany's first republican constitution was drafted in 1919, though there are few reminders of this historic moment (which was centred on the Deutsches Nationaltheater). The ghostly ruins of the Buchenwald concentration camp (p450), on the other hand, still provide haunting evidence of the terrors of the Nazi regime. The Bauhaus and classical Weimar sites are protected as Unesco World Heritage sites.

Weimar's compact and walkable centre is a 20-minute jaunt downhill from the station. There are scores of little book and music shops in town.

Tourist information (☎ **240 00; www.weimar.de; Markt 10; 9.30am-6pm Mon-Fri, to 4pm Sat & Sun**) Discount cards start at €10.

A good place to begin a tour is in front of the neo-Gothic 1841 **Rathaus** on the Markt. Directly east is the **Cranachhaus**, where painter Lucas Cranach the Elder lived for two years before his death in 1553.

The **Goethe Nationalmuseum** (☎ **545 347; Frauenplan 1; adult/child €8.50/6.50; 9am-6pm Tue-Sun**) focuses not so much on the man but his movement, offering a broad overview of German classicism, from its proponents to its patrons. The adjoining **Goethe Haus**, where such works as *Faust* were written, focuses much more on the man himself. He lived here from 1775 until his death in 1832.

The Bauhaus School and movement were founded here in 1919 by Walter

Gropius, who managed to draw artists including Kandinsky, Klee, Feininger and Schlemmer as teachers. The exhibition at the **Bauhaus Museum** (☎ 545 961; Theaterplatz; adult/child €5/4; 10am-6pm) chronicles the evolution of the group and explains its design innovations, which continue to shape our lives.

Housed in the **Stadtschloss**, the former residence of the ducal family of Saxe-Weimar, the **Schlossmuseum** (☎ 545 960; Burgplatz 4; adult/child €5/4; 10am-6pm Tue-Sun Apr-Oct, 10am-4pm Nov-Mar) boasts the Cranach Gallery, several portraits by Albrecht Dürer and collections of Dutch masters and German romanticists. Note that the courtyard was used by both the Nazis and the communists for interrogating political prisoners.

Goethe's fellow dramatist Friedrich von Schiller lived in Weimar from 1799 until his early death in 1805; his house is now the **Schiller Museum** (☎ 545 350; Schillerstrasse 12; adult/child €4/3; 9am-6pm Wed-Mon). The study at the end of the 2nd floor contains the desk where he penned *Wilhelm Tell* and other works.

Liszt Haus (☎ 545 388; Marienstrasse 17; adult/child €4/3; 10am-6pm Tue-Sun Apr-Oct) is on the western edge of Park an der Ilm. Composer and pianist Franz Liszt lived here in 1848 and again from 1869 to 1886, when he wrote *Hungarian Rhapsody* and *Faust Symphony*.

The tourist office can help find accommodation, especially at busy times.

Hotel Anna Amalia (☎ 495 60; www.hotel-anna-amalia.de; Geleitstrasse 8-12; r €60-100;) The 51 rooms are very spacious and quiet in this hotel near Goetheplatz. There's wi-fi, and breakfast in the cheery dining room is free.

Hotel Elephant (☎ 8020; www.starwood.de; Markt 19; r €100-250;) A true classic, the 1937 marble Bauhaus-Deco splendour of the 99-room, five-star Elephant has seen most of Weimar's great and good come and go; just to make the point, a golden Thomas Mann looks out over the Markt from a balcony in front.

Residenz-Café (☎ 594 08; www.residenz-cafe.de; Grüner Markt 4; mains €5-15) Meaty platters let you sample local specialities – all best accented with local mustard.

Zum Weissen Schwan (☎ 908 751; Frauentorstrasse 23; mains €10-18; noon-midnight Wed-Sun) Goethe's favourite dish is served here (broiled beef with herby Frankfurt green sauce, red beet salad and potatoes). Schiller and lots of others have apparently graced the tables of this traditional classic, too.

Deutsches Nationaltheater (German National Theatre; ☎ 755 334; www.nationaltheater-weimar.de; Theaterplatz; closed Jul & Aug) This historic venue hosts a mix of classic and contemporary plays, plus ballet, opera and classical concerts.

Weimar's Hauptbahnhof is on a line with frequent services linking Leipzig (€22, one hour) and Erfurt (€7.50, 15 minutes). Two-hourly ICE/IC services go to Berlin-Hauptbahnhof (€51, 2¼ hours).

Most buses serve Goetheplatz, on the northwestern edge of the Altstadt. Don't have time for the 20-minute walk before the next train? A cab costs €6.

AROUND WEIMAR

The **Buchenwald** (☎ 03643-4300; www.buchenwald.de; 9am-6pm Apr-Oct, 9am-4pm Nov-Mar) concentration camp museum and memorial are 10km north of Weimar. The contrast between the brutality of the former and the liberal humanism of the latter is hard to comprehend.

Between 1937 and 1945, more than one-fifth of the 250,000 people incarcerated here died. Various parts of the camp have been restored and there is an essential museum with excellent exhibits. There's also a heart-breaking display of art created by the prisoners. A visit can occupy several hours.

After the war, the Soviets turned the tables but continued the brutality by establishing Special Camp No 2, in which 7000 so-called anticommunists and ex-Nazis were literally worked to death. Their bodies were found after the reunification in mass graves north of the camp, near the Hauptbahnhof.

In Weimar, Buchenwald Information (☎ 430 200; Markt 10; 9.30am-6pm Mon-Fri, to 3pm Sat & Sun) is an excellent resource.

To reach the camp, take bus 6 (€1.70, 15 minutes, hourly).

BAVARIA

Bavaria (Bayern) can seem like every German stereotype rolled into one. Lederhosen, beer halls, oompah bands and romantic castles are just some Bavarian clichés associated with Germany as a whole. But as any Bavarian will tell you, the state thinks of itself as Bavarian first and German second. And as any German outside of Bavaria will tell you, the *Bavarian* stereotypes aren't representative of the rest of Germany. It's a mostly Catholic place and the politics are often conservative, even if people drink serious quantities of beer (almost 90 years ago this was the land of beer-hall putsches).

Bavaria draws visitors year-round. If you only have time for one part of Germany after Berlin, this is it. Munich, the capital, is the heart and soul. The Bavarian Alps, Nuremberg and the medieval towns on the Romantic Rd are other important attractions.

While not quite as high as their sister summits further south in Austria and Switzerland, the Bavarian Alps (Bayerische Alpen) are still standouts, owing to their abrupt rise from the rolling Bavarian foothills. Road rather than rail routes are often more practical. For those driving, the German Alpine Rd (Deutsche Alpenstrasse) is a scenic way to go.

THOMAS WINZ

Rooftops, Munich

MUNICH

☎ 089 / pop 1.25 million

Munich (München) is truly the capital of all things Bavarian. It's a heady mix of world-class museums, historic sites, cosmopolitan shopping, exhausting nightlife, trendy restaurants, roaring beer halls, vast parks and, of course, Oktoberfest. Against all this urban life is the backdrop of the

Alps, peaks that exude an allure that many locals – and visitors – find inescapable. No visit to Germany is complete without at least some time spent in this storied city.

Munich has been the capital of Bavaria since 1503, but didn't really achieve prominence until the 19th century under the guiding hand of Ludwig I. He was forced to abdicate in favour of his son, Maximilian II, who started a building renaissance, promoting science, industry and education. WWII brought bombing and more than 6000 civilian deaths until American forces entered the city in 1945. Then, in 1972, the Munich Olympics turned disastrous when 11 Israeli athletes were murdered. Today the city is the centre of major German industries such as Siemens and BMW.

ORIENTATION

The main train station is just west of the city centre. From the station, head east along Bayerstrasse, through Karlsplatz, and then along Neuhauser Strasse and Kaufingerstrasse to Marienplatz, the hub of Munich.

North of Marienplatz are the Residenz (the former royal palace), Schwabing (the famous student section) and the parklands of the Englischer Garten through which the Isar River runs. East of Marienplatz is the Platzl quarter for beer houses and restaurants, as well as Maximilianstrasse, a fashionable street that is ideal for simply strolling and window-shopping.

INFORMATION

Bereitschaftsdienst der Münchner Ärzte (☎ 01805-191 212; Elisenhof; 🕑 24hr) Nonemergency medical services with English-speaking doctors.

City Tour Card (www.citytourcard.com; 1/3 days €9.80/18.80) Includes transport and discounts of between 10% and 50% for about 30 attractions. Available at some hotels, MVV (Munich public transport authority) offices and U-Bahn and S-Bahn vending machines.

EurAide (☎ 593 889; www.euraide.de; Hauptbahnhof; 🕑 8am-noon & 1-4pm, longer hours in summer) Validates rail passes, sells train tickets and tours, and dispenses savvy advice in English.

Main post office (Bahnhofplatz 1; 🕑 7.30am-8pm Mon-Fri, 9am-4pm Sat)

Tourist office (☎ 2339 6500; www.muenchen.de) Hauptbahnhof (Bahnhofplatz 2; 🕑 9.30am-6.30pm Mon-Sat, 10am-6pm Sun, longer hours in summer & during holidays); Marienplatz (Neues Rathaus, Marienplatz 8; 🕑 10am-8pm Mon-Fri, to 4pm Sat) Be sure to ask for the excellent and free guides *Young and About in Munich*, *National Socialism in Munich* and various neighbourhood guides.

SIGHTS

PALACES

The huge **Residenz** (Max-Joseph-Platz 3) housed Bavarian rulers from 1385 to 1918 and features more than 500 years of architectural history. Apart from the palace itself, the **Residenzmuseum** (☎ 290 671; www.residenz-muenchen.de; entrance on Max-Joseph-Platz; adult/child €6/free; 🕑 9am-6pm Apr–mid-Oct, 10am-5pm mid-Oct–Mar) has an extraordinary array of 100 rooms containing no end of treasures and artworks. In the same building, the **Schatzkammer** (Treasure Chamber; adult/child €6/free; 🕑 9am-6pm Apr–mid-Oct, 10am-5pm mid-Oct–Mar) exhibits jewels, crowns and ornate gold.

If this doesn't satisfy your passion for palaces, visit **Schloss Nymphenburg** (☎ 179 080; adult/child Apr–mid-Oct €10/8, mid-Oct–Mar €8/6; 🕑 9am-6pm Apr–mid-Oct, 10am-4pm mid-Oct–Mar), northwest of the city centre via tram 17 from the Hauptbahnhof. This was the royal family's equally impressive summer home.

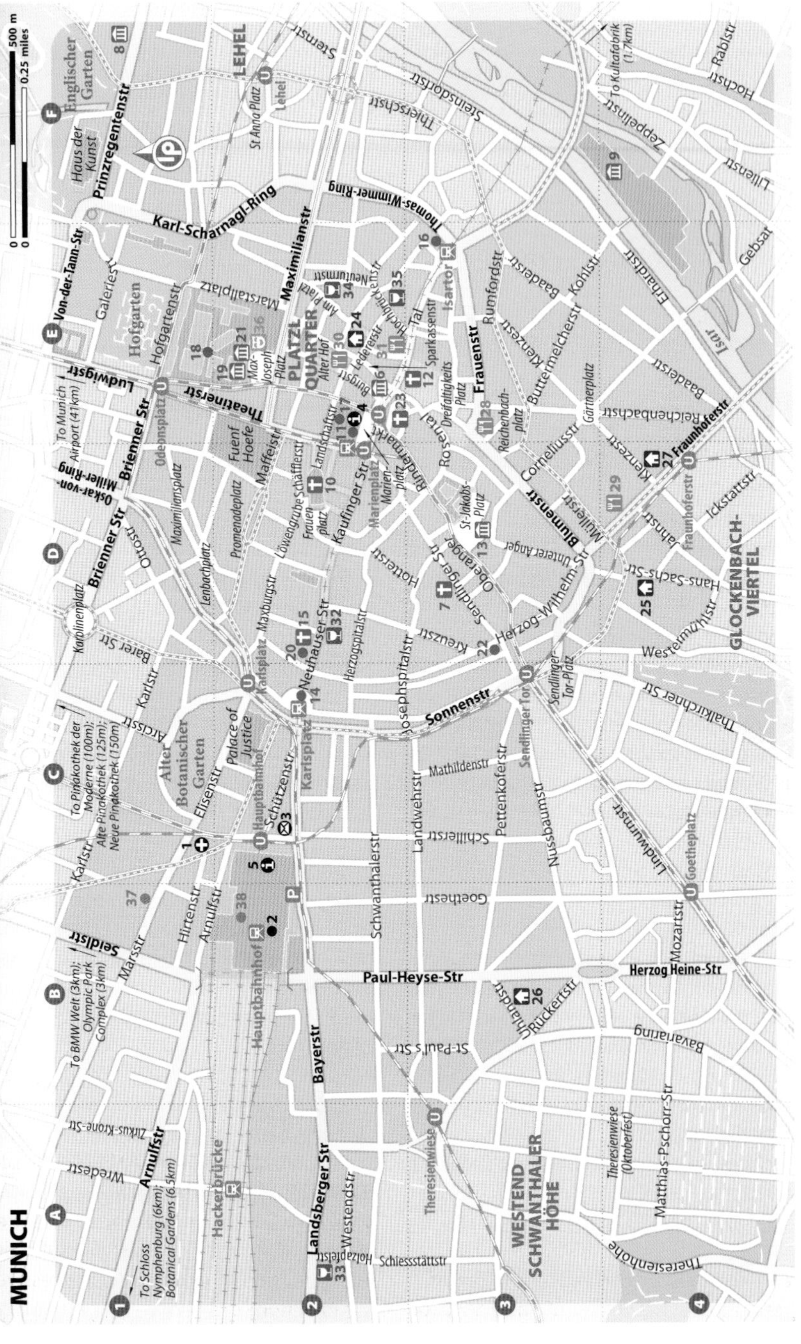
MUNICH
0 500 m
0 0.25 miles
To Schloss Nymphenburg (6km); Botanical Gardens (6.5km)
To BMW Welt (3km); Olympic Park Complex (3km)
To Pinakothek der Moderne (100m); Alte Pinakothek (125m); Neue Pinakothek (150m)
To Munich Airport (41km)
To Kultfabrik (1.7km)
Englischer Garten
Haus der Kunst
Prinzregentenstr
LEHEL
Lehel
St Anna Platz
Sternstr
Thierschstr
Steinsdorfstr
Karl-Scharnagl-Ring
Thomas-Wimmer-Ring
Von-der-Tann-Str
Galeriestr
Hofgarten
Hofgartenstr
Marstallplatz
Maximilianstr
Max-Joseph Platz
PLATZL QUARTER
Alter Hof
Am Platzl
Neuturmstr
Hochbrückenstr
Ledererstr
Burgstr
Sparkassenstr
Tal
Isartor
Dreifaltigkeits Platz
Frauenstr
Rumfordstr
Baaderstr
Kohlstr
Erhardtstr
Isar
Zeppelinstr
Lilienstr
Gebsattelstr
Hochstr
Rablstr
Ludwigstr
Theatinerstr
Odeonsplatz
Brienner Str
Oskar-von-Miller-Ring
Fuenf Hoefe
Maffeistr
Landschaftstr
Marienplatz
Marienplatz
Rindermarkt
Rosental
Reichenbachplatz
Corneliusstr
Gärtnerplatz
Buttermelcherstr
Klenzestr
Reichenbachstr
Fraunhoferstr
Maximiliansplatz
Promenadeplatz
Löwengrube
Schäfflerstr
Frauenplatz
Kaufinger Str
St-Jakobs-Platz
Unterer Anger
Oberanger
Blumenstr
Müllerstr
Jahnstr
Ickstattstr
Hans-Sachs-Str
GLOCKENBACH-VIERTEL
Ottostr
Lenbachplatz
Maxburgstr
Karolinenplatz
Barer Str
Karlstr
Arcisstr
Alter Botanischer Garten
Elisenstr
Palace of Justice
Karlsplatz
Neuhauser Str
Herzogspitalstr
Hotterstr
Sendlinger Str
Kreuzstr
Herzog-Wilhelm-Str
Westermühlstr
Josephspitalstr
Sonnenstr
Sendlinger Tor
Sendlinger-Tor-Platz
Thalkirchner Str
Hauptbahnhof
Schützenstr
Karlsplatz
Mathildenstr
Landwehrstr
Pettenkoferstr
Nussbaumstr
Lindwurmstr
Schillerstr
Goethestr
Goetheplatz
Seidlstr
Marsstr
Hirtenstr
Arnulfstr
Schwanthalerstr
Paul-Heyse-Str
Herzog Heine-Str
Mozartstr
Bayerstr
Uhlandstr
Rückertstr
St-Paul's Str
Bavariaring
Zirkus-Krone-Str
Wredestr
Arnulfstr
Hackerbrücke
Landsberger Str
Westendstr
Holzapfelstr
Schiessstättstr
Theresienwiese
WESTEND SCHWANTHALER HÖHE
Theresienwiese (Oktoberfest)
Matthias-Pschorr-Str
Theresienhöhe

INFORMATION		
Bereitschaftsdienst der Münchner Ärzte	1	C1
EurAide	2	B2
Main Post Office	3	C2
Tourist Office	4	E2
Tourist Office	5	C2
SIGHTS & ACTIVITIES		
Altes Rathaus	6	E2
Asamkirche	7	D3
Bayerisches Nationalmuseum	8	F1
Deutsches Museum	9	F4
Frauenkirche	10	D2
Glockenspiel	11	E2
Heiliggeistkirche	12	E3
Jüdisches Museum	13	D3
Karlstor	14	C2
Michaelskirche	15	D2
Munich Walk Tours	16	E3
Neues Rathaus	17	E2
Residenz	18	E1
Residenzmuseum	19	E2
Richard Strauss Fountain	20	D2
Schatzkammer	21	E2
Sendlinger Tor	22	D3
St Peterskirche	23	E2
SLEEPING		
Hotel Alcron	24	E2
Hotel Olympic	25	D4
Hotel Uhland	26	B3
Pension Gärtnerplatz	27	D4
EATING		
Der Pschorr	28	E3
Fraunhofer	29	D4
Saf Deli	30	E2
Weisses Brauhaus	31	E2
DRINKING		
Augustiner Bierhalle	32	D2
Augustiner Bräustuben	33	A2
Hofbräuhaus	34	E2
Zum Dürnbrau	35	E2
ENTERTAINMENT		
Residenztheater	36	E2
TRANSPORT		
Deutsche Touring	37	B1
Radius Bike Rentals	38	B2

ART GALLERIES

A treasure house of European masters from the 14th to 18th centuries, recently renovated **Alte Pinakothek** (**☎ 2380 5216; www.pinakothek.de; Barer Strasse 27, enter from Theresienstrasse; adult/child €5.50/free, Sun €1; 10am-8pm Tue, to 6pm Wed-Sun**), a stroll northeast of the city, includes highlights such as Dürer's Christ-like *Self Portrait* and his *Four Apostles*, Rogier van der Weyden's *Adoration of the Magi* and Botticelli's *Pietà*.

Immediately north of the Alte Pinakothek, the **Neue Pinakothek** (**☎ 2380 5195; www.pinakothek.de; Barer Strasse 29, enter from Theresienstrasse; adult/child €5.50/free, Sun €1; 10am-5pm Thu-Mon, to 8pm Wed, closed Tue**) contains mainly 19th-century works, including Van Gogh's *Sunflowers*, and sculpture.

Located one block east of the Alte Pinakothek, the **Pinakothek der Moderne** (**☎ 2380 5360; www.pinakothek.de; Barer Strasse 40, enter from Theresienstrasse; adult/child €8/free, Sun €1; 10am-6pm Tue, Wed & Fri-Sun, 10am-8pm Thu**) displays four collections of modern art, graphic art, applied art and architecture in one suitably arresting 2002 building.

MUSEUMS

An enormous science and technology museum, **Deutsches Museum** (**☎ 217 91; www.deutsches-museum.de; Museumsinsel 1; adult/child €8.50/3; 9am-5pm**) celebrates the many achievements of Germans, and humans in general. Take the S-Bahn to Isartor.

The **Bayerisches Nationalmuseum** (**☎ 211 2401; www.bayerisches-nationalmuseum.de; Prinzregentenstrasse 3; adult/child €5/free, Sun €1; 10am-5pm Tue, Wed & Fri-Sun, to 8pm Thu**), east of the Hofgarten, shows the lives of old Bavarians, from peasants to knights.

Tracing the lives of local Jews before, during and after the Holocaust, the **Jüdisches Museum** (**☎ 2339 6096; www.juedisches-museum.muenchen.de; St-Jakobs-Platz 16; adult/child €6/3; 10am-6pm Tue-Sun**) offers insight into Jewish history, life and culture in Munich.

North of the city, auto-fetishists can thrill to the gargantuan **BMW Welt** (**www.bmw-welt.de; admission free, tours adult/child €6/3; 9am-8pm**), adjacent to the BMW headquarters. Take the U3 to Olympiazentrum.

PARKS & GARDENS

One of the largest city parks in Europe, the **Englischer Garten**, west of the city centre, is a great place for strolling, especially along the Schwabinger Bach. In summer nude sunbathing is the rule rather than the exception. It's not unusual for hundreds of naked people to be in the park during a normal business day, with their clothing stacked primly on the grass. If they're not doing this, they're probably drinking merrily at one of the park's three beer gardens (p458).

Munich's beautiful **Botanical Gardens** (☎ 1786 1350; www.botmuc.de; Menzinger Strasse 65; adult/child €3/free; ⏰ varies with season, generally 9am-6pm) are two stops past Schloss Nymphenburg on tram 17.

OLYMPIA PARK COMPLEX

If you like heights, then take a ride up the lift of the 290m **Olympiaturm** (tower) situated in the **Olympia Park Complex** (☎ 3067 2750; adult/child €4/2.50; ⏰ 9am-midnight, last trip 11.30pm). And if you fancy a swim, then the **Olympic Pool Complex** (☎ 3067 2290; Olympic Park; admission €3.60; ⏰ 7am-11pm) will have you feeling like Mark Spitz while you imagine seven gold medals around your neck – or just work on your breaststroke. Take the U3 to Olympia Zentrum.

TOURS

The hordes of visitors and plethora of sights mean there's lots of people willing to show you around – an excellent way to gain background and context on what you see.

Mike's Bike Tours (☎ 2554 3987; www.mikesbiketours.com; tours from €24) Enjoyable (and leisurely) city cycling tours in English.

Munich Walk Tours (☎ 2423 1767; www.munichwalktours.de; Thomas-Wimmer-Ring 1; tours from €10) Walking tours of the city and a tour focused on 'beer, brewing and boozing'.

New Munich Free Tour (www.newmunich.com; tours free; ⏰ 10.45am & 1pm) English-language walking tours tick off all of Munich's central landmarks and historical milestones in three hours.

FESTIVALS & EVENTS

Hordes come to Munich for **Oktoberfest** (www.oktoberfest.de; ⏰ 10am-11.30pm, from 9am Sat & Sun), running the 15 days before the first Sunday in October. Reserve accommodation well ahead and go early in the day so you can grab a seat in one of the hangar-sized beer 'tents'. The action takes place at the Theresienwiese grounds, about a 10-minute walk southwest of the Hauptbahnhof. While there is no entrance fee, those €8 1L steins of beer (called *mass*) add up fast. Although its origins are in the marriage celebrations of Crown Prince Ludwig in 1810, there's nothing regal about this beery bacchanalia now; expect mobs, expect to meet new

CHERYL FORBES

Doorway of the Residenz (p452)

MUNICH WALKING TOUR

The pivotal **Marienplatz** is a good starting point for a walking tour of Munich. Dominating the square is the towering neo-Gothic **Neues Rathaus** (New Town Hall; Marienplatz), with its ever-dancing **Glockenspiel** (carillon), which performs at 11am and noon (also at 5pm from March to October), bringing the square to an expectant standstill (note the fate of the Austrian knight…). Two important churches are on this square: the baroque star **St Peterskirche** (260 4828; Rindermarkt 1; church free, tower adult/child €1.50/0.30; 9am-7pm Apr-Oct, to 6pm Nov-Mar) and, behind the **Altes Rathaus**, the often forgotten **Heiliggeistkirche** (Tal 77; 7am-6pm). Head west along shopping street Kaufingerstrasse to the landmark of Munich, the late-Gothic **Frauenkirche** (Church of Our Lady; 290 0820; Frauenplatz 1; admission free; 7am-7pm Sat-Wed, 7am-8.30pm Thu, 7am-6pm Fri) with its then-trendy 16th-century twin onion domes. Go inside and join the hordes gazing at the grandeur of the place, or climb the tower for majestic views of Munich. Continue west to the large, grey 16th-century **Michaelskirche** (609 0224; Neuhauserstrasse 52; 8am-7pm), Germany's earliest and grandest Renaissance church.

Further west is the **Richard Strauss Fountain** and the medieval **Karlstor**, an old city gate. Double back towards Marienplatz and turn right onto Eisenmannstrasse, which becomes Kreuzstrasse and converges with Herzog-Wilhelm-Strasse at the medieval gate of **Sendlinger Tor**. Go down the shopping street Sendlinger Strasse to the **Asamkirche** (Sendlinger Strasse 34), a flamboyant 17th-century church designed by brothers Cosmas Damian and Egid Quirin Asam. The ornate marble facade won't prepare you for the opulence inside, where scarcely an inch is left unembellished.

and drunken friends, and expect decorum to vanish as night sets in and you'll have a blast.

A few tips: locals call it *Weisn* (meadow), the Hofbrauzelt tent is big with tourists while Augustinerzelt draws traditionalists. Traditional Oktoberfest beer should be a rich copper colour, although the masses demand pale lager.

SLEEPING

Hotel Alcron (228 3511; Ledererstrasse 13; www.hotel-alcron.de, in German; s €60-70, d €80-95, tr €90-105;) Within stumbling distance of the Hofbräuhaus, this quaint hotel has a dizzying spiral staircase leading up to traditionally furnished rooms that don't spoil you with space.

Pension Gärtnerplatz (202 5170; www.pension-gaertnerplatztheater.de; Klenzestrasse 45; s/d from €70/95;) Escape the tourist rabble, or reality altogether, in this eccentric establishment where rooms are a stylish interpretation of Alpine pomp.

Hotel Uhland (543 350; www.hotel-uhland.de; Uhlandstrasse 1; s €75-140, d €85-185;) Three generations of family members are constantly finding ways to improve their guests' experience, be it with wi-fi, bike rentals or mix-your-own breakfast muesli.

Hotel Olympic (231 890; www.hotel-olympic.de; Hans-Sachs-Strasse 4; r €90-180;) If you're into designer decor, Frette linens and chocolates on your pillow, go elsewhere. But if you like a hip location, public areas doubling as an art gallery, and 38 spacious rooms (with wi-fi), give this one a try.

EATING

Clusters of restaurants can be found anywhere there's pedestrian life. The streets in and around Gärtnerplatz and Glockenback-Viertel are the flavour of the moment. You can always do well in and around Marienplatz and the wonderful Viktualienmarkt, while Schwabing is always full of eating delights.

Fraunhofer (**☎ 266 460; Fraunhoferstrasse 9; mains €5-14; 4.30pm-1am**) The old-world atmosphere (mounted animal heads and a portrait of Ludwig II) contrasts with the clued-in, intergenerational crowd and a menu that offers progressive takes on classical fare.

Saf Deli (**☎ 1892 2813; Ledererstrasse 3; mains from €6; 11am-7pm Mon-Sat**) Vegan fair is served in this stylish cafe right in the heart of roasted-meat land.

Weisses Brauhaus (**☎ 290 1380; Tal 7; mains €9-20**) The place for classic Bavarian fare in an ancient beer-hall setting. Everything from *weissewurst* (beloved local white sausage) to hearty traditional fare such as boiled ox cheeks is on offer.

Der Pschorr (**☎ 5181 8500; Viktualienmarkt 15; mains €10-15**) Shining like a jewel box across a square, this modern high-ceilinged restaurant operated by one of the main local brewers is more bistro than beer hall.

ENTERTAINMENT

Munich is one of the cultural capitals of Germany. For tickets, try München Ticket (**☎ 5481 8154; www.muenchenticket.de**).

Residenztheater (**☎ 2185 1920; Max-Joseph-Platz 2**) is home of the Bavarian State Opera (**www.staatsoper.de**) and also the site of many cultural events (particularly during the opera festival in July).

Kultafabrik (**www.kultafabrik.de; Grafingerstrasse 6; 8pm-6am**) There's over 25 clubs in this old potato factory that you can sample before you end up mashed or fried. Electro and house beats charge up the crowd at the loungy apartment 11, the Asian-themed Koi and at the small and red cocktail cantina called Die Bar. It's close to the Ostbahnhof station.

Much of Munich's gay and lesbian nightlife is around Gärtnerplatz and the Glockenback-Viertel. *Our Munich* and *Sergej* are monthly guides easily found in this neighbourhood.

Munich has eight Christmas markets from late November, including a big one on Marienplatz.

GETTING THERE & AWAY

Munich's sparkling white airport (**MUC; www.munich-airport.de**) is second in importance only to Frankfurt-am-Main for international and national connections.

Munich is linked to the Romantic Rd by the popular Deutsche-Touring (**☎ 8898 9513; www.touring.com; Hirtenallee 14**) Munich–Frankfurt service (see p459). Buses stop along the northern side of the train station on Arnulfstrasse.

Train services to/from Munich are excellent. High-speed ICE services from Munich run to Frankfurt (€89, three hours, hourly), Hamburg (€115, 5½ hours, hourly) and Berlin (€113, 5¾ hours, every two hours).

GETTING AROUND

Munich's international airport is connected by the S8 and the S1 to Marienplatz and the Hauptbahnhof (€9.20). The service takes about 40 minutes and there is a train every 10 minutes from 4am until around 12.30am.

BEER HALLS & BEER GARDENS

Beer-drinking is not just an integral part of Munich's entertainment scene, it's a reason to visit. Beer halls can be vast boozy affairs seating thousands, or much more modest neighbourhood hang-outs. The same goes for beer gardens. Both come in all shapes and sizes. What's common is a certain camaraderie among strangers, huge litre glasses of beer (try putting one of those in your carry on) and lots of cheap food – the saltier the better. Note that in beer gardens tradition allows you to bring your own food, a boon if you want an alternative to pretzels, sausages and the huge white radishes served with, you guessed it, salt.

On a warm day there's nothing better than sitting and sipping among the greenery at one of the Englischer Garten's classic beer gardens. **Chinesischer Turm** (☎ 383 8730) is justifiably popular, while the nearby **Hirschau** (☎ 369 942) on the banks of Kleinhesseloher See is less crowded.

our pick **Augustiner Bräustuben** (☎ 507 047; Landsberger Strasse 19) Depending on the wind, an aroma of hops envelops you as you approach this ultra-authentic beer hall inside the actual Augustiner brewery. The Bavarian grub here is superb, especially the *schweinshaxe* (pork knuckles). Giant black draft horses are stabled behind glass on your way to the loo.

Augustiner Bierhalle (☎ 5519 9257; Neuhauser Strasse 27) What you probably imagine an old-style Munich beer hall looks like, filled with laughter, smoke and clinking glasses.

Zum Dürnbrau (☎ 222 195; Tal 21) Tucked into a corner off Tal, this is a great and authentic little alternative to the Hofbräuhaus. There's a small beer garden, and drinkers of dark drafts enjoy pewter-topped mugs.

Hofbräuhaus (☎ 2901 3610; Am Platzl 9) The ultimate cliché of Munich beer halls. Tourists arrive by the busload, but no one seems to mind that this could be Disneyland (although the theme park wasn't once home to Hitler's early speeches, like this place was).

Taxis make the long haul for at least €60.

Pedal power is popular in relatively flat Munich. **Radius Bike Rental** (☎ 596 113; www.radiustours.com; Hauptbahnhof near track 32; 10am-6pm May-Sep) rents out two-wheelers from €15 per day.

Munich's excellent **public transport network** (MVV; www.mvv-muenchen.de) is zone-based, and most places of interest to tourists (except Dachau and the airport) are within the 'blue' inner zone (*Innenraum;* €2.30). MVV tickets are valid for the S-Bahn, U-Bahn, trams and buses, but they must be validated before use. *Tageskarte* (day passes) for the inner zone cost €5, while three-day tickets cost €12.30.

Bus 100, the Museenlinie, runs a route past scores of museums, including all the Pinokotheks, between the Hauptbahnhof (north side) and the Ostbahnhof.

DACHAU

The first Nazi concentration camp was **Dachau** (☎ 08131-669 970; www.kz-gedenkstaette-dachau.de; Alte-Roemerstrasse 75;

admission free; ⌚ 9am-5pm Tue-Sun), built in March 1933. Jews, political prisoners, homosexuals and others deemed 'undesirable' by the Third Reich were imprisoned in the camp. More than 200,000 people were sent here; more than 30,000 died at Dachau, and countless others died after being transferred to other death camps. An English-language documentary is shown at 11.30am and 3.30pm. A visit includes camp relics, memorials and a very sobering museum. Take the S2 (direction: Petershausen) to Dachau and then bus 726 to the camp. A Munich XXL day ticket (€6.70) will cover the trip.

ROMANTIC RD

The popular and schmaltzily named Romantic Rd (Romantische Strasse) links a series of picturesque Bavarian towns and cities. It's not actually one road per se, but rather a 353km route chosen to highlight as many quaint towns and cities as possible in western Bavaria. From north to south it includes the following major stops:

Würzburg Starting point and featuring 18th-century artistic splendour among the vineyards.

Rothenburg ob der Tauber The medieval walled hub of cutesy picturesque Bavarian touring.

Dinkelsbühl Another medieval walled town replete with moat and watchtowers; a smaller Rothenberg. The town is best reached by bus or car.

Augsburg A medieval and Renaissance city with many good places for a beer.

Wieskirche Stunning baroque Unesco-recognised church (p463). Not even the constant deluge of visitors can detract from its charms.

Füssen The southern end of the route, and the cute and over-run home of mad King Ludwig's castles; see p464.

In addition to these principal stops, more than a dozen little towns clamour for attention – and your money. A good first stop is the info-packed English-language website www.romanticroad.de.

GETTING THERE & AROUND

The principal cities and towns listed above are all easily reached by train. With a car, you can blow through places of little interest and linger at those that attract.

A popular way to tour the Romantic Rd is the **Deutsche-Touring Romantic Rd bus** (www.deutsche-touring.com). Starting in Frankfurt in the north and Füssen in the south, a bus runs in each direction each day covering the entire route between Würzburg and Füssen. However, seeing

WAYNE WALTON

Outdoor tables at Hofbräuhaus

MARTIN MOOS

Wurst stand at Nuremberg's Christmas market

the whole thing in one day is only for those with unusual fortitude and a love of buses. Stops are brief (17 minutes for Wieskirche, *Schnell!* 35 minutes for Rothenburg, *Schnell!* etc) so you'll want to choose places where you can break the trip for a day (stopovers are allowed). But of course this leads you to decide between a 30-minute visit and a 24-hour one.

Buses depart April to October south from Frankfurt Hauptbahnhof at 8am and north from Füssen at 8am and Munich Hauptbahnhof (north side) at 11am (about 11 hours). The total fare (tickets are bought on board) is a pricey €150. Railpass-holders get a paltry 20% discount. You can also just ride for individual segments (eg Rothenberg to Augsburg costs €31).

BAMBERG

☎ 0951 / pop 71,000

Off the major tourist routes, Bamberg is worshipped by those in the know. It boasts a beautifully preserved collection of 17th- and 18th-century buildings, palaces and churches. It is bisected by a large canal and a fast-flowing river that are spanned by cute little bridges, and it even has its own local style of beer. No wonder it has been recognised by Unesco as a World Heritage site. Could it be the best small town in Germany?

Start your visit at the **tourist office** (☎ **297 6200; www.bamberg.info; Geyerswörthstrasse 3; 9.30am-6pm Mon-Fri, to 2.30pm Sat year-round, plus 9.30am-2.30pm Sun Apr-Dec**). The Bamberg Card (€8.50) is good for 48 hours of admission to attractions and more.

Bamberg's main appeal is its fine buildings – the sheer number, their jumble of styles and the ambience this creates. Most attractions are spread either side of the Regnitz River, but the **Altes Rathaus** (**Obere Brücke**) is actually solidly perched on its own islet. Its lavish murals are among many around town.

Bamberg's unique style of beer is called *Rauchbier,* which literally means smoked beer. With a bacon flavour at first, it is a smooth brew that goes down easily. Happily, many of the local breweries also rent rooms.

Brauereigasthof Fässla (☎ **265 16; www.faessla.de; Obere Königstrasse 19-21; r €40-70**) Rooms at this snug guesthouse are a mere staircase up from the pub-brewery and covered courtyard.

Hotel Sankt Nepomuk (☎ **984 20; www.hotel-nepomuk.de; Obere Mühlbrücke 9; r €85-130;**) This is a classy yet family-friendly establishment in a half-timbered former mill right on the Regnitz. It has a superb restaurant (mains €15 to €30) and comfy rustic rooms with wi-fi.

our pick **Schlenkerla** (☎ **560 60; Dominikanerstrasse 6;** ⌚ **Wed-Mon**) Decked out with lamps fashioned from antlers, this 16th-century restaurant is famous for tasty Franconian specialities and *Rauchbier*, served directly from oak barrels.

Two trains per hour go to/from both Würzburg (€15.50, one hour) and Nuremberg (€18, one hour). Bamberg is also served by ICE trains running between Munich (€56, two hours) and Berlin (€72, 3¾ hours) every two hours.

NUREMBERG

☎ 0911 / pop 498,000

Nuremberg (Nürnberg) woos visitors with its wonderfully restored medieval Altstadt, its grand castle and its magical *Christkindlesmarkt* (Christmas market). Thriving traditions also include sizzling *Nürnberger bratwürste* (finger-sized sausages) and *lebkuchen* – large, soft gingerbread cookies, traditionally eaten at Christmas time but available here year-round. Both within and beyond the high stone wall encircling the Altstadt is a wealth of major museums that shed light on Nuremberg's significant history.

Nuremberg played a major role during the Nazi years, as documented in Leni Riefenstahl's film *Triumph of the Will* and during the war-crimes trials afterwards. It has done an admirable job of confronting this ugly past with museums and exhibits.

Staff at the **tourist office** (**www.tourismus.nuernberg.de**) Hauptmarkt (☎ **2336 135; Hauptmarkt 18;** ⌚ **9am-6pm Mon-Sat, 10am-4pm Sun May-Oct, 9am-6pm Mon-Sat Nov & Jan-Apr, 10am-7pm daily during Christkindlesmarkt**); Künstlerhaus (☎ **233 6131; Königstrasse 93;** ⌚ **9am-7pm Mon-Sat year-round, plus 10am-4pm Sun during Christkindlesmarkt**) sell the Nürnberg + Fürth Card (€19), which is good for two days of unlimited public transport and admissions.

The scenic **Altstadt** is easily covered on foot. On Lorenzer Platz there's the **St Lorenzkirche**, noted for the 15th-century tabernacle that climbs like a vine up a pillar to the vaulted ceiling.

To the north is the bustling **Hauptmarkt**, where the most famous **Christkindlmarkt** in Germany is held from the Friday before Advent to Christmas Eve (below). The church here is the ornate **Pfarrkirche Unsere Liebe Frau**; the clock's figures go strolling at noon. Near the Rathaus is **St Sebalduskirche**, Nuremberg's oldest church (dating from the 13th century), with the shrine of St Sebaldus.

Climb up Burgstrasse to the enormous 15th-century **Kaiserburg** (☎ **200 9540; adult/child incl museum €6/5;** ⌚ **9am-6pm Apr-Sep, 10am-4pm Oct-Mar**) for good views of the city. The walls spread west to the tunnel-gate

CHRISTMAS MARKETS

Beginning in late November every year, central squares across Germany, especially those in Bavaria, are transformed into Christmas markets or *Christkindlmarkts* (also known as *Weihnachtsmärkte*). Folks stamp about between the wooden stalls, perusing seasonal trinkets (from treasures to schlock) while warming themselves with tasty *glühwein* (mulled, spiced red wine) and treats such as sausages and potato pancakes. The markets are popular with tourists, but locals love 'em too, and bundle themselves up and carouse for hours. Nuremberg's **market** (**www.chriskindlesmarkt.de**) fills much of the centre and attracts two million people.

DENNIS JOHNSON

Wartburg

IF YOU LIKE...

If you like **Neuschwanstein Castle** (p464), the following fortresses might tickle your fancy as well:

- **Wartburg** (☎ 2500; www.wartburg-eisenach.de; tour adult/child €7/4; tours 8.30am-5pm Mar-Oct, 9am-3.30pm Nov-Feb) The only German castle to be named a Unesco World Heritage site is in the small town of Eisenach, outside Efurt.
- **Bellinzona** (Tourist office; ☎ 091 825 21 31; www.bellinzonaturismo.ch; Piazza Nosetto; 9am-6pm Mon-Fri, to noon Sat) This Swiss town near the border with Italy is dominated by three grey-stone, fairytale-worthy medieval castles – also on Unesco's list. You can roam the ramparts of the two larger castles, Castelgrande or Castello di Montebello, both of which are still in great condition and offer panoramic views of the town and countryside.

of **Tiergärtnertor**, where you can stroll behind the castle to the gardens. Nearby is the renovated **Albrecht-Dürer-Haus** (☎ 231 2568; Albrecht-Dürer-Strasse 39; adult/child €5/2.50; 10am-5pm Fri-Wed, to 8pm Thu), where Dürer, Germany's renowned Renaissance draughtsman, lived from 1509 to 1528.

The stunning **Germanisches Nationalmuseum** (☎ 133 10; Kartäusergasse 1; adult/child €6/4; 10am-6pm Tue & Thu-Sun, to 9pm Wed) is the most important general museum of German culture in the country.

Nuremberg has a lot of toy companies and the **Spielzeugmuseum** (Toy Museum; ☎ 231 3164; Karlstrasse 13-15; adult/child €4/2; 10am-5pm Tue-Fri, to 6pm Sat & Sun) presents them in their infinite variety.

Nuremberg's role during the Third Reich is well known. After the war, the Allies deliberately chose Nuremberg as the site for the trials of Nazi war criminals. Don't miss the **Dokumentationzentrum** (☎ 231 5666; www.museen.nuernberg.de; Bayernstrasse 110; adult/child €5/2.50; 9am-6pm Mon-Fri, 10am-6pm Sat & Sun) in the north wing of the massive unfinished Congress Hall, which would have held 50,000 people for Hitler's spectacles. The museum's absorbing exhibits trace the rise of Hitler and the Nazis, and the important role Nuremberg played in the mythology. Take tram 9 or 6 to Doku-Zentrum.

Hotel Elch (☎ 249 2980; www.hotel-elch.com; Irrerstrasse 9; r €55-110;) Tucked up in the antiques quarter, this 14th-century, half-timbered house has morphed into a snug, romantic little 12-room hotel.

Hotel Deutscher Kaiser (☎ 242 660; www.deutscher-kaiser-hotel.de; Königstrasse 55; r €90-125;) A grand sandstone staircase leads to 52 ornately decorated rooms (equipped with wi-fi) in this 1880s-built hotel.

Restaurants line the hilly lanes above the Burgstrasse.

our pick **Bratwursthäusle** (☎ 227 695; Rathausplatz 2; meals €6-12) A local legend and *the* place for flame-grilled and scrumptious local sausages. Get them with *kartoffelsalat* (potato salad). There are also nice tree-shaded tables outside.

Hütt'n (☎ **201 9881; Burgstrasse 19; mains €8-15;** ⌚ **from 4pm Mon-Wed**) Be prepared to queue for a table at this local haunt. The special here is the *ofenfrische krustenbraten:* roast pork with crackling, dumplings and sauerkraut salad. There's also a near-endless variety of schnapps and beers.

Nuremberg's **airport** (**NUE; www.airport-nuernberg.de**) is a hub for budget carrier airberlin, which has services throughout Germany, as well as flights to London. There's frequent service to the airport on the S-2 line (€2, 12 minutes).

The city is also a hub for train services. ICE trains run to/from Berlin-Hauptbahnhof (€89, 4½ hours, every two hours), Frankfurt-am-Main (€48, two hours, hourly) and on the new fast line to Munich (€49, one hour, hourly). Tickets on the bus, tram and U-Bahn system cost €1.80 each. Day passes are €4.

FÜSSEN

☎ 08362 / pop 14,000

Never have so many come to a place with so few inhabitants by comparison. Close to the Austrian border and the foothills of the Alps, Füssen has some splendid baroque architecture, but that is overlooked by the mobs swarming the two castles associated with King Ludwig II in nearby Schwangau. The **tourist office** (☎ **938 50; www.fuessen.de; Kaiser-Maximillian-Platz 1;** ⌚ **9am-5pm Mon-Fri, 10am-2pm Sat, 10am-noon Sun**) is often overrun.

Füssen is a pretty quiet place after dark and most people will stay only long enough to see the castles. There are a couple of cafes in the centre where you can grab lunch.

Altstadt Hotel zum Hechten (☎ **916 00; www.hotel-hechten.com; Ritterstrasse 6; r €50-90**) Set around a quiet inner courtyard, this child-friendly place is one of Füssen's oldest Altstadt hotels, with rustic public areas and bright, modern guest rooms.

Train connections to Munich (€24, two hours) run every two hours. Füssen is the start of the Romantic Rd. Deutsche-Touring buses (p459) start here and are the best way to reach Wieskirche (above; €9, 50 minutes) if you don't have a car.

BERCHTESGADEN

☎ 08652 / pop 7900

Steeped in myth and legend, the Berchtesgadener Land enjoys a natural beauty so abundant that it's almost preternatural. Framed by six formidable mountain ranges and home to Germany's second-highest mountain, the Watzmann (2713m), the dreamy, fir-lined valleys are filled with gurgling streams and peaceful Alpine villages. Much of the terrain is protected by law as the Nationalpark Berchtesgaden, which embraces the pristine Königssee, one of Germany's most photogenic lakes. Yet, Berchtesgaden's history is also indelibly entwined with the Nazi period as chronicled at the Dokumentation Obersalzberg. The Eagle's Nest, a mountaintop lodge

WEISKIRCHE

This Unesco World Heritage **church** (☎ **08862 932 930; www.wieskirche.de;** ⌚ **8am-7pm May-Oct, to 5pm Nov-Apr**) is a truly amazing work of 18th-century rococo excess. Its white pillars tower over a tiny village 25km northeast of Füssen. The church can be reached by the Romantic Rd bus (p459) or via RVO bus 9606 (www.rvo-bus.de), which runs between Füssen and Garmisch-Partenkirchen via Weiskirche and Oberammergau (five to six daily).

ANDREW BAIN

Hohenschwangau castle

NEUSCHWANSTEIN & HOHENSCHWANGAU CASTLES

Neuschwanstein and Hohenschwangau castles provide a fascinating glimpse into the state of mind (or lack thereof) and well-developed ego of the romantic King Ludwig II of Bavaria. Hohenschwangau is where Ludwig lived as a child. It's not as cute, even though both castles are 19th-century constructions, but it draws less crowds and visits are more relaxed. The adjacent Neuschwanstein is Ludwig's own creation (albeit with the help of a theatrical designer). Although it was unfinished when he died in 1886, there is plenty of evidence of Ludwig's twin obsessions: swans and Wagnerian operas. The sugary pastiche of architectural styles, alternatively overwhelmingly beautiful and just a little too much, reputedly inspired Disney's Fantasyland castle.

Tickets may only be bought from the ticket centre. In summer it's worth the €1.80 surcharge per person to reserve ahead. The walk between the castles is a piney 45-minute stroll.

Take the bus from Füssen train station (€2, 15 minutes, hourly) or share a taxi (☎ 7700; €10 for up to four people). Go early to avoid the worst of the rush.

Things You Need to Know: **☎ 930 830; www.ticket-center-hohenschwangau.de; Alpenseestrasse 12, Hohenschwangau; adult/child €9/8, incl Schloss Hohenschwangau €17/15; tickets 8am-5pm Apr-Sep, 9am-3pm Oct-Mar**

built for Hitler, is now a major tourist attraction.

The **tourist office** (**☎ 9670; www.berchtesgaden.de; Königsseer Strasse 2; 8.30am-6pm Mon-Fri, to 5pm Sat, 9am-3pm Sun mid-Jun–Sep, reduced hours other times**) is just across the river from the train station and has internet access.

In 1933, quiet Obersalzberg (some 3km from Berchtesgaden) became the southern headquarters of Hitler's government, a dark period that's given he full historical treatment at the **)okumentation Obersalzberg** (☎ 947 **60; www.obersalzberg.de; Salzbergstrasse 41, bersalzberg; adult/child & student €3/free; 9am-5pm daily Apr-Oct, 10am-3pm Tue-Sun lov-Apr)**. To get there take bus 838 from he Hauptbahnhof in Berchtesgaden.

Berchtesgaden's creepiest – yet im-)ressive – draw is the **Eagle's Nest** ıtop Mt Kehlstein, a sheer-sided peak ıt Obersalzberg. Perched at 1834m, :he innocent-looking lodge (called ‹ehlsteinhaus in German) has sweeping views across the mountains and down nto the valley where the Königssee shimmers. Ironically, Hitler is said to have suffered from vertigo and rarely enjoyed the spectacular views himself. Drive or take bus 849 from the Berchtesgaden Hauptbahnhof to the Kehlstein stop, where you board a special **bus** (**www. ‹ehlsteinhaus.de; adult/child €13/12**) that drives you up the mountain. It runs between 7.20am and 4pm, and takes 35 minutes.

Eagle's Nest Tours (☎ **649 71; www. eagles-nest-tours.com; adult/child 6-12yr €45/30; 1.30pm mid-May–Oct**) has four-hour tours in English that cover the war years.

Crossing the emerald-green Königssee, a beautiful alpine lake situated 5km south of Berchtesgaden (and linked by hourly buses in summer) is sublime. There are frequent boat tours across the lake to the pixel-perfect chapel at St Bartholomä (€12).

The wilds of Berchtesgaden National Park offer some of the best **hiking** in Germany. A good introduction to the area is a 2km path up from St Bartholomä beside the Königssee to the Watzmann-Ostwand, a massive 2000m-high rock face where scores of overly ambitious mountaineers have died.

Hotel Krone (☎ **946 00; Am Rad 5; www. hotel-krone-berchtesgaden.de; s €37-42, d €68-104;**) In a quiet spot, yet close to the centre, this family-run property offers great extras (including wi-fi, a sauna and a steam room) at very reasonable prices. The cosiest rooms are the lodge-style ones, which are clad in knotty pine. The best rooms have stunning mountain panoramas.

There is an hourly service to Berchtesgaden from Munich (€34, 2½ hours), which usually requires a change in Frilassing. There are hourly services to nearby Salzburg in Austria (€9, one hour).

BLACK FOREST

The Black Forest (Schwarzwald) gets its name from the dark canopy of evergreens, which evoke mystery and allure in many. Although some parts heave with visitors, a 20-minute walk from even the most crowded spots will put you in quiet countryside interspersed with enormous traditional farmhouses and patrolled by amiable dairy cows. It's not nature wild and remote, but bucolic and picturesque.

The Black Forest is east of the Rhine between Karlsruhe and Basel. It's shaped like a bean, about 160km long and 50km wide.

Those with a car will find their visit especially rewarding, as you can wander the rolling hills and deep valleys at will. One of the main tourist roads is the Schwarzwald-Hochstrasse (B500), which runs from Baden-Baden to Freudenstadt and from Triberg to Waldshut. Other thematic roads with maps provided by tourist offices include Schwarzwald Bäderstrasse (spa town route), Schwarzwald Panoramastrasse (panoramic view route) and Badische Weinstrasse (wine route). Whatever you do, make certain you have a good commercial regional road map with you.

And, yes, there are many, many places to buy cuckoo clocks (you pay at least €150 for a good one).

Regional specialities include *Schwarzwälder schinken* (ham), which is smoked and served in a variety of ways. Rivalling those ubiquitous clocks in fame (but not price), *Schwarzwälder kirschtorte* (Black Forest cake) is a chocolate and cherry concoction. Most hotels and guesthouses have restaurants serving traditional hearty (but expensive) German fare. Wash it all down with Rothaus, the crisp local pilsener.

The prettiest town in the Black Forest is easily **Schiltach**, where there is the always underlying roar of the intersecting Kinzig and Schiltach Rivers. Half-timbered

THOMAS WINZ

Cuckoo clocks

buildings lean at varying angles along th criss-crossing hillside lanes. The **touris office** (☎ 5850; www.schiltach.de; Hauptstrass 5; 10am-5pm Mon-Fri, to 2pm Sat Apr-Oct) ca help with accommodation and has a lo of English-language information. Be sur not to miss the **Schüttesäge-museu** (Hauptstrasse 1; 11am-5pm Tue-Sun Apr-Oct which is part of an old mill built on th river.

Heir to the Black Forest cake recipe nesting ground of the world's bigges cuckoos and spring of Germany's highest waterfall – **Triberg** is a torrent o Schwarzwald superlatives. Start with a stroll. There's a one-hour walk to the roaring **waterfall**; it starts near the **tourist office** (☎ 866 490; www.triberg.de; Wallfahrtstrass 4; 10am-5pm), which also has a small museum. The duelling oversized cuckoos ar at opposite ends of town (we prefer th one in Schonach).

The iconic glacial lake draws no shortag of visitors to the busy village of **Titisee-Neustadt**. Walking around Titisee o paddle-boating across it are major activities. If you have wheels, ride or drive int the surrounding meadows to see some of the truly enormous traditional house-barn combos. The **tourist office** (☎ 98 40; www.titisee-neustadt.de; Strandbadstrasse 4 9am-6pm Mon-Fri, 10am-1pm Sat & Sun May Oct, 9am-noon & 1.30-5pm Mon-Fri Nov-Apr) ca help you arrange a farm stay.

FREIBURG

☎ 0761 / pop 213,500

Nestled between hills and vineyards Freiburg im Breisgau has a medieva Altstadt made timeless by a thriving university community. There's a sense of fun here exemplified by the *bächle* (tiny medieval canals) running down the middle of streets. Perhaps being Germany's sunniest city contributes to the mood.

Founded in 1120 and ruled for centuries by the Austrian Habsburgs, Freiburg has retained many traditional features, although major reconstruction was necessary following WWII. The monumental 13th-century cathedral is the city's key landmark, but the real attractions are the vibrant cafes, bars and street life, plus the local wines. The best times for tasting are July for the four days of *Weinfest* (Wine Festival) or August for the nine days of *Weinkost* (wine tasting).

The **tourist office** (☎ **388 1880; www.freiburg.de; Rathausplatz 2-4; ⌚ 8am-8pm Mon-Fri, 9.30am-5pm Sat, 10am-noon Sun Jun-Sep, 8am-6pm Mon-Fri, 9.30am-2.30pm Sat, 10am-noon Sun Oct-May**) is well stocked with hiking and cycling maps to the region.

The major sight in Freiburg is the 700-year-old **Münster** (**Cathedral; Münsterplatz; tower adult/child €1.50/1; ⌚ 9.30am-5pm Mon-Sat, 1-5pm Sun**), a classic example of both high- and late-Gothic architecture that looms over Münsterplatz, Freiburg's market square.

The bustling **university quarter** is northwest of the **Martinstor** (one of the old city gates). On the walk in from the station, note the field of **grape vines** from around the world.

The popular trip by **cable car** (**one way/return adult €8/12, child €5/7; ⌚ 9am-5pm Jan-Jun, to 6pm Jul-Sep, 9.30am-5pm Oct-Dec**) to the **Schauinsland peak** (1284m) is a quick way to reach the Black Forest highlands. Numerous easy and well-marked trails make the Schauinsland area ideal for day walks. From Freiburg take tram 4 south to Günterstal and then bus 21 to Talstation.

Hotel Schwarzwälder Hof (☎ **380 30; www.schwarzwaelder-hof.eu; Herrenstrasse 43; r €45-120;** 💻) A wrought-iron staircase sweeps up to snazzy rooms, some with postcard views of the Altstadt.

Hotel zum Roten Bären (☎ **387 870; www.roter-baeren.de; Oberlinden 12; s €100-170;** 💻) Billed as Germany's oldest guesthouse, this blush-wine-pink hotel near Schwabentor dates to 1120.

Hausbrauerei Feierling (☎ **243 480; Gerberau 46; mains €6-12**) Starring one of Freiburg's best beer gardens, this brewpub serves great vegetarian options and humungous schnitzels with *brägele* (chipped potatoes).

Freiburg is on the busy Mannheim to Basel, Switzerland train line. ICE services include Frankfurt (€61, two hours, hourly). Freiburg is linked to Titisee by frequent trains (€10, 40 minutes).

Single rides on the efficient local bus and tram system cost €2. A 24-hour pass costs €5. Trams depart from the bridge over the train tracks.

FRANKFURT-AM-MAIN

☎ 069 / pop 643,000

Called 'Mainhattan' and 'Bankfurt', and much more, Frankfurt is on the Main (pronounced 'mine') River, and, after London, it is Europe's centre of finance. But while all seems cosmopolitan, it is often just a small town at heart. Streets get quiet in the evenings and the long list of museums is devoid of any really outstanding stars. Then again, it has cute old pubs you would only ever find in a small town.

Frankfurt-am-Main is Germany's most important transport hub for air, train and road connections, so you will probably end up here at some point.

ORIENTATION

The airport is 11 minutes by train southwest of the city centre.

Post office Innenstadt (**Zeil 90, ground fl, Karstadt department store; ⌚ 9.30am-8pm**)

Main tourist office (☎ **212 388 00; www.frankfurt-tourismus.de; ⌚ 8am-9pm Mon-Fri,**

DENNIS JOHNSON

Caracalla-Therme

IF YOU LIKE...

If you like soaking with strangers, there's no place better in all of Germany than the storied and ritzy spa town of **Baden-Baden**. The town is on the busy Mannheim–Basel train line, from where you can make connections to much of the country.

- **Tourist Office** (☎ 07221-275 200; www.baden-baden.com; Kaiserallee 3; 🕓 10am-5pm Mon-Sat, 2-5pm Sun) Drink from the hot spring source in the *trinkhalle*.
- **Friedrichsbad** (☎ 07221-275 920; www.roemisch-irisches-bad.de; Römerplatz 1; bathing program €21-29; 🕓 9am-10pm) The 19th-century Friedrichsbad boasts a decadently Roman style and provides a muscle-melting 16-step bathing program. No clothing is allowed inside, and several bathing sections are mixed-gender areas.
- **Caracalla-Therme** (☎ 275 940; Römerplatz 11; per 2hr €13; 🕓 8am-10pm) The more modern, bathing suit–required Caracalla-Therme is a vast complex of outdoor and indoor pools, complete with hot- and cold-water grottoes.

9am-6pm Sat & Sun) In the main hall of the train station.

Römer tourist office (Römerberg 27; 🕓 9.30am-5.30pm Mon-Fri, 10am-4pm Sat & Sun) The Frankfurt-am-Main Card (one day/two days €9/13) gives 50% off admission to important attractions and unlimited travel on public transport.

SIGHTS

Frankfurt has the most skyscraper-filled skyline in Europe. Banks and related firms have erected a phalanx of egotistical edifices along Mainzer Landstrasse and the Taunusanlange. Although postwar reconstruction was subject to the hurried demands of the new age, rebuilding efforts were more thoughtful in the **Römerberg**, the old central area of Frankfurt west of the cathedral, where ersatz 14th- and 15th-century buildings provide a glimpse of the beautiful city this once was.

East of Römerberg, behind the Historischer Garten (which has the remains of Roman and Carolingian foundations), is the **Frankfurter Dom** (Domplatz 14; museum adult/child €3/2; 🕓 9am-noon & 2.30-6pm), the coronation site of Holy Roman emperors from 1562 to 1792.

'Few people have the imagination for reality', uttered Johann Wolfgang von Goethe. Read more quotes at the **Goethe Haus** (☎ 138 800; Grosser Hirschgraben 23-25; adult/child €5/3; 🕓 10am-6pm Mon-Sat, to 5.30pm Sun), where he was born in 1749.

Frankfurt's museum list is long, but a mixed bag. To sample them all, buy a 48-hour Museumsufer ticket (€12). North of the cathedral, the excellent **Museum für Moderne Kunst** (☎ 2123 0447; Domstrasse 10; adult/child €8/4; 🕓 10am-8pm Tue-Sun) features works of modern art by Joseph Beuys, Claes Oldenburg and many others. Also on the north bank there's the **Jüdisches Museum** (Jewish Museum; ☎ 2123 5000;

Untermainkai 14-15; adult/child €4/2; 10am-5pm Tue & Thu-Sun, to 8pm Wed), with exhibits on the city's rich Jewish life before WWII. Numerous museums line the south bank of the Main River along the so-called Museumsufer (Museum Embankment).

SLEEPING

Concorde Hotel (☎ 242 4220; www.hotelconcorde.de; Karlstrasse 9; r €65-120;) Understated and friendly, this establishment in a restored art-deco building near the Hauptbahnhof is a good choice any time, but especially on weekends.

Hotel am Dom (☎ 138 1030; www.hotelamdom.de; Kannengiessergasse 3; r €90-120;) This unprepossessing hotel offers immaculate rooms, suites and apartments just a few paces from the Frankfurter Dom.

Steigenberger Frankfurter Hof (☎ 215 02; www.steigenberger.de; Am Kaiserplatz; r from €160;) Frankfurt's most gracious and traditionally luxurious hotel.

EATING & DRINKING

Apple-wine taverns are Frankfurt's great local tradition. They serve *ebbelwoi* (Frankfurt dialect for *apfelwein*), an alcoholic apple cider, along with local specialities. Anything with the sensational local sauce made from herbs, *grünesauce*, is a winner.

Zur Germania (☎ 613 336; Textorstrasse 16; meals €7-15) This Sachsenhausen apple-wine tavern has a good outdoor area and is well-known for its huge pork roasts.

our pick **Fichte Kränzi** (☎ 612 778; Wallstrasse 5; mains €7-15) Just superb. A smallish place down an alley with a large, shady tree outside. The schnitzels are tops as is the patter from the waiters.

Mutter Ernst (☎ 28 38 22; Alte Rothofstrasse 12; mains €9-18; closed Sun) Grab a wooden table among the panelled walls for some excellent trad German fare.

GETTING THERE & AWAY

Germany's largest airport is **Frankfurt airport** (FRA; ☎ 6901; www.frankfurt-airport.com), a vast labyrinth with connections throughout the world. It's served by most major airlines, although not many budget ones.

Only cynics like Ryanair would say that Frankfurt has another airport. **Frankfurt-Hahn airport** (HHN; www.hahn-airport.de) is 70km west of Frankfurt. Buses from Frankfurt's Hauptbahnhof take about 2¼ hours – longer than the flight from London. Given the journey time it's fitting the bus company is called **Bohr** (☎ 06543-501 90; www.bohr-omnibusse.de; adult/child €12/6; hourly).

The Deutsche-Touring Romantic Rd bus (see p459) leaves from the south side of the Hauptbahnhof.

The Hauptbahnhof handles more departures and arrivals than any station in Germany. Among the myriad train services: Berlin (€111, four hours, hourly), Hamburg (€106, 3½ hours, hourly) and Munich (€89, 3¼ hours).

Many long-distance trains also serve the airport. This station, *Fernbahnhof,* is beyond the S-Bahn station under Terminal 1. S-Bahn lines S8 and S9 run every 15 minutes between the airport and Frankfurt Hauptbahnhof (€3.60, 11 minutes, 4.15am to 1am).

Both single or day tickets for Frankfurt's excellent **transport network** (RMV; www.traffiq.de) can be purchased from automatic machines at almost any train station or stop.

HAMBURG

☎ 040 / pop 1.76 million

The site of Europe's largest urban renewal project is a never-ending forest of cranes that are efficiently transforming old city docks into an extension of the city – it all makes you wonder 'What *can't* this city achieve?' But Germany's leading port city has always been forward-thinking and liberal. Its dynamism, multiculturalism and hedonistic red-light district, the Reeperbahn, all arise from its maritime history. Joining the Hanseatic League trading bloc in the Middle Ages, Hamburg has been enthusiastically doing business with the rest of the world ever since. In the 1960s it nurtured the musical talent of the Beatles. Nowadays, it's also a media capital and the wealthiest city in Germany.

INFORMATION

Hamburg Tourismus Hauptbahnhof (**☎ information 3005 1200, hotel bookings 3005 1300; www.hamburg-tourismus.de; Kirchenallee exit; 🕑 8am-9pm Mon-Sat, 10am-6pm Sun**); Landungsbrücken (**btwn piers 4 & 5; 🕑 8am-6pm Apr-Oct, 10am-6pm Nov-Mar; Ⓜ Landungsbrücken**); airport (**☎ 5075 1010; 🕑 6am-11pm**) Sells the Hamburg Card (€9/19/35 for one/three/five days) giving free public transport and museum discounts.

LIFE'S A BEACH BAR

The city beach season kicks off around April and lasts until at least September, as patrons come to drink, listen to music, dance and generally hang out on the waterfront. A few leading venues, open daily, include **Lago Bay** (**www.lago.cc, in German; Grosse Elbstrasse 150; Ⓜ Königstrasse**), a stylish retreat where you can actually swim while free exercise classes will help you keep fit, er, between cocktails. **StrandPauli** (**www.strandpauli.de, in German; St-Pauli Hafenstrasse 84; 🚌 112**) is a more laid-back stretch of sand with a youthful feel, and **Strandperle** (**www.strandperle-hamburg.de, in German; Övelgönne 1; 🚌 112**) is the original Hamburg beach bar.

SIGHTS & ACTIVITIES

Hamburg's medieval **Rathaus** (**☎ 4283 120 10; tours adult/child €3/0.50, 🕑 tours in English hourly 10.15am-3.15pm Mon-Thu, to 1.15pm Fri, to 5.15pm Sat, to 4.15 Sun; Ⓜ Rathausmarkt or Jungfernstieg**) is one of Europe's most opulent. For many visitors, however, the city's most memorable building is south in the Merchants' District. The 1920s, brown-brick **Chile Haus** (**cnr Burchardstrasse & Johanniswall; Ⓜ Mönckebergstrasse/Messberg**) is shaped like an ocean liner, with remarkable curved walls meeting in the shape of a ship's bow and staggered balconies that look like decks.

The beautiful red-brick, neo-Gothic warehouses lining the Elbe archipelago south of the Altstadt once stored exotic goods from around the world. Now the so-called **Speicherstadt** (**Ⓜ Messberg/Baumwall**) is a popular sightseeing attraction. It's best appreciated by simply wandering through its streets or taking a Barkassen boat up its canals. Another way to see the Speicherstadt is from the **High-Flyer Hot Air Balloon** (**☎ 3008 6968; www.highflyer-hamburg.de; per 15min €15; 🕑 10am-midnight, to 10pm winter, weather permitting**) moored nearby.

Port and Elbe River cruises start in summer at the St Pauli Landungsbrücken. **Hadag** (**☎ 311 7070; www.hadag.de; Brücke 2; 1hr harbour trip adult/child from €9/4.50**) offers some of the best deals and cruises.

No discussion of Hamburg is complete without mentioning St Pauli, home of the **Reeperbahn** (**Ⓜ Reeperbahn**), Europe's biggest red-light district. Sex shops, peep shows, dim bars and strip clubs line the streets, which generally start getting crowded with the masses after 8pm or

9pm. This is also where the notorious **Herbertstrasse** is located (a block-long street lined with brothels that's off-limits to men under 18 and to female visitors of all ages) as well as the **Erotic Art Museum** (☎ 317 4757; www.eroticartmuseum.de; Bernhard-Nocht-Strasse 69; adult/concession €8/5; ⌚ noon-10pm, to midnight Fri & Sat).

Every Sunday between 5am and 10am, curious tourists join locals of every age and from every walk of life at the famous Fischmarkt in St Pauli. The market has been running since 1703, and its undisputed stars are the boisterous *Marktschreier* (market criers) who hawk their wares at full volume.

The **International Maritime Museum** (☎ 300 93 300; www.internationales-maritimes-museum.de; Koreastrasse 1; adult/concession €10/7; ⌚ 10am-6pm Tue, Wed & Fri-Sun, to 8pm Thu; Ⓜ Messberg) is the newest addition to Hamburg's **HafenCity**. This nine-floor, enormous space examines 3000 years of maritime history through displays of model ships, naval paintings, navigation tools and educational exhibits explaining the seas and its tides and currents. Added bonus: sweeping views of the HafenCity development project greet you at every window.

SLEEPING

Hotel Wedina (☎ 280 8900; www.wedina.de; Gurlittstrasse 23; s €70-148, d €118-168; Ⓜ Hauptbahnhof) You might find a novel instead of a chocolate on your pillow at Wedina, a hotel that's a must for bookworms and literary groupies. Jonathan Franzen, Vladimir Nabokov and JK Rowling are just some of the authors who've stayed and left behind signed books.

East (☎ 309 933; www.east-hamburg.de; Simon-von-Utrecht-Strasse 31; d €155-215, ste €250-420, apt €150-550; Ⓜ St Pauli) Pillars, walls and lamps emulate organic forms in the public areas of this warm, richly decorated design hotel.

CRAZY ABOUT EEL

Tired of wurst and dumplings? Well, you're in a port city now so specialities generally involve seafood and definitely veer away from stereotypical German fare. *Labskaus* is a dish of boiled marinated beef put through the grinder with mashed potatoes and herring and served with a fried egg, red beets and pickles. Or perhaps you'd prefer *aalsuppe* (eel soup) spiced with dried fruit, ham, vegetables and herbs? **Deichgraf** (☎ 364 208; www.deichgraf-hamburg.de; Deichstrasse 23; mains €17-27; ⌚ lunch Mon-Sat, dinner Sat) is one leading local restaurant that can acquaint you with these and other local dishes.

GETTING THERE & AWAY

Hamburg's **airport** (HAM; www.flughafen-hamburg.de) has frequent flights to domestic and European cities, including on low-cost carrier **airberlin** (www.airberlin.com). In addition there are EC/ICE trains to Berlin (€65, 1½ to two hours) and Munich (€127, 5½ to six hours).

The **Airport Express** (☎ 227 1060; www.jasper-hamburg.de) runs between the Hauptbahnhof and airport (€5, 25 minutes, every 10 to 20 minutes from 5.45am to midnight).

Hamburg is a fantastic place to explore by bike, with extensive cycle lanes (many along the water). For bike hire, try **Fahrradladen St Georg** (☎ 243 908; Schmilinskystrasse 6; per day €10).

There is an integrated system of buses, U-Bahn and S-Bahn trains. Day tickets, bought from machines before boarding, cost €6, or €5.10 after 9am. From midnight to dawn the night-bus network takes over from the trains, converging on the main metropolitan bus station at Rathausmarkt.

AUSTRIA

VIENNA

☎01 / pop 1.66 million

Vienna is a city that straddles the past and present with ease. Vienna has for centuries been a busy intersection of ethnicities, beliefs and peoples, and this heady mix has attracted a mine of artists, musicians and thinkers. Gustav, Schiele, Beethoven, Mozart, Strauss and Freud (to name but a few) all practised their arts here, and their efforts can be seen and heard in various museums throughout the city. But thankfully it's just as easy to avoid Vienna's cultural trappings as it is to indulge in them. Take a stroll down the Naschmarkt, the city's main market, grab a coffee in a coffee house, head for a *Heurigen* (wine tavern) on the edge of the Vienna Woods, or take a dip in the *Alte Donau* (Old Danube) – and this is just the icing on a very rich cake.

Vienna probably began life as a Celtic camp, but the first solid foundations of the city were laid by the Romans who arrived in 15 BC. It was first officially recorded as 'Wenia' in 881 and became a Babenberg stronghold in the 11th century. The Babenberg's ruled for 200 years until the Habsburgs took control of the city's reigns and held them firm until the end of WWI.

Over the centuries Vienna suffered Ottoman sieges in 1529 and 1683 and occupation in 1805 and 1809 by Napoleon and his armies. In the years in between, it received a major baroque makeover, the remnants of which can be seen in many buildings throughout the city.

ORIENTATION

Many of the historic sights are in the old city, the Innere Stadt. The Danube Canal (Donaukanal) is located to the northeast and a series of broad boulevards called the Ring or Ringstrasse encircle it. Most of the attractions in the city centre are within walking distance of each other.

The main train stations are Franz Josefs Bahnhof to the north, Westbahnhof to the west and Südbahnhof to the south; transferring between them is easy. Most hotels and pensions (B&Bs) are in the city centre and to the west.

INFORMATION

Allgemeines Krankenhaus (General Hospital; ☎40 400-0; 09, Währinger Gürtel 18-20; 24hr)

Main Post Office (☎577 67-71010; 01, Fleischmarkt 19; 6am-10pm)

Tourist Info Wien (☎24 555; www.wien.info; 01, cnr Am Albertinaplatz & Maysedergasse; 9am-7pm) Near the state opera house, with loads of regional information.

Vienna Card (€18.50) Admission discounts and a free 72-hour travel pass; available at tourist offices and hotels.

SIGHTS

Vienna's ostentatious buildings and beautifully tended parks make it a lovely city for strolling. The Ringstrasse (the road circling the city centre) is the perfect place to acquire a taste for the city, and an hour's walk will bring you past the neo-Gothic **Rathaus** (city hall), the Greek Revival–style **Parliament** and the 19th-century **Burgtheater**, among others. You can even glimpse the baroque **Karlskirche** (St Charles' Church) on your meander.

Strolling along the pedestrian-only Kärntner Strasse will take you past plush shops, cafes and street entertainers. The main point of interest in Graben is the

RUSSELL MOUNTFORD

Interior of Stephansdom

VIENNA IN TWO DAYS

Start with **Stephansdom** (below), then head to the **Hofburg** (p476) via Graben and the Kohlmarkt. After a coffee-house lunch break, hop on tram 1 around the Ringstrasse before alighting near the **Museums Quartier** (p476). Spend the evening in the **opera** (p481) or head to a club such as **Flex** (p481).

On your second morning explore a few galleries or museums, then spend a lazy afternoon at **Schloss Schönnbrunn** (p477). At night, venture into the suburbs to Vienna's *Heurigen* (p480).

knobbly **Pestsäule** (Plague Column), designed by Fischer von Erlach and built to commemorate the end of the Great Plague. There's also a concrete **Holocaust memorial** by Rachel Whiteread in Judenplatz, Austria's first monument of its kind.

STEPHANSDOM

The prominent latticework spire and geometric patterned roof tiles of **Stephansdom** (**St Stephen's Cathedral; ☎ 515 52-0; www.stephanskirche.at; 01, Stephansplatz; admission free; 6am-10pm Mon-Sat, 7am-10pm Sun; U-Bahn Stehpansplatz**) make this 13th-century Gothic masterpiece one of the city's key points of orientation. Bearing in mind the significance of the church in daily medieval commerce, run your fingers across over-200-year-old rudimentary circular grooves on the cathedral's face (right side of front), once used for standardising and regulating exact measurements of bread loaves, and over two horizontally fastened iron bars, at one time utilised for gauging proper lengths of cloth.

Inside, you can take the lift up the **north tower** (**adult/child €4.50/1.50; 8.30am-5.30pm**), tackle the 343 steps to the top of the **south tower** (**adult/child €3.50/1; 9am-5.30pm**), and explore the church's **Katakomben** (**catacombs; adult/child €4.50/1.50; 10-11.30am & 1.30-4.30pm Mon-Sat, 1.30-4.30pm Sun**), which contains some of the internal organs of the former Habsburgs rulers. Guided tours (adult/child €4.50/1.50) are also available, as are audio guides (adult/child €3.50/1).

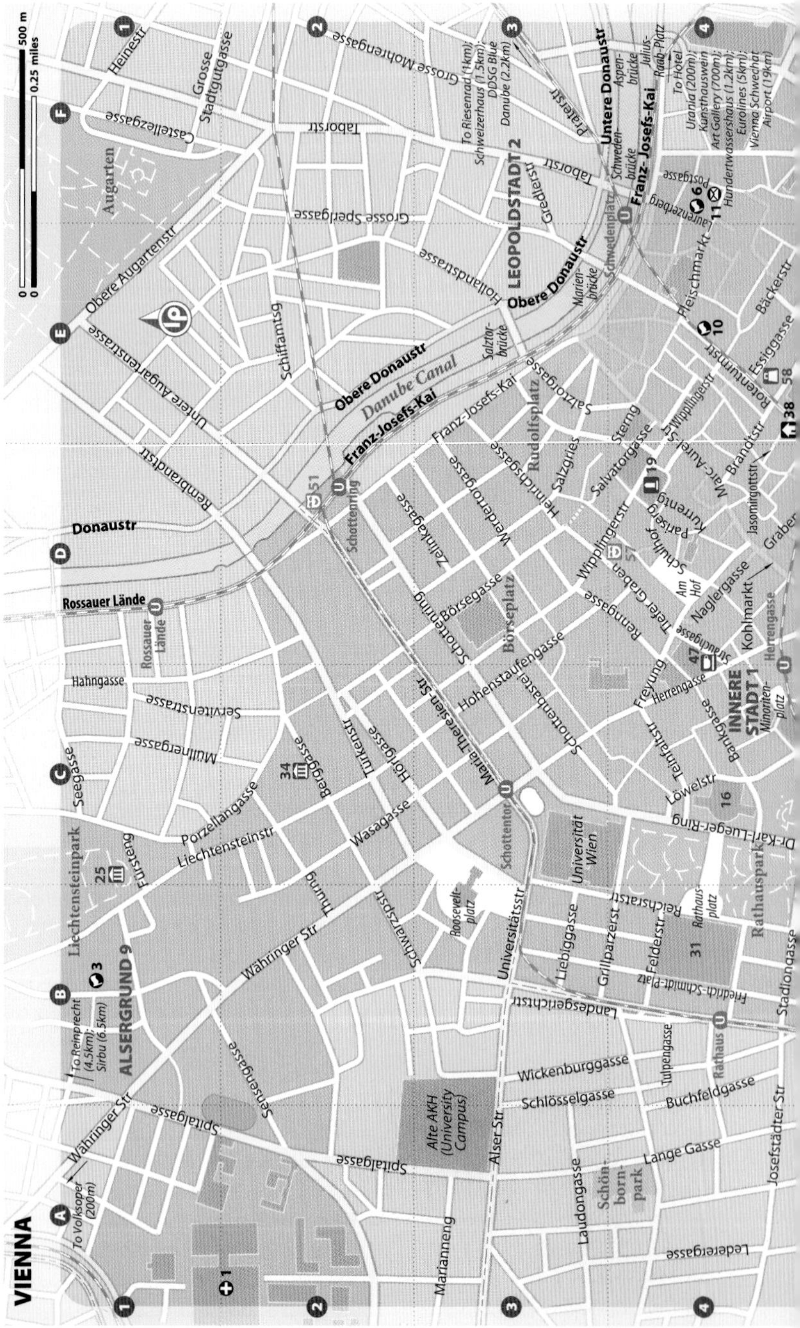
VIENNA
0 500 m
0 0.25 miles
To Volksoper (200m)
To Reinprecht (4.5km); Sirbu (6.5km)
ALSERGRUND 9
Liechtensteinpark
Augarten
LEOPOLDSTADT 2
INNERE STADT 1
Danube Canal
Obere Donaustr
Untere Donaustr
Franz-Josefs-Kai
Donaustr
Rossauer Lände
Schottenring
Schottentor
Schwedenplatz
Herrengasse
Rathaus
Universität Wien
Alte AKH (University Campus)
Rathauspark
Rathausplatz
Roosevelt-platz
Schönbornpark
Börseplatz
Rudolfsplatz
Am Hof
Minoritenplatz
Währinger Str
Spitalgasse
Alser Str
Universitätsstr
Landesgerichtstr
Wickenburggasse
Schlösselgasse
Lange Gasse
Laudongasse
Buchfeldgasse
Lederergasse
Josefstädter Str
Stadiongasse
Reichsratsstr
Felderstr
Grillparzerstr
Liebiggasse
Friedrich-Schmidt-Platz
Dr-Karl-Lueger-Ring
Löwelstr
Teinfaltstr
Bankgasse
Freyung
Schottengasse
Schottenbastei
Hohenstaufengasse
Maria-Theresien-Str
Börsegasse
Zelinkagasse
Werdertorgasse
Heinrichsgasse
Salzgries
Salzorgasse
Sterng
Salvatorgasse
Wipplingerstr
Marc-Aurel-Str
Renngasse
Tiefer Graben
Naglergasse
Kohlmarkt
Graben
Jasomirgottstr
Brandstätte
Rotenturmstr
Essiggasse
Bäckerstr
Fleischmarkt
Laurenzerberg
Postgasse
Schulhof
Parisergasse
Kurrentgasse
Strauchgasse
Wasagasse
Hörlgasse
Türkenstr
Berggasse
Porzellangasse
Liechtensteinstr
Fürsteng
Seegasse
Müllnergasse
Servitengasse
Hahngasse
Thurng
Schwarzspanierstr
Sensengasse
Tulpengasse
Mariannengasse
Rembrandtstr
Untere Augartenstrasse
Obere Augartenstr
Schiffamtsg
Hollandstrasse
Grosse Sperlgasse
Gredlerstr
Taborstr
Grosse Stadtgutgasse
Castellezgasse
Heinestr
Grosse Mohrengasse
Praterstr
Salztorbrücke
Marienbrücke
Schwedenbrücke
Aspernbrücke
Julius-Raab-Platz
To Riesenrad (1km); Schweizerhaus (1.5km); DDSG Blue Danube (2.2km)
To Hotel Urania (200m); Kunsthauswein Art Gallery (700m); Hundertwasserhaus (1.2km); Eurolines (5km); Vienna Schwechat Airport (19km)
A B C D E F
1 2 3 4

Am Stadtpark
Stadtpark
Wien
Stubenring
Weiskirchnerstr
Stubentor
Parkring
Johann Strauss Statue
Kursalon
Wollzeile
Schulerstr
Riemerg
Seilerstätte
Singerstr
Weihburggasse
Himmelpfortgasse
Hegelgasse
Johannesgasse
Schellinggasse
Seilerstätte
Schwarzenbergstr
Stephansplatz
Kärntner Str
Neuer Markt
Annagasse
Krugerstr
Walfischgasse
Mahlerstr
Kärntner Ring
Bösendorferstr
Künstlerhaus
Lothringerstr
Schubertring
Beethoven-platz
Lothringerstr
Schwarzen-bergplatz
Am Heumarkt
Lagergasse
Lisztstr
Salesianergasse
Neulinggasse
Metternichgasse
Strohgasse
Jauresgasse
Rennweg
Schloss Belvedere
Botanic Garden
Prinz-Eugen-Str
Oberes Belvedere & Österreichische Galerie (50m)
Schwindgasse
Wohllebeng
Mattiellistr
Karlsgasse
Gusshausstr
Taubstummengasse
Stadt Wien
Resselpark
Karlsplatz
Paniglgasse
Treitlstr
Floragasse
To Südbahnhof (Train Station; 1km)
WIEDEN 4
Paulanergasse
Schleifmühlgasse
Margaretenstr
Operngasse
Opernring
Friedrichstr
Rechte Wienzeile
Elisabethstr
Schillerplatz
Goethegasse
Burggarten
Albertina-platz
Tegetthoffstr
Maysedergasse
Philharmonikerstr
Augustinerstr
Spiegelgasse
Seilerg
Dorotheergasse
Habsburgergasse
Michaeler-platz
Josefs-platz
In der Burg
Heldenplatz
Neue Burg
Ballhausplatz
Volksgarten
Naturhistorisches Museum
Maria-Theresien-Platz
Burgring
Babenbergerstr
Museumsquartier
Lehárgasse
Gumpendorfer Str
Girardigasse
MARIAHILF 6
Linke Wienzeile
Schikanedergasse
Waaggasse
Pressgasse
Schäffergasse
Margaretenstr
Kettenbrückengasse
Franzensgasse
Wehrgasse
Grüngasse
Rüdigergasse
Hamburgerstr
Linke Wienzeile
Mariahilfer Str
Königsklostergasse
Karl-Schweighofer-Gasse
Windmühlgasse
Gumpendorfer Str
Bellariastr
Volksgartenstr
Hansenstr
Museumstr
Volkstheater
Breite Gasse
Schmerlingplatz
Doblhoffgasse
Josefsgasse
Trautsongasse
Lerchenfelder Str
Piaristengasse
Neustiftgasse
Burggasse
Siebensterngasse
NEUBAU 7
Lindengasse
Mariahilfer Str
Barnabitengasse
Kirchengasse
Zollergasse
Strozzigasse
Neubaugasse
Richtergasse
Andreasgasse
Neubaugasse
Mariahilfer Str
Schadekgasse
Esterházy Park
Gumpendorfer Str
Linnengasse
To Westbahnhof (Train Station; 600m); Schloss Schönbrunn & Schönbrunn Baths (3km)
5
6
7
8
2
4
5
7
8
9
12
13
14
15
17
18
20
21
22
23
24
26
27
28
29
30
32
33
35
36
37
39
40
41
42
43
44
45
46
48
49
50
52
53
54
55
56

INFORMATION
- Allgemeines Krankenhaus (Hospital) **1** A2
- American Consulate **2** E5
- American Embassy **3** B1
- Australian Embassy **4** E7
- British Embassy **5** F7
- Canadian Embassy **6** F4
- Dutch Embassy **7** D6
- French Embassy **8** E7
- German Embassy **9** F7
- Irish Embassy **10** E4
- Main Post Office **11** F4
- Tourist Info Wien **12** D6
- Wiener Festwochen **13** C7

SIGHTS & ACTIVITIES
- Albertina **14** D6
- Burgkapelle **15** C5
- Burgtheater **16** C4
- Haus der Musik **17** E6
- Hofburg **18** C5
- Holocaust Memorial **19** D4
- Kaiserappartements **20** D5
- Kaisergruft **21** D5
- Karlskirche **22** E7
- Kunsthistorisches Museum **23** C6
- Leopold Museum **24** C6
- Liechtenstein Museum **25** C1
- Loos Haus **26** D5
- Museums Quartier **27** B6
- Naschmarkt **28** C7
- Parliament **29** B5
- Pestsäule **30** D5
- Rathaus **31** B4
- Schatzkammer **32** D5
- Schloss Belvedere **33** F7
- Sigmund Freud Museum **34** C2
- Silberkammer (see 20)
- Sisi Museum (see 20)
- Stephansdom **35** E5
- Unteres Belvedere **36** F7

SLEEPING
- Das Tyrol **37** C7
- Hotel am Stephansplatz **38** E4
- Pension Hargita **39** A7
- Pension Pertschy **40** D5
- Pension Suzanne **41** D6

EATING
- DO & CO **42** E5
- Immervoll **43** E5
- Österreicher im MAK **44** F5
- St Josef **45** A6
- Zu den 2 Lieserln **46** A6

DRINKING
- Café Central **47** D4
- Café Sacher **48** D6
- Café Sperl **49** C7
- Demel **50** D5

ENTERTAINMENT
- Burgkapelle (see 15)
- Flex **51** D2
- Musikverein **52** E7
- Porgy n Bess **53** E5
- Spanish Riding School **54** D5
- Staatsoper **55** D6
- Volksgarten **56** C5
- Why Not? **57** D4

SHOPPING
- Manner **58** E4

HOFBURG

The **Hofburg** (**Imperial Palace; www.hofburg-wien.at; U-Bahn Herrengasse**), also known as the Winter Palace, was the Habsburgs' city-centre base. It's been added to many times since the 13th century, resulting in a mix of architectural styles. While not as ornate as Schönbrunn's rooms, the **Kaiserappartements and 'Sisi' Museum** (**☎ 535 75 70; Hofburg; adult/child €9.90/4.90; 9am-5pm; U-Bahn Herrengasse**) are worth seeing because they relate the unusual life story of Empress Elisabeth (Sisi).

Among several other points of interest within the Hofburg you'll find the **Burgkapelle** (Royal Chapel), where the Vienna Boys' Choir performs (see p482), the **Spanish Riding School** (p482), and the **Schatzkammer** (**Treasury; ☎ 525 24-0; Schweizerhof; adult/child €10/7.50; 10am-6pm Wed-Mon; U-Bahn Herrengasse**), which holds all manner of wonders, including the 10th-century Imperial Crown, a 2860-carat Columbian emerald, and even a thorn from Christ's crown.

KAISERGRUFT

Also known as the Kapuzinergruft, the **Kaisergruft** (**Imperial Vault; ☎ 512 68 53; 01 Tegetthofstrasse/Neuer Markt; adult/child €4/1.50; 10am-6pm; U-Bahn Stephansplatz**) is the final resting place of most of the Habsburg elite (although their hearts and organs reside elsewhere). The coffin of Empress Elisabeth's ('Sisi') receives the most attention however: lying alongside that of her husband Franz Josef, it is often strewn with fresh flowers.

MUSEUMS QUARTIER

Small guidebooks have been written on the popular **Museums Quartier** (**☎ 52 58 81; www.mqw.at; 07, Museumsplatz 1; U-Bahn Museumsquartier, Volkstheater**), so only a taster can be given here. The highpoint is undoubtedly the **Leopold Museum** (**☎ 525 700; www.leopoldmuseum.org; adult/student/senior €10/6.50/9; 10am-6pm Fri-Wed, to 9pm Thu; U-Bahn Museumsquartier**), which houses the world's largest collection of Egon Schiele paintings, with some minor Klimts and Kokoschkas thrown in.

:HLOSS BELVEDERE

ıis **palace** (☎ 79 557-0; www.belvere.at; combined ticket adult/student/senior 2.50/8.50/9.50; D or 71 to Belvedere) con-ꞩts of two main buildings. The first is the **beres Belvedere and Österreichische alerie** (Upper Belvedere & Austrian Gallery; , Prinz Eugen Strasse 37; adult/student/senior .50/6/7.50; 10am-6pm), where you'll ıd instantly recognisable works, such Gustav Klimt's *The Kiss*, which is ac-ımpanied by other late-19th to early)th-century Austrian works. The second the **Unteres Belvedere** (Lower Belvedere; , Rennweg 6A; adult/student/senior €9.50/6/7.50; 10am-6pm Thu-Tue, 10am-9pm Wed), which ıntains a baroque museum. The build-gs sit at opposite ends of a manicured arden.

UNSTHAUSWIEN

ıis formerly inconspicuous factory uilding, now fairytale **art gallery** ☎ 712 04 91; www.hundertwasser.at; 03, ıtere Weissgerberstrasse 13; adult/student /7, Mon half price; 10am-7pm; N or O to ıdetzkyplatz) designed and transformed y Friedensreich Hundertwasser into repository for his art, is redolent of ntonio Gaudi's buildings in Barcelona. regular elements, like uneven floors, ıisshapen windows, and amalgama-ons of glass, metal, brick and ceramic le, almost literally sweep you off your et. Down the road there's a block of esidential flats by Hundertwasser, the **undertwassershaus** (03, cnr Löwengasse Kegelgasse; N to Löwengasse).

LBERTINA

imply reading the highlights among s enormous collection – several lichelangelos, some Raphaels and lbrecht Dürer's *Hare* – should have ny art fan lining up for entry into this **gallery** (☎ 53 483-0; www.albertina.at; 01, Albertinaplatz 1a; adult/student/senior €9.50/7/8; 10am-6pm Thu-Tue, 10am-9pm Wed; U-Bahn Karlsplatz). As the collection is so large (1.5 million prints and 50,000 drawings), exhibitions change regularly so check the website to find out what's on show.

SCHLOSS SCHÖNBRUNN

The single attraction most readily associated with Vienna is the Habsburgs' **summer palace** (☎ 81 113-0; www.schoenbrunn.at; 13, Schönbrunner Schlossstrasse 47; self-guided 22-/40-room tour €9.50/12.90; 8.30am-5pm Apr-Oct, to 6pm Jul & Aug, to 4.30pm Nov-Mar; U-Bahn Schönbrunn). Despite being a vast complex, the sumptuous 1441-room palace can at times be uncomfortably crowded, so it's best to arrive early to avoid the throngs.

Other highlights include the formal gardens and fountains, the **maze** (admission €2.90), the **Palmenhaus** (greenhouse; admission €3.30) and the **Gloriette Monument** (admission €2), whose roof offers a wonderful view over the palace grounds and beyond.

LIECHTENSTEIN MUSEUM

The collection of Duke Hans-Adam II of Liechtenstein is on show at Vienna's gorgeous baroque **Liechtenstein Palace** (☎ 319 57 67-0; www.liechtensteinmuseum.at; 09, Fürstengasse 1; adult/child €10/free; 10am-5pm Fri-Tue; D to Bauernfeldplatz). It's one of the largest private collections in the world, and boasts a plethora of classical paintings, including some Rubens.

KUNSTHISTORISCHES MUSEUM

When it comes to classical works of art, nothing comes close to the **Kunsthistorisches Museum** (Museum of Fine Arts; ☎ 52 524-0; www.khm.at; 01, Maria Theresien

WITOLD SKRYP

Oberes Belvedere (p477)

Platz; adult/student €10/7.50; ⌚ 10am-6pm Tue, Wed & Fri-Sun, to 9pm Thu; Ⓤ U-Bahn Volkstheater or Museumsquartier). It houses a huge range of art amassed by the Habsburgs and includes works by Rubens, Van Dyck, Holbein and Caravaggio. Paintings by Peter Brueghel the Elder, including *Hunters in the Snow*, also feature. There is an entire wing of ornaments, clocks and glassware, and Greek, Roman and Egyptian antiquities.

OTHER MUSEUMS

Vienna has so many museums that you might overlook the superlative **Haus der Musik** (**House of Music; ☎ 51 648; www.haus-der-musik-wien.at; 01, Seilerstätte 30; adult/student €10/8.50; ⌚ 10am-10pm; Ⓤ U-Bahn Karlsplatz or Stephansplatz**), but try not to. Interactive electronic displays allow you to create different forms of music through movement and touch, and to connect with something a lot deeper than just your inner child.

Some former homes of the great composers, including one of Mozart's, are open to the public; ask at the tourist offic There is also the fairly low-key **Sigmur Freud Museum** (**☎ 319 15 96; www.freu museum.at; 09, Berggasse 19; adult/student €7/4. ⌚ 9am-6pm Jul-Sep, to 5pm Oct-Jun; Ⓤ U-Ba Rossauer or Schottentor**).

NASCHMARKT

Saturday is the best day to visit this **ma ket** (**06, Linke Wienzeile; ⌚ 6am-6pm Mon-S Ⓤ U-Bahn Karlsplatz or Kettenbrückengass**) when the usual food stalls and occasion tacky clothes stall are joined by a prop flea market.

ACTIVITIES

RIESENRAD

In theory, riding the **Riesenrad** (**gia wheel; www.wienerriesenrad.com; adult/chil student €8/3.50/7; ⌚ 10am-7.45pm; Ⓤ U-Ba Praterstern**) in the Prater amusement pa allows you to relive a classic film momer when Orson Welles ad libbed his immc tal speech about peace, Switzerland ar cuckoo clocks in *The Third Man*. In pra tice, you'll be too distracted by oth assengers and by the views as the Ferris wheel languidly takes you 65m aloft.

WATER SPORTS

here's swimming, sailboarding, boating nd windsurfing in the stretches of water nown as the Alte Donau (Old Danube), ortheast of the Donau Insel (Danube land), and the Neue Donau (New anube), which runs parallel to and just orth of the Donaukanal (Danube Canal). here are stretches of river bank that ffer unrestricted access. Alternatively, isit the **Schönbrunn baths** (**Schönbrunner chlossstrasse 47; full day/afternoon incl locker €9/7; 8.30am-10pm Jun–mid-Aug, 8.30am-8pm mid-ug–late-Aug, 8.30am-7pm May & Sep; U-Bahn chönbrunn**), within the Schloss Schönbrunn rounds.

TOURS

he tourist office publishes a monthly st of guided walks, called *Wiener paziergänge* – online information can e found at www.wienguide.at. **Vienna Walks** (**774 89 01; www.viennawalks.tix.t**) organises **Third Man Tours** (**tour €17; 4pm Mon & Fri**), which explore the locaions of the film, and a tour of **Jewish Vienna** (**tour €13; 1.30pm Mon**).

FESTIVALS & EVENTS

he **Vienna Festival**, from mid-May to nid-June, has a wide-ranging arts proram. Contact **Wiener Festwochen** (**589 2-22; www.festwochen.or.at; 06, Lehárgasse 11; Jan–mid-Jun**) for details.

The free open-air **Opera Film Festival** on Rathausplatz runs throughout July and ugust.

Each year Vienna's traditional **Christkindlmarkt** (Christmas market) akes place in front of the Rathaus between nid-November and 24 December; it's one of a number scattered across the city.

SLEEPING

Pension Hargita (**526 19 28; www.hargita.at; 07, Andreasgasse 1; s/d with shared bathroom from €38/52, with private bathroom €55/66**) One of the cleanest and most charming budget pensions in Vienna. Rooms have aqua blue or sunny yellow features, the friendly Hungarian owner keeps things spotless, and breakfast is included.

Hotel Urania (**713 17 11; www.hotel-urania.at; 03, Obere Weissgerberstrasse 7; s/d/tr/q from €48/70/95/120**) This hotel is tacky, but fun. Not all of the eclectic rooms will be to everyone's taste (a knight's boudoir with animal skins on the floor, anyone?) Others, such as the Hundertwasser and Japanese rooms, are actually quite chic.

Pension Suzanne (**513 25 07; www.pension-suzanne.at; 01, Walfischgasse 4; s/d €77/100;**) Suzanne is only a few steps off Kärnter Strasse and just around the corner from the Staatsoper. Rooms are a little on the small side, but this is mitigated somewhat by attractive antique furniture.

Pension Pertschy (**534 49-0; www.pertschy.com; 01, Habsburgergasse 5; s/d from €90/113;**) Pertschy is a gem of a pension with a peaceful location in the heart of the city.

SPLURGE

Hotel am Stephansplatz (**53 405-0; www.hotelamstephansplatz.at; 01, Stephansplatz 9; s/d/ste from €160/180/260**) With its front windows facing the beauty of Stephansdom, this boutique hotel has arguably the best location for accommodation in the city. Its interior is a perfect complement to the location – spacious, ubercomfortable rooms in warm greens and browns, and ecofriendly duvets and towels. Breakfast is a smorgasbord of organic produce.

Rooms are large, warm and inviting, and staff will welcome both adults and children with equal enthusiasm.

Das Tyrol (☎ 587 54 15; 06, www.das-tyrol.at; Mariahilfer Strasse 15; s/d from €109/149;) For the price, this boutique hotel has some of the best rooms in town. It's handily located on a major shopping thoroughfare and close to the Museums Quartier.

EATING

Zu den 2 Lieserln (07, Burggasse 63; schnitzel from €6) Leiserln has been serving enormous schnitzels for over 100 years to politicians, blue-collar workers, and everyone in between. Take a seat and appreciate a true Viennese institution.

St Josef (07, Mondscheingasse 10; mains €6-7.20; Mon-Sat) St Josef is the choice of the healthy diner. It only serves wholly organic and vegetarian cuisine, and the menu changes daily.

Österreicher im MAK (☎ 714 01 21; 01, Stubenring 5; lunch menu €6.40, mains €12-22) Top chef Helmut Österreicher has channelled his considerable talents into creating a menu here filled with measured portions of classic Viennese dishes and modern takes on traditional Austrian cuisine.

Immervoll (☎ 513 52 88; 01 Weihburggasse 17; mains €8-17) Run by a famous Austrian actor, Immervoll (literally, 'always full') attracts an arty crowd to its uncluttered interior. The menu changes daily; the delicious food often has Hungarian and Italian influences.

Schweizerhaus (02, Strasse des Ersten Mai 116; mains €10-20; mid-Mar–Oct) In the Prater park, this place serves *hintere schweinsstelze* (roasted pork hocks) and the like to a rowdy crowd of international travellers who wash it all down with huge mugs of Czech beer fresh from the barrel.

DO & CO (☎ 535 39 69; 01, Haas Hau Stephansplatz 12; mains €15-30) The foo and the views from seven floors abov Stephansplatz keep this elegant restau rant in business.

DRINKING

COFFEE HOUSES

Vienna's famous *kaffeehäuser* (coffe houses) are like economic forecasts; as two people for a recommendation an you'll get four answers.

our pick **Café Sperl** (☎ 586 41 58; 0 Gumpendorfer Strasse 11) With its scuffed bu original 19th-century fittings and cast c slacker patrons playing chess and read ing newspapers, this is exactly how yo expect an Austrian coffee house to be.

Café Central (☎ 533 37 63; 01, Herrengass 14) A lot more commercialised than whe Herrs Trotsky, Freud and Beethoven dran here, we dare say, but still appealing wit vaulted ceilings, palms and baroque a chitecture.

Café Sacher (☎ 514 56-661; 0 Philharmoniker strasse 4) An institution for it world-famous chocolate cake – the Sache torte, baked here since 1832.

Demel (☎ 535 17 17; 01, Kohlmarkt 14) I operation since 1786. Stop by and gaz longingly at the incredible cake creation in the window.

HEURIGEN (WINE TAVERNS)

Vienna's *Heurigen* are a good way to se another side of the city. Selling 'new' win produced on the premises, they have lively atmosphere, especially as the evenin progresses. Outside tables and picni benches are common, as is buffet food.

Because *Heurigen* tend to be clus tered together, it's best just to head fo the wine-growing suburbs to the north northeast, south and west of the city an to look for the green wreath or branc hanging over the door that identifies a *Heuriger*. Opening times are approximately from 4pm to 11pm, and wine costs less than €2.50 per *viertel* (250mL).

Reinprecht (☎ 320 14 71; 19, Cobenzlgasse 22; mid-Feb–Dec) Reinprecht is the best option in the row of *Heurigen* where Cobenzlgasse and Sandgasse meet in Grinzing. It's in a former monastery and boasts a large paved courtyard and a lively, if somewhat touristy, atmosphere.

Sirbu (☎ 320 59 28; 19, Kahlenberger Strasse 210; Mon-Sat Apr-Oct) This spot has great views of the Danube. Catch bus 38A east to the final stop at Kahlenberg, from where it is a 15-minute walk downhill.

ENTERTAINMENT

Check listings magazine *Falter* (€2.40, in German) for weekly updates. The tourist office has copies of *Vienna Scene* and produces monthly events listings.

CLASSICAL MUSIC

The cheapest deals are the standing-room tickets that go on sale at each venue around an hour before performances. However, you may need to queue three hours before that for major productions.

There are no performances in July and August. Ask at the tourist office for details of free concerts at the Rathaus or in churches.

Staatsoper (State Opera; ☎ 513 1 513; www.staatsoper.at; 01, Opernring 2; standing room €2-3.50, seats €7-254) Performances are lavish, formal affairs, where people dress up.

Volksoper (People's Opera; ☎ 514 44-3318; www.volksoper.at; 09, Währinger Strasse 78; standing room €1.50-4, seats €4-150) Productions are more modern here and the atmosphere is a little more relaxed.

Musikverein (☎ 505 18 90; www.musikverein.at; 01, Bösendorferstrasse 12; standing room €4-6, seats €17-118) The opulent and acoustically perfect (unofficial) home of the Vienna Philharmonic Orchestra.

HANNAH LEVY

Naiad fountain at Schloss Schönbrunn (p477)

NIGHTCLUBS

our pick **Flex** (☎ 533 75 25; www.flex.at; 01, Donaukanal/Augartenbrücke) Time after time this uninhibited shrine to music (it has one of the best sound systems in Europe) puts on great live shows and features the top DJs from Vienna and abroad.

Porgy n Bess (☎ 512 88 11; www.porgy.at; 01, Riemergasse 11; 7pm-late) Vienna's best spot to catch modern, local and international jazz acts.

Volksgarten (☎ 532 42 41; www.volksgarten.at; 01, Burgring 1) There's modern dance and an atmospheric 1950s-style salon that was once a former *Walzer Dancing* venue.

Why Not? (☎ 535 11 58; www.why-not.at; 01, Tiefer Graben 22; Fri & Sat) A popular gay bar-disco for like-minded people.

SPANISH RIDING SCHOOL

The famous Lipizzaner stallions strut their stuff at the **Spanish Riding School** (☎ 533 90 31-0; www.srs.at; 01, Michaelerplatz 1; standing room €20-28, seats €35-165) behind the Hofburg. Performances are sold out months in advance, but you can book online or over the phone. On the day, unclaimed tickets are sold 45 minutes before performances. Travel agents usually charge commission on top of the listed prices.

Same-day **tickets** (adult/senior/student €12/9/6, with entry to the Lipizzaner Museum €25/19/12; 10am-noon Tue-Sat Feb-Jun & Sep-Dec) can be bought to watch the horses train. The best riders go first and queues disappear by 11am.

VIENNA BOYS' CHOIR

The first troupe was put together back in 1498 and the latest bunch of cherubic angels in sailor suits still holds a fond place in Austrian hearts. The choir performs weekly at the **Burgkapelle** (Music Chapel; ☎ 533 99 27; whmk@chello.at; 01, Hofburg, Rennweg 1; standing-room free, seats €5-29, tickets Fri & 8.15am Sun) at 9.15am on Sunday, except from July to mid-September. Concerts are routinely sold out (tickets can be booked in advance via telephone or email) and there's often a crush of fans wanting to meet the choir afterwards. The group also performs regularly in the Musikverein (p481) – check www.wsk.at for more information.

SHOPPING

The Innere Stadt is generally reserved for designer labels and overpriced jewellery – most Viennese head to Mariahilfer Strasse for their High St shopping.

Manner (☎ 513 70 18; 01; Stephansplatz 7) Manner has been producing Vienna's favourite sweets, *Manner schnitten* (wafers filled with hazelnut cream), since 1898, and after one bite, you'll be hooked, too.

GETTING THERE & AWAY

AIR

Austrian Airlines (OS; ☎ 051 766 1000; www.aua.com; Vienna Schwechat airport) regularly links Vienna with Salzburg, Innsbruck, but considering the size of Austria, travelling by train is a highly viable option. There are also daily nonstop flights to all major European destinations. For further details, see p528.

BOAT

Fast hydrofoils travel eastwards to Bratislava (one way €16 to €28, return €32 to €48, bike extra €6, 1¼ hours), daily from April to October and on Saturdays and Sundays in March, and Budapest (one way/return €89/109, bike extra €20, 5½ hours) daily. Bookings can be made through **DDSG Blue Danube** (☎ 58 880-0; www.ddsg-blue-danube.at; 02, Handelskai 265).

Heading west, a series of boats plies the Danube between Krems and Melk, with a handful of services originating in Vienna. Two respectable operators include DDSG Blue Danube (above) and **Brandner** (☎ 07433-25 90; www.brandner.at), the latter located in Wallsee. Both run trips from April through October that start at around €11 one way. For trips into Germany, contact **Donauschiffahrt Wurk + Köck** (☎ 0732 783607; www.donauschiffahrt.de; Untere Donaulände 1, Linz).

BUS

Eurolines (☎ 798 29 00; 03, Erdbergstrasse 202; 6.30am-9pm) is the main bus company operating out of Vienna.

DAMIEN SIMONIS

Lipizzaner horses, bred for the Spanish Riding School

TRAIN

International trains leave from Westbahnhof or Südbahnhof, both of which will be receiving major renovations for the life of this book. Between 2009 and 2013 Südbahnhof will be demolished and a modern station, Wien Hauptbahnhof, will be built in its place. At the time of writing, it was not clear how train services would be affected.

Westbahnhof has trains to northern and Western Europe, and to western Austria. Services to Salzburg (€44, three hours) leave roughly hourly, where a change is normally required if travelling on to Munich (€77, 5½ hours).

For train information, call ☎ 05-17 17.

GETTING AROUND

TO/FROM THE AIRPORT

It is 19km from the city centre to **Wien Schwechat airport**. The **City Airport Train** (**CAT; ☎ 25 250; www.cityairporttrain.com**) takes 16 minutes between Schwechat and Wien Mitte (one way/return €9/16). The **S-Bahn (S7)** does the same journey (single €3.40), but in 26 minutes.

Buses run every 20 or 30 minutes, between 5am and midnight, from the airport (one way/return €7/13). Services run to Südtiroler Platz, Südbahnhof and Westbahnhof, UNO City, and Schwedenplatz.

Taxis cost about €35. **C&K Airport Service** (**☎ 44 444**) charges €27 one way for shared vans.

CAR & MOTORCYCLE

Parking is difficult in the city centre and the Viennese are impatient drivers. Blue parking zones (labelled *Kurzparkzone*) allow a maximum stop of 1½ or two hours from 9am to 10pm on weekdays. Parking vouchers (€0.80/2.40 per one/two hours) for these times can be purchased in *Tabak* (tobacconist) shops and banks. The cheapest parking garage in the city centre is at Museumsplatz.

PUBLIC TRANSPORT

Vienna has a unified public transport network that encompasses trains, trams, buses, and underground (U-Bahn) and suburban (S-Bahn) trains. Routes are outlined on the free tourist-office map.

Before use, all advance-purchase tickets must be validated at the entrance to U-Bahn stations or on trams and buses. Tickets are cheaper to buy from ticket machines in U-Bahn stations or from *Tabak* shops, where single tickets cost €1.70. On board, they cost €2.20. Singles are valid for an hour, and you may change lines on the same trip.

Daily passes *(Stunden-Netzkarte)* cost €5.70 (valid 24 hours from first use); a three-day pass costs €13.60; and an eight-day multiple-user pass *(8-Tage-Karte)* costs €27.20 (validate the ticket once per day per person). Weekly tickets (valid Monday to Sunday) cost €14; the Vienna Card (€18.50) includes travel on public transport for up to three days.

Ticket inspections are not very frequent, but fare dodgers pay an on-the-spot fine of €62.

DANUBE VALLEY

The stretch of Danube between Krems and Melk, known locally as the Wachau, is arguably the loveliest along the entire length of the mighty river. Both banks are dotted with ruined castles, medieval towns, and lined with terraced vineyards.

KREMS AN DER DONAU

☎ 02732 / pop 24,000

Krems is the gateway to the Danube Valley. Despite its pretty cobbled centre and attractive position on the northern bank of the Danube, most people only see it during a stopover on a boat or bike trip through the Danube Valley. The **tourist office** (**☎ 82 676; www.tiscover.com/krems; Kloster Und, Undstrasse 6; 🕑 9am-6pm Mon-Fri, 9am-5pm Sat, 9am-4pm Sun May-Oct, 9am-5pm Mon-Fri Nov-Apr**) can offer accommodation details.

The *Schiffsstation* (boat station) is a 20-minute walk west from the train station along Donaulände. Three buses leave daily from outside the train station to Melk (€6.50, one hour), and frequent trains head in the opposite direction to Vienna (€14, one hour).

MELK

☎ 02752 / pop 5200

With its imposing abbey-fortress rising above the Danube and a small, cobbled town, Melk is the highlight of the Danube Valley. Featured in the epic medieval German poem *Nibelungenlied* and Umberto Eco's best-selling novel *The Name of the Rose,* the impressive Benedictine monastery endures as a major Wachau landmark. It's an essential stop along the Danube Valley route, however, so be prepared to fight through loads of tourists to explore the place.

The train station is 300m from the town centre. The quickest way to the central Rathausplatz is through the small Bahngasse path (to the right of the cow's-head mural at the bottom of the hill), rather than veering left into Hauptplatz.

Turn right from Bahngasse into Rathausplatz and then right again at the end, following the signs to the **tourist office** (**☎ 52 307-410; www.tiscover.com/melk; Babenbergerstrasse 1; 🕑 9am-noon & 2-6pm Mon-Fri, 10am-noon Sat Apr, plus 10am-noon & 4-6pm Sat & Sun May, Jun & Sep, 9am-7pm Mon-Sat, 10am-noon & 5-7pm Sun Jul & Aug, 9am-noon & 2-5pm Mon-Fri, 10am-noon Sat Oct**).

On a hill overlooking the town is the ornate golden abbey **Stift Melk** (**☎ 555 232; www.stiftmelk.at; adult/student €7.70/4.50, with guided tour €9.50/6.30; 🕑 9am-5.30pm May-Sep, 9am-4.30pm mid-Mar–Apr & Oct, guided tours only Nov-Mar**). Home to monks since the 11th century, the current building was erected in the 18th century after a devastating fire. The **Abbey Museum** on the grounds outlines the history of the building and the church with its exhibition topic entitled 'The Path from Yesterday to Today – Melk in its Past and Present'. Various rooms using computer animation, sound and multimedia accurately narrate the 910-year-plus Benedictine monastic history of Melk.

It's helpful to phone ahead if you want a tour in English.

Gasthof Goldener Stern (☎ 52 214; www.sternmelk.at; Sterngasse 17; s/d from €35/42) This charming guesthouse sports individually decorated rooms with more than a touch of romance about them. It's located above the main square and also has a fine restaurant.

Self-caterers should stock up at the **Spar supermarket** (Rathausplatz 9), but those wanting a meal befitting the Wachau can head to **Tom's Restaurant** (☎ 52 475; Hauptplatz 1; mains €20), whose menu heavily features seasonal cuisine and fab regional wines.

Boats leave from the canal by Pionierstrasse, 400m behind the monastery. There are hourly direct trains to Vienna's Westbahnhof (€16.10, 1¼ hours) daily.

SALZBURG

☎ 0662 / pop 149,000

The joke 'if it's baroque, don't fix it' is a perfect maxim for Salzburg; the tranquil Old Town burrowed in below steep hills looks much as it did when Mozart lived here 250 years ago. Second only to Vienna in numbers of visitors, this compact city is centred on a tight grouping of narrow, cobbled streets overshadowed by ornate 17th-century buildings, which are in turn dominated by the medieval Hohensalzburg fortress from high above.

RICHARD NEBESKY

Spiral staircase at Stift Melk

Across the fast-flowing Salzach River rests the baroque Schloss Mirabell, surrounded by gorgeous manicured gardens.

If this doesn't whet your appetite, then bypass the grandeur and head straight for kitsch-country by joining a tour of *The Sound of Music* film locations.

INFORMATION

Tourist offices and hotels sell the Salzburg Card (€21/29/34 for 24/48/72 hours), which provides free museum entry and public transport, and offers various reductions. The tourist office's commission for hotel reservations is €2.20.

Landeskrankenhaus (Hospital; ☎ 44 82-0; Müllner Hauptstrasse 48)

Main post office (Residenzplatz 9; 7am-6.30pm Mon-Fri, 8-10am Sat)

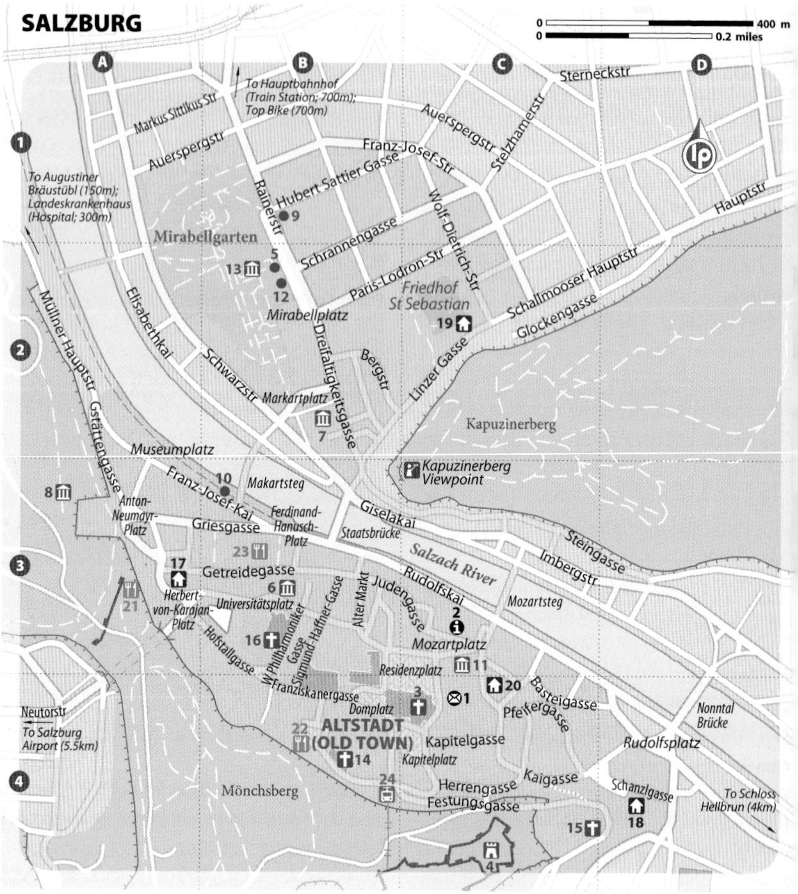

Tourist office (☎ information 88-987 330, hotel reservations 88-987 314; www.salzburg.info; Mozartplatz 5; ⌚ 9am-6pm Mon-Sat Jan-Apr & mid-Oct–Nov, 9am-7pm May–mid-Oct & Dec) A mine of information on the city. Hands out free maps.

SIGHTS

A Unesco World Heritage site, Salzburg's Old Town centre is equally entrancing whether viewed from ground level or the hills above.

Residenzplatz is a good starting point for a wander. The **Dom** (cathedral; Domplatz; admission free; ⌚ 6.30am-5pm Mon-Sat, 8am-5pm Sun), just to the south, is worth checking out for the three bronze doors symbolising faith, hope and charity, and excavations of a medieval cathedral and **Roman remains** (adult/student €2.50/1.50; ⌚ 9am-5pm). From here, head west along Franziskanergasse and turn left into a courtyard for **St Peterskirche** (St Peter Bezirk 1/2; admission free; ⌚ 8am-noon & 2.30-6.30pm), an abbey dating from AD 847. Among lovingly tended graves in the abbey's grounds you'll find the entrance to the **Katakomben** (catacombs;

INFORMATION		
Main Post Office	1	C4
Tourist Office	2	C3
SIGHTS & ACTIVITIES		
Dom	3	C4
Festung Hohensalzburg	4	C4
Fräulein Maria's Cycling Tours	5	B2
Mozart Sound & Film Museum	(see 7)	
Mozarts Geburtshaus	6	B3
Mozart's Wohnhaus	7	B2
Museum der Moderne	8	A3
Panorama Tours	9	B1
River Cruises Start Point	10	B3
Salzburg Museum	11	C3
Salzburg Sightseeing Tours	12	B2
Schloss Mirabell	13	B2
St Peterskirche	14	B4
Stift Nonnberg	15	C4
Universitätskirche	16	B3
SLEEPING		
Arthotel Blaue Gans	17	A3
Gasthaus Hinterbrühl	18	D4
Hotel Amadeus	19	C2
Hotel Wolf	20	C4
EATING		
Stadtalm	21	A3
Stiftskeller St Peter	22	B4
Wilder Mann	23	B3
TRANSPORT		
Festungsbahn Funicular	24	B4

adult/student €1/0.60; 10.30am-5pm May-Sep, 10.30am-3.30pm Wed & Thu, 10.30am-4pm Fri-Sun Oct-Apr). The western end of Franziskanergasse opens out into Max Reinhardt Platz, where you'll see the back of Fisher von Erlach's **Universitätskirche** **(Universitätsplatz; admission free; dawn-dusk)**, an outstanding example of baroque architecture. The **Stift Nonnberg** **(Nonnberg Abbey; admission free; 7am-dusk)**, where *The Sound of Music* first encounters Maria, is back in the other direction, a short climb up the hill to the east of the Festung Hohensalzburg.

FESTUNG HOHENSALZBURG

This **castle fortress** **(☎ 842 430-11; www.salzburg-burgen.at; Mönchsberg 34; adult/student €10/9.10; 9am-7pm May-Sep, 9am-5pm Oct-Apr)**, built in 1077, was home to many archbishop-princes (who ruled Salzburg from 798). Inside are the impressively ornate staterooms, torture chambers and two museums.

It takes 15 minutes to walk up the hill to the fortress, or you can catch the **Festungsbahn funicular** **(Festungsgasse 4; adult/child one way €2.10/1.10, return €3.40/1.80, incl in castle ticket; 9am-10pm May-Aug, 9am-9pm Sep, 9am-5pm Oct-Apr)**.

SCHLOSS MIRABELL

The formal gardens of **Schloss Mirabell** (**dawn-dusk**), with their tulips, crocuses and Greek statues, are the main attraction at this palace built by the archbishop-prince Wolf Dietrich for his mistress in 1606. The gardens were featured in *The Sound of Music*, and are now popular with wedding parties. Concerts are often held in the palace, and there are sometimes open-air performances in the garden (normally at 10.30am and 8.30pm May to August).

MUSEUMS

Although Mozart is now a major tourist drawcard, the man himself found Salzburg stifling and couldn't wait to leave. Consequently, **Mozart's Geburtshaus** **(birthplace; ☎ 844 313; www.mozarteum.at; Getreidegasse 9; adult/student €6.50/5.50; 9am-6pm Sep-Jun, 9am-7pm Jul & Aug, last entry 30min before closing)** and **Mozart's Wohnhaus** **(residence; ☎ 874 227; Makartplatz 8; adult/student €6.50/5.50; 9am-6pm Sep-Jun, 9am-7pm Jul & Aug, last entry 30min before closing)** cover only his early years as a prodigy and young adult, until he left town in 1780 at 24 years of age. The Wohnhaus is more extensive, and houses the **Mozart Sound and Film Museum** **(admission free; 9am-1pm Mon, Tue & Fri, 1-5pm Wed & Thu)**.

The latest entry on Salzburg's list of museums is the aptly named **Salzburg Museum** **(☎ 620 808-700; www.salzburgmuseum.at, in German; Mozartplatz 1; adult/**

student Tue-Sat €7/6, Sun €5.50/4.50; 9am-5pm Tue, Wed & Fri-Sun, to 8pm Thu, plus 9am-5pm Mon Jul, Aug & Dec), which covers the city and its favourite citizens in an interactive way and presents contemporary art exhibitions on a regular basis. The **Museum der Moderne** (☎ 842 220-403; www.museumdermoderne.at; Mönchsberg; adult/student €8/6; 10am-6pm Tue & Thu-Sun, to 9pm Wed) adds a further contemporary touch to historic Salzburg with rotating modern-art shows.

TOURS

SOUND OF MUSIC TOURS

Although these are the tours that interest the greatest number of visitors, how much fun you have depends on whether your fellow passengers enter into the necessary kitsch, tongue-in-cheek attitude. Tours take three to four hours and usually spend most time in neighbouring Salzkammergut, rather than Salzburg itself. Following are some recommended operators:

Fräulein Maria's Bicycle Tours (☎ 0676-342 62 97; www.mariasbicycletours.com; Mirabellplatz; adult/child €22/15; 9.30am May-Sep)

Panorama Tours (☎ 874 029; www.panoramatours.com; Mirabellplatz; adult/child €37/18; 9.30am & 2pm)

Salzburg Sightseeing Tours (☎ 881 616; www.salzburg-sightseeingtours.at; Mirabellplatz; adult/child €37/18; 9.30am & 2pm)

RIVER TOURS

Boats operated by **Salzburg SchiffFahrt** (☎ 825 769-12; www.salzburgschifffahrt.at) cruise along the Salzach (adult/child €13/7, 40 minutes) leaving half-hourly to hourly from around 10.45am to 6pm April to October. Others go to Schloss Hellbrunn (adult/child €16/10), departing at 12.45pm April to September, with an extra sailing at 10.45am in July and August. The company also has atmospheric tours by night in late July and August.

Boats leave from the Salzach Insel, on the city side of the Makart bridge.

FESTIVALS & EVENTS

Austria's most renowned classical music festival, the **Salzburg Festival** (www.salzburgfestival.at), attracts international stars from late July to the end of August. Book on its website before January, or ask the **Festspielhäuser ticket office** (☎ 80 45; Herbert von Karajan Platz 11; from 9am) about cancellations during the festival.

SLEEPING & EATING

Gasthaus Hinterbrühl (☎ 846 798; www.fam-wagner.at; Schanzlgasse 12; s/d €42/58) This small guesthouse may be a bit frayed around the edges, but it's central, cheap, and can trace its history back to the 14th century.

Hotel Wolf (☎ 843 453-0; www.hotelwolf.com; Kaigasse 7; s/d from €80/110;) With its neat living room set off from the main entrance hall, this family-owned hotel immediately feels like a real home.

Hotel Amadeus (☎ 871 401; www.hotelamadeus.at; Linzer Gasse 43; s/d €92/180;) A noteworthy boutique hotel with spacious rooms and huge buffet breakfast.

Arthotel Blaue Gans (☎ 842 491-0; www.blauegans.at; Getreidegasse 41-43; r from €135;) The 'Blue Goose' may be one of Salzburg's oldest inns, but these days it's a contemporary hotel housing modernist art pieces and sleek yet comfortable rooms.

Stadtalm (Mönchsberg 19c; mains €7-11; mid-May–mid-Sep) The dishes here are standard Austrian fare – wurst, *Wiener schnitzel* and *tafelspitz* (boiled beef) – but the view of the Old Town from Mönchsberg is far from standard.

CHRIS MELLOR

Views over Salzburg

Wilder Mann (☎ 841 787; Getreidegasse 20; mains €8-11; ⌚ Mon-Sat) Traditional Austrian food in a friendly, bustling environment, located in the passageway off Getreidegasse. Tables, both inside and out, are often so packed it's almost impossible not to get chatting with fellow diners.

Stiftskeller St Peter (☎ 841 268-34; St Peter Bezirk 1/4; mains €13-23) A favourite of locals and tourists alike, the Stiftskeller is a special spot renowned for its Austrian specialities, vine-clad courtyard, and baroque main salon.

To avoid a large dining bill, make lunch your main meal, or grab a *bosna* (€2.80), a spicy hotdog particular to the city. Sausage stands are scattered around Salzburg.

DRINKING

Salzburg's most famous stretch of bars, clubs and discos remains Rudolfskai, but it's largely patronised by teenagers. Those who've already hit their 20s (or beyond) will probably prefer the scene around Anton Neumayr Platz, where things keep going until 4am on weekends.

Augustiner Bräustübl (☎ 431 246; Augustinergasse 4-6; ⌚ 3-11pm Mon-Fri, 2.30-11pm Sat & Sun) Known locally as Müllnerbräu (after its neighbourhood), this hillside complex of beer halls and gardens is not to be missed. The local monks' brew keeps the huge crowd of up to 2800 humming.

GETTING THERE & AWAY

Salzburg airport (SZG; ☎ 85 80-0; www.salzburg-airport.com) receives scheduled flights from as near as Munich to as far away as Dublin.

Bus services to the Salzkammergut region leave from just to the left of the main Hauptbahnhof exit.

Fast trains leave for Vienna (€44, three hours) hourly. The quickest way to Innsbruck (€35.20, two hours) is by the 'corridor' train through Germany via Kufstein; trains depart at least every two hours. There are trains every hour or so to Munich (€28, two hours).

GETTING AROUND

Salzburg airport is located 4km west of the city centre. Bus 2 goes there from the Hauptbahnhof (€1.80). A taxi costs about €14.

Bus drivers sell single bus tickets for €1.80. Other tickets must be bought from the automatic machines at major stops, *Tabak* shops or tourist offices. Day passes cost €4.20 and weeklies €12.40.

Bicycle hire is available from **Top Bike** (☎ 0676-476 72 59; www.topbike.at; 2hr/4hr/day €6/10/15, 20% discount with all train tickets), which is located just outside the Hauptbahnhof.

AROUND SALZBURG

Four kilometres south of Salzburg's Old Town centre is the popular **Schloss Hellbrunn** (☎ 820 372-0; www.hellbrunn.at; Fürstenweg 37; adult/student €8.50/6; 9am-10pm Jul & Aug, 9am-5.30pm May, Jun & Sep, 9am-4.30pm Mar, Apr & Oct). Built by bishop Markus Sittikus, this 17th-century castle is known for its ingenious trick fountains and water-powered figures. City bus 25 runs to the palace every 30 minutes from Salzburg's Hauptbahnhof, via Rudolfskai in the Old Town. Salzburg tickets are valid.

SALZKAMMERGUT

A picture-perfect wonderland of glassy blue lakes and tall craggy peaks, Austria's Lake District is a long-time favourite holiday destination attracting visitors in droves from Salzburg and beyond. The peaceful lakes offer limitless opportunities for boating, fishing, swimming, or just lazing on the shore. You can also tour the salt mines that made the region wealthy or plunge into the depths of the fantastic Dachstein caves, where glittering towers of ice are masterfully illuminated in the depths of a mountain.

The country's major rail routes bypass the heart of Salzkammergut, but regional trains cross the area north to south. Regular buses connect the region's towns and villages, though they

RICHARD MILLS

Lakeside cafe at Hallstatt

are less frequent on weekends. Passenger boats ply the waters of the Attersee, Traunsee, Mondsee, Hallstätter See and Wolfgangsee.

BAD ISCHL

☎ 06132 / pop 14,000

During the last century of the Habsburg reign, Bad Ischl became the favourite summertime retreat for the imperial family and their entourage. Today the town and many of its dignified buildings still wear an imperial aura, while a shockingly high proportion of the local women still go about their daily business in *dirndl* (Austria's traditional full, pleated skirt). It makes a good base for exploring the entire Salzkammergut region.

The **tourist office** (**Kurdirektion; ☎ 27757-0; www.badischl.at; Bahnhofstrasse 6; 8am-6pm Mon-Fri, 9am-3pm Sat, 10am-1pm Sun**) is helpful.

The **Kaiservilla** (**☎ 23 241; www.kaiservilla.at; Kaiserpark; adult/student €11/10, grounds only €4/3; 9.30am-4.45pm May-Oct, 10am-4pm Wed Jan-Apr**) was Franz Josef's summer residence and shows that he loved huntin', shootin' and fishin' – it's decorated with an obscene number of animal trophies. The teahouse of Franz Josef's wife, Elisabeth, is now a **photo museum** (**☎ 244 422; adult/child €2/1.50; 9.30am-5pm Apr-Oct**).

Hotel Garni Sonnhof (**☎ 23 078; www.sonnhof.at; Bahnhofstrasse 4; s/d from €65/90**) Nestled into a leafy glade of maple trees next to the train station, this is an excellent option – it has cosy, traditional decor, a lovely garden, sunny conservatory, and large bedrooms with attractive antique furniture and wooden floors. There's also a billiard room, sauna and a steam bath on-site.

Bad Ischl also has its fair share of quality private rooms, including those at **Haus Rothauer** (**☎ 23 628; Kaltenbachstrasse 12; s/d €25/44**); both tourist offices can help with accommodation.

Restaurant Zauner Esplanade (**☎ 23 722; Hasner Allee 2; mains €7-18; 10am-9pm May-Oct, to 8pm Wed-Sun Dec–mid-Apr**) Zauner occupies a prime location – right on the banks of the Traun River – and is the perfect place for summer dining. The restaurant's Austrian cuisine is of the highest standard, and often employs organic produce.

Weinhaus Attwenger (**☎ 23 327; Lehárkai 12; mains €7-20; Tue-Sun**) High-quality Austrian food is served at this quaint chalet with a relaxing garden next to the river.

Trains on to Hallstatt depart roughly hourly between 6am and 6pm (€4.50, 30 minutes); be aware that the train station is on the opposite side of the lake from the village.

HALLSTATT

☎ 06134 / pop 900

With pastel-hued homes, swans and towering mountains on either side of a glassy green lake, Hallstatt looks like some kind of greeting card for tranquillity. Boats chug lazily across the water from the train station to the village itself, which clings precariously to a tiny bit of land between mountain and shore. So small is the patch of land occupied by the village that its annual Corpus Christi procession takes place largely in small boats on the lake.

There are up to 12 train services daily from Bad Ischl (€4.50, 30 minutes). The train station is across the lake from the village, but the ferry captain waits for trains to arrive before making the short crossing (€2, six minutes).

TIROL

With converging mountain ranges behind lofty pastures and tranquil meadows, Tirol (also Tyrol) captures a quintessential Alpine panoramic view. Occupying a central position is Innsbruck, the region's jewel, while in the northeast and southwest are superb ski resorts. In the southeast, separated somewhat from the main state since part of South Tirol was ceded to Italy at the end of WWI, lies the protected natural landscape of the Hohe Tauern National Park, which is home to 30 peaks over 3000m, including the country's highest, the Grossglockner (3797m).

INNSBRUCK

☎ 0512 / pop 118,000

Tirol's capital is a sight to behold. The mountains are so close that, within 25 minutes, its possible to travel from the heart of the city to over 2000m above sea level. Summer and winter outdoor activities abound, and it's understandable why some visitors only take a peek at Innsbruck proper before heading for the hills. But to do so is a shame, for Innsbruck has its own share of gems, including an authentic medieval Altstadt (Old Town), inventive architecture, and vibrant student-driven nightlife.

The city centre is compact, with the Hauptbahnhof only a 10-minute walk from the pedestrian-only Altstadt centre.

INFORMATION

Innsbruck Information (**☎ 53 56, hotel reservations 562 00; www.innsbruck.info; Burggraben 3; 9am-6pm Apr-Oct, 8am-6pm Nov-Mar**) Sells ski passes, hands out free maps, books accommodation, and has loads of info on the city and its surrounds.

Main post office (**Maximilianstrasse 2; 7am-9pm Mon-Fri, to 3pm Sat, 8am-7.30pm Sun**)

SIGHTS

Innsbruck's atmospheric, medieval Altstadt is ideal for a lazy stroll. A good starting point is the famous **Goldenes Dachl** (**Golden Roof; Herzog Friedrich Strasse**), which comprises 2657 gilded copper tiles. It was built by Emperor Maximilian I in the 16th century as a display of wealth.

Close by is another former royal dwelling, the **Hofburg** (**Imperial Palace; ☎ 587 186; Rennweg 1; adult/student €5.50/4; 9am-5pm**). A favourite of Maria Theresia, these state apartments betray the wealth of the Habsburgs – each room is lavishly adorned in rococo splendour, the highlight of which is the Riesensaal (Giant's Hall).

The **Hofkirche** (**Imperial Church; Universitätsstrasse 2; adult/child €4/2; 9am-5pm Mon-Sat, 10am-5pm Sun**) contains a memorial to Maximilian, and although his 'sarcophagus' has been restored, it's actually empty. Perhaps more memorable are the 28 giant statues of Habsburgs lining either side of the cask. You're now forbidden to touch the statues, but numerous inquisitive hands have already polished parts of the dull bronze, including Kaiser Rudolf's codpiece!

If you've ever wondered what it feels like to stand on top of an Olympic-sized ski jump, you'll leave the **Bergisel tower** (**☎ 589 259; adult/child €8.30/4; 10am-6.30pm**) with a better idea. And if you've never been curious about such death-defying feats, you'll still be rewarded with truly fantastic views; the tower sits 3km south of the city centre on the crest of the refurbished Winter Olympics ski-jump stadium, overlooking Innsbruck. To get here, take tram 1 (direction Bergisel) from Museumstrasse and then follow the signs to Bergisel – it's a fairly steep path for 15 minutes.

The **Nordkettenbahn** (**Northpark cable car; ☎ 293 344; www.nordpark.com**) connects the centre of Innsbruck with the Hafelekar peak (2256m) in a staggering 25 minutes. The ride is split into three parts: the new **Hungerburgbahn** (**one way/return €3.40/5.60; 7am-7.30pm Mon-Fri, 8am-7.30pm Sat & Sun**), displaying the tell-tale signs of its designer, Zaha Hadid, runs from the Congress Centre to Hungerburg (860m); the **Seegrube cable car** (**Innsbruck–Seegrube one way/return €13.20/22; 8.30am-5.30pm**) connects Hungerburg with the Seegrube station (1905m); and the **Hafelekar cable car** (**Innsbruck–Hafelekar one way/return €14.70/24.50; 9am-5pm**) hauls you up the last leg. The views are breathtaking.

ACTIVITIES

Skiing is a major winter activity around Innsbruck, and the area is constantly being improved each year. Three-/seven-day passes cost €99/188, and equipment hire starts at around €20 per day. However, it's not just a winter pastime in this region – year-round skiing is available at **Stubai Glacier**. The tourist office offers a package for €54 for one day, which includes transport, passes and equipment hire; buses leave from the Hauptbahnhof, with the journey taking about 80 minutes. The last bus back leaves at 5.30pm. It's a good deal in summer, however in winter there's a free ski bus leaving from various hotels, so compare going it alone with taking the tourist-office package first.

The mountains around Innsbruck are criss-crossed with well-marked trails, making them a target for **hiking** in summer. The tourist office offers guided hikes, and the Nordkettenbahn (above) allows hikers to access the mountains with minimum fuss.

GLENN BEANLAND

Early morning in Altstadt, Innsbruck

SLEEPING

our pick **Nepomuks** (**☎ 584 118; www.nepomuks.at; Kiebachgasse 16; dm/d €20/50**) This wonderful establishment has oodles of charm, with CD players and books in rooms and a thoroughly warm welcome.

Weisses Kreuz (**☎ 59 479; www.weisseskreuz.at; Herzog Friedrich Strasse 31; s/d with shared bathroom from €36/66, with private bathroom from €64/100**) It's had the honour of hosting Mozart, and this creaky, atmospheric hotel remains comfortable to this day.

Goldener Adler (**☎ 571 111; www.goldeneradler.com; Herzog Friedrich Strasse 6; s/d from €84/120;**) The grand dame of Innsbruck's hotel scene, the Goldener Adler has been around in one form or another since 1390. The rooms are suitably plush and the location impossible to beat.

Lichtblick (☎ **566 550; 7th fl, Maria Theresien Strasse 18; daytime snacks €7-11, dinner menu €35-45;** 🕑 **Mon-Sat**) This is the city's hot ticket, and little wonder, given both the fabulous views of the surrounding mountains and the delicious modern international food. It's a romantic setting at night. After dinner grab a drink across the foyer in the 360 Bar.

Goldenes Dachl (☎ **589 370; Hofgasse 1; mains €10-18**) The menu features Tirolean specialities, such as *bauerngröstl,* a pork, bacon, potato and egg concoction served with salad, along with *Wiener schnitzel* and various types of *braten* (roasts).

ENTERTAINMENT

The tourist office sells tickets for 'Tirolean evenings' (adult/child €22/10 for alpine music, folk dancing, yodelling and one drink), classical concerts and performances in the **Landestheater** (☎ **520 744; www.landestheater.at, in German; Rennweg 2**). For more entertainment options, pick up a copy of *Innsider,* found in cafes across town.

GETTING THERE & AWAY

EasyJet flies twice a week from London Gatwick to **Innsbruck airport** (**IIN;** ☎ **22 525-0; www.innsbruck-airport.com**), while Austrian Airlines, TUIfly, and Welcome Air connect the city with a handful of other European destinations.

Fast trains depart every two hours to Salzburg (€35.20, two hours).

GETTING AROUND

The airport is 4km west of the city centre. To get there, take bus F, which departs from opposite the Hauptbahnhof half-hourly (hourly on Saturday afternoon and Sunday) and passes through Maria Theresien Strasse. A taxi from the main train station to the airport costs around €10.

Single bus tickets, including to the airport, cost €1.70. A 24-hour pass is €3.80.

MAYRHOFEN

☎ 05285 / pop 3800

Tirol is ribbed by beautiful valleys, but the Zillertal is rated among the best. This long thin, alpine paradise is bristling with high mountain peaks, peaceful meadows, and rural farmhouses. It also has its fair share of towns, villages, and, naturally, tourists, many of whom head for Mayrhofen, a centre where you can base yourself for skiing year-round.

The town's **tourist office** (☎ **676 00; www.mayrhofen.at; Europahaus;** 🕑 **8am-7pm Mon-Fri, 9am-5pm Sat & Sun**) has loads of comprehensive information, including free *Info von A-Z* booklets for both summer and winter in English. There are good **walks** originating from the village; ask at the tourist office for maps or about guided trips. Mayrhofen is home to the steepest piste in Austria, known as the HariKari, and there is year-round **skiing** on nearby **Hintertux Glacier**. A pass costs €39/32 per day in winter/summer; inquire at the tourist office.

To work your taste buds instead of your legs, pay a visit to **Erlebnis Sennerei** (☎ **627 13; www.sennerei-zillertal.at; Hollenzen 116; admission with/without tasting €11.20/5.80;** 🕑 **10-11.30am & 12.30-3pm**), a grass-roots dairy. See how local cheeses are made on the production facility tour and then enjoy the chance to taste them. There's also a fine **restaurant** (**mains €7-14;** 🕑 **10am-6pm**) on-site.

The tourist office has a handy booklet listing all the accommodation in the town and its surrounds. **Traudl** (☎ **625 69; info@traudl.at; Dornaustrasse 612; s/d from €40/70;** 💻)

is a solid Austrian pension, and close to both village amenities and cable cars.

For local grub, try the evergreen drinking and eating hole **Mo's** (**Hauptstrasse 417; mains €6-20**), which offers a selection of fast food from around the world and occasional live music, or **Mamma Mia's** (**Einfahrt Mitte 432; mains €7-10**), where pasta and pizza fill the menu.

To reach Mayrhofen from Innsbruck (€13.40, 1½ hours), a change is required at Jenbach (€5.60, one hour). Trains run at least hourly.

LIENZ

☎ 04852 / pop 12,000

Lienz is the last major Ost Tirol outpost before Italy, only 40km to the southwest. With its pretty centre and busy squares, many visitors find it a charming town, but it's the Dolomite mountain range engulfing the southern skyline that people really come here for. Lienz is also a stopover for skiers and hikers passing through or on the way to the Hohe Tauern National Park.

The **tourist office** (**☎ 652 65; www.lienz-tourismus.at; Europaplatz 1; 8am-6pm Mon-Fri, 9am-noon & 5-7pm Sat Jul–mid-Sep, plus 10.30am-noon Sun Jul & Aug**) will find rooms free of charge, or you can use the hotel board (free telephone) outside.

Lienz has its fair share of hiking and skiing possibilities right on its doorstep. A €30 day pass covers skiing on the nearby **Zettersfeld** and **Hochstein** peaks; however, the area around Lienz is more renowned for its cross-country skiing; the town fills up for the annual **Dolomitenlauf** cross-country skiing race in mid-January.

Cable cars are in action from June to September, and lift passes for either Zettersfeld or Hochstein cost around €10.

Altstadthotel Eck (**☎ 647 85; altstadt hotel.eck@utanet.at; Hauptplatz 20; s/d €42/74**) Atmospheric and spacious, Altstadthotel Eck provides all the comfort you'd expect from one of the town's top hotels.

Adlerstüberl (**☎ 625 50; Andrä Kranz Gasse 5; mains €8-14; 11am-3pm & 6pm-midnight**)

GARETH MCCORMACK

Alpine hiking in Tirol

A central option where tourists and locals alike grab a table to avail of the array of Austrian dishes. The two-course midday menu (€11) will keep you going for days.

Except for the 'corridor' route through Italy to Innsbruck, trains to the rest of Austria connect via Spittal Millstättersee to the east. Trains to Salzburg (€31.40) take at least 3½ hours.

HOHE TAUERN NATIONAL PARK

You wouldn't guess from its small stature, but little Austria actually contains the largest national park in the Alps. Straddling Tirol, Salzburg and Carinthia, the Hohe Tauern National Park stretches over 1786 sq km. At the heart of this protected oasis of flora and fauna (including marmots and some rare ibexes) lies the **Grossglockner** (3797m), Austria's highest mountain. The Grossglockner towers over the 10km-long Pasterze Glacier, which is best seen from the outlook at **Franz Josefs Höhe** (2369m).

MARTIN MOOS

Heiligenblut

The portion of the **Grossglockner Hochalpenstrasse** (Hwy 107; www.grossglockner.at, in German) running through the park is considered one of the most scenic in the world. It winds upwards 2000m past waterfalls, glaciers and Alpine meadows. The highway runs between Lienz and Zell am See, and if you catch a bus from Lienz to Franz Josef's Höhe, you'll be traversing the southern part of this route. If you have your own vehicle, you'll have more flexibility, although the road is open only between May and mid-September, and you must pay tolls (per car/motorcycle €28/18).

The major village on the Grossglockner Rd is **Heiligenblut**, which is dominated not only by mountain peaks, but also by the steep spire of a 15th-century pilgrimage church. Here you'll find a **tourist office** (☎ 04824-20 01; www.heiligenblut.at; 9am-6pm Mon-Fri, 9am-noon & 4-6pm Sat Jul-Aug, 9am-6pm Mon-Fri Dec-Apr, 9am-noon & 2-6pm Mon-Fri, 9am-noon & 4-6pm Sat rest of the year), restaurants, and a spick-and-span **Jugendherberge** (☎ 04824-22 59; www.oejhv.or.at; Hof 36; dm/r €19/26; reception 7-10am, 5-8pm). Although camping is not allowed in the park, there are mountain huts and hiking trails open from May until the first snowfall; the tourist office in Heiligenblut has details.

Eight buses connect Lienz and Heiligenblut from Monday to Saturday year-round (€7.40, one hour); from late June to late September buses make the trip between Heiligenblut and Franz Josefs Höhe (€4.10, 30 minutes, four daily Monday o Friday, three daily Saturday and Sunday). Between mid-June and late September, two buses daily (€10.60, two hours) head north from Franz Josef Höhe to Zell am See, a major holiday resort in the region. Timetables change regularly here though, so it's best to check with the tourist office in Lienz (p495) before setting off.

SWITZERLAND

GENEVA

pop 178,600

Supersleek, slick and cosmopolitan, Geneva (Genève in French, Genf in German) is a rare breed of city. It's one of Europe's priciest. Its people chatter in every language under the sun (184 nationalities comprise 45% of the city's population) and it's constantly thought of as the Swiss capital – which it isn't. This gem of a city superbly strung around the sparkling shores of Europe's largest Alpine lake is, in fact, only Switzerland's second-largest city.

Yet the whole world is here: the UN, International Red Cross, International Labour Organization, World Health Organization – 200-odd governmental and nongovernmental international organisations fill the city's plush hotels with big-name guests, feast on an incredible choice of cuisine and help prop up the overload of banks, jewellers and chocolate shops for which Geneva is known. Strolling manicured city parks, lake sailing and skiing next door in the Alps are weekend pursuits.

The Rhône River divides Geneva into *rive droite* (right bank) – home to central train station Gare de Cornavin and the seedy Pâquis district – and *rive gauche* (left bank), where the Old Town overlooks Geneva's iconic landmark, the giant fountain of the Jet d'Eau.

INFORMATION

Cantonal Hospital (☎ 022 372 33 11; emergency 022 372 81 20; www.hug-ge.ch; Rue Micheli du Crest 24)

Police station (☎ 117; Rue de Berne 6)

Post office (Rue du Mont-Blanc 18; 🕐 7.30am-6pm Mon-Fri, 9am-4pm Sat)

Tourist office (☎ 022 909 70 00; www.geneve-tourisme.ch; Rue du Mont-Blanc 18; 🕐 10am-6pm Mon, 9am-6pm Tue-Sat)

SIGHTS & ACTIVITIES

The city centre is so compact it's easy to see many of the main sights on foot. Start with a coffee on **Île Rousseau**, one of five islands to pierce Europe's largest alpine lake, where a statue honours the celebrated freethinker. Cross to the southern side of the lake and walk west along Quai du Général-Guisan to the **Horloge Fleurie** (Flower Clock) in the **Jardin Anglais** (Quai du Général-Guisan). Geneva's most photographed clock, crafted from 6500 flowers, has ticked since 1955 and sports the world's longest second hand (2.5m). Then dive into the **Old Town**, where the main street here, Grand-Rue, shelters the **Espace Rousseau** at No 40 where the 18th-century philosopher was born.

Nearby, the part-Romanesque, part-Gothic **Cathédrale de St-Pierre** is where the influential Protestant John Calvin preached from 1536 to 1564; you can trace his life in the neighbouring **Musée Internationale de la Réforme** (International Museum of the Reformation; ☎ 022 310 24 31; www.musee-reforme.ch; Rue du Cloître 4; adult/child/student Sfr10/5/7; 🕐 10am-5pm Tue-Sun).

The 140m-tall **Jet d'Eau** on the lake's southern shore is impossible to miss. At any one time there are seven tonnes of water in the air, shooting up with incredible force – 200km/h, 1360 horsepower –

GENEVA

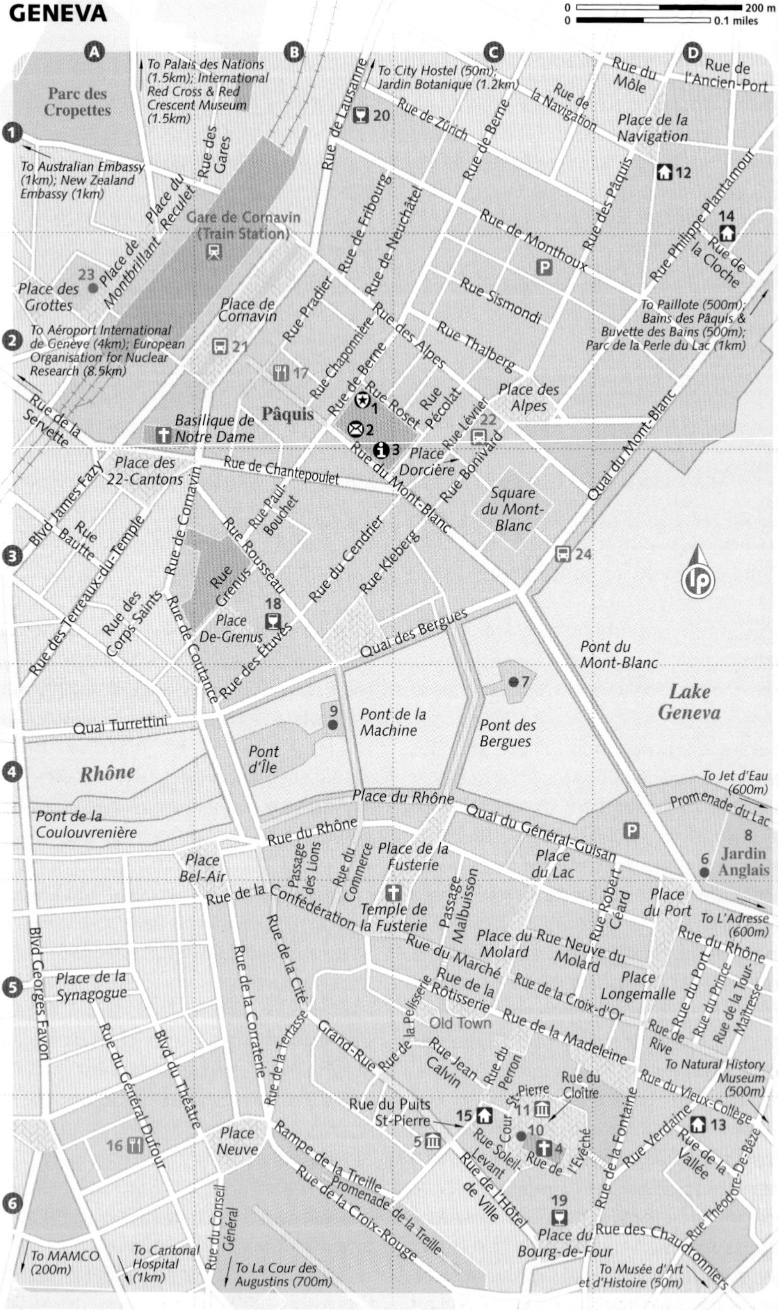
0 200 m
0 0.1 miles
A
B
C
D
1
2
3
4
5
6
Parc des Cropettes
To Palais des Nations (1.5km); International Red Cross & Red Crescent Museum (1.5km)
To City Hostel (50m); Jardin Botanique (1.2km)
To Australian Embassy (1km); New Zealand Embassy (1km)
To Aéroport International de Genève (4km); European Organisation for Nuclear Research (8.5km)
To Paillote (500m); Bains des Pâquis & Buvette des Bains (500m); Parc de la Perle du Lac (1km)
Gare de Cornavin (Train Station)
Place de Cornavin
Place de Montbrillant
Place du Reculet
Place des Grottes
Rue des Gares
Rue de Lausanne
Rue de Zürich
Rue de Berne
Rue du Môle
Rue de la Navigation
Rue de l'Ancien-Port
Place de la Navigation
Rue des Pâquis
Rue Philippe Plantamour
Rue de la Cloche
Rue de Fribourg
Rue de Neuchâtel
Rue de Monthoux
Rue Sismondi
Rue Thalberg
Rue des Alpes
Rue Pradier
Rue Chaponnière
Rue Rosset
Rue Pécolat
Place des Alpes
Quai du Mont-Blanc
Pâquis
Basilique de Notre Dame
Rue de la Servette
Place des 22-Cantons
Rue de Chantepoulet
Rue Lévrier
Place Dorcière
Rue Bonivard
Rue du Mont-Blanc
Square du Mont-Blanc
Blvd James Fazy
Rue Bautte
Rue des Terreaux-du-Temple
Rue de Cornavin
Rue Paul-Bouchet
Rue Rousseau
Rue Grenus
Rue du Cendrier
Rue Kleberg
Rue des Corps Saints
Rue de Coutance
Place De-Grenus
Rue des Étuves
Quai des Bergues
Pont du Mont-Blanc
Lake Geneva
Quai Turrettini
Pont de la Machine
Pont des Bergues
Pont d'Île
Rhône
Pont de la Coulouvrenière
Place du Rhône
Quai du Général-Guisan
To Jet d'Eau (600m)
Promenade du Lac
Jardin Anglais
Rue du Rhône
Place Bel-Air
Passage des Lions
Rue du Commerce
Place de la Fusterie
Temple de la Fusterie
Place du Lac
Passage Malbuisson
Rue Robert Céard
Place du Port
To L'Adresse (600m)
Rue de la Confédération
Rue du Marché
Place du Molard
Rue Neuve du Molard
Rue de la Rôtisserie
Rue de la Croix-d'Or
Place Longemalle
Rue du Port
Rue du Prince
Rue de la Tour-Maîtresse
Rue de Rive
Old Town
Rue de la Madeleine
To Natural History Museum (500m)
Rue du Vieux-Collège
Blvd Georges Favon
Place de la Synagogue
Rue du Général Dufour
Blvd du Théâtre
Rue de la Corraterie
Rue de la Cité
Rue de la Tertasse
Grand-Rue
Rue de la Pélisserie
Rue Jean Calvin
Rue du Perron
Rue du Cloître
Cour St-Pierre
Rue du Puits St-Pierre
Rue Soleil-Levant
Rue de l'Hôtel de Ville
Rue de l'Evêché
Rue de la Fontaine
Rue Verdaine
Rue de la Vallée
Rue Théodore-De-Bèze
Place Neuve
Rampe de la Treille
Promenade de la Treille
Rue de la Croix-Rouge
Rue du Conseil Général
Place du Bourg-de-Four
Rue des Chaudronniers
To MAMCO (200m)
To Cantonal Hospital (1km)
To La Cour des Augustins (700m)
To Musée d'Art et d'Histoire (50m)
1
2
3
4
5
6
7
8
9
10
11
12
13
14
15
16
17
18
19
20
21
22
23
24

INFORMATION		
Police Staton	1	B2
Post Office	2	B2
Tourist Office	3	B3
SIGHTS & ACTIVITIES		
Cathédrale de St-Pierre	4	C6
Espace Rousseau	5	C6
Horloge Fleurie	6	D4
Île Rousseau	7	C4
Jardin Anglais	8	D4
La Cité du Temps	9	B4
Main Entrance to Cathedral	10	C6
Musée Internationale de la Réforme	11	C6
SLEEPING		
Edelweiss	12	D1
Hôtel Bel'Esperance	13	D6
Hôtel de la Cloche	14	D1
Hôtel Les Armures	15	C6
EATING		
Au Grütli	16	A6
Café de Paris	17	B2
RestO by Arthur's	(see 9)	
DRINKING		
La Bretelle	18	B3
La Clémence	19	C6
Scandale	20	B1
TRANSPORT		
City Bus Departures	21	B2
Gare Routière International	22	C2
Genève Roule	23	A2
International Bus Station	24	C3

to create its sky-high plume, kissed by a rainbow on sunny days.

The art-deco **Palais des Nations** (☎ 022 907 48 96; Ave de la Paix 14; tours Sfr10; ⏰ 10am-noon & 2-4pm Apr-Oct, 10am-5pm Jul & Aug, 10am-noon & 2-4pm Mon-Fri Nov-Mar) is the European arm of the UN and the home of 3000 international civil servants. You can see where decisions about world affairs are made on the hour-long tour. ID or passport is obligatory for admission.

There are plenty of museums (many free) to fill rainy days. The **International Red Cross and Red Crescent Museum** (Musée Internationale de la Croix Rouge et du Croissant-Rouge; ☎ 022 748 95 25; www.micr.org; Ave de la Paix 17; admission free; ⏰ 10am-5pm Wed-Mon) is a compelling multimedia trawl through atrocities perpetuated by humanity in recent history. Against the long litany of war and nastiness, documented in films, photos, sculptures and soundtracks, are set the noble aims of the organisation.

Konrad Witz's *La pêche miraculeuse* (c 1440–44) portraying Christ walking on water on Lake Geneva is a highlight of the **Musée d'Art et d'Histoire** (☎ 022 418 26 00; http://mah.ville-ge.ch; Rue Charles Galland 2; permanent/temporary collection admission free/varies; ⏰ 10am-5pm Tue-Sun). The particularly well thought-out **Natural History Museum** (Musée d'Histoire Naturelle; ☎ 022 418 63 00; Route de Malagnou 1; admission free; ⏰ 9.30am-5pm Tue-Sun) buzzes with kids ogling at pretty much every species known to man, stuffed for perpetuity.

Young, international, cross-media exhibitions fill the 1950s factory floor at **MAMCO** (Musée d'Art Moderne et Contemporain; ☎ 022 320 61 22; www.mamco.ch; Rue des Vieux-Grenadiers 10; adult/student & child Sfr8/free; ⏰ noon-6pm Tue-Fri, 11am-6pm Sat & Sun, noon-9pm 1st Wed of month), while every Swatch watch ever designed ticks inside **La Cité du Temps** (☎ 022 818 39 00; www.citedutemps.com; 1 Pont de la Machine; ⏰ 9am-6pm), another old industrial space.

Geneva has loads of parkland, much of it lakefront. Flowers, art installations and soul-stirring views of Mont Blanc on clear days make the northern lakeshore promenade a pleasure to walk: pass hip **Bains des Pâquis** (☎ 022 732 29 74; www.bains-des-paquis.ch; Quai du Mont-Blanc 30; ⏰ 9am-8pm mid-Apr–mid-Sep), where Genevans have frolicked in the sun since 1872 and continue to **Parc de la Perle du Lac**. Further north, peacock-studded lawns ensnare the **Jardin Botanique** (admission free; ⏰ 8am-7.30pm Apr-Oct, 9.30am-5pm Nov-Mar).

The World Wide Web was one of the many creations to come out of the

WITOLD SKRYPCZ

Sunrise views over the lake to Geneva

GENEVA IN TWO DAYS

Explore the left-bank parks, gardens and **Jet d'Eau** (p497), then hit the **Old Town** (p497) for lunch and a stroll. Tummy full, take in a **museum** (p499) followed by a dip in the water and aperitif at **Bains des Pâquis** (p499). Day two: plan a tour of **CERN** (below) or **Palais des Nations** (p499), followed by a spot of stylish shopping.

European Organisation for Nuclear Research (CERN; ☎ 022 767 84 84; visits-service@cern.ch; tours 9am & 2pm Wed & Sat), a laboratory for research into particle physics funded by 20 nations, 8km west near Meyrin. The free three-hour guided visits need to be booked at least one month in advance, and you will need to present your ID or passport.

FESTIVALS & EVENTS

August's two-week **Fêtes de Genève** (www.fetes-de-geneve.ch) ushers in parades, open-air concerts, lakeside merry-go-rounds and fireworks. On 11 December, the **Escalade** celebrates the foiling of an invasion by the Duke of Savoy in 1602 with a costumed parade, the smashing and eating of chocolate cauldrons, and a day of running races around the Old Town.

SLEEPING

When checking-in, ask for your free public transport ticket covering unlimited bus travel for the duration of your hotel stay.

City Hostel (☎ 022 901 15 00; www.cityhostel.ch; Rue de Ferrier 2; dm Sfr32-36, s/d Sfr59-86; reception 7.30am-noon & 1pm-midnight;) Spanking clean is the trademark of this organised hostel, where two-bed dorms give travellers a chance to double up cheaply.

our pick **Hôtel de la Cloche** (☎ 022 732 94 81; www.geneva-hotel.ch/cloche; Rue de la Cloche 6; s with shared bathroom Sfr65-90, with private bathroom Sfr90-120, d with shared bathroom Sfr95-118, with private bathroom Sfr110-148;) Elegant fireplaces, bourgeois furnishings, wooden floors and the odd chandelier add a touch of grandeur to this old-fashioned one-star hotel.

Hôtel Bel'Esperance (☎ 022 818 37 37; www.hotel-bel-esperance.ch; Rue de la Vallée 1; s/d from Sfr98/154; reception 7am-10pm;) This two-star hotel is a two-second flit to the Old Town. Rooms are quiet, cared for and those on the 1st floor share a kitchen.

La Cour des Augustins (☎ 022 322 21 00; www.lacourdesaugustins.com; Rue Jean-Violette 15; s/d from Sfr191/225;) Disguised by a 19th-century facade, the crisp white interior of this 'boutique gallery hotel' sports the latest technology and screams cutting-edge.

Eidelweiss (☎ 022 544 51 51; www.manotel.com; Place de la Navigation 2; d Sfr290-390) Plunge yourself into the heart of the Swiss Alps *en ville* at this Heidi-style hideout, with its big cuddly St Bernard, fireplace and chalet-styled restaurant.

Hôtel Les Armures (☎ 022 310 91 72; www.hotel-les-armures.ch; Rue du Puits-St-Pierre 1; s/d from Sfr395/605;) This slumbering 17th-century beauty oozes history from every last beam. Beautifully placed in the heart of the Old Town, it provides an intimate and refined atmosphere.

EATING

Geneva flaunts ethnic food galore. For the culinarily curious with no fortune to blow, the Pâquis area cooks up cuisine from most corners of the globe in cheap-ish eateries. In the Old Town, terrace cafes and restaurants crowd Geneva's oldest square, medieval Place du Bourg-de-Four. For quintessential Swiss fondue (Sfr32) and yodelling Eidelweiss (above) is *the* address.

Buvette des Bains (☎ 022 738 16 16; www.bains-des-paquis.ch; Quai du Mont-Blanc 30; mains Sfr15; 8am-10pm daily) Meet Genevans at this earthy beach bar at Bains des Pâquis (p499). Dining is on trays and in summer alfresco.

> ### SPLURGE
>
> It's a splurge all right but the water views at **RestO by Arthur's** (☎ 022 818 39 00; La Cité du Temps, 1 Pont de la Machine; mains Sfr35-46; 9am-midnight Mon-Thu, 9am-1am Fri, 11am-1am Sat) are magnificent. The cuisine style is world and every dish comes with its own wine recommendation.

our pick **L'Adresse** (☎ 022 736 32 32; www.ladresse.ch; Rue du 31 Decembre 32; mains Sfr25-35; lunch & dinner Tue-Sat) An urban loft with rooftop terrace and hybrid lifestyle boutique-contemporary bistro, this hip address is at home in converted artist workshops.

Au Grütli (☎ 022 328 98 68; www.cafedugrutli.ch; Rue du Général Dufour 16; mains Sfr28-35; 8am-11pm Mon-Fri, 4-11pm Sat & Sun) Indonesian lamb, moussaka, scallops with ginger and citrus fruits or Provençal chicken are among the international flavours at this razor-sharp theatre restaurant.

Café de Paris (☎ 022 732 84 50; Rue du Mont-Blanc 26; green salad, steak & chips Sfr40; 11am-11pm daily) A memorable dining experience around since 1930. Everyone goes for the same thing here: green salad, beef steak with a killer-calorie herb and butter sauce and as many fries as you can handle.

DRINKING & ENTERTAINMENT

The latest nightclubs, live-music venues and theatre events are well covered in the weekly *Genéve Agenda* (free at the tourist office). Pâquis, the district in between the train station and lake, is particularly well-endowed with bars. In summer the **paillote** (Quai du Mont-Blanc 30; to midnight), with wooden tables inches from the water, gets crammed.

Scandale (☎ 022 731 83 73; www.scandale.ch; Rue de Lausanne 24; 🕑 11am-2am Tue-Fri, 5pm-2am Sat) Retro 1950s furnishings in a cavernous interior with comfy sofas ensures this lounge bar is never empty. Happenings include art exhibitions, Saturday-night DJs and bands.

La Bretelle (☎ 022 732 75 96; Rue des Étuves 17; 🕑 6pm-2am daily) Little has changed since the 1970s, when this legendary bar opened. Live accordion-accompanied French chansons most nights.

La Clémence (☎ 022 312 24 98; www.laclemence.ch; Place du Bourg-de-Four 20; 🕑 7am-1am Mon-Thu & Sun, to 2am Fri & Sat) Indulge in a glass of local wine or an artisanal beer at this venerable cafe-bar located on Geneva's loveliest square.

GREG GAWLOWSKI
Water fountain in the Old Town (p497), Geneva

GETTING THERE & AWAY

Aéroport International de Genève (GVA; ☎ 0900 57 15 00; www.gva.ch), 4km from town, has connections to major European cities and many others worldwide. It is also an easyJet hub.

CGN (Compagnie Générale de Navigation; ☎ 0848 811 848; www.cgn.ch) operates a steamer service from its Jardin Anglais jetty to other villages on Lake Geneva. Many only sail May to September, including those to/from Lausanne (Sfr37.60, 3½ hours). Eurail and Swiss Pass holders are valid on CGN boats or there is a one-day CGN boat pass (Sfr49).

International buses depart from the **bus station** (☎ 0900 320 320, 022 732 02 30; www.coach-station.com; Place Dorcière).

Trains run to most Swiss towns including at least hourly to/from Lausanne (Sfr20.60, 40 minutes), Bern (Sfr46, 1¾ hours) and Zürich (Sfr80, 2¾ hours).

International daily rail connections from Geneva include Paris (Sfr127 by TGV, 3½ hours), Hamburg (Sfr276, 9½ hours), Milan (Sfr97, 4½ hours) and Barcelona (Sfr125, 10 hours).

GETTING AROUND

Getting from the airport is easy with regular trains into Gare de Cornavin (Sfr3, eight minutes). Slower bus 10 (Sfr3) does the same 5km trip. A metered taxi costs Sfr30 to Sfr50.

Pick up a bike at **Genève Roule** (☎ 022 740 13 43; www.geneveroule.ch; Place de Montbrillant 17; 🕑 8am-6pm Mon-Sat) or its seasonal Jetée des Pâquis pick-up point for Sfr12/20 per day/weekend. May to October, borrow a bike carrying publicity for free.

Buses, trams, trains and boats service the city, and ticket dispensers are found at all stops. Tickets cost Sfr2 (within one zone, 30 minutes) or Sfr3 (two zones, one hour) and a city/canton day pass is Sfr7/12. The same tickets are also valid on the yellow shuttle boats known as Les Mouettes (the seagulls) that criss-cross the lake every 10 minutes between 7.30am and 6pm.

LAKE GENEVA REGION

East of Geneva, Western Europe's biggest lake stretches like a giant liquid mirror between French-speaking Switzerland on its northern shore and France to the south. Known as Lake Geneva by many and Lac Léman to Francophones, the Swiss side of the lake cossets the elegant city of Lausanne, pretty palm-tree-studded Riviera resorts such as Vevey and Montreux, and the marvellous emerald spectacle of vines marching up steep hillsides in strict unison.

LAUSANNE

pop 119,200

In a fabulous location overlooking Lake Geneva, Lausanne is an enchanting beauty with several distinct personalities: the former fishing village of Ouchy, with its summer beach-resort feel; Place St-François, with stylish, cobblestone shopping streets; and Flon, a warehouse district of bars, galleries and boutiques. It's also got a few amazing sights. One of the country's grandest Gothic cathedrals dominates its medieval centre.

The **tourist office** (**☎ 021 613 73 21; www.lausanne-tourisme.ch; Place de la Navigation 4; 9am-6pm Oct-Mar, 9am-8pm Apr-Sep**) neighbours Ouchy metro station and has a **branch office** (**Place de la Gare 9; 9am-7pm**) at the train station.

Musée de l'Art Brut (**☎ 021 315 25 70; www.artbrut.ch; Ave des Bergières 11-13; adult/child/student Sfr10/free/5, 1st Sat of month free; 11am-6pm Tue-Sun Sep-Jun, daily Jul & Aug**) is an alluring museum that showcases a fascinating amalgam of 15,000 works of art created by untrained artists – psychiatric patients, eccentrics and incarcerated criminals.

The glorious Gothic **Cathédrale de Notre Dame** (**7am-7pm Mon-Fri, 8am-7pm Sat & Sun Apr-Aug, 7am-5.30pm Sep-Mar**) is arguably the finest cathedral in Switzerland. Built in the 12th and 13th centuries, highlights include the stunningly detailed carved portal, vaulted ceilings and archways, and carefully restored stained-glass windows.

Lausanne is home to the International Olympic Committee, and sports aficionados can immerse themselves in archival footage, interactive computers and memorabilia at the information-packed **Musée Olympique** (**☎ 021 621 65 11; www.museum.olympic.org; Quai d'Ouchy 1; adult/child/student Sfr15/free/10; 9am-6pm daily Apr-Oct, 9am-6pm Tue-Sun Nov-Mar**).

Hotel guests get a Lausanne Transport Card covering unlimited use of public transport for the duration of their stay.

Lausanne GuestHouse (**☎ 021 601 80 00; www.lausanne-guesthouse.ch; Chemin des Épinettes 4; dm Sfr33-38, s/d with shared bathroom Sfr85/95, with private bathroom Sfr94/115;**) An attractive mansion converted into quality backpacking accommodation near the train station. Many rooms have lake views and some of the building's energy is solar.

Hôtel du Port (**☎ 021 612 04 44; www.hotel-du-port.ch; Place du Port 5; s/d Sfr180/230**) A perfect location in Ouchy, just back from the lake, makes this a good choice.

our pick **Café les Alliés** (**☎ 021 648 69 40; www.lesallies.ch; Rue de la Pontaise 48; mains Sfr22-44; lunch & dinner Mon-Fri**) It's not much to look at from the outside, but inside a cosy, warm restaurant with creaky timber floors winds out back towards a pleasant summer garden. Imaginative salads precede mains like *steak de veau poêlé au jus d'abricots* (pan-cooked steak in apricot sauce).

WITOLD SKRYPCZAK

Château de Chillon

Lausanne is one of Switzerland's busier night-time cities. Look for the handy free listings booklet *What's Up* (www.whatsupmag.ch) in bars.

There are trains to/from Geneva (Sfr20.60, 33 to 51 minutes, up to six hourly), Geneva airport (Sfr25, 42 to 58 minutes, up to four hourly) and Bern (Sfr31, 70 minutes, one or two hourly). For boat services see p529.

Buses service most destinations (up to three stops Sfr1.90, one-hour unlimited in central Lausanne Sfr3). The m2 metro line connects Ouchy with the train station and costs the same as the buses.

MONTREUX

pop 23,200

In 1971, Frank Zappa was doing his thing in the Montreux casino when the building caught fire, casting a pall of smoke over Lake Geneva and inspiring the members of Deep Purple to pen their classic rock number 'Smoke on the Water'.

The showpiece of the Swiss Riviera has been an inspiration to writers, artists and musicians for centuries. Famous one-time residents include Lord Byron, Ernest Hemingway and the Shelleys. It's easy to see why: Montreux boasts stunning Alps views, tidy rows of pastel buildings and Switzerland's most extraordinary castle.

Each year crowds throng to the **Montreux Jazz Festival** (**www.montreuxjazz.com**) for a fortnight in early July. Free concerts take place every day, but big-name gigs cost (Sfr40 to Sfr100).

Originally constructed on the shores of Lake Geneva in the 11th century, **Château de Chillon** (**☎ 021 966 89 10; www.chillon.ch; Ave de Chillon 21; adult/child/student Sfr12/6/10; 9am-6pm Apr-Sep, 9.30am-5pm Mar & Oct, 10am-4pm Nov-Feb**) was brought to the world's attention by Lord Byron, and the world has been filing past ever since. Spend at least a couple of hours exploring its myriad courtyards, towers, dungeons and halls filled with arms, period furniture and artwork.

Hôtel La Rouvenaz (**☎ 021 963 27 36; Rue du Marché 1; s/d Sfr130/190;**) A simple, family-run spot with 12 rooms and its own Italian restaurant, you cannot get any closer to the lake or the heart of the action.

ourpick **Hôtel Masson** (☎ **021 966 00 44; www.hotelmasson.ch; Rue Bonivard 5; s/d Sfr180/240)** In 1829, this vintner's mansion was converted into a hotel. Its old charm has remained intact and the hotel, set in magnificent grounds, is on the Swiss Heritage list of most beautiful hotels in the country. Find it in the hills southeast of Montreux.

There are trains to Geneva (Sfr28, 70 minutes, hourly) and Lausanne (Sfr10.20, 25 minutes, three hourly).

VALAIS

Matterhorn country: an intoxicating land that seduces the toughest of critics with its endless panoramic vistas and breathtaking views. Switzerland's 10 highest mountains – all over 4000m – rise to the sky here, while snow fiends ski and board in one of Europe's top resorts, Zermatt. When snows melt and valleys turn lush green, hiking opportunities are boundless.

ZERMATT

pop 5780

Since the mid-19th century, Zermatt has starred among Switzerland's glitziest resorts. Today it attracts intrepid mountaineers and hikers, skiers that cruise at snail's pace, spellbound by the scenery, and style-conscious darlings flashing designer togs in the lounge bars. But all are smitten with the Matterhorn (4478m), the Alps' most famous peak and an unfathomable monolith synonymous with Switzerland that you simply can't quite stop looking at.

The **tourist office** (☎ **027 966 81 00; www.zermatt.ch; Bahnhofplatz 5; ⏲ 8.30am-6pm Mon-Sat, 8.30am-noon & 1.30-6pm Sun mid-Jun–Sep, 8.30am-noon & 1.30-6pm Mon-Sat, 9.30am-noon & 4-6pm Sun rest of year)** has all the bumph.

Views from the cable cars and gondolas are uniformly breathtaking, especially from the cogwheel train to 3090m **Gornergrat** (Sfr38 one way), which takes 35 to 45 minutes with two to three departures per hour. Sit on the right-hand side to gawp at the Matterhorn. Alternatively, hike from Zermatt to Gornergrat in five hours.

The **Alpin Center** (☎ **027 966 24 60; www.alpincenter-zermatt.ch; Bahnhofstrasse 58; ⏲ 8.30am-noon & 3-7pm mid-Nov–Apr & Jul-Sep)** houses the ski school and mountain guides office.

For skiers and snowboarders, Zermatt is cruising heaven, with mostly long, scenic red runs, plus a scattering of blues for ski virgins and knuckle-whitening black runs for experts. The three main skiing areas are **Rothorn**, **Stockhorn** and **Klein Matterhorn** – holding 300km of ski runs in all, with free buses shuttling skiers between areas. Snowboarders make for Klein Matterhorn's freestyle park and half-pipe, while mogul fans enjoy a bumpy glide on Stockhorn.

Klein Matterhorn is topped by Europe's highest cable-car station (3820m), providing access to Europe's highest skiing, Switzerland's most extensive summer skiing (25km of runs) and deep powder at the Italian resort of Cervinia. A day pass covering all ski lifts in Zermatt (excluding Cervinia) costs Sfr67/34/57 per adult/child/student and Sfr75/38/64 including Cervinia.

SLEEPING & EATING

Most places close May to mid-June and again October to mid-November.

Zermatt SYHA Hostel (☎ **027 967 23 20; Staldenweg 5; dm/d with half-board Sfr47.50/100;** 💻) Question: how many hostels have the Matterhorn peeking through the

GLENN VAN DER KNIJFF

Verbier ski fields

IF YOU LIKE...

If you like the skiing at **Zermatt** (p505), we think you might also be interested in:

- **Verbier** (www.verbier.ch) A modern and stylish resort. Here a great variety of easy to challenging slopes combine with a vibrant nightlife to attract the young and the fabulous. Bring your designer duds.
- **Wengen** (www.mywengen.ch) Old-school, chalet-style resort and host to one of the FIS World Cup Alpine ski circuit events.
- **Flims-Laax** (www.flims.com) A mecca for snowboarders and backpackers in the Graubünden region.

window in the morning? Answer: one. And if that doesn't convince you, the modern dorms, sunny terrace and first-rate facilities should.

our pick **Berggasthaus Trift** (☎ 079 408 70 20; dm/d with half-board Sfr63/150; Jul-Sep) It's a trudge to this 2337m-high mountain hut, but the hike is outstanding. The Alpine haven is run by Hugo (a whiz on the alphorn) and Fabienne, who serve treats such as home-cured beef and oven-warm apple tart on the terrace. Get the camera ready for when the sun sets over Monte Rosa.

Whymper Stube (☎ 027 967 22 96; Bahnhofstrasse 80; mains Sfr23-42) The mantra at this Alpine classic serving the tastiest fondue in Zermatt (including variations with pears and gorgonzola): gorge today, climb tomorrow.

DRINKING

Papperla Pub (☎ 027 967 40 40; Steinmattstrasse 34; 11am-11.30pm) Rammed with sloshed skiers, this pub blends pulsating music with lethal Jägermeister bombs and good vibes.

Igloo Bar (Gornergrat; www.iglu-dorf.ch; 10am-4pm) Subzero sippers sunbathe, stare wide-mouthed at the Matterhorn and guzzle *glühwein* amid the ice sculptures at this igloo bar. It's on the run from Gornergrat to Riffelberg.

GETTING THERE & AROUND

Zermatt is car-free. Dinky electric vehicles are used to transport goods and serve as taxis around town. Drivers have to leave their vehicles in one of the garages or the open-air car park in Täsch (Sfr13.50 per day) and take the train (Sfr7.60, 12 minutes) into Zermatt.

Trains depart roughly every 20 minutes from Brig (Sfr35, 1½ hours), stopping at Visp en route. Zermatt is also the starting point of the *Glacier Express* to Graubünden, one of the most spectacular train rides in the world.

BERN

pop 122,400

One of the planet's most underrated capitals, Bern is a fabulous find. With the genteel, old soul of a Renaissance man and the heart of a high-flying 21st century gal, the riverside city is both medieval and modern. The 15th-century Old Town is gorgeous enough to sweep you off your feet and make you forget the century (it's definitely worthy of its 1983 Unesco World Heritage site protection order). But edgy vintage boutiques, artsy-intellectual bars and Renzo Piano's futuristic art museum crammed with Paul Klee pieces slams you firmly back into the present.

INFORMATION

Bern Tourismus (**☎ 031 328 12 12; www.berninfo.com; Bahnhoftplatz; 9am-8.30pm Jun-Sep, 9am-6.30pm Mon-Sat, 10am-5pm Sun Oct-May**) Street-level floor of the train station. City tours, free hotel bookings and internet access (Sfr12 per hour).

BernCard (**per 24/48/72hr Sfr20/31/38**) Discount card providing admission to permanent collections at 27 museums, free public transport and city-tour discounts.

Post office (**Schanzenstrasse 4; 7.30am-9pm Mon-Fri, 8am-4pm Sat, 4-9pm Sun**)

Tourist office (**☎ 031 328 12 12; Bärengraben; 9am-6pm Jun-Sep, 10am-4pm Mar-May & Oct, 11am-4pm Nov-Feb**) Tourist office by the bear pits.

SIGHTS

Bern's flag-bedecked medieval centre is an attraction in its own right, with 6km of covered arcades and cellar shops/bars descending from the streets. After a devastating fire in 1405, the wooden city was rebuilt in today's sandstone.

A focal point is Bern's **Zytglogge** (clock tower) that crowds congregate around to watch its revolving figures twirl at four minutes before the hour, after which the actual chimes begin.

Equally enchanting are the 11 decorative **fountains** (1545) depicting historical and folkloric characters. Most are along Marktgasse as it becomes Kramgasse and Gerechtigkeitsgasse, but the most famous lies in Kornhausplatz: the **Kindlifresserbrunnen** (Ogre Fountain) of a giant snacking…on children.

Inside the 15th-century Gothic **Münster** (**cathedral; audioguide Sfr5, tower admission adult/child Sfr4/2; 10am-5pm Tue-Sat, 11.30am-5pm Sun Easter-Nov, 10am-noon & 2-4pm Tue-Fri, to 5pm Sat, 11.30am-2pm Sun rest of year, tower closes 30 min earlier**), a dizzying hike up the lofty spire – Switzerland's tallest – is worth the 344-step hike.

Bern was founded in 1191 by Berchtold V and named for the unfortunate bear (*bärn* in local dialect) that was his first hunting victim. The bear remains the city's heraldic mascot, hence the **Bärengraben** (**bear pits; www.baerenpark-bern.ch, in German; 9.30am-5pm**) where, to the dismay of some, Pedro has lived his entire life – 28 years. Soon the 3.5m-deep stone pit will

IZZET KERIBAR

Night views along Marktgasse to the Zytglogge

take the shape of a new, spacious, riverside park in which either Pedro (if he makes it) or a new family of bears will live. Don't feed the bears; rather buy a paper cone of fresh fruit (Sfr3) from Walter, his keeper.

The world's most famous scientist developed his theory of relativity in Bern in 1905. Find out more at the **Einstein Haus** (**☎ 031 312 00 91; www.einstein-bern.ch; Kramgasse 49; adult/student Sfr6/4.50; 10am-5pm Mon-Fri, to 4pm Sat Feb-Dec**), in the humble apartment where Einstein lived between 1903 and 1905 while working as a low-paid clerk in the Bern patent office. Multimedia displays now flesh out the story of the subsequent general equation – $E=MC^2$, or energy equals mass times the speed of light squared – which fundamentally changed humankind's understanding of space, time and the universe.

Bern's Guggenheim, the fabulous **Zentrum Paul Klee** (**☎ 031 359 01 01; www.zpk.org; Monument in Fruchtland 3; adult/child Sfr16/6, audioguides Sfr5; 10am-5pm Tue-Sun**) is an eye-catching 150m-long building designed by Renzo Piano on the outskirts of town 3km east. Inside the three-peak structure, the middle 'hill' showcases 4000 rotating works from Paul Klee's prodigious and often playful career. Interactive computer displays built into the seating mean you can get the low-down on all the Swiss-born artist's major pieces, and music audioguides (Sfr5) take visitors on one-hour DIY musical tours of his work.

The 1902 **Bundeshäuser** (**☎ 031 332 85 22; www.parliament.ch; Bundesplatz; admission free; hourly tours 9am-4pm Mon-Sat**), home of the Swiss Federal Assembly, are impressively ornate, with statues of the nation's founding fathers, a stained-glass dome adorned with cantonal emblems and a huge, 214-bulb chandelier. Tours are offered when the parliament is in recess otherwise watch from the public gallery. Bring your passport to get in.

SLEEPING & EATING

The tourist office makes hotel reservation (for free) and has information on 'three nights for the price of two' deals.

Hotel Landhaus (**☎ 031 331 41 66; www.landhausbern.ch; Altenbergstrasse 4; dm from Sfr33 d with shared/private bathroom Sfr120/160;**) Backed by the grassy slope of a city park and fronted by the river and Old-Town spires, this historic hotel oozes character. Its soulful ground-floor restaurant a tad bohemian, draws a staunchly local crowd.

Hotel National (**☎ 031 381 19 88; www.nationalbern.ch, in German; Hirschengraben 24; s/d with shared bathroom from Sfr60/120, with private bathroom Sfr95/140;**) A quaint, charming hotel, the National wouldn't be out of place in Paris, with its wrought-iron lift lavender sprigs and Persian rugs over creaky wooden floors.

Hotel Belle Epoque (**☎ 031 311 43 36 www.belle-epoque.ch; Gerechtigkeitsgasse 18; s/d from Sfr250/350;**) A romantic hotel with art-deco furnishings, standards here are so exacting that modern aberrations are cleverly hidden – dig the TV in the steamer-trunk-style cupboard – so as not to spoil the look.

Bellevue Palace (**☎ 031 320 45 45; www.bellevue-palace.ch; Kochergasse 3-5; s/d from Sfr360/390;**) Bern's power brokers and international statesmen such as Nelson Mandela gravitate towards Bern's only five-star hotel. Near the parliament, it's *the* address to impress.

Altes Tramdepot (**☎ 031 368 14 15; Am Bärengraben; set meals Sfr18-38, mains Sfr16-20; 11am-12.30am, from 10am Sat & Sun**) Even locals recommend this cavernous microbrewery by the bear pits. Swiss specialities

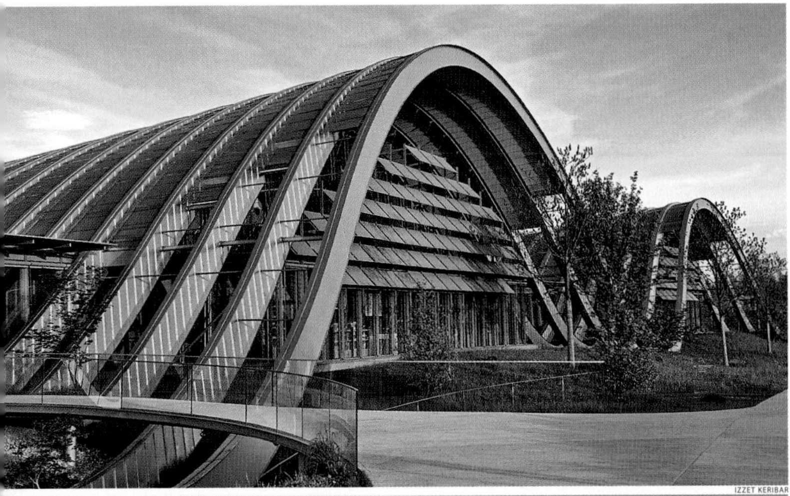
IZZET KERIBAR

Zentrum Paul Klee

nuggle up to wok-cooked stir-fries, pasta nd international dishes on its bistro-tyled menu.

Du Nord (☎ **031 332 23 38; www.du ord-bern.ch; Lorrainestrasse 2; mains Sfr20-35; 8am-11.30pm Mon-Wed, to 12.30am Thu & Fri)** his gay-friendly space with good-value nternational kitchen and bar buzzes with ern's hippest and the occasional gig.

Kornhauskeller (☎ **031 327 72 72; ornhausplatz 18; mains Sfr32-52; lunch & din-er Mon-Sat, dinner Sun, bar 5pm-1am Mon-Wed, o 2am Thu-Sat, to 12.30am Sun)** Dress well nd dine fine beneath vaulted frescoed rches at Bern's former granary, where eautiful people sip cocktails alongside istoric stained-glass on the mezzanine bove.

DRINKING & ENTERTAINMENT

Café des Pyrénées (☎ **031 311 30 63; ornhausplatz 17; Mon-Sat)** With its mix of vine-quaffing trendies and beer-loving tudents, this Bohemian joint feels like a arisian cafe-bar.

Wasserwerk (☎ **031 312 12 31; www.wasser werkclub.ch; Wasserwerkgasse 5; 10pm-late Thu-Sat)** Bern's main techno venue with bar, club and occasional live music.

Klub Elf **(www.klubelf.ch; Ziegelackerstasse 11a; 11pm-late Fri & Sat)** House, techno, trance and minimal do the dance beat at this weekend club, where the real Saturday-night party kicks off after midnight and continues with an 'after' party from 5am on Sunday.

Sous le Pont (☎ **031 306 69 55; www.sousle pont.ch; Neubrückstrasse 8; 11.30am-2.30pm & 6pm-2.30am Tue-Thu, 11.30am-2.30pm & 7pm-2am Fri, 7pm-2.30am Sat)** Delve into the grungy underground scene around the station in the bar of semichaotic alternative-arts centre, Reitschule. Find it in an old stone, graffiti-covered building – an old riding school built in 1897 – by the railway bridge.

SHOPPING

Revel in a lively atmosphere at Bern's open-air **vegetable, fruit & flower markets** **(Bärenplatz, Bundesplatz, Schauplatz**

& Münstergasse; 6am-noon Tue & Sat); and **general market** (**Waisenhausplatz; 8am-6pm Tue, to 4pm Sat Jan-Nov**).

Mooching the Old Town boutiques, many hidden in bunker-style cellars or covered arcades, is delightful. Allow extra time for Gerechtigkeitsgasse, with its art and antique galleries, antiquarian bookshops, small shops specialising in interior design and fashion boutiques.

If truly local souvenirs interest you, grab a Toblerone chocolate – it's made in Bern.

GETTING THERE & AROUND

Bern-Belp airport (**BRN; 031 960 21 21; www.alpar.ch**), 9km southeast of the city centre, is a small airport with direct flights to/from Munich (from where there are onward connections pretty much everywhere) with Lufthansa, and Southampton in the UK with flybe. **Airport shuttles** (**031 971 28 88, 079 651 70 70**) coordinated with flight departures pick up/drop off at the train station (Sfr15, 20 minutes).

Hourly trains connect to most Swiss towns, including Geneva (Sfr46, 1¾ hours), Basel (Sfr37, 70 minutes) and Zürich (Sfr46, one hour).

Walk around – perfectly manageable – or hop on a bus or tram; tickets, available from ticket machines at stops, cost Sfr2 (maximum six stops) or Sfr3.80 for a single journey within zones 1 and 2.

CENTRAL SWITZERLAND & BERNESE OBERLAND

Mark Twain wrote that no opiate compared to walking through this landscape, and he should know. Even when sober, the electric green spruce forests, mountains so big they'll swallow you up, surreal china-blue skies, swirling glaciers and turquoise lakes seem hallucinatory.

LUCERNE

pop 58,400

Recipe for a gorgeous Swiss city: take cobalt lake ringed by mountains of myt add a medieval Old Town and spri kle with covered bridges, sunny plaza candy-coloured houses and waterfro promenades. Lucerne is bright, beautif and has been Little Miss Popular sin the likes of Goethe, Queen Victoria ar Wagner savoured her views in the 19 century. Legend has it that an angel wi a light showed the first settlers where build a chapel in Lucerne, and today it st has amazing grace.

The mostly pedestrian-only Old Town on the northern bank of the Reuss Riv The train station is centrally located c the southern bank; from platform 3 a cess **Luzern Tourism** (**041 227 17 17; ww luzern.com; Zentralstrasse 5; 8.30am-7.30p Mon-Fri, 9am-7.30pm Sat & Sun mid-Jun–mid-Se 8.30am-5.30pm Mon-Fri, 9am-1pm Sat & Sun No Apr, 9am-6.30pm daily rest of year**).

Your first port of call should be th medieval Old Town with ancient rampa walls and towers, 15th-century buil ings with painted facades and the tw much-photographed covered bridge **Kapellbrücke** (Chapel Bridge), datin from 1333, is Lucerne's best-known lan mark. It's famous for its distinctive wat tower and the spectacular 1993 fire th nearly destroyed it. Though it has bee rebuilt, fire damage is still obvious on th 17th-century pictorial panels under th roof. In better condition, but rather da and dour, are the *Dance of Death* pane under the roofline of **Spreuerbrück** (Spreuer Bridge).

Lucerne's blockbuster cultural attra tion is the **Rosengart Collection** (**04 220 16 60; www.rosengart.ch; Pilatusstrasse 1 adult/student Sfr18/16; 10am-6pm Apr-Oc 11am-5pm Nov-Mar**), occupying a gracef eoclassical pile. It showcases the outanding stash of Angela Rosengart, a wiss art dealer and close friend of Picasso. longside works by the great Spanish aster are paintings and sketches by ézanne, Klee, Kandinsky, Miró, Matisse nd Monet. Complementing this collecon are some 200 photographs by David ouglas Duncan of the last 17 years of icasso's life with his family in their home n the French Riviera.

Lucerne's six-day **Fasnacht** celebraon kicks off on 'Dirty Thursday' with e emergence of the character 'Fritschi' om a window in the town hall, when ands of musicians and revellers take to e streets. The carnival moves through ucous celebrations climaxing on Mardi ras (Fat Tuesday), and is over on Ash Vednesday.

June's **Jodler Fest Luzern** is a classic lpine shindig: think 12,000 Swiss yodelers, alphorn players and flag throwers.

Hotel Alpha (☎ 041 240 42 80; www.hotel pha.ch; Zähringerstrasse 24; s/d Sfr70/140; 💻) asy on the eye and wallet, this hotel is in a quiet residential area 10 minutes' walk from the centre. Rooms are simple, light and spotlessly clean.

our pick **Hotel** (☎ 041 226 86 86; www.the-hotel.ch; Sempacherstrasse 14; ste Sfr430-570; ❄ 💻) Streamlined and jet-black, 10 vampy suites reveal stainless-steel fittings, open-plan bathrooms peeking through to garden foliage, and stills from movie classics gracing the ceilings at this Jean Nouvel creation. Downstairs Bam Bou is one of Lucerne's hippest restaurants.

Many places in Lucerne double as bars and restaurants. Places open for breakfast and stay open until late in the evening. Self-caterers should head to Hertensteinstrasse, where cheap eats are plentiful.

Restaurant Schiff (☎ 041 418 52 52; Unter der Egg 8; mains Sfr20-45) Under the waterfront arcades and lit by tealights at night, this restaurant has bags of charm. Try fish from Lake Lucerne and some of the city's most celebrated *chögalipaschtetli* (vol-au-vents stuffed with meat and mushrooms).

IZZET KERIBAR

Kapellbrücke

ROBERTO GEROMETTA

Trümmelbach Falls (p515)

Rathaus Bräuerei (☎ 041 410 52 57; Unter den Egg 2; ⏰ 8am-midnight Mon-Sat, to 11pm Sun) Sip home-brewed beer under the vaulted arches of this buzzy tavern, or nab a pavement table and watch the river flow.

Frequent trains connect Lucerne to Interlaken West (Sfr33.40, two hours, via the scenic Brünig Pass), Bern (Sfr35, 1¼ hours), Geneva (Sfr72, 3¼ hours, via Olten or Langnau) and Zürich (Sfr23, one hour).

INTERLAKEN

pop 5290

Once Interlaken made the Victorians swoon with its dreamy mountain vistas, viewed from the chandelier-lit confines of its grand hotels. Today it makes daredevils scream with its adrenaline-loaded adventures. Though the streets are filled wi enough yodelling kitsch to make Hei cringe, Interlaken still makes a terrif base for exploring the Bernese Oberlan Its adventure capital status has spawne a breed of funky bars and restauran serving flavours more imaginative tha fondue.

ORIENTATION & INFORMATION

Interlaken has two train station Interlaken West and Interlaken Ost; eac has bike rental, money-changing facil ties and a landing stage for boats on Lak Thun and Lake Brienz. The main drag Höheweg, runs between the two station Walk from one to the other in less tha 30 minutes.

Near Interlaken West is the **post offic** (Postplatz; ⏰ 8am-noon & 1.45-6pm Mon-Fri, 8.3 11am Sat) and **tourist office** (☎ 033 826 53 0 www.interlakentourism.ch; Höheweg 37; ⏰ 8an 7pm Mon-Fri, 8am-5pm Sat, 10am-noon & 5-7p Sun Jul–mid-Sep, 8am-noon & 1.30-6pm Mon-Fr 9am-noon Sat rest of year).

ACTIVITIES

Almost every heart-stopping pursuit yo can think of is offered here (althoug the activities take place in the greate Jungfrau Region). You can white-wate raft on the Lütschine, Simme and Saan Rivers, go canyoning in the Saxete Grimsel or Chli Schliere gorges, an canyon-jump at the Gletscherschluch near Grindelwald (see p514). If tha doesn't grab you, there's paragliding glacier bungee jumping, skydiving, ice climbing, hydro-speeding and, phew much more. The latest craze, which yo have to be crazy to try, is zorbing, wher you're strapped into a giant plastic ba and sent spinning down a hill.

Prices are from Sfr90 for rock climbing, Sfr95 for zorbing, Sfr110 for raftin or canyoning, Sfr120 for hydro-speeding, Sfr130 for bungee jumping, Sfr160 for paragliding, Sfr195 for hang-gliding, and Sfr430 for skydiving. Most excursions are without incident, but there's always a small risk and it's wise to ask about safety records and procedures. Major operators able to arrange most sports include the following:

Alpin Center (☎ 033 823 55 23; www.alpincenter.ch; Hauptstrasse 16)

Alpinraft (☎ 033 823 41 00; www.alpinraft.ch; Hauptstrasse 7)

Outdoor Interlaken (☎ 033 826 77 19; www.outdoor-interlaken.ch; Hauptstrasse 15)

Swissraft (☎ 033 821 66 55; www.swissraft-activity.ch; Obere Jungfraustrasse 72)

SLEEPING

our pick **Hotel Rugenpark** (☎ 033 822 36 61; www.rugenpark.ch; Rugenparkstrasse 19; s/d with shared bathroom Sfr65/105, with private bathroom Sfr85/130; closed Nov–mid-Dec;) Chris and Ursula have worked magic to transform this into a sweet B&B. Quiz your knowledgeable hosts for help and local tips.

Post Hardermannli (☎ 033 822 89 19; www.post-hardermannli.ch; s/d Sfr100/155) An affable Swiss-Kiwi couple, Andreas and Kim, run this rustic chalet. The home-grown farm produce at breakfast is a real treat.

Victoria-Jungfrau Grand Hotel & Spa (☎ 033 828 28 28; www.victoria-jungfrau.ch; Höheweg 41; s/d from Sfr560/680, d with Jungfrau views from Sfr780;) The reverent hush and impeccable service evoke an era when only royalty and the seriously wealthy travelled.

EATING

Am Marktplatz is scattered with bakeries and bistros with alfresco seating.

Belvéderè Brasserie (☎ 033 828 91 00; Höheweg 95; mains Sfr18-36) Yes it's attached to the boring-looking Hapimag, but this brasserie has an upbeat modern decor and terrace with Jungfrau views.

Goldener Anker (☎ 033 822 16 72; www.anker.ch, in German; Marktgasse 57; mains Sfr18-38; dinner) This beamed restaurant, locals will whisper in your ear, is the best in town. Globetrotters include everything from sizzling fajitas to red snapper and ostrich steaks. It also has a roster of live bands.

Benacus (☎ 033 821 20 20; www.benacus.ch; Stadthausplatz; mains Sfr20-30; closed Sun, lunch Sat) Supercool Benacus is a breath of urban air with its glass walls, slick wine-red sofas, lounge music and street-facing terrace. The menu stars creative flavours like potato and star anise soup and Aargau chicken with caramelised pak choi.

GETTING THERE & AWAY

The only way south for vehicles without a detour around the mountains is the car-carrying train from Kandersteg, south of Spiez.

Trains to Grindelwald (Sfr10.20, 40 minutes, hourly), Lauterbrunnen (Sfr7, 20 minutes, hourly) and Lucerne (Sfr30, two hours, hourly) depart from Interlaken Ost. Trains to Brig (Sfr41, 1½ hours, hourly) and Montreux via Bern or Visp (Sfr57 to Sfr67, 2¼ hours, hourly) leave from either Interlaken West or Ost.

JUNGFRAU REGION

If the Bernese Oberland is Switzerland's Alpine heart, the Jungfrau Region is where yours will skip a beat. Presided over by glacier-encrusted monoliths Eiger, Mönch and Jungfrau (Ogre, Monk and Virgin), the scenery stirs the soul and strains the neck muscles. A magnet for skiers and snowboarders with its 200km of pistes, a one-day ski pass for Kleine

Scheidegg-Männlichen, Grindelwald-First, or Mürren-Schilthorn costs Sfr59. Come summer, hundreds of kilometres of walking trails allow you to capture the landscape from many angles, but it never looks less than astonishing. The Lauterbrunnen Valley branches out from Interlaken with sheer rock faces and towering mountains on either side. Many visitors choose to visit this valley on a day trip from Interlaken.

GRINDELWALD

pop 3810

Once a simple farming village nestled in a valley under the north face of the Eiger, skiers and hikers cottoned onto Grindelwald's charms in the late 19th century, making it one of Switzerland's oldest and the Jungfrau's largest resorts. And it has lost none of its appeal over the decades, with archetypal Alpine chalets and verdant pastures set against an Oscar-worthy backdrop.

Grindelwald tourist office (**☎ 033 854 12 12; www.grindelwald.ch; Dorfstrasse; 🕒 8am-noon & 1.30-6pm Mon-Fri, 9am-noon & 1.30-5pm Sat & Sun summer & winter, 8am-noon & 1.30-5pm Mon-Fri, 9am-noon Sat rest of year**) is at the Sportzentrum, 200m from the train station.

The shimmering, slowly melting **Oberer Gletscher** (**Upper Glacier; adult/child Sfr6/3; 🕒 9am-6pm mid-May–Oct**) is a 1½-hour hike from the village, or catch a bus (marked Terrasen Weg–Oberer Gletscher) to Hotel-Restaurant Wetterhorn. Walk 10 minutes from the bus stop, then pant up 890 log stairs to reach a terrace offering dramatic vistas. A crowd-puller is the vertiginous hanging bridge spanning the gorge.

The main **skiing** area has runs stretching from **Oberjoch** at 2486m to the village at 1050m. In the summer it caters to **hikers** with 90km of trails above 1200m, 48km of which are open year-round. Catch the longest **cable car** (**☎ 033 854**

ROBERTO GEROMETTA

Views from Schilthorn (p516)

80 80; www.maennlichen.ch) in Europe from Grindelwald-Grund to Männlichen (single/return Sfr31/Sfr51), where there are more extraordinary views and hikes.

SYHA hostel (☎ 033 853 10 09; www.youthhostel.ch/grindelwald; Terrassenweg; dm Sfr31.50-38.50, d with shared bathroom Sfr80, with private bathroom Sfr108; reception 7.30-10am & 4-10pm;) The cosy wooden chalet housing this excellent hostel is perched high on a hill with magnificent views.

Memory (☎ 033 854 31 31; mains Sfr16-28; Dorfstrasse; 11.30am-10.30pm) Always packed, the Eiger Hotel's unpretentious restaurant rolls out tasty Swiss grub such as *rösti* and fondue.

Hourly trains link Grindelwald with Interlaken Ost (Sfr10.20, 40 minutes, hourly).

LAUTERBRUNNEN

pop 2480

Bijou Lauterbrunnen, with its cute main street chock-a-block with quintessential Swiss chalet architecture, is laid-back, down to earth and a hot spot with nature lovers happy to hike and climb. Goethe and Lord Byron penned poems to the ethereal beauty of its wispy **Staubbach Falls** (admission free; 8am-8pm Jun-Oct) – ultra-fine mist from a distance, torrent close up (you'll get wet). But the place is better known for the crash-bang spectacle of its **Trümmelbach Falls** (☎ 033 855 32 32; www.truemmelbach.ch; adult/child Sfr11/4; 9am-5pm Apr-Nov, 8.30am-6pm Jul & Aug). Up to 20,000L of water per second – drained from 24 sq km of Alpine glaciers and snow deposits – corkscrews through ravines and potholes shaped by the swirling waters inside the mountain. The falls are 4km out of town, linked by bus from the train station (Sfr3.40).

Lauterbrunnen's **tourist office** (☎ 033 856 85 68; www.wengen-muerren.ch; 9am-noon & 1-6pm daily May-Sep, 9am-noon & 1-6pm Mon-Fri rest of year) is opposite the train station. Two minutes away is **Valley Hostel** (☎ 033 855 20 08; www.valleyhostel.ch; dm/d Sfr25/70; reception 8am-noon & 3-10pm;), a chilled hostel with open-plan kitchen, garden with waterfall views, free wi-fi and chirpy team who can organise activities.

On the food front, hit **Airtime** (☎ 033 855 15 15; www.airtime.ch; 9am-8pm summer, 9am-noon & 4-8pm winter;), a funky cafe, book exchange, laundry and extreme sports agency inspired by Daniela and Beni's travels in New Zealand.

MÜRREN

pop 440

Arrive on a clear evening when the sun hangs low on the horizon, and you'll think you've died and gone to heaven. Car-free Mürren *is* storybook Switzerland.

In summer, the **Allmendhubel funicular** (single/return Sfr12/7.40) takes you above Mürren to a panoramic restaurant. From here, you can set out on many walks, including the famous **Northface Trail** (1½ hours) via Schiltalp to the west, with spellbinding views of the Lauterbrunnen Valley and monstrous Eiger north face – bring binoculars to spy intrepid climbers. There's also a kid-friendly **Adventure Trail** (one hour).

The **tourist office** (☎ 033 856 86 86; www.wengen-muerren.ch; 8.30am-7pm Mon-Sat, to 8pm Thu, to 6pm Sun high season, to 7pm Mon-Sat, to 5pm Sun shoulder seasons, 8.30am-noon & 1-5pm Mon-Fri low season) is in the sports centre.

Hotel Jungfrau (☎ 033 856 64 64; www.hoteljungfrau.ch; s Sfr88-110, d Sfr270-300;) overlooks the nursery slopes from its perch above Mürren. It dates to 1894 and has a beamed lounge with open fire.

Ten out of 10 to much-lauded chalet, **Hotel Alpenruh** (☎ 033 856 88 00; www.alpenruh-muerren.ch; s/d Sfr145/270; 🖳), for service, food and unbeatable views to Jungfrau massif.

Tham's (☎ 033 856 01 10; mains Sfr15-28; 🕑 dinner) serves Asian dishes cooked by a former five-star chef who's literally taken to the hills to escape.

SCHILTHORN

There's a tremendous 360-degree panorama from the 2970m **Schilthorn** (www.schilthorn.ch). On a clear day, you can see from Titlis to Mont Blanc and across to the German Black Forest. Yet, some visitors seem more preoccupied with practising their delivery of the line, 'The name's Bond, James Bond', than taking in the 200 or so peaks: this is where some scenes from *On Her Majesty's Secret Service* were shot in the 1960s as the fairly tacky **Touristorama** below the **Piz Gloria** revolving restaurant reminds you.

Buy a Sfr116 excursion trip (Half-Fare Card and Eurail Pass 50% off, Swiss Pass 65% off) going to Lauterbrunnen, Grütschalp, Mürren, Schilthorn and returning through Stechelberg to Interlaken. A return from Lauterbrunnen (via Grütschalp) and Mürren costs about Sfr100, as does the return journey via the Stechelberg cable car.

JUNGFRAUJOCH

Sure, the world wants to see Jungfraujoch (3471m) and yes, tickets are expensive, but don't let that stop you. It's a once-in-a-lifetime trip. And there's a reason why two million people a year visit this Holy Grail, Europe's highest train station. The icy wilderness of swirling glaciers and 4000m turrets that unfolds is truly enchanting.

Clear good weather is essential for the trip; check www.jungfrau.ch or call ☎ 033 828 79 31 and don't forget warm clothing, sunglasses and sunscreen. Up top, when you tire (is this possible?) of the view, dash downhill on a snow disc (free), zip across the frozen plateau on a flying fox (Sfr20), enjoy a bit of tame skiing or boarding (Sfr33), drive a team of Greenland dogs, or do your best Tiger-Woods-in-moon-boots impersonation with a round of glacier golf.

From Interlaken Ost, journey time is 2½ hours each way (Sfr177.80 return, Swiss Pass/Eurail Sfr133). However, there's a cheaper 'good morning' ticket of Sfr153.80 (Swiss/Eurail Pass discounts available) if you take the first train (6am from Interlaken Ost) and leave the summit by 12.30pm.

ZÜRICH

pop 350,100

Zürich is the epitome of Swiss efficiency, a savvy finance centre with possibly the densest public transport system in the world. This is a city where Berlin-style grunge jostles for space with swish posh quarters, where fashion fiends feel right at home in its bevy of clubs and lounge bars, where Europe's largest street party lets rip each August. Much of the ancient centre, with its winding lanes and tall church steeples, remains lovingly intact, while urban renovation has transformed the industrial wasteland of Züri-West into a happening space where everyone wants to be.

Zürich is at the northern end of Lake Zürich (Zürichsee), with the city centre split by the Limmat River. Like most Swiss cities it is compact and easy to navigate. The main train station (Hauptbahnhof) is

WITOLD SKRYPCZAK

Street sculpture on Bahnhofstrasse

on the western bank of the river, close to the old centre.

INFORMATION

Police station (☎ 044 216 71 11; Bahnhofquai 3)

Post office (train station; 🕑 7am-9pm daily)

University Hospital (☎ 044 255 11 11, 044 255 21 11; www.usz.ch; Rämistrasse 100) Casualty medical service.

Zürich Tourism (☎ 044 215 40 00, hotel reservations ☎ 044 215 40 40; www.zuerich.com; train station; 🕑 8am-8.30pm Mon-Sat, 8.30am-6.30pm Sun May-Oct; 8.30am-7pm Mon-Sat, 9am-6.30pm Sun Nov-Apr)

ZürichCard (per 24/72hr Sfr17/24) Discount card available from the tourist office and airport train station; provides free public transport, free museum admission and more.

SIGHTS

Explore the cobbled streets of the pedestrian **Old Town** lining both sides of the river.

The bank vaults beneath **Bahnhofstrasse**, the city's most elegant street, are said to be crammed with gold and silver. Indulge in affluent Züricher-watching and ogle at the luxury shops selling watches, clocks, chocolates, furs, porcelain and fashion labels galore.

On Sundays it seems all of Zürich strolls around the lake. Do the same.

Standing on the west bank of the Limmat River, the 13th-century **Fraumünster** (cathedral; www.fraumuenster.ch; Münsterplatz; 🕑 9am-6pm May-Sep, 10am-5pm Oct-Apr) is Zürich's most noteworthy attraction, with some of the most distinctive and attractive stained-glass windows in the world.

Across the river is the dual-towered **Grossmünster** (Grossmünsterplatz; www.grossmuenster.ch; 🕑 9am-6pm daily mid-Mar–Oct, 10am-5pm Nov–mid-Mar, tower closed Sun morning mid-Mar–Oct & all Sun Nov–mid-Mar). This was where, in the 16th century, the Protestant preacher Huldrych Zwingli first spread his message of 'pray and work' during the Reformation – a seminal period in

ZÜRICH

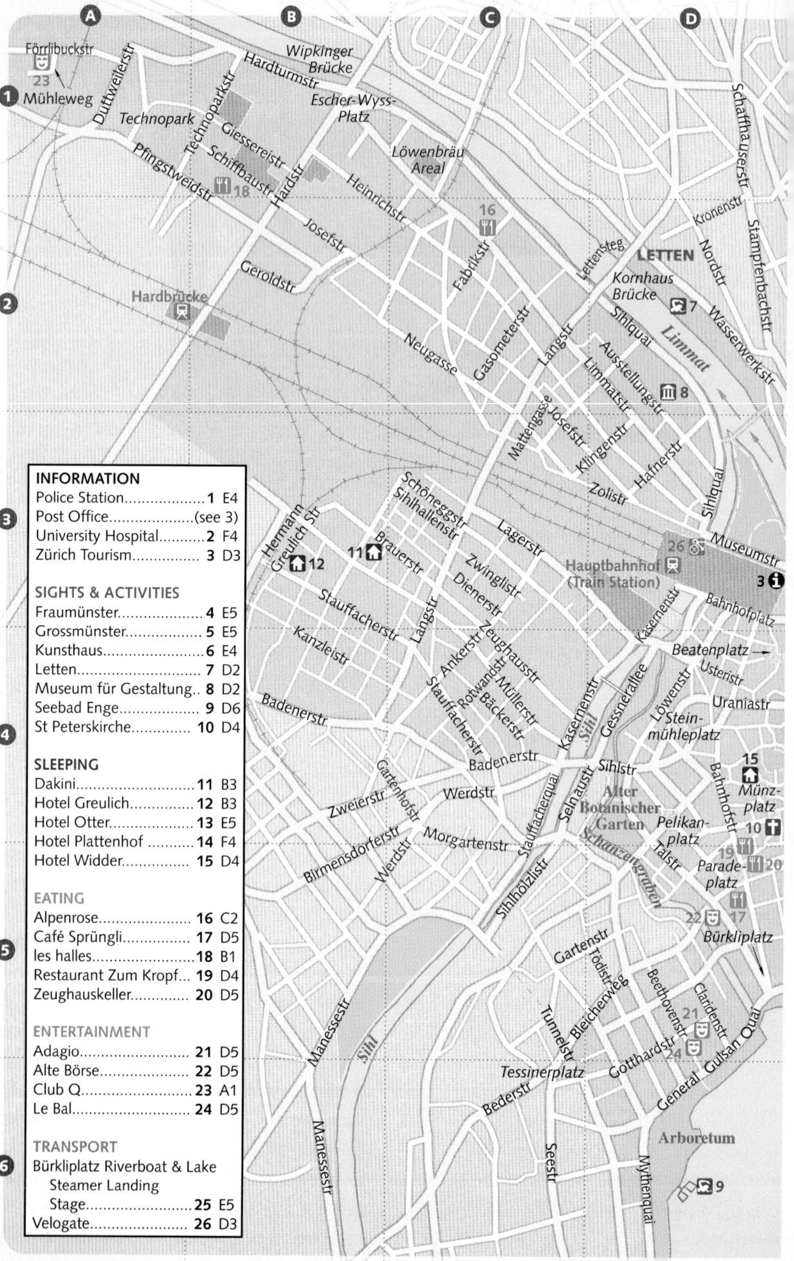

INFORMATION
Police Station ... 1 E4
Post Office ... (see 3)
University Hospital ... 2 F4
Zürich Tourism ... 3 D3

SIGHTS & ACTIVITIES
Fraumünster ... 4 E5
Grossmünster ... 5 E5
Kunsthaus ... 6 E4
Letten ... 7 D2
Museum für Gestaltung ... 8 D2
Seebad Enge ... 9 D6
St Peterskirche ... 10 D4

SLEEPING
Dakini ... 11 B3
Hotel Greulich ... 12 B3
Hotel Otter ... 13 E5
Hotel Plattenhof ... 14 F4
Hotel Widder ... 15 D4

EATING
Alpenrose ... 16 C2
Café Sprüngli ... 17 D5
les halles ... 18 B1
Restaurant Zum Kropf ... 19 D4
Zeughauskeller ... 20 D5

ENTERTAINMENT
Adagio ... 21 D5
Alte Börse ... 22 D5
Club Q ... 23 A1
Le Bal ... 24 D5

TRANSPORT
Bürkliplatz Riverboat & Lake Steamer Landing Stage ... 25 E5
Velogate ... 26 D3

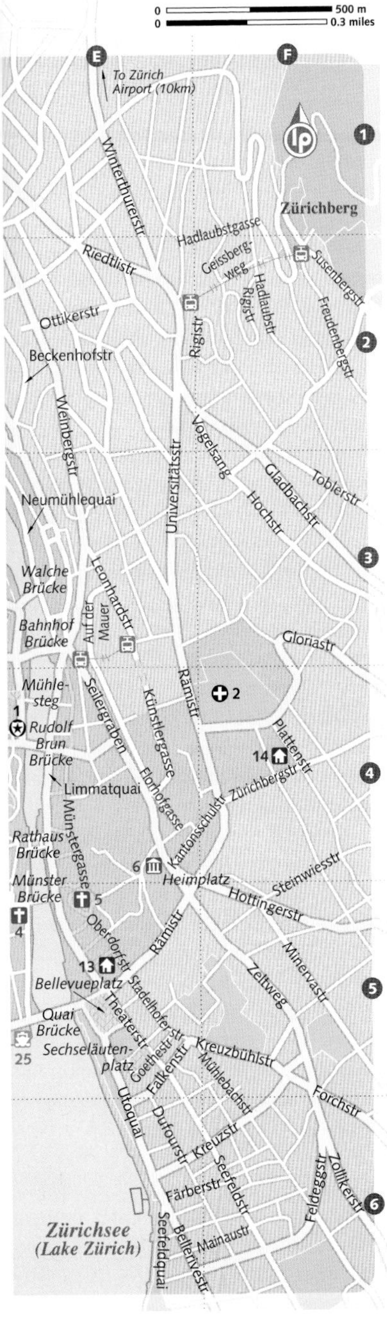

Zürich's history. The figure glowering from the south tower of the cathedral is Charlemagne, who founded the original church at this location.

From any position in the city, it's impossible to overlook the 13th-century tower of **St Peterskirche** (**St Peter's Church; St Peterhofstatt; 8am-6pm Mon-Fri, 8am-4pm Sat, 11am-5pm Sun**). Its prominent clock face, 8.7m in diameter, is Europe's largest.

KUNSTHAUS

Zürich's impressive **Fine Arts Museum** (**044 253 84 84; www.kunsthaus.ch; Heimplatz 1; adult/child/student Sfr18/free/8, Sun free; 10am-8pm Wed-Fri, to 6pm Tue, Sat & Sun**) boasts a rich collection of Alberto Giacometti stick-figure sculptures, Monets, Van Goghs, Rodin sculptures and other 19th- and 20th-century art. Swiss artist Ferdinand Hodler is also represented.

MUSEUM FÜR GESTALTUNG

The exhibitions at this **Design Museum** (**043 446 67 67; www.museum-gestaltung.ch; Ausstellungstrasse 60; adult/student Sfr9/6; 10am-8pm Tue-Thu, to 5pm Fri-Sun**) are consistently impressive and wide-ranging – anything from Bollywood to photographic short stories.

ACTIVITIES

Zürich comes into its own in summer, when its green lakeshore parks are abuzz with bathers, sun-seekers, in-line skaters, footballers, lovers, picnickers, party animals, preeners and police patrolling on rollerblades! From May to mid-September, **outdoor swimming areas** (**admission Sfr6; 9am-7pm May & Sep, to 8pm Jun-Aug**) – think a rectangular wooden pier partly covered by a pavilion – open around the lake and up the Limmat River. Many offer massages, yoga and saunas, as well as snacks. Our favourites are trendy **Seebad Enge** (**044 201 38 89; www.seebadenge.ch; Mythenquai 95**),

GLENN VAN DER KNIJFF

Flower beds by Lake Zürich (p516)

where the bar opens until midnight in fine weather; and **Letten** (☎ 044 362 92 00; Lettensteg 10; admission free) where hip Züri-Westers swim, barbecue, skateboard, play volleyball or just drink and hang on the grass and concrete.

FESTIVALS & EVENTS

Zürich celebrates spring with **Sechseläuten** (www.sechselaeuten.ch), which sees guild members in historical costume parade down the streets on the third Monday in April, climaxing with the burning of a fireworks-filled 'snowman' (Böögg) to mark winter's end.

August's **Street Parade** (www.street-parade.ch) is Europe's largest street party in any given year, attracting well over half a million ravers.

SLEEPING

Dakini (☎ 044 291 42 20; www.dakini.ch; Brauerstrasse 87; s/d Sfr75/130; 💻) This relaxed B&B attracts a bohemian crowd of artists and performers, academics and trendy tourists who don't bat an eyelid at its location near the red-light district. Take tram 8 to Bäckeranlange.

Hotel Otter (☎ 044 251 22 07; www.wueste.ch; Oberdorfstrasse 7; s/d from Sfr115/150) A true gem, the Otter has 17 rooms variously decorated with pink satin sheets and plastic beads, raised beds, wall murals and in one instance a hammock. A popular bar, the Wüste, is downstairs.

Hotel Greulich (☎ 043 243 42 43; www.greulich.ch; Hermann Greulich Strasse 56; s/d from Sfr190/255) The curving blue-grey walls lend these designer digs in a quieter part of Kreis 4 a retro art-deco touch. Minimalist, off-white rooms are laid out in facing bungalows along two sides of an austere courtyard.

Hotel Plattenhof (☎ 044 251 19 10; www.plattenhof.ch; Plattenstrasse 26; s/d from Sfr205/245) This place manages to be cool without looking pretentious. It features a youthful, vaguely Japanese style, with low beds and mood lighting in its newest rooms. Take tram 6 to Platte.

Hotel Widder (☎ 044 224 25 26; www.widderhotel.ch; Rennweg 7; s/d from Sfr523/725; ❄ 💻) A stylish hotel in the equally grand Augustiner district, the Widder is a pleasing fusion of modernity and traditional charm. Rooms and public areas across the eight town houses that make up this place are stuffed with art and designer furniture.

EATING

Zürich has a thriving cafe culture and hundreds of restaurants – explore Niederdorfstrasse and its nearby backstreets.

Zeughauskeller (☎ 044 211 26 90; www.zeughauskeller.ch; Bahnhofstrasse 28a; mains Sfr17.50-33.50; 11.30am-11pm) The menu at this huge, atmospheric beer hall offers 20 different kinds of sausages in eight languages, as well as numerous other Swiss specialities of both a carnivorous and vegetarian variety.

Restaurant Zum Kropf (☎ 044 221 18 05; www.zumkropf.ch; In Gassen 16; mains Sfr21.50-45.50; 11.30am-11.30pm Mon-Sat) Notable for its historic interior, with marble columns, stained glass and ceiling murals, Kropf has been favoured by locals since 1888 for its hearty Swiss staples and fine beers.

les halles (☎ 044 273 11 25; www.les-halles.ch; Pfingstweidstrasse 6; mains Sfr22-29; 11am-midnight Mon-Wed, to 1am Thu-Sat) One of several chirpy bar-restaurants in revamped factory buildings, this is the best place in town to tuck into *moules mit frites* (mussels and fries). Hang at the bustling bar and shop at the market.

our pick **Alpenrose** (☎ 044 271 39 19; Fabrikstrasse 12; mains Sfr 24-42; Mon-Sat) With its timber-clad walls, No Polka-dancing warning and fine cuisine from regions all over Switzerland, this place makes for an inspired meal out. Try risotto from Ticino, *pizokel* (a kind of long and especially savoury *spätzli*, or dumpling) from Graubünden or freshly fished local perch fillets.

Café Sprüngli (☎ 044 224 47 31; www.spruengli.ch; Bahnhofstrasse 21; 7am-6.30pm Mon-Fri, 8am-6pm Sat, 9.30am-5.30pm Sun) Indulge in cakes, chocolate and coffee at this epicentre of sweet Switzerland, in business since 1836.

DRINKING

Buzzing drinking options congregate in the happening Kreis 4 and Kreis 5 districts, together known as Züri-West. Langstrasse, directly behind the station, is a minor red-light district – safe to wander though you may be offered drugs or sex – with loads of popular bars quietly humming off its side streets. Mid-May to mid-September, Wednesday to Sunday, the trendy water bars at the **lake baths** (see p519) are hot places to hang bare-footed.

Clubbers dress well and be prepared to cough up Sfr15 to Sfr30 admission.

our pick **Club Q** (☎ 044 444 40 50; www.club-q.ch; Förrlibückstrasse 151; admission up to Sfr30; 11pm-7am Fri, 11pm-8am Sat, 10pm-4am Sun) In a car park, Club Q is for serious dancers only, be it house, hip-hop or R&B.

Alte Börse (www.alteboerse.com; Bleicherweg 5; 10pm-late Thu-Sat) In a respectable town-centre building, hundreds of dance fanatics cram in to this recently opened club for intense electronic sessions with DJs from all over the world.

Two adjacent clubs for a well-dressed over-25s crowd lie just back from the northwest end of the lake: **Adagio** (☎ 044 206 36 66; www.adagio.ch; Gotthardstrasse 5; 9pm-2am Tue-Wed, to late Thu, to 4am Fri & Sat) seems like a scene from a medieval thriller with its vaulted and frescoed ceiling, while neighbouring **Le Bal** (☎ 044 206 36 66; www.lebal.ch; Beethovenstrasse 8; 9pm-2am Tue-Wed, to late Thu-Sat) swings between Latin and house.

GETTING THERE & AWAY

Zürich airport (ZRH; ☎ 043 816 22 11; www.zurich-airport.com), 10km north of the centre, is a small international hub with two terminals.

Direct daily trains run to Stuttgart (Sfr76, three hours), Munich (Sfr104, 4½ hours) and Innsbruck (Sfr79, four hours) and many other international destinations. There are regular direct departures to most major Swiss towns, such as

Lucerne (Sfr23, 46 to 50 minutes) and Bern (Sfr46, 57 minutes).

GETTING AROUND

Up to nine trains an hour yo-yo between the airport and main train station between 6am and midnight (Sfr6, nine to 14 minutes).

There is a comprehensive, unified bus, tram and S-Bahn service in the city, which includes boats plying the Limmat River. Short trips under five stops are Sfr2.40. A 24-hour pass for the centre is Sfr7.80. For unlimited travel within the canton, including extended tours of the lake, a day pass costs Sfr30.40.

April to October **lake steamers** (☎ 044 487 13 33; www.zsg.ch) depart from Bürkliplatz.

City bikes (www.zuerirollt.ch) can be picked up at **Velogate** (train station; 🕑 8am-9.30pm) for free if you bring the bike back after six hours or pay Sfr5 per day.

GRAUBÜNDEN

Don't be fooled by Graubünden's diminutive size on a map. This is topographic origami at its finest. Unfold the rippled landscape to find an outdoor adventurer's paradise riddled with more than 11,000km of walking trails, 600-plus lakes and 1500km of downhill ski slopes. Linguistically wired to flick from Italian to German to Romansch, locals keep you guessing, too.

ST MORITZ

pop 5060

Switzerland's original winter wonderland and the cradle of Alpine tourism, St Moritz (San Murezzan in Romansch) has been luring royals, the filthy rich and moneyed wannabes since 1864. With its smugly perfect lake and aloof mountains, the town looks a million dollars. Yet despite the Gucci set propping up the bars and celebs bashing the pistes (Kate Moss and George Clooney included), this resort isn't all show. The real riches lie outdoors with superb carving on Corviglia, hairy black runs on Diavolezza and miles of hiking trails when the powder melts.

Hilly St Moritz Dorf is above the train station, with luxury hotels, restaurants and shops. To the southwest, 2km around the lake is the more downmarket St Moritz Bad; buses run between the two. St Moritz is seasonal and becomes a ghost town during November and from late April to early June.

The **tourist office** (☎ 081 837 33 33; www.stmoritz.ch; Via Maistra 12; 🕑 9am-6.30pm Mon-Fri, 9am-noon & 1.30-6pm Sat, 4-6pm Sun Dec-Easter & mid-Jun–mid-Sep, 9am-noon & 2-6pm Mon-Fri, 9am-noon Sat rest of the year) has all the usual traveller info.

Skiers and snowboarders will revel in the 350km of runs in three key areas. For groomed slopes with big mountain vistas, head to **Corviglia** (2486m), accessible by funicular from Dorf. From Bad a cable car goes to Signal (shorter queues), giving access to the slopes of **Piz Nair**. A ski pass for both areas costs Sfr67 (child/youth Sfr23/45) for one day. Silhouetted by glaciated 4000ers, **Diavolezza** (2978m) is a must-ski for free-riders and fans of jaw-dropping descents.

See www.skiengadin.ch for the complete skiing low-down.

You can hike or try your hand at golf (including on the frozen lake in winter), tennis, in-line skating, fishing, horse riding, sailing, windsurfing and river rafting, to mention just a few.

Chesa Chantarella (☎ 081 833 33 55; www.chesachantarella.ch; Via Salastrains; s/d Sfr95/190; 🕑 Jun-Sep & Dec-Apr) Sitting above the town, this is a lively choice with bright, modern

CHRIS MELLOR

Gruyères

IF YOU LIKE...

If you like getting off the beaten path, head for the small towns and villages in the **Fribourg, Neuchâtel** and **Jura** cantons of western Switzerland. From the evocative medieval cantonal capitals to the mysterious green hills and deep dark forests, travel here is discovery. Highlights include:

- **Neuchâtel** (**Tourist office; ☎ 032 889 68 90; www.neuchateltourism.ch; Hôtel des Postes, Pl du Port; 9am-noon & 1.30-5.30pm Mon-Fri, 9am-noon Sat**) The old-town sandstone elegance, airy Gallic nonchalance of cafe life and the vibrant lakeside air makes this small university town charming.
- **Valley train ride** Swilling the modern version of the green fairy (aka absinthe), which was first distilled in this region, is particularly evocative at the bar aboard an old steam train. Jump aboard in Neuchâtel with **Vapeur Val de Travers** (**☎ 032 863 24 07; www.rvt-historique.ch; Rue de la Gare 19, Travers; day trips with lunch Sfr75**).
- **Val de Travers** Hikers come to this valley to marvel at the enormous Creux du Van abyss reached on foot from Noiraigue, 22km southwest of Neuchâtel.
- **Gruyères** Cheese and featherweight meringues drowned in thick cream is what this village, so dreamy even Sleeping Beauty wouldn't wake up, is all about. The beans about its hard AOC-protected cheese, made for centuries in its surrounding Alpine pastures, are spilled at the **Maison du Gruyère** (**☎ 026 921 84 00; www.lamaisondugruyere.ch; adult/child under 12yr Sfr7/3; 9am-7pm Apr-Sep, 9am-6pm Oct-Mar**) in Pringy, 1.5km away.
- **St Ursanne, the Jura** (**Tourist office; ☎ 032 420 47 73; Place Roger Schaffter; 10am-noon & 2-5pm Mon-Fri, 10am-4pm Sat & Sun**) Deep, mysterious forests and impossibly green clearings succeed one another along the 1200km of paths in the low mountains of the Jura. You'll find heaps of information on walking in St Ursanne, a drop-dead-gorgeous medieval village.

rooms. Sip hot chocolate on the terrace, venture down to the wine cellar or dine on hearty local fare in the restaurant.

Hotel Waldhaus am See (☎ 081 836 60 00; www.waldhaus-am-see.ch; s/d Sfr170/320; 🖳) Overlooking the lake, this friendly pad has light-flooded rooms with pine furnishings and floral fabrics, many with enticing lake and mountain views. There's a sauna and a restaurant serving appetising grill specialities.

our pick **Hatecke** (☎ 081 864 11 75; www.hatecke.ch; snacks & mains Sfr15-25; ⏲ 9am-6.30pm Mon-Fri, to 6pm Sat) Edible art is the only way to describe the organic, locally sourced delicacies at Hatecke. Sit on a sheepskin stool in the funky cafe next door to lunch on delicious Engadine beef carpaccio or *Bündnerfleisch* with truffle oil.

Engiadina (☎ 081 833 32 65; Plazza da Scuola 2; fondue Sfr29-46; ⏲ Mon-Sat) A proper locals' place, Engiadina is famous for fondue, and that's the best thing to eat here. Champagne gives the melted cheese a kick. It's open year-round.

Around 20 bars and clubs pulsate in winter. While you shuffle to the beat, your wallet might also waltz itself wafer-thin, because nights out in St Moritz can be nasty on the banknotes.

The **Glacier Express** (www.glacierexpress.ch) plies one of Switzerland's most famous scenic train routes, connecting St Moritz to Zermatt (Sfr138 plus Sfr15 or Sfr30 reservation fee in summer, 7½ hours, daily) via the 2033m Oberalp Pass. It covers 290km and crosses 291 bridges. Novelty drink glasses in the dining car have sloping bases to compensate for the hills – remember to keep turning them around!

The *Palm Express* postal bus runs to Lugano (Sfr69 or Sfr20 with Swiss Travel pass, four hours, daily summer; Friday, Saturday and Sunday winter); advance reservations (☎ 058 386 31 66) are obligatory.

SWISS NATIONAL PARK

The road west from Müstair stretches 34km over the Ofenpass (Pass dal Fuorn, 2149m), through the thick woods of Switzerland's only **national park** (www.nationalpark.ch; ⏲ Jun-Oct) and on to **Zernez** and the brand-new, hands-on **Swiss National Park Centre** (☎ 081 851 41 41; www.nationalpark.ch; adult/child Sfr7/3; ⏲ 8.30am-6pm Jun-Oct, 9am-noon & 2-5pm Nov-May), where you can explore a marmot hole, eyeball adders in the vivarium and learn about conservation and environmental change.

The national park was established in 1914 – the first such park in Europe – and spans 172 sq km. 'Nature gone wild' pretty much sums it up: think dolomite peaks, shimmering glaciers, larch woodlands, gentian-flecked pastures, clear waterfalls, and high moors strung with topaz lakes. Zernez **tourist office** (☎ 081 856 13 00; Chasa Fuchina) has hike details, including the three-hour tramp from S-chanf to Trupchun (popular in autumn when you might spy rutting deer) and the Naturlehrpfad circuit near **Il Fuorn**, where bearded vultures can be sighted.

Trains run regularly from Zernez to St Moritz (Sfr17.40, 50 minutes).

DIRECTORY

ACTIVITIES

HIKING & MOUNTAINEERING

The rugged alpine scenery and fairytale forests in Germany, Austria and Switzerland are ideal for hiking and mountaineering. There are well-marked trails criss-crossing the countryside, especially in popular areas such as the Black

Forest and the Bavarian Alps in Germany. Good sources of information on hiking and mountaineering are **Verband Deutscher Gebirgs-und Wandervereine** (Federation of German Hiking Clubs; ☎ 0561-938 730; www.wanderverband.de); and **Deutscher Alpenverein** (German Alpine Club; ☎ 089-140 030; www.alpenverein.de).

In Austria options include a central route from Feldkirch to Hainburger Pforte, via Hohe Tauern National Park. Don't try mountaineering without having the proper equipment or experience. The **Österreichischer Alpenverein** (ÖAV, Austrian Alpine Club; ☎ 0512-59 547; www.alpenverein-ibk.at, in German; Wilhelm Greil Strasse 15, A-6010 Innsbruck) has touring programs and also maintains a list of alpine huts in hill-walking regions.

And there is simply no better way to enjoy Switzerland's spectacular scenery than to walk through it. There are 50,000km of designated paths, often with a convenient inn or cafe located en route. The **Schweizer Alpen-Club** (SAC; ☎ 031 370 1818; www.sac-cas.ch, in German; Monbijoustrasse 61, Bern) maintains huts for overnight stays at altitude and can also help with extra information.

SKIING & SNOWBOARDING

The Bavarian Alps are the most extensive area in Germany for winter sports. Cross-country skiing is also good in the Black Forest.

Austria's most popular ski region is Tirol, but Salzburg province offers cheaper possibilities. Unusually, skiing is possible year-round at the famous Stubai Glacier near Innsbruck.

There are dozens of ski resorts throughout the Alps, pre-Alps and Jura, and 200-odd different ski schools. Equipment hire is available at resorts and ski passes allow unlimited use of mountain transport.

DANGERS & ANNOYANCES

Although the usual cautions should be taken, theft and other crimes against travellers are relatively rare in these Alpine nations. Africans, Asians and southern Europeans may encounter racial prejudice. However, the animosity is usually directed against immigrants, not tourists.

EMBASSIES & CONSULATES

GERMANY

The following embassies are all in Berlin.

Australia (Map pp438-9; ☎ 030-880 0880; www.australian-embassy.de; Wallstrasse 76-79)
Canada (Map pp438-9; ☎ 030-203 120; www.kanada-info.de; Leipziger Platz 17)
France (Map pp438-9; ☎ 030-590 039 000; www.botschaft-frankreich.de; Pariser Platz 5)
Ireland (Map pp438-9; ☎ 030-220 720; www.botschaft-irland.de; Friedrichstrasse 200)
Netherlands (Map pp438-9; ☎ 030-209 560; www.dutchembassy.de; Klosterstrasse 50)
New Zealand (Map pp438-9; ☎ 030-206 210; www.nzembassy.com; Friedrichstrasse 60)
UK (Map pp438-9; ☎ 030-204 570; www.britischebotschaft.de; Wilhelmstrasse 70)
USA (Map pp438-9; ☎ 030-238 5174; www.us-botschaft.de; Pariser Platz 2)

AUSTRIA

The following diplomatic missions are located in Vienna unless otherwise stated:

Australia (Map pp474-5; ☎ 01-506 740; www.australian-embassy.at; 04, Mattiellistrasse 2-4)
Canada (Map pp474-5; ☎ 01-53 138-3000; www.kanada.at; 01, Laurenzerberg 2)
France (Map pp474-5; ☎ 01-50 275-0; www.ambafrance-at.org; 04, Technikerstrasse 2)
Germany (Map pp474-5; ☎ 01-71 154-0; www.wien.diplo.de; 03, Metternichgasse 3)
Ireland (Map pp474-5; ☎ 01-715 42 46-0; 01, Rotenturmstrasse16-18)

Netherlands (Map pp474-5; ☎ 01-58 939; www.mfa.nl/wen; 01, Opernring 5)
New Zealand (Map pp438-9; ☎ 49-30-206 210; www.nzembassy.com; Friedrichstrasse 60, D-10117 Berlin, Germany) Berlin has the nearest New Zealand embassy.
UK (Map pp474-5; ☎ 01-71 613-0; www.britishembassy.at; 03, Jauresgasse 12)
USA Embassy (Map pp474-5; ☎ 01-31 339-0; www.usembassy.at; 09, Boltzmanngasse 16); Consulate (Map pp474-5; ☎ 512 58 35; 01, Parkring 12a) Visas at the consulate only.

SWITZERLAND

For a comprehensive list, see www.eda.admin.ch. Embassies are in Bern unless otherwise noted:
Australia (off Map p498; ☎ 022 799 91 00; www.australia.ch; Chemin des Fins 2, Geneva)
Austria (☎ 031 356 52 52; www.aussenministerium.at/bern, in German; Kirchenfeldstrasse 77-79)
Canada (☎ 031 357 32 00; www.canada-ambassade.ch; Kirchenfeldstrasse 88)
France (☎ 031 359 21 11; www.ambafrance-ch.org, in German & French; Schosshaldenstrasse 46)
Germany (☎ 031-359 41 11; www.bern.diplo.de, in German & French; Willadingweg 83)
New Zealand (off Map p498; ☎ 022 929 03 50; Chemin des Fins 2, Grand-Saconnex, Geneva)
UK (☎ 031 359 77 00; http://ukinswitzerland.fco.gov.uk/en; Thunstrasse 50)
USA (☎ 031 357 70 11; http://bern.usembassy.gov; Sulgeneckstrasse 19)

FESTIVALS & EVENTS

Check the national tourist board websites for more event listings: www.austria.info, www.cometogermany.com and www.switzerland.com.

JANUARY & FEBRUARY

Karneval/Fasching (Carnival) The pre-Lent season is celebrated with colourful parades, costumed street partying, and general revelry in the Black Forest and Munich.

MARCH

Combats de Reines March to October, the lower Valais, Switzerland stages traditional cow fights known as the Combats de Reines.

MAY

Vienna Festival (www.festwochen.or.at) The Wiener Festwochen focuses on classical music, theatre and other performing arts in Vienna.

JUNE

Christopher Street Day (www.csd-germany.de) Major gay celebration with wild street parades and raucous partying, especially in Berlin and Hamburg but also in Dresden, Munich, Stuttgart and Frankfurt.

JULY & AUGUST

Love Parade (www.loveparade.net) No longer techno only, but all types of electronic music at the world's largest rave in mid-July; Berlin.
Salzburg Festival (www.salzburgfestival.at) Austria's leading classical-music festival attracts major stars, like Simon Rattle and Placido Domingo to Salzburg.
Montreux Jazz Festival Big-name rock/jazz acts hit town for this famous festival (www.montreuxjazz.com) held during the first two weeks of July.
Street Parade (www.streetparade.ch) Zürich lets its hair down in the second week of August with an enormous techno parade with 30 love mobiles and more than half a million excited ravers.

SEPTEMBER & OCTOBER

Oktoberfest (www.oktoberfest.de) Legendary beer-swilling party, enough said. Actually starts in mid-September; Munich.

Frankfurt Book Fair (Frankfurter Buchmesse; www.buchmesse.de) October sees the world's largest book fair, with 1800 exhibitors from 100 countries.

DECEMBER

Christmas Markets Quaint stalls selling traditional decorations, foodstuffs, mulled wine and all manner of presents heralding the arrival of the festive season in cities across all three countries.

HOLIDAYS

GERMANY

Neujahrstag (New Year's Day) 1 January

Ostern (Easter) March/April – Good Friday, Easter Sunday and Easter Monday

Christi Himmelfahrt (Ascension Day) Forty days after Easter.

Maifeiertag/Tag der Arbeit (Labour Day) 1 May

Pfingsten (Whit/Pentecost Sunday and Monday) May/June; 50 days after Easter.

Tag der Deutschen Einheit (Day of German Unity) 3 October

Weihnachtstag (Christmas Day) 25 December

Zweite Weihnachtstag (Boxing Day) 26 December

AUSTRIA

New Year's Day 1 January

Epiphany 6 January

Easter Monday March/April

May Day 1 May

Ascension Five and a half weeks after Easter

Whit Monday Seven weeks after Easter

Corpus Christi Ten days after Whit Monday

Assumption of the Virgin Mary 15 August

National Day 26 October

All Saints' Day 1 November

Immaculate Conception 8 December

Christmas Day 25 December

St Stephen's Day 26 December

SWITZERLAND

New Year's Day 1 January

Easter March/April; Good Friday, Easter Sunday and Easter Monday

Ascension Day 40th day after Easter

Whit Sunday and Monday Seventh week after Easter

National Day 1 August

Christmas Day 25 December

St Stephen's Day 26 December

TELEPHONE

German phone numbers consist of an area code followed by the local number, which can be between three and nine digits long. In Austria, don't worry if a telephone number you are given has only four digits, as many as nine digits, or some odd number in between. Area codes do not exist in Switzerland; numbers must always be dialled in full, including city prefixes, even when calling from next door – literally.

MOBILE PHONES

Mobile phones ('Handys') are ubiquitous in all three nations. You can pick up a prepay SIM card at major providers' stores from €30; top-up cards are available from kiosks and various shops.

PAY PHONES

Most pay phones in Germany, administered by Deutsche Telekom, accept only phonecards, available for €5, €10 and €20 at post offices, news kiosks, tourist offices and banks.

Telekom Austria (☎ 0800-100 100; www.aon.at, in German) maintains the public phones throughout that country; they take either coins or phonecards. It's also possible to make calls from phone booths inside post offices.

The National telephone provider, **Swisscom** (http://fr.swisscom.ch), operates the world's densest network of public phone booths. Phones take Swiss franc or euro coins, and phonecards, which are sold at post offices, newsagencies etc. Many booths also accept major credit cards.

PHONECARDS

A range of phonecards are sold across Germany, Austria and Switzerland, usually available from post offices, train stations and newsstands.

TRANSPORT

GETTING THERE & AWAY

AIR

GERMANY

The main arrival and departure points in Germany are Frankfurt-am-Main and Munich. But with the explosion of budget carriers, places such as Berlin, Nuremberg and even Baden-Baden have cheap flights to parts of Europe.

Ryanair, easyJet, airberlin and germanwings are among the foremost cheap options in Germany, but don't count Lufthansa out: it has been aggressively competing on price as well.

The following are tops among airlines flying to Germany from Europe:

airberlin (AB; ☎ 01805-737 800; www.airberlin.de)
easyJet (BH; ☎ 01803-654 321; www.easyjet.com)
germanwings (4U; ☎ 01805-955 855; www.germanwings.com)
Lufthansa (LH; ☎ 01803-803 803; www.lufthansa.com)
Ryanair (FR; ☎ 0190-170 100; www.ryanair.com)

AUSTRIA

Vienna is served by flights from around the globe and across Europe, Innsbruck and Salzburg are also connected to cities across Europe. The top big-name and budget carriers include:

airberlin (AB; ☎ 0820-600 830; www.airberlin.com)
Austrian Airlines (OS; ☎ 05-17 66-1000; www.aua.com)
easyJet (U2; www.easyjet.com)
germanwings (4U; ☎ 0820-240 554; www.germanwings.com)

SWITZERLAND

The main international airports are in Zürich and Geneva. More than 100 scheduled airlines fly to/from Switzerland. Among them, the following are most helpful for getting around Europe:

airberlin (AB; www.airberlin.com)
Baboo (F7; www.flybaboo.com)
Helvetic (2L; www.helvetic.com)
Swiss International Air Lines (LX; ☎ 0848 852 000; www.swiss.com)
Jet2.com (LS; www.jet2.com)

LAND

BUS

Travelling by bus between the three Alpine countries and the rest of Europe may be cheaper than travelling by train or plane, but journeys will take a lot longer. **Eurolines** (www.eurolines.com) is a consortium of national bus companies operating routes throughout the continent.

TRAIN

As elsewhere in Europe, a favourite way to get around is by train. The unsurpassed scenery adds to the attraction in these rugged countries.

The main German hubs with the best connections for major European cities are Hamburg (for Scandinavia); Frankfurt (high-speed trains to Paris) and Munich (high-speed trains to Paris and regular trains to southern and southeastern Europe).

The main rail services in and out of Austria from the west normally pass through Innsbruck or Salzburg on their way to Vienna's Westbahnhof. Trains to eastern destinations like Budapest and Bratislava invariably leave from Südbahnhof in Vienna.

Zürich is the busiest international terminus in Switzerland. There are several trains daily from Paris to Swiss cities including Geneva (3½ hours) and Bern (4½ hours).

Night trains are often available for longer routes, but if you're travelling via the Alps, think twice before deciding to sleep through the views.

RIVER, LAKE & SEA

Hydrofoils run to Bratislava and Budapest from Vienna (see p482).

Switzerland can be reached by steamer from several lakes: from Italy via Lago Maggiore (☎ **091 751 61 40; www.navigazionelaghi.it**); and from France along Lake Geneva (☎ **0848 811 848; www.cgn.ch**).

GETTING AROUND

AIR

Given Germany's larger size, it is the country in the trio you're most likely to traverse by air. There are lots of flights within the country, many by budget carriers such as airberlin and germanwings (see opposite). But note that with check-in and transit times, flying may not be as efficient as a fast train.

Vienna is connected with Innsbruck by air, and you can fly from Geneva to Zürich or Lugano, but it hardly seems worth the bother.

BOAT

Boats are most likely to be used for basic transport in Germany when travelling on tours along the Rhine, Elbe and Moselle Rivers.

Services along the Danube in Austria are mainly scenic pleasure cruises, but provide a leisurely way of getting from Krems to Melk. For more information on boat services along the river, see p482.

BUS

The bus networks in Germany, Austria and Switzerland function primarily in support of the train networks. Consider using buses when you want to cut across two train lines and to avoid long train rides to and from a transfer point. A good example of where to do this is in the Alps, where the best way to follow the peaks is by bus.

Between major cities in environmentally friendly Austria, only train services exist.

CAR & MOTORCYCLE

In Switzerland and Germany, your home licence will suffice for driving. Same for Austria if you're visiting from the US or EU; other nationalities require an international driving permit.

You usually must be at least 21 years of age to hire a car. Multinational car-hire firms **Avis** (**www.avis.at**), **Budget** (**www.budget.at**), **Europcar** (**www.europcar.co.at**) and **Hertz** (**www.hertz.at**) are well represented in cities across the three nations.

Competitive rates are often found on Auto Europe (www.autoeurope.com).

Germany, Austria and Switzerland are served by excellent highway systems. Motorways often require toll stickers, which may already be affixed to rental cars; check with the company. In Switzerland some Alpine tunnels incur additional tolls.

The usual speed limits are 50km/h in towns, 120 km/h to 130km/h on motorways and 80 km/h to 100km/h on other roads. The speed on *autobahns* in Germany is unlimited, though there's an advisory speed of 130km/h; exceptions are clearly signposted. Germany also has one of the highest concentrations of speed cameras in Europe.

In all three countries the blood alcohol limit is 0.05%; penalties include on-the-spot fines or even imprisonment.

Automobile associations:

Allgemeiner Deutscher Automobil-Club (ADAC; ☎ for roadside assistance 0180-222 2222, if calling from mobile phone 222 222; www.adac.de, in German)

Austrian Automobile Club (Österreichischer Automobil; ☎ 0810-120 120; www.oeamtc.at)

Swiss Touring Club (Touring Club der Schweiz; ☎ 022 417 24 24; www.tcs.ch)

TRAIN

The railways are operated almost entirely by state-run companies: the **Deutsche Bahn** (DB; www.bahn.de), **ÖBB** (www.oebb.at) and **Swiss Federal Railways** (www.rail.ch, www.sbb.ch/en), in Germany, Austria and Switzerland, respectively. In addition to domestic information, the DB website has an excellent schedule feature that works for the whole of Europe.

Prices are especially high in Switzerland. If you're taking more than one or two train trips it's best to purchase a four- or eight-day **Swiss Pass** (www.swisstravelsystem.ch), which allows unlimited travel on almost every train, boat and bus service, and on trams and buses in 38 towns. DB offers German rail passes also. Eurail and InterRail, single and multicountry passes (see p796) are valid in all three countries.

CZECH REPUBLIC, SLOVAKIA & HUNGARY

CZECH REPUBLIC

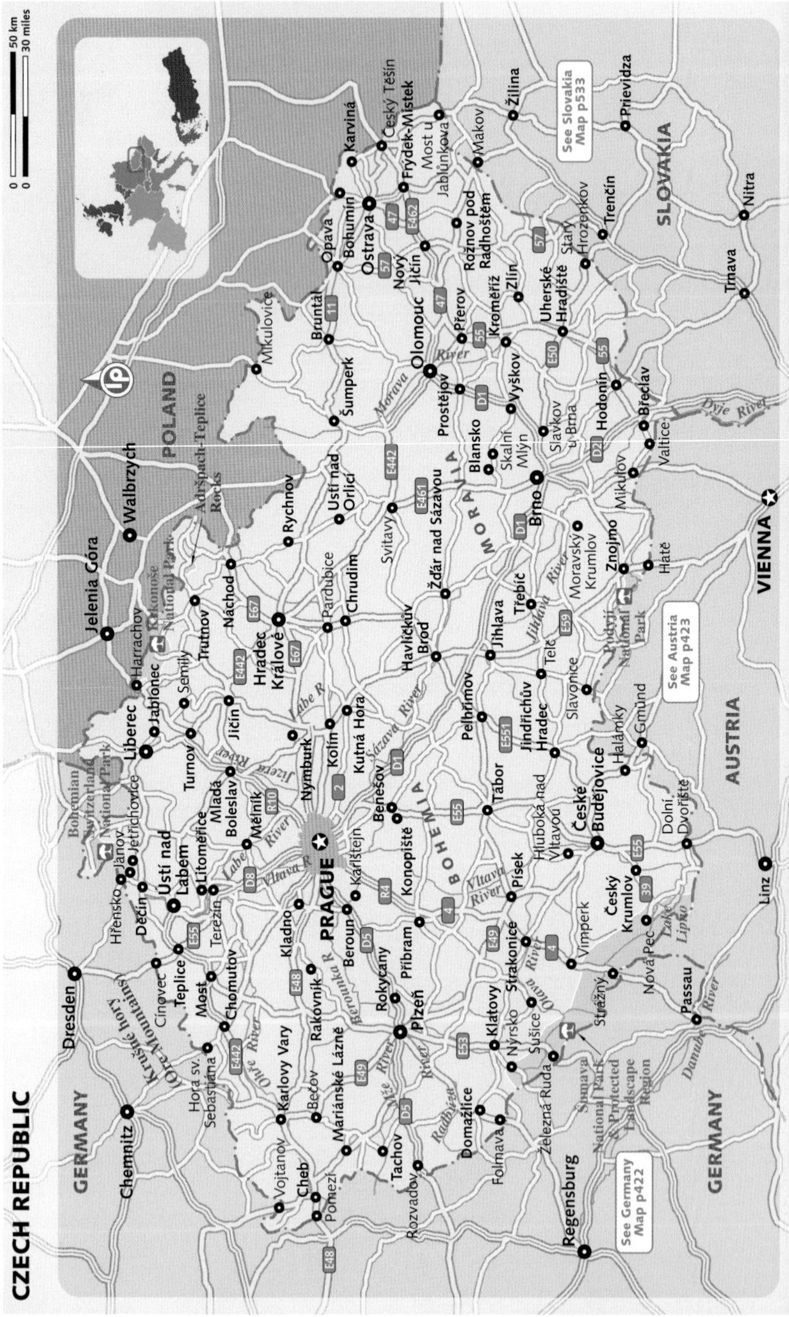

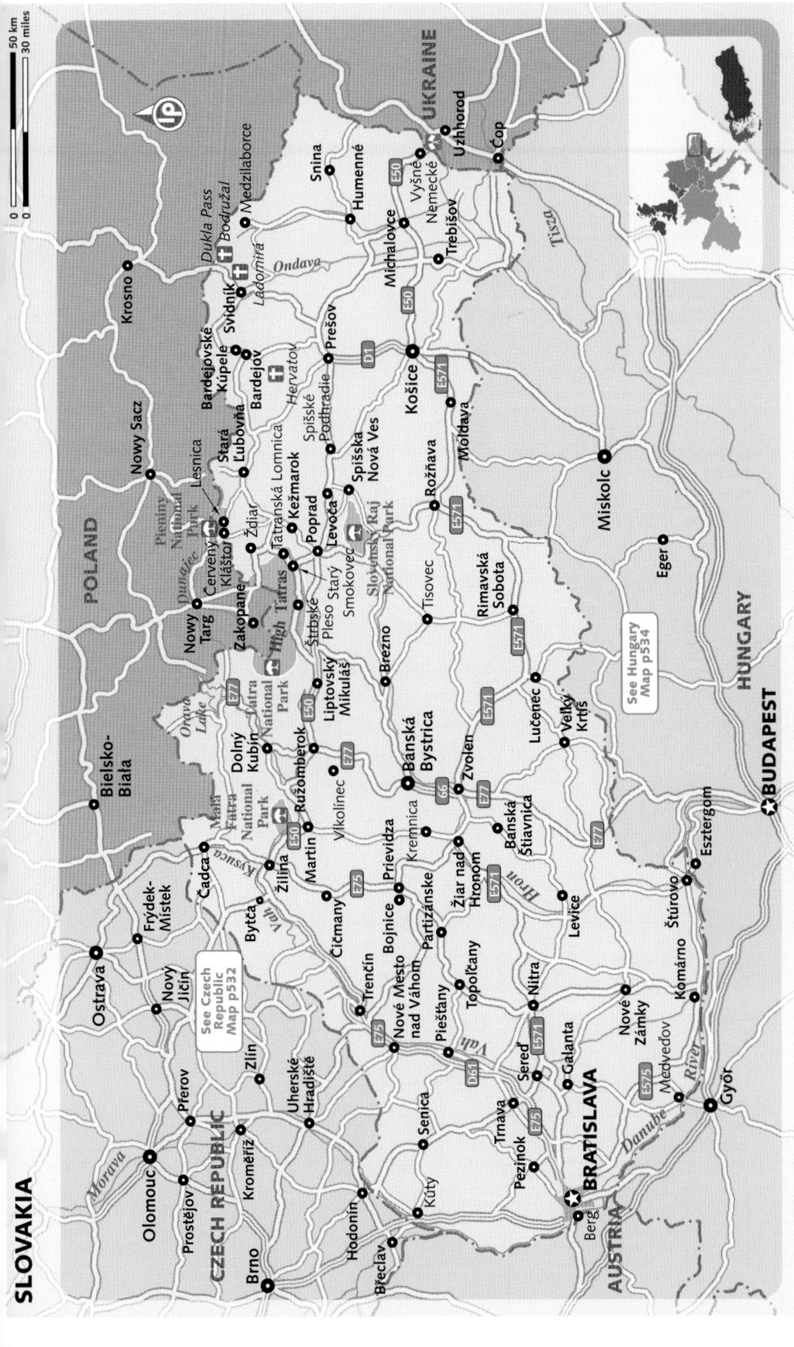
SLOVAKIA
0 50 km
0 30 miles
POLAND
CZECH REPUBLIC
UKRAINE
HUNGARY
AUSTRIA
BRATISLAVA
BUDAPEST
See Czech Republic Map p532
See Hungary Map p534
Brno
Olomouc
Prostějov
Přerov
Kroměříž
Zlín
Uherské Hradiště
Ostrava
Nový Jičín
Frýdek-Místek
Bielsko-Biała
Čadca
Bytča
Žilina
Martin
Čičmany
Trenčín
Nové Mesto nad Váhom
Piešťany
Topoľčany
Nitra
Bojnice
Prievidza
Partizánske
Ziar nad Hronom
Kremnica
Banská Štiavnica
Levice
Zvolen
Banská Bystrica
Vlkolínec
Ružomberok
Dolný Kubín
Liptovský Mikuláš
Brezno
Tisovec
Rimavská Sobota
Lučenec
Veľký Krtíš
Štrbské Pleso
Starý Smokovec
Tatranská Lomnica
Poprad
Levoča
Kežmarok
Ždiar
Červený Kláštor
Lesnica
Stará Ľubovňa
Spišská Nová Ves
Spišské Podhradie
Hervatov
Bardejov
Bardejovské Kúpele
Svidník
Ladomirá
Bodružal
Dukla Pass
Medzilaborce
Prešov
Košice
Rožňava
Moldava
Michalovce
Humenné
Snina
Trebišov
Vyšné Nemecké
Uzhhorod
Čop
Krosno
Nowy Sacz
Nowy Targ
Zakopane
Miskolc
Eger
Esztergom
Štúrovo
Komárno
Nové Zámky
Galanta
Sereď
Trnava
Pezinok
Senica
Kúty
Hodonín
Břeclav
Berg
Medveďov
Győr
Malá Fatra National Park
Tatra National Park
High Tatras
Pieniny National Park
Slovenský Raj National Park
Orava Lake
Dunajec
Váh
Hron
Kysuca
Morava
Danube River
Ondava
Tisza
E50
E75
E77
E571
E575
D1
D61
66

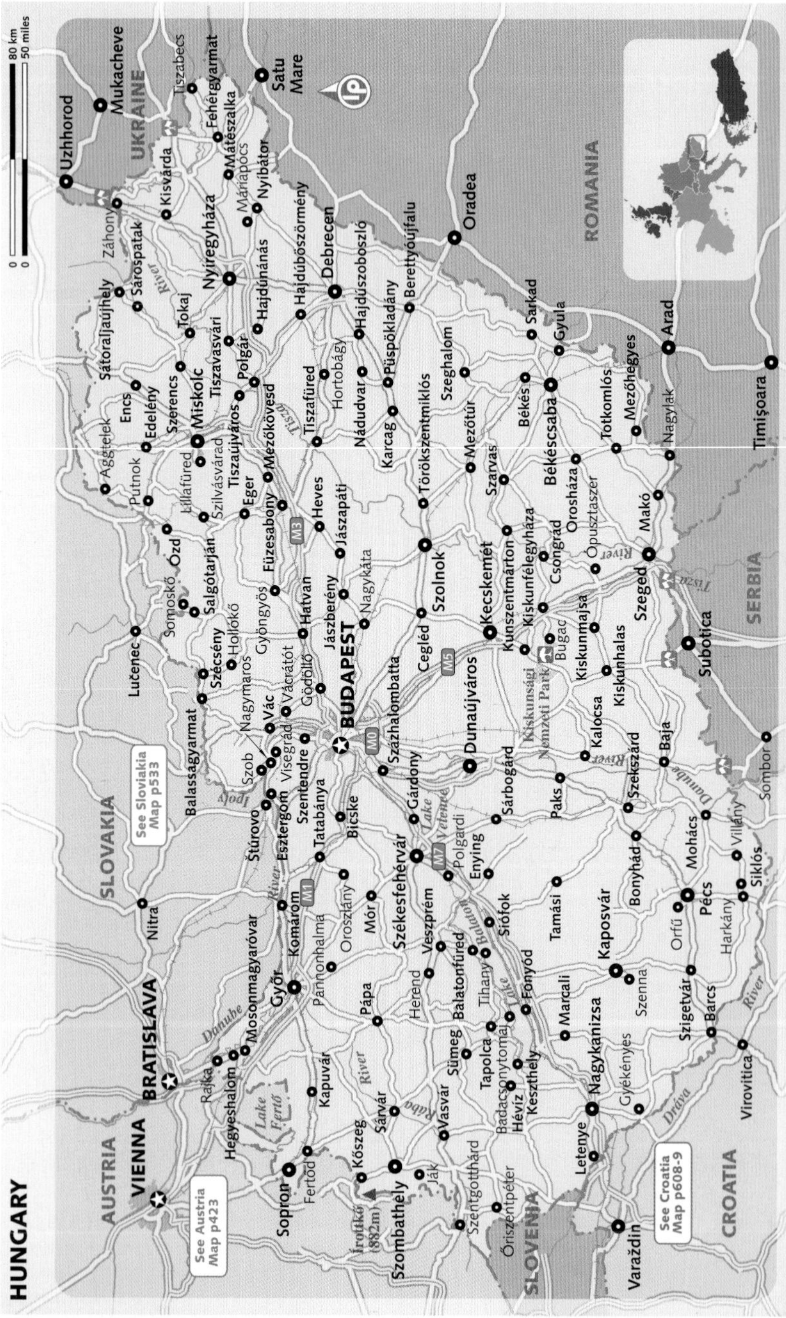
HUNGARY
0 80 km
0 50 miles
AUSTRIA
VIENNA
See Austria Map p423
SLOVAKIA
BRATISLAVA
See Slovakia Map p533
UKRAINE
ROMANIA
SERBIA
CROATIA
See Croatia Map p608-9
SLOVENIA
BUDAPEST
Uzhhorod
Mukacheve
Satu Mare
Tiszabecs
Fehérgyarmat
Mátészalka
Máriapócs
Nyírbátor
Kisvárda
Záhony
Sárospatak
Sátoraljaújhely
Tokaj
Nyíregyháza
Hajdúnánás
Hajdúböszörmény
Debrecen
Hajdúszoboszló
Püspökladány
Berettyóújfalu
Oradea
Sarkad
Gyula
Arad
Timişoara
Mezőhegyes
Nagylak
Tótkomlós
Békéscsaba
Békés
Szeghalom
Mezőtúr
Túrkeve
Karcag
Nádudvar
Hortobágy
Tiszafüred
Polgár
Tiszavasvári
Miskolc
Szerencs
Edelény
Encs
Aggtelek
Putnok
Lillafüred
Szilvásvárad
Tiszaújváros
Mezőkövesd
Eger
Füzesabony
Heves
Jászapáti
Törökszentmiklós
Szolnok
Szarvas
Orosháza
Ópusztaszer
Makó
Szeged
Csongrád
Kiskunfélegyháza
Kecskemét
Kunszentmárton
Bugac
Kiskunmajsa
Kiskunhalas
Kiskunsági Nemzeti Park
Subotica
Özd
Salgótarján
Somoskő
Gyöngyös
Hatvan
Jászberény
Nagykáta
Cegléd
Lučenec
Szécsény
Hollókő
Nagymaros
Vác
Vácrátót
Gödöllő
Balassagyarmat
Szob
Visegrád
Szentendre
Százhalombatta
Dunaújváros
Kalocsa
Baja
Sombor
Štúrovo
Esztergom
Ipoly
Tatabánya
Bicske
Gárdony
Lake Velence
Polgárdi
Enying
Sárbogárd
Paks
Szekszárd
Bonyhád
Mohács
Villány
Siklós
Harkány
Pécs
Orfű
Tamási
Dombóvár
Kaposvár
Szenna
Szigetvár
Barcs
Virovitica
Dráva River
Danube River
Tisza River
Maros River
Nitra
Komárom
Oroszlány
Mór
Székesfehérvár
Veszprém
Herend
Balatonfüred
Tihany
Siófok
Lake Balaton
Fonyód
Marcali
Nagykanizsa
Gyékényes
Letenye
Varaždin
Keszthely
Hévíz
Badacsonytomaj
Tapolca
Sümeg
Pápa
Pannonhalma
Győr
Mosonmagyaróvár
Rajka
Hegyeshalom
Lake Fertő
Kapuvár
Rába River
Sárvár
Vasvár
Fertőd
Sopron
Kőszeg
Szombathely
Ják
Írottkő (882m)
Szentgotthárd
Őriszentpéter
M0
M1
M3
M5
M7

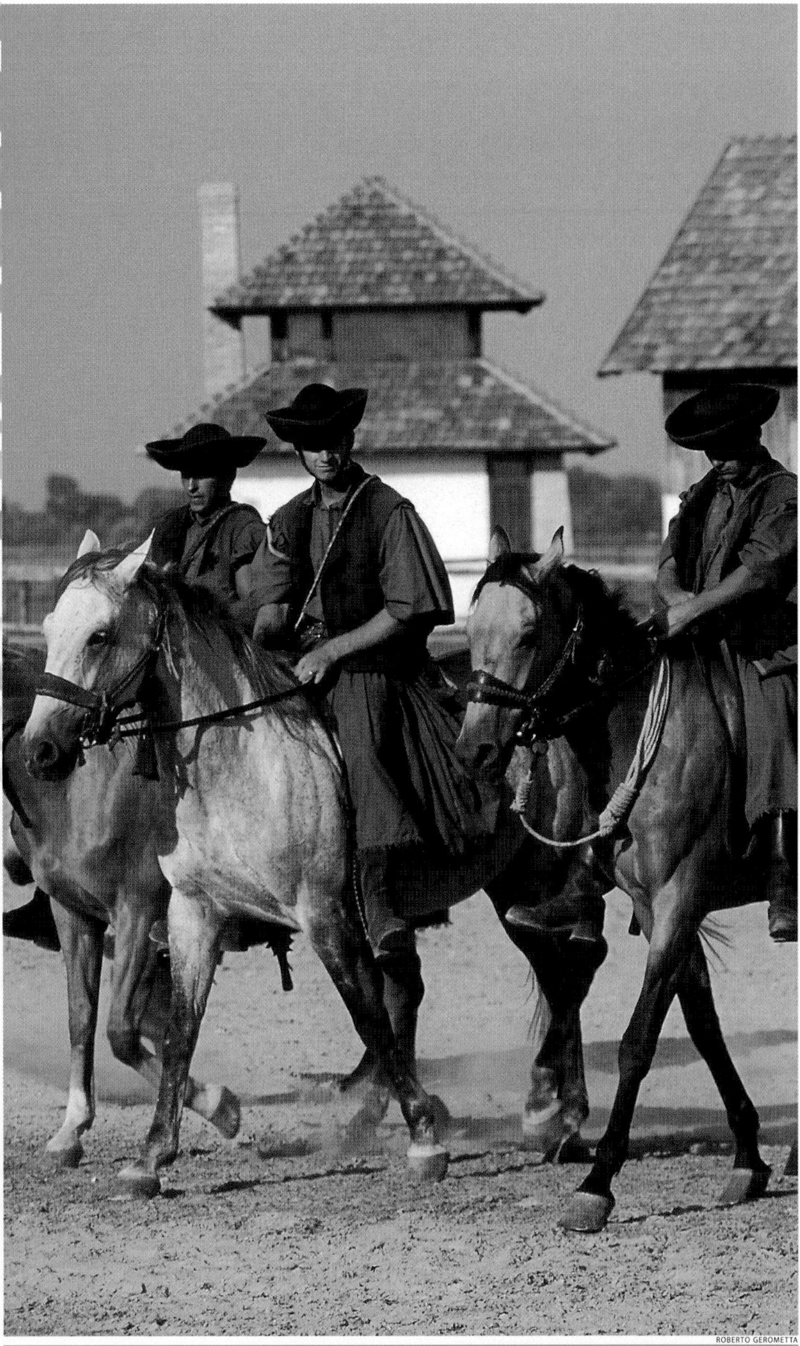

ROBERTO GEROMETTA

Riders in a horse show, Hungary

HIGHLIGHTS

1 KECSKEMÉT & KISKUNSÁGI NP

ZSUZSA FÁBIÁN, GUESTHOUSE CO-OWNER & MANAGER

Kecskemét is big enough to have great international festivals and an exciting cultural life, but it's a relaxed place with a countryside feel. And if I drive half hour to Kiskunsági Nemzeti Park, I'm in another world. Sitting on top of a sand dune, watching the blue sky… it's like being in the desert.

ZSUZSA FÁBIÁN'S DON'T MISS LIST

❶ ART-NOUVEAU ARCHITECTURE

Art nouveau is an amusing style with lots of colours, flowers and folklore motifs on the buildings, even on the roofs. In Kecskemét this style is not just for museums and tourists, it's part of daily life. You can even find fanciful details on locals' homes.

❷ MINIMUSEUMS

You can wander through the Bozso Museum and its unique Hungarian folklore collection, the Leskowsky Musi Museum of traditional instruments, o the toy, photography or naive-arts ex hibitions. Like all the other museums i town, they're tiny but worth visiting.

❸ FESTIVALS GALORE

There are so many festivals locally. Hirö Week, the town's anniversary celebra tion in July, and the Wine and Palink Festival in August are the biggest an most exciting. At those times the whol town meets on the main square t

Clockwise from top: Statue of Kossuth before the Town Hall (p599); Pulpit in the Great Church (p599); Bugac horse rider (p600); Chillies for sale at the Kecskemét market; House of Science & Technology (p599)

CLOCKWISE FROM TOP: MARTIN MOOS; MARTIN MOOS; TIBOR BOGNAR / ALAMY; MARTIN MOOS; MARTIN MO

aste the finest wines of Hungary, eat ausages and enjoy live concerts.

4 BUGAC HORSE SHOW

Passing by old farmsteads or a lonely pole well, it's like time has stopped on the *puszta* (great plain). At the famous **horse show** (p600) in Kiskunság National Park, you see herdsmen in traditional costumes riding acrobatically on the plains. Riders stand astride two horses while holding the reins of two or three others. And horses sit and lay on command like obedient puppies.

5 NATURE AT YOUR DOORSTEP

Kiskunsági Nemzeti Park (p600) has nine islands of protected land totalling 760 sq km. Most travellers are surprised to find a nature reserve so close to a large town. Getting lost hiking in the ancient juniper groves is a truly unforgettable experience. More and more people come for the birdwatching. You can spot the great bustard, the biggest land bird in Europe, and tens of thousands of migrating birds rest at the park's salt lakes on their way to warmer countries.

THINGS YOU NEED TO KNOW

Top tip English-speaking guides and educational trails in English are found in the national park **Timing** The Kecskemét city website (www.kecskemet.hu) has a list of festivals and goings-on **See our author's reviews on p598 & p600**

HIGHLIGHTS

2

MYSTICAL PRAGUE

Plan on spending several days in magical **Prague** (p546). Take a morning stroll before the crowds arrive on **Charles Bridge** (p555), enjoy a big glass of Budvar in a summer beer garden, picnic overlooking the Vltava River at **Vyšehrad fortress** (p556) and learn about cubism, the indigenous Czech architecture. The longer you stay, the easier it is to escape the crowds and experience the city's essence.

3

TAKE A BATH

Taking a bath in **Budapest** (p584): whether you soak in luxurious surrounds at the **Gellért Baths** (p587) or in sprawling neoclassical **Széchenyi Baths** (p589), it's an experience not to miss. Once you've changed into your swimsuit, take your choice of different temperature thermal mineral pools. Plunging from hot to cold gets your circulation going – just ask the life-long regulars.

4

THIS BUD'S FOR YOU

The Czech Republic is known worldwide for its Pilsner Urquell and Budvar (aka Budweiser) beers. They're available in almost any pub. But taking a brewery tour in **Plzeň** (p567) or **České Budějovice** (p565) is a real experience. The beers' taste seems to intensify when drunk deep in a brewery's cellar.

5

MAIN SQUARE EVENTS

Something's always going on in Bratislava's **Hlavné nám** (p573). During summer months, at weekends especially, there's often a free concert or folk dance performance on. In November and December the usual number of craft stands doubles, and food booths pop up selling sausages and hot wine for the Christmas market.

6

BRING A COKE BOTTLE

Go from table to table sampling Bull's Blood wine by the decilitre (100mL) in the dozens of tiny cellars of **Szépasszony völgy** (Valley of the Beautiful Women, p601). Decide which you prefer and the proprietor will be happy to fill your empty plastic bottle with cask wine to go.

2 RICHARD NEBESKY; 3 DAVID GREEDY; 4 RICHARD NEBESKY; 5 GLENN BEANLAND; 6 DANITA DELIMONT / ALAMY

2 Views over Charles Bridge (p555) to Staré Město; 3 Széchenyi Baths (p589); 4 Beer hall in Prague (p558); 5 Souvenirs for sale in Hlavné nám (p573); 6 Szépasszony völgy (p601)

THE BEST...

CASTLES & CHATEAUX

- **Prague Castle** (p551) Europe's largest castle complex.
- **Konopiště Chateau** (p562) Archduke Franz Ferdinand d'Este's country estate.
- **Spiš Castle** (p583) Four hectares of fortress ruins.
- **Castle Hill** (p585) Meandering back lanes in Budapest's crowning glory.

VANTAGE POINTS WITH A VIEW

- **Malá Strana Bridge Tower** (p555) A Gothic wonderland view in Prague.
- **Citadella** (p587) Sweeping panorama of both Buda and Pest.
- **Fishermen's Bastion** (p586) A view of Budapest's nine bridges through a fanciful arcade.

PLACES TO TAKE A BATH

- **Karlovy Vary** (p564) Modern spa complexes in an age-old town.
- **Chodová Planá** (p566) Beer bathing at the Czech Republic's newest theme spa.
- **Széchenyi Baths, Budapest** (p589) Dozens of pools and saunas, indoors and out.
- **Gellért Baths, Budapest** (p587) Surrounded by sumptuous marble and stained glass.

FREE THRILLS

- **Charles Bridge** (p555) At dawn it's just you, St John of Nepomuk and 29 other statues.
- **Vyšehrad** (p556) Hilltop fortress overlooking the Vltava River.
- **Bratislava** (p571) Rabbit-warren-like streets of a compact Old Town.
- **Hősök tere** (p587) Watch skaters throw tricks beneath a pantheon of Hungarian greats.

LEFT: GAVIN GOUGH; RIGHT: GLENN BEANLA

Left: Fishermen's Bastion (p586), Budapest; Right: Cobbled laneway in Bratislava's Old Town (p571)

THINGS YOU NEED TO KNOW

AT A GLANCE

- **Population** 10.2 million (Czech Republic), 5.44 million (Slovakia), 10 million (Hungary)
- **Official languages** Czech (Czech Republic), Slovak (Slovakia), Hungarian (Hungary)
- **Currency** Czech crown (Kč, Czech Republic), euro (€, Slovakia), forint (Ft, Hungary)
- **Telephone codes** ☎420 (Czech Republic), ☎421 (Slovakia), ☎36 (Hungary)
- **When to go** May to June, September and October
- **Tipping** 5% to 10%

REGIONS IN A NUTSHELL

- **Bohemia** (p563) Spa towns, medieval enclaves and barrels of beer.
- **Moravia** (p569) Quiet Old Town centres removed from the crowds.
- **East Slovakia** (p577) Unesco-listed towns beneath the 2000m-plus High Tatra mountains.
- **South Hungary** (p597) Interesting architecture and a horse show on the plains.
- **Northeast Hungary** (p601) Hungary's hill country, complete with baroque town and vineyards.

ADVANCE PLANNING

- **A month ahead** For summer travel in Prague, Budapest and the High Tatras, book a month or more in advance.
- **One week ahead** In July and August make dinner reservations in Česky Krumlov and Prague.

BE FOREWARNED

- **Museums** Closed Monday
- **Castle ruins & outdoor attractions** May close November to April.

BUSINESS HOURS

- **Banks** (8am-4.30pm Mon-Fri)
- **Bars** (11am-midnight) Sometimes later on weekends.
- **Grocery stores** (7am-6pm Mon-Fri, to noon Sat) Hypermarkets such as Tesco often have extended hours.
- **Nightclubs** (4pm-2am Thu-Sat) Clubs in Prague have longer hours.
- **Post offices** (8am-6pm Mon-Fri, to noon Sat)
- **Restaurants** (11am-10pm or 11pm)
- **Specialty shops** (8.30am-5pm or 6pm Mon-Fri, to noon Sat)

COSTS

Provincial towns and villages are an average of 20% to 40% cheaper than the capital city costs listed here.

CZECH REPUBLIC

- **1000Kč per day** A bed in a dorm, some self-catered meals, a few beers a night.
- **3500Kč** A midrange guesthouse outside the centre, eating two restaurant meals a day
- **8000Kč+** A central hotel with all the amenities and fancy food three times a day.

SLOVAKIA

- **€60 per day** Dormitory or cheap guesthouse accommodation, some grocery-store picnics and occasional dinners out.

THINGS YOU NEED TO KNOW

- **€100** An average guesthouse, eating most meals out, all museum admissions and public transport.
- **€250+** Bratislava's finest lodging and dining, plus car hire.

HUNGARY

- **19,000Ft per day** Private rooms or dorms, a few meals at cheap restaurants.
- **32,00Ft** A guesthouse room, restaurant dining with wine, museums and nightclub entry.
- **80,000Ft+** Four- to five-star grand hotels, top-tier dining, opera tickets.

EMERGENCY NUMBERS

- **Ambulance** (☎ Czech Republic 155, Slovakia 112, Hungary 104)
- **Fire** (☎ Czech Republic 150, Slovakia 112, Hungary 105)
- **Police** (☎ Czech Republic 156, Slovakia 112, Hungary 107)

GETTING AROUND

For more on getting around this region, see p605.

- **Train travel** Extensive train networks in all three nations make riding the rails the best way to go.
- **Gateway airports** Prague, Budapest, and Vienna, Austria.
- **Flying around** Little to no domestic air service exists, but you can fly between Prague and Bratislava or Budapest.

MEDIA

- **Prague Post** (www.praguepost.cz) Newspaper with events and visitor information in English.
- **Slovak Spectator** (www.slovakspectator.sk) English-language weekly with current affairs and event listings.
- **Budapest Sun** (www.budapestsun.com) Weekly English-language paper with a useful arts and entertainment section.

RESOURCES

- **Association of Information Centres of Slovakia** (AICES; ☎ 16 186; www.aices.sk) Extensive network of city information centres.
- **Czech Tourism** (www.czechtourism.com) Offices provide info about tourism, culture and business.
- **Hungarian National Tourist Office** (HNTO; www.hungarytourism.hu) Extensive destination website.
- **Slovak Tourist Board** (www.slovakiatourism.sk)
- **Tourinform** (☎ 30 30 30 600; www.tourinform.hu) Network of 140 tourist offices across Hungary.

VISAS

- **EU citizens** Stay indefinitely in these Schengen-affiliated member states.
- **US, Canadian, Australian, New Zealand & Japanese citizens** Stay for up to 90 days visa free.
- **More information** Available at www.czech.cz, www.mzv.sk and www.mfa.gov.hu.

;ET INSPIRED

BOOKS

- **Feast in the Garden** Péter Nádas' book about a small Jewish community in Hungary.
- **Prague** Arthur Phillip's account of early 1990s expat life – in Budapest.
- **Time's Magpie: A Walk in Prague** Best-selling novelist Myla Goldberg's Prague adventure.
- **Unbearable Lightness of Being** Milan Kundera's novel evokes 1960s Czechoslovakia.

FILMS

- **Citizen Havel** (2008) A documentary look at playwright and president Václav Havel's life.
- **Kontroll** (2003) A dark comedy-thriller set in the Budapest metro.
- **Krajinka** (2000) Rural life vignettes span WWII to the 1990s in rural Czechoslovakia.
- **Latcho Drom** (1994) Follows the Roma through their music from India to central Europe.

MUSIC

- **Bartered Bride** Bedřich Smetana's comic opera.
- **Hungarian Rhapsodies** Classical composer Ferenc Liszt's Roma-influenced music.
- **Live from Hungary** Slovak jazz legend Peter Lipa jams.
- **Magor's Shem** Fortieth anniversary tour of Prague's revolutionary Plastic People of the Universe band.

WEBSITES

- **Budapest Daily Photo** (www.budapestdailyphoto.com) A photo-filled blog.
- **Prague Information Service** (http://webcam.pis.cz) Watch Charles Bridge live on a webcam.
- **Prague Life** (www.prague-life.com) Czech out culture in the capital.
- **Slovakia Document Store** (www.panorama.sk) Inspiring books and photos.

RICHARD NEBESKY

P Pavlova metro station, Prague

ITINERARIES

DAY TRIPPING PRAGUE Three Days

With only three nights in the region, we'd be hard pressed to tell y to stay anywhere but the Czech capital. After a full day exploring t ancient architecture of **(1) Prague** (p546), wake up ready to day-trip o You should see the moving, but not pleasant, fortress-concentrati camp at **(2) Terezín** (p563). Make sure to read the poetry and see t drawings made by the young children held captive there.

On day three you have a choice to make. You can either visit t turreted **(3) Karlštejn Castle** (p562), which wouldn't be out of pla on Disneyland's main street. Or, our favourite, excursion out to be bo enchanted and spooked at **(4) Kutná Hora** (p562) and around. T magnificent Cathedral of St Barbara trumps anything in Prague f all-in-one Gothic splendour. The **Sedec Ossuary** (p562) is a bit mo on the creepy side of the coin – the bones of 40,000 humans ha been artistically stacked into vaulted ceilings and hung as chandelie Together the two make up a Unesco-recognised heritage site.

A CAPITAL TOUR Five Days

Two days in **(1) Prague** (p546) hardly seems like enough, but in th time you can easily cover the castle, **Charles Bridge** (p555) and t **Old Town Sq** (p549) on foot. You'll have to be in front of the **astr nomical clock** (p549) on the half hour to see the mechanical m do their dance. Make sure to book ahead for some fine dining in th cultural capital, or order tickets for an evening show.

A little over a four-hour train ride brings you to **(2) Bratislava** (p57 A wander around the rabbit-warren Old Town is a must, but the aren't many superlative sights. Content yourself relaxing in one ou door cafe after another. If you really must do something, climb t castle ramparts for a rooftop view.

Then quick, quick, you're on to **(3) Budapest** (p584). Take the y low line metro, one of the oldest in Europe, up Andrássy út to t **Terror House museum** (p589) to learn about the secret, spy-fill past. Continue up the stately avenue to **Hősök tere monument** (p58 and a soak at the **Széchenyi Baths** (p589). Your last day is reserv for the sights of **Castle Hill** (p585), and the view of the river and ni bridges below.

ANICIENT OLD TOWNS One Week

Gothic, baroque, rococo and Renaissance – smaller towns in the three nations boast some spectacular age-old architecture. The na row lanes and footbridges of romantic **(1) Český Krumlov** (p566) a hardly unknown. But you can get more out of the beautiful old city you slow down, spend a couple nights and canoe on the Vltava Rive

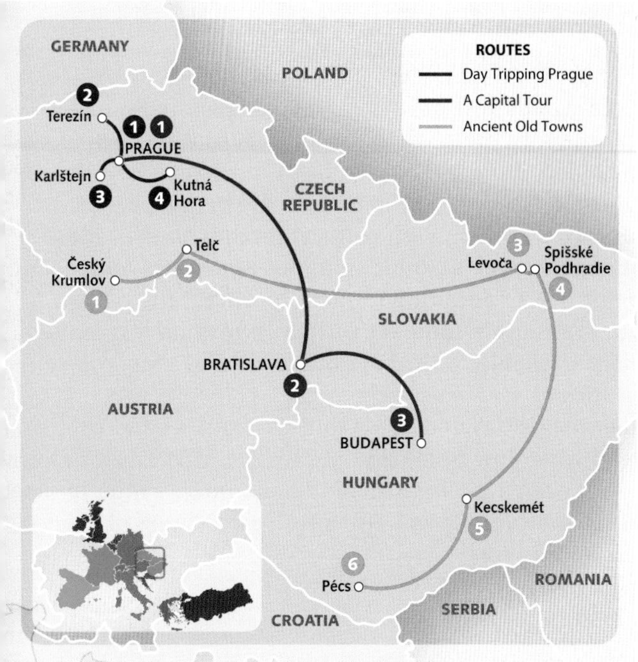

Next stop is a night in the Moravian town of (2) Telč (p569), with its Unesco-noted medieval buildings and fish ponds.

Moving on to Slovakia, (3) Levoča (p581) is another Unesco-recognised old town filled with 13th-century buildings that contain hotels and restaurants. The 4-hectare ruins of (4) Spiš Castle (p583) are just 15km away.

South of Budapest, art nouveau is the architecture of choice in colourful little (5) Kecskemét (p598). Most weekends in summer, festival concerts and food stands enliven the pedestrian centre. Moorish minarets and the Mosque Church (p597) add interest to the southern city of (6) Pécs (p597), where you can also find Roman tombs and a medieval bishopric.

DISCOVER CZECH REPUBLIC, SLOVAKIA & HUNGARY

The spectre of the communist past in repressed 'Eastern European' nations may still come to mind when some think of the Czech Republic, Slovakia and Hungary, but it's been more than two decades since the Iron Curtain lifted. All three nations are well a part of an integrated European Union, with cultural capitals to rival those across the continent. Prague's Gothic, spindles-and-spires appeal and Budapest's vibrant mix of ancient and modern attract the masses – for good reason. Bratislava's compact Old Town may be less lauded, but it's supremely strollable, with more outdoor cafes than you can shake a swizzle stick at.

Go beyond the main cities and you'll find that castles and chateaux abound, beer and wine flow freely and impressive medieval cities are ubiquitous. There's even a pocket-size alpine mountain range to hike. And getting out of the capitals will also save you a chunk of change. So what are you waiting for?

CZECH REPUBLIC

PRAGUE

pop 1.22 million

It's the perfect irony of Prague. You are lured there by the past, but compelled to linger by the present and the future. Fill your days with its artistic and architectural heritage – from Gothic and Renaissance to art nouveau and cubist – but after dark move your focus to the here and now in the lively restaurants, bars and clubs in emerging neighbourhoods like Vinohrady and Žižkov. And if Prague's seasonal army of tourists sometimes wears you down, that's OK. Just drink a glass of the country's legendary Bohemian lager, relax and be reassured that quiet moments still exist: a private dawn on Charles Bridge, a chilled beer in Letná as you gaze upon the glorious cityscape of Staré Město or getting reassuringly lost in the intimate lanes of Malá Strana or Josefov. Every day you'll uncover plenty of reasons to reinforce Prague's reputation as one of Europe's most exciting cities.

ORIENTATION

Central Prague nestles on the Vltava River separating Hradčany (the medieval castle district) and Malá Strana (Little Quarter) on the west bank from Staré Město (Old Town) and Nové Město (New Town) on the east. Prague's up-and-coming neighbourhoods include leafy Vinohrady, with good cafes and restaurants, and the grungier, more energtic after-dark scene of Žižkov.

INFORMATION

The major banks are best for changing cash, but using a debit card in an ATM gives a better rate of exchange. Avoid *směnárna* (private exchange booths), which advertise misleading rates and have exorbitant charges.

Canadian Medical Care (off Map pp548-9; ☎ 235 360 133, after hr 724 300 301; www.cmcpraha.cz; Veleslavínská 1, Veleslavín; 🕑 8am-

5pm Mon, Wed & Fri, to 8pm Tue & Thu) Expat centre with English-speaking doctors, 24-hour medical aid and pharmacy.

Main post office (Map pp552-3; Jindřišská 14, Nové Město; 2am-midnight) Collect a ticket from the automated machines outside the main hall (press 1 for stamps and parcels, 4 for Express Mail Service – EMS).

Prague 1 Police Station (Map pp552-3; ☎ 224 222 558; Jungmannovo nám 9, Nové Mesto; 24hr) If your passport or valuables are stolen, obtain a police report and crime number from here. You'll need this for an insurance claim. There's usually an English-speaker on hand.

Prague Information Service (Pražská infor mační služba, PIS; Map pp552-3; ☎ 12 444, in English & German 221 714 444; www.pis.cz; Staroměstské nám 5, Staré Město; 9am-7pm Mon-Fri, to 6pm Sat & Sun Apr-Oct, to 6pm Mon-Fri, to 5pm Sat & Sun Nov-Mar) Provides free tourist information with good maps and detailed brochures including accommodation. This main branch is at the Old Town Hall.

DANGERS & ANNOYANCES

Pickpockets work the crowds at the astronomical clock, Prague Castle and Charles Bridge, and on the central metro and tram lines, especially crowded trams 9, 22 and 23.

Most taxi drivers are honest, but some operating from tourist areas overcharge their customers (even Czechs). Phone a reputable taxi company (see p561) or look for the red and yellow signs for the 'Taxi Fair Place' scheme, indicating authorised taxi stands.

Bogus police sometimes approach tourists and ask to see their money, claiming they're looking for counterfeit notes. They then run off with the cash. If in doubt, just ask the 'policeman' to accompany you to the nearest police station.

SIGHTS

All the main sights are in the city centre, and are easily reached on foot. You can take in the Castle, Charles Bridge and Old Town Sq in a couple of days.

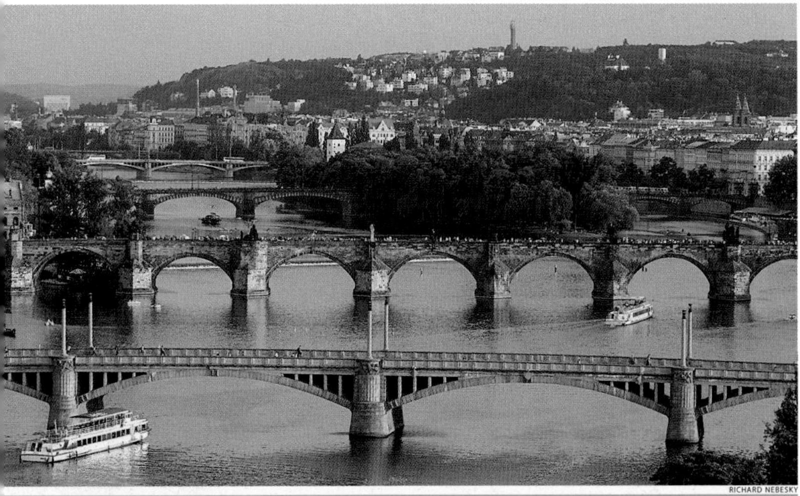

RICHARD NEBESKY

Bridges spanning the Vltava River, Prague

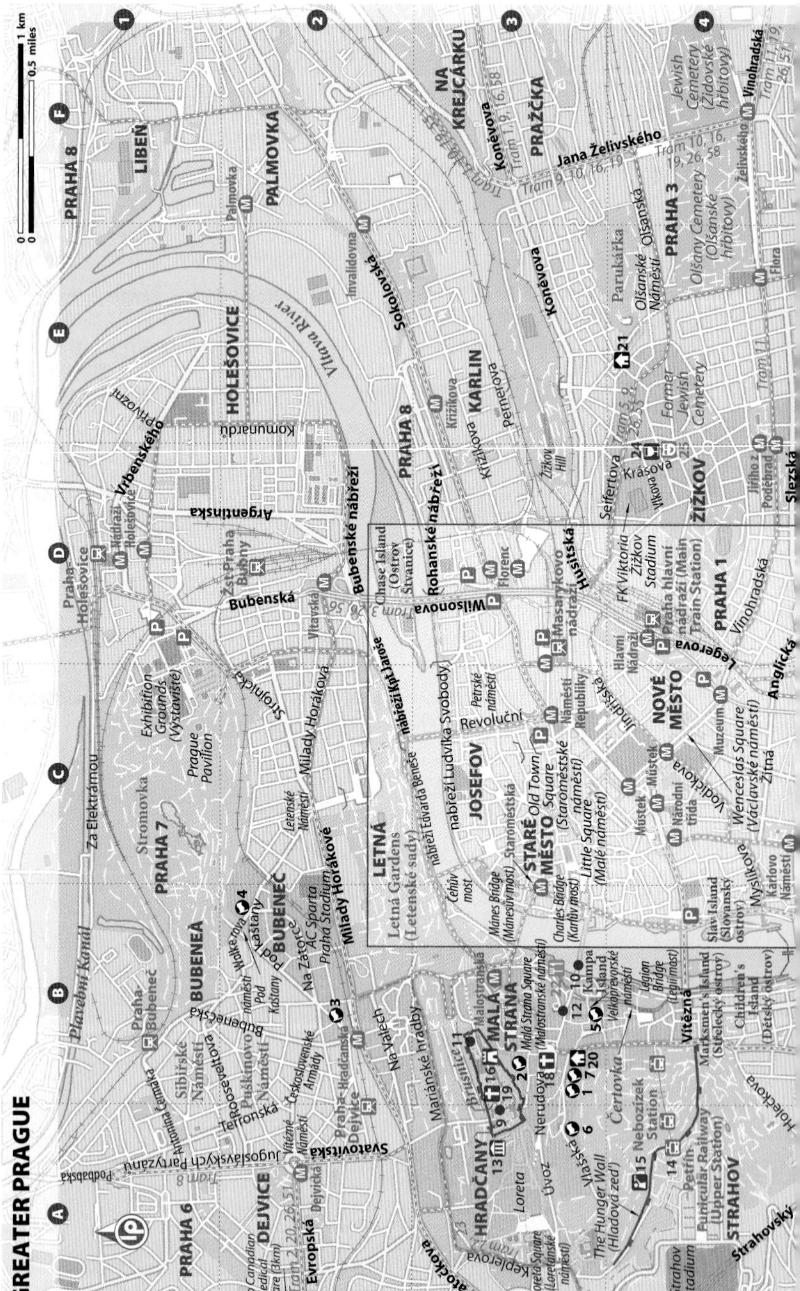
GREATER PRAGUE
0 0.5 miles
0 1 km
PRAHA 6
DEJVICE
HRADČANY
MALÁ STRANA
STRAHOV
BUBENEČ
BUBENEČ
PRAHA 7
LETNÁ
JOSEFOV
STARÉ MĚSTO
NOVÉ MĚSTO
PRAHA 1
ŽIŽKOV
PRAHA 3
KARLÍN
PRAHA 8
HOLEŠOVICE
PALMOVKA
LIBEŇ
PRAHA 8
NA KREJCÁRKU
PRAŽČKA
Vltava River
Stromovka
Exhibition Grounds (Výstaviště)
Prague Pavilion
Letná Gardens (Letenské sady)
Old Town Square (Staroměstské náměstí)
Little Square (Malé náměstí)
Wenceslas Square (Václavské náměstí)
Charles Bridge (Karlův most)
Mánes Bridge (Mánesův most)
Čechův most
Legion Bridge (Legií most)
Kampa Island
Slav Island (Slovanský ostrov)
Marksmen's Island (Střelecký ostrov)
Children's Island (Dětský ostrov)
Chase Island (Ostrov Štvanice)
Malá Strana Square (Malostranské náměstí)
Loreta Square (Loretánské náměstí)
The Hunger Wall (Hladová zeď)
Petřín Funicular Railway (Upper Station)
Nebozízek Station
Strahov Stadium
AC Sparta Praha Stadium
FK Viktoria Žižkov Stadium
Žižkov Hill
Praha hlavní nádraží (Main Train Station)
Masarykovo nádraží
Olšany Cemetery (Olšanské hřbitovy)
Jewish Cemetery (Židovské hřbitovy)
Former Jewish Cemetery
Mariánské hradby
Plavební kanál
Za Elektrárnou
Patočkova
Evropská
Svatovítská
Milady Horákové
Bubenská
Wilsonova
Revoluční
Sokolovská
Koněvova
Jana Želivského
Vinohradská
Legerova
Argentinská
Strahovský
To Canadian Medical Care (3km)

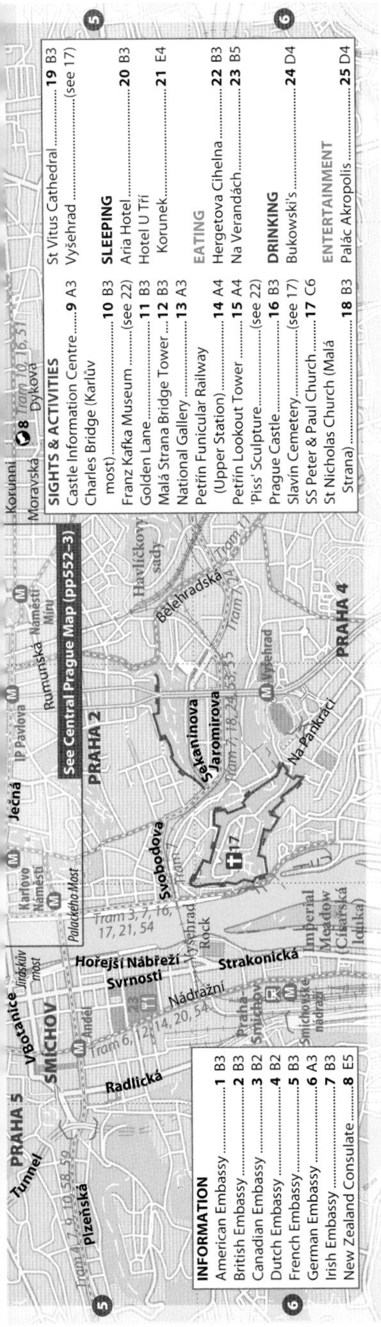

STARÉ MĚSTO

Kick off in Prague's **Old Town Sq** (Staroměstské nám), dominated by the twin Gothic steeples of **Týn Church** (Map pp552-3; 1365), the baroque **St Nicholas Church** (Map pp552-3; 1730s), not to be confused with the more famous St Nicholas Church in Malá Strana, and the **Old Town Hall clock tower** (**Map pp552-3; ☎ 224 228 456; Staroměstské nám 12; adult/child 60/40Kč; 11am-6pm Mon, 9am-6pm Tue-Sun**). From the top spy on the crowds below watching the **astronomical clock** (Map pp552-3; 1410), which springs to life every hour with assorted apostles and a bell-ringing skeleton. Don't be too surprised to hear random mutterings of the 'Is that it?' variety. In the square's centre is the **Jan Hus Monument** (Map pp552-3), erected in 1915 on the 500th anniversary of the religious reformer's execution.

The shopping street of Celetná leads east to the art-nouveau **Municipal House** (**Obecní dům; Map pp552-3; www.obecni-dum.cz; nám Republiky 5; guided tours adult/child 190/140Kč; 11am-5pm**), decorated by the early 20th century's finest Czech artists.

To the south of the Old Town Sq is the neoclassical 1783 **Estates Theatre** (Stavovské divadlo; Map pp552-3), where Mozart's *Don Giovanni* was premiered on 29 October 1787, with the maestro himself conducting.

North and northwest of the Old Town Sq, **Josefov** was Prague's Jewish quarter. Six monuments form the **Prague Jewish Museum** (**☎ 221 711 511; www.jewishmuseum.cz; adult/child 300/200Kč; 9am-6pm Sun-Fri Apr-Oct, to 4.30pm Nov-Mar**). The museum's collection exists only because in 1942 the Nazis gathered objects from 153 Jewish communities in Bohemia and Moravia, planning a 'museum of an extinct race' after completing their extermination program.

Part of the museum, the **Klaus Synagogue** (Map pp552-3; U Starého hřbitova 1) features an exhibition on Jewish customs and traditions, and the **Pinkas Synagogue** (Map pp552-3; Široká 3) is now a memorial to the Holocaust. Its walls are inscribed with the names of 77,297 Czech Jews, including Franz Kafka's three sisters. A few blocks northeast is the **Spanish Synagogue** (Map pp552-3; Dušní 12), built in a Moorish style in 1868. Now the ornate interior is used occasionally for concerts.

The oldest still-functioning synagogue in Europe, the early Gothic **Old-New Synagogue** (Map pp552-3; Červená 1; adult/child 200/140Kč; 9.30am-5pm Sun-Thu, 9am-4pm Fri), dates from 1270. Opposite is the Jewish town hall, with its picturesque 16th-century clock tower.

The **Old Jewish Cemetery** (Map pp552-3; entered from the Pinkas Synagogue) is Josefov's most evocative corner. The oldest of its 12,000 graves date from 1439. Use of the cemetery ceased in 1787 as it was becoming so crowded that burials were up to 12 layers deep.

Tucked away in the northern part of Staré Město's narrow streets is one of Prague's oldest Gothic structures, the magnificent **Convent of St Agnes** (Map pp552-3; ☎ 221 879 111; www.ngprague.cz; U Milosrdných 17; adult/child 150/80Kč; 10am-6pm Tue-Sun), now housing the National Gallery's collection of Bohemian and central European medieval art, dating from the 13th to the mid-16th centuries.

More contemporary is the **Museum of Czech Cubism** (Map pp552-3; ☎ 221 301 003; www.ngprague.cz; Ovocný trh 19; adult/child 100/50Kč; 10am-6pm Tue-Sun). Located in Josef Gočár's **House of the Black Madonna**, the angular collection of art and furniture is yet another branch of Prague's National Gallery. On the ground floor is the Grand Café Orient.

NOVÉ MĚSTO

Dating from 1348, Nové Město (New Town) is only 'new' when compared with the even older Staré Město. The sloping avenue of **Wenceslas Sq** (Václavské nám; Map pp552-3), lined with shops, banks and restaurants, is dominated by a **statue of St Wenceslas** (Map pp552-3) on horseback. Beneath the statue is a shrine to the victims of communism, including students Jan Palach and Jan Zajíc, who burned themselves alive in 1969 protesting against the Soviet invasion.

The nearby **Lucerna pasáž** (Map pp552-3; Lucerna Passage) is an art-nouveau shopping arcade now graced with David Černý's 'Horse' sculpture, a sly upside-down reflection of the statue of St Wenceslas in the square.

At the uphill end of the square is the imposing **National Museum** (Map pp552-3; ☎ 224 497 111; www.nm.cz; Václavské nám 68; adult/child 100/50Kč; 10am-6pm May-Sep, to 5pm Oct-Apr, closed 1st Tue of month), with a brand new annex also open across the street. In 2011, the museum is scheduled to close for five years for major renovations.

Fans of artist Alfons Mucha, renowned for his art-nouveau posters of garlanded Slavic maidens, can admire his work at the **Mucha Museum** (Map pp552-3; ☎ 221 451 333; www.mucha.cz; Panská 7; adult/child 120/60Kč; 10am-6pm), which features an interesting video on his life and art. Mucha also painted the magnificent *Slav Epic*, a series of paintings the size of billboards depicting Slavic history and mythology.

The **Museum of Communism** (Map pp552-3; ☎ 224 212 966; www.muzeumkomunismu.cz; Na příkopě 10, Nové Město; adult/child 180/140Kč; 9am-9pm) is tucked (ironically) behind McDonald's. The fascinating exhibition uses simple, everyday objects to illuminate the restrictions of life under communism.

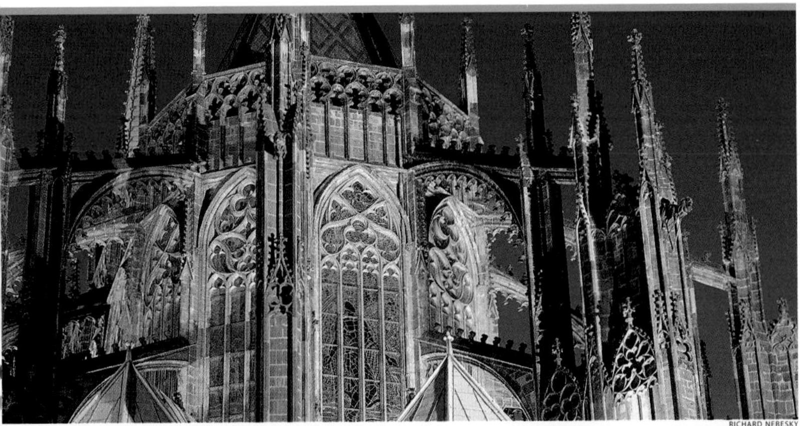

St Vitus Cathedral (p554)

PRAGUE IN TWO DAYS

Beat the tourist hordes with an early-morning stroll across **Charles Bridge** (p555) and continue uphill to Hradčany and the glories of **Prague Castle** (below). Head back down to the **Franz Kafka Museum** (p556), and cross the river again to the **Charles Bridge Museum** (below).

On day two, explore **Josefov** (p549), Prague's original Jewish quarter, and then pack a hilltop picnic for the view-friendly fortress at **Vyšehrad** (p556). Make time for a few Czech brews at the excellent **Pivovarský Klub** (p558) before kicking on for robust Czech food at **Kolkovna** (p557) or **Na Verandách** (p557).

Before or after strolling across Charles Bridge (p555), examine the history of the Vltava's famous crossing at Prague's newest museum, the **Charles Bridge Museum** (**Map pp552-3; ☎ 739 309 551; www.muzeumkarlovamostu.cz; Křížovnické nám, Staré Město; adult/child 150/100Kč; 🕐 10am-8pm**). When you know the bridge's tumultuous 650-year history, it's surprising it's still standing.

PRAGUE CASTLE

The biggest castle complex in the world, **Prague Castle** (**Pražský hrad; Map pp548-9; ☎ 224 373 368; www.hrad.cz; 🕐 castle 9am-5pm Apr-Oct, 9am-4pm Nov-Mar, grounds 5am-midnight Apr-Oct, 9am-11pm Nov-Mar**) feels more like a small town. The **long tour** (**adult/child 350/175Kč**) includes the Old Royal Palace, the Story of Prague Castle exhibit, the Basilica of St George, the Convent of St George and the Golden Lane with the Daliborka Tower. The **short tour** (**adult/child 250/125Kč**) omits a visit to the Old Royal Palace. Buy tickets at the **Castle Information Centre** (Map pp548-9) in the Second Courtyard. Count on about three hours for the long tour and two hours for the short tour. Tickets are valid for two days, but you can only visit each attraction once. DIY audio guides can also be rented. Entry to the castle courtyards and the gardens is free. The main entrance is at the western end.

The **changing of the guard**, with stylish uniforms created by Theodor Pistek

CENTRAL PRAGUE

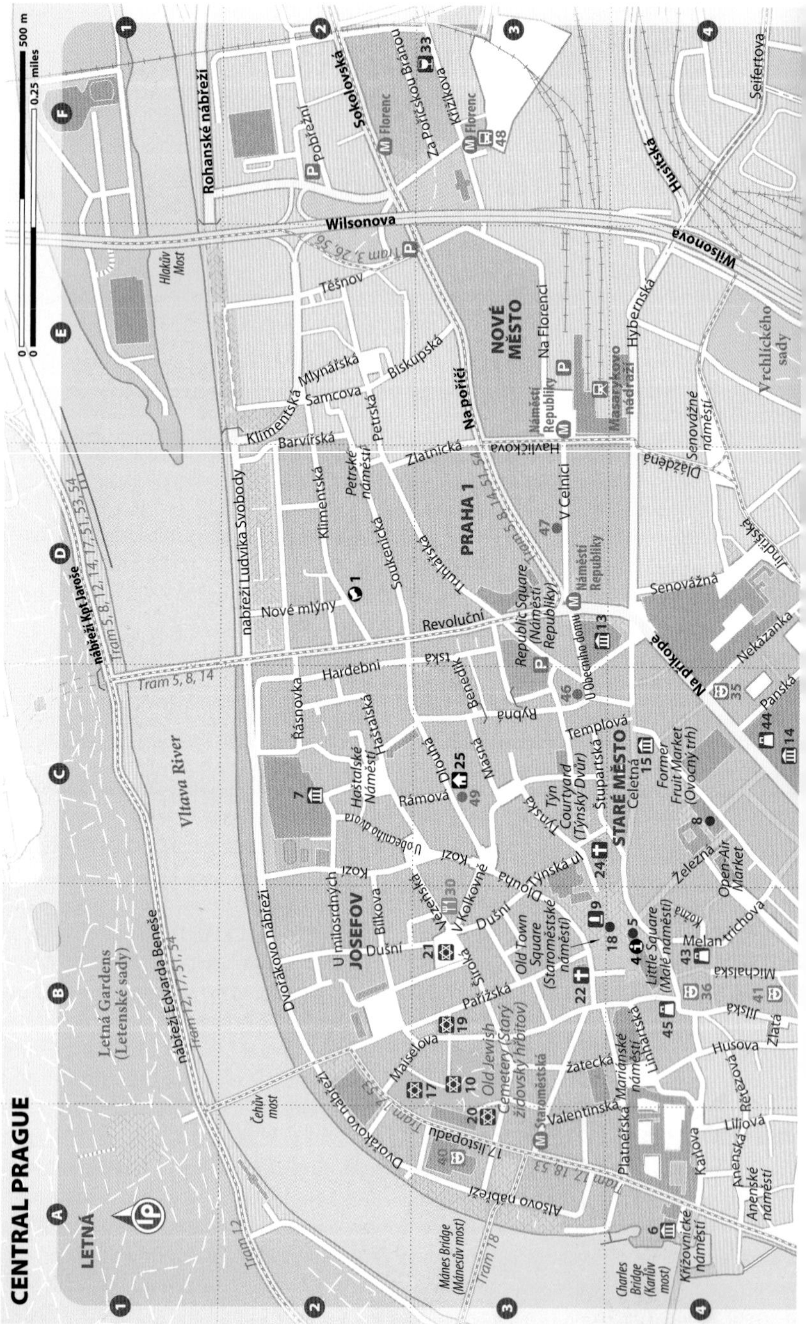

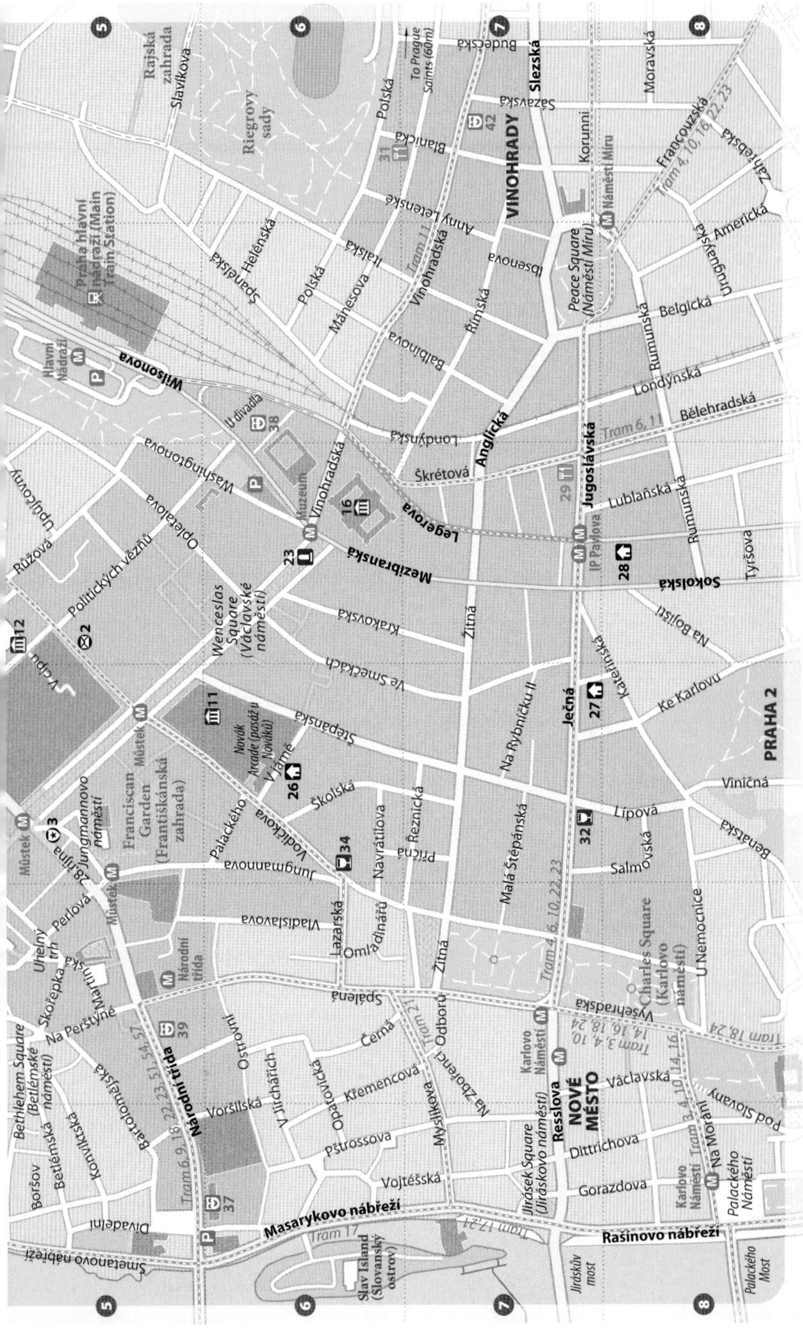
Praha hlavní nádraží (Main Train Station)
Hlavní Nádraží
Wilsonova
Rajská zahrada
Slavíkova
Riegrovy sady
To Prague Saints (60m)
Polská
Budečská
Slezská
Sázavská
Blanická
Vinohrady
Korunní
Náměstí Míru
Peace Square (Náměstí Míru)
Francouzská
Tram 4, 10, 16, 22, 23
Záhřebská
Americká
Uruguayská
Belgická
Rumunská
Londýnská
Bělehradská
Tram 6, 11
Jugoslávská
Lublaňská
IP Pavlova
Sokolská
Tyršova
Na Bojišti
Ke Karlovu
Kateřinská
Praha 2
Viničná
Benátská
Lípová
Salmovská
U Nemocnice
Charles Square (Karlovo náměstí)
Vyšehradská
Tram 18, 24
Tram 3, 4, 10, 14, 16, 18, 24
Václavská
Pod Slovany
Na Moráni
Palackého Náměstí
Karlovo Náměstí
Rašínovo nábřeží
Palackého Most
Jiráskův most
Jiráskovo Square (Jiráskovo náměstí)
Resslova
Nové Město
Dittrichova
Gorazdova
Vojtěšská
Pštrossova
Myslíkova
Na Zbořenci
Odborů
Křemencova
Opatovická
V Jirchářích
Ostrovní
Černá
Tram 21
Spálená
Masarykovo nábřeží
Tram 17
Tram 17, 21
Slav Island (Slovanský ostrov)
Smetanovo nábřeží
Divadelní
Národní třída
Tram 6, 9, 18, 22, 23, 51, 54, 57
Voršilská
Bartolomějská
Na Perštýně
Skořepka
Martinská
Uhelný trh
Perlová
Bethlehem Square (Betlémské náměstí)
Betlémská
Konviktská
Boršov
Vladislavova
Lazarská
Omladinářů
Žitná
Jungmannova
Palackého
Jungmannovo náměstí
28.října
Můstek
Franciscan Garden (Františkánská zahrada)
Vodičkova
Školská
Navrátilova
Řeznická
Příčná
Malá Štěpánská
Na Rybníčku II
Ječná
Štěpánská
V Jámě
Novák Arcade (pasáž u Nováků)
Ve Smečkách
Krakovská
Wenceslas Square (Václavské náměstí)
V cípu
Politických vězňů
Růžová
Opletalova
Washingtonova
Jindřišská
Muzeum
Vinohradská
Mezibranská
Legerova
Škrétová
Anglická
Římská
Balbínova
Mánesova
Italská
Anny Letenské
Ibsenova
Helénská
Španělská
U divadla
Tram 11

INFORMATION
Australian Consulate ... 1 D2
Main Post Office ... 2 D5
Prague 1 Police Station ... 3 C5
Prague Information Service (Old Town Hall) ... 4 B4

SIGHTS & ACTIVITIES
Astronomical Clock ... 5 B4
Charles Bridge Museum ... 6 A4
Convent of St Agnes ... 7 C2
Estates Theatre ... 8 C4
Jan Hus Monument ... 9 B3
Klaus Synagogue ... 10 B3
Lucerna pasáž ... 11 C6
Mucha Museum ... 12 D5
Municipal House ... 13 D3
Museum of Communism ... 14 C4
Museum of Czech Cubism ... 15 C4
National Museum ... 16 D6
Old Jewish Cemetery ... 17 B3
Old Town Hall Clock Tower ... (see 4)
Old Town Square (Staroměstské Náměstí) ... 18 B4
Old-New Synagogue ... 19 B3
Pinkas Synagogue ... 20 A3
Spanish Synagogue ... 21 B3
St Nicholas Church (Staré Město) ... 22 B3
Statue of St Wenceslas ... 23 D6
Týn Church ... 24 C3

SLEEPING
Hotel Antik ... 25 C3
Icon Hotel ... 26 C6
Miss Sophie's ... 27 C7
Pension Březina ... 28 D8

EATING
Café FX ... 29 D7
Kolkovna ... 30 B3
Pastička ... 31 F6

DRINKING
Pivovarský Dům ... 32 C7
Pivovarský Klub ... 33 F3
U Sudu ... 34 C6

ENTERTAINMENT
Black Theatre of Jiří Srnec ... (see 39)
Bohemia Ticket International (BTI) ... 35 C4
Bohemia Ticket International (BTI) ... 36 B4
Laterna Magika ... 37 A6
Prague State Opera ... 38 E6
Reduta Jazz Club ... 39 B5
Rudolfinum ... 40 A3
USP Jazz Lounge ... 41 B4
Valentino ... 42 F7

SHOPPING
Manufaktura ... 43 B4
Moser ... 44 C4
Rott Crystal ... 45 B4

TRANSPORT
Cedaz Minibus Stop ... (see 47)
City Bike ... 46 C3
Czech Airlines ... 47 D3
Eurolines ... (see 48)
Florenc Bus Station ... 48 F3
Praha Bike ... 49 C3
Student Agency ... (see 48)

(costume designer for the film *Amadeus*) takes place every hour, on the hour. At noon a band plays from the windows above.

The **Matthias Gate** leads to the Second Courtyard and the **Chapel of the Holy Cross** (concert tickets on sale here). The Third Courtyard is dominated by **St Vitus Cathedral** (Map pp548-9), a French Gothic structure begun in 1344 by Emperor Charles IV, but not completed until 1929. Stained-glass windows created by early 20th-century Czech artists illuminate the interior, including one by Alfons Mucha (third chapel on the left as you enter the cathedral) featuring SS Cyril and Methodius. In the apse is the **tomb of St John of Nepomuk** – two tons of baroque silver watched over by hovering cherubs.

The 14th-century chapel on the cathedral's southern side with the black imperial eagle on the door contains the **tomb of St Wenceslas**, the Czechs' patron saint and the Good King Wenceslas of Christmas-carol fame. On the other side of the transept, climb the 287 steps of the **Great Tower** (**adult/child 50/25Kč; 9am-4.15pm Apr-Oct**).

Also on the southern side is the **Story of Prague Castle** (**www.story-castle.cz; adult/child 140/70Kč, incl with long-tour tickets**) exhibition. This multimedia take on history includes a 40-minute **documentary** (**in English 9.45am, 11.14am, 12.45pm, 2.15pm & 3.45pm**). The exhibit is a good way to get a handle on Prague Castle's sprawling location and history before or after you go exploring.

Opposite is the entrance to the **Old Royal Palace** (included with long- and short-tour tickets) with the elegantly vaulted **Vladislav Hall**, built between 1486 and 1502. Two Catholic councillors were thrown out the window of the adjacent **Chancellery** by irate Protestant nobles on 23 May 1618. This infamous Second Defenestration of Prague ignited the Thirty Years' War.

Leaving the palace, the Romanesque **Basilica of St George** (1142; included with long- and short-tour tickets), and the nearby **Convent of St George** (**www.ngprague.cz; adult/child 100/50Kč; 1am-6pm Tue-Sun**) has an extensive Renaissance art collection administered by the National Gallery.

Beyond, the crowds surge into the **Golden Lane** (Map pp548-9; included with long- and short-tour tickets), a 16th-century tradesmen's quarter of tiny houses in the castle walls. Kafka lived and wrote at his sister's place at number 22 from 1916 to 1917.

There are two main routes to the castle. Either catch the metro to Malostranská or tram 12, 20, 22 or 23 to Malostranska nám and look forward to a brisk walk up Nerudova, or take tram 22 or 23 to the Pražský hrad stop, from where you can enter at the Second Courtyard.

HRADČANY

The Hradčany area west from Prague Castle is mainly residential, with shops and restaurants on Loretánská and Pohořelec. In 1598, Hradčany was almost levelled by Hussites and fire, and the 17th-century palaces were built on the ruins.

The 18th-century Šternberg Palace, outside the castle entrance, houses the **National Gallery** (**Map pp548-9; ☎ 220 514 598; www.ngprague.cz; adult/child 150/80Kč; 10am-6pm Tue-Sun**), with the country's principal collection of 14th- to 18th-century European art.

MALÁ STRANA

Downhill are the baroque backstreets of Malá Strana (Little Quarter), built in the 17th and 18th centuries by victorious Catholic clerics and nobles on the foundations of their Protestant predecessors' Renaissance palaces.

Near the cafe-crowded main square of Malostranské nám is the beautiful baroque **St Nicholas Church** (**Map pp548-9; www.psalterium.cz; adult/child 70/35Kč; 9am-5pm Mar-Oct, to 4pm Nov-Feb**). From April to October the church is used for **classical music concerts** (**adult/child 490/300Kč; 6pm Wed-Mon**).

JOHN ELK III

Oriel window in the Old Town, Olomouc

IF YOU LIKE...

If you like the ornate architecture in **Prague**, but don't love the crowds, travel to **Olomouc** (**☎ tourist office 585 513 385; www.olomouc-tourism.cz; Horní nám; 9am-7pm**). The quiet Moravian town has a smaller, though no less impressive Old Town square – complete with its own 17th-century town hall and astronomical clock; here worker figures trundle out to mark the hour instead of pious saints. The impressive renaissance churches, numerous fountains and the Unesco-recognised Holy Trinity Column, one of the largest baroque plague columns in Europe, are quite the sight. Plus this university town has a laid-back vibe a world apart from the capital city buzz.

Malá Strana is linked to Staré Město by **Charles Bridge** (Karlův most; Map pp548-9). Built in 1357, and graced by 30 18th-century statues, until 1841 it was the city's only bridge. Climb the **Malá Strana bridge tower** (**Map pp548-9; adult/child 50/30Kč; 10am-6pm Apr-Nov**) for excellent views. In the middle of the bridge is a bronze statue (1683) of St John of Nepomuk, a priest thrown to his death from the bridge in 1393 for refusing to reveal the queen's confessions to King Wenceslas IV. Visit the bridge at dawn, before the tourist hordes arrive. An after-dark crossing with an illuminated Prague Castle is also an essential Prague experience. From 2006 to 2010, Charles Bridge has undergone significant reconstruction. Visit the **Charles Bridge Museum** (p551) to understand why, after 650 years of history, a makeover was overdue.

North of Charles Bridge is the **Franz Kafka Museum** (Map pp548-9; ☎ 257 535 507; www.kafkamuseum.cz; Cihelná 2b; adult/child 120/60Kč; 10am-6pm). Kafka's diaries, letters and first editions provide a poignant balance to the T-shirt cliché the writer has become in tourist shops.

In front is the **'Piss' sculpture** by Czech artist David Černý, with its two animatronic figures piddling in a puddle shaped like the Czech Republic. Interrupt the flow of famous Prague literary quotations by sending your own message via SMS to ☎ 420 724 370 770.

RICHARD NEBESKY

Malá Strana bridge tower (p555)

Escape the throngs on the **funicular railway** (Map pp548-9; tram ticket 26Kč; every 10-20 min 9.15am-8.45pm) from Újezd to the rose gardens on **Petřín Hill**. Climb 299 steps to the top of the view-friendly iron-framed **Petřín Lookout Tower** (Map pp548-9; adult/child 50/40Kč; 10am-10pm May-Sep, to 7pm Apr & Oct, to 5pm Sat & Sun Nov-Mar), built in 1891 in imitation of the Eiffel Tower. Behind the tower a staircase leads to lanes winding back to Malostranské nám.

VYŠEHRAD

Pack a picnic and take the metro (Vyšehrad station) to the ancient clifftop fortress **Vyšehrad** (Map pp548-9; www.praha-vysehrad.cz; admission free; 9.30am-6pm Apr-Oct, to 5pm Nov-Mar), perched above the Vltava. Dominated by the towers of **SS Peter & Paul Church** (Map pp548-9) and founded in the 11th century, Vyšehrad was rebuilt in the neo-Gothic style between 1885 and 1903. Don't miss the art-nouveau murals inside. The adjacent **Slavín Cemetery** (Map pp548-9) contains the graves of many Czechs, including the composers Smetana and Dvořák. The view from the citadel's southern battlements is superb.

TOURS

Prague Tours (☎ 777 816 849; www.praguer.com; per person 300-450Kč) Including an Old Town Pub Tour and Ghost Trail.

Prague Walks (☎ 608 339 099; www.praguewalks.com; per person 300-450Kč) From Franz Kafka to microbreweries, communism, and a fashion tour (300Kč).

Wittmann Tours (☎ 603 426 564; www.wittmann-tours.com; per person from 750Kč) Specialises in tours of Jewish interest, including day trips (1150Kč) to the Museum of the Ghetto at Terezín.

FESTIVALS & EVENTS

Prague Spring (www.festival.cz) From 12 May to 3 June, classical music kicks off summer.

Prague Fringe Festival (www.praguefringe.com) Eclectic action in late May.

Khamoro (www.khamoro.cz) Late May's annual celebration of Roma culture.

SLEEPING

Miss Sophie's (Map pp552-3; ☎ 296 303 530; www.miss-sophies.com; Melounova 3; dm 560Kč, s/d from 1790/2050Kč, apt from 2290Kč; 💻) 'Boutique hostel' sums up this converted apartment building. Polished concrete blends with oak flooring, and the basement lounge is all bricks and black leather. Good restaurants await outside.

Pension Březina (Map pp552-3; ☎ 296 188 888; www.brezina.cz; Legerova 39-41, Nové Město; s/d economy 1400/1600Kč, luxury 2700/2900Kč) A friendly pension in a converted art-nouveau apartment block with a small garden. Ask for a quieter room at the back.

Hotel Antik (Map pp552-3; ☎ 222 322 288; www.antikhotels.com; Dlouhá 22, Staré Město; s/d 2590/2990Kč) A recent makeover has given the popular Antik a modern tinge, but heritage fans can still celebrate its 15th-century building (no lift) beside an antique shop. It's a great area for bars and restaurants, so ask for a quieter back room.

Hotel U Tří Korunek (Map pp548-9; ☎ 222 781 112; www.three-crowns-hotel-prague.com; Cimburkova 28, Žižkov; s/d/tr from €85/105/130) The 'Three Crowns' rambles across three buildings. Up-and-coming Žižkov is a good area for bars, and the city centre is just a few tram stops away.

our pick **Icon Hotel** (Map pp552-3; ☎ 221 634 100; www.iconhotel.eu; V jámě 6, Nové Město; d €165-210; 💻) Design-savvy cool concealed down a quiet laneway. The handmade beds are extra-wide, and the crew at reception is unpretentious and hip.

Aria Hotel (Map pp548-9; ☎ 225 334 111; www.ariahotel.net; Tržiště 9, Malá Strana; d from €215; 💻) Choose your favourite composer or musician and stay in a luxury themed room with a selection of their tunes in a music database.

EATING

Prague has many cuisines and price ranges. Choose from good-value beer halls with no-nonsense fare, or enjoy a chic riverside restaurant with a high-flying clientele and prices to match.

Café FX (Map pp552-3; ☎ 224 254 776; Bělehradská 120, Vinohrady; mains 120-230Kč; 🕑 11.30am-2am) Café FX is chiffon and chandelier chic, with Prague's best vegetarian flavours from Mexico, India and Thailand.

Na Verandách (Map pp548-9; ☎ 257 191 200; Nádražní 84, Smichov; meals 150-300Kč) Across the river in Smichov, the Staropramen brewery's restaurant is a modern spot crowded with locals enjoying superior versions of favourite Czech dishes and an 'it could be a long night' selection of different brews.

Pastička (Map pp552-3; ☎ 222 253 228; Blanikcá 24, Vinohrady; mains 150-350Kč; 🕑 11am-midnight Mon-Fri, from 5pm Sat & Sun) Vinohrady's emerging dining scene around Mánesova now features the unpretentious 'Mousetrap'. Locals come to drink excellent Bernard beer, to eat huge meaty meals, and to feel good about living in the funky part of town.

Kolkovna (Map pp552-3; ☎ 224 819 701; Kolkovně 8, Staré Město; meals 160-400Kč) Kolkovna's contemporary spin on the traditional beer hall serves up classy versions of Czech dishes like *gulaš* and roast pork. Try Pilsner Urquell's delicious unpasteurised *tankovna* beer.

Hergetova Cihelna (Map pp548-9; ☎ 257 535 534; Cihelná 2b, Malá Strana; mains 220-550Kč; 🕑 9am-2am) A restored *cihelná* (brickworks)

RICHARD NEBESKY

Bartender at Pivovarský Dům

is now a hip space with a riverside terrace looking back to Charles Bridge and Staré Město.

DRINKING

Bohemian beers are among the world's best. The most famous brands are Budvar, Plzeňský Prazdroj (Pilsner Urquell) and Prague's own Staropramen. An increasing number of independent microbreweries also offer a more unique drinking experience.

our pick **Pivovarský Dům** (**Map pp552-3; ☎ 296 216 666; cnr Ječná & Lipová, Nové Město**) The 'Brewery House' microbrewery conjures everything from a refreshing wheat beer to coffee- and banana-flavoured styles – even a beer 'champagne'.

Pivovarský Klub (**Map pp552-3; ☎ 222 315 777; Křižíkova 17, Karlín**) Submit to your inner hophead at this pub-restaurant-beer-shop with interesting limited-volume draught beers, and bottled brews from around the Czech Republic. Come for lunch, as it gets full of loyal regulars later on.

Bukowski's (**Map pp548-9; Bořvojova 86, Žižkov; from 6pm**) This new late-night cocktail bar is driving grungy Žižkov's inevitable transformation into Prague's hottest after-dark neighbourhood.

U Sudu (**Map pp552-3; ☎ 222 232 20; Vodičkova 10, Nové Město**) Moravian wines are growing in reputation and this labyrinth of cellar bars and lounges is a good spot to fast-track your knowledge of the local wine scene.

Prague's summer streets are crammed with outdoor tables, and good-quality tea and coffee are widely available.

ENTERTAINMENT

For current listings, see *Culture in Prague* (available from PIS offices; see p547), www.prague.tv or the monthly free *Provokátor* magazine (www.provokator.org), available from clubs, cafes and art-house cinemas.

Try the following ticket agencies:

Bohemia Ticket International (**☎ 224 227 832; www.ticketsbti.cz**) Nové Město (**Map pp552-3; Na příkopě 16; 10am-7pm Mon-Fri,**

to 5pm Sat, to 3pm Sun); Staré Město (Map pp552-3; Malé nám 13; 9am-5pm Mon-Fri, to 1pm Sat)

Ticketstream (www.ticketstream.cz) Online bookings for events in Prague and the Czech Republic.

PERFORMING ARTS

You'll see fliers advertising concerts for tourists. It's a good chance to relax in old churches and historic buildings, but performances can be of mediocre quality. Prices begin around 400Kč.

Rudolfinum (Map pp552-3; ☎ 227 059 352; www.rudolfinum.cz; nám Jana Palacha, Staré Město; box office 10am-12.30pm & 1.20-6pm Mon-Fri plus 1hr before performances) One of Prague's main concert venues is the Dvořák Hall in the neo-Renaissance Ruldolfinum, home to the Czech Philharmonic Orchestra.

Prague State Opera (Státní opera Praha; Map pp552-3; ☎ 224 227 266; www.opera.cz; Legerova 75, Nové Město; box office 10am-5.30pm, 10am-noon & 1-5pm Sat & Sun) Opera, ballet and classical drama (in Czech) are performed at this neo-Renaissance theatre.

Laterna Magika (Map pp552-3; ☎ 224 931 482; www.laterna.cz; Nová Scéna, Národní třída 4, Nové Město; tickets 540-680Kč; box office 10am-8pm Mon-Sat) A multimedia show combining dance, opera, music and film.

Black Theatre of Jiří Srnec (Map pp552-3; ☎ 257 921 835; www.blacktheatresrnec.cz; Reduta Theatre, Národní 20, Nové Město; tickets 620Kč; box office 3-7pm Mon-Fri, shows at 9.30pm) Prague is awash in 'black light theatre' shows combining mime, ballet, animated film and puppetry. Jiří Srnec's Black Theatre is the original and the least touristy.

LIVE MUSIC

Prague has jazz clubs varying in style from traditional to avant-garde.

Palác Akropolis (Map pp548-9; ☎ 296 330 911; www.palacakropolis.cz; Kubelikova 27, Žižkov; club 7pm-5am) Get lost in the labyrinth of theatre, live music, clubbing, drinking and eating that makes up Prague's coolest venue. Hip hop, house, reggae, or rocking Roma bands from Romania – anything goes.

Reduta Jazz Club (Map pp552-3; ☎ 224 912 246; www.redutajazzclub.cz; Národní třída 20, Nové Město; 9pm-3am) Founded in 1958 and one of the oldest jazz clubs in Europe. Bill Clinton jammed here in 1994.

USP Jazz Lounge (Map pp552-3; ☎ 603 551 680; www.jazzlounge.cz; Michalská 9, Staré Město; 8pm-3am) A less traditional venue with modern jazz from 10pm. DJs kick on from midnight.

GAY & LESBIAN VENUES

The inner suburb of Vinohrady is developing as a gay quarter, and the city enjoys a relaxed scene.

Prague Saints (Map pp552-3; ☎ 222 250 326; www.praguesaints.cz; Polska 32, Vinohrady) Online information on Prague's gay scene. The on-site Saints Bar (open from 5pm to 4am) is a good intro to what's happening. Thursdays from 8pm is lesbian night.

Valentino (Map pp552-3; ☎ 222 513 491; www.club-valentino.cz; Vinohradská 40, Vinohrady; from 11am) Welcome to Prague's gay superclub, with three floors containing two dance areas, four bars, and other rooms with exceedingly low lighting.

SHOPPING

Prague's main shopping streets are in Nové Město – Wenceslas Sq, Na příkopě, 28.října and Národní třída – and there are many tourist-oriented shops on Celetná, the Old Town Sq, Pařížská and Karlova in Staré Město. Local souvenirs include Bohemian crystal, ceramics, marionettes and garnet jewellery.

Moser (Map pp552-3; ☎ 224 211 293; Na příkopě 12, Nové Město; 10am-8pm Mon-Fri,

to 7pm Sat & Sun) Top-quality Bohemian crystal.

Rott Crystal **(Map pp552-3; ☎ 224 229 529; Malé nám 3, Staré Město; ⏰ 10am-8pm)** Housed in a neo-Renaissance building that's worth a look even if you're just browsing.

Manufaktura **(Map pp552-3; ☎ 221 632 480; www.manu faktura.biz; Melantrichova 17, Staré Město)** Sells traditional Czech handicrafts, wooden toys and handmade cosmetics.

GETTING THERE & AWAY

See also p605.

BUS

The main terminal for international and domestic buses is **Florenc Bus Station** **(ÚAN Florenc; Map pp552-3; ☎ 12 999; Křižíkova 4, Karlín)**, 600m northeast of the main train station (ÚAN is short for *Ústřední autobusové nádraží,* or 'central bus station').

Eurolines **(Map pp552-3; ☎ 245 005 245; www.bei.cz; ÚAN Florenc Bus Station; ⏰ 8am-7pm Mon-Fri)** Buses to all over Europe.

Student Agency **(☎ 224 894 430; www.studentagency.cz; ⏰ 9am-6pm Mon-Fri)** Linking major Czech cities and services throughout Europe.

TRAIN

Prague's main train station is **Praha-hlavní nádraží** **(Map pp552-3; ☎ 221 111 122; Wilsonova, Nové Město)**. Some international trains stop at Praha-Holešovice station on the northern side of the city, while some domestic services terminate at Praha-Masarykovo in Nové Město, or Praha-Smíchov south of Malá Strana. Also buy train tickets and get timetable information from **ČD Centrum** **(⏰ 6am-7.30pm)** at the southern end of level 2 in Praha-hlavní nádraží.

There are direct trains from Praha-hlavní nádraží to České Budějovice (211Kč, 2½ hours, hourly), Karlovy Vary (292Kč, three hours, three daily) and Kutná Hora (95Kč, 55 minutes, seven daily).

Check train timetables and depature points online at www.idos.cz.

GETTING AROUND

TO/FROM THE AIRPORT

Prague's Ruzyně airport is 17km west of the city centre. To get into town, buy a ticket from the public transport (Dopravní podnik; DPP) desk in arrivals and take bus 119 (26Kč, 20 minutes, every 15 minutes) to the end of the line (Dejvická), then continue by metro into the city centre (another 10 minutes, no extra ticket needed). Alternatively, the **Airport Express** **(adult/child 45/25Kč; ⏰ 5am-9pm)** bus service goes direct to the Holešovice metro station.

The **Cedaz minibus** **(☎ 221 111 111; www.cedaz.cz)** leaves from outside arrivals (20 minutes, every half-hour from 6am to 9pm). Buy your ticket from the driver. The minibus stops at the **Czech Airlines** **(Map pp552-3; V Celnici 5)** office near the Hilton around nám Republiky (120Kč) or further out at the Dejvická metro station (90Kč). You can also get a Cedaz minibus from your hotel or any other address (480Kč for one to four people, 960Kč for five to eight).

Prague Airport Taxis, with airport-regulated prices, charge 650Kč into central Prague. Drivers speak good English.

BICYCLE

City Bike **(Map pp552-3; ☎ 776 180 284; www.citybike-prague.com; Králodvorská 5, Staré Město; ⏰ 9am-7pm May-Sep)** Independent hire is 300Kč for the first two hours and 500Kč for all day.

Praha Bike **(Map pp552-3; ☎ 732 388 880; www.praha bike.cz; Dlouhá 24, Staré Město; ⏰ 9am-8pm)** A range of different tour routes including rail and bike combos to Karlštejn Castle.

CAR & MOTORCYCLE

Challenges to driving in Prague include cobblestones, trams and one-way streets. Try not to arrive or leave on a Friday or Sunday afternoon or evening, when Prague folk are travelling to and from their weekend houses. Central Prague has many pedestrian-only streets, marked with Pěší Zoná (Pedestrian Zone) signs, where only service vehicles and taxis are allowed; parking can be a nightmare.

PUBLIC TRANSPORT

All public transport is operated by **Dopravní podnik hl. m. Prahy** (DPP; ☎ 800 191 817; www.dpp.cz), with information desks at **Ruzyně airport** (🕑 7am to 7pm) and in four metro stations – **Muzeum** (🕑 7am to 9pm), **Můstek** (🕑 7am to 6pm), **Anděl** (🕑 7am to 6pm) and **Nádraží Holešovice** (🕑 7am to 6pm) – where you can get tickets, directions, a multilingual system map, a map of *Noční provoz* (night services) and a detailed English-language guide to the whole system.

Buy a ticket before boarding a bus, tram or metro. Tickets are sold from machines at metro stations and major tram stops, at news-stands, Trafiky snack shops, PNS and other tobacco kiosks, hotels, all metro station ticket offices and DPP information offices.

A *jízdenka* (transfer ticket) is valid on tram, metro, bus and the Petřín funicular and costs 26Kč (half-price for six- to 15-year-olds); large suitcases and backpacks (anything larger than 25cm by 45cm by 70cm) also need a 13Kč ticket. Validate (punch) your ticket by sticking it in the little yellow machine in the metro station lobby or on the bus or tram the first time you board; this stamps the time and date on it. Tickets remain valid for 75 minutes from the time of stamping, if validated between 5am and 10pm on weekdays, and for 90 minutes at other times. Within this period, you can make unlimited transfers between all types of public transport (you don't need to punch the ticket again). Tickets for 24 hours (100Kč) and three/five days (330/500Kč) are also available. Before shelling out on a pass, note much of central Prague can be explored on foot.

TAXI

Try to avoid getting a taxi in tourist areas such as Wenceslas Sq. To avoid being ripped off, phone a reliable company such as **AAA** (☎ 14 014; www.aaa.radiotaxi.cz) or **City Taxi** (☎ 257 257 257; www.citytaxi.cz). Both companies also offer online bookings.

STEPHEN SAKS

Karlštejn Castle (p562)

Prague recently introduced the 'Taxi Fair Place' scheme, with authorised taxis in tourist areas. Drivers can charge a maximum of 28Kč/km and must announce the estimated price in advance. Look for the yellow and red signs.

If you do feel cheated, keep the receipt and email the details to taxi@cityofprague.cz.

AROUND PRAGUE

KARLŠTEJN

Erected by the Emperor Charles IV in the mid-14th century, **Karlštejn Castle** (☎ **274 008 154; www.hradkarlstejn.cz; Karlštejn; 🕑 9am-6pm Tue-Sun Jul & Aug, to 5pm May, Jun & Sep, to 4pm Apr & Oct, to 3pm Mar & Nov, closed Jan, Feb & Dec**), crowns a ridge above Karlštejn village. It's a 20-minute walk from the train station.

The highlight is the **Chapel of the Holy Rood**, where the Bohemian crown jewels were kept until 1420. The 55-minute guided tours (in English) on Route I costs 200/120Kč for adult/child tickets. Route II, which includes the chapel (June to October only), are 300/150Kč adult/child and must be prebooked.

Trains from Praha-hlavní nádraží station to Beroun stop at Karlštejn (46Kč, 45 minutes, hourly).

KONOPIŠTĚ

The assassination of the heir to the Austro-Hungarian throne, Archduke Franz Ferdinand d'Este, sparked off WWI. For the last 20 years of his life he hid away southeast of Prague in **Konopiště Chateau**, his country retreat.

Three guided tours are available. **Tour III** (**adult/child 300/200Kč**) is the most interesting, visiting the archduke's private apartments, unchanged since the state took over the chateau in 1921. **Tour II** (**adult/child 190/110Kč**) takes in the **Great Armoury**, one of Europe's most impressive collections. The castle is a testament to the archduke's twin obsessions of hunting and St George.

There are direct trains from Prague's hlavní nádraží to Benešov u Prahy (66Kč, 1¼ hours, hourly). Konopiště is 2.5km west of Benešov. Local bus 2 (11Kč, six minutes, hourly) runs from a stop on Dukelská, 400m north of the train station (turn left out of the station, then first right on Tyršova and first left) to the castle car park. Otherwise it's a 30-minute walk. Turn left out of the train station, go left across the bridge over the railway, and follow Konopištská street west for 2km.

KUTNÁ HORA

In the 14th century, the silver-rich ore under Kutná Hora gave the now-sleepy town an importance in Bohemia second only to Prague. The local mines and mint turned out silver *groschen* for use as the hard currency of central Europe. The silver ore ran out in 1726, leaving the medieval townscape largely unaltered. Now with several fascinating and unusual historical attractions, the Unesco World Heritage–listed town is a popular day trip from Prague.

The **information centre** (☎ **327 512 378; www.kutnahora.cz; Palackého nám 377; 🕑 9am-6pm Apr-Sep, 9am-5pm Mon-Fri, 10am-4pm Sat & Sun Oct-Mar**) books accommodation, provides internet access (1Kč per minute), and rents bicycles (220Kč per day).

Walk 10 minutes south from Kutná Hora hlavní nádraží to the remarkable **Sedlec Ossuary** (**Kostnice; ☎ 327 561 143; www.kostnice.cz; adult/child 50/30Kč; 🕑 8am-6pm Apr-Sep, 9am-noon & 1-5pm Oct & Mar, 9am-noon & 1-4pm Nov-Mar**). When the Schwarzenberg family purchased Sedlec monastery in 1870, a local woodcarver got creative with the bones of 40,000 people from the centuries-old crypt. Skulls and femurs are strung from the vaulted ceiling, and the central chandelier contains at least one of each bone in the human body. Four giant pyramids of stacked bones squat in the corner chapels, and crosses of bone adorn the altar.

From the Kutná Hora bus station catch bus 1B and get off at the Tabak stop. From Sedlec it's another 2km walk (or five-minute bus ride) to central Kutná Hora.

There are direct trains from Prague's hlavní nádraží to Kutná Hora hlavní nádraží (98Kč, 55 minutes, seven daily).

BOHEMIA

The ancient land of Bohemia makes up the western two-thirds of the Czech Republic. The modern term 'bohemian' comes to us via the French, who thought that Roma came from Bohemia; the word *bohémien* was later applied to people living an unconventional lifestyle. The term gained currency in the wake of Puccini's opera *La Bohème* about poverty-stricken artists in Paris.

TEREZÍN

The massive fortress at Terezín (Theresienstadt in German) was built by the Habsburgs in the 18th century to repel the Prussian army, but the place is better known as a notorious WWII prison and concentration camp. Around 150,000 men, women and children, mostly Jews, passed through en route to the extermination camps of Auschwitz-Birkenau: 35,000 of them died here of hunger, disease or suicide, and only 4000 survived. From 1945 to 1948 the fortress served as an internment camp for the Sudeten Germans, who were expelled from Czechoslovakia after the war.

Ironically, Terezín played a tragic role in deceiving the world of the ultimate goals of the Nazi's 'Final Solution'. Official visitors were immersed in a charade, with Terezín being presented as a Jewish 'refuge', complete with shops, schools and cultural organisations – even an autonomous Jewish 'government'. As late as April 1945, Red Cross visitors espoused positive reports.

The **Terezín Memorial** (☎ **416 782 225; www.pamatnik-terezin.cz**) consists of the Museum of the Ghetto in the Main Fortress, and the Lesser Fortress, a 10-minute walk east across the Ohře River. Admission to one part costs 160/130Kč for an adult/child; a combined ticket is

MARTIN MOOS

Human bones at Sedlec Ossuary

RICHARD NEBESKY

Garden statue at Konopiště Chateau

200/150Kč. Most poignant are the copies of *Vedem* ('In the Lead') magazine, published by 100 boys from 1942 to 1944. Only 15 of the boys survived the war.

Buses between Prague and Litoměřice stop at both the main square and the Lesser Fortress. Many Prague tour companies offer day trips to Terezín.

KARLOVY VARY

pop 60,000

According to legend, Emperor Charles IV discovered Karlovy Vary's hot springs accidentally in 1350 when one of his hunting dogs fell into the waters. Now the fashionable town is the closest the Czech Republic has to a glam resort, but Karlovy Vary is definitely glam with a small 'g'.

The **Karlovy Vary International Film Festival** in early July is well worth attending. More than 200 films are shown, tickets are easy to get, and a funky array of concurrent events, including buskers and world-music concerts, gives the genteel town an annual energy transfusion.

Trains from Prague arrive at Horní nádraží. Take bus 11, 12 or 13 (12Kč) from across the road to the Tržnice station; 11 continues to Divadelni nám in the spa district.

The **Infocentrum** (Dolni nádraží ☎ 353 232 838; www.karlovyvary.cz; Západni; 9am-5pm Mon-Fri, 10am-4pm Sat & Sun; Lázeňska ☎ 353 224 097; Lázeňska 1; 10am-6pm Mon-Fri, to 5pm Sat & Sun) has loads of information on the town, plus maps, accommodation help and pricey internet (2Kč per minute).

At the central spa district is the neoclassical **Mill Colonnade** (Mlýnská Kolonáda), with occasional summer concerts. Other elegant colonnades and 19th-century spa buildings are scattered along the Teplá River, with the 1970s concrete **Hotel Thermal** spoiling the effect slightly. Purchase a *lázenské pohár* (spa cup) and some *oplátky* (spa wafers) and sample the various hot springs (free).

Just out of town, the newly expanded **Moser Glass Museum** (Sklářské muzeum Moser; ☎ 353 416 242, www.moser-glass.com; Kpt Jaroše 19; adult/child 80/50Kč; 9am-5pm) has more than 2000 items on display.

STEPHEN SAKS

Mill Colonnade

Afterwards get hot under the collar at the adjacent **glassworks** (adult/child 120/70Kč; 9am-2.30pm).

Although the surviving traditional *lázně* (spa) centres are basically medical institutions, many of the town's old spa and hotel buildings have been renovated as 'wellness' hotels with cosmetic treatments, massages and aromatherapy. **Castle Spa** (Zámecké Lázně; ☎ 353 222 649; http://english.edenhotels.cz; Zámechý vrch; treatments from €25; 7.30am-7.30pm Mon-Fri, from 8.30am Sat & Sun) is a modernised spa centre, complete with a subterranean thermal pool. It still retains a heritage ambience.

For a cheaper paddle head to the **open-air thermal pool** (per hr 80Kč; 8am-8pm Mon-Sat, to 9pm Sun). Follow the 'Bazén' signs up the hill behind Hotel Thermal.

Accommodation is pricey, and can be tight during weekends and festivals; book ahead. Infocentrum (opposite) can find hostel, pension and hotel rooms.

Hotel Kavalerie (☎ 353 229 613; www.kavalerie.cz; TG Masaryka 43; s/d incl breakfast from 950/1225Kč) Friendly staff abound in this cosy spot above a cafe. It's located near the bus and train stations, and nearby eateries can help you avoid the spa district's high restaurant prices.

Embassy Hotel (☎ 353 221 161; www.embassy.cz; Nová Luka 21; s/d incl breakfast from 2260/3130Kč;) KV's not short of top-end hotels, but most lack the personal touch inherent in the Embassy's family-owned combination of a riverside location and perfectly pitched heritage rooms.

Steakhouse Sklipek (☎ 353 229 197; Zeyerova 1; meals 140-180Kč) Red-checked tablecloths and an emphasis on good steak, fish and pasta give this place an honest, rustic ambience lacking in the more expensive chichi spots down in the spa district.

Student Agency (www.studentagency.cz) and **Megabus** (www.megabus.cz) run frequent buses to/from Prague Florenc (130Kč, 2¼ hours, eight daily) departing from the main bus station beside Dolní nádraží train station.

There are direct (but slow) trains from Karlovy Vary to Prague Holešovice (288Kč, three hours). Heading west from Karlovy Vary to Nuremberg, Germany (4½ hours, two a day), and beyond, you'll have to change at Cheb (Eger in German). Check online at www.idos.cz and www.bahn.de.

ČESKÉ BUDĚJOVICE

pop 100,000

The regional capital of South Bohemia is also a picturesque medieval city. Arcing from the town square are 18th-century arcades leading to bars that get raffishly rowdy on weekends – most fuelled by the town's prized export, of course.

The **Municipal Information Centre** (Městské Informarční Centrum; ☎ 386 801 413; www.c-budejovice.cz; nám Přemysla Otakara II 2; 8.30am-6pm Mon-Fri, 8.30am-5pm Sat, 10am-4pm Sun May-Sep, 9am-5pm Mon-Fri, to 1pm Sat Oct-Apr) books tickets, tours and accommodation, and has free internet access.

The **Budweiser Budvar Brewery** (☎ 387 705 341; www.budvar.cz; cnr Pražská & K Světlé; adult/child 100/50Kč; 9am-4pm) is 3km north of the main square. Group tours run every day and the 2pm tour (Monday to Friday only) is open to individual travellers. The highlight is a glass of real-deal Budvar deep in the brewery's chilly cellars. Catch bus 2 to the Budvar stop (12Kč).

In 1876, the founders of US brewer Anheuser-Busch chose the brand name Budweiser because it was synonymous with good beer. Since the late 19th century, both breweries have used the name and a legal arm wrestle over the brand continues. The legal machinations subsided slightly in 2007, with Anheuser-Busch signing a deal to distribute Budvar

MARIÁNSKÉ LÁZNĚ & CHODOVÁ PLANÁ

For a more relaxed Bohemian spa experience than bustling Karlovy Vary (p564), consider Mariánské Lázně. Perched at the southern edge of the Slavkov Forest (Slavkovský Les), the spa town formerly known as Marienbad drew luminaries such as Goethe, Thomas Edison and King Edward VII. Even old misery-guts Franz Kafka was a regular visitor, enjoying the pure waters and getting active on the walking trails that criss-cross the rolling forest. In contemporary times the appeal of spa services, heritage hotels and gentle exercise is complemented by a busy summertime cultural program, including mid-August's **Chopin Music Festival** (www.chopinfestival.cz). You can also catch a local bus (18Kč, 20 minutes) to nearby Chodová Planá and bath in giant hoppy tubs of lager in the Czech Republic's only **beer spa** (www.chodovar.cz).

From Prague, Mariánské Lázně can be reached by train (390Kč, five hours) via Cheb from Prague's main train station (Praha-hlavní nádraží). Buses (160Kč, three hours) run from platform 18 at Prague's Florenc bus station. There are also trains (98Kč, 1½ hours, eight per day) and buses (69Kč, one hour, four daily) to/from Plzeň. From the adjacent bus and train stations at the southern end of Mariánské Lázně, catch trolleybus 5 to the spa area's main bus stop. The **information office** (www.marianskelazne.cz) is 200m uphill on the left.

(as 'Czechvar') in the United States. To confuse matters, České Budějovice's second brewery Samson, produces a beer called BB Budweiser.

Penzión Centrum (☎ 387 311 801; www.penzion centrum.cz; Biskupská 130/3; s/d incl breakfast 1000/1400Kč) Huge rooms with queen-size beds and crisp linen make this an excellent reader-recommended spot near the main square. Right next door there's a good organic restaurant.

Hotel Savoy (☎ 387 201 719; www.hotel-savoy-cb.cz; B Smetany; s/d/tr 1350/1850/2350Kč; 💻) Newly opened, the Savoy is already making an impression with spacious, modern rooms decorated with art-deco-style furniture – trust us, the combination works – and a quiet location just outside the Old Town.

U Tři Sedláku (☎ 387 222 303; Hroznová 488; mains 101-170Kč) Locals celebrate that nothing much has changed at U Tři Sedláku since opening in 1897. Tasty meaty dishes go with the Pilsner Urquell that's constantly being shuffled to busy tables.

Singer Pub (Česká 55) With Czech and Irish beers, plus good cocktails, don't be surprised if you get the urge to rustle up something on the Singer sewing machines on every table. If not, challenge the regulars to a game of *foosball* with a soundtrack of noisy rock.

There are trains from České Budějovice to Prague (211Kč, 2½ hours, hourly) and Plzeň (172Kč, two hours, five daily). Frequent trains trundle to Český Krumlov (44Kč, 45 minutes).

Heading for Vienna (620Kč, four hours, two daily) you'll have to change at Gmünd, or take a direct train to Linz (420Kč, 2¼ hours, one daily) and change there.

ČESKÝ KRUMLOV

pop 14,600

Crowned by a stunning castle, and centred on an elegant Old Town square, Český

Krumlov's Renaissance and baroque buildings enclose the meandering arc of the Vltava River. During summer, countless camera memory cards are filled as pigeons dart through busloads of day-tripping tourists exploring the town's narrow lanes and footbridges.

The town's original Gothic fortress was rebuilt as an imposing Renaissance chateau in the 16th century. Since the 18th century the town's appearance is largely unchanged, and careful renovation and restoration has replaced the architectural neglect of the communist era. In 1992 Český Krumlov was granted Unesco World Heritage status.

For too many travellers, Český Krumlov is just a hurried day trip, but its combination of glorious architecture and watery fun on the Vltava deserve more attention.

ORIENTATION

The train station is 1.5km north of the town centre; buses 1, 2 and 3 go from the station to the Špičák bus stop. From the bridge over the main road beside the bus stop, Latrán leads south into town.

Infocentrum (☎ 380 704 622; www.ckrumlov.cz; nám Svornosti 1; 9am-6pm) Transport and accommodation info, maps, internet access (5Kč per five minutes) and audio guides (100Kč per hour). A guide for disabled visitors is available. A good source of information on the Šumuva region.

Krumlov Tours (☎ 723 069 561; www.krumlovtours.com; nám Svornosti; per person 200-250Kč) Has walking tours with regular departure times; good for solo travellers.

SIGHTS & ACTIVITIES

The Old Town, almost encircled by the Vltava River, is watched over by **Český Krumlov Castle** (☎ 380 704 721; www.castle.ckrumlov.cz; 9am-6pm Tue-Sun Jun-Aug, to 5pm Apr, May, Sep & Oct) and its ornately decorated **Round Tower** (45/30Kč). Three different guided tours are on offer. Wandering through the courtyards and gardens is free.

The path beyond the fourth courtyard leads across the spectacular **Most ná Plášti** to the castle gardens. A ramp to the right leads to the **former riding school**, now a restaurant. The relief above the door shows cherubs offering the head and boots of a vanquished Turk – a reference to Adolf von Schwarzenberg, who conquered the Turkish fortress of Raab in the 16th century. From here the Italian-style **Zámecká zahrada** (castle gardens) stretch away towards the **Bellarie summer pavilion**.

Across the river is nám Svornosti, the Old Town square, overlooked by the Gothic **town hall** and a baroque **plague column** (1716). Above is the striking Gothic **Church of St Vitus** (1439), and

RICHARD NEBESKY

Pilsner drinkers in a Czech beer hall

IF YOU LIKE...

If you like beer, we mean, **České Budějovice** (p565), you might also have a taste for **Plzeň** (☎ information centre 378 035 330; www.plzen.eu; nám Republiky 41; 9am-6pm). Near the spa towns in western Bohemia, Plzeň is home to the **Pilsner Urquell Brewery** (☎ 377 062 888; www.prazdroj.cz; guided tour adult/child 150/80Kč; 10am-6pm) and associated tour and museum.

CZECH REPUBLIC

BOHEMIA

ČESKÝ KRUMLOV

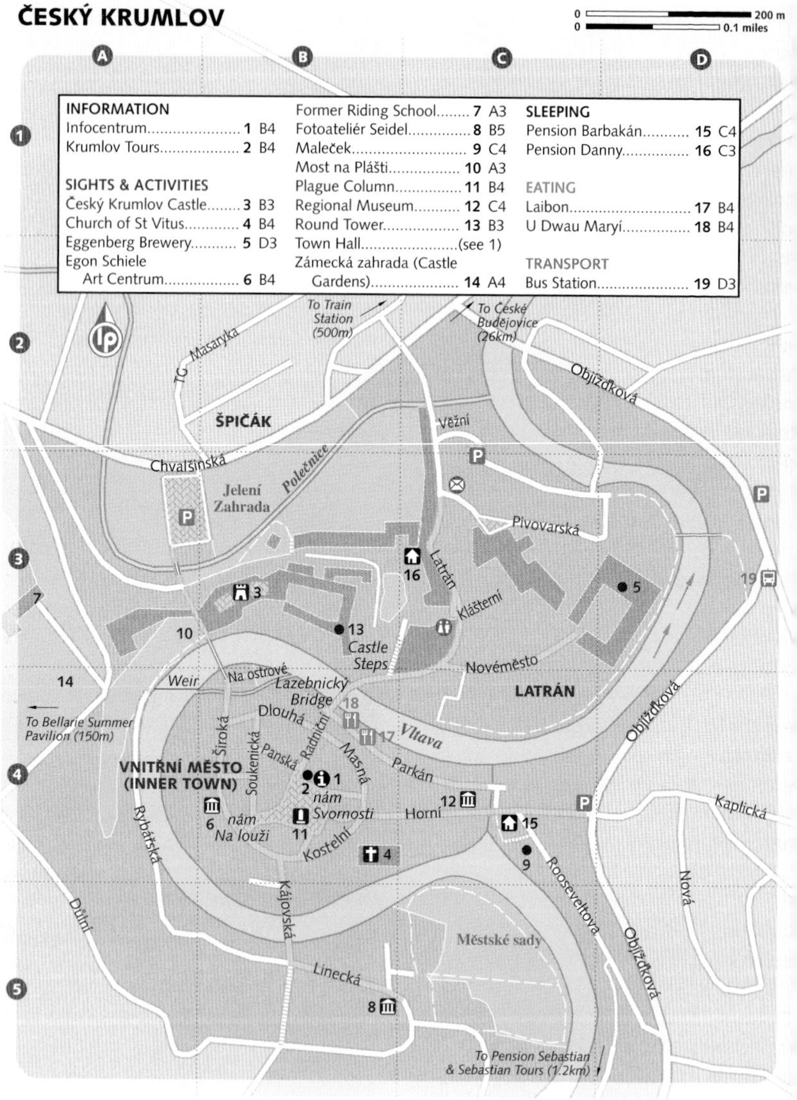

nearby is the **Regional Museum** (☎ 380 711 674; Horní 152; adult/child 50/25Kč; ⌚ 10am-6pm Jul & Aug, 10am-5pm May, Jun & Sep, 9am-4pm Tue-Fri, 1-4pm Sat & Sun, Mar, Apr & Oct-Dec), with an interactive model of the town c 1800.

The **Egon Schiele Art Centrum** (☎ 380 704 011; www.schielartcentrum.cz; Široká 70-72; adult/child 120/700Kč; ⌚ 10am-6pm) is an excellent gallery showcasing the Viennese painter Egon Schiele (1890–1918). The attached **cafe** (⌚ 10am-7pm) is appropriately rty and has a good selection of Moravian vines.

Newly opened in 2008, the **Fotoateliér Seidel** (☎ 380 704 611; Linecká 272; www.seiel.ckrumlov.cz; admission 130Kč; ⌚ 9am-6pm) presents a retrospective of the work of local photographers Josef Seidel and his son František. Especially poignant are the images recording early-20th-century life in nearby mountain villages.

The **Eggenberg Brewery** (☎ 380 711 225; www.eggenberg.cz; Latrán 27; tours with/without tasting 130/100Kč; ⌚ tours 11am) is also where most canoeing and rafting trips end. Relive your experiences on the Vltava's gentle rapids in the brewery's beer garden. Book brewery tours at Infocentrum.

Rent canoes, rafts and rubber rings from **Maleček** (☎ 380 712 508; http://en.malecek.cz; Rooseveltova 28; ⌚ 9am-5pm). Maleček also has sedate river trips through Český Krumlov on giant wooden rafts seating up to 36 people (290Kč, 45 minutes).

Sebastian Tours (☎ 607 100 234; www.sebastianck-tours.com; 5 Května Ul, Plešivec; per person 450Kč) can get you discovering southern Bohemia on guided tours including stops at Hluboká nad Vltavou and České Budějovice.

SLEEPING & EATING

Booking for dinner in July and August is recommended.

our pick **Pension Sebastian** (☎ 608 357 381; www.sebastianck.com; 5 Května Ul, Plešivec; s/d/tr incl breakfast 790/990/1490Kč; ⌚ Apr-Oct) An excellent option just 10 minutes' walk from the Old Town, and therefore slightly cheaper. The well-travelled owners also run tours of the surrounding region.

Pension Danny (☎ 380 712 710; www.pensiondanny.cz; Latrán 72; d incl breakfast from 990Kč) Exposed timber beams and refurbished bathrooms add up to a good-value Old Town location. Have breakfast in your room and enjoy views of romantic CK at the same time.

Pension Barbakán (☎ 380 717 017; www.barbakan.cz; Horní 26; s/d incl breakfast from 1700Kč; 💻) Originally the town's gunpowder arsenal, Barbakán now creates fireworks of its own, with supercomfy rooms featuring bright and cosy wooden decor. Sit in the grill restaurant (mains 140Kč to 210Kč) and watch the tubing and rafting action below.

our pick **Laibon** (☎ 728 676 654; Parkán 105; mains 90-180Kč) Candles and vaulted ceilings create a great boho ambience in the best little vegetarian teahouse in Bohemia. Order the blueberry dumplings for dessert and don't miss the special 'yeast beer' from the Bernard brewery.

U Dwau Maryí (☎ 380 717 228; Parkán 104; mains 100-200Kč) The 'Two Marys' medieval tavern recreates old recipes and is your best chance to try dishes made with buckwheat and millet; all tastier than they sound. In summer it's a tad touristy, but the stunning riverside castle views easily compensate.

GETTING THERE

Buses depart from Prague Florenc to Český Krumlov (160Kč, three hours, daily) via České Budějovice. **Student Agency** (www.student agency.cz) leaves from Prague Ná Knížecí (140Kč). In July and August this route is very popular and booking a couple of days ahead is recommended.

MORAVIA

Away from the tourist commotion of Prague and Bohemia, Moravia provides a quietly authentic experience.

TELČ

pop 6000

Telč is a quiet town with a gorgeous old centre ringed by medieval fish ponds and unspoilt by modern buildings. Unwind with a good book and a glass of Moravian wine at one of the local cafes.

The bus and train stations are a few hundred metres apart on the eastern side of town. A 10-minute walk along Masarykova leads to nám Zachariáše z Hradce, the Old Town square.

The **information office** (☎ 567 243 145; www.telc-etc.cz; nám Zachariáše z Hradce 10; 8am-5pm Mon-Fri, 10am-5pm Sat & Sun) books accommodation in private homes (around 350Kč to 400Kč per person).

In a country full of gorgeous Old Town squares, Telč's Unesco World Heritage–listed and cobblestoned **nám Zachariáše z Hradce** may outshine the lot. When the day trippers have departed, the Gothic arcades and elegant Renaissance facades are a magical setting.

At the square's northwestern end is the **Water Chateau** (☎ 567 243 943; www.zamek-telc.cz). **Tour A** (1hr adult/child90/45Kč, in English 180Kč; 9am-5pm Tue-Sun May-Sep, to 4pm Apr & Oct) visits the Renaissance halls, while **Tour B** (45min adult/child 80/40Kc; 9am-5pm Tue-Sun May-Sep) visits the private apartments, inhabited by the aristocratic owners until 1945. A new exhibition focuses on the chateau's **portrait gallery** (adult/child 40/20Kč; 9am-5pm Tue-Sun May-Sep, to 4pm Apr & Oct, to 3pm Nov-Mar).

At the castle's entrance is the **Chapel of All Saints**, where angels guard the tombs of Zacharias of Hradec, the castle's founder, and his wife. The **historical museum** (adult/child 30/15Kč; 9am-5pm Tue-Sun May-Sep, to 4pm Apr & Oct), in the courtyard has a model of Telč from 1895. More than a century later, not much has changed.

A pretty merchant's house on the main square conceals friendly **Penzión u Rudolfa** (☎ 567 243 094; nám Zachariáš z Hradce 58; s/d 300/600Kč; Jul & Aug), with shared kitchen facilities.

Three-star charm showcases 12 romantic rooms with decor varying from cosy wood to wedding-cake kitsch at **Hotel Celerin** (☎ 567 243 477; www.hotelcelerin.cz; nám Zachariáše z Hradce 43; s/d incl breakfast from 980/1530Kč;). Have a look before you hand over your passport.

SLAVONICE

Barely hanging onto the Czech Republic's coat-tails – the border with Austria is just 1km away – Slavonice is a little town any country would be proud to own. Slavonice's initial prosperity during the Thirty Years' War produced two squares dotted with stunning Renaissance architecture. Economic isolation followed when the main road linking Prague and Vienna was diverted in the 18th century, and in the 20th century, Slavonice's proximity to the Cold War border with Austria maintained its isolation. The town's architectural treasures were spared the socialist makeover other parts of the country endured and now, once the Austrian day trippers have left, Slavonice resurrects its compellingly moody atmosphere like nowhere else.

Slavonice is on a little-used train line from Telč (43Kč, one hour). The sleepy **tourist office** (☎ 384 493 320; www.mesto-slavonice.cz) is on the main square, nám Miru. Just off nám Miru, **Beśidka** (☎ 606 212 070; www.besidka.cz; d 1290-1490Kč) has spacious loft-style rooms and a cosmopolitan downstairs cafe that might just serve the Czech Republic's best wood-fired pizzas.

Sizzling grills and live music are the big drawcards at cosy **Šenk Pod Věži** (☎ 603 526 999; Palackého 116; mains 100-200Kč; 11am-3pm & 6-9pm Mon-Sat, 11am-4pm Sun) under the tower.

Telč's hipper younger citizens crowd buzzy **U Marušky** (☎ 605 870 854; Palackého) for cool jazz and tasty eats.

Five buses daily travel from Prague Roztyly to Telč (124Kč, 2½ hours). Buses running between České Budějovice and Brno also stop at Telč (92Kč, two hours, two daily). Trains rumble south to the beautiful village of Slavonice.

Hračky Cyklo Sport (nám Zachariáše z Hradce 23; per day 100Kč; 8am-5pm Mon-Fri, 9am-noon Sat) rents bicycles.

Rent **rowboats** (per 30min 20Kč; 10am-5pm Jul & Aug) from outside the East gate.

SLOVAKIA

BRATISLAVA

☎ 02 / pop 426,091

The capital city is a host of contrasts – a charming Old Town across the river from a communist concrete-block city, an age-old castle sharing the skyline with the 1970s, UFO-like New Bridge. Still, narrow pedestrian streets, pastel 18th-century rococo buildings and sidewalk cafes galore make for a supremely strollable – if miniscule – historic centre. You may want to pop into a museum if it's raining, but otherwise the best thing to do is meander the mazelike alleys, stopping regularly for coffee or drinks. There's sure to be some chichi restaurant just opened. Try to ignore the gangs of inebriated English-speaking blokes roaming about on weekends.

The city flourished during the reign of Maria Theresa of Austria (1740–80), when many of the imposing baroque palaces you see today were built. From the Turkish invasion until 1830, Hungarian monarchs were crowned in St Martin's cathedral, and Hungarian parliament met in Bratislava (then known as Pressburg or Poszony in German or Hungarian) until 1848.

INFORMATION

Bratislava City Card (1/2/3 days €6/10/12) Provides discounted museum admission and city transport; it's sold at the Bratislava Culture & Information Centre (below).

Bratislava Culture & Information Centre (BKIS; ☎ 16 186; www.bkis.sk) Airport (MR Štefánika; 8am-7.30pm Mon-Fri, 10am-6pm Sat); Centre (Klobučnícka 2; 8.30am-7pm Mon-Fri, 10am-5pm Sat) Staff hide brochures behind the central tourist office counter and seem uninterested, but keep pressing and they'll help – a little.

Bratislava Tourist Service (BTS; ☎ 2070 7501; www.bratislava-info.sk; Ventúrska 9; 10am-8pm) A tiny, tiny place, but it has a much more obliging staff than BKIS, and lots of maps and knick-knacks.

Main police station (☎ 159; Gunduličova 10)

Main post office (Nám SNP 34-35)

Poliklinika Ruzinov (☎ 4823 4113; Ružinovská 10) Hospital with emergency services and a 24-hour pharmacy.

SIGHTS & ACTIVITIES

Bratislava Castle (Bratislavský hrad; admission free; 9am-9pm Apr-Sep, to 6pm Oct-Mar) lords over the west side of the Old Town on a hill above the Danube. Winding ramparts provide a great vantage point for comparing ancient and communist Bratislava. A fire devastated the fortress in 1811; what you see today is a reconstruction from the 1950s. Except for a small archaeology exhibit, most of the interiors that make up the **Historical Museum** (Historické múzeum; ☎ 5441 1441; www.snm.sk; adult/concession €3/1.50; 9am-5pm Tue-Sun) are closed for

WAYNE WALTON

Devín Castle (p577)

BRATISLAVA IN TWO DAYS

Spend a day roaming the pedestrian streets, stopping for nibbles at one of Bratislava's many eateries, such as **Prašná Bašta** (p574). Ascend castle hill or the New Bridge for a citywide view, contrasting the charming Old Town with the ugly new. The next day, trip out to **Devín Castle** (p577) at the confluence of two rivers and three countries.

reconstruction until 2011. To see a more historically complete castle, take the bus beneath the New Bridge to Devín (p577), 8km outside the city.

A series of old homes winds down the castle hill along Židovská in what was once the Jewish quarter. The **Museum of Clocks** (**Múzeum hodín; ☎ 5441 1940; Židovská 1; adult/concession €2/0.70; 🕑 10am-5pm Tue-Sun**) is housed in the skinniest house in Slovakia. Further down, the **Museum of Jewish Culture** (**Múzeum Židovskej kultúry; ☎ 5441 8507; Židovská 17; adult/concession €6.70/2; 🕑 11am-5pm Sun-Fri**) displays moving exhibits about the community lost during WWII. Black-and-white photos show the old ghetto and synagogue ploughed under by the communists to make way for a highway and bridge.

A relatively modest interior belies the elaborate history of **St Martin's Cathedral** (**Dóm sv Martina; ☎ 5443 1359; Rudnayovo nám; admission €1.50; 🕑 8-11.30am & 1.30-4.30pm Mon-Sat**). Eleven ruling monarchs (10 kings and one queen, Maria Theresa) were crowned in this 14th-century church. The busy motorway almost touching St Martin's follows the moat of the former city walls and is shaking the building to its core.

An 18th-century palace and a Stalinist-modern building make interesting co-hosts for the **Slovak National Gallery** (**Slovenská Národná Galéria; ☎ 5443 4587; www.sng.sk; Rázusovo nábr 2; adult/concession €3.30/1.70; 🕑 10am-5pm Tue-Sun**). The nation's eclectic art collection ranges from Gothic to graphic design.

Two of Old Town's opulent theatres are off Hviezdoslavovo nám, a broad, tree-lined plaza. The gilt, neobaroque 1914 **Reduta Palace** hosts the nation's philharmonic orchestra (see p575), and he ornate 1886 Slovak National Theatre (p575) is the city's opera house. Neither is open for tours, but ticket prices aren't prohibitive.

Bustling, narrow **Rybárska brána** (Fisherman's Gate) street runs from Hviezdoslavovo nám to **Hlavné nám**, a main square which is filled with cafe tables in summer and a craft market that grows exponentially at Easter and Christmas times. Flanking one side of the square is the 1421 **old town hall** (Stará radnica), and the city museum contained within, under indefinite reconstruction at the time of writing.

A sizeable chunk of the old city, including the synagogue, was demolished to create **New Bridge** (Nový most; ☎ 6252 300; www.u-f-o.sk; Viedenská cesta; observation deck adult/concession €6.70/3.30; 10am-11pm), colloquially called the UFO (pronounced ew-fo) bridge. This modernist marvel from 1972 has a viewing platform, an overhyped nightclub and a restaurant with out-of-this-world prices.

SLEEPING

Bratislava's lodging market is giving nearby Vienna's rates a run for its money these days, but don't expect comparable services. To book an apartment, check out www.bratislavahotels.com and www.apartmentsbratislava.com.

Hostel Blues (☎ 09204020; www.hostelblues.sk; Špitálska 2; dm/d €20/63;) Friendly, professional staff not only help you plan your days, they offer free city sightseeing tours weekly. Choose from single-sex or mixed dorms, or those with double bunk beds. Apartments sleep four to six (from €108).

Hotel-Penzión Arcus (☎ 5557 2522; www.hotelarcus.sk; Moskovská 5; s/d incl breakfast €68/100) Because this family-run hotel was once an apartment building, rooms are quite varied in size (some with balcony, some with courtyard views).

Penzión Chez David (☎ 5441 3824; www.chezdavid.sk; Zámocká 13; s/d incl breakfast €74/102;) With the cool-blue colour scheme, great old photos of synagogues on the walls, and primo Old Town location, you'll hardly even notice the building's boxiness (though the rooms are small). Kosher restaurant on site; free wi-fi in restaurant and garden.

Arcadia Hotel (☎ 5949 0500; www.arcadia-hotel.sk; Františkánska 3; s/d incl breakfast €250/280;) Pains were taken when turning a 13th-century palace into Bratislava's first five-star hotel: an ornate stained-glass skylight tops the interior courtyard and hand-painted designs grace the dining room's vaulted arches.

EATING

The Old Town certainly isn't lacking for dining options or international cuisines. Most cater to visitors, and are priced accordingly.

MAN AT WORK

The most photographed sight in Bratislava is a bronze statue called the **Watcher** (Čumil). He peeps out of an imaginary manhole at the intersection of Panská and Rybarska, below a 'Man at Work' sign. But he's not alone. There are other quirky statues scattered around the pedestrian Old Town. Can you find them? The **Frenchman** leans on a park bench, the **Photographer** stalks his subject paparazzi-style around a corner and the **Schöner Náci** tips his top hat on a square. Look up for other questionable characters, such as a timepiece-toting monk and a rather naked imp, decorating building facades.

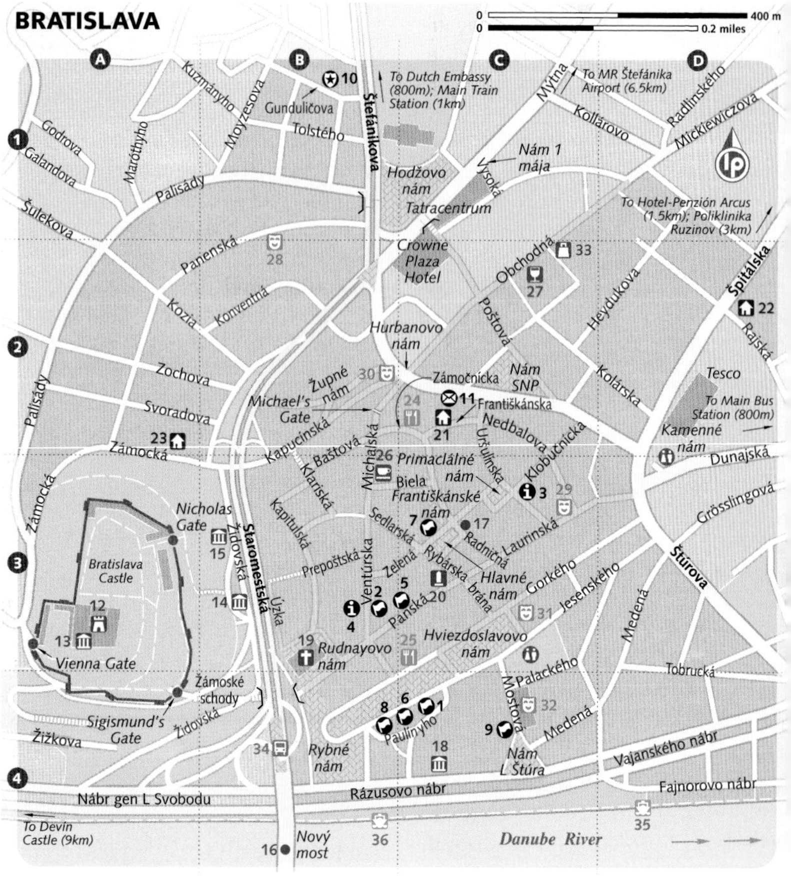

Verne (☎ 5443 0514; Hviezdoslavovo nám 18; mains €5-8; 🕑 8.30am-midnight Mon-Fri, 11am-midnight Sat & Sun) Thoroughly reasonable prices, long hours (breakfast, too) and sidewalk seating attract expats and locals alike. Slovak-international food served.

U Remeselníka (☎ 5273 1357; Obchodná 64; mains €5-10) This folksy cafe, associated with the traditional craft store upstairs, is a great place to try a trio of *halušky* – dumplings with sheep's cheese and bacon, with *klobasa* (sausage), and with cabbage.

our pick Prašná Bašta (☎ 5443 4957; Zámočnicka 11; mains €8-15) The round, vaulted interior oozes old-Bratislava charm, bu the hidden courtyard seating with a view of Michael's Gate is even better. Dishe range from traditional (potato-dough crusted schnitzel) to modern easter European (pork medallions with cream leak and mustard sauce).

DRINKING

From mid-April to October, sidewal tables fill with folks settling in for a cockta or two. Any one will do for a drink.

Čokoládovňa (☎ 5433 3945; Michalská 6 🕑 9am-9pm) This tiny 'chocolate cafe' ha

INFORMATION		
American Embassy	1	C4
Austrian Embassy	2	B3
Bratislava Culture & Information Centre	3	C3
Bratislava Tourist Service	4	B3
British Embassy	5	C3
Czech Embassy	6	C4
French Embassy	7	C3
German Embassy	8	B4
Irish Embassy	9	C4
Main Police Station	10	B1
Main Post Office	11	C2
SIGHTS & ACTIVITIES		
Bratislava Castle	12	A3
Historical Museum	13	A3
Museum of Clocks	14	B3
Museum of Jewish Culture	15	B3
New Bridge	16	B4
Old Town Hall	17	C3
Reduta Palace	(see 32)	
Slovak National Gallery	18	C4
St Martin's Cathedral	19	B3
Watcher	20	C3
SLEEPING		
Arcadia Hotel	21	C2
Hostel Blues	22	D2
Penzión Chez David	23	A2
EATING		
Prašná Bašta	24	C2
U Remeselníka	(see 33)	
Verne	25	C3
DRINKING		
Čokoládovňa	26	B3
Kréma Gurmánov Bratislavy	27	C2
ENTERTAINMENT		
Apollon Club	28	B2
Café Štúdio Club	29	C3
Channels	30	B2
Slovak National Theatre	31	C3
Slovak Philharmonic	32	C4
SHOPPING		
Úľuv	33	C2
TRANSPORT		
Bus to Devín Castle	34	B4
Hydrofoil Terminal	35	D4
Propeller Terminal	36	B4

liqueurs, coffees and desserts made with the dark ambrosia.

Kréma Gurmánov Bratislavy (**KGB; ☎ 5273 1279; Obchodná 52; 10am-2am Mon-Fri, 4pm-3am Sat, 4pm-midnight Sun**) Drink a dark and smoky toast to a statue of Stalin under a Soviet flag at the cellar KGB bar.

ENTERTAINMENT

Check **What's On** (**www.whatsonslovakia**) and **Kam do Mesta** (**www.kamdomesta.sk**) for the latest bands and theatre events. We know of a few Brits who've been turned away by bouncers; backlash from stag party antics. Be respectful, and know that Bratislavans themselves are pretty conservative.

NIGHTCLUBS

Café Štúdio Club (**☎ 5443 1796; cnr Laurinská & Radničná; 10am-1am Mon-Wed, to 3am Thu & Fri, 4pm-3am Sat**) Bop to the oldies or chill out to jazz; most nights there's live music of some sort.

Channels (**☎ 0911447323; Župné nám 2; 9.30am-4am**) Each of two stories has a bar and a dance floor for grooving to a techno DJ beat.

Apollon Club (**☎ 091548031; www.apollongay-club.sk; Panenská 24; 6pm-3am Mon-Thu & Sun, 6pm-5am Fri & Sat**) The only gay disco in town has two bars and three stages. Monday is karaoke; Sunday, boys only.

PERFORMING ARTS

Slovak National Theatre (**Slovenské Národné Divadlo, SND; www.snd.sk; Hviezdoslavovo nám; 8am-5.30pm Mon-Fri, 9am-1pm Sat**) The local company stages both Slavic and international operas, along with ballets, at the state theatre. Buy tickets online or at the ticket office around the back of the building.

Slovak Philharmonic (**Slovenská Filharmónia; ☎ 5920 8233; www.filharmonia.sk; cnr Nám L Štúra & Medená; ticket office 1-7pm Mon, Tue, Thu & Fri, 8am-2pm Wed**) Listen to the state opera in gilt splendour at its Reduta Palace theatre home.

SHOPPING

There are several crystal, craft and jewellery stores, as well as souvenir booths, in and around Hlavné nám. More and more artisan galleries are popping up in Old Town alleys; check out the side streets.

Úľuv (**☎ 5273 1351; www.uluv.sk; Obchodná 64**) For serious folk-art shopping head to Úľuv, where there are two stores and a courtyard filled with artisans' studios.

GETTING THERE & AWAY

The best source for both domestic and international train and bus schedules is http://cp.atlas.sk.

PIEŠŤANY

Thermal waters bubble under much of the country. Slovakia's premier spa site, **Piešťany** (☎ **33-775 7733; www.spa-piestany.sk**), is only 87km northeast of Bratislava. A few years back Slovak spas were medical facilities requiring a doctor's note. Not so today. OK, there's still a slightly antiseptic look to some treatment rooms, but many of Piešťany's lovely 19th-century buildings sport a new coat of Maria Theresa yellow paint and others are under reconstruction. On Kúpelne ostrov (Spa Island) you can swim in thermal pools, breathe seaside-like air in a salt cave and be wrapped naked in hot mud. Head to the *kasa* (cashier) at Napoleon 1 to book a service, or go online. There are several island hotels, which can be reserved on the spa website, and many more in town across the river. Trains from Bratislava take 1¼ hours (€4, 12 daily) and you can continue on the same line to Trenčín (€2, 45 minutes).

Most of the destinations from **MR Štefánika airport** (**BTS;** ☎ **3303 3353; Ivanska cesta 1; www.airportbrati slava.sk**), 7km northeast of the centre, are outside the region.

Plying the waters is a cruisy way to get to Bratislava from neighbouring Danube cities. From mid-April to September, **Slovenská plavba a prístavy** (☎ **5293 2226; www.lod.sk**) runs one or two daily hydrofoils to Vienna (€22 one way, 1½ hours) and to Budapest (€79 one way, four hours) from the **hydrofoil terminal** (**Fajnorovo nábr 2**). From June to October the **Twin City Liner** (☎ **0903610716; www.twincityliner.com**) operates up to six boats a day between Vienna (€28 one way, 1½ hours) and the Bratislava **propeller terminal** (**Rázusovo nábr**).

The **main bus station** (**autobusová stanica, AS;** ☎ **reservations 5556 7349; www.slovaklines.sk; Mlynské Nivy**) is 1.5km east of the Old Town. Buses leave from here heading to towns across Slovakia.

At least 12 daily trains depart the **main train station** (**Hlavná stanica; www.zsr.sk**), 1km north of the centre, for Poprad (€14, 4¾ to eight hours). Direct trains connect Bratislava with Prague (€27, 4½ hours, six daily), Budapest (€21, three hours, seven daily) and Vienna (€9, one hour, 30 daily).

GETTING AROUND

Bus 61 links the airport with the main train station (€0.75, 20 minutes). To get to the centre by taxi costs up to €15; services that operate out of the airport legitimately charge more than in town.

The main train station, Hlavná stanica, is just 1km north of the centre. Tram 13 runs from the station to Nám L Štúra, immediately south of Hviezdoslavovo nám, and bus 93 stops at Hodžovo nám. If you arrive by bus, you can take bus 206 to Hodžovo nám or bus 210 to the train station.

Dopravný Podnik Bratislava (**DPB;** ☎ **5950 5950; www.dpb.sk**) runs an extensive tram, bus and trolleybus network. You can buy tickets (€0.50/0.60/0.75 for 10/30/60 minutes) at news-stands. Check routes and schedules at www.imhd.sk.

The Bratislava City Card (one/two/three days for €6/10/12) includes all city transport, among other benefits. It's sold by Bratislava Culture & Information Centres; see p571 for details.

Bratislava's taxis have meters, but there still seems to be a slight English-speaking surcharge. Within the Old Town a trip should cost no more than €10. Try **ABC Taxi** (☎ **16 100**) or **Fun Taxi** (☎ **16 777**).

AROUND BRATISLAVA

Hard-core castle aficionados should don their daypack and head to **Devín Castle** (☎ **02-6573 0105; Muranská; adult/concession €3/1.50;** 🕑 **10am-5pm Tue-Fri, to 6pm Sat & Sun mid-Apr–Oct**), 9km west of Bratislava. Once the military plaything of 9th-century warlord Prince Ratislav, the castle withstood the Turks but then was blown up in 1809 by the French. Peer at the older bits that have been unearthed and tour a reconstructed palace museum. Bus 29 links Devín with Bratislava's New Bridge stop, under the bridge. Austria is just across the river.

EAST SLOVAKIA

Alpine peaks in Slovakia? As you look upon the snow-strewn jagged mountains rising like an apparition east of Liptovský Mikuláš, you may think you're imagining things, but there they are. Hiking the High Tatras is undoubtedly the highlight of the region, but in eastern Slovakia you can also admire ancient architecture, explore castle ruins, visit the second city and seek out small villages.

HIGH TATRAS

☎ 052

OK, this isn't exactly Switzerland, but the High Tatras (Vysoké Tatry) is the tallest range in the Carpathian Mountains. The massif is only 25km wide and 78km long; about 600 of the 726 sq km area falls within Slovakia. Photo opportunities at higher elevations might get you fantasising about a career with *National Geographic* – pristine snowfields, ultramarine mountain lakes and crashing waterfalls.

When planning your trip, keep in mind that the higher trails are closed from November to mid-June, and avalanches may close lower portions as well.

Poprad is the nearest sizeable town (with main-line train station and airport), 15km south of Starý Smokovec. Tatranská Lomnica, the smallest and quaintest resort, lies 5km to the east of Smokovec and the bustling lakeside Štrbské Pleso is 11km west. A narrow-gauge electric train connects Poprad with Štrbské Pleso via Starý Smokovec, where you have to change to get to Tatranská Lomnica.

INFORMATION

All three main resort towns have ATMs.

Post office (**off Cesta Slobody**) Above Starý Smokovec train station.

Tatra Information Office (**TIK**) Starý Smokovec (☎ **4423 440; www.tatry.sk; Starý Smokovec 23;** 🕑 **8am-8pm Mon-Fri, to 1pm Sat**); Štrbské Pleso (☎ **4492 391; Hotel Toliar;** 🕑 **8am-4pm**); Tatranská Lomnica (☎ **4468 118; Cesta Slobody;** 🕑 **10am-6pm Mon-Fri, 9am-1pm Sat**) The Štrbské Pleso branch is good for trail information, Smokovec has the largest office, and overall, the staff in Lomnica are the most helpful.

T-Ski Travel (☎ **4423 200; www.slovakiatravel.sk; Starý Smokovec 46, Starý Smokovec;** 🕑 **9am-4pm Mon-Thu, to 5pm Fri-Sun**) Books lodging, including some hikers' huts, in person and online. Can arrange ski and mountain-bike programs. Located at the funicular station.

SIGHTS & ACTIVITIES

A 600km network of trails reaches all the alpine valleys and some peaks, with mountain huts for hikers to stop at along the way. Routes are colour coded and easy to follow. Park regulations require you to keep to the marked trails and to refrain from picking flowers. For the latest weather and trail conditions stop by the **Mountain Rescue Service** (**Horská Záchranná Služba;** ☎ **emergency 18 300; http://his.hzs.sk/; Starý Smokovec 23, Starý Smokovec**).

STARÝ SMOKOVEC

From Starý Smokovec a **funicular railway** (☎ 4467 618; www.vt.sk; adult/concession return €7/5.50; 🕑 7.30am-7pm), or a 55-minute hike on the green trail, takes you up to **Hrebienok** (1280m). From here you have a great view of the Velká Studená Valley and a couple of hiking options. Following the red trail, past the restaurant and lodging at Bilíkova chata, to **Obrov Waterfalls** (Obrovsky vodopad) takes about an hour. Continuing on from the falls, it's a 35-minute hike to Zamkovského chata, and Skalnaté pleso (see right), with its cable car and trails down to Tatranská Lomnica. An excellent day hike, this is part of the **Tatranská Magistrála Trail** that follows the southern slopes of the High Tatras for 65km.

Rent mountain bikes at **Tatrasport** (☎ 4425 241; www.tatry.net/tatrasport; per day €15; 🕑 8am-noon & 1-6pm), above the bus-station parking lot.

TATRANSKÁ LOMNICA

While in the Tatras, you shouldn't miss the ride to the precipitous 2634m summit of **Lomnický štít** (bring a jacket!). Fron Lomnica, a large **gondola** (☎ 0903112200 www.vt.sk; adult/concession return €12/6 🕑 8.30am-7pm Jul & Aug, to 3.30pm Sep-Jun stops at mid-station Štart before it take you to the winter sports area, restauran and lake at **Skalnaté pleso**. From there, smaller **cable car** (☎ 0903112200; www.vt.sk adult/concession return €20/16; 🕑 8.30am-7pn Jul & Aug, to 3.30pm Sep-Jun) goes on to th summit, where there's a viewing platforn and Warhol-esque cafe-bar. Queues forn early and timed tickets sometimes sel out.

Alternatively, you can huff it up t Skalnaté by foot (2½ hours), where there' also a **chairlift** (☎ 0903112200; www.vt.sk adult/concession €5/4; 🕑 8.30am-5.30pm Jul & Aug, 8.30am-4.30pm Sep-Jun) running up t **Lomnické sedlo**, a 2190m saddle and sk area and trailhead below the summit.

Get off the cable car at Štart and you'r at **Funtools** (☎ 0903112200; www.vt.sk; cabl car plus 1 ride €9; 🕑 noon-6.30pm May-Sep), fron where you can take a fast ride down th mountain on a two-wheeled scooter,

MARK DAF

Hiker looking over the High Tatras

ugelike three-wheel cart or a four-wheel nodified skate board.

ŠTRBSKÉ PLESO

'alk about development: if it's not a new :ondo-hotel going up, it's an old one being revamped. Day hikes are extremely popular here, where you can follow the ed-marked **Magistrála Trail** (uphill from he train station) for 3km (about an hour) o **Popradské pleso**, an even more idylic pond at 1494m. From Popradské pleso he Magistrála zigzags steeply up the nountainside then traverses east towards Sliezsky dom and the Hrebienok funicular above Starý Smokovec (four hours).

There is also a year-round **chairlift** (☎ 4492 343; www.parksnow.sk; adult/concession eturn €7.50/5; ⏰ 8am-3.30pm) up to Chata od Soliskom, from where it's a 2km (one our) walk north along the red trail to the 093m summit of **Predné Solisko**.

Park Snow (☎ 4492 343; www.parksnow.k; Areál FIS; day lift ticket adult/concession €26/18; ⏰ 8.30am-3.30pm) in Štrbské pleso is the nost poplar ski and snowboard area, with wo chairlifts, four tow lines, 12km easy o moderate runs, one jump and a snowubing area.

LEEPING

or the quintessential Slovak mountain xperience, you can't beat hiking from ne *chata* (a mountain hut, could be nything from shack to chalet) to the ext, high up among the peaks. Food (opional meal service or restaurant) is always vailable. Beds in these hikers' huts fill up ast; reserve ahead. No wild camping is ermitted.

TARÝ SMOKOVEC & AROUND

Bilíkova chata (☎ 4422 439; www.bilikovachata., in Slovak; Hrebienok; r with shared bathroom €53) 10 minute walk downhill from the upper funicular station brings you to the closest of the higher elevation (1220m) *chaty*. Stay among the clouds at this basic log-cabin hotel with a full-service restaurant.

Grand Hotel (☎ 4870 000; www.grandhotel.sk; Starý Smokovec 38; s/d €86/112; 🅿) More than 100 years of history are tied up in the most prominent lodging in Starý Smokovec. For full effect, splash out in the imperial grandeur of the royal suite (€230).

TATRANSKÁ LOMNICA & AROUND

Look for private room (*privat* or *zimmer frei*) signs on the back streets south and east of the train station.

Penzión Encian (☎ 4467 520; www.tatry.sk/encian; Tatranská Lomnica 36; s/d €33/66) Owners Zdenka and Štefan Unák have created a warm and welcoming main-street inn. The small restaurant has a fire in the hearth and antique skiing memorabilia on display.

Grandhotel Praha (☎ 4467 941; www.grandhotelpraha.sk; s/d incl breakfast €105/145; 💻 🅿) Remember when travel was elegant and you dressed for dinner? No? Well the 1899 Grandhotel does. Rooms are appropriately classic, if uninspired, and there's a snazzy spa.

ŠTRBSKÉ PLESO & AROUND

Rabid development and crowds make staying in Štrbské pleso a last choice, with one grand exception.

Grand Hotel Kempinski (☎ 3262 222; www.kempinski-hightatras.com; Kupelna 6; r €255-300; ✖ 💻 🅿) After seamlessly blending several remodelled villas and new buildings, Kempinski opened its lap-of-luxury lakeside chateau in spring of 2009. Far and away the swankiest Tatra accommodation, the chain is hoping to entice high-end travellers into Poprad-Tatry airport with their Zen spa awaiting after the limousine service to the hotel.

Mountain huts above Štrbské pleso:

Chata pod Soliskom (☎ **0905652036; www.chata solisko.sk; dm €10**) Nine beds, ugly concrete building, nice terrace. No hiking required – it's next to the chair-lift; at 1800m.

Chata Popradské pleso (☎ **4492 177; www.poprad skepleso.sk; dm/d €15/53**) Sizeable log lodge with restaurant and bar. Reserve ahead and you can drive here (road requires permission); at 1500m.

EATING & DRINKING

The villages are close enough that it's easy to sleep in one and eat in another, but the restaurant offerings in general aren't great. All of the hotels, and some of the guesthouses, have OK eateries; the grand ones have bars and discos. Look for the local *potraviny* (supermarket) on the main road in each village.

Tatry Pub (☎ **4422 448; Tatra Komplex, Starý Smokovec;** ⏲ **1pm-midnight**) Refresh yourself at the official watering hole of the Mountain Guide Club. A full schedule of events includes DVD presentations, karaoke and DJ nights; pub food, too.

Scattered among the villages are numerous, often touristy, *koliba* restaurants. Our favourites are **Koliba Patria** (☎ **4492 591; Southern lake shore, Štrbske pleso; mains €6-15**), for it's lakeside terrace, and **Zbojnícka Koliba** (☎ **4467 630; road to Grand Hotel Praha, Tatranská Lomnica; mains €10-20;** ⏲ **4pm-midnight**), where some weekend evenings musicians play gypsy songs on the cimbalom while your chicken roasts over the open fire (it'll take an hour to cook).

GETTING THERE & AROUND

To reach the Tatras by public transport from most destinations you need to switch in Poprad to an electric train that makes numerous stops along the main Tatra road, or buses that go to off-lin destinations as well.

Buses from Poprad travel to Stary Smokovec (€0.80, 20 minutes, every 3 minutes), Tatranská Lomnica (€1.20, 3 minutes, every 60 minutes) and Štrbsk pleso (€1.50, 50 minutes, every 4 minutes).

A narrow-gauge electric train connect Poprad and the main High Tatra resor towns at least hourly. A €1.50 ticket cov ers up to a 29km ride, but it's easier t buy a one-/three-/seven-day pass fo €3.30/6.70/12. If there's not a ticket win dow, buy tickets from the conductor; vali date on board.

BELÁ TATRAS

☎ 052

Travel east over the High Tatra mountai ridges and you start to hear Slovak spoke with a Polish accent. The Goral folk cul ture is an intricate part of the experienc in the small *Belianské Tatry* (Belá Tatras Decorated timber cottages line long an narrow **Ždiar**, the only mountain settle ment inhabited since the 16th century Goral traditions have been both bolstere and eroded by tourism. Several sections c the village are historical reservations, ir cluding the **Ždiar House Museum** (**Ždiarsk dom;** ☎ **4498 142; adult/concession €3/1.5** ⏲ **10am-4pm Tue-Sun**), a tiny place with col ourful local costumes and furnishings.

Cross over the main road from th museum and a green trail skirts the rive through Monkova Valley (880m) for a 2½ hour return hike with very little elevatio change.

Ždiar has a huge number of *privat* (here they are large lodgings with share facility rooms for rent, about €11 per pe son), so odds are good if you just show u and knock. Otherwise, check www.zdia sk (in Slovak), under *ubytovanie*.

our pick **Ginger Monkey Hostel** (☎ 4498 844; www.gingermonkey.eu; Ždiar 294; dm/d €13/30; 💻) Crushing mountain views from an old Goral-style house, hot tea at any hour, laundry, wi-fi and a surprising sense of community among adventurous English-speakers… Don't just book one night, you'll end up extending.

Goral Krčma (☎ 4498 138; Ždiar 460; mains €3-6) A traditional 'village pub' restaurant associated with an inn, this *krčma* serves all the regional specialities, such as potato pancakes stuffed with a spicy sauté.

There are up to six buses daily between Ždiar and Poprad (€1.80, 50 minutes) via Starý Smokovec (€1.10, 45 minutes) and Tatranská Lomnica (€1, 30 minutes).

POPRAD

☎ 052 / pop 55,185

Poprad is an important air and land transfer point for the High Tatras. Otherwise, the modern, industrial city's attraction is limited. Oh, there is a HUGE water park here.

The **City Information Centre** (☎ 7721 700; www.poprad.sk; Dom Kultúry Štefániková 72; 🕑 8am-5pm Mon-Fri, 9am-noon Sat) has town info only.

Poprad's thermal water park, **Aqua City** (☎ 7851 222; www.aquacitypoprad.sk; Športová 1397; 🕑 9am-9pm), is admirably green. Among other initiatives, the water, heat and electricity here come from geo-thermal and solar sources. Prices for sauna, swim and slide zones differ; access to the outdoor thermal complex is €18/15 per day for adult/concession.

Poprad-Tatry International airport (☎ 7763 875; www.airport-poprad.sk; Na Letisko 100) is currently served by flights from Prague and Bratislava. London service may start again someday.

Intercity (IC) or Eurocity (EC) trains are the quickest way to get in and out of Poprad; four a day run to Bratislava (€16, four hours).

LEVOČA

☎ 053 / pop 14,677

High medieval walls surround ancient town buildings and cobblestone streets – so this is what Slovakia looked like in the

JANE SWEENEY

Pool and slides at Aqua City

13th century. Today Levoča is one of the few Slovak cities to have its historic defences largely intact. At the Old Town centre is the pride of the country's religious art and architecture collection, the Gothic Church of St Jacob and its 18m-high alter by Master Pavol. During the Middle Ages the king of Hungary invited Saxon Germans to colonise the eastern frontiers and Levoča became central to the resulting Slavo-Germanic Spiš cultural region.

RICHARD NEBESKY

Bojnice Castle

IF YOU LIKE...

If you like **Spiš Castle** (opposite), we think you'll enjoy exploring the following more complete castle complexes. If you visit on a weekend in July or August, don't miss the chance to take a night tour.

- **Trenčín Castle** (**☎ 032-7435 657; www.muzeumtn.sk; Trenčín, adult/concession €4/2; 9am-5.30pm May-Sep, to 4.30pm Apr & Oct, to 3.30pm Nov-Mar**) Sitting high atop a rocky crag overshadowing the town, this mighty fortress has several complete palaces to tour.
- **Bojnice Castle** (**☎ 046-5430 633; www.bojnicecastle.sk; Bojnice; adult/concession €5.30/2.70; 9am-5pm daily Jun-Sep, 9am-5pm Tue-Sun May, 10am-3pm Tue-Sun Oct-Apr**) Straight out of a fairytale dream filled with towers, turrets and tunnels.

Ask for the free photocopied map at the **tourist information office** (**☎ 4513 763; www.levoca.sk; Nám Majstra Pavla 58; 9am-6pm May-Sep, 9am-4pm Mon-Fri, 10am-2pm Sat Oct-Apr**).

The spindles-and-spires **Church of St Jacob** (**Chrám sv Jakuba; ☎ 4512 347; www.chramsvjakuba.sk; Nám Majstra Pavla; adult/concession €2/1; 1pm, 2pm, 3pm & 4pm Apr-Oct**), built in the 14th and 15th centuries, elevates your spirit with its soaring arches, precious art and rare furnishings. Everyone comes to see the splendid golden Gothic altar (1517) created by Master Pavol of Levoča. On it the mysterious master carved and painted cherubic representations of the Last Supper and the Madonna and Child. (This Madonna's face appeared on the original 100Sk banknote.) Buy tickets at the **cashier** (**kasa; 11am-5pm**) inside the **Municipal Weights House** across the street from the north door. Entry is limited to certain hours, so check online or in person for additional times in the high season – we've listed the minimum.

Hotel Arkáda (**☎ 4512 372; www.arkada.sk; Nám Majstra Pavla 26; s/d €35/53;**) Pine timbers and furnishings are the norm, but you can upgrade to an apartment with antiques for just €67. The hotel restaurant (mains €5 to €8) serves heaping grilled meat platters and fondue for two among its offerings. Free wi-fi.

Reštaurácia Slovenka (**☎ 4512 339; Nám Majstra Pavla 66; mains €3-7**) The only place in town to get homemade *pirohy* (dumplings stuffed with potato, somewhat akin to ravioli) topped with sheep's cheese and crackling.

Bus travel is most practical in the area: frequent services take you to Spišské Podhradie (€1, 20 minutes) and Poprad (€1.60, 30 minutes), which has the onward, main-line train connections best for travelling to Bratislava.

SPIŠSKÉ PODHRADIE

☎ 053 / pop 3826

Stretching for 4 hectares above the village of Spišské Podhradie, the Spiš Castle ruins are undoubtedly one of the largest in Europe. They're certainly the most photographed sight in Slovakia. A kilometre away, the medieval Spiš Chapter ecclesiastical settlement helps make this a favourite day trip from Levoča or the mountains. The village itself is pretty hohum, not worth a stay-over unless you're doing a castle night tour.

From far down the E50 motorway you catch glimpses of eerie outlines and stony ruins crowning the ridge on the eastern side of Spišské Podhradie. Can it really be that big? Indeed, **Spiš Castle** (Spišský hrad; ☎ 4541 336; www.spisskyhrad.com; adult/concession €4.50/2.50; 9am-5pm May-Oct) seems to go on forever. Sitting 200m above a broad valley floor, if the reconstructed ruins are this impressive, imagine what the fortress once was.

Chronicles first mention Spiš Castle in 1209, and the remaining central residential tower is thought to date from that time. Few structures are whole, but there's a cistern, a chapel and a rectangular Romanesque palace, which holds the museum. Night tours are available some summer weekends.

From the spur line train station, the castle is a healthy hike up. Cross the tracks near the station and follow the yellow markers. One kilometre south is Spišské Podhradie's bus stop. If you're driving or cycling, the easiest access is off the Prešov highway east of the castle.

The castle has a food stand, and the village has a little grocery store.

Buses connect with Levoča (€1, 20 minutes) and Poprad (€2.20, 50 minutes) at least hourly.

BARDEJOV

☎ 054 / pop 33,374

Muted hues and intricately painted facades set apart each of Bardejov's Gothic-Renaissance burgher houses. And yet the remarkable homogeneity of uniformly steep roofs and flat fronts helps make the main square the prettiest in Slovakia. Bardejov has been enthusiastically well preserved since the 15th century (there's always some scaffolding signalling upkeep) and deservedly made Unesco's World Heritage list in 2000. Today the quiet square is the tourist draw, but there are a few museums, including one that sheds light on this region's Eastern-facing religious art. Wooden churches in the area reflect the Carpatho-Rusyn heritage that the area shares with neighbouring parts of Ukraine and Poland.

The **tourist information centre** (☎ 4723 013; www.bardejov.sk; Radničné nám 21; 9am-6.30pm Mon-Fri, to 4pm Sat & Sun May-Sep, 9am-5pm Mon-Fri, to 4pm Sat, 1-4pm Sun Oct-Apr) has loads of info, souvenirs and guide services.

There are two branches of the **Šariš Museum** (☎ 4724 966; www.muzeumbardejov.sk; 8am-noon & 12.30-4pm Tue-Sun) worth seeing. In the centre square, the **town hall** (radnica; Radničné nám 48; adult/concession €2/1) contains altarpieces and a historical collection. Built in 1509, it was the first Renaissance building in Slovakia. At the **Icon Exposition** (Expozícia ikony; Radničné nám 27; adult/concession €2/1), more than 130 dazzling icons from the 16th to 19th centuries are on display. The religious art originally decorated Greek Catholic and Orthodox churches east of Bardejov.

Penzión Semafor (☎ 0905830984; www.penzionsemafor.sk; Kellerova 13; s/d €24/32, apt s/d €28/38) The five bright doubles in this family-run guesthouse share a communal

WOODEN CHURCHES

Travelling east from Bardejov, you come to the crossroads of Western and Eastern Christianity. The Greek Catholic (or Uniate) and Orthodox faithful living in the region in the 17th to 19th centuries built intricate onion-domed wooden churches (many without nails) and decorated them with elaborate icon screens and interior paintings. In July of 2008, eight eastern Slovak wooden churches were added to the Unesco World Heritage list, including one Catholic and two Protestant, but there are many more to see than that. (The Greek Catholic Presov Diocese website, www.grkatpo.sk/drevenecerk, has an extensive list.) Most of the churches are in isolated villages with limited bus connections and fewer services. Buy a *Wooden Churches Around Bardejov* booklet at the Bardejov tourist information centre (p583) for a self-driving tour of vernacular architecture in that area, including the oldest listed church at **Hervatov** (c 1500). Others, such as the listed churches at **Ladomirá** and **Bodružal**, are closer to Svidník.

kitchen and laundry; two more-spacious 'apartment' rooms have small kitchens of their own.

Hotel Bellevue (☎ 4728 404; www.bellevuehotel.sk; Mihalov 2503; s/d €64/84;) Glass-enclosed pool, landscaped gardens and leafy surrounds are the main selling points for this hotel on a hill, 3km south of centre. There is a special-evening-out restaurant and great views.

Bardejov is on a spur train line from Prešov, so buses are most convenient. They run between Bardejov and Poprad (€5, 2½ hours, eight daily).

AROUND BARDEJOV

Three short kilometres to the north, with frequent local bus connections, you'll find the parklike spa town of **Bardejovské Kúpele**. If you want to book a service (mineral bath €10, 15-minute massage €7), you have to go in person to the **Spa House** (Kúpelny dom; ☎ 4774 225; 8am-noon & 1-5pm Mon-Sat) at the top of the main pedestrian street. Across the way is the **Museum of Folk Architecture** (Múzeum Ľudovej Architektúry; ☎ 4722 070; adult/concession €1.30/0.70; 9am-5pm Tue-Sun, to 3pm Oct-Apr), the oldest *skanzen* (open-air museum) in Slovakia. One of the Unesco-listed wooden churches is among the many traditional buildings relocated here. If you have a car, park in the lot by the bus station at the base of the village and walk up; the whole village is pedestrian-only.

HUNGARY

BUDAPEST

☎ 1 / pop 1.7 million

There's no other Hungarian city like Budapest in terms of size and importance. But it's the beauty of Budapest – both natural and constructed – that makes it stand apart. Straddling a gentle curve in the Danube, the city is flanked by the Buda Hills on the west bank and the beginnings of the Great Plain to the east. Architecturally it is a gem, with enough baroque, neoclassical, eclectic and art nouveau elements to satisfy anyone. In recent years, Budapest has taken on the role of the region's party town. In the warmer months outdoor entertainment areas called *kertek* (gardens) are heaving with party-goers, and the world-class

Sziget Music Festival in August is a cultural magnet.

Strictly speaking, the story of Budapest begins only in 1873 with the administrative union of three cities that had grown together: Buda, west of the Danube; Óbuda (Buda's oldest neighbourhood) to the north; and Pest on the eastern side of the river. But the area had already been occupied for thousands of years.

In the late 19th century, under the dual Austro-Hungarian monarchy, the population of Budapest soared. Many notable buildings date from that boom period. The city suffered some damage in the two world wars, and the 1956 revolution left structures pockmarked with bullet holes. Today many of the city's grand buildings have been restored, and Budapest is the sophisticated capital of a proud nation with a distinctive heritage.

ORIENTATION

The city's aquatic artery, the Danube, is spanned by nine bridges that link hilly, residential Buda with bustling, commercial and very flat Pest. The most central square in Pest is Deák tér, where the three metro lines meet. Buda is dominated by Castle and Gellért Hills; its main square is Moszkva tér.

INFORMATION

Budapest Card (☎ 266 0479; www.budapestinfo.hu; 48/72hr card 6500/8000Ft) Offers access to many museums; unlimited public transport; and discounts on tours and other services. Buy it at hotels, travel agencies, large metro station kiosks and tourist offices.

Discover Budapest (Map p590; ☎ 269 3843; VI Lázár utca 16; 9.30am-6.30pm Mon-Fri, 10am-4pm Sat & Sun) Visit this one-stop shop for helpful tips and advice, accommodation bookings, internet access, and cycling and walking tours.

District V Police Station (Map p590; ☎ 373 1000; V Szalay utca 11-13) Pest's most central police station.

FirstMed Centers (Map p588; ☎ 224 9090; I Hattyú utca 14, 5th fl; 8am-8pm Mon-Fri, 9am-2pm Sat) On call 24/7 for emergencies.

Main post office (Map p590; V Petőfi Sándor utca 13-15; 8am-8pm Mon-Fri, to 2pm Sat) Just minutes from Deák Ferenc tér.

Tourinform main office (Map p590; ☎ 438 8080; V Sütő utca 2; 8am-8pm); Castle Hill (Map p588; ☎ 488 0475; I Szentháromság tér; 9am-7pm May-Oct, 10am-6pm Nov-Apr); Liszt Ferenc Square (Map p590; ☎ 322 4098; VI Liszt Ferenc tér 11; 10am-6pm Mon-Fri)

DANGERS & ANNOYANCES

Overall, Hungary is a very safe country with little violent crime, but scams can be a problem in the capital. Those involving attractive young women, gullible guys, expensive drinks in nightclubs and a frogmarch to the nearest ATM accompanied by in-house security have been all the rage in Budapest for well over a decade now, so be aware. Overcharging in taxis is also not unknown. Watch out for pickpockets.

SIGHTS & ACTIVITIES

Budapest is an excellent city for sightseeing, especially on foot. The Castle District in Buda contains a number of museums, both major and minor, but the lion's share is in Pest.

BUDA

Surfacing at the M2 metro station of the Socialist-style Moszkva tér, continue left up Várfok utca, or board bus 16A to reach **Castle Hill** (Várhegy; Map p588), where most

RICHARD NEBESKY

Fishermen's Bastion, Castle Hill

BUDAPEST IN TWO DAYS

The best way to start your day in Budapest is to have an early-morning soak alfresco at **Széchenyi Baths** (p589). Then stroll down Andrássy út and grab a late breakfast or coffee at **Lukács** (p593), next to the infamous and ever-popular spy museum, the **Terror House** (p589). Take an afternoon tour around the grand **Hungarian State Opera House** (p589) and have cake at the legendary **Gerbeaud** (p593), before hitting the shops on **Váci utca** (p589). Then go dancing at **Merlin** (p593).

On day two grab breakfast at **Centrál Káveház** (p593) before getting the funicular to **Castle Hill** (p585) in Buda. Tour **Matthias Church** (below) and explore the many museums, including the **Budapest History Museum** (opposite).

of Budapest's remaining medieval buildings are clustered. **Magdalene Tower** (Magdolona toronye; Map p588; Kapisztrán tér) is all that's left of a Gothic church destroyed here during WWII.

Don't miss the gorgeous neo-Gothic **Matthias Church** (Mátyás Templom; Map p588; www.matyas-templom.hu; I Szentháromság tér 2; adult/concession 700/480Ft; 9am-5pm Mon-Sat, 1-5pm Sun), with a colourful tiled roof and lovely murals inside. Franz Liszt's *Hungarian Coronation Mass* was played here for the first time at the coronation of Franz Joseph and Elizabeth in 1867.

Step across the square under the gaze of Hungary's first king, immortalised in the equestrian **St Stephen statue** (Szent István szobor; Map p588). Behind the monument, walk along **Fishermen's Bastion** (Halászbástya; Map p588; I Szentháromság tér; adult/concession 330/160Ft; 8.30am-11pm). The fanciful neo-Gothic arcade built on the fortification wall is prime picture-taking territory, with views of the river and the parliament beyond.

Tárnok utca runs southeast to Dísz tér, past which is the entrance for the **Sikló** (Map p588; I Szent György tér; one way/return adult 800/1400Ft, child 500/900Ft; 7.30am-10pm, closed 1st & 3rd Mon of month), a funicular railway. The views from the little capsule, across the Danube and over to Pest, are glorious. The Sikló takes you down the hill to Clark Ádám tér. The massive **Royal Palace** (Királyi Palota; Map p588) occupies the far end of Castle Hill; inside are the **Hungarian National Gallery** (Nemzeti Galéria; Map p588; www.mng.hu; I Szent György tér 6; adult/concession 800/400Ft; ⌚ 10am-6pm Tue-Sun) and the **Budapest History Museum** (Budapesti Történeti Múzeum; Map p588; www.btm.hu; I Szent György tér 2; adult/concession 900/450Ft; ⌚ 10am-6pm daily mid-Mar–mid-Sep, 10am-4pm Wed-Mon mid-Sep–mid-Mar).

Nearby is the **Royal Wine House & Wine Cellar Museum** (Borház és Pincemúzeum; Map p588; www.kiralyiborok.com; I Szent György tér, Nyugati sétány; adult/concession 900/500Ft; ⌚ noon-8pm), situated in what were once the royal cellars, dating back to the 13th century. Tastings cost 1350/1800/2700Ft for three/four/six wines. You can also elect to try various types of Hungarian champagne and *pálinka* (fruit brandy).

The 'other peak' overlooking the Danube, south of Castle Hill, is Gellért Hill. The **Liberty Monument** (Szabadság szobor; Map p588), a gigantic statue of a lady with a palm frond proclaiming freedom throughout the city, sits at its top and is visible from almost anywhere in town.

West of the monument is the **Citadella** (Map p588; www.citadella.hu; admission free; ⌚ 24hr). Built by the Habsburgs after the 1848 revolution to 'defend' the city from further Hungarian insurrection, it was never used as a fortress. Excellent views, exhibits, a restaurant and a hotel can be enjoyed here.

Bellow Gellért Hill is the city's most famous thermal spa, the **Gellért Baths** (Gellért Fürdő; Map p590; ☎ 466 6166; Danubius Hotel Gellért, XI Kelenhegyi út; admission 3400Ft; ⌚ 6am-7pm May-Sep, 6am-7pm Mon-Fri & 6am-5pm Sat & Sun Oct-Apr), where majestic domes hang above healing waters. This art-nouveau palace has dreamy spas where you can soak for hours while enjoying its elegant and historic architecture.

In Buda's southwest is **Memento Park** (off Map p590; www.mementopark.hu; XXII Balatoni út 16; adult/concession 1500/1000Ft; ⌚ 10am-dusk), a kind of historical dumping ground for socialist statues deemed unsuitable since the early '90s. It's a major tourist attraction and there's a direct bus from Deák tér in Pest at 11am daily (adult/concession return 3950/2450Ft, including admission).

PEST

HŐSÖK TERE & AROUND

The leafy Andrássy út, Pest's northeastern artery, is the best place to start your sightseeing. From Deák tér, Bajcsy-Zsilinszky ut becomes Andrássy út, which ends at the wide, tiled **Hősök tere** (Heroes' Sq; Map p590). This public space holds a sprawling monument constructed to honour the millennial anniversary (in 1896) of the Magyar conquest of the Carpathian Basin. Across the street, the **Museum of Fine Arts** (Szépmüvészeti Múzeum; Map p590; www.mfab.hu; XIV Dózsa György út 41; adult/concession 1200/600Ft; ⌚ 10am-5.30pm Tue, Wed & Fri-Sun, 10am-10pm Thu) houses a collection of foreign art, including an impressive number of El Grecos. Don't miss the **Palace of Art** (Műczarnok; off Map p590; www.mucsarnok.hu; XIV Hősök tere; adult/concession 1200/600Ft; ⌚ 10am-6pm Tue-Wed & Fri-Sun, to 8pm Thu), a large contemporary-art gallery, opposite the museum.

Adjacent is the oasis of **City Park** (Városliget; off Map p590), which has boating on a small lake in the summer, ice skating in winter, and duck-feeding year round. The park's schizophrenic **Vájdahunyad Castle** (Vájdahunyad Vár; off Map p590) was built in varied architectural styles typical of historic Hungary,

BUDA

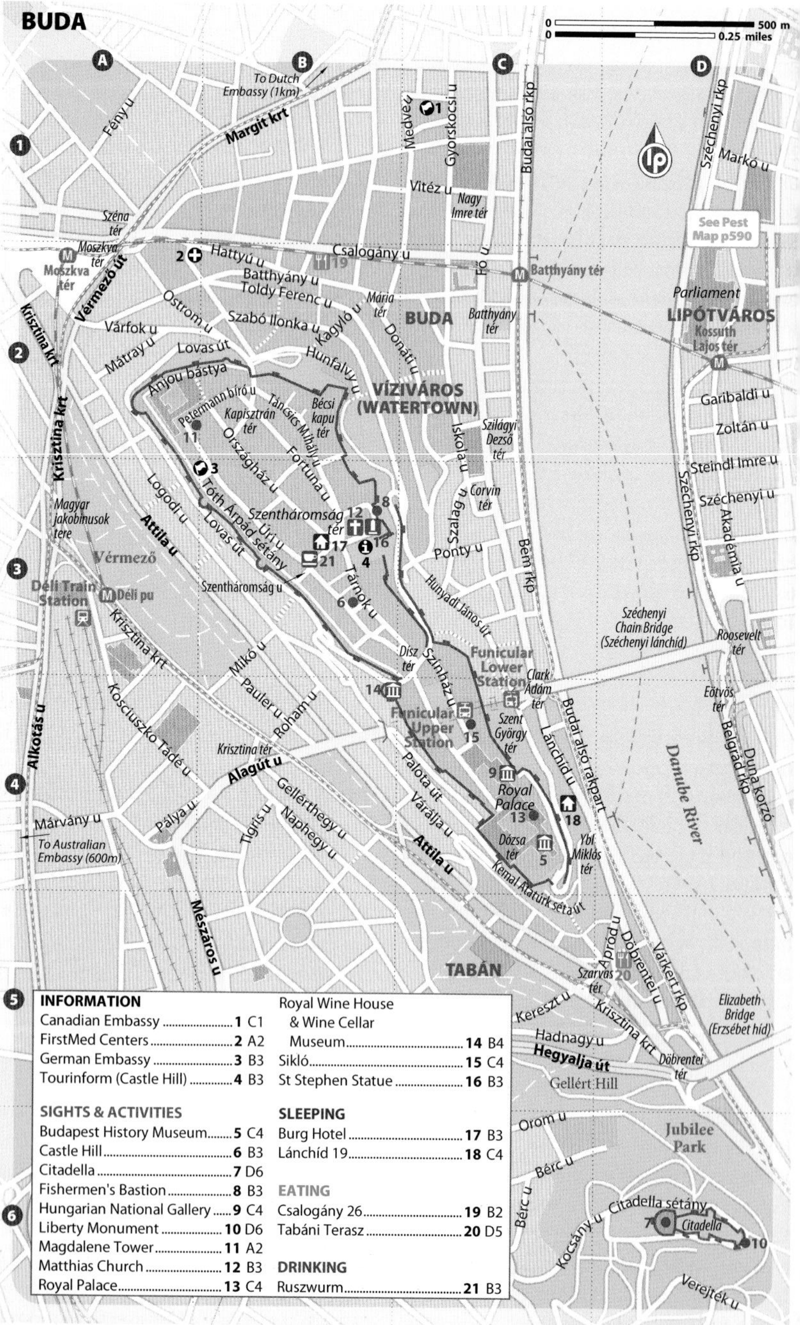

INFORMATION	
Canadian Embassy	1 C1
FirstMed Centers	2 A2
German Embassy	3 B3
Tourinform (Castle Hill)	4 B3

SIGHTS & ACTIVITIES	
Budapest History Museum	5 C4
Castle Hill	6 B3
Citadella	7 D6
Fishermen's Bastion	8 B3
Hungarian National Gallery	9 C4
Liberty Monument	10 D6
Magdalene Tower	11 A2
Matthias Church	12 B3
Royal Palace	13 C4
Royal Wine House & Wine Cellar Museum	14 B4
Sikló	15 C4
St Stephen Statue	16 B3

SLEEPING	
Burg Hotel	17 B3
Lánchíd 19	18 C4

EATING	
Csalogány 26	19 B2
Tabáni Terasz	20 D5

DRINKING	
Ruszwurm	21 B3

including baroque, Romanesque, Gothic and Tudor. In the park's northern corner is **Széchenyi Baths** (**Széchenyi Fürdő; off Map p590; ☎ 363 3210; XIV Állatkerti út 11; admission 2600Ft; ⏲ 6am-10pm**), its cupola visible from anywhere in the park. Built in 1908, this place has a dozen thermal baths and five swimming pools. The peaceful atmosphere of the indoor thermal baths, saunas and massage area contrasts with the buzzing atmosphere of the main pool.

Walk southwest from Hősök tere on Andrássy út to see many grand, World Heritage-listed 19th-century buildings. Stop for coffee and cake at Lukács (p593), the old haunt of the dreaded secret police, whose headquarters have now been turned into the **Terror House** (**Terror Háza; Map p590; www.terrorhaza.hu; VI Andrássy út 60; adult/concession 1500/750Ft; ⏲ 10am-6pm Tue-Fri, to 7.30pm Sat & Sun**), almost next door. The museum focuses on the crimes and atrocities committed by Hungary's fascist and Stalinist regimes.

Further down on Andrássy út, the opulence of the 1884 neo-Renaissance **Hungarian State Opera House** (**Magyar Állami Operaház; Map p590; ☎ 332 8197; www.operavisit.hu; VI Andrássy út 22; tours adult/concession 2800/1400Ft; ⏲ 3pm & 4pm**) is a real treat; try to make it to an evening performance here. **Váci utca**, in Pest's touristy centre, is an extensive pedestrian shopping street. It begins at the southwest terminus of the yellow line, Vörösmarty tér.

PARLIAMENT & AROUND

The huge, riverfront **Parliament** (**Parlament; Map p590; ☎ 441 4904; www.parlament.hu; V Kossuth Lajos tér 1-3; adult/concession 2520/1260Ft; ⏲ 8am-6pm Mon & Wed-Fri, to 4pm Sat, to 2pm Sun May-Sep, 8am-4pm Mon & Wed-Sat, to 2pm Sun Oct-Apr**) dominates Kossuth Lajos tér. English-language tours are at 10am, noon and 2pm daily.

Across the park is the **Ethnography Museum** (**Néprajzi Múzeum; Map p590; www.neprajz.hu; V Kossuth Lajos tér 12; adult/concession 800/400Ft; ⏲ 10am-6pm Tue-Sun**), which has an extensive collection of national costumes among the permanent displays on folk life and art. Look for the mummified right hand of St Stephen in the chapel of the colossal **St Stephen's Basilica** (**Szent István Bazilika; Map p590; V Szent István tér; adult/concession 400/300Ft; ⏲ 9am-5pm Apr-Sep, 10am-4pm Oct-Mar**) near Bajcsy-Zsilinszky út.

JEWISH QUARTER

Northeast of the Astoria metro stop is what remains of the Jewish quarter. The twin-towered 1859 **Great Synagogue** (**Nagy Zsinagóga; Map p590; VII Dohány utca 2; synagogue & museum adult/concession 1600/750Ft; ⏲ 10am-6.30pm Mon-Thu, to 2pm Fri, to 5.30pm Sun mid-Apr–Oct, 10am-3pm Mon-Thu, to 2pm Fri, to 4pm Sun Nov–mid-Apr**) has a museum with a harrowing exhibit on the Holocaust, and behind the synagogue is the **Memorial of the Hungarian Jewish Martyrs** (Map p590) in the shape of a weeping willow. Funded by the actor Tony Curtis, it's dedicated to those who perished in the death camps. A few blocks south along the *kis körút* (little ring road) is the **Hungarian National Museum** (**Magyar Nemzeti Múzeum; Map p590; www.hnm.hu; VIII Múzeum körút 14-16; adult/concession 1000/500Ft; ⏲ 10am-6pm Tue-Sun**), with its historic relics, from archaeological finds to coronation regalia.

TOURS

To tour the Danube, hop on one of the cruises operated by **Mahart PassNave** (**Map p590; ☎ 484 4005; www.mahartpassnave.hu; Vigadó tér Pier; ⏲ Apr-Oct**). There are regular two-hour sightseeing cruises (adult/concession 2900/1490Ft), and lunch- and

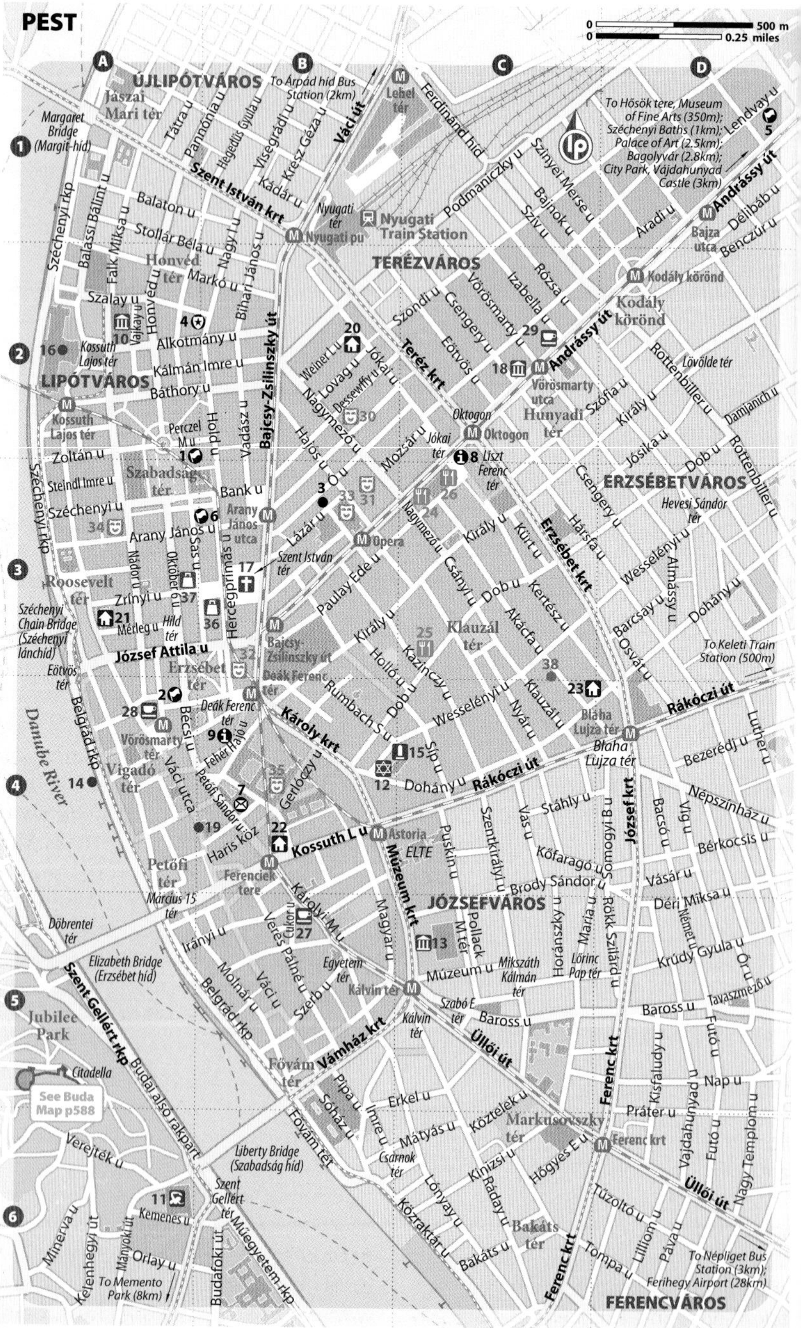
PEST
0 500 m
0 0.25 miles
A
B
C
D
1
2
3
4
5
6
ÚJLIPÓTVÁROS
Jászai Mari tér
To Árpád híd Bus Station (2km)
Lehel tér
Margaret Bridge (Margit-híd)
To Hősök tere, Museum of Fine Arts (350m); Széchenyi Baths (1km); Palace of Art (2.5km); Bagolyvár (2.8km); City Park, Vájdahunyad Castle (3km)
Nyugati tér
Nyugati Train Station
Nyugati pu
TERÉZVÁROS
Kodály körönd
Kodály körönd
LIPÓTVÁROS
Honvéd tér
Kossuth Lajos tér
Szabadság tér
Arany János utca
Oktogon
Vörösmarty utca
Hunyadi tér
Liszt Ferenc tér
Jókai tér
Lövölde tér
ERZSÉBETVÁROS
Hevesi Sándor tér
Opera
Szent István tér
Roosevelt tér
Széchenyi Chain Bridge (Széchenyi lánchíd)
Eötvös tér
Erzsébet tér
Bajcsy-Zsilinszky út
Deák Ferenc tér
Klauzál tér
To Keleti Train Station (500m)
Blaha Lujza tér
Danube River
Vörösmarty tér
Vigadó tér
Astoria
ELTE
Petőfi tér
Ferenciek tere
Március 15 tér
JÓZSEFVÁROS
Döbrentei tér
Elizabeth Bridge (Erzsébet híd)
Egyetem tér
Kálvin tér
Mikszáth Kálmán tér
Lőrinc Pap tér
Szabó E tér
Jubilee Park
Citadella
See Buda Map p588
Fővám tér
Markusovszky tér
Ferenc krt
Liberty Bridge (Szabadság híd)
Szent Gellért tér
Csarnok tér
Bakáts tér
To Memento Park (8km)
To Népliget Bus Station (3km); Ferihegy Airport (28km)
FERENCVÁROS
Váci út
Szent István krt
Teréz krt
Andrássy út
Erzsébet krt
Károly krt
Rákóczi út
József krt
Kossuth L u
Múzeum krt
Vámház krt
Üllői út
Szent Gellért rkp
Budai alsó rakpart
Ferdinánd híd
József Attila u
Széchenyi rkp
Belgrád rkp
Váci utca

INFORMATION
- American Embassy 1 A2
- British Embassy 2 A4
- Discover Budapest 3 B3
- District V Police Station 4 A2
- French Embassy 5 D1
- Irish Embassy 6 B3
- Main Post Office 7 B4
- Tourinform (Liszt Ferenc Square) 8 C2
- Tourinform (Main Office) 9 B4

SIGHTS & ACTIVITIES
- Ethnography Museum 10 A2
- Gellért Baths 11 A6
- Great Synagogue 12 B4
- Hungarian National Museum 13 C5
- Hungarian State Opera House (see 33)
- Mahart PassNave 14 A4
- Memorial of the Hungarian Jewish Martyrs 15 C4
- Parliament 16 A2
- St Stephen's Basilica 17 B3
- Terror House 18 C2
- Váci utca 19 B4

SLEEPING
- Cotton House 20 B2
- Four Seasons Gresham Palace Hotel 21 A3
- Leo Panzió 22 B4
- Soho Hotel 23 C4

EATING
- Klassz 24 C3
- Köleves 25 C3
- Menza 26 C3

DRINKING
- Centrál Kávéház 27 B5
- Gerbeaud 28 A4
- Lukács 29 C2

ENTERTAINMENT
- Alter Ego 30 B2
- Café Eklektika 31 B3
- Gödör Klub 32 B3
- Hungarian State Opera House 33 B3
- Kalamajka Táncház 34 A3
- Merlin 35 B4

SHOPPING
- Bortársaság 36 B3
- Mester Pálinka 37 A3

TRANSPORT
- BKV Office 38 C3
- Mahart PassNave (see 14)

dinner-buffet cruises (adult/concession 5990/2990Ft). Tickets can be purchased at the pier before departure.

FESTIVALS & EVENTS

Many festivals and events are held in and around Budapest. Look out for the tourist board's annual *Events Calendar* for a complete listing.

Sziget Music Festival (www.sziget.hu) On Óbudai hajógyári-sziget (Óbuda Shipbuilding Island), from late July to early August.

Hungarian Formula One Grand Prix (www.hungaro ring.hu) At Mogyoród, 24km northeast of Budapest, in mid-August.

SLEEPING

Leo Panzió (Map p590; ☎ 266 9041; www.leopanzio.hu; V Kossuth Lajos utca 2/a; s/d from €49/76;) Just steps from Váci utca, this B&B with a lion motif is in the middle of everything. A dozen of its 14 immaculate rooms look down on busy Kossuth Lajos utca, but they all have double glazing and are quiet.

Cotton House (Map p590; ☎ 354 2600; www.cotton house.hu; Jókai utca 26; r €70-150;) This 23-room guesthouse has a jazz/speakeasy theme, complete with vintage telephones and old radios that actually work. Prices vary depending on the season and whether there's a shower, tub or spa in the bathroom.

Burg Hotel (Map p588; ☎ 212 0269; www.burghotelbudapest.com; I Szentháromság tér 7-8; s/d/ste from €85/99/109;) The affordable Burg is at the centre of Castle Hill, just opposite Matthias Church. The 26 partly refurbished rooms are fairly ordinary, but location is everything here.

Soho Hotel (Map p590; ☎ 872 8292; www.sohohotel.hu; VII Dohány utca 64; s/d/ste from €99/109/169;) This delightfully stylish boutique hotel sports a foyer bar in eye-popping reds, blues and lime greens. The nonallergenic rooms have bamboo matting on the walls, parquet floors and a music/film theme throughout (check out the portraits of Bono, George Michael and Marilyn).

our pick **Lánchíd 19** (Map p588; ☎ 419 1900; www.lanchid19hotel.hu; I Lánchíd utca 19; s/d/ste from €120/140/300;) This new boutique number facing the Danube won the European Hotel Design Award for Best Architecture in 2008.

Four Seasons Gresham Palace Hotel (Map p590; ☎ 268 6000; www.fourseasons.com; V Roosevelt tér 5-6; s/d/ste from €305/340/1090;) Restored to its bygone elegance, with whimsical ironwork, mushroom-

HOLGER LEUE

Thermal pool at Gellért Baths (p587)

shaped windows, and glittering gold decorative tiles on the exterior, the Four Seasons inhabits the art nouveau Gresham Palace (1907) and provides superb views of the Danube through Roosevelt Park.

EATING

Ráday utca and Liszt Ferenc tér are the two most popular traffic-free streets. The moment the weather warms up, tables and umbrellas spring up on the pavements and the people of Budapest crowd the streets. Both areas have oodles of cafes, restaurants, snack shops and bars.

Köleves (Map p590; ☎ 322 1011; Kazinczy utca 35 & Dob utca 26; mains 1280-3680Ft; ⌚ noon-midnight) Always buzzing, 'Stone Soup' attracts a young crowd with its delicious matzo-ball soup, tapas, lively decor and reasonable prices. It's a great place to first try Hungarian food.

our pick **Klassz** (Map p590; ☎ 413 1545; www.klassz.eu; VI Andrássy út 41; mains 1490-3490Ft; ⌚ 11.30am-11pm Mon-Sat, to 6pm Sun) Varieties of foie gras and native *mangalica* pork are permanent stars on the menu, with dishes such as Burgundy-style leg of rabbit and lamb trotters with vegetable ragout playing cameo roles.

Menza (Map p590; ☎ 413 1482; VI Liszt Ferenc tér 2; mains 1890-2490Ft; ⌚ 10am-1am) This stylish restaurant on Budapest's most lively square takes its name from the Hungarian for a drab school canteen – something it is anything but.

Tabáni Terasz (Map p588; ☎ 201 1086; I Apród utca 10; mains 2600-4900Ft; ⌚ noon-midnight) This delightful terrace and cellar restaurant at the foot of Castle Hill has a modern take on Hungarian cuisine, with lighter dishes and an excellent wine selection.

Csalogány 26 (Map p588; ☎ 201 7892; I Csalogány utca 26; mains 2800-4000Ft; noon-3pm & 7pm-midnight Tue-Sat) One of the best restaurants in Budapest turns out superb international dishes.

Bagolyvár (Map p590; ☎ 468 3110; XIV Állatkerti út 2; mains 2850-4250Ft; ⌚ noon-11pm) Serving imaginatively reworked Hungarian classics, the 'Owl's Castle' attracts the Budapest foodie cognoscenti.

DRINKING

Budapest in the 19th century rivalled Vienna in its cafe culture, though cafe numbers waned under communism. The majority of the surviving traditional cafes are in Pest, but Buda can still lay claim to a handful. Budapest is also loaded with pubs and bars, and there's enough variation to satisfy all tastes. In summer the preferred drinking venues are the *kerteks*, outdoor entertainment zones.

Ruszwurm (Map p588; I Szentháromság utca 7; ⌚ 10am-7pm) This is the perfect place for coffee and cake in the Castle District, though it can get pretty crowded.

Centrál Kávéház (Map p590; V Károlyi Mihály utca 9; ⌚ 8am-midnight) One of the finest coffee houses in the city, with high, decorated ceilings, lace curtains, pot plants, elegant coffee cups and professional service.

For more coffee in exquisite art-nouveau surroundings, two places are particularly noteworthy. **Gerbeaud** (Map p590; V Vörösmarty tér 7; ⌚ 9am-9pm;), Budapest's cake-and-coffee-culture king, has been serving since 1870. Or station yourself at **Lukács** (Map p590; VI Andrássy út 70; ⌚ 8.30am-8pm Mon-Fri, 9am-8pm Sat, 9.30am-8pm Sun) where Hungary's dreaded ÁVH secret police once had its HQ.

ENTERTAINMENT

To find out what's on, check out the free **Budapest Funzine** (www.funzine.hu), published every second Thursday and available at hotels, bars, cinemas and various tourist spots. The free *Koncert Kalendárium*, published monthly (bimonthly in summer), covers the performing arts, including classical concerts, opera and dance. A hip little publication with all sorts of insider's tips is the *Budapest City Spy Map*. It's available free at pubs and bars.

GAY & LESBIAN VENUES

Alter Ego (Map p590; www.alteregoclub.hu; VI Dessewffy utca 33; ⌚ 10pm-5am Fri & Sat) Budapest's premier gay club, with the coolest crowd (think attitude) and the best dance music.

Café Eklektika (Map p590; V Semmelweiss utca 21; ⌚ noon-midnight) This lesbian-owned cafe and restaurant (lunch buffet 990Ft) in stunning new digs is a great place for a meal and a little LGBT information gathering. Attracts a youthful, arty crowd.

PERFORMING ARTS

Hungarian State Opera House (Magyar Állami Operaház; Map p590; ☎ 331 2550; www.opera.hu; VI Andrássy út 22) Take in a performance while admiring the incredibly rich interior decoration. The ballet company performs here as well.

Kalamajka Táncház (Map p590; ☎ 354 3400; V Arany János utca 10; ⌚ 8.30pm-midnight Sat) The Kalamajka is an excellent place to hear authentic Hungarian music, especially on its dance nights, when everyone gets up and takes part.

Classical concerts are held regularly in the city's churches, including Matthias Church (p586) on Castle Hill in Buda.

NIGHTCLUBS

Merlin (Map p590; www.merlinbudapest.org; V Gerlóczy utca 4; ⌚ 10am-midnight Sun-Thu, to 5am Fri & Sat) One of those something-for-everyone places, with everything from jazz and breakbeat to techno and house. It's most visitors' first port of call in Budapest.

Gödör Klub (Map p590; V Erzsébet tér; ⌚ 9am-late) This large underground club is a real mixed bag, offering a mix of folk, world, rock and pop, played to an audience of all ages.

SHOPPING

There's an excellent selection of Hungarian wines at **Bortársaság** (Map p590; ☎ 328 0341; V Szent István tér 3; ⌚ noon-8pm Mon-Fri, 10am-4pm Sat) in Pest, and you can pick up the Hungarian fruit-flavoured brandy, *pálinka*, at **Mester Pálinka** (Map p590; ☎ 374 0388; V Zrínyi utca 18).

GETTING THERE & AWAY

AIR

The main international carriers fly in and out of Terminal 2 at Budapest's **Ferihegy airport** (www.bud.hu), 24km southeast of the centre on Hwy 4; low-cost airlines use the older Terminal 1 next door. For carriers flying to Hungary, see p605.

BOAT

Mahart PassNave (Map p590; ☎ Belgrád rakpart 484 4010, Vigadó tér Pier 484 4005; www.marhartpassnave.hu) runs ferries and hydrofoils from Budapest. A hydrofoil service on the Danube River between Budapest and Vienna (5½ to 6½ hours) operates daily from late April to early October; passengers can disembark at Bratislava with advance notice (four hours).

There are ferries departing at 10.30am daily for Szentendre (one way/return 1490/2235Ft, 1½ hours) from May to September, decreasing to 9am departures on weekends only in April and October. Esztergom (one way/return 3290/4990Ft, 1½ hours) can be reached by fast hydrofoil from Budapest at 9.30am on weekends between May and September (and also on Friday from June to August).

BUS

Volánbusz (☎ 382 0888; www.volanbusz.hu), the national bus line, has an extensive list of destinations from Budapest. All international buses and some buses to/from southern Hungary use **Népliget bus station** (off Map p590; IX Üllői út 131). Most buses to the northern Danube Bend arrive at and leave from the **Árpád híd bus station** (off Map p590; off XIII Róbert Károly körút). All stations are on metro lines, and all are in Pest. If the ticket office is closed, you can buy your ticket on the bus.

CAR & MOTORCYCLE

Car rental is not recommended if you are staying in Budapest. The extensive public transport network is cheap, parking is scarce and road congestion is high.

GAVIN GOUGH

Views over Széchenyi Chain Bridge and Danube River to the Parliament (p589)

TRAIN

The Hungarian State Railways, **MÁV** (☎ 06 40 494949; www.mav.hu) covers the country well and has its schedule online.

Keleti train station (Eastern; off Map p590; VIII Kerepesi út 2-4) handles international trains from Vienna and most other points west, plus domestic trains to/from the north and northeast. For the Danube Bend, head for **Nyugati train station** (Western; Map p590; VI Nyugati tér). For trains bound south, go to **Déli train station** (Southern; Map p588; I Krisztina körút 37). All three train stations are on metro lines.

GETTING AROUND

TO/FROM THE AIRPORT

The simplest way to get to town is to take the **Airport Minibus** (☎ 296 8555; www.airportshuttle.hu; 1-way/return 2990/4990Ft) directly to the place you're staying. Buy tickets at the clearly marked stands in the arrivals halls.

An alternative is travelling with **Zóna Taxi** (☎ 365 5555), which has the monopoly on picking up taxi passengers from the airport. Fares to most central locations range from 5100Ft to 5700Ft.

PUBLIC TRANSPORT

Public transport is run by **BKV** (☎ 461 6500; www.bkv.hu). The underground metro lines (M1 yellow, M2 red, M3 blue) meet at Deák tér in Pest. The HÉV above-ground suburban railway runs north from Batthyány tér in Buda. There's also an extensive network of buses, trams and trolleybuses.

A transfer ticket (420Ft) is valid for one trip with one validated transfer within 90 minutes. The three-day *turista* pass (3400Ft) or the seven-day pass (4000Ft) make things easier, allowing unlimited travel inside the city limits. Keep your ticket or pass handy; the fine for 'riding black' is 6000Ft on the spot, or 12,000Ft if you pay later at the **BKV Office** (Map p590; ☎ 461 6800; VII Akácfa utca 22; 6am-8pm Mon-Fri, 8am-1.45pm Sat).

TAXI

Taxi drivers overcharging foreigners in Budapest has been a problem for some time. Never get into a taxi that lacks an official yellow licence plate, the logo of the taxi firm and a visible table of fares. If you have to take a taxi, it's best to call one; this costs less than if you flag one down. Dispatchers usually speak English. **City** (☎ 211 1111), **Fő** (☎ 222 2222) and **Rádió** (☎ 377 7777) are reliable companies.

THE DANUBE BEND

North of Budapest, the Danube breaks through the Pilis and Börzsöny Hills in a sharp bend before continuing along the Slovak border. Today the easy access to historic monuments, rolling green scenery – and vast numbers of souvenir craft shops – lure many day trippers from Budapest.

SZENTENDRE

☎ 26 / pop 24,000

Once an artists colony, now a popular day trip 19km north of Budapest, pretty little Szentendre (*sen*-ten-dreh) has narrow, winding streets and is a favourite with souvenir shoppers. The charming old centre has plentiful cafes and art-and-craft galleries, and there are several Orthodox churches that are worth a peek. Expect things to get crowded in summer and at weekends. Outside town is the largest open-air village museum in the country.

Tourinform (☎ 317 965; szentendre@tourinform.hu; Dumtsa Jenő utca 22; 9.30am-4.30pm Mon-Fri year-round, 10am-2pm Sat & Sun mid-Mar–Oct) has information about the numerous small museums and galleries in town.

Don't miss the **Open-Air Ethnographic Museum** (Szabadtéri Néprajzi Múzeum; www.skanzen.hu; Sztaravodai út; adult/concession 1000/500Ft;

JONATHAN SMITH

Greek Orthodox Blagoveštenska Church, Szentendre

9am-5pm Tue-Sun late Mar-Oct), 3.5km outside town. Walking through the ancient wooden and stone homes, churches and working buildings brought here from around the country, you can see what rural life was – and sometimes still is – like in different regions of Hungary.

Seeing Szentendre on a day trip from Budapest is probably your best bet. The most convenient way to get to Szentendre is to take the commuter HÉV train from Buda's Batthyány tér metro station to the end of the line (one way 370Ft, 45 minutes, every 10 to 15 minutes).

For ferry services from Budapest, see p594.

ESZTERGOM

33 / pop 29,800

It's easy to see the attraction of Esztergom, even from a distance. The city's massive basilica, sitting high above the town and Danube River, is an incredible sight, rising magnificently from its rural setting.

The significance of this town is greater than its architectural appeal. The 2nd-century Roman emperor-to-be Marcus Aurelius wrote his famous *Meditations* while here. In the 10th century, Stephen I, founder of the Hungarian state, was born and crowned at the cathedral. Nowadays it's an attractive riverside town, with much spiritual and temporal attraction for both Hungarians and international visitors.

Gran Tours (**502 001; Rákóczi tér 25; 8am-5pm Mon-Fri, 9am-noon Sat Jun-Aug, 8am-4pm Mon-Fri Sep-May**) is the best source of information in town.

Hungary's largest church is the **Esztergom Basilica** (**Esztergomi Bazilika; www.bazilika-esztergom.hu; Szent István tér 1; 6am-6pm**). Perched on Castle Hill, its 72m-high central dome can be seen for many kilometres around. Reconstructed in the neoclassical style, much of the building dates from the 19th century; the oldest section is the red-marble **Bakócz Chapel** (Bakócz Kápolna; 1510). The **treasury** (**kincsház; adult/concession 600/300Ft; 9am-4.30pm Mar-Oct, 11am-3.30pm Sat & Sun Nov-Dec**) contains priceless objects, including ornate vestments and the 13th-century Hungarian coronation cross. Among those buried in the **crypt** (**altemplom; admission 150Ft; 9am-4.45pm**) under the cathedral is the controversial Cardinal Mindszenty, who was imprisoned by the communists for refusing to allow Hungary's Catholic schools to be secularised.

At the southern end of the hill is the **Castle Museum** (**Vár Múzeum; adult/concession 800/400Ft; 10am-6pm Tue-Sun Apr-Oct, to 4pm Tue-Sun Nov-Mar**), inside the reconstructed remnants of the medieval royal palace (1215), which was built upon previous castles. The earliest excavated sections on the hill date from the 2nd to 3rd centuries.

Csülök Csárda (☎ **412 420; Batthyány Lajos utca 9; mains 1800-3900Ft**) The Pork Knuckle Inn – guess the speciality here – is a charming eatery popular with visitors and locals alike. It serves up good home cooking (try the bean soup), with huge portions.

Hourly buses link Esztergom to Szentendre (750Ft, 1½ hours). The most comfortable way to get here from Budapest is by rail. Trains depart from Budapest's Nyugati train station (900Ft, 1½ hours) at least hourly. For ferry services from Budapest, see p594.

SOUTH HUNGARY

Southern Hungary is a place to savour life at a slower pace. Passing through the region, you'll spot whitewashed farmhouses whose thatched roofs and long colonnaded porticoes decorated with floral patterns seem unchanged over the centuries. The weather always seems to be a few degrees warmer here than in other parts of the country; the sunny clime is great for grape growing, and oak-aged Villány reds are well regarded, if highly tannic.

PÉCS

☎ 72 / pop 156,000

Blessed with a mild climate, an illustrious past and a number of fine museums and monuments, Pécs (pronounced *paich*) is one of the most pleasant and interesting cities to visit in Hungary. For those reasons and more – a handful of universities, the nearby Mecsek Hills, a lively nightlife – many travellers put it second only to Budapest on their Hungary must-see list.

History has far from ignored Pécs. The Roman settlement of Sopianae on this site was the capital of the province of Lower Pannonia for 400 years. Christianity flourished here in the 4th century and in 1009 Stephen I made Pécs a bishopric. City walls were erected after the Mongol invasion of 1241, but 1543 marked the start of almost a century and a half of Turkish domination. In the 19th century the manufacture of Zsolnay porcelain and other goods, such as Pannonia sparkling wine, helped put Pécs back on the map.

Tourinform (☎ **213 315; baranya-m@tourinform.hu; Széchenyi tér 9; ⌚ 8am-6pm Mon-Fri, 10am-8pm Sat & Sun Jun-Aug, 8am-5.30pm Mon-Fri, 10am-2pm Sat May, Sep & Oct, 8am-4pm Mon-Fri Nov-Apr**) has internet access (100Ft per hour) and tons of local info, including a list of museums.

SIGHTS & ACTIVITIES

The curiously named **Mosque Church** (**Mecset Templom; Széchenyi tér; ⌚ 10am-4pm Mon-Sat, 11.30am-4pm Sun mid-Apr–mid-Oct, 10am-noon Mon-Sat, 11.30am-2pm Sun mid-Oct–mid-Apr**) dominates the central square. It has no minaret and has been a Christian place of worship for a long time, but the Islamic elements inside, such as the mihrab on the southeastern wall, reveal its original identity. Constructed in the mid-16th century from the stones of an earlier church, the mosque underwent several changes of appearance over the years – including the addition of a steeple. In the late 1930s the building was restored to its medieval form.

West along Ferencesek utcája, you'll pass the ruins of the 16th-century Turkish **Pasa Memi Baths** (Memi Pasa Fürdője) before you turn south on Rákóczi utca to get to the 16th-century **Hassan Jakovali Mosque** (**Hassan Jakovali Mecset; adult/concession 500/250Ft; ⌚ 9.30am-5.30pm Wed-Sun late Mar-Oct**). There's a small museum of Ottoman history inside.

Continue west to Dóm tér and the walled bishopric complex containing the four-towered **Basilica of St Peter** (**Szent Péter Bazilika; Dóm tér; adult/concession 800/500Ft; ⌚ 9am-5pm Mon-Sat, 1-5pm Sun Apr-Oct, 10am-4pm Mon-Sat, 1-4pm Sun Nov-Mar**). The oldest part of the building is the 11th-century crypt. The 1770 **Bishop's Palace** (Püspöki Palota; adult/concession 1500/700Ft; tours 2pm, 3pm & 4pm Thu late Jun-mid-Sep) stands in front of the cathedral. Also near the square is a nearby 15th-century **barbican** *(barbakán)*, the only stone bastion to survive from the old city walls.

On the southern side of Dom tér is the new **Cella Septichora Visitors Centre** (Janus Pannonius utca; adult/concession 1500/800Ft; 10am-6pm Tue-Sun Apr-Oct, 10am-4pm Tue-Sun Nov-Mar), which illuminates a series of early-Christian burial sites that have been on Unesco's World Heritage list since 2000. The highlight is the so-called **Jug Mausoleum** (Korsós Sírkamra), a 4th-century Roman tomb whose name comes from a painting of a large drinking vessel with vines.

SLEEPING

Ábrahám Kishotel (510 422; www.abrahamhotel.hu; Munkácsy Mihály utca 8; s/d/tr 9100/12,000/14,000Ft;) Excellent little guesthouse with blue rooms, a well-tended, peaceful garden and a friendly welcome. It's owned by a religious establishment, so head elsewhere if you're looking for a party.

Hotel Diána (328 594; www.hoteldiana.hu; Tímár utca 4/a; s/d/tr from 9500/13,000/18,300Ft;) This very central pension offers 20 spotless rooms, comfortable kick-off-your-shoes decor and a warm welcome.

Palatinus Hotel (889 400; www.danubiushotels.com; Király utca 5; s/d from €60/80;) For art-nouveau glamour, Palatinus is *the* place in Pécs. An amazing marble reception has a soaring Moorish-detailed ceiling. It's a shame that the rooms are not as luxurious, but still, in Pécs, it's as good as it gets.

EATING & DRINKING

Pubs, cafes and fast-food eateries line pedestrian-only Király utca.

Minaret (311 338; Ferencesek utcája 35; mains 1200-2100Ft; noon-4pm Sun-Mon, to 9pm Tue-Thu, to 11pm Fri & Sat) Boasting one of the loveliest gardens in the city, this eatery in the shadow of the Pasa Memi Baths serves tasty Hungarian favourites.

our pick **Áfium** (511 434; Irgalmasok utca 2; mains 1400-1900Ft; 11am-1am) With Croatia and Serbia so close, it's a wonder that more restaurants don't offer cuisine from south of the border.

Aranykacsa (518 860; Teréz utca 4; mains 1620-3240Ft; 11.30am-10pm Tue-Thu, to midnight Fri & Sat, to 3pm Sun) This stunning wine restaurant takes pride in its silver service and beautiful venue. The menu offers at least eight duck dishes, including such memorables as duck ragout with honey and vegetables.

SHOPPING

Zsolnay (310 220; Jókai tér 2) has a porcelain outlet south of Széchenyi tér.

GETTING THERE & AWAY

Pécs is on a main rail line with Budapest's Déli train station (3230Ft, 3½ hours, nine daily).

KECSKEMÉT

76 / pop 103,000

Kecskemét (*kech*-kah-mate) is a green, pedestrian-friendly city with interesting art-nouveau architecture. Colourful buildings, fine small museums and the region's excellent *barackpálinka* (apricot brandy) beckon. And Kiskunsági Nemzeti Park, the *puszta* of the Southern Plain, is right at the back door. Day-trip opportunities include hiking in the sandy, juniper-covered hills, a horse show at Bugac, or a visit to one of the area's many horse farms.

Central Kecskemét is made up of squares that run into one another, and consequently it's hard to tell them apart.

A 10-minute walk southwest along Nagykőrösi utca brings you to the first of the squares, Szabadság tér.

The **Tourinform** (☎481 065; kecskemet@tourinform.hu; Kossuth tér 1; 8am-7pm Mon-Fri, 10am-8pm Sat & Sun Jul-Aug, 8am-6pm Mon-Fri Sep-Jun) is located in the northeastern corner of the large Town Hall.

Walk around the parklike squares, starting at Szabadság tér, and admire the eclectic buildings, including the Technicolor art-nouveau style of the 1902 **Ornamental Palace** (Cifrapalota; Rákóczi út 1), recently refurbished and covered in multicoloured majolica tiles. Check out the wonderful interiors of the **Kecskemét Gallery** (Kecskeméti Képtár; Rákóczi út 1; adult/concession 300/150Ft; 10am-5pm Tue-Sat, 1.30-5pm Sun) here. Across the street, the Moorish building is the **House of Science & Technology** (Tudomány és Technika Háza; Rákóczi út 2; adult/concession 200/100Ft; 8am-4pm Mon-Fri). This former synagogue is now an exhibition hall.

Kossuth tér is dominated by the massive 1897 art-nouveau **Town Hall** (Városháza), which is flanked by the baroque **Great Church** (Nagytemplom; Kossuth tér 2; 9am-noon & 3-6pm Tue-Sun May-Sep, 9am-noon Tue-Sun Oct-Apr) and the earlier **Franciscan Church of St Nicholas** (Szent Miklós Templom), dating from the 13th century. Nearby is the magnificent 1896 **József Katona Theatre** (Katona József Színház; ☎483 283; Katona József tér 5), a neobaroque performance venue with a statue of the Trinity (1742) in front of it.

The town's museums are scattered around the main squares' periphery. Go first to the **Hungarian Museum of Naive Artists** (Magyar Naive Müvészek; Gáspár András utca 11; adult/concession 200/100Ft; 10am-5pm Tue-Sun mid-Mar–Oct), in the Stork House (1730) northwest off Petőfí Sándor utca. It has an impressive small collection. Further to the southwest, the **Hungarian Folk Craft Museum** (Népi Iparmüvészeti Múzeum; Serfőző utca 19/a; adult/concession 300/150Ft; 10am-5pm Tue-Sat Feb-Nov) has a definitive collection of regional embroidery, weaving and textiles, as well as some furniture, woodcarving and agricultural tools. A few handicrafts are for sale at the entrance.

DAVID GREEDY

Vineyards at Tokaj

IF YOU LIKE...

If you like the forest surrounds and wine tasting in **Eger** (p601), we think you might also be interested in these:

- **Szilvásvárad** (www.szilvasvarad.hu; information stand on Szalajka-völgy; 10am-6pm Jun-Oct) An excellent excursion 28km from Eger. This forest village is home to the graceful white Lipizzaner stallions, a narrow-gauge train and many trails.
- **Tokaj** (☎047-552 070; www.tokaj.hu; Serház utca 1; 9am-6pm Mon-Fri, 10am-7pm Sat & Sun Jun-Aug, 9am-5pm Mon-Fri Sep-May) A northeastern Hungarian town known for its sweet dessert wines and cellars.

Barokk Antik Panzió (☎260 3215; www.barokkantik-panzio.hu; Fráter György utca 17; s/d 7500/10,500Ft) A sombre painting or two lends a bit of an old-world feel, but we wouldn't say the rooms have actual antiques.

our pick **Fábián Panzió** (☎477 677; www.panzio fabian.hu; Kápolna utca 14; s/d from

AS STRONG AS A BULL

The story of the Turkish attempt to take Eger Castle is the stuff of legend. Under the command of István Dobó, a mixed bag of 2000 soldiers held out against more than 100,000 Turks for a month in 1552. As every Hungarian kid in short trousers can tell you, the women of Eger played a crucial role in the battle, pouring boiling oil and pitch on the invaders from the ramparts.

If we're to believe the tale, it seems that Dobó sustained his weary troops with a ruby-red vintage of the town's wine. When they fought on with increased vigour – and stained beards – rumours began to circulate among the Turks that the defenders were gaining strength by drinking the blood of bulls. The invaders departed, and the legend of Bikavér (Bull's Blood) was born.

8800/11,000Ft;) The world-travelling family that owns this pretty-in-pink guesthouse knows how to treat a visitor well. Friendly staff help their guests plan each day's excursions, teapots are available for in-room use, wireless internet is free, and bikes are available for hire.

our pick **Liberté Étterem** (**☎ 509 175; Szabadság tér 2; mains 1200-2000Ft**) Artistic presentations come with your order, whether it's the traditional stuffed cabbage or the mixed sautéed chicken with aubergine. This is modern Hungarian done well. Its outside tables have the best seats in town for people-watching.

Kecskeméti Csárda (**☎ 488 686; Kölcsey utca 7; mains 1500-2000Ft**) Restaurant trading on folksy charm. It goes over the top with rustic fishing gear on the walls and Romani music at weekends.

A direct rail line links Kecskemét to Budapest's Nyugati train station (1770Ft, 1½ hours, hourly).

KISKUNSÁGI NEMZETI PARK

Totalling 760 sq km, **Kiskunsági Nemzeti Park** (**Kiskunság National Park; www.knp.hu**) consists of half a dozen 'islands' of protected land. Much of the park's alkaline ponds and sand dunes are off limits. **Bugac** (*boo-gats*) village, about 30km southwest of Kecskemét, is the most accessible part of the park.

From the village, walk, drive, or ride a **horse-driven carriage** (**adult/concession incl horse show 2900/1700Ft; 11.15pm & 12.15pm May-Oct**) along the 1.5km-long sandy track to the **Herder Museum** (**admission free; 10am-5pm May-Oct**), a circular structure designed to look like a horse-driven dry mill. The highlight of the museum is the popular **horse show** (**admission 1400Ft; 12.15pm & 1.15pm May-Oct, extra show 3.15pm Jun-Aug**). Once the show starts, the horse herders crack their whips, race one another bareback and ride 'five-in-hand', a breathtaking performance in which one *csikós* (cowboy) gallops five horses at full speed while standing on the backs of the rear two.

Afterwards, the food is surprisingly good at the kitschy **Bugaci Karikás Csárda** (**☎ 575 112; Nagybugac 135; mains 1600-2100Ft; 8am-8pm May-Oct**), next to the park entrance. The *gulyás* is hearty and the accompanying folk-music ensemble will get your feet tapping on the terrace.

The best way to get to Bugac is by bus from Kecskemét (600Ft, 50 minutes). The 11am bus from the main terminal gets you to the park entrance around noon. A bus returns directly from Bugac to Kecskemét at 3.50pm on weekdays.

NORTHEAST HUNGARY

If ever a Hungarian wine were world-famous, it would be tokay. And this is where it comes from, a region of Hungary containing microclimates conducive to wine production. The chain of wooded hills in the northeast constitutes the foothills of the Carpathian Mountains, which stretch along the Hungarian border with Slovakia.

EGER

☎ 36 / pop 58,300

Filled with preserved baroque architecture, Eger (*egg*-air) is a jewel box of a town containing gems aplenty. Explore the bloody history of Turkish conquest and defeat at its hilltop castle and climb a Turkish minaret…but best of all, go from cellar to cellar in the Valley of Beautiful Women (yes, it's really called that), tasting the celebrated Bull's Blood wine where it's made.

It was here in 1552 that Hungarian defenders temporarily stopped the Turkish advance into Western Europe and helped preserve Hungary's identity (see boxed text, opposite). However, the persistent Ottomans returned in 1596 and finally captured Eger Castle. They were evicted in 1687.

ORIENTATION & INFORMATION

The main train station is a 15-minute walk south of town, on Vasút utca, just east of Deák Ferenc utca. The bus station is west of Széchenyi István utca, Eger's main drag.

Post office (**Széchenyi István utca 22; 8am-8pm Mon-Fri, to 1pm Sat**)

Tourinform (**☎ 517 715; eger@tourinform.hu; Bajcsy-Zsilinszky utca 9; 9am-5pm Mon-Fri, to 1pm Sat & Sun mid-Jun–mid-Sep, closed Sun mid-Sep–mid-Jun**)

SIGHTS & ACTIVITIES

The most striking attraction and the best views of town are from **Eger Castle** (**Egri Vár; www.egrivar.hu; Vár 1; adult/concession incl museum 1200/600Ft; 9am-5pm Tue-Sun Apr-Oct, 10am-4pm Tue-Sun Nov-Mar**), a huge walled complex at the top of the hill off Dósza tér. First fortified after an early Mongol invasion in the 13th century, the earliest ruins on site are the foundations of St John's Cathedral, built in the 12th century and destroyed by the Turks. The excellent

DANITA DELIMONT / ALAMY

Open-air restaurants, Szépasszony völgy

SZÉPASSZONY VÖLGY

To sample Eger's wine, visit the extravagantly named Szépasszony völgy (Valley of the Beautiful Women), home to dozens of small wine cellars that truck in, store and sell Bull's Blood and other regional red and white wines. Walk the horseshoe-shaped street through the valley and stop in front of one that strikes your fancy and ask ('*megkosztólhatok?*') to taste their wares (100Ft per decilitre). If you want wine to go, you can bring an empty bottle and have it filled for about 350Ft per litre. The cellar's outdoor tables fill up on a late summer afternoon as locals cook *gulyás* in the park and strains from a gypsy violinist float up from the restaurants at the valley's entrance. A taxi back to the centre costs about 1000Ft.

Things you need to know: **off Király utca**

István Dobó Castle Museum (Dobó István Vármuzeum), inside the Bishop's Palace (1470) within the castle grounds, explores the history and development of the castle and the town.

A surprise awaits you west of the castle hill: a 40m-high **minaret** (Knézich Károly utca; admission 200Ft; 10am-6pm Apr-Oct), minus the mosque, is allegedly Europe's northernmost remains of the Ottoman invasion in the 16th century. The **Minorite Church** (Minorita Templom; Dobó István tér; admission free; 9am-5pm Tue-Sun), built in 1771, is a glorious baroque building. In the square in front are statues of national hero István Dobó and his comrades-in-arms routing the Turks in 1552.

The first thing you see as you come into town from the bus or train station is the neoclassical **Eger Basilica** (Egri Bazilika; Pyrker János tér 1), built in 1836. Directly opposite is the Copf-style **Lyceum** (Líceum; Esterházy tér 1; admission free; 9.30am-3.30pm Tue-Sun Apr-Sep, 9.30am-1pm Sat & Sun Oct-Mar), dating from 1765, with a 20,000-volume frescoed **library** (könyvetár; adult/concession 700/350Ft) on the 1st floor and an 18th-century observatory in the **Astronomy Museum** (Csillagászati Múzeum; adult/concession 800/650Ft) on the 6th floor. Climb three more floors up to the observation deck for a great view of the city and to try out the camera obscura, the 'eye of Eger', designed in 1776 to entertain the locals.

The Archbishop's Garden was once the private reserve of papal princes, but today the park is open to the public. Inside the park, the **City Thermal Baths** (Városi Térmalfürdő; 413 356; Fürdő utca 1-3; adult/concession 1250/1050Ft; 6am-8pm Apr-Oct, 9am-7pm Nov-Mar) has both open-air and covered pools with different temperatures and mineral contents. From June to August you can pay 700Ft extra to get into the modern 'adventure' complex, with bubbling massage pool and a castle-themed kids' pool. By the time you read this, the 1617 Turkish Bath (Török Fürdő) should have reopened after a total reconstruction.

SLEEPING

Atrium Apartmanház (418 427; www.atriumapart ment.eu; Neumayer János út 8; s/d/t apt 6500/10,000/12,500Ft) Your home in the city. Each loft apartment has at least one bedroom, a kitchenette, and cool tile floors.

Hotel Villa Völgy (321 664; www.hotelvillavolgy.hu; Tulipánkert utca 5; s/d 12,900/17,500Ft) Awaken to a view of the vineyards in this classy, modern-design villa situated in the wine valley. Neoclassical columns surround the glass-enclosed pool.

Hotel Senator Ház (320 466; www.senatorhaz.hu; Dobó István tér 11; s/d 15,000/19,000Ft) Warm and cosy rooms with traditional white furnishings fill the upper floors of this delightful 18th-century inn on Eger's main square. The ground floor is shared by a quality restaurant and a reception area that could easily moonlight as a history museum.

EATING & DRINKING

At the base of Szépasszony völgy utca there are numerous small terrace *büfé* (snack bars) that resemble food stands but employ a waiter to serve you at your picnic table. There are also lots of restaurants and cafes along pedestrianised Széchenyi István utca in town. The area is known for its *pistrang* (trout) dishes.

our pick **Palacsintavár** (413 986; Dobó István utca 9; mains 1400-1600Ft) Entrée-sized *palacsintak* (crêpelike pancakes) are served with an abundance of fresh vegetables and range in flavour from Asian to Italian.

Szántófer Vendéglő (517 298; Bródy utca 3; mains 1400-1800Ft; 8am-10pm) The est choice in town for hearty, homestyle lungarian food.

GETTING THERE & AWAY

lourly buses make the trip from Eger to .ecskemét (2060Ft, 4½ hours, three daily) nd Szeged (3220Ft, 5¾ hours, two daily). Jp to seven direct trains a day head to udapest's Keleti train station (2290Ft, ½ hours).

DIRECTORY

ACTIVITIES

Canoeing and rafting are popular on the 'ltava River around Český Krumlov (p569) nd the whole of the Czech Republic is ideal or cycling and cycle touring. **Greenways Travel Club** (☎ 519 511 572; www.visitgreenways.com) offers everything from cycling and valking itineraries to beer and wine, Czech glass and Czech music tours.

The High Tatra mountains (p577) in Slovakia are a great hiking destination.

Hungary has more than 100 thermal baths open to the public, and many are attached to hotels with guest packages. For locations, ask Tourinform for the *Spa & Wellness* booklet. For more about Budapest pas, check out www.spasbudapest.com.

DANGERS & ANNOYANCES

Pick-pocketing can be a problem in the main tourist zones of Prague and Budapest. Never leave anything on the eat of an unattended vehicle, even a ocked one; apparently that's advertising ou don't want it any more.

EMBASSIES & CONSULATES

CZECH REPUBLIC

Embassies are located in Prague.

Australia (Map pp552-3; ☎ 296 578 350; www.embassy.gov.au/cz.html; 6th fl, Klimentká 10, Nové Město) Honorary consulate for emergency assistance only; nearest Australian embassy is in Vienna.

Canada (Map pp548-9; ☎ 272 101 800; www.canada.cz; Muchova 6, Bubeneč)

France (Map pp548-9; ☎ 251 171 711; www.france.cz, in French & Czech; Velkopřerovské nám 2, Malá Strana)

Germany (Map pp548-9; ☎ 257 113 111; www.deutschland.cz, in German & Czech; Vlašská 19, Malá Strana)

Ireland (Map pp548-9; ☎ 257 530 061; www.embassyofireland.cz; Tržiště 13, Malá Strana)

Netherlands (Map pp548-9; ☎ 233 015 200; www.netherlandsembassy.cz; Gotthardská 6/27, Bubeneč)

New Zealand (Map pp548-9; ☎ 222 514 672; egermayer@nzconsul.cz; Dykova 19, Vinohrady) Honorary consulate providing emergency assistance only (eg stolen passport); the nearest NZ embassy is in Berlin. Visits only by appointment.

UK (Map pp548-9; ☎ 257 402 111; www.britain.cz; Thunovská 14, Malá Strana)

USA (Map pp548-9; ☎ 257 022 000; www.usembassy.cz; Tržiště 15, Malá Strana)

SLOVAKIA

Australia and New Zealand do not have embassies in Slovakia; the nearest are in Vienna and Berlin respectively. The following are all in Bratislava:

Austria (Map p573; ☎ 02-5443 1334; www.embassyaustria.sk; Ventúrska 10)

Czech Republic (Map p573; ☎ 02-5920 3303; www.mzv.cz/bratislava/; Hviezdoslavovo nám 8)

France (Map p573; ☎ 02-5934 7111; www.france.sk; Hlavné nám 7)

Germany (Map p573; ☎ 02-5920 4400; www.pressburg.diplo.de; Hviezdoslavovo nám 10)

Ireland (Map p573; ☎ 02-5930 9611; www.dfa.ie; Carlton Savoy Bldg, Mostová 2)

Netherlands (off Map p573; ☎ 02-5262 5081; www.holandskoweb.com; Frana Krála 5)

UK (Map p573; ☎ 02-5998 2000; www.britishembassy.sk; Panská 16)

USA (Map p573; ☎ 02-5443 0861; http://slovakia.usembassy.gov; Hviezdoslavovo nám 4)

HUNGARY

Embassies in Budapest include the following:

Australia (off Map p588; ☎ 1-457 9777; XII Királyhágó tér 8-9)
Canada (Map p588; ☎ 1-392 3360; II Ganz utca 12-14)
France (Map p590; ☎ 1-374 1100; VI Lendvay utca 27)
Germany (Map p588; ☎ 1-488 3505; I Úri utca 64-66)
Ireland (Map p590; ☎ 1-301 4960; V Szabadság tér 7-9)
Netherlands (off Map p588; ☎ 1-336 6300; II Füge utca 5-7)
UK (Map p590; ☎ 1-266 2888; V Harmincad utca 6)
USA (Map p590; ☎ 1-475 4164; V Szabadság tér 12)

HOLIDAYS

CZECH REPUBLIC

New Year's Day 1 January; also anniversary of the founding of the Czech Republic.
Easter Monday March/April
Labour Day 1 May
Liberation Day 8 May
SS Cyril & Methodius Day 5 July
Jan Hus Day 6 July
Czech Statehood Day 28 September
Republic Day 28 October
Struggle for Freedom & Democracy Day 17 November
Christmas 24 to 26 December

SLOVAKIA

New Year's & Independence Day 1 January
Three Kings Day 6 January
Good Friday & Easter Monday March/April
Labour Day 1 May
Victory over Fascism Day 8 May
SS Cyril & Methodius Day 5 July
SNP Day 29 August
Constitution Day 1 September
Our Lady of Sorrows Day 15 September
All Saints' Day 1 November
Christmas 24 to 26 December

HUNGARY

New Year's Day 1 January
1848 Revolution Day 15 March
Easter Monday March/April
International Labour Day 1 May
Whit Monday May/June
St Stephen's Day 20 August
1956 Remembrance Day 23 October
All Saints' Day 1 November
Christmas Holidays 25 and 26 December

TELEPHONE

All Czech phone numbers have nine digits – you have to dial all nine for any call, local or long distance. Slovakian and Hungarian numbers have seven or eight digits and you must dial the area code if calling from outside the city.

Payphones are abundant in all three nations, but most take telephone cards only. Buy them from news-stands and post offices.

Mobile-phone coverage (GSM 900) is excellent in the Czech Republic and Hungary, less so in Slovakia.

TRAVELLERS WITH DISABILITIES

Ramps for wheelchair users are becoming more common, but cobbled streets, steep hills and stairways often make getting around difficult in all three countries. Public transport is still problematic, but a growing number of trains and trams have wheelchair access.

TRANSPORT

GETTING THERE & AWAY

AIR

CZECH REPUBLIC

The Czech Republic's main international airport is **Prague-Ruzyně** (☎ 220 113 314; www.csl.cz/en). The national carrier, **Czech Airlines** (ČSA; Map pp552-3; ☎ 239 007 007; www.csa.cz; V celnici 5, Nové Město), has direct flights to Prague from many European cities.

Budget carriers include the following:

easyJet (EZY; www.easyjet.com)
Ryanair (FR; www.ryanair.com)
SmartWings (QS; www.smartwings.net)
Wizzair (W6; www.wizzair.com)

SLOVAKIA

There is no national carrier in Slovakia. Flights connect Bratislava to limited destinations across Europe. The main gateway airport, however, is **Vienna International airport** (VIE; www.viennaairport.com), only 60km from Bratislava in Austria. Buses connect from there to Bratislava's bus station almost hourly.

Airlines flying to and from Slovakia:

Austrian Airlines (OS; www.aua.com)
Czech Airlines (OK; www.czechairlines.com)
Danube Wings (V5; www.danubewings.com)
Ryanair (FR; www.ryanair.com)
Wizz Air (W6; www.wizzair.com)

HUNGARY

The vast majority of international flights land at **Ferihegy International Airport** (☎ 1-296 7000; www.bud.hu) on the outskirts of Budapest. Hungary's national carrier is **Malév Hungarian Airlines** (MA; ☎ 06 40 212121; www.malev.hu).

Discount airlines servicing Hungary include the following:

easyJet (EZY; www.easyjet.com)
germanwings (4U; ☎ 1-526 7005; www.germanwings.com)
Ryanair (FR; www.ryanair.com)
Wizz Air (W6 ☎ 06 90 181 181; www.wizzair.com)

LAND

BUS

International buses do head for Prague, Bratislava and Budapest, and may be a bit cheaper, but train trips will be much shorter, and more comfortable.

CAR & MOTORCYCLE

You will need to buy a *nálepka* (motorway tax coupon) – on sale at border crossings, petrol stations and post offices – in order to use Czech motorways (220/330Kč for one week/month). See www.ceskedalnice.cz for more information.

TRAIN

International trains travel from Prague to Vienna (4½ hours), Bratislava (4½ hours), Berlin (five hours), Munich (six hours), Budapest (seven hours) and Frankfurt (7½ hours), among other destinations. Check train timetables and departure points online at www.idos.cz.

Direct trains connect Bratislava with Prague (4½ hours), Budapest (three hours) and Vienna (one hour). The website http://cp.atlas.sk has international and domestic schedules.

The Hungarian State Railways, **MÁV** (☎ 1-371 9449; www.mav.hu) links up with international rail networks in all directions, and its schedule is available online. Some direct train connections from Budapest include Vienna (three hours), Bratislava (three hours), Prague (€38, seven hours), Venice (€55, 14 hours) and Thessaloniki, Greece (23 hours).

RIVER

A hydrofoil service on the Danube River between Budapest (p594), Bratislava (p576) and Vienna (p482) operates daily from late April to early October.

GETTING AROUND

AIR

The Czech Republic, Hungary and Slovakia are so small, there's really no domestic air service to speak of.

BOAT

In summer there are regular passenger ferries on from Budapest to the Danube Bend. Details of the schedules are given in the relevant destination sections.

BUS

Within the Czech Republic buses may be more convenient than trains, though not as comfortable. Most services are operated by the national bus company **CŠAD** (☎ **information line 900 144 444**). Check bus timetables and prices at www.idos.cz. Private companies include **Student Agency** (**www.studentagency.cz**), with destinations including Prague, České Budějovice, Český Krumlov and Karlovy Vary, and **Megabus** (**www.megabus.cz**), linking Prague with Karlovy Vary.

Slovak national buses run by **Slovenská autobusová doprava** (**SAD; www.sad.sk**) are comparably priced to trains, but take longer for most cities in this chapter. Search schedules at http://cp.atlas.sk.

Domestic Hungarian buses run by **Volánbusz** (☎ **1-382 0888; www.volanbusz.hu**) cover an extensive nationwide network.

CAR & MOTORCYCLE

Foreign driving licences are valid in all three countries. The main international car-rental chains all have offices in th[e] capitals and at the airports.

Road rules are the same as the rest o[f] Europe. Speed limits are 30km/h or 50km/[h] in built-up areas, 90km/h on open road[s] and 130km/h on motorways; motorbike[s] are limited to 80km/h. The most importan[t] rule to remember is that there's a 100% ban on alcohol when you are driving, an[d] this rule is *very* strictly enforced.

You need a motorway tax coupon o[r] sticker to use the motorways. This is included with most rental cars in the Czech Republic and Slovakia. In Hungary, you can buy a ticket for the duration of you[r] stay at petrol stations.

LOCAL TRANSPORT

Prague and Budapest have underground metro train systems. Bratislava and other cities only have trams and buses. Tickets must be purchased in advance – they're sold at bus and train stations, news-stands and vending machines – and must be validated in the time-stamping machines on buses and trams and at the entrance to metro stations. Tickets are hard to find at night, on weekends and in residential areas, so carry a good supply. Public transport generally runs from 4.30am to 11.30pm.

TRAIN

The national rail companies **Czech Railways** (**ČD; www.cd.cz**), **Slovak Republic Railways** (**ŽSR;** ☎ **18 188; www.zsr.sk**) and **Hungarian State Railways** (**MÁV;** ☎ **1-371 9449; www.mav.hu**) run efficient and comprehensive train networks covering thousands of kilometres.

Eurail and Inter-Rail, single and multi-country passes (see p796) are valid in all three countries.

CROATIA

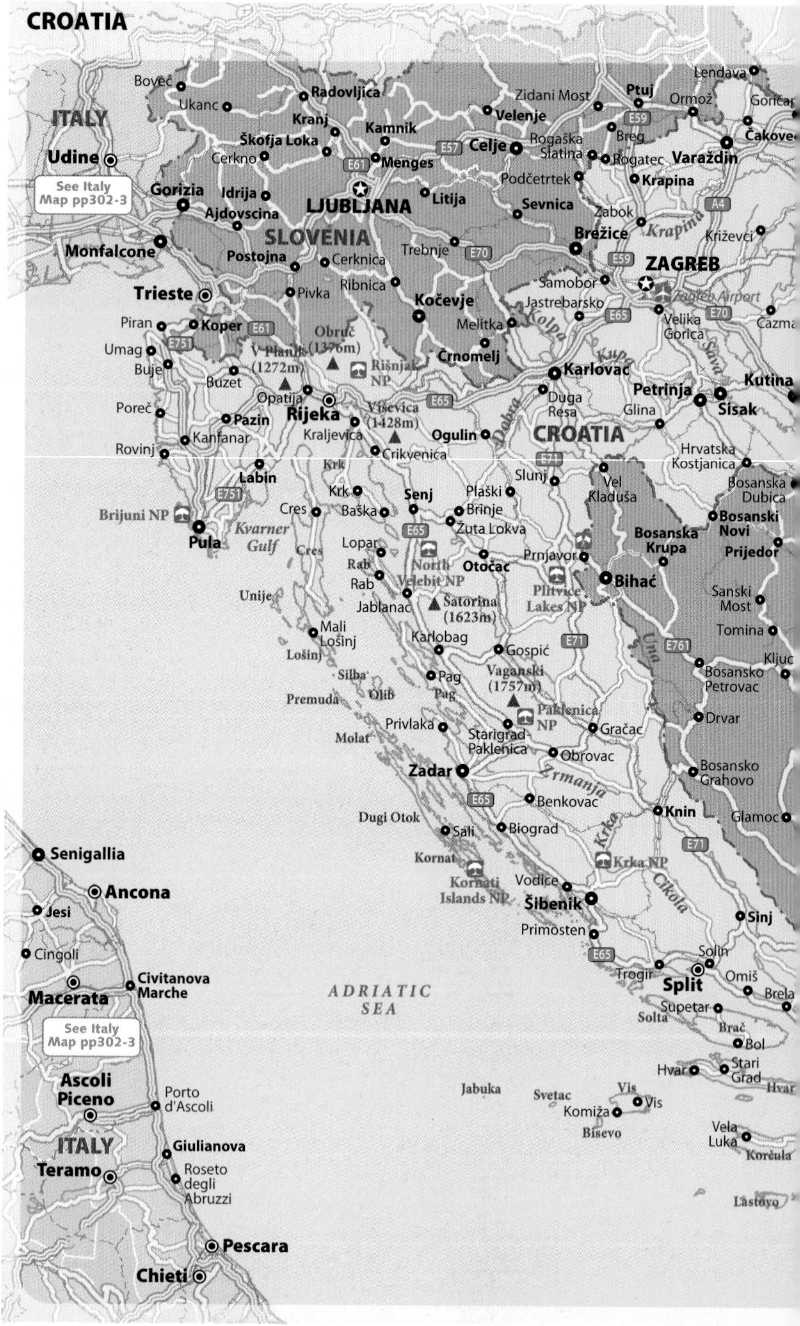
CROATIA
ITALY
Udine
See Italy Map pp302-3
Gorizia
Monfalcone
Trieste
Bovec
Ukanc
Radovljica
Kranj
Škofja Loka
Cerkno
Idrija
Ajdovscina
Kamnik
Menges
LJUBLJANA
SLOVENIA
Postojna
Cerknica
Pivka
Ribnica
Kočevje
Litija
Trebnje
Velenje
Celje
Zidani Most
Ptuj
Ormož
Lendava
Čakovec
Varaždin
Rogaška Slatina
Rogatec
Breg
Podčetrtek
Krapina
Sevnica
Zabok
Brežice
Krapina
Križevci
ZAGREB
Samobor
Zagreb Airport
Jastrebarsko
Velika Gorica
Čazma
Melitka
Kolpa
Črnomelj
Piran
Koper
Umag
Buje
Buzet
V Planik (1272m)
Obruč (1376m)
Rišnjak NP
Opatija
Rijeka
Poreč
Pazin
Kanfanar
Rovinj
Višvica (1428m)
Kraljevica
Crikvenica
Karlovac
Kupa
Duga Resa
Dobra
Ogulin
CROATIA
Petrinja
Sisak
Kutina
Glina
Sava
Hrvatska Kostjanica
Slunj
Labin
Krk
Krk
Senj
Cres
Baška
Plaški
Brinje
Žuta Lokva
Vel Kladuša
Bosanska Dubica
Bosanski Novi
Bosanska Krupa
Prijedor
Brijuni NP
Pula
Kvarner Gulf
Cres
Lopar
Rab
Rab
North Velebit NP
Otočac
Prnjavor
Plitvice Lakes NP
Bihać
Sanski Most
Unije
Jablanac
Šatorina (1623m)
Mali Lošinj
Lošinj
Karlobag
Gospić
Tomina
Una
Ključ
Silba
Pag
Pag
Vaganski (1757m)
Bosansko Petrovac
Premuda
Olib
Paklenica NP
Privlaka
Starigrad Paklenica
Gračac
Drvar
Molat
Obrovac
Zadar
Zrmanja
Bosansko Grahovo
Benkovac
Dugi Otok
Sali
Biograd
Knin
Glamoc
Krka
Kornat
Krka NP
Kornati Islands NP
Vodice
Šibenik
Cikola
Sinj
Primosten
Solin
Trogir
Split
Omiš
Brela
ADRIATIC SEA
Supetar
Solta
Brač
Bol
Hvar
Stari Grad
Hvar
Jabuka
Svetac
Vis
Vis
Komiža
Biševo
Vela Luka
Korčula
Lastovo
Senigallia
Ancona
Jesi
Cingoli
Macerata
Civitanova Marche
See Italy Map pp302-3
Ascoli Piceno
Porto d'Ascoli
ITALY
Giulianova
Teramo
Roseto degli Abruzzi
Pescara
Chieti
E59
E57
E61
A4
E70
E59
E65
E70
E61
E751
E65
E71
E751
E65
E761
E71
E65
E71
E65

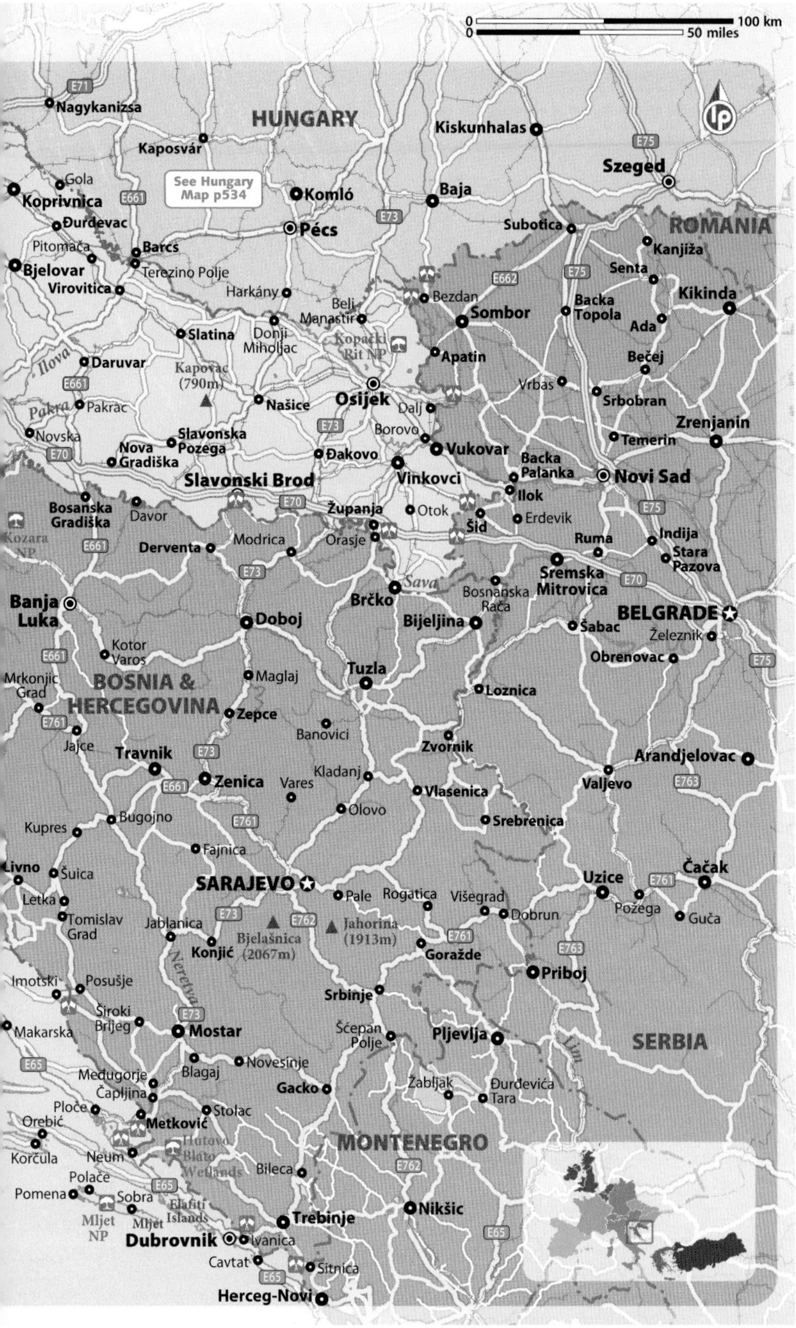
0 100 km
0 50 miles
HUNGARY
ROMANIA
BOSNIA & HERCEGOVINA
SERBIA
MONTENEGRO
See Hungary Map p534
Nagykanizsa
Kaposvár
Kiskunhalas
Szeged
Gola
Koprivnica
Komló
Baja
Đurđevac
Pécs
Subotica
Pitomača
Barcs
Kanjiža
Bjelovar
Terezino Polje
Senta
Virovitica
Harkány
Bezdan
Backa Topola
Kikinda
Beli Manastir
Sombor
Ada
Slatina
Donji Miholjac
Kopački Rit NP
Apatin
Bečej
Daruvar
Kapovac (790m)
Vrbas
Osijek
Srbobran
Ilova
Pakra
Pakrac
Našice
Dalj
Zrenjanin
Novska
Slavonska Požega
Borovo
Temerin
Nova Gradiška
Đakovo
Vukovar
Backa Palanka
Novi Sad
Slavonski Brod
Vinkovci
Ilok
Bosanska Gradiška
Davor
Županja
Otok
Šid
Erdevik
Kozara NP
Modrica
Orasje
Ruma
Indija
Derventa
Stara Pazova
Sremska Mitrovica
Sava
Bosnanska Rača
Banja Luka
Brčko
BELGRADE
Doboj
Bijeljina
Šabac
Železnik
Kotor Varos
Obrenovac
Tuzla
Mrkonjic Grad
Maglaj
Loznica
Zepce
Jajce
Banovici
Zvornik
Arandjelovac
Travnik
Kladanj
Zenica
Vares
Valjevo
Vlasenica
Olovo
Bugojno
Srebrenica
Kupres
Fajnica
Livno
Šuica
Uzice
Čačak
SARAJEVO
Pale
Rogatica
Višegrad
Letka
Požega
Tomislav Grad
Dobrun
Guča
Jablanica
Bjelašnica (2067m)
Jahorina (1913m)
Konjić
Goražde
Priboj
Neretva
Imotski
Posušje
Srbinje
Široki Brijeg
Makarska
Mostar
Šćepan Polje
Pljevlja
Lim
Blagaj
Novesinje
Međugorje
Čapljina
Gacko
Žabljak
Đurđevića Tara
Ploče
Orebić
Metković
Stolac
Korčula
Neum
Hutovo Blato Wetlands
Bileca
Polače
Pomena
Sobra
Elafiti Islands
Mljet NP
Mljet
Trebinje
Nikšic
Dubrovnik
Ivanica
Cavtat
Sitnica
Herceg-Novi
E71
E75
E661
E73
E662
E70
E761
E763
E762
E65

HIGHLIGHTS

1 COASTAL CULTURE

MERI MATESIC, NATIVE OF ZADAR

Croatia is a country of more than 1000 islands. You can find hot spots like Hvar or Brač, but there are also small places that are pure tranquillity – the Mediterranean as it once was. Growing up in Zadar was beautiful... the sea is great source of inspiration and strength for me.

MERI MATESIC'S DON'T MISS LIST

❶ PORT TOWNS

I think the allure of the port towns is the unique Mediterranean lifestyle, the relaxed and beautiful scenery combined with the urban energy of vibrant cities. People live and work here. At the same time these are the places to relax with the most beautiful sunsets and enjoy traditional Croatian food and wine with the fascinating sea all around you. You must have realized by now, it's all about the magic of the sea.

❷ PEBBLY STRETCHES

Croatia is not known as a sandy-beach destination, but all along the coast especially on islands, there is at leas one sandy stretch. Personally I prefe pebble beaches: south of Split, the 'Makarska Riviera' is the absolute win ner, with its long beautiful pebble beaches and Biokovo mountain jus behind it. **Zlatni Rat** (p637), on Brač changes its shape due to the wind and sea. Koločep, one of the **Elafiti Islands** (p640), is also popular.

Clockwise from top: Port at Rovinj (p626); Rab beach; Jadrolinija ferry (p647) on the Adriatic Sea; Coastline, Elafiti Islands (p640); Zlatni Rat, Brač (p637)

CLOCKWISE FROM TOP: JEAN-PIERRE LESCOURRET; CRAIG PERSHOUSE; TIM HUGHES; WAYNE WALTON; RACHEL LEW

HIDDEN GEMS

Vith so many islands everyone can ind a special one. Silba, a small green sland in the Zadar archipelago, is quite lifferent from other islands because of he special spirit and tranquillity, and here are no cars so the whole island eels like yours. Rab, in the northern varner region, has a sandy beach just eneath historic city walls.

TRACES OF ANCIENT TIMES

ince time immemorial the Adriatic ea has been the shortest maritime route leading from the central 1editerranean and the centres of the reat civilizations of antiquity to the entral European mainland. Having een such a vital route, both on land nd beneath its blue waters are found relics from all periods in the development of European and world civilizations. For example, the **Baron Gautsch** (p627), an Austrian passenger ship sunk in 1914, is the most popular diving destination in Istria.

THINGS YOU NEED TO KNOW

When to dive deep Diving season runs from May through November; the Adriatic is relatively calm, no high waves or strong currents **Routing around** Most ferries travel from the mainland to islands, not between islands, so the easiest way to see multiple islands in a day is with a tour company

HIGHLIGHTS

2

↘ HVAR ISLAND

Hvar Town (p634) is home to posh yachties and a see-and-be-seen crowd. You'll certainly find a luxurious place to lay your head here – when you're not out partying. But the sunniest place in the country (2724 hours a year) also holds a few surprises. Lavender plants and aromatic herbs fill the inland fields, and Jelsa is an intimate port town within easy reach of swimming coves and sandy spots.

3

↘ DIOCLETIAN'S PALACE

One of the most impressive Roman ruins in existence, **Diocletian's Palace** (p631) in Split, is more like a small walled city than a traditional royal abode or museum. The labyrinthine streets contain shops, restaurants and local residences. One of the best things to do is just get lost wandering. When you tire, stop for a beverage at the cafe tables that line the exterior walls and soak up the ambiance.

ZADAR

You may not have heard as much about **Zadar** (p628) as other coastal towns, but you should have. A lively cafe scene and bustling market bring this little town to life. The marble-clad, traffic-free old town follows the old Roman street plan, complete with ruins. Don't miss the circular Church of St Donat, one of the most outstanding monuments in Dalmatia.

CRUISING THE DALMATIAN COAST

Croatia's most scenic **ferry ride** (p647) is the nine hours spent cruising between Split and Dubrovnik. Sunbathe while you soak in the rugged shoreline views. Islands like Hvar and Korčula pass by at a leisurely pace. The boat trip takes about twice as long as the bus, but it sure is worth it.

CAFE CULTURE, ZAGREB

One of the nicest ways to experience *špica,* the Saturday morning and prelunch coffee drinking ritual, is on a terrace in **Zagreb** (p620), a year-round outdoor city. Order your macchiato (strong espresso-like *kava* diluted with milk) and watch the world go by. On summer nights the scene resembles a vast outdoor party.

2 JEAN-PIERRE LESCOURRET; 3 CHRISTOPHER GROENHOUT; 4 JOHN ELK III; 5 WAYNE WALTON; 6 ANDREW BURKE

2 Square in Hvar Town (p634); 3 Diocletian's Palace (p631); 4 Pedestrian street with outdoor cafe, Zadar (p628); 5 Korčula waterfront (p636); 6 Tkalčićeva (p625), Zagreb

THE BEST...

DALMATIAN BEACHES

- **Banje Beach, Dubrovnik** (p645) Rent beach chairs from the East-West Club by day and buy beach drinks there at night.
- **Zlatni Rat, Brač Island** (p637) Dramatic cliffs and shady pines back more than 500m of smooth white stones.
- **Lokrum Island** (p644) Peaceful beach perfect for naturists.

NATIONAL WONDERS

- **Plitvice Lakes National Park** (p624) Sixteen turquoise lakes linked by a series of waterfalls and cascades.
- **Mljet Island National Park** (p639) Encompassing the western third of the forested island, the park surrounds two saltwater lakes.
- **Kornati Islands National Park** (p629) Startling rock formations on rugged islands.

CROATIAN CUISINE

- **Kerempuh, Zagreb** (p625) A daily set menu changes based on the freshest ingredients from the market.
- **Kornat, Zadar** (p630) Elegant, modern restaurant with knock-out food.
- **Konoba Trattoria Bajamont, Split** (p633) Enjoy authentic seafood stew at one of a handful of tables.

HOLY GROUND

- **Church of St Euphemia, Rovinj** (p627) The massive cathedral, with its 60m-high tower, punctuates the Istrian peninsula.
- **St Donatus Church, Zadar** (p628) A Byzantine structure constructed over an ancient forum still has Roman remnants.
- **Franciscan Monastery, Dubrovnik** (p642) Beautiful mid–14th century late-Romanesque cloister.

LEFT: RICHARD NEBESKY; RIGHT: CHRISTOPHER GROENHOUT

Left: Plitvice Lakes National Park (p624); Right: Banje Beach, Dubrovnik (p640)

THINGS YOU NEED TO KNOW

AT A GLANCE

- **Population** 4.5 million
- **Official language** Croatian
- **Currency** Kuna (KN)
- **Telephone code** ☎ 385
- **When to go** May through June and September
- **Tipping** Service charges are always included, just round up the bill

REGIONS IN A NUTSHELL

- **Zagreb** (p620) Culture, arts, music, architecture, nightlife, gastronomy and all the other things that make a quality capital.
- **Istria** (p626) Continental Croatia meets the Adriatic on a peninsula near Italy. Vast hotel complexes line most of its rocky beaches.
- **Dalmatia** (p628) The jagged coast is speckled with lush offshore islands such as Hvar and dotted with historic cities including Zadar, Split and Dubrovnik. Simply unforgettable.

ADVANCE PLANNING

- **One week before** Book cabins on overnight ferries.
- **A day or two before** Book long-distance bus tickets.

BE FOREWARNED

- **Avoid the sea urchins** These spiny little creatures live on the Adriatic sea bed and do sting if you step on them. Wearing water shoes is your best protection.
- **Coastal time** Along the coast, life is relaxed: shops and offices may occasionally close around noon for an afternoon break and reopen around 4pm.
- **Gay & lesbian travellers** Homosexuality is tolerated, but public displays of affection between members of the same sex may be met with hostility, especially outside major cities.

BUSINESS HOURS

- **Banks** (7am-7pm Mon-Fri, 8am-noon Sat)
- **Post offices** (7am-7pm Mon-Fri, 8am-noon Sat)
- **Shops** (8.30am-7pm Mon-Fri, 8am-noon Sat)
- **Restaurants** (11am or noon to 11pm or midnight, closed Sun Oct-Apr)
- **Cafes & bars** (8am-midnight)

COSTS

- **750KN per day** Midrange lodging, restaurant meals, museum entry and public transport.
- **1500KN +** Top-end digs and top-star eats.

EMERGENCY NUMBERS

- **Ambulance** (☎ 94)
- **Fire** (☎ 93)
- **Police** (☎ 92)
- **Roadside Assistance** (☎ 987)

THINGS YOU NEED TO KNOW

GETTING AROUND

- **By land** Travelling by bus is the cheapest and most efficient method of getting around mainland Croatia; there are few trains.
- **By sea** Ferry transport between coastal cities is definitely more atmospheric, but it takes twice as long as buses. Island ferries shuttle fairly frequently to the mainland, but few travel between islands. Ferry schedules are more limited from October through April.
- **Gateway airport** Zagreb; European carriers and charters link seaside airports.

MEDIA

- **Newspaper** *Vjesnik* is the most respected daily newspaper.
- **Online** Croatian Times (www.croatiantimes.com) has local news in English.
- **Radio** Narodni Radio broadcasts only Croatian music.

RESOURCES

- **Croatia Homepage** (www.hr.hr) Hundreds of links to everything you want to know about Croatia.
- **Croatian National Tourist Board** (☎ 01-45 56 455; www.htz.hr; Iblerov Trg 10, Importanne Gallerija, 10000 Zagreb) A good source of information with an excellent website.
- **Split-Dalmatian Tourist Region** (www.dalmatia.hr) All about Dalmatia, including reservations for private accommodation.

VISAS

- **Australian, Canadian, New Zealand, EU and US citizens** No visa required for stays of less than 90 days.
- **Other nationalities** Visas are issued free of charge at Croatian consulates.

LEFT: WITOLD SKRYPCZAK; RIGHT: WAYNE WALTON

Left: Rovinj (p626); Right: St Mark's Church (p623), Zagreb

GET INSPIRED

BOOKS

- **Black Lamb and Grey Falcon** Rebecca West's rollicking, WWII-era Yugoslavian travelogue.
- **How We Survived Communism and Even Laughed** Slavenka Drakulić's intellectual exposé.
- **Croatia: Aspects of Art, Architecture and Cultural Heritage** Full colour pictorial.
- **Croatian Nights** A collection of short stories by contemporary Croatian writers.

FILMS

- **How the War Started on My Island** (1996) Vinko Brešan's humorous take on the Yugoslavian war.
- **A Wonderful Night in Split** (2004) A darkly comic modern film set over a New Year's Eve in Split.
- **Armin** (2007) Critically acclaimed film about a Bosnian boy journeying to Zagreb to be a movie star.
- **From Russia With Love** (1963) James Bond meets his Soviet double in Zagreb.

MUSIC

- **Croatia: Music of Long Ago** Runs the gamut of Croatian music.
- **Pripovid O Dalmaciji** Traditional *klapa*, an outgrowth of choir singing.
- **Lijepa naša tamburaša** Chants accompanied by mandolin.
- **Zdravo Marijo** Pop-music queen Severina Vučković's recent album.

WEBSITES

- **Culturenet** (www.culturenet.hr) A rundown of festivals and exhibitions in Croatia.
- **Croatia Beaches** (www.croatia-beaches.com) Best beaches broken down by activity.
- **Croatian Traveller** (http://croatiatraveller.com/blog/) Croatian travel blog.
- **Croatia Report** (www.croatiareport.com) Croatian videos, recipes and more.

ITINERARIES

DUBROVNIK & AROUND Three Days

This age-old Adriatic seaport also serves as a great base for island explorations. The red roofs and stone buildings of **(1) Dubrovnik** (p640) became world famous when they fell victim to the bombs of the 'Homeland War' in 1991 and 1992. Thankfully all's restored. Don't miss a stroll down Stradum, the town's pedestrian promenade.

Overall you'll stay in Dubrovnik all three nights, but by day you'll be adventuring out. First take the ferry **(2) Mljet Island** (p638) and its national park. A short boat ride brings you to the monastery of **Veliko Jezero** (p639) on an islet-within-an-island, and there's hiking around the two salt lakes.

Then the next day you could take a water taxi to **Lokrum Island** (p644), a national park with a rocky nudist beaches and a botanical garden. Or, better yet, hook up with a guide for an activity-filled tour of **(3) Elafiti Islands** (p640). Sea kayaking is a favourite pastime and a terrific way to see the sparsely inhabited archipelago. Other options include simple cruises and fishing excursions.

A DALMATIAN DALLIANCE Five Days

Tour two of the region's top seaside cities – and the islands in between. Always buzzing, **(1) Split** (p630), Croatia's second largest city, achieves an admirable balance of old and new. Dozens of shops and eateries reside within the ancient Roman palace walls. After you've spent two days exploring the old city, its flourishing beach life and nearby ruins, hop on a boat to groovy **(2) Hvar Island** (p634), just an hour away. Your night here can be one of plush partying in upmarket Hvar Town or the more leisurely pace of cultured Stari Grad on the northern coast. The former offers all sorts of waterborne activities, from diving to beach-hopping excursion boats.

Catch the Jadrolinija ferry the next day from Stari Grad. You may want to stop for a night on the large and lush **(3) Korčula Island** (p636), where folk traditions are still strong. The main town is a striking walled city and there are plenty of quiet coves and small beaches. Then move on to ever-popular **(4) Dubrovnik** (p640). All in all you'll have spent nine hours cruising, but little compares to the sight of these atmospheric old city walls coming into view. Just don't expect to have the place to yourself.

ZAGREB THROUGH ZADAR One Week

From land to sea, the Zs have it all. Wondering if stopping in the Croatian capital of **(1) Zagreb** (p620) is worth it? Doubt not. Though far inland from the dazzling waterfronts, here you get the opportunity to explore Croatia's Austro-Hungarian history through a lively cafe

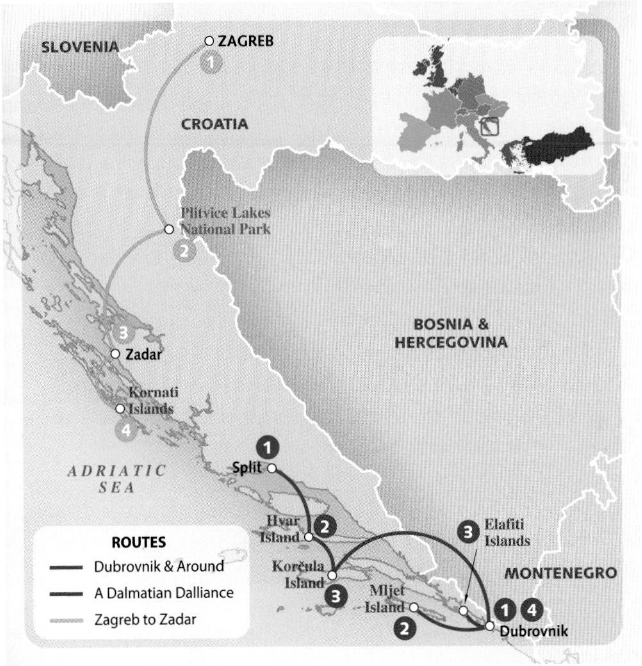

culture and imposing architecture. Spend a few nights because you'll have plenty of museums and a bustling market to explore.

The next day move on to the Unesco Heritage–listed **(2) Plitvice Lakes National Park** (p624), where nearly 20 hectares of forested hills encapsulate some extraordinary natural beauty. Follow wooden foot bridges and paths past lakes, streams and rumbling waterfalls.

Three and a half hours southwest, you reach the Adriatic at **(3) Zadar** (p628), one of Croatia's most underrated cities, with Roman ruins and a stunning Byzantine church and art. The second day of your stay here, take an excursion to the rugged nature of **(4) Kornati Islands** (p629). If you have more time, extend your tour south to include a Dalmatian Dalliance, opposite.

DISCOVER CROATIA

Touted as the 'new this' and the 'new that' for years since its re-emergence on the world tourism scene, it is now clear that Croatia is a unique destination that can hold its own and then some: this is a country with a glorious 1778km-long coast and a staggering 1185 islands. The Adriatic coast is a knockout: its limpid sapphirine waters draw visitors to remote islands, hidden coves and traditional fishing villages, all while touting the glitzy beach and yacht scene. Istria is captivating, thanks to its gastronomic delights and wines, and the bars, clubs and festivals of Zagreb, Zadar and Split remain little-explored gems. Eight national parks protect pristine forests, karst mountains, rivers, lakes and waterfalls in a landscape of primeval beauty. Punctuate all this with breathtaking Dubrovnik in the south – a country couldn't wish for a better finale.

ZAGREB

☎01 / pop 780,000

Everyone knows about Croatia, its coast, beaches and islands, but a mention of the country's capital still draws confused questions of whether it's nice or worth going to for a weekend. Well, here it is, once and for all: yes, Zagreb is a great destination, weekend or week-long. Zagreb is made for strolling, drinking coffee in almost permanently full cafes, popping into museums and galleries and enjoying theatres, concerts, cinema and music. It's a year-round outdoor city.

HISTORY

Medieval Zagreb developed from the 11th to the 13th centuries in the twin villages of Kaptol and Gradec, which make up the city's hilly Old Town. The two communities merged and became Zagreb, capital of the small portion of Croatia that hadn't fallen to the Turks in the 16th century. As the Turkish threat receded in the 18th century, the town expanded and the population grew. It was the centre of intellectual and political life under the Austro-Hungarian empire and became capital of the Independent State of Croatia in 1941 after the German invasion. The 'independent state' was in fact a Nazi puppet regime in the hands of Ante Pavelić and the Ustaša movement, even though most Zagrebians supported Tito's partisans.

In postwar Yugoslavia, Zagreb took second place to Belgrade but continued expanding. Zagreb has been capital of Croatia since 1991, when the country became independent.

ORIENTATION

The city is divided into Lower Zagreb, where most shops, restaurants, hotels and businesses are located, and Upper Zagreb, defined by the two hills of Kaptol and Gradec. As you come out of the train station, you'll see a series of parks and pavilions directly in front of you and the twin neo-Gothic towers of the cathedral in Kaptol in the distance. Trg Jelačića, beyond the northern end of the parks, is the main city square of Lower Zagreb. The bus station is 1km east of the train station.

INFORMATION

Atlas Travel Agency (☎ 48 13 933; Zrinjevac 17) The Amex representative in Zagreb.

Croatia Express (☎ 49 22 237; www.zug.hr; Trg Kralja Tomislava 17; 9.30am-7pm Mon-Fri, 9am-3pm Sat) At this office opposite the train station you can change money, make train reservations, rent cars, buy air tickets and ferry tickets, plus book hotels around the country.

KBC Rebro (☎ 23 88 888; Kišpatićeva 12; 24hr) Provides emergency aid.

Main post office (Branimirova 4; 24hr Mon-Sat, 1pm-midnight Sun)

Main tourist office (☎ 48 14 051; www.zagreb-touristinfo.hr; Trg Josipa Jelačića 11; 8.30am-8pm Mon-Fri, 9am-5pm Sat, 10am-2pm Sun) Distributes city maps and free leaflets. It also sells the Zagreb Card.

Plitvice National Park Office (☎ 46 13 586; Trg Kralja Tomislava 19; 9am-5pm Mon-Fri) Has details on Croatia's national parks.

Zagreb Card (www.zagrebcard.fivestars.hr/page_hr_onlinecatalogue.htm; 24/72hr 60/90KN) Provides free travel on all public transport, and a 50% discount on museum and gallery entries.

SIGHTS

KAPTOL

Zagreb's colourful **Dolac** (Market; 6am-3pm) is just north of Trg Josipa Jelačića. It's the buzzing centre of Zagreb's daily activity, with traders coming from all over Croatia to sell their products. The main part of the market is on an elevated square; the street level has indoor stalls selling meat and dairy products and, a little further towards the square, flowers. The stalls at the northern end of the market are packed with local honey and handmade ornaments.

The twin neo-Gothic spires of the 1899 **Cathedral of the Assumption of the Blessed Virgin Mary** (Katedrala Marijina Uznešenja; formerly known as St Stephen's Cathedral) are nearby. Elements of the medieval cathedral on this site, destroyed by an earthquake in 1880, can be seen inside, including 13th-century frescos, Renaissance pews, marble

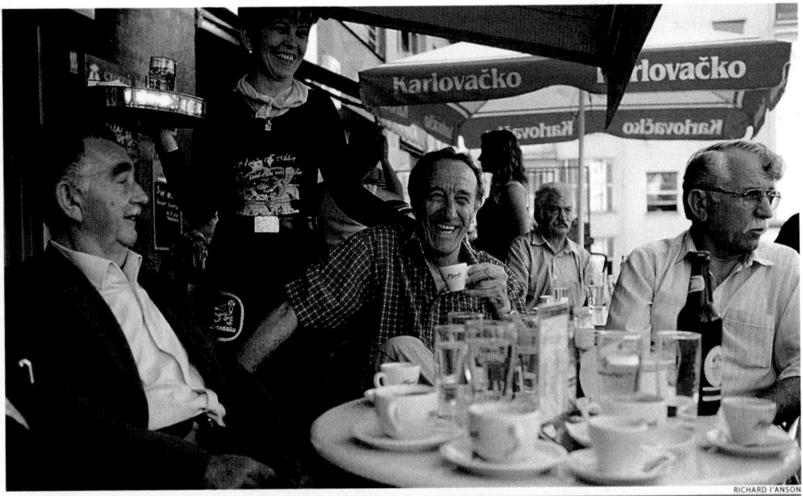

RICHARD I'ANSON

Outdoor cafe, Zagreb

CROATIA
ZAGREB

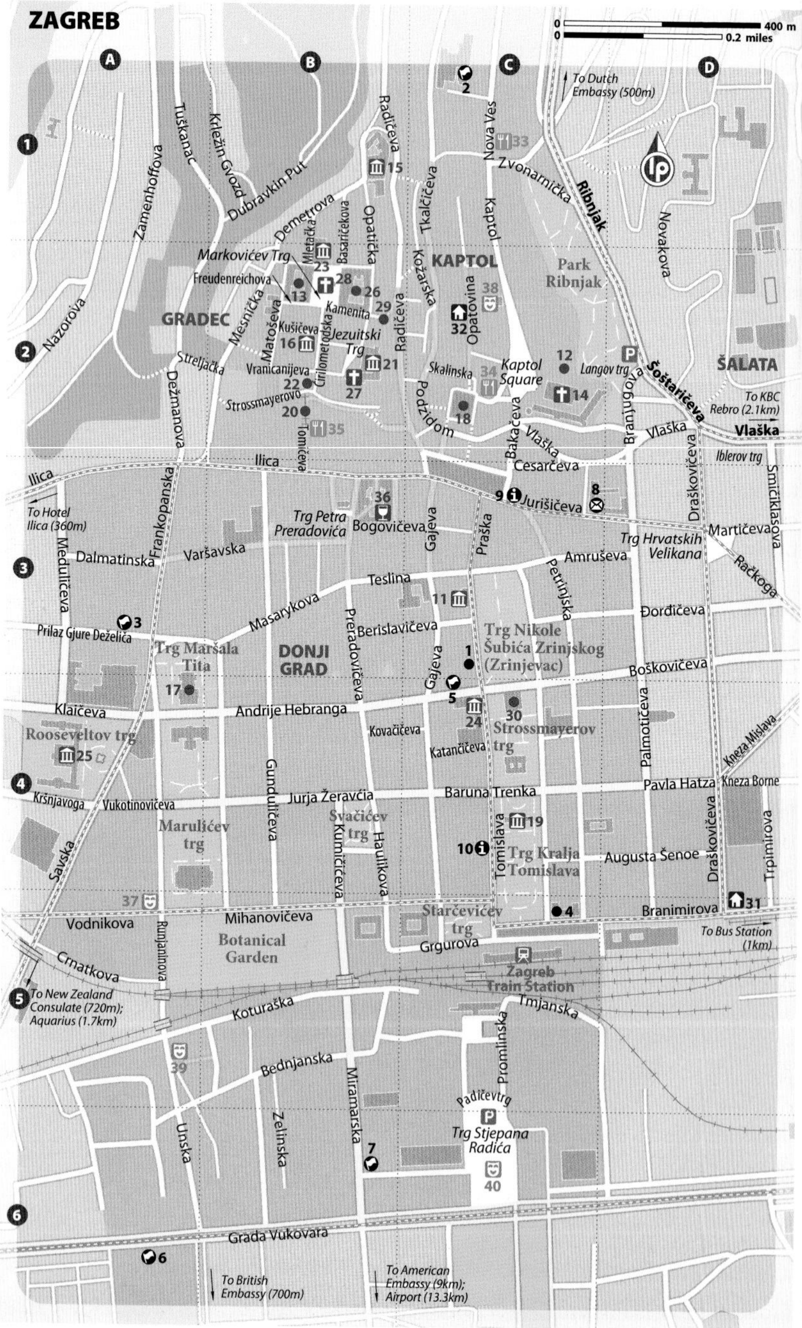
ZAGREB
0 400 m
0 0.2 miles
A
B
C
D
1
2
3
4
5
6
To Dutch Embassy (500m)
Tuškanac
Krležin Gvozd
Dubravkin Put
Zamenhoffova
Nazorova
Radićeva
Nova Ves
Zvonarnička
Ribnjak
Novakova
Demetrova
Mletačka
Basaričekova
Opatička
Tkalčićeva
Kaptol
Markovićev Trg
Freudenreichova
Kožarska
KAPTOL
Park Ribnjak
GRADEC
Mesnička
Matoševa
Kamenita
Kušićeva
Jezuitski Trg
Ćirilometodska
Opatovina
Vranicanijeva
Strossmayerovo
Streljačka
Dežmanova
Tomićeva
Skalinska
Kaptol Square
Podzidom
Langov trg
Šoštarićeva
ŠALATA
To KBC Rebro (2.1km)
Vlaška
Bakačeva
Branjugova
Cesarčeva
Ilica
To Hotel Ilica (360m)
Frankopanska
Iblerov trg
Jurišičeva
Trg Petra Preradovića
Bogovićeva
Gajeva
Praška
Draškovićeva
Smičiklasova
Martićeva
Trg Hrvatskih Velikana
Račkoga
Medulićeva
Dalmatinska
Varšavska
Amruševa
Teslina
Petrinjska
Masarykova
Preradovićeva
Berislavićeva
Đorđićeva
Prilaz Gjure Deželića
Trg Maršala Tita
DONJI GRAD
Trg Nikole Šubića Zrinjskog (Zrinjevac)
Boškovićeva
Klaićeva
Andrije Hebranga
Kovačićeva
Katančićeva
Strossmayerov trg
Palmotićeva
Rooseveltov trg
Kneza Mislava
Kršnjavoga
Vukotinovićeva
Jurja Žeravćia
Baruna Trenka
Pavla Hatza
Kneza Borne
Gundulićeva
Marulićev trg
Svačićev trg
Kumičićeva
Hauliková
Tomislava
Trg Kralja Tomislava
Augusta Šenoe
Trpimirova
Savska
Vodnikova
Mihanovićeva
Starčevićev trg
Branimirova
To Bus Station (1km)
Runjaninova
Botanical Garden
Grgurova
Crnatkova
Zagreb Train Station
To New Zealand Consulate (720m); Aquarius (1.7km)
Koturaška
Tmjanska
Promlinska
Bednjanska
Miramarska
Zelinska
Unska
Padićevtrg
Trg Stjepana Radića
Grada Vukovara
To British Embassy (700m)
To American Embassy (9km); Airport (13.3km)
1
2
3
4
5
6
7
8
9
10
11
12
13
14
15
16
17
18
19
20
21
22
23
24
25
26
27
28
29
30
31
32
33
34
35
36
37
38
39
40

INFORMATION
Atlas Travel Agency........ 1 C3
Australian Embassy........ 2 C1
Canadian Embassy........ 3 A3
Croatia Express........ 4 C5
French Embassy........ 5 C4
German Embassy........ 6 A6
Irish Consulate........ 7 B6
Main Post Office........ 8 C3
Main Tourist Office........ 9 C3
Plitvice National Park Office........ 10 C4

SIGHTS & ACTIVITIES
Archaeological Museum........ 11 C3
Archbishop's Palace........ 12 C2
Banski Dvori........ 13 B2
Cathedral of the Assumption of the Blessed Virgin Mary........ 14 C2
City Museum........ 15 B1
Croatian Museum of Naive Art........ 16 B2
Croatian National Theatre........ 17 A4
Dolac Fruit & Vegetable Market........ 18 C2
Exhibition Pavilion........ 19 C4
Funicular Railway........ 20 B2
Galerija Klovićevi Dvori........ 21 B2
Lotrščak Tower........ 22 B2
Meštrović Atelier........ 23 B2
Modern Gallery........ 24 C4
Museum Mimara........ 25 A4
National Assembly........ 26 B2
St Catherine's Church........ 27 B2
St Mark's Church........ 28 B2
Stone Gate........ 29 B2
Strossmayer Gallery of Old Masters........ 30 C4

SLEEPING
Arcotel Allegra........ 31 D5
Krovovi Grada........ 32 C2

EATING
Baltazar........ 33 C1
Kerempuh........ 34 C2
Vallis Aurea........ 35 B2

DRINKING
Škola........ 36 B3

ENTERTAINMENT
David........ 37 A5
Komedija Theatre........ 38 C2
KSET........ 39 A5
Vatroslav Lisinski Concert Hall........ 40 C6

altars and a baroque pulpit. The baroque **Archbishop's Palace** surrounds the cathedral, as do 16th-century fortifications constructed when Zagreb was threatened by the Turks.

GRADEC

From Radićeva 5, off Trg Jelačića, a pedestrian walkway called stube Ivana Zakmardija leads to the **Lotrščak Tower** (**Kula Lotrščak; ☎ 48 51 768; admission 10KN; 🕑 11am-7pm Tue-Sun**) and a **funicular railway** (**one way 3KN; 🕑 6.30am-9pm**) built in 1888, which connects the Lower and Upper Towns. The tower has a sweeping 360-degree view of the city. To the east is the baroque **St Catherine's Church** (Crkva Svete Katarine), with Jezuitski trg beyond. The **Galerija Klovićevi Dvori** (**☎ 48 51 926; Jezuitski trg 4; adult/student 40/20KN; 🕑 11am-7pm Tue-Sun**) is Zagreb's premier exhibition hall, where superb art shows are staged. Further north and to the east is the 13th-century **Stone Gate**, with a painting of the Virgin, which escaped the devastating fire of 1731.

Gothic **St Mark's Church** (**Crkva Svetog Marka; ☎ 48 51 611; Markovićev trg; 🕑 11am-4pm & 5.30-7pm**) marks the centre of Gradec. Inside are works by Ivan Meštrović, Croatia's most famous modern sculptor. On the eastern side of St Mark's is the Croatia's 1908 **National Assembly** (Sabor).

West of the church is the 18th-century **Banski Dvori**, the presidential palace, with guards at the door in red ceremonial uniform. Between April and September there is a changing of the guard ceremony at noon at the weekend.

Not far from the palace is the former **Meštrović Atelier** (**☎ 48 51 123; Mletačka 8; adult/concession 30/15KN; 🕑 10am-6pm Tue-Fri, to 2pm Sat**), now housing an excellent collection of some 100 sculptures, drawings, lithographs and furniture created by the artist. There are several other museums nearby. The best is the **City Museum** (**Muzej Grada Zagreba; ☎ 48 51 364; Opatička 20; adult/concession 20/10KN; 🕑 10am-6pm Tue-Fri, to 1pm Sat & Sun**), with a scale model of old Gradec, atmospheric background music and interactive exhibits that fascinate kids. There's also the lively and colourful **Croatian Museum of Naive Art** (**Hrvatski Muzej Naivne Umjetnosti; ☎ 48 51 911; Ćirilometodska 3; adult/concession 10/5KN; 🕑 10am-6pm Tue-Fri, to 1pm Sat & Sun**).

LOWER TOWN

Zagreb really is a city of museums. There are four in the parks between the train

PLITVICE LAKES NATIONAL PARK

Midway between Zagreb and Zadar, **Plitvice Lakes National Park** (☎ 053 751 015; www.np-plitvicka-jezera.hr; adult/student Apr-Oct 110/50KN, Nov-Mar 70/35KN; 🕑 7am-8pm) is 19.5 hectares of wooded hills and 16 turquoise lakes, all connected by a series of waterfalls and cascades. The mineral-rich waters carve new paths through the rock, depositing tufa (new porous rock) in continually changing formations. Wooden footbridges follow the lakes and streams over, under and across the rumbling water for an exhilaratingly damp 18km. Swimming is not allowed. Your park admission (prices vary by season) is valid for the entire stay and also includes the boats and buses you need to use to see the lakes. There is hotel accommodation only on-site, and private accommodation just outside the park. Check the options with the National Parks information office in Zagreb (see p621).

station and Trg Jelačića. The yellow **exhibition pavilion** (1897) across the park from the station presents changing contemporary art exhibitions. The second building north, also in the park, houses the **Strossmayer Gallery of Old Masters** (Strossmayerova Galerija Starih Majstora; ☎ 48 95 115; www.mdc.hr/strossmayer; Zrinjevac 11; adult/concession 10/5KN; 🕑 10am-1pm & 5-7pm Tue, 10am-1pm Wed-Sun). When it's closed you can still enter the interior courtyard to see the Baška Slab (1102) from the island of Krk, one of the oldest inscriptions in the Croatian language.

The fascinating **Archaeological Museum** (Arheološki Muzej; ☎ 48 73 101; www.amz.hr; Trg Nikole Šubića Zrinjskog 19; adult/concession 20/10KN; 🕑 10am-5pm Tue-Fri, to 1pm Sat & Sun) has a wide-ranging display of artefacts from prehistoric times through to the medieval period. Behind the museum is a garden of Roman sculpture that is turned into a pleasant open-air cafe in the summer.

The **Museum Mimara** (Muzej Mimara; ☎ 48 28 100; Rooseveltov trg 5; adult/concession 20/15KN; 🕑 10am-5pm Tue, Wed, Fri & Sat, to 7pm Thu, to 2pm Sun) has a diverse collection amassed by Ante Topić Mimara and donated to Croatia. Housed in a neo-Renaissance palace, the collection includes icons, glassware, sculpture, Oriental art and works by renowned painters such as Rembrandt, Velázquez, Raphael and Degas.

The neobaroque **Croatian National Theatre** (☎ 48 28 532; Trg Maršala Tita 15; 🕑 box office 10am-1pm & 5-7.30pm Mon-Fri, to 1pm Sat, 30min before performances Sun) dates from 1895 and has Ivan Meštrović's sculpture *Fountain of Life* (1905) in front.

FESTIVALS & EVENTS

Zagreb's highest profile music event is **INmusic Festival** (www.inmusicfestival.com), a two-day extravaganza on 3 and 4 June, taking place on Jarun Lake's island. In July and August the **Zagreb Summer Festival** presents a cycle of concerts and theatre performances on open stages in the upper town. For a complete listing of Zagreb events, see www.zagreb-convention.hr.

SLEEPING & EATING

Krovovi Grada (☎ 48 14 189; Opatovina 33; s/d/tr 200/300/400KN) Possibly the most charming of Zagreb's central options, this place is right in the Upper Town. The restored old house is set back from the street and has creaky-floor rooms with pieces of vintage furniture and grandma blankets.

Hotel Ilica (☎ 37 77 522; www.hotel-ilica.hr; Ilica 102; s/d/tr/apt 399/499/599/849KN;) A great option, with rooms ranging from super kitsch to lushly decorous – there are gilded motifs, plush beds, wall-long paintings and lots of reds.

our pick **Arcotel Allegra** (☎ 46 96 000; www.arcotel.at/allegra; Branimirova 29; d €152-162;) The Arcotel Allegra is Zagreb's first designer hotel, with airy, elegant rooms and a plush, marble-and-exotic-fish reception.

Vallis Aurea (☎ 48 31 305; Tomićeva 4; mains from 30KN) This is a true local eatery that has some of the best home cooking you'll find in town, so it's no wonder that it's chock-a-block at lunchtimes.

our pick **Kerempuh** (☎ 48 19 000; Kaptol 3; mains 50-70KN) Overlooking Dolac market, this is a fabulous place to taste a) Croatian cuisine cooked well and simply, and b) the market's ingredients on your plate.

Baltazar (☎ 46 66 999; www.restoran-baltazar.hr; Nova Ves 4; mains from 120KN; Mon-Sat) Meat – duck, lamb, pork, beef and turkey – is grilled and prepared the Zagorje and Slavonia way in this upmarket old-timer with a good choice of local wines.

DRINKING

In the Upper Town, the chic Tkalčićeva is throbbing with bars. In the Lower Town, Trg Petra Preradovića is the most popular spot for street performers and occasional bands in mild weather. One of the nicest ways to see Zagreb is to join in on the *špica* – the Saturday morning and prelunch coffee drinking on the many terraces along Preradovićeva and Tkalčićeva.

our pick **Škola** (☎ 48 28 197; www.skolaloungebar.com; Bogovićeva 7) This has to be the best-designed bar in the whole of Zagreb, with its huge, differently themed rooms, lounge sofas, an olive tree in the middle of the main room, and notebook-style menus (it's called School, you see?). There are DJ nights, various 'after-school' parties and it's packed with the trendiest of people (and, of course, students).

ENTERTAINMENT

Zagreb is definitely a happening city. Its theatres and concert halls present a great variety of programs throughout the year. Many (but not all) are listed in the monthly brochure *Zagreb Events & Performances,* which is available from the main tourist office.

NIGHTCLUBS

The dress code is relaxed in most Zagreb clubs. It doesn't get lively until near midnight.

KSET (☎ 61 29 999; www.kset.org; Unska 3; 8pm-midnight Mon-Fri, to 3am Sat) Zagreb's best music venue, with everyone who's anyone performing here.

Aquarius (☎ 36 40 231; Jarun Lake) A truly fab place to party, this enormously popular spot has a series of rooms that open onto a huge terrace on the lake.

The gay and lesbian scene in Zagreb is finally becoming more open than it had previously been, although 'free-wheeling' it isn't. Many gays discreetly cruise the south beach around Jarun Lake and are welcome in most discos. **David** (☎ 091 533 7757; Marulićev Trg 3) is a sauna, bar and video room, popular on Zagreb's gay scene.

PERFORMING ARTS

A small office marked 'Kazalište Komedija' (look out for the posters) sells theatre tickets; it's in the Oktogon, a passage connecting Trg Petra Preradovića to Ilica 3.

The neobaroque Croatian National Theatre (p624) was established in 1895. It stages opera and ballet performances.

Komedija Theatre (☎ 48 14 566; Kaptol 9) Near the cathedral, the Komedija Theatre stages operettas and musicals.

Vatroslav Lisinski Concert Hall (☎ ticket office 61 21 166; Trg Stjepana Radića 4; 9am-8pm Mon-Fri, to 2pm Sat) Just south of the train station, this concert hall is a prestigious venue where symphony concerts are held regularly.

GETTING THERE & AWAY

For information about international flights to and from Croatia, see p647.

Zagreb's big, modern **bus station** (☎ 61 57 983; www.akz.hr, in Croatian) has a large waiting room and a number of shops. You can buy most international tickets at windows 17 to 20.

Domestic trains depart from **Zagreb train station** (☎ 060 33 34 44; www.hznet.hr); see p648 for more information.

There are also four daily trains from Zagreb to Budapest (€60, 5½ to 7½ hours). Between Venice and Zagreb (€60, 6½ to 7½ hours) there are two daily direct connections and several more that run through Ljubljana.

GETTING AROUND

Zagreb is a fairly easy city to navigate, whether by car or public transport. Traffic isn't bad, there's sufficient parking and the efficient tram system should be a model for other polluted, traffic-clogged European capitals.

The Croatia Airlines bus to Pleso airport leaves from the bus station every half-hour or hour from about 4am to 8.30pm, depending on flights, and returns from the airport on about the same schedule (50KN one way). A taxi would cost about 300KN.

Public transport is based on an efficien network of trams, though the city centr is compact enough to make them un necessary. Controls are frequent on th tram system, with substantial fines for no having the proper ticket.

ISTRIA

☎ 052

Continental Croatia meets the Adriatic i Istria (Istra to Croatians), the heart-shape 3600-sq-km peninsula just south of Triest in Italy. Vast hotel complexes line much o the coast and its rocky beaches are no Croatia's best, but the facilities are wide ranging, the sea is clean and seclude spots still aplenty.

ROVINJ

pop 14,200

Rovinj (Rovigno in Italian) is coastal Istria' star attraction. While it can get overru with tourists in the summer months an residents are developing a sharp eye fo maximising their profits (by upgradin the hotels and restaurants to four-sta status), it remains one of the last true Mediterranean fishing ports. Woode hills and low-rise hotels surround the Ol Town, webbed by steep, cobbled street and piazzas.

Private accommodation, excursions an transfers can be booked through **Futura Travel** (☎ 817 281; www.futura-travel.hr; Matte Benussi 2; 8.30am-9pm Mon-Sat, 8.30am-1pm & 5-9pm Sun May-Sep).

Globtour (☎ 814 130; www.globtour-turiz am.hr; Alda Rismonda 2; 9am-10pm Jul & Aug, reduced hr rest of year) offers excursions, private accommodation and bike renta (60KN per day).

Just off Trg Maršala Tita, the **tourist office** (☎ 811 566; www.tzgrovinj.hr; Pina Budicina 12; 8am-10pm Jul & Aug, to 9pm Sep

DIANA MAYFIELD

Hilltop town in Istria

& Jun) has plenty of brochures, maps and materials.

The town's showcase is the imposing **Church of St Euphemia** (Sveta Eufemija; ☎ 815 615; Petra Stankovića; 10am-6m Jul & Aug, 11am-3pm Sep-Jun), which dominates the Old Town from its hilltop location. On the harbour, **Batana House** (☎ 812 593; www.batana.org; Pina Budicina 2; admission free, with guide 15KN; 10am-1pm & 7-10pm Tue-Sun May-Sep, 10am-1pm Tue-Sun Oct-Apr) is a multimedia museum dedicated to the *batana,* a flat-bottomed fishing boat that stands as a symbol of Rovinj's seafaring and fishing tradition.

When you've seen enough of the town, follow the waterfront on foot or by bike past Hotel Park to the verdant **Golden Cape Forest Park** (Zlatni Rt, or Punta Corrente) about 1.5km south. Here you can swim off the rocks or just sit and admire the offshore islands.

Diver Sport Center (☎ 816 648; www.diver.hr; Villas Rubin) is the largest operation in Rovinj, offering boat dives from 210KN, with equipment rental. The main dive attraction is the wreck of the *Baron Gautsch,* an Austrian passenger-steamer sunk in 1914 by a mine.

Most travel agencies (see opposite) sell day trips to Venice (450KN to 520KN) and Plitvice (580KN). There are also fish picnics (250KN), panoramic cruises (100KN) and trips to Limska Draga Fjord (150KN).

Rovinj has become Istria's destination of choice for hordes of summertime tourists, so reserving accommodation in advance is strongly recommended.

our pick **Casa Garzotto** (☎ 811 884; www.casa-garzotto.com; Via Garzotto 8; s 510-760KN, d 650-1015KN;) has four nicely outfitted studio apartments with original detail, stylish touches and up-to-the-minute amenities. Bikes are complimentary.

Hotel Villa Angelo D'Oro (☎ 840 502; www.angelodoro.hr; Vladimira Švalbe 38-42; s 619-990KN, d 1005-1762KN;), in a renovated Venetian townhouse, has 24 plush rooms and (pricier) suites. This boutique hotel has lots of antiques plus mod perks aplenty.

Most of the restaurants that line the harbour offer the standard fish and meat mainstays at similar prices. For a more gourmet experience you'll need to bypass the water vistas. Note that many restaurants shut their doors between lunch and dinner. For an evening snack of local cheese, cured meats and tasty small bites, head to **Ulika** (**Vladimira Švalbe 34; dinner only**), a tiny tavern a few doors down from Angelo d'Oro.

Eurostar Travel (**813 144; Pina Budicina 1; 9am-9pm Mon-Sat, 9am-1pm & 5-8pm Sun**) has schedules and tickets for boats to Venice and Trieste.

There are buses from Rovinj to Dubrovnik (593KN, 16 hours, one daily), Zagreb (173KN to 255KN, five hours, four daily) and Split (417KN, 11 hours, one daily).

The closest train station is at Kanfanar, 20km away on the Pula–Divača line.

DALMATIA

Roman ruins, spectacular beaches, old fishing ports, medieval architecture and unspoilt offshore islands make a trip to Dalmatia (Dalmacija) unforgettable. Split is the largest city in the region and a hub for bus and boat connections along the Adriatic, as well as home to the late-Roman Diocletian's Palace. Nearby are the early Roman ruins in Solin (Salona). Zadar has yet more Roman ruins and a wealth of churches. The architecture of Hvar and Korčula recalls the days when these places were outposts of the Venetian empire. None can rival majestic Dubrovnik, a cultural and aesthetic jewel.

ZADAR

023 / pop 72,700

It's hard to decipher the mystery of why Zadar (ancient Zara), the main city of northern Dalmatia, is an underrated tourist destination. It wouldn't be because of its compact, marble, traffic-free Old Town that follows the old Roman street plan and contains Roman ruins and medieval churches. Or because it's recently been dubbed as Croatia's 'city of cool' for its clubs, bars and festivals run by international music stars.

In the past 2000 years Zadar has escaped few wars. Its strategic position on the Adriatic coast made it a target for the Romans, the Byzantine, Venetian and Austro-Hungarian empires and Italy. Although it was damaged by Allied bombing raids in 1943–44 and Yugoslav rockets in 1991, this resilient city has been rebuilt and restored, retaining much of its old flavour. Don't forget to sample Zadar's famous maraschino-cherry liqueur.

INFORMATION

Aquarius Travel Agency (**/fax 212 919; www.jureskoaquarius.hr; Nova Vrata bb**) Books accommodation and excursions.

Main post office (**Poljana Pape Aleksandra III**) You can make phone calls here.

Miatours (**/fax 212 788; www.miatours.hr; Vrata Sveti Krševana**) Books accommodation and excursions.

Tourist office (**316 166; www.tzzadar.hr; Mihe Klaića 5; 8am-8pm Mon-Sat, to 1pm Sun Jun-Sep, to 6pm Mon-Sat Oct-May**)

SIGHTS & ACTIVITIES

Most attractions are near **St Donatus Church** (**Sveti Donat; 250 516; Šimuna Kožičića Benje; admission 10KN; 9.30am-1pm & 4-6pm Mar-Oct**), a circular 9th-century Byzantine structure built over the Roman forum. The outstanding **Museum of Church Art** (**Trg Opatice Čike bb; adult/student 20/10KN; 10am-12.30pm daily, 6-8pm Mon-Sat**), in the Benedictine monastery opposite St Donatus, offers three floors of elaborate old and silver reliquaries, religious paint-ıgs, icons and local lacework.

The 13th-century Romanesque **:athedral of St Anastasia** (Katedrala Svete tošije; Trg Svete Stošije; Mass only) has some ne Venetian carvings in the 15th-century hoir stalls. The **Franciscan Monastery** ranjevački Samostan; Zadarskog Mira 1358; admis-on free; 7.30am-noon & 4.30-6pm) is the old-st Gothic church in Dalmatia (consecrated 1 1280), with lovely interior Renaissance eatures and a large Romanesque cross in he treasury, behind the sacristy.

The most interesting museum is the **rchaeological Museum** (Arheološki Muzej; rg Opatice Čike 1; adult/student 10/5KN; 9am-pm & 6-9pm Mon-Fri, 9am-1pm Sat), across from t Donatus, with an extensive collection of artefacts, from the Neolithic period hrough the Roman occupation to the levelopment of Croatian culture under he Byzantines.

Any of the many travel agencies around own can supply information on tourist ruises to the beautiful **Kornati Islands** Kornati Islands National Park is an archi-pelago of 147 mostly uninhabited islands), nd river-rafting and half-day excursions o the Krka waterfalls.

LEEPING & EATING

Most visitors head out to the 'tourist set-lement' at Borik, 3km northwest of Zadar, n the Puntamika bus (6KN, every 20 min-ıtes from the bus station).

Venera Guest House (☎ 214 098; www.hotel-venera-zd.hr; Šime Ljubića 4a; d 300-50KN) Venera – also known as the Jović Guesthouse – is the centre's only option. Although the rooms are miniscule, have oversized wardrobes and no numbers on he doors, all have private bathrooms, he beds are good and the atmosphere is retty relaxed.

JOHN ELK III

Children before St Donatus Church

our pick **Villa Hrešć** (☎ 337 570; www.villa-hresc.hr; Obala Kneza Trpimira 28; s 550-650KN, d 750-850KN;) Zadar's plushest choice is in a cheery pink building on a bay. The stylish rooms are in pastel colours, the beds are luxurious dreaming spots, and as you lounge by the swimming pool you can admire views of the Old Town.

Zalogajnica Ljepotica (☎ 311 288; Obala Kneza Branimira 4b; mains from 35KN) The food is great and home cooked, and the dishes are usually squid-ink risotto, tomato and seafood pasta, plus something meaty.

Trattoria Canzona (☎ 212 081; Stomorića 8; mains 40KN) A great little trattoria in the Old Town, with red-and-white chequered tablecloths, friendly waiters and tons of locals who love the menu of daily specials.

SEA SONGS

Zadar's incredible (and world's only) **Sea Organ** (Morske Orgulje), designed by local architect Nikola Bašić, is bound to be one of the more memorable sights you'll see in Croatia. Set within the perforated stone stairs that descend into the sea is a system of pipes and whistles that exudes wistful sighs when the movement of the sea pushes air through the pipes. Right next to it is the newly built **Sun Salutation** (Pozdrav Suncu), another wacky and wonderful Bašić creation.

You can swim from the steps off the promenade and listen to the sound of the Sea Organ. There's a swimming area with diving boards, a small park and a cafe on the coastal promenade off Zvonimira.

our pick **Kornat** (☎ 254 501; Liburnska Obala 6; mains from 80KN) This is without a doubt Zadar's best restaurant. There's the smooth Istrian truffle monkfish, a creamy squid and salmon risotto (70KN), and the fresh fish (around 350KN per kilogram) is prepared with simple ingredients to maximum deliciousness.

our pick **Garden** (☎ 450 907; www.thegardenzadar.com; Bedemi Zadarskih Pobuna; late May-Oct) One of the reasons many of Croatia's youngsters rate Zadar as 'a really cool place' is basically because it has the Garden. It's owned and run by UB40's producer Nick Colgan and drummer James Brown. Daytime here is relaxed, while night-time is when the fun really begins. Don't miss it if you're in town.

Zadar's morning **market** (6am-3pm) is one of Croatia's best. In summer the many cafes along Varoška and Klaića place their tables on the street; it's great for people watching.

GETTING THERE & AWAY

Zadar's airport, 12km east of the city, served by **Croatia Airlines** (☎ 250 10 Poljana Natka Nodila 7) and **Ryanair** (ww ryanair.com). A Croatia Airlines bus mee all flights and costs 15KN; a taxi into tow costs around 175KN.

The office of **Jadrolinija** (☎ 254 80 www.jadrolinija.hr) is on the harbour an has tickets for all local ferries, or you ca buy ferry tickets from the Jadrolinija sta on Liburnska Obala. The company rur car ferries from Ancona, Italy (€49.50, s to eight hours, daily). Ferries are less fre quent during winter months.

The **bus station** (☎ 211 035; www.liburni -zadar.hr, in Croatian) is a 10-minute walk fro the centre and has daily buses to Zagre (100KN to 140KN, 3½ to seven hours, 2 daily).

The **train station** (☎ 212 555; www.hzne hr; Ante Starčevića 3) is adjacent to the bus sta tion. There are five daily trains to Zagre two fast trains (150KN, seven hours) an three slower ones (134KN, 9¾ hours).

SPLIT

☎ 021 / pop 188,700

The second-largest city in Croatia, Spl (Spalato in Italian), is a great place to se Dalmatian life as it's really lived. Free c mass tourism and always buzzing, this i a city with just the right balance of tra dition and modernity. Just step insid Diocletian's Palace – a Unesco Worl Heritage site and one of the world's mos impressive Roman monuments – an you'll see dozens of bars, restaurants an shops thriving amid the atmospheric ol walls where Split life has been going o for thousands of years. Split's unique se ng and exuberant nature make it one of he most delectable cities in Europe.

Split achieved fame when Roman emperor Diocletian (AD 245–313) had his etirement palace built here from 295 to 05. After his death the great stone palace ontinued to be used as a retreat by Roman ulers. When the neighbouring colony of alona was abandoned in the 7th century, nany of the Romanised inhabitants fled to plit and barricaded themselves behind he high palace walls, where their descendnts continue to live to this day.

ORIENTATION & INFORMATION

he bus, train and ferry terminals are djacent on the eastern side of the harbour, a short walk from the Old Town. The eafront promenade, Obala Hrvatskog Narodnog Preporoda, better known as Riva, is the best central reference point.

Change money at travel agencies or the post office. You'll find ATMs around the bus and train stations.

Daluma Travel (☎/fax 338 484; www.daluma.hr; Obala Kneza Domagoja 1) Finds private accommodation and has information on boat schedules.

Turist Biro (☎/fax 342 142; turist-biro-split@st.t-com.hr; Obala Hrvatskog Narodnog Preporoda 12) This office arranges private accommodation and sells guidebooks and the Split Card (€5, offers free and discounted admission to Split attractions).

Turistička Zajednica (☎/fax 342 606; www.visitsplit.com; Peristile; 9am-8.30pm Mon-Sat, 8am-1pm Sun) Has information on Split; sells the Split Card.

SIGHTS

The Old Town is a vast open-air museum and the new information signs at the important sights explain a great deal of Split's history. **Diocletian's Palace** (entrance Obala Hrvatskog Narodnog Preporoda 22), facing the harbour, is one of the most imposing Roman ruins in existence. It was built as a strong rectangular fortress, with walls measuring 215m from east to west, 181m wide at the southernmost point and reinforced by square corner towers. The imperial residence, mausoleum and

WAYNE WALTON

Cathedral campanile, Diocletian's Palace

JOHN ELK III

Waterfront, Split

temples were south of the main street, now called Krešimirova, connecting the east and west palace gates.

Enter through the central ground floor of the palace. On the left are the excavated **Basement Halls** (⌚ 10am-6pm), which are empty but impressive. Go through the passage to the **Peristyle**, a picturesque colonnaded square, with a neo-Romanesque cathedral tower rising above. The **Vestibule**, an open dome above the ground-floor passageway at the southern end of the peristyle, is overpoweringly grand and cavernous. A lane off the peristyle opposite the cathedral leads to the **Temple of Jupiter**, which is now a baptistery.

On the eastern side of the peristyle is the **Cathedral**, originally Diocletian's mausoleum. The only reminder of Diocletian in the cathedral is a sculptu of his head in a circular stone wreat below the dome which is directly abo the baroque white-marble altar. For small fee you can climb the tower.

In the Middle Ages the nobility an rich merchants built their residenc within the old palace walls; the Papal Palace is now the **Town Museum** (**Grads Muzej; ☎ 341 240; Papalićeva ul 5; adul concession 10/5KN; ⌚ 9am-noon & 5-8pm Tue-F 10am-noon Sat & Sun Jun-Sep, 10am-5pm Tue-F 10am-noon Sat & Sun Oct-May**). It has a tic collection of artefacts, paintings, furni ture and clothes from Split. Captions a in Croatian.

The **East Palace Gate** leads to the ma ket area. The **West Palace Gate** oper onto medieval Narodni Trg, dominate by the 15th-century Venetian Gothic **Ol Town Hall**.

Go through the **North Palace Gate** t see Ivan Meštrović's powerful 1929 **statu of Gregorius of Nin**, a 10th-century Slav religious leader who fought for the righ to perform Mass in Croatian. Notice th his big toe has been polished to a shin it's said that touching it brings goo luck.

The **Archaeological Museum** (**Arheološ Muzej; ☎ 318 720; Zrinjsko-Frankopanska 2 adult/student 20/10KN; ⌚ 9am-2pm Tue-Fri, 1pm Sat & Sun**), north of town, is a fasc nating supplement to your walk aroun Diocletian's Palace, and to the site c ancient Salona.

The finest art museum in Split i **Meštrović Gallery** (**Galerija Meštrović; ☎ 35 450; Šetalište Ivana Meštrovića 46; adult/stude 30/15KN; ⌚ 9am-9pm Tue-Sun Jun-Sep, 9am-4p Tue-Sat, 10am-3pm Sun Oct-May**). You'll see comprehensive, well-arranged collec tion of works by Ivan Meštrović, Croatia' premier modern sculptor.

LEEPING & EATING

rivate accommodation is again the best ption and in the summer you may be eluged at the bus station by women ffering *sobe* (rooms available). The best hing to do is to book through the **Turist iro** (☎/fax 342 142; www.turistbiro-split.hr; bala Hrvatskog Narodnog Preporoda 12; 9am-pm Mon-Fri, to 4pm Sat).

our pick **B&B Kaštel 1700** (☎343 912; www.astelsplit.com; Mihovilova Širina 5; s 290-510KN, 400-660KN;) Among Split's best alue for money places, it's near the bars, verlooks Radićev Trg and has sweet and idy rooms and friendly, efficient service.

Hotel Adriana (☎340 000; www.hoteladriana.com; Obala Hrvatskog Narodnog Preporoda Riva) 9; s 550-650KN, d 750-900KN;) Good alue, excellent location. The rooms are ot massively exciting, with their navy urtains and beige furniture, but some ave sea views, which is a real bonus in plit's Old Town.

Buffet Fife (☎345 223; Trumbićeva Obala 11; nains around 40KN) Dragomir presides over motley crew of sailors and misfits who rop in for the simple home-cooking (esecially the *pašticada*) and his own brand f grumpy but loving hospitality.

our pick **Konoba Trattoria Bajamont** ☎091 253 7441; Bajamontijeva 3; mains from 0KN) The food is excellent and the menu sually features things such as small fried ish, squid-ink risotto, *brujet* (fish/seafood tew with wine, onions and herbs, served vith polenta) and octopus salad.

The **market** (6am-2pm), outside the ast palace gate, has a wide array of fresh ocal produce.

RINKING & ENTERTAINMENT

plit is great for nightlife, especially or more so) in the spring and summer nonths. The palace walls are generally throbbing with loud music on Friday and Saturday nights.

Le Porta (Majstora Jurja) Next door to Teak Caffe, Le Porta is renowned for its cocktails. On the same square – Majstora Jurja – are Kala, Dante, Whisky Bar and Na Kantunu, all of which end up merging into one when the night gets busy.

Café Puls (Mihovilova Širina) and **Café Shook** (Mihovilova Širina) are pretty much indistinguishable late on Friday or Saturday night, when the dozen steps that link these two bars are chock-a-block with youngsters.

Croatian National Theatre (Trg Gaje Bulata; best seats about 60KN) During winter, opera and ballet are presented here. Erected in 1891, the theatre was fully restored in 1979 in its original style; it's worth attending a performance for the architecture alone.

GETTING THERE & AWAY

The country's national air carrier, **Croatia Airlines** (☎062-777 777; Obala Hrvatskog Narodnog Preporoda 8), operates flights between Zagreb and Split (170KN to 350KN, 45 minutes) up to four times every day. Rates are lower if you book in advance. There's also **easyJet** (www.easyjet.com).

The following companies have ferries to/from Italy:

Jadrolinija (www.jadrolinija.hr) Croatia's national boat line runs car ferries from Ancona to Split (€51, nine or 10 hours, six weekly), as well as a route from Bari to Dubrovnik (€51, eight hours, six weekly), which continues on to Split. Ferries are less frequent during winter months.

SNAV (☎322 252; www.snav.com) Has a fast car ferry that travels from Ancona to Split (4½ hours, daily).

Split Tours (www.splittours.hr) Connects Ancona and Split (nine hours), continuing on to Stari Grad (Hvar, 12 hours).

There are also several agents in the large ferry terminal opposite the bus station that can assist with boat trips from Split, including **Jadrolinija** (☎ 338 333), which handles all car-ferry services that depart from the docks around the ferry terminal; and **SEM agency** (☎ 060 325 523), which handles tickets between Ancona, Split and Hvar.

Advance bus tickets with seat reservations are recommended. There are buses from the main **bus station** (☎ 060 327 327; www.ak-split.hr, in Croatian) beside the harbour to a variety of destinations.

From the train station there are three fast trains (138KN, six hours) and three overnight trains (138KN, 8½ hours) between Split and Zagreb.

GETTING AROUND

There's an airport bus stop at Obala Lazareta 3. The bus (30KN, 30 minutes) leaves about 90 minutes before flight times, or you can take bus 37 from the bus station on Domovinskog (11KN for a two-zone ticket).

Buses run about every 15 minutes from 5.30am to 11.30pm. A one-zone ticket costs 9KN for one trip in central Split. You can buy tickets on the bus and the driver can make change.

SOLIN

The ruins of the ancient city of Solin (known as Salona by the Romans), among the vineyards at the foot of mountains 5km northeast of Split, is the most interesting archaeological site in Croatia. Salona was the capital of the Roman province of Dalmatia from the time Julius Caesar elevated it to the status of colony. It held out against the barbarians and was only evacuated in AD 614 when the inhabitants fled to Split and neighbouring islands in the face of Avar and Slav attacks. Solin is the site of a summer **Ethnoambien** (www.ethnoambient.net) music festival eac August.

A good place to begin your visit is a the main entrance, near Caffe Bar Salon. There's a small **museum and informatio centre** (admission 10KN; 9am-6pm Mon-Sa Jun-Sep, to 1pm Mon-Sat Oct-May) at the en trance, which also provides a helpful ma and some literature about the complex

The ruins are easily accessible on Spl city bus 1, which runs direct to Soli every half-hour from the city bus sto at Trg Gaje Bulata. Alternatively, you ca catch most Sinj-bound buses (15KN, 1 daily) from Split's main bus station t take you to Solin.

HVAR ISLAND

☎ 021 / pop 12,600

Hvar is the number-one carrier of Croatia' superlatives: it's the most luxurious islanc the sunniest place in the country (272 sunny hours each year) and, along wit Dubrovnik, the most popular tourist des tination. Hvar is also famed for its ver dancy and its lavender fields, as well a other aromatic herbs such as rosemar and heather.

The island's hub and busiest destina tion is Hvar Town, estimated to drav around 30,000 people a day in the hig season. It's odd that they can all fit in th small bay town, but fit they do. Visitor wander along the main square, explor the sights on the winding stone streets swim on the numerous beaches or pop of to nudist Pakleni Islands. There are severa good restaurants and a number of grea hotels, as well as a couple of hostels.

Car ferries from Split deposit you i Stari Grad but local buses meet most fer ries in summer for the trip to Hvar Town The town centre is Trg Sv Stjepana, 100n west of the bus station. Passenger ferrie e up on Riva, the eastern quay, across om Hotel Slavija.

IFORMATION

tlas travel agency (☎ 741 670) On the estern side of the harbour.

elegrini Travel (☎/fax 742 250; pelegrini@et.hr) Also finds accommodation.

ost office (Riva) You can make phone alls here.

ourist office (☎/fax 742 977; www.tzhvar.; 8am-1pm & 5-9pm Mon-Sat, 9am-noon Sun n-Sep, 8am-2pm Mon-Sat Oct-May) In the arenal building on the corner of Trg Sv tjepana.

IGHTS & ACTIVITIES

he full flavour of medieval Hvar is best avoured on the backstreets of the Old own. At each end of Hvar Town is a ionastery with a prominent tower. The ominican **Church of St Marko** at the ead of the bay was largely destroyed by urks in the 16th century but you can visit ne local **Archaeological Museum** (admison 10KN; 10am-noon Jun-Sep) in the ruins. it's closed you'll still get a good view of ne ruins from the road just above, which eads up to a stone cross on a hilltop offerng a picture-postcard view of Hvar.

At the southeastern end of Hvar ou'll find the 15th-century Renaissance **ranciscan Monastery** (10am-noon & -7pm Jun-Sep, Christmas week & Holy Week), vith a wonderful collection of Venetian aintings in the church and adjacent **mueum** (admission 15KN; 10am-noon & 5-7pm Ion-Sat Jun-Sep), including *The Last Supper* y Matteo Ingoli.

Smack in the middle of Hvar Town is the mposing Gothic **arsenal**, and upstairs is Ivar's prize, the first **municipal theatre** n Europe (1612) – both under extensive enovations at the time of research. On the ill high above Hvar Town is a **Venetian fortress** (1551), and it's worth the climb up to appreciate the lovely, sweeping panoramic views. The fort was built to defend Hvar from the Turks, who sacked the town in 1539 and 1571.

HOLGER LEUE

Views from the Venetian fortress, Hvar Island

SLEEPING & EATING

Accommodation in Hvar Town is extremely tight in July and August: a reservation is highly recommended.

Jagoda & Ante Bracanović Guesthouse (☎ 741 416, 091 520 3796; http://hvar-jagoda.com; Poviše Škole; s 100-120KN, d 190-220KN) The Bracanović family has turned a traditional stone building into a small pension. Rooms come with balconies, private bathrooms and access to a kitchen, and the family goes out of its way for guests.

Hotel Croatia (☎ 742 400; www.hotelcroatia.net; Majerovica bb; per person 245-575KN;) Only a few steps from the sea, this medium-size, rambling 1930s building is among gorgeous, peaceful gardens.

our pick **Hotel Riva** (☎ 750 750; www.suncanihvar.hr; Riva bb; s €176-380, d €187-391;) Now the luxury veteran on the Hvar Town hotel scene, the Riva is a 100-year-old hotel that's a picture of modernity. The location is right on the harbour, perfect for watching the yachts glide up and away.

Konoba Menego (☎ 742 036; mains from 70KN) This is a rustic old house where everything is decked out in Hvar antiques and the staff wears traditional outfits. Try the cheeses and vegetables, prepared the old-fashioned Dalmatian way.

Luna (☎ 741 400; mains from 70KN) Climb the 'stairway to heaven' (you have to guffaw) to the rooftop terrace. Luna has dishes such as gnocchi with truffles, and seafood and wine pasta.

Yakša (☎ 277 0770; www.yaksahvar.com; mains from 80KN) A top-end restaurant where many come not just for the food but also for its reputation as the place to be seen in Hvar.

ENTERTAINMENT

Hvar has some of the best nightlife on the Adriatic coast, and it's mainly famous for **Carpe Diem** (☎ 742 369; www.carpe-diem-hvar.com; Riva), the mother of all Dalmatian clubs. The music is smooth, the drinks aplenty and there's lots of dancing on the tables in bikinis.

GETTING THERE & AWAY

The Jadrolinija ferries between Rijeka and Dubrovnik stop in Stari Grad before continuing to Korčula. The Jadrolinija agency sells boat tickets. Car ferries from Split call at Stari Grad (42KN, one hour) three times daily (five daily in July ar August). The speedy catamaran goes fiv times a day between Split and Hvar Tow in the summer months (22KN, one hou The **Jadrolinija agency** (☎ 741 132; ww jadrolinija.hr; Riva) is beside the landing i Stari Grad.

It's possible to visit Hvar on a (hecti day trip from Split by catching the mor ing Jadrolinija ferry to Stari Grad, a bus t Hvar town, then the last ferry from Sta Grad directly back to Split.

Ferries to/from Italy:

Jadrolinija (www.jadrolinija.hr) Runs c ferries from Bari to Dubrovnik (€5 eight hours, six weekly), continuing o to Rijeka, Stari Grad and Split.

SNAV (www.snav.com) Has a car ferry th travels from Pescara to Hvar (3½ hour daily) and on to Split (6½ hours).

Split Tours (www.splittours.hr) Connect Ancona to Split (nine hours) and Sta Grad (12 hours). In summer, ferries leav twice daily Saturday to Monday an daily on other days.

GETTING AROUND

Buses meet most ferries that dock at Sta Grad in July and August, but if you com in the low season it's best to check a the tourist office or at Pelegrini to mak sure the bus is running. A taxi costs fro 150KN to 200KN. **Radio Taxi Tihi** (☎ 09 338 824) is cheaper if there are a numbe of passengers to fill up the minivan. It' easy to recognise with the picture of Hva painted on the side.

KORČULA ISLAND

☎ 020 / pop 16,200

Rich in vineyards and olive trees, the islan of Korčula was named Korkyra Melain (Black Korčula) by the original Greek set tlers because of its dense woods and plan life. Swimming opportunities aboun ı the many quiet coves and secluded eaches, while the interior produces some f Croatia's finest wine, especially dessert /ines made from the *grk* grape cultivated round Lumbarda. On a hilly peninsula ıtting into the Adriatic sits Korčula Town, striking walled town of round defensive owers and red-roofed houses.

The big Jadrolinija car ferry drops you ff either in the west harbour next to the Hotel Korčula or the east harbour next o Marko Polo Tours. The Old Town lies etween the two harbours. The large otels and main beach lie south of the ast harbour, and the residential neighbourhood Sveti Nikola (with a smaller each) is southwest of the west harbour. The town bus station is 100m south of the Old Town centre.

There are ATMs in the town centre t HVB Splitska Banka and Dubrovačka Banka.

Atlas travel agency (☎ 711 231; Trg Kralja Tomislava) represents Amex, runs excursions and finds private accommodation.

Marko Polo Tours (☎ 715 400; markopolo-tours@du.t-com.hr; Biline 5) finds private accommodation and organises excursions.

Located on the west harbour, the **tourist office** (☎ 715 701; tzg-korcule@du.t-com.hr; Obala Franje Tudjmana bb; 8am-3pm & 5-9pm Mon-Sat, 8am-3pm Sun Jun-Sep, 8am-1pm & 5-9pm Mon-Sat Oct-May) is an excellent source of nformation.

Other than following the circuit of the former city walls or walking along the shore, sightseeing in Korčula centres on Trg Sv Marka. The Gothic **St Mark's Cathedral** (Katedrala Svetog Marka; 10am-noon & 5-7pm Jul & Aug, Mass Sep-Jun) features two paintings by Tintoretto (*Three Saints* on the altar and *Annunciation* to one side).

WAYNE WALTON

Vis waterfront buildings

↘ IF YOU LIKE...

If you like **Hvar Island** (p634), consider venturing to these other central Dalmatian islands around Split:

- **Vis** (www.tz-vis.hr) Fairly far from mainland Croatia (2½ hours by ferry), Vis' lack of development is its drawcard. Come seeking authenticity, nature, peace – and some of Croatia's most well-known wines and freshest fish.
- **Brač** A dramatic landscape with steep cliffs and evocative coves supports two main towns and a handful of interior villages. The island is known for its white stone (used to build Diocletian's Palace in Split, and the White House in Washington, DC), for the old town of Bol (www.bol.hr) and for its fabulous white-pebble beach, Zlatni Rat, which graces many Croatia tourism posters.

The **Town Museum** (Gradski Muzej; ☎ 711 420; Trg Sv Marka Statuta; admission 10KN; 10am-1pm Nov-Mar, 10am-2pm Apr & May, 10am-2pm & 7-9pm Jun & Oct, 10am-9pm Jul & Aug) in the 15th-century Gabriellis Palace opposite the cathedral has exhibits of Greek pottery, Roman ceramics and home furnishings, all with English captions. The **treasury** (☎ 711 049; Trg Sv Marka; admission 15KN; 9am-2pm & 5-8pm May-Oct), in the 14th-century Abbey

Palace next to the cathedral is also worth a look. It's said that Marco Polo was born in Korčula in 1254; you can visit what is believed to have been his **house** (Depolo; admission 10KN; 10am-1pm & 5-7pm Mon-Sat Jul & Aug) and climb the tower.

In the high summer season, water taxis at the east harbour collect passengers to visit various points on the island, as well as to **Badija Island**, which features a historic 15th-century Franciscan Monastery in the process of reconstruction, plus **Orebić** and the nearby village of **Lumbarda**, which both have sandy beaches. Both Atlas travel agency and Marko Polo Tours offer a variety of boat tours and island excursions.

Pansion Marinka (712 007, 098 344 712; marinka.milina-bire@du.t-com.hr; d 150-230KN) is a working farm and winery situated in Lumbarda, in a beautiful setting within walking distance of the beach.

In the residential neighbourhood close to the Old Town and 100m west of the bus station, **Villa DePolo** (/fax 711 621; tereza.depolo@du.t-com.hr; d 240/290KN;) has four modern, clean rooms, some wit sea views. Note that there is a 30% extr charge for one-night stays.

OREBIĆ

Orebić, on the southern coast of the Pelješac Peninsula between Korčula and Ploče, offers better beaches than those found at Korčula, 2.5km across the water. The easy access by ferry from Korčula makes it the perfect place to go for the day. The best beach in Orebić is Trstenica cove, a 15-minute walk east along the shore from the port.

In Orebić the ferry terminal and the bus station are adjacent to each other. Korčula buses to Dubrovnik, Zagreb and Sarajevo stop at Orebić.

Right in the heart of the medieval Ol Town, the family-run and marine-theme **Konoba Marinero** (711 170; Mark Andrijića; mains from 50KN) has the sons catc the fish and the parents prepare it accord ing to a variety of traditional recipes.

Konoba Maslina (711 720; Lumbarajsk cesta bb; mains from 50KN) is well worth th walk for the authentic Korčulan home cooking. It's about a kilometre pas the Hotel Marko Polo on the road t Lumbarda, but you can often arrange t be picked up or dropped off in town.

Between June and October there' **moreška sword dancing** (tickets 100KN show 9pm Thu) by the Old Town gate performances are more frequent durin July and August. Atlas, the tourist offic and Marko Polo Tours sell tickets.

Transport connections to Korčul are good. There's one bus every day t Dubrovnik (87KN, three hours), one t Zagreb (195KN, 12 hours).

There's a **Jadrolinija office** (715 410 about 25m up from the west harbour. A regular afternoon car ferry runs between Split and Vela Luka (35KN, three hours), on the island's western end, that stops a Hvar most days.

The daily fast boat running from Split to Hvar and Korčula is great for locals working in Split but not so great for tourists who find themselves leaving Korčula at 6am. Get tickets at Marko Polo.

Next to Marko Polo, **Rent a Đir** (711 908; www.korcula-rent.com) hires autos, scooters and small boats.

MLJET ISLAND

020 / pop 1110

Of all the Adriatic islands, Mljet (Meleda in Italian) may be the most seductive. Over

2% of the island is covered by forests, nd the rest is dotted by fields, vineards and villages. Created in 1960, Mljet ational Park occupies the western third f the island and surrounds two saltwater kes, Malo Jezero and Veliko Jezero. Most eople visit the island on excursions from orčula or Dubrovnik.

The island is 37km long, and has an verage width of about 3km. The main oints of entry are Pomena and Polače, wo tiny towns about 5km apart. Tour oats from Korčula and the Dubrovnik atamarans arrive at Polače wharf in the igh season. Pomena is the site of the land's only conventional hotel, Hotel disej. There's a good map of the island osted at the wharf. Jadrolinija ferries top only at Sobra but catamarans from)ubrovnik and Korčula stop at Polače.

Goveđari, the national park's entry oint, is just between Pomena and Polače. he **national park** (adult/concession 90/30KN) neasures 54 sq km and the entry price ncludes a bus and boat transfer to the enedictine monastery. If you stay overight on the island you only pay the park dmission once.

The **tourist office** (☎ 744 186; www.nljet.hr; 8am-8pm Mon-Sat, 8am-1pm Sun un-Sep, 8am-1pm & 5-8pm Mon-Fri Oct-May) is n Polače and there is an ATM next door. here's another ATM at the Hotel Odisej n Pomena.

The administrative centre of the island s at Babino Polje, 18km east of Polače, vhere there is another **tourist office** (☎/ax 745 125; www.mljet.hr; 9am-5pm Mon-Fri) nd a post office.

From Pomena it's a 15-minute walk to a jetty on **Veliko Jezero**, the larger of the wo lakes. Here you can board a boat to a small lake islet and have lunch at a 12th-century **Benedictine monastery**, which now houses a restaurant.

WAYNE WALTON
Village on Mljet Island

Mljet is good for cycling; several restaurants along the dock in Polače and the Odisej Hotel in Pomena hire bicycles (10/100KN per hour/day). If you plan to cycle between Pomena and Polače be aware that the two towns are separated by a steep mountain. The bike path along Veliko Jezero is an easier pedal but it doesn't link the two towns.

The island offers some unusual opportunities for **diving**. There's a Roman wreck dating from the 3rd century in relatively shallow water. There's also a German torpedo boat from WWII and several walls to dive. Contact **Kronmar diving** (☎ 744 022; Hotel Odisej).

Jadrolinija ferries stop only at Sobra (32KN, two hours) but the **Melita catamaran** (☎ 313 119; www.gv-line.hr; Vukovarska 34)

Hillside village, Mljet Island (p638)

IF YOU LIKE...

If you like **Mljet Island** (p638), we think you may enjoy this:

- **Elafiti Islands** These are tiny, forested islands northwest of Dubrovnik. Many in-town tour companies operate cruises or kayaking or trips to the area. The three main islands Koločep (20 minutes), Lopud (35 minutes) and Šipan (1¼ hours) are connected by Jadrolinija ferry (www.jadrolinija.hr). The latter two have old 15th-and 16th-century buildings as well as villages and sand and pebble beaches.

goes to Polače (70KN) after Sobra (50KN) in the summer months, leaving Dubrovnik at 9.45am daily and returning from Polače at 4.55pm, making it ideal for a day trip from Dubrovnik. From Sobra, you can get to Pomena on a bus (1½ hours) and from Polače you can either cycle or walk there.

DUBROVNIK

☎020 / pop 43,800

No matter whether you are visiting Dubrovnik for the first time or if you're returning again and again to this marvellous city, the sense of awe and beauty when you set eyes on the Stradun never fades. It's hard to imagine anyone, even the city's inhabitants, becoming jaded by its marb streets and baroque buildings, or failin to be inspired by a walk along the ancie city walls that once protected a civilise sophisticated republic for five centurie and that still look out onto the endles shimmer of the peaceful Adriatic.

Founded 1300 years ago by refugee from Epidaurus in Greece, mediev Dubrovnik (Ragusa until 1918) shoo off Venetian control in the 14th centur becoming an independent republic an one of Venice's more important maritim rivals, trading with Egypt, Syria, Sicil Spain, France and later Turkey.

The deliberate shelling of Dubrovni by the Yugoslav army in 1991 sent shock waves through the international commu nity but, when the smoke cleared in 199 traumatised residents cleared the rubbl and set about repairing the damage Reconstruction has been extraordinaril skilful.

The Jadrolinija ferry terminal and th bus station are next to each other at Gruž several kilometres northwest of the Ol Town, which is closed to cars. The mai street in the Old Town is Placa (bette known as Stradun). Most accommoda tion is on the leafy Lapad Peninsula, wes of the bus station.

INFORMATION

You can change money at any trave agency or post office. There are numer ous ATMs in town, near the bus statio and near the ferry terminal.

Atlas Travel Agency Obala Papa Ivana Pavla II (**Map p641; ☎418 001; Obala Pap Ivana Pavla II 1**); Sv Đurđa (**Map p641; ☎44 574; Sv Đurđa 1**) All excursions are run by Atlas.

Hospital (**Map p641; ☎431 777; Dr Roka Mišetića bb**) Emergency services are available 24 hours.

DUBROVNIK

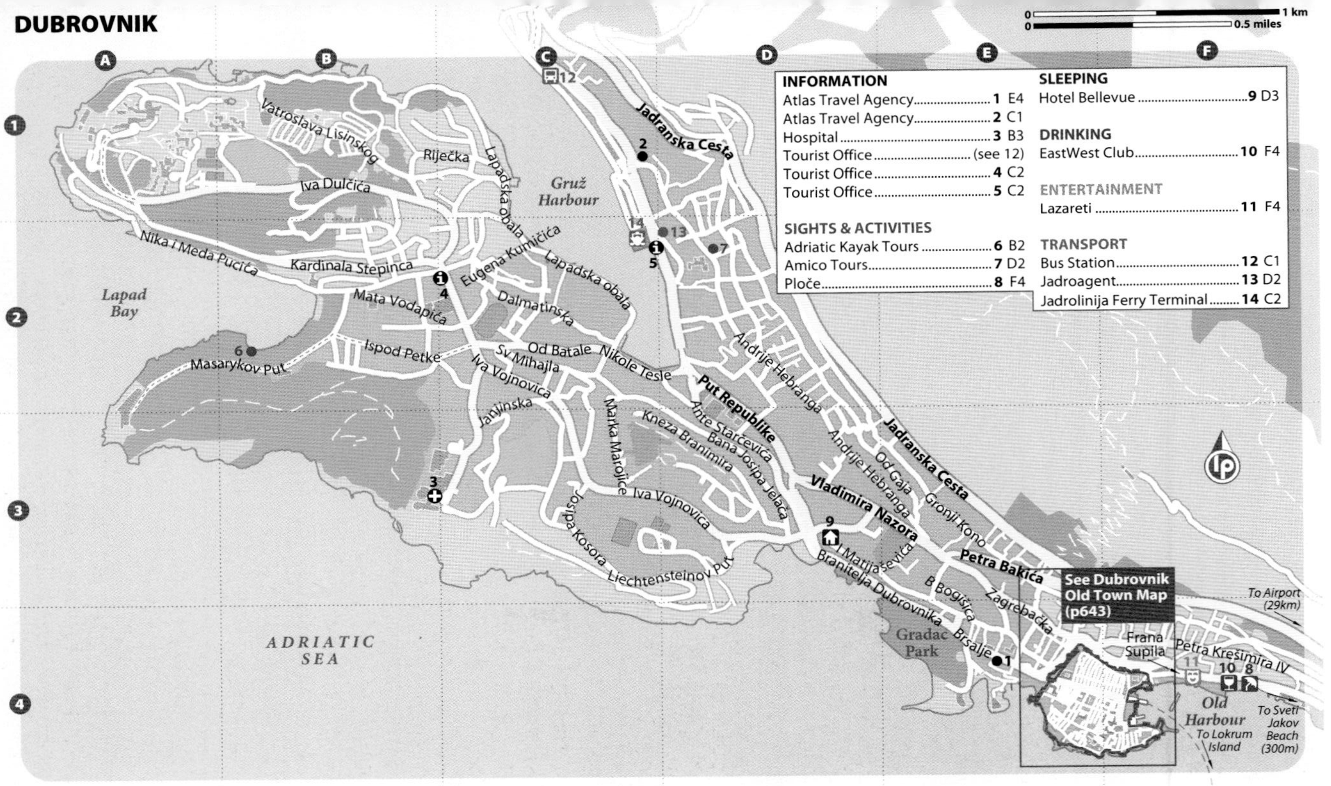

INFORMATION

Atlas Travel Agency 1 E4
Atlas Travel Agency 2 C1
Hospital 3 B3
Tourist Office .... (see 12)
Tourist Office 4 C2
Tourist Office 5 C2

SIGHTS & ACTIVITIES

Adriatic Kayak Tours 6 B2
Amico Tours 7 D2
Ploče 8 F4

SLEEPING

Hotel Bellevue 9 D3

DRINKING

EastWest Club 10 F4

ENTERTAINMENT

Lazareti 11 F4

TRANSPORT

Bus Station 12 C1
Jadroagent 13 D2
Jadrolinija Ferry Terminal 14 C2

Main post office (Map p643; cnr Široka & Od Puča)

Tourist office (www.tzdubrovnik.hr) Bus Station (Map p641; ☎ 417 581; Obala Pape Ivana Pavla II 24; 🕒 8am-8pm Jun-Sep, 8am-3pm Mon-Fri, 9am-2pm Sat, closed Sun Oct-May); Gruž Harbour (Map p641; ☎ 417 983; Obala Stjepana Radića 27; 🕒 8am-8pm daily Jun-Sep, 8am-3pm Mon-Fri, 9am-2pm Sat, closed Sun Oct-May); Lapad (Map p641; ☎ 437 460; Šetalište Kralja

HOLGER LEUE

Old Town walls

↘ OLD DUBROVNIK CITY WALLS

Spend a morning taking a leisurely walk around the city walls (Gradske Zidine), which have entrances just inside Pile Gate, across from the Dominican monastery and near Fort St John. Built between the 13th and 16th centuries, these powerful walls are the finest in the world and Dubrovnik's main claim to fame. They enclose the entire city in a protective veil over 2km long and up to 25m high, with two round and 14 square towers, two corner fortifications and a large fortress. The views over the town and sea are great – this walk could be the high point of your visit.

Things you need to know: Map p643; adult/child 50/20KN; 🕒 9am-7.30pm Apr-Oct, 10am-3.30pm Nov-Mar

Zvonimira 25; 🕒 8am-8pm daily Jun-Sep, 8an 3pm Mon-Fri, 9am-2pm Sat, closed Sun Oct-May Old Town (Map p643; ☎ 323 587; Široka 🕒 8am-8pm daily Jun-Sep, 8am-3pm Mon-Fr 9am-2pm Sat, closed Sun Oct-May); Pile Gat (Map p643; ☎ 427 591; Dubrovačkih Branitelja 🕒 8am-8pm daily Jun-Sep, 8am-3pm Mon-Fr 9am-2pm Sat, closed Sun Oct-May) Maps, ir formation and the indispensable *Du brovnik Riviera* guide.

SIGHTS

OLD TOWN

You will probably begin your visit c Dubrovnik's World Heritage–listed Ol Town at the city bus stop outside **Pi Gate** (Map p643). As you enter the city Dubrovnik's wonderful pedestrian prom enade, Placa, extends before you all th way to the **clock tower** at the other en of town.

Just inside Pile Gate is the huge 143 **Onofrio Fountain** (Map p643) an **Franciscan Monastery** (Muzej Franjevačko Samostana; Map p643; ☎ 321 410; Placa adult/concession 20/10KN; 🕒 9am-6pm), wit a splendid cloister and the third-oldes functioning **pharmacy** (🕒 9am-5pm) i Europe; it's been operating since 139 The **church** (Map p643; 🕒 7am-7pm) has re cently undergone a long and expensiv restoration to startling effect. The **mon astery museum** (Map p643; adult/concessio 20/10KN, 🕒 9am-5pm) has a collection of li turgical objects, paintings and pharmac equipment.

In front of the clock tower at the easter end of Placa (on the square called Luža) i the 1419 **Orlando Column** (Map p643) a favourite meeting place. On opposit sides of the column are the 16th-centur **Sponza Palace** (Map p643) – originally customs house, later a bank, and whic now houses the **State Archives** (Državn Arhiv u Dubrovniku; ☎ 321 032; admission 15K

DUBROVNIK OLD TOWN

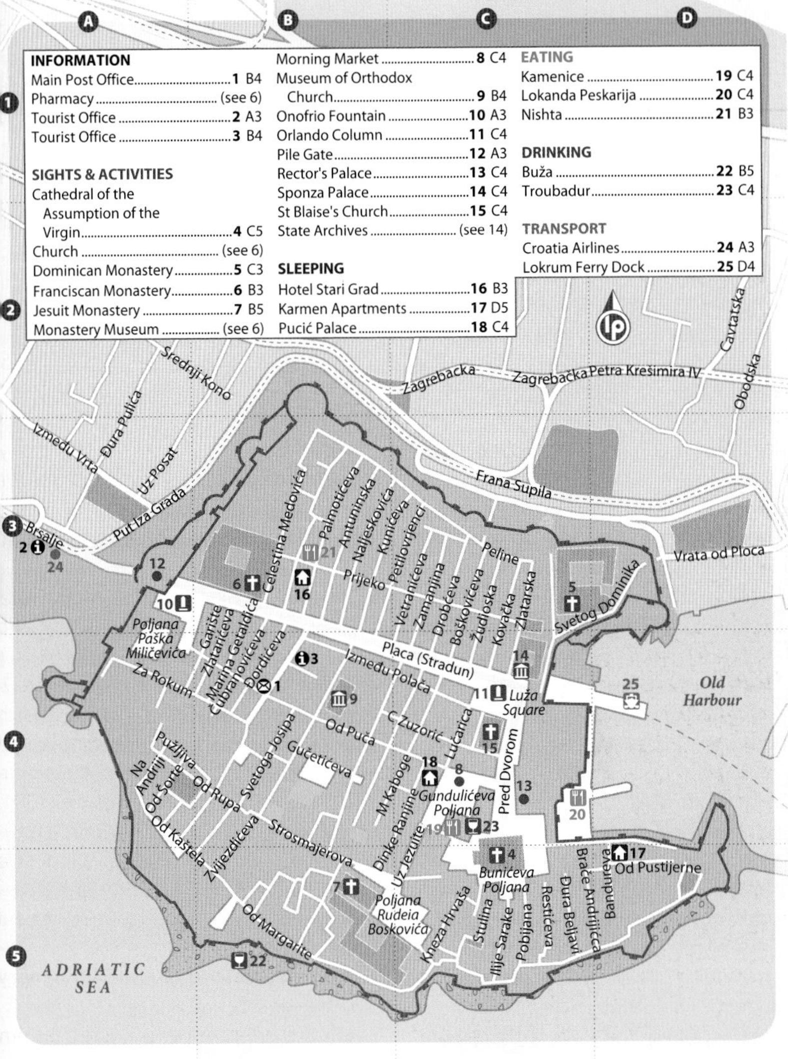

⌚ 8am-3pm Mon-Fri, to 1pm Sat) – and **St Blaise's Church** (Map p643), a lovely Italian baroque building built in 1715 to replace an earlier church destroyed in the 1667 earthquake. At the end of Pred Dvorom, the wide street beside St Blaise, is the baroque **Cathedral of the Assumption of the Virgin** (Map p643). Located between the two churches, the 1441 Gothic **Rector's Palace** (**Map p643; ☎ 321 437; Pred Dvorom 3; adult/student 35/15KN, audio guide 30KN; ⌚ 9am-6pm**) houses a museum with furnished rooms, baroque paintings and historical exhibits. The elected rector was not permitted to leave the building during his one-month term without the permission of the senate. The narrow street opposite opens onto Gundulićeva Poljana, a bustling **morning market** (Map p643). Up the stairs south of the square is the 1725 **Jesuit Monastery** (Map p643; Poljana Ruđera Boškovića).

As you proceed up Placa, make a detour to the **Museum of the Orthodox Church** (Muzej Pravoslavne Crkve; Map p643; ☎ 323 283; Od Puča 8; adult/concession 10/5KN; ⏲ 9am-2pm Mon-Sat) for a look at a fascinating collection of 15th- to 19th-century icons.

Wherever you go in Dubrovnik, you'll notice the 14th-century **Dominican Monastery** (Muzej Dominikanskog Samostana; Map p643; ☎ 322 200; off Svetog Dominika 4; adult/child 20/10KN; ⏲ 9am-5pm) in the northeastern corner of the city, whose forbidding, fortresslike exterior shelters a rich trove of paintings from Dubrovnik's finest 15th- and 16th-century artists.

BEACHES

Ploče (Map p641), the closest beach to the Old Town, is just beyond the 17th-century **Lazareti** (p645; a former quarantine station) outside **Ploče Gate**. Another good, local beach is **Sveti Jakov**, a 20-minute walk down Vlaho Bukovac or a quick ride on bus 5 or 8 from the northern end of the Old Town. There are also hotel beaches along the **Lapad Peninsula**, which you are able to use without a problem.

An even better option is to take the ferry that shuttles half-hourly in summer to lush **Lokrum Island** (return 40KN), a national park with a rocky nudist beach (marked FKK), a botanical garden and the ruins of a medieval Benedictin monastery.

TOURS

Adriatic Kayak Tours (Map p641; ☎ 312 77 www.kayakcroatia.com; Frankopanska 6) offers great series of kayak tours for experience and beginner kayakers.

Amico Tours (Map p641; ☎ 418 24 www.amico-tours.com; Od Skara 1) offers da trips to Mostar and Međugorje (390KN Montenegro (390KN), Albania (990KN Korčula and Pelješac (390KN), and th Elafiti Islands (250KN), as well as nume ous kayaking, rafting and jeep safari da trips (590KN).

SLEEPING & EATING

Karmen Apartments (Map p643; ☎ 323 43 098 619 282; www.karmendu.com; Bandureva 1; ap €55-145; ❄) Set inside an old stone hous in the middle of the Old Town, the fou apartments are beautifully decorated wit original artwork and imaginative use c recycled materials.

Hotel Stari Grad (Map p643; ☎ 32 244; www.hotelstarigrad.com; Palmotićev s 650-1180KN, d 920KN-1580KN; ❄) Staying i the heart of the Old Town in a lovingl restored stone building is an unmatch able experience. The eight rooms ar elegantly and tastefully furnished t feel simple and luxurious at the sam time.

Pucić Palace (Map p643; ☎ 326 22 www.thepucicpalace.com; Od Puča 1; s €206-31 d €290-505; ❄) Right in the heart of th Old Town and inside what was once nobleman's mansion, this five-star hote is Dubrovnik's most exclusive and hottes property.

OUR PICK **Hotel Bellevue** (Map p641; ☎ 33 000; www.hotel-bellevue.hr; Petra Čingrije 7 d from €250; ❄ 💻 🏊) Although not withi the borders of the Old Town, but a five ninute walk west from Pile Gate, Hotel Bellevue's location – on a cliff that overlooks the open sea and the lovely bay underneath – is pretty much divine.

Nishta (Map p643; ☎ 091 896 7509; Prijeko 30; mains from 30KN) Head here for a refreshing gazpacho, a heart-warming miso soup, Thai curries, vegies and noodles, and many more vegie delights.

Kamenice (Map p643; ☎ 421 499; Gundulićeva Poljana 8; mains from 40KN) It's been here since the 1970s and not much has changed: the socialist-style waiting uniforms, the simple interior, the massive portions of mussels, grilled or fried squid and griddled anchovies, and *kamenice* – oysters – too.

our pick **Lokanda Peskarija** (Map p643; ☎ 324 750; Ribarnica bb; mains from 40KN) Located on the Old Harbour right next to the fish market, this is undoubtedly one of Dubrovnik's best eateries. The quality of the seafood dishes is unfaltering, the prices are good, and the location is gorgeous.

DRINKING & ENTERTAINMENT

our pick **Buža** (Map p643; Ilije Sarake) The Buža is just a simple place on the outside of the city walls, facing out onto the open sea, with simple drinks and blissful punters.

EastWest Club (Map p641; ☎ 412 220; Frana Supila bb) By day this outfit on Banje Beach rents out beach chairs and umbrellas and serves drinks to the bathers. When the rays lengthen, the cocktail bar opens.

Troubadur (Map p643; ☎ 412 154; Bunićeva Poljana 2) A legendary Dubrovnik venue; come here for live jazz concerts in the summer.

Lazareti (Map p641; ☎ 324 633; www.lazareti.du-hr.net; Frana Supila 8) Dubrovnik's best art and music centre, Lazareti hosts cinema nights, club nights, live music, masses of concerts and pretty much all the best things in town.

GETTING THERE & AWAY

Daily flights to/from Zagreb are operated by **Croatia Airlines** (Map p643; ☎ 413 777; Brsalje 9). There are also nonstop flights to Rome, London and Manchester between April and October.

In addition to the **Jadrolinija** (Map p641; ☎ 418 000; Gruž) coastal ferry north (Split–Hvar 1¾ hours, Hvar–Korčula 3¾ hours, Korčula–Dubrovnik 3¼ hours), there's a local ferry that leaves from Dubrovnik for Sobra on Mljet Island (50KN, 2½ hours) throughout the year. There are several ferries a day year-round to the outlying islands of Šipanska, Suđurađ, Lopud and Koločep.

Jadroagent (Map p641; ☎ 419 009; fax 419 029; Radića 32) handles ticketing for most international boats from Croatia.

For international connections:

Azzurra Lines (www.azzurraline.com) Sails from Bari, Italy to Dubrovnik (€65).

Jadrolinija (www.jadrolinija.hr) Runs car ferries from Bari to Dubrovnik (€51, eight hours, six weekly), which continue on to Stari Grad and Split.

In a busy summer season and at weekends buses out of Dubrovnik can be crowded, so book a ticket well before the scheduled departure time.

GETTING AROUND

Čilipi international airport is 24km southeast of Dubrovnik. The Croatia Airlines airport buses (25KN, 45 minutes) leave from the main **bus station** (Map p641; ☎ 357 088) 1½ hours before flight times. Buses meet Croatia Airlines flights but not all others. A taxi costs around 200KN.

Dubrovnik's buses run frequently and generally on time. The fare is 10KN if you buy from the driver but only 8KN if you buy a ticket at a kiosk.

DIRECTORY

ACTIVITIES

The clear waters and varied underwater life of the Adriatic have led to a flourishing dive industry along the coast. Cave diving is the real speciality in Croatia; night diving and wreck diving are also offered and there are coral reefs in some places, but they are in rather deep water. Most of the coastal resorts mentioned in this chapter have dive shops. See **Diving Croatia** (www.diving-hrs.hr) for contact information.

There are countless possibilities for anyone carrying a folding sea kayak, especially among the Elafiti and Kornati Islands.

EMBASSIES & CONSULATES

The following addresses are in Zagreb (area code ☎01):

Australia (Map p622; ☎48 91 200; www.auembassy.hr; Kaptol Centar, Nova Ves 11) North of the centre.

Canada (Map p622; ☎48 81 200; zagreb@dfait-maeci.gc.ca; Prilaz Đure Deželića 4)

France (Map p622; 48 93 680; consulat@ambafrance.hr; Hebrangova 2)

Germany (Map p622; ☎61 58 105; www.deutschebotschaft-zagreb.hr in German; ul grada Vukovara 64) South of the centre.

Ireland (Map p622; ☎66 74 455; Turinina 3)

Netherlands (off Map p622; ☎46 84 880; nlgovzag@zg.t-com.hr; Medveščak 56)

New Zealand (off Map p622; ☎61 51 382; Trg Stjepana Radića 3) Southwest of the centre.

UK (off Map p622; ☎60 09 100; I Lučića 4)

USA (off Map p622; ☎66 12 200; www.usembassy.hr; Ul Thomasa Jeffersona 2) South of the centre.

FESTIVALS & EVENTS

In July and August there are summer festivals in Dubrovnik, Split, Pula and Zagreb. Dubrovnik's summer music festival emphasises classical music, while Pula hosts a variety of pop and classical stars in the Roman amphitheatre and also hosts a film festival. Mardi Gras celebrations have recently been revived in many towns with attendant parades and festivities, but nowhere is it celebrated with more verve than in Rijeka.

GAY & LESBIAN TRAVELLERS

Homosexuality has been legal in Croatia since 1977 and is tolerated, but public displays of affection between members of the same sex may be met with hostility, especially outside major cities. Exclusively gay clubs are a rarity outside Zagreb, but many of the large discos attract a mixed crowd.

Most Croatian websites devoted to the gay scene are in Croatian only, but a good starting point is the English-language www.touristinfo.gay.hr, which has articles on the gay scene and links to other relevant websites.

HOLIDAYS

New Year's Day 1 January
Epiphany 6 January
Easter Monday March/April
Labour Day 1 May
Corpus Christi 10 June
Day of Antifascist Resistance 22 June marks the outbreak of resistance in 1941
Statehood Day 25 June
Victory Day and National Thanksgiving Day 5 August
Feast of the Assumption 15 August
Independence Day 8 October
All Saints' Day 1 November
Christmas 25 and 26 December

MONEY

Amex, MasterCard, Visa and Diners Club cards are widely accepted in large hotels, stores and many restaurants, but don't count on cards to pay for private accommodation or meals in small restaurants. You'll find ATMs accepting MasterCard, Maestro, Cirrus, Plus and Visa in most bus and train stations, airports, all major cities and most small towns.

TELEPHONE

Croatia uses GSM 900/1800. If your mobile is unlocked, SIM cards are widely available.

To make a phone call from Croatia, go to the town's main post office. You'll need a phonecard to use public telephones, but calls using a phonecard are about 50% more expensive. Phonecards are sold according to *impulsa* (units), and you can buy cards of 25 (15KN), 50 (30KN), 100 (50KN) and 200 (100KN) units. These can be purchased at any post office and most tobacco shops and newspaper kiosks.

TOURIST INFORMATION

The **Croatian National Tourist Board** (**Map p622; ☎ 45 56 455; www.htz.hr; Iblerov Trg 10, Importanne Gallerija, 10000 Zagreb**) is a good source of information. There are regional tourist offices that supervise tourist development and municipal tourist offices that have free brochures and good information on local events. Some arrange private accommodation.

TRANSPORT

GETTING THERE & AWAY

Connections into Croatia are in a constant state of flux, with new air and boat routes opening every season. Following is an overview of the major connections into Croatia.

AIR

The following airlines fly to Croatia:

Croatia Airlines (**OU; ☎ 01-48 19 633; www.croatiaairlines.hr; Zrinjevac 17, Zagreb**)
easyJet (**EZY; www.easyjet.com**)
Germanwings (**GWI; www.germanwings.com**)
Turkish Airlines (**TK; ☎ 01-49 21 854; www.turkishairlines.com**)
Wizzair (**W6; www.wizzair.com**)

LAND

There are train services from Budapest to Zagreb. Trains also run between Venice and Zagreb.

SEA

Regular boats from several companies connect Croatia with Italy from towns including Zadar (p630), Split (p633), Stari Grad (p636) on Hvar Island, and Dubrovnik (p645).

GETTING AROUND

AIR

Croatia Airlines is the one and only carrier for flights within Croatia. Seniors and people aged under 26 get discounts.

BOAT

Year-round Jadrolinija car ferries operate along the Bari–Rijeka–Dubrovnik coastal route, stopping at Zadar, Split and the islands of Hvar, Korčula and Mljet. Services are less frequent in winter. The most scenic section is Split to Dubrovnik, which all Jadrolinija ferries cover during the day. With a through ticket, deck passengers can stop at any port for up to a week, provided they notify the purser beforehand and have their ticket validated. This is much cheaper than buying individual sector tickets but is only good for one stopover. Cabins should be booked a week ahead, but deck space is usually available on all sailings.

You must buy tickets in advance at an agency or the Jadrolinija office, as they are not sold on board. Cabins can be arranged at the reservation counter aboard the ship, but advance bookings are recommended if you want to be sure of a place. Bringing a car means checking in at least two hours in advance, more in the summer.

BUS

Bus services are excellent and relatively inexpensive. There are often a number of different companies handling each route so prices can vary substantially. Generally, the cheaper fares are on overnight buses.

It's generally best to call or visit the bus station to get the complete schedule but the following companies are among the largest:

Autotrans (☎ 051-660 360; www.autotrans.hr)
Brioni Pula (☎ 052-502 997; www.brioni.hr, in Croatian)
Contus (☎ 023-315 315; www.contus.hr)

At large stations bus tickets must be purchased at the office; book ahead to be sure of a seat. Tickets for buses that arrive from somewhere else are usually purchased from the conductor. Buy a one-way ticket only or you'll be locked into one company's schedule for the return

CAR & MOTORCYCLE

You have to pay tolls on the motorways around Zagreb. The motorway connecting Zagreb and Split has cut travel time to the coast to around four hours. Tolls add up to about 160KN. Over the ne[xt] few years, look for completion of the fin[al] leg running from Split to Dubrovnik. Fo[r] general news on Croatia's motorways an[d] tolls, see www.hac.hr.

The large car-hire chains represente[d] in Croatia are Avis, Budget, Europcar an[d] Hertz. Throughout Croatia, Avis is allie[d] with the Autotehna company, while Hert[z] is often represented by Kompas.

Independent local companies are ofte[n] much cheaper than the internationa[l] chains, but Avis, Budget, Europcar an[d] Hertz have the big advantage of offerin[g] one-way rentals that allow you to drop th[e] car off at any one of their many stations i[n] Croatia free of charge.

LOCAL TRANSPORT

Zagreb has a well-developed tram system as well as local buses, but in the rest of the country you'll only find buses.

Taxis are available in all cities and towns but they must be called or boarded at a taxi stand. Prices are rather high (meters start at 25KN).

TRAIN

Train travel is about 15% cheaper than bus travel and often more comfortable although slower. The main lines run from Zagreb to Zadar and Split. There are no trains along the coast. Local trains usually have only unreserved 2nd-class seats. Reservations may be required on express trains. 'Executive' trains have only 1st-class seats and are 40% more expensive than local trains.

For train information check out **Croatian Railway** (www.hznet.hr).

GREECE
ΕΛΛΑΔΑ

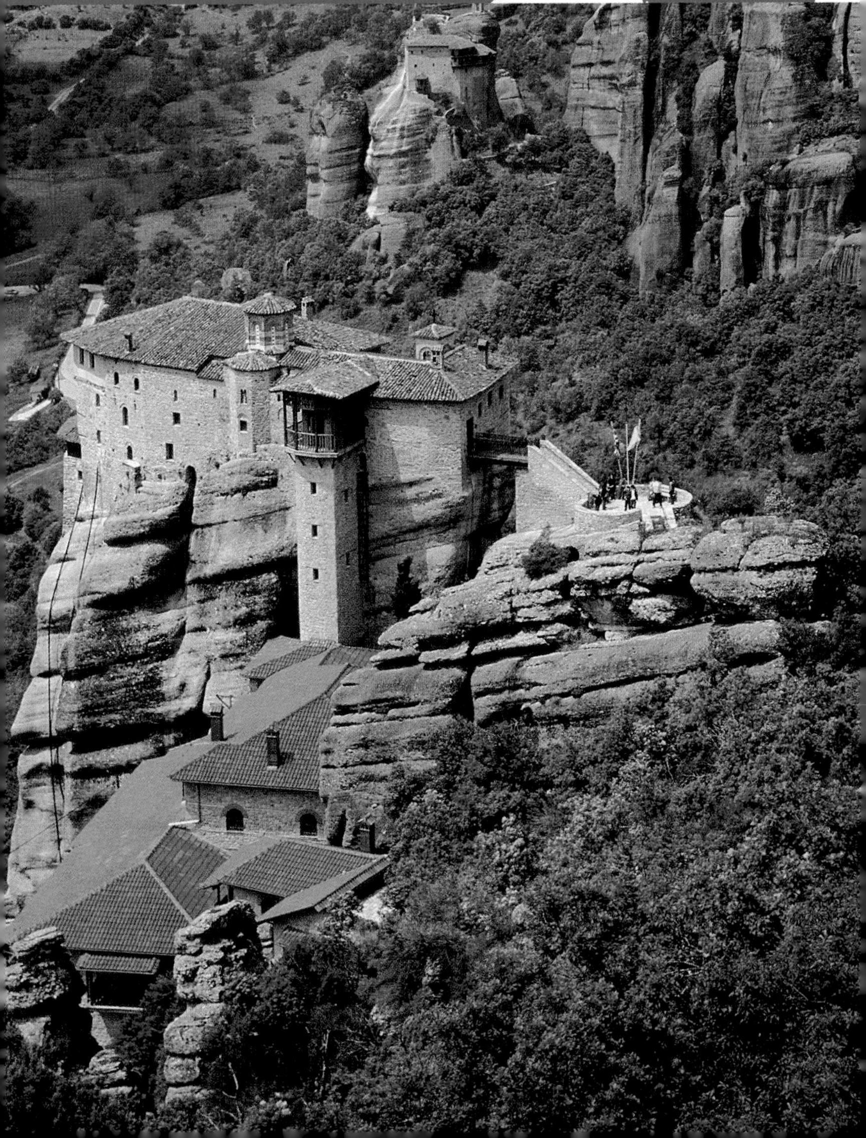

GREECE

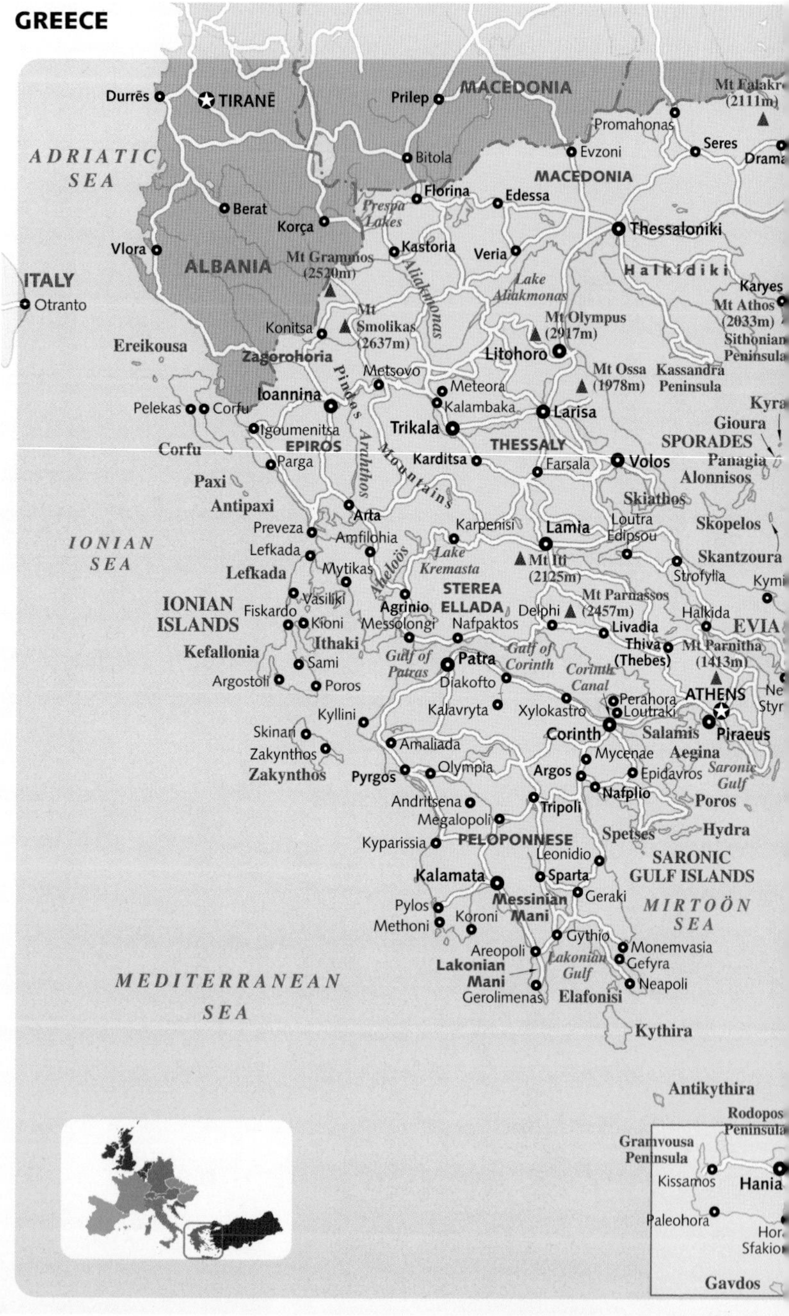

Durrës
TIRANË
Prilep
MACEDONIA
Mt Falakro (2111m)
Promahonas
Seres
Drama
ADRIATIC SEA
Bitola
Evzoni
MACEDONIA
Florina
Edessa
Berat
Prespa Lakes
Korça
Thessaloniki
Vlora
Kastoria
Veria
Mt Grammos (2520m)
ALBANIA
Halkidiki
ITALY
Otranto
Aliakmonas
Lake Aliakmonas
Karyes
Mt Athos (2033m)
Mt Smolikas (2637m)
Mt Olympus (2917m)
Konitsa
Sithonian Peninsula
Ereikousa
Zagorohoria
Litohoro
Metsovo
Mt Ossa (1978m)
Kassandra Peninsula
Pindos Mountains
Meteora
Ioannina
Kalambaka
Pelekas
Corfu
Larisa
Kyra
Trikala
Gioura
Igoumenitsa
EPIROS
THESSALY
SPORADES
Corfu
Arahthos
Karditsa
Volos
Panagia
Parga
Farsala
Alonnisos
Paxi
Skiathos
Antipaxi
Arta
Loutra Edipsou
Preveza
Karpenisi
Skopelos
IONIAN SEA
Amfilohia
Lamia
Lefkada
Lake Kremasta
Skantzoura
Lefkada
Mytikas
Mt Iti (2125m)
Strofylia
Acheloös
Kymi
STEREA ELLADA
Vasiliki
IONIAN ISLANDS
Mt Parnassos (2457m)
Agrinio
Fiskardo
Delphi
Halkida
Kioni
Messolongi
Nafpaktos
Livadia
EVIA
Ithaki
Kefallonia
Thiva (Thebes)
Mt Parnitha (1413m)
Gulf of Corinth
Gulf of Patras
Patra
Sami
Argostoli
Poros
Diakofto
Corinth Canal
Perahora
ATHENS
Kalavryta
Xylokastro
Loutraki
Kyllini
Corinth
Salamis
Piraeus
Skinari
Amaliada
Mycenae
Aegina
Zakynthos
Epidavros
Zakynthos
Pyrgos
Olympia
Argos
Saronic Gulf
Nafplio
Andritsena
Tripoli
Poros
Megalopoli
Spetses
Hydra
Kyparissia
PELOPONNESE
Leonidio
SARONIC GULF ISLANDS
Kalamata
Sparta
Messinian Mani
Geraki
MIRTOÖN SEA
Pylos
Koroni
Methoni
Gythio
Monemvasia
Areopoli
Lakonian Gulf
Gefyra
Lakonian Mani
MEDITERRANEAN SEA
Gerolimenas
Elafonisi
Neapoli
Kythira
Antikythira
Rodopos Peninsula
Gramvousa Peninsula
Kissamos
Hania
Paleohora
Hora Sfakion
Gavdos

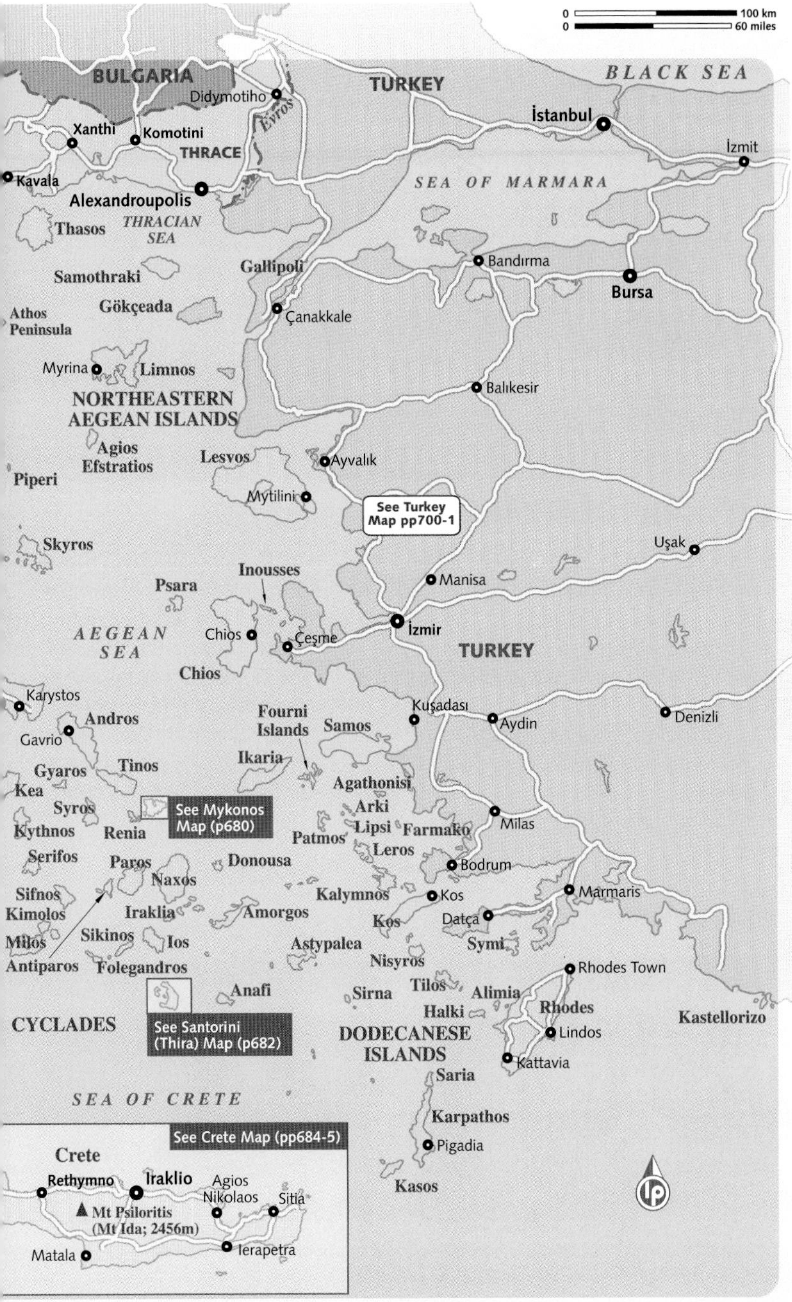
0 100 km
0 60 miles
BLACK SEA
BULGARIA
TURKEY
Didymotiho
Xanthi
Komotini
THRACE
Evros
İstanbul
İzmit
Kavala
Alexandroupolis
SEA OF MARMARA
Thasos
THRACIAN SEA
Gallipoli
Bandırma
Bursa
Samothraki
Athos Peninsula
Gökçeada
Çanakkale
Myrina
Limnos
NORTHEASTERN AEGEAN ISLANDS
Balıkesir
Agios Efstratios
Piperi
Lesvos
Ayvalık
Mytilini
See Turkey Map pp700-1
Skyros
Uşak
Inousses
Psara
Manisa
AEGEAN SEA
Chios
Çeşme
İzmir
TURKEY
Chios
Karystos
Andros
Gavrio
Fourni Islands
Samos
Kuşadası
Aydin
Denizli
Ikaria
Gyaros
Tinos
Kea
Agathonisi
Syros
See Mykonos Map (p680)
Arki
Lipsi
Milas
Kythnos
Renia
Patmos
Farmako
Leros
Serifos
Paros
Donousa
Bodrum
Naxos
Sifnos
Kalymnos
Kos
Marmaris
Kimolos
Iraklia
Amorgos
Datça
Kos
Milos
Sikinos
Ios
Astypalea
Symi
Antiparos
Folegandros
Nisyros
Rhodes Town
Anafi
Tilos
Sirna
Alimia
Rhodes
Kastellorizo
Halki
CYCLADES
See Santorini (Thira) Map (p682)
DODECANESE ISLANDS
Lindos
Kattavia
Saria
SEA OF CRETE
Karpathos
See Crete Map (pp684-5)
Crete
Pigadia
Rethymno
Iraklio
Agios Nikolaos
Sitia
Kasos
Mt Psiloritis (Mt Ida; 2456m)
Matala
Ierapetra

HIGHLIGHTS

1 CRETE

IOANNIS SAATSAKIS, MANAGING DIRECTOR SOLMAR TOURS, CRETE

Crete is unlike anywhere else in Greece. There are natural places that are very beautiful, it has harbour cities like Rethymno, and Crete is the birthplace of Minoan civilisation – one of the oldest cultures in Europe.

➘ IOANNIS SAATSAKIS' DON'T MISS LIST

❶ RETHYMNO

First came the Venetians, then the Turks and then the Greeks. In the old city of **Rethymno** (p685) you have a sense of how things were ages ago. The restaurants around the old town, the small shops, the narrow streets… it's a wonderful combination of the old and the new.

❷ MINOAN ANTIQUITIES

To see what the Minoan culture produced so many millennia ago is just amazing; around 2000 BC they even had their own baths. The palace at **Knossos** (p685) is the most important Minoan site, but there's also Phaistos, Malia and other ruins. You have to see the **archaeology museum** (p684) in Iraklio – it's the most comprehensive museum of Minoan civilisation.

Clockwise from top: Harbourside cafes, Hania (p686); Samaria Gorge (p687); Palace fresco, Knossos (p685); Visitors at Knossos (p685); Playing backgammon in Rethymno (p685)

CLOCKWISE FROM TOP: NEIL SETCHFIELD; GREG GAWLOWSKI; NEIL SETCHFIELD; NEIL SETCHFIELD; NEIL SETCHFIELD

TAKING A LOCAL TASTE

ı Sfakia or the small villages toward ania, you can try real Cretan food in ıe small tavernas. It's almost always ıade with olive oil. One dish that is nown worldwide is the Cretan salad – ke a 'Greek' salad it's made with toıatoes and cucumbers, but also has local bread in the mix. At traditional estaurants you will sometimes see 'retan folk music and dancing, which ; very different from that in the rest f Greece.

NATURAL BEAUTY

ry not to miss the lovely **Samaria iorge** (p687) – it's one of the longest ı Europe. You can hike down and take boat and a bus ride back to town. 'here are also many smaller natural places that are different and beautiful. At the western end of the island, just 100m off shore, there is a small islet, Elafonisi, which you can walk to. With very white sand, it's like your own tropical oasis. And on Mt Psiloritis (Mt Ida), the highest mountain on Crete, there is a cave that is reputed to be the birthplace of Zeus.

THINGS YOU NEED TO KNOW

Best photo op The palace of Knossos is known for its frescos. Don't miss the opportunity to photograph the school of dolphins in the Queen's room **When to start** If you're hiking the Samaria Gorge, start by 8am to miss the crowds **See our author's review on p683**

HIGHLIGHTS

2

THE ACROPOLIS

People lived in the 'upper city', or **Acropolis** (p663), until around 500 BC, when it was declared the province of the gods. When you're there, wander around the ancient temple ruins and consider the glory of Greece from so long ago. If you happen to be there during the full moon in August, entering the site at night is a quietly festive experience, and not to be missed.

3

A GREEK TAVERNA

Greeks often travel great distances to eat in village tavernas where they know the meat is local and the produce is from the owner's garden. Follow suit. Peer into the pots to see what's cooking, pull up a plate of *medzedhes* (mixed appetizers) and meet the locals. Dining al fresco at a neighbourhood taverna, whether by the sea or high in the hills, is always an adventure.

4

➘ DREAM PHOTOGRAPHY

Much of Greece is a photographer's dream – ancient ruins, old town ports, rugged hillsides...but **Santorini** (p680) beats all. Here you can frame a shot of stark white, cliff-top architecture in vivid contrast to azure seas. Expect the cobalt roofs of Oia's church domes to figure prominently in the pictures you bring home.

5

➘ ISLAND HOPPING

Whether you speed along the major routes on a superferry or chug along the backwaters in an ageing open boat, **island hopping** (p696) is an experience not to miss. You can plop your sleeping bag in deck class or splash out on a cruise-ship cabin. Just be sure to skip the catamarans if you hope to leave your seat and roam around deck – they have none.

6

➘ METEORA

The massive pinnacles of rock in **Meteora** (p676) first came to be inhabited by monks in the 11th century. Today the monasteries are linked by roads, but hiking the ancient paths provides a more authentic experience. Luckily, you no longer have to use pulley windlasses to visit; stairs were carved into the cliffsides in the 1920s.

2 GEORGE TSAFOS; 3 ANDERS BLOMQVIST; 4 DIANA MAYFIELD; 5 ADINA TOVY AMSEL; 6 PAOLO CORDELLI

2 The Acropolis (p663); 3 Athens taverna (p668); 4 Views of Oia (p682), Santorini; 5 Ferry (p696), Ionian Islands; 6 Agias Varvaras Rousanou (p676), Meteora

THE BEST...

CLASSICAL AGE ARCHITECTURE

- **Parthenon, Athens** (p663) The mother of all Doric structures, completed in 438 BC.
- **Temple of Olympian Zeus, Athens** (p665) Greece's largest temple took more than 700 years to build.
- **Sanctuary of Athena, Delphi** (p675) A graceful, circular dome-style temple from the 4th century BC.
- **Theatre of Dionysos, Athens** (p664) Built to hold 17,000 people, way back in 342 BC.

OLD TOWN CHARM

- **Nafplio, Peloponnese** (p673) Elegant Venetian houses and hillside neoclassical mansions.
- **Rhodes Town** (p688) Largest walled medieval town still inhabited in Europe.
- **Rethymno, Crete** (p685) A romantic Venetian harbour with Ottoman influences.
- **Corfu Town** (p693) A tangle of winding alleys and surprising plazas, watched over by two fortresses.

STYLISH SLEEPS

- **Central Athens Hotel** (p668) Chic modernity with Acropolis views.
- **Hotel Atlantis** (p682) Crisp white-and-blue Santorini style.
- **Amphora Hotel** (p687) Elegant rooms occupy a Venetian mansion in Hania, Crete.

BEACHES

- **Paradise, Mykonos** (p679) Party beach to see and be seen.
- **Perissa, Santorini** (p681) Black sand on southern Santorini.
- **Halkidiki** (p678) More than 500km of golden sand.

LEFT: DENNIS JONES; RIGHT: DIANA MAYFIELD

Left: Perissa beach (p681), Santorini; Right: Parthenon (p663), Athens

THINGS YOU NEED TO KNOW

VITAL STATISTICS

- **Population** 11.1 million
- **Official language** Greek
- **Currency** Euro (€)
- **Telephone code** ☎ 30
- **When to go** April through mid-June, mid-September through mid-November
- **Tipping** In restaurants a service charge is always included in the price of the meal, but rounding the bill for a small tip is expected

REGIONS IN A NUTSHELL

- **Athens** (p662) Amazing antiquities situated in a modern metro-polis.
- **Peloponnese** (p673) Peninsula of varied landscapes, romantic towns and ancient ruins.
- **Central Greece** (p674) Rugged terrain that's home to rock-top monasteries and the ancient oracle.
- **Northern Greece** (p677) Think Greece's cosmopolitan second city, Thessaloniki.
- **Cyclades** (p678) Sun-kissed, sybaritic islands like Mykonos and Santorini.
- **Crete** (p683) Ancient Minoan sites, Venetian-Turkish port towns and dramatic landscapes are all found on Greece's largest island.
- **Dodecanese** (p688) An island chain dominated by Rhodes, off the west coast of Turkey.
- **Aegean Islands** (p690) Far-flung, lesser-visited islands such as Lesvos attract intrepid explorers.
- **Ionian Islands** (p692) Idyllic evergreen-covered islands such as Corfu, off the western coast of mainland Greece.

ADVANCE PLANNING

- **As far as possible ahead** If you're taking a car on a ferry, be sure to book as early as possible.
- **A month ahead** If you're travelling in July and August, especially on weekends, book accommodation ahead of time.

BE FOREWARNED

- **Watch your step** Many Athenian footpaths are made from marble, which gets slippery when it's wet – ridged rubber soles are the safest option.
- **Schedules change** Be aware that ferry schedules will change, and rarely is there a single portside agency that sells passage on all available boats. You'll have to check the timetable posted outside each agency to find out which ferry departs next.

BUSINESS HOURS

- **Banks** (8am-2pm Mon-Thu, to 1.30pm Fri) Later in big cities.
- **Post offices** (7.30am-2pm Mon-Fri) Later in big cities.
- **Shops** (8am-1.30pm & 5.30-8.30pm Tue & Thu-Fri, 8am-2.30pm Mon/Wed/Sat)

THINGS YOU NEED TO KNOW

- **Restaurants** (11am-2pm & 7pm-midnight, in tourist areas 11am-midnight)
- **Nightclubs** From between 8pm and 10pm to 4am or later.

COSTS

Room rates can be 20% to as much as 40% less outside the July and August high season, especially on the islands.

- **€70 per day** Staying in cheap rooms, taking few ferries, some self-catering.
- **€130** High-season travel, comfortable midrange rooms, restaurant meals, museum admission and some flights or ferry passage.
- **€225+** Chichi lodgings, top-end restaurants and frequent ferry rides.

EMERGENCY NUMBERS

- **Ambulance** (☎ 166)
- **Fire** (☎ 199)
- **Police** (☎ 100)
- **Roadside Assistance** (ELPA; ☎ 104)
- **Tourist Police** (☎ 171)

GETTING AROUND

For more on getting around, see p695.

- **Float your boat** Catamarans and ferries criss-cross the Adriatic and the Aegean, but departures are much more regular in summer months.
- **Airport** Athens is the gateway airport.
- **Air alternatives** If you book ahead, flying budget carriers around Greece can easily beat the price of cabin accommodation on ferries.
- **Rolling right along** A comprehensive system of bus routes is the way to roll through the mainland.

MEDIA

- **Newspapers** The *Kathimerini* supplement inside the *International Herald Tribune* contains daily event listings and a cinema guide for Athens.

RESOURCES

- **Greek National Tourist Organisation** (www.gnto.gr) Concise tourist information.
- **Greek Travel Pages** (www.gtp.gr) Useful directory for travel businesses.
- **Greek Ferries** (www.greekferries.gr) International and domestic schedules and fares.

VISAS

- **Up to 90 days** No visa is necessary for citizens of all EU countries, Australia, New Zealand, the USA, Canada and Japan.

GET INSPIRED

BOOKS

- **Hill of Kronos** Peter Levi's cerebral look at Greece life.
- **The Summer of My Greek Taverna** Tom Stone lives the dream.
- **The Iliad and the Odyssey** Homer's classic tales of the Trojan War and Odysseus' wanderings.
- **Zigzag Through the Bitter Orange Trees** Ersi Sotiropoulos' darkly comic novel set in Athens.

FILMS

- **Zorba the Greek** (1964) Nikos Kazantzakis' iconic story brought to film in Crete.
- **Shirley Valentine** (1989) A British housewife's escape fantasy lived out on Mykonos.
- **Ulysses' Gaze** (1995) A Greek-American filmmaker returns home to Ptolemas for a screening.
- **A Touch of Spice** (2003) A tale about food and life from Athens to Istanbul.

MUSIC

- **Ta Rembetika** A two-CD set of the folk-traditional Greek 'blues'.
- **Score from Zorba the Greek** Prolific composer Mikis Theodorakis' most well-known work.
- **40 Hronia Tsitsais** Original artists' recordings of Vasilis Tsitsanis' Greek classics.
- **Sta Hamila Kai Sta Psila** From contemporary singer-songwriter Dimitris Zervoudakis.

WEBSITES

- **Greek Mediterranean Gastronomy** (www.kerasma.gr) Food-oriented travel articles and recipes.
- **Rebetiko** (www.rebetiko.gr) More than 10,000 Greek folk songs.
- **Odysseus** (http://odysseus.culture.gr) The history of Greek archaeological sites.
- **Hellenic Yachting** (www.yachting.gr) All about sailing in Greece.

LEFT: GEORGE TSAFOS; RIGHT: DIANA MAYFIELD

Left: DJ in an Athens bar (p669); Right: Mykonos (p678)

ITINERARIES

AROUND ANCIENT ATHENS Three Days

Antiquities and ancient sites fill your days and nights. With only three days, the first two should be spent in **(1) Athens** (p662). Start at the **Acropolis Museum** (p664), which brings together the surviving art treasures unearthed at the namesake site, before hiking up to the **Parthenon** (p663). Continue your promenade down the pedestrian way to the **Ancient Agora** (p664). Don't miss seeing the ruins illuminated at night. The next day, see sites you missed, like the **Roman Agora** (p665), or spend the day studying Greece's ancient cultures at the **National Archaeological Museum** (p665).

On day three, take a tour to **(2) Ancient Delphi** (p675) and feel the potent spirit on the slopes of Mt Parnassos. The ancient Greeks considered this the centre of the world. The oracle sat on a tripod in front of a fume-emitting chasm here to prophesy the future. Follow the **Sacred Way** (p675) uphill to the most impressive ruin, the 20-column **Sanctuary of Athena** (p675). The museum on site is quite the treasure trove – don't skip it.

INLAND PASSAGE Five Days

Landlubbers rejoice: you can enjoy a lot of Greece without ever needing your sea legs. During your two days in **(1) Athens** (p662) experience ancient Plaka, then see the lively side of the modern city by dining out in swank surrounds or listening to traditional music in Psyrri.

From there, head north. If there's time, take a detour to the ancient temples at **(2) Delphi** (p675). Otherwise, continue on to **(3) Meteora** (p676). Use **Kastraki** (p676) as your base for exploring the rock-top monasteries and interesting geological formations. Take a bus up to the top and work your way back down or walk the ancient paths; you can usually visit at least four of the religious communities in a day.

Spend the last night and day indulging in the fine food, sinful sweets and chic shopping of **(4) Thessaloniki** (p677). The ancient walls and Byzantine churches form a perfect backdrop for the cafe-lined waterfront.

THREE-ISLAND TOUR One Week

Spend seven days cruising through harbour towns and along watery ways (but make sure you keep in mind that seafaring schedules change frequently and most ferries run primarily in summer). From **(1) Piraeus** (p672), the closest port to Athens, it's a seven-hour sojourn to **(2) Iraklio** (p684) on Crete. The largest city is a good base for exploring the Minoan site at **Knossos** (p685), but smaller

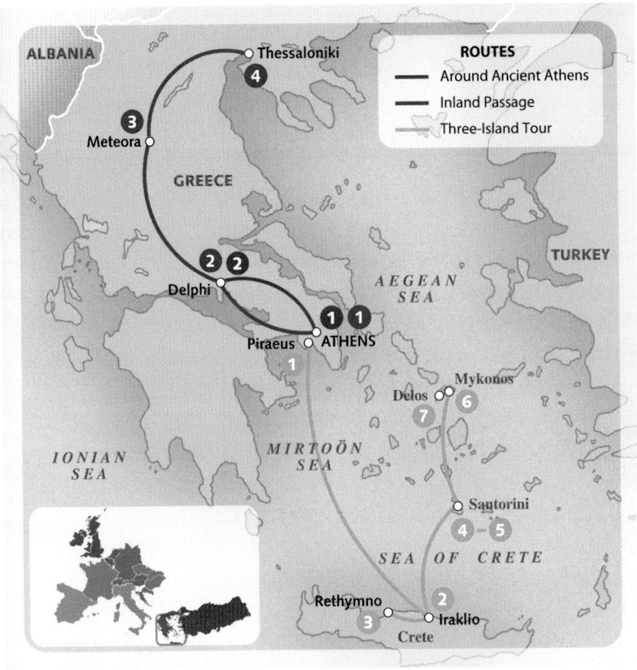

(3) Rethymno (p685), with its ancient Venetian harbour, is an even more atmospheric place to stay.

From Iraklio, head to Santorini – a mere 4½ hours by ferry. The multitude of fellow admirers won't diminish the impact of the views from the volcanic caldera overlooking the cliff town of (4) Fira (p681). Make sure to day-trip to the village of (5) Oia (p682). The stunning architecture here gets longer sunsets and fewer tourists than the larger town.

Time it right to catch one of the two-weekly, six-hour ferries to (6) Mykonos Town (p679). Small boats depart for the best sunny southern beaches; with names like Paradise and Super Paradise, how can you go wrong? Save a day for an excursion to the sacred island of (7) Delos (p681). The birthplace of Apollo has ancient temples and excellent hiking, but no overnighting is allowed.

DISCOVER GREECE ΕΛΛΑΔΑ

There is something mystical and magical about Greece that makes it one of the most popular destinations on the planet. Within easy reach of magnificent archaeological sites are breathtaking beaches and relaxed tavernas serving everything from octopus to ouzo. It's a combination that makes for guilt-free travel – throw in welcoming locals with an enticing culture and captivating music, and it's easy to see why most visitors head home vowing to come back.

Adrenalin-focussed travellers can mountain climb, hike, windsurf, dive and even hit the ski slopes. Party types can enjoy pulsating nightlife in Greece's vibrant modern cities and on islands such as Mykonos and Santorini. Wanderers can just island-hop to their heart's content. No matter what you are there for, however, you cannot go far without stumbling across a broken column, a crumbling bastion or a tiny Byzantine church, some neglected and forgotten but all retaining an aura of their former glory.

ATHENS ΑΘΗΝΑ

pop 3.7 million

Stroll around a corner in Athens and you'll come face-to-face with breathtaking archaeological treasures, evocations of classical mythology and reminders of the city's enormous historical influence on all of Western civilisation. With the makeover that accompanied the 2004 Olympics, Athens also presented its cosmopolitan, chic side on the world stage. Though the city still suffers from traffic congestion, pollution and urban sprawl, take the time to look beneath her skin and you'll discover a complex metropolis full of vibrant subcultures – a city of contradictions, sometimes as frustrating as it is seductive. Couture-clad fashionistas ply the streets alongside leather-bedecked punks. Elegant Michelin-star restaurants abut traditional family tavernas, funky new cafes sit beside neighbourhood *ouzeria,* and *rembetika* is performed at one bar while a DJ spins some trance at the club across the street.

ORIENTATION

Athens is a sprawling city but most sights are within a manageable distance. Syntagmatos Sq, or Syntagma (*syn*-tag-ma), is the city's heart. Surrounded by luxury hotels, banks and travel offices, it's dominated by the Greek parliament building. Omonia Sq (Plateia Omonias) lies to the north of Syntagma; Gazi, Psyrri and Monastiraki Sq (Plateia Monastirakiou) are to its west and Kolonaki is at its east. Plaka, a charming old neighbourhood of labyrinthine streets (now inundated with souvenir shops and tavernas) nestles on the northeastern slope of the Acropolis, with most ancient sites nearby.

INFORMATION

Athens Central Police Station (Map pp666-7; ☎ 210 770 5711/17; Leoforos Alexandras 173, Ambelokipi; Ⓜ Ambelokipi) With a branch at Syntagma Sq (☎ 210 725 7000).

Athens Central Post Office (Map pp666-7; Eolou 100, Omonia; 🕑 7.30am-8pm Mon-Fri, to 2pm Sat; Ⓜ Omonia)

Eurochange Omonia (Map pp666-7; ☎ 210 552 0314; Omonia Sq; ⏰ 9am-9pm; Ⓜ Omonia); Syntagma (Map p670; ☎ 210 331 2462; Karageorgi Servias 2; ⏰ 8am-9pm; Ⓜ Syntagma)

Greek National Tourist Organisation/ EOT Syntagma (Map p670; ☎ 210 331 0392; Amalias 26; ⏰ 9am-7pm Mon-Fri, 10am-6pm Sat & Sun; Ⓜ Syntagma); airport (☎ 210 353 0445; arrivals hall; ⏰ 9am-7pm Mon-Fri, 10am-4pm Sat & Sun); head office (Map pp666-7; ☎ 210 870 7000; www.gnto.gr; Tsoha 7; ⏰ 9am-2pm Mon-Fri; Ⓜ Ambelokipi)

Tourist police (☎ 171; ⏰ 24hr) General tourist info and emergency help.

DANGERS & ANNOYANCES

Like any big city, Athens has its hot spots. Omonia is home to pickpockets, prostitutes and drug dealers. Women should avoid walking alone here at night. Also watch for pickpockets on the metro and at the Sunday market.

When taking taxis, establish whether the driver's going to use the meter or negotiate a price in advance.

Bar scams are commonplace, particularly in Plaka and Syntagma. Women appear, more drinks are served and the crunch comes at the end of the night when traveller is hit with an exorbitant bill.

KRZYSZTOF DYDYNSKI

Detail of Doric columns in the Parthenon

THE PARTHENON

The Parthenon epitomises the glory of ancient Greece. Completed in 438 BC, it's unsurpassed in grace and harmony. To achieve the appearance of perfect form, columns become narrower towards the top and the bases curve upward slightly towards the ends – effects that make them look straight. The Parthenon was built to house the great statue of Athena commissioned by Pericles, and to serve as the new treasury. In AD 426 the gold-plated 12m-high statue was taken to Constantinople, where it disappeared. The best surviving artefacts are the controversial Elgin Marbles, carted off to Britain by Lord Elgin in 1801.

SIGHTS

ACROPOLIS

Arguably the most important ancient monument in the Western world, the **Acropolis** (Map p670; ☎ 210 321 0219; sites & museum adult/concession €12/6; ⏰ 8am-7pm Apr-Oct, to 5.30pm Nov-Mar; Ⓜ Akropoli) attracts multitudes of tourists, so visit in the early morning or late afternoon.

The site was inhabited in Neolithic times and the first temples were built during the Mycenaean era in homage to the goddess Athena. Enter near the **Beule Gate**, a Roman arch added in the 3rd century AD. Beyond this lies the **Propylaea**, the enormous columned gate that was the city's entrance in ancient times. Damaged in the 17th century when lightning set off a Turkish gunpowder store, it's since been restored. South of the Propylaea, the small, graceful **Temple of Athena Nike** was recently restored.

To the north lies the **Erechtheion** and its much-photographed Caryatids, the six maidens who support its southern portico. These are plaster casts – the originals

GEORGE TSAFOS

National Archaeological Museum

ATHENS IN TWO DAYS

Walk the morning streets of the charming Plaka district to reach the **Acropolis** (p663) and **Agora** (below) before the crowds. Dig in to *mezedes* before spending the afternoon at the **National Archaeological Museum** (opposite). Enjoy Parthenon views and haute cuisine with dinner at **Varoulko** (p669).

On the second day, visit the wonderful **Benaki Museum** (opposite) or **Museum of Cycladic Art** (opposite).

(except for the one taken by Lord Elgin) are in the new, superb **Acropolis Museum** (**Map pp666-7; ☎ 210 321 0219; Makrigianni 2-4; 8am-7pm Apr-Oct, to 5pm Nov-Mar; M Akropoli**), designed by renowned architect Bernard Tschumi, on the southern base of the hill.

SOUTH OF THE ACROPOLIS

The importance of theatre in the everyday lives of Athenians is evident from the dimensions of the enormous **Theatre of Dionysos** (**Map p670; ☎ 210 322 4625; 8am-7pm Apr-Oct, to 5.30pm Nov-Mar; M Akropoli**); enter via Dionysiou Areopagitou and Thrasillou Sts. Built between 340 BC and 330 BC on the site of an earlier theatre dating to the 6th century BC, it held 17,000 people. The **Stoa of Eumenes** (Map p670), built as a shelter and promenade for theatre audiences, runs west to the **Theatre of Herodes Atticus** (Map p670), built in Roman times (open only for performances).

ANCIENT AGORA

The **Ancient Agora** (**Map p670; ☎ 210 321 0185; Adrianou 24; adult/concession €4/2; 8am-6.30pm Apr-Oct, to 5pm Nov-Mar; M Monastiraki**) was the marketplace of early Athens and the focal point of civic and social life. Socrates spent time here expounding his philosophy. The main monuments of the Agora are the well-preserved **Temple of Hephaestus** (Map pp666-7), the 11th-century **Church of the Holy Apostles** (Map p670) and the reconstructed **Stoa of Attalos** (Map p670), which houses the site's excellent museum.

ROMAN AGORA

The Romans built their **agora** (Map p670; ☎ 210 324 5220; cnr Pelopida Eolou & Markou Aureliou; adult/concession €2/1; ⏲ 8am-7pm Apr-Oct, to 5pm Nov-Mar; Ⓜ Monastiraki) just east of the ancient Athenian Agora. The wonderful **Tower of the Winds** was built in the 1st century BC by a Syrian astronomer, Andronicus. Each side represents a point of the compass and has a relief carving depicting the associated wind.

TEMPLE OF OLYMPIAN ZEUS & PANATHENAIC STADIUM

Begun in the 6th century BC, Greece's largest **temple** (Map pp666-7; ☎ 210 922 6330; adult/concession €2/1; ⏲ 8am-7pm Apr-Oct, to 5pm Nov-Mar; Ⓜ Akropoli), behind **Hadrian's Arch** (Map p670), took more than 700 years to build, with Emperor Hadrian overseeing its completion in AD 131. It's impressive for the sheer size of its Corinthian columns – 17m high with a base diameter of 1.7m. East of the temple, the **Panathenaic Stadium** (Map pp666-7), built in the 4th century BC as a venue for the Panathenaic athletic contests, hosted the first modern Olympic Games in 1896.

NATIONAL ARCHAEOLOGICAL MUSEUM

One of the world's great museums, the **National Archaeological Museum** (Map pp666-7; ☎ 210 821 7717; www.culture.gr; Patission 44; adult/concession €7/3; ⏲ 1-7.30pm Mon, 8am-7.30pm Tue-Sun Apr-Oct, 1-7.30pm Mon, 8.30am-3pm Tue-Sun Nov-Mar; Ⓜ Viktoria) contains significant finds from major archaeological sites throughout Greece. The vast collections include exquisite gold artefacts from Mycenae, spectacular Minoan frescoes from Santorini and intricate Cycladic figurines.

BENAKI MUSEUM

This superb **museum** (Map pp666-7; ☎ 210 367 1000; www.benaki.gr; cnr Leof Vasilissis Sofias & Koumbari 1, Kolonaki; adult/concession €6/3; ⏲ 9am-5pm Mon, Wed, Fri & Sat, to midnight Thu, to 3pm Sun; Ⓜ Syntagma) houses the extravagant collection of Antoine Benaki, the son of an Alexandrian cotton magnate. The splendid displays include ancient sculpture, Persian, Byzantine and Coptic objects, Chinese ceramics, icons, El Greco paintings and fabulous traditional costumes.

GOULANDRIS MUSEUM OF CYCLADIC & ANCIENT GREEK ART

This wonderful private **museum** (Map pp666-7; ☎ 210 722 8321; www.cycladic-m.gr; Neofytou Douka 4, Kolonaki; adult/concession €5/2.50; ⏲ 10am-4pm Mon & Wed-Fri, to 3pm Sat; Ⓜ Evangelismos) was custom-built to display its extraordinary collection of Cycladic art, with an emphasis on the early Bronze Age. It's easy to see how the graceful marble statues influenced the art of Modigliani and Picasso.

FESTIVALS & EVENTS

The annual **Hellenic Festival** (www.greekfestival.gr; ☎ 210 928 2900), the city's most important cultural event, runs from mid-June to August. International music, dance and theatre go on at venues across the city.

SLEEPING

Popular Plaka is close to the sights. Book well ahead for July and August.

Hotel Acropolis House (Map p670; ☎ 210 322 2344; hotel@acropolishouse.gr; Kodrou 6-8, Plaka; d with shared bathroom €65, s/d/tr with private bathroom & incl breakfast from €50/78/113; Ⓜ Syntagma; ❄) This well-situated hotel in a 19th-century house feels more pension

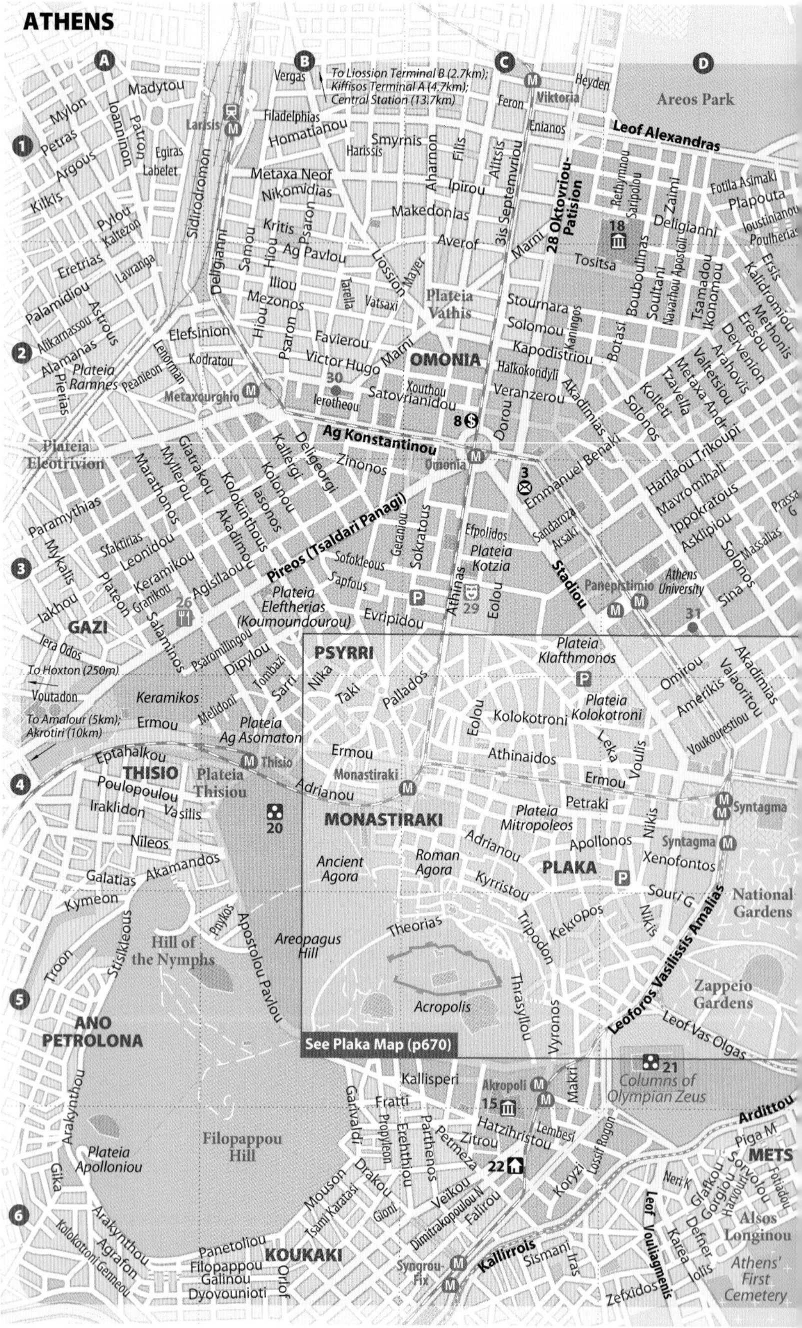
ATHENS
A
B
C
D
1
2
3
4
5
6
To Liossion Terminal B (2.7km); Kiffisos Terminal A (4.7km); Central Station (13.7km)
Vergas
Viktoria
Heyden
Areos Park
Feron
Madytou
Mylon
Petras
Ioanninon
Patron
Egiras
Labelet
Larisis
Filadelphias
Homatianou
Smyrnis
Harissis
Aharnon
Filis
Alitsis
3is Septemvriou
Enianos
Leof Alexandras
Argous
Kilkis
Sidirodromon
Metaxa Neof
Nikomidias
Ipirou
28 Oktovriou-Patision
Rethymnou
Saripolou
Zaimi
Fotila Asimaki
Plapouta
Ioustinianou
Poulherias
Pylou
Kaltezon
Kritis
Psaron
Samou
Hiou
Ag Pavlou
Makedonias
Averof
Marni
18
Deligianni
Eretrias
Lavranga
Deligianni
Tosítsa
Bouboulinas
Navarhou Apostoli
Soultani
Tsamadou
Ikonomou
Kalidromiou
Ersis
Palamidiou
Astrous
Iliou
Mezonos
Tarella
Vatsavi
Liossion
Mayer
Plateia Vathis
Stournara
Solomou
Kaningos
Botasi
Eresou
Methonis
Alikarnassou
Alamanas
Elefsinion
Lenorman
Kodratou
Plateia Ramnes
Pierias
Peanieon
Hiou
Psaron
Favierou
Victor Hugo
Marni
OMONIA
Kapodistriou
Halkokondyli
Derveniou
Arahovis
Metaxourghio
30
Ierotheou
Satovrianidou
Xouthou
Veranzerou
Akadimias
Valtetsiou
Metaxa Andr
Tzavella
Kolleti
Solonos
8
Dorou
Ag Konstantinou
Plateia Eleotrivion
Giatrakou
Myllerou
Marathonos
Kallergi
Deligeorgi
Zinonos
Omonia
3
Emmanuel Benaki
Harilaou Trikoupi
Mavromihali
Ippokratous
Kolokinthous
Iasonos
Kolonou
Akadimou
Pireos (Tsaldari Panagi)
Geraniou
Sokratous
Efpolidou
Plateia Kotzia
Sandaroza
Arsaki
Asklipiou
Prassa
Massalias
Paramythias
Mykalis
Sfaktirias
Leonidou
Keramikou
Granikou
Agisilaou
Sofokleous
Sapfous
Athinas
Eolou
29
Stadiou
Panepistimio
Athens University
Solonos
Sina
Iakhou
Plateon
Salaminos
26
Plateia Eleftherias (Koumoundourou)
Evripidou
31
GAZI
Iera Odos
Psaromilingou
Dipylou
Tombazi
PSYRRI
Plateia Klafthmonos
Akadimias
To Hoxton (250m)
Voutadon
Keramikos
Melidoni
Sarri
Nika
Taki
Palladou
Eolou
Kolokotroni
Plateia Kolokotroni
Omirou
Amerikis
Valaoritou
Voukourestiou
To Amalour (5km); Akrotiri (10km)
Ermou
Plateia Ag Asomaton
Leka
Voulis
Eptahalkou
Thisio
Ermou
Athinaidos
Ermou
THISIO
Plateia Thisiou
Monastiraki
Adrianou
Petraki
Syntagma
Poulopoulou
Iraklidon
Vasilis
20
MONASTIRAKI
Plateia Mitropoleos
Nikis
Apollonos
Syntagma
Nileos
Adrianou
Xenofontos
Galatias
Akamandos
Ancient Agora
Roman Agora
PLAKA
Kyrristou
Souri G
National Gardens
Kymeon
Pnykos
Apostolou Pavlou
Areopagus Hill
Theorias
Tripodon
Kekropos
Nikis
Leoforos Vasilissis Amalias
Hill of the Nymphs
Troon
Stisikleous
Acropolis
Thrasyllou
Vyronos
Zappeio Gardens
ANO PETROLONA
See Plaka Map (p670)
Leof Vas Olgas
21
Kallisperi
Makri
Akropoli
Columns of Olympian Zeus
Arakynthou
Fratti
Garivaldi
15
Arditou
Propyleon
Erehthiou
Parthenos
Petmeza
Hatzihristou
Zitrou
Lembesi
Iossif Rogon
Piga M
METS
Plateia Apolloniou
Filopappou Hill
22
Gika
Mouson
Drakou
Veikou
Koryzi
Leof Vouliagmenis
Neri K
Sorvolou
Fotiadou
Harvouri
Gorgiou
Glafkou
Tsami Karatasi
Gioni
Dimitrakopoulou N
Falirou
Alsos Longinou
Arakynthou
Agrafon
Kolokotroni Genneou
Panetoliou
Filopappou
Galinou
Dyovouniotí
KOUKAKI
Orlof
Syngrou-Fix
Kallirrois
Sismani
Iras
Karea
Defner
Iolis
Zefxidos
Athens' First Cemetery

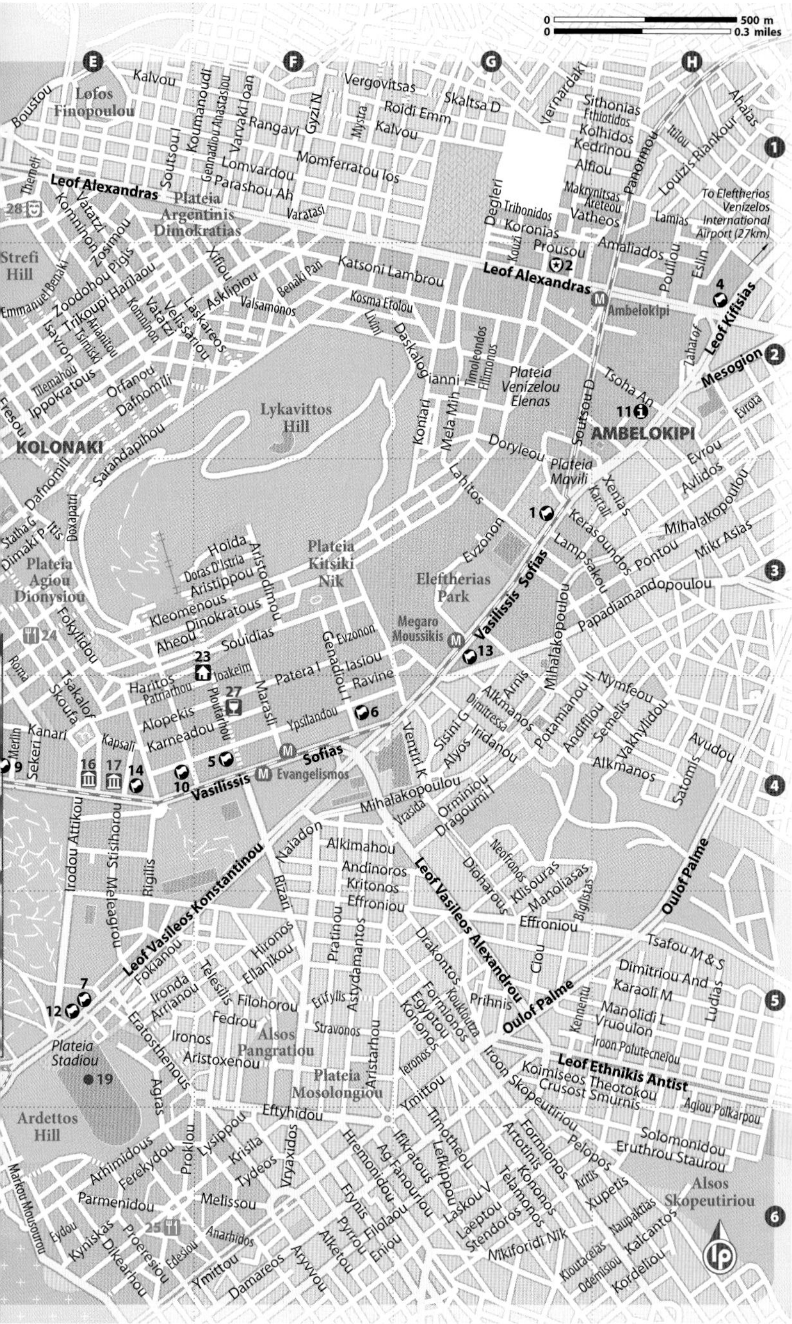
0 500 m
0 0.3 miles
E
F
G
H
1
2
3
4
5
6
Lofos Finopoulou
Strefi Hill
Plateia Argentinis Dimokratias
Leof Alexandras
Lykavittos Hill
KOLONAKI
Plateia Agiou Dionysiou
Plateia Kitsiki Nik
Eleftherias Park
Megaro Moussikis
Plateia Venizelou Elenas
AMBELOKIPI
Ambelokipi
Plateia Mavili
To Eleftherios Venizelos International Airport (27km)
Leof Kifisias
Mesogion
Vasilissis Sofias
Evangelismos
Leof Vasileos Konstantinou
Leof Vasileos Alexandrou
Oulof Palme
Leof Ethnikis Antist
Plateia Stadiou
Ardettos Hill
Alsos Pangratiou
Plateia Mosolongiou
Alsos Skopeutiriou
Kalvou
Boustou
Koumanoudi
Gennadiou Anastasiou
Varvaki Ioan
Soutsou I
Rangavi
Gyzi N
Vergovitsas
Skaltsa D
Roidi Emm
Mystra
Momferratou Ios
Lomvardou
Parashou Ah
Varatasi
Themeli
Vatatzi
Komninon
Zosimou
Zoodohou Pigis
Emmanuel Benaki
Trikoupi Harilaou
Xifiou
Asklipiou
Benaki Pan
Katsoni Lambrou
Kosma Etolou
Valsamonos
Laskareos
Velissariou
Isavron
Tsimiski
Ariantou
Tilemahou
Ippokratous
Orfanou
Dafnomili
Fresou
Sarandapihou
Doxapatri
Dimaki P
Itis
Fokylidou
Roma
Tsakalof
Skoufa
Kanari
Merlin
Sekeri
Kapsali
Hoida
Doras D'Istria
Aristippou
Aristodimou
Kleomenous
Dinokratous
Aheou
Souidias
Haritos
Patriarhou
Ioakeim
Ploutarhou
Alopekis
Karneadou
Marasli
Patera I
Genadiou I
Evzonon
Iasiou
Ravine
Ypsilandou
Sofias
Daskalogianni
Timoleondos Filimonos
Koniari
Mela Mih
Lahitos
Doryleou
Evzonon
Vernardaki
Sithonias
Fthiotidos
Kolhidos
Kedrinou
Alfiou
Panormou
Makrynitsas
Areteou
Vatheos
Degleri
Trihonidos
Koronias
Kouzi
Prousou
Amaliados
Itilou
Louizis Riankour
Ahaias
Lamias
Pouliou
Eslin
Zaharof
Soutsou D
Tsoha An
Evrota
Evrou
Avlidos
Xenias
Karrali
Kerasoundos
Lampsakou
Mihalakopoulou
Mikr Asias
Pontou
Papadiamandopoulou
Nymfeou
Potamianou II
Andifilou
Semelis
Vakhylidou
Avudou
Alkmanos
Satomis
Arnis
Alkmanos
Dimitressa
Iridanou
Sisini G
Alyos
Ventiri K
Mihalakopoulou
Vrasida
Orminiou
Dragoumi I
Irodou Attikou
Stisihorou
Meleagrou
Rigillis
Naiadon
Rizari
Alkimahou
Andinoros
Kritonos
Effroniou
Neofronos
Klisouras
Manoliasas
Biglistas
Dioharous
Effroniou
Ciou
Tsafou M & S
Dimitriou And
Karaoli M
Manolidi L
Vruoulon
Iroon Polutecneiou
Ludias
Kennentu
Prihnis
Koukloutza
Formionos
Egyptou
Kononos
Drakontos
Fokianou
Hironos
Ellanikou
Telesilis
Iironda
Arrianou
Filohorou
Fedrou
Erifylis
Astydamantos
Pratinou
Stravonos
Aristarhou
Ieronos
Ironos
Aristoxenou
Eratosthenous
Agras
Eftyhidou
Ymittou
Iroon Skopeutiriou
Koimiseos Theotokou
Crusost Smurnis
Agiou Polkarpou
Solomonidou
Eruthrou Staurou
Pelopos
Formionos
Artotinis
Kononos
Telamonos
Antis
Xupetis
Naupaktias
Kalcantos
Kordeliou
Odemisiou
Kioutaeias
Nikiforidi Nik
Stendoros
Laeptou
Laskou V
Timotheou
Lefkippou
Ifikratous
Ag Fanouriou
Hremonidou
Filolaou
Eniou
Frynis
Pyrrou
Alketou
Aryvvou
Damareos
Ymittou
Vryaxidos
Tydeos
Krisila
Lysippou
Proklou
Melissou
Anarhidos
Edesiou
Proeresiou
Dikearhou
Kyniskas
Eydou
Markou Mousourou
Parmenidou
Arhimidous
Ferekydou
1
2
4
5
6
7
9
10
11
12
13
14
16
17
19
23
24
25
27
28

Name	No.	Grid
INFORMATION		
Aliens Bureau	(see 2)	
American Embassy	1	G3
Athens Central Police Station	2	G2
Athens Central Post Office	3	C3
Australian Embassy	4	H2
British Embassy	5	F4
Canadian Embassy	6	F4
Dutch Embassy	7	E5
Eurochange	8	C2
French Embassy	9	E4
German Embassy	10	E4
Greek National Tourist Organisation (EOT Head Office)	11	H2
Irish Embassy	12	E5
Japanese Embassy	13	G3
New Zealand Embassy	14	E4
SIGHTS & ACTIVITIES		
Acropolis Museum	15	C5
Benaki Museum	16	E4
Goulandris Museum of Cycladic & Ancient Greek Art	17	E4
National Archaeological Museum	18	D1
Panathenaic Stadium	19	E5
Temple of Hephaestus	20	B4
Temple of Olympian Zeus	21	D5
SLEEPING		
Hera Hotel	22	C6
Periscope	23	F3
EATING		
Entryfish	24	E3
Spondi	25	E6
Varoulko	26	A3
DRINKING		
Mai Tai	27	F4
ENTERTAINMENT		
Decadence	28	E1
Rembetika Stoa Athanaton	29	C3
TRANSPORT		
OSE Office	30	B2
OSE Office	31	D3

than hotel, with a comfy sitting room and hospitable management.

Hotel Adonis (**Map p670; ☎ 210 324 9737; www.hotel-adonis.gr; Kodrou 3, Plaka; s/d/tr incl breakfast from €66/92/120; Ⓜ Syntagma;**) Stroll up the peaceful, pedestrianised street to this immaculate wee hotel. Guests return for the friendly welcome, great location and super Acropolis views from the roof garden.

our pick **Central Athens Hotel** (**Map p670; ☎ 210 323 4357; www.centralhotel.gr; Apollonos 21, Plaka; s/d incl breakfast from €99/121; Ⓜ Syntagma;**) Pass through the sleek, modern lobby and by the attentive staff to spacious white rooms hung with original art and decked out with all the mod cons. Some balconies have Acropolis views, as does the rooftop where you can sunbake and relax in the jacuzzi.

Hera Hotel (**Map pp666-7; ☎ 210 923 6682; www.hera hotel.gr; Falirou 9, Makrigianni; s/d incl breakfast €135/155; Ⓜ Akropoli;**) The interior of this exquisite boutique hotel matches its lovely neoclassical facade. The rooftop garden, restaurant and bar boast spectacular views and it is a short walk to the Acropolis and Plaka.

Periscope (**Map pp666-7; ☎ 210 729 7200; www.peri scope.gr; Haritos 22, Kolonaki; r from €160; Ⓜ Evangelismos;**) A hip hotel with a cool, edgy look (and Mini Cooper seats for chairs in the ground-floor cafe-bar), this place has comfortable minimalis rooms with all the mod cons and a quie location in chic Kolonaki.

Hotel Grande Bretagne (**Map p670 ☎ 210 333 0000; www.grandebretagne.gr; Vasileo Georgiou 1, Syntagma; r/ste from €345/480; Ⓜ Syntagma;**) Dripping with eleganc and old-world charm, the place to stay i Athens has always has been the delux Hotel Grande Bretagne. Built in 1862 to ac commodate visiting heads of state, it rank among the great hotels of the world.

EATING

In addition to the mainstay tavernas Athens has developed a flock of bistros swank eateries, and high-end *mezede* bars. Many popular top restaurants li outside the heavily touristed neighbour hoods but are worth the walk or cab ride Wear your most stylish outfits at night, a Athenians dress up to eat out.

O Platanos (**Map p670; ☎ 210 322 0666 Diogenous 4; mains €7-9; Ⓜ Monastiraki**) Laid back O Platanos (Plane Tree) serve tasty, home-style Greek cuisine. The lam dishes are delicious and we love the leaf courtyard.

Eat (**Map p670; ☎ 210 324 9129; Adrianou 9 mains €8-17; Ⓜ Syntagma**) A sleek alterna tive to the endless traditional tavernas Eat serves interesting salads and pasta and modern interpretations of Gree lassics such as shrimp dolmas with sun-lried tomatoes (€9).

Taverna tou Psarra (Map p670; ☎ 210 321 734; Eretheos 16; mains €8-23; Ⓜ Monastiraki) On path leading up towards the Acropolis, his gem of a taverna is one of Plaka's best, erving scrumptious *mezedes* and excel-ent fish and meat classics on a tree-lined errace.

Café Avyssinia (Map p670; ☎ 210 321 '407; Kynetou 7, Monastiraki; mains €8.50-14.50; Ⓜ Monastiraki) Hidden away on the edge of grungy Plateia Avyssinias in the middle of he Flea Market, this *mezedhopoleio* gets op marks for atmosphere, and the food s not far behind. Often has live music on veekends.

our pick **Entryfish** (Map pp666-7; ☎ 210 361 '666; Skoufa 52, Kolonaki; mezedes €11-20; Ⓜ Syn-agma) Brush shoulders with CEOs at this packed, new, swank seafood salon. Funky newsprint and art glass line the walls, and he *mezedes* all have exquisitely delicate lavours.

Amalour (off Map pp666-7; ☎ 210 933 '710; N Plastira Nikolau 45 cnr Filadelfeias St, Nea Smyrni; mains €11-24) In a beautiful restored mansion in a residential neighbourhood, he warmly modern upstairs dining area serves up delicious Mediterranean cuisine.

DRINKING

Athenians know how to party. To be around locals, head to Psyrri (around Agatharchou St), Gazi (around Voutadon St and the Keramikos metro station) and Kolonaki (around Ploutarhou and Haritos Sts or Skoufa and Omirou Sts) and explore! In summer most of the ac-tion heads to Piraeus, Glyfada and the slands.

Athens' cafes have some of the high-est prices for coffee in Europe, yet if you do what the locals do and sit on a frappé for hours, you can laze the day away. Kolonaki has a mind-boggling array of cafes off Plateia Kolonakiou, on Skoufa and Tsakalof Sts.

our pick **Hoxton** (off Map pp666-7; ☎ 210 341 3395; Voutadon 42, Gazi; Ⓜ Keramikos) Kick back on overstuffed leather couches under modern art in this industrial space that fills up late with bohemians, ruggers and the occasional pop star.

Mai-Tai (Map pp666-7; Ploutarhou 18, Kolonaki; Ⓜ Evange lismos) Jam-packed with well-heeled young Athenians, this is just one in a group of happening spots in the middle of Kolonaki.

ENTERTAINMENT

The *Kathimerini* supplement inside the *International Herald Tribune* contains daily event listings and a cinema guide.

SPLURGE

Competition is fierce for the honor-ary title of Athens' best restaurant. These are the two front-runners at the time of writing:

Varoulko (Map pp666-7; ☎ 210 522 8400; www.varoulko.gr; Pireos 80, Gazi; mains €22-30; closed Sun; Ⓜ Keramikos) For a magical Greek dining experi-ence, you can't beat the winning combination of Acropolis views and delicious seafood by celebrated Greek chef Lefteris Lazarou.

Spondi (Map pp666-7; ☎ 210 756 4021; www.spondi.gr; Pyrronos 5, Pangrati; mains €36-50; 8pm-midnight) Chef Arnaud Bignon has won two Michelin stars creating extravagant seasonal menus using local ingredients. The world-class haute cuisine stays true to French technique but embodies vibrant Greek flavours.

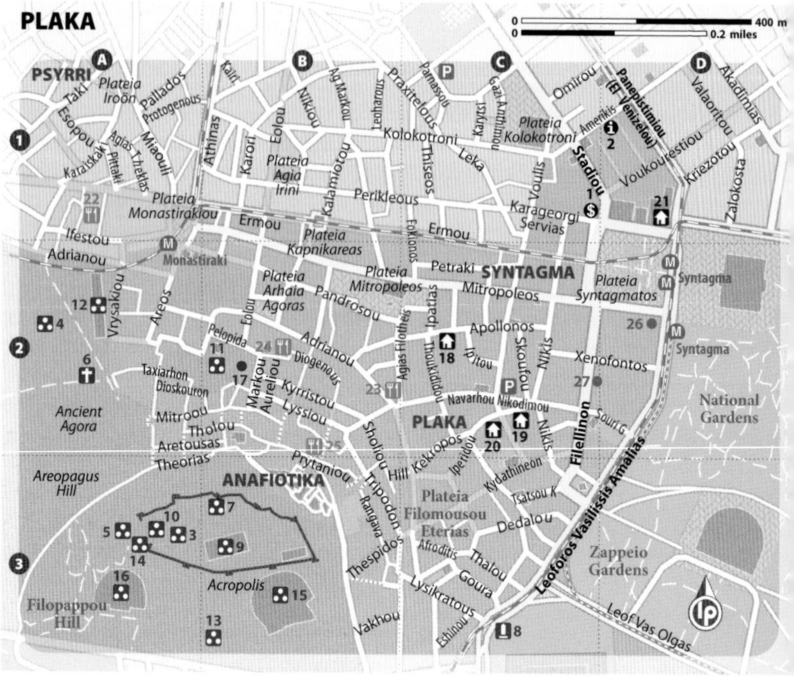

NIGHTCLUBS

Athenians go clubbing after midnight and dress up. Head to beachfront venues in summer.

Decadence **(Map pp666-7; ☎ 210 882 3544; cnr Pouliherias & Voulgaroktonou 69, Lofos Strefi; admission €6-8)** For indie and alternative music lovers, a quieter bar scene occupies the lower floor and a club the upper.

Akrotiri **(off Map pp666-7; ☎ 210 985 9147; Vasileos Georgiou B 5, Agios Kosmas; admission €10; 10pm-5am)** This massive beach club has a capacity for 3000, features bars and lounges over different levels, and hosts great party nights with top DJs.

REMBETIKA

Traditional *rembetika* is hard to catch during the summer months when most of the authentic venues close, but you can see a popularised version at some taverna in Psyrri.

Rembetika Stoa Athanaton **(Ma pp666-7; ☎ 210 321 4362; Sofokleous 19; 3.30 6pm & midnight-late Mon-Sat Oct-May)** Locate above the meat market, this is still *th* place to listen to *rembetika*.

GAY & LESBIAN VENUES

The greatest number of gay bars cluste in Makrigianni, south of the Temple o Olympian Zeus, Exarhia, Psyrri and Gazi Check out www.gay.gr or a copy of th *Greek Gay Guide* booklet at *peripter* (street kiosks).

SHOPPING

Athens is the place to shop for coo jewellery, chic clothes and shoes, a well as souvenirs such as backgammo sets, hand-woven textiles, olive-oil skir products, worry beads and colourful ceramics. You'll find boutiques on Ermou; designer brands and cool shops in Kolonaki; and souvenirs, folk art and leather in Plaka and Monastiraki.

GETTING THERE & AWAY

AIR

Athens is serviced by **Eleftherios Venizelos International airport** (ATH; ☎ 210 353 0000; www.aia.gr) at Spata, 27km east of Athens.

The majority of domestic flights are handled by Greece's much-maligned national carrier, **Olympic Air** (OA; Map p670; ☎ 210 926 4444; www.olympicairlines.com; Filellinon 15, Syntagma). Crete-based **Aegean Airlines** (A3; Map p670; ☎ 210 626 1000; www.aegeanair.com; Othonos 10, Syntagma) offers flights to many of the same destinations. Several European budget carriers, such as **easyJet** (☎ 210 353 0300; www.easyjet.com), **Blue 1** (☎ 210 353 0373; www.blue1.com) and **Vueling** (www.veuling.com) serve Athens.

BUS

Athens has two main intercity **KTEL** (www.ktel.org) bus stations, one 5km and one 7km to the north of Omonia. Timetables are available at EOT offices (see p663).

FERRY

See p696 for information on ferries travelling to and from the islands.

TRAIN

Intercity trains to central and northern Greece depart from the central **Larisis train station** (Map pp666-7), about 1km northwest of Omonia Sq (metro Line 2).

For information or bookings, call or visit an **OSE office** (Omonia Map pp666-7; ☎ 210 524 0647; Karolou 1; 8am-3pm Mon-Fri; Syntagma Map pp666-7; ☎ 210 362 4402; Sina 6; 8am-3.30pm Mon-Fri, 8am-3pm Sat).

For the Peloponnese, take the suburban rail (www.isap.gr) to Kiato and change for other OSE services there, or check for available lines at the Larisis station. A new rail hub is going to be located about 20km north of the city.

GETTING AROUND

The metro system makes getting around central Athens and to Piraeus easy, but Athens' road traffic is still horrendous.

TO/FROM THE AIRPORT

Line 3 of the metro links the airport to the city centre in around 30 minutes.

Taxi fares vary according to the time of day and level of traffic, but you should expect to pay from €25 to €30 to get from the airport to the city centre, and €30 from the airport to Piraeus, depending on traffic. Both trips can take up to an hour.

PUBLIC TRANSPORT

Route numbers and destinations are listed on the free EOT map. Get timetables at

EOT tourist offices or the **Athens Urban Transport Organisation** (OASA; ☎ 210 883 6076; www.oasa.gr).

Special buses to Piraeus operate 24 hours, running every 20 minutes from 6am to midnight, and then hourly until 6am. Bus 040 leaves from the corner of Syntagma and Filellinon, and bus 049 leaves from the Omonia end of Athinas. The metro operates from 5am to midnight. For metro timetables visit www.ametro.gr. Tickets must be validated before travelling.

A fast **suburban rail** (☎ 1110; www.proastiakos.gr; 24hr) connects Athens with the airport, Piraeus, the outer regions and the Peloponnese.

PIRAEUS ΠΕΙΡΑΙΑΣ

pop 175,700

The highlights of Greece's main port and ferry hub, Piraeus, are the otherworldly rows of ferries, ships and hydrofoils filling its seemingly endless quays. It takes around 25 minutes to get here from the centre of Athens by metro (avoid taking a bus or taxi – the streets are even mo[re] clogged than they are in Athens), s[o] there's no reason to stay in shabby Piraeu[s]. However, a trip to tranquil Mikroliman[o] (Small Harbour), with its cafes and fis[h] restaurants, reveals a gentler Piraeus.

The largest of its three harbours is th[e] Megas Limin (Great Harbour) on the wes[t]ern side, from where all the ferries leav[e] along with hydrofoils and catamarans t[o] the Cyclades. Zea Marina (Limin Zeas) an[d] Mikrolimano, on the eastern side of th[e] peninsula, are for private yachts.

If you're killing time in Piraeus, tak[e] Trolleybus 20 to Mikrolimano for a goo[d] harbour-front seafood feed.

GETTING THERE & AWAY

BUS

Two 24-hour bus services operate be[-]tween central Athens and Piraeus. Bu[s] 049 runs from Omonia to the bus sta[-]tion at the Great Harbour, and bus 04[0] runs from Syntagma to the Great Harbou[r] bus station and the tip of the Piraeu[s] peninsula.

GEORGE TSAF

Mikrolimano, Piraeus

FERRY

The following information is a guide to ferry departures between June and mid-September. There are fewer ferries running in April, May and October, and they are radically reduced in winter – especially to smaller islands. The main branch of EOT in Athens (p663) has a reliable schedule, updated weekly. All ferry companies make timetables available online (see p696). When buying your ticket, confirm the departure point. See the Getting There & Away sections for each island for more details.

Crete There are two boats a day to Hania and Iraklio, a daily service to Rethymno.

Cyclades There are daily ferries to Mykonos, Santorini.

Dodecanese There are daily ferries to Rhodes.

Northeastern Aegean Islands Daily ferries to Lesvos (Mytilini).

HYDROFOIL & CATAMARAN

Hellenic Seaways (www.hellenicseaways.gr) operates high-speed hydrofoils and catamarans to the Cyclades from early April to the end of October.

METRO

The fastest and most convenient link between the Great Harbour and Athens is the metro (€0.80, 25 minutes). The station is close to the ferries, at the northern end of Akti Kalimassioti.

THE PELOPONNESE ΠΕΛΟΠΟΝΝΗΣΟΣ

The Peloponnese encompasses a breathtaking array of landscapes, villages and ruins. Home to Olympia, birthplace of the Olympic Games, much of Greek history has played out here.

PATRA ΠΑΤΡΑ

Greece's third-largest city, Patra is the principal ferry port for the Ionian Islands and Italy. Despite its 3000-year history, ancient sites and vibrant social life, few travellers linger longer than necessary. Laid out on a grid stretching uphill from the port to the old *kastro* (castle), Patra is easy to negotiate.

Tourist office (☎ 26104 61741; www.infocenterpatras.gr; Othonos Amalias 6; 8am-10pm) Friendly multilingual staff run easily the best tourist office in Greece, with plentiful info on transport and free stuff to do in town, free bicycles and internet access.

NAFPLIO ΝΑΥΠΛΙΟ

pop 14,500

Elegant Venetian houses and neoclassical mansions dripping with crimson bougainvillea cascade down Nafplio's hillside to the azure sea. Vibrant cafes, shops and restaurants fill winding pedestrian streets. Crenulated Palamidi Fortress perches above it all. What's not to love?

At Syngrou, the English-speaking staff at the **Kasteli Travel & Tourist Agency** (☎ 27520 29395; 38 Vas Konstantinou; 9am-2pm year-round & 6-8pm Jun-Sep) book rooms, rent cars, and sell transport tickets.

The **Municipal tourist office** (☎ 27520 24444; 25 Martiou; 9am-1pm & 4-8pm) is generally unhelpful. A kiosk in Fillenon Sq offers free headsets for walking tours (10am to 1pm and 6pm to 8pm).

Enjoy spectacular views of the town and surrounding coast from the magnificent hilltop **Palamidi Fortress** (☎ 27520 28036; admission €4; 8.30am-6.45pm Jun-Aug, to 2.45pm Sep-May), built by the Venetians between 1711 and 1714. The **Vasilios Papantoniou Museum** (☎ 27520 28379; 1 Vas Alexandrou St; adult/concession €4/2; 9am-2.30pm & 5.30-10.30pm) is one of Greece's best small museums, with its displays of vibrant regional costumes and rotating exhibits. The **Alexandros Soutzos Museum** (Sidiras Merarhias 23; adult/concession €3/1.50, admission free Mon; 10am-3pm & 5-8pm Wed-Mon, 10am-2pm Sun) showcases the 1821 Greek War of Independence in a stunningly restored neoclassical building.

Per capita, Nafplio has some of the most exquisite hotels in Greece. The Old Town is *the* place to stay, with plenty of pensions, but limited budget options.

Pension Marianna (☎ 27520 24256; www.pensionmarianna.gr; Potamianou 9; s/tr incl breakfast €60/100, d incl breakfast €70-85; P) Up a steep set of stairs, and tucked under the fortress walls, a dizzying array of rooms intermix with sea-view terraces.

Hotel Grande Bretagne (☎ 27520 96200; www.grandebretagne.com.gr; Filellinon Sq; s/d incl breakfast €120/170) In the heart of Nafplio's cafe action and overlooking the sea, this splendidly restored hotel with high ceilings, antiques and chandeliers radiates plush opulence.

Nafplio's Old Town streets are loaded with restaurants; the tavernas on Staïkopoulou and those overlooking the port on Bouboulinas get jam-packed on weekends.

Nafplio shopping is a delight, with jewellery workshops, boutiques and wonderful regional products, such as honey, wine and handicrafts.

The **KTEL Argolis bus station** (☎ 27520 27323; Syngrou 8) has hourly buses to Athens (€11.30, 2½ hours) via Corinth. Buses go to Argos (for Peloponnese connections), Mycenae and Epidavros; these cost about €2.50 and take 30 to 45 minutes.

OLYMPIA ΟΛΥΜΠΙΑ

pop 1000

Tucked along the Klados River, in fertile delta country, the modern town of Olympia supports the extensive ruins of the same name. The first Olympics wer staged here in 776 BC, and every four yea thereafter until AD 394 when Emper Theodosius I banned them. During th competition the city-states were boun by a sacred truce to stop fighting an take part in athletic events and cultur exhibitions.

The folks at the **Olympia Municipa Tourist Office** (☎ 26240 23100; Praxitelou Kondyli) don't speak much English but hav transport schedules.

Ancient Olympia (☎ 26240 22517; adul concession €6/3, site & museum €9/5; 8am-7p May-Oct, to 5pm Nov-Apr) is dominated b the immense ruined **Temple of Zeus**, t whom the games were dedicated. Don miss the statue of **Hermes of Praxiteles** a classical sculpture masterpiece, at th exceptional **museum** (adult/concession €6/ 10.30am-7pm Mon, 8am-7pm Tue-Sun May-Oc to 5pm Nov-Apr).

Family-run **Best Western Europ** (☎ 26240 22650/23850; www.hoteleuropa.g Drouva 1; s/d €90/130; P) perche on a hill above town and has gorgeou sweeping vistas from rooms' balconie and the wonderful swimming poo Tucked beneath the trees, **Taverna Gefsi Melathron** (☎ 26240 22916; George Douma mains €5-8) is by far the best place to ea delicious traditional cuisine, includin scrumptious vegetarian options, such a fried baby zucchini balls.

Trains run daily to Pyrgos (€0.70, 3 minutes) where you can switch for Athen and Patra.

CENTRAL GREECE ΚΕΝΤΡΙΚΗ ΕΛΛΑΔΑ

This dramatic landscape of deep gorge rugged mountains and fertile valley is home to the magical stone pinnacle topping monasteries of Meteora an the iconic ruins of ancient Delphi, wher

\lexander the Great sought advice from he Delphic Oracle.

)ELPHI ΔΕΛΦΟΙ

op 2800

Лodern Delphi and its adjoining ruins ıang stunningly on the slopes of Mt 'arnassos overlooking the shimmering Gulf of Corinth.

The bus station, post office, OTE, banks ınd **EOT** (☎ 22650 82900; Vasileon Pavlou 44; 7.30am-2.30pm Mon-Fri) are all on modern)elphi's main street, Vasileon Pavlou.

The ancient Greeks regarded Delphi ıs the centre of the world. According o mythology, Zeus released two eagles ıt opposite ends of the world and they net here. By the 6th century BC, **ancient)elphi** (☎ 22650 82312; site or museum €6 year-ound, combined adult/concession €9/5 year-round, ree Sun Nov-Mar; site 7.30am-7.30pm Apr-Oct, am-5pm Nov-Mar, museum 7.30am-7.30pm daily pr-Oct, 8.30am-6.45pm Mon-Fri, 8.30am-3pm Sat, un & public holidays Nov-Mar) had become the ianctuary of Apollo. Thousands of pilgrims flocked here to consult the female oracle, who sat at the mouth of a fume-emitting chasm. After sacrificing a sheep or goat, pilgrims would ask a question, and a priest would translate the oracle's response into verse. From the entrance, take the **Sacred Way** up to the **Temple of Apollo**, where the oracle sat. From here the path continues to the **theatre** and **stadium**.

Opposite the main site and down the hill some 100m, don't miss the **Sanctuary of Athena** and the much-photographed **Tholos** – a 4th-century-BC columned rotunda of Pentelic marble.

In the town centre, the welcoming **Hotel Hermes** (☎ 22650 82318; Vasileon Pavlou-Friderikis 27; s/d incl breakfast €55/70;) has spacious rooms sporting balconies with stunning valley views.

Locals pack **Taverna Gargadouas** (☎ 22650 82488; Vasileon Pavlou & Friderikis; mains €4-7) for grilled meats and slow-roasted lamb (*provatina;* €6.50).

Six buses a day go from the **bus station** (☎ 22660 82317) on the main road to Athens (€13, three hours). Take a bus to

ANTHONY PIDGEON

Views of ancient Delphi from the top of the theatre

LEFT: PAOLO CORDELLI; RIGHT: MARK DAFFI

Left: Monks' skulls, Megalou Meteorou; Right: Kastraki

Lamia (€7.80, two hours, two to three per day) or Trikala (€13.80, 4½ hours, two per day) to transfer for Meteora.

METEORA ΜΕΤΕΩΡΑ

Meteora (meh-*teh*-o-rah) should be a certified Wonder of the World, with its magnificent late-14th-century monasteries perched dramatically atop enormous rocky pinnacles. Try not to miss it. Meteora's stunning rocks are also a climbing mecca.

While there were once monasteries on all 24 pinnacles, only six are still occupied: **Megalou Meteorou** (Grand Meteoron; 9am-5pm Wed-Mon), **Varlaam** (9am-2pm & 3.20-5pm Fri-Wed), **Agiou Stefanou** (9am-2pm & 3.30-6pm Tue-Sun), **Agias Triados** (Holy Trinity; 9am-12.30pm & 3-5pm Fri-Wed), **Agiou Nikolaou Anapafsa** (9am-3.30pm Sat-Thu) and **Agias Varvaras Rousanou** (9am-6pm). Admission is €2 for each monastery and strict dress codes apply (no bare shoulders or knees and women must wear skirts; borrow a long skirt at the door if you don't have one). Walk the footpaths between monasteries or drive the bac road.

The tranquil village of **Kastraki**, 2km from Kalambaka, is the best base for visiting Meteora.

our pick **Doupiani House** (☎ 2432 75326; doupi ani-house@kmp.forthnet.gr; s/d/t €30/45/55) Around 500m from the town square, gregarious hosts Thanassis and Toula Nakis offer this comfy home from which to explore or simply sit and enjoy the panoramic views. Ask for a room with a balcony, and reconfirm your booking.

Taverna Gardenia (Kastrakiou St; main €3-8) You'll find the freshest Greek food served with aplomb here; the splendid views of Meteora and fragrant scent of gardenias are a bonus. The owners also have good-value and spacious rooms (some with views) at Plakjas (☎ 2432 22504; single/double/triple €30/40/50) behind the restaurant.

Local buses shuttle between Kalambaka and Kastraki (€1.90), two of which go to Moni Megalou Meteoron. From Kalambaka, there are also express train

› Athens (€20, five hours, two daily) and ›essaloniki (€17, four hours, two daily) a Paliofarsalos.

IORTHERN GREECE ΒΟΡΕΙΑ ΕΛΛΑΔΑ

orthern Greece is stunning, graced as is with magnificent mountains, thick ›rests, tranquil lakes and archaeological tes. Most of all, it's easy to get off the eaten track and experience aspects of reece noticeably different to other mainnd areas and the islands.

HESSALONIKI ΘΕΣΣΑΛΟΝΙΚΗ

›p 800,800

odge cherry sellers in the street, smell ›ices in the air and enjoy waterfront reezes in Thessaloniki (thess-ah-lo-*nee*-h), also known as Salonica (Saloniki). The econd city of Byzantium and of modrn Greece boasts countless Byzantine hurches, a smattering of Roman ruins, ngaging museums, shopping to rival thens, fine restaurants and a lively cafe cene and nightlife.

Tourist information office (☎ 23102 1100; the-info_office@gnto.gr; Tsimiski 136; 8am-2.45pm Mon-Fri, to 2pm Sat)

Tourist police (☎ 23105 54871; 5th fl,)dekanisou 4; 7.30am-11pm)

Check out the seafront **White Tower** ☎ 2310 267 832; Lefkos Pyrgos; adult €2; 8am-›m Tue-Sun, 12.30-7pm Mon) and wander the hurches and *hammams* (Turkish baths) efore stopping in at the award-winning **Iuseum of Byzantine Culture** (☎ 23108 3570; Leoforos Stratou 2; admission €4; 1-30pm Mon, 8am-3pm Tue-Fri), one of Greece's est, with splendid sculptures, mosaics, cons and other intriguing artefacts beaufully displayed. The exquisite finds at the **rchaeological Museum** (☎ 23108 30538; anoli Andronikou 6; admission €4; 8.30am-3pm) include Macedonian gold from Alexander the Great's time.

City Hotel (☎ 23102 69421; www.cityhotel.gr; Komninon 11; s/d incl breakfast €115/135;) Ask for a light-filled front room in this excellently located sleek, stylish hotel.

Electra Palace Hotel (☎ 23102 94011; www.electra hotels.gr; Plateia Aristotelous 9; d €135-220;) Dive into five-star seafront luxury: impeccable service, plush rooms, a rooftop bar, indoor and outdoor swimming pools, and a *hammam*.

Tavernas dot Plateia Athonos, funky bars line Plateia Aristotelous and cafes and bars pack Leof Nikis.

Zythos (☎ 23105 40284; Katouni 5; mains €5-10) Popular with locals, this excellent taverna with two locations and friendly staff serves up delicious traditional Greek food, interesting regional specialities, good wines by the glass and beers on tap.

Krikela's (☎ 23105 01600; Salaminos 6; mains €12-30) The iconic Krikela's offers a superlative, refined dining experience for gastronomes, with dishes ranging from wild game to Cretan snails and other local Greek specialities.

Thessaloniki's **Makedonia airport** (SKG; ☎ 23104 73700) is 16km southeast of the centre. **Olympic Air** (☎ 23103 68666; Navarhou Koundourioti 3) and **Aegean Airlines** (☎ 23102 80050; El Venizelou 2) have several flights a day to Athens. Between them they fly to Lesvos, Corfu, Mykonos, Crete, Rhodes and Santorini.

The **train station** (☎ 23105 17517; Monastiriou) has seven daily express services to Athens (€36, 5½ hours). All international trains from Athens (to Belgrade, Sofia, İstanbul etc) stop at Thessaloniki. Get schedules from the **train ticket office** (OSE; ☎ 23105 98120; Aristotelous 18) or the station.

Karaharisis Travel & Shipping Agency (☎ 23105 24544; fax 23105 32289; Navarhou Koundourioti 8) handles tickets for all ferries and hydrofoils.

From the airport to town, take bus 78 (€0.50, one hour, from 5am to 10pm) or a taxi (€20, 20 minutes).

HALKIDIKI ΧΑΛΚΙΔΙΚΗ

Beautiful pine-covered Halkidiki is a three-pronged peninsula that extends into the Aegean Sea, southeast of Thessaloniki. Splendid, if built-up, sandy beaches rim its 500km of coastline.

MT ATHOS ΑΓΙΟΣ ΟΡΟΣ

Halkidiki's third prong is occupied by the all-male Monastic Republic of Mt Athos (known in Greek as the Holy Mountain), where monasteries full of priceless treasures stand amid an impressive landscape of gorges, wooded mountains and precipitous rocks. While the process for obtaining a four-day visitor permit is becoming easier, only 10 non-Orthodox adult males may enter Mt Athos per day, so the summer waiting list is long. Start by contacting the **Mt Athos Pilgrims' Office** (☎ 23102 52578; fax 23102 22424; pilgrimsbureau@c-lab.gr; Egnatia 109, Thessaloniki; 🕑 9am-2pm Mon-Fri, 10am-noon Sat) to make a booking. You can visit 20 monasteries on foot, but you may only stay one night at each of the monasteries you've booked.

MT OLYMPUS ΟΛΥΜΠΟΣ ΟΡΟΣ

Greece's highest mountain, Mt Olympus, was the ancient home of the gods. The highest of its eight peaks is Mytikas (2917m), popular with trekkers, who use Litohoro (5km inland from the Athens–Thessaloniki highway) as their base. The main route to the top takes two days, with a stay overnight at one of the refuges (open May to October). Good protective clothing is essential, even in summer. you trek outside the official season, yo do so at your own risk. The **EOS offic** (☎ 23520 84544; Plateia Kentriki; 🕑 9.30ar 12.30pm & 6-8pm Mon-Sat, Jun-Sep) has info mation on treks.

CYCLADES ΚΥΚΛΑΔΕΣ

The Cyclades (kih-*klah*-dez) are Gree islands to dream about. Named after th rough *kyklos* (circle) they form around th island of Delos, they are rugged outcrop of rock in the azure Aegean, speckled wit white cubist buildings and blue-dome Byzantine churches. Throw in sun-blaste golden beaches, a dash of hedonism an a fascinating culture, and it's easy to se why many find the Cyclades irresistible

MYKONOS ΜΥΚΟΝΟΣ

pop 9700

Sophisticated Mykonos glitters happi under the Aegean sun, shamelessly su viving on tourism. The island has some thing for everyone, with marvellou beaches, romantic sunsets, chic bou tiques, excellent restaurants and bars, an its long-held reputation as a mecca fo gay travellers. The maze of white-walle streets in Mykonos Town was designed t confuse pirates, and it certainly manage to captivate and confuse the crowds th consume the island's capital in summe

ORIENTATION & INFORMATION

Mykonos Town has two ferry quays. Th old quay, where the smaller ferries an catamarans dock, is 400m north of th town waterfront. The new quay, whe the bigger boats dock, is 2.5km north o town. Buses meet arriving ferries.

The **Tourist Information Offic** (☎ 22890 25250; www.mykonos.gr; 🕑 9am-9p Jul & Aug, 10am-5pm Easter-Jun, Sep & Oct) is a the western end of the waterfront. **Islan**

SHANIA SHEGEDYN

Windmills, Mykonos

Mykonos Travel (☎ 22890 22232; www.discovergreece.org), on Taxi Sq, where the port road meets the town, is helpful for travel information.

SIGHTS & ACTIVITIES

A stroll around **Mykonos Town**, shuffling through snaking streets with blinding white walls and balconies of flowers is a must for any visitor. Don't forget your sunglasses! **Little Venice**, where the sea laps up to the edge of the restaurants and bars, and Mykonos' famous hilltop row of **windmills** should be included in the spots-to-see list. You're bound to run into one of Mykonos' famous resident pelicans on your walk.

The island's most popular beaches are on the southern coast. **Platys Gialos** has wall-to-wall sun lounges, while nudity is not uncommon at **Paradise Beach**, **Super Paradise**, **Agrari** and gay-friendly **Elia**.

SLEEPING

Hotel Apollon (☎ 22890 22223; fax 22890 24237; Paralia, Mykonos Town; s/d with shared bathroom €50/65) Prepare for some old-world Mykonian charm in the middle of the main waterfront. Rooms are traditional and well kept, and the owner is friendly.

Hotel Philippi (☎ 22890 22294; chriko@otenet.gr; 25 Kalogera, Mykonos Town; s €60-90, d €75-120; ❄) In the heart of the *hora*, Philippi has spacious, bright, clean rooms that open onto a railed veranda overlooking a lush garden. An extremely pleasant place to stay.

Hotel Lefteris (☎ 22890 27117; www.lefterishotel.gr; 9 Apollonas, Mykonos Town; s/d €90/115, studios €180-230; ❄) Tucked away just up from Taxi Sq, Lefteris has bright and comfy rooms, and a relaxing sun terrace with superb views over town. A good international meeting place.

EATING & DRINKING

There is no shortage of places to eat and drink in Mykonos Town. If you're on a budget, steer clear of the waterfront and head into the back of the maze that is Mykonos Town, where there are plenty of cheap eats.

MYKONOS

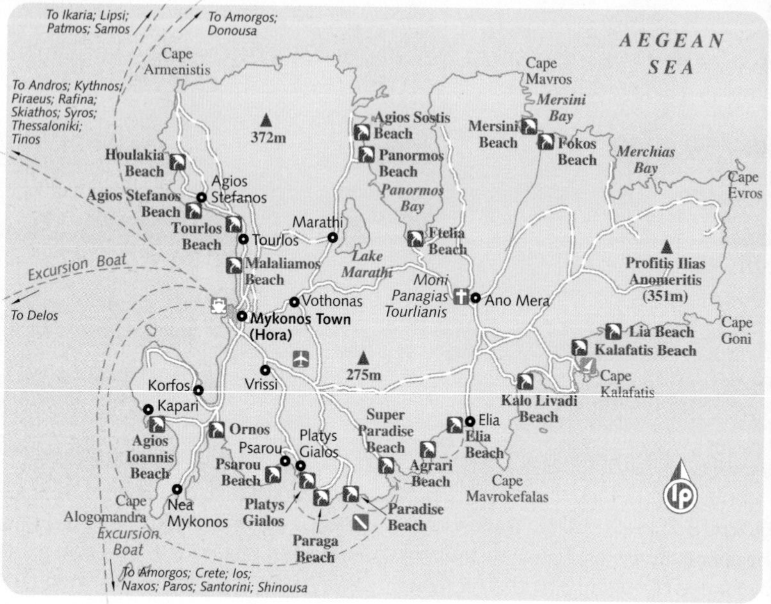

Paraportiani (☎ 22890 23531; mains from €7) Just above the western end of the waterfront, Paraportiani does superb seafood and benefits from having the town's top tout, one of Mykonos' resident pelicans.

Cavo Paradiso (☎ 22890 27205; www.cavoparadiso.gr) For those who want to go the whole hog, this club 300m above Paradise Beach picks up around 2am and boasts a pool the shape of Mykonos. A bus transports clubbers from town in summer.

Long feted as a gay travel destination, Mykonos has plenty of gay-centric clubs and hang-outs. In Little Venice, **Kastro** (☎ 22890 23072; Agion Anargion) is the spot to start the night with cocktails as the sun sets. **Pierro's** (☎ 22890 22177), just near Taxi Sq, is a popular dance club for rounding off the night.

GETTING THERE & AROUND

There are daily flights connecting Mykonos airport (JMK) to Athens (€65), Santorini and Rhodes with varying regularity.

Daily ferries arrive from Piraeus (€25, six hours). From Mykonos, there are daily ferries and hydrofoils to most major Cycladic islands, daily services to Crete, and less-frequent services to the northeastern Aegean Islands and the Dodecanese. Head to Island Mykonos Travel (p678) for details and tickets.

SANTORINI (THIRA) ΣΑΝΤΟΡΙΝΗ (ΘΗΡΑ)

pop 13,500

Stunning Santorini is unique and should not be missed. The startling sight of the submerged caldera almost encircled by sheer lava-layered cliffs – topped off by clifftop towns that look like a dusting of cing sugar – will grab your attention and not let it go. If you turn up in the high eason though, be prepared for relentess crowds and commercialism because Santorini survives on tourism.

ORIENTATION & INFORMATION

Fira, the main town, perches on top of the caldera, with the new port of Athinios, where most ferries dock, 10km south by road. The old port of Fira Skala, used by cruise ships and excursion boats, is directly below Fira and accessed by cable car (adult/child €4/2 one way), donkey (€4, up only) or by foot (588 steps).

The bus station and taxi station are just south of Fira's main square, Plateia Theotokopoulou.

Dakoutros Travel (☎ 22860 22958; www.dakoutrostravel.gr; 8.30am-10pm), opposite the taxi station, is extremely helpful, and there is a batch of other agencies around the square. Check out www.santorini.net for more info.

SIGHTS & ACTIVITIES

The stunning caldera views from Fira are unparalleled.

The exceptional **Museum of Prehistoric Thira** (☎ 22860 23217; admission €3; 8.30am-3pm Tue-Sun), which has wonderful displays of artefacts predominantly from ancient Akrotiri, is two blocks south of the main square. **Megaron Gyzi Museum** (☎ 22860 22244; admission €3.50; 10.30am-1pm & 5-8pm Mon-Sat, 10.30am-4.30pm Sun), behind the Catholic cathedral, houses local memorabilia, including photographs of Fira before and after the 1956 earthquake.

Santorini's black-sand **beaches** of **Perissa** and **Kamari** sizzle – beach mats are essential. It's a strange feeling to walk over black sand then out onto smooth lava when going for a dip.

DELOS ΔΗΛΟΣ

Southwest of Mykonos, the island of **Delos** (☎ 22890 22259; sites & museum €5; 9am-3pm Tue-Sun) is the Cyclades' archaeological jewel. The opportunity to clamber among the ruins shouldn't be missed.

According to mythology, Delos was the birthplace of Apollo – the god of light, poetry, music, healing and prophecy. The island flourished as an important religious and commercial centre from the 3rd millennium BC, reaching its apex of power in the 5th century BC.

Ruins include the **Sanctuary of Apollo**, containing temples dedicated to him, and the **Terrace of the Lions**. These proud beasts were carved in the early 6th century BC using marble from Naxos to guard the sacred area. The original lions are in the island's museum, with replicas on the original site. The **Sacred Lake** (dry since 1926) is where Leto supposedly gave birth to Apollo, while the **Theatre Quarter** is where private houses were built around the **Theatre of Delos**.

The climb up **Mt Kynthos** (113m), the island's highest point, is a highlight. The view of Delos and the surrounding islands is spectacular, and it's easy to see how the Cyclades got their name.

Overnighting on Delos is forbidden. Numerous boat companies offer trips from Mykonos to Delos.

Excavations in 1967 uncovered the remarkably well-preserved Minoan settlement of **Akrotiri** at the south of the island with its remains of two- and three-storey buildings. A section of the roof collapsed in 2005 killing one visitor, and at the time of research the site's future as a visitor attraction was up in the air.

On the north of the island, the flawless village of **Oia** (ee-ah), famed for its postcard sunsets, is less hectic than Fira and a must-visit. Its caldera-facing tavernas are superb spots for brunch. There's a path from Fira to Oia along the top of the caldera that takes three to four hours to walk.

Of the surrounding islets, only **Thirasia** is inhabited. Visitors can clamber around on volcanic lava on **Nea Kameni** then swim into warm springs in the sea at **Palia Kameni**; there are various excursions available to get you there.

SLEEPING

Fira has spectacular views, but is miles from the beaches. Perissa has a great beach but is on the southeast coast, away from the caldera views.

Stelio's Place (☎ 22860 81860; www.steliosplace.com; r €30-80; P ✱ ☒) Stelio's is an excellent option just back from Perissa's black-sand beach on the southeast coast. There's a refreshing pool, very friendly service, and free port and airport transfers. Rates halve out of the high season.

Hotel Keti (☎ 22860 22324; www.hotelketi.gr; Agiou Mina; d/tr €80/105; ✱ ☐) Overlooking the caldera, with views to die for, Hotel Keti has traditional rooms carved into the cliffs. Half of the rooms have jacuzzis.

our pick **Hotel Atlantis** (☎ 22860 22232; www.atlantishotel.gr; s/d incl breakfast €200/284; P ✱ ☐ ☒) Perfectly positioned and

SANTORINI (THIRA)

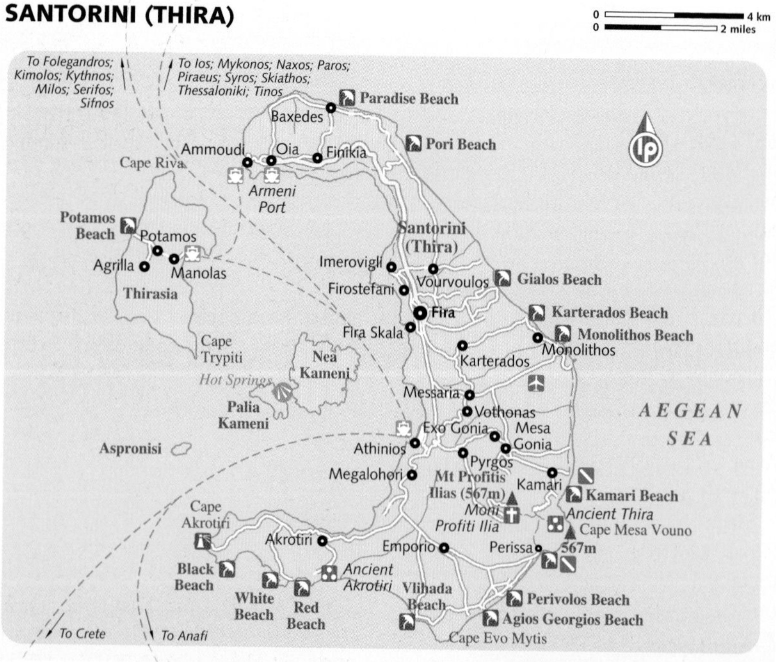

epitomising Santorini style, Atlantis is the oldest and most impressive place in Fira. With bright, airy rooms, relaxing terraces and lounges, it is a superb place to stay.

EATING & DRINKING

Cheap eateries are in abundance around the square in Fira. Great eating and drinking options line the waterfront in Perissa. Most of the more popular bars and clubs are clustered along Erythrou Stavrou.

Taverna Lava (☎ 22860 81776; mains €3-8) On Perissa's waterfront, this islandwide favourite has a mouth-watering menu. You can visit the kitchen and pick what looks good.

Fanari (☎ 22860 25107; www.fanari-restaurant.gr; mains from €5) On the street leading down to the old port, Fanari's serves up both tasty traditional dishes and superlative views.

Nikolas (☎ 22860 24550; Erythrou Stavrou; mains €5-10) This long-established place serving Greek cuisine in the heart of Fira receives rave reviews from diners.

GETTING THERE & AROUND

Santorini airport (JTR) has daily flight connections with Athens (€60). **Sky Express** (SEH; ☎ 28102 23500; www.skyexpress.gr) has connections with Crete, Mykonos and Rhodes with varying regularity.

There are daily ferries (€28, nine hours) and fast boats (€45, 5¼ hours) to Piraeus; daily connections in summer to Mykonos, Ios and Iraklio; and ferries to the smaller islands in the Cyclades. Large ferries use Athinios port, where they are met by buses (€1.20) and taxis.

Buses go frequently to Oia, Kamari, Perissa and Akrotiri from Fira. Port buses usually leave Fira, Kamari and Perissa one to 1½ hours before ferry departures. A rental car or scooter is a great option on Santorini.

ALLAN MONTAINE

Naxos

IF YOU LIKE...

If you like **Mykonos** (p678), we have some other islands in the Cyclades to recommend:

- **Paros** A friendly, attractive laid-back island with an enticing main town, good swimming beaches and terraced hills that build up to Mt Profitis Ilias (770m).
- **Naxos** The biggest and greenest of the Cyclades group, Naxos produces olives, grapes, figs, citrus, corn and potatoes. The island is worth taking the time to explore for its fascinating main town, excellent beaches and striking interior.
- **Ios** This island's long-held reputation as 'Party Island' holds true. There are wall-to-wall bars and nightclubs in 'the village' (Hora) that thump all night, and fantastic fun activities at Milopotas Beach that entertain all day.

CRETE ΚΡΗΤΗ

pop 540,000

Crete is Greece's largest and most southerly island, and its size and distance from the rest of Greece gives it the feel of a different country. The island is split by a spectacular chain of

CRETE

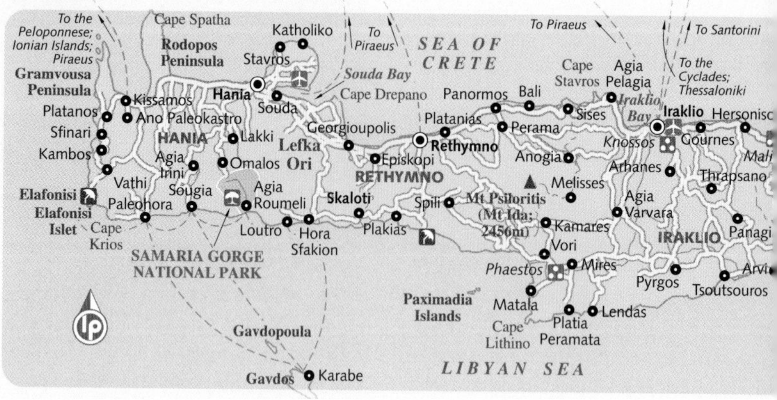

mountains running east to west. Major towns are on the more hospitable northern coast, while most of the southern coast is too precipitous to support large settlements. The rugged, mountainous interior, dotted with caves and sliced by dramatic gorges, offers rigorous hiking and climbing.

While Crete's proud, friendly and hospitable people have enthusiastically embraced tourism, they continue to fiercely protect their traditions and culture – and it is the people that remain a major part of the island's appeal.

Good websites on Crete include www.interkriti.org, www.infocrete.com and www.explorecrete.com.

Crete was the birthplace of Minoan culture, Europe's first advanced civilisation, which flourished between 2800 and 1450 BC. Very little is known of Minoan civilisation, which came to an abrupt end, possibly destroyed by Santorini's volcanic eruption in around 1650 BC.

IRAKLIO ΗΡΑΚΛΕΙΟ

pop 131,000

Iraklio (ee-*rah*-klee-oh; often spelt Heraklion), Crete's capital, is a bustling modern city and the fifth-largest ir Greece. It has a lively city centre, an excellent archaeological museum and i: close to Knossos, Crete's major visito attraction.

The **tourist office** (☎ 28102 46299 **Xanthoudidou 1; 8.30am-8.30pm Apr-Oct, tc 3pm Nov-Mar**) is opposite the archaeological museum. There is good information at www.heraklion-city.gr. **Skoutelis Travel** (**☎ 28102 80808; www.skoutelis.gr; 25 Avgoustou 20**), between Plateia Venizelou and the olc harbour, handles airline and ferry bookings, and rents cars.

Iraklio's **archaeological museum** (**☎ 28102 79000; Xanthoudidou 2; adult/student €6/3; 12.30-7pm Mon, 8am-7pm Tue-Sun**) has an outstanding Minoan collection, second only to the national museum in Athens.

Protecting the old harbour is the impressive **Koules Venetian Fortress** (**☎ 28102 46211; adult/student €2/1; 9am-6pm Tue-Sun**), also known as Rocca al Mare, which, like the city walls, was built by the Venetians in the 16th century.

The **Battle of Crete Museum** (**☎ 28103 46554; cnr Doukos Beaufort & Hatzidaki; admission free; 8am-3pm**) chronicles the historic

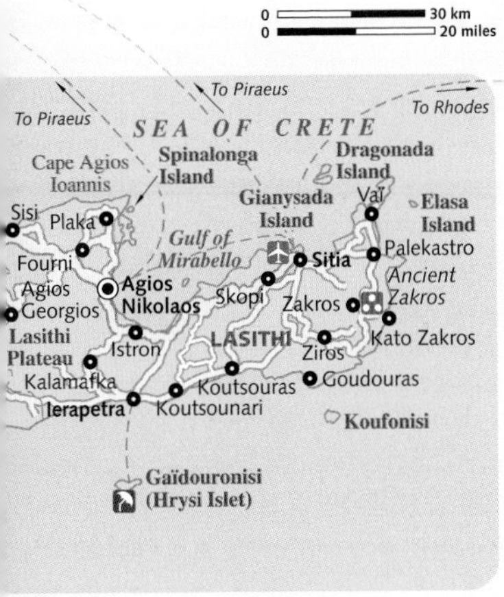

WWII battle with photographs, letters, uniforms and weapons.

Hotel Kronos (☎ 28102 82240; www.kronoshotel.gr; Sofokli Venizelou 2; s/d €49/65;) Down by the old harbour, this well-maintained older hotel has large, airy rooms that come with phone and TV.

our pick **Lato Boutique Hotel** (☎ 28102 28103; www.lato.gr; Epimenidou 15; s/d €100/127;) A top place to stay is this stylish boutique hotel overlooking the waterfront. The contemporary interior design extends to the bar, breakfast restaurant and Brilliant (☎ 28103 34959), the superb fine-dining restaurant on the ground floor.

There's a congregation of cheap eateries in the Plateia Venizelou and El Greco Park area, as well as a bustling, colourful market all the way along 1866.

Giakoumis Taverna (☎ 28102 80277; Theodosaki 5-8; mains €2.50-8; closed Sun) With its full menu of Cretan specialities, Giakoumis is the best of a bunch of cheap tavernas in the market area.

There are many flights daily from Iraklio's Nikos Kazantzakis airport (HER) to Athens (€60) and, in summer, regular flights to Thessaloniki and Rhodes.

Daily ferries service Piraeus (€30, seven hours), and most days boats go to Santorini and continue on to other Cycladic islands.

Bus Station A is just inland from the new harbour and serves eastern Crete. The Hania and Rethymno terminal is opposite Bus Station A.

KNOSSOS ΚΝΩΣΣΟΣ

Five kilometres south of Iraklio, **Knossos** (☎ 28102 31940; admission €6; 8am-7pm Jun-Oct, to 5pm Nov-May) was the capital of Minoan Crete, and is now the island's major tourist attraction.

Knossos (k-nos-*os*) is the most famous of Crete's Minoan sites and is the inspiration for the myth of the Minotaur. According to legend, King Minos of Knossos was given a magnificent white bull to sacrifice to the god Poseidon, but decided to keep it. This enraged Poseidon, who punished the king by causing his wife Pasiphae to fall in love with the animal. The result of this odd union was the Minotaur – half-man and half-bull – who lived in a labyrinth beneath the king's palace, munching on youths and maidens.

In 1900 Arthur Evans uncovered the ruins of Knossos. Although archaeologists tend to disparage Evans' reconstruction, the buildings – incorporating an immense palace, courtyards, private apartments, baths, lively frescoes and more – give a fine idea of what a Minoan palace might have looked like.

Buses to Knossos (€1.15, three per hour) leave from Bus Station A.

RETHYMNO ΡΕΘΥΜΝΟ

pop 29,000

Rethymno (*reth*-im-no) is Crete's third-largest town. It's also one of the island's architectural treasures, due to its stunning fortress and mix of Venetian and Turkish

NEIL SETCHFIELD

Ancient pottery, Malia

IF YOU LIKE...

- If you like the ancient archaeological site at **Knossos** (p685), you could also seek out these smaller Minoan sites:
- **Phaestos** (☎ 29820 42315; admission €4; 8am-7pm May-Oct, to 5pm Nov-Apr) Sixty-three kilometres southwest of Iraklio, the layout is similar to Knossos, if a little less impressive, but with stunning views of the surrounding Mesara plain and Mt Psiloritis (Mt Ida).
- **Malia** A palace complex and adjoining town, 34km east of Iraklio.
- **Zakros** The last Minoan palace to be discovered (in 1962). It's 40km southeast of Sitia.

houses in the old quarter. A compact town, most spots of interest are within a small area around the old Venetian harbour.

The **municipal tourist office** (☎ 28310 29148; www.rethymno.gr; Eleftheriou Venizelou; 9am-8.30pm Mar-Nov), on the beach side of El Venizelou, is convenient and helpful. **Ellotia Tours** (☎ 28310 24533; www.rethymnoatcrete.com; Arkadiou 155) will answer all transport, accommodation and tour inquiries.

Rethymno's 16th-century **Venetian fortress** (fortezza; ☎ 28310 28101; Paleokastro Hill; admission €3; 8am-8pm) is the site of the city's ancient acropolis and affords great views across the town and mountains. The main gate is on the eastern side of the fortress, opposite the interesting **archaeological museum** (☎ 28310 54668; admission €3; 8.30am-3pm Tue-Sun), which was once a prison.

Sea Front (☎ 28310 51981; www.rethymnoatcrete.com; Arkadiou 159; d €35-45;) has all sorts of options and is ideally positioned with beach views and spacious rooms. **Hotel Fortezza** (☎ 28310 55551; www.fortezza.gr; Melissinou 16; s/d incl breakfast €57/69; P) is more upmarket; with a refreshing pool, it's in a refurbished old building in the heart of the Old Town.

There are plenty of eating options, but **Samaria** (☎ 28310 24681; El Venizelou 39; mains from €4) is one of the few waterfront tavernas where you'll see local families eating. **Restaurant Symposium** (☎ 28310 50538; www.symposium-kriti.gr; mains from €5), near the Rimondi fountain, takes its food seriously (check out the website) but has good prices.

There are regular ferries between Piraeus and Rethymno (€29, nine hours), and a high-speed service in summer. Buses depart regularly to Iraklio (€6.5, 1½ hours) and Hania (€6, one hour).

HANIA ΧΑΝΙΑ

pop 53,500

Crete's most romantic, evocative and alluring town, Hania (hahn-*yah;* often spelt Chania) is the former capital and the island's second-largest city. There is a rich mosaic of Venetian and Ottoman architecture, particularly in the area of the old harbour, which lures tourists in droves. Modern Hania retains the exoticism of a city caught between East and West. Hania is an excellent base for exploring nearby idyllic beaches and a spectacular mountainous interior.

The **tourist information office** (☎ 28210 36155; Kydonias 29; 8am-2.30pm), under the Town Hall, is helpful and provides practical information and maps. The city's website at www.chania.gr is worth a look for more information and upcoming events. **Tellus Travel** (☎ 28210 91500; www.tellustravel.gr; Halidon 108; 8am-11pm) can help with schedules and ticketing, and also rents out cars.

A stroll around the **old harbour** is a must for any visitor to Hania. It is worth the 1.5km walk around the sea wall to get to the Venetian **lighthouse** at the entrance to the harbour.

The **archaeological museum** (☎ 28210 90334; Halidon 30; admission €2; 8.30am-3pm Tue-Sun) is in a 16th-century Venetian church that the Turks made into a mosque.

Pension Lena (☎ 28210 86860; www.lenachania.gr; Ritsou 5; s/d €35/55;) For some real character in where you stay, Lena's pension in an old Turkish building near the mouth of the old harbour is the place to go.

our pick **Amphora Hotel** (☎ 28210 93224; www.amphora.gr; Parodos Theotokopoulou 20; s/d €75/90;) Amphora is in an impressively restored Venetian mansion with elegantly decorated rooms around a courtyard. The hotel also runs the waterfront restaurant, which ranks as the best along that golden mile.

The entire waterfront of the old harbour is lined with restaurants and tavernas, many of which qualify as tourist traps.

Taverna Tamam (☎ 28210 58639; Zambeliou 49; mains €4-6.50; 1pm-12.30am) A taverna in an old converted Turkish bathhouse, with tables that spill out onto the street, this place has tasty soups and a superb selection of vegetarian specialities.

our pick **Michelas** (☎ 28210 90026; mains €5-7; 10am-4pm Mon-Sat) For some authentic Cretan specialities at reasonable prices head to Michelas in the eastern wing of the food market. This family-run place uses only Cretan ingredients and cooks up a great selection each day that you can peruse, then choose from.

There are several flights a day between Hania airport (CHQ) and Athens (€65) and five flights a week to Thessaloniki (€80). The airport is 14km east of town on the Akrotiri Peninsula.

Frequent buses run along Crete's northern coast to Iraklio (€11, 2¾ hours, 21 daily), Rethymno (€6, one hour, 21 daily).

Buses for the beaches west of Hania leave from the eastern side of Plateia 1866.

SAMARIA GORGE
ΦΑΡΑΓΓΙ ΤΗΣ ΣΑΜΑΡΙΑΣ

The **Samaria Gorge** (☎ 28250 67179; admission €5; 6am-3pm May–mid-Oct) is one of Europe's most spectacular gorges and a superb hike. Walkers should take rugged footwear, food, drinks and sun protection for this strenuous five- to six-hour trek.

You can do the walk as part of an excursion tour, or do it independently by taking the Omalos bus from the main bus station in Hania (€5.90, one hour) to the head of the gorge at Xyloskalo (1230m) at 6.15am, 7.30am, 8.30am or 2.00pm. It's a 16.7km walk out (all downhill) to Agia Roumeli on the coast, from where you take a boat to Hora Sfakion (€7.50, 1¼ hours, three daily) and then a bus back to Hania (€5.40, two hours, four daily). You are not allowed to spend the night in the gorge, so you need to complete the walk in a day.

DODECANESE ΔΩΔΕΚΑΝΗΣΑ

Strung out along the coast of western Turkey, the 12 main islands of the Dodecanese (*dodeca* means 12) have suffered a turbulent past of invasions and occupations that has endowed them with a fascinating diversity.

In 1291 the Knights of St John, having fled Jerusalem, came to Rhodes and established themselves as masters of the Dodecanese. In 1522 Süleyman I staged a massive attack and took Rhodes Town, claiming the islands for the Ottoman Empire. In 1947 the Dodecanese became part of Greece. These days, tourists rule.

RHODES ΡΟΔΟΣ

pop 98,000

Rhodes (Rodos in Greek) is the largest island in the Dodecanese. According to mythology, the sun god Helios chose Rhodes as his bride and bestowed light, warmth and vegetation upon her. The blessing seems to have paid off, for Rhodes produces more flowers and sunny days than most Greek islands. Throw in an east coast of virtually uninterrupted sandy beaches and it's easy to understand why sun-starved northern Europeans flock here.

GETTING THERE & AWAY

There are plenty of flights daily between Rhodes airport (RHO) and Athens (€77), and one daily to Iraklio (€65). Call **Olympic Air** (OA; ☎ 22410 24571; Ierou Lohou 9) or **Aegean Airlines** (A3; ☎ 22410 98345; Diagoras airport). **Sky Express** (SEH; ☎ 28102 23500; www.skyexpress.gr) has options to Iraklio and Santorini.

Rhodes is the main port of the Dodecanese and there is a complex array of departures. There are daily ferries from Rhodes to Piraeus (€40, 15 to 18 hours). Most sail via the Dodecanese north of Rhodes, but at least three times a week there is a service Crete and the Cyclades.

There are boats between Rhodes and Marmaris in Turkey (one way/return €50/70, 1¼ hours). Check www.marmarisinfo.com for up-to-date details.

For details on all your options, contact Triton Holidays (below).

RHODES TOWN

pop 56,000

Rhodes' capital is Rhodes Town, on the northern tip of the island. Its World Heritage–listed Old Town, the largest inhabited medieval town in Europe, is enclosed within massive walls and is a joy to explore. To the north is New Town, the commercial centre.

The main port, Commercial Harbour, is east of the Old Town, and north of here is Mandraki Harbour, the supposed site of the Colossus of Rhodes, a 32m-high bronze statue of Apollo built over 12 years (294–282 BC). The statue stood for a mere 65 years before being toppled by an earthquake.

For information about the island, visit www.ro dos.gr. The **Tourist information office** (EOT; ☎ 22410 35226; cnr Makariou & Papagou; 🕑 8am-2.45pm Mon-Fri) has brochures, maps and *Rodos News*, a free English-language newspaper.

In the New Town, **Triton Holidays** (☎ 22410 21690; www.tritondmc.gr; Plastira 9, Mandraki) is exceptionally helpful, handling accommodation bookings, ticketing and rental cars.

The Old Town is reputedly the world's finest surviving example of medieval fortification, with 12m-thick walls. The Knights of St John lived in the Knights' Quarter in the northern end of the Old Town.

The cobbled **Odos Ippoton** (Ave of the Knights) is lined with magnificent medieval buildings, the most imposing of which is the **Palace of the Grand Masters** (☎ 22410 23359; admission €6; 8.30am-7.30pm Tue-Sun), which was restored, but never used, as a holiday home for Mussolini.

The 15th-century Knight's Hospital now houses the **archaeological museum** (☎ 22410 27657; Plateia Mousiou; admission €3; 8am-4pm Tue-Sun). The splendid building was restored by the Italians and has an impressive collection that includes the ethereal marble statue *Aphrodite of Rhodes*.

The pink-domed **Mosque of Süleyman**, at the top of Sokratous, was built in 1522 to commemorate the Ottoman victory against the knights, then rebuilt in 1808.

Hotel Andreas (☎ 22410 34156; www.hotelandreas.com; Omirou 28d, Old Town; s/d €50/75;) Tasteful, with individually decorated rooms and terrific views from its roof-terrace, rates differ by the room at Hotel Andreas.

Marco Polo Mansion (☎ 22410 25562; www.marcopolomansion.gr; Agiou Fanouriou 40, Old Town; d €90-170) In a 15th-century building in the Turkish quarter of the Old Town, this place is rich in Ottoman-era colours and features in glossy European magazines. Take a look at the rooms online.

There is food and drink every way you look in Rhodes. Outside the city walls, there are a lot of cheap places in the New Market, at the southern end of Mandraki Harbour.

Taverna Kostas (☎ 22410 26217; Pythagora 62, Old Town; mains €5-10) This good-value spot has stood the test of time and can't be beaten for its quality grills and fish dishes.

To Meltemi (☎ 22410 30480; Kountourioti 8; mains €5-12) Gaze out on Turkey from this beachside taverna at the northern end of Mandraki Harbour. The seafood is superb.

Rhodes Town has two bus stations. The west-side bus station, next to the

WAYNE WALTON

Old fortifications, Rhodes Town

New Market, serves the airport and the west coast. The **east-side bus station** (**Plateia Rimini**) serves the east coast, Lindos (€4.70, 1½ hours) and the inland southern villages.

AROUND THE ISLAND

The **Acropolis of Lindos** (☎ **22440 31258; admission €6;** 🕑 **8.30am-6pm Tue-Sun**), 47km from Rhodes Town, is an ancient city spectacularly perched atop a 116m-high rocky outcrop. Below is the town of **Lindos**, a tangle of streets with elaborately decorated 17th-century houses.

The extensive ruins of **Kamiros** (**admission €4;** 🕑 **8am-5pm Tue-Sun**), an ancient Doric city on the west coast, are well preserved, with the remains of houses, baths, a cemetery and a temple, but the site should be visited as much for its lovely setting on a gentle hillside overlooking the sea.

AEGEAN ISLANDS ΤΑ ΝΗΣΙΑ ΤΟΥ ΑΙΓΑΙΟΥ

One of Greece's best-kept secrets, these far-flung islands are strewn across the northeastern corner of the Aegean, closer to Turkey than mainland Greece. They harbour unspoilt scenery, welcoming locals and fascinating independent cultures, and remain relatively calm even when other Greek islands are sagging with tourists at the height of summer.

LESVOS (MYTILINI) ΛΕΣΒΟΣ (ΜΥΤΙΛΗΝΗ)

pop 93,500

Lesvos, or Mytilini as it is often called, tends to do things in a big way. The third-largest of the Greek Islands after Crete and Evia, Lesvos produces half the world's ouzo and is home to over 11 million olive trees. Mountainous yet fertile, the island presents excellent hiking and birdwatching opportunities, but remains relatively untouched in terms of tourism development. An excellent source of information on the island is www.greeknet.com.

The two main towns on the island are the capital of Mytilini on the southeast coast, and attractive Mithymna on the north coast.

GETTING THERE & AWAY

Written up on flight schedules as Mytilene, Lesvos' Odysseas airport (MJT) has daily connections with Athens (€78) and Thessaloniki (€88). **Sky Express** (**SEH;** ☎ **28102 23500; www.skyexpress.gr**) operates to Iraklio, Crete and Thessaloniki.

In summer there are daily boats to Piraeus (€30, 12 hours), and one boat a week to Thessaloniki (€35, 13 hours). There are four ferries a week to Ayvalik in Turkey (one way/return €30/45). Stop by Zoumboulis Tours (below) for ticketing and schedules.

MYTILINI ΜΥΤΙΛΗΝΗ

pop 27,300

The capital and main port, Mytilini is built between two harbours (north and south) with an imposing fortress on the promontory to the east. All ferries dock at the southern harbour, and most of the town's action is around this waterfront. With a large university campus, Mytilini is a lively place year-round.

The **tourist office** (☎ **22510 42511; 6 Aristarhou;** 🕑 **9am-1pm Mon-Fri**), 50m up Aristarhou inland from the quay, offers brochures and maps, but its opening hours are limited. **Zoumboulis Tours** (☎ **22510 37755; Kountourioti 69**), on the waterfront, handles flights, boat schedules, ticketing and excursions to Turkey.

Mytilini's excellent neoclassical **archaeological museum** (☎ **22510 22087; 8 Noemvriou; adult/child €3/2;** 🕑 **8am-7.30pm**)

GEORGE TSAFOS

Village on Samos

IF YOU LIKE...

- If you like **Rhodes** (p688), these other islands off the Turkish coast might be worth exploring.
- **Kos** (**Tourist office** ☎ **22420 24460; www.kosinfo.gr; Vasileos Georgiou 1;** 🕒 **8am-2.30pm & 3-10pm Mon-Fri, 9am-2pm Sat**) Popular with history buffs as the birthplace of Hippocrates (460–377 BC), the father of medicine. Kos also attracts an entirely different crowd – sun-worshipping beach lovers from northern Europe who flock in on summer charter flights.
- **Chios** (**Tourist office** ☎ **22710 44389; infochio@otenet.gr; Kanari 18, Chios Town;** 🕒 **7am-10pm Apr-Oct, to 4pm Nov-Mar**) Off-the-beaten-track travellers take note. Unesco-listed Nea Moni (New Monastery), 14km west of Chios Town, has 11th-century mosaics, including some of the finest Byzantine art in the country. Ancient villages await inland, including the *mastihohoria* (mastic villages), where mastic was harvested for chewing gum.
- **Samos** (**Tourist office** ☎ **22730 61389; deap5@otenet.gr; Pythagorio;** 🕒 **8am-9.30pm**) Just 3km from Turkey, Samos was an important centre of Hellenic culture, and the mathematician Pythagoras and storyteller Aesop are among its sons. The island has beaches that bake in summer, and a hinterland that is superb for hiking.
- **Patmos** (**Tourist office** ☎ **22470 31666; Skala Town;** 🕒 **8am-6pm Mon-Fri Jun-Sep**) Christians have long made pilgrimages to Patmos, for it was here that John the Divine ensconced himself in a cave and wrote the Book of Revelation. There are great beaches and a relaxed atmosphere.

has a fascinating collection from Neolithic to Roman times.

A superb place for a stroll or a picnic is the pine forest surrounding Mytilini's impressive **fortress** (**adult/student €2/1;** 🕒 **8am-2.30pm Tue-Sun**), which was built in early Byzantine times and enlarged by the Turks.

SAPPHO, LESBIANS & LESVOS

Sappho, one of Greece's great ancient poets, was born on Lesvos during the 7th century BC. Most of her work was devoted to love and desire, and the objects of her affection were often female. These days, Lesvos is visited by many lesbians paying homage to Sappho. The whole island is very gay-friendly, in particular the southwestern beach resort of Skala Eresou, which is built over ancient Eresos where Sappho was born. The village is well set up to cater to lesbian needs and has a 'Women Together' festival held annually in September. Check out www.sapphotravel.com for details.

Hotel Sappho (☎ 22510 22888; Kountourioti 31; s/d/tr €35/55/66) On the waterfront, rooms here are simple but clean. It's easy to find, and has the attraction of a 24-hour reception as ferries into Mytilini tend to arrive at nasty hours.

Porto Lesvos 1 Hotel (☎ 22510 41771; www.portolesvos.gr; Komninaki 21; s/d €60/90;) This hotel has good rooms and service – right down to robes and slippers – in a restored building one block back from the waterfront.

our pick **Diavlos** (☎ 22510 22020; Ladadika 30; mains from €4) Head straight to Diavlos for the best in both local cuisine and art; paintings by local artists line the walls and can be purchased should you get the urge.

Kalderimi (☎ 22510 46577; Thasou 3; mains from €6) Popular with locals, Kalderimi has an excellent ambience with tables in a vine-covered pedestrian street just back from the Sappho statue on the main harbour.

MITHYMNA ΜΗΘΥΜΝΑ

pop 1500

The gracious, preserved town of Mithymna (known by locals as Molyvos) is 62km north of Mytilini. Cobbled streets canopied by flowering vines wind up the hill below the impressive castle. The town is full of cosy tavernas and genteel stone cottages.

From the bus stop, walk straight ahead towards the town for 100m to the helpful **municipal tourist office** (☎ 22530 71347; www.mithymna.gr; 8am-9pm Mon-Fri, 9am-7pm Sat & Sun), which has good maps. The noble **Genoese castle** (☎ 22530 71803; admission €2; 8am-7pm Tue-Sun) perches above the town like a crown and affords tremendous views out to Turkey. Don't forget to stroll down to the harbour.

Eftalou hot springs (☎ 22530 71245; public/private bath per person €3.50/5; public bath 10am-2pm & 4-8pm, private bath 9am-6pm), 4km from town on the beach, is a superb bathhouse complex with a whitewashed dome and steaming, pebbled pool.

Buses to Mithymna (€5) take 1¾ hours from Mytilini, though a rental car is a good option.

IONIAN ISLANDS ΤΑ ΕΠΤΑΝΗΣΑ

The idyllic cypress- and fir-covered Ionian Islands stretch down the western coast of Greece. Mountainous, with dramatic cliff-backed beaches, soft light and turquoise water, they're more Italian in feel, offering a contrasting experience to other Greek islands. Invest in a hire car to get to small villages tucked along quiet back roads.

CORFU ΚΕΡΚΥΡΑ

pop 114,000

Many consider Corfu to be Greece's most beautiful island – the unfortunate consequence of which is that it's often overrun with crowds.

Ioannis Kapodistrias airport (CFU; ☎ 26610 30180) is 3km from Corfu Town. Olympic Air (☎ 26610 22962) and **Aegean Airlines** (☎ 26610 27100) fly daily to Athens. Olympic flies a few times a week to other Ionian islands and Thessaloniki.

CORFU TOWN

pop 39,500

Built on a promontory and wedged between two fortresses, Corfu's Old Town is a tangle of narrow walking streets through gorgeous Venetian buildings. Explore the winding alleys and surprising plazas in the early morning or late afternoon to avoid the hordes of day trippers searching for souvenirs.

The Palaio Frourio (Old Fortress) stands on an eastern promontory, separated from the town by seafront gardens known as the Spianada. The Neo Frourio (New Fortress) lies to the northwest. Ferries dock at the new port, just west of the Neo Frourio. The **long-distance bus station** (☎ 26610 28900; Avrami) lies inland from the port. The **tourist police** (☎ 26610 30265; 3rd fl, Samartzi 4) provide helpful info. Check email at **Netoikos** (Kaloheretou 14; per hr €3), behind the Church of Agios Spyridon.

The **Archaeological Museum** (☎ 26610 30680; Vraïla 5; admission €3; 8.30am-3pm Tue-Sun) houses a collection of finds from Mycenaean to classical times. The richly decorated **Church of Agios Spiridon** (Agios Spiridonos) displays the remains of St Spiridon, paraded through town four times a year.

Accommodation prices fluctuate wildly depending on season; book ahead. If you're after a bite, cafes and bars line the arcaded Liston.

Hotel Astron (☎ 26610 39505; hotel_astron@hol.gr; Donzelot 15, Old Port; s €45-55, d €55-65) Recently renovated and with some sea views, light-filled rooms are managed by friendly staff.

our pick **Bella Venezia** (☎ 26610 46500; www.bellaveneziahotel.com; N Zambeli 4; s/d incl breakfast from €85/105) Impeccable and understated contemporary rooms

JOHN ELK III

Plateia Dimarchiou (Town Hall Sq), Corfu Town

are decked out in cream linens and marbles.

To Tsipouzadiko (☎ 26610 82240; mains €5-8; ⌚ dinner) Old 45 *rembetika* records line the walls, and the gregarious owner serves up generous portions of fresh (cheap) Greek food. It's on the lane behind the courthouse and Hotel Konstantinoupolis in Old Port.

To Dimarchio (☎ 26610 39031; Plateia Dimarchio; mains €8-25) Relax in a luxuriant rose garden on a charming square. Attentive staff serve elegant, inventive Italian and Greek dishes, prepared with the freshest ingredients.

DIRECTORY

ACTIVITIES

HIKING

Greece is a hiker's paradise, but outside the main popular routes the trails are generally overgrown and poorly marked. Several companies run organised hikes; **Trekking Hellas** (Map p670; ☎ 21033 10323; www.outdoorsgreece.com; Filellinon 7, Athens) has options throughout Greece. **Cretan Adventures** (☎ 28103 32772; www.cretanadventures.gr; Evans 10, Iraklio) specialises in activities on Crete.

YACHTING

Set aside any prejudices about those who wear deck shoes and knot their cardigans around their neck: yachting is a brilliant way to see the Greek Islands. The **Hellenic Yachting Server** (www.yachting.gr) is packed with information.

EMBASSIES & CONSULATES

All foreign embassies in Greece are in Athens and its suburbs.

Australia (Map pp666-7; ☎ 210 870 4000; Leoforos Alexandras & Kifisias, Ambelokipi, GR-115 23)

Canada (Map pp666-7; ☎ 210 727 3400; Genadiou 4, GR-115 21)

France (Map pp666-7; ☎ 210 361 1663; Leoforos Vasilissis Sofias 7, GR-106 71)

Germany (Map pp666-7; ☎ 210 728 5111; cnr Dimitriou 3 & Karaoli, Kolonaki GR-106 75)

Ireland (Map pp666-7; ☎ 210 723 2771; Vasileos Konstandinou 7; Athens GR-106 74)

Japan (Map pp666-7; ☎ 210 775 8101; Athens Tower, Leoforos Messogion 2-4, GR-115 27)

Netherlands (Map pp666-7; ☎ 210 725 4900; Vasileos Konstandinou 5-7, GR-106 74)

New Zealand (Map pp666-7; ☎ 210 687 4701; Kifissias 268, Halandri)

UK (Map pp666-7; ☎ 210 723 6211; Ploutarhou 1, GR-106 75)

USA (Map pp666-7; ☎ 210 721 2951; Leoforos Vasilissis Sofias 91, GR-115 21)

FESTIVALS & EVENTS

In Greece, the number of celebrations means it is probably easier to list the dates when festivals and events are *not* on! Some festivals are religious, some cultural, and others are seemingly just an excuse to party. It is worth timing at least part of your trip to coincide with one festival or event, as you will be warmly invited to join in the revelry. The following list is by no means exhaustive, and further details can be found at www.cultureguide.gr and www.whatsonwhen.com.

Carnival Season The three-week period before the beginning of Lent is celebrated all over Greece with fancy dress, feasting and traditional dance.

Easter The most important festival of the Greek Orthodox religion occurs March/April. The emphasis is on the Resurrection rather than the Crucifixion so it's a celebratory event. The most significant part of the event is midnight on Easter Saturday when candles are lit (symbolising the Resurrection) and a ireworks and candlelit procession hits he streets. Orthodox Easter is usually at different time than Easter celebrated y the Western churches.

HOLIDAYS

lew Year's Day 1 January
piphany 6 January
irst Sunday in Lent February
ireek Independence Day 25 March
iood Friday/Easter Sunday March/ pril
lay Day (Protomagia) 1 May
east of the Assumption 15 August
)hi Day 28 October
hristmas Day 25 December
it Stephen's Day 26 December

POST

ahydromia (post offices) are easily identiied by the yellow sign outside. Regular ost boxes are yellow; red post boxes are or express mail.

TELEPHONE

he Greek telephone service is mainained by Organismos Tilepikoinonion llados, always referred to by its acroym OTE (o-*teh*). Public phones are easy o use and pressing the 'i' button brings p the operating instructions in English. ublic phones are everywhere and all use honecards.

Mobile phones have become the musthave accessory in Greece. If you have a ompatible GSM phone from a country vith a global roaming agreement with ireece, you will be able to use your hone there. Make sure you have gloal roaming activated before you leave our country of residence. There are several mobile service providers in Greece; **CosmOTE** (www.cosmote.gr) has the best overage. You can purchase a Greek SIM ard for around €20 and cards are available everywhere to recharge the SIM card.

Telephone codes are part of the 10-digit number within Greece. The landline prefix is ☎ 2 and for mobiles it's ☎ 6.

All public phones use OTE phonecards, sold at OTE offices and *periptera* (kiosks).

VISAS

Visitors from most countries don't need a visa for Greece. The list of countries whose nationals can stay in Greece for up to three months include Australia, Canada, all EU countries, Iceland, Israel, Japan, New Zealand and the USA. For longer stays, apply at a consulate abroad or at least 20 days in advance to the **Aliens Bureau** (Map pp666-7; ☎ 210 770 5711; Leoforos Alexandras 173, Athens; 🕑 8am-1pm Mon-Fri) at the Athens Central Police Station. Elsewhere in Greece, apply to the local authority.

TRANSPORT

GETTING THERE & AWAY

AIR

There are 16 international airports in Greece, but most of them handle only summer charter flights to the islands. **Eleftherios Venizelos airport** (ATH; ☎ 21035 30000; www.aia.gr), near Athens, handles the vast majority of international flights and has regular scheduled flights to all the European capitals. National carrier **Olympic Air** (OA; ☎ 80111 44444; www.olympicairlines.com) and **Aegean Airlines** (A3; ☎ 80111 20000; www.aegeanair.com) are Greek companies operating a growing number of international routes.

LAND

Daily trains operate between İstanbul and Thessaloniki (around 12 hours).

SEA

You'll find all the latest information about ferry routes, schedules and services online at www.ferries.gr. This site will also provide links to individual ferry company websites.

ITALY

There are ferries between the Italian ports of Brindisi and Venice and Patra, Corfu. If you want to take a vehicle across, it's a good idea to make a reservation beforehand.

TURKEY

Five regular ferry services operate between Turkey's Aegean coast and the Greek Islands. For more information about these services, see Rhodes (p688), Chios (p691), Kos (p691), Lesvos (p691) and Samos (p691).

GETTING AROUND

Greece is a relatively straightforward destination to travel around thanks to its comprehensive transport system. On the mainland, buses travel to just about every town on the map and trains offer a good alternative where available. Island-hopping is what most people think of when travelling within Greece and there are myriad ferries that criss-cross the Adriatic and Aegean Seas. There is also an extensive and well-priced domestic air network. Note that timetables are seasonal and change in at least some way every year.

AIR

Domestic air travel is becoming very price competitive, and it's sometimes cheaper to fly than take the ferry, especially if you book ahead online.

Greece's national carrier, **Olympic Air** (OA; ☎ 801 114 4444; www.olympicairlines.com) has the most extensive network. Privat company **Aegean Airlines** (A3; ☎ 8011 20000; www.aegeanair.com) is their big com petition, offering newer aircraft and similar prices on popular routes. A recen addition to the skies over Greece is **Sky Express** (SHE; ☎ 28102 23500; www.skyexpress gr), based in Iraklio, Crete, which mainl flies routes that the big two don't.

BOAT

Island-hopping by boat in the Gree Islands is great fun. Keep in mind thoug that domestic sea travel options are con stantly changing. Operations are highl seasonal and changes to schedules ca take place at the last minute. Be pre pared to be flexible. Boats seldom ar rive early, but often arrive late! And som don't come at all. Think of it as part o the fun.

Check out www.ferries.gr for sched ules, costs and links to individual boa company websites.

FERRY

Every island has a ferry service of som sort, although in winter these are pare back. Services pick up from April, an during July and August Greece's sea are a mass of wake and wash. The fer ries come in all shapes and sizes, from the state-of-the-art 'superferries' tha run on the major routes to the agein open ferries that operate local service to outlying islands.

The newer high-speed ferries ar slashing travel times on some of th longer routes, but generally cost muc more.

CLASSES

'Classes' on ferries are largely a thing o the past. Basically, you have the option o 'deck class', which is the cheapest ticke nd is the class that most travellers use, r 'cabin class' with air-con cabins and a ecent lounge and restaurant. It doesn't nake much difference on short trips, but n overnight trips you might want to go or one of the cabin options.

Children under four travel free, those etween four and 10 years pay half-fare. hildren over 10 pay full fare. When buyng tickets you will automatically be given eck class.

OUTES

he hub of the vast ferry network is iraeus, the main port of Athens. It as ferries to the Cyclades, Crete, the odecanese and the northeastern egean Islands. Patra is the main port or ferries to the Ionian Islands.

ATAMARAN

igh-speed catamarans have become an nportant part of the island travel scene. hey are just as fast as hydrofoils and are nuch more comfortable. They are also nuch less prone to cancellation in rough veather and the fares are generally the ame as hydrofoils. The main players re Hellas Flying Dolphins and Blue Star erries.

YDROFOIL

ydrofoils offer a faster alternative to erries on some routes. They take half he time, but cost twice as much. Most outes will operate only during the high eason. **Hellenic Seaways** (☎ 21041 9000; www.hellenicseaways.gr) travels rom Piraeus to the ports of the eastrn Peloponnese. **Aegean Hydrofoils** (☎ 22410 24000), based in Rhodes, serves he Dodecanese.

Tickets for hydrofoils must be bought n advance and there is often seat llocation.

BUS

All long-distance buses on the mainland and the islands are operated by regional collectives known as **KTEL** (Koino Tamio Eispraxeon Leoforion; www.ktel.org). Fares are fixed by the government and service routes can be found on the company's website.

Tickets should be bought at least an hour in advance to ensure a seat. Buses don't have toilets and refreshments, but stop for a break every couple of hours.

CAR & MOTORCYCLE

A great way to explore areas in Greece that are off the beaten track is by car. However, it's worth bearing in mind that Greece has the highest road-fatality rate in Europe. The road network has improved dramatically in recent years and places that were little more than a one-lane dirt track masquerading as a road have now been widened and asphalted. Freeway tolls are fairly hefty.

Almost all islands are served by car ferries, but they are expensive. Costs vary by the size of the vehicle.

The Greek automobile club, **ELPA** (www.elpa.gr), generally offers reciprocal services to members of other national motoring associations. If your vehicle breaks down, dial ☎ 104.

HIRE

Hire cars are available just about anywhere in Greece. The major multinational companies are represented in most major tourist destinations.

Mopeds and motorcycles are available for hire everywhere; however, regulations stipulate that you need a valid motorcycle licence stating proficiency for the size of motorcycle you wish to rent – from 50cc upwards.

If you plan to hire a motorcycle or moped, check that your travel insurance covers you for injury resulting from motorcycle accidents.

ROAD RULES

While it sometimes appears that there aren't any road rules in Greece, you are apparently supposed to drive on the right and overtake on the left. Drink-driving laws are strict; a blood alcohol content of 0.05% incurs a fine of around €150 and over 0.08% is a criminal offence.

PUBLIC TRANSPORT

Most Greek towns are small enough to get around on foot. All major towns have local bus systems, but the only places that you're likely to need them are Athens and Thessaloniki.

Athens is the only city large enough t warrant a metro system.

Taxis are widely available in Greece an they are reasonably priced. Yellow cit cabs are metered.

TRAIN

Trains are operated by the **Gree Railways Organisation** (OSE; www.os gr). Greece has only two main line Athens north to Thessaloniki an Alexandroupolis, and Athens to th Peloponnese. In addition, there are number of branch lines, such as th Pyrgos–Olympia line.

Inter-Rail and Eurail passes are valid i Greece, but you still need to make a re ervation. In summer make reservations a least two days in advance.

➘ TURKEY

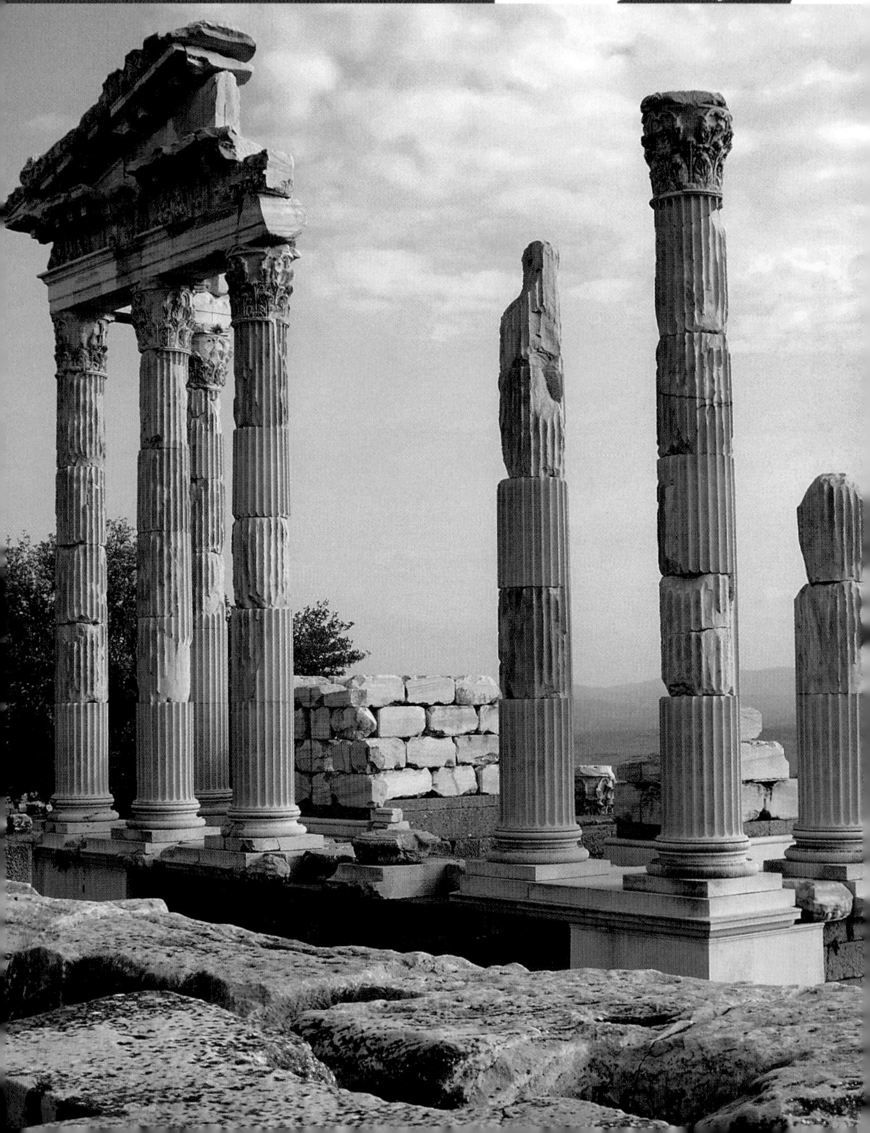

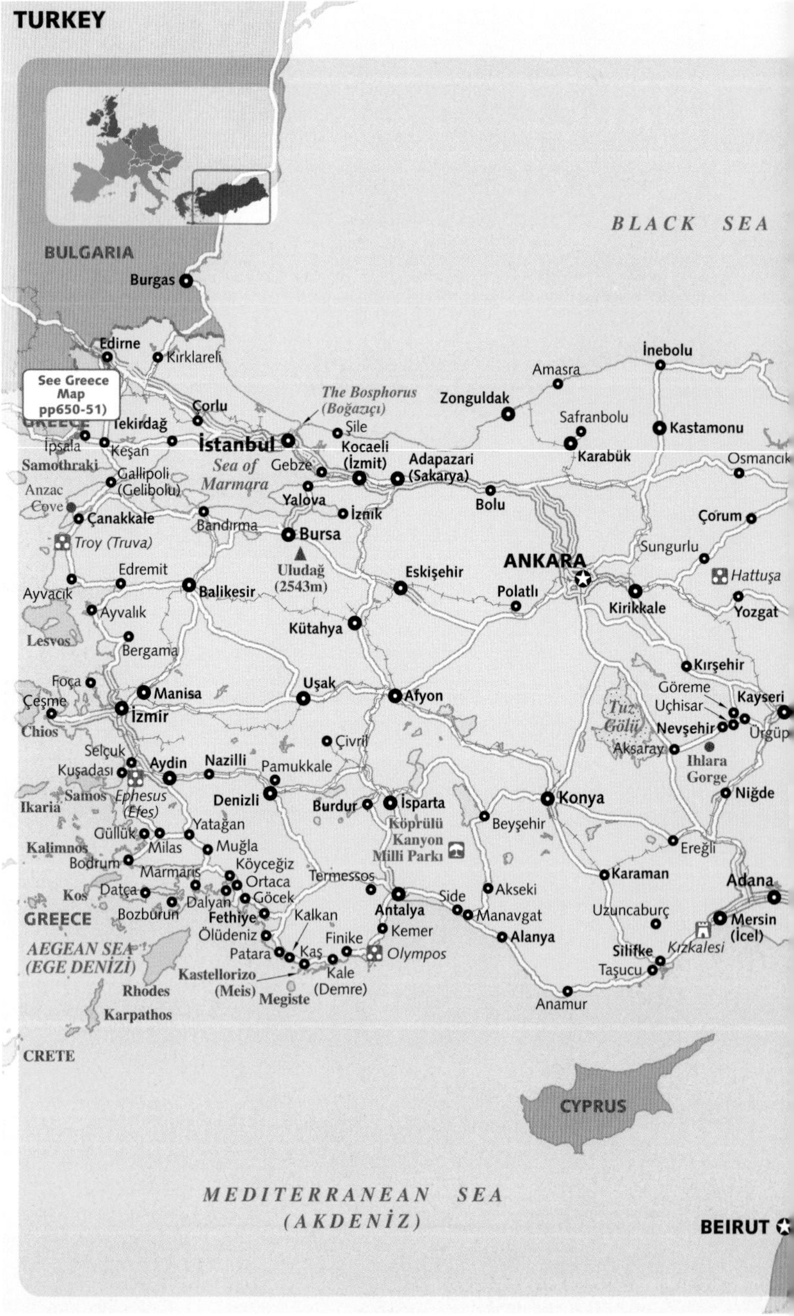
TURKEY
BLACK SEA
BULGARIA
Burgas
Edirne
Kirklareli
See Greece Map pp650-51)
Çorlu
Tekirdağ
İpsala
Keşan
İstanbul
The Bosphorus (Boğazıçı)
Şile
Kocaeli (İzmit)
Gebze
Sea of Marmara
Samothraki
Gallipoli (Gelibolu)
Anzac Cove
Çanakkale
Bandırma
Yalova
İznik
Bursa
Adapazari (Sakarya)
Bolu
Zonguldak
Amasra
İnebolu
Safranbolu
Karabük
Kastamonu
Osmancık
Çorum
Sungurlu
Troy (Truva)
Uludağ (2543m)
Edremit
Balikesir
Ayvacık
Ayvalık
Lesvos
Bergama
Eskişehir
ANKARA
Polatlı
Kirikkale
Hattuşa
Yozgat
Kütahya
Kırşehir
Foça
Çeşme
Chios
Manisa
İzmir
Uşak
Afyon
Tuz Gölü
Göreme
Uçhisar
Kayseri
Nevşehir
Ürgüp
Aksaray
Ihlara Gorge
Çivril
Selçuk
Kuşadası
Aydin
Nazilli
Pamukkale
Samos
Ephesus (Efes)
Ikaria
Denizli
Burdur
Isparta
Konya
Niğde
Köprülü Kanyon Milli Parkı
Beyşehir
Güllük
Milas
Yatağan
Muğla
Kalimnos
Bodrum
Köyceğiz
Marmaris
Ortaca
Termessos
Ereğli
Karaman
Kos
Datça
Dalyan
Göcek
Antalya
Side
Akseki
Adana
Bozburun
Fethiye
Kalkan
Manavgat
Uzuncaburç
Mersin (İcel)
GREECE
Ölüdeniz
Finike
Kemer
Alanya
AEGEAN SEA (EGE DENİZİ)
Patara
Kaş
Olympos
Silifke
Kızkalesi
Taşucu
Kastellorizo (Meis)
Megiste
Kale (Demre)
Rhodes
Anamur
Karpathos
CRETE
CYPRUS
MEDITERRANEAN SEA (AKDENİZ)
BEIRUT

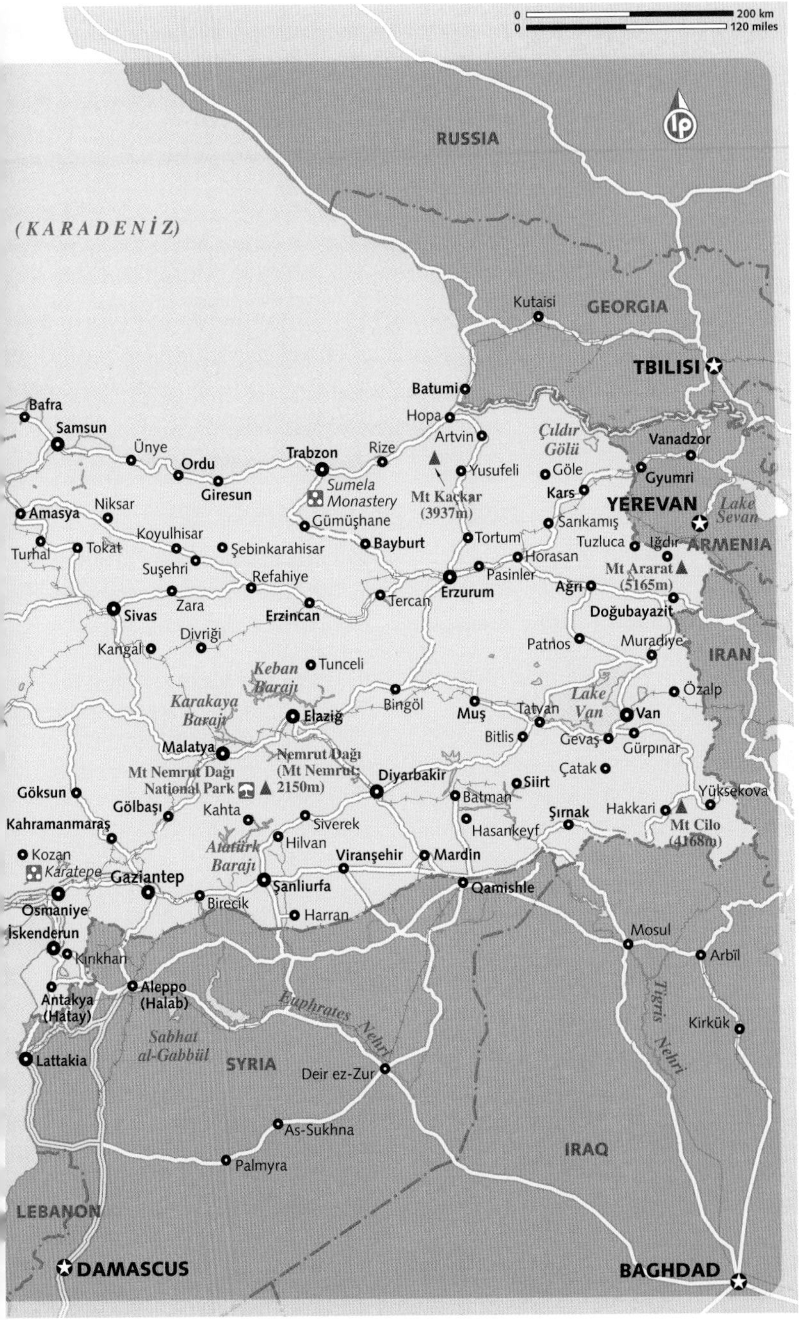
0 200 km
0 120 miles
RUSSIA
(KARADENİZ)
GEORGIA
Kutaisi
TBILISI
Batumi
Hopa
Artvin
Bafra
Samsun
Ünye
Ordu
Giresun
Trabzon
Rize
Sumela Monastery
Gümüşhane
Yusufeli
Mt Kaçkar (3937m)
Çıldır Gölü
Göle
Kars
Vanadzor
Gyumri
YEREVAN
Lake Sevan
ARMENIA
Amasya
Niksar
Tokat
Turhal
Koyulhisar
Şebinkarahisar
Suşehri
Bayburt
Tortum
Sarıkamış
Tuzluca
Iğdır
Horasan
Pasinler
Erzurum
Mt Ararat (5165m)
Ağrı
Doğubayazit
Refahiye
Zara
Sivas
Erzincan
Tercan
Divriği
Kangal
Patnos
Muradiye
IRAN
Keban Barajı
Tunceli
Karakaya Barajı
Elazığ
Bingöl
Muş
Tatvan
Lake Van
Van
Özalp
Bitlis
Gevaş
Gürpınar
Malatya
Nemrut Dağı (Mt Nemrut; 2150m)
Mt Nemrut Dağı National Park
Diyarbakir
Siirt
Çatak
Batman
Yüksekova
Göksun
Gölbaşı
Kahta
Siverek
Hasankeyf
Şırnak
Hakkari
Mt Cilo (4168m)
Kahramanmaraş
Hilvan
Atatürk Barajı
Kozan
Karatepe
Gaziantep
Viranşehir
Mardin
Şanliurfa
Qamishle
Osmaniye
Birecik
Harran
İskenderun
Kırıkhan
Mosul
Arbil
Antakya (Hatay)
Aleppo (Halab)
Euphrates Nehri
Tigris Nehri
Kirkük
Sabhat al-Gabbül
SYRIA
Lattakia
Deir ez-Zur
As-Sukhna
Palmyra
IRAQ
LEBANON
DAMASCUS
BAGHDAD

HIGHLIGHTS

1 İSTANBUL

SAFFET EMRE TOGUC, AUTHOR OF 101 MUST-SEE PLACES IN İSTANBUL

Napoleon exclaimed *'Constantinople! C'est l'empire du monde'* (Constantinople! It's the empire of the world!), and he was quite right. İstanbul is the only city that has been the capital of three huge empires – the Roman, Byzantine and Ottoman. To make it even more unique, the sea runs right through the city, splitting it into two.

SAFFET EMRE TOGUC'S DON'T MISS LIST

❶ EAST MEETS WEST

Located in the most beautiful of geographic settings, İstanbul is also the only city in the world built on two continents. In this cosmopolitan place the peal of the church bells mixes with the call to prayer, which echoes across the skies five times a day from thousands of mosques. In İstanbul, East meets West, and they rub along together rather well.

❷ OLD CITY, NEW CITY

In **Old İstanbul** (p717), the incredibl monuments of the empires can hardl fail to dazzle visitors. On what was onc the city's first hill, Aya Sofya, the Blu Mosque, Topkapı Palace and the Basilic Cistern reveal their history. In contras the new city reflects a very European flavour. **İstiklal Caddesi** (p719), the mos crowded pedestrian street, welcome everyone and offers a nonstop line-u of cafes, bars, restaurants, bookstore movie theatres and shops.

Clockwise from top: Crowds in the Grand Bazaar (p717); Spices and sweets at the Spice Bazaar; Bebek apartment buildings; The Blue Mosque (p717); Graffiti in İstanbul's Nevizade Sokak (p720)

CLOCKWISE FROM TOP: HOLGER LEUE; GEORGE TSAFOS; ADINA TOVY AMSEL; PHILIP & KAREN SMITH; TIM HUGH

MARKET MADNESS

ie **Grand Bazaar** (p717) is one of e world's oldest and largest mar- ets, with nearly 60 streets stuffed ith around 4,000 shops. Despite the ouristy veneer, Kalpakçılar Caddesi, e wide, vaulted main street, houses umberless jewellery shops, which are ill very popular with the locals. At the **pice Bazaar** **(Mısır Çarşıs, Egyptian Market; 8.30am-6.30pm Mon-Sat)** visitors enjoy iopping for many of the same herbs id spices as locals have for 350 years, us tourist souvenirs. For a more au- ientic experience explore the stalls on ther side of the bazaar, where many cals still come to stock up on their uit, vegies and cheese.

❹ BEST-KEPT SECRETS

The Bosphorus suburbs of Bebek, Arnavutköy, Boyacıköy and Büyükdere on the European side, and Kanlıca, Kandilli and Kuzguncuk on the Asian side are some of the city's best-kept secrets. Here, the İstanbul of old still breathes down your neck in the shape of wooden buildings hidden in secre- tive side streets.

THINGS YOU NEED TO KNOW

Braving the bazaar There's no doubt that the Grand Bazaar is a tourist trap par excellence. Your best bet is to explore back streets. Take your time and don't worry about getting lost – there's still plenty to be discovered here. **See our author's review on p712**

TURKEY

HIGHLIGHTS

HIGHLIGHTS

2

FAIRY CHIMNEYS

The fanciful-looking rock pyramids and pinnacles – the fairy chimneys – of **Cappadocia** (Kapadokya; p735) are certainly a sight to behold. But the fact that you can sleep in the hotels and guesthouses carved into many of them adds a whole other dimension to the experience. For a loftier perspective, take an early morning hot-air balloon flight and enjoy unforgettable views of the valleys.

3

THE ART OF NEGOTIATION

Turkish rugs are known the world over, but the experience of purchasing one is almost as good as the product. Typically a patron entering a shop will be offered a comfortable seat and a glass of apple tea, or appropriate beverage. To bargain effectively, take your time and enjoy the banter. An offer 20% to 50% below the original price is not an insult. Agreeing and then changing your mind is.

4

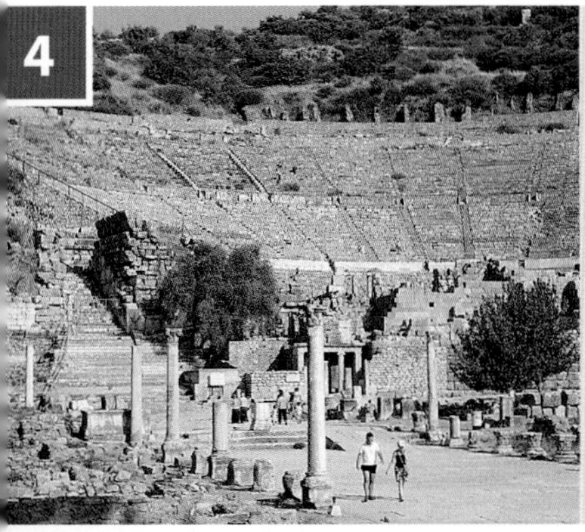

↘ ROMAN RUINS AT EPHESUS

Ephesus (Efes; p727) is *the* place in Turkey to get a feel for what Roman times were really like. It's hard not to be dazzled by this classical city: with a theatre, temples, terraced houses, a marketplace and all those other visitors, it's not a stretch to imagine this as a thriving metropolis.

5

↘ CRUISING THE MED

Author and painter Cevat Şakir Kabaağaçlı wrote in his famous book *Mavi Yolculuk* of an idyllic, early 20th-century sailing excursion. Today for many travellers a 'blue cruise' on a gület (wooden yacht) out of **Fethiye** (p728) is a highlight of their Turkish trip. Be warned, with some operators it's more 'booze' than blue cruise (though alcohol costs extra).

6

↘ NEMRUT DAĞI

The spellbinding peak of **Nemrut Dağı** (Mt Nemrut; p739) rises to 2150m, but it's the quizzical figures at the summit that attract all the attention. Outsiders didn't stumble on the more-than-2000-year-old temple, tomb and giant seated-god statues (their heads alone are 2m tall) until 1881. The area remains remote, so take a tour from **Göreme** (p736).

2 SHANIA SHEGEDYN; 3 WES WALKER; 4 HOLGER LEUE; 5 JOHN ELK III; 6 IZZET KERIBAR

2 Fairy chimneys of Cappadocia (p735); 3 Carpet shopping in İstanbul; 4 Ephesus (p727); 5 Cruising out of Fethiye (p728); 6 Ruins at Nemrut Dağı (p739)

THE BEST...

↘ COASTAL CITIES

- **İstanbul** (p712) Big city, Bosphorus views.
- **Çanakkale** (p724) Sprawling harbour town a stone's throw from the Gallipoli battlefields.
- **Fethiye** (p728) Blue cruise departure point, on a broad bay with nearby islands.
- **Antalya** (p731) Stylishly modern and classically beautiful, with a pristine Roman harbour.

↘ ANCIENT WONDERS

- **Ephesus** (p727) A complete Roman city, with a 25,000-seat theatre.
- **Ancient Olympos** (p731) Ruins peek out of a wildly abandoned place.
- **Nemrut Dağı** (p739) Massive, pre-Roman statues of the gods high on a mountain.
- **Pergamum** (p725) An ancient centre of medicine, including an excellent Asclepion.

↘ OFFBEAT ACCOMMODATIONS

- **Fairy chimneys, Cappadocia** (p735) Sleep in caves and carved-out rock formations – really, we're not kidding.
- **Tree houses, Olympos** (p731) Rustic living among the treetops; dig the commune-like vibe.
- **Tuvana, Antalya** (p732) Ottoman royal houses turned into a hotel.

↘ FESTIVITIES TO ENJOY

- **Camel wrestling, Selçuk** (p740) Male camels square off in January...
- **Kırkpınar Oil Wrestling Championship, Edirne** (p723) ...then slippery men tangle in July.
- **İstanbul International Music Festival** (p720) International artists play at interesting venues.

IZZET KERI

Antalya (p731)

THINGS YOU NEED TO KNOW

AT A GLANCE

- **Population** 71.9 million
- **Official language** Turkish
- **Currency** Turkish lira (TL)
- **Telephone code** ☎ 90
- **When to go** April to May and September to October
- **Tipping** About 10% of the bill

REGIONS IN A NUTSHELL

- **İstanbul** (p712) Age-old monuments *and* a vibrant, modern city on the sea.
- **The Aegean Coast** (p723) Ruins, ruins and more seaside ruins.
- **The Mediterranean Coast** (p728) The 'Turquoise Coast' with pebble-beach coves and lively harbours.
- **Central Anatolia** (p732) A heavy sense of history surrounds Turkey's capital on the plains.
- **Cappadocia** (p735) Valleys of cascading white cliffs surround otherworldly rock formations.

ADVANCE PLANNING

- **A week ahead** If you're arriving in Cappadocia by air, book a bus from Kayseri airport to Göreme a week ahead – or ask your lodging to arrange it.
- **Three days ahead** If you're taking a sleeper train from Ankara to İstanbul, book ahead.

BE FOREWARNED

- **Get in line** Citizens that need a visa (see below) need to get in the line to buy one before getting in the customs line to exit the airport.
- **Run man, run** Some İstanbullus drive like rally drivers, and there is no such thing as right of way for pedestrians, despite the little green man.

BUSINESS HOURS

Opening hours in Turkey are never set in stone, but in general:

- **Banks** (🕑 8.30am-noon & 1.30-5pm Mon-Fri)
- **Post offices** (🕑 7.30am-2pm Mon-Fri) Later in big cities.
- **Shops** (🕑 9am-6pm Mon-Fri) In tourist areas, shops are open extended hours.
- **Restaurants** (🕑 8am-10pm)
- **Bars** (🕑 5pm-8pm) In tourist areas, they may be open all day.

COSTS

- **TL70 per day** Stay in hotels with shared bathrooms, eat only one meal out a day.
- **TL130** Midrange accommodations, meals in restaurants, bus transport, entry to a sight or two.
- **TL300** Live like a sultan – boutique hotels, internal flights, wining and dining daily.

EMERGENCY NUMBERS

- **Ambulance** (☎ 112)
- **Fire** (☎ 110)
- **Police** (☎ 155)

THINGS YOU NEED TO KNOW

GETTING AROUND

For more on getting around Turkey, see p742.

- **Gateway airport** İstanbul
- **Rail travel** Trains don't cover the coast at all; the İstanbul to Ankara fast train is the only line of real use to travellers.
- **Rolling along** Cheap and comfortable, the extensive bus network is the way to roll in the country.

MEDIA

- **Turkish Daily News** (**www.turkishdailynews.com**) Turkey's English daily.
- **Time Out İstanbul** Monthly English edition with a large listings section. It's available at newsstands.
- **Cornucopia magazine** Published three times a year, it has interesting English articles about İstanbul.

RESOURCES

- **İstanbul Gay** (**www.istanbulgay.com**) Gay accommodation and tours.
- **Tourism Turkey** (**www.tourismturkey.org**) Government website with grab-bag of info.
- **My Merhaba** (**www.mymerhaba.com**) Expat resource giving the low-down on the country.
- **Turkey Travel Planner** (**www.turkeytravelplanner.com**) Regularly updated travel information.

VISAS

- **90 days visa free** Citizens of Denmark, Finland, France, Germany, Ireland, Israel, Italy, Japan, New Zealand, Sweden and Switzerland can enter visa-free for 90 days
- **Rubber-stamp visa required** Although nationals of Australia, Austria, Belgium, Canada, the Netherlands, Norway, Portugal, Spain, the UK and the USA need a visa, this is just a stamp in the passport that you buy on arrival.
- **More information** Contact the Ministry of Foreign Affairs (www.mfa.gov.tr).

LEFT: CHRIS MELLOR; RIGHT: IZZET KERIBAR

Left: Carving lamb for *kebaps*; Right: A silk market

GET INSPIRED

BOOKS

- **My Name is Red** Nobel Laureate Orhan Pamuk's Ottoman-era murder mystery.
- **Portrait of a Turkish Family** Irfan Orga's autobiography about the collapse of his wealthy İstanbullus family.
- **Birds Without Wings** Superbly researched historical fiction from Louis de Bernières.
- **İstanbul: the Imperial City** An impressive history of an impressive city, by John Freely.

FILMS

- **Climates** (Iklimer, 2006) Renowned director Nuri Bilge Ceylan's take on relationships between Turkish men and women.
- **Hamam** (1997) A Turk living in Italy returns to İstanbul after inheriting a *hamam*.
- **Yol** (1982) Once-banned political film following five prisoners in Turkey.
- **Troy** (2004) Brad Pitt's blockbuster about ancient Troy (unfortunately, though, it was filmed in Malta).

MUSIC

- **Işık Doğudan Yükselir** Contemporary folk from megastar Sezen Aksu.
- **Come Closer** Heart-throb Tarkan sings all in English.
- **Gipsy Rum** Burhan Öçal's knee-slapping introduction to Turkish gypsy music.
- **Su** Sufi-electronic-techno-fusion from Mercan Dede.

WEBSITES

- **Turkish Culture Foundation** (www.turkishculture.org) A virtual arts encyclopaedia.
- **Turkish Book Review** (www.planb.com.tr/tbr) Literary reviews and articles by up-and-coming writers.
- **Mehmetefendi Coffee** (www.mehmetefendi.com) Learn about Turkish coffee and fortune telling from the grounds.
- **Skylife Magazine** (www.thy.com) Turkish Airlines' inflight magazine serves up inspirational articles.

ITINERARIES

BOATING, BUYING & BATHING Three Days

Sure, you need to see the superlative sights, but you also want t *experience* **(1) İstanbul** (p712). The Bosphorus strait is the major thor oughfare in town: on one side is Asia, on the other is Europe. Start you first day with a cruise on a **Public Bosphorus Excursion Ferry** (p720) A 90-minute journey ends at Anadolu Kavağı village at the ruins o a medieval castle. You can take the bus back, but it's better to poke around and enjoy the return boat journey.

The next day is reserved for your shopping pleasure. In **Old İstanbul** (p717) the streets behind the Blue Mosque are the place to look for carpets, textiles and ceramic shops. But most will brave the kilometres-long **Grand Bazaar** (p717); be prepared to swap friendly banter with hundreds of shopkeepers. The **Old Book Bazaar** (p713 is a highlight. Over in modern **Beyoğlu** (p719), İstiklal Caddesi is lined with shops.

All that's on your agenda for day three is to visit the city's most beautiful bath house, **Cağaloğlu Hamamı** (p719). Cover yourself in the provided cloth and clogs and prepare to steam then be scrubbed and massaged on a marble – all in exquisite surrounds.

HISTORICAL HIGHLIGHTS Five Days

Explore a plethora of historical sights travelling down the Aegean coast. From İstanbul, start early for Çanakkale so you can be at the **(1) Gallipoli battlefields** (p723), site of the devastating WWI battle, by noon. The next morning head to famous **(2) Troy** (p724), worth a visit even if the ruins require a little imagination. Then on day three, head to the classical ruins at **(3) Pergamum** (p725). At the **Archaeology Museum** (p726) look for the 'Pergamum school' statues, among the first to start representing gods as recognisable human figures.

You've saved the best for last. Move on to your next base, fairly low-key **(4) Selçuk** (p726), which has its own fine archaeological museum and **Temple of Artemis** (p727) to explore. You'll want to spend a full day at nearby **(5) Ephesus** (p727), a one-time Roman provisional capital and the best-preserved classical city in the eastern Mediterranean. The ruins are a lot to take in; we'd buy the audio tour, or even hire one of the guides who linger around the ticket barriers.

WHAT IN THE WORLD? One Week

You'll have to cover a lot of ground to see these two curious sights in the Turkish interior. The easiest way to get from İstanbul to Cappadocia is by plane to Kayseri, but there are also overnight buses. It's hard not to be dumbstruck when you first see the fanciful rock formations around **(1) Göreme** (p736). You'll be staying for three days, preferably

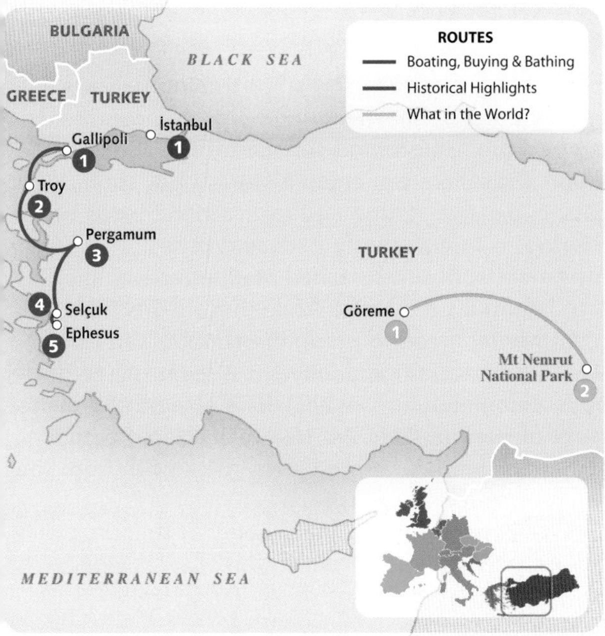

a cave or fairy chimney guesthouse. From there you can adventure ıt to see the rock-cut churches, monasteries and villages set in and nong the cones and pinnacles of volcanic tuff in the surrounding lleys.

Then hook up with one of the tour operators in Göreme for a four-ıy trip to see the giant mountain-top statues in **(2) Mt Nemrut ational Park** (p739). A pre-Roman king cut two impossible ledges to the summit to hold his monuments. The area has been shaken earthquakes, so colossal statue bodies sit silently in rows while n-high god heads look on from the ground.

DISCOVER TURKEY

While many Turks see their country as European, the nation packs in as many towering mosques and spice-trading bazaars as neighbouring Iran, Iraq and Syria. This bridge between continents has absorbed Europe's modernism and sophistication, and Asia's culture and tradition. Travellers can enjoy historical hot spots, mountain outposts, expansive steppe and caravanserai-loads of the exotic, without having to forego comfy beds and buses.

Turkey's charms range from sun-splashed Mediterranean and Aegean beaches to İstanbul's minarets. While these gems fit its reputation as a continental meeting point, the country can't be easily pigeonholed. Cappadocia (Kapadokya) is a dreamscape dotte with fairy chimneys, completely unlike anywhere else on the planet. The ethereal beauty of Nemrut Dağı (Mt Nemrut), littered with giant stone heads, and Olympos, where Lycian ruins peek from the undergrowth, is quintessentially Turkish.

And that's before you lace up your hiking boots or pull on a dive mask…

İSTANBUL

☎ 0212 / pop 16 million

Here you can retrace the steps of the Byzantine emperors when visiting Sultanahmet's monuments and museums, marvel at the magnificent Ottoman mosques on the city's seven hills, and wander the cobbled streets of ancient Jewish, Greek and Armenian neighbourhoods. The feeling of *hüzün* (melancholy) that the city once had is being replaced with a sense of energy, innovation and optimism not seen since the days of Süleyman the Magnificent. Stunning contemporary art galleries are opening around the city, and the possibility of a European-flavoured future is being embraced in the rooftop bars of Beyoğlu and the boardrooms of Levent. There has never been a better time to visit.

HISTORY

Late in the 2nd century AD, the Roman Empire conquered the small city-state of Byzantium, which was renam Constantinople in AD 330 after Emper Constantine moved his capital there. Wh Constantinople fell for the first time 1204, it was ransacked by the loot-hung Europeans of the Fourth Crusade.

İstanbul only regained its former glo after 1453, when it was captured b Mehmet the Conqueror and made capit of the Ottoman Empire. During the gli tering reign of Süleyman the Magnifice (1520–66), the city was graced with ma beautiful new buildings, and retaine much of its charm even during the em pire's long decline.

Occupied by Allied forces after WW the city came to be thought of as the de adent playpen of the sultans, notorio for its extravagant lifestyle and insidio spy games. As a result, when the Turkis Republic was proclaimed in 1923, Anka became the new capital, in an attempt wipe the slate clean.

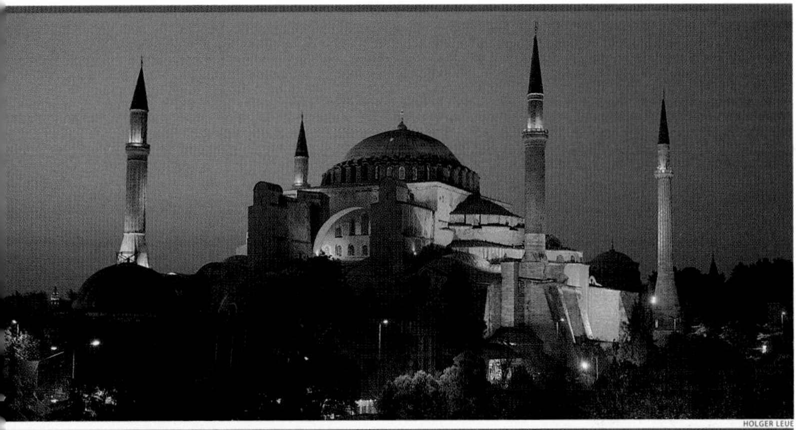

HOLGER LEUE

Aya Sofya (p718)

İSTANBUL IN TWO DAYS

Starting in Sultanahmet, **Topkapı Palace** (p717) could easily fill your first day; try to also fit in **Aya Sofya** (p718) and the **Blue Mosque** (p717). In the evening, head to a *hamam* (Turkish bath).

On the second day, spend the morning in the chaos of the **Grand Bazaar** (p717), then head over to **Beyoğlu** (p719) for a glimpse of modern İstanbul.

ORIENTATION

The Bosphorus strait, between the Black Sea and the Sea of Marmara, divides Europe from Asia.

Sultanahmet is the heart of Old İstanbul and boasts many of the city's famous sites. The adjoining area, which has hotels to suit all budgets, is called Cankurtaran, although if you say 'Sultanahmet' most people will understand where you mean. Beyoğlu, located on the northern side of the Golden Horn, was once the 'new', or 'European', city. The Tünel funicular railway runs uphill from Karaköy to the southern end of Beyoğlu's pedestrianised main street, İstiklal Caddesi.

INFORMATION

BOOKSHOPS

Bibliophiles will want to head towards the Byzantine **Old Book Bazaar** (Map pp714-15; Sahaflar Çarşısı, Beyazıt), in a shady little courtyard west of the Grand Bazaar; İstanbul's best range of bookshops is along or just off İstiklal Caddesi in Beyoğlu.

EMERGENCY

Tourist police (Map p716; ☎ 527 4503; Yerebatan Caddesi 6, Sultanahmet)

MEDICAL SERVICES

American Hospital (Amerikan Hastanesi; Map pp714-15; ☎ 444 3777; Güzelbahçe Sokak 20, Nişantaşı)

MONEY

Banks, ATMs and exchange offices are widespread, including in Sultanahmet's Aya Sofya Meydanı (Map p716) and along İstiklal Caddesi in Beyoğlu. The exchange rates offered at the airport are usually as good as those offered in town.

İSTANBUL

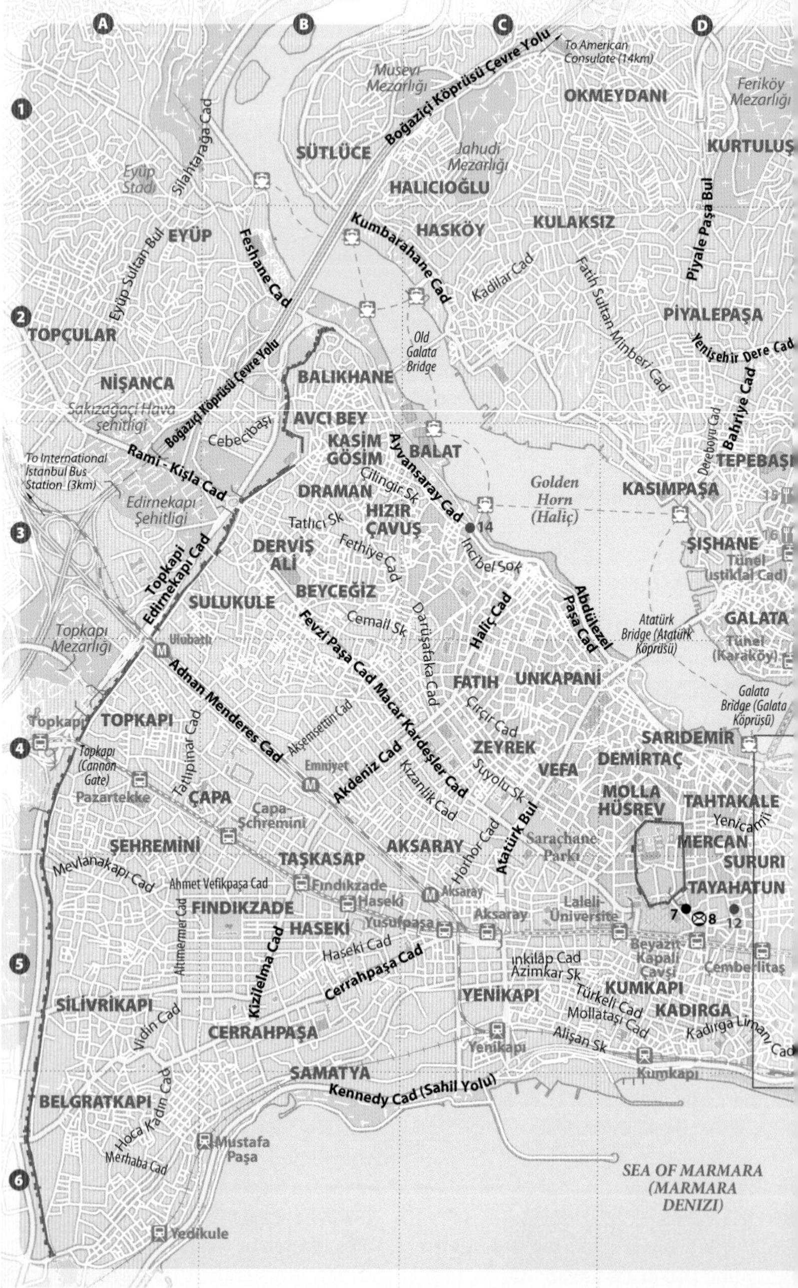
A
B
C
D
1
2
3
4
5
6
To American Consulate (14km)
Musevi Mezarlığı
Boğaziçi Köprüsü Çevre Yolu
OKMEYDANI
Feriköy Mezarlığı
KURTULUŞ
SÜTLÜCE
Jahudi Mezarlığı
HALICIOĞLU
Eyüp Stadı
Silahtarağa Cad
EYÜP
Feshane Cad
Kumbarahane Cad
HASKÖY
KULAKSIZ
Piyale Paşa Bul
Eyüp Sultan Bul
Kadılar Cad
Fatih Sultan Minberi Cad
Old Galata Bridge
TOPÇULAR
PİYALEPAŞA
Yenişehir Dere Cad
NİŞANCA
BALIKHANE
Sakızağacı Hava Şehitliği
AVCI BEY
Cebecibaşı
Bahriye Cad
Dereboyu Cad
To International İstanbul Bus Station (3km)
Rami - Kışla Cad
KASİM GÖSİM
BALAT
TEPEBAŞI
Ayvansaray Cad
DRAMAN
Çilingir Sk
Golden Horn (Haliç)
KASIMPAŞA
Edirnekapı Şehitliği
HIZIR ÇAVUŞ
Tatlıcı Sk
14
15
16
DERVİŞ ALİ
Fethiye Cad
İncibel Sok
ŞİŞHANE
Tünel (İstiklal Cad)
Topkapı Edirnekapı Cad
BEYCEĞİZ
SULUKULE
Abdülezel Paşa Cad
Cemail Sk
Haliç Cad
GALATA
Atatürk Bridge (Atatürk Köprüsü)
Darüşşafaka Cad
Tünel (Karaköy)
Topkapı Mezarlığı
Ulubatlı
Fevzi Paşa Cad
Macar Kardeşler Cad
FATİH
UNKAPANI
Galata Bridge (Galata Köprüsü)
Adnan Menderes Cad
Topkapı
TOPKAPI
Tatlıpınar Cad
Akşemsettin Cad
Çırçır Cad
SARIDEMİR
Topkapı (Cannon Gate)
ZEYREK
Emniyet
Akdeniz Cad
Kızanlık Cad
VEFA
DEMİRTAÇ
Pazartekke
ÇAPA
Suyolu Sk
MOLLA HÜSREV
TAHTAKALE
Çapa-Şehremini
Horhor Cad
Atatürk Bul
Yeni Camii
ŞEHREMİNİ
AKSARAY
Saraçhane Parkı
MERCAN
Mevlanakapı Cad
TAŞKASAP
SURURİ
Ahmet Vefikpaşa Cad
Fındıkzade
Aksaray
TAYAHATUN
FINDIKZADE
Haseki
Laleli-Üniversite
Altımermer Cad
HASEKİ
Yusufpaşa
7
8
12
Beyazıt-Kapalı Çarşı
Çemberlitaş
Haseki Cad
Kızılelma Cad
Cerrahpaşa Cad
İnkilâp Cad
Azimkar Sk
YENİKAPI
KUMKAPI
Türkeli Cad
KADIRGA
SİLİVRİKAPI
Mollataşı Cad
Kadırga Limanı Cad
Vidin Cad
CERRAHPAŞA
Alişan Sk
Yenikapı
Kumkapı
SAMATYA
Kennedy Cad (Sahil Yolu)
BELGRATKAPI
Hoca Kadın Cad
Mustafa Paşa
Merhaba Cad
SEA OF MARMARA (MARMARA DENİZİ)
Yedikule

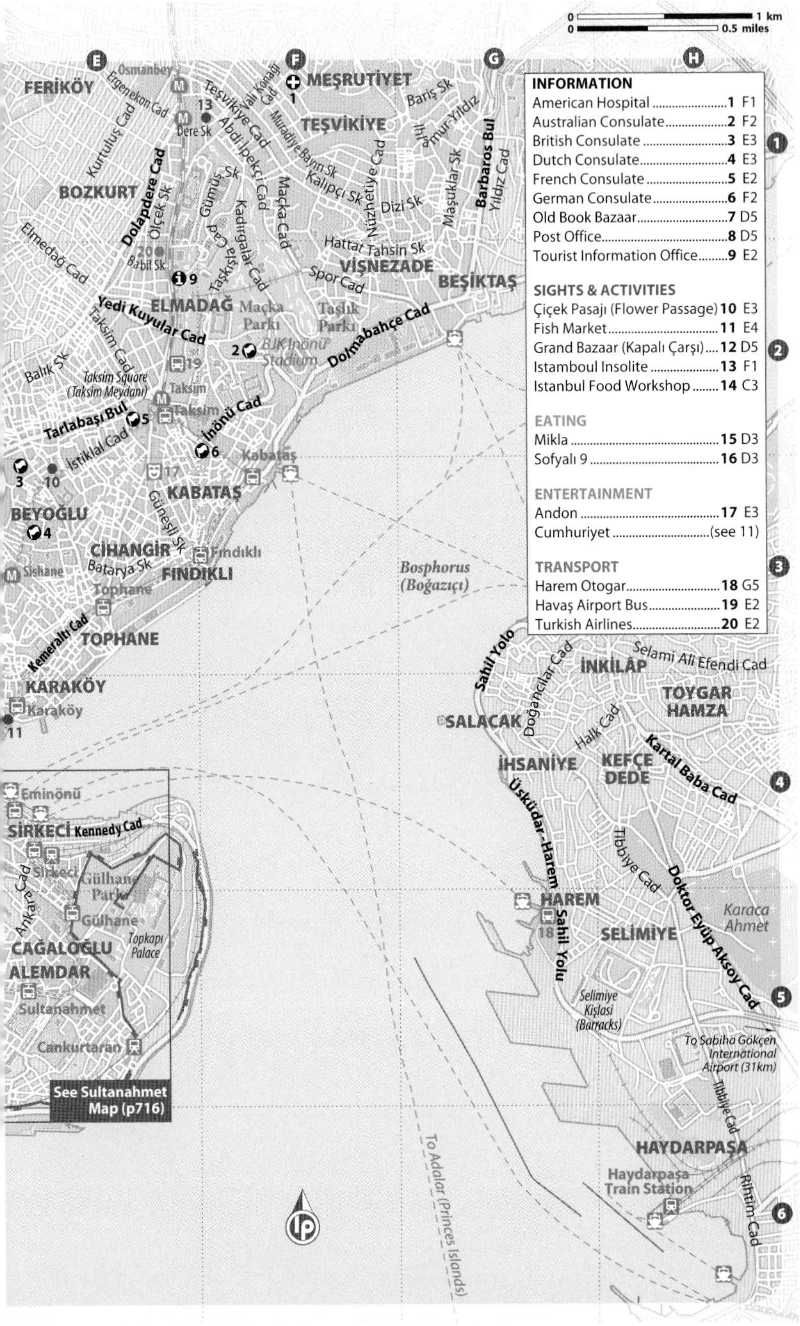
0 1 km
0 0.5 miles
INFORMATION
American Hospital 1 F1
Australian Consulate 2 F2
British Consulate 3 E3
Dutch Consulate 4 E3
French Consulate 5 E2
German Consulate 6 F2
Old Book Bazaar 7 D5
Post Office 8 D5
Tourist Information Office 9 E2
SIGHTS & ACTIVITIES
Çiçek Pasajı (Flower Passage) 10 E3
Fish Market 11 E4
Grand Bazaar (Kapalı Çarşı) 12 D5
Istamboul Insolite 13 F1
Istanbul Food Workshop 14 C3
EATING
Mikla 15 D3
Sofyalı 9 16 D3
ENTERTAINMENT
Andon 17 E3
Cumhuriyet (see 11)
TRANSPORT
Harem Otogar 18 G5
Havaş Airport Bus 19 E2
Turkish Airlines 20 E2
FERİKÖY
Osmanbey
MEŞRUTİYET
TEŞVİKİYE
BOZKURT
VİŞNEZADE
BEŞİKTAŞ
ELMADAĞ
Maçka Parkı
Taşlık Parkı
BJK İnönü Stadium
Taksim Square (Taksim Meydanı)
Taksim
Kabataş
KABATAŞ
BEYOĞLU
CİHANGİR
FINDIKLI
Fındıklı
Şişhane
Tophane
TOPHANE
KARAKÖY
Karaköy
Bosphorus (Boğazıcı)
İNKİLÂP
TOYGAR HAMZA
SALACAK
İHSANİYE
KEFÇE DEDE
HAREM
SELİMİYE
Karaca Ahmet
Selimiye Kışlasi (Barracks)
To Sabiha Gökçen International Airport (31km)
HAYDARPAŞA
Haydarpaşa Train Station
To Adalar (Princes Islands)
Eminönü
SİRKECİ
Sirkeci
Gülhane Parkı
Gülhane
Topkapı Palace
CAĞALOĞLU
ALEMDAR
Sultanahmet
Cankurtaran
See Sultanahmet Map (p716)
Kennedy Cad
Ankara Cad
Dolapdere Cad
Yedi Kuyular Cad
Tarlabaşı Bul
İstiklal Cad
İnönü Cad
Dolmabahçe Cad
Barbaros Bul
Kemeraltı Cad
Sahil Yolu
Selami Ali Efendi Cad
Kartal Baba Cad
Üsküdar - Harem Sahil Yolu
Doktor Eyüp Aksoy Cad
Tıbbiye Cad
Rıhtım Cad

SULTANAHMET

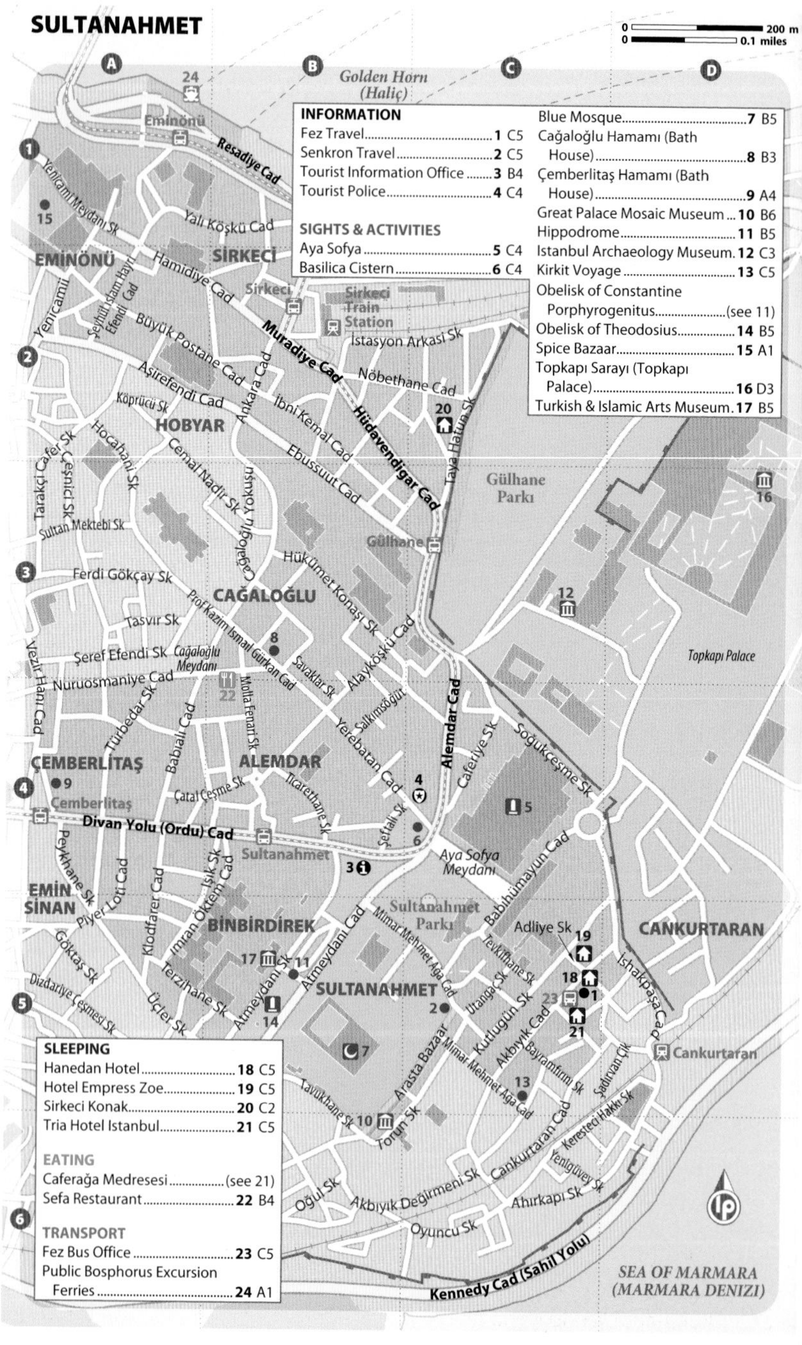

INFORMATION

- Fez Travel....1 C5
- Senkron Travel....2 C5
- Tourist Information Office....3 B4
- Tourist Police....4 C4

SIGHTS & ACTIVITIES

- Aya Sofya....5 C4
- Basilica Cistern....6 C4
- Blue Mosque....7 B5
- Cağaloğlu Hamamı (Bath House)....8 B3
- Çemberlitaş Hamamı (Bath House)....9 A4
- Great Palace Mosaic Museum....10 B6
- Hippodrome....11 B5
- Istanbul Archaeology Museum....12 C3
- Kirkit Voyage....13 C5
- Obelisk of Constantine Porphyrogenitus....(see 11)
- Obelisk of Theodosius....14 B5
- Spice Bazaar....15 A1
- Topkapı Sarayı (Topkapı Palace)....16 D3
- Turkish & Islamic Arts Museum....17 B5

SLEEPING

- Hanedan Hotel....18 C5
- Hotel Empress Zoe....19 C5
- Sirkeci Konak....20 C2
- Tria Hotel Istanbul....21 C5

EATING

- Caferağa Medresesi....(see 21)
- Sefa Restaurant....22 B4

TRANSPORT

- Fez Bus Office....23 C5
- Public Bosphorus Excursion Ferries....24 A1

POST

İstanbul's central **post office** (Map pp714-15) is a few blocks southwest of Sirkeci Railway Station.

TOURIST INFORMATION

Tourist offices can be found at several locations:

Elmadağ (**Map pp714-15; ☎ 233 0592; ⏰ 9am-5pm Mon-Sat**) In the arcade in front of the İstanbul Hilton Hotel, just off Cumhuriyet Caddesi. About a 10-minute walk north of Taksim Sq.

Sultanahmet (**Map p716; ☎ 518 8754; ⏰ 9am-5pm**) At the northeast end of the Hippodrome.

TRAVEL AGENCIES

Fez Travel (**Map p716; ☎ 516 9024; www.feztravel.com; Akbıyık Caddesi 15, Sultanahmet**)

Senkron Travel (**Map p716; ☎ 638 8340; www.senkrontours.com; Arasta Bazaar 51, Sultanahmet**)

DANGERS & ANNOYANCES

İstanbul is no more nor less safe a city than any large metropolis, but there are some dangers worth highlighting. Bag-snatching is a slight problem, especially on Galipdede Sokak in Tünel and on İstiklal Caddesi's side streets. Probably most importantly, however, you should be aware of the long-standing scam involving men, bars and women.

The PKK (Kurdistan Workers Party) separatist group sporadically targets İstanbul with bombings, normally aimed at affluent, touristy neighbourhoods; the most recent was a double bomb attack in July 2008.

SIGHTS & ACTIVITIES

OLD İSTANBUL

The Sultanahmet area is 'Old İstanbul', a Unesco-designated World Heritage site packed with so many wonderful sights you could spend several weeks here and still only scratch the surface.

BLUE MOSQUE

A striking monument, the **Blue Mosque** (**Sultan Ahmet Camii; Map p716; Hippodrome, Sultanahmet; ⏰ closed during prayer times**) is a voluptuous architectural feat. It was built between 1606 and 1616, and is light and delicate compared with its squat neighbour, Aya Sofya. The graceful exterior is notable for its six slender minarets and a cascade of domes and half domes; the inside is a luminous blue, created by the tiled walls and painted dome.

Rents from the *arasta* (row of shops) to the east provide support for the Blue Mosque's upkeep, and it's also a great hassle-free spot to shop. Nearby the *arasta* is the entrance to the **Great Palace Mosaic Museum** (**Büyüksaray Mozaik Müzesi; Map p716; ☎ 518 1205; Torun Sokak; admission TL8; ⏰ 9am-6.30pm Tue-Sun**), a spectacular stretch of ancient Byzantine pavement featuring hunting scenes.

TOPKAPI SARAYI

Possibly İstanbul's most iconic monument, opulent **Topkapı Sarayı** (**Topkapı Palace; Map p716; ☎ 512 0480; Babıhümayun Caddesi; palace TL20, harem TL15; ⏰ 9am-7pm Wed-Mon summer**) is a highlight of any trip. The palace was begun by Mehmet shortly after the Conquest in 1453, and Ottoman sultans lived in this impressive environment until the 19th century. Make sure you visit the mind-blowing **harem**, the palace's most famous sight, and the **treasury**, which features an incredible collection of precious objects.

GRAND BAZAAR

Hone your haggling skills before dipping into the truly enormous **Grand Bazaar**

PHIL WEYMOUTH

Aya Sofya interior

AYA SOFYA (CHURCH OF HOLY WISDOM)

No doubt you will gasp at the overblown splendour of **Aya Sofya**, one of the world's most glorious buildings. Built as part of Emperor Justinian's (527–65) effort to restore the greatness of the Roman Empire, it was completed in AD 537 and reigned as the grandest church in Christendom until the Conquest in 1453. The exterior does impress, but the interior, with its sublime domed ceiling soaring heavenward, is truly over the top.

Things you need to know: Map p716; ☎ 522 0989; Aya Sofya Meydanı, Sultanahmet; adult/child under 6 TL20/free; ⏲ 9am-7.30pm Tue-Sun, upper gallery closes 15-30 min earlier

(Kapalı Çarşı; Map pp714-15; ⏲ 9am-7pm Mon-Sat) covered market. Just north of Divan Yolu, this labyrinthine medieval shopping mall consists of some 4000 shops selling everything from carpets to clothing, including silverware, jewellery, antiques and belly-dancing costumes. Starting from a small masonry *bedesten* (market enclosure) built during the time of Mehmet the Conqueror, the bazaar has grown to cover a vast area. It's probably the most discombobulating and manic shopping precinct you could hope to experienc Sure, the touts are ubiquitous, but com in the right frame of mind and you' realise it's part of the fun. With severa kilometres of lanes, it's also a great plac to ramble and get lost – which you wi certainly do at least once.

BASILICA CISTERN

Across the tram lines from Aya Sofya i the entrance to the majestic Byzantin **Basilica Cistern** (Yerebatan Sarnıçı; Map p71 ☎ 522 1259; Yerebatan Caddesi 13, Sultanahme admission TL10; ⏲ 9am-6.30pm Apr-Sep), bui by Justinian in AD 532. This vast, atmos pheric, column-filled cistern stored up t 80,000 cubic metres of water for regula summer use in the Great Palace, as we as for times of siege.

İSTANBUL ARCHAEOLOGY MUSEUM

Downhill from the Topkapı Palace, this su perb **museum complex** (Arkeoloji Müzeler Map p716; ☎ 520 7740; Osman Hamdi Bey Yokuşu Gülhane; admission TL10; ⏲ 9am-5pm Tue-Sun is a must-see for anyone interested i the Middle East's ancient past. The mai building houses an outstanding collectio of Greek and Roman statuary, includin the magnificent sarcophagi from the roya necropolis at Sidon in Lebanon.

In a separate building, the **Museum o the Ancient Orient** houses Hittite an other older archaeological finds. Also o the grounds is the **Tiled Pavilion** (Çini Köşk), one of İstanbul's oldest Ottoma buildings.

HIPPODROME

In front of the Blue Mosque is th **Hippodrome** (Atmeydanı; Map p716 where chariot races once took place It was also the scene of a series of riot during Justinian's rule. While construc tion started in AD 203, the Hippodrom was later added to and enlarged by Constantine.

The **Obelisk of Theodosius** (Map p716) is an Egyptian column from the temple of Karnak. It features 3500-year-old hieroglyphics and rests on a Byzantine base. The 10m-high **Obelisk of Constantine Porphyrogenitus** (Map p716) was once covered in bronze, subsequently stolen by the Crusaders. The base rests at the former level of the Hippodrome, several metres below the ground.

TURKISH & ISLAMIC ARTS MUSEUM

On the Hippodrome's western side, this **museum** (Türk ve İslam Eserleri Müzesi; Map p716; ☎ 518 1805; At Meydanı 46, Sultanahmet; admission TL10; 9am-4.30pm Tue-Sun) is housed in the former palace of İbrahim Paşa, son-in-law of Süleyman the Magnificent. Inside, you'll be wowed by one of the world's best collections of antique carpets and some equally impressive manuscripts and miniatures. The coffee shop in the lovely green courtyard is a welcome refuge from the crowds and touts.

HAMAMS

The **Cağaloğlu Hamamı** (Map p716; Yerebatan Caddesi 34; bath services €15-50; men 8am-10pm, women 8am-8pm) is the city's most beautiful *hamam* (Turkish bath). It's pricey and pretty touristy, but the surroundings are simply exquisite. Separate baths for men and women each have a large *camekan* (reception area) with private, lockable cubicles where it's possible to have a nap or a tea at the end of your bath. The **Çemberlitaş Hamamı** (Map p716; Vezir Hanı Caddesi 8, Çemberlitaş; bath services €14.50-39.50; 6am-midnight) was designed by the great Ottoman architect Mimar Sinan in 1584, and is one of İstanbul's most atmospheric *hamams*.

BEYOĞLU

The neighbourhood is a showcase of cosmopolitan Turkey at its best – miss Beyoğlu and you haven't seen İstanbul. Stretching from Tünel Sq to Taksim Sq, **İstiklal Caddesi** (Independence Ave; Map pp714-15) was known as the Grande Rue de Péra in the late 19th century, and now it carries the life of the modern city up and down its lively promenade. There's a plethora of sights, but the **fish market** (*balık pazar;* Map pp714-15) and, in the Cité de Pera building, the **Çiçek Pasajı** (Flower Passage; Map pp714-15) are absolute must-sees; both are near the Galatasaray Lisesi (a prestigious public school). These days locals bypass the touts and the mediocre food on offer at Çiçek Pasjı and make their way behind the

GEORGE TSAFOS

Inside the Basilica Cistern

IZZET KERIBAR

Cruising on the Bosphorus

passage to one of İstanbul's most colourful and popular eating and drinking precincts, Nevizade Sokak.

BOSPHORUS CRUISE

Don't leave the city without exploring the Bosphorus. Most day trippers take the much-loved **Public Bosphorus Excursion Ferry** (Map p716; one way/return TL10/17; 10.35am, noon & 1.35pm) trip up its entire length (90 minutes one way). These depart from Eminönü and stop at various points before turning around at Anadolu Kavağı. The shores are sprinkled with monuments and various sights, including the monumental Dolmabahçe Palace, the majestic Bosphorus Bridge, the waterside suburbs of Arnavutköy, Bebek, Kanlıca, Emirgan and Sarıyer, as well as lavish *yalı*s (waterfront wooden summer residences) and numerous mosques.

COURSES

İstanbul Food Workshop (Map pp714-15; ☎ 534 4788; www.istanbulfoodworkshop.com; Yıldırım Caddesi 111, Fener) A well-respected outfit running walking tours as well as Turkish and Ottoman cooking classes.

TOURS

İstamboul Insolite (Map pp714-15; ☎ 241 2846; www.istanbulguide.net/insolite; Bahtiyar Sokak 6, Nışantaşı; full-day tours per person €50-150) This small agency runs a variety of offbeat tours.

Kirkit Voyage (Map p716; ☎ 518 2282; www.kirkit.com; Amiral Tafdil Sokak 12, Sultanahmet; half- & full-day tours €23-50) Kirkit specialises in small-group walking tours of the must-see sights.

FESTIVALS & EVENTS

The **İstanbul International Music Festival** (www.iksv.org/muzik), from early June to early July, attracts big-name artists from around the world, who perform in venues that are not always open to the public (such as Aya İrini Kilisesi).

SLEEPING

İstanbul's accommodation is becoming quite pricey. For the time being, the best area to stay remains Cankurtaran, where the quiet streets have moderate hotels with stunning views from their roof terraces, as well as some more luxurious options. Unless otherwise stated, rates include breakfast and private bathrooms.

Hanedan Hotel (Map p716; ☎ 516 4869; www.hanedanhotel.com; Adliye Sokak 3, Cankurtaran; s €40, d €60-65;) Pale lemon walls and polished wooden floors give the Hanedan's rooms an elegant feel, and the roof terrace offers views of the sea and Aya Sofya.

Hotel Empress Zoe (Map p716; ☎ 518 2504; www.emzoe.com; Adliye Sokak 10, Cankurtaran; s €75, d €110-135, ste €120-240;) This American-owned boutique hotel has individually and charmingly decorated rooms and suites. Breakfast is served in a flower-filled garden, and there's a rooftop lounge-terrace with excellent views.

Tria Hotel İstanbul (Map p716; ☎ 518 4518; www.triahotelistanbul.com; Terbıyık Sokak 7, Cankurtaran; s €180, d €218-280;) Extremely comfortable and quiet rooms offer tea- and coffee-making equipment, flat-screen TVs, work desks and large beds; all are attractively decorated with polished floorboards, silk curtains, embroidered bedspreads and objets d'art.

Sirkeci Konak (Map p716; ☎ 528 4344; Taya Hatun Sokak 5, Sirkeci; r €190-320;) Sirkeci's owners know what keeps guests happy: large, well-equipped rooms, with extras such as tea- and coffee-making equipment, satellite TV, quality toiletries and luxe linen. There's also a wellness centre with pool, gym and *hamam*, as well as complimentary afternoon teas and Anatolian cooking lessons.

EATING

Unfortunately, Sultanahmet has the least impressive range of eating options in the city, so we recommend crossing the Galata Bridge to join the locals.

SPLURGE

Mikla (Map pp714-15; ☎ 0212-293 5656; Marmara Pera Hotel, Meşrutiyet Caddesi 15, Tepebaşı; mains TL36-46.25; noon-3pm & 7pm-1am Mon-Fri, 7pm-1am Sat) is the city's best restaurant – bar none. Local celebrity chef Mehmet Gürs is a master of perfectly executed Mediterranean cuisine, and the Turkish accents he employs make his food truly memorable. Extraordinary views, luxe surrounds and exemplary service complete the experience.

Caferağa Medresesi (Map p716; ☎ 513 3601; Cafariye Sokak; soup TL3, köfte TL10; 8.30am-6pm) This teensy *lokanta* in the gorgeous courtyard of a Sinan-designed *medrese* near Topkapı Palace is a rare treat in Sultanahmet, allowing you to nosh in stylish surrounds without paying through the nose.

Sefa Restaurant (Map p716; ☎ 520 0670; Nuruosmaniye Caddesi 17, Cağaloğlu; mains TL6.50-16; 7am-5pm) Locals favour this place on the way to the Grand Bazaar. You can order from an English-language menu or choose from the bain-marie.

our pick **Sofyalı 9** (Map pp714-15; ☎ 245 0362; Sofyalı Sokak 9, Tünel; mains TL10-16; 11am-1am Mon-Sat) Tables at this gem are hot property at weekends. It serves some of the city's best *meyhane* (tavern) food – notably the *Arnavut ciğeri* (Albanian fried liver), fried fish and meze – in surroundings as welcoming as they are attractive.

DRINKING

There's a healthy and thriving bar scene in Beyoğlu, which is almost permanently crowded with locals who patronise the atmosphere-laden *meyhaneler* (taverns)

GREG ELMS

Turkish coffee

IZZET KERIBAR

Turkish cemetery, Gallipoli

lining the side streets. There's nothing better than swigging a few glasses of *rakı* around Balo Sokak and Sofyalı Sokak, or in the sleek rooftop bars on both sides of İstiklal Caddesi.

Sultanahmet isn't as happening but it has a few decent watering holes, particularly on Akbıyık Caddesi in summer. The area's alcohol-free, atmosphere-rich *çay bahçesis* (tea gardens) or *kahvehanes* (coffee houses) are great for relaxing and sampling that great Turkish institution, the *nargileh* (water pipe), along with a cup of *Türk kahvesi* (Turkish coffee) or *çay*.

ENTERTAINMENT

A classic İstanbul night out involves carousing to live *fasıl*, a raucous local form of Romani music. Two good *meyhaneler* for indulging in this time-honoured activity are **Cumhuriyet** (Map pp714-15; Sahne Sokak 4; music 8.30pm-midnight most nights) in Beyoğlu's Balık Pazar; and **Andon** (Map pp714-15; Sıraselviler Caddesi 51, Taksim; music 9pm-2am most nights) just off Taksim Sq.

GETTING THERE & AWAY

AIR

Turkish Airlines (Map pp714-15; ☎ 252 1106; www.thy.com; Cumhuriyet Caddesi 7) is the main domestic carrier, and Onur Air, Atlasjet and Fly Air also operate domestic flights from İstanbul.

For more details on flying to/from and within Turkey, see p742.

BUS

The huge **International İstanbul Bus Station** (Uluslararası İstanbul Otogarı; off Map pp714-15; ☎ 658 0505) is the city's main *otogar* for intercity and international routes. It's in Esenler, about 10km northwest of Sultanahmet. The Light Rail Transit (LRT) service stops here en route to/from the airport. Many bus companies offer a free *servis* (shuttle bus) to or from the *otogar*.

If you're heading east to Anatolia, you might want to board at the smaller **Harem Otogar** (Map pp714-15; ☎ 0216-333 3763), north of Haydarpaşa Railway Station on the Asian shore, but the choice of services here is more limited.

TRAIN

For services to Edirne and Europe go to **Sirkeci Railway Station** (Map p716; ☎ 527 0051). Daily international services from Sirkeci include the *Dostlu/Filia Ekspresi* service to Thessaloniki (Greece; TL101 to TL178). European trains will terminate at Yenikapı after the completion of Marmaray, an ambitious public transport project aimed at relieving İstanbul's woeful traffic congestion, but this will not come about until 2012 at the earliest.

Trains from Anatolia and from countries to the east and south terminate at **Haydarpaşa Railway Station** (Map pp714-15; ☎ 0216-336 4470), on the Asian shore of the Bosphorus.

GETTING AROUND

There is a quick, cheap and efficient LRT service from Atatürk International Airport to Zeytinburnu, from where you connect with the tram that takes you directly to Sultanahmet. If you are staying near Taksim Sq, the **Havaş airport bus** (Map pp714-15; ☎ 244 0487) is your best bet. Buses leave Atatürk (TL9) every 15 to 30 minutes from 4am until 1am, and Sabiha Gökçen (TL10) 25 minutes after planes land. A taxi to Atatürk from Sultanahmet costs from TL35; to Sabiha Gökçen, at least TL80.

The cheapest and most scenic way to travel any distance in İstanbul is by ferry. The main ferry docks are at the mouth of the Golden Horn (Eminönü, Sirkeci and Karaköy) and at Beşiktaş, a few kilometres northeast of the Galata Bridge, south of Dolmabahçe Palace.

İstanbul's efficient bus system has major bus stations at Taksim Sq, Beşiktaş, Aksaray, Rüstempaşa-Eminönü, Kadıköy and Üsküdar. You must have a ticket before boarding; buy tickets from the white booths near major stops or, for a small mark-up, from some nearby shops (look for 'İETT *otobüs bileti satılır*' signs).

There is a one-stop Tünel funicular system between Karaköy and İstiklal Caddesi (every 10 or 15 minutes from 7.30am to 9pm). A newer funicular railway runs through a tunnel from the Bosphorus shore at Kabataş (where it connects with the tram) up to the metro station at Taksim Sq.

AROUND İSTANBUL

EDİRNE

☎ 0284 / pop 136,000

One of the world's oldest and most bizarre sporting events takes place annually in late June/early July at Sarayiçi in northern Edirne. At the 650-year-old **Tarihi Kırkpınar Yağlı Güreş Festivali** (Historic Kırpınar Oil Wrestling Festival), muscular men, naked except for a pair of heavy leather shorts, coat themselves with olive oil and throw each other around. For more information, visit the **Kırpınar Evi** (Kırpınar House; ☎ 212 8622; www.kirkpinar.com; 🕑 10am-noon & 2-6pm) in Edirne or check out www.turkishwrestling.com.

There are regular bus services for İstanbul (TL20, 2½ hours, 235km) and Çanakkale (TL25, four hours, 230km).

AEGEAN COAST

Turkey's Aegean coast can convincingly claim more ancient ruins per square kilometre than any other region in the world. Here you'll see the famous ruins of Troy, Ephesus and Pergamum (Bergama), and you can contemplate the devastation of war at the battlefield sites of Gallipoli.

GALLIPOLI (GELIBOLU) PENINSULA

☎ 0286

Antipodeans and many Britons won't need an introduction to Gallipoli; it is the backbone of the 'Anzac legend', in which an Allied campaign in 1915 to knock Turkey out of WWI and open a relief route to Russia turned into one of the war's greatest fiascos. Some 130,000 men died, a third from Allied forces and the rest Turkish.

Today the Gallipoli battlefields are peaceful places, covered in brush and pine forests. But the battles fought here nearly a century ago are still alive in many memories, both Turkish and foreign, especially Australians and New Zealanders, who view the peninsula as a place of pilgrimage. The Turkish officer responsible for the defence of Gallipoli was Mustafa Kemal (the future Atatürk); his victory is commemorated in Turkey on 18 March. On Anzac Day (25 April), a dawn service marks the anniversary of the Allied landings.

The easiest way to see the battlefields is with your own transport or on a minibus tour from **Hassle Free Tours** (☎ 213 5969; www.hasslefreetour.com; Anzac House Hostel, Çanakkale; TL45-55), **Trooper Tours** (☎ 217 3343; www.troopertours.com; Yellow Rose Pension, Çanakkale; TL55) or **TJs Tours** (☎ 814 3121; www.anzacgallipollitours.com; TJs Hotel, Eceabat; TL45). With a tour you get the benefit of a guide who can explain the battles as you go along.

ÇANAKKALE

☎ 0286 / pop 86,600

The liveliest settlement on the Dardanelles, this sprawling harbour town would be worth a visit for its sights, nightlife and overall vibe even if it didn't lie opposite the Gallipoli Peninsula. Its sweeping waterfront promenade heaves during the summer months.

A good base for visiting Troy, Çanakkale has become a popular destination for weekending Turks; if possible plan your visit for midweek. The **tourist office** (☎ 217 1187; Cumhuriyet Meydanı; 8am-noon & 1-7pm Jun-Sep, to 5pm Oct-May) is 150m from the ferry pier, and you can access the internet at **Maxi Internet** (Fetvane Sokak 51; per hr TL1.50).

Built by Sultan Mehmet the Conqueror in 1452, the **Ottoman castle** at the southern end of the waterfront now houses the **Military Museum** (Askeri Müze; admission TL3; 9am-noon & 1.30-5pm Tue, Wed & Fri-Sun). About 1.5km south of the *otogar* on the road to Troy, the **Archaeological Museum** (Arkeoloji Müzesi; admission TL2; 8am-5pm) holds artefacts found at Troy (below) and Assos.

Rooms are expensive around Anzac Day and are usually booked solid months before 25 April arrives.

Yellow Rose Pension (☎ 217 3343; www.yellowrose.4mg.com; Aslan Abla Sokak 5; dm/s/d/tr TL17/30/55/60;) This bright, attractive guest house has a central but quiet location and extras including a laundry service and fully equipped kitchen.

our pick **Kervansaray Hotel** (☎ 217 8192; www.otelkervansaray.com; Fetvane Sokak 13; s/d/tr €35/50/60;) Çanakkale's only boutique hotel is as lovely as you could hope for, laying on Ottoman touches in keeping with the restored house it occupies.

To eat on the hoof, browse the stalls along the waterfront, which offer corn on the cob, mussels and other simple items.

Doyum (☎ 217 1866; Cumhuriyet Meydanı 13; dishes TL4.50-10) Generally acknowledged to be the best *kebap* and pide joint in town, a visit to Doyum is worth it for the good cheer alone.

Köy Evi (☎ 213 4687; Yalı Caddesi 13; menu TL5) Proper home cooking rules in this tiny eatery, where local women make *mantı*, *börek* and *gözleme* (TL1.50).

There are regular buses to İstanbul (TL30, six hours).

TROY (TRUVA)

☎ 0286

Of all the ancient sites in Turkey, the remains of the great city of Troy are in fact among the least impressive; you'll have to use your imagination. It's an important stop for history buffs, however, and if you have read Homer's *Iliad*, the ruins have a romance few places on Earth can match.

Pergamum ruins

The ticket booth for the ruins of **Troy** (☎ 283 0536; per person/parking TL10/3; ⌚ 8.30am-7pm May-15 Sep, to 5pm 16 Sep-Apr) is 500m before the site. The site is rather confusing for nonexpert eyes (guides are available), but the most conspicuous features, apart from the reconstruction of the Trojan Horse, include the **walls** from various periods; the Graeco-Roman **Temple of Athena**, of which traces of the altar remain; the Roman **Odeon**, where concerts were held; and the **Bouleuterion** (Council Chamber), built around Homer's time (c 800 BC).

From Çanakkale, *dolmuşes* to Troy (TL2, 35 minutes, 30km) leave every hour on the half-hour from 9.30am to 5.30pm from a station under the bridge over the Sarı River and drop you by the ticket booth. *Dolmuşes* run back to Çanakkale on the hour, until 5pm in high season and 3pm in low season.

The travel agencies offering tours to the Gallipoli battlefields (p724) also offer tours to Troy (around €25 per person).

BERGAMA (PERGAMUM)

☎ 0232 / pop 58,200

As Selçuk is to Ephesus, so Bergama is to Pergamum: a workaday market town that's become a major stop on the tourist trail because of its proximity to the remarkable ruins of Pergamum, site of the pre-eminent medical centre of Ancient Rome. During Pergamum's heyday (between Alexander the Great and the Roman domination of Asia Minor) it was one of the Middle East's richest and most powerful small kingdoms.

İzmir Caddesi (the main street) is where you'll find banks with ATMs and the PTT. There is a basic **tourist office** (☎ 631 2851; İzmir Caddesi 54; ⌚ 8.30am-noon & 1-5.30pm), just north of the museum, and most pensions and hotels offer free internet access.

One of the highlights of the Aegean coast, the well-proportioned **Asclepion** (Temple of Asclepios; admission/parking TL10/3; ⌚ 8.30am-5.30pm), about 3km from the city centre, was a famous medical school with a library rivalling that of Alexandria in Egypt. The ruins of the **Acropolis** (**admission TL10; 8.30am-5.30pm**), 6km from the city, are equally striking. The hilltop setting is absolutely magical, and the well-preserved ruins are magnificent, especially the vertigo-inducing 10,000-seat **theatre** and the marble-columned **Temple of Trajan**, built during the reigns of Emperors Trajan and Hadrian and used to worship them as well as Zeus.

The excellent **Archaeology Museum** (**Arkeoloji Müzesi; İzmir Caddesi; admission TL2; 8.30am-5.30pm Tue-Sun**) has a small but substantial collection of artefacts from both of these sites, including a collection of 4th-century statues from the so-called 'Pergamum School'.

Gobi Pension (**633 2518; www.gobipension.com; Atatürk Bulvarı 18; s/d €20/32**) On the main road behind a greenery-draped terrace, this is a great family-run place with bright, cheery rooms, most with new private bathrooms.

our pick **Akropolis Guest House** (**631 2621; www.akropolisguesthouse.com; Kayalik Caddesi 5; s/d €20/49**) This 150-year-old stone house is the closest Bergama gets to boutique, with eight attractively decorated rooms surrounding a pool and garden, a restaurant set in a barn and a terrace with Acropolis views.

Sağlam Restaurant (**632 8897; Cumhuriyet Meydanı 47; mains TL6-11**) This large, simple place is well known in town for its high-quality home cooking. It does a good selection of meze, which change daily, and delicious *kebaps*.

Bergama's new *otogar* lies 7km from the centre at the junction of the highway and the main road into town. From here a *dolmuş* service shuttles into town (TL2).

There's no public transport to the archaeological sites. A taxi tour of sites including the Acropolis, the Asclepion and the museum costs from TL40 to TL60, depending on the time of year.

SELÇUK

0232 / pop 27,300

Selçuk boasts one of the Seven Wonders of the Ancient World, an excellent museum, a fine basilica and mosque, a stork-nest-studded aqueduct and,

HOLGER LEUE

Tourists at the ruins of Ephesus

ght on the town's doorstep, Ephesus. ompared to the vast tourism factory of earby Kuşadası, however, Selçuk's tourm industry is a small-scale, workshopzed affair.

Selçuk's *otogar* lies just east of the mir-Aydın road (Atatürk Caddesi), with ne town centre and some pensions imediately north of it. On the western side f the main road a park spreads out in ont of one wing of the Ephesus Museum. he **tourist office** (☎ 892 6945; www.selcuk.ov.tr; Agora Caddesi 35; 🕑 8am-noon & 1-5pm lon-Fri winter, daily in summer) is opposite he museum.

Selçuk is not only close to Ephesus, it s also blessed with superb monuments cattered around the centre. Don't miss he conspicuous **Basilica of St John** (St ean Caddesi; admission TL2; 🕑 8am-5pm Oct-Apr, o 7pm May-Sep), atop Ayasuluk Hill. It was uilt in the 6th century on the site where was believed St John the Evangelist had een buried. The less-impressive **Temple f Artemis** (admission free; 🕑 8am-5pm Oct-pr, to 7pm May-Sep), between Ephesus nd Selçuk, was once one of the Seven Vonders of the Ancient World. In its rime, it was larger than the Parthenon n Athens. Unfortunately, little more than ne pillar now remains.

The **Ephesus Museum** (☎ 892 6010; ğur Mumcu Sevgi Yolu Caddesi; admission €2.50; 🕑 8am-5pm Oct-Apr, to 7pm May-Sep) houses striking collection of artefacts, including the effigy of Priapus, the Phallic God, vhich pops up in postcard racks through-ut Turkey.

Tuncay Pension (☎ 892 6260; www.tuncay ension.com.tr; 2019 Sokak 1; d with/without air-on €50/35; ❄) It's a touch expensive for pension, but a good, friendly choice onetheless. There's a cool courtyard with fountain where generous breakfasts are erved.

Naz Han (☎ 892 8731; nazhanhotel@gmail.com; 1044 Sokak 2; r €50-70; ❄ 💻) Living up to its name, which means 'coy', the Naz Han hides behind high walls. This 100-year-old Greek house has five simple but comfortable rooms arranged around a courtyard.

Okumuş Mercan Restaurant (☎ 892 6196; 1006 Sokak 44; mains TL7-9) This place is loved locally for its traditional home fare, served in a courtyard beside a fountain in the shade of a mulberry tree.

Garden Restaurant (☎ 892 6165; Garden Motel & Camping, Kale Altı 5; mains TL7-11) About as organic as it gets in Selçuk, the Garden enjoys a bucolic setting amid plots where the majority of the produce on your plate is grown. The meze selection is particularly good.

EPHESUS (EFES)

Even if you're not an architecture buff, you can't help but be dazzled by the sheer beauty of the ruins of **Ephesus** (☎ 892 6010; admission/parking TL15/3; 🕑 8am-5pm Oct-Apr, to 7pm May-Sep), the best-preserved classical city in the eastern Mediterranean. If you want to get a feel for what life was like in Roman times, Ephesus is an absolute must-see.

There's a wealth of sights to explore, including the **Great Theatre**, reconstructed between AD 41 and 117, and capable of holding 25,000 people; the marble-paved **Sacred Way**; the 110-sq-m **agora** (marketplace), heart of Ephesus' business life; and the **Library of Celsus**, adorned with niches holding statues of the classical Virtues. Going up Curetes Way, you can't miss the impressive Corinthian-style **Temple of Hadrian**, on the left, with beautiful friezes in the porch; the magnificent **Terraced Houses** (admission TL15; 🕑 9am-4.30pm); and the **Fountain of Trajan**. Curetes Way ends at the two-storey **Gate of Hercules**, constructed in the 4th century AD, which has reliefs of Hercules on both main pillars. Up the hill on the left are the very ruined remains of the **prytaneum** (municipal hall) and the **Temple of Hestia Boulaea**, in which a perpetually burning flame was guarded. Finally, you reach the **Odeum**, a small theatre dating from AD 150 and used for musical performances and town council meetings.

Audioguides are available – as are water and snacks, but bring your own as prices are high. Heat and crowds can be problematic so come early or late and avoid weekends and public holidays.

Many pensions in Selçuk offer free lifts to the main Ephesus admission gate; a taxi costs about TL12. You may prefer to be dropped off at the upper entrance (the southern gate or *güney kapısı*) so that you can walk back downhill (roughly 3km) through the ruins and out through the lower main entrance.

It's a 30- to 45-minute walk from the tourist office to the main Ephesus admission gate. The first 20 minutes are easy enough, along a tree-shaded road, but th next uphill section is much harder wo with no pavement and little shade (n to mention constant attention from ta drivers).

MEDITERRANEAN COAST

The Western Mediterranean, known as th 'Turquoise Coast', is a glistening stretch clear blue sea where Gods once played sublime pebble coves, and where spe tacular ruins abound. In villages too pret to postcard, sun-kissed locals yawn an smile at travellers' never-ending quest f the 'Med Life'.

FETHİYE

☎ 0252 / pop 50,700

In 1958 an earthquake levelled the o harbour city of Fethiye, sparing only th ancient remains of Telmessos (400 BC from its wrath. Fifty years on and Fethiy is once again a prosperous and proud hu of the Western Mediterranean. Its natu ral harbour, tucked away in the souther reaches of a broad bay scattered wit

PAMUKKALE

East of Selçuk, Pamukkale's gleaming white ledges (travertines), with pools that flow over the plateau edge, used to be one of the most familiar images of Turkey. Sadly, the water supply has dried up and it is no longer possible to bathe in the pools. Next to this fragile wonder, you can tour the magnificent ruins of the Roman city of **Hierapolis** (admission TL5; ⌚ daylight), an ancient spa resort with a theatre, colonnaded street, latrine building and necropolis.

Afterwards, swim amid sunken columns at Hierapolis' **Antique Pool** (adult/child TL18/9; ⌚ 9am-7pm), and visit the **Hierapolis Archaeology Museum** (admission TL3; ⌚ 9am-12.30pm & 1.30-7.15pm Tue-Sun).

Frequent buses connect local hub Denizli with Selçuk (TL18, three hours). Buses run between Denizli and Pamukkale every 15 minutes (TL2, 30 minutes). We've heard of travellers buying tickets to Pamukkale, but being offloaded in Denizli. If this happens, insist you're reimbursed the additional TL2 you'll need to travel on to Pamukkale.

ɔretty islands, is perhaps the region's ınest.

Fethiye's *otogar* is 2.5km east of the :entre. Atatürk Caddesi, the main street, ıas banks with ATMs. Most pensions are ɜither up the hill or west of the marina; he **tourist office** (☎ 614 1527; İskele Meydanı; 10am-noon & 1-5.30pm) is opposite the narina, just past the Roman theatre.

In central Fethiye, little remains of the ɔriginal town of Telmessos other than a **Roman theatre** and several **Lycian ;arcophagi**. The cliffs hold several rock-:ut tombs, including the Ionic **Tomb ɔf Amyntas** (admission TL5; 8am-7pm). **Fethiye Museum** (505 Sokak; admission TL5; 8.30am-5pm Tue-Sun) has some small statues and votive stones.

Most people enjoy the well-promoted 12-island boat tour (TL25 per person), the Butterfly Valley tour (TL20) via Ölüdeniz, the Saklıkent Gorge tour (TL40) and the Dalyan tour (TL40).

Dolmuşes run to the nearby evocative Ottoman Greek 'ghost town' of **Kayaköy** (admission TL5; 9am-7pm), abandoned after the population exchange of 1923.

Fethiye is the starting (or finishing) point for the **Lycian Way**, a superb scenic walking trail along the coast. The town also makes a good base for day trips to the beautiful **Saklıkent Gorge**, an 18km-long crack in the Akdaglar mountains too narrow for even sunlight to squeeze through; and to the ruins at **Tlos** (admission TL8; 8am-6pm) and **Pınara** (admission TL3).

Fethiye has some good-value midrange digs, but not much at the deluxe end.

Tan Pansiyon (☎ 614 1584; fax 614 1676; 30 Sokak 43; s/d TL30/50) When the backpacker grind wears thin, try this traditional Turkish pension run by a charming elderly couple.

Villa Daffodil (☎ 614 9595; www.villadaffodil.com; Fevzi Çakmak Caddesi 115; s/d TL50/90;) This large Ottoman-designed guesthouse is one of the few surviving older buildings in town. The rooms have slanted ceilings and a homely feel; the best have sea views and anterooms.

Meğri Lokantasi (☎ 614 4047; Çarşı Caddesi 26; mains TL14-25) Packed with locals who spill onto the streets, the Meğri does excellent and hearty home-style cooking. The *güveç* (casseroles) are a speciality.

Hilmi et Balık Restaurant (☎ 612 6242; Hal ve Pazar Yeri 53; 400g fish TL15-20; 10am-midnight) Set inside the fish market

BLUE CRUISE

Fethiye is the hub of Turkey's cruising scene, dispatching dozens of yachts on a daily basis in summer. The most popular voyage is the 'Blue Cruise' to Kale (Demre), 1¼ hours by bus from Olympos – a four-day, three-night journey on a *gület* (traditional wooden yacht) that attracts young party animals. You call in at bays along the way for swimming, sunbathing and variable amounts of boozing. A less common route is between Marmaris and Fethiye, also taking four days and three nights. Aficionados say this is a much prettier route, but for some reason it's not as popular.

Make sure you shop around for a service that suits – there are many shoddy operators working the waters (and your wallet). Recommended operators include **Almila Boat Cruise** (☎ 0535-636 0076; www.beforelunch.com), **Big Backpackers** (☎ 0252-614 9312; www.bluecruisefethiye.com) and **Olympos Yachting** (☎ 0242-892 1145; www.olymposyachting.com).

MARTIN MOC

Tomb of Amyntas (p729), Fethiye

IF YOU LIKE...

- If you like **Fethiye** (p728), and other towns along the coast, you might also want to check out the following settlements:
- **Bodrum** The Aegean's premier party town – dive intensely, dine stylishly and dance wildly.
- **Marmaris** The unashamedly brash harbour city swells to over 200,000 people, including many package tourists, during summer.
- **Dalyan** A laid-back river-mouth community makes an entertaining base for exploring the popular turtle-nesting grounds of İztuzu Beach and Lake Köyceğiz.
- **Patara** After you explore the extensive ruins in scruffy little Patara (Gelemiş), take advantage of the 20-odd km of wide, golden beach.
- **Kalkan** A stylish hillside harbour town that slides steeply into a sparkling blue bay. It's as rightly famous for its restaurants as for its sublimely pretty beach.
- **Kaş** While Kaş proper may not sport the finest beach culture in the region, it's a yachties' haven, the atmosphere of the town is wonderfully mellow, and a plethora of adventure sports are on offer. The 500m-high mountain known as 'Sleeping Man' (Yatan Adam) forms a beautiful backdrop.

building, this place does meat dishes as well as fish (which is its speciality) and is a firm favourite locally.

Fethiye's bars and nightclubs are mostly cheek by jowl on one little street, Hamam Sokak, just off İskele Meydanı.

Buses from the *otogar* to Antalya (TL20, 7½ hours) head east along the coast *(sahil)* via Olympos (TL15, five hours). The inlanc *(yayla)* road to Antalya (TL16, four hours is quicker but less scenic.

OLYMPOS

☎ 0242

Olympos has long had an ethereal holc over its visitors. It was an importan

Lycian city in the 2nd century BC, when the Olympians devoutly worshipped Hephaestus (Vulcan), the god of fire. No doubt this veneration sprang from reverence for the mysterious Chimaera, an eternal flame that still springs from the earth nearby.

The drive here is a treat, strewn with mountain views all the way from Kaş. Don't miss the fascinating ruins of **ancient Olympos** (**admission TL2**). A skip away from the beach, it's a wild, abandoned place where ruins peek out from forested coppices, rocky outcrops and riverbanks.

Most pensions in Olympos run tours (TL10) to **Chimaera**, a cluster of flames that blaze from crevices on the rocky slopes of Mt Olympos. It's located about 7km from Olympos.

Staying in an Olympos tree house has long been the stuff of travel legend – it offers fabulous value, community-minded accommodation in a stunning natural setting. The tree-house dream is fading in the face of modern conveniences, but all camps include breakfast and dinner in the price, although drinks are extra.

Kadir's Yörük Top Treehouse (**☎ 892 1250; www.kadirstreehouses.com; dm/bungalow TL20/40;**) Kadir's started the tree-living trend. But the fun has not gone away: there are three bars (including the time-honoured Bull Bar) and a rock-climbing wall.

Şaban (**☎ 892 1265; www.sabanpansion.com; dm/tree house TL20/30, bungalow TL35-40;**) Şaban is not a party place, and instead sells itself on tranquillity, space, a family feel, and great home cooking. It's a good choice for single women.

Orange Pension (**☎ 892 1317; www.olymposorangepension.com; bungalow TL40;**) The wooden rooms upstairs have a futuristic Swiss Family Robinson feel, while the concrete rooms downstairs are perhaps the future of Olympos. It's got a great communal dining area, and the same guys run a nightclub hidden in the valley.

Varuna (**☎ 892 1347; mains TL10-15**) Next to Bayram's, this popular restaurant serves snacks and mains including fresh trout, *gözleme* and *şiş kebaps* (roast skewered meat) in attractive open cabins.

Buses and minibuses plying the Fethiye–Antalya road will drop you at a roadside restaurant from where hourly minibuses go on to Olympos (TL2.75, 20 minutes). From October to April they wait until enough passengers arrive, which can sometimes take a while.

The most pleasant way to get from Fethiye to Olympos is on a cruise (see p729).

ANTALYA

☎ 0242 / pop 603,200

Once seen by travellers as the gateway to the 'Turkish Riviera', Antalya is generating a buzz among culture vultures. Situated directly on the Gulf of Antalya (Antalya Körfezi), the largest Turkish city on the Mediterranean is both stylishly modern and classically beautiful. It boasts the creatively preserved Roman-Ottoman quarter of Kaleiçi, a pristine Roman harbour, plus stirring ruins in the surrounding Beydağları (Bey Mountains). The city's restaurants and boutique hotels rival those throughout the country, the archaeological museum is world class, and there is a smattering of chic Med-carpet clubs.

The city centre is at Kale Kapısı, a major intersection marked by a clock tower. To get into Kaleiçi, head south down the hill from the clock tower or cut in from Hadrian's Gate (Hadriyanüs Kapisi), just off Atatürk Caddesi. There are several post offices within walking distance of Kaleiçi, and a **tourist information booth** (**☎/fax 241 1747; Yavuz Ozcan Parkı; 8am-7pm**).

Around the harbour is lovely historic **Kaleiçi** (Old Antalya), whose walls once repelled raiders. It's a charming area full of twisting alleys, atmosphere-laden courtyards, souvenir shops and lavishly restored mansions. Heading down from the **clock tower** you will pass the **Yivli Minare** (Grooved Minaret), which rises above an old church that was converted into a mosque. In the southern reaches of Kaleiçi, the quirky **Kesik Minare** (Cut Minaret) is built on the site of a ruined Roman temple. Just off Atatürk Caddesi, the monumental **Hadrian's Gate** was erected during the Roman emperor Hadrian's reign (AD 117–38).

Don't miss the excellent **Suna & İnan Kıraç Kaleiçi Museum** (Kocatepe Sokak 25; admission TL1.70; 9am-noon & 1-6pm Thu-Tue), in the heart of Kaleiçi. It houses a fine collection of Turkish ceramics, together with rooms set up to show important events in Ottoman family life.

Excursion yachts tie up in the Roman Harbour in Kaleiçi, offering **boat trips** that visit the Gulf of Antalya islands and some beaches for a swim (TL20 to TL80).

There are pensions aplenty in Kaleiçi, and most are housed in renovated historic buildings.

Tuvana (☎ 247 6015; www.tuvanahotel.com; Karanlýk Sokak 7; s/d TL100/150;) This hidden, once-royal compound of Ottoman houses has been converted into a fine old city inn. Rooms are suitably plush, with *kilims*, linen and light fittings emitting soft oranges and yellows.

Hotel Alp Paşa (☎ 247 5676; www.alppasa.com; Hesapçı Sokak 30-32; s/d from €65/190;) The outdoor courtyard displays Roman columns and other artefacts unearthed during the hotel's construction. There's an on-site *hamam* and an atmospheric stone-walled restaurant.

A nearly endless assortment of cafe and eateries are tucked in and around th harbour area; those perched over the ba command the highest prices.

Hasanağa Restaurant (☎ 242 810 Mescit Sokak 15; meals TL10-20) Expect to fin the garden here absolutely packed o Friday and Saturday nights, when trad tional Turkish musicians and folk dancer entertain.

Parlak Restaurant (☎ 241 6553; Kazı Özlap Qvenue Zincirlihan 7; meals TL12-25) Thi sprawling, open-air patio is a local leg end for its slow-roasted chicken. A goo choice if you're looking to relax for a whil and just steps from Kale Kapısı.

Antalya's airport is 10km east of the cit centre on the Alanya highway. Turkis Airlines offers frequent flights to/fron İstanbul and Ankara. Atlasjet also ha flights to/from İstanbul.

From the *otogar,* buses head t Olympos (TL8, 1½ hours).

CENTRAL ANATOLIA

On central Turkey's hazy plains, the sens of history is so pervasive that the aver age *kebap* chef can remind you that th Romans preceded the Seljuks. This is after all, the region where the Whirlin Dervishes first swirled, Atatürk bega his revolution, Alexander the Great cu the Gordion Knot and King Midas turne everything to gold. Julius Caesar cam here to utter his famous line, *'Veni, vid vici'* ('I came, I saw, I conquered').

ANKARA

☎ 0312 / pop 4.5 million

İstanbullus may quip that the best viev in Ankara is the train home, but th Turkish capital has more substance thar its reputation as a staid administrativ centre suggests. The capital establishe by Atatürk offers a mellower, mor manageable vignette of urban Turkey than İstanbul, and claims two of the country's most important sights: the Anıt Kabir, Atatürk's hilltop mausoleum; and the Museum of Anatolian Civilisations. Ankara can be a disjointed place, but two or three neighbourhoods have some charm: the historic streets in the hilltop citadel; the chic Kavaklıdere district; and Kızılay, one of Turkey's hippest urban quarters.

Ankara's *hisar* (citadel) crowns a hill 1km east of Ulus Meydanı (Ulus Sq), the heart of Old Ankara and near most of the inexpensive hotels. The newer Ankara lies further south, with better hotels, restaurants and nightlife in Kızılay and Kavaklıdere. The **tourist office** (☎ 310 8789/231 5572; Anafartalar Caddesi 67, Ulus; ⏰ 9am-5pm Mon-Fri, 10am-5pm Sat), southeast of Ulus Meydanı, plans to move to a new office at the train station.

With the world's richest collection of Hittite artefacts, the state-of-the-art **Museum of Anatolian Civilisations** (Anadolu Medeniyetleri Müzesi; ☎ 324 3160; admission TL15; ⏰ 8.30am-5pm), housed in a beautifully restored 15th-century *bedesten*, is Turkey's best museum outside İstanbul. Just up the hill, it's also well worth exploring the side streets of the **citadel**, the most scenic part of Ankara. Inside it, local people still live as if in a traditional Turkish village.

About 400m north of Ulus Meydanı, it's worth taking a look at the surprisingly well-preserved remains of the **Roman baths** (Roma Hamaları; admission TL3; ⏰ 8.30am-12.30pm & 1.30-5.30pm), dating back to the 3rd century.

Pay your respects to the founder of modern Turkey and observe the Turks' enduring reverence for Atatürk at his mausoleum, the **Anıt Kabir** (admission free; ⏰ 9am-5pm mid-May–Oct, to 4pm Nov-Jan, to 4.30pm Feb–mid-May), 2km northwest of Kızılay Meydanı.

WES WALKER

Statues in front of Anıt Kabir

SLEEPING & EATING

Locals advise against wandering Ulus' streets after about 9pm, so you may prefer to stay in Kızılay, which is pricier but has better restaurants and bars.

Hotel Metropol (☎ 417 3060; www.hotelmetropol.com.tr; Olgunlar Sokak 5, Kızılay; s/d TL70/100; ❄) Quite a snip at these prices, the three-star Metropol provides quality and character across the board. The breakfast is excellent, but laundry rates are high.

our pick **Angora House Hotel** (☎ 309 8380; angorahouse@gmail.com; Kalekapısı Sokak 16-18, Ulus; s/d/tr €45/60/75; ⏰ Mar-Oct; 💻) Ankara's original boutique hotel is in

SAFRANBOLU & AMASYA

Safranbolu and Amasya, respectively 145km north and 270km northeast of Ankara, are slightly off the beaten track, but beckon savvy travellers with their ethereal settings and historic atmosphere. Both retain many of their original Ottoman buildings.

Safranbolu is such an enchanting city that it was declared a Unesco World Heritage site in 1994. It boasts a wonderful old Ottoman quarter bristling with 19th-century half-timbered houses; as part of the ongoing restoration, many have been turned into hotels or museums.

Blissfully located on riverbanks beneath cliffs carved with Pontic tombs, **Amasya** is one of Turkey's best-kept secrets, harbouring historic sites including a lofty citadel, Seljuk buildings and enough picturesque Ottoman piles to satisfy the fussiest sultan.

Both towns boast excellent accommodation, with a profusion of delightful B&Bs set in skilfully restored Ottoman mansions. In Safranbolu, travellers love **Bastoncu Pansiyon** (☎ 0370-712 3411; www.bastoncupension.com; Hıdırlık Yokuşu Sokak, Safranbolu; dm TL20, s/d/tr TL35/50/70; 💻). In Amasya, **Grand Pasha Hotel** (☎ 0358-212 4158; www.grandpashahotel.com; Tevfık Hafız Çıkmazı 5, Amasya; s/d TL50/100) is a good deal. There are a few direct buses from Ankara to both Safranbolu (TL20, three hours) and Amasya (TL30, five hours); the latter is closer to Sivas.

a great location inside the citadel and offers beautiful, individually decorated rooms in a restored house, benefiting from some fine half-timbering and a walled courtyard.

Zenger Paşa Konağı (☎ 311 7070; www.zengerpasa.com; Doyran Sokak 13, Ulus; mains TL12-17; 🕐 noon-12.30am; ❄) It looks at first like a deserted ethnographic museum, but the pide, meze and grills, cooked in the original oven, and the perfect citadel views attract wealthy Ankaralıs.

Köşk (☎ 432 1300; İnkılap Sokak 2, Kızılay; mains TL15-30) Ankara's best fish restaurant has a glass-fronted dining room with views of the pedestrianised boulevards, and a chanteuse warbling away.

GETTING THERE & AROUND

Ankara's Esenboğa airport, 33km north of the city centre, is the hub for Turkish Airlines' domestic flight network; there are daily nonstop flights to most Turkish cities with Turkish Airlines or Atlasjet. International flights to İstanbul are generally cheaper. Havaş buses depart from Gate B at 19 May Stadium every half-hour between 4.30am and midnight daily (TL10, 45 minutes). They may leave sooner if they fill up, so get there early to claim your seat. Don't pay more than TL50 for a taxi.

Train services between İstanbul and Ankara are the best in the country, with eight departures daily from TL23.

Buses marked 'Ulus' and 'Çankaya' run the length of Atatürk Bulvarı. Those marked 'Gar' go to the train station.

Ankara's underground train network currently has two lines. The two lines interconnect at Kızılay.

:APPADOCIA (KAPADOKYA)

entral Anatolia's mountain-fringed plains ive way to a land of fairy chimneys and nderground cities. The fairy chimneys – ɔck columns, pyramids, mushrooms and ven a few shaped like camels – were ɔrmed, alongside the valleys of cascadꞁg white cliffs, when Erciyes Daği (Mt rciyes) erupted. The intervening millenia added to the remarkable Cappadocian anvas, with Byzantines carving out cave hurches and subterranean complexes to ouse thousands of people.

You could spend days touring the rockut churches and admiring their frescos technically seccos; one of many factoids isitors learn on a hike through the canons). Alternatively, view the troglodyte rchitecture from far above on a dawn ot-air balloon ride or from a panoramic otel terrace. Whether it's a pension or boutique hideaway with as few rooms s it has fairy chimneys, Cappadocia's ac:ommodation rates as some of Turkey's est and allows guests to experience cave lwelling first hand.

TOURS

The following Göreme-based agencies ɔffer good daily tours (costing around TL60) of local highlights. There are also gencies in nearby Urgup.

Heritage Travel (☎ 0384-271 2687; www.urkishheritagetravel.com; Yavuz Sokak 31, Göreme)

Middle Earth Travel (☎ 0384-271 2559; www.middleearthtravel.com; Cevizler Sokak 20, Göreme) Intrepid outfit offering walking tours and activities such as abseiling.

Neşe Tour (☎ 0384-271 2525; www.nesetour.com; Avanos Yolu 54, Göreme)

Nomad Travel (☎ 0384-271 2767; www.nomadtravel.com.tr; Müze Caddesi 35, Göreme)

Yama Tours (☎ 0384-271 2508; www.yamatours.com; Müze Caddesi 2, Göreme)

Tours usually start at a lookout point with a view across the valleys, then continue to locations such as Ihlara Valley, a pottery workshop in Avanos, the rock formations in Devrent Valley, Uçhisar's rock citadel and one of the fascinating underground cities at **Kaymaklı** or **Derinkuyu** (admission €7.50; 8am-5pm, last admission 4.30pm). Many companies also offer trips further afield, for example to eastern Turkish locations such as Nemrut Dağı (Mt Nemrut; see p739).

GETTING THERE & AWAY

Transfer buses operate between Kayseri airport and accommodation in central Cappadocia for passengers leaving or arriving on flights between the

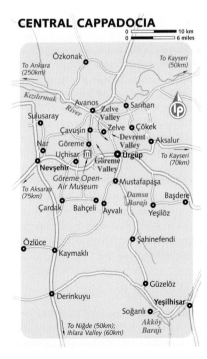

CENTRAL CAPPADOCIA

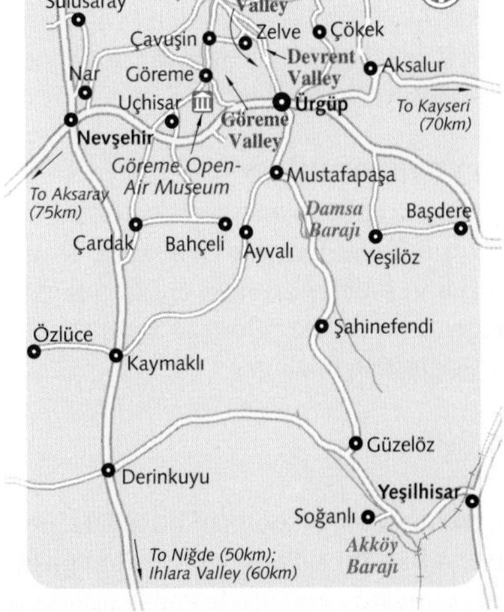

SHANIA SHEGED

Ballooning over Cappadocia

mid-morning and evening. The buses pick up from and drop off at hotels and pensions in Ürgüp (TL15), Göreme, Uçhisar and Avanos. Prebook the buses by phone or email with **Argeus Tours** (☎ 0384-341 4688; www.argeus.com.tr, www.cappadociaexclusive.com; İstiklal Caddesi 7, Ürgüp) if you fly Turkish Airlines; or with **Peerless Travel Services** (☎ 0384-341 6970; www.peerlessexcursions.com; İstiklal Caddesi 59a, Ürgüp) if you fly Onur Air. Alternatively, you can easily request your hotel or pension in Cappadocia to book a seat for you.

GETTING AROUND

The most convenient bases for exploring central Cappadocia are Göreme or Ürgüp. Bus and *dolmuş* services are frequent in high summer, apart from on Sundays, and much less so in winter.

GÖREME

☎ 0384 / pop 2250

Göreme is the archetypal travellers' utopia: a beatific village where the surreal surroundings spread a fat smile on everyone's face. Beneath the honeycomb cliffs the locals live in fairy chimneys – or increasingly, run hotels in them. The wav white valleys in the distance, with thei hiking trails, panoramic viewpoints and rock-cut churches, look like giant tub of vanilla ice cream. Rose Valley, mean while, lives up to its name; watching it pink rock slowly change colour at sunse is best accompanied by meze in one o the excellent eateries.

Tourism is having an impact on this village, where you can start the day in a hot air balloon (see opposite), before touring a valley of rock-cut Byzantine churches a Göreme Open-Air Museum. Nonetheless you can still see rural life continuing in a place where, once upon a time, if a man couldn't lay claim to one of the rock hewn pigeon houses, he would struggle to woo a wife.

All the services useful to traveller are in the centre, including the *otogar* where there are four ATMs and a **tourist information booth** (☎ 271 2558; www.goreme.org).

Cappadocia's number one attraction, **öreme Open-Air Museum** (**Göreme Açık ava Müzesi; admission TL10; 8am-5pm**), may e pricey but it's worth every lira. Medieval rescos can be seen in the rock-hewn nonastic settlement where some 20 nonks lived. The best-preserved churches re from the 10th to 13th centuries, alhough some are even older than that. The tunning **Karanlık Kilise** (Dark Church) is ne of the most famous and fresco-filled f the churches, and it is worth paying he extra TL5 admission fee to enter. cross the road from the main entrance, he **Tokalı Kilise** (Buckle Church) is also mpressive, with an underground chapel nd fabulous frescos.

With about 100 hostels, pensions and otels in Göreme, competition keeps rices low. If you're visiting between)ctober and May, pack warm clothes as gets very cold at night.

Kelebek Hotel & Cave Pension (**271 531; www.kelebekhotel.com; Yavuz Sokak 31; s/d rom €28/35;**) More than the *hamam,* arden and small swimming pool, it's the elpful staff and Yavuz's passion for vilage life that make this a magical spot.

Fairy Chimney Inn (**271 2655; www.airychimney.com; Güvercinlik Sokak 5/7; s/d/tr rom €44/55/66;**) Rooms are beautifully lecorated, with simple furniture, cushions nd carpets everywhere, and a refreshing ack of TVs and jacuzzis.

Kismet Cave House (**271 2416; www.ismetcavehouse.com; Kağnı Yolu 9; d standard/deıxe €60/80**) The arched rooms up top have he edge on the chimney chambers, but fghani bedspreads, jacuzzis and views of ose Valley feature throughout.

Most of Göreme's pensions provide ood, cheap meals, but you could also take dvantage of some fine eateries in town.

Cappadocia Pide Salonu (**271 2858; akki Paşa Meydanı; pide TL5-9**) Göreme's pide hotspot has a more local feel than most of the village's eateries.

our pick **Dibek** (**271 2209; Hakkı Paşa Meydanı 1; mains TL10-15; 9am-11pm**) Dibek is one of Göreme's most original restaurants, and the best place to try a *testi kebap* (kebab cooked in a terracotta pot, broken at the table to serve). You must give three hours' notice before eating, so the dish can be slow-cooked in an oven in the stone floor.

A'laturca (**271 2882; Müze Caddesi; mains TL10-25**) Style meets substance at this elegant eatery.

ÜRGÜP

0384 / pop 15,500

If you have a soft spot for upmarket hotels and fine dining, look no further. The ever-growing battalion of boutique

BALLOONS AT DAWN

If you've never taken a flight in a hot-air balloon, Cappadocia is one of the best places in the world to do it. Flight conditions are especially favourable here, with balloons operating most mornings from the beginning of April to the end of November. The views across the valleys and fairy chimneys are simply unforgettable and it's a magical way to start the day.

The various operators offer different packages (and safety standards), so do shop around. The following have good credentials:

Kapadokya Balloons (**0384-271 2442; www.kapadokyaballoons.com; Adnan Menderes Caddesi, Göreme**)

Sultan Balloons (**0384-353 5249; www.sultanballoons.com; Sarıgüvercinlik Mevkii, Mustafapaşa Kasabası, Ürgüp**)

TIM HUGHES

Uçhisar viewed from a wheat field

IF YOU LIKE...

If you like the fairy-chimney setting of **Göreme** (p736), these quieter Cappadocian places might pique your interest as well:

- **Uçhisar** Picturesque, laid-back, yet stylish, Uçhisar is built around a rock citadel that offers panoramic views from its summit.
- **Zelve Valley** Less visited than the Göreme Valley (though the monastic seclusion once offered here is certainly long gone), Zelve has rock-cut churches, a rock-cut mosque and opportunities for serious scrambling.
- **Mustafapaşa** The sleeping beauty of Cappadocia – a peaceful village with pretty old stone-carved houses, some minor rock-cut churches and a few good places to stay.

hotels in Ürgüp's honey-coloured stone buildings (left over from the pre-1923 days when the town had a large Greek population) win over discerning travellers. With a spectacular natural setting and a wonderful location at the very heart of central Cappadocia, this is one of the most seductive holiday spots in the whole of Turkey.

The **tourist office** (☎ 0384 341 4059; Kayseri Caddesi 37; 8am-5pm Mon-Fri Oct-Apr, to 5.30pm Mon-Fri May-Sep) gives out a walking map and has a list of hotels.

Local travel agencies Argeus Tours and Peerless Travel Services (see p736) can arrange tours and transfers.

Cappadocia Palace (☎ 341 2510; www.hotel-cappadocia.com; Duayeri Mahallesi Mektep Sokak 2; s/d/tr from TL35/70/85;) This comfortable hotel is housed in a converted Greek mansion near Cumhuriyet Meydan. There's a lovely arched restaurant-lounge and an attractive foyer area.

Esbelli Evi (☎ 341 3395; www.esbelli.com; Esbelli Mahallesi Sokak 8; s/d/ste €80/90/200;) Having bought surrounding properties to preserve Esbelli's atmosphere of hilltop serenity, consummate host Süha Ersöz's complex now has 10 rooms and five suites in nine houses.

Melekler Evi (☎ 341 7131; www.meleklerevi.com.tr; Dereler Mahallesi Dere Sokak 59; d €90-145) Restored by an architect and an interior designer, the cave and arch rooms are tastefully decorated in subtle shades.

Şömine Cafe & Restaurant (☎ 341 8442; Cumhuriyet Meydanı; mains TL9-15) This popular restaurant on the main square has a roof terrace and an attractive indoor dining room. Start with a salad or a meze choice such as *sosyete mantısı* (one large ravioli), then attack a *kiremit* (clay-baked meat or vegetable dish).

Dimrit (☎ 341 8585; Yunak Mahallesi, Teyfik Fikret Caddesi 40; mains TL10-21) With meze served in curvy dishes and three types of *rakı* (anise-flavoured spirit), Dimrit's hillside terraces are top spots to spend a sunset.

IHLARA VALLEY

☎ 0382

A beautiful canyon full of greenery and rock-cut churches dating back to Byzantine times, **Ihlara Valley** (Ihlara Vadısı dmission TL5; 8am-6.30pm) is a definite must-see. Footpaths follow the course of the river, Melendiz Suyu, which flows for 3km between the narrow gorge at Ihlara village and the wide valley around **Selime Monastery** (dawn-dusk).

The easiest way to see the valley is on day tour from Göreme (p735), which allows a few hours to walk through the central part of the gorge.

MT NEMRUT NATIONAL PARK

Nemrut Dağı (Mt Nemrut; 2150m) is one of the country's most awe-inspiring sights. Two thousand years ago, right on top of the mountain and pretty much in the middle of nowhere, an obscure Commagene king chose to erect fabulous temples and funerary mound. The fallen heads of the gigantic decorative statues of gods and kings, toppled by earthquakes, form one of the country's most enduring images.

Some people take a two-day tour from Göreme to Cappadocia (about TL250; p735), but it's a tedious drive. If you have enough time, it's better to opt for a three-day tour, which should also include few stops, such as Harran, Şanlıurfa and Gaziantep.

DIRECTORY

ACTIVITIES

The spectacular valleys of central Cappadocia are also excellent for hiking. All sorts of water sports, including diving, waterskiing, rafting and kayaking, are available on the Aegean and Mediterranean coasts. Those of a lazier disposition may want to take a *gület* (wooden yacht) trip along the coast, stopping off to swim in bays along the way (see p729). The laziest 'activity' of all consists of paying a visit to a *hamam*, where you can get yourself scrubbed and massaged for a fraction of what it would cost in most Western countries.

DANGERS & ANNOYANCES

Although Turkey is in no way a dangerous country to visit, it's always wise to be a little cautious, especially if you're travelling alone. Conceal your money in a safe place (such as a discreet money belt, or in a zippable shirt pocket) and be wary of pickpockets on buses, in markets and in other crowded places. Keep an eye out for anyone suspicious lurking near ATMs.

More commonly, the hard-sell tactics of carpet sellers can drive you to distraction. 'Free' lifts and other suspiciously cheap services often lead to near-compulsory visits to carpet showrooms or hotel commission for touts.

Visitors should also note that sporadic bombings, often linked to the PKK Kurdish separatists, target affluent areas frequented by tourists, including a double-bomb attack in İstanbul in 2008. Again, check advisories for the latest information.

EMBASSIES & CONSULATES

Foreign embassies are in Ankara but many countries also have consulates in İstanbul. For more information, visit http://tinyurl.com/6ywt8a.

Australia Ankara (☎ 0312-459 9521; www.embaustralia.org.tr; Uğur Mumcu Caddesi 88/7, Gaziosmanpaşa); İstanbul (Map pp714-15; ☎ 0212-243 1333; 2nd fl, Suzer Plaza, Asker Ocağı Caddesi 15, Elmadağ, Şişli)

Canada (☎ 0312-409 2700; Cinnah Caddesi 58, Çankaya, Ankara)

France Ankara (☎ 0312-455 4545; Paris Caddesi 70, Kavaklıdere); İstanbul (Map pp714-15; ☎ 0212-334 8730; İstiklal Caddesi 8, Taksim)

Germany Ankara (☎ 0312-455 5100; Atatürk Bulvarı 114, Kavaklıdere); İstanbul (Map pp714-15; ☎ 0212-334 6100; İnönü Caddesi 16-18, Taksim)
Ireland Ankara (☎ 0312-446 6172; fax 0312-446 8061; Uğur Mumcu Caddesi, MNG Binasi B-Bl 88/3, Gaziosmanpaşa); İstanbul (☎ 0212-482 2434; fax 0212-482 0943; Ali Riza Gurcan Caddesi 2/13, Merter)
Netherlands Ankara (☎ 0312-409 1800; fax 0312-409 1898; Hollanda Caddesi 3, Yıldız); İstanbul (Map pp714-15; ☎ 0212-393 2121; fax 0212-292 5031; İstiklal Caddesi 393, Beyoğlu)
New Zealand Ankara (☎ 0312-467 9054; www.nzembassy.com/turkey; İran Caddesi 13/4, Kavaklıdere); İstanbul (☎ 0212-244 0272; nzhonconist@hatem-law.com.tr; İnönü Caddesi 48/3, Taksim)
UK Ankara (☎ 0312-455 3344; fax 0312-455 3320; Şehit Ersan Caddesi 46/A, Çankaya); İstanbul (Map pp714-15; ☎ 0212-334 6400; fax 0212-334 6401; Meşrutiyet Caddesi 34, Tepebaşı, Beyoğlu)
USA Ankara (☎ 0312-455 5555; fax 0312-467 0019; Atatürk Bulvarı 110, Kavaklıdere); İstanbul (Map pp714-15; ☎ 0212-335 9000; fax 0212-335 9019; Kaplıcalar Mevkii 2, İstiniye)

FESTIVALS & EVENTS

Following are some of the major annual festivals and events in Turkey:
Camel Wrestling Hoof it to Selçuk (p726) on the last Sunday in January.
Nevruz Kurds and Alevis celebrate the ancient Middle Eastern spring festival on 21 March. Banned until recent years, Nevruz is now an official holiday.
Anzac Day The WWI battles at Gallipoli (p723) are commemorated with dawn services on 25 April.
İstanbul International Music Festival (www.iksv.org/muzik) Every June to July, İstanbul (p720) hosts world-class classical concerts.
Kırkpınar Oil Wrestling Championship Huge crowds watch oil-covered men wrestling in a field near Edirn (p723) in late June or early July.
Aspendos Festival Opera and ballet i the Roman theatre near Antalya (p731 from mid-June to early July.

HOLIDAYS

Public holidays in Turkey:
New Year's Day 1 January
Nevruz 21 March
Children's Day 23 April
Youth and Sports Day 19 May
Victory Day 30 August
Republic Day 29 October
Anniversary of Atatürk's Death 10 November

Turkey also celebrates all of the mai Islamic holidays, the most important c which are the month-long **Ramada** (September/October) and, about tw months later, **Kurban Bayramı**. Due t the fact that these holidays are celebrate according to the Muslim lunar calenda the exact dates change from year t year.

MONEY

Inflation is an ongoing problem in Turke and many businesses quote prices in th more-stable euro. We have used bot lira and euros in listings, according t the currency quoted by the business i question.

ATMs readily dispense Turkish lira t Visa, MasterCard, Cirrus, Maestro an Eurocard holders; there's hardly a tow without a machine. Some tellers also dis pense euros and dollars.

Turkey is fairly European in its ap proach to tipping and you won't be pe tered by demands for baksheesh. Leav waiters and bath attendants aroun 10% of the bill; in restaurants, check tip hasn't been automatically added t ne bill. It's usual to round up metered axi fares.

Hotel and transport prices are sometimes negotiable, and you should always argain for souvenirs, even if prices are ixed'.

POST

he Turkish postal service is known as the TT. *Postanes* (post offices) are indicated y black-on-yellow 'PTT' signs.

RESPONSIBLE TRAVEL

especting Muslim sensibilities should e a point of principle, even when you're urrounded by half-naked sun-seekers. Vomen should keep their legs, upper rms and neckline covered, except on the each. When entering a mosque, women hould cover their heads, shoulders and rms, while everyone should cover their egs and remove their shoes.

Equally, though, there's no need to go verboard: obvious non-Muslims wearing headscarves and the like will probably ttract just as much curious attention as hose without!

TELEPHONE

he Turks just love *cep* (mobile) phones, ut calling a mobile costs roughly three mes the cost of calling a landline, no matter where you are. Mobile phone numbers tart with a four-figure code beginning ith ☎ 05. If you set up a roaming facility ith your home network, most mobiles an connect to the Turkcell, Vodafone and vea networks.

We have listed local area codes at the tart of each city or town section. Note hat İstanbul has two codes: ☎ 0212 for he European side and ☎ 0216 for the sian side. Telephone numbers that start vith ☎ 444 are national, so they don't equire an area code.

Türk Telekom's public telephones mostly require telephone cards, which can be bought at telephone centres or, for a small mark-up, from some shops and street vendors. The cheapest option for international calls is with phonecards such as Bigalo.

TOURIST INFORMATION

Local tourist offices can rarely do more than hand out glossy brochures and sketch maps. That said, some staff have a genuine interest in their region and make a real effort to help you with any specific queries.

VISAS

Make sure you join the queue to buy your visa before joining the one for immigration. How much you pay depends on your nationality; at the time of writing, Australians and Americans paid US$20 (or €15), Canadians US$60 (or €45), and British citizens UK£10 (or €15 or US$20). Customs officers expect to be paid in one of these currencies, in cash, and may not accept Turkish lira. They also don't give change.

See the **Ministry of Foreign Affairs** (**www.mfa.gov.tr**) for the latest information.

WOMEN TRAVELLERS

Things may be changing, but Turkish society is still basically sexually segregated, especially once you get away from the big cities and tourist resorts. Although younger Turks are questioning the old ways and women do hold positions of authority (there's even been a female prime minister), foreign women can find themselves being harassed. It's mostly just catcalls and dubious remarks, but serious assaults do occasionally occur.

Travelling with companions usually improves matters, and it's worth remembering that Turkish women ignore men who speak to them in the street. Wearing a wedding ring and carrying a photo of your 'husband' and 'child' can help, as can wearing dark glasses to avoid eye contact.

Men and unrelated women are not expected to sit beside each other in long-distance buses, and lone women are often assigned seats at the front of the bus near the driver.

Women can sit where they like in eateries in tourist areas. Elsewhere, restaurants that aim to attract women often set aside a section for families. Look for the term *aile salonu* (family dining room). The same applies to *çay bahçesi* (tea gardens).

TRANSPORT

GETTING THERE & AWAY

AIR

The cheapest fares for Turkey are usually to İstanbul's **Atatürk International Airport** (IST; ☎ 0212-465 5555; www.ataturkairport.com), 25km west of the city centre and, increasingly, **Sabiha Gökçen International Airport** (SAW; ☎ 0216-585 5000; www.sgairport.com), some 50km east of Sultanahmet on the Asian side of the city. Turkey's national carrier, **Turkish Airlines** (Türk Hava Yolları, THY; ☎ İstanbul 0212-252 1106; www.thy.com), and European carriers fly to İstanbul from most major European cities.

The following are a few of the airlines flying to/from Turkey:

easyJet (U2; www.easyjet.com)
germanwings (4U; www.germanwings.com)
Olympic Airlines (OA; ☎ 0212-296 7575; www.olympicairlines.com)

Also see Getting Around (right) for details of more Turkish airlines, many of which run international flights.

LAND

At the time of writing there were no direct trains to/from Western Europe, other than the comfy overnight *Filia-Dostluk Expre*[ss] between Thessaloniki (Greece) an[d] İstanbul. For more information, conta[ct] **Turkish State Railways** (www.tcdd.gov.t[r]) or the **Hellenic Railways Organisatio[n]** (www.ose.gr). The *Bosphorus Express* run[s] between İstanbul and Eastern Europe.

SEA

Ferrylines (www.ferrylines.com) is a goo[d] starting point for information about fer[ry] travel in the region.

Marmara Lines (www.marmaralines.com[)] ferries connect Brindisi and Ancona i[n] Italy with Çeşme.

Private ferries link Turkey's Aegea[n] and Mediterranean coasts and the Gree[k] islands, which are in turn linked by a[ir] or boat to Athens. In summer, boat[s] run roughly daily on a variety of route[s:] Kos–Bodrum, Samos–Kuşadası, Rhodes[–]Bodrum. See the individual destinatio[ns] for information about the services.

GETTING AROUND

AIR

Turkish Airlines (Türk Hava Yolları, TH[Y;] ☎ İstanbul 0212-252 1106; www.thy.com) co[n]nects all the country's major cities and re[]sorts, often via one of its two main hub[s,] İstanbul and Ankara.

Cheaper domestic flights are als[o] available:

Atlasjet (KK; www.atlasjet.com)
Onur Air (8Q; www.onurair.com.tr) Flie[s] from İstanbul to Antalya, Bodru[m,] Kayseri, among others.
Pegasus Airlines (H9; www.pegasusairline[s.]com)

BUS

The Turkish bus network is a very plea[s]ant surprise: coaches go just about every[]where, they're cheap and comfortabl[e,] smoking isn't permitted, drinks an[d] snacks are often provided, regular toilet stops are built into longer routes, and drivers even use the stops to wash down their vehicles!

The premium companies have nationwide networks offering greater speed and comfort for slightly higher fares. They also have the best safety records. A town's *otogar* is often on the outskirts, but most bus companies provide free *servis* minibuses to ferry you into the centre and back again. Besides intercity buses, *otogars* often handle *dolmuşes* (see Local Transport) to outlying districts or villages. Larger bus stations have an *emanetçi* (left luggage) room, which you can use for a nominal fee.

An easy option, geared towards backpackers (don't expect to meet many Turks on it), is the **Fez Bus** (**Map p716; ☎ 0212-516 9024; www.feztravel.com; Akbıyık Caddesi 15, Sultanahmet, İstanbul**). The hop-on, hop-off bus service links the main resorts of the Aegean and the Mediterranean with İstanbul, Cappadocia and Nemrut Dağı.

The best bus companies, with extensive route networks:

Boss Turizm (**☎ 444 0880; www.bossturizm.com, in Turkish**) Specialises in superdeluxe İstanbul–Ankara services.

Ulusoy (**☎ 444 1888; www.ulusoy.com.tr**)

Varan (**☎ 444 8999; www.varan.com.tr**)

CAR & MOTORCYCLE

In the major cities, plan to leave your car in a parking lot and walk – traffic is terrible. **Türkiye Turing ve Otomobil Kurumu** (**Turkish Touring & Automobile Association; ☎ 0212-282 8140; www.turing.org.tr**) can help with questions and problems.

Hiring a car is quite expensive (often around TL70 to TL120 per day with unlimited mileage, less for a longer period). All the main car-hire companies are represented in the main towns and resorts. It's better to stick to the well-established companies (such as Avis, Budget, Europcar, Hertz and Thrifty) as they have bigger fleets and better emergency backup. You can get great discounts through **Economy Car Rentals** (**www.economycarrentals.com**), which covers most of the country, but you need to book at least 24 hours in advance.

Drink-driving is a complete no-no.

LOCAL TRANSPORT

Short-distance and local routes are usually served by medium-sized 'midibuses' or smaller *dolmuşes* (minibuses that follow prescribed routes), run by private operators. Most towns have an internal bus network funded by the council; this may be supplemented by underground, tram, train and even ferry services in the largest cities. Taxis are plentiful; they have meters – just make sure they're switched on.

TOURS

Areas where an organised tour makes sense, particularly with limited time, include Troy (p724) and the Gallipoli battlefields (p723), and Cappadocia (p735).

TRAIN

Turkish State Railways (**☎ 444 8233; www.tcdd.gov.tr**) runs services throughout the country. Although most people still opt to travel by bus, as train journey times are notoriously long and the system is being overhauled, several fast lines, such as the one between İstanbul and Ankara, are now in service. The sleeper trains linking İstanbul, İzmır and Ankara are well worth considering.

RISTORANTE
ISTORANTE
DA
IVO

EUROPE IN FOCUS

ACCOMMODATION

RICHARD NEBESK

Hostel suite, Berlin, Germany

Where you stay in Europe may be one of the highlights of your trip. Quirky family-run inns, manic city hostels and languid and low-key beach resorts are just some of the places where you'll make both new memories and, more than likely, new friends.

The cheapest places to stay in Western Europe are camping grounds, followed by hostels and accommodation in student dormitories. Cheap chain hotels are popping up across the region, but pensions, private rooms and B&Bs have much more character and are often good value. Self-catering apartments and cottages are worth considering when travelling with a group, especially if you plan to stay somewhere for a while. During peak holiday periods, accommodation can be seriously hard to find, and it's advisable to book ahead.

HOSTELS

Hostels offer the cheapest roof over your head in Europe, and you don't have to be a youngster to use them (with the rather bizarre exception of Bavaria, where the strict maximum age is 26 unless you're a group leader or parent accompanying a child). Most countries don't adhere to an age limit, although there is sometimes a surcharge for over 26s.

Most hostels are part of the national Youth Hostel Association (YHA), which is affiliated with the **Hostelling International** (HI; www.hihostels.com) umbrella organisation. Technically, you're supposed to be a YHA or HI member to use affiliated hostels, but you can often stay by paying an extra charge; stay enough nights as a non-member and you automatically become a member. You can join HI at any affiliated hostel or by contacting your local or national hostelling association.

At a hostel, you get a bed for the night plus the use of communal facilities, which often include a kitchen where you can prepare your own meals. You are usually required to have a sleeping sheet; sleeping bags are now banned in many hostels. If you don't have your own sleeping sheet, you can usually hire or buy one.

Hostels vary widely in character, but the growing number of travellers and increased competition from other forms of accommodation, particularly the emergence of private backpacker hostels, have prompted many places (especially in Western Europe) to improve their facilities and cut back on rules and regulations. Increasingly, hostels are open all day, strict curfews are disappearing and 'wardens' with sergeant-major mentalities are becoming an endangered species. Polish hostels tend to be extremely basic, but they're inexpensive and friendly; in the Czech Republic and Slovakia, many hostels are actually fairly luxurious junior hotels with double rooms, and are often fully occupied by groups.

Dormitory accommodation is still the norm, although the trend is increasingly towards smaller dorms with between four and six beds. Most hostels also have a limited selection of single and double rooms with private bathrooms, or you can just rent out an entire dorm if you're travelling in a group – an increasingly popular option for family travellers. Even if you've never contemplated staying in a hostel before, it's worth considering if your funds are limited – a private room in a hostel is usually much cheaper than a comparable room in a hotel or B&B.

There are many hostel guides and websites with listings, including the hostel bible, HI's *Europe*. Many hostels accept reservations by phone, fax or email, but not always during peak periods. You can also book hostels through national hostel offices. You can book accommodation up to six months in advance through the HI website.

HOSTEL WEBSITES

The following websites are recommended resources; all of them have booking engines, helpful advice from fellow travellers and excellent tips for novice hostellers.

Europe's Famous Hostels (www.famoushostels.com)
Hostel Planet (www.hostelplanet.com)
Hostel World (www.hostelworld.com)
Hostelling International (www.hihostels.com)
Hostels.com (www.hostels.com)
Hostelz (www.hostelz.com)

PRIVATE HOSTELS

In addition to the HI-affiliated hostels, there are many private hostelling organisations in Europe and hundreds of unaffiliated backpacker hostels. Private hostels have fewer rules (eg no curfew, no daytime lockout), more self-catering kitchens and a much lower number of large, noisy school groups. They often also have a bit more character and charm than the official HI hostels.

However, whereas HI hostels must meet minimum safety and cleanliness standards, facilities vary greatly in private hostels. Dorms in some private hostels, especially in Germanic countries, can be mixed gender.

KRZYSZTOF DYDYNSKI
B&B, Venice, Italy

B&BS, GUESTHOUSES & PENSIONS

The traditional B&B (bed & breakfast) (aka guesthouse, pension, *gasthaus, zimmerfrei, chambre d'hôte* etc) is an institution throughout much of Europe. At its simplest level, you'll essentially just get a spare room in somebody's house, but with a bit of digging you'll often be able to find more sophisticated places that match up favourably with many similarly priced hotels. The UK, Ireland, Spain and France have particularly good B&B scenes, while small private pensions are now very common in Austria, Hungary, Slovakia, the Czech Republic and Croatia. Breakfast is usually included in the room price, but it's always worth checking on the location if you're staying in a big city (B&Bs are often tucked away in suburbs). And don't automatically assume your host will be able to speak English – they might not, so a few words of the local lingo might well come in handy to make sure you're au fait with the house rules.

HOMESTAYS & PRIVATE ROOMS

Homestays are often a great way to see daily life and meet local people. Travel agencies can arrange homestays in many European countries, and in Hungary you can get a private room almost anywhere.

Some rooms are like mini apartments, with cooking facilities and private bathrooms for the sole use of guests. Prices are low, but there's often a 30% to 50% surcharge if you stay fewer than three nights. In Hungary, the Czech Republic and Croatia, higher taxation has made staying in a private room less attractive, but it's still cheaper than a hotel.

You don't have to go through an agency or an intermediary for a private room. Any house, cottage or farmhouse with *zimmer frei* (German), *sobe* (Slovak) or *szoba kiadó* (Hungarian) displayed outside is advertising private rooms; just knock on the door and ask if any are available. You might also be approached at train or bus stations with offers of a private room or a hostel bed – but to avoid any unwelcome surprises, it's probably worth sticking to the official agencies. Obviously, if you are staying with strangers, you shouldn't leave your valuables behind when you go out; certainly don't leave your money, credit cards or passport.

Make sure you bring some small gifts for your hosts – it's a deeply ingrained cultural tradition in many areas.

FARMSTAYS

Staying out in the countryside at a local farmhouse can be a fine way to experience local life. It's very common in many parts of Europe, especially in Hungary, France and Italy (where it's known as *agriturismo*). You will usually need your own wheels, but farms are often located in picturesque rural areas and may offer activities nearby such as horse riding, kayaking and cycling. Tourist offices nearly always keep comprehensive lists of local farmstays.

FARMSTAY SITES

Agriturismo (www.agriturismo.com) Ideas for Italian farmstays.

Aventure sur la Paille/Schlaf im Stroh (☎ 041 678 12 86; www.abenteuer-stroh.ch) The ultimate Swiss adventure – stay in a real-life Alpine hay-barn (bring a sleeping bag and pocket torch).

Bienvenue à la Ferme (www.bienvenue-a-la-ferme.com) Specialising in French farmstays.

Worldwide Opportunities on Organic Farms (www.wwoof.org) For information about working on organic farms in exchange for room and board.

HOTELS

Above the B&B and guesthouse level are hotels. At the bottom end of the scale, cheap hotels may be no more expensive than private rooms or guesthouses, while at the other extreme you'll find beautifully designed boutique hotels and five-star hotels with price tags to match. You'll often find inexpensive hotels clustered around bus and train stations, which are always good places to start hunting; however, these areas can be charmless and scruffy.

European hotels are often a lot smaller compared to those of many countries (especially if you're used to travelling in the US and Canada). It's always a good idea to check your room before you agree to stay, although this obviously won't be possible if you're booking from overseas, so pre-trip research is always a good idea. Ask about breakfast; sometimes it's included, but other times it may be obligatory and you'll have to pay extra for it. Check where the fire exits are, especially in older hotels.

Hotel prices in some countries are sometimes quoted per person rather than per room, so what looks like a reasonable rate can become rather less tempting if there are two of you staying. Single travellers usually have to pay a premium – generally around 75% of the standard cost for a double room. Opting for a shared bathroom down the hall can be a good way of cutting costs, although they're becoming less and less common; even the cheapest rooms usually have their own washbasin.

Whether breakfast is included in the price of a room really depends on the country

HOTEL SITES

Besides big booking sites such as **Travelocity** (www.travelocity.com) and **Hotels.com** (www.hotels.com) and the community-reviewed **TripAdvisor** (www.tripadvisor.com), you could also try the following discount sites:

Direct Rooms (www.directrooms.com)
GTA (www.gtahotels.com)
Hotel Club (www.hotelclub.net)
Hotel Info (www.hotel.info)
HRS (www.hrs.com)
LateRooms (www.laterooms.com)
Last Minute (www.lastminute.com)

RENTAL ACCOMMODATION SITES

Try the following websites for rental accommodation, just a few of scores:

HolidayHavens.co.uk (www.holidayhavens.co.uk)
Holiday-Rentals (www.holiday-rentals.com)
Homelidays (www.homelidays.com)
Vacations-Abroad.com (www.vacations-abroad.com)

you're staying in – it's almost unheard of in France, but is still relatively common in many UK hotels. You'll often find the more expensive the hotel, the less likely they are to include breakfast – go figure.

RESERVATIONS

Cheap hotels in popular destinations fill up quickly. It's a good idea to make reservations ahead, at least for the first night or two. You can prebook online – via the hotel's website or via one of the many online agencies. The drawback is that you can't view your room before you book – but if you stick to our recommendations, you shouldn't go too far wrong.

If you arrive without a reservation, airport accommodation desks and tourist offices can usually help you. The fee for this service is generally low, and it can be a good way to get around any language problems.

RENTAL ACCOMMODATION

The last option for accommodation is to rent your own apartment, villa or holiday home – it's great value and great fun for families travelling together, or for travellers staying in the same place for at least one week. You'll have the freedom of coming and going when you like without worrying about curfews and strict checkout times, plus a feeling of coming 'home' after a hard day of sightseeing. All rentals should be equipped with kitchens (or at least a kitchenette), which can save on the food bill and allow you to peruse the neighbourhood markets and shops. Some short-term rental properties are a little more upmarket, with laundry facilities, parking pads, daily maid services and even a concierge. Check with local tourist offices noted in individual country chapters for a list of rental properties.

ARCHITECTURE

HOLGER LEUE

Stonehenge (p103), Britain

With an architectural heritage stretching back over seven millennia, Europe is one long nonstop textbook for building buffs. From Greek temples to venerable mosques and modern skyscrapers, Europe's fascinating and complex architectural environment is bound to be one of the main highlights of your visit.

Some of the earliest examples of human habitation are the prehistoric cave paintings found in Spain, France and several other areas of Europe; the most famous examples are those of the Vézère Valley (p215) in France and Altamira in Spain.

As the centuries wore on, the first recognisable settlements began to emerge as humans began to practise rudimentary agriculture, crop cultivation and cattle farming. Neolithic settlements have been discovered across much of Europe and the Mediterranean, along with hundreds of stone circles, henges, barrows, burial chambers and alignments, including impressive examples at Stonehenge (p103), Brú Na Bóinne in Ireland (p150) and Carnac (p209). Meanwhile, on the opposite side of the continent, some of Europe's earliest complex civilisations were beginning to flourish around ancient Turkey; traces of their existence can still be seen throughout much of central Turkey.

By around 2500BC and the advent of the Bronze Age, many corners of Europe had developed their own distinct cultures, but it was the advanced Cycladic, Minoan and Mycenaean civilisations, followed by the ancient Greeks, who left the most enduring architectural mark. Athens (p662) is the best place to appreciate Greece's golden age: the monuments of the Acropolis (p663) perfectly illustrate the ancient Greeks'

THE BEST

BARBARA VAN ZANTEN

Cathédral de Notre Dame de Paris (p187), France

GOTHIC LANDMARKS

- **Cathédrale de Notre Dame de Paris** (p187)
- **Chartres Cathedral** (p203)
- **Münster Cathedral** (p467)
- **York Minster** (p116)
- **Catedral de Léon** (p290)
- **St Vitus Cathedral** (p551)

sophisticated understanding of geometry, shape and form, along with many architectural principles that continue to exert an enduring influence through to the present day.

By the 3rd century BC, ancient Greece's star was beginning to wane and a new empire was on the rise. Over the next few centuries, the power of the Roman empire extended across most of Europe, from the imperial city at Byzantium (modern İstanbul, p712) to the great engineering project of Hadrian's Wall (p121) in northern Britain. Obviously, Rome has the greatest concentration of architectural treasures, including the Colosseum (p318) and the Forum (p318), but you'll find fascinating Roman remains scattered all over the continent.

The fall of the Roman empire in the late 5th century AD led to the advent of the Dark Ages throughout Western Europe, and it wasn't until the early Middle Ages when the next great period of European construction began. The first significant development was the advent of Romanesque architecture, an architectural style designed to convey a sense of religious strength, permanence and solidity, characterised by rounded arches, vaulted roofs and massive columns and walls. Even more influential was the development of Gothic architecture, which gave rise to many of Europe's most spectacular cathedrals. Tell-tale characteristics of Gothic architecture include the advent of pointed arches, ribbed vaulting, great showpiece windows and flying buttresses.

At the same time, the Muslim rulers in several areas of Spain created some of the great achievements of Moorish architecture, including Granada's Alhambra (p293) and Cordoba's Mezquita (p292). Later, as the Ottoman empire reached its peak, a distinctive Turkish style emerged. The Topkapı Sarayı (p717) in İstanbul is perhaps the most glittering example.

Between the 15th and 17th centuries, the Renaissance represented a revolution not just for European art, but for architecture, too. Pioneering Italian architects such as Brunelleschi, Michelangelo and Palladio shifted the emphasis away from Gothic austerity towards a more humanist architectural approach, blending elements from classical Greece and Rome with new building materials, new engineering techniques and specially commissioned sculpture and artworks. The centre of the Italian Renaissance is undoubtedly Florence (p352), closely followed by Venice (p341), but its influence can be felt practically everywhere, with each country interpreting the distinctive tropes and tics of the Renaissance style in their own unique way.

The flamboyance and showiness of the Baroque movement was a logical extension of the Renaissance, and resulted in a new rash of stunningly ambitious buildings, including countless country estates, castles and townhouses: Castle Howard (p119), Prague's Church of St Nicholas (p555), Paris' Hôtel des Invalides, London's St Paul's Cathedral (p81), the Residenz in Wurzbürg (p459) and practically all of Salzburg's buildings (p485) bear the hallmarks of the Baroque movement, but the style reached its zenith with Louis XIV's mindbogglingly lavish weekend getaway, the Château de Versailles (p203). Turkey enjoyed its own golden architectural period during the 16th and 17th centuries, largely thanks to the work of the pioneering architect Mimar Sinan; iconic buildings of the period include İstanbul's Blue Mosque (p717), built by one of Sinan's pupils, Sedefhar Mehmet Aga.

Following on from the flamboyant showpieces of the Baroque movement, the Rococo style favoured more delicate forms. But it was the advent of the industrial age that led to Europe's next great process of architectural reinvention. Architects began to reject the showiness and ornamentation of the Baroque and Rococo periods in favour of the pure lines, solidity and symmetry of classical architecture. The chaotic streets and higgledy-piggledy buildings of many European cities were swept away in favour of carefully planned urban architecture, incorporating factories, public buildings, museums and residential suburbs into a seamless integrated whole. One of the most obvious examples of urban remodelling was Baron Haussman's dramatic reinvention of Paris during the late 19th century, which resulted in the city's great boulevards and many of its landmark buildings.

The Gothic revival in the late 19th century led to a host of grand new buildings using new industrial materials, especially iron, brick and glass – Amsterdam's Rijksmuseum (p385) and London's Natural History Museum (p84) are both iconic examples of the neo-Gothic movement.

But by the turn of the 20th century, architects had begun to experiment with new approaches to shape and form. The flowing shapes and architectural quirks of art nouveau

DIEGO LEZAMA

Blue Mosque (p717), İstanbul, Turkey

THE BEST

JOHN HAY

Detail of door of the Duomo (p354), Florence, Italy

RENAISSANCE LANDMARKS

- **Duomo, Florence** (p354)
- **St Peter's Basilica, Rome** (p320)
- **Palazzo Pitti, Florence** (p355)
- **Sistine Chapel, Vatican City** (p322)
- **Château de Chambord, Loire Valley** (p208)

had a profound influence on the work o Charles Rennie Mackintosh in Glasgow (p135), the Belgian architect Victor Hort (p404) and the Modernista buildings o Antonio Gaudí (whose most ambitiou project, the Sagrada Familia in Barcelona still remains unfinished eighty years afte his death – see p273). Meanwhile, othe architects stripped their buildings bac to the bare essentials, emphasising stric function over form: Le Corbusier, Ludwig Mies van der Rohe and Walter Gropiu (founder of the German Bauhaus movement) are among the most influentia figures of the period.

Functional architecture continued to dominate much of 20th-century architecture, especially in the rush to reconstruc Europe's shattered cities in the wake o the two world wars. The 'concrete box style of architecture certainly isn't to everyone's taste, and the more extreme expressions of modernist architecture – epitomised by London's Southbank Centre (p94) the New Bridge (Nový most, p573) in Bratislava and many eastern European city centres – have largely fallen out of fashion over recent decades.

In their place have come a rash of imaginative and exciting structures, from soaring skyscrapers such as London's Gherkin and the Sapphire in İstanbul (currently unde construction) to groundbreaking buildings such as Frank Gehry's Guggenheim Museum in Bilbao (p281) and IM Pei's controversial glass pyramid outside the Louvre (p189) Europeans often have a love–hate relationship with modern architecture, but the more imaginative, enduring structures eventually find their place – a good example of this is the inside-out Centre Pompidou (p188) in Paris, which initially drew howls of protest, but is now considered one of the icons of 20th-century architecture. Regardless of whethe or not you approve of the more recent additions to Europe's architectural landscape one thing's for sure – you certainly won't find them boring.

FAMILY TRAVEL

DOMINIC BONUCCELLI

-amily at entrance to the Museo Guggenheim (p281), Bilbao, Spain

et's face it: travelling with your kids can be one long dventure or a nonstop nightmare. The key to fun and ewarding family travel is planning – mugging up on the laces and pitfalls you're likely to experience on your European rip is not just an excellent way to avoid any unwelcome urprises, it's also an excellent way to get everyone excited bout the adventure ahead.

he number-one guideline for travelling with children is to avoid trying to do too much ı too little time. (Actually, this should be the number-one guideline for travelling 'ithout children, too.) Trying to pack too much sightseeing into the available time is uaranteed to cause problems – you'll get tired, the kids will get irritable and tantrums re sure to follow.

Always try to break up your holiday into small, achievable chunks – planning to see ıe whole of London in a day simply isn't sensible, but by limiting yourself to one specific area (Covent Garden, Westminster, Kensington or Greenwich, for example) you'll et much more out of your explorations. It's also a good idea to mix up the museums /ith things the kids are guaranteed to like – balance that visit to the Tate Modern or ıe Louvre with a trip to the London Aquarium or a day at Disneyland Paris. Including hildren in the planning process is also a great idea. They may not have an opinion bout Paris versus Prague, but they'll certainly have an opinion about how they would ke to spend the day when they get there…

The other common cause of family trouble is travel time. If you're covering a large rea – especially if you're visiting several countries in a single trip – you'll spend a lot

THE NITTY GRITTY

- **Baby-changing facilities** Found at most supermarkets and major attractions
- **Cots and highchairs** Available in many restaurants and hotels, but ask ahead
- **Health standards** Generally good, but pack a well-stocked first-aid kit for emergencies
- **Nappies (diapers)** Sold everywhere
- **Strollers** Bring your own
- **Transport** Trains are fine, but they'll get bored on buses

of time and effort trying to keep the kic entertained en route. Traffic is at its wor during popular holiday seasons, especiall between June and August, and train jou neys in Europe can be long and (depen ing where you are) sometimes slow, to Despite the travel times, trains can actu ally be a great option for family travel the kids will have much more space t move around than in buses or cars, an can pack books, puzzles and compute games to keep them entertained whe the appeal of staring at the scenery star to wane. Again, it's all a question of plar ning – instead of trying to drive a hug distance in a single day, it's a much bette idea to break up the trip into bite-size bi with things to see and do en route.

Most of Europe is fairly child-friendly. Car-hire firms have children's safety seats fc hire at a nominal cost, but you'll probably have to book them in advance. Baby foo infant formulas, soy and cows' milk, disposable nappies and so on are widely availab in supermarkets, and many major tourist sights and museums provide baby-changin facilities or mother-and-baby bathrooms. High chairs and cots (cribs) are also fairly cor mon, but it's always worth asking in advance whether hotels are happy to accept kids some smarter establishments impose a minimum age limit on guests, while others ar fully geared for family travel, with childrens' activities, child-minding services and th like. The same goes for restaurants, pubs and bars – asking in advance will avoid an uncomfortable moments along the line.

FOOD & DRINK

GIORGIO COSULICH

:arving meat in a restaurant, Italy

ıne sure-fire way to understand what makes a country tick by thinking with your stomach. Sampling some (or lots!) f Europe's cuisines will be one of the most memorable spects of your European expedition. The range of food you'll ncounter will be wonderfully varied, from the fiery flavours nd spicy ingredients of Mediterranean cuisine to Turkish ebabs, French cheeses, Swiss fondues and German sausages. ome of the ingredients and flavours might not always be) your taste, but you won't know till you try – so open your nind, swallow your preconceptions, do as the locals do and ıst tuck in. *Bon appetit…*

TAPLES & SPECIALITIES

REAKFAST

ney say breakfast's the most important meal of the day, but quite what you'll find n the table depends on where in Europe you happen to be. Every nation has its own ıke on the breakfast question.

In Britain and Ireland, the traditional start to the day consists of a cooked breakfast ıtherwise known as a 'fry-up'), an artery-hardening concoction of fried eggs, bacon, ausages, black pudding (blood sausage) and tomatoes. Cereals and toast are also opular. In the same vein, cold meats and cheeses very often grace the breakfast tables f Germany, Austria, Switzerland and many Eastern European nations.

THE BEST

Sweet pastries at a French patisserie

MUST-TRY THINGS

- A British fry-up
- French patisseries
- Spanish tapas
- German sausage
- Turkish kebap
- Italian pizza
- Hungarian goulash
- Greek mezedes
- Czech beer

The Mediterranean approach is alt gether lighter: Spaniards usually sta the day with a light *desayuno* (breakfas perhaps coffee with a *tostada* (piece toast) or *pastel/bollo* (pastry), while tl French usually opt for a *petit déjeun* (breakfast) of coffee and baguette wi jam, occasionally accompanied by croissant or a *pain au chocolat* (chocola croissant). The Italians tend not to eat sit-down *colazione* (breakfast), prefe ring instead a cappuccino and *cornet* (croissant) at a cafe.

STREET FOOD & QUICK EATS

Perhaps the most famous street foc has its roots either in Belgium or tl Netherlands (depending on who you li ten to). The *friet* (fry; known in Britain the chip) is a national passion in the Lo Countries, and you'll find street stalls se ing perfectly cooked fries practically an where you go (although overseas visito are often surprised to find that Europeans prefer to dip their chips in mayonnai rather than ketchup). One of Britain's staple takeaway foods is fish and chips – battered fillet of cod that is fried, sprinkled with salt and vinegar and served wi thick-cut chips (rather than the thin chips you'll find served in most other Europea countries).

Sandwiches are another staple snack. Legend has it that the sandwich was invented the 18th century by John Montagu, the 4th Earl of Sandwich, although in reality peop have probably been slapping ingredients between two hunks of bread since Neolith times. In the UK, a sandwich is usually made with a square-sized loaf, cut in two; acro the Channel in France and Belgium, they're more likely to make their sandwiches usir a long baton-shaped baguette. The Italians favour the *panini*, a pocket-shaped parc of bread usually served piping hot; the pitta, a flatbread served widely in Greece ar Turkey, is a close relation.

Pizza is another ubiquitous street food. For the real McCoy you'll obviously want head to Italy, although many other countries have their own variations: *lahmacun* a paper-thin Arabic pizza topped with chopped onion, lamb and tomato sauce, whi a French version served around Nice and Marseille is *pissaladière*, a thin pizza toppe with caramelised onions, olives, garlic and anchovies.

Spain and Greece have a sophisticated snack culture based around small bite-si dishes (known as tapas and meze respectively). A selection of three or four starte represents a good meal and makes an excellent vegetarian option. *Pintxos* is the Basq version of tapas.

The ubiquitous Turkish *dürüm döner kebap* consists of compressed meat (usually hicken or lamb) cooked on a revolving upright skewer over coals, then thinly sliced. /hen laid on pide bread, topped with tomato sauce and browned butter and with yohurt on the side, *döner kebap* becomes *İskender kebap,* primarily a lunchtime delicacy. qually ubiquitous are *köfte* (meatballs).

In Greece, large kebabs are known as *gyros*, while souvlaki is made from small cubes f meat individually cooked on a skewer; both are served wrapped in pitta bread with alad and served with lashings of tzatziki (a yoghurt, cucumber and garlic dip). Felafel :hickpea balls) are another much-loved Greek snack.

The Netherlands' colonial legacy has introduced Indonesian and Surinamese cooking o the Dutch palate, and you'll find lots of takeaways specialising in Far Eastern–style treet dishes. Bratwurst and pretzel stands (sometimes stuffed with meats and cheeses) bound in Germany, while the French often munch on crêpes and *galettes* (paper-thin ancakes served both savoury and sweet). Tortillas (like omelettes) are an inexpensive tandby snack in Spain.

'ISH & SEAFOOD

ish and other seafood feature heavily in much Mediterranean cooking, usually cooked vith tomatoes, spices, herbs, onions, garlic and, of course, the essential ingredient of lediterranean cuisine, olive oil.

Spain's most characteristic dish, paella, is typical of the predominant flavours of lediterranean cooking, consisting of rice, seafood, the odd vegetable and often hicken or meat, simmered together in a large steel pan and traditionally coloured ellow with saffron.

Another seafood staple you'll encounter all over Europe is mussels, usually cooked n white wine or cream and served in steaming hot cauldrons. France and the Low

GREG ELMS

Pasta with seafood in an Italian restaurant

PASTA

The home of pasta is, of course, Italy, where it's so much more than a simple foodstuff. The art of pasta-making is passed down through the generations; you're as likely to find Italians getting into a heated debate about the merits of a particular pasta as they are about their politicians' latest exploits. Pasta comes in a myriad of different shapes and forms, with each region maintaining its own special traditions and sauces – for example, Genoa for pesto and Bologna for *ragù* (bolognese sauce). But while Italy is undoubtedly where you'll still taste the top pasta, this versatile ingredient has infiltrated practically all of Europe's major cuisines these days.

Countries are particularly keen on mussels, while other super-fresh shellfish such as prawns, oysters, clams, cockles and winkles are popular all over the Mediterranean.

There are far too many fish in the sea to mention here, although there are a few you're almost guaranteed to encounter, including calamari (fried squid), swordfish, shark, red and grey mullet, monkfish, cod, haddock and bass, as well as crustaceans such as lobster, crab, crayfish and langoustine. If you don't speak the local lingo, a good-quality dictionary can help you avoid any unexpected seafood surprises.

MEAT

Carnivores will be spoilt for choice. This is one of the world's great meat-eating continents, and most nations aren't terribly fussy about which bits of the animal they eat – kidney, liver, tongue and even brains are often just as much of a delicacy as a fillet steak or a prime rib. Every region has its distinctive meaty cuisine but broadly speaking the hot south tends to favour dishes based around olive oil, garlic and tomatoes, while the cooler north favours hearty country flavours based around root vegetables, rich gravies and creamy or buttery sauces.

The countries of central and northern Europe are perhaps the biggest meat-eaters, favouring hearty dishes such as casseroles, stews, hotpots, large mixed grill platters and seemingly endless types of sausage. Pork and ham are widely eaten, often in dried or cured form such as *jamón serrano* (Spanish cured ham), *Bündnerfleisch* (Swiss dried beef, smoked and thinly sliced) or *charcuterie* (a catch-all term for various French cured meats).

Throughout Austria, Switzerland and Germany *wurst* (sausage) is available in hundreds of different forms, including bratwurst (spiced sausage), *weissewurst* (veal sausage), *blutwurst* (blood sausage) and many forms of schnitzel (breaded pork or veal cutlet), including Austria's signature dish, *Wiener schnitzel*. Some staples such as *wurst* and regional dishes such as *Tiroler bauernschmaus* (a selection of meats served with sauerkraut, potatoes and dumplings) can be very fatty and stodgy.

Central and Eastern European nations offer similarly hearty fare, often revolving around various schnitzels and stews. Dutch food is just as filling; dishes include *stamppot* (mashed pot) – potatoes mashed with kale, endive or sauerkraut and served with smoked sausage or pork strips. *Hutspot* (hotchpotch) is similar, but with potatoes, carrots, onions and braised meat.

The omnipresent seasoning in Hungarian cooking is paprika, a mild red pepper that ɔpears on restaurant tables as a condiment beside the salt and black pepper, as well in many recipes.

HEESE

ırope is world famous for its cheeses. Every country has its favourites, but the king European cheese-making has to be France, which produces literally hundreds of fferent types (the French general and president Charles de Gaulle famously quipped ow can you govern a country which has 246 varieties of cheese?'). Some of the big ımes you're bound to encounter are camembert, brie, Livarot, Roquefort, Époisses, eu d'Auvergne and Pont l'Évêque.

Only just behind the French in the cheese stakes are the Italians: again, there are ındreds of different types to choose from, but among the biggest names are parme-ın, ricotta and mozzarella.

Switzerland, the Netherlands and Germany tend to favour hard rather than soft ıeeses, especially emmental, gruyère, gouda and edam. One of the best-known Swiss shes is fondue, in which melted emmental and gruyère are combined with white wine a large pot and eaten with bread cubes. Another popular artery-hardener is *raclette*, elted cheese served with potatoes.

Britain's top cheese is cheddar – a matured hard cheese with a pungent flavour – but ıere are others to discover including Wensleydale, Red Leicester and Stilton. Greece's rong, salty feta cheese is also a highlight.

ESSERTS & SWEET TREATS

om pralines to puddings, Europe provides endless opportunities to indulge in some-ıing sweet, sticky and sinful. Germans and Austrians are particularly known for their

GLENN BEANLAND

Chocolate on display, Switzerland

sweet tooth – popular choices include *Salzburger nockerl* (a fluffy soufflé), *Schwarzwälc kirschtorte* (Black Forest cherry cake), plus endless varieties of *apfeltasche* (apple past and strudel (filo pastry filled with a variety of fruits, poppy seeds or cheese). The Bri are another big cake-eating nation – a slice of cake or a dunked biscuit is still a teatin ritual in many corners of the British Isles.

Not far behind are the Belgians, who have been making some of the world's fine chocolate for well over a century. The Italians are perhaps best known for their *gelateri* or ice-cream stalls (the very best will be labelled *produzione propria*, indicating that i been handmade on the premises).

Most Greek desserts are Turkish in origin and are variations on pastry soaked honey, such as baklava (thin layers of pastry filled with honey and nuts). Delicio Greek yoghurt also makes a great dessert, especially served with honey, while Turkey famously chewy sweet, *lokum* (Turkish delight) has been made here since the 18 century.

But it's the French who have really turned dessert into a fine art. Stroll past the windo of any *boulangerie* (bakery) or patisserie and you'll be assaulted with a Wonkaesqu selection of sweet temptations, from creamy éclairs and crunchy *macarons* (macaroon to fluffy madeleines (shell-shaped sponge cakes) and spicy *pains d'épices* (a type French gingerbread).

Go on – you know you want to.

THAT'S THE SPIRIT

Europeans need no excuse for a good stiff drink. Aniseed-flavoured ouzo is a way of life in Greece – it's been the favourite afternoon drink for gentlemen of a certain age since time immemorial. It's traditionally mixed with water and ice (turning a cloudy white). Similar traditions exist in the south of France (where pastis is the tipple), Spain (grappa) and Turkey (raki).

Whisky-lovers should head to Scotland and Ireland, where single and blended malts have been brewed in the time-honoured fashion for centuries. Other spirits to look out for are *pálinka,* a strong Hungarian brandy, Croatian *rakija* (flavoured brandy), and Dutch *jenever,* a powerful juniper-flavoured spirit.

DRINKS

BEER

No country in the world has a brewin tradition as rich and diverse as Belgium which boasts somewhere betwee 400 and 800 different beers, incluc ing dark Trappist beers, potent golde nectars such as Duuvel and the tang champagne-style *lambic* beers brewe around Brussels.

Germany and Austria also have lots different beer types: *vollbier* is 4% alcoh by volume, *export* is 5% and *bockbier* 6%. *Helles bier* is light beer, while *dunkle bier* is dark. *Export* is similar to, but muc better than, typical international brew while the *pils* is more bitter. *Alt* is darke and more full-bodied. A speciality *weizenbier*, which is made with whe instead of barley malt and served in a ta 500mL glass.

Most other European countries (incluc ing France, Spain, Hungary, the Czec Republic and Slovakia) favour lager-sty eer, but the traditional British brew is ale – erved warm and flat in order to bring ut the intense, hoppy flavours. Similarly, eland's trademark ale is stout – usually uinness, although in Cork stout can ean a Murphy's or a Beamish, too.

WILL SALTER

Beer pulls in a Scottish pub

VINE

urope's top wine-producing nation is rance, where the principal regions of lsace, Bordeaux, Burgundy, Champagne, anguedoc-Roussillon, the Loire region nd the Rhône still produce the vast ajority of Europe's whites, reds and hampagnes.

Close behind is Italy, with many excel- ent vineyards based in the principal wine- rowing areas of Piedmont, Tuscany and icily, and Spain (where the major areas re Penedès, Priorat, Ribera del Duero and ioja). Sangria, a sweet punch made of red ine, fruit and spirits, is a popular Spanish ummer drink.

Germany is principally known for its ugely popular white wines – inexpen- ive, light and intensely fruity. The Rhine nd Moselle Valleys are the classic wine- rowing regions. Greek and Croatian wines are less well-known, although decent rapes are available in both countries. Retsina, wine flavoured with pine-tree resin, s a tasty alternative in Greece – though an acquired taste for some. Croatians often nix their wine with water, calling it *bevanda*.

VEGETARIANS & VEGANS

'egetarians will have a tough time in many areas of Europe – meat-eating is still ery much the norm, especially in France, Germany and Hungary, while vegans vill probably want to avoid the dairy-obsessed nations of Austria and Switzerland ltogether.

Having said that, things have come on in leaps and bounds over recent years, and ou'll usually be able to find at least something meat-free on most menus (even if your hoice is rather limited). Vegetable-based antipasti (starters), tapas, meze, pastas, side lishes and salads are all good ways of ensuring a meat-free diet. Shopping for yourself n local markets can also be a good way of avoiding awkward meat moments.

HISTORY

ANDERS BLOMQ

Statue of Plato before the Town Hall, Athens (p662), Greece

It's thought the first humanoid settlers set foot on the landmass now known as Europe around two million years ago. The oldest known remains of *Homo erectus* (the prehistoric predecessor of *Homo sapiens*) outside Africa were found in Dmanisi, Georgia, and have been dated to approximately 1.6 to 1.8 million years old. More recent human remains have been discovered in various locations around Europe, along with the remains of prehistoric Neanderthals, a separate humanoid species who probably co-existed alongside our prehistoric ancestors.

The last major ice age ended sometime between 12,000BC and 8000 BC, and roughl coincides with the first stage of colonisation of Europe by 'modern' humans. Over th next few millennia, human hunter-gatherer tribes extended their reach northwards i search of new land and fresh hunting grounds as the ice sheets thawed.

4500–2500 BC	2500–500 BC	1st century BC–4 AD
Neolithic tribes spread throughout Europe, building many burial tombs, barrows, stone circles and alignments.	Emergence of the first great European civilisations. Ancient Greeks break new ground in technology, science, art and architecture.	The Romans conquer much of Europe. The Republic is founded in 510 BC, followed by the Roman Empire under Augustus and his successors.

GREEKS & ROMANS

urope's first recognisable society is generally considered to be the Cucuteni-Trypillian ulture, which emerged in the Carpathian Mountains between 5000BC and 2000BC. urther civilisations developed in Mycenae (about 90km southwest of Athens) and ncient Crete, but it was the Greeks and the Romans who really kickstarted Europe.

The civilisation of Ancient Greece emerged around 2000BC and made huge leaps orward in science, technology, architecture, philosophy and democratic principles. Many of the writers, thinkers and mathematicians of ancient Greece, from Pythagoras o Plato, still exert a profound influence on us to this day.

Hot on the heels of the Greeks came the Romans, who promptly set about conquering most of Europe and devised the world's first recognisable democratic republic. At its eight, Roman power extended all the way from Celtic Britain to ancient Persia (Iran), nd the Romans' achievements are almost too myriad to mention: they founded cities, aised aqueducts, constructed roads, laid sewers and built baths all over the continent, nd produced a string of brilliant writers, orators, politicians, philosophers and military eaders who laid the foundations for modern Europe.

THE DARK AGES

pin the clock forward a few centuries, and both the Greek and Roman empires had already seen their golden ages come and go. Greece had been swallowed by the kingdom f Macedonia, led by Alexander the Great, then by Rome itself in AD 146. Meanwhile, Rome's empire-building ambitions eventually proved too much, and a series of political roubles and military disasters resulted in the sacking of Rome (in 410) at the hands of he Visigoths. Although Roman emperors clung on to their eastern Byzantine empire or another 1000 years, founding a new capital at Constantinople, Rome's period of dominance over western Europe was well and truly over. A new era, the Dark Ages, had begun.

Meanwhile, out in the east, new empires were rising. A warlike people known as the Huns arrived from central Asia and set about making incursions into parts of the territory left behind by the fallen Romans, led by their charismatic leader, Attila. Struggles or power were breaking out elsewhere in Europe, too, with rival peoples vying for post-Roman supremacy. Eventually, in 768, Charlemagne, King of the Franks, brought ogether much of Western Europe under what would later become known as the Holy Roman Empire. The new territory came under attack from various fronts – including from Vikings (from present-day Scandinavia), Magyars (from Hungary) and Muslims (from Northern Africa, Turkey and the Middle East) – although the majority of the invaders were eventually either driven out or encouraged to put down roots.

410

The sacking of Rome brings an end to Roman dominance, although the Eastern Empire lives on in Constantinople until 1453.

800

Charlemagne becomes the first Holy Roman Emperor, although the title is not officially employed until the coronation of Otto I in 962.

1066

William the Conqueror invades England and defeats the English King Harold at the Battle of Hastings.

THE BEST

HOLGER LEUE

Grand Canal, Venice (p341), Italy

PHOTOGENIC TOWNS

- **Venice** (p341)
- **Bruges** (p412)
- **Edinburgh** (p130)
- **Salzburg** (p485)
- **Carcassonne** (p214)

Meanwhile, an alliance of Christia nations repeatedly sent troops to reclai the Holy Land from Islamic control in series of campaigns collectively know as the Crusades. Later centuries saw o going conflict between European powe and the powerful Turkish Ottoman empi as it slowly consolidated control of As Minor, Eastern Europe and parts of th Balkans.

RENAISSANCE, REFORMATION & REVOLUTION

Europe's troubles rumbled on into th 14th and 15th centuries. In the wake c further conflicts and political upheaval as well as the devastating outbreak of th Black Death (which is estimated to hav wiped out between a third and half of Europe's population), control over the Hol Roman Empire passed into the hands of the Austrian Habsburgs, a political dynast that was to become one of the continent's dominant powers from around the 14t century onwards. Out in the east, the Ottomans took control over the Byzantine empir after the fall of Constantinople in 1453, effectively cutting off Europe's lucrative trad ing links with the Orient. Meanwhile, the Italian city-states of Genoa, Venice, Pisa an Amalfi consolidated their control over the Mediterranean.

In the mid-15th century, a new age of artistic and philosophical development brok out across the continent. The Renaissance, as it came to be known, encouraged writer artists and thinkers all over Europe to challenge the accepted doctrines of theolog philosophy, architecture and art. The centre of this artistic tsunami was Florence, wher inspirational figures such as Michelangelo and Leonardo da Vinci broke new ground i art and architecture. Meanwhile, another epoch-changing development was underwa in Germany, thanks to the invention of the printing press, which had been devised b Johannes Gutenburg around 1440. The advent of 'moveable type' made printed book available to the masses for the first time.

While the Renaissance largely challenged artistic ideas, the Reformation was almos entirely a question of religion. Challenging Catholic 'corruption' and the divine author ity of the Pope, the German theologian Martin Luther established his own breakawa

1096	1340s	1453
Pope Urban II calls for the First Crusade to recover the Holy Land from Muslim control. The Crusades continue until 1291.	The Black Death reaches its peak in Europe. By 1400 between 30% and 60% of Europe's population has been killed.	Constantinople falls to the Ottomans, who establish the city as a base from which to expand their growing empire.

anch of the church, Protestantism, in ;17. His stance was soon echoed by ie English monarch Henry VIII, who cut f ties with Rome in 1534 and founded s own (Protestant) Church of England, wing the seeds for several centuries of oody conflict between Catholics and 'otestants in Europe.

The schisms of the church certainly eren't the only source of trouble. The iscovery of the 'New World' in the mid-5th century led to a colonial arms race etween the major European nations (es-ecially France, Britain and Spain). More ouble was to follow during the Thirty ears' War (1618–48), which began as a onflict between Catholics and Protestants nd eventually sucked in most of Europe's rincipal powers. The war was eventually nded by the Peace of Westphalia in 1648, nd Europe entered a period of compara-ve stability.

MARTIN HUGHES
Artworks outside the Uffizi (p354), Florence, Italy

But in the wake of the Enlightenment ;ee boxed text, p768), people in many reas of Europe became increasingly issatisfied with the political status uo, which consolidated the majority of vealth, prestige and power in the hands of a few unelected aristocrats and all-powerful ionarchs. Things came to a head in 1789, when armed mobs stormed the Bastille rison in Paris, kickstarting the French Revolution.

Before long, heads began to roll. Scores of aristocrats met their end under the guil-otine's blade, including the French monarch Louis XVI, who was publicly executed in anuary 1793 in Paris' Place de la Concorde. But the ideals of revolution quickly soured: he Reign of Terror between September 1793 and July 1794 saw religious freedoms evoked, churches closed, cathedrals turned into 'Temples of Reason' and thousands eheaded. In the chaos, a dashing young Corsican general named Napoleon Bonaparte 1769–1821) stepped from the shadows.

15th century	1517	1789
The Renaissance brings about a revolution in art, architecture and science, spearheaded by da Vinci and Michelangelo.	Martin Luther nails his demands to the church door in Wittenburg, sparking the start of the Reformation and the development of Protestantism.	The French Revolution results in the establishment of a new French republic. Thousands of aristocrats are executed by guillotine.

THE AGE OF REASON

If there's one era that's defined Europe's philosophical landscape over the last few centuries, it's the Enlightenment (also known as the 'Age of Reason'). This was the period in the 18th century when science and rationality took supremacy over religious belief for the first time. Its emphasis on logic, education and liberal social values over the constraints of religious doctrine has influenced the work of countless poets, philosophers and politicians, and contributed to the outbreak of the French Revolution. Key figures of the movement include the antimonarchist, antireligious French writer Voltaire (1694–1778) and the German philosopher Immanuel Kant (1724–1804).

Napoleon assumed power in 1799 and in 1804 was crowned Emperor. His attemp to colonise Europe under French rule eventually ended in defeat by British forces at th Battle of Waterloo in 1815, but the civil laws he introduced in France set the framewor for political reform across much of Europe, spreading ideas of liberty, equality an universal freedom across the globe.

INDUSTRY, EMPIRE & WWI

Having vanquished Napoleon, Britain became Europe's predominant power. With i novations such as the steam engine, the railway and the factory, Britain unleashed th Industrial Revolution and, like many of Europe's big powers (including France, Spai Belgium and the Austro-Hungarian empire) set about developing its colonies acros much of Africa, Australasia and the Middle and Far East.

Before too long these competing empires clashed again, with predictably cata strophic consequences. When the heir to the Austro-Hungarian throne, Archduke Fran Ferdinand, was assassinated in 1914, the blame fell on a Serbian nationalist by the nam of Gavrilo Princip. Tensions broke out into open warfare just a month later, heraldin the beginning of the bloodiest war ever fought on European soil. Allies lined up o opposing sides; Germany and Turkey sided with the Austro-Hungarians, while Britai France, Russia and Italy (later joined by the USA) sided with the Serbians.

By the end of hostilities in 1918, huge tracts of northern France and Belgium ha been razed, and over 16 million people across Europe had been killed. In the Treaty o Versailles, the defeated powers of Austro-Hungary and Germany lost large areas of terri tory and found themselves crippled with a massive bill for reparations, sowing seeds o discontent that would be exploited a decade later by a young Austrian house-painte by the name of Adolf Hitler.

18th & 19th centuries	1914–1918	1939–1945
The Industrial Revolution brings about a sea change in European society, resulting in mass migration and environmental change.	The assassination of Archduke Franz Ferdinand leads to the outbreak of WWI.	WWII rages across most of Europe.

WWII & THE IRON CURTAIN

Hitler's rise to power was astonishingly swift. By 1936 he had risen to the role of Chancellor and, as the head of the Nazi Party, assumed total control of Germany's power structures. Having spent much of the 1930s building up a formidable war machine – as well as assisting General Franco's nationalist forces during the Spanish Civil War – Hitler then annexed former German territories in Austria and parts of Czechoslovakia, before extending his reach onwards into Poland in 1939.

The occupation of Poland proved the final straw. Britain, France and its Commonwealth allies declared war on Germany, who had formed its own alliance of convenience with the other Axis powers of Italy and Japan. Hitler unleashed his blitzkrieg on an unsuspecting Europe and within a few short months had conquered huge areas of territory across eastern and central Europe, forcing the French into submission and driving the British forces into a humiliating retreat at Dunkirk.

The Axis retained the upper hand until the Japanese attack on Pearl Harbour forced a reluctant USA into the war in 1941. Hitler's subsequent decision to invade Russia in 1941 proved to be a catastrophic error of judgment, resulting in devastating German losses and eventually paving the way for the Allied invasion of Normandy in June 1944.

After several months of bitter fighting, Hitler's remaining forces were pushed back towards Berlin. Hitler committed suicide on 30 April 1945 and the Russians took the city, crushing the last pockets of German resistance. By 8 May, Germany and Italy had unconditionally surrendered to the Allied powers, bringing the long war in Europe to an end.

Tragically, the cessation of hostilities wasn't the end of Europe's troubles. Differences of opinion between the Western powers and the communist Soviet Union soon led to a stand-off. The USSR closed off its assigned sectors – including East Berlin, East Germany and much of Eastern Europe – heralding the descent of the figurative Iron Curtain and the beginning of the Cold War, a period of political tension and social division in Europe that was to continue for the next forty years.

THE BEST

RICHARD NEBESKY

Vltava River, Prague (p546), Czech Republic

CLASSIC CAPITALS

- **Rome** (p314)
- **Paris** (p178)
- **London** (p72)
- **Prague** (p546)
- **Madrid** (p248)

1957

The European Economic Community (EEC) is established by Belgium, France, Italy, Luxembourg, the Netherlands and West Germany.

1973

The EEC is enlarged to include the UK, Ireland and Denmark.

1989

The fall of the Berlin Wall heralds the downfall of oppressive regimes across much of Eastern Europe.

KRZYSZTOF DYDYN

Checkpoint Charlie (p443), Berlin, Germany

The era finally came to an end in 1989, when popular unrest in Germany resulted in th fall of the Berlin Wall. Germany was reunified in 1990; a year later the USSR was dissolvec and shortly afterwards Romania, Bulgaria, Poland, Hungary and Albania had implemente multiparty democracy. Perhaps the most astonishing transition of power occurred i Czechoslovakia, where the so-called 'Velvet Revolution' brought about the downfall of th communist government through mass demonstrations and other nonviolent means.

EUROPE UNITED

Elsewhere in Europe, the process of political and economic integration has continue apace since the end of WWII. The formation of the EEC (European Economic Communit in 1957 began as a loose trade alliance between six nations, but since its rebrandin as the European Union at the Treaty of Maastricht in 1993 its core membership has ex panded to 27 countries. Sixteen nations have so far chosen to adopt the single currenc the euro, although divisions over the future direction and democratic accountabilit of Europe continue to rumble on in many of its constituent states.

After a long period of discussion and debate concerning a new pan-Europea Constitution, the controversial treaty was finally ratified in late 2009, paving the wa for the appointment of Europe's first ever fixed-term President. It's strictly an honorar title at this stage, but perhaps a sign of things to come.

1993	2002	2009
The Maastricht Treaty leads to the formation of the European Union (EU).	Twelve member states of the EU ditch their national currencies in favour of the euro.	The new European Constitution paves the way for the first permanent President of the EU Belgian Prime Minister Herman Van Rompuy.

SPORTS & ACTIVITIES

BRIAN CRUICKSHANK

Football fans at a match in Germany

With a long history of sporting prowess under its belt and a landscape taking in everything from snow-flecked mountains to sapphire seas, Europe offers endless ways to get active. Hardcore hikers, bike nuts, diving devotees and adrenaline junkies will all find plenty to keep them occupied, and if you really want to get under a nation's skin, you could do a lot worse than head for the nearest football ground…

FOOTBALL

Football (*not* soccer, please) is Europe's number-one spectator sport, and is tantamount to a religion in many corners of the continent. Europe's big nations battle it out every four years (with varying degrees of success) in the knockout European Championships; the most recent winner was Spain in 2008, with the next tournament scheduled to be jointly hosted by Poland and Ukraine in 2012.

Each country has it own top-flight domestic league (the Premier League in Britain, the Bundesliga in Germany, Serie A in Italy, La Liga in Spain and so on) plus a series of lower divisions. The top teams from each league battle it out in the hotly contested Champions League in a bid to be crowned European champions, while lower-placed teams contest the UEFA Europa League. The football season varies from country to country, but it generally runs from sometime in August or September to anytime between May and July. Tickets for top sides such as Manchester United, Chelsea, Barcelona, Real Madrid, Bayern Munich, Juventus and Inter Milan are seriously expensive (if you can get hold of one, that is) – so if you're desperate to catch a match you'll probably have much more luck by going to see one of the lesser-ranked sides.

For more info on European football clubs and competitions, the official site for **UEFA** (www.uefa.com) is the best place to start.

HIKING

Keen hikers can spend a lifetime exploring Western Europe's many exciting trails. Probably the most spectacular are to be found in the Alps and the Italian Dolomites, which are criss-crossed with well-marked trails; food and accommodation are available along the way in season. The equally sensational Pyrenees are less developed, which can add to the experience as you'll often rely on remote mountain villages for rest and sustenance. Hiking areas that are less well known, but nothing short of stunning, are Corsica and Sardinia, as well as many areas in eastern Europe including Slovakia's High Tatras. The Picos de Europa range in Spain is also rewarding, while the Lake District, the Yorkshire Dales and the Scottish Highlands are among the UK's top hiking spots.

The best months for hiking are generally from June to September, although the weather can be unpredictable at practically any time of year. Be prepared, check the weather forecast and wear the appropriate clothing, especially if you're planning on hiking through remote areas – if you get into trouble, help can be a long, long way away.

Most countries in Europe have national parks and other interesting areas that qualify as a hiker's paradise. Guided hikes are often available for those who aren't sure about their physical abilities or who simply don't know what to look for – local tourist offices can provide all the info you need.

For really hardcore hikers, Europe now has eleven long distance paths covering various countries, mostly making use of existing GR (*grande randonnée*) trails – contact the **European Ramblers' Association** (www.era-ewv-ferp.org) for further information.

LONG DISTANCE TRAILS

- **Camino de Santiago** (St James' Way; www.santiago-compostela.net) Spain's best-known long-distance trail traces the old pilgrimage route to Santiago de Compostela.
- **Grand Italian Trail** Hiking trail that cuts 6166km across Italy.
- **Haute Randonnée Pyrénéenne** High-altitude hiking through the Pyrenees.
- **Lycian Way** (www.lycianway.com) Thirty-day, 509km walk around Turkey's coast and mountains.
- **South West Coast Path** (www.swcp.org.uk) Most of Britain's stunning south-west coastline is accessible via this 630km trail.
- **Via Alpina** (www.via-alpina.org) Network of five long-distance routes across the alpine regions of Slovenia, Austria, Germany, Liechtenstein, Switzerland, Italy, France and Monaco.
- **West Highland Way** (www.west-highland-way.co.uk) Classic route through southern Scotland.

CHRISTIAN ASLUND

Snowboarder in the Alps, France

SKIING & SNOWBOARDING

Winter sports are a way of life for many European nations – the Austrians, Swiss, Germans, French and Slovakians are particularly snow-mad, and have collectively produced many of the great names in skiing and snowboarding over the last century.

If you fancy taking to the pistes, you'll find hundreds of resorts located in the Alps and Pyrenees for downhill skiing and snowboarding. Cross-country skiing is also very popular in some areas, and many resorts also offer other snowbound activities such as luge, bobsleigh and ice-climbing.

A skiing holiday can be expensive once you've added up the costs of ski lifts, accommodation and the inevitable après-ski sessions. Equipment hire, on the other hand, can be relatively cheap, and the hassle of bringing your own skis may not be worth it.

The skiing season generally lasts from early December to late March, though at higher altitudes it may extend an extra month either side. Snow conditions can vary greatly from one year to the next and from region to region, but January and February tend to be the best (and busiest) months.

Ski resorts in the French and Swiss Alps offer great skiing and facilities, but are also by far the most expensive. Expect high prices in the German Alps, too, though Germany has cheaper (but far less spectacular) options in the Black Forest and Harz Mountains. Austria is generally slightly cheaper than France and Switzerland (especially in Carinthia). Prices in the Italian Alps are similar to Austria (with some upmarket exceptions), and can be relatively cheap given the right package.

Possibly the cheapest skiing in western Europe is to be found in the Pyrenees in Spain and Andorra, and in the Sierra Nevada range in the south of Spain.

For comprehensive reports on ski conditions across Europe, try **On The Snow** (**www.onthesnow.com**).

WATER SPORTS

With the Mediterranean, the Atlantic, the Adriatic and the English Channel right on the doorstep, you won't be surprised to discover that messing about on the water is a popular European pastime.

DIVING

Tropical it isn't, but that doesn't mean Europe isn't a great place to dive. Topaz waters and a spiky, volcanic geology make for spectacular diving all along the Mediterranean coast, while the clear waters and varied underwater life of the Adriatic have led to a flourishing dive industry there, too, especially in Croatia. Wreck-diving is a particular highlight – Europe's long maritime history (as well as its war-torn past) mean that the coastline is littered with underwater vessels. The many islands of the Mediterranean offer some of Europe's finest diving – Sicily's Aeolian Islands (p362), Sardinia (p362), Corsica (p299) and the Greek Islands (p678) all provide fantastic opportunities for underwater exploring.

If you're a novice diver, diving schools offering introductory dives and longer courses are available in many areas; **PADI** (**www.padi.com**) has listings of accredited operators all around Europe. If you're an experienced diver, make sure you remember your accreditation certificates and any other relevant paperwork if you're planning on renting equipment or undertaking more complex dives.

BOATING, CANOEING & KAYAKING

Europe's lakes, rivers and diverse coastlines offer a variety of boating options unmatched anywhere in the world. You can kayak in Switzerland, row on a peaceful Alpine lake, join a Danube River cruise from Amsterdam to Vienna, rent a sailing boat on the Côte d'Azur or putter along the extraordinary canal network of Britain (or Ireland, or France) – the possibilities are endless.

DAVID TOMLINSON

Kayaking the Mediterranean coast, France

WEIRD SPORTS

- **Yağı güreş** (oil wrestling) Burly Turkish men grease themselves up and go at it near Edirne (p723) every June.
- **Camel wrestling** This Turkish pastime is as mad as it sounds. Selçuk hosts a major tournament in January.
- **Cotswold Olimpicks** Every year since 1612, locals have been competing in British sports including welly-wanging, pole-climbing and shin-kicking.
- **Cheese-rolling** (www.cheese-rolling.co.uk) This Gloucestershire contest involves foolhardy contestants running downhill at full-pelt in pursuit of a circular cheese.
- **Highland Games** Traditional Scots sports including caber-tossing, stone-putting and sheaf-throwing feature at the Cowal Highland Gathering (www.cowalgathering.com) and the Braemar Gathering (www.braemar gathering.org).

SURFING & WINDSURFING

The best surfing in Europe is on the Atlantic coastline. Top spots include the Atlantic Coast in France (especially around Biarritz), the west coasts of Wales, Ireland, Scotland and southwest England, and Spain's Basque Country (San Sebastián, Zarautz and Mundaka).

Windsurfing is less dependent on geography, so you'll be able to catch a break anywhere there's some wind and open water. With its long beaches and ceaseless wind, Tarifa, near Cádiz in Spain, is considered to be Europe's windsurfing capital, but you'll find windsurfing spots all over the Med and Adriatic.

SAILING

Sailing is a brilliant way to see Europe's coastline. Eastern Europe's most famous yachting area is the passage between the long, rugged islands off Croatia's Dalmatian coast, while sailing between the Mediterranean's coast and islands is hugely popular.

SUSTAINABLE TRAVEL

GLENN VAN DER KNIJF

Train at a mountain-pass station in the Bernese Oberland (p510), Switzerland

It's not always easy to travel and still keep your carbon footprint to a minimum, but in Europe it's a lot easier than many places. The major advantage of travelling in Europe is that unless you're planning on crossing from one side of the continent to the other, the distances involved are relatively small – especially when compared to the US, Australia and Asia.

Air travel, while fast, convenient and often relatively cheap, is by far the most damaging way to travel, and once you factor in commuting to the airport, checking in and waiting for your flight to take off, you might well find it's not always the fastest way to get from A to B. The same can be said for road travel – while it's convenient and will allow you to reach the more out-of-the-way spots that aren't served by public transport, the costs mount up quickly once you factor in hire charges, motorway tolls and fuel.

Thankfully, there's really no need to fly or drive too far. Europe has one of the world's best integrated public transport networks, with fast, efficient high-speed trains connecting nearly all the major cities. With a bit of pre-planning and route-juggling, most areas of Europe can be reached in a single day by train, and if you book your tickets in advance, ticket prices often compare very favourably with flying. We've listed full details for all Europe's international rail networks on p795, and you'll find detailed train travel information for each country in the relevant destination chapter.

The next main way of reducing your environmental impact is to change where you stay. If you're mainly visiting towns and cities, you can nearly always find a hotel that's handily positioned within walking distance of the main sights. For destinations further

GREEN TRAVEL RESOURCES

- **International Friends of Nature** (www.nfi.at) Supports sustainable travel ideas throughout Europe.
- **Sustainable Travel International** (www.sustainabletravelinternational.org) US-based information service, but useful for everyone.
- **Man in Seat 61** (www.maninseat61.com) Find out how to get practically anywhere in Europe by train.
- **Responsible Travel** (www.responsibletravel.com) Comprehensive ideas for eco-friendly travel all over the globe.
- **Gentle Tours** (www.gentle-tours.org) Database of green businesses and providers.
- **Atmosfair** (www.atmosfair.com) One of several companies where you can offset those carbon emissions.
- **Roadsharing** (www.roadsharing.com) Catch a ride and make a new friend.

afield, most places have a decent system of buses, metros or trams to help get you around, although out in the countryside things can get a bit trickier.

Steering clear of the big multinational chain hotels is another good way of making your travel more sustainable. With a bit of pre-trip research you can usually turn up some form of eco-friendly accommodation in most areas, whether that means a green-accredited British B&B, a French farmstay or an Italian *agriturismo* – handing over your money straight to a local business means you'll be directly supporting the local economy. The same goes for food shopping and eating out: buying your supplies at a local market rather than a supermarket, or choosing to eat at a small *taverna* rather than a fast-food chain, might seem like small choices, but they often make a big difference to the lives of local people.

It's also worth looking out for local environmental certificates, eco labels and awards given by local tourism bodies to businesses that have committed to reducing their environmental impact (whether by using local suppliers, reducing energy use or sourcing power from renewable resources). One example of this is the UK's **Green Tourism Business Scheme** (www.green-business.co.uk), but there are many others to look out for in other parts of Europe.

VISUAL ARTS

MARTIN MOC

Detail of statue, Rome, Italy

If there were a global league table measuring artistic importance, Europe would surely take the top prize. Practically every major art movement of the last millennia can trace its origins back to European shores, and you'll find many of the world's top artistic institutions dotted across the continent.

Some of Europe's greatest artistic treasures were left behind by its earliest civilisations – Greeks, Romans, Etruscans and many other ancient cultures have left us with a wealth of artworks (particularly sculptures, monuments and pottery) that provide a fascinating window onto the ancient world.

But after the fall of the great empires, it wasn't until the Middle Ages that Europe really rediscovered its artistic feet. The power of the church and its growing importance as an artistic patron meant that the majority of subjects in the early Middle Ages dealt with religious subjects and biblical iconography.

Some of the finest artworks of the period are literally woven into the fabric of Europe's great churches and cathedrals in the form of intricate carvings, sculpture and carpentry. Meanwhile, Flemish and German painting produced several important figures, including Jan van Eyck (1390–1441), Hans Memling (1430–1494) and Hieronymus Bosch (1450–1516).

But it was during the Renaissance that Europe's golden age of art began in earnest. Leonardo da Vinci (1452–1519), Michelangelo Buonarroti (1475–1564) and other like-minded artists broke free of the constraints of traditional painting and introduced ambitious new techniques, colours and forms into the artistic lexicon, while simultaneously drawing inspiration from the great sculptors and artists of the classical 'orld. Landscape and the human form, in particular, gained increasing importance ɹuring the Renaissance – Michelangelo's masterpiece, *David*, is often cited as one f the most perfect representations of the human figure ever created (despite the ıct that the artist deliberately distorted its proportions in order to make it more leasing to the eye). The sculpture is now on display at the Galleria dell'Accademia)355) in Florence.

In the wake of the Renaissance came the great names of the Baroque period, epitoıised by the Dutch artists Rembrandt (1606–1699), Rubens (1577–1640) and Johannes ermeer (1632–75). The Baroque artists introduced new levels of lifelike realism into ıeir work, lending their best paintings an almost photographic intensity.

During the 18th century, Romantic artists such as Rouen-born Théodore Géricault 1791–1824) and Eugène Délacroix (1798–1863) moved away from classical scenes ı favour of more contemporary subjects, drawing inspiration from recent French istory and prominent people of the day. Other artists such as Caspar David Friedrich 1774–1840) and JMW Turner (1775–1851), experimented with the drama and power f the natural landscape – cloud-capped mountains, lonely hilltops, peaceful meadws, pastoral countryside and moody sunsets. One of Spain's most important artists, rancisco Goya (1746–1828), also emerged during the period: his work encompasses verything from royal portraits to anguished war scenes, bullfight etchings and tapstry designs.

During the late 19th century, the Impressionists took bold new strides, experimentıg with light, subject and form. Artists such as Claude Monet (1840–1926), Edgar)egas (1834–1917), Camille Pissarro (1830–1903), Edouard Manet (1832–1883) and 'ierre-Auguste Renoir (1841–1919) used lisjointed brushstrokes and impressionisic colours to capture the general sense of scene rather than its strictly naturalistic epresentation. The Impressionists also lrew inspiration from ordinary, everyday cenes, often painted *en plein air* (literally, open-air', on location). Their work segued nto that of their successors, including the ikes of Paul Cézanne (1839–1906), Vincent /an Gogh (1853–90) and Paul Gauguin 1848–1903).

The upheavals of the 20th century brought great change and a rash of new artistic movements. The Fauvists used colour to suggest figures and motion, typified by the work of Henri Matisse (1869–1954), while the Cubists, such as Georges Braque 1882–1963) and Pablo Picasso (1881–1973), threw out the artistic rulebook and nstead focused on highly abstract forms, drawing inspiration from everything from

THE BEST

ORIEN HARVEY

Tate Modern (p82) at night, London, Britain

PLACES TO SEE MODERN ART

- **Tate Modern, London** (p82)
- **SMAK, Ghent** (p411)
- **Museu Picasso, Barcelona** (p269)
- **Guggenheim Museum, Bilbao** (p281)
- **Teatre-Museu Dalí** (p279)

THE BEST

IZZET KERIBAR

Musée du Louvre (p189), Paris, France

GREAT ART MUSEUMS

- **National Gallery, London** (p77)
- **Musée du Louvre, Paris** (p189)
- **Rijksmuseum, Amsterdam** (p385)
- **Prado, Madrid** (p249)
- **Uffizi Gallery, Florence** (p354)

primitive art to the emerging science psychoanalysis.

The Dadists and Surrealists took the ideas to their illogical extreme, explorir representations of dreams and the su conscious: key figures include Belgia Réné Magritte (1898–1967), German Ma Ernst (1891–1976) and the Spaniar Joan Miró (1893–1983) and Salvador Da (1904–1989).

Spin forward to the late 20th centu and you'll pass through a myriad of arti tic movements: abstract expressionisr neoplasticism, minimalism, formalism ar pop art, to name a few, not to mention th advent of one of the twentieth century most influential artistic innovations photography. All have left an endurin mark on Europe's artistic landscape, bu it's the explosion in conceptual art tha has perhaps done the most to reinvigorate public interest (both good and bad) in th contemporary art scene. From Brit bad boy Damien Hirst's pickled sharks and diamon encrusted skulls to the bizarre sculptures of the Belgian avant-garde artist Panamarenk Europe's art scene is still capable of stirring up controversy and debate.

DIRECTORY & TRANSPORT

DIRECTORY

The country directories appear at the end of each country chapter and are a round-up of specific details pertaining to that country. This chapter provides an overview of conditions, and includes information that applies to the whole of Europe. Given the vast size of the region, this has meant some generalisation. For specifics on any given topic, see the individual country directories.

CLIMATE CHARTS

Our climate charts (opposite) provide a snapshot of Europe's weather patterns.

CUSTOMS REGULATIONS

Duty-free goods are not sold to those travelling from one EU country to another. For goods purchased at airports or on ferries *outside* the EU, the usual allowances apply for tobacco (200 cigarettes, 50 cigars or 250g of loose tobacco) – although some countries have reduced this to curb smoking – and alcohol (1L of spirits or 2L of liquor with less than 22% alcohol by volume; 4L of wine). The total value of these goods cannot exceed €300.

Do not confuse these with duty-paid items (including alcohol and tobacco) bought at normal shops and supermarkets in another EU country, where certain goods might be cheaper. (Booze in France, for example, is cheaper than in the UK.)

DANGERS & ANNOYANCES

Europe is as safe – or unsafe – as any other part of the developed world. But do exercise common sense. Look purposeful, keep alert and you'll be OK. Also, leave a record (ie a photocopy) of your passport, credit and ATM cards and other important documents in a safe place. If things are stolen or lost, replacement is much easier wh you have the vital details available.

DRUGS

Always treat drugs with caution. There a a lot of drugs available in Western Euro sometimes quite openly (particularly the Netherlands), but that doesn't me they're legal. Even a little hashish c cause a great deal of trouble in so places. Don't even think about bringi drugs home with you either: if you ha what energetic customs officials may thi are 'suspect' stamps in your passport (Amsterdam's Schiphol airport), they m well decide to take a closer look.

SCAMS

See the individual chapters for scams country.

A word of warning about credit car fraudulent shopkeepers have been kno to make several charge-slip imprints wi your credit card when you're not looki and then simply copy your signature fro the authorised slip. There have also be reports of these unscrupulous peop making quick and very hi-tech duplicat of credit- or debit-card information with machine. If you'll be travelling for a whi you might consider having a trusted pers at home who can go online to check yo bank account from time to time, as ide tity thieves can steal your details and lo your account. Prompt action can stop th and get you restitution. (One main reas not to check your bank account yours from internet cafes is that spyware that c record keystrokes – and thus your accou login details – is all too common.)

THEFT

Theft is definitely a problem in Europe, a nowadays you also have to be wary of the by other travellers. The most importa

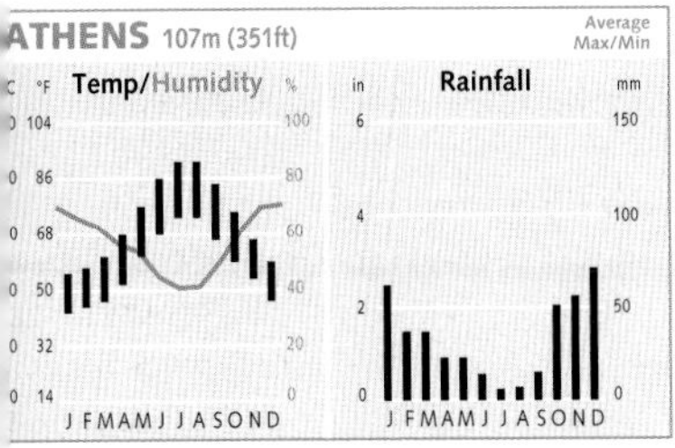
ATHENS 107m (351ft)
Average Max/Min
Temp/Humidity
Rainfall
J F M A M J J A S O N D

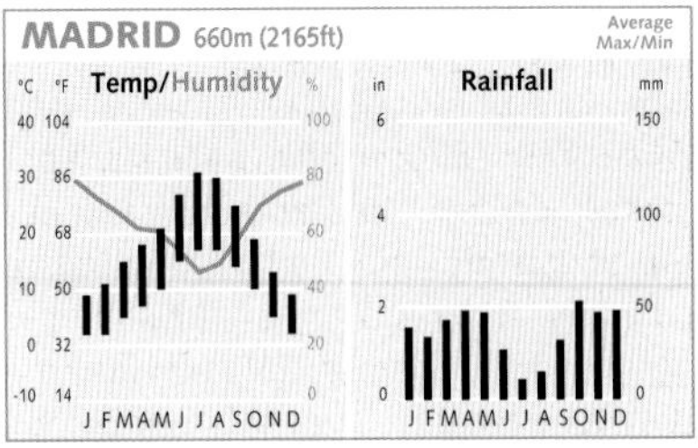
MADRID 660m (2165ft)
Average Max/Min
Temp/Humidity
Rainfall
J F M A M J J A S O N D

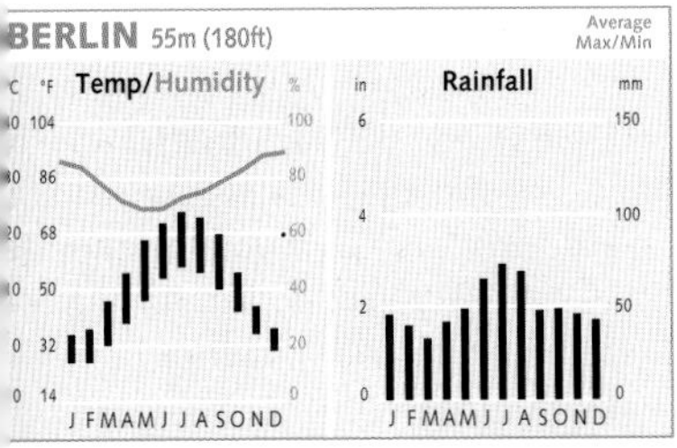
BERLIN 55m (180ft)
Average Max/Min
Temp/Humidity
Rainfall
J F M A M J J A S O N D

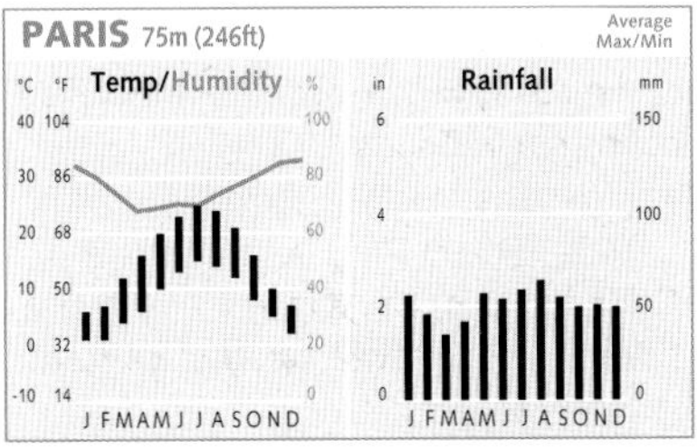
PARIS 75m (246ft)
Average Max/Min
Temp/Humidity
Rainfall
J F M A M J J A S O N D

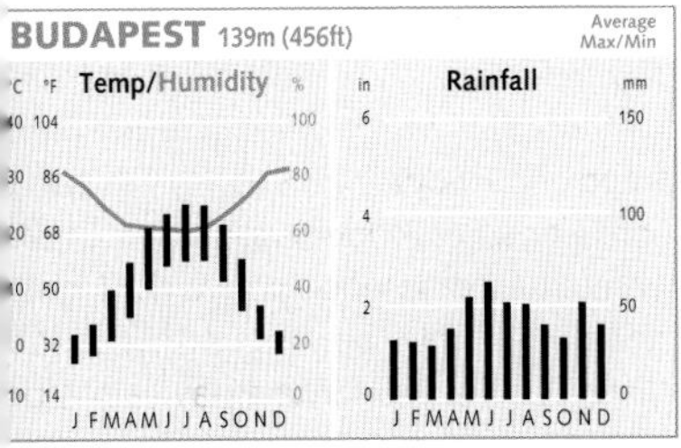
BUDAPEST 139m (456ft)
Average Max/Min
Temp/Humidity
Rainfall
J F M A M J J A S O N D

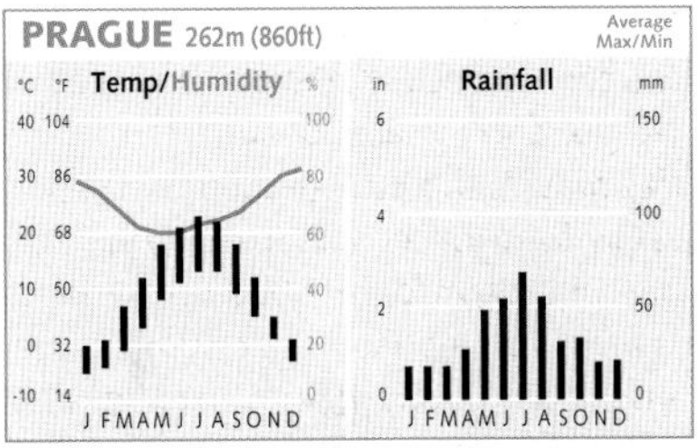
PRAGUE 262m (860ft)
Average Max/Min
Temp/Humidity
Rainfall
J F M A M J J A S O N D

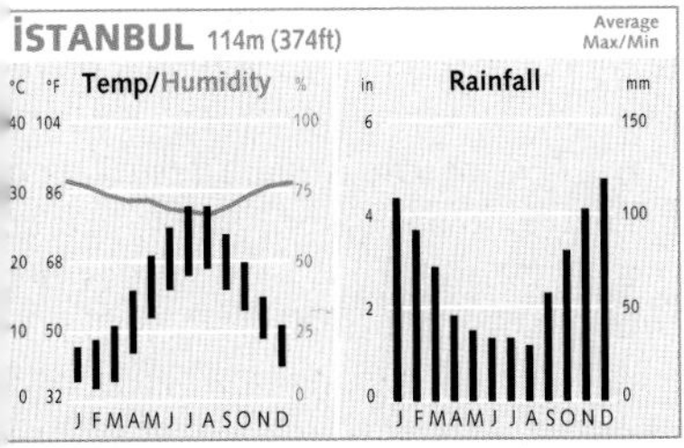
İSTANBUL 114m (374ft)
Average Max/Min
Temp/Humidity
Rainfall
J F M A M J J A S O N D

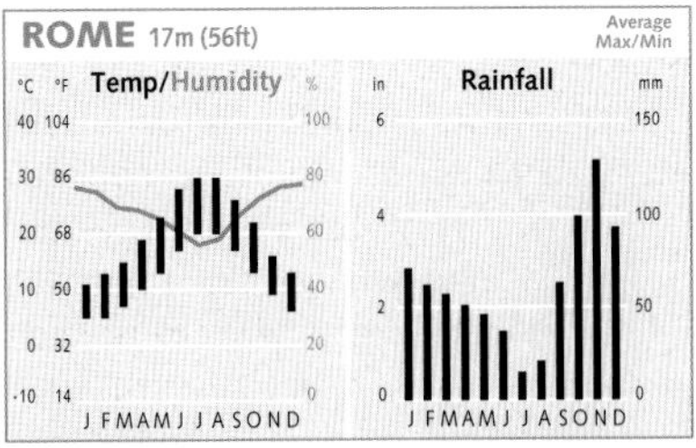
ROME 17m (56ft)
Average Max/Min
Temp/Humidity
Rainfall
J F M A M J J A S O N D

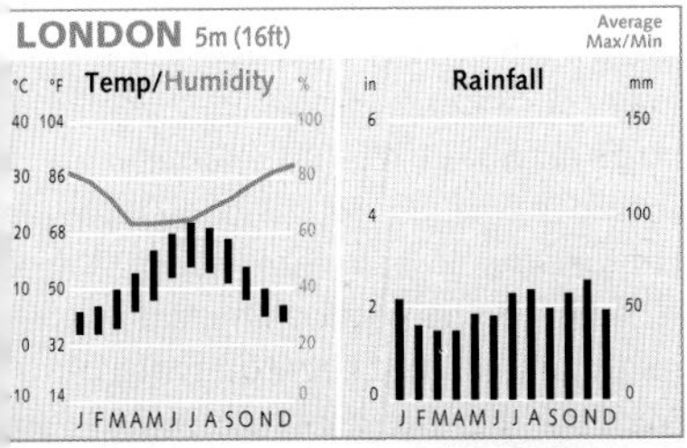
LONDON 5m (16ft)
Average Max/Min
Temp/Humidity
Rainfall
J F M A M J J A S O N D

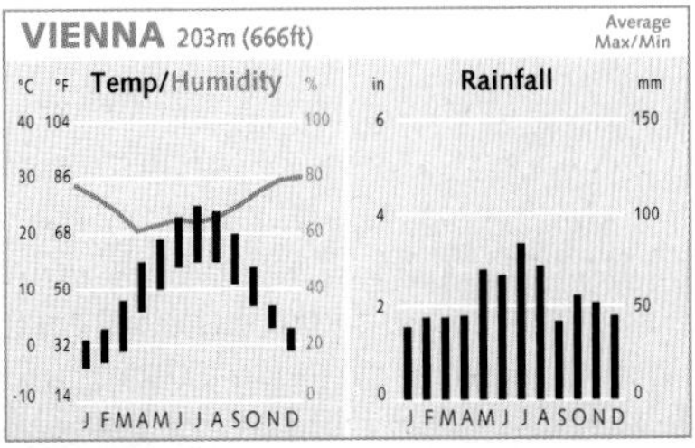
VIENNA 203m (666ft)
Average Max/Min
Temp/Humidity
Rainfall
J F M A M J J A S O N D

things to guard are your passport, tickets and money – in that order. It's always best to carry these next to your skin inside your clothes. Train-station lockers or luggage-storage counters are useful places to store your bags (but *never* valuables) while you get your bearings in a new town.

You can lessen the risks further by being careful of snatch thieves. Cameras or shoulder bags are an open invitation for these people, who sometimes operate from motorcycles or scooters and expertly slash the strap before you have a chance to react. Pickpockets are most active in dense crowds, especially in busy train stations and on public transport during peak hours. A common ploy is for one person to distract you while another zips through your pockets. Beware of gangs of kids – who can look either dishevelled or well dressed – madly waving newspapers and demanding attention. In the blink of an eye, a wallet or camera can go missing. And a jacket or purse left on the back of a chair is an invitation for theft.

Be careful even in hotels; don't leave valuables lying around in your room.

Parked cars containing luggage and other bags are prime targets for petty criminals in most cities, particularly cars with foreign number plates and/or rental-agency stickers. While driving in cities, beware of snatch thieves when you pull up at the lights – keep doors locked and windows rolled up high.

In case of theft or loss, always report the incident to the police and ask for a statement. Otherwise your travel-insurance company won't pay up.

DISCOUNT CARDS

SENIOR CARDS

Many attractions offer reduced-price admission for people over 60 or 65 (or sometimes 55 for women). EU residents, especially, are eligible for discounts i many EU countries. Make sure you brin proof of age; that suave signor in Italy o that polite Parisian mademoiselle is nc going to believe you're a day over 39.

For a fee of around €20, European resi dents aged 60 and over can get a Railplu Card as an add-on to their national ra senior pass. It entitles the holder to trair fare reductions of around 25%.

STUDENT & YOUTH CARDS

The **International Student Trave Confederation** (ISTC; www.istc.org) issue three cards for students, teachers anc under-26s, offering thousands of world wide discounts on transport, museum entry, youth hostels and even some restaurants. These cards are: the ISIC (International Student Identity Card), the ITIC (International Teacher Identity Card and the IYTC (International Youth Trave Card). You can check the full list of dis counts and where to apply for the card on the ISTC website. Issuing offices in clude **STA Travel** (www.statravel.com). Mos places, however, will also accept regula student identity cards.

For people under 30, there's also a spe cific – and inaccurately named – card, the **Euro<26**, which has scores of discounts. Fo information, check out www.euro26.org.

GAY & LESBIAN TRAVELLERS

Consensual homosexual sex is legal in al of the countries of Europe. But in many countries, society frowns on overt dis plays of affection in any case – and even more so when it's between members of the same gender. In cosmopolitar centres in Western Europe you'll finc very liberal attitudes toward homo sexuality. London, Paris, Berlin, Madrid Lisbon and Amsterdam have thriving gay ommunities and pride events. The Greek slands of Mykonos and Lesvos are popu- r gay beach destinations.

The following websites are useful:

amron (www.damron.com) The USA's eading gay publisher offers guides to vorld cities.

ay Journey (www.gayjourney.com) A nishmash of travel-related information, ncluding lists of gay-friendly hotels in urope.

partacus International Gay Guide vww.spartacusworld.com) A male-only di- ectory of gay entertainment venues in urope and the rest of the world.

HEALTH

BEFORE YOU GO

ring medications in their original, clearly abelled containers. If carrying syringes r needles, be sure to have a physician's etter documenting their medical neces- ity. If you need vision correction, it is rec- mmended that you carry a spare pair of ontact lenses and glasses, and take your ptical prescription with you.

RECOMMENDED VACCINATIONS

he World Health Organization (WHO) ecommends that all travellers be covered or diphtheria, tetanus, measles, mumps, ubella and polio, regardless of their desti- ation. Since most vaccines don't produce mmunity until at least two weeks after hey're given, visit a physician at least six veeks before departure.

AVAILABILITY OF HEALTH CARE

Good health care is readily available and harmacists can give valuable advice nd sell over-the-counter medication or minor illnesses. They can also advise vhen more specialised help is required nd point you in the right direction. The tandard of dental care is usually good; however, it is sensible to have a check-up before a long trip.

HOLIDAYS

Throughout Europe, children get the summer months (usually July and August) off from school, which is one reason why this is the busiest time to go to the beach and other resorts. There are also usually breaks for Easter and Christmas; keep in mind that dates for Orthodox Christmas and Easter are different to those of their Catholic and Protestant counterparts.

INSURANCE

A travel-insurance policy to cover theft, loss and medical problems is always a good idea.

The policies handled by **STA Travel** (www.statravel.com) and other student travel agencies are usually good value. Emergency insurance from companies such as **Travel Guard** (www.travelguard.com) is for those who have coverage at home that does not extend to where they're travelling. More and more airline companies are offering trip-cancellation insurance when you get your tickets.

Some insurance policies will specifically exclude 'dangerous activities', which can include scuba diving, motorcycling and

BOOK YOUR STAY ONLINE

For more accommodation reviews and recommendations by Lonely Planet authors, check out the online booking service at www.lonelyplanet.com. You'll find the true, insider lowdown on the best places to stay. Reviews are thorough and independent. Best of all, you can book online.

even trekking. Some policies even exclude certain countries, so read your fine print. Also check that your policy covers ambulances and an emergency flight home.

Worldwide cover to travellers from over 44 countries is available online at www.lonelyplanet.com/travel_services.

INTERNET ACCESS

As broadband access in homes becomes common in Europe, the number of internet cafes is shrinking. When in doubt, ask at a tourist office; it's a top question after 'Where are the toilets?'.

Hostels, hotels and other accommodation usually have some sort of internet access. This can range from a computer in the corner to wi-fi access in every room (which is becoming common). Note that the latter is often free in hostels and budget joints, while costing €20 or more at top-end hotels.

To find wi-fi hot spots, try sites such as www.jiwire.com.

LEGAL MATTERS

Most European police are friendly and helpful, especially if you have been a victim of a crime. You are required by law to prove your identity if asked by police, so always carry your passport, or an identity card if you're an EU citizen.

The age of consent for heterosexual and homosexual intercourse is generally 16. You can generally purchase alcohol (beer and wine) between 16 and 18 (usually 18 for spirits) but, if in doubt, ask. Although you can drive at 17 or 18, you might not be able to hire a car until you reach 25 years of age.

MAPS

Good maps are easy to find when you're in Europe, and in bookshops before you leave. In general, buying city maps in advance is unnecessary, as nearly all larg towns produce them locally for a fractio of the price you'll pay at home.

Road atlases are essential if you a driving or cycling. Tourist offices are a excellent source for maps. Some are fre and fairly basic while others are comme cial products offered for sale.

Maps published by European automo bile associations such as Britain's **AA** (**www theaa.com**) and Germany's **ADAC** (**www.ada de**) are usually excellent and sometime free if membership of your local associa tion gives you reciprocal rights.

MONEY

For security and flexibility, diversif your source of funds. Carry an ATM car credit card, cash and possibly travelle cheques.

ATMS

Every country in this book has internation ATMs that allow you to withdraw cash d rectly from your home account, and th is the most common way European trave lers access their money. When you with draw money from an ATM the amounts ar converted and dispensed in local currenc However, there will be fees (see the boxe text, opposite). In some remote village ATMs might be scarce, too.

You will have problems if you don have a four-digit PIN number – chec with your bank. If your card is rejecte try again in a few hours' time. Make su you bring your bank's phone number, an if your card fails again, call them.

Finally, always cover the keypad whe entering your PIN and make sure ther are no unusual devices attached to th machine; these can copy your card's de tails or cause it to stick in the machine. your card disappears and the screen goe blank before you've even entered you

N, don't enter it – especially if a 'helpful' ystander tells you to do so. If you can't trieve your card, call your bank's emerency number as soon as possible.

REDIT CARDS

sa and MasterCard/Eurocard are more idely accepted in Europe than Amex and iners Club; Visa (sometimes called Carte eue) is particularly strong in France and ain. There are, however, regional differnces in the general acceptability of credit rds. In the UK, for example, you can usuly flash your plastic in the most humble f budget restaurants; in Germany some staurants don't take credit cards. Cards e not widely accepted off the beaten ack.

As they have with ATM cards, banks ave loaded up credit cards with hiden charges for foreign purchases. Cash ithdrawals on a credit card are almost ways a much worse idea than using an TM card due to the fees and high interst rates. Plus, purchases in currencies ifferent from home are likely to draw arious currency conversion surcharges at are simply there to add to the bank's rofit. These can run up to 5% or more. our best bet is to check these things efore leaving and try to use a card that ffers the best deal. The website www.fly rtalk.com has a forum called 'Best Card r Foreign Exchange', which has many seful tips.

NTERNATIONAL TRANSFERS

nternational bank transfers are good r secure one-off movements of large mounts of money, but they might take ree to five days and there will be a fee bout £25 in the UK, for example). Be ure to specify the name of the bank, plus e sort code and address of the branch here you'd like to pick up your money.

MINIMISING ATM CHARGES

When you withdraw cash from an ATM overseas there are several ways you can get hit. Firstly, most banks add a hidden 2.75% loading to what's called the 'interbank' exchange rate. Additionally, some banks charge their customers a cash withdrawal fee (at least 2%, with a minimum €2 or more). If you're really unlucky, the bank at the foreign end might charge you as well. Triple whammy.

Most experts agree that having the right bankcard is still cheaper than exchanging cash directly. If your bank levies fees, then making larger, less frequent withdrawals is better. It's also worth seeing if your bank has reciprocal agreements with banks where you are going that minimise ATM fees (eg Bank of America and Barclay's Bank in the UK have such a deal).

In an emergency, it's quicker and easier to have money wired via **Western Union** (**www.westernunion.com**) or **MoneyGram** (**www.moneygram.com**). All are quite costly.

MONEYCHANGERS

In general, US dollars and UK pounds are the easiest currencies to exchange in Western Europe. Most airports, central train stations, big hotels and many border posts have banking facilities outside regular business hours, at times on a 24-hour basis. Post offices in Europe often perform banking tasks, tend to be open longer hours, and outnumber banks in remote places. While they always exchange cash, they might baulk at handling travellers cheques that are not in the local currency.

THE EURO

A common currency, the euro is the official currency used in 16 EU states: Austria, Belgium, Cyprus, Finland, France, Germany, Greece, Ireland, Italy, Luxembourg, Malta, the Netherlands, Portugal, Slovakia, Slovenia and Spain. Denmark, Britain, Switzerland and Sweden have held out against adopting the euro for political reasons.

The euro has the same value in all EU member countries. The euro is divided into 100 cents. There are seven euro notes (five, 10, 20, 50, 100, 200 and 500 euros) and eight euro coins (one and two euros, then one, two, five, 10, 20 and 50 cents). One side of the coin is standard for all euro coins and the other side bears a national emblem of participating countries.

The best exchange rates are usually at banks. *Bureaux de change* usually – but not always – offer worse rates or charge higher commissions. Hotels are almost always the worst places to change money.

When changing money, work out what you should be getting before you hand over your cash. Behind a seductively high rate may lurk a punishing commission charge. Then again, an enticing 'no commission' sign may hit you hard with a lousy, uncompetitive exchange rate.

TAXES & REFUNDS

Luckily, when non-EU residents spend more than a certain amount (around €75) they can usually reclaim that tax when leaving the country.

Making a tax-back claim is straightforward. First, make sure the shop offers duty-free sales. (Often a sign will b displayed reading 'Tax-Free Shopping When making your purchase ask the sho attendant for a tax-refund voucher, fill in with the correct amount and the dat This can be used to claim a refund direct at international airports, or be stamped ferry ports or border crossings and maile back for a refund.

None of this applies to EU residen Even an American citizen living in Londo is not entitled to rebate on items boug in Paris. Conversely, an EU passport hold living in New York is.

TIPPING

Tipping practices vary from country country, and often from place to plac Tipping has become more complicate with 'service charges' of 5% to 10% bei added to bills. In theory, this mea you're not obliged to tip. In practice, th money often doesn't go to the serv and they might make it clear they st expect a gratuity. In general, you car go wrong if you add 10% onto your b at a restaurant.

For more details about tipping, see th individual country chapters.

TRAVELLERS CHEQUES

Travellers cheques have been replaced b international ATMs and it's often difficu to find places that cash them.

That said, having a few travelle cheques might be a good back-up. If the are stolen you can claim a refund, pro vided you have a record of cheque num bers, but it is vital to store these numbe away from the cheques themselves.

Amex and Thomas Cook representativ cash their own travellers cheques witho commission, but both give poor rates exchange. If you're changing more tha US$20, you're usually better off going bank and paying the standard 1% to 2% ommission to change there.

PHOTOGRAPHY, VIDEO & DVD

Be aware that museums often demand that you buy permission to photograph or video their displays.

PHOTOGRAPHY

Oh those memories, oh those treasured images, oh those pictures designed to make others drool on your Facebook page. Be sure your camera has at least a 2GB memory card so you can take lots of high-definition snaps and not worry about downloading.

If you do run out of memory, your best bets are to burn your photos onto a CD or upload to the web at an internet cafe (if you can find one).

If you are travelling with a laptop, you can download your own pictures and with a wi-fi connection be quickly posting your images online or emailing them to jealous friends and loved ones. There you are, topless on the Mediterranean for the world to see – almost in real time.

VIDEO

Properly used, a video camera can give a fascinating (or often mind-numbing) record of your holiday. Unlike still photography, video means you can record scenes such as countryside rolling past the train window. Make sure you keep the batteries charged and have the necessary charger, plugs and transformer for the country you are visiting. If your camera uses cassettes, it's still possible to obtain them easily in large towns and cities in most countries. And do us just one favour – stop shooting long enough to view your scene outside of the tiny monitor.

DVD

European DVD discs and players are formatted for the PAL (Secam in France) TV system as opposed to the NTSC system used in the USA and Japan.

DVDs are encoded with a regional code (code 1 for America and Canada, 2 for Europe and South Africa, and 4 for Australia and New Zealand). If you buy a disc in Europe, check that its code corresponds with that of your DVD player at home; a player coded 1 or 3 will not play a disc that is coded 2. One way around this is to look for universally compatible players and discs carrying a 0 code.

TELEPHONE

You can ring abroad from almost any phone box in Europe. Public telephones accepting stored-value phonecards (available from post offices, telephone centres, newsstands and retail outlets) are virtually the norm now; in some countries (eg France), coin-operated phones are almost impossible to find. Many people also use internet cafes or places aimed at immigrants to make cheap calls home. Treat your hotel phone and its often hidden and outrageous rates the same way you'd treat a thief.

Internet and phone shops in train stations often allow Skype and other cheap VoIP internet calling for small fees.

MOBILE PHONES

Travellers can easily purchase prepaid mobile phones or SIM cards with international capabilities. GSM cellular phones are compatible throughout all the countries in Western Europe, but prices vary. As in your home country no doubt, mobile shops are everywhere.

If you bring your mobile phone from home, check in advance to see what your international roaming rates are. Often they are extortionate. Users of smart phones such as the iPhone can get socked with huge roaming fees for data usage for email and web connections.

You can bring your mobile phone from home and buy a local SIM card to enjoy cheap local calling rates if it is a) unlocked, and b) compatible with GSM networks. Check first.

PHONECARDS

For most calls from public phones you're usually better off with a local phonecard. Reverse-charge (collect) calls are often possible, but not always. From many countries, however, Country Direct schemes (such as AT&T's USADirect) let you phone home by billing the long-distance carrier you use at home (at rates higher than a local phonecard). The numbers can often be dialled from public phones without even inserting a phonecard. Calls made using a credit card are almost always very expensive.

TIME

Most of the countries covered in this book are on Central European Time (GMT/UTC plus one hour). Britain and Ireland are on GMT/UTC, and Greece and Turkey are on Eastern European Time (GMT/UTC plus two hours).

Clocks are advanced on the last Sunda in March by one hour for daylight-savin time, and set back on the last Sunday i October. During daylight-saving tim Britain and Ireland are GMT/UTC plus on hour, Central European Time is GMT/UT plus two hours and Greece is GMT/UT plus three hours.

TOURIST INFORMATION

The provision of tourist information varie enormously. You'll find the details for th local office in almost every city and tow listing in this book.

TRAVELLERS WITH DISABILITIES

Picturesque cobblestone streets an medieval Old Towns are charming in deed – but they can also be awkward fo travellers with disabilities. Rental cars an taxis may be accessible, but public trans port rarely is. Train facilities, however, ca be OK, and some destinations boast nev tram services or lifts to platforms. The fo lowing websites can help with specifi details:

Lonely Planet Thorn Tree (**www.lone planet.com/thorntree**) Share experiences o the Travellers with Disabilities branch o this forum.

CLIMATE CHANGE & TRAVEL

Travel – especially air travel – is a significant contributor to global climate change. At Lonely Planet, we believe that all who travel have a responsibility to limit their personal impact. As a result, we have teamed with Rough Guides and other concerned industry partners to support Climate Care, which allows people to offset the greenhouse gases they are responsible for with contributions to energy-saving projects and other climate-friendly initiatives in the developing world. Lonely Planet offsets all staff and author travel.

For more information, turn to the responsible travel pages on www.lonelyplanet.com. For details on offsetting your carbon emissions and a carbon calculator, go to www.climatecare.org.

Mobility International USA (www.miusa.org) Publishes guides and advises travellers with disabilities on mobility issues.

Royal Association for Disability & Rehabilitation (www.radar.org.uk) Publishes a comprehensive annual guide, *Holidays in Britain & Ireland – A Guide for Disabled People.*

Society for Accessible Travel & Hospitality (www.sath.org) Reams of information for travellers with disabilities.

VISAS

Citizens of the USA, Australia, New Zealand, Canada and the UK need only a valid passport to enter most of the countries in this guide for up to three months, provided they have some sort of onward or return ticket and/or 'sufficient means of support' (ie money). In line with the Schengen Agreement, there are no passport controls at borders between Andorra, Austria, Belgium, Czech Republic, Denmark, Finland, France, Germany, Greece, Hungary, Iceland, Italy, Liechtenstein, Luxembourg, the Netherlands, Norway, Portugal, Spain, Sweden and Switzerland.

Of the non-Schengen countries in this book, only Turkey requires visas from Australian, Canadian, British and US nationals. They can be bought at any point of entry into the country.

For those who do require visas, it's important to remember that these will have a 'use-by' date, and you'll be refused entry after that period has elapsed. It may not be checked when entering these countries overland, but major problems can arise if it is requested during your stay or on departure and you can't produce it.

For additional details, see the Visa section of the directory in each country chapter.

WOMEN TRAVELLERS

Women travellers, in general, will find Europe relatively enlightened and shouldn't often have to invent husbands or boyfriends that will be back any minute. If you do find yourself in an uncomfortable situation or area, leave, or pipe up and make a racket. In parts of Spain, Italy and Greece, you may find men more aggressive in their stares or comments.

TRANSPORT

GETTING THERE & AWAY

Europe is well connected to the rest of the world by air. With intense competition between long-haul and no-frills carriers, there are plenty of tickets available to a variety of cities. Major gateways include London's Heathrow and Gatwick airports; the two Paris airports, Orly and Roissy Charles de Gaulle; Rome's Leonardo da Vinci airport (better known as Fiumicino); Madrid's Barajas airport; and Atatürk International Airport in İstanbul.

Expect to pay high-season prices between June and September; the two months either side of this period are the shoulder seasons. Low season is November to March.

Flights, tours and rail tickets can be booked online at www.lonelyplanet.com/travel_services.

GETTING AROUND

Getting around Europe poses no great difficulties. There's a comprehensive transport network, and relations between countries are generally good. The proliferation of low-cost carriers has made short air hops across the region possible.

AIR

Flying around Europe is definitely an option. A few low-cost carriers have gone out of business due to the global economic downturn, but others have added routes. It is possible to go from London to Berlin at times for less than €30; fares around Europe for less than €100 are common. More interestingly, dozens of tiny airports across Europe now boast airline service, so that a trip to Italy doesn't mean choosing between Milan and Rome, but rather scores of airports up and down the 'boot'.

It is possible to put together a practical itinerary that might bounce from London to the south of Spain to Florence to Amsterdam in a two-week period, all at an affordable price and avoiding endless train rides. But with cheap fares come many caveats. First, some of the barebones carriers are just that. Discount leader Ryanair prides itself on nonreclining seats, nonexistent legroom and nonexistent window shades. In-flight meals, hold baggage, airport check-in, priority boarding – these are all things you might be charged extra for. When booking online, always ensure that you untick any add-on options you don't want, as the default page settings of many airline websites have them automatically ticked.

A second caveat involves the airports. Many no-frills airlines use secondary provincial airports – see the individual country chapters for details. For example, if you really want to go to Carcassonne in the south of France, then getting a €20 Ryanair ticket from London will be a dream come true. But if you want to go to Frankfurt in Germany and end up buying a ticket to 'Frankfurt-Hahn', you'll find yourself at a small airport 70km west of Frankfurt and two hours away by bus.

BICYCLE

A tour of Western Europe by bike may seem like a daunting prospect but help is at hand. The **European Cyclists' Federation** (☎ **in Belgium 02 234 38 74; www.ecf.com**) advocates bike-friendly policies and organises tours. The federation also manages EuroVelo, a project to create bike routes across the continent.

The key to a successful bike trip is to travel light. There are no special road rules for cyclists, although it's advisable to carry a helmet, lights and a basic repair kit. This might contain spare brake and gear cables, spanners, Allen keys, spare spokes and some strong adhesive tape. Take a good lock and make sure you use it when you leave your bike unattended. The wearing of helmets is not compulsory in most European countries, but is certainly advised.

A seasoned cyclist can average about 80km a day, but this depends on the terrain and how much weight is being carried. Don't overdo it – there's no point burning yourself out during the initial stages.

Outside certain areas there are very few dedicated cycle lanes, and drivers tend to regard cyclists as an oddity. Poor road conditions, particularly in the Eastern European countries, and mountainous terrain provide further obstacles.

Transporting your bike to the region poses no great problems. Different airlines apply different rules – some insist that you pack it in a bike bag, others simply require you to remove the pedals and deflate the tyres, some even sell special bike boxes. Remember that the bike's weight will be included in your luggage allowance.

Bikes can generally be carried on slower trains, subject to a small supplementary fee. On fast trains they might need to be sent as registered luggage and will probably end up on a different train from the one you take.

BOAT

Major ferry routes for users of this book include the thicket of services between

Britain and France. There are routes between the UK, Ireland, Spain and France; between Italy, Spain, Greece, Croatia, and Turkey; and between the hundreds of Mediterranean islands. See the relevant country chapters for further details. Popular routes get very busy in summer, so try to book ahead.

Multiple ferry companies compete on all the main ferry routes, and the resulting service is comprehensive but complicated. The same ferry company can have a host of different prices for the same route, depending upon the time of day or year, the validity of the ticket or the length of your vehicle. It is worth planning (and booking) ahead where possible, as there may be special reductions on off-peak crossings and advance-purchase tickets. Most ferry companies adjust prices according to the level of demand (so-called 'fluid' or 'dynamic' pricing), so it may pay to offer alternative travel dates. Vehicle tickets usually include the driver and a full complement of passengers.

BUS

Buses sometimes have the edge in terms of costs, but are generally slower and less comfortable than trains and not as quick or sometimes as cheap as airlines. Europe's biggest network of international buses is provided by a group of bus companies that operates under the name **Eurolines** (www.eurolines.com).

CAR

Travelling with your own vehicle allows increased flexibility and the option to get off the beaten track. Unfortunately, cars can be the proverbial ball and chain in city centres when you have to negotiate one-way streets or find somewhere to park amid a confusing concrete jungle.

DRIVING LICENCE & DOCUMENTATION

Proof of ownership and insurance should always be carried when touring the region. Many non-European driving licences are valid in Europe. Some travel websites and auto clubs advise carrying an International Driving Permit (IDP), but this costly multilingual document sold by national auto clubs is rarely necessary – especially to rent a car.

HIRE & LEASE

Hiring a vehicle is a relatively straightforward procedure. The minimum rental age is between 21 and 25, and you'll need a credit card. It is imperative to understand exactly what is included in your rental agreement (unlimited mileage? collision waiver?). Make sure you are covered by an adequate insurance policy. Ask in advance if you are allowed to drive a rented car across borders (and if so, which ones). Note that less than 4% of European cars have automatic transmissions, so if you need this, request ahead and expect to pay more for your car.

The big international firms will give you reliable service and a good standard of vehicle. You may also have the option of returning the car to a different outlet (for a substantial fee). National or local firms often undercut the big companies. When comparing rates, beware of printed tariffs intended only for local residents, as they may be lower than the prices foreigners are charged. When in doubt, ask.

You will find the most rental options near airports and in capital cities. Prices at airport rental offices are usually higher than at branches in the city centres, but in general rates range from €25 to €75 per day. Prebook for the lowest cost – you will pay more if you walk into an office and ask for a car on the spot, even allowing for special weekend deals. Smaller towns, especially in the east, may not have rental outlets. Check the Transport section of individual country chapters for more details. You can make advance reservations online with the following international companies:

Avis (www.avis.com)
Budget (www.budget.com)
Europcar (www.europcar.com)
Hertz (www.hertz.com)

Brokers such as **Kemwel Holiday Autos** (www.kemwel.com) and **Auto Europe** (www.autoeurope.com) can arrange Europe-wide deals. If you're coming from North America, Australia or New Zealand, fly/drive packages may also be worth looking into. Ask your airline if it has any special deals for rental cars in Europe.

Motorcycle and moped rental is common in countries such as Italy, Spain, Greece and in the south of France.

ROAD CONDITIONS

Conditions and types of roads vary across the region, but it is possible to make some generalisations. The fastest routes are four- or six-lane highways (motorways, autobahns, autoroutes etc). These roads are great for speed, though some require a tariff for usage, often in the form of a motorway sticker or pass. There will usually be an alternative route you can take. Motorways and other primary routes are almost always in very good condition.

ROAD RULES

You drive on the right-hand side of the road throughout the region and overtake on the left. Use your indicators for any change of lane and when pulling away from the kerb. Take care with speed limits, as they vary from country to country. Speed limits are signposted, and are generally 110km/h or 120km/h on motorways, 100km/h on other highways, 80km/h on secondary and tertiary roads and 50km/h or 60km/h in built-up areas. Motorcycles are usually limited to 90km/h on motorways, and vehicles with trailers to 80km/h. In towns you may only sound the horn to avoid having an accident. There is usually no speed limit on autobahns; exceptions are clearly signposted.

The use of seat belts is mandatory everywhere in central Europe. In most countries, children aged under 12 and intoxicated passengers are not permitted in the front seat. Driving after drinking any alcohol is a very serious offence – European countries have a blood-alcohol-concentration (BAC) limit of between 0% and 0.08%.

PUBLIC TRANSPORT

Most European cities have excellent public transport systems, which comprise some combination of subways, trains, trams and buses. Service is usually comprehensive. Major airports generally have fast-train or subway links to the city centre. See the country chapters for more information.

TOURS

Tours exist for all ages, interests and budgets. Specialist operators offer everything from tours of the region's gardens to island-hopping cruises, walking holidays and adventure-sports packages.

Established outfits include the following:

Busabout (www.busabout.com) Best known for its European bus tours, London-based Busabout also offers tours to Italy (UK£159), Spain (UK£439), and cruises in Greece (from UK£199) and Croatia (from UK£389).

CBT Tours (☎ in the USA 800 736 24 53; www.cbttours.com) A US operator specialising in walking and cycling holidays, including a six-day bike ride through Tuscany.

Contiki (www.contiki.com) Contiki runs a range of European tours for 18 to 35-year olds, including city breaks, camping trips and island-hopping journeys. Also has its own resort on Mykonos.
Ramblers Holidays (☎ UK 01707 33 11 33; www.ramblersholidays.co.uk) A British-based outfit that offers hiking holidays, ski packages and much more.
Saga Holidays (☎ in the UK 0800 096 00 74; www.saga.co.uk) Serving people aged over 50, Saga sells everything from travel insurance to bus tours, river cruises and special-interest holidays.
Top Deck (☎ in the UK 020 8987 3300; www.topdeck travel.co.uk) A youth specialist, this London-based outfit offers everything from Croatian coastal cruises to festival weekends and tapas trails.

TRAIN

Trains are the most atmospheric, comfortable and fun way to make long overland journeys in central Europe. All of the major, and most of the minor, cities are on the rail network. It's perfectly feasible for train travel to be your only form of intercity transport. Overnight trains have the added benefit of saving you a night's accommodation. Think before you schedule, however – a daytime train journey through the Alps is definitely a trip highlight.

Every national rail company has a website with a vast amount of schedule and fare information. For international details, German national railway company Deutsche Bahn (www.bahn.de) has excellent schedule and fare information in English for trains across Europe. The website Man in Seat 61 (www.seat61.com) has invaluable train descriptions and details. You can find links of all kinds to Europe's railways (including maps, schedules and more) at www.railfaneurope.net/links.html.

Note that European trains sometimes split en route in order to service two destinations, so even if you're on the right train, make sure you're also in the correct carriage.

CLASSES

On most trains there are 1st- and 2nd-class carriages. As a rough guide, a 1st-class ticket generally costs about double the price of a 2nd-class ticket. In 1st-class carriages there are fewer seats and more luggage space. But note that the traditional image of compartments with little wine-bottle holders and various characters roaming the corridor is being replaced by fast and modern trains that are more like especially comfortable versions of airliners.

On overnight trains, your comfort depends less on which class you're travelling than on whether you've booked a regular seat, couchette or sleeper. Couchette bunks are comfortable enough; there are four per compartment in 1st class or six in 2nd class. Sleepers are the most comfortable option, offering beds for one or two passengers in 1st class, and two or three passengers in 2nd class. Charges vary depending on the journey, but they are significantly more expensive than couchettes. Expect to pay at least €100 per person.

RESERVATIONS

On many local services it's not possible to reserve a seat – just jump on and sit where you like. On faster, long-distance trains it's sometimes obligatory to make a reservation; regardless of whether it's necessary, it's often a good idea to do so, especially in peak periods. Most international trains require a seat reservation, and you'll also need to book sleeping accommodation on overnight trains. Bookings can be made for a small, nonrefundable fee (usually about €3) when you buy your ticket.

Supplements and reservation costs are not covered by most rail passes.

TRAIN PASSES

European rail passes are worth buying if you plan to do a fair amount of intercountry travelling within a short space of time. Research your options before committing to a particular pass – find the one out there that best fits your plans and budget. Which pass you choose depends on a number of factors – how many countries you want to see, how flexible you want to be, and whether you want to go 1st or 2nd class – but the most important factor is where you hold residency. Non-European residents can buy Eurail passes; for European residents, there are Inter-Rail passes.

Available online or at travel agents, passes vary in price, so shop around before committing yourself. Once you've purchased a pass, take care of it, as it cannot be replaced or refunded if it is lost or stolen. Pass-holders must always carry their passport for identification purposes.

Comprehensive information and online bookings are available at **Rail Europe** (**www.raileurope.com, www.raileurope.co.uk**), **Rail Pass** (**www.railpass.com**) and **Rail Plus** (**www.railplus.com.au**).

EURAIL

Passes that are sold by **Eurail** (**www.eurail.com**) are available to non-European residents only, and are best bought before you leave home. The Eurail Global pass allows unlimited travel in 21 countries. The pass is valid for a designated period of time, ranging from 15 days (adult/under 25 €511/332) to three months (adult/under 25 €1432/933).

Alternatively, if you don't plan to travel quite so intensively but you still want the range of countries, consider the Eurail Global Flexi, which allows for 10 or 15 travel days over the course of two months. The Flexi is suitably more affordable: the 10-day pass goes for US$826/545/414 per adult/youth/child from Rail Europe or A$1319/824/662 from Rail Plus.

The Eurail Selectpass allows for travel between three to five contiguous countries for five, 10 or 15 days per two months. Options are myriad; as a guide, an adult can travel between Austria, the Czech Republic, Germany, Hungary and Switzerland for 10 days within two months for €564. Youth and 'saver' discounts still apply.

INTER-RAIL

Passes that are sold by **Inter-Rail** (**www.interrail.net**) are only available to European residents of at least six months' standing (passport identification is required). There are two types of pass: the Global Pass and the One Country Pass. Adult passes are available in 1st and 2nd class, while the youth passes (under 26) are for 2nd class only. Child fares are available for One Country Passes for kids between four and 11; kids aged under three travel free.

The Global Pass is valid for travel in 30 countries. You can opt for five days of travel in a 10-day period (adult/youth €249/159); 10 days in a 22-day period (adult/youth €359/239); 22 days of continuous travel (adult/youth €469/309); or one month of continuous travel (adult/youth €599/399).

NATIONAL RAIL PASSES

Some discounted one-country rail passes are available from Eurail and Inter-Rail, as well as from the national train service itself. These are not always great value, but they do save the time and hassle of having to buy individual tickets. In a large, expensive country such as Germany, a pass can make sense; in a small, relatively inexpensive country such as Slovakia, it makes none whatsoever.

LANGUAGE

Don't let the language barrier get in the way of your travel experience. This section offers basic phrases and pronunciation guides to help you negotiate your way around Europe. Note that in our pronunciation guides, the stressed syllables in words are indicated with italics.

CROATIAN

Hello.	*Bog.*	bog
Goodbye.	*Do viđenja.*	do vee·*je*·nya
Yes./No.	*Da./Ne.*	da/ne
Please.	*Molim.*	*mo*·leem
Thank you.	*Hvala.*	*hva*·la
Help!	*Upomoć!*	*oo*·po·moch

I don't understand.
Ne razumijem. ne ra·*zoo*·mee·yem
How much is this?
Koliko stoji? ko·*lee*·ko *sto*·yee
Where's (the toilet)?
Gdje je (zahod)? gdye ye (*za*·hod)

CZECH

Hello.	*Ahoj.*	*uh*·hoy
Goodbye.	*Na shledanou.*	*nuh*·skhle·duh·noh
Yes./No.	*Ano./Ne.*	*uh*·no/ne
Please.	*Prosím.*	*pro*·seem
Thank you.	*Děkuji.*	*dye*·ku·yi
Help!	*Pomoc!*	*po*·mots

I don't understand.
Nerozumím. *ne*·ro·zu·meem
How much is this?
Kolik to stojí? *ko*·lik to *sto*·yee
Where's (the toilet)?
Kde je (záchod)? gde ye (*za*·khod)

DUTCH

Hello.	*Dag.*	dakh
Goodbye.	*Dag.*	dakh
Yes./No.	*Ja./Nee.*	yaa/ney
Please.	*Alstublieft.*	al·stew·*bleeft*
Thank you.	*Dank u.*	dangk ew
Help!	*Help!*	help

I don't understand.
Ik begrijp het niet. ik buh·*khreyp* huht neet
How much is this?
Hoeveel kost het? hoo·*veyl* kost huht
Where's (the toilet)?
Waar zijn (de toiletten)? waar zeyn (duh twa·*le*·tuhn)

FRENCH

Hello.	*Bonjour.*	bon·zhoor
Goodbye.	*Au revoir.*	o·rer·vwa
Yes./No.	*Oui./Non.*	wee/non
Please.	*S'il vous plaît.*	seel voo play
Thank you.	*Merci.*	mair·see
Help!	*Au secours!*	o skoor

I don't understand.
Je ne comprends pas. zher ner kom·pron pa
How much is this?
C'est combien? say kom·byun
Where's (the toilet)?
Où sont (les toilettes)? oo son (lay twa·let)

GERMAN

Hello.	*Guten Tag.*	*goo*·ten taak
Goodbye.	*Auf Wiedersehen.*	owf *vee*·der·zey·en
Yes./No.	*Ja./Nein.*	yaa/nain
Please.	*Bitte.*	*bi*·te
Thank you.	*Danke.*	*dang*·ke
Help!	*Hilfe!*	*hil*·fe

I don't understand.
Ich verstehe nicht. ikh fer·*shtey*·e nikht
How much is this?
Was kostet das? vas *kos*·tet das
Where's (the toilet)?
Wo ist (die Toilette)? vaw ist (dee to·a·*le*·te)

GREEK

Hello.	Γεια σου.	yia su
Goodbye.	Αντίο.	a·*di*·o
Yes./No.	Ναι./Όχι.	ne/*o*·hi
Please.	Παρακαλώ.	pa·ra·ka·*lo*
Thank you.	Ευχαριστώ.	ef·kha·ri·*sto*
Help!	Βοήθεια!	vo·*i*·thia

I don't understand.
Δεν καταλαβαίνω. dhen ka·ta·la·*ve*·no

How much is this?
Πόσο κάνει; *po*·so *ka*·ni

Where's (the toilet)?
Που είναι (η τουαλέτα); pu *i*·ne (i tu·a·*le*·ta)

HUNGARIAN

Hello.	*Szervusz.* (sg)	*ser*·vus
	Szervusztok. (pl)	*ser*·vus·tawk
Goodbye.	*Viszlát.*	*vis*·lat
Yes./No.	*Igen./Nem.*	*i*·gen/nem
Please.	*Kérem.*	*key*·rem
Thank you.	*Köszönöm.*	*keu*·seu·neum
Help!	*Segítség!*	*she*·geet·sheyg

I don't understand.
Nem értem. nem *eyr*·tem

How much is this?
Mennyibe kerül? *men'*·nyi·be *ke*·rewl

Where's (the toilet)?
Hol van (a vécé)? hawl von (o *vey*·tsey)

ITALIAN

Hello.	*Buongiorno.*	bwon·*jor*·no
Goodbye.	*Arrivederci.*	a·ree·ve·*der*·chee
Yes./No.	*Sì./No.*	see/no
Please.	*Per favore.*	per fa·*vo*·re
Thank you.	*Grazie.*	*gra*·tsye
Help!	*Aiuto!*	a·*yoo*·to

I don't understand.
Non capisco. non ka·*pee*·sko

How much is this?
Quanto costa? *kwan*·to *ko*·sta

Where's (the toilet)?
Dove sono (i gabinetti)? *do*·ve *so*·no (ee ga·bee·*ne*·ti)

SLOVAK

Hello.	*Dobrý deň.*	*do*·bree dyen'
Goodbye.	*Do videnia.*	do *vi*·dye·ni·yuh
Yes./No.	*Áno./Nie.*	*a*·no/*ni*·ye
Please.	*Prosím.*	*pro*·seem
Thank you.	*Ďakujem.*	*dyuh*·ku·yem
Help!	*Pomoc!*	*po*·mots

I don't understand.
Nerozumiem. *nye*·ro·zu·myem

How much is this?
Koľko to stojí? *kol'*·ko to *sto*·yee

Where's (the toilet)?
Kde je (záchod)? kdye ye (*za*·khod)

SPANISH

Hello.	*Hola.*	*o*·la
Goodbye.	*Adiós.*	a·*dyos*
Yes./No.	*Sí./No.*	see/no
Please.	*Por favor.*	por fa·*vor*
Thank you.	*Gracias.*	*gra*·thyas
Help!	*¡Socorro!*	so·*ko*·ro

I don't understand.
No entiendo. no en·*tyen*·do

How much is this?
¿Cuánto cuesta? *kwan*·to *kwes*·ta

Where's (the toilet)?
¿Dónde están (los servicios)? *don*·de es·*tan* (los ser·*vee*·thyos)

TURKISH

Hello.	*Merhaba.*	*mer*·ha·ba
Goodbye.	*Hoşçakalın.*	hosh·*cha*·ka·luhn
Yes./No.	*Evet./Hayır.*	e·*vet*/*ha*·yuhr
Please.	*Lütfen.*	*lewt*·fen
Thank you.	*Teşekkür ederim.*	te·shek·*kewr* e·*de*·reem
Help!	*İmdat!*	*eem*·dat

I don't understand.
Anlamıyorum. an·*la*·muh·yo·room

How much is this?
Şu ne kadar? shoo ne ka·*dar*

Where's (the toilet)?
(Tuvalet) nerede? (too·va·*let*) *ne*·re·de

BEHIND THE SCENES

THE AUTHORS

LISA DUNFORD

Coordinating Author; This is Europe; Europe's Top 25 Experiences; Europe's Top Itineraries; Planning Your Trip; Germany, Austria & Switzerland; Czech Republic, Slovakia & Hungary; Croatia; Greece; Turkey; Directory & Transport

Lisa's fascination with the continent began when she learned one grandfather was born in Hungary, a grandmother emigrated from County Cork and she had cousins living in England. During university Lisa studied in Budapest, but her first grand tour came in the months she travelled before moving to Bratislava, Slovakia. While working for the US Agency for International Development she continued to experience as many of the cultures of Europe as possible. Though Lisa, her husband and dogs now call a riverfront in southeast Texas home, personal ties and writing assignments bring her back regularly – and she wouldn't have it any other way.

Author Thanks A big thanks goes to family friends Carol, Stephan and Christian Von Düring in Geneva for helping get me connected. Alex Konstantinou and Jelena Bestak Fowles at the Greek and Croatian tourist boards were a big help. Putting this project together has been monumental; I am so grateful to my coauthor Olly, commissioning editor Will Gourlay, project manager Rachel Imeson, managing cartographer Herman So and editor Barbara Delissen, who made *Discover Europe* what it has been – a lot of fun.

OLIVER BERRY

Britain & Ireland; France; Spain; Italy; The Netherlands & Belgium; Europe in Focus

Since graduating from University College London with a degree in English, Oliver has spent most of the last decade getting lost in unfamiliar places. He joined Lonely Planet in 2002 and has contributed to many of the company's best-selling European guidebooks, including *France, Great Britain, Western Europe* and *Europe on a Shoestring*. When he's not on the road, he lives and works in Cornwall as a writer and photographer.

LONELY PLANET AUTHORS

Why is our travel information the best in the world? It's simple: our authors are passionate, dedicated travellers. They don't take freebies in exchange for positive coverage so you can be sure the advice you're given is impartial. They travel widely to all the popular spots, and off the beaten track. They don't research using just the internet or phone. They discover new places not included in any other guidebook. They personally visit thousands of hotels, restaurants, palaces, trails, galleries, temples and more. They speak with dozens of locals every day to make sure you get the kind of insider knowledge only a local could tell you. They take pride in getting all the details right, and in telling it how it is. Think you can do it? Find out how at lonelyplanet.com.

Author Thanks As always, too many people to thank and too little space – but a special mention has to go to Will Gourlay for giving me the *Discover* gig in the first place and Lisa Dunford for sage advice, moral support and an impeccable mastery of word counts. Thanks also to Barbara, Jess, Herman and Corey for making sense of things and knocking everything into shape. But the biggest thanks goes to all the other talented Lonely Planet writers who provided the text on which this book is based – we literally couldn't have done it without you, fellas.

BRETT ATKINSON
Czech Republic

Brett has been travelling to Eastern Europe for more than 20 years. On his second extended research trip to the Czech Republic, he attempted to really get off the beaten track, especially if this meant seeking out interesting out-of-the-way microbreweries. When he's not on the road for Lonely Planet, Brett lives with Carol in Auckland, New Zealand.

ALEXIS AVERBUCK
Greece

A California native and a travel writer for two decades, Alexis Averbuck lives in Hydra, Greece, and makes any excuse she can to travel the isolated back roads of her adopted land. She is committed to dispelling the stereotype that Greece is simply a string of beaches.

JAMES BAINBRIDGE
Turkey

James first visited Turkey as a student, and subsisted on cheese triangles for a week in İstanbul and the Princes' Islands. When he's not charging around with a notebook in hand, James lives in London – right on Green Lanes, the city's 'little Turkey'. He has contributed to a dozen Lonely Planet books and to media worldwide.

NEAL BEDFORD
Austria, Hungary

In his heart Neal will always be a New Zealander, but after living in Austria for the past decade, part of him now calls this rugged land home. He is constantly amazed at the country's beauty. With Hungary only a short train ride away, Neal has seen almost every corner of the country, but Hungary will always remain foreign and fascinating.

GEERT COLE
Belgium

An avid traveller since his late teens, Geert left his native Belgium behind and combed continents for years before realising that only one nation on earth is founded on beer, chocolate and chips. Then Leanne entered the scene and offered Geert life on the road with Lonely Planet. Perfect really, and it's all now shared with two young daughters.

DAVID ELSE
Britain

As a backpacker, David has travelled widely in Europe, Africa, India and beyond. His knowledge of Britain comes from a lifetime of travel around the country – often on foot or by bike. Originally from London, David is currently based in the south Cotswolds.

STEVE FALLON
Hungary

Steve first visited Magyarország in the early 1980s and immediately fell in love with thermal baths, Tokaj wine and the voice of Márta Sebestyén. Not happy with just the occasional fix, he moved to Budapest in 1992, where he could enjoy all three in abundance. Now based in London, Steve returns to Hungary regularly for all these things and more.

DUNCAN GARWOOD — Italy, Directory, Transport

Following work experience in a newspaper office in Slough and three years as a corporate journalist, Duncan moved to Bari in 1997. Since then he's travelled up and down Italy various times, contributing to several Italian guides, including *Rome*, *Naples & the Amalfi Coast*, and *Piedmont*. He currently lives in a small town just south of Rome.

LEANNE LOGAN — Belgium

Leanne's first taste of Belgium was a cone of mayonnaise-smothered chips at the age of 12. Many years later, en route around Belgium and Luxembourg for Lonely Planet, she found an appetite for beer, chocolate and a Flemish man. She now introduces her half-Flemish daughters to the fine things Belgium has to offer – including chips.

VESNA MARIC — Croatia

Vesna was born in Bosnia and Hercegovina while it was still a part of Yugoslavia and, as a result, she has never been able to see Croatia as a foreign country. A lifelong lover of Dalmatia's beaches, pine trees, food and wine, she expanded her knowledge during this book by exploring Zadar and Zagreb, two cities she discovered anew.

VIRGINIA MAXWELL — Italy

After working for many years at Lonely Planet's Melbourne headquarters, Virginia decided she'd be happier writing guidebooks than commissioning them. She's written or contributed to Lonely Planet books about nine countries, eight of which are on the Mediterranean. Virginia has covered Rome and ventured to the north of Italy for Lonely Planet's *Italy*.

CRAIG McLACHLAN — Greece

A Kiwi with a bad case of wanderlust, Craig enjoys nothing more than visiting the Greek Isles – he leads hiking tours to Greece and has even taken a group of doctors to Kos to see where Hippocrates came from. Craig runs an outdoor-activity company in Queenstown, New Zealand, in the southern hemisphere summer, then heads north for the winter.

TIM RICHARDS — Hungary

Tim first visited Hungary in 1993. He was fascinated by the traces remaining from the communist era, and by three delightful aspects of Hungarian life: paprika appearing as a condiment on every table; delicious cherry strudel available on every corner; and the country's marvellous Tokaj wine. Tim is a freelance journalist based in Melbourne, Australia.

CAROLINE SIEG — Germany

Half-American and half-Swiss, Caroline Sieg has spent most of her life moving back and forth across the Atlantic Ocean, with lengthy stops in Zürich, Miami and New York City. When not cycling around Berlin's Tiergarten or Hamburg's waterways in an effort to work off a daily dose of *Kaffee und Kuchen* (coffee and cakes), Caroline can be found commissioning and writing guidebooks for Lonely Planet.

DAMIEN SIMONIS — Spain

The spark was lit on a short trip over the Pyrenees to Barcelona during a holiday in France; it was Damien's first taste of Spain and he found something irresistible about the place. Damien came back years later, living in Toledo, Madrid and finally settling in Barcelona. He has travelled to all corners of the country.

RYAN VER BERKMOES — Germany, The Netherlands, Directory, Transport

Ryan once spent three years in Frankfurt, during which time he got the chance to write for Lonely Planet. One of his first jobs was researching Germany for *Western Europe*, and later he worked on the very first edition of Lonely Planet's *The Netherlands*, a country where they pronounce his name better than he can. He now lives in Portland, Oregon.

MARA VORHEES — Directory, Transport

Mara took her first trip to Eastern Europe in 1988, riding a bus from Helsinki to Leningrad. She has since travelled throughout the region, acting as an au pair in Ukraine, bussing through the Baltics, journeying by train across Russia and drifting down the Danube. When not in the east, she lives in Somerville, Massachusetts.

NICOLA WILLIAMS — Switzerland

Ever since Nicola moved to a village on the southern side of Lake Geneva, she has never quite been able to shake off that uncanny feeling she's on holiday. Nicola has lived and worked in France since 1997, and when not flitting to Geneva, skiing, or dipping into the Swiss countryside, she can be found writing at her desk.

NEIL WILSON — Ireland

Neil's first round-the-world trip was way back in 1983, but despite living in Scotland he never made it to Ireland until 1990, with a visit to Kinsale and the south coast. Trips to Northern Ireland followed, and his interest in the history and politics of the place intensified a few years later when he found out that most of his mum's ancestors were from Ulster.

THIS BOOK

This 1st edition of *Discover Europe* was coordinated by Lisa Dunford, with contributions from Oliver Berry, and was researched and written by Lisa and Oliver, Brett Atkinson, Alexis Averbuck, James Bainbridge, Neal Bedford, Geert Cole, David Else, Steve Fallon, Duncan Garwood, Leanne Logan, Vesna Maric, Virginia Maxwell, Craig McLachlan, Tim Richards, Caroline Sieg, Damien Simonis, Ryan Ver Berkmoes, Mara Vorhees, Nicola Williams and Neil Wilson. This guidebook was commissioned in Lonely Planet's Melbourne office, and produced by the following:

Commissioning Editor Will Gourlay
Coordinating Editor Barbara Delissen
Coordinating Cartographer Corey Hutchison
Coordinating Layout Designers Paul Iacono, Margaret Jung
Managing Editor Laura Stansfeld
Managing Cartographers David Connolly, Hunor Csutoros, Herman So
Managing Layout Designer Laura Jane

Assisting Editors David Carroll, Daniel Corbett, Jessica Crouch, Rowan McKinnon, Saralinda Turner
Assisting Cartographers Xavier Di Toro, Birgit Jordan, Joelene Kowalski
Cover Naomi Parker, lonelyplanetimages.com
Internal Image Research Aude Vauconsant, lonelyplanetimages.com
Project Manager Rachel Imeson
Language Content Branislava Vladisavljevic

Thanks to Sasha Baskett, Glenn Beanland, Yvonne Bischofberger, Sally Darmody, Eoin Dunlevy, Jane Hart, Suki Gear, Joshua Geoghegan, Mark Germanchis, Chris Girdler, Michelle Glynn, Brice Gosnell, Imogen Hall, James Hardy, Steven Henderson, Jim Hsu, Lauren Hunt, Chris Lee Ack, Nic Lehman, Alison Lyall, John Mazzocchi, Jennifer Mullins, Wayne Murphy, Darren O'Connell, Naomi Parker, Piers Pickard, Howard Ralley, Lachlan Ross, Julie Sheridan, Jason Shugg, Caroline Sieg, Cara Smith, Kerrianne Southway, Naomi Stephens, Geoff Stringer, Jane Thompson, Sam Trafford, Stefanie Di Trocchio, Gerard Walker, Tashi Wheeler, Clifton Wilkinson, Juan Winata, Emily K Wolman, Nick Wood

Internal photographs p10 Tuscan landscape near San Gimignano, Italy, Diana Mayfield; p3, p12 Street scene, Edinburgh, Scotland, Will Salter; p31 Masked Carnevale patron, Venice, Italy, Juliet Coombe; p43 Paris metro sign, France, Richard Nebesky; p3, p58 Giant's Causeway, Northern Ireland, Gareth McCormack; p3, p165 Eiffel Tower, Paris, France, Will Salter; p3, p235 Casa Batlló, Barcelona, Spain, Krzysztof Dydynski; p3, p301 Vespa parked in narrow laneway, Ravello, Italy, Glenn Beanland; p3, p369 Woman cycling on frozen river, the Netherlands, Frans Lemmens; p3, p421 Neuschwanstein Castle, Bavaria, Germany, David Tomlinson; p3, p531 Astronomical clock and Týn Church, Prague, Czech Republic, Richard Nebesky; p3, p607 Waterfront buildings, Rovinj, Croatia, Jean-Pierre Lescourret; p3, p649 Agias Varvaras Rousanou and Nikolaou Anapafsa monasteries, Meteora, Greece, Andrew Bain; p3, p699 Acropolis, Pergamum, Turkey, Shania Shegedyn; p3, p744 Gondola passing a restaurant, Venice, Italy, Tony Burns; p781 Covered central courtyard, Berlin, Germany, Krzysztof Dydynski.

SEND US YOUR FEEDBACK

We love to hear from travellers – your comments keep us on our toes and help make our books better. Our well-travelled team reads every word on what you loved or loathed about this book. Although we cannot reply individually to postal submissions, we always guarantee that your feedback goes straight to the appropriate authors, in time for the next edition. Each person who sends us information is thanked in the next edition and the most useful submissions are rewarded with a free book.

To send us your updates – and find out about Lonely Planet events, newsletters and travel news – visit our award-winning website: lonelyplanet.com/contact.

Note: we may edit, reproduce and incorporate your comments in Lonely Planet products such as guidebooks, websites and digital products, so let us know if you don't want your comments reproduced or your name acknowledged. For a copy of our privacy policy visit lonelyplanet.com/privacy.

INDEX

D

000 Map pages
000 Photograph pages

000 Map pages
000 Photograph pages

000 Map pages
000 Photograph pages

INDEX

T-Z

MAP LEGEND

ROUTES

Tollway
Freeway
Primary
Secondary
Tertiary
Lane
Under Construction
Unsealed Road
One-Way Street
Mall/Steps
Tunnel
Pedestrian Overpass
Walking Tour
Walking Tour Detour
Walking Path
Track

TRANSPORT

Ferry
Metro
Monorail
Rail/Underground
Tram
Cable Car, Funicular

HYDROGRAPHY

River, Creek
Intermittent River
Swamp/Mangrove
Reef
Canal
Water
Dry Lake/Salt Lake
Glacier

BOUNDARIES

International
State, Provincial
Disputed
Regional, Suburb
Marine Park
Cliff/Ancient Wall

AREA FEATURES

Area of Interest
Beach, Desert
Building/Urban Area
Cemetery, Christian
Cemetery, Other
Forest
Mall/Market
Park
Restricted Area
Sports

POPULATION

CAPITAL (NATIONAL)
LARGE CITY
Small City
CAPITAL (STATE)
Medium City
Town, Village

SYMBOLS

Sights/Activities

Buddhist
Canoeing, Kayaking
Castle, Fortress
Christian
Confucian
Diving
Hindu
Islamic
Jain
Jewish
Monument
Museum, Gallery
Point of Interest
Pool
Ruin
Sento (Public Hot Baths)
Shinto
Sikh
Skiing
Surfing, Surf Beach
Taoist
Trail Head
Winery, Vineyard
Zoo, Bird Sanctuary

Information

Bank, ATM
Embassy/Consulate
Hospital, Medical
Information
Internet Facilities
Police Station
Post Office, GPO
Telephone
Toilets
Wheelchair Access

Eating

Eating

Drinking

Cafe
Drinking

Entertainment

Entertainment

Shopping

Shopping

Sleeping

Camping
Sleeping

Transport

Airport, Airfield
Border Crossing
Bus Station
Bicycle Path/Cycling
FFCC (Barcelona)
Metro (Barcelona)
Parking Area
Petrol Station
S-Bahn
Taxi Rank
Tube Station
U-Bahn

Geographic

Beach
Lighthouse
Lookout
Mountain, Volcano
National Park
Pass, Canyon
Picnic Area
River Flow
Shelter, Hut
Waterfall

LONELY PLANET OFFICES

Australia
Head Office
Locked Bag 1, Footscray, Victoria 3011
☎ 03 8379 8000, fax 03 8379 8111
talk2us@lonelyplanet.com.au

USA
150 Linden St, Oakland, CA 94607
☎ 510 250 6400, toll free 800 275 8555,
fax 510 893 8572
info@lonelyplanet.com

UK
2nd fl, 186 City Rd,
London EC1V 2NT
☎ 020 7106 2100, fax 020 7106 2101
go@lonelyplanet.co.uk

Published by Lonely Planet
ABN 36 005 607 983

Printed by Fabulous Printers Pte Ltd
Printed in Singapore